ZHOU ENLAI

ZHOU ENLAI

A Life

CHEN JIAN

THE BELKNAP PRESS OF HARVARD UNIVERSITY PRESS
Cambridge, Massachusetts · London, England · 2024

Printed in the United States of America
First printing

Library of Congress Cataloging-in-Publication Data
Names: Chen, Jian, 1952– author.
Title: Zhou Enlai : a life / Chen Jian.
Description: Cambridge, Massachusetts ; London, England : The Belknap Press of Harvard University Press, 2024. | Includes bibliographical references and index.
Identifiers: LCCN 2023034792 | ISBN 9780674659582 (cloth)
Subjects: LCSH: Zhou, Enlai, 1898–1976. | Prime ministers—China—Biography. | China—Politics and government—1949–1976.
Classification: LCC DS778.C593 C4433 2024 | DDC 951.05092 [B]—dc23/eng/20230808
LC record available at https://lccn.loc.gov/2023034792

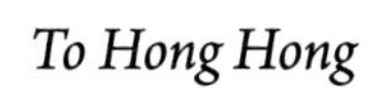

To Hong Hong

Contents

Abbreviations in Text

CC	Central Committee
CCP	Chinese Communist Party
CCRG	Central Cultural Revolution Group
CMC	Central Military Commission
DRV	Democratic Republic of Vietnam
ERA	Eighth Route Army
FEB	The Comintern's Far Eastern Bureau
GMD	Guomindang (Nationalist Party)
ICP	Indonesian Communist Party
JCP	Japanese Communist Party
KPA	Korean People's Army
NFA	New Fourth Army
NPPCC	New People's Political Consultative Committee
PKU	Peking University
PLA	People's Liberation Army
PPCC	People's Political Consultative Committee
PRC	People's Republic of China
SAB	Soviet Area Bureau
SWRRH	Shanghai Workers' Revolutionary Rebellion Headquarters
UN	United Nations

MAP 1: China in the Republican Period (1911–1949)

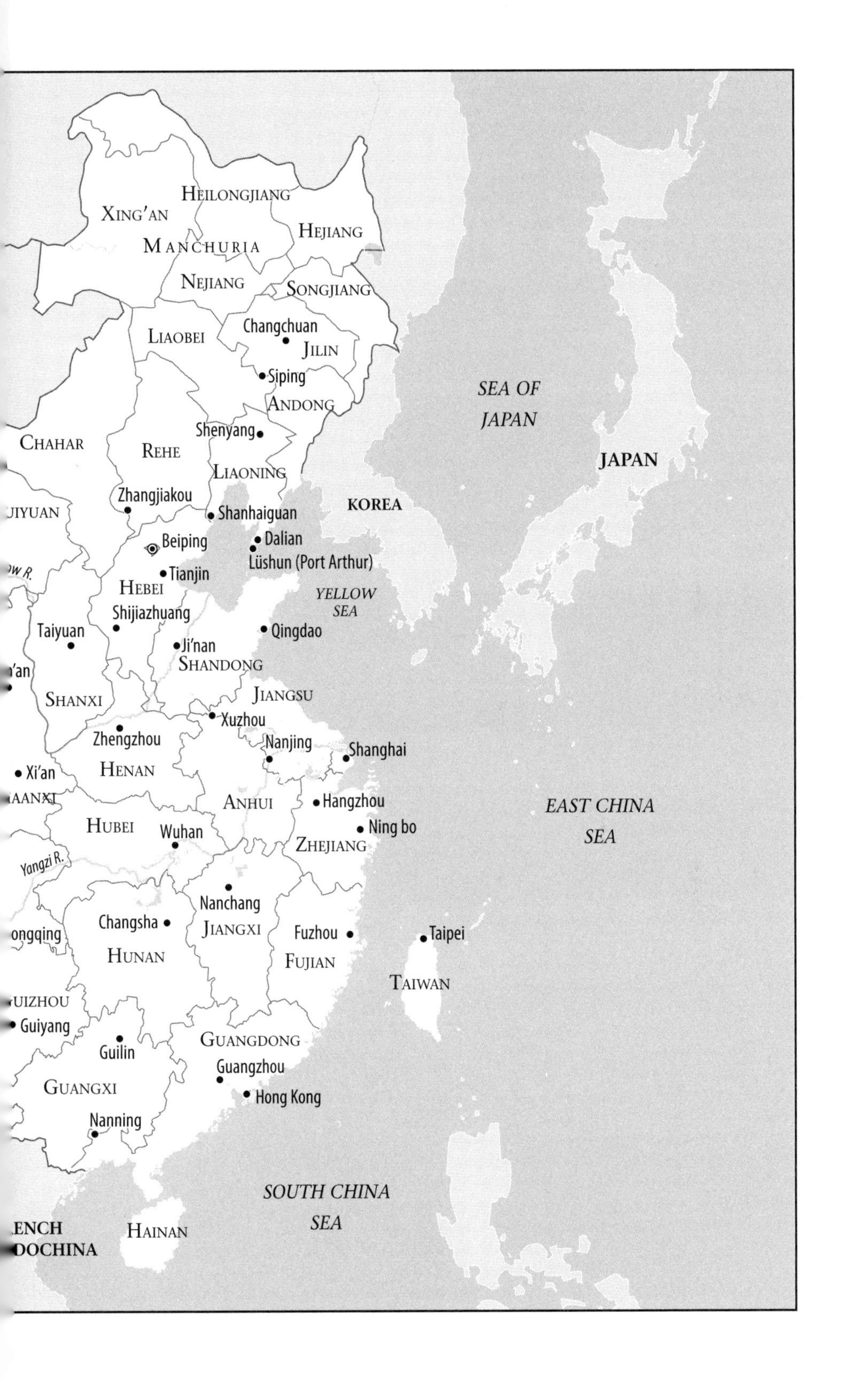
HEILONGJIANG
XING'AN
HEJIANG
MANCHURIA
NEJIANG
SONGJIANG
Changchuan
LIAOBEI
JILIN
Siping
ANDONG
SEA OF JAPAN
Shenyang
CHAHAR
REHE
JAPAN
LIAONING
Zhangjiakou
KOREA
Shanhaiguan
Dalian
Beiping
Lüshun (Port Arthur)
Tianjin
HEBEI
YELLOW SEA
Shijiazhuang
Taiyuan
Qingdao
Ji'nan
SHANDONG
SHANXI
JIANGSU
Xuzhou
Zhengzhou
Nanjing
Shanghai
Xi'an
HENAN
ANHUI
Hangzhou
EAST CHINA SEA
HUBEI
Wuhan
Ning bo
ZHEJIANG
Yangzi R.
Nanchang
Changsha
JIANGXI
Fuzhou
Taipei
HUNAN
FUJIAN
TAIWAN
Guiyang
Guilin
GUANGDONG
Guangzhou
GUANGXI
Hong Kong
Nanning
SOUTH CHINA SEA
HAINAN

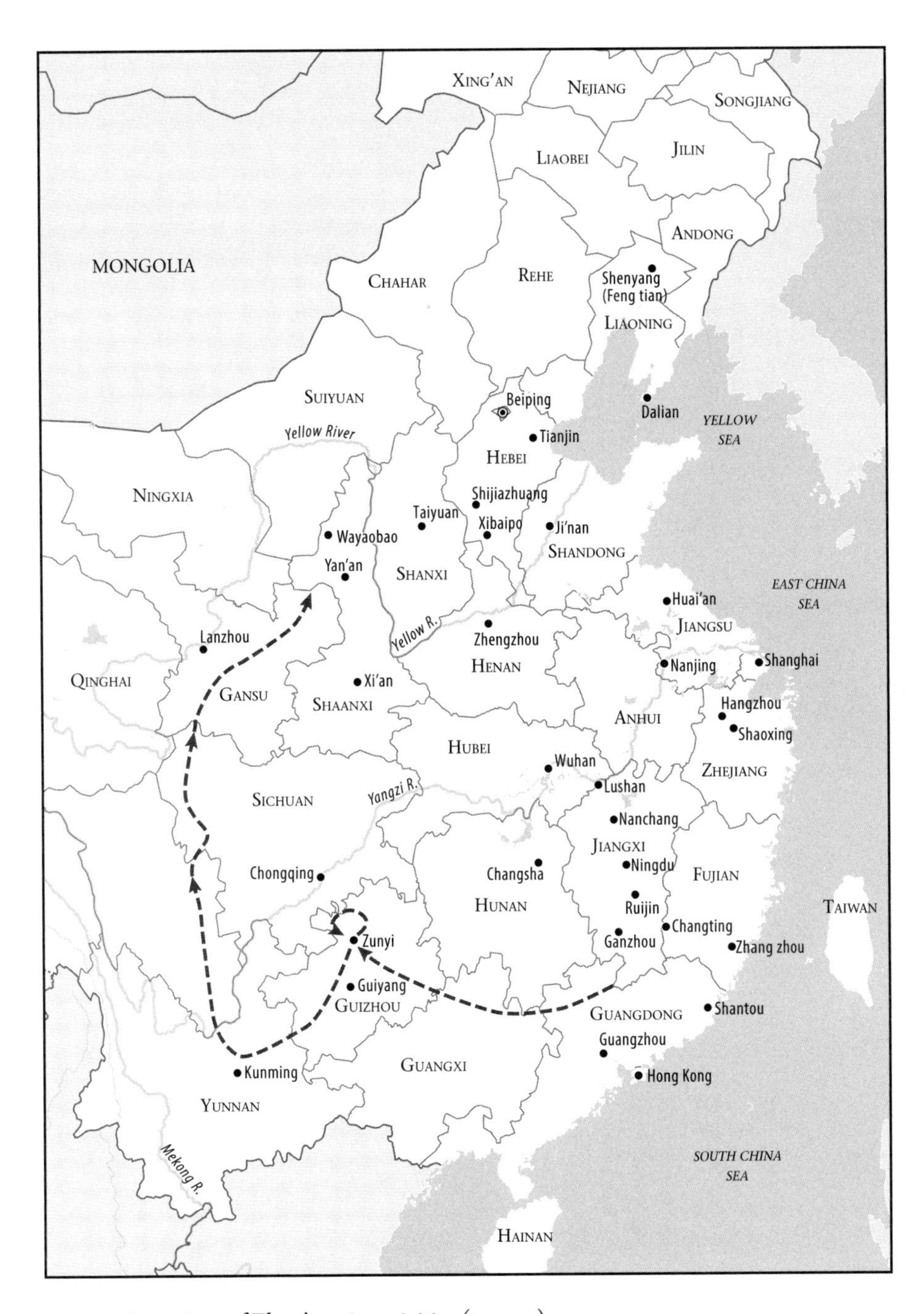

MAP 2: Locations of Zhou's main activities (to 1949)

MAP 3: The People's Republic under Mao (1949–1976)

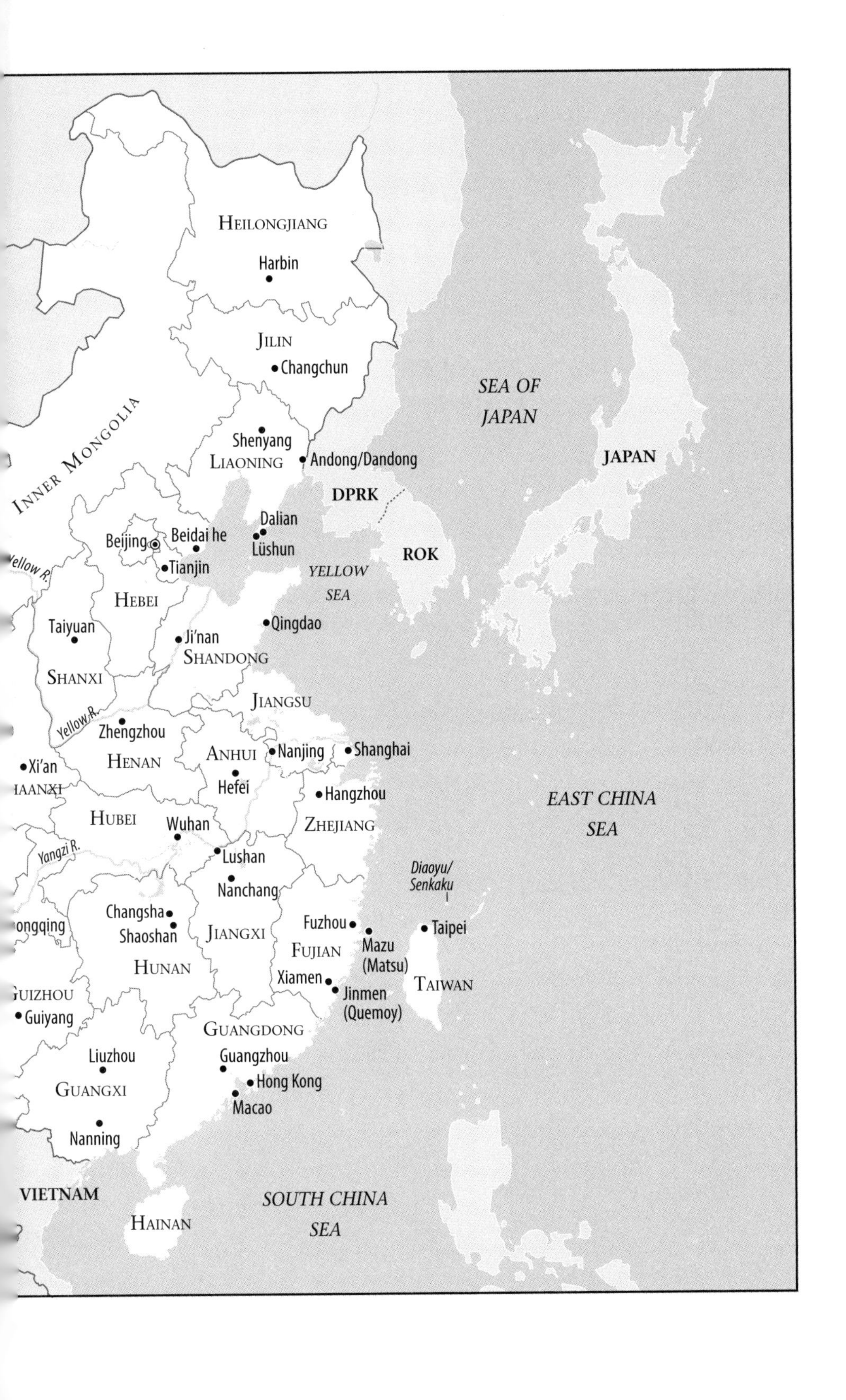
HEILONGJIANG
Harbin
JILIN
Changchun
INNER MONGOLIA
Shenyang
LIAONING
Andong/Dandong
SEA OF JAPAN
JAPAN
DPRK
ROK
Dalian
Lüshun
Beijing
Beidai he
Tianjin
Yellow R.
YELLOW SEA
HEBEI
Taiyuan
Ji'nan
SHANDONG
Qingdao
SHANXI
JIANGSU
Yellow R.
Zhengzhou
HENAN
ANHUI
Nanjing
Shanghai
Xi'an
Hefei
Hangzhou
EAST CHINA SEA
HUBEI
Wuhan
ZHEJIANG
Yangzi R.
Lushan
Diaoyu/ Senkaku
Nanchang
Changsha
Shaoshan
JIANGXI
Fuzhou
Mazu (Matsu)
Taipei
FUJIAN
HUNAN
Xiamen
Jinmen (Quemoy)
TAIWAN
Guiyang
GUANGDONG
Liuzhou
Guangzhou
Hong Kong
GUANGXI
Macao
Nanning
VIETNAM
SOUTH CHINA SEA
HAINAN

ZHOU ENLAI

PROLOGUE

January 11, 1976, a day of bone-chilling cold in Beijing.

From predawn hours, men and women of all ages began to gather along Chang'an Avenue, the city's main east-west artery and China's "Number One Boulevard" that runs past the legendary Tiananmen Square. By early afternoon, hundreds of thousands of people had gathered along a section of the street over a dozen miles in length. They were there to bid farewell to Zhou Enlai, China's premier of twenty-seven years, who had passed away three days before. Unlike at so many mass rallies and other state-sponsored events that had been held at the square and on Chang'an Avenue, the mourners who had assembled there on this day did so on their own accord. The prevailing sentiment among them was genuine sadness tinged with deep frustration and anger.

The people who lined up along Chang'an that day probably did not recognize the historical significance of the moment. In retrospect, their gathering had transmitted an important signal: China's revolutionary era was approaching its end; the light of an age of great transformations was glimmering on the horizon.

In the afternoon, snow began to fill the sky. Shortly after four o'clock, a stream of cars left Beijing Hospital in the city center, where Zhou's body had lain in state for the past several days. Thousands had visited the hospital to pay tribute to the late premier. A white-and-black hearse carried Zhou's coffin. As the motorcade drew near, many of the citizens lining the street began to weep. Their tears gave way to loud cries the instant the fleet of cars passed before them. Around five o'clock, Zhou's body was cremated following a brief ceremony at Babaoshan Revolutionary Funeral Home in the city's western suburbs.

Four days later, the official memorial service for Zhou was held at the Great Hall of the People, on the west side of Tiananmen Square. Chairman Mao Zedong, Zhou's patron and colleague for over a half century, was notably absent.[1] Vice Premier Deng Xiaoping read the eulogy in what was to be his last public appearance before he was purged for the second time during the Cultural Revolution. Zhou was extolled as "a great proletarian revolutionary, an outstanding Communist, and an extraordinary leader of China's party and state."[2]

The ceremony concluded the official ritual procedures for mourning the late premier. Zhou's ashes, in accordance with his wishes, were scattered among China's mountains and waters.

• • •

Yet the mass mourning of Zhou did not stop. Across China, in the cities and the countryside, people continued to organize myriad activities to commemorate the "beloved premier." These activities then evolved into covert and even overt protests against the "Gang of Four"—headed by Jiang Qing, Mao's wife, and composed of radical Maoist leaders Wang Hongwen, Zhang Chunqiao, and Yao Wenyuan. The implied fifth target of the rebuke was none other than the "great leader" himself.

On March 25, *Wenhui bao* (Wenhui daily), a Shanghai-based newspaper, published an article on "repulsing the rightist trend of negating the Cultural Revolution." Its text included a suspicious sentence which many believed to imply that Zhou, a "capitalist roader" (a leader who follows the path of capitalism), had supported the "unrepentant capitalist roader" Deng Xiaoping in the latter's endeavor to reclaim counterrevolutionary power.[3] As Shanghai had been the Gang of Four's political base, people immediately linked the article to a vicious plot by those anti-Zhou radicals to slander him. In Nanjing, students and many others spontaneously assembled to hold rallies and protests, at which demonstrators displayed banners emblazoned with such slogans as "Defend Zhou Enlai" and "Down with those who oppose Premier Zhou."[4]

On April 1, the Chinese Communist Party (CCP) Center telephoned party organs throughout the country, characterizing the events in Nanjing as a "serious political conspiracy aiming at splitting the party led by Chairman Mao." Party officials were ordered to "investigate the sources of rumor spreading" and to find and punish the "plotters behind the curtain."[5] However, popular protests in many parts of the country showed no sign of abating.

Finally, in early April, the Tiananmen Incident of 1976 erupted. Tens of thousands of ordinary men and women came to and eventually occupied Tiananmen Square, ostensibly to pay their respects to Zhou during *Qingming,* an annual holiday dedicated to the commemoration of the spirits of departed loved ones. What they openly expressed was widespread dismay over economic stagnation as felt by their own lived experience, and the political terror resulting from Mao's "continuous revolution."[6] Hundreds of poems were posted on nearby walls and circulated among the occupiers of the square. One read:

> The era of Qin Shi Huang's dictatorship has passed away forever
> And the people are no longer so easy to fool![7]

Nowhere in its lines did the chairman's name appear. However, no reader would fail to link the poem's mention of Qin Shi Huang, the notorious first emperor of China who established a unified but highly autocratic and oppressive empire in 221 B.C., to the chairman. The crowds at the square began to spread similar expressions and ideas to other parts of Beijing and, eventually, to the whole country. This was a mass rebellion on a scale never before seen in the history of the People's Republic.

The aging and ailing Mao, who would himself "go to meet Karl Marx" only a few months later, considered the activities at Tiananmen Square "reactionary in essence." In response, he approved a dramatic crackdown on the crowds.[8] By early morning on April 6, all those who had assembled at the square had been expelled by force, with hundreds beaten or imprisoned. By moving to quash the gathering, though, the chairman essentially acknowledged that, despite the extraordinary power and authority he had acquired during the Cultural Revolution, his revolutionary programs aimed at placing a new social order in the hearts and minds of the Chinese people had failed.

This was the funeral of China's revolutionary era. At that moment, the curtain was lifted on the postrevolutionary age.

• • •

0.1 In early April 1976, tens of thousands of everyday Chinese gathered at Tiananmen Square, mourning the late premier Zhou Enlai. *Top Photo Corporation / Alamy Stock Photo*

Mao died on September 9, 1976. China has since experienced a comprehensive process of derevolutionization and, indeed, de-Maoization. Beginning in the late 1970s, Deng Xiaoping, who upon his return to politics had emerged as China's paramount leader, launched a grand campaign of "reform and opening-up." The Chinese leadership's gradual adoption of a "market-oriented socialist economy" has produced phenomenal economic growth in China, accompanied by broad, deep, and continuous transformations of Chinese society and popular mind-sets. These changes also released powerful new social and intellectual forces unprecedented in China's history.[9] As a result, the legitimacy of the Chinese *Communist* state, which has become anything but Communist, has been constantly called into question.

These changes have also tested Zhou's image and legacy. Once upon a time, a broad consensus existed among the Chinese authorities, the general public, and even academics that Zhou's legacy would be seen in a positive light. This was particularly true in the days immediately after Mao's Cultural Revolution. Praise and admiration of Zhou's character, integrity, political wisdom, and leadership style came from all corners of Chinese society.

Zhou was heralded as the "moral example of the revolution," the symbol of the "consciousness of the people and the nation," and the bearer of "hopes of the future."[10] Within this context, Han Suyin, an internationally renowned writer and biographer of Zhou Enlai, found it virtually impossible "to find faults (or) defects" in Zhou.[11]

The efforts of the Chinese authorities undoubtedly played a role in the outpouring of praise for Zhou. Chinese leaders of the post-Mao era would find it useful for coping with the serious legitimacy challenges they faced to glorify or even deify Zhou. Moreover, they hoped that invoking Zhou would help them cultivate popular support for the party's ambitious plans to modernize China.

At the same time, however, the enthusiastic and widespread admiration for Zhou among everyday Chinese was not insincere. Their adoration of the late premier revealed that they both desired and expected to cast off China's Maoism-dominated revolutionary era. Indeed, the collective memory of Zhou as a nearly perfect individual served as an imaginary bridge linking people's painful recollections of an excruciating past and their boundless hope for a bright future.

• • •

But the exalted image of Zhou Enlai has been increasingly contested in the forty-plus years since his death. The reform and opening-up process has also prompted a profound reexamination of China's modern history, and of Mao and the Maoist era in particular. Not surprisingly, Zhou, who had been with Mao and served the Maoist revolutionary cause for almost half a century, became a target of exhaustive scrutiny. The surfacing of details concerning the darkest chapters of the Chinese Communist Revolution and the emergence of an increasingly critical approach among Chinese intellectuals toward China's revolutionary era have muddied Zhou's posthumous reputation.

China's party- and state-controlled official discourse has consistently praised Zhou, describing him as an extraordinary human being, a devoted and altruistic revolutionary, a wise and farsighted statesman, and a first-class diplomat. In the mainstream collective memory, Zhou seems to have retained his status as a positive historical figure. In the main, he has been remembered as an initiator and planner of, and a principal actor in, China's prolonged rise over the course of the twentieth century to the status as a prominent world power.

In the meantime, the continuous uncovering of negative records of Mao's revolution has tested the durability of Zhou's popularity. A growing number of people have begun to question his reputation as an exemplary leader. Generally speaking, criticism of Zhou, including the most pointed rebukes, centers on three issues. First, Zhou has been criticized for his unfailing loyalty to Mao and Mao's disastrous revolutionary programs, especially the Great Leap Forward and the Great Proletarian Cultural Revolution. Frank Dikötter, a renowned historian, described him in one account as Mao's "faithful dog."[12] Second, Zhou has been called "hypocritical" and "selfish" for adopting a political philosophy that prioritized self-protection above all other political goals. Third, the most serious criticism of Zhou concerns his character, integrity, and morality; this criticism in particular has tarnished and, ultimately, severely damaged Zhou's once impeccable public image.[13] Indeed, when prominent authors like Jung Chang and Jon Halliday portray Mao as a Hitler-type villain and the Chinese Communist Revolution as one of the darkest chapters in human history, how could Zhou, who had stood with the chairman through his revolution and "continuous revolution," remain generally a "good man" and bright historical figure?[14]

The change in attitude of Gao Wenqian, whose highly influential Zhou biography (in Chinese) among Chinese readers, is quite revealing. Gao was the son of a Communist cadre. His wife was the daughter of Pu Shouchang, an interpreter and close associate of Zhou's. In the 1980s, as a researcher at the CCP Central Institute of Historical Documents and one of the principal authors of the official Zhou biography, Gao also published several essays in which he praised Zhou as a farsighted leader with an exceptional sense of responsibility and an extraordinary capacity for leadership.[15] Gao left China in the wake of the Tiananmen tragedy of 1989. The violent crackdown had compelled him to rethink what he had previously taken for granted, and he became increasingly critical of Zhou and the Chinese Communist Revolution.[16] In his widely acclaimed Zhou biography *Wannian Zhou Enlai* (Zhou Enlai in his later years), he presents a sharply critical perspective of Zhou's political career in general and his experience during the Cultural Revolution in particular, sharply questioning Zhou's character and moral integrity.[17]

The story of Yu Changgeng, who coauthored another Zhou biography, is equally telling. A longtime member of China's diplomatic service, Yu was once a loyal supporter of Zhou and China's foreign policy. His attitude changed after careful examination of Maoist policies, in whose implementation Zhou had served as a driving force. Yu found it impossible to continue to accept the high regard in which Chinese authorities had held Zhou. Consequently, in the Zhou biography that he coauthored with Barbara Barnouin, he goes so far as to denounce Zhou for "being loyal to one of the most brutal tyrants of the century—comparable to Hitler and Stalin."[18]

* * *

What kind of person was Zhou Enlai? Why did he, along with so many of his contemporaries, embark on the path to revolution? How should his life and career be evaluated? Why did a country of a billion people so fervently mourn him after his death? How and why, four-plus decades after Zhou's passing, did the public image of one of the most important leaders of twentieth-century China and the world become the source of such radical divergence and controversy?

These are the questions I explore in this biography, by tracing Zhou's life as a Communist revolutionary, an influential politician and statesman, a diplomatic giant, and, in the final analysis, a human being. Supporting this effort is extensive research (including many interviews) that I have conducted over the last quarter century on the Chinese Communist Revolution and China's changing relations with the world, in both of which Zhou played a key role. This is the first comprehensive biography of Zhou published in English written with the support of many years of multilingual, multiarchival, and multisource research.

At the center of my endeavor lies the challenge of correctly placing the Chinese Communist Revolution within the annals of history. Revolution is no sin, I believe. Revolutions happen for a reason. A revolution would not have erupted if the old regime that nurtured it had not deteriorated beyond repair. This is also the case of the Chinese Communist Revolution, which came as a dramatic response to the total failure of the Chinese old regime in the face of the daunting internal and external crises engulfing China's state, society, and even civilization. Therefore, the coming of a revolutionary era in China was not in any way an accident; rather, there must have been historically justifiable factors for its occurrence.

Yet all revolutions have their downsides. They are inevitably destructive, cruel, and bloody—and radical and transformative revolutions in particular. This was especially true of China's Communist Revolution and Mao's "continuous revolution," both of which, in order to reach the grand aim of the "creation of [a] new human being," nevertheless embraced their share of sinister moments, often characterized by unspeakable violence against humanity.

The "New China" created by the Chinese Communist Revolution was no exception. Since its birth, it has faced profound legitimacy challenges as the result of persistent discordance between ideals and reality, ends and means, and rampant power and the absence of laws and institutions to check and balance that power. Mao, who stood center stage in the revolution for half a century, complicated this disjuncture. Buoyed by vast, unchecked, and unbalanced political power, he fused utopian visions with grand plans for political, social, and cultural transformation through prolonged mass mobilization campaigns unprecedented in Chinese and world history.

Consequently, the Chinese Communist Revolution, especially Mao's "continuous revolution," unfolded as a phenomenon mixing hope and despair, success and failure, progress and setbacks, and bright times and dark moments. The revolution began as an intellectual, political, and social drive—as the revolutionaries claimed—to enlighten popular political consciousness and promote the emancipation of the people. It ended up in tyranny, the total suppression of the consciousness it had once championed, and the extraordinary suffering of the people. Zhou played an integral role in all of the above.

To achieve a deeper understanding of Zhou, it is essential to examine him within the complex context of China's revolutionary era. Zhou was an active participant in this era, and he was also a product of it. He and his comrades made the revolution, and they were remade by it. As the revolution's protagonists, they were also its prisoners. The many paradoxes of Zhou and his experience epitomize the dilemmas and tragedies of China's revolutionary era. Such an understanding, in my view, should serve as the point of departure for exploring and narrating Zhou's life and career.

Throughout his career, Zhou took on challenging roles, and he often had to make difficult choices. Yet none was comparable to the ordeals he endured during the tumultuous years of the Great Proletarian Cultural Revolution. When Mao, the great helmsman, steered the giant ship of China into a violent storm, Zhou, as the ship's first officer, fought valiantly to prevent the vessel from sinking. Moreover, China not only survived the storm but was able to move forward, albeit slowly and tortuously, paving the way for the country's painful and prolonged rise. Here, Zhou's contributions should be critically assessed and duly credited.

At the end of the day, if we seek to reject revolution in general and to China's revolutionary era in particular, and if we are determined to prevent such tragedies in the future, we cannot merely reject revolution. The most crucial course of action is to articulate the historical conditions and scenarios under which a revolution begins. We must also identify why, where, and how the revolution went wrong and ran counter to the goal of the revolutionaries—the liberation of the people.

This is a complicated project, to be sure. I fully understand that it is probably beyond the capacity of one person and one book to provide definitive answers on how Zhou's position in history should be illustrated and defined. Therefore, in writing this book, I try to treat Zhou's life and career as a test case, one that symbolizes—and, in many key senses, even embodies—not only the constructive results of China's revolutionary era but also its deep paradoxes and enduring complexities. There exists no single or straightforward formula with which I may tell and make sense of Zhou's story. This understanding forms the historical and intellectual starting point of my work.

PART I

EARLY YEARS

1

CHILDHOOD

1898–1910

North of the Yangzi River, amid the plains of eastern China, sits the small city of Huai'an.[1] A stone's throw away, the Grand Canal intersects the Huai River. For centuries, Huai'an was a hub of commerce in Jiangsu Province. There was also a large floating population in Huai'an, many of whom eventually chose to settle there, attracted by the city's peacefulness and its convenient location as a local transportation center.

In 1898, on the fifth day of March, Zhou Enlai was born into a declining mandarin's family in Huai'an.[2] He was the eldest son of Zhou Yineng and Wan Dong'er, as well as the seventh male child of his generation in the extended Zhou family. The whole family rejoiced at the baby's birth, and they also had very high expectations of him. They gave him the nickname Da Luan, which literally means "Big Male Phoenix." Later, when Enlai reached school age, he, like many Chinese then, received a courtesy name, which in his case was Xiangyu, meaning "flying in the universe." At the time, however, none of the elders of the Zhou family could have imagined that this boy would one day rank among the most important and influential figures of the twentieth century.

The Zhou clan, native not to Huai'an but to Shaoxing, in Zhejiang Province, had a long and prominent history.[3] A grand ancestor, Zhou Dunyi (1017–1073), was one of China's most influential and distinguished gentry-officials and Confucian scholars during the Song Dynasty (960–1279).[4] Zhou Shuren (pen name Lu Xun), arguably China's greatest writer and literary critic of the modern era, probably was Zhou Enlai's distant uncle.[5]

1.1 Zhou Enlai's birthplace in Huai'an, Jiangsu, China. *Liang Zhao / Alamy Stock Photo*

But by the time Enlai came into the world, the family's prominence had long declined. His grandfather, Zhou Qikui (courtesy name Zhou Panlong), while serving as a staff member for various provincial or prefectural officials, left Shaoxing in the early 1860s to pursue career opportunities elsewhere, including in neighboring Jiangsu Province. Later, he himself was appointed to several county magistrate posts in Jiangsu. The Zhou family also moved from Shaoxing to Huai'an in the 1870s.[6] In Zhou Panlong's whole career, however, he never achieved a position above the county level. He passed away only a few days after Enlai's birth, so Enlai had no personal memory of his grandfather.[7]

Enlai's father had an even less impressive resume. With no outstanding talent or ambition to speak of, and burdened by a personality that was by no means strong or aggressive, he held only low positions at the county staff level or the equivalent, earning a meager income throughout his life. Unlike most other Chinese fathers at the time, he never had a dominant voice, let alone governing authority, in the household.[8]

At the time of Enlai's birth, it was the women of the Zhou family who held the power and influence in domestic and even external affairs. As a child, "Big Phoenix" grew up under the care of two women: his mother and, in particular, his adoptive mother (who actually was his aunt).

Enlai's mother, Madame Wan, was also born of scholar-official stock. Her father (Enlai's maternal grandfather) held county magistrate positions in Jiangsu, too. She herself had only a few years of education, and so she was barely literate. However, she was widely known as a warmhearted, open-minded, caring, and also quite capable person. After her marriage to Enlai's father, Madame Wan moved into the Zhou household in Huai'an, where she quickly emerged as the manager of all of the extended family's important matters. Zhou Enlai would later recall that it was from his mother that he had cultivated the qualities of diligence, attentiveness, and effective use of his talents, which would benefit him his whole life.[9]

Enlai's adoptive mother, his aunt Madame Chen, had the greatest impact on him as a young boy. When Enlai was six months old, a younger brother of his father, who did not have a son, fell terminally ill. A Chinese custom suggested that a man who died without a male heir had failed his duty of filial piety; but if he produced a son, his illnesses might heal faster. So, at the persistent urging of Enlai's grandmother, he was adopted by his uncle and aunt and moved to live with them (still in the same Zhou family compound, and in close proximity to his biological mother). However, in spite of the family's following the old custom, his uncle died a few months later.

The aunt was said to be a devout Buddhist. However, as revealed by her education of Enlai, her devotion to Buddhism was more a stance toward this worldly life than a true religious, otherworldly belief. Now a widow in her early twenties, she found in Buddhism a spiritual and mental refuge. As Enlai's adoptive mother, she devoted to Enlai all of her love and attention. After her husband's death, she, together with Enlai and his parents, moved to nearby Qinghe County, the birthplace of Enlai's biological mother. With the help of a nanny (a Ms. Jiang, yet another woman!), Madame Chen took exceptional care of Enlai, and the bond between adoptive mother and son grew extremely close.[10]

An educated woman by the standards of the time, Madame Chen tried her best to provide Enlai with a decent early education. When Enlai was only four years old, she began to teach him to write Chinese characters. When Enlai turned five, she sent him to a private school for the children of the family. At home, she directed him to read classic Chinese literature and developed his understanding of Confucian ethics. It seemed that Madame Chen had never read any Buddhist classics or texts, so she never instructed

Enlai to study any. The education that young Enlai received was, in essence, reflective of a traditional Chinese culture that lacked religious heritage or concerns with the "other shore." His character thus was imbued with Confucian ethics that emphasized, as life's ultimate goal, "cultivating oneself, keeping the family in harmony, managing the country well, and bringing peace to the sphere all under heaven."[11]

Among the books that Enlai studied were selected chapters of the Four Books (*Analects, Mencius, The Great Learning,* and *The Doctrine of the Mean*), as well as *The Book of Songs.* He also read classic novels, including *Journey to the West, Water Margin,* and *Romance of the Three Kingdoms.* These laid the foundation of his knowledge of traditional Chinese culture. Many years later, Zhou Enlai told *New York Times* correspondent Henry R. Lieberman, "Even today I am still truly appreciative of the enlightening teaching of my (adoptive) mother. Had there not been her love and care, I would not have received such good education."[12]

When Enlai was nine years old, both his adoptive mother and his biological mother passed away, and he left Qinghe and returned to the Zhou family compound in Huai'an. He grew up, as he himself later recalled, almost overnight.[13] The Zhou family had fallen on hard times for a while, and the deaths of the two women drove the family into even deeper debt. Enlai's father had to take up another low-paying administrative job in remote Hubei Province, from which he hardly ever made it back to the Zhous' Huai'an home. Enlai oftentimes had no choice but to assume the duties of the "man of the family." As he later remembered, he paid frequent visits to the local pawnshops to get some cash to pay for the family's most urgent needs, which was an unfitting or even humiliating experience for him.[14] But he was thus given ample opportunities to learn to cope with complicated situations, even those that far exceeded all expectations for a young boy.

Despite all the adversity that Enlai encountered, he did not quit learning and reading. He attended a private school near the family compound run by Mr. Gong Yinsun, a cousin of his biological mother. Gong was known as a Confucian scholar who had been exposed to new ideas, especially as he had studied in Japan, a rare experience for the majority of Chinese at the time. In addition to Confucian classics, Gong also introduced to the students, most of whom were Enlai's distant cousins, books and other reading materials about modern Western civilization. Zhou remembered Gong as "a teacher of my intellectual and political enlightenment."[15]

1.2 The room in which Zhou Enlai was born. *Liang Zhao / Alamy Stock Photo*

Zhou Enlai's early life and education seem to have left two indelible stamps on his personality and approach to challenges. First, he could be very tolerant, considerate, flexible, and, if necessary, extremely resilient or even tough. Second, there was always a place reserved in his mind for the teachings of the ancient Chinese sages that he learned in his childhood, even once he seemed to have wholeheartedly embraced Communist ideologies and revolutionary philosophies. It would become clear that these qualities had prepared Zhou for a distinguished political and diplomatic career. Yet probably these qualities simultaneously sowed the seed of his unwillingness, as well as inability, to claim a top leadership role in the Chinese Communist Revolution, which was steeped in, and even dominated by, the age-old tradition of an authoritarian political culture.

2

MANCHURIA TO NANKAI

1910–1917

Zhou Enlai could have lived the rest of his life in Huai'an had a big change not come in 1910, when Gong Yinsun decided to leave Huai'an. Gong's family school, where Enlai had been a student, closed.[1]

For a few years, Enlai corresponded with another uncle, his father's elder brother, Zhou Yigeng. Among the four siblings (including one who passed away shortly after Enlai's birth), Zhou Yigeng had a relatively successful career. Like Enlai's father, he also had taken up staff positions throughout China. Yet his job was more stable, and he also earned the promotions that always eluded Enlai's father. Zhou Yigeng did not have any children, so he had long treated Enlai as his own son. When Enlai spoke of his intention to pursue further study outside Jiangsu, Zhou Yigeng invited his nephew to live and study under his patronage in Manchuria (the Northeast), where he was then working.[2]

One day in spring 1910, Enlai left Huai'an. For the rest of his life, he would never return, even for a brief visit.

Enlai lived with Zhou Yigeng for the next seven years, first in Manchuria and then, from 1913 to 1917, in Tianjin, one of China's major coastal treaty ports. This provided him with the opportunity to receive formal and modern education, while exposing him to the world beyond his provincial hometown. Zhou Enlai later said that if he had not left Huai'an, his life would have been completely different, "ending up with accomplishing nothing."[3]

* * *

The experience of traveling to, studying in, and living in remote Manchuria was immediately eye opening for young Zhou Enlai. Away from home, he saw a backward China sinking into an ever-deepening national crisis in the face of incursions by Western powers and Japan.

He would learn that in 1894–1895, China had been defeated by Japan and forced to sign the humiliating Treaty of Shimonoseki. The treaty dictated that China pay a huge indemnity, cede Taiwan to Japan, and give up its suzerainty over Korea. In the year Zhou was born, China witnessed the 1898 Reform, which aimed to bring about political, economic, and educational improvements to the country. However, the reform efforts failed after just three months. The hardline conservatives surrounding the aging but still powerful Empress Dowager Cixi carried out a coup that placed the proreform Guangxu Emperor under house arrest, and also forced prominent reformers such as Kang Youwei and Liang Qichao into exile.[4] Two years later, the Boxer Rebellion erupted in Beijing, which resulted in the capital city of China's occupation by an international army composed of troops from Western powers and Japan. The Qing court then signed an even more damaging treaty, the Boxer Protocol, with these powers. The Qing government had to pay another massive indemnity and sign over China's maritime customs tariff, the most important source of the Qing's revenues, as the security bond for the debt. Chinese in that age felt that the crises facing China were grave.

Zhou Yigeng was then serving as a senior staff member at the Bureau of Finance in Fengtian (also known as Shenyang). However, in the middle of the school year, he simply could not find a good school there for his nephew to attend. At that time, Zhou Yigeng's elder cousin, Zhou Yiqian, was serving as director of the Municipal Tax Bureau in a nearby town, Tieling (Yinzhou), where Zhou Enlai's father probably was, too. With Zhou Yiqian's help, Enlai traveled to Tieling to attend the Yingang Academy, which offered elementary education.[5]

After spending six months in Tieling, in October 1910, Zhou moved back to Fengtian. This was a big city far removed from Huai'an, especially as there were educational opportunities that Zhou could have only dreamed of in his hometown. Zhou Yigeng decided to send his nephew to a newly established elementary school, the Sixth Primary School (it would be renamed Dongguan Model School the next year, after the 1911 Revolution). There, for the first time, Zhou studied what many contemporaries regarded as "new education." In addition to Chinese language, literature and history, and classical knowledge, the students were also required to learn mathematics, English, geography, physics, and music and to take a class in physical education.[6] Through this new curriculum, Zhou saw emerging before him a much broader horizon than he had ever conceived of.

The two teachers at Dongguan who influenced Zhou the most were a progressive history teacher, Gao Gewu, and a conservative geography teacher, Mr. Mao. Teacher Gao was a member of the Tongmenghui, the revolutionary alliance that Sun Yat-sen formed to overthrow the Qing and establish a new republic. He directed Zhou to read the works of Zhang Bingling and Zou Rong, both of whom were famous for their radical idea of carrying out a nationalist revolution to save China. Zou, the author of *Revolutionary Army,* was particularly influential among China's educated youth, as he advocated that Chinese use violence to destroy Manchu rule in China. His early death at the age of thirty made him a martyr, even a legend, in the eyes of young students like Zhou Enlai.

On the other hand, Teacher Mao—an ethnic Manchu—was a firm supporter of the Qing's imperial reign. But he also admired the writings of Kang Youwei and Liang Qichao, both of whom were initiators of the 1898 Reform and, after its failure, strove to transform the empire into a constitutional monarchy. Under Mao's tutelage, Zhou familiarized himself with Kang's and Liang's gradualist political ideas.[7]

In October 1911, the second year after Zhou moved to Manchuria, the revolution that brought down the Qing Dynasty erupted. A boy of thirteen, Zhou was among the very first in his school to cut off his queue, the very symbol of loyalty to the Qing.[8] Did this act foreshadow Zhou's interest in politics and his inclination, though still vague, toward revolutionary change?

Manchuria was much colder than Huai'an (especially in the winter) and the diet was dramatically different. Sorghum replaced rice as Zhou's food for nearly every meal. Zhou would later mention that his years in Manchuria accustomed him to tough living conditions. He believed this was good for him both physically and mentally, making him healthier and stronger.[9]

Zhou's study at school would be augmented by his personal experience in Manchuria, leading to the awakening in him of raw patriotic sentiment. Shenyang was at the center of the sphere of influence that Japan claimed after its victories in the First Sino-Japanese War of 1894 and the Russo-Japanese War of 1904–1905. Zhou visited the sites of battles belonging to

2.1 Zhou Enlai at Dongguan Model School in Shenyang, 1912.
Sovfoto / Universal Images Group via Getty Images

those wars. In an essay he wrote in October 1912, he asked, "Who are we?" "Isn't it true that we will be citizens responsible for the country in the future? Isn't it true that we will be shouldering arduous responsibilities for our country?" His answer was, "We have to study, to question, and to think."[10] A classmate of Zhou's recalled that on one occasion, when a teacher asked what goal they would like to pursue as students, Zhou answered, "For the rise of China!"[11]

· · ·

Zhou Enlai probably would have stayed in Shenyang, living with his uncle and completing his high-school education there, had Zhou Yigeng continued to work there. But another big change came in February 1913. Zhou Yigeng was transferred from Shenyang to Tianjin, where he assumed a new position at the Bureau of Salt Transportation.[12] Zhou followed his uncle to the new city, which would come to represent another landmark in his education and growth.

* * *

Tianjin, a coastal city about seventy-five miles south of Beijing, had been designated an open "treaty port" since the mid-nineteenth century. Foreign concessions, where legislation, jurisdiction, and administrative powers were primarily controlled by foreigners, covered broad swaths of the city. Tianjin was more westernized, commercialized, cosmopolitan, and generally more modern than Shenyang. The city's environment thus opened a whole new world for young Zhou Enlai.

Almost immediately after Zhou moved to Tianjian, he began to prepare to enter the newly established Nankai School there. How could he have failed to do so? Nankai enjoyed a reputation as an unconventional yet excellent institution of education. Yan Xiu (1860–1929), a Qing educational official, founded the school in 1904. A prominent Confucian scholar, he had also long aspired to create an institution of modern Western education. In 1905, he was one of the scholar-officials who petitioned, successfully, for the Qing court to abolish the age-old imperial examination system. After the Qing's downfall, the Republican government repeatedly invited him to take up high official posts. He turned all of them down, as he preferred to concentrate on developing Nankai into a model institution of China's modern education and a vanguard of educational reforms.[13]

Yan and Nankai's board were fortunate to have found Zhang Boling (1876–1951) to serve as Nankai's inaugural principal. Zhang began his career as a naval officer. In 1898, he witnessed the turning over of Weihaiwei, a naval port in Shandong, to the British, who had forced the Qing court to let them "lease" it. The moment he saw the lowering of the Chinese flag at the port, he felt deeply humiliated and decided to leave the navy to dedicate himself to the development of Chinese education. He soon earned the status of a pioneer who enthusiastically favored instilling new knowledge, new ideas, and a new national consciousness into the minds of Chinese students. Nankai thus afforded him a golden opportunity to realize his ideals.[14]

In August 1913, Zhou passed Nankai's entrance examination. He enrolled in the class of 1917, as each Nankai student would graduate after four years of study. He immediately fell in love with this new school, finding Nankai's curriculum design fresh and attractive. The major subjects included Chinese language and literature, English, and mathematics; minor subjects included physics, chemistry, Chinese history and geography, Western history and geography, biology, legal knowledge, and physical education.[15] Beginning in the second year, all courses, except for Chinese literature and Chinese history and geography, used English-language textbooks. In science courses, students could conduct experiments in laboratories that were stocked with equipment imported from Japan.

Zhou's strongest subjects were Chinese and mathematics, and he showed great interest in history. He also diligently applied himself in other courses. At first, he found classes taught in English particularly daunting, and he thus labored greatly to improve his English proficiency. Although English was never his most accomplished subject, this did not impede him from becoming one of Nankai's most outstanding students. Beginning in his second year at Nankai, his tuition and fees were waived by the school.[16]

Nankai encouraged students to participate in extracurricular activities. The school's policy was that every weekday, no student would be allowed to stay in the classroom or the dorm while classes weren't in session, and all students had to participate in sports, student organizations, or other activities.[17] Shortly after entering Nankai, Zhou began to take full advantage of this school policy.

Newspapers had meanwhile become increasingly widespread in China. Zhou, in keeping with the habit he had developed in Manchuria, became a keen newspaper reader. In particular, he showed a robust appetite for news of national and international politics. Like many of his educated contemporaries, he longed sincerely to find ways to save China and strengthen the country. He read the works of Gu Yanwu and Wang Fuzhi, two of China's great thinkers of the transformative times of the Ming and Qing. He also read Chinese translations of works by various important Western authors, including Jean-Jacques Rousseau's *The Social Contract,* Charles-Louis Montesquieu's *The Spirit of the Laws,* Thomas Henry Huxley's *Evolution and Ethics and other Essays,* and Adam Smith's *The Wealth of Nations.* While it is difficult to tell to what extent these works influenced him intellectually, the fact that he had read them indicates that he was open minded about all kinds of ideas and thoughts.[18]

Zhou also actively participated in student organizations. During his second year at Nankai, he and several friends decided to organize the Jingye Lequn Hui, which literally meant "The Society for Cherishing Professionalism and Favoring Collectivism." Its defined goals were "to take intellectual development as the main mission, moral development as the foundation, connect fellow students with affection, so as to supplement what is not taught in the classroom."[19] The society began with about twenty members but gradually blossomed into one of Nankai's largest student organizations, reaching close to three hundred members, almost one-third of Nankai's enrolled students. Zhou charmed his fellow students as he combined a modest and earnest attitude with a good work ethic, capacity and efficiency, and attention to both the big picture and minute details. He was first elected as the society's director of intellectual development, and he would later serve as its vice president and president.[20]

One activity that the society enthusiastically promoted was drama performance, which, buoyed by the encouragement and support of Yan Xiu and Zhang Boling, was very popular among Nankai students. Zhou loved it and soon busied himself with performances. Many of Zhou's fellow students were deeply impressed by his acting as the heroine in the play *Yi Yuan Qian* (One dollar).

Does Zhou's performance of a woman in the play possibly reveal peculiar sexual tendencies? Or was this even an indication that he was gay? No direct evidence from Zhou's career at Nankai, or any other episode of his life, supports such an allegation. Zhou attended Nankai at a time when young students encountered a diversity of new ideas. And the age-old tradition of cursing "ambiguous distinction and relationship between men and women" met serious pushback from young students. Further, the Zhou clan originated in Shaoxing, Zhejiang Province, the birthplace of Yue opera, in which all roles are played by women. All of these provide useful clues as to why Zhou acted as a heroine in *Yi Yuan Qian*.[21]

Many years later, when Zhou had already established himself as a highly sophisticated politician and statesman with global influence, Henry R. Lieberman, a *New York Times* correspondent who had conducted extensive interviews with Zhou in the 1940s and met him again in the 1970s, said that "he was one of the world's greatest actors."[22] Any politician, as a public figure, has to be an actor in some sense. Yet, if Zhou indeed deserved this accolade as "one of the world's greatest actors," his years at Nankai with the society and his performance in stage plays must have enabled him to practice those performing arts that would benefit him tremendously in his political and diplomatic career.

* * *

During Zhou's years at Nankai, China's state and society, as well as its external relations, faced constant threats. The new Republic of China that emerged in the wake of the Qing's downfall proved to be an extremely difficult enterprise to construct. Efforts to erect a parliamentary democracy encountered powerful resistance from political and military leaders such as Yuan Shikai, the republic's president from 1912 to 1916, as well as many large and small warlords who exercised provincial and local political power and controlled financial resources throughout the country. China's society, which had been dominated by the gentry and landlords for millennia, was left largely untouched in the wake of the 1911 Revolution. Many Chinese intellectuals and young students felt an ever-deepening sense of uncertainty about the prospects of China's state and society.

This doubt turned into a sense of profound crisis as China's international experience was brought into the picture. China entered the First World War on the side of the Entente Powers. However, the "unequal treaties" that China had been coerced into accepting during the second half of the nineteenth century remained. Worse, imperialist Japan, capitalizing on the Western powers' preoccupation with the war in Europe, was aggressively pursuing its exclusive spheres of influence in China, thus translating its gains in the First Sino-Japanese War and Russo-Japanese War into political and economic dominance. All this, in turn, nurtured conditions for the rise of modern nationalism, especially among Chinese intellectuals and young students.

Zhou and his fellow students at Nankai were deeply affected by the prevailing sense of China's national crisis and the emergence of Chinese nationalism. During the first two years of his study at Nankai, however, Zhou's everyday life remained largely apolitical. He was engrossed in his coursework and relished all kinds of academic and nonpolitical activities outside the classroom. Occasionally, he discussed how "the nation's affairs" (*guoshi*) would be mismanaged if young students like him failed to innovate reformist ideas and actions.[23] Eventually, he wrote, "We should work for the society, serve the country, and use the knowledge that we have learned to benefit the world."[24] For the moment, though, he was no revolutionary. Also, he almost never, during his first two years at Nankai, linked national affairs or crises to any personal action he might need to take.

A turning point came in 1915, the third year of Zhou's study at Nankai. In January, Japan imposed the notorious "Twenty-One Demands" on China. In addition to claiming Japanese spheres of influence in Manchuria, Shandong, and the Yangzi River Valley, the demands also stipulated that the Chinese political, financial, police, and military administrations employ Japanese advisors.[25] The exposure of these terms inflamed the Chinese public. On May 7, Japan delivered an ultimatum to the Chinese government demanding acceptance of the terms. This ultimatum triggered an outburst of nationalism among young Chinese students; those at Nankai were no exception. Like many of his classmates and teachers, Zhou was alarmed and angered by Japan's attempt to impinge upon China's sovereignty and integrity. Never before had he felt that China and Chinese culture faced such urgent threats.

Wu Guozhen was a close friend of Zhou's at Nankai who later would hold elite positions in the Nationalist government, including mayor of Shanghai and governor of Taiwan. In his memoir, he vividly described how he and other Nankai students felt when they learned that the Beijing Government had been forced to accept the Japanese demands:

> On the fateful days of May 8th and 9th, we forgot about all our classes and talked about nothing but Japan's ultimatum. We passed by each other in depressing silence and a sense of shame, as if we ourselves were the cause of the national humiliation. I remember that, at sunset on May 9, I looked at Zhou Enlai and Li Jingfu, and we said nothing to each other. We wished either the Earth would be destroyed, so that all pain would end, or a miracle would happen, so that the country would be saved from suffering in an unknown way. Our mood was so desperately grave . . . and we so strongly felt that the world was unfair. We would rather go to the extreme, even by collectively committing suicide.[26]

Zhou could no longer just concentrate on his own academic studies. In one essay, which he wrote after learning of the contents of the Twenty-One Demands, he made a passionate appeal to his teachers and classmates, and to his own consciousness:

> Oh, we are living in a time that China is approaching the urgent moment of a life-and-death challenge. Our neighbor in the East, who is of the same race as us, is shamelessly ambitious. When the bad news arrived, the whole country was shocked. Everyone is willing to fight, and this we have taken as our very last resort, as well as our plan facing a situation of no return. My emotion of patriotism has reached the boiling point.[27]

This was not the first time that Zhou, like many of his contemporaries, had worried about the fate of the motherland. However, never before had Zhou felt so strongly and emotionally that the motherland's very survival was at stake, and that it was his and his classmates' responsibility to rescue the Chinese nation. For the first time in his Nankai years, Zhou took politically oriented action. On June 6, 1915, he participated in a mass rally alongside people from all walks of life in Tianjin that called for donations to a "Bond of Saving the Country." As a student of seventeen, he made his very first public political speech at the rally. He asked, "How can the humiliation of today be washed out?" "Only by devoting our red blood," he answered. So everyone should make his contribution, no matter how trivial, to make the country strong and to allow the "fate of the nation to flourish."[28]

· · ·

This was only the beginning of Zhou's involvement in politics as a Nankai student. By then, he was already a well-known figure at school. Subsequently, in the last two years of his study at Nankai, he repeatedly directed people's attention to the severity of China's crisis and to how urgent it was to save the Chinese nation.

In October 1916, he was one of the finalists in a school-wide speech competition. In front of the whole school community, he talked about "China's current crisis." He began the speech by asking the audience, "What an extremely dangerous situation has China sunk into today? Isn't this something

2.2 Zhou Enlai with his teacher and friends at Nankai School, 1916. *Album / Alamy Stock Photo*

that all of us know very well?" He then stated that China faced domestic and international, practical and spiritual crises. He was disappointed by the failed effort to democratize China's political institutions in the wake of the 1911 Revolution; he was alarmed by the rise of warlordism in various parts of China; and he was deeply frustrated by the "collapse of the moral standard of our people." In particular, "external threats" had pushed "our country into a disastrous situation," he noted. "Japan, although not a country with sufficient power, has been pursuing one foot after gaining one inch, and, step by step, has brought our nation into great danger." How should all of this be dealt with? As though he were talking not to the audience, but to himself, he said, "It is every man's responsibility to be concerned about the rise and fall of his country. . . . Let us begin with concentrating on what we must do now."[29]

When Zhou, in his last year at Nankai, ruminated on how to deal with the challenges that China faced, ideas of socialism had begun to penetrate his worldview. Early in 1917, after a short visit to Beijing, he recorded in one essay "how much I have been enraged by how ugly the society and how dark the government are."[30] In May, in one of the last essays he wrote as a Nankai student, he discussed what "genuine republicanism" should be, and he stated that "unless social classes are eliminated, there is no hope for equality to be achieved."[31] This was one of the first times—if not the first time—that Zhou adopted the concept of "social class" in discussing how to deal with challenges facing Chinese society.

If Zhou had always had ideals and aspirations for his life and career, it was in his Nankai years that the rudiments of his worldview—especially his sense of responsibility to serve society and save the nation—took form and hardened. His political tendencies were still quite vague, and he was by no means a radical revolutionary. Yet the foundation of a possible development of revolutionary beliefs had been laid. No wonder Zhou would maintain a profound sense of attachment to Nankai throughout his life.[32]

Zhou Enlai graduated from Nankai in June 1917 with highest academic honors. By then, he firmly believed that it should be his mission to help save China and make the country strong. "Let us hope to meet at the time that China has risen high again in the world."[33] These were the words that he wrote to his friends on the eve of graduation. Indeed, these were also the words that he selected as his—as well as his generation's—motto.

3

JAPAN

1917–1919

One day in September 1917, Zhou Enlai boarded at the port of Tianjin a ship bound for Japan.[1] For months, Zhou had been considering what to do after he graduated from Nankai. He could have stayed in China to attend a good university there, or he could have gone to study in Europe, as many of his fellow students had elected to do. He settled on Japan, largely because he wanted to know why Japan, a country with cultural traditions and an early modern experience similar to China's, could have risen to become a recognized power in East Asia—and the world—in a few short decades. Further, the Chinese and Japanese governments had signed an agreement that stipulated that the Chinese government would cover both tuition and living expenses of a Chinese student who was admitted to a recognized Japanese university.[2] Zhou was not from a rich family, so it was essential that he receive such support to study in a foreign country.

Before he boarded the ship for Japan, Zhou wrote a poem, which he later shared with several of his friends:

> Singing the song of the Great River, I sail the East,
> Delving in all schools vainly for ideas to save the world;
> Facing a wall for ten years for awakening in consciousness,
> Daring to tread the sea, or die an avowed hero.[3]

This poem is widely regarded as one of the most important that Zhou ever wrote. It was more than a poem; it was a young man's declaration of his determination to embrace the world around him in ways that would imbue his life with enduring meaning and worth. Zhou spelled out in the poem's lines his aspirations and hopes, while taking his first step beyond Nankai and China.

* * *

Despite Zhou's rosy outlook on his prospects in Japan, his experience there was plagued from the outset by hardship and stagnation. In fact, his time in Japan was marked by some of the most difficult and depressing episodes of his life.

The first challenge Zhou faced was to improve his Japanese language proficiency. This was a new experience for him, as courses at Nankai were taught either in Chinese or English, and he knew virtually no Japanese. After he arrived and, with the help of several Nankai alumni, settled in Tokyo, Zhou began intensive language study almost immediately. In October, he enrolled in a college preparatory program, Toa (East Asia) School, in the Kanda district, not far from his cramped rented room on the second floor of a furniture store.[4]

Zhou's goal was to enter Tokyo Higher Normal School or Tokyo First Higher School, which were leading institutions of higher education in Japan. To realize this goal, he needed first to pass either school's entrance exam. A modest sum of funds raised by several of his relatives, teachers, and close friends at Nankai subsidized Zhou's study in Japan.[5] He knew very well that his family, including Zhou Yigeng, the uncle who had supported him for the last seven years, could not possibly cover his expenses abroad. Only by formally enrolling in a Japanese public university could he qualify for the Chinese government scholarship. This was for him more than a question of his academic success; this was a question of whether he could survive in Japan.

However, the challenge that Zhou met was much more difficult than he expected. Although he toiled over his studies during his first months in Japan, his progress was slow and insignificant. He grew increasingly anxious with each passing day. "I must always remember the sacrifice that my family has made for me, and must study diligently every hour and every minute," he wrote on January 11, 1918. "If indeed I can succeed in obtaining the government scholarship, I will feel greatly relieved then, and I will move forward one step after another, so maybe I will one day be able to repay my family."[6]

Yet diligence and optimism alone proved fruitless in Zhou's endeavor to improve his Japanese, especially as it gradually became clear that he had no gift for language learning, despite the many days and nights that he had spent studying Japanese.

"By now I have been here for over four months, but I have made almost no progress in learning Japanese," he lamented on January 29. "The examination for the Higher Normal School is quickly approaching. If I do not push myself to study even harder, not only will I have no hope for this examination but also will there be little hope for the next one (for the First Higher School)."[7]

What followed was the intrusion of a grave strain of frustration, or even depression, into Zhou's mind. He felt as though life was hopeless and ultimately meaningless. By that time, Zhou confessed in his diary, he had embraced a Buddhist-style nihilism (*Wusheng zhuyi*). "The sea of bitterness has no bounds, to reach the shore one must turn around," he wrote. "It would be better for me to abandon everything, and to adopt the path of 'doing nothing.' At least my life will be made easier."[8]

Never before during Zhou's time in Japan had he felt so lonely. He had been in contact ever since he arrived in the country with other Nankai graduates who had come to study in Japan, and he had enjoyed all kinds of help from them. Now, in early 1918, he began to spend more time with the "Nankai circle" in Tokyo.[9] This helped to mitigate his anxiety but simultaneously heightened his sense of guilt—he was fully aware that his priority should be to spend time studying Japanese and preparing for the exam, not getting together with his Nankai friends. But he simply could not bear to lock himself in a room to study a language that, by then, he neither enjoyed learning nor seemed capable of quickly mastering.

• • •

A change came in the first half of February. Zhou deviated from his study of Japanese and indulged in readings unrelated to his exam preparation. Fortuitously, he picked a copy of the journal *Xin Qingnian* (The new youth) that he had obtained from Yan Zhikai (son of Yan Xiu, Nankai's founder) and began to read it. He was hooked. *Xin Qingnian,* an influential intellectual and political forum for new ideas and new ways of thinking in China, advocated that liberty replace servility, progressivism replace conservatism, cosmopolitanism replace "closed-doorism," practicality replace fantasy, science replace imagination, and the tactic of retreating and hiding give way to advancing.[10] The journal's editor was Chen Duxiu, a Peking University professor who later became one of the founders and the principal leader of the Chinese Communist Party (CCP). Zhou had known of the journal since his Nankai days, and he had even bought and read several issues. However, as he was then "too busy with other things at school," he did not "pay much attention to [*Xin Qingnian*]."[11]

But this time it was different. When Zhou began to read *Xin Qingnian* anew, he grew quickly engrossed in the ideas and viewpoints it introduced. In particular, he found himself "in complete agreement with anti-Confucianism, celibacy, and revolutionary literary critique" as presented in the journal.[12] His sentiments had changed.

Since Zhou's time at Nankai, he had developed a very strong belief in celibacy, which was known by almost all of his close friends. Not surprisingly, *Xin Qingnian*'s vigorous advocacy of celibacy immediately caught his eyes, triggering his thinking on the relationship between "marriage" and "love." In his diary entry of February 9, he wrote, "There exists no difference between male and female in a free love; in life, it is not necessary to get married." He called marriage "indeed the thing that is most painful," and he elaborated that "love grows out of affection" between any two; "regardless of male or female, or between anything, when one expresses one's affection and the other can feel what is love. Therefore, even horses and dogs may respond to each other's affection." Obviously in order to defend his embrace of celibacy, Zhou further declared that "the union of husband and wife is purely for organizing a family to carry on one's ancestral lines. Only a pair of husband and wife that is the result of love is a genuine marriage."[13] Similar discussions appeared in several of his diary entries in the next months. These were a young man's attempt to thoroughly explore the essence of "marriage" and "love." In particular, if we put these expressions into the context that Zhou had been a believer in and practitioner of celibacy since his Nankai years, we clearly see how hard he was trying to justify the choice of not marrying.[14]

In a broader perspective, Zhou's untraditional discussion of "love" and "marriage" and the relationship between them was an integral part of his deep and comprehensive thinking about meanings of and attitudes toward life. This was an intellectual process that Zhou called "grand awakening," characterized by one word, "new"—and its scope far surpassed that of marriage and love. "Since the beginning of this month, I have felt that my mind has become more eased," wrote Zhou in his diary. "In the past several days, I have carefully read three volumes of *Xin Qingnian*. I now realize that what I had in mind back at home was all greatly mistaken. . . . Instead, I should pursue 'new thinking,' seek 'new knowledge,' and do 'new things.'" He felt "as if I had experienced a 'rebirth' or 'new birth.'"[15]

All this helped change Zhou's mood and his outlook on life. On Chinese New Year's Day, February 11, 1918, he set for himself three new goals: "First, when I think, I should think in the newest way, even newer than that which is cutting-edge; second, when I do things, I should do the newest things; and, third, when I study, I should study the newest knowledge."[16] On February 15, he achieved a state he described as "reawakening." He recorded his thoughts and feelings in response to his *Xin Qingnian* reading, and he also described how silly and immature he had been to succumb to nihilism, and how delightful and "much more relaxed" he felt to envision a life that would "follow a progressive path" and "do things that are closest to the newest ideas of great commonwealth." He ended this day's long diary entry with the following lines:

> Windy and rainy time is coming to an end,
> The red sun is already rising in the East.[17]

Zhou's excitement was profound. Two days later, on February 17, he was still basking in the joy that flowed from his sense of self-awakening: "Since the awakening the day before yesterday," he wrote, "I have felt so happy from the bottom of my heart. My behavior of the past has died like the passing of yesterday."[18] He compared his transcendent experience to the "new birth" and "rebirth" one experiences when he or she converts to a religion. "What I have thought, studied, and done in the past are of no use and no value at all," he reflected, "and I hope that my thought, learning and action will move forward along a progressive path."[19]

Zhou's "self-awakening" prompted a shift in his perspective toward Japan. He now regarded the country of Japan in general and Japanese militarism in particular in a critical light. When Zhou arrived in Japan, he had hoped to find in Japan an ideal model through which to learn ways to rescue and modernize China. Despite his strong opposition to Japan's imperialist ambition and activities in China during the last two years of his time at Nankai, Zhou remained deeply impressed by the effectiveness of Japan's modernization drive. He also thought that a "powerful militarist state" and "benign and effective elite politics" were the main factors that contributed to Japan's success, from which China might learn.[20]

In Japan, Zhou had witnessed such widespread social inequality that he began to reconsider whether China should follow the same path as Japan toward modernity. In the course of his "self-awakening," Zhou further reflected on militarism and elite politics in Japan. On February 20, he wrote in his diary:

> Japan is a country which follows militarism, the principal requisite of which is the belief in "power without justice." . . . Militarism also takes territorial expansion as a matter of utmost importance. . . . After the end of the war in Europe, it seems that militarism in Germany is not to continue, but how about militarism in Japan? In my opinion, militarism in the 20th century absolutely should not continuously be in existence. In the past, I had thought that it was militarism and elitism that might save China. Now I have realized that this is completely wrong![21]

With this revelation, Zhou considered whether study at a Japanese university was actually the most desirable way to obtain a deep understanding of Japan, develop a blueprint for China's own path toward modernity, and, in a broader sense, explore the meaning of life. He would not give up his study of the Japanese language and preparation for university entrance exams. At the heart of his decision lay a practical reason: he still needed to justify why he should stay in Japan and continue to receive financial support from his friends and family. In the meantime, he was no longer wholeheartedly committed to entering a university. "Knowledge can be pursued everywhere," wrote Zhou. "Why should one, then, treat studying textbooks all the time as the only way to acquire knowledge? . . . We should pay attention to every initiative and every move of the Japanese, as well as their ways of dealing with things. . . . We should know and understand Japan's national conditions."[22]

In early March 1918, Zhou finally sat for Tokyo Normal Higher School's entrance exam. Unsurprisingly, he failed. Despite the time and effort he had dedicated to his study of Japanese, his poor grasp of the language barred him from higher education in Japan. Although he was not unprepared for such a failure, it still was a rare embarrassing moment in his life. He was deeply disappointed. "After failing the examination for the Normal Higher School," he wrote, "I am in great anxiety. I know if I do not prepare well for the examination of the First Higher School in July, absolutely I will have no hope to succeed."[23] He formulated a new "study plan": each day he would spend thirteen and a half hours studying for the exam, allowing himself only three and a half hours for breaks and "doing other things" and around six hours to sleep.[24]

However, Zhou's serious implementation of his new regimen did not last long. Politics again intruded into his daily life. The international situation in East Asia was shifting in the wake of the Russian Bolshevik Revolution, especially after Bolshevik Russia unilaterally signed the Treaty of Brest-Litovsk with Germany in March 1918 and withdrew from the Great War. Japan then urged the Chinese government to secretly negotiate the signing of a joint Chinese-Japanese defense agreement that ostensibly targeted Communist Russia.

By early April, news of the secret negotiations had been leaked and reported in the media. Many Chinese students in Japan were alarmed by the development, viewing this as just another indication of Japan's imperialist ambition—already exposed in the Twenty-One Demands that Japan had tried to impose upon China a few years before—of striving for new privileges in China.

Zhou was also shocked. He wrote in his diary, "Reading English newspapers, I have learned that the Japanese government has put forward twenty requests to China. . . . And the attitude of our government has been dubious."[25] Like many of his fellow Chinese students in Japan, Zhou now found it impossible to maintain the daily routine that he had just begun and continue his full-time preparation for the university exam. He also found it impossible not to participate in the students' activities for "saving China."

In early May, more reports came out indicating that the signing of the Chinese-Japanese agreement was imminent. Zhou's anxiety and anger spiked. "I spent much time reading the newspaper," he wrote on May 2, "the situation facing our country is deteriorating continuously."[26] At the moment, the Chinese students attending the First Higher School (where Zhou was then eager to study) decided to quit their studies in Japan and return to China.[27] Zhou did not join these students, probably because he still wanted to prove his ability to himself as well as others by taking and passing the university entrance examination. Nonetheless, he was actively involved in the protests. Throughout May, his diaries kept a detailed account of new developments in Chinese-Japanese relations. On May 10, he wrote, "The Chinese-Japanese treaty was like a loud thunder, when we have lost our country, what is the meaning of living a slave's life?"[28]

The Chinese government, ignoring the protests of students and people of different backgrounds in many Chinese cities, signed with Japan the Sino-Japanese Military Agreement for Common Defense on May 16. Zhou and his fellow Chinese students in Japan were enraged. On May 19, Zhou joined the New China Study Society, a patriotic organization of Chinese students in Japan, many of whom were Nankai graduates. That day, Zhou made a speech:

> The reason why China has been so weak is because we can neither preserve tradition nor carry out reform. . . . I have just joined this society. When I see the word 'new' in its name, I feel so overjoyed and encouraged. I hope that all of our comrades should always remember this word 'new,' and China will then be hopeful.[29]

At the time, Zhou should have devoted all of his energy and effort to prepare for Tokyo First Higher School's examination. But, throughout May, he did almost nothing else but protest against Japan's act of aggression against China.

In early June, Zhou decided once more to pick up the study plan that he had devised in March and return to intensive examination preparation. It was the last time he did so in Japan. We do not know to what extent he actually carried out the plan. However, we do know that in early July, he failed the Tokyo First Higher School entrance exam.

Although the failure did not surprise Zhou, it must have come to him as another big blow. In his diary entry on July 4, he wrote, "I failed again in exams yesterday and the day before yesterday. I am so deeply disappointed."[30] Despite his reputation as one of Nankai's finest graduates, he was unable to pass the examination, while many other Nankai alumni studying in Japan did, which embarrassed Zhou. He even wrote, "If I could not pass the exam for entering a public university, this would be a shame of my whole life."[31]

But might this event have also compelled him further to reconsider whether studying at a university was the best and most suitable path of life for him, especially after he contemplated the problems he faced? In turn, could all of this have stimulated his desire to devote himself to political activities?

Zhou needed a break. From the end of July to early September, he took a six-week vacation trip back to China, during which he visited family members, including his father. On August 7, he visited Nankai. Other than this, we do not know much about what he did in China. But there is reason to believe that he also made the visit to get some sense about whether he should end his stay in Japan and return to China.

Zhou was back in Japan on September 4. He did not make a serious effort to compete in another university entrance examination until he returned to China the next spring.

* * *

While Zhou was away from Japan, the "rice riots" erupted and swept across vast swaths of the country. Workers and peasants throughout Japan, including many women, protested against sharply rising rice prices and high inflation sometimes violently. Dismally low incomes and low social status, as well as what protesters saw as the government's protection and support of the exploitative rice merchants, enraged the workers and peasants. By then, Zhou already strongly disapproved of the oppressive and exploitative features of Japan's state and society. The rice riots further drove him to pay attention to such radical, transformative theories as socialism.

The Russian Bolshevik Revolution happened in November 1917, shortly after Zhou came to Japan. A keen newspaper reader, he was aware of the developments in Russia and had noticed the activities of the "Reds" there. "The aims of these radicals (in Russia) are very attractive to the workers and peasants," he wrote on April 23, 1918, "and their strength thus has increased day by day, breaking up the system of capitalism and the restrictions of religion. Countries adopting socialism in the world probably will treat Russia as the first test ground."[32] However, as his mind was then preoccupied with the more urgent issues of Japan's imperialist behavior in China, he did not pay much attention to the Bolsheviks, let alone think about how Russia's development might be of any relevance to China's future transformation. When he became increasingly disillusioned with Japan as a possible model of modernity for China, Zhou again turned his attention to the Russian Bolshevik Revolution. In the meantime, he eagerly learned about various new schools of thought, including socialism.

Thus, in late 1918, Zhou read John Reed's *Ten Days that Shook the World,* an eyewitness account that offered him a clearer understanding of what occurred in Russia after Lenin and the Bolsheviks took over political power there. He also read the Japanese Marxist economist Kawakami Hajime's *Tale of Poverty* and Kotoku Shusui's *The Essence of Socialism.* After the inaugural publication of the journal *Study of Social Issues,* edited and published by Kawakami, in January 1919, Zhou immediately became a reader of it. In a diary entry, Zhou wrote, "At the age of twenty I begin to learn what the truth is; although late, this is not too late for me."[33] He did not spell out that "the truth" referred to the ideas of socialism. However, given his critical perspectives on Japan's capitalist society and imperialist foreign policy, it is probable that his encounters with socialism in Japan had at least opened for him a path of intellectual and political development toward socialism or even Communism. In particular, he might have already felt, if only vaguely, that socialism could offer the right solutions to China's problems.

During this period, Zhou made little effort to prepare to enter a Japanese university or even study Japanese. Finally, in March 1918, when he learned that a new Nankai University, as an outgrowth of the Nankai School, would open the coming fall, he decided instantly to return to China. This was, in Zhou's mind, an excellent reason to leave Japan. At the time of his departure, he seemed to be in high spirits. He visited the mountain Arashiyama while passing through Kyoto, writing several poems during his visit. One of them was "Arashiyama in the Rain":

> In rain, coming to Arashiyama again,
> Blue pines on sides, cherry trees in between.
> A peak rises at the road's end,
> A spring winds around rocks,
> Glittering, and flows in jade green.
> Drizzle rustling, mist thickening,
> A beam of sunlight breaks through the clouds.
> How more beautiful it is to be seen!
>
> In search of truths in life,
> As if the more the effort, the more hazy one feels.
> All a sudden a beam of light breaks through the haze,
> How exquisitely enchanting it is![34]

3.1 Zhou Enlai and his Nankai friends in Kyoto, Japan, April 6, 1919.
Album / Alamy Stock Photo

How should we decipher the meaning of this poem—and, for that matter, that of numerous other poems similar to this one that Zhou wrote almost at the same time? Zhou's delight was quite visible in the words and lines. Many scholars, especially those in China, have identified the "beam of light" in Zhou's poem as an implicit reference to ideas of socialism and Marxism. While this is not implausible, Zhou's joyfulness probably should not be attributed exclusively to his being enlightened by these new ideas. In fact, as will be further discussed in Chapters 4 and 5, as late as 1919, when Zhou arrived in Europe, he still claimed that he had not committed to any "ism" and would continuously compare "different schools of thoughts and ideas."[35] So, might not the poem have also reflected Zhou's joy and relief at being able to finally, gracefully, leave Japan and return to China?

A few days later, Zhou ended his "study life" of eighteen months in Japan, boarded a ship in the port of Kobe, and headed back to China. As far as Zhou's original goal of studying at a Japanese university was concerned, his experience in Japan was a failure. However, if Zhou had succeeded in entering and studying at a Japanese university, might he have taken an entirely different approach to "saving China and making China strong" through academic activities? Had that been the case, he would not have returned to China, positioned himself at the center of China's gathering political storms, and risen from them as a highly influential political figure. At the very least, the Zhou Enlai we know today would probably have never existed.

4

MAY FOURTH ACTIVIST

1919–1920

Zhou Enlai arrived in Tianjin in late April 1919 with the plan to spend another several years at Nankai—this time as a student at the newly established Nankai University. But his plan would soon be shelved. He could not have expected that the May Fourth Movement, a landmark event in modern Chinese history, would erupt a few days later; or that he would find himself, wholly unprepared, near the center of this huge political storm and come to actively participate in it. His political perspectives, in turn, would transform toward an embrace of revolutionary nationalism and some version of socialism, which further opened the door to his later conversion to Communism. Zhou eventually decided to travel to Europe, where he would finally declare himself a Communist and busy himself with creating the European branch of the Chinese Communist Party (CCP). Zhou's May Fourth activities served as a critical starting point for these developments.

• • •

When Zhou set foot on Chinese soil after his return from Japan, the country was gripped by a tense political atmosphere, especially among intellectuals and students. In France, the Versailles Peace Conference had been underway since mid-January 1919. Many informed Chinese, like Zhou, felt optimistic that the conference might deliver for China certain benefits; in particular, they expected that the Western Powers—and the United States in particular—would help China reclaim the rights, interests, and privileges it had lost in modern times. After all, wasn't China also an Entente country, one of the victors of the Great War? Many, including Zhou, paid attention to the Fourteen Points that US president Woodrow Wilson had introduced at the opening of the conference. They found especially inspiring Wilson's notions of national self-determination and democracy, as well as the guarantees enumerated in his statement of the independence and territorial integrity of weaker countries. Chen Duxiu, a Peking University professor who later became a founder of the CCP, even hailed Wilson as "the number one 'good man' under heaven."[1] For young people like Zhou, Versailles could have meant the dawn of a new age in international relations, one in which China would gain a more equal position in the international community.

This outburst of a new consciousness of nationalism occurred amid an intellectual and cultural upheaval, known as the New Culture Movement, that prevailed in China throughout much of the 1910s, as many radical Chinese intellectuals leveled sharp, even iconoclastic, criticism against the deficiencies of China's "old culture."[2] (*Xin Qingnian,* the journal that triggered Zhou's intellectual rebirth in Japan, was a main forum of the movement.) Radical Chinese intellectuals' sense of humiliation and anger, stemming from Japan's imperialist bullying of China during the Great War, constantly informed and fueled their criticism. In their view, the Versailles Conference should help China guard against Japan's aggressive and expansionist ambition in China, and they were very hopeful that this would be the case.[3]

As the developments at Versailles unfolded, however, many Chinese intellectuals, and young students in particular, grew increasingly worried. The Chinese delegation to the conference raised such questions as abolishing foreign spheres of influence in China, repatriating foreign troops and police, regulating foreign postal and telegraphic services, eliminating foreign extraterritoriality rights, returning foreign settlements to China, and allowing the Chinese government to set customs tariffs.[4] Yet at the conference, only the Shandong question, which concerned whether Japan would take over former German "rights and privileges" in Shandong, on China's eastern coast, was formally included on the agenda.

Shandong, the birthplace of the great Chinese sage Confucius, had long been regarded as the holy land of Chinese civilization. In the late 1890s, Germany brought the Shandong Peninsula into its sphere of influence. In 1915, during the Great War, Japan put forward the Twenty-One Demands, and in 1918, Tokyo forced the Chinese government to sign a common defense agreement (which, as described in Chapter 3, enraged Zhou and many other Chinese students in Japan). Shandong became a hot spot in Japan's ambitious plan to establish dominance over China. At Versailles, the Chinese delegates pleaded repeatedly with their Japanese counterparts to fully restore China's sovereignty in Shandong, but Japan refused to make any concessions. Japan's position was further enhanced when it was revealed that Britain, France, and Italy had secretly endorsed "Japan's claim in regard to the disposal of Germany's rights in Shandong."[5] President Wilson originally showed sympathy for the Chinese request. However, after Japan threatened to withdraw from the conference, an act that would jeopardize Wilson's plan to establish the League of Nations, he yielded to Japan's pressure. On April 30, Washington joined London and Paris to accept Tokyo's terms for taking over German "rights" in Shandong.[6]

When the news of China's failure to reclaim full sovereignty in Shandong reached Beijing, a profound sense of national humiliation emerged among the population, combined with an increasingly radical sentiment of nationalism. On May 4, more than three thousand students took to the streets of Beijing to hold a large-scale protest. The demonstrators set fire to the house of Cao Rulin, China's minister of foreign affairs and transportation, who was widely blamed for selling out China's interests to Japan. The wave of protests spread rapidly to cities around the country.

• • •

The public protests in Beijing erupted only days after Zhou's return to Tianjin. He paid close attention to the protests' development from the very moment he first heard about them, and he also tried to actively participate in related activities. As a Nankai alumnus, he came to the Nankai campus almost every day after May 4.[7]

At the moment, for the first time in his life, Zhou found himself in disagreement with Nankai's principal, Zhang Boling, Zhou's longtime patron and admirer. Once the student protesters had burned down his residence in Beijing, Cao Rulin fled to Tianjin, where he hid in another of his houses in the foreign concessions there. Eager to improve his public image, Cao had earlier offered to make a substantial monetary donation to Nankai. Zhang was willing to accept the donation, and he also planned to make Cao a member of Nankai's board of trustees. Nankai's students, including Zhou, strongly opposed this arrangement once news of it leaked after the May Fourth demonstrations in Beijing. In a letter to Nankai alumni in Japan, Zhou sharply criticized Zhang: "About Nankai . . . if the situation is examined from all angles, I must frankly say that it looks very dangerous. The principal may have had his own reasons, but I cannot understand what has been in his mind." Zhou linked his disappointment in Principal Zhang to several larger issues concerning the trajectory that Nankai, as a school and a university-to-be, might choose. Nankai, Zhou thought, needed "to pursue new things" rather than "maintain a close relationship with the (Chinese) traitors and assist them in robbing the money of the government and the people, which is most shameful." He also commented that Principal Zhang "has been managing the cause of education by applying Chinese-style political methods. . . . He talks about democracy every day, but has done things in arbitrary ways, leading to people's loss of confidence in him." Zhou believed that "the only hope of creating the 'new' (at Nankai) lies in us, the students."[8]

Guided by the belief that it was up to the students to take action to save Nankai and, more broadly, to save China, Zhou was ready to engage in student activities in Tianjin. On May 14, college and high school students in Tianjin established a Tianjin Higher School and College Students Union. Ma Jun, a close friend of Zhou's at Nankai, was named the union's vice president. As Zhou had not enrolled in Nankai as a student, he was ineligible to become a formal member of the union; however, he still attempted to join its activities. On May 17, he attended a gathering of a group of Nankai alumni and members of the Jingye Society to discuss political issues.[9]

At the same time that the Tianjin Students Union was established, a group of radical female students also formed a Tianjin Association of Patriotic Female Comrades. Among its founding members was Deng Yingchao, a girl of fifteen. She was born into a Qing prefectural-level official's family in Guangxi Province. After the death of her father, Deng moved with her mother, a medical doctor and schoolteacher, to Tianjin. When the May Fourth Movement erupted, Deng was a student at Zhili First Women's Normal School. She partook enthusiastically in political and patriotic activities, being named to the association's executive committee and becoming head of its speech team.

Yingchao did not know Enlai at the time. But they would eventually meet and, several years later, the two would marry.[10]

• • •

As Zhou was not an enrolled student at Nankai University, he had not formally participated in the activities of the Tianjin Students Union; however, a change came in late June, when the union decided to publish a daily paper of its own, *Tianjin Student Union Bulletin.* Two of the union's leaders—Zhen Zhiduo and Ma Jun—still remembered Zhou's reputation as a fine essayist and an acclaimed editor of Nankai's student journals, *Jingye* (Dedication) and *Xiaofeng* (School spirit), and thus invited Zhou to serve as the *Bulletin*'s editor. Zhou accepted the offer, promising that he would ensure that the *Bulletin*'s publication would help "the persistent development of the students' patriotic movement."[11] Almost immediately he began to prepare for the newspaper's inauguration.

On July 12, Zhou published an essay, in which he highlighted the goals he believed the *Bulletin* should pursue: "We should make the spirit of 'Gexin' (革心, to pursue transformation of hearts and minds) and 'Gexin' (革新, to achieve reformation of society) the main purpose of this daily newspaper" so as to "explore the meanings of everyone's new life."[12] Nine days later, the inaugural issue of the *Bulletin* was launched. In its first issue, the paper's mission was indeed defined as to "achieve reformation of society" and to "pursue transformation of hearts and minds."[13]

Why were these two aims introduced? What was the relationship between them? Both goals were quite popular among young students and intellectuals at the time. Here, the logic was that achieving the transformation of society and the nation was next to impossible unless culture and minds were successfully transformed simultaneously. In retrospect, this was where Zhou and his later comrades embarked on the conceptual path toward their eventual embrace of such radical ideas as socialism and Communism.

Under Zhou's editorship, the *Bulletin* quickly emerged as an influential political forum in Tianjin and across the nation. The paper's circulation soon ballooned from just five thousand copies printed per day at the outset of its publication to over twenty thousand copies per day. This was no small feat.

Zhou, as the paper's editor, paid close attention to national and international political issues, focusing continuously on the Shandong question.

In July 1919, around the time of the *Bulletin*'s inauguration, Japanese troops stationed in Ji'nan and Qingdao, two cities in Shandong Province, reportedly beat and arrested several local Chinese. In early August, a crowd of demonstrators gathered in Ji'nan in front of the provincial government to protest the violence by Japanese soldiers. Ma Liang, the commander of the provincial military headquarters, ordered his soldiers to open fire on the protesters. Three were killed.[14] When the news of the bloody suppression reached Tianjin, Zhou and his comrades were incensed. "My fellow citizens, my fellow citizens! The force of darkness is sweeping forward like a tidal wave. . . . We must take action," Zhou wrote in an essay published on August 6 in the *Bulletin.* "It is time for all of us, the citizens, to be wakened in the consciousness of ourselves."[15]

On August 23, the Tianjin Students Union dispatched a delegation of ten to Beijing, who joined student representatives from various schools in Beijing and other parts of China to protest against the brutality in Shandong and demand the punishment of Ma Liang and others responsible for the bloodshed. The government, however, arrested the representatives. The *Bulletin* immediately published a special issue about the incident in Beijing. Three days later, a demonstration led by over two thousand students took place in Beijing; Zhou's friend Ma Jun acted as the protest's general commander. After a standoff that lasted for three days, the government sent armed soldiers and policemen to disperse the students, and Ma Jun and several others were arrested. Zhou joined several hundred Tianjin students who rushed to Beijing and held sit-in protests in front of the Presidential Office. On August 30, all students who had been arrested were released.[16]

. . .

On September 2, Zhou and six friends held an informal meeting on their train ride back from Beijing to Tianjin. A female student, Zhang Ruoming, opined that male and female students should break down the "feudal fence" between them and jointly take part in political activities. Zhou echoed Zhang's suggestion, proposing the establishment of a new and more tightly structured organization, one that would include activists from both the Tianjin Students Union and the Tianjin Female Students Association. Other attendees of the meeting enthusiastically supported the idea.[17]

Two weeks after Zhou and his friends returned to Tianjin, on September 16, the "Awakening Society" (Juewu She) formally came into being. Zhou was elected the society's coordinator, and he was also responsible for editing its journal, *Juewu* (Awakening). Again, as he had done for the *Bulletin,* Zhou persuaded his comrades in the society to accept "reformation of society" and "transformation of hearts and minds" as the group's primary goal. In the manifesto he drafted for the society, Zhou wrote:

> In accordance with the spirit of "transforming hearts and minds" and "reforming society," we are striving to achieve the self-consciousness and self-determination of every one of us.

As far as the goals of the society's political activities were concerned, Zhou announced that it would strive to eliminate "militarism, the capitalist class, party lords, bureaucrats, inequality between genders, obstinate ideas, obsolete morals, and old ethics."[18]

In a sense, the Awakening Society was a Chinese-style fraternity. Among the original twenty charter members, ten were male and ten were female. To demonstrate solidarity and gender equality, members regarded one another as brothers and sisters. They did not call each other by names. Instead, everyone was given a number from one to fifty through a random drawing. Zhou Enlai was number five, which in Chinese was "Wu Hao." This would become one of the pseudonyms that Zhou used on many other occasions, including his time performing underground Communist Party duties, in the years to come.

Number one, or "Yi Hao," was a girl of fifteen years of age: Deng Yingchao. This was the beginning of an increasingly intimate relationship between her and Zhou. From the time of their involvement in the Awakening Society, both Wu Hao and Yi Hao left a deep impression on one another. They would regard each other as closest comrades-in-arms for the rest of their lives.

By then, Zhou had been admitted into Nankai University as a liberal arts student. He was already an enthusiastic political activist, and it was very difficult for him to devote his attention solely to academic studies. Shortly after he enrolled at Nankai, Tianjin police authorities ordered that the *Bulletin* be discontinued, charging that its reports had been "detrimental to public safety and social order."[19] As the paper's editor, Zhou, along with his classmates who also worked for the paper, decided to disobey the order. The authorities suspended the paper's publication on September 22, but, thanks to Zhou's persistent efforts, the *Bulletin* resumed publishing on October 7. The paper's coverage focused consistently on important political issues, particularly the Shandong problem, and Zhou penned essays that reflected his firsthand experience as a political activist.

On October 1, student representatives from Tianjin, together with their counterparts from Shanghai, Shandong, and four other provinces, traveled to Beijing to submit a petition to the Presidential Office. Zhou served as the representatives' liaison. They demanded that the government adopt a more resolute stance on the Shandong question and punish the "traitor" Ma Liang. All the representatives were arrested and imprisoned for a week.[20] The students were incensed. To protest the government's behavior, students throughout China organized coordinated demonstrations on October 10. In Tianjin, it was reported that as many as forty to fifty thousand students and citizens held a mass rally on Nankai's campus. Zhou participated in the rally and also served as a student representative to meet with Tianjin's police chief.[21]

On November 16, guards and residents at the Japanese Consulate in Fuzhou, the capital city of Fujian Province, wounded several Chinese students who were participating in a rally to boycott Japanese goods. A Chinese policeman was also killed in the fray. Reports about the "Fuzhou Incident" immediately ignited widespread rage across China. On December 20, over one hundred thousand students and citizens of various backgrounds gathered at Nankai's campus to decry the "bandit-style behavior of the Japanese imperialists."[22] After the rally, students organized pickets to ensure that all Japanese goods had been taken off store shelves in Tianjin.

In early January, the governor of Zhili Province (of which Tianjin was officially a part at that time) ordered that all schools begin their winter break immediately and that all students return home. Zhang Boling, the then president of Nankai University, supported the decision and closed Nankai's campus. Zhou and a few of his closest comrades called an emergency meeting of the Awakening Society. Despite their general respect for Zhang, they decided to oppose and challenge his directive.[23]

On January 23, 1920, when a group of student inspectors discovered some Japanese goods at a Chinese shop in Tianjin, the owner called in three "Japanese hooligans" who, it was alleged, savagely beat the students. Zhou and his fellow members of the board of the Students Union decided not only to continue the anti–Japanese imperialism protest but to expand it. A few days later, when the students gathered in front of the city hall to hold a mass rally, the city authorities summoned the police to disperse the students. The students resisted, and twenty of them were arrested.[24]

Six days later, with Zhou as the general commander, around five to six thousand students again demonstrated in front of the Zhili Provincial Government. They condemned the government's "surrenderist attitudes toward Japanese outrages" in China and demanded that the provincial authorities entreat the government in Beijing to devise a "reasonable solution" for the Fuzhou tragedy. Zhou and three other students were elected as representatives. Though police barricaded the building's entrance, the students entered it nonetheless to demand a meeting with the governor. They were all arrested.[25] Subsequently, Zhou was officially expelled from Nankai University.[26]

* * *

Zhou was imprisoned for the first and only time in his life. For a future revolutionary such as him, no environment would better serve as a school than a prison. He and his fellow students were initially held at the Detention Center of the Tianjin Police Bureau; after a week, they were moved to the Detention Center of the Tianjin Local Procuratorate. Since both locations were prisons, Zhou's movement was restricted. However, except for the first several days of their imprisonment, the students found the two prisons rather hospitable, especially by Chinese standards. Upon successfully petitioning and debating with the authorities at the second prison, the students were not only given access to newspapers, journals, and books, but were also allowed to stay in the same cell.

Consequently, the six months that Zhou was imprisoned became a prolonged "study session." He read widely, touching upon many different schools of thoughts and ideas, and he and his fellow inmates organized a series of discussion sessions on "various social issues" to get familiar with "all kinds of new thoughts."[27] They shared their opinions on their reading and, later, even organized discussion sessions and seminars on the books that they had read. They were all young, and they were enraged at their treatment at the hands of the authorities. They held the profound conviction that, politically and morally, they were correct and the authorities were wrong. They thus were readily swayed by radical sentiments and ideas during their time in prison. As one of Zhou's inmates recalled, a main theme and, indeed, the conclusion of several of their study sessions was that it should be their mission in the future "to emphasize and pursue a fundamental transformation of society."[28] Within this context, Zhou hosted several discussions and gave presentations on the subjects on which he "had been regarded as a kind of expert." He elected to give several lectures on Marx and Marxism. Specifically, he discussed the history of class struggle, Marx's theory of surplus value of labor, and the theory of historical materialism.[29] While all of this did not necessarily mean that Zhou already was a Marxist or a communist, it demonstrates his increasing willingness to study or even embrace Marxist ideas.

Zhou and his comrades received continuous support during their time in prison from the media and students at Nankai and other schools. The cases against Zhou and the students quickly became an embarrassment to the authorities, who were eager to dismiss the charges in a face-saving way. Beginning on July 6, the students' trial began in a packed room at the Tianjin Local Court. The judges knew that public opinion overwhelmingly supported the defendants. Moreover, the Tianjin Students Union had also planned to hold "unprecedented massive protests" if Zhou and his fellow students were punished harshly. On July 16, the judges issued their verdicts. Zhou was convicted of "conduct of harassment"; he and ten other male inmates were given two months' imprisonment. Two female students were only fined sixty yuan with no prison term imposed. As the students had already served longer time than required by their sentences, they were released immediately after the trial.[30] An enormous crowd composed of people of all backgrounds warmly welcomed Zhou and his fellow inmates as they walked out of the prison.

Zhou clearly felt that there had been some significant change in his conceptual realm. "My thought has changed from favoring revolution toward the direction of embracing socialism," he later recalled.[31] He was more committed than ever to the idea of transforming China and the world in revolutionary ways. What he needed to do, he believed, was further clarify his ideas and thoughts, and then put them into action. Thus, Zhou made another important decision: to study in Europe for the purpose of "investing and understanding the social realities of those countries and the ways of resolving problems, and identifying those that could be used to solve the problems of our own nation."[32]

5

BECOMING A COMMUNIST IN EUROPE

1920–1924

Europe had long fascinated Zhou Enlai. He had thought of Europe as an alternative destination for his studies even before he left for Japan in 1917. In the days of the May Fourth Movement, Zhou became increasingly engrossed in such radical ideas as socialism and anarchism, both of which originated in Europe. In June 1920, when Zhou was still in prison, he wrote a poem for a friend who was about to depart to study in France:

> On the seashore of Marseilles,
> Or in the outskirts of Paris,
> Maybe the two of us
> Will see each other in three months.[1]

Zhou's keen desire to be in Paris manifests vividly in the poem. When, shortly after he was released from prison, Zhou received an opportunity to travel to Europe, he immediately seized it. This time, he again benefitted from his Nankai connections. Yan Xiu, Nankai's founder, specifically designated Zhou and Li Jingfu as the two recipients of his newly created scholarship of 7,000 Chinese silver dollars.[2] Both Zhou and Li had been regarded as Nankai's most outstanding graduates. Under the auspices of Yan's foundation, the two would receive monetary support to cover, mostly, tuition and fees. Li was a close friend of Zhou's, who was singularly interested in science and, indeed, later became a scientist. Zhou expressed that he wished to use the scholarship to "pursue true knowledge and endeavor to establish oneself" in Europe.[3]

Zhou's editorship of the Tianjin Students Union's *Bulletin* also caught the attention of *Yishi bao* (Social welfare), an influential newspaper based in Tianjin and sponsored by the Catholic Church. The paper, upon learning that Zhou would be going to Europe, invited him to serve as its correspondent in Europe.[4] This would provide Zhou with an additional source of income.

Thus, in financial terms, Zhou's experience in Europe was different from his stay in Japan: he had at his disposal a good income to cover his living expenses. Also, unlike his time in Japan, language study or enrolling in a college or university was not a precondition for him to stay in Europe. He had much greater freedom to set up his own agenda of activities.

On November 7, 1920, Zhou boarded a French steamship, *Porthos,* at the port of Shanghai. For reasons still unclear, he used a different name—John Knight—in the passport he held at the time.[5] The ship stopped at Saigon, Singapore, Colombo, and several other ports of call in the Indian Ocean and the Mediterranean Sea. En route to France, Zhou felt deeply humiliated when he witnessed "discrimination against overseas Chinese." Instead of blaming others, however, he believed that "the fault is also in ourselves as China has been such a backward country. . . . It is every man's responsibility to care about the rise and fall of his own country."[6]

During the journey, Zhou completed a detailed account of his experience in prison. He titled it "Jianting rilu" (A chronological record at the public execution prison), which would later be published, first in a newspaper, *Xin minyi bao* (New public opinion), and then as a pamphlet.[7]

• • •

Zhou arrived in Marseilles in mid-December after over a month at sea. Then he came to Paris, a temporary stop in his original plan, as his final destination was the United Kingdom. But he was ill, so his stay in the French capital extended to longer than three weeks. Finally, on January 5, 1921, he arrived in London.[8]

Before he set off for Europe, Zhou had written to the University of Edinburgh for conditional admission, whereby he might obtain a waiver for the entrance examination. After arriving in Europe, he again inquired with the university. The response came quickly: his Nankai School coursework was accepted. So long as he could pass an English proficiency test, he would be qualified to enroll in the university without taking any other test.[9] As he had spent four years studying and practicing English at Nankai, he should have felt confident in his ability to meet the requirement. The pressure on him to engage in intensive academic preparation further lessened when he discovered that he had until the coming fall to pass Edinburgh's English proficiency test.[10]

At that moment, the United Kingdom faced serious social instability, economic difficulty, and political turmoil in the wake of the Great War. As a correspondent for *Yishi bao,* Zhou had accepted an assignment to write about "anything" he deemed "important, significant, or interesting." As in Japan, he also saw his experiences in Europe in general and Britain in particular as educational opportunities. He wanted to take advantage of living in London to dig deeper and learn more about British society. "London is the largest metropolis in the world," he wrote. "To pursue study in London should be a matter of more than just attending lectures in the classroom. The multiple dimensions of the city as a phenomenon should also be taken as a worthy subject to explore."[11] Beginning in early February, Zhou published a series of "reports from London" in *Yishi Bao.* In the first report, which appeared in the paper on February 1, 1921, he described what a shocking "first impression" he had had "stepping onto the soil of Europe." "The European societies have been under the huge impact of the Great War, and the instability of the current situation is obvious," he wrote. What were the causes of this instability? "Low productivity, anxiety in the economic world, and poverty in everyday life. . . . in addition to all of this there is the spiritual loss, and the conditions of the society thus have been made even more unstable." Near the end of his report, Zhou made a radical prediction: "If the crisis in Europe goes out of control, then the tide of social revolutions will move eastward, and even our country will not be able to avoid it."[12] Zhou did not deploy the method of "class analysis" in this published report. However, in a private letter, he mentioned that "prices are high, and unemployment is widespread; what has been the biggest headache of those in power in Europe is that the class struggle between the laborers and the capitalists has continued with no sign of ending."[13]

Yet, despite his discussion of the prospect of "social revolutions" and application of Marxist concepts to his writing, Zhou was not yet a Communist. He still endeavored to "conduct a comparison of all 'isms,'" so as to test and establish his own beliefs.[14] On January 30, he penned a lengthy letter to Chen Shizhou, his elder cousin and close childhood friend, in which he described in great detail his conceptual and ideological dilemmas at the time. "I will try to understand the true faces of social conditions in other countries, and think about how the knowledge and understanding that I have obtained might be used to serve our own nation," Zhou wrote to Chen. "As far as the adoption of a specific 'ism' is concerned, it is now still beyond my superficial capacity of knowledge to make the final judgment." In the letter, he also compared the different "roads of reforms and changes" adopted by Russia and England. Which one was better? And which one was more suitable for China? He conveyed his sympathy for the Russian path, but he did not completely reject the English model as an alternative. Again, he had not reached his final conclusion. He weighed the compatibility of the Russian and English paths, respectively, in the context of what he understood as China's special conditions. "In our country," Zhou wrote, "the problems have accumulated to such depth that, unless we follow the example of a Russian-style revolution, it would be difficult to reach the effect of reforms and changes." But Zhou also worried that the eruption of a revolution in China would provoke very strong reactions from such "powerful neighbors" as Japan and Russia. "We are surrounded by strong neighbors, and every move on our part thus must be very cautious, as any violent action would provide them with excuses. Therefore, the ideas favoring steady and gradual changes seem to be more persuasive." Between the two, Zhou continued, "whether to follow the example of Russia or that of England, I have no fixed opinion. But I believe that instead of choosing to go to the extreme, it should be better to find a way of compromises, so as to properly direct the people of our country."[15]

As his stay in London continued to extend, Zhou increasingly found that living expenses in Britain were too high. He mentioned this issue repeatedly to Yan Xiu and Chen Shizhou. In one letter, he asked Yan Xiu to help him obtain a government scholarship, though he knew it was unlikely that he would receive one.[16] Since he would not need to enroll at the University of Edinburgh for another eight months, Zhou left London and returned to the much cheaper Paris in mid-February.[17]

• • •

Zhou's financial calculations, though, might not have been the sole or even main reason behind his decision to return to Paris. In addition, two of his Tianjin friends, Zhang Shenfu and Liu Qingyang, who were a couple, had been in Paris since New Year's Day of 1921.[18] Liu, who was also a member of the Awakening Society, had been a close friend of Zhou's, and through her, Zhou had met Zhang in Tianjin. Zhang, five years Zhou's senior, participated in the May Fourth Movement and was a close confidant of Chen Duxiu and Li Dazhao, professor and head of Peking University Library and a co-founder of the CCP. By the time he arrived in Europe, Zhang, like Chen and Li, was already a self-proclaimed Communist and had discussed with Chen the idea of establishing a Communist party in China.[19] Ostensibly, Zhang came to France to take up a well-paid lectureship (with a monthly salary of 800 francs) at the Chinese-French University in Lyon. In reality, Zhang had another important and secret mission—Chen, "with full confidence" in him, had asked him to recruit in Paris members for the Communist party that they planned to form.[20]

Zhang was a legendary figure in the history of the Chinese Communist movement. His interest in and devotion to Communism seemed quite genuine, but he also aspired to combine theories of Communism with the philosophy of Bertrand Russell (whom Zhang greatly admired and had met) and the ideas of Confucianism.[21] Zhou had long considered Zhang a teacher in an intellectual and political sense. By the time he returned to Paris, Zhang already persuaded Liu, his newlywed wife, to join his Communist cell in Europe. Then, with both Zhang and Liu serving as references, sometime in spring 1921, the cell absorbed Zhou as a new member.[22] Many years later, in 1985, the CCP Central Committee formally acknowledged that "Comrade Zhou joined the party in spring 1921," although this was several months before the formal establishment of the party itself.[23]

This was by no means a formal or well-regulated process. According to Zhang's account, there was no paperwork done and no oath taken, nor was any formal procedure performed for Zhou to join the cell. Zhang sent only a brief personal note to Chen Duxiu following Zhou's initiation for Chen's records. Zhang believed that he had brought Zhou into a "small circle of friends with shared interests and ideas." The circle would remain small. Only two more members, Zhao Shiyan and Chen Gongpei, both of whom had been Zhang's friends, would be added to the cell's rolls after Zhou.[24]

Zhou's activities in the following months did not appear to be those of a party member. For a short while, he entered a French-language program in the suburbs of Paris. Then, along with four other work-study students from China, he moved to Blois in central France. Apart from taking some French-language classes, he did not enroll at any school; in fact, he never even attempted, as he had in Japan, to enter a college or university. After February 1921, he apparently never revisited the prospect of enrolling in the University of Edinburgh. His full-time job was as a *Yishi Bao* correspondent, and, when it came to writing reports for the paper, he focused his energy on an "investigation of the society and its problems." In the meantime, it seems, he continued his exploration of "isms."

The period from February 1921 to March 1922 was Zhou's most productive time as a journalist. Altogether he published fifty-plus reports in *Yishi Bao,* some of them lengthy ones. In addition to his own name, Zhou Enlai or Enlai, he also used such pen names as Wu Hao (the code name he had obtained as an Awakening Society member), Xiangyu (his courtesy name), and Fei Fei. These reports, supported by Zhou's extensive and careful reading and research of newspapers published in the United Kingdom, covered a wide range of issues, including the massive miners' strike in the United Kingdom, the reparations issue after the war, the Pacific question and the Washington Conference of 1921–1922, and the uneasy relations between Britain and France.[25]

Among these issues, Zhou paid special attention to the British miners' strike that began in late spring 1921. From May to July 1921, he published nine lengthy essays in which he described and analyzed the causes and development of the strike. He showed great sympathy for the miners, becoming increasingly critical of Britain's capitalist system. "The capitalists will do anything to pursue profits, and to reach a compromised conclusion of the strike thus is truly difficult," he wrote in his last essay on the strike. "Unless a fundamental solution is to be sought and achieved, there exists no other way to end the class war between the laborers and the capitalists."[26]

As a *Yishi Bao* correspondent, Zhou also paid close attention to the situation and activities of the Chinese students in France, who numbered over two thousand at the time. Most of these students were from Hunan and Sichuan and had come to France on various work-study programs. Moreover, many of them had participated in the May Fourth Movement. Now, in France, they struggled to find employment in a country that had been torn apart during the war and still suffered from the postwar recession, and they endured serious hardship in their daily lives. In spring 1921, when the Chinese-French Education Association stopped the meager aid it had provided the students because of its own financial difficulties, and the government in Beijing refused to help, the students held protests in front of the Chinese Legation in Paris.[27] In the summer, when the students learned that secret talks for high-interest loans and military purchases were underway between the Chinese and French governments, they again protested what they regarded as "wracking the county and bringing misfortune to the people."[28] Finally, in September, the Chinese Legation announced the termination of financial aid to the Chinese work-study students. The Chinese-French University also stopped admitting those work-study students who were already in France, instead bringing new students directly from China. The aggrieved students occupied the university's campus. The French authorities, in turn, suppressed the demonstration and forcibly deported 104 students, including Cai Hesen, Li Lisan, and Chen Yi, who would all go on to become leaders of the Chinese Communist Revolution.[29]

Zhou was not a work-study student, and he did not directly participate in the students' protests. But he was associated with these student activities in two respects. First, from March to December 1921, he wrote and published four series of reports (including two lengthy pieces, each published in installments lasting for more than ten days) in *Yishi bao,* providing detailed coverage and analysis of the development of the student movement. In particular, he emphasized that the significance of the activities transcended the students' defense of their own interests; they involved issues related to China's dignity, fate, and sovereignty.[30]

Second, he was active in mediating and resolving the differences between students of different backgrounds or from different regions to bring them together. Some of the students were Zhou's friends. For the writing of his *Yishi Bao* reports, he mingled with the students and conducted thorough interviews with many of them. Subsequently, he became more deeply involved in the planning and organization of the students' activities. As the students planned their occupation of the Chinese-French University campus, he proposed to them that they should not send all of their people there but should keep "some core members" back to deal with contingencies and continue the struggle.[31] His involvement elevated his status and influence among Chinese students in France. As many of the students would later become activists in and leaders of the Chinese Communist Party, this also served to strengthen the foundation of Zhou's own future leadership role in the Chinese Communist Revolution.

• • •

Zhou's school of thought and political orientation reached a critical turning point in spring 1922.[32] Until then, although he had shown great interest in, or even a strong sense of attachment to, Communism, he had never explicitly declared himself a Communist. His membership in Zhang Shenfu's Paris Communist cell did not involve much political activity. Zhou's reading list was long, and his thinking was earnest, to be sure. He aimed to derive a conclusion about which "ism" should become his intellectual and ideological lodestar.

Finally, the point of breakthrough arrived in February and March 1922. In a letter to two former Awakening Society comrades, Chen Xiaocen and Li Yitao, Zhou wrote:

> Concerning the question of ism. . . . We should believe in the theory of Communism as well as the principles of class revolution and proletarian dictatorship, and the implementation of them, of course, needs to be adjusted in accordance with specific times and conditions. . . . The principles of the Awakening Society obviously are not sufficient and not clear. The truth is that it is sufficient just to believe in Communism.[33]

In another letter written around the same time, Zhou announced:

> My commitment to Communism will not change, and I will more resolutely propagate and strive for it.[34]

Why and how did this breakthrough occur? Unlike during his time in Japan, Zhou did not keep a diary while he was in Europe. However, a path of intellectual and conceptual growth characterized by three outstanding yet interrelated features can be identified in the letters and many essays that he wrote during this period. First, on the most practical and urgent level, Zhou was genuinely ashamed of China's backwardness and deeply worried that the very survival of China and the Chinese nation was imperiled. The fate of China and the Chinese nation thus manifested as a persistent theme of his thinking. He angrily condemned the imperialist aggression of the West and Japan against China, and he believed that it was essential to "save China and make China strong."

But Zhou was not simply a nationalist. What linked him with other young Communists (such as Ho Chi Minh, whom Zhou met in Paris) were what he considered to be the most effective ways to save China, and how the country's salvation should be associated with greater meanings and purposes. Zhou embraced the ideas of development and national independence, but he was even more attracted to the concept of national liberation. To that end, he found that Communism was the right intellectual and political instrument with which to achieve his ideals and goals.

On an even deeper level, though, Zhou did not take as his ultimate mission or goal the salvation of the Chinese nation and the transformation of China's state and society through revolutionary means. For him, none of these objectives was cogent unless the process of transformation also left an impression on, as he had envisioned since his Nankai years, the hearts and souls of the people, leading to their "rebirth" or "new birth." In the final analysis, it is here one may identify the ultimate reason for Zhou's turning to Marxism-Leninism in his intellectual pursuit of the truth and meaning of life. When he first arrived in Europe, he still harbored the concern that a revolution could prove disastrous for China, given the fact that China was "surrounded by neighbors" hostile to radical political and social change. However, as his stay in Europe continued, and especially after he witnessed what he regarded as the fundamental problems of capitalism and imperialism, he decided that a Communist revolution, despite its potential of causing significant harm, was nevertheless the only way to achieve a "new China" and a "new world." For this, any sacrifice was justified, and any price was worth paying.[35]

• • •

In early March 1922, Zhou moved from France to Germany with Zhang Shenfu and Liu Qingyang. They stayed in a small town in the southern

5.1 Zhou Enlai in Europe, ca. 1922–1923. *World History Archive / Alamy Stock Photo*

suburbs of Berlin to save on living expenses. By this time, Zhou had already been actively involved in the forming of a new Communist organization of Chinese activists in Europe. In June, a Chinese Youth Communist Party in Europe was formed in Paris; Zhou traveled from Germany to attend the party's first congress. He urged all members to take oaths as they joined the party, so that they would be a "politically bound and committed force." Unlike Zhang Shenfu's "liberal practice," Zhou favored adopting a Leninist method to develop the party. At the congress, Zhou was elected to the party's three-person executive committee, in charge of personnel and organizational matters.[36] A few months later, after Zhou took up this initiative, the fledgling organization applied to join the Chinese Socialist Youth League, which had been established in Guangzhou the previous May, as its European branch.

While Zhou and his comrades awaited the league's response, they learned that Chen Duxiu had arrived in Moscow to attend the Comintern's Fourth Congress. They immediately sent a letter to Chen, obviously with the hope of drawing the CCP leadership's attention to their own organization. Chen's reply came in January 1923. He proposed that the name of Zhou and his comrades' organization be changed to the "European Branch of the Chinese Communist Youth League," and he also instructed them to establish direct connections with the CCP and the league in China.[37] Zhou and his comrades then held another congress in Paris on February 17–20, when they changed the organization's name to the Chinese Communist Youth League in Europe. Taking the Bolshevik Party as a model, Zhou drafted for the league a constitution, which the congress adopted. The congress also elected a five-person executive committee. Zhou was elected to the committee and assumed the role of its secretary.[38] Shortly after the congress's conclusion, Zhou and his comrades received a letter from the Chinese Communist Youth League Central Committee, accepting their organization as its European branch. On March 13, on behalf of the committee, Zhou sent his first formal report to the League Center, in which he promised that he and his comrades would spare no effort in fighting "under the unified banner of Communism."[39]

Zhou was, by this time, a full-fledged professional revolutionary, who had fully devoted himself to the cause of a Communist revolution aimed at transforming China and the world. And he was willing and ready to sacrifice his life for such a noble cause. Zhou composed a poem of commendation for a comrade and close friend, Huang Ai, who was killed for organizing a textile factory workers' strike in Hunan, becoming one of the first martyrs of the Chinese Communist Revolution. In the poem, Zhou wrote:

> Parted in life or separated by death—
> The worst that could happen to me.
> . . . .
>
> No sowing done,
> No reaping possible.
> No sowing the seed of revolution,
> No blossoming of the flower of communism!
> Dreaming of Red Flags flying high,

Without sacrificing them in blood.
Such a cheap gain—could there ever be?[40]

Beginning in mid-1922, Zhou stopped writing for *Yishi Bao* and devoted all his time and energy to working for the party. In doing so, he demonstrated both great vision and cautiousness, as he believed that only the very best, capable, and devoted revolutionaries should be allowed to join the party. Among those who had been admitted to Zhou's organization with him as a formal reference was Zhu De. Zhu, a former military officer who had participated in the 1911 Revolution, forfeited his lucrative position and, at the age of almost forty, came to study in Europe. He met Zhou in Berlin in October 1922 and expressed his strong desire to join the Communist organization. After a lengthy and engaging conversation, Zhou thought that he should accept him. In November 1922, with Zhou and Zhang Shenfu as the references, Zhu De became a member of the party.[41] Later, Zhu—along with Mao, Zhou, and other top CCP leaders—would emerge as a central figure of the Chinese Communist Revolution.

In October 1922, Zhou added an additional item—one with which he had considerable experience—to his working agenda: to edit and publish a journal, *Shaonian* (The youth, which changed to *Chi Guang*, or Red light, in February 1924), which would serve as the organization's mouthpiece. He hoped to use the journal as a vehicle for the party's propaganda work; he also wanted to turn it into a forum for theoretical exploration. The editorial office was located in a small room on the third floor of 17 Rue Godefroy, near Place d'Italie in Paris.[42]

Zhou published in the journal a series of essays, including "Communism and China"; "Religious Spirit and Communism"; "A Letter to Labor Friends"; "The October Revolution"; "On the Trade Union Movement"; and "Has the Russian Revolution Failed?" One point he underscored was that discipline was of critical importance for a vanguard Communist organization. Therefore, generally Zhou was in support of the viewpoint put forward by Zhang Shenfu. "Discipline is the soul of a Communist party. Without discipline, a Communist party won't be able to survive at all," wrote Zhang in one essay published in *Shaonian*. "If there is discipline, there is the party; if there is no discipline, the party will be gone. . . . For anyone who does not understand this, he is not qualified to join the party, let alone to organize the party."[43] But at the same time, Zhou did not believe that the emphasis upon discipline meant the necessity of blind obedience or the elimination of critical thinking. Thus, in an essay also published in *Shaonian,* Zhou stressed that

> the Communist Party surely should not include such liberals who "are neither capable nor willing to accept instructions." However, the Communist Party must never try to produce members who are as uncritical as pigs, and who know nothing but obedience.[44]

Apparently, even when he was becoming a loyal Communist, Zhou still earnestly hoped to keep his independent personality while also keeping space for critical thinking.

In the process of editing and publishing the journal, Zhou met a young man who was six years his junior. He was short, barely five feet in height, and spoke with a heavy Sichuan accent; but he was full of energy and also a quick learner. Under Zhou's direction, he contributed to the journal's publication, mostly by serving as a stencil cutter, and also by handling the mimeograph machine, thus winning the nickname "Doctor of Mimeograph." He was Deng Xiaoping.[45] He was from a "petty bourgeoisie family that was nearly broken" in Guang'an in Sichuan Province. His father was once a successful "small bureaucrat." In his childhood, he lived a "rich and happy life," and, as he acknowledged, "my specialty was that I did not like reading." After his father's side was defeated in Sichuan's provincial politics, the quality of Deng's life worsened dramatically. To "[glorify] the ancestors" of the Deng family, his father exhausted his resources to send his son to study in France. Yet, when Deng's father tried to impose upon him an arranged marriage, he "almost cut off all relationship" with his family. Because of the hardship he had endured in his work-study experience in France, and also influenced by reading *New Youth* and other progressive literature, he began to embrace Communist thought. In June 1923, he joined the Chinese Communist Youth League in Europe; then, he came to Paris to work, under Zhou's leadership, for *Shaonian* and *Chi Guang.*[46] This would be the beginning of a half century of collaboration and friendship between two giants of the Chinese Communist Revolution, as well as two great statesmen of twentieth-century China and the world.

How did Zhou support himself and his activities? According to Zhou's official biography, "the main source for Zhou to pay for his living expenses was his royalties."[47] However, as mentioned earlier, beginning in mid-1922,

Zhou no longer wrote for *Yishi Bao,* and his contributions to *Shaonian* and *Chi Guang* did not yield any royalties. Moreover, Yan Xiu recorded in his diary that the financial support he provided to Zhou would end in late 1922.[48]

In fact, after Zhou became a professional revolutionary, he and the organization received financial support from the Comintern through the French Communist Party, and they probably obtained funding from the Chinese Communist Party Center as well.[49] On occasion, monetary support came from other sources. For example, a sum of 1,000 francs given to Zhang Shenfu by his personal friend Zhang Shizhao effectively brought *Shaonian* into being.[50] But the funding Zhou and his comrades received was limited. Therefore, there was only a single bed and a small desk in that small room of about sixty square feet on the third floor of 17 Rue Godefroy that served as Zhou's bedroom and the editorial office of *Shaonian.* When people came to meet and talk with Zhou, or when he needed to host several people for a meeting, he would have to go to a nearby restaurant.[51]

During Zhou's last year in Europe, the emphasis of his work increasingly tilted in the direction of pursuing cooperation with the Guomindang (GMD; the Nationalist Party). As early as June 1922, under mounting pressure from Moscow, the CCP leadership, headed by Chen Duxiu, had issued a statement about the party's perspective on the current situation, in which the CCP stated that it was "willing to work with the Guomindang and other revolutionary democratic parties to establish a united front of democracy."[52] Two months later, the CCP Central Executive Committee decided that, in principle, CCP members might join the Guomindang as individuals.[53]

Zhou decided at once to support the party's new policy orientation once he learned of it. In issue 2 of *Shaonian,* he published an essay by Zhang Shenfu, "The Chinese Communist Party and Its Current Policy," which firmly endorsed the idea of CCP-GMD cooperation. Early in 1923, Sun Yat-sen, leader of the Nationalist Party, dispatched Wang Jingqi to France to establish the party's branch there. Wang himself had been a student in France, and Zhou had known him for some time. He had actively participated in occupation of the Chinese-French University and was thus expelled from France, after which he returned to China. When Zhou learned that Wang had returned to France as Sun Yat-sen's representative, he immediately resumed contact with him. On June 16, Zhou, alongside two of his comrades, reached an agreement with Wang, according to which all members of the European Branch of the Chinese Communist Youth League were free to join the Nationalist Party as individuals.[54] Zhou then wrote to Wang, proposing that "three main tasks" be established as top priorities: "First, to propagate the necessity of the democratic revolution in present-day China and the strategies and policies of it; second, to attract to the Guomindang people with revolutionary spirit among Chinese in Europe; and third, to strive for enhancing organizational work and personnel training for the Guomindang."[55] Sun and the Guomindang appointed Zhou as a preparatory envoy of the GMD's Paris liaison office.[56]

In November, the Nationalist Party's France Branch was formally established in Lyon. Zhou and quite a few of his Communist comrades joined the branch, and they immediately became dominant in the organization. Wang became the director of the branch, and Zhou was in charge of its general office. During Wang's absence in France, Zhou would assume his duties as acting director.[57]

• • •

During Zhou's times attending the Nankai School, studying in Japan, and participating in the May Fourth Movement, he was known by many of his classmates and friends as a practitioner of celibacy, who did not plan to marry. After he arrived in Europe, his attitude toward love and marriage quietly changed. In mid-1923, toward the beginning of his fourth year in Europe, Zhou wrote more frequently to Deng Yingchao, whom he had known since their time as Awakening Society comrades in the days of the May Fourth Movement.

Deng was not Zhou's first romantic target. Zhou and Zhang Ruoming, another Awakening Society comrade, had become fast friends during Zhou's first two years in Europe. Zhang was born in 1902, four years later than Zhou. Like Zhou, she was one of the founders of the Awakening Society, and she was imprisoned together with Zhou in 1920. In *Jinting Juliu Ji* (The record of detention at the police station), Zhou cited Zhang's diary from January 29 to February 6, which clearly revealed the intimate relationship between them.[58] After their release from prison, Zhou and Zhang had grown closer to each other. But Zhou was then still known for being celibate. Even Deng Yingchao later recounted to Zhou's niece, "At that time, there was a girl, Zhang Ruoming, who had a much closer relationship with your uncle. I had thought then that if your uncle was willing to marry someone, she would have been the most suitable one for him to marry. All of our friends felt the same."[59]

In late 1920, Zhou and Zhang took the same French ship, *Porthos,* from China to France.[60] Zhang was a pretty girl, also widely recognized as the most accomplished among her fellow students from China in France. She and Zhou had been comrades, and the cultural challenges of living in a foreign environment must have brought them even closer together. Everyone who knew them thought that they were heading toward engagement and marriage. But Zhou finally took the initiative to distance himself from Zhang, feeling that there was too much "petty bourgeois smell" on Zhang's part. Many years later, Zhou explained to his niece why he had made such a decision: "When I was determined to devote myself to the revolution, I also felt that she (Zhang Ruoming) was not suitable as a lifetime companion for a revolutionary."[61]

Zhou turned to Deng Yingchao, with whom he had corresponded since he arrived in Europe. Beginning in mid-1923, Zhou's letters to Deng arrived one after another. The interval between each letter grew shorter and shorter, until one day in late 1923 or early 1924, Zhou proposed to Deng. In an essay, Deng, writing as if she were talking to Zhou, recalled their relationship as follows:

> Three years have passed. Although you have written me more frequently than before, I have not really paid attention to the underlying meanings of the letters. At the moment when you explicitly proposed in a letter, asking to turn our friendship into love, you suddenly caught my heart. I have to consider this. And I had considered this. Then we were engaged.[62]

At that moment, China itself was perched on the eve of the "Great Revolution," one that was initiated and pushed forward by the CCP-GMD united front. The Chinese Communist Youth League decided to send its members back to China to participate in the Great Revolution, including Zhou. The European Branch of the Chinese Communist Youth League's official reference letter for Zhou read as follows:

> Zhou Enlai, a Zhejiang native, is twenty-six years of age. He is sincere and modest, energetic and with rich and sufficient capacity, eloquent

> and persuasive in verbal presentation, witty and quick in writing, and has a profound knowledge of (Commun)ism. Therefore, he has been fully proletarianized. His command of English is very good, and he can also read books and newspapers in French and German. He is one of the founders of the [European] Branch. He has been a member of the branch's executive committee for three terms. He is passionate and hardworking, and he has had outstanding accomplishments.[63]

These are comments written very much in the fashion of a Communist party. We do not know who wrote them. But the letter clearly demonstrated the extent to which Zhou had earned the trust of the party and his comrades.

• • •

In late July 1924, after almost four years in Europe, Zhou boarded a ship for China. The time that Zhou spent in Europe was critical in the development of his political career. When he first arrived in France, he was still a young student fresh out of school. Although he had participated in political activities during the May Fourth Movement and had won a reputation among radical youth in Tianjin, he was one of tens of thousands of minor figures in a time of great political turmoil. His activities and influence were essentially no more than local. Further, despite his tendency to embrace radical, transformative ideas, he had not committed to any "ism" in his conceptual and intellectual search for the ultimate truth.

It was in Europe that Zhou had fully accepted Communism as his ideological lodestar. By throwing himself wholeheartedly into the work of establishing and developing Communist organizations, he had made himself part of the vanguard and a core member of this new and highly energetic—though still small—political force. Most crucially, by taking advantage of Europe's geographical proximity to the Comintern center in Moscow, he had established a series of relationships highly advantageous to his future political development and had been placed on the Comintern's list of prospective cadres for future appointment. As a result, he had built up political influence with the potential to stretch far beyond the locality of his activities. In retrospect, all of this represented a lofty and promising point of departure in Zhou's rapid rise in the political stage of China's radical revolutions.

PART II

MAKING REVOLUTION

6

INTO STORMS OF THE GREAT REVOLUTION

1924–1927

In southern China, at the center of the Pearl River Delta about 120 miles west of Hong Kong, lies the semitropical city of Guangzhou, capital of Guangdong Province. Known by westerners as Canton, the city was the only Chinese port officially open to foreign trade from the mid-eighteenth through the mid-nineteenth centuries. In 1839, the British-Chinese Opium War erupted in Guangzhou. The Qing's decisive defeat in the war opened the door for China to enter the Western power–dominated treaty system, initiating an "era of humiliation" for the Chinese in their encounters with the outside world.[1] Guangzhou witnessed a clash of cultures between the East and the West, coupled with the impact of crises, wars, and, as the twentieth century began to unfold, revolution.

Zhou Enlai arrived in Guangzhou in early September 1924 after a month-long maritime journey. There, he saw a city rapidly transforming into a powerhouse of the Great Revolution led by a "united front" that the CCP had entered into with Sun Yat-sen's Guomindang, ostensibly to pursue a genuine Chinese republic free from the yoke of Western and Japanese imperialism.[2]

Zhou was just twenty-six years old. He had no previous experience as a military or political leader; nor was his name known beyond a small group of young Communists in Europe. However, he was buoyed by his accumulated political capital and the reputation he had earned during his years carrying out revolutionary activities in Europe as a dedicated and capable Communist. Moreover, he also seemed to have the endorsement of Moscow and the Comintern. (It was probably around this time that he, like many other Chinese Communist leaders, was given the alias "Moskvin" in Moscow.[3]) All of this laid the groundwork for Zhou's speedy emergence in the young Chinese Communist Party and his simultaneous entry into the inner circle of the CCP-GMD united front.

In the ensuing quarter century, during the CCP's struggles that culminated in its seizure of political power in China in 1949, Zhou would have his share of bright times and dark moments, but he would remain a main figure of the Chinese Communist Revolution. Indeed, the impact of Zhou's role manifested in almost every important episode of the revolution's development. Guangzhou was a starting point of all of this.

It was in Guangzhou that Zhou first met a man named Mao Zedong.[4] Mao had come to the city to host a training program for prospective activists and organizers of peasant movements.[5] As the city provided the future chairman with a theoretical testing ground for his rural-oriented brand of Communist revolution, Guangzhou was also Mao's starting point.

Zhou was no Mao, however. He never became the top leader of the CCP, nor did he ever demonstrate Mao's utopian idealism and charisma. In comparison, Zhou might be characterized as more a man of action than of ideas. Yet it would be mistaken, as the previous and the following chapters attest, to describe Zhou as a person with no vision or thought of his own. What differentiated Zhou and Mao was not Zhou's absence of ideas or vision, but his lack of the requisite will and determination to rise to and maintain the position of the revolution's supreme leader.

* * *

Zhou stopped for a few days in Hong Kong before he arrived in Guangzhou. On September 1, he wrote to the CCP Central Committee, asking the party leaders in Shanghai to decide upon his assignment and stating that he would "be traveling to and staying in Guangzhou to wait for the Central Committee's order."[6] The letter reached the Party Center at the right time. The party leadership, eager to expand its influence, was then in great need of qualified cadres. Given Zhou's good credentials, the Central Committee, in an effort to reorganize the party's Guangdong district committee, appointed him the committee's head and director of propaganda affairs.[7]

In the meantime, Zhou became an instructor at the Whampoa Military Academy, where he taught a course on political economy.[8] Established in 1923 by Sun Yat-sen with massive military, financial, and other support from the Comintern and Soviet Russia, the academy had the main mission of training revolutionary officers and cadres. It would thus come to be known as the leading source of China's twentieth-century military leadership. The person who recommended Zhou for the position was Zhang Shenfu, who had returned to China in 1923 and thereafter served for a short while as Whampoa's deputy director of political affairs. When Liao Zhongkai, a close associate of Sun and a pro-Communist, left-wing leader of the GMD, asked Zhang to nominate candidates for open positions at Whampoa, Zhang gave him fifteen names. Zhou was number one on the list.[9]

Soon, in November 1924, Zhou encountered another major opportunity. The position of Whampoa's director of political affairs was vacant. The job had not garnered much attention within the organization, nor had it been associated with any substantial political power. The position had been held by Shao Yuanchong, a veteran GMD member, who likely considered it more a liability than an asset. So, when Sun Yat-sen asked Shao to accompany him on his expedition to Beijing for talks on "important national affairs" with the warlord-controlled government there, Shao immediately resigned from Whampoa. Zhou took over the Department of Political Affairs as Shao's replacement.[10]

This appointment, though on the surface quite routine, would turn out to be a pivotal step in Zhou's political rise. To be sure, the position was not the most distinguished or powerful that Zhou occupied in his long career. But it probably was a crucial post for Zhou in accumulating political capital. The most important factor was that so many of Whampoa's graduates would later become high-ranking commanders in the CCP and GMD. Zhou's experience at Whampoa thus won him an unusual degree of seniority in both parties' military and political hierarchies. Zhou's growing prestige proved especially valuable in China's political culture—in which one's influence and power were often based on seniority.

Zhou began to transform the director's position as soon as he assumed it. When he defined his mission and work, he emphasized that as a revolutionary institution, Whampoa would have to highlight the importance of

6.1 Zhou Enlai at Whampoa Military Academy, ca. 1925. *AFP via Getty Images*

instilling both a sense of discipline and a "revolutionary spirit" into its curriculum, educating the students in a political as well as a military sense.[11] Zhou presented the CCP as a party of political correctness, stressing that the CCP's cooperation with the GMD and the critical role that it played in the united front were indispensable to the triumph of the Great Revolution.[12] Wielding his newly acquired power, he appointed his CCP comrades to various key positions at Whampoa, and also managed to recruit Communists and Communist-sympathizing cadets for the academy.[13]

A student of Zhou's at Whampoa was Lin Biao. Born in 1907, Lin was from a rich merchant's family in Huanggang County, Hubei Province. At the age of sixteen, he joined the Socialist Youth League while attending a middle school in Wuhan. In 1925, he was admitted to Whampoa and became a CCP member there. After graduating from Whampoa in October 1926, he emerged in the Northern Expedition, China's war against Japan, and the CCP-GMD civil war as a military genius, making significant contributions to the Communist seizure of China's political power in 1949. After 1959, his unique "favoring Mao in any circumstances" approach won him Mao's trust, opening his path to become China's number two leader and Mao's designated successor in the Cultural Revolution. His legend, however, ended abruptly in September 1971, when he betrayed Mao and died miserably in an airplane crash in Öndörkhaan, Outer Mongolia. Guangzhou was also the starting point of Lin's career.

Zhou also strove to pursue a good working relationship with his GMD colleagues, including Chiang Kai-shek, Whampoa's founding commander.[14] Chiang also seemed to have had a fine impression of Zhou. In April 1925, Chiang appointed Zhou to another important position at Whampoa—director of the school's Department of Military Discipline.[15] "In Chiang's eyes," according to the leading Chiang biographer Jay Taylor, Zhou was "a sincere man." After their time working together at Whampoa, "over forty-seven years of competition, struggle, and violent conflict between the KMT (GMD) and the CCP, an unusual relationship would develop between the two men, including a mutual respect that during times of bitter interparty conflict would sporadically manifest itself."[16]

Zhou also established close working relationships with Comintern representatives and Soviet advisors in Guangzhou, who were then gaining influence and power as a result of Sun Yat-sen's adoption of a policy of "allying with the Soviet Union".[17] As observed by Zhang Guotao, a CCP founder and, at that time, a prominent party figure, Zhou maintained an "intimate relationship" with Mikhail Borodin, Sun Yat-sen's chief Soviet advisor, thus earning Borodin's support.[18]

Also among those Zhou worked with was Ho Chi Minh (Nguyen Ai Quoc), the Vietnamese Communist whom he had known since his time in Paris. Ho, who spoke fluent Chinese, was then serving as Borodin's interpreter. At Ho's invitation, Zhou gave guest lectures at the Vietnamese Revolutionary Youth Training Program that Ho was then sponsoring in Guangzhou. At Ho's request, Zhou also helped admit several Vietnamese revolutionaries to Whampoa.[19]

In early 1925, Zhou embraced another fortuitous opportunity when the revolutionary government in Guangzhou decided to launch a military campaign, known as the First Eastern Expedition. At the time, two-thirds of Guangdong's territory, especially areas east of Guangzhou, remained under the control of Chen Jiongming, a warlord whose one-time alliance with Sun Yat-sen had turned into fierce enmity and who presented a threat to Guangzhou. Late in January 1925, the revolutionary government gave the order to launch an attack on Chen's forces. Newly formed units with Whampoa's cadets serving as officers comprised a main part of Guangzhou's troops. This "Whampoa Student Army," showing great discipline and very high morale, played a major role in defeating Chen's forces. Zhou was in charge of political mobilization in the expedition. Victory not only helped prove Zhou's methods of political indoctrination an effective way to heighten troops' morale, but also prompted many to begin to recognize him as a man of admirable military talent.[20]

• • •

Indeed, Zhou's mood in these days was one of celebration. Along with his ascendancy on the political stage, his romance and love with Deng Yingchao had also reached "harvest time."

By then, Deng had also joined the CCP and become a devoted party activist in Tianjin (as Zhou expected she would), where she had stayed throughout Zhou's four-year stay in Europe.[21] The two young activists maintained frequent correspondence during this period. Altogether, according to Deng's recollection, Zhou wrote more than 250 letters to her, none of which seems to have survived. "We fell in love . . . writing to each other," she told the writer Han Suyin in an interview sixty years later.[22] Now, as Zhou had returned to China and established himself in Guangzhou, he was ready and eager to bring his long-distance romance with Deng to a close and marry her. In January 1925, at the CCP's fourth national congress, following the party's established policy that a high-ranking cadre's marriage would have to be endorsed by the party leadership, he asked permission of Peng Shuzhi, a Central Committee member who was in charge of such matters, to marry Deng. Peng smiled and nodded in assent.[23]

The story that followed reflected Zhou and Deng's understanding of the relationship between revolution and love—for them, the former must always precede the latter. Deng arrived in Guangzhou by ship from Tianjin in July 1925. No one was waiting for her at the dock. Zhou was too busy with his work, so he sent Chen Geng, a party member and Whampoa cadet, to meet her. But Chen missed Deng, and Deng had to navigate to Zhou's quarters by herself.[24]

This "small episode," however, seemed to have meant nothing for the young bride- and groom-to-be. On August 8, 1925, Zhou invited about two dozen close comrades and friends to a dinner; in truth, the occasion was his and Deng's "wedding banquet." Zhou was visibly excited. Glass after glass, he drank three bottles of whisky, a personal record. When, near midnight, the dinner came to an end, he was totally drunk. When Zhou woke up the next morning, Deng told him, "For the sake of revolution, never drink so much in the future." Zhou promised that he would not.[25] Zhou and Deng had become a "revolutionary couple," but this did not mean that theirs was not a loving bond. From that moment onward, Zhou, by using the third syllable of Deng's name, would forever call her "Xiao Chao" ("Little Chao"), a very intimate nickname used only for a loved one.

For Zhou, this marriage also lay at the nexus of love, rationality, and political calculation. Throughout Zhou's life, Deng Yingchao was his most intimate comrade-in-arms, as well as a firm defender of his best political interests. She remained so even after Zhou's death.[26]

This practice of regarding political considerations as a key condition for marriage has since become embedded in the family heritage of Zhou and Deng. Many years later, Zhou Bingde, Zhou's niece whom he and Deng had raised, dated a young man who had studied in the Soviet Union. The two admired each other, and their commitment to each other strengthened as their romance blossomed. Meanwhile, however, Sino-Soviet relations were quickly deteriorating. When Zhou and Deng learned of Bingde's love affair, they advised her, not as her uncle and aunt but as her "comrades," to separate from her boyfriend.[27] This was because the interest of the revolution was paramount, even in romantic matters.

• • •

Zhou had no time for a honeymoon. On August 20, Liao Zhongkai, who was the most fervently pro-Communist of all the GMD's top leaders, was assassinated. Zhou, like all of his CCP comrades, was shocked. His intuition told him that Liao's death could change the political balance of power between the pro-CCP and anti-CCP forces within the GMD, in turn profoundly impacting the GMD's own development as well as the future orientation of the united front between the Communists and the Nationalists. He was deeply worried.[28]

But before Zhou and his comrades could deal with the deepening tensions within the GMD and between the CCP and the GMD, they had to organize and carry out the Second Eastern Expedition, the aim of which was to eliminate Chen Jiongming's remaining troops in Guangdong. In late August, the "Whampoa Student Army" was reorganized, expanded, and designated as the First Army of the newly established National Revolutionary Army. Zhou was appointed director of the First Army's Political Department as well as the political commissar of the army's First Division. As he had done in the First Eastern Expedition a few months before, Zhou again emphasized the importance of political mobilization for improving the soldiers' morale and combat capacity. By mid-November, the First Army had won a series of victories, and the whole of Guangdong Province was now placed under Guangzhou's control.[29]

Victory on the battlefield presented yet another opportunity for Zhou. On November 21, the revolutionary government appointed him to serve as administrative commissar of the Dongjiang District, which covered most of the territory that the First Army had just occupied, including twenty-five counties.[30] The district provided the Guangzhou government with additional outlets to the sea while, at the same time, functioning as a much-needed base for taxation and other support. This was also the first time that a CCP member would occupy such a critical political and administrative position. That Zhou was chosen for the role clearly demonstrated his growing political power and influence in the CCP-GMD united front.

To dedicate himself to his new position in Dongjiang, Zhou resigned as Whampoa's director of political affairs, but he was still bogged down by his involvement with the First Army. He envisioned that he would concentrate his work in Dongjiang on two tasks. The first was to continuously suppress any remaining influence of the "reactionary forces" through organizing and mobilizing the masses, especially among the peasants. The second, to which he assigned even higher priority, was to devise plans for development in "such important areas as education, business, water projects, and transportation" to transform Dongjiang into a "consolidated base area for the ongoing revolution."[31]

Before Zhou could carry out his plans in Dongjiang, however, he was dismissed from his district position on March 16, 1926.[32] Ostensibly, the decision was made because Zhou had complained that he found his simultaneous positions with the First Army and in Dongjiang to be overwhelming. The underlying reason, though, seems to have been the significant heightening of tensions between the CCP and the GMD, as well as between the GMD's left- and right-wing factions, concerning whether CCP members should be allowed to hold important GMD positions while retaining their CCP membership. This source of friction became increasingly visible after Sun Yat-sen's untimely death due to liver cancer in March 1925. When Sun was alive, he had leveraged his authority to suppress debates on the issue to pave the way for his policy of "allying with Soviet Union and the CCP." When Sun was gone, the breach within the GMD continued to widen.

Chiang Kai-shek, who laid claim to a singular military and political leadership role in the GMD after Sun's death, had long been regarded as a key figure in the party's left wing. However, as he witnessed the expansion of the CCP's influence in his own party, even Chiang feared that the CCP might emerge as a "party within a party" inside the GMD. Therefore, as he once told Zhou, he believed that all CCP members in the GMD should either forfeit their membership in the CCP or withdraw from both the GMD and the Whampoa Academy.[33] Zhou was alarmed by this. In early 1926, he brought this particular issue to the attention of Borodin, proposing that "due actions" be taken to check Chiang's power. He also reported this matter to the CCP leadership, headed by Chen Duxiu. However, Zhou later recalled that after a long delay, his petitioning was met only with indifference, and no steps were pursued along the lines of his proposal.[34]

* * *

Zhou's worry was not without ground. A mere four days after his dismissal from his Dongjiang position, a major crisis in the CCP-GMD relationship, the Gunboat *Zhongshan* Incident (also known as the March 20th Incident), erupted almost instantaneously. On March 19, Chiang Kai-shek received a report that the *Zhongshan,* under the command of captain Li Zhilong, a CCP member, had been traveling without authorization from Whampoa to Guangzhou. Unaware of the journey and its purpose, Chiang was startled by the news.

At that moment, he received two phone inquiries from Wang Jingwei, head of the GMD's pro-Communist left-wing contingent and contender for Chiang's leadership position in the GMD, about his whereabouts. Chiang grew more alarmed; he suspected that Wang might have colluded with his CCP friends and the Soviet advisers in a plot to kidnap and send him to the Soviet Far East.[35] Chiang decided almost immediately to leave Guangzhou and seek refuge at a safe haven. But on his way out of the city, he had second thoughts. If he left Guangzhou, he reasoned, wouldn't other people regard his fleeing as evidence of his culpability? After all, he controlled a substantial share of Guangzhou's military power. Why shouldn't he use it? Moreover, why should he cower in the face of his political enemies' plot?[36] On this premise, he returned to Guangzhou and ordered Li Zhilong's arrest. On the morning of March 20, Chiang declared that martial law be instituted in Guangzhou and that the CCP-controlled workers' pickets be disarmed. By the day's end, he had taken a series of other actions, including besieging the Soviet advisors' residence and cleaning up the First Army, ordering the Communists, Zhou included, to withdraw from it.[37]

Zhou was shocked. As he recalled nearly twenty years later, he rushed to Chiang's office to protest these developments. However, Chiang refused to meet with Zhou, and Chiang "kept" him in the office against his will for twenty-four hours. Not until Chiang realized that no such conspiracy existed to kidnap him did he lift martial law and let Zhou go.[38]

The March 20th Incident was long one of the most mysterious and controversial events in twentieth-century Chinese history. The Nationalists persistently claimed that the Communists had, in fact, conspired to kidnap Chiang. On the other hand, the Communists attributed the incident to Chiang's deliberate concocting and spreading of a rumor with the aim of expelling the Communists from the GMD and the revolutionary army.

In the past quarter century, studies by Chinese scholars such as Yang Tianshi and Yang Kuisong convincingly have proven that the March 20th Incident mostly likely happened accidentally. On the evening of March 18, a commercial ship from Shanghai to Guangzhou was attacked by pirates near Whampoa and sent an emergency request for help to the nearby Whampoa Academy. *Zhongshan,* with the approval of the Bureau of the Navy, traveled to Whampoa. The next day, Li Zhilong was informed that a delegation from

Soviet Russia sought to visit Guangzhou, and he then reported to Chiang for approval to move the ship from Whampoa to Guangzhou. Unaware that *Zhongshan* had steamed to Whampoa following the pirate incident and had done so by order of the Bureau of the Navy, Chiang suspected at once that this was a Communist plot to kidnap him, and he then took the course of action he deemed necessary.[39]

But there were deeper reasons underlying the March 20th Incident. Conflict had been intensifying between the CCP and the GMD, and also between the GMD's right- and left-wing factions, prior to the incident. Chiang himself remained eager to promote a "Nationalist Revolution" aimed at struggling against imperialism and pursuing China's national independence. In the meantime, he also felt increasingly suspicious of the ideas and practices of Communism. In addition, there existed a widening rift between Chiang and Wang Jingwei, as well as between Chiang and the chief Soviet military advisor known as "Kissarka" (N. V. Kuibyshev). After Sun Yat-sen's death, Chiang and Wang became the two principal competitors for the position of paramount leader within the GMD. They were like two tigers competing to occupy the same mountain. Kissarka, who was reportedly quite arrogant, held the highest rank of any Soviet military commander in China. Upon his arrival in Guangzhou, he looked down upon Chiang's qualifications as a commander, which Chiang had sensed. The two truly disliked each other. This was the time that the revolutionary government in Guangzhou was preparing to launch a Northern Expedition against the government in Beijing and various regional warlords in eastern, central, and northern China. On the eve of the March 20th Incident, the two had disagreed on strategies for the Northern Expedition, neither one willing to compromise, further straining their already fraught relationship.[40] Once something happened, it was easy for the suspicious Chiang to make a mountain out of a molehill.

By nightfall on March 20, Chiang had already realized that there had been no such conspiracy to kidnap him, and that he had gone too far by imposing martial law and placing Communist officers under "coercive protection." Throughout the long night of March 20, and until sometime the next day, Chiang's mood shifted from anger to panic, as he now became extremely worried about how he might settle the chaos that had resulted from his indiscreet management of the events the day before.[41]

The challenge that Zhou and his CCP comrades now faced was how to deal with Chiang. Despite his amicable relations with Chiang, Zhou preferred an aggressive approach. He believed that the Communists, together with the pro-Communist left wing of the GMD, were well positioned to "firmly repulse Chiang's attack." This was particularly true of Wang Jingwei, who was incensed by Chiang's "outrageous behavior" and determined to bring Chiang down. Kissarka, the chief Soviet military advisor, also strongly endorsed the idea of "dealing Chiang a serious blow." Moreover, Zhou believed that widespread support could also be found among commanders of various units of the revolutionary army for "teaching Chiang a bitter lesson."[42]

According to an account by Zhou almost twenty years later, in the wake of the March 20th Incident, he met Mao for the first time in his life. "I met Mao at (Li) Fuchun's home," recalled Zhou. "Mao inquired about the balance of strength between various armies, and he favored waging a resolute counteroffensive (against Chiang). Following Mao's advice, I went to see the Soviet advisor Kissarka, who emphasized that we should split (with Chiang). In fact, our military strength at the time should have allowed us to challenge Chiang."[43] This was Zhou's narrative; Mao never recalled when and where he and Zhou met for the first time. If Zhou's memory was accurate, this episode marked the beginning of his half-century-long bond with the future chairman, a relationship chiefly defined by his living and working in the shadow of the latter's ideas, programs, authority, and power.

However, the situation did not develop as Zhou and Mao had hoped. A Soviet general, Andrei S. Bubnov, a Soviet Bolshevik Party Central Committee member, was then heading a high-ranking Soviet delegation of inspectors to China and had just arrived in Guangzhou. Following what he understood as Moscow's established policy of "uniting with Chiang," he decided to pursue a compromise with the generalissimo.[44] Then things changed rapidly opposite to Zhou's expectations. Kissarka was dismissed from his post and sent back to the Soviet Union. Wang Jingwei, deeply disappointed with Bubnov's decision, opted to leave China for France. The political and military power in Guangzhou fell into Chiang's hands.[45]

Once Chiang had further consolidated his gains, he moved swiftly to drive the Communists out of the GMD's decision-making circle. On the one hand, by excluding the Communists or curtailing their numbers, he installed his own people in a series of key GMD positions. On the other hand, Chiang loudly announced his intention to struggle against the GMD's anti-Communist, right-wing elements, showcasing his steadfast willingness to work together with the Soviets and the Communists.[46]

Chiang's words were no more than lip service. In May, the GMD Central Committee held a plenary session at Chiang's discretion. First on the meeting's agenda was a "Resolution on Rectifying Party Affairs," which stipulated that all CCP members within the GMD either voluntarily withdraw from it or give up their CCP membership. The session adopted the resolution.[47]

In the wake of the session, top CCP leaders began to regard Chiang as belonging to the GMD's "new right wing" or, at best, as a "centrist leaning toward the right." However, it was not the party itself but Moscow that devised the CCP's strategy. The Soviet leaders, driven primarily by their own intraparty struggles, still hoped to "cooperate with Chiang," despite his consistently odd behavior toward the CCP.[48] Under these circumstances, the CCP leaders chose a strategy of neither trying to overthrow Chiang nor giving him support. What exactly did such a strategy mean, and how would it work? No one in the CCP leadership, Zhou included, could offer an answer at the moment.[49]

All of this had a huge impact on Zhou. In April, he was discharged from his position as the First Army's deputy party representative and director of political affairs.[50] Several other prominent CCP members were also fired from their posts. The CCP leadership, who now treated Zhou as a military expert, appointed him to head a military commission under the party's Guangdong Provincial Committee. Zhou's main task was to coordinate preparations for the forthcoming Northern Expedition. In July, over two hundred Communist officers who had left Whampoa and the First Army gathered at a Buddhist temple in Guangzhou to attend a special political training program, of which Zhou served as director and principal instructor.[51] The Northern Expedition War began almost simultaneously.

* * *

In December 1926, the CCP Central Committee formally transferred Zhou from Guangzhou to Shanghai, making him a member of the party's Central Military Commission (CMC) and a secretary of the Party's Central Personnel Department. Thus, Zhou was entrusted to help manage two of the CCP's most important tasks, its military and organizational affairs.[52] Deng Yingchao, then already several months pregnant, stayed in Guangzhou.

By then, the Communists had already organized two armed uprisings by the workers in Shanghai to seize control of the city—both had ended in failure. After Zhou's arrival, the party leadership immediately assigned him to oversee preparations for another uprising in Shanghai. From the outset, Zhou placed particular emphasis on the importance of "making careful preparation and catching the right moment to act."[53]

On May 19, the advance units of the Northern Expedition Army arrived in Shanghai's suburbs. Early that morning, Zhou chaired and spoke at an urgent meeting by the CCP's Shanghai District Committee. He realized that the right time to launch the uprising had arrived. If the enemy forces "show sign of collapse," Zhou said, "orders should immediately be issued to begin a general strike while, at the same time, taking action (to launch the uprising)."[54]

At nine o'clock the next morning, Zhou issued the order for the uprising to start. Shanghai's workers, who allegedly numbered over 800,000, began a general strike. The CCP-led workers' military pickets launched attacks on various key targets in the city, including the Shanghai Train Station, police bureaus, and postal and communication facilities. By the afternoon of March 22, the Shanghai Train Station, which was the enemy forces' last stronghold, had fallen into the hands of the workers' pickets. Zhou pronounced the uprising a success. A pro-CCP provisional municipal government was then established.

By then, however, the troops under Chiang's command had already entered Shanghai. On March 26, Chiang himself also arrived. He wasted no time in demanding that the workers' pickets be immediately disarmed. He also refused to recognize and work with Shanghai's Communist-controlled provisional government. Zhou, who had accumulated much experience in dealing with Chiang in Guangzhou, was deeply troubled. "All circumstantial evidence has clearly shown that he (Chiang) is ready to deal a blow to us," Zhou warned his comrades at a CCP special committee meeting on March 30. "In the future, when they try to . . . fully control Shanghai, surely they will use force to deal with us."[55] However, Zhou was unable to come up with a workable plan to prevent Chiang from taking the initiative to attack the Communists.

At the start of April, Chiang further enhanced his control of Shanghai as more of his troops arrived in the city. Subsequently, he declared martial law in Shanghai, strictly banning mass rallies, strikes, and unauthorized demonstrations.[56] Every sign indicated that a huge storm, one that could destroy the GMD-CCP united front, was approaching.

The big showdown came on April 12, 1927. Members of Shanghai's Green Gang, an underworld society, who had had close connections with Chiang, conducted an early-morning raid on the offices of Communist-led union organizations throughout the city. Then, Chiang's troops, under the pretext of "stopping street fighting," disarmed almost all workers' pickets in Shanghai. The next day, Chiang's soldiers opened fire on thousands of demonstrating workers who had heeded the Communist-led union's call for a general strike. Three days later, Chiang formally announced his intention to split with the CCP and "cleanse the Guomindang." His troops and agents began to arrest and massacre Communists and Communist sympathizers throughout the city.

All this put Zhou in grave danger. On the evening of April 11, Zhou received a dinner invitation from Si Lie, a division commander of Chiang's troops and the younger brother of a former colleague of Zhou's. When Zhou attended the dinner, however, he was not allowed to leave until late the next day.[57] By then, all pro-Communist pickets had been disarmed. Though Chiang's move enraged him, Zhou found himself and his party without a card to play against the generalissimo. Many years later, when Zhou related the circumstances of that day, he still lamented, "We were truly very young at that time, and truly inexperienced. . . . The most serious mistake on our part was that we had had no mental preparation at all, and we had never thought of what the next step should be."[58]

In the days following Chiang's April 12 coup, Shanghai descended into a "white terror," as Chiang's soldiers continuously rounded up Communists and Communist supporters. With each passing day, the upheaval in Shanghai grew increasingly dangerous for Zhou and his CCP comrades. To conceal himself from Chiang's agents, Zhou went underground.[59]

On April 16 and 19, a special committee formed after Chiang's coup, composed of Zhou, Li Lisan, Chen Yannian, Zhao Shiyan, and Gregory Voitingsky (a representative from the Comintern's Oriental Department), held two urgent meetings to draw up a strategy to grapple with the grave challenge facing the CCP. At that time, Wuhan was still under the control of the GMD's left wing, but its troops were engaged in fierce fighting with the forces of warlords in the North. Should Wuhan continue to focus on the Northern Expedition, or should it turn to fight against Chiang? For Zhou, the answer was obvious: Chiang was now the main enemy of the revolution. Thus, the Communists, along with the GMD's left wing, should expose Chiang's "reactionary face" and immediately launch an anti-Chiang campaign. Moreover, Zhou believed that Wuhan should adopt the strategy of "fighting Chiang first, waging the Northern Expedition second" and pursue military actions to counter Chiang.[60] The committee adopted Zhou's recommendation. Zhou then drafted a telegram to the CCP leadership, which several other attendees of the meeting also signed, urging the Party Center to implement the strategy of "immediately launching an offensive against Chiang."[61]

At this perilous moment, Deng Yingchao was due to give birth to her and Zhou's baby in Guangzhou. The delivery was an ordeal, and the baby did not survive. Deng herself immediately went underground to evade the enemies' purge. Not until several weeks later did she receive a message from Zhou, who asked her to come join him in Shanghai. Once she managed to get to Shanghai, Deng used Zhou's code name from his Awakening Society days, Wu Hao, to run a missing person column in Shanghai newspapers. Zhou saw it, and Deng and Zhou were secretly reunited in Shanghai's political underground.[62]

Now, there was little that Zhou could do in Shanghai. One night in mid-May, he left Shanghai on a ship flying the Union Jack.[63] Around May 20, he arrived in Wuhan, the new center of the Great Revolution, where the united front still lingered between the CCP and the GMD's left wing headed by Wang Jingwei.

The CCP held its Fifth Congress in Wuhan just days prior to Zhou's arrival in the city. Though Zhou missed the congress, he was still elected to the Central Committee and the Politburo and was made head of the Central Committee's secretarial staff. On May 25, Zhou was invited to attend a Politburo Standing Committee meeting, at which he was named head of the Central Committee's Department of Military Affairs, authorized to attend Standing Committee meetings "if necessary."[64] Four days later, Zhou earned an additional role as an acting member of the Standing Committee. Thus, less than two weeks after he arrived in Wuhan, Zhou joined the innermost circle of the party's central leadership.

In the second half of May, the Comintern's Executive Committee adopted a "Resolution on the China Question," which was known as the "May Instruction." Moscow ordered the Chinese Communists to carry out armed struggles aimed chiefly at the "promotion of land revolutions." In particular, the Comintern instructed the CCP to "organize eight to ten divisions, composed of revolutionary workers and peasants and commanded by those who are absolutely reliable."[65]

Indeed, from the Communists' perspective, the situation in Wuhan was rapidly deteriorating. Wang Jingwei, who had earned a reputation as the leader of the pro-Communist left wing within the GMD, seriously considered splitting with the CCP too. Wang would never forget his experience a year earlier, during and after the March 20th Incident. Then, he had felt certain that the Soviet advisers would back him in his standoff with Chiang. But he was betrayed; he left the country disappointed and in disgrace. How could Moscow and the CCP have hoped that, this time, he would take their side in another major confrontation with Chiang, one in which the generalissimo already held the upper hand?[66]

In mid-July, the CCP leadership was restructured according to the Comintern's instructions. Chen Duxiu was removed from his position as the party's general secretary with the establishment of a new Provisional Standing Committee. On July 13, the CCP announced that it would withdraw from the government in Wuhan and stop cooperating with Wang Jingwei. Two days later, on July 15, Wang in turn decided to split with the CCP. Akin to what had happened in Shanghai three months before, Wang began a bloody suppression of Communists and Communist supporters in areas under his control.

As Chiang and Wang both moved to split with the Communists, the two revolutionary trends—Nationalist revolution and Communist revolution—that had converged during the Great Revolution would embark on separate paths. To be sure, the Chinese Communists and Nationalists still held much in common. Most importantly, they both still held high the banner of anti-imperialism and emphasized the critical importance of "saving China" and empowering the Chinese to stand up in the world. However, in the political and military confrontations that would soon consume them, both the Communists and Nationalists would make the elimination of the other party their top priority, leading in the decades to come to a bloody civil war.

• • •

Did this mean that the Great Revolution had failed? Neither the CCP nor the Comintern in distant Moscow was willing to accept this as a reality. The CCP Central Committee, following Moscow's instructions, decided to mobilize pro-CCP troops to catalyze a military uprising in Nanchang, the capital city of Jiangxi Province. By then, Zhou had consolidated his reputation as a party leader "with good military expertise"; he was thus appointed to organize and serve as secretary for the Frontal Committee, which would oversee the uprising.[67]

In late July, Zhou left Wuhan along with virtually all other CCP leaders in the city. Zhou and several of his comrades in the party leadership moved to Jiujiang, a municipality not far from Wuhan, where they held a meeting on July 24. Zhou and others in attendance decided to mobilize the troops under the party's influence to launch an armed uprising in Nanchang.[68] Concerning their general strategy, Zhou and his colleagues decided to follow the advice of the Soviet advisor General Vasilli K. Bliukher (known by the pseudonym of "Galen"). According to the plan, the troops involved in the uprising would immediately move southward toward Guangdong, try to establish base areas there, control seaports, and obtain "international support." Then they would launch another Communist-led northern expedition from their newly formed base in Guangzhou.[69] On July 27, Zhou secretly arrived in Nanchang.

Early in the morning of August 1, the Nanchang Uprising began. Within a few short hours, the pro-Communist troops had seized control of the whole city. A Revolutionary Committee—of which Zhou was a member—was established to serve as Nanchang's new political and military authority. Zhou and his comrades, however, had no intention of keeping the city. According to their plans, their troops would immediately move south toward Guangdong, where they would establish a new base area, seizing seaports along the way.[70]

The troops under Zhou and his comrades' command left Nanchang on August 3. After a series of bloody battles during which they sustained heavy casualties, they finally crossed into Guangdong in mid-September. On September 24, they occupied Shantou, a seaport city in eastern Guangdong. Zhou and his comrades were delighted by the troops' progress.

Yet, although the troops seemed to have been making headway toward their objectives, their luck had begun to falter. By the time they arrived in Guangdong, Zhou's troops had been greatly diminished in numbers. Also, after they entered the province, they did not win the expected "local support" from workers and peasants there. What made the situation even more daunting to Zhou and his comrades was that an ever-expanding enemy force had followed them throughout their trek from Nanchang to Guangdong. When Zhou's troops occupied Shantou, the enemy force, which by then had grown to be several times larger and more powerful than Zhou's troops, encircled them. An offensive on Shantou followed. By October 1, Zhou's troops were defeated, and Shantou was lost.[71]

Zhou once thought of leading his remaining troops to the countryside to carry out guerrilla warfare. However, as Shantou was so tightly surrounded by enemies, there was no way for them to escape and implement the plan. At this critical moment, Zhou suffered a vicious case of malaria. He had a very high fever and was in a coma for several days. A local party member found a small boat and, after tossing in choppy waves for two days, brought Zhou to Hong Kong, where he received medical treatment and survived.[72]

Many of Zhou's comrades had died in the days and weeks after Shantou's fall. In hindsight, only by sheer luck had Zhou narrowly avoided the same fate. He hid in Hong Kong for almost a month, where, by late October, he was beginning to gradually regain his health. On October 23, he received a notice from the Central Committee, delivered to him via a surviving party organ in Guangdong, which instructed him to attend an urgent meeting in Shanghai.[73] In early November, he boarded a ship in Hong Kong bound for Shanghai.

From the perspective of the Chinese Communists, the Great Revolution ended in failure. For Zhou, this was a blood-soaked learning experience. Most importantly, he had developed a deeper understanding of the relationship between pursuing the "united front" strategy and resorting to armed struggles. Indeed, Zhou was among the first CCP leaders to put into practice the concept that "political power comes out the barrel of a gun" in the wake of Chiang's anti-Communist coup. The CCP's failure in the Great Revolution thus offered Zhou the rare, painful, yet valuable lessons that helped him grow into a more mature leader of the Chinese Communist Revolution in the years to come.

7

SHANGHAI UNDERGROUND

1927–1931

Shanghai, the "Paris of the Orient," was also known as a paradise of adventurers. A fishing village in the distant past, Shanghai gradually developed into a small walled city by the mid-nineteenth century. In the wake of the Qing's defeat in the Opium War and the Chinese Empire's subsequent signing of a series of "unequal treaties" with Western powers, Shanghai rapidly transformed into a major treaty port and one of the principal commercial centers in China and East Asia. A main feature of the city—divided into the Chinese zone and various foreign concessions—was its lack of a unified judicial and administrative structure. Any modern metropolis offered conditions for underground activities by organized political forces in opposition to the prevailing order. Shanghai offered even better conditions for these activities due to the inability of its fragmented authorities to coordinate the policing of the city.[1]

Zhou Enlai sneaked into Shanghai in early November 1927, a time of grave crises, challenges, and anxieties for the nascent CCP. Zhou's comrades had anxiously awaited his arrival. On November 9, he attended a two-day enlarged meeting of the Politburo chaired by Qu Qiubai, who had replaced Chen Duxiu as the party's general secretary three months before. However, Vissarion Lominadze, the Comintern representative from Moscow, was actually in charge. Although there was latent danger in every sound outside the house, CCP leaders boasted that the Chinese revolution should be "uninterrupted" and that "the whole country is on the eve of a more thorough revolution." Zhou echoed these sentiments. Due to the defeat of the

Nanchang Uprising, Zhou was given a warning. In the meantime, however, he was made a member of the Politburo Standing Committee and appointed chief of the Central Committee's secretariat. In contrast, Mao Zedong was criticized for "not following the Party's strategies." Moreover, unlike Zhou, he was deprived of his alternate membership in the Politburo.[2]

In the next four years, Zhou would make Shanghai his main base of activities. During this period, several others would occupy the top leadership position within the CCP. Zhou actually had the opportunity to climb to that post, as he controlled almost all of the party's organizational links and its intelligence network. However, he did not seem willing to seize the opportunity. He was even blamed on several occasions for giving too much attention to the trivia of the party's everyday operations at the expense of "big issues."[3] Nonetheless, Zhou never lost his influence or power. No matter who became the party's top leader or who was the Comintern's representative in Shanghai, they had to depend on Zhou to keep pace with the party's routine operations.

When Zhou arrived in Shanghai, he knew well that he and his comrades would be acting in an extremely dangerous environment. For them, Shanghai was a city of rampant "white terror." Since Chiang Kai-shek's anti-Communist coup in April, tens of thousands of Communists and Communist supporters had been murdered or jailed. Now, both the Nationalist government and foreign concession authorities would be more than eager to destroy CCP organs in hiding. In the meantime, however, uncoordinated forces controlled the city's judiciary and police power. Thus, the Communists had sufficient space for their underground activities.[4]

As soon as Zhou assumed his new posts, he established the party's security and intelligence services, known as the "Section of Special Service" or *Teke,* as a top priority. This endeavor had its origins in a "special work section" that had been formed within the CCP's Military Affairs Department in Wuhan as early as May 1927, when Zhou was in charge of the department. Gu Shunzhang was chosen to head the new section. A Shanghai native with a blue-collar background, Gu was a legendary figure, a self-taught master magician who at one time had connections with the Green Gang, a notorious underworld society. Gu and his colleagues' primary responsibilities were to collect intelligence information and carry out "unconventional and special assignments" for the party.[5]

Gu and his comrades moved to Shanghai in the wake of Wang Jingwei's purge of the Communists in Wuhan in mid-July 1927. When Zhou reorganized the special work section into the *Teke,* Gu headed the new unit, which was assigned tasks relating to intelligence, security, elimination of traitors, and radio communication.[6] In November 1928, over a year after the formation of the *Teke,* the CCP Center decided to establish a special committee, headed by Zhou, to supervise the *Teke*'s operation and to handle communications with the Comintern in Moscow.[7]

It was almost a miracle that Zhou survived the powder keg filled with explosives that was Shanghai. On one hand, it certainly helped that a substantial part of the city was under foreign authorities' jurisdiction. On the other hand, Zhou's survival should also be attributed to his skillful management of the dangerous environment in which he operated. Throughout his years in Shanghai, he always regarded security as an issue of utmost importance, paying attention to small details. He frequently moved between residences (which were almost always located in foreign concessions), never staying in one place longer than a month. Every time he moved to a new location, he would use a new name. He would not go out except before dawn or after dark, unless in an emergency. He would carefully apply makeup before he ventured out, and he sometimes sported a large beard. Often, even Zhou's close friends could not recognize him.[8]

In the autumn and winter of 1927, Zhou and his fellow CCP leaders were puzzled by the question of where the Chinese revolution then stood and what sort of future it would have. In December 1927, the party launched an armed uprising in Guangzhou. At one point, the party-led rebels seized control of many parts of the city. In a few days, however, enemy forces arrived in huge waves. Overwhelmed, the Communists failed miserably. Several of Zhou's close comrades died. Members of the Soviet consulate in Guangzhou were also involved in the violent coup and were met with a fierce retaliatory attack by Guomindang troops. Half a dozen Soviets were killed and their bodies lay in the street for days. The Nationalist Government severed diplomatic relationship with the Soviet Union. How to assess such a huge blow, plot the direction of future action, and make strategies and policies accordingly became urgent matters for Zhou and other CCP leaders.

Against this background, preparations for the only CCP congress held abroad began in late 1927. Moscow was selected to host the congress. Security considerations certainly influenced this decision; after all, it was truly difficult to find a safe place within China's borders where almost all of the party's leaders could gather. But a more important reason was that CCP elites, in devising strategies at a time of great uncertainty, needed the Comintern's guidance nearby.

In early May 1928, Zhou and Deng Yingchao left Shanghai disguised as an antiques-dealing couple on a business trip. They first boarded a Japanese steamship bound for Dalian. At the port in Dalian, the two were stopped by several plainclothes Japanese agents who brought Zhou to the police station for interrogation. "What do you do?" asked one agent. "I am a merchant of antiques," Zhou calmly replied. "Why do you bring with you so many newspapers?" "For reading aboard the ship." "Why do you come to Manchuria?" "To visit my uncle." After Zhou had answered all their questions, the agents decided to let him go. The couple left Dalian the same afternoon.[9] They traveled by train across Manchuria enroute to the Soviet Union.

Zhou and Deng arrived in Moscow in mid-May. Stalin had recently won a series of victories in his fierce conflicts with Leon Trotsky and other opposition leaders within the Bolshevik Party. The "China question" had been an issue neither side could afford to ignore. Now, it became an important tool in Stalin's hands with which to confront the opposition and consolidate his "victory."[10] On June 9, Stalin met with a group of CCP representatives, including Zhou, for whom this was his first meeting with the Soviet dictator. When Stalin spoke with the group, he obviously kept in mind the issues over which he had quarreled with Trotsky. He stressed that China could not engage in an "uninterrupted revolution" (which was exactly what Trotsky had favored). "Imperialism has remained a main force in China, very powerful militarily, and this is completely different from the Russian Revolution," said Stalin. "Now we cannot say that the Chinese Revolution is in its high times." But the CCP should not sit idly by and wait for the coming of a revolutionary high tide. Rather, the party should "strive to create its own military force, as nothing can be done without it."[11]

Zhou, who served as the note taker, did not speak at the meeting. Li Lisan, a CCP leader who also attended the meeting, tried to share his own views with Stalin. "There are still struggles of the workers and peasants in China, so the revolution is still at high tide," said Li. "Even in low tide, there could be a few errant waves," the Soviet dictator replied, coldly rebutting Li.[12] Zhou looked on, saying nothing.

Zhou and his comrades were gripped by persistent and deep confusion. They dearly hoped to obtain more concrete answers to their questions in the mecca of the world revolution. Therefore, upon arriving in Moscow, they submitted to the Comintern a series of questions. Among them were theoretical ones: What kind of bourgeoisie class was there in China? How should the CCP deal with the petty bourgeoisie class? They also raised questions about the state of China's revolution: What was the difference between the *rising* tide of a revolution and its *high* tide? At a time when the world revolution was at a low ebb, could the Chinese revolutionaries achieve victory in their own campaign? One of their sharpest questions was: Why did the Comintern representatives in China often swing between the Right and the Left during the Great Revolution?[13]

These were tough questions. The person who answered them on behalf of the Comintern was Nikolai Bukharin, who was known as the master theorist of the Bolshevik Party and was then still an ally of Stalin. Bukharin told Zhou and his comrades that the Chinese revolution had yet to reach its "high tide." Indeed, Bukharin asserted, it lay in the trough that occurs between two cresting waves in the making of revolutionary tides.[14] Although CCP delegates reported that Bukharin's answers had enlightened them, they did not seem to have clearly understood what he really meant. For example, how might they turn the theoretical understanding proposed by Bukharin into strategies and policies? This issue remained unresolved.

The CCP held its Sixth Congress at an old plantation in Moscow's suburbs from June 18 to July 11. Zhou was a central figure at the congress, serving as head of the secretariat in charge of its organization.[15] At the congress, he gave two reports on personnel and military matters, respectively, and most importantly, also delivered a lengthy response to Qu Qiubai's political report, which was actually a comprehensive speech in itself. Zhou prepared the response assiduously—the outline alone covered several long pages. Revealed in the report were Zhou's anxiety, confusion, and aspiration. Zhou seemed to contradict himself, however, in his assessment of the situation and description of the party's mission. On the one hand, he supported abandoning the "uninterrupted revolution" thesis, especially as it was easily confused with Trotsky's mistaken ideas. On the other hand, he contended that the revolution should always advance toward the coming of another high tide.

Zhou's dilemma was not exceptional. For example, Qu also stressed in his political report that "our revolution is continuously moving toward another high tide."[16] What seemed clear in Zhou's presentation was his willingness to learn from the lessons of the Great Revolution. He thus argued for the need to mobilize the masses, prepare for armed uprisings, and establish Soviet regimes in China.[17]

In comparison, Zhou's report on personnel matters was much clearer. Tens of thousands of CCP members and supporters had been murdered or were still imprisoned in the wake of the GMD's anti-Communist coups in Shanghai and Wuhan. How to reorganize the party was a critical challenge facing Zhou and his comrades. Zhou spoke emphatically about the extreme importance of "iron discipline" and centralized leadership. Ever since the party's birth, Zhou had firmly believed that it should be made a Leninist party in the style of the Bolsheviks. Now, as "white terror" was sweeping across China, imposing discipline on the party became an issue of life-and-death importance for him.[18]

Zhou's report on military affairs at the congress reinforced his image as a military expert among his comrades. The lessons for the CCP to draw were painful ones. In a sense, the party's defeat in the Great Revolution was the result of its failure to brandish guns of its own. "Given the new situation that we are now facing," Zhou stressed, "it is essential to prepare and conduct armed uprisings . . . and the premise is to establish our own military force."[19]

The new CCP Central Committee held its first plenary session on July 19. Zhou was elected to the Politburo and, along with Xiang Zhongfa, Su Shaozheng, Cai Hesen, and Xiang Ying, to the Politburo's Standing Committee. He also was appointed head of the Central Committee's Secretariat and director of its Personnel Department.[20] Of the five members of the new Standing Committee, only Zhou would live to see the victory of the Chinese Communist Revolution.

Zhou cherished throughout his life his experience of attending the Sixth Congress. He had been made a target of harsh criticism during the Rectification Movement in Yan'an in the 1940s, when he was compelled to make "self-criticisms" on many issues. However, he insisted that the Sixth Congress was correct in direction and orientation. After he endured the trial of the Rectification Campaign, the first major presentation he gave to party cadres concerned the Sixth Congress.[21]

From mid-July to early September, Zhou attended the Comintern's Sixth Congress in Moscow. He was elected an alternate member of the Comintern's Executive Committee, thus emerging as a noticeable figure in the entire international Communist movement.[22] After this congress, Zhou stayed in the Soviet Union for another month. During this period, he met with

CCP military personnel who had been trained in the Soviet Union, and he helped investigate and resolve disputes among Chinese students at Sun Yat-sen University in Moscow.[23] Apart from these activities, what else did he do? As the party leader in charge of the *Teke,* he likely used this opportunity to obtain special training in intelligence matters and related technological skills, and he may also have discussed cooperation with the GPU (the predecessor of the KGB).[24] All this should have greatly enhanced his capacity as the CCP's spymaster after his return to China.

• • •

Zhou was back in Shanghai in early November 1928. Again, he treated the safety of the CCP headquarters in Shanghai as an absolute priority. Next in importance was to maintain communication with Moscow. Barely had Zhou rested from his travels before he set out to enhance the *Teke;* in October 1929, under his supervision, the CCP established its first secret radio transmitter station in Shanghai.[25]

Zhou also endeavored to plant his own agents and informants in the enemies' intelligence services. Thus emerged the three outstanding heroes of the early years of the CCP's intelligence activities: Qian Zhuangfei, Li Kenong, and Hu Di. By leveraging special connections, Qian managed to infiltrate the Investigation Section of the GMD's Central Personnel Department (which would later become one of the GMD's two main intelligence services). He gained the trust of Xu Enzeng, a GMD spymaster and head of the Investigation Section, and became a close assistant of Xu. Qian then referred Li to join the Investigation Section to work at one of its key branches, the Shanghai Radio Management Bureau. In the meantime, Hu assumed a position at the section's radio transmitter station in Tianjin. All three reported to Zhou.[26]

Zhou's biggest gain was to have successfully recruited Yang Dengying, a GMD special envoy in Shanghai with deep links to the police authorities in the British concession. Yang was not a CCP member; he agreed to work for the CCP mainly because Zhou compensated him generously. He became the most important informant planted by Zhou and the *Teke* in Shanghai's enemy camp.[27]

The *Teke* also established within its organization a "Red Squadron," whose primary objective was to use "abnormal means" to deal with those enemy agents regarded as the most dangerous, and also to punish party traitors.[28] Gu Shunzhang, who remained in charge of the *Teke,* reported directly to Zhou. Oftentimes, Zhou personally intervened in the *Teke*'s decision-making and activities. He kept to himself some of the most important intelligence links, unknown even to Gu. The *Teke* also received substantial financial and technological support from Moscow, and many of its members had been trained in the Soviet Union.[29] Consequently, the *Teke* not only survived for a long time but also sometimes held the upper hand against the GMD and foreign concession authorities in late-1920s and early-1930s Shanghai.

• • •

Zhou met his toughest challenge in trying to manage his relations with Mao Zedong. After Chiang's anti-Communist coup in 1927, several party members, such as Peng Bai and Mao, went to the countryside to mobilize the peasants to carry out armed struggles. At one point, Peng—who established a base area and a Soviet regime in Guangdong—enjoyed a greater reputation than Mao. By May 1928, however, the Guangdong base had been lost to overwhelming enemy forces. Peng escaped and fled to Shanghai. Later, he was arrested and executed by GMD authorities.[30]

In late 1927, Mao organized an "Autumn Harvest Uprising" in Hunan, his home province; the revolt was quickly suppressed by a much stronger enemy. Mao managed to lead a group of about one thousand defeated soldiers to Mount Jinggang in Jiangxi Province, where they established a new base. Then, in the wake of the unsuccessful Nanchang Uprising, another group of remnant troops, led by Zhu De, arrived at Jinggang to join forces with Mao's. Together, they established the Red Fourth Army. Originally, Mao had neither ideas nor plans about how to establish base areas in the countryside. After he and his troops occupied Jinggang, it occurred to Mao that this was a spot on the periphery of Jiangxi and Hunan provinces, which was not well controlled by the provincial authorities of either. Mao's Red Army won the support of the area's peasants through confiscating and redistributing land held by landlords. With the gradual expansion of their impact and influence, Mao's activities even captured Moscow's positive attention.[31]

However, in January 1929, under pressure from a superior enemy force, Mao's troops abandoned Mount Jinggang and trekked into southern

Jiangxi. There they suffered a bad defeat in a battle in the small town of Dayu. Subsequently, Mao lost contact with party headquarters in Shanghai.[32]

Zhou oversaw military affairs at the Party Center, so it was his duty to maintain communication with Mao and the Red Army. On February 7, he drafted a letter to Mao and Zhu. Since Zhou had not received responses from Mao and Zhu to several of his previous letters, the tone of this message was pessimistic. He instructed Mao and Zhu to divide the Red Army into small squadrons so that it could not be completely eliminated by the enemy. He also requested that Mao and Zhu leave the Red Army and report to the Party Center in Shanghai.[33] On April 7, Zhou dispatched another letter to Mao and Zhu, again asking them to "temporarily leave the Red Army and come to Shanghai."[34]

Before Zhou's February letter was delivered to Mao and Zhu, the Red Army under their command won several battles. By the time they finally received Zhou's letter in early April, their situation had already greatly improved. Two days later, Mao claimed in a response letter that Zhou and others at the Party Center were seriously mistaken, as they had felt "too pessimistic about the situation and our own strength." Hence Mao refused to leave the Red Army and come to Shanghai.[35] The Politburo discussed Mao's report on June 12. Zhou, while rebutting Mao's claim that he had been "too pessimistic," acknowledged that it was inappropriate to ask the Red Army to disperse. Zhou also withdrew the request for Mao or Zhu to come to Shanghai; instead, they were given the option to dispatch to the Party Center a "capable person as their representative."[36]

This was Zhou's most important encounter with Mao since his time in Guangzhou. Although he was then Mao's absolute superior within the party, his attitude toward the future chairman was remarkably shrewd. Unwilling to use his power and authority to compel Mao's obedience, he showed Mao patience and respect. Indeed, mixed with his prudence toward Mao was a subtle fearfulness. While it is difficult to identify the sources of such a feeling, this was probably an early manifestation of the unique and even mysterious chemical reaction that would characterize the relationship between the two men who, in the half century to come, would lead the Chinese Communist Revolution to victory and then rule the Chinese Communist state.

One wave rose before an earlier one subsided. In April 1929, a major war erupted between Chiang Kai-shek and warlords in Guangxi Province. As

Chiang shifted the bulk of his attention to Guangxi, Mao and Zhu seized a providential opportunity to defeat a much-weakened enemy force and recover Mount Jinggang. Despite the improved situation, however, the long-existing yet hitherto concealed differences between Mao and Zhu surfaced to spoil their relations. Earlier, before the Red Army gave up Jinggang, Zhu was secretary of the Party Committee of the Fourth Army; above it was a Party Frontal Committee with Mao as the secretary. After it abandoned Jinggang, Zhu's Army Committee temporarily halted its activities, relinquishing its power to Mao's Frontal Committee for more efficient decision-making and implementation in a daunting environment. Mao thus controlled all of the army's power. Once the Red Fourth Army had recovered Jinggang, Zhu's Army Committee resumed functioning, which Mao was reluctant to see.

Then, the Party Center dispatched Liu An'gong, who had recently returned from the Soviet Union, to the Fourth Army and appointed him provisional secretary of the Army Committee. Liu hailed from the same hometown as Zhu, with whom he had also studied in Germany. After taking up his new role, Liu collaborated with Zhu to gradually strengthen the Army Committee's power. Mao, offended, attempted to permanently dissolve the Army Committee, which Zhu firmly opposed. Consequently, two competing groups, one supporting Mao and another favoring Zhu, came into being within the Fourth Army. A showdown came in June at a party congress of the Fourth Army. Chen Yi, who leaned toward Zhu (he had known Zhu since their years in Europe), chaired the congress. Although he criticized both Mao and Zhu for promoting disunity, he held that "Mao should bear the main responsibility for causing the dispute." Chen also blamed Mao for his "patriarchal style as a leader." At the congress's conclusion, Mao was voted down as secretary of the Frontal Committee, and Chen was elected to replace Mao.[37]

Mao flew into a wild rage. Alone, he departed for "medical treatment" while he filed a complaint to the Party Center.[38] Chen also rushed to Shanghai to make his report. At the Party Center, Zhou was responsible for settling the dispute. In August, when the Politburo met to discuss how to avoid a split between Mao and Zhu, Zhou had already developed a plan. He believed the key was to appease Mao and bring him back into the fold. Therefore, he took an ambiguous attitude toward the Fourth Army Party Congress in June that had dethroned Mao as the virtual emperor of the Red

Zone (areas controlled by the Red Army), declaring that some of its resolutions were correct but others were wrong. He also proposed to transfer Liu An'gong back to Shanghai, thus bringing the Army Committee into dysfunction.[39] Zhou had a lengthy conversation with Chen after the latter arrived in Shanghai, in which he stressed that it was essential "to bring Mao back." At a Politburo meeting on August 29, Zhou, while criticizing Mao's "patriarchal tendency," emphasized that "extreme democracy" was not acceptable either. He proposed to include both Mao and Zhu in the Frontal Committee, with Mao serving as its secretary.[40] After the meeting, Zhou had several lengthy talks with Chen, in which he persuaded him to accept a compromise. Then, Zhou asked Chen to draft a letter to this effect on behalf of the Party Center; Zhou personally revised the letter. He asked Chen to take the letter back to the Fourth Army.[41]

This letter, later known as the "September Instruction," was another document bearing Zhou's hallmark centrist style. He criticized both Mao and Zhu yet leaned more toward Mao. He criticized Mao's abdicating his responsibility in order to pressure his comrades for concessions as "incompatible with a true Communist's consciousness." He also implied that Mao's style was too dictatorial. But he supported Mao's notion that the Red Army's main tasks were to carry out land revolution, wage guerrilla warfare, and take over the countryside before seizing cities. Zhou also affirmed that the Fourth Army had to be led by the Frontal Committee, and that Mao's authority should be enhanced, not weakened. Zhou concluded the letter by formally reinstating Mao as secretary of the Frontal Committee.[42]

Zhu De willingly accepted the September Instruction once Chen brought the document back to the Red Zone. Together, they invited Mao to return. Upon learning that he would resume his leadership role at the Frontal Committee, Mao immediately announced, "I have recovered from my illness." Then he rushed back to Fourth Army headquarters.[43]

Mao did not stop at this victory. In late December, he took a big step forward. At another Fourth Army Party congress held at Gutian, a small town in Fujian, Mao convinced the congress to adopt what would later become a central text of the Maoist military doctrine, "Resolutions of the Gutian Conference." The message it conveyed was that "the gun must be placed under the Party's absolute command."[44] With his thesis adopted,

Mao greatly enhanced his reputation and power in the Red Army. However, in retrospect, Zhou had played a crucial role in the making of the resolutions.

• • •

In early March 1930, Zhou suddenly disappeared from Shanghai. "Following a decision by the Politburo," he traveled to Moscow.[45] He made the trip in the wake of a series of disputes between the CCP leadership and the Comintern's Far Eastern Bureau (FEB). Zhou, as a CCP Center representative, would "report the CCP's work since the Sixth Congress and its disputes with the FEB."[46]

The CCP leadership's relations with the Shanghai-based FEB had been tense for some time. The bureau, then composed of a Pole and a German, had engaged in a series of quarrels with CCP leaders since 1929 concerning concrete strategies and policies. For example, in October 1929, two CCP-leaning GMD generals in Guangxi, Yu Zuobai and Li Mingrui, announced their intention to split with Chiang. Zhou and the CCP Center dispatched Deng Xiaoping as a representative to work with the two generals, who then launched an anti-Chiang armed uprising. The FEB representatives disapproved of Zhou's approach toward Yu and Li, accusing him of making a "rightist mistake" that had "obscured class lines." The accusation genuinely offended Zhou and his fellow CCP leaders, who in turn condemned the criticism for "ignoring China's specific condition by blindly adopting Russia's experience."[47] The undertone of the disputes, in reality, was the FEB's ambition to dominate the CCP's decision-making process, which Zhou and his comrades were unwilling to accept.

Tensions further escalated in December 1929. The FEB quoted a resolution that the Comintern had adopted two months before to again accuse Zhou and his comrades of having committed "rightist mistakes." Zhou, along with Xiang Zhongfa and Li Lisan, held several meetings with FEB representatives. Neither side was willing to yield to the other, and relations between them became even more strained.[48] On December 14, the CCP Politburo decided to send Zhou to Moscow to report to the Comintern directly.[49] But Zhou was then too busy to leave Shanghai; he also remained hopeful that he could reach a compromise with his comrades from the FEB.

The delay lasted until March 1930, when CCP leaders and the FEB entered into another round of fierce mutual attacks, each castigating the other for following a "rightist policy line." Zhou determined that he had no choice but to make another trip to the Soviet Union.

Unlike on his first trip to the Soviet Union in 1928, this time Zhou took the maritime route to Europe and then travelled by train to Moscow. We know little about his exact itinerary, but we do know that when he passed through Paris, he paid an unexpected visit to Zhang Ruoming, whom he had dated during his first two years in Europe.[50] In late April, he attended a small gathering of party members and supporters in Berlin, where he gave a speech on the international situation and the development of the Chinese Red Army.[51] In addition, he published an article about the Chinese Soviet Republic in *Red Flag,* the mouthpiece of the German Communist Party.[52]

Zhou arrived in Moscow around May 10. To settle the differences between the CCP and the FEB, he tried his best to tell Comintern leaders that the CCP had followed strategies and policies "best fitting China's conditions." Meanwhile, he also endeavored to clarify the Comintern's assessment of China's situation and, accordingly, how the CCP was expected to embrace an emerging revolutionary situation in China.[53]

Zhou and Qu Qiubai met with Stalin for more than an hour in late July. This was Zhou's second time meeting the Soviet dictator. The discussion was dominated by Stalin's monologue. He did not criticize the CCP leadership after listening to Zhou's briefing on China's situation and the CCP's efforts to "catch the right moment to embrace a coming revolutionary high tide." Instead, he asserted that China was a big and backward country with imbalanced development in political and economic realms. Therefore, stressed Stalin, the Chinese revolution would experience an uneven progress. Whereas in Germany, a general uprising by workers in Berlin could lead the Communists to seize national power, in China, the CCP had to first pursue victory in one or a few provinces, and establish and expand revolutionary base areas there, before it could attempt to occupy big cities. It was essential to have a strong Red Army to carry out such a strategy. "This is where the hope of the Chinese revolution lies," Stalin emphasized, "and you must make it a central task of yours."[54]

For Zhou, Stalin's words were more an endorsement than a critique of the CCP's strategies. In fact, in mid-July he gave a speech at a Bolshevik Party congress on how the CCP would promote the coming revolutionary outburst. He stated that, given China's uneven internal developments, "Soviet regimes and the Red Army exist in some areas before the revolutionary high tide" and that "the revolution could first achieve victory in one or a few provinces."[55] On July 23, the Comintern adopted a resolution on China.[56] Its content further convinced Zhou that Stalin and Moscow had maintained their neutrality in the CCP leadership's quarrels with the FEB representatives. His main objective in Moscow, he thought with delight, was accomplished.

There was another important item on Zhou's Moscow wish list: to secure from the Comintern more substantial financial support for the CCP. The party had received funding from Moscow since its inception. After 1927, with the CCP moving completely underground, that support became ever more critical; indeed, the party's very survival depended upon it. However, financial support from Moscow was unstable and was often interrupted for all kinds of reasons. The CCP leadership repeatedly tried to settle this issue; nonetheless, it lingered until Zhou's trip to Moscow.[57]

Now, when Stalin urged CCP leaders to strive to develop the Red Army and the Red Zone, he understood that he should provide the Chinese Communists with more aid. In early August, Stalin met with Zhou again, informing him that the funding issue would be "satisfactorily resolved." He promised Zhou that, "from now on, you will receive the funds calculated in gold prices." Following Stalin's instruction, Osip A. Piatnitsky, head of the Comintern's International Department, notified Zhou that the Comintern's representatives in Shanghai would pay off all the funds owed to the CCP. "I will personally be in charge of sending the funds to the CCP," Piatnitsky stated, which would be delivered in cash, calculated according to the price of gold, "before you return to China."[58] This was another of Zhou's extraordinary achievements, albeit for the moment only on paper.

There was more to come. Shortly after Zhou returned to China, he reportedly invented a new secret code, dubbed "Hao Mi" (the Hao codes), which corresponded to one of Zhou's aliases, "Wu Hao." This was a code system that would be used only in telecommunications of the highest level with utmost confidentiality, and only by top CCP leaders.[59] How did Zhou acquire the knowledge and expertise to create this code? No Chinese source has provided any explanation; Zhou was simply described as a genius. But this is knowledge too specific to be acquired even by a rare genius. Since he invented Hao Mi immediately after his return from the Soviet Union, it is reasonable to assume that he obtained relevant intelligence training in the Soviet Union, which enabled him to invent the code system.

• • •

Zhou returned to Shanghai on August 19, 1930. He immediately realized that tensions between the CCP Center and FEB had further deteriorated. During his absence from Shanghai, Xiang Zhongfa, and Li Lisan in particular, temporarily controlled CCP decision-making. To compete for the political and moral high ground vis-à-vis FEB representatives, Li put forward a series of radical plans to embrace an "imminent revolutionary situation." In mid-May, Li claimed that "China belonged to the weakest link in the chain of world imperialism, where the volcano of the world revolution is most likely to erupt first."[60] Then, in mid-June, the CCP Center, in a resolution for "a revolutionary outburst" across the country, demanded "powerful support from proletariats of the Soviet Union."[61] FEB representatives, realizing that such a demand contravened Stalin's grand strategy of "building socialism in one country" (i.e., the Soviet Union), immediately expressed their firm opposition to it.[62]

Around the same time, a major war erupted between Chiang Kai-shek's troops and two warlords, Yan Xishan and Feng Yuxiang, in central China. The conflict attracted the attention of almost all of the enemy forces attacking the Red Zones. The Red troops, capitalizing on this rare opportunity, temporarily occupied Changsha, the capital of Hunan Province, in late July. Li and Xiang took this as evidence that the rapid surge of the Chinese revolution was indeed imminent. In early August, the CCP Politburo again demanded Moscow's full support for unleashing the revolutionary tide upon the whole country, even though this might trigger a "war between (the Soviets) and Japan in Manchuria."[63] The FEB at once charged that Li had meant to "wage a struggle against the Comintern" by "forcing the Soviet Union to declare a war on world imperialism."[64]

This was the situation that Zhou faced upon his arrival in Shanghai. To try to reduce the tensions, he immediately called a meeting with Li and Xiang, stressing that it was crucial to strictly follow Moscow's orders rather than to try to direct Moscow's action.[65] At two Politburo meetings in late August, Zhou relayed what he understood as the Comintern's instructions. To persuade

Li to issue a "self-criticism," he earnestly downplayed the differences between the CCP Center and the Comintern. After all, Zhou emphasized, between the CCP and the Comintern "there existed little difference about political lines," and the CCP's "mistakes exist in only one or two isolated issues in the party's policymaking." In light of his talks with Stalin, he reminded his comrades that "more attention should be given to the Red Army and Red Zones than in the past.[66]

Zhou's soft tone revealed his failure to recognize the dangerous situation that the CCP leadership faced. And it was not difficult at all for Li and Xiang to accept the Comintern's views as conveyed to them by Zhou. Li acknowledged that the Comintern "indeed has been somewhat different with the CCP Center in strategies and tactics." Xiang proposed to send a telegram to the Comintern, admitting that "misunderstandings on our part have existed in the past" but asserting that "all problems have been resolved."[67]

In late September, Zhou, together with Qu Qiubai, chaired an enlarged Central Committee Plenum to criticize the "(Li) Lisan line." Li again conceded that his "policies and work arrangement had gone to the wrong direction of adventurism." As he relayed the Comintern's instructions, Zhou emphasized once more that there had existed "no big difference" between the CCP's policy lines and the instructions of the Comintern. Li's mistake was nothing more than "an overestimation of the degree and pace of the current situation of the revolution."[68] Quoting Zhou's conversation with Stalin, the Politburo emphasized that "the task of utmost importance . . . was to build the Red Zone, and to create a Red Army led by the politically and militarily fully prepared proletariat."[69]

Around that time, Zhou expressed his desire to leave Shanghai and be transferred to the Red Zone. Why did he do so? Was this due to his premonition that a big storm would soon come to Shanghai? Or was this because he wanted to take a leading role in implementing Stalin's call to strengthen the Red Army and Red Zone? The Central Committee established a Soviet Area Bureau (SAB) with Zhou as its secretary.[70] However, as Zhou was still dealing with too much unfinished business in Shanghai to leave the city, the Politburo decided to appoint Xiang Ying as the SAB's acting secretary on Zhou's behalf.[71]

A big storm indeed came before long. After he received the FEB's reports, Stalin erupted in rage, convinced that the CCP leadership had violated Moscow's instructions and that Zhou had not helped the CCP Center correct its mistakes, either. In a November 16 instruction, the Comintern dramatically escalated its accusations against the CCP, characterizing Li Lisan's problem as a "serious one involving general lines." Indeed, according to the Comintern, Li's mistakes were not "randomly committed" but "systematically made," exposing his "hostility to Leninism as well as to the Comintern."[72] To Li, accusations like these meant that his political career would be finished. This barrage of rhetoric must have also come as a huge surprise for Zhou, as this meant that everything he had done after returning to China had been wrong.

On January 7, 1931, the CCP leadership convened one of the most important conferences in its history, the Fourth Plenum of the Central Committee (elected at the Sixth Congress). Directing the conference was "Pavel Mif" (Mikhail Alexandrovich Fortus), the Comintern's special envoy, who previously had been the president of Sun Yat-sen University in Moscow. Although he did not actually attend the plenum, he behaved like a "super Czar." As Zhou later recalled, "Mif arranged and controlled everything."[73] With Mif's support from behind the curtain, Wang Ming, a former student of Mif's, was unexpectedly elected to the Central Committee and the Politburo.

The plenum's main mission, announced Mif, was to "thoroughly criticize the Lisan Line" and the "rightist-leaning reconciliatory attitude" of some party leaders toward the line, which should be regarded as "the most serious danger facing the party." Naturally, Li was the number one target of criticism at the plenum. As Zhou had failed to correct Li's mistakes after his return from Moscow, he became another main target of criticism. Labeled as a person "lacking a sense of principle," Zhou had to take "major responsibility" for the CCP Center's adoption of the "Lisan Line."

These developments must have shocked Zhou. He doubtless had a lot of grievances and complaints, but he did little to defend himself. He had to make "serious self-criticism," he knew; and he had to put all the blame on himself. "The party is now facing a very difficult challenge," he told his comrades. "The Lisan Line has demoralized the party. We are in desperate need of bringing the party back to a healthy status." In a note attached to the text of his self-criticism, which he asked to be relayed to the whole party, Zhou wrote, "I have asked that this document be distributed to let the whole party know about and criticize my mistakes."[74] After all, Zhou was the party's man.

At the heart of his mind-set was the belief that "the party's interests should always be placed above anything else."[75]

But Zhou was a "getting things done" person, and without him, even the Party Center's daily operations could be in serious jeopardy. Therefore, Mif did not want to get rid of him. Alexander Al'brecht, another Comintern representative who attended the meeting, thus showed lenience toward Zhou: "We must kick Comrade Zhou Enlai's buck [*sic*]. But we do not mean to knock him out. Instead, we should allow him to correct his mistakes in the future."[76] There was a call at the plenum for Zhou's removal from the Politburo, but the motion was defeated, with eighteen "nays" to six "yeas."[77] Despite the round of attacks directed at Zhou, he would continue to manage the Party Center's day-to-day operations.

The outcome of the Fourth Plenum—especially the impact of Mif and his associates' harsh actions—produced huge repercussions within the party. Wang Ming was so new and so young; with only shallow roots in the party, he lacked influence and authority. After the plenum, a series of separatist activities within the party challenged Mif and the party leadership. In late January 1931, the dissidents established a special committee independent of the Party Center. Although Zhou had endured severe criticism at the recent plenum, he firmly opposed these separatists from the outset and quickly joined in suppressing their activities. Zhou held a powerful weapon, which was to cut off the separatists' supply lines, closing any channel through which they might receive aid from Moscow and the Comintern.[78] Consequently, the opposition factions within the CCP all gradually withered. The party maintained its unity. And Zhou had every reason to claim the credit.

* * *

At that moment, CCP organs faced a rapidly worsening environment in Shanghai. GMD intelligence services, by upgrading their own capacity and bolstering their coordination with foreign concession authorities, redoubled their efforts to flush out Communists in hiding. Zhou and his comrades found themselves left with almost no space for activities or even survival. The coming of a major catastrophe for them, it seemed, was only a matter of time.

Disaster finally struck in April 1931. On the twenty-fourth of that month, Gu Shunzhang, *Teke* chief and Zhou's right-hand man in the party's intelligence services, was arrested by Nationalist agents in Wuhan. Gu told his interrogators almost immediately that he would give away all CCP secrets in exchange for his life and favorable treatment.[79]

But Gu made a fatal mistake. He demanded a face-to-face meeting with Chiang, refusing to disclose any information before that.[80] By doing so, Gu meant to show his importance, as well as to test how Chiang and the GMD regarded him. What he had failed to realize was that this also had left time for the news of his arrest to leak. The telegram reporting Gu's arrest arrived at the Nanjing office of Xu Enzeng, head of the GMD Investigation Section, on the evening of April 25, a Saturday, when Xu was already out at a dancing party. Qian Zhuangfei, Zhou's most deeply embedded agent on Xu's side, intercepted the telegram. He immediately sent his son-in-law, also a Communist agent, to rush to Shanghai on an overnight train, and managed to report Gu's arrest and treason to Zhou.[81] Zhou, though shocked, wasted no time in attempting to evacuate party leaders and organs, severing their connections with Gu. He also ordered the party to cease all the methods and procedures with which Gu was familiar.[82]

Three precious days had passed when, once Gu had met with Chiang in person, GMD special agents began the cleanup operation in Shanghai. However, they found nothing in most places they searched. While the CCP's underground network still suffered serious damage, the party avoided a catastrophe. Also, Zhou's long-held reservations about Gu proved farsighted, as there were critical holes in Gu's knowledge of the CCP's underground organizations and activities. Had he known more, it would have been impossible for Zhou and the CCP Center to remain in Shanghai after Gu's betrayal.

Any revolution is brutal. In the name of "justice" and "necessity," a revolution is capable of fully exposing the most barbaric aspects of human nature. In managing the Gu case, Zhou revealed a quite cruel and ruthless aspect of his character. He knew that Gu's wife, Zhang Xinghua, and several relatives of Gu had been involved in CCP underground activities. Zhou personally ordered *Teke* agents to kill Zhang and eight other members of the Gu family, including a two-year-old boy. The corpses were buried on site. The only survivor was Gu's three-year-old daughter, who happened to be away from home.[83]

Why did Zhou decide to kill all members of Gu's extended family? It seems that he did so for the sake of "killing a chicken to warn monkeys," so that other potential "traitors" would know that anyone who dared to follow in Gu's footsteps would be most severely punished. This, to be sure, was extremely inhumane. When Zhou ordered the killings, his usual calm demeanor gave way. Reportedly, he confided in his subordinates that he was unsure whether this was a good or a bad decision. "Let history judge," he said.[84]

* * *

By late 1931, Shanghai's environment had become increasingly hopeless for the CCP despite Zhou's efforts. The GMD's special services continuously tightened their encirclement of CCP underground organs. One after another, party cadres and activists were caught; many then defected. Zhou had no choice but to act ever more cautiously. He never left his hiding place in daylight; even after dark, he would not go out unless it was absolutely necessary. He moved to a new residence once every two to three days, if not more frequently. On the very rare occasions that he had to go out onto the street, he would extensively apply makeup. In such terrifying circumstances, the safety of Zhou and other CCP leaders had aroused Moscow's attention. On May 12, the Comintern met to discuss the security threat that CCP leaders faced. The meeting resolved that Zhou should come to Moscow for six months to a year.[85]

Soon after, Zhou and the CCP were dealt another blow. On June 22, 1931, Xiang Zhongfa, then CCP general secretary, was arrested by GMD intelligence services. Alarmed, Zhou immediately relocated to a new shelter. He also ordered all party organs to evacuate at once. Meanwhile, he mobilized all agents embedded in the enemy's intelligence and other services to obtain information about Xiang's whereabouts. At first, he meant to organize a mission to rescue Xiang, but he quickly learned that Xiang had already surrendered to the enemy. A few days later, for reasons still unclear, Xiang was executed by a direct order from Chiang Kai-shek.[86]

Almost at the same time, a Comintern spy in Shanghai, Hilaire Noulens, a Ukrainian member of the Bolshevik Party since 1917 whose real name was Jakob Rudnik, was arrested along with his wife. On orders from the Comintern, they had come to China in March 1930 to establish a secret liaison station in Shanghai.

The lead-up to the Noulenses' exposure came from Singapore, where, in early 1931, a Comintern messenger was arrested. The documents he brought with him pointed to Noulens and his activities in Shanghai. On June 15, concession police arrested the Noulenses and discovered at their home a large amount of documents, including Comintern instructions, CCP reports to Moscow, and FEB balance sheets. The Noulenses were put on trial, causing a huge media shockwave.[87] By then, Zhou had gone completely underground, and he did not participate in the rescue operation of the Noulenses organized by the Comintern. However, this incident and the coordinated efforts of GMD intelligence services and foreign concession authorities made it even more difficult for Zhou to survive in Shanghai. Zhou did not leave Shanghai immediately, but he was forced to cut off almost all connection with others.[88]

Still, in September 1931, Zhou had a meeting with Richard Sorge, the legendary spy dispatched to Shanghai by the Comintern. Sorge had been in Shanghai since January 1931, maintaining a close working relationship with *Teke* personnel. At the meeting, Sorge reportedly asked Zhou for recommendations of reliable intelligence agents who might work for him.[89]

As Shanghai became a hell on earth for the Communists, the Comintern fixed its attention on Zhou's precarious safety. Moscow again instructed Zhou to either decamp to the Red Zone or travel to Moscow.[90] Zhou did not want to leave China. Since both the Comintern and the CCP leadership were then repeatedly emphasizing the importance of the Red Army for the Chinese revolution, Zhou chose to go to the Red Zone.

By then, Zhou had been in Shanghai for four years. His biggest gain in those years, in retrospect, was his consolidation of firm control over the party's routine operations. He thus had institutionalized his own administrative power and intelligence connections within the party apparatus.

In the ensuing decades, the Chinese Communist Revolution and Zhou himself would follow a tortuous path. Yet Zhou's control over the administrative power and intelligence network of the party, and then the party-state, would endure. An interesting pattern emerged from this: Although Zhou never became the paramount leader of the party, he consistently stood at the center of the party's operational network and, after 1949, that of the Communist state as well. Zhou was a person, to be sure; but he was also a phenomenon. It is no exaggeration to say that, without him, the very operation of the party and the party-state could have become paralyzed. This largely explains why Zhou could hold on to his role in the Chinese Communist Revolution despite the gauntlet of challenges, difficulties, and ordeals that he faced.

• • •

A big tree invites blowing wind. Shortly after Zhou left Shanghai, there occurred what would later be known as the "Wu Hao Incident." In February 1932, two months after Zhou departed the city, *Shengbao*, a Shanghai-based newspaper, published a statement by "243 persons including Wu Hao to denounce the Communist Party." As the reader may remember, "Wu Hao" was an alias that Zhou adopted during the May Fourth Movement, which eventually became his code name. The statement was actually fabricated by GMD intelligence services to undermine the morale of the underground Communist movement. In order to rebut the phony article, CCP organs in Shanghai succeeded in publishing a note in *Shengbao* on February 22, which read as follows: "Mr. Wu Hao: The rebuttal statement that you sent to us on the 18th of this month has been received. It has not been published for lacking a proper company warrant."[91] This was all that the CCP underground organs could then do to indicate that the earlier statement by Wu Hao was not Zhou's. All of this occurred without Zhou's knowledge.

What Zhou could not have imagined at the time was that this matter would not go away. Indeed, it would be mentioned a decade later, during the Rectification Campaign in Yan'an. Then, in the Cultural Revolution years, it would resurface to entangle Zhou again. Even when Zhou was terminally ill, he was unable to ward off the specter of the "Wu Hao Incident."[92] Revealed here is how ugly the CCP's intraparty politics and struggles under Mao could become.

8

JIANGXI COUNTRYSIDE

1931–1934

One moonless night in early December 1931, Zhou Enlai, disguised as a skilled blue-collar worker, left Shanghai on a steam launch registered with a British company.[1] A few days later, he disembarked from the boat at the port of Shantou in Guangdong and then traveled to one of the Red Zones (areas controlled by the Red Army) through secret CCP routes. By the end of the month, he had arrived at Ruijin, a previously little-known town at the zone's center in Jiangxi Province, immediately taking over the position of secretary of the Soviet Area Bureau (SAB) there to which he had been appointed the previous year.[2]

After Chiang's anti-CCP coup in 1927, Mao and other Communists waged a series of armed uprisings under the banner of "land revolution." By the early 1930s, a dozen or so Red Zones had appeared in southern China, where revolutionary regimes were established. Following the Soviet Union's example, the Communists named them "Soviets," so the Red Zones became "Soviet Areas." The Chinese Soviet Republic was established in November 1931. The Soviet Area across Jiangxi and Fujian, with Ruijin as the capital, became the Central Soviet Area. At its peak, it covered the entirety of seven counties and included parts of another twenty-eight, inhabited by a population of over three million.

The Shanghai that Zhou had left behind was a city of death, where he lived a life of dark nights. Now, as he set foot on the sunlit land controlled by his comrades, his delight was visible.[3] Meanwhile, however, he felt quite uneasy thinking of the challenges that lay ahead. Indeed, he was about to enter a completely new environment. Although he had been Whampoa's director of political affairs and had participated in the two Eastern Expeditions, he was not a battlefield commander. He acquired his only combat experience in the Nanchang Uprising and the march to Guangdong after it, which had ended in total failure. Since 1927, he had presided over military affairs at the Party Center, a job he did from a lofty position. Zhou knew that he would have to deal with all kinds of tough matters in the Red Zone, including how to handle relations with Mao.

Zhou and Mao had not had much direct contact since their exchanges in 1929. But Zhou had paid close attention to Mao's activities, especially after Zhou was named SAB secretary in Jiangxi in late 1930. Tied up by his duties in Shanghai, he could not go to Jiangxi then. At the end of 1930, Xiang Ying was dispatched to the Soviet Area to serve as acting SAB secretary on Zhou's behalf. In April 1931, a three-person Central Committee delegation, composed of Ren Bishi, Wang Jiaxiang, and Gu Zuolin, also arrived in the Soviet Area, where they joined Xiang and Mao as SAB members. Though Zhou was in Shanghai, his indirect relationship with Mao was inevitably marked by tense episodes, as he had to handle matters in the Red Zone fraught with complications.

Xiang arrived at Ruijin as the campaign to unearth an "Anti-Bolshevik Clique" (or the "AB Clique") raged, fueled by Mao's ruthless urging. The clique in question, once a small group within the GMD, had dissolved long before. However, in early 1930, Mao launched a "suppression of reactionaries" campaign in the Red Zone in the name of fighting an imagined enemy. The Red Zone leadership was then composed of both individuals with local backgrounds and those (such as Mao) from other regions. It was difficult for the leaders to work together due to their different social connections. In the wake of the Gutian Conference, Mao was determined to pursue a "dictatorship by the party secretary" (e.g., by himself), believing himself infallible, especially after victories in battles. However, he frequently encountered friction when dealing with comrades of different backgrounds. Mao responded by labeling his opponents "AB Clique" enemies, and his agents subsequently carried out one wave after another of arrests, torture, and killings of those who disagreed with him. Consequently, the death toll climbed, and the purge grew out of control.[4]

Shortly before Xiang's arrival, an anti-Mao mutiny by the Red Twentieth Army erupted in Futian, a small town in western Jiangxi. In early

December 1930, Mao dispatched Li Shaojiu, a loyalist of his, to Futian to "wipe out hidden reactionaries" in the Twentieth Army, authorizing him to "kill them in large numbers."[5] Hence, immediately after Li arrived in Futian, he ordered the arrest and execution of many Twentieth Army officers, most of whom were locals. On December 12, Liu Di, a regiment commander, launched a mutiny and arrested Li and his associates. The next day, Liu and others announced their separation from Mao's First Frontal Army.[6] Then, several leaders of the party's Jiangxi Provincial Committee who supported the mutiny established a committee of their own, publicly denouncing "serious wrongdoings in the Anti-AB Clique campaign" and dispatching an envoy to convey their grievances to the Party Center in Shanghai.[7]

At first, Xiang had hoped to cooperate with Mao in managing the Futian Incident. Therefore, "in principle," he endorsed Mao's "line of struggle."[8] In practice, however, Xiang favored settling the incident through negotiations with Twentieth Army commanders, a plan Mao firmly opposed. The two became locked in a fierce dispute, with neither willing to yield to the other.

All of this was brought to Zhou's attention at a time when the political atmosphere within the party leadership was very tense in the aftermath of the Fourth Plenum. Zhou was cautious, as he dared not commit any mistake on "matters concerning principles." After carefully reading reports from the Red Zone, he had come to the understanding that the Futian Incident probably occurred as a natural consequence of "(Mao's) Frontal Committee's attempt to arrest 'AB Clique members' within the Provincial Committee," who were forced to take action. In late February, when the Politburo met to discuss this matter, Zhou acted tactfully. The AB Clique was indeed a reactionary organization, he said, and the Futian Incident was a "reactionary event." However, he added that among AB Clique members were some "wavering and less-committed ones." Hence, not all involved were reactionaries. Therefore, all sides "should stop the dispute and unite to fight the enemy."[9] In late March 1931, the Comintern's Far Eastern Bureau (FEB) intervened, declaring that the Futian Incident was "definitely reactionary in essence," and that, categorically, all those involved were reactionaries. The CCP Center accepted this arbitrary judgment.[10]

This was when Ren, Wang, and Gu arrived in the Red Zone to manage the dispute between Mao and Xiang. Following the Party Center and the FEB's instructions, they quickly pronounced the Futian Incident a "reactionary riot." On April 18, leaders of the rebelling Twentieth Army were summoned to a meeting with Mao and Party Center representatives, where they were arrested and then executed.[11]

In settling the Futian Incident Ren, Wang, and Gu stood in Mao's corner and criticized Xiang. At one point, they even favored letting Mao take over Xiang's position as SAB acting secretary. But Mao also had left them with an odd impression, in particular because they were bound by the same instructions that the Comintern had given the CCP: to pursue victory first in one or a few provinces, yet Mao had failed to do this in the Red Zone. Further, over time they also had grown extremely uncomfortable with Mao's practice of shutting out all different voices in the name of a "dictatorship by the party secretary." In this respect, they found common ground with Xiang.

Negative comments about Mao by Xiang, and then Ren, Wang, and Gu, alerted Zhou and the Party Center. Zhou had dealt with Mao before, so he knew that Mao was not an easy person to get along with. However, Mao's authority and power in the Red Zone were then at their zenith. Indeed, even Moscow and the Comintern had watched his progress carefully. Zhou had to act shrewdly and cautiously.

• • •

Zhou knew by the summer of 1931 that he would soon leave Shanghai for Jiangxi. By then, Wang Ming was about to leave Shanghai to serve as head of the CCP delegation to the Comintern in Moscow. The Party Center's work would be charged by Bo Gu (Qin Bangxian), a Soviet returnee only twenty-four years of age. Because his outstanding performance in the struggles against the Li Lisan Line, Bo Gu was named secretary of the Communist Youth League in the wake of the Fourth Plenum in early 1931. After Xiang Zhongfa's death, the FEB proposed to establish a provisional Politburo. Although Bo Gu was not even a member of the Central Committee, he was made a Politburo Standing Committee member. With both Wang Ming and Zhou leaving Shanghai soon, he was asked to "take up overall responsibility" at the Party Center.[12] Zhou's attitude toward Mao became even subtler. He knew that Wang Ming, Bo Gu, and other "Soviet returnees" disliked Mao, finding Mao's behavior far too "rightist-leaning" compared with the Comintern's instructions. Zhou was inclined to agree with them. But he also knew that he had to rely upon Mao's support, even as he attempted to control Mao, to perform his own duties in the Red Zone. As Zhou later acknowledged in his "self-criticism" during the Yan'an Rectification, his "dubious attitudes" toward Mao flowed from this calculation.[13]

Earlier, Zhou and the Party Center had also dispatched Ouyang Qin to the Red Zone as an associate of Ren, Wang, and Gu. In early July, before Ouyang returned to Shanghai to report to the Central Committee, Ren and Wang prepared on behalf of the SAB a report for Ouyang to bring to Shanghai. The content of the report has not been declassified except for a few paragraphs.[14] However, it was after reading the report that Zhou wrote an instructional letter, representing the Central Committee, to the SAB, in which he harshly criticized Mao. Therefore, the report must have included negative comments on Mao.

Zhou's instruction letter, dated August 30, was dozens of pages in length. In it, he leveled a series of accusations against Mao without naming him. "The most serious mistake in the Central Soviet Area," Zhou wrote in the letter, "is the lack of a clearly-defined class line and absence of effective mass work," which had caused other mistakes. Militarily, "as of now, the Red Army has not cast away old-fashioned guerrillas' habits or narrow-minded small-group actions, which is incompatible with its designated tasks of engaging in large-scale operations for achieving victory in one or several provinces." Zhou also cited missteps in the anti-AB Clique campaign. "The AB Clique threat" and "the enemy's sabotage capacity," according to the letter, "have been exaggerated," eroding "confidence in our own class." The letter's attack on Mao's patriarchal style of handling party and military decision-making must have been most offensive for the future chairman. The above grievances, Zhou stressed, revealed Mao's exposure to the "heavy influence of the Guomindang's working method and style."[15]

Zhou drafted the letter on behalf of the Party Center, so the ideas in it were not necessarily all his. He also spoke for Bo Gu and Wang Ming, who virtually controlled the Party Center. However, even their views were not entirely original; they were following what they understood to be the Comintern's instructions. In the final analysis, however, Zhou authored the letter, which triggered a series of anti-Mao events in the following months, resulting in Mao's loss of his superior position in the party and Red Army in the Red Zone.

When Zhou's letter was being delivered to the Red Zone, Mao put another difficult matter in front of Zhou and the Party Center. On October 11, with Mao's backing, the SAB cabled the Party Center with two requests: First, that the SAB move in tandem with the First Frontal Army; and second, that, as Xiang Ying "has been completely wrong in managing the Futian Incident . . . and thus had lost others' trust and shown his incompetence, the bureau . . . make Comrade Mao Zedong its acting secretary."[16] These two requests presented a tough test for Zhou, the SAB's new secretary.

At the time, Zhou was hidden deep in Shanghai's political underground. Yet this was a matter too important for him not to intervene. The Party Center's reply came in mid-October. The first request was rejected, as the Central Committee regarded it "inappropriate for the SAB to move around together with the Frontal Army." The second request was approved, permitting Mao to temporarily serve as acting secretary of the SAB: "The Party Center's new representative (namely, Zhou) will soon depart for the Soviet Area, and will work together with you to resolve all issues."[17] This response helped to stabilize Mao while paving the way for Zhou to seize all power in the Red Zone after his arrival.

The Central Committee, worrying that the SAB might have not received Zhou's August 30 letter, dispatched a telegram to the SAB around October 20, stressing that Zhou's letter was extremely important. The forthcoming party congress of the Soviet Area, according to the telegram, "must follow the instructions in the letter, adopt the resolutions accordingly, and send them to the Party Center for approval."[18]

Ren, Wang, Gu, and others in the SAB had long been at odds with Mao. But Mao was a strong-willed man who held tightly to his power, so they could do little to check him, apart from reporting their complaints to the Party Center. Now, Zhou's letter provided them with the much-needed ammunition to "wage struggles" face to face with Mao. They began to act immediately.

On November 1, the Gannan (Southern Jiangxi) Conference, a five-day gathering by Red Zone leaders, began. Mao attended it in his capacity as acting secretary of the SAB. But it was Ren and Wang who were really in charge. Ren relayed Zhou's August 30 letter to the conference attendees, immediately making Mao a target of harsh criticism. Ideologically, Mao was said to have exhibited a tendency for "narrow-minded experimentalism"; with respect to land-reform policy, he had pursued an approach of favoring "rich peasants"; and militarily, he had failed to "abandon the old-fashioned method of guerrilla warfare" and ignored the importance of "positional and city warfare."[19] Refusing to accept any of these accusations, Mao held a fierce debate with Ren, Wang, and others. He also mobilized a group of cadres to support him at the conference. All this, however, only invited more criticism and exacerbated Mao's isolation.[20]

The conference passed several resolutions in line with Zhou's letter. Mao's land-distribution policies were criticized for "mistakenly favoring rich peasants." A central Maoist text, the "Resolution of the Gutian Conference," was accused of allowing Mao to justify his consolidation of personal control over the Red Army, resulting in the "total loss of independence of Red Army military and political officers." The new resolutions called for an end to Mao's "monopoly of the executive power in the Red Zone and Red Army."[21] Mao suffered a more serious setback when he was not elected a member of the Central Revolutionary Military Commission. He also lost his position as the Red Army's general political commissar.[22]

But Zhou and the Party Center did not mean to totally discredit Mao. The Chinese Soviet Republic was formally established a few days after the Gannan Conference, and Zhou and the Central Committee insisted upon naming Mao as chairman of the republic.[23] From that point on, Mao became "Chairman Mao." Ostensibly, this new title elevated Mao's influence and reputation to a new height. In reality, however, his power and authority in the Red Zone were in sharp decline.

* * *

Zhou, still in Shanghai, remained aloof throughout these events. After he arrived in Ruijin, he had to encounter Mao face to face. He already had a plan. To win others' trust and support, he would begin with exposing Mao's "excessive implementation" of "suppression of reactionaries," forcing Mao on the moral defensive. Zhou believed that such a plan would help consolidate his authority and reputation while simultaneously limiting those of Mao.

Zhou quickly discovered that the campaign to crush "reactionaries" had indeed gone out of control, resulting in massive killings and yielding grave consequences. In a letter to the Party Center on December 18, he reported that, after just three days in the Red Zone, he already saw that many innocent people had been arrested and tortured. The Party Center, he suggested, should immediately adopt a resolution to correct these wrongdoings.[24] Obviously, he was ready to have a showdown with Mao.

In Ruijin, Zhou's first action as SAB secretary was to stop the "ridiculous development" of purging "reactionaries." He devised a clever strategy: affirm the campaign in rhetoric, but negate it in substance. In criticizing the campaign, he also avoided publicly shaming or embarrassing Mao. Under Zhou's guidance, the SAB passed a resolution to recognize the Futian Incident as "a counterrevolutionary mutiny led by the AB Clique" and the struggle against "the AB Clique as necessary and correct." Then the resolution turned to mistakes committed in the campaign. Indeed, the campaign had been "ignorant of both the class line and the mass line." Because of these mistakes, the "anti AB-Clique" struggle had been reduced to "no more than arresting, interrogating, and settling AB Clique members, . . . relying merely upon confessions by the suspects." All of this, according to the resolution, arose from "wrong perceptions, namely, lack of confidence in one's own class, and in the strength of our victorious revolution."[25]

Nowhere in the resolution was Mao named. However, every word of it pointed to Mao's behavior. Mao kept silent, knowing that this was not a matter about which he could or should argue with Zhou. Armed with his well-prepared and shrewdly enacted plan, Zhou won a clear victory in his first encounter with Mao in the Red Zone. As a result, though Mao developed feelings of rancor concerning Zhou, in appearance their relations did not worsen dramatically, certainly not beyond repair.

But Mao would never forget this "debt" that Zhou owed him. Years later, when Zhou made a self-criticism during the Yan'an Rectification Movement, he explicitly stated that one of his "serious crimes" had been his opposing Mao on the issue of suppressing reactionaries in the Red Zones.[26] Decades later, in June 1972, Zhou heeded Mao's request to "review his own history" in the wake of Lin Biao's death. He again highlighted this early 1930s episode as a "criminal mistake" that he had committed.[27] Throughout Mao's life, he would never endow Zhou with his full trust or make Zhou his prospective successor in his "great cause of revolution."

• • •

When Zhou arrived at Ruijin, the Red Army was in a critical situation. With the establishment of his Nationalist government in Nanjing while renaming Beijing to Beiping in 1928, Chiang Kai-shek achieved nominal unification of the whole country. However, conflict persisted between Nanjing and various provincial warlords, leading to a series of wars. As it was next to impossible for Chiang to turn all his attention to suppressing the Red Army, the Soviet Areas expanded continuously between 1929 and 1931.

By late 1931, Chiang thought that he had subdued almost all dissident warlords; then he began to amass forces for another major campaign against the Central Soviet Area. Chiang's troops had previously carried out three such campaigns, each of which failed due to serious flaws in strategy, troop mobilization, operation coordination, logistical support, and intelligence collection. Chiang's troops simply could not match Mao's Red Army in these respects. After the failure of the third Nationalist campaign in late 1931, the Central Soviet Area, as well as several other Soviet Areas, reached the peak of its development.

Chiang then faced another major challenge. On September 18, 1931, the Japanese Kwantung Army provoked the Mukden Incident and subsequently occupied the whole of Manchuria. In late January 1932, Japanese troops engaged in fierce fighting with the Chinese Nineteenth Army stationed in Shanghai. Chinese throughout the country were enraged, and outcries to resist Japanese aggression could be heard everywhere. Chiang was caught in a huge dilemma. Faced with the urgent task of dealing with the "Japanese bandits," he was unable to simultaneously cope with the Red Army, who took advantage of this fact to further develop and expand.

All this caused great optimism among the Comintern and CCP leaders. Zhou and his comrades believed that the Red Army should "take advantage of the favorable political and military conditions, and occupy one or two major cities and pursue victory of the revolution in one or more provinces."[28] In January 1932, the SAB, under Zhou's direction, discussed plans to attack several cities in Jiangxi, as required by the Party Center. Mao, concerned that superior enemy forces would overwhelm the Red Army, opposed these plans. Zhou shared some of Mao's concerns, but he had no intention of disobeying the Party Center's instructions.[29] Finally, ignoring Mao's disagreement, Zhou decided to attack Ganzhou, a city in southern Jiangxi. Occupying Ganzhou, Zhou reasoned, would expand the Central Soviet Area and link it with other Soviet areas.[30] Mao, however, offended by Zhou's decision, requested sick leave and moved to the suburbs of Ruijin.[31] Mao would remember this as another "debt" that Zhou owed him.

The Red Army's attack on Ganzhou began on February 4. The city, solidly walled and surrounded on three sides by water, was easier to defend than to attack. After almost a month, Zhou's troops, lacking proper equipment and firepower, still could not make much progress. In early March, Nationalist reinforcements gradually arrived, threatening to encircle or even eliminate the Red troops. Zhou was compelled to order his troops to abandon their siege of Ganzhou. Realizing that Mao was indeed a visionary military strategist, Zhou decided to invite Mao back to Red Army headquarters. When Mao received the invitation, his "illness" evaporated, and he was on his way back to Ruijin that same evening.[32]

In mid-March, Zhou chaired a discussion to review the Ganzhou defeat and make plans for future actions. Mao proposed that the Red Army move to areas between Jiangxi and Fujian, where, he contended, lay the enemy's weak spots. He also tried to convince Zhou and other comrades that this move would allow the Soviet Areas to further expand and link together. Although Mao's military vision in the wake of the Ganzhou defeat had impressed Zhou, he was not ready to accept every suggestion Mao put forward. When most attendees at the meeting rejected Mao's ideas as too "opportunistic," Zhou stood on their side. They decided to dispatch part of the Red Army to areas in the Gan River valley, and Mao was assigned to lead another part of the Red Army to march northward to "search for opportunities of rapid expansion."[33]

Mao was unhappy with this arrangement. He approached Zhou after the meeting, proposing that, as the enemy's strength appeared relatively weak in western Fujian (a province next to Jiangxi), the Red Army should seek development opportunities there. Finally, Zhou agreed to follow Mao's idea.[34]

At the Fujian front, when Mao was trying to put his ideas into practice, he found a prime target in Zhangzhou, a commercial city in southern Fujian. Zhangzhou was rich and boasted an abundance of resources, and it was also poorly defended. By occupying it, the Red Army would gain much-needed supplies of grain, money, weapons and ammunition, and other resources. He immediately cabled Zhou, proposing that the Red Army attack Zhangzhou.[35] Zhou saw Mao's point. To confirm Mao's judgment, Zhou rushed from Ruijin to Changting, where Mao's frontal headquarters was located. After the two met, Zhou accepted Mao's suggestion, also deciding to stay in Changting to supervise the operation.[36]

Working together, Zhou and Mao gathered two Red Army corps at Zhangzhou. The attack on the city began in the early morning of April 19, and by the next day, the Red Army had taken Zhangzhou. Zhou was jubilant, as this was the Red Army's biggest victory since his arrival in the Red Zone.

For Mao, however, this moment of celebration was quickly spoiled by a telegram from the Party Center. On April 14, the center, in accordance with its understanding of the Comintern's political line, had dispatched new instructions to party organs in various Soviet Areas. Mao was not mentioned by name in the instructions, but he seemed to be the target of every accusation enclosed therein. The Party Center claimed that the problem of Soviet areas was far more serious than "narrow-minded experimentalism." Indeed, the main danger facing Soviet Areas was pervasive "conservatism" and "defensivism" that permeated policymaking and implementation. Therefore, criticism of these mistaken tendencies should be brought to the level of "the struggle against rightist opportunism," a task that was far from accomplished.[37]

The Red Army had just won a big victory at Zhangzhou, and Mao's arrogance had soared to an all-time high. Enraged, he angrily rebutted the Party Center's instructions in a response on May 3. "The Central Committee's political assessment and military strategy are totally wrong," he declared. It was "absolutely correct" for the troops under his command to attack and occupy Zhangzhou, which meant "adopting an offensive strategy by leading the war into the enemy's territory."[38]

All this put Zhou in a quandary. It was he who had initiated the landslide of criticism against Mao. He did so to teach Mao a lesson—in order to make him accept Zhou's leadership role. With Mao's errors exposed during and after the Gannan Conference, Zhou had achieved his objective, and he saw no point in going too far in attacking Mao. Nonetheless, the Party Center and many of Zhou's comrades obviously did not want to let Mao off the hook so easily.

On May 11, Zhou chaired an SAB meeting in Changting, a town in western Fujian. Following the Party Center's demands, he promised to "thoroughly correct the erroneous tendency of rightist opportunism committed by the SAB in the past."[39] Mao, "busy with military affairs on the front," missed the meeting. Still, he was made the main target of a series of accusations all aimed at his "wrongdoings." He was labeled not only as a "narrow-minded experimentalist" but also, more seriously, as a "rightist opportunist." A resolution passed at the meeting urged the SAB leadership to "thoroughly correct" its "mistake" of failing to rectify Mao's transgressions.[40]

The meeting also decided to reinstall Zhu De as the First Frontal Army's commander in chief; Mao, however, did not get back his position as the general commissar.[41]

Not until June did Mao learn what had happened in Changting two months before. He was furious and would always remember this episode as a source of great personal shame. Nine years later, when he was launching the Yan'an Rectification Movement, Mao cynically complained that he was not given the "fantastic verdict" of the Changting meeting until two months after its passage, and that the "official sentence" had been made without giving him an opportunity to appeal.[42] Mao believed that Zhou was the one who had done this behind his back. Indeed, in his view, the actor who should ultimately be held responsible for this ugly drama was neither the Party Center in Shanghai nor his other colleagues at the SAB. It was Zhou Enlai.

The feud between Mao and Zhou erupted while the Red Zones again faced serious challenges. In May 1932, Chiang's government reached a cease-fire agreement with Japan, which greatly lessened the Japanese threat to Nanjing at the moment. Meanwhile, Chiang had further subdued challenges to the Nationalists by local and provincial strongmen. Once more, he could concentrate on dealing with Communist rebellions in Jiangxi and elsewhere. In June, he began to gather a force, reportedly, of half a million soldiers to wage another suppression campaign against the Red Zones. Rather than attacking all of them simultaneously, though, he would first mobilize his main force to invade two of them; one, led by Zhang Guotao, straddling Hubei, Henan, and Anhui; and another, commanded by He Long, at the periphery of Hunan and western Hubei. He would deploy another strong force to check the Red Army in the Central Soviet Area. After "pacifying" the areas commanded by Zhang and He, Chiang would marshal all of his troops for an all-out attack on the Central Soviet Area.

Faced with such a complex situation, Zhou again saw the need to work closely with Mao. On July 21, he left Ruijin for the front line in southeastern Jiangxi. Ren Bishi and Xiang Ying would stay in Ruijin to lead the charge in the rear area. Leaders in the Central Soviet Area were thus divided into two parts, including a "front group," comprising Zhou, Mao, and Zhu De, and one "rear group," composed of Ren, Xiang, and others.

Zhou's first course of action was to put forward a motion to reinstall Mao as the general political commissar "for the military commanding needs at the front."[43] The rear group did not immediately respond. Zhou pressed them, stressing that "we are so much in need of taking full advantage of Mao's military experience and strength. . . . With Mao in charge, we are putting the commanding power into the right hands."[44] On August 8, the SAB appointed Mao as political commissar of the First Frontal Army.[45]

All the while, however, the Red troops led by Zhang and He suffered a series of defeats against Chiang's overwhelming forces. In late August, Chiang's troops occupied several centrally located towns in Zhang's Soviet area. In despair, Zhang sent an emergency cable to the Party Center, urging the party leadership to dispatch Zhou and Mao "to provide us with the support that we need urgently and desperately."[46] The Party Center wasted no time to send several telegrams to the SAB, and to Mao and Zhou in particular, ordering them to come at once to the rescue of the other two Soviet areas. Without such "direct support," the Party Center emphasized, Chiang's "unprecedented endeavors" to destroy the Red Zones and Red Army could prevail.[47]

The messages reached Zhou and Mao while the two were battling to seize more resources while consolidating and expanding the territory under their control in southeastern Jiangxi. Moreover, they found that Chiang had held a sizeable force along the borders of the Central Soviet Area, blocking their way to aid the two other Soviet areas. Zhou and Mao thus cabled the Party Center, writing that it was unfeasible to render direct support to Zhang "in the current situation." Instead, they contended, their troops should continue with their operations in southeastern Jiangxi, "waiting for the situation to change, and getting fully prepared to strike and eliminate the enemy's main forces." Although this would not be "an immediate attack on the enemy, this nevertheless is a strategic move of positive offensive." On the other hand, Mao and Zhou stressed, they would be "committing a serious mistake" to "hurriedly engage in the operation" to rescue the other two Soviet areas, a mission they deemed both totally unworkable and undesirable.[48]

In Ruijin, Ren and Xiang of the rear group were extremely worried about the fate of the Soviet areas led by Zhang and He. They immediately rebutted Mao and Zhou's plans, lamenting that their scheme would delay efforts to rescue the other two Soviet areas "for at least a month," which would lead to "serious consequences."[49] Zhou and Mao, however, were unwilling to deviate from the path they had chosen.[50]

Ren and Xiang, totally offended, cabled Mao and Zhou on September 29, criticizing their behavior as "completely in violation of principles and most dangerous." In the name of SAB, they asked Zhou and Mao to "stop all operations" and to "hold an SAB meeting immediately to settle the disputes."[51] The next day, Ren and others cabled Zhou, quoting Zhou's earlier suggestion that "if necessary an SAB meeting can be convened." They demanded that such a meeting be called to "correct all the mistakes."[52] The same afternoon, Ren and his comrades left Ruijin, rushing to the front.

The actions taken by Ren and others reflected the anti-Mao tone of Zhou's letter of August 30, 1931. Now, the meeting that they sought to call also followed the footsteps that had led from the Gannan to the Changting conferences. Indeed, the meeting would bring to the surface the tensions that had begun to swirl around Mao since then. Zhou had ignited the anti-Mao fire. He now lost control of the spreading flame.

* * *

Beginning on October 3, Zhou chaired a five-day meeting of the SAB in Ningdu, a small town in southeastern Jiangxi; thus, the meeting was titled the Ningdu Conference. From the start, Mao encountered a barrage of harsh attacks from a majority of the participants, who characterized the event as "a struggle between two opposing political lines unprecedented in SAB history."[53]

Zhou, as a central figure at the conference, had a big say in defining its trajectory and orientation. If he wanted to crush Mao, given that Mao was disliked—even hated—by so many of his colleagues, and that Mao had already set the precedent of settling intraparty struggles by labeling his opponents as reactionaries, Zhou could have treated Mao the same way.[54] However, Zhou refused to steer the conference in that direction. Instead, he adopted a more reconciliatory approach. "My stand was a wavering one at the Ningdu Conference," he recalled decades later.[55] On the one hand, he severely criticized Mao, saying that many of Mao's ideas and actions were "unacceptable." In particular, Mao had demonstrated that "he has been unwilling to accept the Party Center's instructions." On the other hand, Zhou also defended Mao, underscoring Mao's experience in military affairs, the area in which Mao was most interested. Therefore, Zhou argued, if Mao could continue to contribute to military affairs, "it would greatly benefit our war effort." Zhou thus proposed that "Comrade Mao should stay at the front." He presented two options: First, he would take overall responsibility for the war, and Mao would stay at the front and serve as his associate. Second, Mao would assume overall responsibility for the war, and Zhou would serve as Mao's associate, "supervising the implementation of operational plans."[56]

Zhou's reconciliatory attitude toward Mao at Ningdu was compatible with his usual style of maintaining the role of compromiser in intraparty disputes. He might have also chosen this balanced approach because he understood that Mao, a founding member of the CCP whose name was regarded favorably by Moscow, still had deep roots and connections within the Red Army and the Red Zones. It would be almost impossible to eliminate Mao without paying a very high price.

Further, having in the past collaborated with Mao, Zhou was deeply impressed by Mao's military genius. He probably realized that the Red Army, as Mao had repeatedly stressed, lacked the capacity to attack major cities or fight a regular war and thus was better suited to engage in a guerrilla war. If Mao were to be removed, Zhou himself would be forced to take up heavier duties as the Red Army's paramount military decision-maker, while dealing directly with the Party Center. Zhou was uncertain about his own ability with respect to the former, and reluctant to see the latter come to be. Therefore, it would be better to allow Mao to bear some responsibility or, at least, to keep him at the front as an associate.

Zhou's comrades, however, did not understand his predicament or underlying considerations. At the end of the conference, the Revolutionary Military Commission dismissed Mao as general commissar of the First Frontal Army.[57] Zhou's reconciliatory attitude also backfired after Ningdu; Ren, Xiang, and others cabled the Central Committee to complain about Zhou. "In an unprecedented struggle between two lines," they claimed, Zhou "not only had failed to criticize Mao, but also tried to cover some of Mao's mistakes or even speak on Mao's behalf." This revealed one of Zhou's main weak spots, they announced: he was "not resolute in waging struggles."[58]

Zhou had no choice but to defend himself. "I admit that I have been lukewarm in criticizing Comrade (Mao) Zedong," Zhou wrote in a telegram to the Central Committee. "I have not done enough to criticize his mistake of maintaining a rather ambiguous concept about the party." He argued, however, that his SAB colleagues had criticized Mao too harshly, and that what he had done was no more than an attempt to strike a balance between the two sides. He firmly rejected the notion that he "had failed to carry out the necessary struggle, or had obscured the political line in the struggle."[59]

The dispute between Zhou and his SAB colleagues mired the Party Center in a dilemma. After much deliberation, the center decided to side with Zhou. "The line and general policies" that Zhou adopted at the Ningdu Conference were sensible and correct, announced the center. Furthermore, as "Comrade (Mao) Zedong had acknowledged his mistakes at the conference, it is possible to help him correct his attitude and play a more active role in his work." Zhou was not "a nonrespecter of principles" as some of his comrades claimed. "For the purpose of breaking up the enemy's suppression campaign," the center concluded, "the most important is to keep all leaders united."[60]

It was strange for the Party Center to mention that Mao "had acknowledged his mistakes," as Mao had not done so at the Ningdu Conference, nor did he do so after it. This was most likely Zhou's doing. Though Mao refused to make any self-criticism, Zhou told the center that Mao had done so, anyway. This was Zhou's tactic to prevent the intraparty struggle in the Red Zone from spiraling out of control.

Indeed, at Ningdu, Zhou played a significant role in reducing the pressure upon Mao. In truth, given that Mao had been disliked by the Party Center and also opposed by many of his colleagues in the Red Zone, he would have become the target of harsh attacks anyway. The Ningdu Conference had actually served to protect Mao to the extent that it was chaired by Zhou, who demonstrated his prowess as a master compromiser. Otherwise, though his military commanding power had been rescinded, Mao could have been more severely purged (such as he had done to his own adversaries) by those who opposed him.

Still, in many of his later "self-criticisms," Zhou described the Ningdu Conference as "the biggest mistake and crime" that he had ever committed.[61] Why so? There were probably two reasons for this. First, Zhou was the person who initiated criticism of Mao in the Soviet Areas. From his August 30, 1931, letter to a series of anti-Mao events, such as the Gannan and Changting conferences, he effectively cleared the path toward Ningdu. Second, Zhou took over the position of political commissar of the First Frontal Army after Mao's dismissal.[62] For Mao, the loss of his military commanding power, which he had cherished the most, was extraordinarily offensive. In the wake of Ningdu, Mao said, he did nothing but "eat, sleep, and shit."[63] Ningdu, in Mao's memory, was a nightmare that plagued him ceaselessly. No matter what Zhou had actually done at the Ningdu Conference itself, in Mao's eyes, ultimately he was the one to blame.

But Mao's "eat, sleep, and shit" statement was an exaggeration. After Ningdu, he remained chairman of the Chinese Soviet Republic, and much administrative power was still within his reach. However, Mao, who believed that "political power grows out of the barrel of a gun," had little interest in power of secondary importance. He was politically too ambitious to take up smaller duties.

From a longer perspective, though, Zhou had actually done Mao a big favor, albeit unintentionally. After Ningdu, Mao spent a great deal of time reading and thinking. Both were important for Mao to come up with a new profile when he reemerged in CCP high politics. From this angle, Zhou looked even more like a "creditor" of Mao's, although Mao would never have looked upon Zhou and Ningdu this way.

• • •

The CCP's war against the GMD continued despite these intraparty struggles. In late December 1932, Chiang, after subduing the two other Soviet Areas, trained his sights on the Central Soviet Area. Chiang's troops would invade the Central Soviet Area from three directions: Jiangxi, Fujian, and Guandong.

As soon as Ningdu was over, Zhou concentrated all of his attention on resisting Chiang's suppression campaign. This was to be Zhou's first time commanding such a major battle. Luckily for him, he had Zhu De as his partner. Zhou had known Zhu since their time in France, and he served as a reference when Zhu joined the CCP. The two had worked alongside each other during the Nanchang Uprising. Zhu had been in the Soviet Area for several years; his experience was of great help to Zhou.

Zhou and Zhu disagreed with the Party Center on military strategy. The center had ordered them to amass their strength to attack and seize Nanfeng—a county seat where the enemy had assembled a sizeable force of troops—in order to undermine Chiang's offensive with one decisive strike. But Zhou and Zhu found it more desirable to eliminate enemy forces in a mobile war, rather than to "expose our intent by focusing on attacking

Nanfeng."[64] However, the center refused to listen to Zhou and, finally, ordered him to obey, which Zhou and Zhu did.[65]

On February 12, 1933, Zhou and Zhu led the First Frontal Army to attack Nanfeng. Chen Cheng, commander of the Guomindang forces there, ordered the troops in Nanfeng to defend it to the death. Meanwhile, he would move his main force to Nanfeng along three routes, with the intention to surround and wipe out Zhou's troops there. Zhou and Zhu, without asking for approval from the Party Center, decided to "change Nanfeng from the target of the main attack to a feint, and use our main force first to eliminate the enemy's reinforcements."[66] They ordered a tripartite maneuver: only a small portion of their troops would continuously attack Nanfeng; another portion would masquerade as the main force and move toward Lichuan, in order to lure Chen Cheng's main force to follow them there; and their main force would move into and hide in areas southwest of Nanfeng, where they would await opportunities to eliminate the enemy's reinforcements.

Thus Zhou had prepared a huge trap for his enemy. Chen fell for the bait, dispatching his best troops to Lichuan, where he believed Zhou's main force was. Two of his other divisions fell into Zhou's trap as they rushed to save Nanfeng. Fierce fighting began on February 27 and lasted for two days; the two divisions were almost totally lost. Chen dispatched two more divisions to attack Zhou's troops, but Zhou set a new trap. One of Chen's divisions was nearly wiped out and another was hit hard in an ensuing battle that erupted on March 20. Chen immediately ordered the rest of his troops to disengage from their battles. Chiang's fourth campaign to attack the Central Soviet Area had failed.

This was Zhou's most glorious moment of his years in Jiangxi. His power and reputation were ascendant. But he was unable to enjoy his growing clout. Instead, deep anxiety filled his mind. He had glimpsed the worrying reality of the Red Zone lurking behind the Red Army's victories. Indeed, a series of structural problems were eroding the zone's foundation, sinking it into ever-worsening economic and social conditions.

On the military side of things, although Chiang's most recent suppression campaign had failed to conquer the Central Soviet Area, he had succeeded in occupying the two other main Soviet areas, leaving the Central Area isolated. Moreover, repeated battles resulted in heavy casualties for the Red Army, draining the Soviet Area's manpower and other resources. When

Chiang gave up his fourth campaign, Zhou and his comrades found that almost no men of suitable age in the Red Zone remained to be drafted.[67]

More damaging to the Red Zone were the party's increasingly radical land-distribution policies and "killing a chicken for the egg" methods of extracting resources, which placed Zhou and his comrades in an even direr environment. The Red Zone's land-distribution practices were never consistent, having gone from confiscating land from landlords, to giving only bad land to rich peasants, and then to denying rich peasants land, in a muddled flurry of repeated measures. Confiscations of the land and other property of new "landlords" and "rich peasants," who had been identified as "class enemies," accompanied the changing land policy. Yet, these "class struggles" were waged largely to obtain resources needed for the war effort, rather than to serve the Communists' ideological convictions. The "class struggle" language used here provided the much-needed legitimacy for the CCP's prolonged and excessive war mobilization efforts. Did Zhou truly support such a practice of self-destruction? In reality, did he have a better alternative?

Chiang's continuing attacks on the Red Zone also made it impossible for the Communists to consolidate their base areas. When Chiang's fourth suppression campaign failed, Zhou and his comrades thought that, as in previous times, they would have some breathing space for regrouping and rectification. However, Chiang instantly began to plan and implement another, much larger, offensive. And the Red Zone, as Zhou could clearly see, faced serious shortages of manpower, ammunition, and other basic resources to sustain a prolonged war. Zhou was gravely worried.

• • •

Zhou's time as the Red Army's practical supreme commander did not last long. The CCP Center could no longer stay in Shanghai as the situation there deteriorated. Bo Gu arrived in Ruijin in January 1933. Otto Braun, the Comintern's German military advisor, followed a few months later. Zhou's military commanding power was at stake.

Zhou chose to cooperate with the new arrivals from the CCP Center from the beginning. He shared his political leadership role with Bo Gu with no hesitation and yielded much of his military decision-making power to Braun. Zhou was appointed vice chairman of the Central Revolutionary Military Commission in February 1934. This promotion represented a practical demotion, though mainly by his own choosing, as he no longer possessed ultimate authority over the troops' deployment and movement on the front.[68]

Zhou's attitude toward Mao also became subtler. He had kept a "respectful distance" from Mao in the wake of Ningdu. With the Party Center entering the Central Soviet Area, he readily sensed Bo Gu's disdain for Mao and Braun's underestimation of Mao in military matters. Zhou and Mao still saw each other occasionally, but it was usually Mao, not Zhou, who took the initiative.

At this moment, CCP leaders committed a huge mistake by failing to take advantage of an anti-Chiang rebellion in Fujian. Chiang had earlier sent the Nineteenth Army—although it was not a unit under his direct control—to Fujian to participate in attacks on the Red Army. However, its commanders, generals Cai Tingkai and Jiang Guangnai, complained that Chiang had failed to lend them sufficient support during their fight against Japanese troops in Shanghai. Unwilling to attack the Red Army, they established an anti-Chiang "People's Government" in Fujian in late November 1933, interrupting Chiang's invasion of the Red Zone.

Zhou immediately saw this as an opportunity to improve the Red Army's military posture. In a cable to the Party Center on November 24, he observed that "Chiang is moving his troops into Fujian to suppress the Fujian People's Government, postponing his attacks on the Central Soviet Area." The Red Army, he proposed, "should act at once to attack Chiang's troops entering Fujian from their flanks."[69] Bo Gu also shared Zhou's views.

But the CCP had to listen to the Comintern's instructions. Through a "class analysis" lens, Moscow viewed the events in Fujian in a very negative light. Those generals who were against Chiang, the Comintern warned, were actually "opportunists" within the reactionary Guomindang and could thus prove even more dangerous than Chiang himself. Therefore, under no circumstances should the Red Army lift a finger to help them.[70] Zhou and his comrades had to obey the Comintern's directive. They offered almost no help to the anti-Chiang generals in Fujian. Therefore, when Chiang's troops were fighting the rebels in Fujian, he did not need to worry too much about the Red Army. In the end, the anti-Chiang generals failed.

Chiang quickly focused his attention exclusively on the much-delayed suppression campaign against the Central Soviet Area. This time, Chiang adopted the same political and military strategies that had proven effective in destroying two other Soviet Areas. Chiang acted patiently, advancing his troops one step after another, to avoid being ensnared by the Red Army's traps. Chiang's troops were steadily occupying the Red Zone's territory.

Zhou, Bo Gu, and Braun were faced with a dilemma: Should they fight the war in the Red Zone, or try to lead the war into enemy territory? In fact, they had considered bringing the war to the enemy's rear to obtain more resources and create a larger space for maneuvering. But this was easier said than done. If such a plan was carried out, the Red Zone's territory would have inevitably shrunk, and the Red troops would have encountered daunting supply challenges. After weighing the pros and cons of both plans, the three finally decided to pursue a "trench warfare" strategy, whereby the Red Army would compete with the enemy for every inch of land, although this meant that the Red troops would have to engage in a frontal war with Chiang's superior troops.

Beginning in late April 1934, the Red Army was engaged in fierce fighting over Guangchang, regarded as "the gate of the Central Soviet Area," with an enemy force that both outmanned and outgunned it. To remedy this, Zhou and his comrades amassed nine divisions of Red troops in Guangchang. Though the Red Army fought valiantly, losing over 5,500 soldiers in the battle, it was unable to hold on to Guangchang, which was lost on April 28.

Chiang was not in a hurry, however. He continuously adhered to the strategy of steady advance, and his troops relentlessly pushed the Red Army into an ever-shrinking corner. Zhou, Bo Gu, and Braun were unable to come up with an effective response. The Red Zone shrunk day by day, and its structural problems also became more severe. Facing such challenges as shortage of labor, economic depression, and resource exhaustion, Zhou and his comrades could not devise any solution other than to squeeze as much as possible out of anything that remained.

As the summer of 1934 came to an end, it became evident to Zhou and his comrades that the Central Soviet Area's collapse was only a matter of time. They had to search for an alternative.

9

THE LONG MARCH

1934–1935

It was October 10, 1934. On a dark and windy night, Zhou Enlai set out on a long journey.

The Central Red Army, with a claimed total strength of 86,000 soldiers, began to depart the Central Soviet Area along with cadres from the party and the Red Army headquarters. The trek they embarked on was a strategic maneuver that would later be famously called the "Long March." At the time, however, the endeavor was no more than a last resort, as the Communists saw no better alternative. One might describe the journey as an evacuation, or simply as an escape. But most important of all was how it would end. Had it resulted in the Red Army's demise—which was quite possible given the grave situation they faced—the story of modern Chinese history would have been rewritten.

Zhou had to deal with an array of issues before the journey began. One was whether Mao should stay in the Jiangxi Red Zone or go with the main force. This was a question of enormous consequence for Mao's fate. Otto Braun and Bo Gu, who respectively presided over military and political decision-making at the Party Center, had considered leaving Mao behind to lead "a guerilla war" from within the Red Zone.[1] If Mao had stayed in Jiangxi, though, his chances of survival would likely have been slim, as most CCP and Red Army leaders who remained there ultimately died. At the very least, he would have been separated from the CCP leadership and thus would have lost the opportunity to reemerge and claim the position of the party's top leader. Mao recognized these threats and so, when he learned of the evacuation plan, he refused to stay in the doomed Red Zone. Zhou had a big say in the matter, firmly supporting Mao's going with the Party Center on the march.[2] In the end, Zhou's voice prevailed, and Mao joined the main force. Had Zhou not spoken on Mao's behalf, would the future chairman's life, like those of Qu Qiubai and so many others who stayed behind, have come to a miserable end?

The Red Army did not set out on the expedition in a hurry. Initial planning for the operation began shortly after the army's defeat in Guangchang. As the military situation continued to deteriorate, preparations for the expedition accelerated. The CCP Center also reported its plan to abandon the Jiangxi Soviet Area to the Comintern, which gave its approval on June 16.[3] The journey was not purposeless. The Red Army was supposed to pass through the border region between southern Jiangxi and northern Guangdong, then enter western Hunan, where it would join forces with the Red Second and Sixth Army Corps. Together, they would try to establish and expand new base areas. As they laid out the original plan for the operation, the notion of "marching northward to join the resistance against Japan," as Zhou and his comrades claimed after the Long March, did not occur to them, nor had they any idea that the Red Army's trek was to become a "Long March" that would pass through eleven provinces in all.

To direct the march, the CCP and Red Army leadership formed a "three-person group," which comprised Zhou, Bo Gu, and Braun. According to Braun, the evacuation plan was drafted and revised by Zhou before the Politburo approved it. Additionally, it was Zhou's idea to evacuate the entire Central Soviet Area.[4] Before the expedition began, Zhou sent Pan Hannian and He Changgong, two of his special envoys, to negotiate with Chen Jitang, a Guangxi warlord who had long been at odds with Chiang Kai-shek.[5] The two sides agreed to a cease-fire. According to the agreement, they would avoid fighting against each other and exchange intelligence information, and Chen would let the Red Army pass through areas under his control.[6] Chen honored the deal. By mid-November, the Red troops had crossed three of the enemy's blockade lines without facing combat (except for a few small battles due to poor communication from lower officers on both sides).

A big operation such as this should be sudden and swift. However, heeding the orders of the three-person group, the Red troops left Jiangxi with "all institutions, rear-line services, and installations" in tow, and even brought along "machines for printing paper money and propaganda materials."[7] The three-person group calculated that by bringing these resources with them, the Red government could resume operations almost immediately after it arrived in western Hunan. However, this reasoning also came with a heavy burden for the Red Army, which moved at a much slower pace—only about a dozen miles each day.

The Red Army began to arrive at the Xiang River on November 25. The situation then took a drastic turn. Chiang had correctly anticipated that the Reds would attempt to merge with the Communist forces on the other side of the river. Thus Chiang's well-prepared forces lay in wait for the Communists, under orders to try to eliminate them "east of the Xiang River."[8] Finally, after eight days' fierce fighting, Zhou's troops crossed the river after suffering very heavy casualties. The soldiers' morale was dealt a severe blow.

• • •

After they crossed the Xiang River, Zhou and the Red Army command faced the tough question of what to do next. Should they stick to the original plan and try to join forces with the Second and Sixth Red Army Corps in western Hunan? Zhou and many of his comrades knew well that this would be next to impossible. As the Xiang River battle had clearly revealed, Chiang had shrewdly predicted the Red Army's intentions.[9] Furthermore, the GMD forces from Hunan had shown that they were a tough enemy. If the Red Army now tried to intrude on their home province, they would surely fight to the death. Without a well-configured strategic aim, the Reds first marched toward Guangxi. After they were stopped there, they deviated from the plan, opting instead to occupy the gaps between enemy troops they found in the region straddling Sichuan, Yunnan, and Guizhou. Zhou and his comrades keenly sensed that their troops—now lacking the support of a base area—were being pushed into a shrinking corner.

By then, the CCP Center had lost telegraphic communication with Moscow. Thus, the party and the Red Army were unable to receive any instructions or advice from the Comintern. This also meant that they would not need to obey any order from Moscow.[10]

Amid prevailing despair, some party and Red Army leaders began to engage in "abnormal activities." In the wake of recurring military defeats in the late Jiangxi days, Braun and Bo Gu had lost much of their authority and credibility among top Red Army commanders, leading to increasing desire for a change in military leadership. Mao took note of all this. Since the Ningdu Conference two years before, he had been an "unwilling idler." Now, he went to work. Driven by his goal to reemerge at the top of the party and army leadership, Mao spoke with various colleagues to solicit their support. He later recalled that, after the Xiang River battle, he lay on a stretcher specifically assigned for him and talked to other leaders who were also lying on stretchers. In particular, he worked on Zhang Wentian and Wang Jiaxiang, two Politburo members who had been sidelined by Bo Gu and Braun, trying to pull them to his side. Gradually, Zhang and Wang leaned toward Mao.[11]

But Mao understood that it was crucial to get Zhou's support. Zhou had high seniority in the army and maintained good working relations with others in the party leadership, including Bo Gu and Braun (despite his dissatisfaction with their military leadership role). His voice counted. Zhou's stand on the issue had the potential to determine the direction of a possible leadership change.

In fact, Zhou already knew that Mao had been hard at work on his comeback after the Red troops had suffered repeated military defeats. For a while, he was quite reluctant to allow Mao to stage his reemergence. He knew Mao well. "As a person, Mao's biggest problem is that he is very ambitious, suspicious, subjective, and does not listen to others," Zhou once told Bo Gu.[12] Zhou could not easily support Mao's reemergence without prompting stiff resistance from other party and army leaders who did not want to let him seize big power. Further, if Zhou had had any ambition to control the supreme power himself, this moment was heaven-sent. Indeed, Zhou had many reasons to reject Mao's political resurrection.

For weeks, as Zhou rode on horseback, he thought through nearly every facet of this critical matter. Finally, a turning point came in mid-December, when the debate and dispute among party and army leaders at the Liping Conference pushed Zhou to make up his mind in favor of Mao.

In the face of a desperate situation, Zhou knew that the Red Army needed a clear sense of direction. If they were to make another big mistake, the Red troops would inch even closer to their demise. After crossing the Xiang River, however, the central leaders of the CCP and Red Army differed on how to proceed. Should they adhere to the original plan of merging with the Second and Sixth Corps, or should they change course in accordance with the changing situation? Braun supported sticking to the original plan.[13] Mao, however, contended that doing so would cause the Red Army to fall into the enemy's trap, a conclusion his access to "intercepted enemy intelligence information" enabled him to draw. He favored turning westward, toward Guizhou, where the enemy appeared to be weaker and less prepared. Neither side could persuade the other.[14]

On December 12, at a preparatory meeting attended by CCP and Red Army leaders, Mao's ideas gained the support of Wang Jiaxiang, Zhang Wentian, and several others. Zhou also cast a "yea" vote for Mao's plan, despite Braun's strong opposition.[15] Three days later, the Red Army entered Guizhou and occupied a small town named Liping, where CCP leaders again convened a meeting chaired by Zhou. The debate over the direction of the Communists' next move became more heated. Braun was sick and missed the meeting; Bo Gu spoke on his behalf.[16] Wang and Zhang strongly supported Mao's plan of turning west toward Guizhou—a proposal that Zhou also endorsed.[17] In the end, the meeting rejected Braun's idea of "creating a new Soviet area" by adhering to the original plan, which was regarded as "no longer possible to be carried out." Instead, it was decided that the Red Army should "resolutely turn to the west to establish new base areas "in the border regions of Sichuan and Guizhou provinces, beginning by occupying areas surrounding Zunyi."[18]

That evening, Zhou delivered to Braun the English translation of the resolution adopted at the day's meeting. The German advisor, Zhou recalled, was "outraged as he had lost the debate."[19] Blaming Zhou for failing to support him, Braun lost his temper. Though Braun's views were often different from his own, Zhou had long been quite polite toward him. But this evening, Zhou allowed himself to get involved in a face-to-face showdown with the German. The two were so incensed with each other that, at one point, Zhou even pounded the table with his fist, whereupon "the lantern on the table jumped up and the fire went off."[20] This was a clear indication that Zhou had made up his mind to split with Braun.

Why did Zhou's mind-set change? Zhou fully understood that the Red Army was teetering on the brink of destruction. "The matter of utmost importance now is how to win in battles, and all other matters must obey this principle," Zhou repeatedly told his comrades.[21] Zhou was swayed by his deep conviction that Mao was a military genius. He also knew that Mao would not offer wholehearted service if he was not granted real decision-making power. Zhou felt he had no choice but to bring Mao back into the decision-making circle, just as someone on the verge of death would turn to any available doctor for help.

In addition, Zhou probably also predicted that if his troops could climb out of the abyss they found themselves in, they would join forces with Zhang Guotao's Fourth Frontal Army in western Sichuan.[22] Zhou knew Zhang well; he understood that Zhang, like Mao, was extraordinarily ambitious, and equally difficult to deal with.[23] Zhou also understood that, of all his comrades, Mao was probably the only one who could match Zhang in ambition and trickery. Zhou would need Mao on his side if he was to deal with Zhang. Thus, restoring Mao's power gave Zhou a certain amount of room for maneuvering in intraparty politics, if only for the moment.

Unbeknownst to Zhou at the time, however, was how extraordinarily abusive a leader Mao would eventually be. Mao would lead the Chinese Communist Revolution to national victory. But, enabled by unchecked and unlimited power, he would also drag China into such cataclysmic disasters as the Great Leap Forward, the Great Famine, and the Great Proletarian Cultural Revolution. Zhou would serve for twenty-seven years as China's premier under Mao, but he would also repeatedly fall victim to Mao's psychological torture and political purges. If Zhou could have foreseen these later developments during the days of the Long March, would he still have supported Mao's claim to supreme power over the CCP?

* * *

After Liping, the Central Red Army moved deeper into Guizhou facing only weak enemy resistance along the way. The more powerful units of Chiang's "Central Army" commanded by General Xue Yue ceased following the Red Army, after having pursued it all the way from Jiangxi to Guizhou. Instead, following Chiang's orders, they turned southwest and occupied Guiyang, capital of Guizhou Province, which had been controlled by Guizhou warlord Wang Jialie. This move betrayed Chiang's plan to use the objective of "chasing the Reds" as a pretext to penetrate into and control areas held by various provincial warlords.[24] But this also greatly reduced the military pressure on the Red Army. Zhou began to prepare intensively for Mao's return to the Red Army's decision-making circle.

On January 7, 1935, the Red Army occupied Zunyi, Guizhou's second-largest city. The only enemy troops nearby were the weak soldiers of Guizhou and Yunnan warlords, while Chiang's elite forces remained far away. It seemed that the Red Army would not be engaged in a major battle for the time being.

In the wake of Liping, disputes among CCP and Red Army leaders about the Communists' next move continued to simmer. Braun, supported by Bo Gu, was unwilling to accept the views of Mao, Zhou, and others. Thus, another enlarged meeting of the Politburo, organized by Zhou, was called. As a precaution, Zhou deployed a garrison unit not controlled by Braun and Bo Gu to maintain order at the meeting, recognizing that nothing unexpected should be allowed to happen during the meeting.[25]

The conference at Zunyi began on January 15, and it lasted three days.[26] At the outset, Bo Gu delivered a report on the military defeats in the late Jiangxi days, but he "did not admit his own mistakes."[27] This approach backfired, causing Bo Gu and Braun to become even more isolated from the other CCP leaders.

Zhou spoke next. He attributed the loss of the Jiangxi Red Zone to mistakes committed by the military leadership, of which he was a part. Unlike Bo Gu, who put the blame on others and attributed the failure to objective reasons, Zhou stressed "subjective reasons," telling everyone that he also should bear responsibility for the loss. This was an expression of Zhou's political wisdom. The moment he admitted to a share of the blame, he occupied a favorable position to further speak out at the conference.

Following Zhou, Zhang Wentian made a presentation on behalf of himself, Wang Jiaxiang, and Mao. He sharply attacked the "ultra-leftist-leaning" tendency of the party and the Red Army leadership, an attack aimed at Bo Gu and Braun. Mao delivered a lengthy address, in which he assigned various labels to the "leaders of leftist-leaning lines," accusing them of adopting "adventurism in times of offensives, conservativism in times of defensives, and escapism in times of breaking up the enemies' encirclement."[28]

Zhou had specially arranged the meeting to allow for these presentations. According to Bo Gu's recollection, Zhou, wielding his power as the conference's main organizer, suddenly changed the agenda of the meeting (which he had set up with Bo Gu) to let Zhang, Wang, and Mao deliver their coordinated speeches. Bo Gu and Braun were caught off guard.[29] Zhou further put his weight behind the accusations leveled by Mao, Zhang, and Wang, saying that he "fully endorsed the outlines and opinions presented by them."[30]

The conference adopted several decisions, the most important of which was to elect Mao to the Politburo Standing Committee, thus making him a member of the CCP's innermost decision-making circle. The three-person group composed of Bo Gu, Otto Braun, and Zhou was dissolved. The conference decided that "Zhu (De) and Zhou (Enlai) will be commanders in military affairs, and Comrade (Zhou) Enlai is the person entrusted by the party to make the final decision in military matters." After the conference, the Standing Committee met to discuss the division of responsibility. It was decided that Zhang Wentian would "replace Comrade Bo Gu as the person with overall responsibility" and that "Comrade (Mao) Zedong will assist Comrade (Zhou) Enlai in military commanding matters."[31] As a result, Bo Gu and Braun were removed from their leadership roles in the CCP, which opened the door for Mao to deepen his pursuit of control over the party's military and political command.

Still, Zhou was concerned about the reactions that Bo Gu and others might have to the power shuffle. After the Zunyi Conference, he took the initiative to find Bo Gu and had a "heart-touching" conversation with him, in order to persuade him to voluntarily step down from his position or, at a minimum, to lower the chances that Bo Gu would retaliate angrily.[32] Once Bo Gu accepted the result of the conference, Braun would almost certainly not cause any more trouble. Thus, another barrier was removed from Mao's path toward his political reemergence.

The Zunyi Conference did not, as the official history of the CCP has long claimed, result in "the establishment of Mao's commanding position in the Party and the military leadership." Documents from the conference clearly indicate that it was actually Zhou, not Mao, who emerged from it as the Red Army's ultimate decision-maker. Given that military affairs took precedence over all other matters, Zhou could have easily put all power into his own hands, if he so wished. But Zhou did not do this. As he implemented the conference's resolutions, Zhou demonstrated a modest attitude toward Mao, pushing Mao to the center of the Red Army's inner circle. Indeed, he was always willing to listen to Mao's opinions and did everything in his power to ensure that Mao's intentions would be turned into actions. Consequently, Mao's practical status changed from that of a "helper" to that of the final decision-maker. In retrospect, Zhou's attitude and actions made it possible for Mao eventually to seize ultimate power over the army and the party.

* * *

However, the Central Red Army was not immediately victorious on the battlefield under Mao's leadership. Following a resolution adopted at Zunyi, the Red Army abandoned its plan to establish bases in Guizhou; instead, it would attempt to cross the Yangzi River into Sichuan, where it would unite with the Fourth Frontal Army led by Zhang Guotao.[33] In late January 1935, under Mao's direct command, the Red troops engaged in a major battle in the town of Tucheng, with the purpose of clearing the path to cross the Yangzi. However, this time, the intelligence report that Mao and Zhou had received was inaccurate, and their soldiers encountered an overwhelming enemy force. Finally, the Reds had to hurriedly withdraw from the battle to avoid being encircled by the enemy. As a result, Mao and Zhou had to put off the plan to rendezvous with Zhang Guotao's troops.[34]

Despite the embarrassing outcome of this battle, Mao did not lose confidence in his own ability, and he certainly did not give up his ambition. Moreover, he still had Zhou's support. Over the next three months, the Central Red Army followed Mao's orders to zigzag along the borders of Yunnan, Guizhou, and Sichuan provinces, striving to find and take advantage of gaps between various units of Guomindang troops. They crossed the Chishui River, back and forth, a total of four times. The Red troops marched briskly almost every day of the first month. The soldiers, who were utterly exhausted, did not understand why they had to be on the road every day. Mao's hard-earned new position thus faced challenges. Even Lin Biao, who had long been loyal to Mao, openly challenged him and asked for a thorough explanation. "The army will collapse under the current leadership," lamented Lin. "How can Mao command the Red Army if this situation is to continue?"[35]

Zhou saw the trouble that Mao faced. Yet, as he still believed that Mao was the only person who could save the Red Army from complete destruction, he had to continuously justify his support for Mao. Hence, he continuously did Mao a big favor. Since the late Jiangxi years, the Red Army intelligence under Zhou's leadership had been able to decode the enemy's encoded communications. Zhou's intelligence personnel retained this capacity during the

Long March.[36] Thus, Zhou often knew the enemy's movements in advance. Zhou now decided to share this information with Mao alone; he did not disclose it to any other colleague. Consequently, the myth that Mao was a military genius began to spread among Red Army officers and soldiers, enhancing Mao's power and authority.[37]

Finally, back in Zunyi, the Central Red Army achieved the "biggest victory since the Long March [began]." In late February, after they crossed the Chishui River for another time and again approached Zunyi, they caught the enemy there by surprise and easily occupied the city. Enemy casualties numbered several thousand. The Red Army also captured large amounts of weapons, ammunition, and other badly needed supplies.[38]

The victory greatly boosted Mao's credibility and reputation within the Red Army. After the Red Army's triumph at Zunyi, Mao wasted no time to propose that a new top decision-making body be formed to guarantee that timely decisions would be made in urgent circumstances. Thus, on March 10, a new "three-person group" was established, comprising Zhou (who would head the group), Mao, and Wang Jiaxiang.[39] But Zhou was uncomfortable holding such a position, as he knew well that he was not as shrewd and talented as Mao in military judgment and decision-making. Therefore, he suggested, along with Zhang Wentian, that the Central Military Commission appoint Zhu De as commander and Mao as political commissar of the Frontal Headquarters.[40] Zhu, like Zhou, had long been accustomed to not competing with Mao for power, and he had worked closely with Mao in the Jiangxi years. In the end, although Zhou would remain the head of the new three-person group for months to come, Mao held all actual military power.

The fortunes of Zhou and the Red Army did not just depend on Mao's wise vision and clever tactics. They all benefited from an unexpected source—Chiang Kai-shek himself. As the generalissimo believed that the "remnants of the Red bandits" were doomed, hoping all the while to penetrate into areas controlled by provincial warlords, he failed to go all out to "chase a dying enemy to his death."[41] Chiang had other serious concerns. This was the time that "Japanese aggression in northern China was turning increasingly more rampant," reaching the extent of "threatening Beiping and Tianjin." Chiang was compelled to turn much of his attention and resources to dealing with "the outrageous push of the Japanese bandits," lest it produce "mounting crises and even the demise (of China)."[42] On top of this was Chiang's own repeated misjudgment of the direction of the Red Army's movement. Chiang grew so frustrated after constantly making wrong troop deployment decisions that, at one point, he even lamented that he had "fallen into one trap after another" set by the Reds.[43] Consequently, in the mountainous region between Guizhou, Yunnan, and Sichuan, Mao, Zhou, and the Red Army miraculously survived the encirclement of overwhelming Guomindang forces.

Zhang Guotao also lent Mao and Zhou a hand. As their soldiers fought to avoid annihilation, Mao and Zhou repeatedly urged Zhang to come to their rescue. Zhang was not an unselfish person. But at the time, he also faced daunting pressure from enemy forces encroaching on his bases in northern Sichuan. In May, primarily because of that pressure, he ordered his Fourth Frontal Army to abandon its base areas and embark on a small "long march."[44] This move, as it turned out, meant that in their attempt to prevent superior enemy forces from encircling them, Zhang's troops also came closer to the Reds led by Mao and Zhou. In the meantime, Zhang's troops also further made themselves one of Chiang's primary targets, thus greatly mitigating the threat facing Mao and Zhou.

In late spring and early summer 1935, the Red Army operated continuously throughout Guizhou and Yunnan, exploiting gaps between enemy forces as they found them. At one point, it feigned a sudden attack on Guiyang, where Chiang was stationed, before suddenly changing course and turning in the opposite direction. At another moment, it bluffed a speedy advance toward Kunming, the capital of Yunnan Province, then once more magically veered away not far from the city. Chiang and his generals were genuinely confused by these feints, but not so worried—why should they have been? After all, Mao and Zhou's tactics, Chiang believed, were no more than the last throes of a dying patient on his deathbed.

In early May, Mao and Zhou's troops completely defied Chiang's expectations when they crossed the Jinsha River, an upper tributary of the great Yangzi, after a fierce fight. They now entered western Sichuan, an area mainly inhabited by the ethnic Yi people. When Zhou learned that the Red Army commander Liu Bocheng had liaised earlier with Yi aristocrats, he sent Liu to negotiate with them. Liu managed to persuade Xiaoyedan, a Yi princeling, to swear an oath of brotherhood with him. The Red Army passed through the Yi region with almost no trouble at all.[45]

In late May, Mao and Zhou's troops, after another deadly fight, crossed the legendary Dadu River, where, seven decades before, a once-powerful army of the Taiping rebels had been wiped out. But this time the Dadu did not stop—let alone destroy—the Red Army. Now, Jiajin Mountain, also known as the Great Snow Mountain, lay before Mao, Zhou, and their troops. The mountain's peak was a towering three thousand meters high. The Communists' enemy was nature itself. As the Long Marchers trekked over the mountain, many soldiers, already exhausted, perished in the freezing cold and thin air. The majority of the Reds, however, made it to the other side of the mountain. The Guomindang troops that chased them were now left far behind them, separated from their quarry by two torrential rivers, the Jinsha and Dadu, plus the Great Snow Mountain. Although the fate of Mao, Zhou, and their fighters remained uncertain, for the moment, at least, they faced no prospect of immediate destruction.

* * *

On June 12, 1935, remnants of the Central Red Army were met at Maogong, a small town in Sichuan mostly inhabited by ethnic Tibetans, by an advance unit of Zhang Guotao's Fourth Frontal Army. The officers and soldiers of the two armies were overjoyed. A few days later, Mao and Zhou warmly embraced Zhang, and then together they enjoyed a feast and a lot of drinking overnight. They seemed to bask in an atmosphere of harmony and solidarity.[46]

Yet this moment of sheer joy was superficial and short lived. Before long, serious problems surfaced between the two forces. Their contradictions were first revealed in their different military and political approaches. Mao and Zhou contended that, upon merging, the two armies should carry out a strategy of "marching northward" toward the border regions of Sichuan, Shaanxi, and Gansu, and establish a new base area there. They reasoned that the "reactionary reign" in this region was "relatively weak" and that the area was also "closer to the Soviet Union and Mongolia"; thus it would be easier for the Red Army to "receive international support."[47] Zhang, however, was not enthusiastic about such a plan. He preferred to either stay closer to northern Sichuan, where his old bases had been, or turn southward, establishing and expanding new base areas in Sichuan and Xikang.[48]

These strategic differences posed difficult challenges; yet the competition between Mao and Zhang for control of political and military decision-making proved even tenser. Both men were master power players, and both were eager to become the CCP's paramount leader. Neither would allow "two tigers to live in the same mountain." Shortly after the two armies joined forces, Zhou and Zhang Guotao had a chat, during which Zhang inquired about the actual strength of Zhou's troops. "We have a little more than ten thousand soldiers," replied Zhou. Zhang's "face changed immediately," Zhou noticed.[49] How could Zhou's reply fail to touch a nerve with Zhang? While the Central Red Army had been reduced to only ten thousand exhausted and poorly equipped soldiers, Zhang's army had maintained a strength of fifty thousand much better-armed fighters. In addition, the new CCP leadership established at the Zunyi Conference had yet to be approved by the Comintern. In Zhang's view, therefore, its legitimacy remained questionable.

Zhang took action at once. He began demanding, both implicitly and explicitly, that the "reality" of the difference in strength between the two armies be "truthfully reflected" in the structure of the central leadership. This meant, in his own words, that "personnel issues should be duly resolved."[50] After carefully weighing the pros and cons of the situation, Mao and Zhou concluded that they had to yield to Zhang's demand. At a Politburo meeting on July 18, Zhou resigned his position as general commissar of the Red Army. Zhang took up the position while assuming the responsibility of heading the Central Military Commission.[51] Then, several other Fourth Frontal Army commanders also took over top positions at the Red Army general headquarters.

Yet neither the relationship between Mao and Zhou on one side, and Zhang on the other, nor that between the two armies, had improved. Tensions worsened continuously. On August 6, at another Politburo meeting attended by Mao, Zhou, Zhang, and others, Mao again emphasized that a northward move was the only right option, as it would bring the Red Army "geographically closer to the Soviet Union." This proximity to the Soviet Union held an enormous advantage, Mao emphasized. In addition to "receiving political and material support, including obtaining deliveries of planes and artillery pieces, it will also produce a big impact on our country's domestic political development."[52] Again, Zhang disagreed. He clearly spelled out another plan: the Red Army, instead of heading north, should pursue development in the south, establishing, consolidating, and expanding base areas in the region straddling Sichuan and Xikang provinces.[53]

At this critical time, Zhou became seriously ill. He came down with a high fever, which he endured nearly constantly from mid-August, and even suffered periodic comas. Two doctors accompanying the Red Army surmised that Zhou was suffering from amebic dysentery from which he could die. Fortunately for Zhou, the Red Army was in possession of some quinine, a medicine especially effective for treating the disease. Deng Yingchao, who had previously suffered from pulmonary tuberculosis, had been with a recuperation squadron since the beginning of the Long March. She came to Zhou's side and stayed to help care for him. After wavering between life and death for over two weeks, Zhou began to get better, and he would survive.[54]

By then, the Red Army had been reorganized into two columns, comprising a mix of units from the former Central Red Army and the Fourth Frontal Army. The Left Route Column was led by Zhang Guotao, and Mao and Zhou commanded the Right Route Column. While the two columns were marching northward parallel to one another, a controversial "telegram incident" occurred, in which Zhang allegedly intended to "use military means to subdue the CCP Center."[55]

A version of the story told by Mao is as follows: On September 9, Zhang telegraphed Chen Changfeng and Xu Xiangqian, two Fourth Frontal Army commanders who had been marching alongside Mao and Zhou, ordering them to lead the Right Route Column southward while carrying out "a thorough settlement of the intraparty struggle." When Ye Jianying, chief of staff of the Right Route Column and a Mao loyalist, saw the telegram by chance, he immediately went to Mao and showed it to him. Mao quickly wrote down the contents of the telegram. That evening, Mao called an urgent meeting with Zhang Wentian, Bo Gu, and Wang Jiaxiang. Though he was still feverish, Zhou also attended the meeting. They concluded that Zhang Guotao meant to "harm the Party Center." Thus, they decided to order the troops loyal to them in the Right Route Column immediately to set off and move northward, "leaving this dangerous environment."[56] At 2:00 A.M., the troops gathered and departed. Mao and the others cabled Zhang on behalf of the Party Central Committee, pointing out that "in the Party Center's view, the order for the Right Route Column to move southward is totally inappropriate." They emphasized that "it is the Party Center's opinion that the strategy of moving northward should in no circumstance be altered, and that the Left Route Column should also rapidly move northward."[57]

As with so many other important and mysterious events in CCP history, many people have raised a host of questions about this "telegram incident." The original text of the telegram has never been located, and Mao's own copy did not survive either. Therefore, no definitive answer exists as to the content of the telegram. Mao's own descriptions of it were not always consistent. Chen Changhao, one of the telegram's designated recipients, firmly asserted that he had never seen the telegram. And Zhang Guotao, the telegram's alleged author, categorically denied that he wrote and dispatched it.[58] It is likely that the truth about the telegram will never be known.

Regardless of what exactly had happened with the telegram, more important was that the CCP and the Red Army divided into two parts with the sudden departure of Mao, Zhou, and soldiers of the Right Route Column under their command. This was the most serious crisis faced by the Red Army during the Long March. However, the fragmenting of the army provided Mao and Zhou with a series of opportunities, when their immediate interests were identical, to closely cooperate with each other. Zhou was at Mao's side every step of the way in the struggle against Zhang; at this time, they were the closest they would ever be in the half century of their working relationship.

* * *

On September 12, Mao and Zhou convened an enlarged meeting of the Politburo at Ejie, a Tibetan-inhabited village in Gansu, to discuss strategies for their next move. Mao characterized the split with Zhang Guotao as embodying "struggles between two political lines, and between Bolshevism and the tendency toward warlordism." Then, on the subject of "the basic policy principles for the current situation," Mao emphasized that "through guerrilla warfare, we should fight to make thorough connections with international aid, rectify and regroup our troops, and expand the Red Army, so as to, as the first step, create a base area not far from the territory of the Soviet Union, which we will further develop toward the East."[59]

The meeting also adopted another important decision, which was to reorganize the remaining troops of the Right Route Column into a new "Shaanxi-Gansu Brigade," of which Peng Dehuai was to be the commander, Lin Biao the vice commander, Mao the political commissar, and Wang Jiaxiang the director of political affairs. In the meantime, a "five-person leadership group" was formed, composed of Mao, Zhou, Peng, Lin, and Wang, who would be in charge of important military decision-making.[60] Zhou lost his position in the Red Army as a result of this arrangement. Indeed, he was the only one among the five who did not hold an actual combat position. With his declining influence in the military, Zhou was no longer in a position to strive for a top leadership role within the party and the Red Army—if he ever sought to do so. However, wasn't this exactly what he had longed for?

Mao and Zhou were still facing a big problem, however. Although they knew that they would march northward, they did not know where exactly their northern destination should be. They had only about five to six thousand exhausted soldiers. No matter which route they took, they would be facing an uncertain situation. With almost no local knowledge or support, if the brigade encountered a strong enemy force anywhere along their trek, they could easily meet their demise.

Again, luck was on their side. After they entered Gansu Province, the Shaanxi-Gansu Brigade arrived at a small town called Hadapu in late September. By chance, Zhou picked up an old newspaper at the local post office. He glanced at a report in the paper: a Red Army detachment led by Liu Zhidan, a former student of Zhou's at the Whampoa Military Academy, had established a small yet substantial Soviet area in northern Shaanxi. This was almost a gift from heaven. Overjoyed, Mao, Zhou, and their comrades immediately made a critical decision: Instead of marching toward areas bordering the Soviet Union and Mongolia, they would head for northern Shaanxi, to "defend and expand the Soviet areas there."[61]

They also made another critical decision, to change the brigade's name to "The Advance Brigade to March North to Fight Japan." For the first time since the beginning of the Long March, they aligned their journey with the cause of "resistance against Japan." A few days later, Mao announced at a meeting of brigade cadres, "We intend to march north, and Zhang Guotao wants to go south. . . . The Japanese imperialists are invading China, and we are going north to resist Japanese invasion."[62]

Chiang, in an unintentional yet ironic twist, also did Mao and Zhou yet another big favor. After the split, Mao and Zhou commanded far fewer troops than did Zhang Guotao. Moreover, Zhang's troops were operating in areas closer to the interior of Sichuan. Chiang thus viewed Zhang as a more dangerous and urgent threat.[63] At the same time, he eased his chase after Mao and Zhou. After all, as Chiang now saw it, it was only a matter of time before their troops were liquidated once and for all. Why should he, then, do all he could to pursue that end? As history later proved, however, this was a fatal mistake on the part of Chiang and the Guomindang.

9.1 Zhou Enlai on horseback in Northern Shaanxi after the Long March, ca. 1936. *Sovfoto / Universal Images Group via Getty Images*

All of this afforded Mao, Zhou, and their "North March Brigade" precious space for survival. In late October, they entered the territory controlled by Liu Zhidan's Red Army detachment in northern Shaanxi. After the long journey crossing eleven provinces, the brigade that had once called itself the "Central Red Army" had shrunk to a few thousand soldiers. But they finally found a location where they could rest, if only for the moment.

On October 22, Mao announced in Wuqi, a small town in Shaanxi, that "the headquarters of the revolution in the whole country has now moved here."[64] In early November, the CCP leadership decided to establish a Revolutionary Military Committee of the Northwest. Mao became the committee's chairman, and Zhou was named its vice chairman. For the first time since his working relationship with Mao began, Zhou's position was formally and clearly defined as Mao's associate.[65]

Zhou's attitude toward Mao also underwent subtle changes. In the second half of 1935, when he and Mao were engaged in a fierce struggle against Zhang Guotao, Zhang had repeatedly presented them with daunting and mind-boggling challenges. Zhou witnessed Mao's extraordinary capacity and skills in his handling of each and every crisis. This was something Zhou could not and would not do. Mao, on the other hand, could not only think about *how* to deal with the dilemmas he faced, but endeavor to solve them, and ultimately succeed. This inevitably led to the further deepening of Zhou's internalized obedience to Mao.

However, was this the end of the legendary Long March? The place at which Mao and Zhou's troops had arrived at the end of their arduous journey was the barren land of northern Shaanxi. There, they possessed neither the resources nor the manpower to support their mission. Meanwhile, the nearby Northeast and Southeast Armies of the Guomindang were on high alert due to the Red troops' arrival. In addition, larger and more powerful units from Chiang Kai-shek's Central Army were en route to the Communists' new base area.

Although Mao announced that the Long March had come to a successful conclusion, the fate of the CCP and the Red Army still hung in the balance.

10

"AS CHINESE, WE MUST FIGHT AS ONE NATION"

1935–1937

Chilling winds from the Gobi Desert stirred up sandstorms in the Loess Plateau in northern Shaanxi (also known as Shaanbei). It was winter again.

Hardly had their soldiers settled down when Mao, Zhou, and their comrades faced another dilemma. Deep down, they knew that Shaanbei, with its barren soil and poor, sparse population, was not a good location for nurturing a great cause. It was not even suitable for survival. Ever since they split with Zhang Guotao, Mao and Zhou had planned to lead their troops to areas bordering Mongolia and the Soviet Union. This remained their top option.[1] Also, their struggle with Zhang Guotao for supremacy in the party leadership showed no sign of abating.[2] They had to tread cautiously.

In mid-November 1935, Lin Biao's cousin Liu Yutang (who went by the alias "Zhang Hao") suddenly appeared in Shaanbei. He was a Comintern messenger who brought secret codes for communicating with Moscow, which he had memorized.[3] For Mao and Zhou, this was a gift from heaven. If they could resume telegraphic communication with Moscow, they would be able to act in the Comintern's name and subdue Zhang's "Party Center."

When Zhang Hao arrived at Wayaobao, the small town where Mao and Zhou's headquarters was located, they were away defending against an enemy offensive in Shaanbei. They showed utmost interest in another message that Zhang Hao delivered: Moscow had agreed to allow Mao and Zhou's troops to move north into "areas close to the Soviet Union."[4] After returning to Wayaobao in early December, they quickly persuaded Zhang Hao, acting as a "Comintern envoy," to cable Zhang Guotao, demanding that he dissolve his "bogus central committee."[5] In the next weeks, Zhang Hao sent Zhang Guotao two more telegrams, informing him that he possessed the codes for communicating with Moscow and that the Comintern had instructed him to "help settle the problems" between the two Red Army units. He suggested that Zhang Guotao name his party organ the "Southwestern Bureau," which would subject itself "directly to the leadership of the Party delegation (in Moscow)," and that Zhang's disputes with Mao and Zhou "can be judged and resolved by the Comintern."[6] If Zhang Guotao were to accept the proposals unconditionally, his "Party Center" would lose its status. By making Zhang Hao speak in such a voice, Mao and Zhou demonstrated their combined ability to manage intraparty struggles.

Zhang Guotao received these telegrams at a very bad time. His troops had suffered a series of setbacks in northwestern Sichuan and Xikang as the result of constant attacks by GMD forces and troubles caused by complicated ethnic conflict. Furthermore, the areas where Zhang was operating were too poor to support his troops. As he was unable to establish new bases, his situation grew increasingly grim. He thus decided to take a step back in his competition with Mao and Zhou, agreeing to rename his "Party Center" as the "Southwestern Bureau" if Mao and Zhou would rename theirs the "Northwestern Bureau." Mao and Zhou rejected his offer.[7] This instance of successful cooperation between Mao and Zhou established another important precedent in their relationship for the decades to come.

Zhang Hao's usefulness to Mao and Zhou transcended the CCP's intraparty politics. He also relayed to them the Comintern's new grand strategy of pursuing a worldwide "antifascist united front."[8] Mao and Zhou in particular immediately embraced the Comintern's vision, as it meant—if only by coincidence—that they could now highlight the Long March as an endeavor by which the Reds would join the "resistance against Japan." The united front strategy could also allow them to pivot toward an anti-Japanese united front with the GMD. Mao and Zhou could not have foreseen such a turn of events when they split with Zhang Guotao only a few months before. Seemingly in an instant, their space for strategic maneuvering widened considerably.

The pivot to the new strategy, however, did not happen overnight. In a statement issued in late November, the CCP leadership continued to equate Chiang with the "Japanese bandits," regarding him as the most dangerous enemy.[9] After they learned of the Comintern's new united front strategy, their attitude toward the civil war began to change. A week-long enlarged meeting of the CCP Politburo convened on December 17 to discuss the party's military and strategic options. When many of Zhou's comrades demonstrated that they still viewed Chiang as well as the Japanese imperialists as the main enemies, he reminded them of the dangers involved in an "exclusionist approach." Therefore, he declared, the CCP should transform its war against the GMD into "a war to save the nation."[10] The conference finally adopted a resolution reflecting Zhou's ideas, which pointed out that "exclusionism is the main danger facing the party" and called for the "establishment of a national defense government and a united anti-Japanese army."[11]

CCP leaders' changing assessment of the situation was more obvious at another Politburo meeting on January 2, 1936. Zhou again emphasized the necessity of discarding the "exclusionist approach," telling his comrades, "At the center of the political situation now is how to fight a war to defend our nation. . . . Our party should play a leading role in uniting the masses to carry out a revolutionary *national* war."[12] These developments opened the door for the CCP to adopt "resistance against Japan" as the backbone of its grand strategy, which also enabled the party to pursue an anti-Japanese partnership with the GMD.

At the Wayaobao Conference, Zhou was also named secretary of the newly established "Northeastern Army Work Committee."[13] Though this appointment did not seem particularly significant at the moment, it would change the fate of the Red Army and, indeed, of modern Chinese history.

The Northeastern Army, commanded by Zhang Xueliang, who was known as the "Young Marshal," was the biggest GMD force stationed near Shaanbei. Zhang, in his mid-thirties, was the son of the powerful warlord Zhang Zuolin, the "Old Marshal" of Manchuria (or northeastern China). After Japanese agents assassinated Zhang Zuolin in early 1928, Zhang Xueliang succeeded his father as the "strongman of the Northeast," and that December, he declared his allegiance to Chiang's Nanjing government. He was a patriot and hated the Japanese. However, Zhang lost his home territory to the Japanese in the wake of the Mukden Incident of 1931. His Northeastern Army eventually settled in Shaanxi after evacuating from Manchuria and moving across different parts of China. Zhang's troops lost several battles with Mao and Zhou's Red Army after it arrived in Shaanbei. One of Zhang's officers, who had been captured by the Red Army, upon his release delivered

10.1 From right, Mao Zedong, Zhu De, Zhou Enlai, and Qin Bangxian (Bo Gu) in northern Shaanxi, ca. 1936. *CPA Media Pte. Ltd. / Alamy Stock Photo*

to the Young Marshal a proposal from Mao and Zhou for a truce. Zhang was quite willing to accept it. Thus, the CCP formed the Northeastern Army Work Committee to handle the matter.

• • •

CCP leaders' shifting strategic thinking came at a time of dramatic transformation for China. The scenario facing Chiang featured both good and bad news. The Communists had been his most dangerous enemy for a decade. Despite Japan's aggressive actions in China, he decided to make his top priorities defeating the Reds and containing the warlords who refused to obey him. This "domestic first" strategy seemed to be working. By late 1935, Chiang was delighted to see that the "red bandits" had been almost totally defeated and that China's domestic situation as a whole had also improved greatly in his favor.

But Chiang's worries about Japan deepened. Since the Japanese imperial army's occupation of Manchuria in 1931, he had tried—and failed—to check Japan's expansion with the help of the League of Nations. In 1933, Japan even withdrew from the League of Nations. As Chiang shifted his focus to domestic challenges, the Japanese threat continuously worsened, endangering China's very survival, as he saw it, and forcing him to reconsider his strategic priorities. While he persisted in his efforts to eliminate the Reds, he now saw negotiating with the CCP as a plausible means to solve the Japanese problem.[14] He declared, "As of now, the effort taking the suppressing of Communist bandits as the central task has achieved 70 percent success. Beginning next year, we may take resisting the Japanese bandits as the main task, while continuously wiping out the Communist bandits."[15]

Chiang believed that he would need international support for China to confront Japan. He thus set his sights on Moscow, because "the Japanese bandits fear the Soviets the most."[16] Since 1927, Chiang had treated Moscow as an enemy. Even after the resumption of diplomatic relations between Nanjing and Moscow in 1932, suspicion and hostility between them persisted. At the beginning of 1935, however, Chiang began to carefully explore channels through which he could contact the Soviets, led by the hope that they might help him settle the CCP issue while bolstering his leverage against Japan. Nonetheless, he still stood firm in his belief that he would "connect with Russia, but never tolerate the CCP!"[17]

In late 1935, Chiang took a series of steps to explore ways of "politically settling" the CCP issue while liaising with the Soviet Union. He sent his close associate Chen Lifu to Europe to investigate how to gain access to the Comintern. In Moscow, Deng Wenyi, the Chinese military attaché there, repeatedly met with Soviet officials, as well as with Wang Ming, the CCP delegate to the Comintern, to discuss conditions for formal negotiations between the CCP and the Nationalist government. Meanwhile, Zeng Yangpu, one of Chen Lifu's most trusted associates, approached CCP underground organs in northern China through an intermediary to seek closer contact with the CCP Center.[18]

Mao and Zhou knew nothing of Chiang's moves. For them, survival remained the most urgent task. At the Wayaobao Conference, they made another decision—the main force of the Red Army would march into Shanxi, a province abutting Shaanxi. This, they calculated, would allow them to expand their territory and personnel in Shanxi, with the prospect of "further penetrating into nearby Suiyuan and getting closer to the Soviet Union and Outer Mongolia." They would justify the expedition by describing it as a move aimed at "opening a path to fight against Japan."[19] To avoid being stabbed in the back when the bulk of the Red Army left Shaanbei, it was essential for Mao and Zhou to work out a truce with the Northeastern Army commanded by Zhang Xueliang, the Young Marshal.[20]

Thus Zhou, as secretary of the Northeastern Army Work Committee, extended several peace overtures to the Young Marshal. He soon found out that Zhang was also interested in a cease-fire with the Red Army. In the previous two months, two of his divisions had been wiped out in battles with the Reds. The losses shocked Zhang, who did not want to face more such defeats. On the last day of 1935, under Zhou's direction, Red Army frontal commanders worked out a truce with officers from the Northeastern Army.[21]

The Red Army's Shanxi expedition began in mid-January 1936. CCP leaders divided their responsibilities as follows: Mao would lead the main force across the Yellow River into Shanxi in mid-February, while Zhou would stay in Shaanbei, taking care of logistical matters and negotiating with the Northeastern Army.[22] In late February, the Red Army won a series of battles after crossing the Yellow River. The Shanxi campaign seemed to be off to a good start.

In Shaanbei, Zhou's endeavors to engage the Northeastern Army also made solid progress. Zhou's associate Li Kenong (one of the three heroes of *Teke*) secretly met with the Young Marshal on January 20. In a telegram to Zhou and Mao, Li reported that many officers from the Northeastern Army were sympathetic to the CCP's plans to establish a national defense government. "If we show our genuine sincerity," Li wrote, Zhang was willing to hold formal discussions with CCP leaders.[23] In early February, Zhou decided after speaking with Li to send him back for another meeting with Zhang. "In no circumstance should you allow the meeting to fail," Zhou instructed Li. "You must try your best to make it a success."[24]

Just before Li left, two of Zhou's former *Teke* subordinates, Dong Jianwu and Zhang Zihua, arrived at the Young Marshal's headquarters in Xi'an bearing a message from Chiang about "resolving the CCP problem politically." After checking with Chiang, who confirmed that the message was indeed his, the Young Marshal arranged for Dong and Zhang to be escorted to Wayaobao.[25] Upon reading the message, Zhou immediately cabled Mao. "We should tell Chiang that we will dispatch a formal negotiator to Nanjing," Zhou stressed. "We absolutely should seize this rare opportunity," Mao agreed.[26] CCP leaders would convene a Politburo meeting in Shanxi to draft a formal response. Zhou immediately departed for the meeting.

Meanwhile, Li and Zhang Xueliang met again. The Young Marshal reiterated his hope that the CCP would help connect him with Moscow and expressed his wish to meet with a top CCP leader in the near future to discuss this objective. Li replied to Zhang that either Mao or Zhou could meet with him in Yan'an, which was then under Zhang's control.[27] Once Li informed Zhou of the meeting, Zhou instructed him to travel to Shanxi to report to the Politburo.[28]

In late March, at a politburo meeting at Shilou in Shanxi, Zhou underscored the importance of the party reaching a consensus on negotiations with the GMD. "To begin with," Zhou said, "we must oppose closed-doorism, and not be bound by our past experience." He told his comrades that "some GMD leaders have already realized the necessity of fighting Japan," but there was still some disagreement among the GMD elite. Therefore, Zhou argued, the CCP should pursue "a united front strategy from both the top and the bottom, promoting the establishment of a national defense government and a united army of resistance against Japan." The politburo endorsed Zhou's ideas, as well as his plan to meet with Zhang.[29]

* * *

Zhou, accompanied by Li, set out for Yan'an on April 7 and arrived the next evening. Wasting no time, he had an overnight meeting with the Young Marshal at a Catholic church there.

Zhou was well prepared for the meeting. He told Zhang that "the Red Army is sincere in fighting against Japan" and that "suppression of the Communists cannot go hand in hand with resisting Japan." Thus, Zhou stressed, the civil war must end, and "a national defense government and a united army against Japan" must be established. Zhang's response was enthusiastic. He agreed to maintain "economic and commercial exchanges" with the CCP, providing the Communists with radio transmitters, medicine, and even ammunition. Zhou found that Zhang was eager to communicate directly with Moscow. The CCP would assist him, Zhou said, "in sending his representatives to the friendly Soviet Union." Zhang candidly told Zhou that "it [was] not yet possible for him to openly oppose Chiang." Zhou replied, "I understand completely."[30]

Zhou had worked his way into the Young Marshal's heart. After the meeting, Zhang told a close associate, "Mr. Zhou has helped me solve my conundrums, and he strengthened my confidence in fighting Japan. I am completely satisfied with the meeting."[31] Sensing Zhang's friendly inclination, Zhou wrote to Zhang after their discussion, "For the sake of the resistance against Japan, we should support Chiang, but we cannot support Chiang at the expense of the resistance against Japan. For the resistance against Japan, and for the Northeastern Army, you must prepare accordingly."[32] Zhang's attitude toward Chiang began to change. "If I want to take action, I will do it resolutely," he wrote.[33] The seed of his later kidnapping of Chiang was sown.

While Zhou's relationship to Zhang grew closer, the Red Army's Shanxi expedition suffered a series of defeats at the hands of the reinforcements that Chiang had sent to Shanxi. Indeed, the GMD's victories threatened even the CCP's Shaanbei base area. In late April, the Red Army was forced to return to Shaanbei, its plan to open an "international pathway" through Shanxi a failure.

Mao and Zhou turned to give more emphasis to their newly established connections with the Northwestern Army. With Zhou's support, Mao put forward the idea of pursuing a "Grand Northwestern Plan" at a Politburo meeting. According to the plan, the Red Army would cooperate with the Northeastern Army under the banner of resistance against Japan to expand into Ningxia and northern Gansu. The goal of the expansion was to further blaze a trail through Xinjiang linking the Reds to the Soviet Union.[34]

When Zhou met with the Young Marshal again on May 12, he explained in detail the Grand Northwestern Plan. Impressed, Zhang decided to cooperate with the CCP in carrying out the plan. They agreed to "work closely with each other, realize the 'great union' in the Northwest, establish a Northwestern National Defense Government, and connect with the Soviet Union."[35]

Zhou's successful meeting with Zhang made the prospects of the Grand Northwestern Plan brighter than ever before. On May 20, Mao and Zhou cabled Zhang Guotao and He Long, the commander of another major Red Army force, the Red Second Frontal Army, informing them that "the Comintern has sent several envoys to us with the hope that we may seize a big opportunity emerging in the Northwest."[36] They urged Zhang and He to bring their troops to Shaanbei to carry out "the Comintern's instruction on creating a grand new vista in the Northwest." They particularly wooed Zhang, emphasizing that "there now exists no political or strategic difference between us and Comrade (Zhang) Guotao," and that "our task is to be united to fight against the Japanese imperialists and Chiang."[37]

Meanwhile, Zhou also made significant progress in recruiting General Yang Hucheng to the Northwestern Plan. Yang, a Shaanxi native, was commander of the Seventeenth Army, which was called the Northwestern Army because it originated in Shaanxi. Yang had long leaned to the left politically; he had once even applied to join the CCP. Over the years, he had developed a deep antagonism to the generalissimo, to whom he was never close. Beginning in spring 1936, Zhou's agents had connected Yang with Zhou. While Zhou engaged Zhang in secret talks, he also continuously worked on Yang. At a Politburo meeting on May 28, Zhou reported that "neither Zhang Xueliang nor Yang Hucheng will accept Chiang's command."[38]

June 1936 was a good time for Zhou and the CCP. Early in the month, the warlords in Guangdong and Guangxi launched a military campaign to challenge Chiang's position as generalissimo, forcing Chiang to turn his attention away from the Reds. In Nanjing, CCP negotiators reached a "draft accord" with representatives from the GMD.[39] In the Northwest, the Communists signed a series of secret agreements with Zhang Xueliang, who even submitted an application to join the CCP, which the Party Center approved. Most exciting for Mao and Zhou was that Zhang Guotao finally decided to disband his own "Party Center."[40] The nearly year-long split of the Red Army ended with a major victory for Mao and Zhou.

In mid-June, the CCP resumed its long-interrupted telegraphic communication with Moscow. CCP leaders cabled the Comintern, relaying news of the Grand Northwestern Plan and of Zhang Xueliang's application to join the party, and soliciting Moscow's "strong support."[41] Preparing for and implementing the Great Northwestern Plan became Mao and Zhou's priority.

Moscow's instructions came in August. Early in the month, Pan Hannian arrived in Shaanbei from Moscow, bearing the Comintern's instruction that the CCP should abandon its slogan of "opposing Chiang while resisting Japan." Two days later, on August 10, Zhou proposed at a Politburo meeting that the slogan be discarded.[42] Mao and other CCP leaders endorsed the suggestion, but they still believed it was desirable to cooperate with Zhang Xueliang as a step toward the "creation of a Northwestern National Government."[43]

On August 15, the Comintern's response to the CCP leadership's mid-June telegram finally arrived. It was "politically mistaken" for the CCP to regard "Chiang Kai-shek and the Japanese bandits in equal terms," emphasized the Comintern. Therefore, the CCP "must formally propose to the GMD and Chiang Kai-shek to immediately begin negotiations on stopping military action and signing concrete agreements on the joint resistance against Japan." The Comintern categorically rejected the CCP's plan to "accept Zhang Xueliang as a party member" and sternly ordered the CCP not to admit Zhang to its ranks.[44]

Mao, Zhou, and other CCP leaders could not have expected a worse response from the Comintern in its first telegram to them. Moscow's rejection of the Grand Northwestern Plan meant that the strategy they had worked so hard to bring into being was no longer feasible. The Comintern's response dealt the most crushing blow to Zhou. After all, his successfully inducing Zhang to join the CCP had been a brilliant achievement, but now his efforts had been nullified, which he considered a personal failure. More seriously, Zhang's exclusion from the party instantly darkened the Red Army's strategic prospects, as Chiang's superior forces were attempting to destroy their base areas in Shaanbei. How could they repel Chiang without the Young Marshal's wholehearted help? On August 25, Zhou and Mao cabled Wang Ming, the CCP representative in Moscow, proposing an alternative plan. In order to avoid a showdown with Nanjing's forces and to defend its base areas, "the Red Army's main force must occupy western Gansu, Ningxia, and Suiyuan," in order to get close to the Soviet Union and improve the Red Army's financial situation and food supply.[45]

Meanwhile, the CCP's secret negotiations with Nanjing continued as planned. On August 27, Zhou received a message from Chen Lifu and his brother Chen Guofu via Zeng Yangpu. inviting him to "come out to negotiate."[46] In response, Zhou wrote a personal letter to the Chens, promising that when the conditions were ripe, he would be "very much willing to have concrete negotiations with representatives of your side."[47] The CCP leadership also formally decided to abandon the slogan of "fighting Chiang while resisting Japan," replacing it with "compelling Chiang to resist Japan."[48]

Moscow did not want to see the Red Army caught in a death trap. On September 10, Stalin personally approved the CCP's request for aid. Georgi Dimitrov, the Comintern's general secretary, approved the CCP's plan to receive Soviet weapons and ammunition in Ningxia and Gansu, close to the border with Mongolia.[49] Mao and Zhou were delighted, but they also knew that the Red Army's numbers in Shaanbei were quite thin, especially after Moscow vetoed their plan to ally with the Northeastern Army. They thus considered calling all Red Army forces to Shaanbei for the expedition to the Mongolian border. They hoped that by doing so, they might also conclusively end the split with Zhang Guotao. From mid- to late September, they dispatched several telegrams to Zhang and He Long, urging them to rush their forces to Shaanbei.[50]

The Politburo met again in mid-September to discuss how to implement the Comintern's instruction to change the party's political and military strategies. In his speech, Zhou emphasized the necessity of working with Chiang to fight against Japan. It was wrong "to exclude Chiang's forces in the past," he said. "Chiang's attitude has changed, and is moving toward resisting Japan."[51] The meeting adopted a resolution to abandon the banner of the Soviets and favored establishing a democratic republic based on a united front against Japan.[52]

But the path toward a partnership with Nanjing was rather bumpy. When Pan Hannian, the CCP representative, met with Chen Lifu in Nanjing in November, he found the terms Chen presented to be exceedingly stringent: The CCP must dissolve its regime and disband its army except for no more than three thousand soldiers; and all commanders at the division level and above must "be dismissed and sent abroad." These were not "terms for negotiations," Pan immediately told Chen, but "conditions for surrender." Chen refused to retreat a single inch. "If Zhou Enlai is willing to come to the negotiations and meet with Chiang," Chen said, these conditions could probably be softened. Unless a temporary truce was reached, Pan replied, "I do not believe that he will come to Nanjing to join the negotiation."[53]

Chiang's change of attitude was not surprising. After all, he had agreed to talk to the Communists for the sake of "settling the CCP issue" politically. From the outset, he had prepared for two possibilities. If negotiations would work, then he would pursue them. But if military means were necessary, he was ready to use them. At the moment, Chiang found it a good time to fight. In September, he had successfully suppressed the military challenge that the Guangdong and Guangxi warlords had presented to him. He thus was able to turn his main attention back to dealing with the Red Army. The two Red forces, led by Zhang Guotao and He Long, respectively, arrived in Shaanbei in November. The massing of the entire Red Army greatly strengthened its forces' impact and power. However, as Chinese historian Yang Kuisong has argued, it was in this moment that the Red Army actually faced its greatest peril.[54] For years, Chiang had strived to suppress Communist rebellions around the country. Now, the "red bandits" had all gathered in Shaanbei. Not surprisingly, Chiang immediately moved his forces to Shaanxi, hoping to eliminate the Red Army once and for all.

Mao, Zhou, and other Red Army leaders knew that their negotiations with Chiang would go nowhere unless the Red Army could show its strength on the battlefield. On November 21, the Red Army annihilated a GMD brigade at Shanchengbao, a strategically important spot in Gansu, forcing the enemy to retreat. Chiang was stunned. He realized that the Red Army remained a formidable enemy, and that more defeats of that kind could "produce an enormous negative impact in our own camp."[55]

Chen Lifu appeared "more reasonable" when Pan met with him again in early December.[56] Chiang, however, was determined to adhere to his general strategy toward the CCP: while continuing to negotiate with CCP representatives, he would also accelerate the mobilization for a final battle of "bandit suppression." On December 4, he arrived in Xi'an to supervise preparations for what was to be a decisive battle.

By implementing this strategy, though, Chiang also pushed Zhang and Yang, who had colluded with the Red Army, into a corner. Chiang was not politically naïve. He firmly rejected Zhang's final plea to end the civil war. Atop his desk sat intelligence reports detailing Zhang's collusion with the Communists. But he simply did not believe that the Young Marshal would go so far as to harm him.[57] In comparison, Zhou's knowledge and understanding of Zhang and how to deal with him were far more sophisticated and shrewder than Chiang's.

• • •

Before daybreak on December 12, Zhang Xueliang and Yang Hucheng launched a coup in Xi'an and kidnapped Chiang. This, the conspirators hoped, would force Chiang to end the civil war and unite the whole country to resist Japan. Zhang and Yang did not consult with CCP leaders about the coup in advance. Yet shortly after they carried it out, Zhang cabled Mao and Zhou twice, informing them that Chiang had been arrested and asking the Communist leaders for "farsighted advice."[58]

Mao and Zhou had known of Zhang's staunch opposition to Chiang for a while, but they did not expect Zhang to act so quickly and dramatically. They were jubilant. In a reply, they told Zhang that "(Zhou) Enlai will come to discuss this important matter with you." They also suggested that Zhang and Yang move their best units to areas surrounding Xi'an to prepare for attacks from Chiang's troops. The Red Army, they promised, "absolutely will not occupy a single inch of your territory."[59]

The same evening, CCP leaders cabled the Comintern, seeking instruction from Moscow on whether the CCP might join forces with Zhang and Yang while working with some "progressive figures" in Nanjing to form a "revolutionary government of national defense."[60] When they met to discuss the Xi'an Incident the next morning, CCP leaders overwhelmingly agreed that "Chiang must step down and be put on public trial by the people."[61] Mao was quite emotional. He praised the action taken by Zhang and Yang as a "righteous revolutionary move, which has saved us from the disastrous fate of imprisonment." He believed that "there is every reason to execute Chiang" and to "make Xi'an the center of the whole country."[62]

Zhou, like Mao and other CCP leaders, was excited about Chiang's capture. But, as Zhou had been the one to deal with Zhang Xueliang and coordinate negotiations with Nanjing, he had his own opinion about how to manage and settle the incident. In a lengthy presentation, he analyzed factional divisions within the GMD. While they should prepare to fight, Zhou argued, the Communists should also consider "the possibility of adopting a nonconfrontational approach toward Nanjing." Therefore, they should strive to work with those GMD factions willing to put resisting Japan above all other concerns.[63] In the following days, CCP leaders debated about how to respond to Chiang's arrest. Radio broadcasts from Moscow ultimately helped them reach a near consensus on the matter. They learned from the broadcasts that Soviet reports on the events in Xi'an were quite negative.[64] Zhou's view of resolving the incident through "nonconfrontational ways" gradually began to prevail among party leaders.

In Xi'an, Chiang refused to talk to anyone, let alone make any concessions, after his capture. On December 14, William Henry Donald, an American journalist and one-time advisor to the Young Marshal, arrived in Xi'an. He brought with him a written message from Meiling Soong (Song Meiling), Chiang's wife, who urged her husband to "choose to fight Japan rather than die at the hands of your enemies." After he spoke with Donald, Chiang's attitude softened. On December 17, he dispatched a close associate to fly back to Nanjing and deliver his order that there should be no bombardment of or attack on Xi'an for the moment.[65]

Early on the morning of December 15, Zhou left for Yan'an leading a team of eighteen. There, they boarded a plane prepared by Zhang, arriving in Xi'an on the afternoon of December 17.[66] He was cautiously excited. Although Chiang was in custody, Zhou told an associate, his position was different from that of the Russian czar after the Bolshevik Revolution or of Napoleon after Waterloo, as Chiang still controlled a powerful military force. Therefore, it was vital to make the utmost efforts to prevent the current situation from descending into a larger civil war.[67]

Zhou's conversation with the Young Marshal began shortly after he arrived at the latter's residence; the two talked through the night. How might they deal with Chiang? Zhou asked. Zhang replied that if Chiang agreed to stop the civil war and unite the country to resist Japan, he should be released and continue to be endorsed as China's national leader. Only when there absolutely was no other option left would Chiang be executed. Zhou agreed and shared his own thoughts with the Young Marshal: Chiang's detention had not affected his actual power and strength. Therefore, "in handling him, we should be extremely cautious." There were basically two options: either release Chiang or execute him. "If Chiang could be persuaded to stop the civil war and unite the nation to resist Japan, China would avoid being destroyed by Japan." Conversely, if they were to "denounce Chiang and eventually kill him," Zhou elaborated, "not only will the civil war continue, but the Japanese imperialists will also be given more favorable conditions to destroy China." The first option was thus the best.[68] Consequently, Zhou and Zhang agreed on five conditions for resolving the incident: stopping the civil war; mobilizing the whole country to resist Japan; establishing a transitional government excluding pro-Japanese elements; forming an anti-Japanese united army; and releasing all political prisoners and practicing democracy.[69]

These five conditions reflected Zhou's political vision and wisdom. At once he put the banners of "nationalism" and "democracy" firmly into the hands of Zhang and the CCP. Chiang's arrest also changed in meaning from an act of "rebellion" to one of "positive admonition by force." That evening, Zhou proposed to the Party Center that if Nanjing agreed to stop the civil war, "it is acceptable to guarantee Chiang's safety."[70] The next day, the CCP leadership cabled GMD leaders in Nanjing, offering to stop the civil war and unite to resist Japan. If the Xi'an Incident was settled peacefully, CCP leaders promised, "Chiang's safety and freedom will not be a problem at all."[71]

Zhou also met with General Yang Hucheng, another main figure behind the Xi'an Incident. The CCP had decided to pursue a peaceful solution to the incident, Zhou told Yang. Knowing what kind of person Chiang was, Yang was deeply worried. He did not directly challenge Zhou, but said that he feared Chiang would retaliate. "Resisting Japan is the main trend," said Zhou. "So long as the three forces in the Northwest stand together, while uniting with the people of the whole country, it will be impossible for Chiang to retaliate.[72]

• • •

CCP leaders were still waiting for Moscow's instructions. The Comintern had already sent a telegram to the CCP leadership on December 16. However, the CCP side, unable to decode the message, had to ask Moscow to resend it. Nonetheless, CCP leaders already knew Moscow's attitudes from reading Soviet news reports. While continuing to regard the events in Xi'an in a positive light, CCP leaders also realized that if they mishandled the matter, it could "spell extreme danger for the Chinese nation and cause a full-scale civil war." They thus decided at a Politburo meeting on December 19 to "go all out to unite with the leftists in Nanjing, attract middle-of-the-roaders, and oppose the pro-Japanese faction, so as to promote the establishment of a nationwide united front to resist Japan."[73]

On December 20, CCP leaders finally received the Comintern's resent telegram and successfully decoded it, which urged them to "strive for a peaceful settlement" of the Xi'an Incident. More concretely, Moscow ordered the CCP to resolve the incident if Chiang accepted the following terms: that he would reorganize the government by absorbing representatives of the anti-Japanese movement, guarantee the people's democratic rights, stop his persecution of the Red Army and unite with it to resist Japan, and cooperate with countries sympathetic to China's resistance against Japan (but not under slogans put forward by the Soviet Union).[74] These terms were quite compatible with Zhou's ideas about peacefully resolving the Xi'an Incident. After he received the telegram—which Mao had conveyed to him—Zhou immediately relayed it to Zhang and Yang (after deleting the sentence blaming the Young Marshal for the crisis).[75]

It was at this time that Chiang's brother-in-law T. V. Soong (Song Ziwen) arrived in Xi'an. Zhou immediately asked Zhang to help arrange a meeting for him with Soong.[76] But Soong refused to see Zhou. After speaking with Soong, Chiang's attitude softened further, "gradually becoming more reasonable."[77] Soong promptly flew back to Nanjing. On December 22, he flew back to Xi'an along with his sister Meiling Soong. After a long conversation with them, Chiang agreed that if Zhou and the CCP would agree to abolish the Chinese Soviet government, stop using the name "Red Army," abandon class struggle, and obey Chiang's command, he would be willing to "reorganize the government, convene within three months a conference to save the country, and unite with the Soviet Union and the CCP."[78] Chiang also permitted Soong to meet with Zhou, providing Soong the opportunity to "explore Zhou's exact attitude, so as to make our policies accordingly."[79]

Zhou, accompanied by the Young Marshal, met with Soong the next day. Zhou laid out six conditions: that there would be a cease-fire and GMD troops would be withdrawn; that the Nanjing government would be reorganized to exclude pro-Japanese elements and absorb anti-Japanese ones; that political prisoners would be released; that the suppression of the CCP would be halted; and that Chiang would cooperate with countries sympathetic to China. Soong said that he personally supported all these conditions and promised to "relay them to Chiang."[80] Zhou was then more hopeful than before that the Xi'an Incident would be peacefully settled.

At the urging of his wife and T. V. Soong, Chiang made a series of verbal promises to the Young Marshal on December 24. He agreed to withdraw Nanjing's troops, appoint anti-Japanese figures to the government, send pro-Japan officials abroad, release prodemocracy leaders from prison, unite with the CCP, and ally with the Soviet Union as well as with Britain and America. Zhang immediately conveyed Chiang's reply to Zhou.[81]

That evening, Zhou paid a brief visit to the generalissimo. As the two "had not seen each other for many years, naturally they both were emotional."

Chiang was already in bed at the time of Zhou's arrival, so Zhou "said goodbye and left the room" soon after he exchanged greetings with Chiang.[82] At around 10 o'clock the next morning, Zhou and Chiang met again for a substantial conversation. He assured Chiang that the CCP did not want to fight a civil war, "so that the strength of our country might be maintained."[83] According to Chiang's diary, when Zhou asked Chiang to promise "not to suppress the Communists in the future," they had the following exchange:

CHIANG: "Do you know what kind of person I am?"

ZHOU: "Of course I know; you are a revolutionary. So, I dare not to impose anything upon you."

CHIANG: "As you know my character well, how can you ask me to promise that I 'will not suppress the Communists in the future'? I absolutely cannot say this at the moment! If you do not continue to sabotage unification, and completely obey my command, I will not only stop suppressing you, I will also treat you the same as I treat my other subordinates."

ZHOU: "The Red Army will absolutely obey your command and support the central government's unification efforts, and will in no circumstance sabotage them."[84]

Zhou's summary of the conversation differed somewhat from Chiang's account. He did promise Chiang that the CCP would "support Chiang in unifying China" and "obey Chiang's commands." But Zhou also recalled Chiang promising to "stop suppressing the CCP, and unite with the Red Army to fight against Japan." Toward the end of the conversation, Chiang invited Zhou to "go to Nanjing for direct negotiations."[85]

When Zhou walked out of Chiang's room, Soong pleaded with him and the Young Marshal to let Chiang "leave now, today." Zhou insisted that Chiang "must sign a political document" before he departed for Nanjing.[86] But the Young Marshal was worried about Chiang's safety in Xi'an. Without consulting Zhou, Zhang decided to let Chiang go, and even decided to accompany him on his flight to Nanjing.[87] "This is bad! Bad!" Zhou exclaimed when he learned that Zhang would fly with Chiang to Nanjing. He rushed to the airport, but it was too late. The plane carrying Chiang and Zhang had already left.[88]

What concerned Zhou the most was not Zhang's physical safety. He knew Chiang well, and he judged that Zhang's life was not in danger. Rather, he was most worried that Zhang's absence would cause the Northeastern Army to lose a leader who was capable of uniting its commanders and soldiers. Without Zhang, the "three-in-one" framework in the Northwest, comprising the Red Army, the Northeastern Army, and the Northwestern Army, would face serious challenges. Although the Xi'an Incident had been resolved peacefully, it had not ended as Zhou would have liked. At the end of 1936, he knew that a long and difficult path still lay ahead for CCP-GMD cooperation.

• • •

As Zhou had predicted, Chiang was not grateful for the earnest efforts of the CCP—and Zhou in particular—that led to the peaceful resolution of the Xi'an Incident. On the contrary, the episode revealed to Chiang that he had greatly underestimated the political influence of his enemy. If he did not contain the CCP's further expansion, he worried, it would continue to pose a grave danger to him and his government. But in the prevailing peaceful atmosphere of the time, he knew that it would be unwise for him to continue his campaign of "bandit suppression." What he could and should do, he calculated, was to use his position as China's paramount leader and the GMD's superior military strength to subdue the CCP and the Red Army through negotiations with the backing of a military threat.

As the CCP's chief negotiator and someone who had ample experience dealing with Chiang, Zhou knew the generalissimo so well that he could practically read his mind. So, after Xi'an, Zhou shifted his focus to keeping the "three-in-one" structure in the Northwest intact, in order to use it as leverage in his negotiations with Chiang. For his part, Chiang regarded dismembering the northwestern "three-in-one" structure as an urgent task. He thus decided to subject Zhang Xueliang to a "military trial," which ended with the sentencing of the Young Marshal to ten years' imprisonment. Then Chiang offered Zhang a "special pardon" but ordered that Zhang be put under "strict restriction for reeducation" in Nanjing.[89] As a result, the Northeastern Army lost the only person who could glue its various elements together.

Chiang's behavior enraged many officers of the Northeastern and Northwestern armies, who "favored resolutely confronting Chiang." Yang Hucheng, commander of the Northwestern Army, also "intended to fight."[90] Zhou had pushed emphatically for settling the Xi'an Incident in a peaceful way. Now, in the face of such a complicated situation, he still believed that it was necessary to avoid a military confrontation with Chiang and the government in Nanjing. Moreover, the Comintern instructed the CCP that "the party's principal task now is to end the civil war and strive to unite with Nanjing to oppose the Japanese aggressors."[91] Finally, CCP leaders decided to "make concessions to Nanjing," advising the commanders of the Northeastern and Northwestern armies to accept Chiang's conditions.[92] Disappointed and angry, a group of radical young officers from the Northeastern Army launched a munity on February 2, 1937, killing General Wang Yizhe, the only person who could preserve whatever unity still remained in the Northeastern Army. Zhou tried his best to pacify the situation, and the munity was stopped. However, the northwestern "three-in-one" structure collapsed.

Chiang, again, was unappreciative of the CCP's help, this time in quelling the chaos in the Northwest stemming from the Young Marshal's continued detention. Indeed, the influence that Zhou and the CCP had shown in resolving a troublesome situation further reminded Chiang of the urgency of resolving the "Communist issue." In Zhou's negotiations with Chiang's representatives, he followed the Comintern's instructions to recognize the GMD's leading position in the country, offer to stop armed uprisings and put an end to the policy of "land revolution," abolish the Soviet system, reorganize the Red Army, and accept Chiang's unified command.[93] However, Chiang's envoys kept pressuring the CCP for more concessions. In February, a GMD plenum adopted a resolution on "thoroughly eliminating the Red menace," demanding that the CCP disband the Red Army and discard communism. Chiang made it clear that the CCP and the Red Army must be "restructured" on his terms.[94] Zhou realized that instead of "recognizing GMD-CCP cooperation," Chiang actually wanted "the Red Army to surrender." He thus told Chiang's representatives that the CCP would "not give up its belief in Communism," "dissolve the Party," or "disband the Red Army" and place it under the command of GMD "political commissars."[95] Gradually, Zhou's negotiations with his GMD counterparts narrowed to two critical issues: the "political transformation" of the CCP and the "reorganization" of the Red Army. While Zhou insisted that the CCP must retain command over its troops, Chiang's negotiators firmly opposed allowing the Red Army to remain a force outside Chiang's control.[96] Finally, Zhou was told, he had to discuss these issues with Chiang in person.

On March 26, Zhou met with Chiang in Hangzhou. Their conversation went smoothly. Zhou once again assured Chiang that the CCP sincerely supported Chiang's leadership of China's resistance against Japan, as well as his efforts to secure domestic peace and improve the people's livelihood. But he also emphasized that "the CCP will not surrender, and the Red Army will not dissolve." He offered to change the name of "the Soviet areas" to "border regions" and to reorganize the Red Army into three divisions with a total strength of forty thousand soldiers. However, Zhou also asserted that the CCP should be allowed to "establish a general headquarters to command these troops, with representatives from the central government serving mainly in the capacity as liaisons." With a smile, Chiang commented that these were all "small matters which should not become problems," and that "even if the negotiations do not go well, surely there will be no further fighting." He even praised the CCP as "a new force with national consciousness and revolutionary spirit." What he cared about most, Chiang emphasized, were his own relations with the CCP, and to what extent the Communists would obey him as the supreme leader. Chiang asked Zhou to come up with concrete suggestions on these matters and told him they would meet again once he had done so.[97]

Zhou returned to Yan'an in early April, bringing with him a set of secret codes that Chiang gave him for directly communicating with him. On April 9, Zhou reported back to Chiang: "Since returning to Yan'an, I have expressed to others your sincerity in cooperating with us; everyone is extremely excited. Now our party is discussing plans to permanently cooperate with you."[98] At that moment, it seemed that the negotiations were approaching success.

Despite Chiang's encouraging words, however, Zhou's negotiations with the GMD representatives in Xi'an remained extremely difficult. The two sides bargained back and forth over almost every detail, and a final agreement seemed remote. Once again, Zhou found it necessary to meet with Chiang. On May 23, he reported to the Party Center that he would soon see Chiang at Lushan.[99]

When Zhou met with Chiang again in early June, he found that Chiang presented a different face to him. In fact, the generalissimo had decided that, in his approach to the CCP, he would be "lenient in economics," "less lenient in politics," and "most restrictive in military matters." In addition to asking the CCP to "cut off relations with the Comintern," Chiang insisted that the CCP's troops should be significantly reduced in number and not be controlled by CCP commanders.[100] He urged Mao to "serve in the Government," while pushing the GMD and CCP to merge into an "Alliance of National Revolution," which Chiang would command. Zhou rejected all of these conditions, leading him and Chiang into "a prolonged dispute."[101]

But the negotiations did not fail. Both sides had reasons to keep them going. The CCP, still heavily depending on support from Moscow, had to follow the Comintern's instructions to try its best to cut a deal with Chiang. Zhou fully understood this. When he returned to Yan'an, he stressed the positive aspects of his talks with Chiang while deemphasizing the difficulties he had encountered. After listening to Zhou, his comrades agreed to make as many concessions to Chiang as possible; and Zhou would remain the CCP's chief negotiator.[102]

• • •

On July 7, 1937, Japanese troops held an exercise close to the Lugou Bridge (Marco Polo Bridge) in the western suburbs of Beijing. They then alleged that one of their soldiers had disappeared and demanded to conduct a search in the nearby town of Wanping, which was controlled by Chinese troops. When the demand was rejected, the Japanese attacked Wanping, encountering fierce resistance from the Chinese. This was the Lugou Bridge or July 7th Incident, which ultimately triggered the Second Sino-Japanese War.[103]

On that day, Zhou was traveling to Lushan for another meeting with Chiang. One week later, Zhou personally handed the CCP's declaration of cooperation with the GMD to Chiang at Lushan. Yet the negotiations that followed were still not easy. The two parties were still far apart on such central issues as "restructuring" the Red Army and legalizing the CCP. But the clock was ticking, as the danger of an all-out Sino-Japanese war mounted. While the Japanese were increasingly more determined to bring Chiang to his knees, the outcries by the Chinese to firmly resist Japan intensified. On August 1, Chiang invited Mao, Zhu De, and Zhou to Nanjing to "discuss important national issues." One week later, Zhou arrived in Nanjing. He began another round of negotiations with Chiang almost immediately thereafter.

On August 7, the Japanese government announced that it would not negotiate with the Nationalist government. Six days later, when the fighting reached Shanghai, an all-out Chinese war of resistance against Japan became a reality. Zhou's negotiations with Chiang moved forward rapidly. On August 22, the Nationalist government announced that the Red Army would be reorganized as the Eighth Route Army (ERA). In late September, Chiang recognized the CCP's legal status, and an anti-Japanese CCP-GMD united front formally came into being.

• • •

When the war broke out, Mao contended that the CCP, while carrying the banner of resistance, should strive to develop its own military strength and expand its political influence.[104] Zhou quickly found himself involved in a major dispute with Mao about the grand strategies and policies of the CCP.

The CCP Politburo met in Luochuan, a small town about sixty miles south of Yan'an, beginning on August 22. Zhou rushed back from Nanjing to attend the meeting. Mao had much to say; he warned his comrades that Chiang's final goal was still "to restrict us as well as to undermine us." Therefore, Mao argued, the CCP must maintain a keen "sense of class independence" and a "high degree of alertness" about Chiang's moves. The party's priorities must be to expand its territory and enlarge its military force while avoiding costly battles with the Japanese. Instead, Mao asserted that the Communists should wage "independent guerilla warfare in hilly and mountainous regions."[105] Zhou did not necessarily view Mao's perspectives as wrong, but he saw the whole picture from a different angle. He believed that Chiang "will not compromise with Japan" and that "the CCP's independence should not be overemphasized to the extent of openly violating Nanjing's orders." With respect to military strategy, Zhou contended that when necessary, "our troops should still be amassed to wipe out the enemy" in cooperation with government forces. Although the CCP-led troops "may suffer heavy casualties in such actions, they are worth it, as they will prove to the people of the whole country that we are making our utmost effort in fighting against the enemy."[106] But Zhou was unable to persuade Mao, although a majority of attendees at the meeting did support his points. Tension thus emerged between him and Mao.

However, Mao still controlled the CCP's military power. He remained chairman of the Central Military Commission; Zhou and Zhu De were both vice chairmen of the CMC. On August 23, the CCP leadership decided to name Zhou secretary of a committee responsible for managing united front work involving Chiang and the GMD.[107] This was the work Zhou was most willing to do.

After the Luochuan Conference, Zhou went to Shanxi, the front line of the war against Japan. Yan Xishan, the warlord who had controlled Shanxi for over two decades, demonstrated his eagerness to cooperate with the CCP. Zhou thus believed that he could play a key role in expanding the CCP's strength and influence by staying in Shanxi.

Zhou developed a good working relationship with Yan over the three months he spent in Shanxi. On September 25, the CCP-led ERA, fighting alongside Yan's troops, won a battle in Pingxiangguan in which it reportedly killed more than one thousand enemy soldiers. This was one of the few victories that the Chinese won in the early days of the war against Japan. Zhou now felt even more confident that he could make a positive impact in Shanxi. He thus asked the Party Center to permit him to prolong his stay in Shanxi, which he intended to use as his base for "war commanding matters."[108] His determination to promote a CCP-GMD united front grew stronger. He would stay in Shanxi until mid-November, when the province's capital, Taiyuan, fell to the Japanese.

Zhou returned to Yan'an on November 12. A few days later, Wang Ming—who had served as the CCP's head delegate in Moscow—also flew back to Yan'an. A five-day Politburo meeting, known as the "December Conference," began on December 9. Wang, regarded as an envoy from the Comintern, was the star of the meeting. He almost instantly posed a serious challenge to Mao's political and military leadership.

Wang delivered a lengthy speech at the conference's opening. "The central issue is that everything should serve the war against Japan," he told his comrades, "and should go through the united front." As China's political system had "begun to be democratized" with the outbreak of the war against Japan, Wang stressed, it was no longer correct to divide the GMD into "left, middle, and right" factions. The criterion to judge an enemy from a friend was whether they were for or against Japan. With respect to the military, Wang argued that it was necessary to establish a "unified national defense army" with "unified command, unified discipline, unified weapon systems, and unified supplies and combat plans."[109] Wang had the Comintern's backing. From Moscow's perspective, it was important for China to continue its fight against Japan, as this would allow the Soviet Union to avoid fighting simultaneous wars to its east and its west.

Wang's words appealed to CCP elites, including Zhou, at a time when China was facing an enormous national crisis. Informed by his own dealings with Chiang, Zhou believed that the generalissimo was fundamentally a nationalist. In his presentation, Zhou criticized the tendency within the party to overemphasize the party's independence, while failing to "place the war against Japan above all else." He cited his experience in Shanxi in particular: "As revealed by the situation in Shanxi, due to the failure to follow the principle of treating resistance against Japan as a top priority, and the overemphasis given to maintaining the party's independence and self-reliance, both by military and among civilian leaders, there have emerged ideas, opinions, and actions that are not good for the War of Resistance, or for the united front."[110] Zhou contended that the CCP must correct these mistakes and further improve relations with the GMD. Although he did not name anyone in the presentation, Mao was apparently one of the targets of his criticism.

Zhou's presentation, which proved influential at the conference, echoed Wang's. Mao found himself isolated at the conference. More seriously, in light of the actual alliance that had formed between Zhou and Wang, Mao feared he could lose the power that he had seized after the Zunyi Conference. It was no wonder Mao lamented after the conference that "my orders cannot reach beyond my own cave residence."[111]

In fact, Mao exaggerated his plight. He did not lose power or influence. At the conference, he was named chairman of a committee in charge of preparing for the party's Seventh Congress, while Wang was appointed the secretary of this committee. Hence, they actually shared power evenly. The restructured Central Secretariat comprised Mao, Wang, Zhang Wentian, Chen Yun, and Kang Sheng. Zhou was not included.[112]

After the December Conference, Zhou went to Wuhan to take charge of the party's Yangzi River Bureau, which commanded CCP operations in southern China, and worked with Chiang and the Nationalist government there. Rather than stay in Yan'an, Wang Ming decided to go to Wuhan, too. As he had given such emphasis to the CCP's cooperation with the GMD, he believed that Wuhan was the place where he could play a major role in enhancing the united front. However, in terms of the CCP's intraparty politics, Wang's decision was a fatal mistake. His absence from Yan'an would allow Mao to control the Party Center's telegraphic communication with Moscow while issuing orders, in the name of the Party Center, to party organs throughout the country.

In retrospect, it was at this moment that the balance in the CCP began to shift in Mao's favor in his competition with Wang for supreme power in the party. Mao would never give Wang any opportunity to recover his lost authority. These were also the circumstances that saw the gradual emergence of Zhou's support for Mao. Yet Mao would never forget Zhou's "huge mistakes" of standing on Wang Ming's side and taking a "rightist-leaning approach" toward Chiang and the GMD. Zhou would live for the rest of his life in the enormous shadow of Mao's thought and power, from which he would never escape.

11

CHONGQING FOG

1938–1943

Chongqing is a hilly city located at the confluence of the Yangzi and Jialing Rivers. Heavy fog often blankets the city the whole day between October and April. In the war years, bad weather offered the city a natural barrier against bombing from Japanese planes. The foggy weather was the city's protector.

The Nationalist government announced on November 20, 1937, that China's capital would be preemptively moved to Chongqing, as Nanjing was under siege at the time. When Nanjing fell to Japanese troops in December, most government agencies moved to Wuhan, the biggest city in central China, or to other inland cities and towns. Few went directly to Chongqing. Zhou arrived in Wuhan with Deng Yingchao on December 18. The city would serve as his main base for the next ten months. By then, the Nationalists and Communists had vowed to cooperate; yet the memory of the bloody, decade-long civil war was difficult to erase. Chiang Kai-shek proclaimed that he would embrace the Communists "with open arms" for the sake of saving the motherland.[1] In his mind, though, they were "still untrustworthy."[2]

Zhou conferred with Chiang on December 21, accompanied by Wang Ming and Bo Gu. The generalissimo said that he had "long waited to see them." Zhou put forward a series of proposals, such as "forming a two-party committee, drafting a common program, jointly publishing newspapers and establishing agencies to coordinate the two parties' activities, and transforming the National Consultative Council into a parliament-style entity." Chiang commented that "if these proposals can materialize, the future will be bright."[3]

Nevertheless, mutual distrust persisted between the two parties. Chiang hoped that cooperating with the CCP would "help enhance relations with Russia, allowing us to better cope with the changing international situation."[4] He thus wanted the CCP to merge with the GMD to form a "big party." Meanwhile, calls for "one ideology," "one leader," and "one army" still abounded within the GMD, and the CCP was labeled a "feudal force of warlords" that should be disbanded.[5]

Zhou was eager to cooperate with the GMD, but he opposed merging the two parties. In February 1938, Chiang invited Zhou to serve as deputy director of politics under the Military Commission. Zhou was willing to accept the offer, as the position would enable him "to expand our party's influence."[6] But he also told the generalissimo that problems between the two parties could only be resolved "through continuous cooperation and unity," not by merging the CCP and GMD. Chiang expressed his disappointment in a diary entry: "This is a blow to the plans to transform our party."[7]

Given the complexity of the CCP's relations with the GMD, Zhou and Wang Ming repeatedly cabled Yan'an, suggesting that the Politburo convene to discuss "many new problems recently emerging."[8] Yet Mao's attitude toward the meeting was lukewarm. Only after Zhou and Wang repeatedly urged him did he reluctantly give his assent to the meeting. Zhou and Wang returned to Yan'an in late February. At the Politburo meeting, Zhou contended that the CCP should continuously strive to expand and consolidate the united front, rather than merge with the GMD. Mao viewed the matter from a different angle. He felt that the "Zhou-Wang alliance" represented an obstacle to his pursuit of absolute leadership in the party.[9]

Back in Wuhan, Zhou continued to fret about the deteriorating situation of China's war against Japan. Chinese troops had lost far more battles than they had won. In mid-May, the Japanese army occupied Xuzhou and then immediately began to march toward Wuhan. On June 27, the Nationalist government issued a call for "defending greater Wuhan." Implementing this directive became a central task for Zhou.

Zhou and Wang returned to Yan'an again in early September to attend another important meeting, the CCP Sixth Central Committee's Sixth Plenum. At the conference, Wang Jiaxiang conveyed instructions from Georgi Dimitrov, general secretary of the Comintern: The CCP's political line in the past years had been correct, and the party should resolve the leadership issue under Mao.[10] Dimitrov's words came as a shock to Zhou. He should have stayed throughout the conference, but he was worried that if Wuhan fell, the CCP's relations with the GMD would face new challenges. Mao, by his own calculation, also urged Zhou to return to Wuhan. Thus, Zhou left Yan'an in the middle of the Sixth Plenum.[11]

Wuhan indeed was in danger. A major evacuation of the city began as Japanese troops approached. The fighting lasted until October 25. Zhou stayed in the city until a few hours before it fell to the Japanese. He arrived in Changsha, the capital of Hunan Province, on the evening of October 27.[12]

A fire broke out in Changsha around midnight on November 12. An ocean of flames engulfed the city mere hours later. By the time Zhou's associates awakened him, the city was in a state of total chaos, as panicked crowds were blocking all the roads. Zhou barely managed to escape the city. Later, he learned that Chiang had ordered that the city be burned to ashes if it fell into the hands of the Japanese. Military and civilian leaders had set the blaze that night, believing the untrue rumor that the Japanese were approaching Changsha. "The principal criminals responsible for the fire," Zhou demanded, "must be brought to justice."[13] Ultimately, though, only three lower-level officials were put to death.

* * *

Zhou and Deng Yingchao arrived in Chongqing in mid-December. From that point until he was called back to Yan'an in 1943, the wartime capital served as his base, from which he commanded CCP organizations and activities in GMD-ruled areas, the "Great Rear."

At the time of Wuhan's fall, the CCP CC's Sixth Plenum was still underway. In Zhou's absence, Mao and the CCP leadership decided to name Zhou and Liu Shaoqi, respectively, as secretaries of the newly established Southern and Central Bureaus.[14] Liu, a Hunan native, joined the party in late 1921 in Moscow. He accumulated useful experience and a strong reputation by leading the workers' movement in Anyuan, a coal mining town in Hunan, and quickly emerged as a prominent leader of China's labor movement.[15] In 1931, he was elected to the CCP Politburo. During the Long March, he firmly supported Mao at the Zunyi Conference and after, becoming a firm Maoist. With Mao's trust, he would emerge as the CCP's number two leader.

Zhou's main duty at the Southern Bureau was to handle relations with Chiang and the Nationalist government. By then, the honeymoon between the CCP and GMD had ended, as Chiang again pushed the CCP to disband. "The CCP should abandon its name and merge with the GMD," he stated. "Otherwise, the War of Resistance will be meaningless."[16] Zhou rebutted Chiang's suggestion, calling it "absurd." But Chiang was persistent. When he met Zhou on January 20, 1939, he pressed Zhou on the issue of "unifying the two parties." "This is impossible," replied Zhou. Chiang insisted that Zhou "telegraph the CCP Center to report the matter."[17] The reply came the next day; in it, the CCP Center emphasized that the merging of the CCP and GMD "is a violation of our fundamental principles" and that this matter should not be confused with the two parties' cooperation in the War of Resistance.[18] Zhou wrote Chiang, reiterating that the CCP had no intention to overthrow the GMD and that the GMD should not fear the CCP's development either.[19] Upset, Chiang told a GMD plenum that the CCP "must be disciplined and regulated."[20] To contain the CCP, the GMD leadership adopted a "resolution on restricting the activities of alien parties."

While treating management of relations with Chiang as a top priority, Zhou did not ignore other forces in Chongqing, including those known as "middle parties." He diligently tried to make new friends to expand the CCP's influence. He also paid considerable attention to propaganda and cultural affairs. Zhou had been asking Chiang for some time to permit the CCP to publish a newspaper in the Great Rear. Chiang had said "yes" to Zhou but instructed his subordinates not to act on the matter. After he arrived in Wuhan, Zhou personally raised the issue with Chiang, who again gave his approval. Zhou immediately used his newly acquired power as deputy director of politics under the Military Commission to complete the paper's registration. *Xinhua ribao* (New China daily) was launched in Wuhan in January 1938. When Wuhan fell, the paper moved to Chongqing. Zhou worked tirelessly to spread the party's policies and ideas through the paper, which served as the CCP's main mouthpiece in the Great Rear. He sought to use the *Xinhua ribao* to enhance the CCP's image among everyday people while hampering Chiang's efforts to suppress the CCP. From the CCP's perspective, under Zhou's direction, the party occupied the political and moral high ground vis-à-vis the GMD by highlighting the themes of "nationalism" and "democracy."

Zhou also extended his activities into the area of diplomacy. In April 1939, the Southern Bureau established an international propaganda group under Zhou's direction. Wang Bingnan, who would become one of Zhou's main diplomatic associates, was appointed head of the group.[21] A foreign affairs section, also led by Wang, was set up in the Southern Bureau in December. Its members included Qiao Guahua, Gong Peng, Chen Jiakang, and Zhang Wenjin, who would later form the core of Zhou's diplomatic "inner circle."[22] Under Zhou's direction, the Foreign Affairs Section of the Southern Bureau became an important channel for the CCP to engage the outside world. These efforts helped the CCP establish a new international image, different from that of "Communist bandits."

While carrying out all of these activities, secretly Zhou was intensively engaged in another mission. Since the late 1920s, Zhou had been the leader of the CCP's intelligence activities. When he, as well as the Party Center, left Shanghai due to the deteriorating security environment there, the CCP's underground organs in the GMD-ruled areas were repeatedly sabotaged and almost destroyed. Zhou, as the CCP's spymaster, was based first in the Jiangxi countryside, then went through the Long March, and finally arrived in the remote land of Shaanbei. It was beyond his capacity during those years to reconstruct the party's intelligence services in GMD-ruled areas.

The establishment of the CCP-GMD united front offered favorable conditions for Zhou to launch new intelligence endeavors. After arriving in Chongqing, he immediately began planning to reestablish and expand the party's underground network in the Great Rear. In fact, Zhou had begun to work on this important matter when he was still in Wuhan. On January 21, 1938, in a telegram to the Party Center on behalf of the Yangzi River Bureau, Zhou promised that he would take immediate action to recover the CCP's underground organs and intelligence network in the Great Rear, especially in Sichuan, while "striving to develop confidential military work" there.[23] Then, he dispatched Qian Zhiguang, Zhou Yi, Zhang Yuqin, and several other talented intelligence officers to Chongqing to set up an office for the CCP-led ERA there.[24] In January 1939, after the Southern Bureau's establishment, Zhou was personally in charge of intelligence work. In March, the intelligence and communication staff who had worked at Zhou's Wuhan office moved to Chongqing, where they served as the core of a new Office of Confidential Matters within the Southern Bureau. Zhou appointed Tong Xiaopen, a close associate of his, to head the office. In addition, a Telegraphic

Communication Office was also established, which was headed by another of Zhou's trusted subordinates, Qian Songfu.[25]

In May 1939, the Southern Bureau moved into a new three-story building in Hong Yan. Zhou's intelligence staff occupied the whole third floor, which alone demonstrated the extraordinary emphasis that Zhou gave to their work. On both strategic and operational levels, Zhou basically adopted the methods of the *Teke* era, with some necessary changes and renovations. He emphasized three major intelligence endeavors. First, he strove to restore or reconstruct the CCP's underground organizations and intelligence network in the Great Rear. To fulfill this critical task, he transferred many of the most capable, experienced, and devoted party cadres into the CCP's intelligence services. Second, he strove to implant Communist agents in the political and military apparatus of the GMD and the Nationalist government, especially inside the GMD's intelligence services. Meanwhile, he never ignored the importance of maintaining contacts within the Japanese intelligence network. Third, he was personally involved in establishing and maintaining reliable telecommunications and other communication channels with Yan'an. In particular, he tried extremely hard to make sure that the CCP's secret codes would never be broken by the Nationalist or Japanese intelligence experts. Consequently, only a few short months after he arrived in Chongqing, Zhou already had established the institutions and networks required for carrying out intelligence activities, which he would constantly improve and enhance. All this became a key component of his overall work arrangement in his years in Chongqing.

• • •

Zhou and the CCP leadership saw dramatic changes in China's external situation after March 1939. Moscow began to restructure its policies toward Berlin in the wake of the British-German pact at Munich the previous September, as Stalin feared the threat of Hitler spreading German power to the east. The Comintern ordered all communist parties, including the CCP, to be prepared to resist reactionary forces in their own countries that might attempt to suppress the Communists. Meanwhile, Japan's enhanced "peace offensive" toward Chiang gave rise to fears among Mao and his fellow CCP leaders that China could be the site of a "Far Eastern Munich."[26] Mao again called on the whole party to prepare for Chiang's surrender to Japan. For

Mao, Chiang's drive to "oppose Communism" and "confine the CCP" exposed his true intention to collude with Japan, as "the CCP stood as the biggest barrier to his attempt to surrender to Japan."[27] Zhou found Mao's opinions difficult to accept, but he did not challenge them directly.

Chiang also felt increasingly uneasy about the CCP's development. Once more, he told Zhou that the CCP must dissolve its organization and cease its activities. "Otherwise," Chiang warned, "the CCP must bear all responsibility."[28] Zhou realized that the GMD's pressure on the CCP was mounting.

Zhou returned to Yan'an at the end of June to attend Politburo meetings on managing relations with Chiang. By then, he could clearly sense that the political atmosphere in Yan'an had changed dramatically over the six months he had been away from the Communist base. Mao's star was quickly rising, which put Zhou on alert. He knew that he had to tread cautiously during the upcoming Politburo meetings, especially as they would concentrate on CCP-GMD relations, a subject on which he and Mao often differed.

Zhou's life, however, was struck by an accident on July 10. At sunset that day, he and Jiang Qing, Mao's new wife, rode on horseback to the Party Central School to give a speech. Jiang lost control of her horse as she and Zhou were crossing the Yan River. Her wildly galloping horse scared a dog, which in turn frightened Zhou's horse. Zhou fell from his horse, suffering a supracondylar fracture in his right arm.[29] Doctors from an Indian medical team in Yan'an examined Zhou with a portable X-ray machine and found that Zhou's "right elbow was bent to an acute angle." They applied a plaster cast to Zhou's arm. The next day, Dr. Atel, a member of the Indian medical team, rushed to Yan'an. Using "a method he learned in London," he "unbandaged and put the fractured arm and elbow in a straight splint," assuring Zhou "an early recovery." Two days later, however, another X-ray exam showed that Zhou's "fractured ends of humerus above elbow were not aligned properly."[30]

Zhou had no time to rest. He needed to attend the Politburo meetings, which began on July 30. In early August, he delivered a lengthy report on CCP-GMD relations. China's united front involved nationalism, democracy, and society, he said. Chiang "was basically anticommunist," and he never treated the united front as a "legal entity comprising equal partners." But Chiang's attitude was complicated. It was true that "he had tried to contain the CCP," but he was also "willing to adhere to unity in the War of Resistance, rather than push the country to a total division." Therefore, Zhou argued, the CCP should deal with Chiang by abiding by its principles while remaining

11.1 Zhou Enlai with Liu Shaoqi after his arm injury, 1939.
Historic Collection / Alamy Stock Photo

flexible in tactics and methods. This, Zhou stressed, meant that "we should help him when he is in difficulty, reject him when he is unreasonable, criticize him while providing him with concrete suggestions, and unite with the progressive elements and oppose those backward ones around him." While the CCP "should not place too much hope in Chiang," Zhou concluded, its policy toward the generalissimo should "balance competition with necessary concessions."[31]

Mao praised the Southern Bureau's "good job" under Zhou's leadership. But he also pointed to Zhou's shortcomings, namely that party organs in the Great Rear "have not been consolidated," the "work on organizing the masses remains weak," and the "middle elements within the united front have not been sufficiently developed."[32] Zhou delivered his concluding remarks on August 25. He was in complete agreement with Mao in "assessing the current situation," he said, as it was indeed possible to reach a partial compromise with Chiang. In response to Mao's criticism, Zhou acknowledged that he "had paid too much attention to uniting with Chiang" while "not doing enough to unite the middle forces" and not "working enough with the masses." He promised that he would give more attention to "pursuing development" while "consolidating our own ground."[33] At the end of the conference, both Mao and Zhou had reason to feel satisfied.

* * *

Medical care in Yan'an was poor, and the initial treatment that Zhou had received was inadequate. He was still in pain several weeks after the accident, and he could not move his right arm. Another X-ray exam confirmed that "his right elbow remained ankylosed, in spite of vigorous physiotherapy." Zhou faced "the danger of permanent handicap."[34] The CCP Center cabled Stalin on August 1, reporting Zhou's condition and asking for a plane to take him to Moscow for treatment.[35] Moscow approved the request but explained that "for political considerations, instead of sending a plane to Yan'an, it is better for Zhou to travel to Lanzhou by car, and then transfer to the Soviet Union."[36]

Zhou, accompanied by Deng Yingchao, left Yan'an on August 27 and arrived in Moscow in mid-September. The Soviet doctors immediately conducted a detailed examination of his condition. They concluded that "instead of performing a major surgery for him," which could make things "even worse," it was more desirable to give him a smaller surgery "in two to three days."[37] On September 19, Soviet doctors performed a corrective surgery on his arm, hoping to restore as much of its functionality as possible. The operation was only partially successful. "The operative incision heals quickly," Georgi Dimitrov reported to the CCP on October 8, but "the degree of the arm's bending is larger than expectation, and its mobility cannot be fully recovered."[38] Zhou stayed in the hospital until late December. He would live with a moveable yet bent right arm for the rest of his life.

Zhou went to Moscow also in order to report to the Comintern. While he was still in the hospital, he began working on a summary of China's situation and the CCP's strategies and policies. This was a matter of enormous importance for both Zhou and the party.

Zhou was unable to meet with Stalin, unlike in his previous two visits to Moscow. On January 23, 1940, he wrote to Stalin, stating that China's War of Resistance was at a critical juncture, and that serious friction existed within the CCP-GMD united front. Apparently he wished to meet with the Soviet leader.[39] Stalin still did not see him.[40] Instead, Zhou had many discussions with two Comintern leaders, Dimitrov and Dmitriy Manuisky.[41] Reportedly, Stalin felt it was inconvenient to see Zhou because he had not formally met with representatives of the Nationalist government.[42] But there might have been another reason why Stalin did not meet Zhou in Moscow. Zhou had come to the Soviet capital at the time of Stalin's Great Purge. Among the victims of the purge was Guo Shaotang, a member of the Comintern secretariat staff, who in his confession had named numerous CCP leaders—including Zhou—as his "accomplices."[43]

Zhou, however, had no idea of what was happening behind the Kremlin's high walls. For weeks, he concentrated on writing a lengthy report, "Memorandum on the China Question." Zhou offered a CCP perspective on the party's relations with the GMD, the united front, and the prospects of China's War of Resistance. In his defense of CCP policies, Zhou placed particular emphasis on the importance of Mao's leadership.[44] He submitted the report to the Comintern on December 29, knowing that Stalin would read it.

Another of Zhou's missions was to secure financial support from the Comintern, a most important funding source for the CCP since its founding. CCP operations expanded rapidly during the war against Japan, depleting the party's cash reserves. When he met with Dimitrov, Zhou stressed the CCP's financial difficulties and asked the Comintern to help. Dimitrov said that the CCP had to try its best to overcome the hardship on its own. Meanwhile, he wrote Stalin, "In 1940, it should be appropriate to provide the CCP with the financial support of 350,000 dollars." "We will give them 300,000 US dollars," Stalin decided.[45] For the CCP, the cash infusion was much-needed rain after a long drought.

Zhou was called to speak at a meeting of the Comintern's executive committee in January.[46] In early March, he finally received the Comintern's response to his speech, in which it confirmed that "the CCP's political line has been correct."[47] Dimitrov told Zhou that the resolution was made under Stalin's direction.[48] Zhou was immensely relieved. He and Deng Yingchao knew that the time was approaching to return to China.[49]

· · ·

In Moscow, Zhou's time had always been busy or even tense. Their step-daughter, Sun Weishi, brought joy to him and Deng Yingchao. Weishi was born in 1921; her father was Sun Bingwen, a close comrade of Zhou's. In 1922, together with Zhu De, Sun Bingwen joined the CCP in Germany with Zhou as their reference. In 1927, he was arrested and executed by the GMD in the wake of Chiang Kai-shek's anti-CCP coup. In late 1937, Weishi, at the age of sixteen, came to the ERA's office in Wuhan, seeking to go to Yan'an to join the revolution, where she met Zhou. When Zhou learned that she was Sun Bingwen's daughter, he immediately approved her request. Zhou and Deng had no children of their own, and they both liked Weishi very much. After consulting with Weishi's mother and getting her consent, they adopted Weishi as their daughter.[50] In May 1938, Weishi joined the CCP in Yan'an. In September 1939, when Zhou was departing for Moscow for medical treatment, "with Chairman Mao's approval," Weishi joined Zhou and Deng at the airport and traveled to Moscow with them. She wanted to "study a special skill" in the Soviet Union for the sake of "serving my country in the future."[51] After Zhou and Deng returned to China, Weishi stayed in the Soviet Union to pursue her studies for seven years, finally returning to China in September 1946. First in Manchuria and then in Beijing, she devoted herself to theater acting and directing, emerging as one of China's most famous theater directors.[52] In the war years, Zhou and Deng took care of quite a few surviving children of deceased comrades, but Weishi was the only one they formally adopted.[53] She called them "dad" and "mom." In many letters to Weishi, Deng called her "my dear daughter." And Zhou in his letter to Deng called Weishi "our daughter."[54]

· · ·

Zhou and Deng Yingchao left Moscow on February 25, 1940, along with Ren Bishi and Okano Susumu (Nosaka Sanzo), a Japanese Communist leader. Dimitrov informed Mao in a cable that Zhou was returning to China and would "personally inform you about everything we discussed and agreed upon regarding Chinese affairs." He urged Mao "to seriously consider everything and take decisive measures completely on your own," but he also instructed Mao that if he "disagreed with us on some questions, please inform us promptly with your reasons."[55]

11.2 Zhou Enlai and Deng Yingchao with their stepdaughter Sun Weishi in Moscow, late 1939 or early 1940. From left to right, front row, Sun, Deng, Ren Bishi, and Cai Chang; from left to right, back row, Zhou, Chen Congying (Ren's wife), and Zhang Mei (Lin Biao's wife then). *Historic Collection / Alamy Stock Photo*

Zhou and his entourage took a train from Moscow to Almaty. Then they flew to Lanzhou, from where they drove in cars to Yan'an. Accompanying Zhou was Shi Zhe, who had lived in the Soviet Union for fifteen years and would later become the CCP leaders' chief Russian-language interpreter. Zhou left Moscow, Shi recalled, with a new radio transmitter and two sets of telegraphic codes, as well as a large amount of foreign currency. He carried a case that he never let out of his sight. When they were stopped by police and GMD special agents, he acted in his capacity as deputy director of politics of the Military Commission to fend them off.[56] On March 25, Zhou arrived in Yan'an.

• • •

The CCP's relations with the GMD had deteriorated dramatically in the six months that Zhou was abroad. The two parties were constantly involved in military conflict, especially in northwestern and northern China, over control of territory and the number of troops under the CCP's command.

By the time Zhou returned to Yan'an, the GMD had turned its strategic attention to containing the expansion of the CCP-led New Fourth Army (NFA) in eastern China. At first, Chiang and the GMD military command ordered NFA units in the lower reaches of the Yangzi to move to southern Anhui. They issued a new order a few months later, this time urging NFA units positioned south of the Yangzi to cross the river, join the CCP-led ERA there, and penetrate further into areas north of the Yellow River that were mainly controlled by the Japanese.[57]

The orders alarmed Mao and the CCP leadership. The chairman believed that the generalissimo meant "to expose CCP troops to the (Japanese) enemy, while blocking their path of retreat and starving them to death." Mao emphatically warned, "We must never fall into such a trap."[58] Representing the CCP Center, he instructed the NFA on May 4 not to obey Chiang's order or confine itself to one area, but instead strive to expand its forces and create new bases. "We must emphasize the struggle with Chiang," Mao concluded. "Otherwise, we will commit a huge mistake."[59]

Zhou felt that Mao had put too much emphasis on competing with Chiang. But he did not challenge Mao. After he returned to Chongqing, he told Chiang at a meeting that the Communists supported him and hoped to cooperate with the GMD. In the main, Zhou stressed, the CCP had expanded in enemy-occupied zones by fighting the Japanese and their puppets, rather than by competing with the GMD. Chiang said that so long as the CCP obeyed his orders, all questions between the two parties could be easily resolved. "We are willing to obey you," Zhou promised, but he cautioned Chiang that the GMD should not use its authority to pressure the CCP. Zhou stated in his report to the Party Center, "Although there is still the danger of Chiang surrendering (to Japan), he is not determined to split with us."[60]

On June 19, Zhou submitted to Chiang a general proposal, written after discussions with Mao, intended to ease tensions between the CCP and the GMD. In the proposal, Zhou asked Chiang to "legalize all anti-Japanese parties," "release imprisoned CCP members," and "practice democracy." He also requested that Chiang recognize the CCP's "liberated zones" and accept a reasonable expansion of the CCP's military forces.[61] Chiang countered with further demands to reduce the number of CCP troops and restrict the expansion of CCP territory. Zhou's talks with Chiang stalemated. On July 16,

Chiang issued a "Central Instruction," in which he ordered the CCP to move all its troops to areas north of the Yellow River within a month, while dramatically contracting its forces.[62] Zhou and the CCP regarded these demands as an alarming ultimatum.

Zhou flew back to Yan'an on July 27 for Politburo discussions on the escalating conflict with the GMD.[63] Zhou acknowledged in his presentations that relations between the two parties faced serious difficulties. Nonetheless, they had not broken up, he stressed, and "it is impossible for Chiang to surrender to Japan." Therefore, the CCP should continue to unite with other progressive parties and groups, pressuring Chiang to carry out political reforms. Zhou suggested that the CCP should, in dealing with Chiang, "criticize his anticommunist behavior while pushing him to resist Japan."[64] In line with Zhou's report, the CCP Center issued a circular to the whole party on August 12. Although talks between the two parties had been "in limbo," according to the circular, their cooperation had not collapsed. The party thus should take it as a "central task" to "win over the forces in the middle," while "isolating and dividing the most reactionary elements."[65]

Mao praised Zhou for "making the united front grow significantly and paying good attention to the middle forces." He also acknowledged that Zhou's work in the Great Rear was vital in the CCP's strategic deployment. Therefore, Mao declared, "all party organs in the Great Rear should be commanded by Zhou Enlai."[66] For Zhou, Mao's praise, especially his recognition of Zhou's dominant position in managing the CCP's relations with the GMD, was important. Zhou echoed Mao's tone in response, stressing that the CCP should continuously struggle with Chiang and the GMD while avoiding the collapse of CCP-GMD relations. Zhou's ideas emerged as the party leadership's consensus at the meetings.

Zhou returned to Chongqing on August 25. He told Chiang that the CCP was willing to make further concessions on regulating the territories under its control and establishing an upper limit to the size of its army. Chiang, however, took a hard line, insisting that unless all Communist troops moved north of the Yellow River, "no problem can be resolved." He also made it clear that CCP guerrilla units staying behind must be commanded by "the headquarters of the regions where they belong."[67]

At the same time as Zhou was negotiating with Chiang, the NFA nearly eliminated a large GMD unit in a battle at Huangqiao in northern Jiangsu. Zhou neither knew about the battle in advance nor wanted it to happen.

Although the battle had significantly strengthened the NFA's position in Jiangsu, it severely strained overall CCP-GMD relations. Zhou had the onerous task of cleaning up the mess. Not surprisingly, the anti-CCP hardliners within the GMD saw the crisis as a good excuse to crush the CCP militarily. He Yingqing and Bai Chongxi, respectively the chief and deputy chief of staff of GMD forces, cabled three top CCP military commanders—Zhu De, Peng Dehuai, and Ye Ting—on October 19, accusing the ERA and NFA of committing a series of regulatory and disciplinary violations. He and Bai ordered the two armies to move to the areas designated by the Nationalist government "within one month."[68]

This was a shocking development for CCP leaders, and Zhou bore the brunt of the pressure it put on them. Mao suspected that Chiang's "ardent anti-Communism was a step toward preparing to surrender to Japan, Germany, and Italy." The CCP Center even planned to respond to He and Bai's telegram with a "bomblike declaration."[69] Zhou, though deeply worried, kept calm. The telegram by He and Bai was particularly troublesome, he analyzed, because it demonstrated that "anti-Communist sentiment had been rising within the GMD" and that Chiang might behave more aggressively toward the Communists. However, he stressed, the two parties' relations were not on the verge of a total breakdown. The CCP should reject the telegram in practice, while promising to make some concessions in words. And the main force of the NFA might also act flexibly, either moving north or staying put to carry out guerrilla raids.[70]

Zhou's opinions were influential among CCP leaders. Even Mao changed his tone, saying that although the CCP should get ready for an all-out attack from Chiang, as well as "a very dark scenario," it should "deal with the GMD's attacks in a steady way" and "adopt a defensive position militarily." Therefore, "if they do not attack us, we should not attack them at will, and, politically, we should emphasize resisting against Japan in unity."[71] Mao and the CCP Center thus agreed that the NFA's headquarters might move north of the Yangzi. Zhou then offered his assessment of the current situation: While there "indeed is the danger of the GMD launching an anti-Communist war, thus leading to a split," a "Chinese-Japanese compromise will not succeed." Therefore, Zhou continued, the CCP must "quickly measure various options, weighing the pros and cons," and "come up with due decisions and instructions soon."[72]

CCP leaders decided to make additional concessions to Chiang at Zhou's urging. On November 9, Mao sent a telegram to He and Bai on behalf of Zhu

De and other top CCP commanders. The CCP leadership refused to move CCP troops to areas north of the Yellow River but offered to transfer NFA units north of the Yangzi River.[73] Chiang and the GMD high command soon replied, giving the CCP until the end of the year to carry out the move.[74]

* * *

The deadline for the NFA's northward move was fast approaching as the end of 1940 loomed. Zhou was overcome with burning anxiety. He met with Chiang on December 25 to discuss the matter. Chiang appeared very sincere, saying that although he had been extremely busy, the day marked the fourth anniversary of "our common suffering" in Xi'an: hence he had to see Zhou. Chiang assured Zhou that he absolutely did not want to fight a civil war or tear the parties' fragile partnership asunder. As both the ERA and NFA were "under my command," he reasoned, "why do I want to see killing between brothers?" Then, Chiang showed his true colors, demanding that all CCP troops eventually "move north of the Yellow River, otherwise I will not be in a position to command my troops." By the same token, if the NFA failed to obey his orders, "conflict will be inevitable, and I can say with certainty that you will be defeated."[75] Alarmed, Zhou stressed in a telegram to Mao that Chiang was untrustworthy. "In addition to scaring us, he also tries to use good words to coax us."[76]

NFA commanders Ye Ting and Xiang Ying had not decided upon how their troops might cross the Yangzi River, though Chiang's deadline was rapidly drawing nearer. On December 30, Zhou received an intelligence report that Chiang and his generals had set a trap in northern Anhui for the NFA. Zhou suggested that "it is better for the troops to move through southern Jiangsu." Mao and the CCP Center immediately conveyed the information to the NFA.[77]

Xiang and Ye, however, hesitated for several days. Finally, instead of moving north or east, they decided to first take a detour through GMD-controlled areas to the south, before turning northeast to cross the Yangzi River. Thus, NFA headquarters secretly set out on January 4, 1941, when the best timing to make such a move had already passed. In the preceding days, the GMD command, not knowing of the NFA's plans, had gathered a large force south of the Yangzi to force the NFA northward and across the river. On January 6, NFA units unexpectedly encountered a sizeable force of GMD troops. Gu Zhutong, the commander of the GMD force, judged that the NFA meant to push south. As the NFA group "had failed to follow the order to move north and cross the Yangzi along designated routes," he ordered his troops to encircle and eliminate the "rebellious troops."[78]

Ye and Xiang shut down their radio transmitters—thus cutting off communication with the Party Center—as the enemy encircled them. By January 9, the resistance of their troops was on the verge of collapse. Zhou and his intelligence network, however, were effectively "deaf and blind" during these critical days, receiving no report about the encirclement. Not until January 11, when NFA headquarters resumed indirect telegraphic exchange with the Party Center, did CCP leaders learn that NFA headquarters was facing certain destruction.[79]

Mao cabled Zhou on January 12 with an urgent message that NFA headquarters had been "almost eliminated" and instructed him to "immediately contact the GMD," demanding that its troops "stop the attack and allow our troops to move north."[80] Shocked, Zhou knew that he would inevitably be held responsible for the NFA's dire circumstances; he was even more worried that the fighting would strike a fatal blow to the beleaguered CCP-GMD united front. He soon managed to reach a GMD commander in charge of the attack. The explanation the commander gave Zhou was that the incident originated in the "NFA's failure to move north following the designated route, . . . thus causing a misunderstanding with the GMD troops."[81] Zhou at once conveyed the information to Mao.

NFA headquarters was by then almost gone. Ye was arrested by the GMD; Xiang had deserted the troops and would later be murdered by his bodyguard. Zhou knew nothing of these developments. In fact, Zhou even felt optimistic, after speaking with his GMD counterparts, that the incident could be settled. He asked the Party Center to inquire with Ye and Xiang about what they planned to do next, so that he could conduct more concrete negotiations with the GMD side.[82] The following day, the CCP Center confirmed that almost all the surrounded NFA units had been wiped out. Mao cabled Zhou, instructing him to immediately demand Chiang to stop the offensive.[83] But it was too late—there was nothing Zhou could do.

• • •

The NFA Incident brought the CCP's relations with the GMD to a breaking point. CCP leaders were in shock and Mao was especially enraged. Mao had warned his comrades since the beginning of the war to always remain vigilant when dealing with Chiang. However, many of Mao's colleagues, including Zhou, had not fully heeded his warnings. This time was different. During a Politburo meeting on January 15, Mao branded Xiang Ying a "political prisoner of the GMD" who never dared to "wage necessary struggles while adhering to independence and self-reliance." He claimed that Xiang's approach had "long enjoyed support from some comrades in our leadership."[84] Here, Mao kept his criticism of Zhou implicit. His comments in a telegram he sent to Zhou were more straightforward: "Chiang's offensives can only be repulsed by a radical, resolute, and comprehensive counterattack. We must not be afraid of splitting with Chiang and must wage a counteroffensive with determination. You should immediately abandon the moderate approach of yours."[85]

The NFA Incident had dealt Zhou a heavy blow indeed. As he was the person in charge of negotiations with Chiang, Zhou had persistently sought compromise with the GMD. Zhou still tried to stop Mao and the Party Center from responding excessively. He cabled Mao on January 16, stating that while politically the CCP should seriously criticize Chiang, militarily it was inappropriate to take bold action against him. Zhou argued that an offensive against Chiang would easily backfire, putting the CCP in an even more disadvantageous position.[86] Liu Shaoqi voiced his support for Zhou's opinion: "Though politically we should carry out a comprehensive counteroffensive throughout the whole country, militarily, except for in a few locations, we should not push for counteroffensives." This was not the right time to split with the GMD, Liu stressed.[87] Mao, having listened to Zhou and Liu, began to calm down.

The situation changed again on January 17. Chiang, encouraged by the GMD troops' victory and under great pressure from hard-liners within the GMD, denounced the NFA as "rebels," abolished its code designation, and court-martialed Ye Ting.[88] Yan'an was awash in outrage. Mao angrily told the Politburo that Chiang had "exposed the GMD's intent to break with us," a move which, he asserted, "was surely backed by the imperialists."[89] Again, Mao implicitly criticized Zhou: "The assessment that we had held before December 17 no longer works. . . . We should not be ambiguous about, tolerant, or fearful of a split, otherwise we will commit a serious mistake."[90] The next day, the Central Secretariat cabled Zhou, claiming that "it is now proven that Chiang has used all kinds of nonsense to cheat you during the talks in Chongqing." Given that "the environment in Chongqing is rapidly deteriorating," and his role there "is shrinking day by day," the secretariat continued, Zhou "should immediately try to find an excuse to leave Chongqing and return to Yan'an." Two days later, the secretariat again urged Zhou "to depart Chongqing as soon as possible."[91]

Zhou was unwilling to leave Chongqing at such a time of crisis. He reacted fiercely to Chiang's decision to dissolve the NFA. Ignoring the Nationalist government's orders, he published a poem in the January 18 edition of *Xinhua ribao:*

> The injustice of a thousand years is prevailing,
> A lone leaf floating in Jiangnan;
> Brothers attacked by brothers,
> Why in such a hurry to try to kill the others?!"

The front page of the newspaper that day featured Zhou's calligraphy of the phrase "Mourning the martyrs who sacrificed for the country in Jiangnan."[92] Zhou made this loud outcry to protest Chiang's behavior, as well as to win public sympathy and support. He also did so to bolster his endangered position within the CCP leadership.

On January 20, the CCP Center—without consulting Zhou—issued twelve terms drafted by Mao to settle the NFA Incident. The terms stipulated that Chiang must "take back his reactionary order of January 17 and acknowledge that he has been totally wrong," "punish those responsible for the NFA Incident," and "abolish his one-party dictatorship and implement democratic politics."[93] Mao then informed Zhou that "unless Chiang invalidates his order and takes other necessary steps, we will have to confront him, as we have no other path to go on."[94] Zhou immediately submitted the twelve terms to Chiang.

Zhou had by then lost control over negotiations with the GMD. Mao repeatedly stressed to the CCP leadership that "it is necessary to redefine CCP-GMD relations" and that it was "no longer beneficial at all to cooperate with Chiang."[95] In telegrams to Zhou, he emphasized that "once we have made our attitudes clear, we should leave Chiang to deal with everything; either he should honor the twelve terms, thus leading to reconciliation, or there will be a total split."[96]

• • •

At this critical moment, the Japanese provided Zhou with unexpected help. Mao had concluded that Chiang's "total split" with the CCP was related to his "peacemaking plot with Japan."[97] Zhou had long held his own view of Chiang, and he would have passionately disagreed with Mao's assessment of the generalissimo's intentions. The political climate of the time, however, made it difficult for Zhou to openly express his disagreement. While Mao's warning about collusion between Chiang and the Japanese was still fresh, Japanese troops suddenly launched a massive offensive against GMD troops in Henan. In an instant, the anti-Communist hard-liners within the GMD lost their momentum. Chiang hurriedly sent Zhang Chong to see Zhou, hoping that making concessions such as allowing CCP troops to delay moving north would catalyze the resumption of negotiations toward a compromise. Negotiations would not restart, Zhou replied, unless the GMD carried out the CCP's twelve conditions.[98]

The events proved that Zhou's insistence that Chiang would not collude with Japan had been correct. Mao now acknowledged that "we have ignored all of this [deep conflict between Chiang and the Japanese] in the past." Consequently, Mao's basic assessment of the situation began to change. He now agreed that "our policy should be centered on taking advantage of contradictions between Chiang and Japan" and that Chiang and the GMD "could possibly reduce their efforts to oppose the CCP."[99] The huge pressure that Zhou had endured in the wake of the NFA Incident gradually lessened.

The Americans offered additional help when CCP-GMD relations showed signs of improving. In Chongqing, Zhou had tried for some time to influence the British and the Americans and had established a good working relationship with Archibald Kerr, the British ambassador to China. Zhou maintained his connections with Western diplomats after the outbreak of war in Europe, even when the CCP was harshly criticizing the "anti-Soviet policies" of Western countries. Tensions between the United States and Japan rapidly intensified with Japan's invasion of Indochina in late 1940. In February 1941, President Roosevelt dispatched Lauchlin Currie to China as his special envoy. Currie's duties in China were to investigate China's war against Japan and help mediate GMD-CCP relations.[100] Zhou immediately recognized the opportunity this gave the CCP. In comparison, Chiang was uneasy about Currie's coming, which he feared would make Washington "even more bewitched by Communist propaganda."[101]

Currie met with Chiang on February 10. The generalissimo told the American envoy that the CCP was not an active force in the war against Japan. Yet, the more he said so, the more Currie felt that Chiang "was full of hatred of the

Communists" and that "he distrusts them extremely." Eager for direct contact with the CCP, Currie told Chiang that the United States was ready to provide China with $45 million worth of weapons and equipment in addition to financial support to help stabilize the Chinese currency. But, he stressed, Washington was very concerned about the conflict between the Nationalists and the Communists, as it benefited only Japan. He told Chiang that he wanted to meet with Zhou; Chiang had no choice but to accept Currie's request.[102]

Zhou and Currie met on February 14 at the residence of British ambassador Kerr. Zhou knew precisely what to tell Currie. The CCP was absolutely not America's enemy, Zhou said in a sincere voice, and the party hoped that America would not treat it as an enemy either. The CCP, anxious to unite with the GMD to fight the Japanese, always regarded Chiang as China's leader. But Chiang refused to view the CCP as friendly, producing mounting difficulties between the two parties. Currie found Zhou not a "particularly radical" man, and "considered him interesting and sympathetic." He told Zhou that Washington supported China's internal unity and believed that the Chinese government should be reformed.[103] After the meeting, he again urged Chiang to cooperate with the CCP. "I now know that the Communist propaganda has deeply penetrated US government and society," Chiang wrote in his diary, "and Currie has been so deeply influenced. He could not be saved."[104]

The outcome of Currie's visit to China was exactly what Zhou had hoped for. He was giving more weight to developing the CCP's relations with the United States, which became another major emphasis of his work in Chongqing and beyond.

• • •

The CCP's relations with the GMD showed more signs of amelioration in mid-February. After all, given that the War of Resistance was still underway, neither party could afford a total confrontation. A National Assembly plenum scheduled to begin in early March became a test case for whether GMD-CCP cooperation could be saved. In previous years, the assembly had been the site of CCP-GMD cooperation. When the convening of the next assembly plenum was put on the table in February, Zhou realized that the plenum would provide the CCP with an opportunity to press the GMD for substantial concessions. On February 10, after consulting with several small parties, Zhou cabled Mao, proposing that the CCP's seven representatives to the National Assembly bring the twelve terms to the plenum. Alternatively, Zhou suggested, they could boycott it.[105] The CCP Center approved Zhou's proposal, calculating that Chiang would absolutely not accept these terms. Mao hoped to "use our political offensive to crush Chiang's offensive," thus seizing the political initiative.[106]

Chiang rejected the terms, as Zhou and Mao expected he would. However, Chiang came under mounting pressure as the assembly plenum approached. His representative, Zhang Chong, visited Zhou on three consecutive days from February 25, imploring the Communists to "remember the interests of the whole country" and attend the plenum, rather than adhering to the twelve terms. Zhang even told Zhou that "for the sake of the country, I am willing to kowtow to you."[107] No matter how earnestly Zhang begged him, though, Zhou followed the Party Center's instructions and did not yield a single inch. Enraged, Chiang declared that if the CCP would "boycott the assembly, there surely will be a total split." Several small parties and groups were also extremely worried; they held back-to-back meetings with Zhou, urging the CCP to attend the assembly. Zhou was unmoved.[108] On February 28, a day before the assembly plenum was scheduled to begin, the CCP Center decided to put forward twelve new provisional conditions, which omitted the party's previous demands for Chiang to withdraw his order to dissolve the NFA, penalize He Yingqing and others, and abolish the GMD's one-party dictatorship. In the new set of conditions, the CCP proposed that the plenum be postponed for two weeks.[109] In fact, Mao had included this last suggestion to once more put the blame on Chiang, as he did not expect that Chiang would accept the new terms. Not surprisingly, when Zhang Chong saw these conditions, he refused to convey them to Chiang, as he knew that the generalissimo would reject them.[110]

Several smaller parties proposed on March 1 that the assembly plenum be postponed for a day, so that they might persuade the CCP to attend it. Zhou urgently cabled the CCP Center, stating that "we have earned a great deal of face as well as huge influence in handling the opening of this assembly . . . and Chiang has been beaten like a drowning dog in the river." Now, "the whole of Chongqing is waiting for our response and hoping that we will attend the assembly." Zhou suggested that "it is time to make the turnaround," as the CCP had taken the "maximum advantage" in the matter.[111]

Mao refused to compromise. "Chiang," he contended, "is putting the utmost pressure on us to attend the assembly. If we yield to the pressure and change our position, we will lose all the political advantage that we have gained."[112] Consequently, CCP representatives did not appear at the National Assembly.

This was a huge blow to CCP-GMD relations. Yet, in the final analysis, neither side wanted to see a total split between the two parties. At the assembly plenum, Chiang stated that he would not commit to "suppressing the CCP"; rather, he said, he sought to "sincerely unite with the Communists and jointly overcome the danger facing the nation." On March 14, he again summoned Zhou for a conversation aimed at "lessening the mood of hostility." But the two knew that "this [was] not the time to resolve big issues." Chiang gave a "vague and perfunctory" response to Zhou's mention of such critical questions as the CCP's territorial sphere and the expansion of CCP military forces. Zhou then raised "a few small issues," such as allowing the *Xinhua ribao* to be published, stopping the arrests of CCP members, issuing passports to CCP representatives, and resuming shipments of supplies to CCP troops. Chiang did not rebut the issues that Zhou raised, but he sensed that Chiang merely sought a "superficial and temporary relaxation" of relations with the CCP.[113] While a total GMD-CCP split had been averted for the moment, the limited mutual trust that once existed between the leaders of the two parties had faded, and prospects for their future relations were not optimistic.

• • •

Early in May, Japanese troops launched a sudden large-scale offensive against GMD troops on Mount Zhongtiao in southern Shanxi. GMD forces there suffered a series of miserable defeats. On May 5, Chiang sent a representative to Zhou inquiring if CCP troops could be sent to help the GMD troops at Zhongtiao. He urged Zhou to "reply in two days."[114] Zhou's response came four days later. Following Mao's instructions, he said that it was "no problem at all" for CCP troops to engage in the fighting in Shanxi, provided that Chiang accept such CCP conditions as immediately resolving the NFA issue, resuming supply shipments to CCP troops, and stopping anti-Communist activities.[115] Chiang met with Zhou on May 11, urging CCP troops to help cut the Japanese transportation and supply lines. "If you are cooperative," Chiang promised, "surely I will reward you, and I will provide you with ammunition once you have made progress."[116]

The national interest always carried great weight to Zhou. He sent telegrams to Mao and the CCP Center, providing detailed reports of his conversation with Chiang. He also relayed the opinion of General V. I. Chuikov, the chief Soviet military advisor in Chongqing, which was that

CCP troops should immediately engage in fighting the Japanese. Further, Zhou reported that widespread criticism of the CCP's inaction on the front had emerged in Chongqing.[117] Apparently, Zhou was trying to push Mao to offer support to GMD troops.

Mao refused to listen to Zhou. He repeatedly asked Zhou to tell Chiang that the CCP leadership had already ordered its troops to cooperate with GMD forces. It was Chiang who should keep his promise to supply the CCP with ammunition and stop anti-Communist activities. Mao also requested that Zhou "tell the (Soviet) chief advisor not to make groundless statements. The GMD has accused us of failing to engage in fighting . . . we should never be pushed around by such nonsense."[118] Mao was determined to sit with his arms folded on the sidelines, watching the GMD fight the Japanese. He stated in a telegram to Peng Dehuai, ERA deputy commander, "Now we must fight the Japanese, but we should not fight them too diligently. If we do not fight them, the GMD will attack us, and the middle forces will also blame us. But if we fight the Japanese too hard, they will turn to attack us, and the GMD will thus benefit or even attack our border regions." Mao also asked Peng to treat Zhou's opinion as no more than a suggestion and not, as Zhou had suggested, to allow "our operation to be directed by pressure from the GMD and foreigners."[119]

CCP troops in northern China acted in accordance with Mao's calculations. In Chongqing, Zhou submitted to Chiang "the ERA's operation plans" while loudly propagating the narrative of CCP troops' heroic fighting against the Japanese and repeatedly asking Chiang to supply CCP troops with weapons and ammunition.[120]

Fierce enemy offensives dealt the GMD troops more bad defeats while Zhou and his GMD counterparts were still bargaining back and forth. Finally, Chiang evacuated his troops from the Mount Zhongtiao front. Chiang angrily accused the CCP of "sitting there without lending a hand," while Zhou rebuked him, claiming that it was "all rumor to say that CCP troops have not been cooperative in battles."[121] CCP-GMD relations, which had never been good, became worse still.

• • •

Hitler's Germany invaded the Soviet Union in late June 1941. Fearing that Japan might attack the Soviet Far East, Stalin cabled Yan'an, demanding that CCP troops "immediately wage large-scale operations to help check a possible attack by Japan (on the Soviet Union.)." Meanwhile, he quickly approved Mao's request, which had been sitting on his desk for months, for $1 million in financial aid.[122] But Mao did not want to go along with Stalin's call for mobilization. He would accept the Soviet money but use all kinds of excuses not to engage CCP troops in any major fighting. He shared his thoughts with Zhou: "If Japan were to attack the Soviet Union, I am afraid that we won't be able to play a big role in waging a coordinated military operation. If we try to act regardless of the consequences, we will likely be miserably defeated and even unable to keep our base areas. This would be disadvantageous to everyone. Therefore, we should concentrate on consolidating our base areas, carry out guerrilla operations, and prolong the struggles against the Japanese bandits by enduring for the time being. We should never put all our strength into one attempt." Mao also asked Zhou to ask General Chuikov to tell Moscow that CCP troops were short on ammunition and equipment, especially machine guns and artillery.[123] Zhou fully understood Mao's tricks. Every time Soviet advisors urged the CCP to engage in fighting to check Japanese troops, Zhou would request Moscow to accelerate deliveries of weapons and ammunition.[124]

The United States declared war on Japan in December 1941, after the attack on Pearl Harbor, hugely affecting the prospects of China's war against Japan. Mao now believed that "it would be unlikely for the GMD to attack CCP-controlled regions, and it would be more likely for them to neither surrender to Japan nor continue to suppress the CCP." Therefore, Mao expected CCP-GMD relations to improve.[125]

Lin Biao returned to China in January 1942 from a medical leave in the Soviet Union. As soon as he arrived in Xi'an, he spoke enthusiastically about the necessity of CCP-GMD cooperation to jointly build a new China. Chiang was taken by Lin's words, and it seemed as if a new trend was growing in favor of a CCP-GMD partnership.

But Zhou was not optimistic. In a telegram to Mao on January 20, he reasoned that Britain and the United States, following their military defeats in the South Pacific, did not want to offend Chiang. Thus, Zhou argued, Chiang was behaving rather arrogantly. Although CCP-GMD relations were unlikely to collapse, the CCP might have to face more difficult challenges.[126] Indeed, Zhou stated in another telegram to Mao that the year 1942 would likely be "the most difficult year in domestic politics, although probably not the darkest." Throughout the spring of 1942 he believed that "Chiang's arrogance is second to none" and that he "will challenge us here and there, and will not relax comprehensive political oppression against us."[127]

Zhou's pessimism largely stemmed from the terrible losses that the CCP's underground network under his command had recently suffered at the hands of GMD intelligence services. The trouble began in July 1941. Two CCP leaders in Jiangxi, Xie Yucai and Luo Qixun, were arrested in an operation planned and directed by Feng Qi (Xu Xigen), a GMD intelligence chief in Jiangxi and a CCP defector who was once a member of the CCP Politburo. Luo immediately cooperated and provided leads that led to the capture of Yan Fuhua, another CCP leader in Jiangxi. The arrests led to the total destruction of the CCP's underground network in the province. Then, to catch "bigger fish," Feng ordered the CCP Jiangxi Committee's radio transmitter to stay in constant contact with that of its superior agency, the CCP Southern China Work Committee.[128] Neither Zhou nor his agents detected any of this.

CCP underground organs in the Great Rear suffered a series of additional blows at the beginning of 1942. Yuan Xiaoxian, director of the ERA's office in Luoyang, surrendered himself to the GMD secret police in early February. Guo Qian, personnel director of the CCP Southern China Work Committee, was arrested three months later. Subsequently, GMD agents captured almost all CCP underground leaders in southern China using information given by Guo. By July, more than seven thousand CCP members had been arrested, and the CCP's underground network in southern China, which was under Zhou's command, collapsed.[129]

Zhou had been hospitalized at that critical moment to undergo surgery on an intestinal hernia. His father passed away in mid-July while Zhou was still in the hospital; Deng Yingchao kept the news from him. Zhou openly wept when he heard of his father's death after his discharge from the hospital, scolding Deng and others.[130] In addition to the pain of losing his father, might Zhou's loss of control have also been caused by the deep frustration he felt as the result of his enormous intelligence failure? In August, Zhou ordered all CCP underground organs in southern China to cease operation. All agents who had been exposed were transferred elsewhere. He further ordered in December that the Southern China Work Committee be dissolved.[131]

It is no wonder Zhou felt pessimistic about negotiations with the GMD. Even the Comintern noted his gloomy outlook on CCP-GMD relations. Dimitrov received a report from Alexander Panyushkin, Soviet ambassador to China, on June 7, in which Panyushkin mentioned that CCP leaders, especially Zhou, had failed to "make the utmost effort to prevent the further worsening of the GMD's attitude toward the CCP." Indeed, Chiang was even "unwilling to see Zhou" and had "not met with him for seven months."[132] Dimitrov intervened, stressing in a telegram to Mao that "under the current situation, it is absolutely necessary for the CCP to make every effort and exhaust all means to improve relations with Chiang, so as to strengthen China's united front." But "Zhou has failed to take this into consideration."[133] "We fully agree with you," Mao immediately replied. "We have already asked Zhou to thoroughly carry out your instructions."[134]

The CCP resumed negotiations with the GMD under pressure from Moscow, promising the GMD that the party would "obey the generalissimo and abide by the Three Principles of the People."[135] On July 21, Zhou met with Chiang, who said that he already had assigned Zhang Zhizhong and Liu Wei to handle negotiations with Zhou.[136] Chiang met with Zhou again on August 14, mentioning that he would be traveling to Xi'an in a week and hoped to meet Mao there.[137] Although he did not "detect an evil intention in Chiang's attitude," Zhou told Mao, he was "not sure about Chiang's purpose." Zhou suggested that Mao "feign sickness and send Lin Biao as his representative to see Chiang in Xi'an."[138] Mao, however, believed that "in the current situation, I should meet with Chiang." Zhou further advised Mao that "it is not yet the right time for you to meet with Chiang" and that Mao should wait until Zhou had taken "some concrete action." It was better for Lin to talk to Chiang, and Mao should wait until "a more concrete negotiation agenda is worked out" to meet with Chiang in Chongqing.[139] The Politburo approved of Zhou's suggestion, but Mao still wished to "take advantage of the favorable international situation now" to "improve relations with the GMD" by meeting with Chiang.[140] Zhou dispatched a lengthy telegram to Mao, explaining why such a meeting was "still premature." Finally, he raised a point that Mao could not ignore: if Mao indeed came to Chongqing, "Chiang may find an excuse to keep Mao there for a prolonged time." Finding Zhou's point compelling, Mao gave up the idea to see Chiang.[141]

Flooding delayed Lin on his way to Xi'an, and he missed the chance to meet with Chiang there. Lin finally arrived in Chongqing on October 7. Zhou, who would accompany Lin in meeting with Chiang, sensed that it was premature to try to settle concrete problems between the two parties, although Lin might "relax tensions between them" and "reopen the door for negotiation." Any pursuit beyond these limited goals would force the CCP to "make bigger concessions in territory under its control," Zhou predicted. This time Mao replied, "I agree."[142]

As Zhou had predicted, the differences between the two sides were as great as before when Lin met with Chiang on December 12.[143] Mao then decided to abandon his plan to meet with Chiang. Zhou held several meetings with Zhang Zhizhong, which also ended with no result. Chiang fiercely attacked the CCP in his new book, *China's Destiny,* published in March 1943, and CCP-GMD talks again stalemated.

The Comintern announced in late May 1943 that it would dissolve. Chiang decided to formally suspend negotiations with the CCP, informing Zhou on June 4 that the talks would be "put aside" indefinitely.[144] At that moment, Zhou received the call to return to Yan'an to participate in the Rectification Campaign. Zhou met with Chiang on June 7 and obtained permission to leave Chongqing.[145] He set off for Yan'an three weeks later. Zhou would not return to Chongqing for a year and a half, when he accompanied General Patrick J. Hurley of the US Army for CCP-GMD negotiations. He would visit the city in the future only for a few short stays.

• • •

Zhou had been in Chongqing for over four years, throughout which China's war against Japan had persisted. With the Allies' offensives in the Asia-Pacific region, at last the light of victory was flashing at the end of a long and dark tunnel. The CCP's united front with the GMD, which Zhou had so diligently managed, had survived too, even though it had nearly collapsed on so many occasions. Zhou had good reason to celebrate his achievements. However, Mao's Rectification Campaign dominated politics in Yan'an during the war years. Zhou had never ignored the signs that Mao's red sun was rising, even when he was in the Great Rear. Now, as he was called back to the red capital to participate in the campaign, he probably realized that another unprecedented experience in his political career as a Communist awaited him in Yan'an.

12

YAN'AN SUNRISE

1941–1945

In northwestern China, in the heart of the Loess Plateau and about 240 miles north of Xi'an, sits the small city of Yan'an. Historically known as Fushi, Yan'an had never been widely known, nor would its name ever have become known across China and the world had the Red Army not seized the city after the Xi'an Incident, and had the CCP Center not relocated there. Between 1937 and 1947, Yan'an became China's "red capital" while it played host to the CCP headquarters.[1]

With the exception of the two years that he participated in the Maoist Rectification Campaign in Yan'an, Zhou Enlai spent most of that decade elsewhere, mainly in Wuhan, Chongqing, Nanjing, and Shanghai. However, no change that took place in Yan'an, especially Mao's ascent to the position of top leader of the CCP, escaped his notice. As the chairman's "red sun" rose, Yan'an increasingly took on a sacred meaning to Zhou.

Yet Zhou did not view Yan'an as the political center during the early stages of the war against Japan. On December 18, 1937, four days after the December Conference, Zhou arrived in Wuhan, where he ceaselessly championed enhancing the CCP's united front with the Guomindang to strengthen China's resistance against Japan. This was what the Comintern had instructed the CCP to do, and this was, in Zhou's mind, what he and the party ought to do. Chiang endorsed many of Zhou's ideas about CCP-GMD cooperation.[2]

This honeymoon between the Communists and Nationalists was short lived, however. Before long, a series of rifts appeared between them, undermining their cooperation. Zhou, like Wang Ming, found himself at odds with Mao about the CCP-GMD united front. Zhou believed that the front should be strengthened, despite the GMD's many problems. He also firmly rejected the possibility that Chiang might "surrender to Japan."[3] Conversely, Mao stressed the importance of preserving the CCP's independence in the united front.[4] At the March Conference in early 1938, Zhou and Wang's viewpoints won the support of most CCP leaders.[5] Though he was upset, Mao did not confront Zhou and Wang about the matter. But years later, Mao admitted that he had been "extremely unhappy" with the March Conference's agenda as dictated by Zhou and Wang.[6]

Although Mao was compelled for the moment to retreat to the background in CCP strategy and policymaking, he maintained his influence on the assignment of top positions in the party. The March Conference had not diminished Mao's capacity for manipulating the party's decision-making; in fact, the conference may have even strengthened it. Zhang Wentian, general secretary of the CCP, backed Mao at the time. Ren Bishi, once opposed to Mao, had joined Mao's side. Moreover, Liu Shaoqi, who then controlled the party's Northern Bureau, also was tending to embrace Maoism.

Furthermore, Mao strove to dominate the making of the party's mainstream discourse. Mao wrote more prolifically in this period—as he waited for the situation to improve and prepared to enact his plans—than he would at any other point in his life. His writings included, among many other works, the essays *On Protracted War, On Contradiction, On Practice,* and *The Chinese Revolution and the Chinese Communist Party,* which burnished his image as a revolutionary thinker. These works would be made the core texts of Maoism, laying the theoretical groundwork for the CCP's adoption of "Mao Zedong Thought" as its ideological lodestar.

The trajectory of China's war against Japan also echoed Mao's predictions. Although the Japanese Imperial Army occupied almost all of China's coastal cities and important transportation lines, China's War of Resistance persisted and, as Mao had expected, became a protracted struggle. CCP troops had won few battles against the Japanese, despite suffering heavy casualties. Many CCP leaders and military commanders realized that they should avoid frontal showdowns with the Japanese simply to avoid risking their own annihilation. Mao had also foreseen the troubles the CCP would face in its cooperation with the GMD. Thus, he increasingly found himself in a position to tell his comrades, including Zhou, that it was dangerous to have illusions about the GMD. "We must conduct class education in the party," Mao declared in a remark implicitly aimed at Zhou and Wang.[7]

The balance of strength within the CCP leadership was quietly, albeit steadily, turning in Mao's favor. Most telling was Ren Bishi's change of allegiance. Although Ren had opposed Mao during the Jiangxi years, his attitude toward the chairman had changed since the later phase of the Long March. He supported nearly every decision Mao made in handling the party's policies; hence, Ren's relationship with Mao became much closer.[8] As Ren had long enjoyed a reputation among high-ranking CCP members as an insightful and prudent person, his turning to support Mao clearly reflects the fact that party elites increasingly recognized Mao as the leader of the CCP.

Ren travelled to Moscow in March after the Politburo decided that he would replace Wang Jiaxiang as the CCP's representative to the Comintern.[9] As it turned out, this development would serve to further enhance Mao's standing in the Party Center. Once he arrived in the Soviet capital, Ren submitted two reports to the Comintern. In the reports, Ren highlighted the CCP's dedication to the anti-Japanese united front with the GMD and emphasized Mao's belief that the party had to maintain its independence in the united front and preserve its freedom to criticize.[10] When Ren met with Comintern leaders, he did everything he could to promote Mao's image and views.[11] The Comintern's response came in mid-June. "We fully approve the CCP's political lines," it stated, endorsing the CCP's efforts to pursue "political and organizational independence and space for its activities" in the united front with the GMD.[12] This was a big victory for Mao.

Ren had the support of Wang Jiaxiang. Before Wang departed for China, he and Ren met with Georgi Dimitrov, the general secretary of the Comintern. Dimitrov told them, "Comrade Mao Zedong is the leader emerging in the struggle of the Chinese revolution. Tell Wang Ming not to compete with him!"[13] Mao was thus delivered another triumph.

In September 1938, the CCP Central Committee held an important meeting, the Sixth Plenum. This was another turning point for Mao. In his own words, "it was at the Sixth Plenum that China's fate was determined."[14]

The plenum began with a bombshell, when Wang Jiaxiang relayed Dimitrov's instruction to his comrades: "In the environment today, it is hard for CCP leaders to gather in one place. Therefore, problems easily appear. They should be resolved in an atmosphere of intimacy and unity among the leadership under Comrade Mao Zedong's command."[15] Mao relished the moment.

He later confessed, "Without the Comintern's instructions (as relayed by Wang), it would have been very difficult for the Sixth Plenum to resolve the problems."[16] Indeed, the "Dimitrov Message" dealt a major blow to Wang Ming, undermining his reputation as "the Comintern's guy" while crippling his prospects of attaining the party's top leadership role.

Zhou attended only part of the plenum, and his attitude remained ambiguous. "I fully support the Comintern's instruction," he stated. He also agreed it was necessary "to keep our party's independence." Yet he continued to argue that it was essential to endorse Chiang's resistance against Japan and consolidate the united front.[17] He outlined twelve principles at the plenum. The first was "to take the War of Resistance as the absolute top priority," and the second was "to maintain the party's political independence."[18] Obviously, at that moment Zhou was still not fully convinced of the correctness of all of Mao's strategies and policies. Mao took note of all this, and as later events in his relationship with Zhou showed, he remembered it, too.

But Zhou could also sense that the general feeling among the party leadership was turning in Mao's favor. His own attitude toward Mao also subtly changed. He and Wang Ming went to Wuhan again after the plenum. At first, Mao contended that "given today's situation, Wang should not go to Wuhan again." But a majority of party leaders overrode Mao's opposition.[19] Mao was clearly worried that if Wang went to Wuhan, he might once more join forces with Zhou and form another virtual "Party Center" there, challenging his leadership of the party.

Yet soon it became evident that Mao's concern was unwarranted. Zhou showed no interest in allying with Wang Ming. The Party Center decided that Wang should return to Yan'an within one month.[20] But Wang did not want to leave Wuhan. Meanwhile, Mao did not push Wang to leave, as he already realized that there would be no such a Zhou-Wang alliance set up to challenge him. Zhou later said he felt that Wang was trying to "organize a clique of his own."[21] He knew that he should keep his distance from Wang.

Zhou's change in attitude reflected a broader phenomenon of the time: Mao's authority and power within the CCP leadership had been sharply increasing after the Sixth Plenum. From now on, Mao would never, under any circumstances, allow his paramount power to slip away from him while he lived.

* * *

As Mao's political star rose, he began to envision and implement a grand plan to remake the CCP, its cadres, and its members. He wanted to turn the party into his party, to guide it toward the "liberation" of China, and to continuously lead the party while wielding it as a tool to transform China, the Chinese people, and "all under heaven."

In May 1941, Mao delivered a speech titled "Reform Our Study" at a meeting of CCP elites in Yan'an. In the speech, he discussed the importance of combining the "universal truth of Marxism-Leninism" with the realities facing China. Yet, he stressed, many party leaders and members blindly worshiped "foreign doctrines" and knew little about conditions in China. It was thus necessary, Mao emphasized, to carry out a program of rectification within the party to render it ready and qualified to lead the great mission of defeating all reactionary forces at home and abroad and to build a "new China."[22] Mao wanted to set the tone for the "Rectification Campaign" in the political, ideological, and discursive senses. That July and August, the CCP leadership adopted a series of resolutions that enunciated and endorsed Mao's ideas.[23] In Yan'an, Maoist rectification was looming on the horizon.

The international situation at the time also gave Mao the space he needed to launch such a campaign. After Nazi Germany's massive attack on the Soviet Union on June 22, 1941, surviving the German invasion became the absolute priority for Stalin and the Comintern. For Mao, this meant that although the CCP remained a branch of the Comintern, it had gained greater leeway in policymaking than ever before.

Beginning in early September, the CCP Politburo convened another meeting, the September Conference of 1941. Five prolonged sessions were held over six weeks. This represented another critical step in Mao's preparation for his long-envisioned Rectification Campaign. Wang Ming was a target of fierce criticism and accusations at the conference; he was labeled as both a "leftist opportunist" and a "rightist opportunist." In one way or another, each of Wang's "mistakes" or even "crimes" exposed implicitly—and sometimes explicitly—at the conference implicated Zhou.

Zhou did not return to Yan'an, and he missed the conference. One obvious explanation for his absence was that he was truly busy with a host of important responsibilities in Chongqing. But it is likely that Zhou missed the conference in part because Mao did not want him there. If Zhou were present at the conference and joined forces with Wang, it would have been more difficult or even embarrassing for Mao to carry out his grand plans.

On September 10, Mao delivered a speech on "opposing subjectivism and factionalism," defining the agenda of the conference and, more broadly, the Rectification Campaign that he intended to launch. What was "subjectivism"? According to Mao, it was making policy decisions that accorded with "empty doctrines," while completely ignoring the practical feasibility of the policies, as well as real-world circumstances. One example that Mao highlighted was a resolution on the international situation adopted by the Soviet Area Bureau on May 11, 1932, which Mao characterized as "completely a product of subjectivism." The chief author of the document was none other than Zhou—the bureau's secretary at the time.[24]

Two weeks later, the CCP Center decided to establish an "advanced-level study group" headed by Mao.[25] All party cadres were required to study selected party documents issued since the Sixth Congress in 1928, taking them as models for a process of "thought remodeling" in order to "overcome" the "subjectivism and formalism" in one's mind.[26] Following the example set in Yan'an, CCP organs elsewhere quickly established study groups of their own. Zhou did not lag behind, either. The Southern Bureau established its study group, led by Zhou, even before the CCP Center formally ordered that these groups be set up.[27]

At the September Conference, Wang Ming endured a relentless barrage of fierce attacks from his comrades. Then, there came—as it seemed—a moment of opportunity for him. On October 4, Mao conveyed to him a telegram from Dimitrov in which the general secretary of the Comintern inquired about the CCP's situation in fifteen questions. In particular, Dimitrov mentioned Wang in a favorable tone.[28] After he read the telegram, Wang decided to challenge Mao and then delivered a lengthy address at a meeting of the CCP Central Secretariat. In his last wave of criticism against Mao, Wang blamed the chairman for carrying out policies toward the GMD, various provincial political forces, and the national bourgeoisie that were excessively leftist leaning.[29]

The CCP was then still a branch of the Comintern, so Mao could not afford to ignore Dimitrov's "inquiry." On October 13, he ordered a halt to all "discussion of Wang Ming's problems" as "he is ill."[30] But Mao stressed that this did not mean Wang had not committed grave mistakes; in fact, he had, "although they were not yet mistakes in political lines."[31] As a consequence, Wang was temporarily excused from attending additional "education sessions." It is worth noting that Zhou was closely linked to many of the "serious mistakes" Mao accused Wang of having committed, foreshadowing the ruthless criticism that Zhou would later be subjected to during the Rectification Movement.

By the time the September Conference ended in late October 1941, CCP leaders had adopted two important decisions. They elected to establish a committee—to be chaired by Mao—on "settling historical records," and also adopted a decision to "reexamine the cases of cadres who had been purged in the past."[32] These would become central texts in the Rectification, revealing that reckoning with old historical debts would be a focus of the campaign.

Because he had not attended the September Conference, Zhou knew little about what had happened at it until two years later, when he returned to Yan'an to participate in the Rectification. When he found that Mao repeatedly used cases associated with him as examples of subjectivism, factionalism, and "leftist-leaning" or "rightist-leaning" opportunism, Zhou likely became keenly aware that he was a principal target of Mao's rectification drive.

Mao wrote nine critical commentaries following the September Conference about nine key Party Center documents issued between September 1931 and May 1932. He directed the bulk of his sharp criticism at Zhou, Li Lisan, Wang Ming, and Bo Gu. Raging, the chairman wrote his tirades as though he were venting years of accumulated frustration. In the words of Mao's secretary Hu Qiaomu, the tone of the commentaries was "spicy, acrimonious, and sarcastic." These texts were products of Mao's "flaming passion."[33]

It is probably for this reason that these essays—although they were among the chairman's favorites and were revised on several occasions, such as on the eve of the Cultural Revolution and the "Criticizing Lin Biao and Confucius Campaign"—were never formally declassified. The nine essays were locked away in drawers after Mao's death. Periodically, rumors surfaced that the writings would be declassified, but their contents were never revealed. That Mao's essays attacked Zhou seems to be an important reason for their remaining classified.

• • •

With the conclusion of the September Conference of 1941, Mao launched his Rectification Campaign. Basically, he had two closely interconnected goals for the campaign. The first was "to unify thought" within the party ranks, and the second was "to eliminate factions" in the party. Both objectives served Mao's larger purpose of establishing absolute control over the party and solidifying his ultimate domination of the Chinese Communist Revolution. "Rectification" was the instrument that Mao would use to achieve these two goals. Their realization, Mao calculated, would not only allow him to establish unchecked power and authority in the party, but would also make the party more united and better equipped to jockey with the GMD for control of political power in China. Meanwhile, of the many reasons Mao was ultimately able to defeat Chiang, one of the most important was Chiang's inability to resolve these two basic problems—"unification of thought" and "elimination of factions"—in the GMD.

From the start, Mao demanded that all party organs and cadres conduct both "thought rectification" and "organization rectification." "Thought rectification," according to Mao, meant that every party cadre had to wage "a revolution in one's own soul" and would therefore willingly embrace the process as a step toward transforming themselves into "a new man of the proletarian class." Mao highlighted the necessity of the "sinification of Marxism," effectively granting himself the discursive power to define and interpret the party's official ideology. In practice, thought rectification would combine "soft procedures"—characterized by documentary study and criticism, as well as self-criticism—with "hard procedures," which included the forced exposing and denunciation of the "dark sides" of one's experiences and behavior. In Mao's mind, both procedures were indispensable to the rectification process. Not surprisingly, the implementation of these procedures inevitably resulted in physical and psychological torture—assaulting and even destroying the basic rights, dignity, and decency of those involved. But for Mao, this was exactly the purpose of rectification: only by crushing the sense of "self" could the concept of the "collective," as embodied by the party and indeed, by Mao himself, be firmly established.

Mao designed "organizational rectification" in the image of "thought rectification." In the final analysis, "organizational rectification" was intended to eliminate all voices of dissent, whether real or imagined, from the party, thus achieving "absolute unity" within the party under Mao's leadership. Central to "organizational rectification" was a process known as the "examination of cadres" or *shen'gan.* This was essentially a witch hunt that everyone in Yan'an had to go through. The purges employed means so harsh and brutal, such as "hunting for GMD special agents," that they erased whatever sense of reason and rationality remained. Consequently, thousands of party members would be given the spurious label of "class enemy."

To carry out *shen'gan* in such a way served Mao's desire to create an atmosphere pervaded by fear, in which all would be aware of and yield to his superior authority and ultimate power. The chairman had his pawns, the most notorious of whom was Kang Sheng, a Soviet returnee. However, unlike so many others who had studied or worked in the Soviet Union, Kang managed to win Mao's trust. He knew how to read Mao, and he thoroughly understood Mao's ideas and intentions. As *shen'gan* vanguards, Kang and his henchmen claimed to have unmasked thousands of "enemy special agents" and uncovered hundreds of "hidden GMD cells" within the party.

As they carried out *shen'gan,* Mao and Kang paid special attention to cadres from the Great Rear, areas for which Zhou was responsible. Kang's "discovery" was astonishing. On April 30, 1943, shortly before Zhou was called back to Yan'an to participate in the Rectification Campaign, he received a top-secret telegram from Mao. "During *shen'gan,*" the chairman asserted, "many of the cadres and even the delegates designated to attend the Seventh Congress from the Great Rear have been identified as the enemy's special agents." Indeed, Mao even claimed, "the majority or even overwhelming majority of our Party's organs in the Great Rear have fallen to agencies controlled by the enemy." The chairman demanded that Zhou "immediately take action" to deal with this severe situation.[34]

As Southern Bureau secretary and the CCP's spymaster in the Great Rear, Zhou had to treat Mao's warning with the utmost urgency. We do not know what exactly Zhou did, or what transpired in his further exchanges with Mao. But we do know the "final answer" he gave to the Party Center once he returned to Yan'an. A thorough investigation, Zhou reported, had revealed that the claim of widespread enemy infiltration of party organs in the Great Rear was completely unfounded.[35]

How could Mao and Kang have been so wrong? In fact, what Zhou had endured was not an isolated incident, but just one instance of a widespread phenomenon in the Rectification. As it later turned out, almost none of Kang's discoveries of "enemies" among the cadres in Yan'an was verified. Moreover, his witch hunt eventually provoked a great deal of anger among party comrades, as well as serious repercussions in Yan'an that endangered the legitimacy of Mao's rectification efforts. The chairman, realizing that

Kang had probably gone too far, issued a public apology for "harming those comrades loyal to the party" and asked for their "understanding" and "cooperation."[36] But Kang was not punished, although for a while Mao had to sideline him from the center stage of CCP politics. But Mao did not forget him. When the time was right, Mao would unhesitatingly entrust him with important duties. Kang Sheng recovered his political prominence and again became Mao's pawn in the Cultural Revolution.

It is also striking that the excesses of the *shen'gan* campaign did not result in fiercer resistance by its victims. In retrospect, this was largely because of a critical difference between Mao's Rectification and the "suppression of the AB Clique" campaign in the Jiangxi years. Rather than execute the perceived "class enemies," Mao introduced the principle of "while the majority would not be arrested, not even one would be executed."[37] So, during the Rectification, no matter how severely one was accused, one's life would not be taken away and, in most cases, one would not be imprisoned. Mao hoped to bring about a "revolution" deep in the hearts and minds of people, not one predicated on their liquidation. In this sense, the Rectification Campaign served as the predecessor to a series of "thought transformation" campaigns that took place throughout the Maoist era and that would reach their peak during the Great Proletarian Cultural Revolution.

Shen'gan had another important feature. Although the program involved tens of thousands of party members, Mao made it clear at the onset of *shen'gan* that the emphasis of the Rectification was not on "cadres of the low and middle levels" but on party leaders. "The main thrust of the Rectification should cover high-ranking cadres, so as to settle the problems in their conceptual realm," Mao proclaimed. "Once their thought issues have been resolved, lower-levels cadres' rectification will make good progress."[38]

Zhou was a top party leader. Since the mid-1920s, he had occupied crucial positions at the Party Center and wielded significant decision-making power in political, military, and intelligence matters. Over the years, he and Mao from time to time had held different views. Not surprisingly, he would become a primary target of the Rectification Campaign. Indeed, he was later labeled as a main representative of the "experimentalist faction" in the party, and he became a principal target of myriad accusations during the Rectification Movement.

However, Zhou managed to avoid the Rectification for the first two years of the campaign. One major reason was that he was then in charge of dealing with the Nationalist government as well as the world outside China. When a serious conflict broke out between the CCP and GMD in the wake of the NFA Incident of 1941, Zhou was the best suited of the CCP leaders to handle the dispute. Meanwhile, the CCP was badly in need of "international intervention" to check Chiang's "anti-CCP plots." Again, Zhou proved adept at managing such a challenge. In fact, no one within the party leadership had Zhou's skill and capacity for handling the complicated situations of the time. It was truly hard for him to leave Chongqing and return to Yan'an.

Yet there was another important reason—perhaps a more important one—for Zhou's emerging from the first two years of Rectification unscathed. Mao knew well that it would be tactically unwise to make too many enemies at the beginning of the Rectification. By then, the chairman had become highly sophisticated in his manipulation of the CCP's intraparty struggle. Mao shrewdly decided to first aim his attacks toward such "dogmatists" as Wang Ming and Bo Gu, particularly Wang.

Here, Mao's political acuity was on full display. Wang, a very ambitious person, had long enjoyed the Comintern's support, and thus he presented a more dangerous challenge to Mao's own ambition than anyone else within the party. Yet Wang's connections and popularity with party leaders paled in comparison to Zhou's. Zhou enjoyed high seniority in the military stemming from his tenure as director of the Political Department at the Whampoa Military Academy. He also controlled the party's personnel matters and intelligence network and had long been known for getting things done. For Mao to make Zhou a premature victim of the Rectification would not only have diverted the attacks against Wang but might have also caused the whole campaign to face stronger resistance from within the party and the army. Mao was not willing to take those risks.

Wang and other "Soviet returnees" were comparatively easier targets. They had all gained top positions in the CCP leadership only after returning from Moscow; hence, unlike Zhou, they lacked deep roots and connections in the party and the army. They had all committed various mistakes in the creation and implementation of important policies, rendering them vulnerable to Mao's accusations.

Mao adopted a gradualist strategy. In February 1942, he attacked what he called "stereotype writing" in the drafting of party documents.[39] He sternly criticized those "dogmatists" within the party who had treated "Marxism-Leninism as a religious doctrine," ridiculing them as "even more foolish than pigs."[40] In late May, the CCP established a Central General Study Committee—with Mao serving as its chairman and Kang Sheng as the vice chairman—which assumed overall responsibility for directing the Rectification Campaign.[41] For a while, the committee even stood above the Politburo, to ensure that Politburo members would undergo rectification, too. Mao ordered all cadres in Yan'an to write self-criticisms in the form of "reflection notes," and keep a "journal of thought evolution," which they would submit to the party for evaluation.[42] Mao kept Zhou abreast of the measures as they were put into place. In Chongqing, Zhou followed the example set by Yan'an and established his own Study Committee.[43]

While the Rectification Campaign unfolded, Mao managed to restructure the party leadership, letting his personal likes and dislikes dominate the process. In early 1942, Zhang Wentian left the Party Center to "conduct an investigation" in the countryside, though he had been a Maoist since the mid-1930s.[44] Mao never liked Zhang, and he consistently remembered him as a "Soviet returnee" who had been deeply involved in the making of "wrong policy lines" before the mid-1930s. Wang Jiaxiang was also a Maoist at the time; nonetheless, he was never one of Mao's favorites. He became the target of sharp criticism for the role he played in shaping the "opposition to Mao" movement during the early Jiangxi years.[45] On the other hand, Ren Bishi was one individual whom Mao liked. Despite having been at odds with Mao in the past, Ren had been a staunch Maoist since the mid-1930s, so he was given more power and important appointments. Liu Shaoqi, who was "historically clean" and had also repeatedly demonstrated himself to be a Mao loyalist, was summoned back to Yan'an and quickly emerged as Mao's second-in-command.[46]

Against this backdrop, the CCP Politburo passed a resolution on March 20, 1943, making Mao its chairman. A new Central Secretariat composed of Mao, Liu Shaoqi, and Ren Bishi was established, with Mao at its head. The secretariat would adopt the following principle:

> Comrade (Mao) Zedong, as the Chairman, can call meetings—which will not be held regularly—at any time, and for any question discussed at those meetings. He has the final power to make the decision.[47]

Thus, Mao's position in the party leadership changed from that of a top decision-maker to the indisputable ultimate decision-maker.

This arrangement effectively excluded Zhou from the party's innermost circle. As it soon turned out, the change also signaled the rapid approach of Zhou's days as a direct target of the Rectification Campaign.

At this critical time, in late May 1943, the Comintern announced that it would be dissolved. This was a godsend for Mao. Although the Comintern had endorsed Mao over the years, and despite Moscow's significantly relaxing its control over the CCP after the outbreak of the Soviet-German War, Mao did not like its looming presence. He still worried that he could face big trouble if he had somehow offended Moscow in the past. Therefore, in the preceding years, Mao had tightly controlled the telegraphic communication between Yan'an and Moscow.[48]

Now that the Comintern was gone, Mao knew that the opportunity had come for him to further rectify the CCP at his will. The Rectification Campaign would enter a new phase. The time of Zhou's reckoning had arrived.

. . .

On May 24, Zhou received a telegram from Mao and the CCP Central Committee: "The Comintern has been dissolved, and the Central Committee will discuss our policies in China. Please rush back to Yan'an immediately."[49] But Zhou was then busy with a variety of tasks in Chongqing. Additionally, as he was also a high-ranking official in the Nationalist government, he needed Chiang's permission to leave Chongqing. Chiang delayed his response to Zhou's request, and it was not until June 7 that he met with Zhou and agreed to grant him a passport to leave the city.[50] Mao was anxious; he cabled Zhou repeatedly, inquiring "when, exactly" would he "be departing" and urging him "not to have any delay on the way."[51]

Zhou did not seem to be in a hurry to return to Yan'an. Chiang's slow response was certainly a factor. But Zhou probably also had a hunch that this trip back to Yan'an would be different from the ones before it, and so he needed time to prepare. He was to participate in the Rectification Movement, and he likely would not come back to Chongqing for a while.

Zhou finally set out from Chongqing on June 28, 1943. He had not been based in Yan'an for almost six years. He knew that Mao's Rectification Campaign awaited him there, but he did not know what his experience in Yan'an would be like. Perhaps he was not even certain whether he would ever have the chance to return to Chongqing.

A fresh crisis faced the CCP and the GMD while Zhou was on his way back to Yan'an. Chiang and the GMD seized the opportunity provided by the Comintern's dissolution to demand that the CCP also dissolve itself, placing its troops under the command of the Nationalist government.[52] Xiong Xianghui, a superspy whom Zhou had planted next to Hu Zongnan, one of the leading GMD generals, sent Yan'an a top-secret intelligence report that Chiang was amassing troops for an attack on Yan'an.[53] The CCP leadership decided to publicize the report, openly denouncing Chiang for trying to subdue the CCP by attacking its base area.[54] Mao also sent several telegrams to Zhou, instructing Zhou to stop in Xi'an on his way to Yan'an and meet with Hu in person to "try to turn things around and to avoid military conflicts."[55] Accordingly, Zhou stopped in Xi'an for a week. After meeting with Hu, he notified the chairman that although Chiang had ordered Hu to attack Yan'an, "he [was] still preparing" to implement the order, so there was no need for Yan'an "to be on high alert" for the moment.[56] The crisis between the two sides gradually subsided.

On July 16, Zhou was back in Yan'an. Upon his arrival, he instantly sensed that the sentiment of "favoring Mao" pervaded the red capital's political atmosphere. He decided at once to act, explicitly expressing his firm support for Mao as the party's paramount leader. At a reception for him on August 3, Zhou stated enthusiastically:

> Nothing has been more evident than the developments of the past three years. For anyone who had opposed or doubted Comrade Mao Zedong's leadership role and his opinions in the past, it is now proven that they had been completely wrong. The twenty-two-year history of our party has made it clear that Comrade Mao Zedong's ideas span the entire history of the party, and have developed into the line that has sinicized Marxism-Leninism; that is the line of the Chinese Communist Party. Comrade Mao Zedong's direction is the direction of the Chinese Communist Party! Comrade Mao Zedong's line is the line of the Chinese Bolsheviks![57]

This was Zhou's manifesto of his ultimate loyalty to Mao. To what extent Zhou's words were sincere remains unknown. Yet one thing seems clear: his statement represented the outcome of his constant observation and cogitation in the preceding two to three years. Although this statement did not save Zhou from severe criticism, it did allow him to survive and remain a leader of the CCP. Most important of all, the statement formed the basis on which Zhou was to work with Mao in the decades to come.

Zhou pored over party documents in the ensuing months as he got ready to "actively participate in" the Rectification. He also wrote a series of self-critical "thought notes" about the party's mistakes in policy lines and the Comintern's "erroneous guidance" since the late 1920s, which he linked to his own experience and duties. This was his preparation for joining the Rectification Campaign and making self-criticism about his own mistakes. Emulating the tone Mao used in his attacks, Zhou fiercely condemned the "criminal mistakes" that Li Lisan, Wang Ming, and Bo Gu had made.[58] During this process, he likely reviewed all the party documents, including the harsh attack Mao had directed at him. Zhou must have realized that the experience awaiting him was one that would etch its mark on his bones and leave an imprint on his heart.

• • •

Beginning on September 7, 1943, the CCP Politburo held a series of meetings about bringing Rectification to "deeper levels." In a presentation, Mao highlighted the necessity of criticizing two factional tendencies—dogmatism and experimentalism. Of these two labels, "dogmatism" had been the one assigned to Wang Ming, who by then had been thoroughly demonized. Although Wang had never acknowledged his own mistakes, Mao and most of the party elite regarded him as a "dying tiger." There was no need for them to treat him as a main target of the Rectification as they had done in the past two years.

The case of experimentalism was different. To grapple with this issue required a great deal of attention and energy for Mao. According to Hu Qiaomu, Mao's longtime secretary, after Wang's dogmatism and his "dogmatist faction" were meticulously examined, it became more urgent to deal with "the danger involved in the experimentalist faction," as "leaders associated with this faction [remained] dangerous figures."[59] Here, "experimentalism" actually referred to a label that Mao had specifically tailored to entangle Zhou. Mao's use of the term was intended to imply that Zhou, despite his reputation within the party leadership for getting things done, frequently moved in the wrong direction. Evidently, Zhou had been identified as the principal target of the next phase of Rectification among high-ranking party cadres.

On September 13, Kang Sheng, now Mao's Rectification lieutenant, spoke at a Politburo meeting. While elaborating on the topic of Wang Ming's "mistakes and crimes," Kang abruptly mentioned the issue of newspaper publication, and he took *Xinhua ribao* as an example. He claimed that in the past years, *Xinhua* had not only completely lost its direction but had even deteriorated to the point of becoming a mouthpiece of the GMD. "There have been many anti-Communist pieces published in it, such as the ones claiming that Chiang Kai-shek has been an anti-Japanese patriot, and therefore at any time, on any occasion, and in any circumstance, one should endorse his government. This is nothing but naked surrenderism."[60] As everyone in the CCP leadership knew, it was Zhou who had launched *Xinhua,* and he had always directed the newspaper since its inception. Kang's accusation against the paper was actually a veiled criticism of Zhou. But Zhou did not try to rebut Kang, knowing that Mao stood behind Kang, and that he would soon face his own trial of "criticism and self-criticism."

Mao meant to keep Zhou in Yan'an for a while. The chairman personally answered Chiang Kai-shek's repeated inquiries as to when Zhou would return to Chongqing. Mao asked Dong Biwu, Zhou's replacement in Chongqing, to tell Chiang that "Zhou had had nothing to do in Chongqing for three years, so for the moment he does not plan to return to Chongqing." Mao authorized Dong to discuss all matters with the GMD, making it no secret that Zhou would not return to Chongqing—at least not for a while.[61]

• • •

On October 10, Mao announced on behalf of the Central Committee that all high-ranking party cadres should begin another round of "study of the party's history and policy lines." The Rectification would accordingly enter a new phase through which everyone would be "elevated to a higher level" of political consciousness.[62] Zhou, as the perceived representative of the "experimentalist faction," would be brought to center stage in the Rectification.

On November 13, Mao chaired a series of Politburo meetings that would last three weeks. The purpose of the meetings, as the chairman made it clear, was to thoroughly expose and criticize the "leftist opportunist mistakes" of the Jiangxi years and the "rightist opportunist mistakes" during the early stage of the war against Japan. Mao had actually crafted this agenda particularly with Zhou in mind, as Zhou was the designated target of this Politburo gathering.

Zhou had known for some time that this moment would come, and he had prepared for it with all his heart and soul. On November 15, the third day of the meetings, he finished an "outline of self-criticism" of twenty-five thousand characters in length, which he submitted to the party leadership. In the document, Zhou hewed to the tone that Mao had set for the campaign, calling himself the representative and head of the "experimentalist faction" and an "accomplice of the domination of the doctrinist faction." Taking "opposing Mao and trying to seize power from Mao" as the main thread of the outline, Zhou criticized himself by enumerating every case in which he had had a difference with Mao. Without exception, he took responsibility for each of them, relentlessly criticizing himself to the point of slashing his own face.[63]

Beginning on November 27, Zhou spoke for five days (yes, five days!) straight before the Politburo, criticizing the "mistakes and crimes" that he had made during the Jiangxi period and the early stage of the war against Japan. He did this, first and foremost, for Mao to hear. The chairman seemed to enjoy each and every minute of Zhou's tortured soul-searching.

In the Jiangxi years, Zhou confessed, he made "unpardonable criminal mistakes" as reflected in his "planning, implementing, and completing" of conspiracies aimed at depriving Mao of "the power of the party, the Red government, and the Red Army." Zhou divided his "anti-Mao experience" in Jiangxi into four phases. The first "reached its peak with the nullifying of the suppression of reactionaries campaign," which was a Maoist program; the second phase resulted in the Gannan Conference, at which Mao was put on trial; the third, which culminated in the Ningdu Conference, witnessed Mao's loss of military power; the fourth consolidated the reign of Bo Gu and the leftist opportunists in the party as well as in the Jiangxi Red Zone after sidelining Mao.[64] Zhou said that he had played a key role throughout these four phases. Indeed, he was the culprit behind the anti-Mao attacks, so he surely should be the one to take full responsibility for Mao's suffering. In particular, after Ningdu, he replaced Mao to become the supreme military leader in the Red Zone. His "responsibility as a criminal" who stripped Mao of his power, therefore, was both overwhelming and inexcusable.

Zhou's self-criticism also emphasized his "criminal mistakes" during the early phase of the war against Japan. This criticism centered on the confluence of the "experimentalist faction" headed by Zhou and the "doctrinist faction" represented by Wang Ming. Indeed, Zhou said, "this was the second time that such a confluence of these two factions occurred." He and Wang had joined forces and challenged the "correct policy lines" represented by Mao, resulting in serious mistakes in the direction of "rightist opportunism."[65]

Following what had become general practice in the culture of the CCP, Zhou also tried to "dig deep into his own mind and soul" to identify the origins of such serious "criminal mistakes":

> I came from the family of a bankrupt feudal mandarin, which imparted me with such bad characteristics as vanity, favoritism, face-saving, selfishness, tactfulness, overcautiousness, egocentric perfectionism, and poor taste and ugly motivation, which had not been fully eliminated. Further, when I was a child, I was nurtured with excessive mothering, which further increased my softness and sense of blind obedience within the party, and which served as a source when I grew up of my character of reconciliation and lacking a sense of principle.[66]

Zhou was obviously eager to earn a passing grade in the Rectification, so he presented his self-criticism in this exceedingly humble, even self-abasing manner. Yet he did not pass the test immediately. He continued to face criticism and accusations, which showed no sign of stopping.

When Zhou was under immense pressure, and just as it seemed that he would finally sink to the nadir of his political disgrace, Mao actually was ready to let him off the hook. But Mao still needed an occasion that would allow both Zhou and him to save face. One such occasion soon presented itself to Mao. On December 22, Dimitrov "personally" cabled Mao, saying that he could not "fail to tell you of my alarm at the situation in the Chinese Communist Party." "Kang Sheng's role seems dubious to me," Dimitrov admitted, implicitly voicing his resentment of the purges in Yan'an. Then, he explicitly stated that

> I consider politically mistaken the campaign being waged against Zhou Enlai and Wang Ming, who are being incriminated with the Comintern-endorsed national front policy, as a result of which they have allegedly led the party to schism. Persons such as Zhou Enlai and Wang Ming must not be severed from the party.[67]

Dimitrov tried his utmost to support Zhou and Wang. He mentioned Zhou ahead of Wang, demonstrating the special attention that Moscow had paid to Zhou. And anyone who knew about the political structure in Moscow would understand that Dimitrov would not have written such a letter without Stalin's approval.

The Comintern had already been dissolved for months by then, so Mao did not necessarily need to heed directions from Moscow. But neither was he in a position to completely ignore Moscow's input. Furthermore, he had never meant to permanently deal a fatal blow to Zhou politically. Mao, now a master of intraparty struggles, had handled such matters like the criticism of Zhou in increasingly sophisticated ways. He knew well that he should set limits on his actions. Therefore, after he received Dimitrov's telegram, Mao immediately decided to do him a "favor" and let off both Zhou and Wang Ming.

Mao treated Zhou and Wang differently, however. He allowed Zhou, who had exhibited a "profound understanding of his own mistakes" and made "genuine and sincere self-criticism," to retain the important positions that he had held before. As for Wang, who had been stubborn and "unwilling to acknowledge his own mistakes," Mao would never let him hold any position of real power. Not surprisingly, Mao described Zhou and Wang differently. "Our relationship with Comrade Zhou Enlai has been very good," Mao stated in his reply to Dimitrov. "We have no intention to exclude him." Mao reserved nastier words for Wang, however: "Wang Ming has carried out all sorts of antiparty activities, and all of this has been relayed to cadres throughout the party." As if this were not enough, Mao further claimed that Wang was "unrealiable," having once "confessed that he was a party member" after being arrested in Shanghai. Furthermore, he also had a "dubious connection with [Pavel] Mif [formerly the Comintern's special envoy to the CCP]."[68] To those who might have remained unwilling to accept Mao's leadership, the stark difference in the ways Mao treated Zhou and Wang came as a very real warning.

• • •

In early May 1944, Zhou delivered a speech at the Central Party School. Based on the understanding of the intraparty struggles that he had obtained during Rectification, he highlighted, unsurprisingly, how Mao had been "forever correct" throughout the history of the party.[69] Zhou's speech meant that his ordeal in the Rectification Campaign had finally come to a close.

Mao allowed Zhou to make such a speech for two purposes. One was to let Zhou's voice be added to the chorus of praise for him. The second was to show his lenience toward an old comrade who had committed serious mistakes yet shown remorse for them. The chairman had "most generously," as his followers claimed, offered Zhou an opportunity to emerge from the abyss that Mao himself had created, allowing Zhou to continue to serve the party and the revolution and—first and foremost—to serve Mao, the great leader. This would become the foundation of Mao and Zhou's work together in the decades to come.

To conclude the Rectification Campaign, in April 1945 the CCP leadership adopted a resolution on a series of controversial issues in the party's history. According to the resolution, the CCP leadership had repeatedly committed mistakes in political lines since the failure of the Great Revolution. These transgressions included the rightist-leaning mistakes under Chen Duxiu; the leftist-leaning mistakes by Li Lisan, Wang Ming, and Bo Gu; and the rightist-leaning mistakes in the early stage of the war against Japan. Mao had always stood on the right side of history and struggled against each of these mistakes, not only saving the party, but also guiding the revolution toward victory in the process.[70] Although Zhou was not named in the text of the resolution, it was apparent that Zhou had often stood on the side of wrong lines, which was a "sin" that Zhou would forever have to live with. By confirming all of these mistakes and Mao's singular leadership in such a formal resolution, the CCP officially ended the Rectification Campaign.

* * *

This experience of being wrapped around Mao's finger was a lesson that Zhou never forgot for the rest of his life. Although he had willingly accepted Mao's leadership since the Long March and was fully prepared to embrace Mao as the party's paramount leader when he returned to Yan'an to participate in the Rectification, Mao's way of purging him far exceeded his expectations. In the end, he survived, and he was more determined than ever before to subject himself to Mao's authority and power. He understood that he was not Mao's peer when it came to playing intraparty politics. More importantly, he found in Mao a mastermind in whose perception he could place his faith.

Zhou's experience revealed some basic features and characteristics of the CCP's "party culture," which was especially shaped during the Rectification.

The most important aspects of the party culture were as follows: individual party members must always obey the organization; the whole party must always obey the Central Committee; and the Central Committee must always obey the great leader, that is, Chairman Mao. Stemming from this was the absolute dominance of "Mao worship" or "Mao cult" in the party culture, which deprived all party members and cadres, including Zhou, of their individuality. In hindsight, what was most frightening was not that Zhou and so many of his comrades had lost their faith in the party after enduring the Rectification Campaign, but that in its wake, they simply came up with a new faith, one that left no room for critical thinking and drove them to blindly worship Mao and embrace Mao Zedong Thought.

In that moment, the lofty cause of the Chinese Communist Revolution became centered on a single person's "greatness" and the supposed brilliance of his ideas. Zhou and his comrades had handed Mao total power to make and define the revolution's legitimacy narrative and created no institutions to check and balance such power. This was a critical point in the history of the Chinese Communist Revolution. The day of the revolution's victory—if indeed Mao, Zhou, and their comrades could achieve it—would mark the day that uncontrolled power was allowed to run rampant and ultimately prevail. The revolution would degenerate into an enterprise standing in opposition to the goal that the revolutionaries had once so loudly proclaimed, the emancipation of humanity.

But, at the moment, Mao still needed to prove that he deserved to enjoy such unchecked power, by using it to lead the Chinese Communist Revolution to victory. In this case, the truth would be proven or disproven by the result. Mao knew this, and he seemed quite confident that he would pass the test. As the chairman saw it, the CCP had emerged from the Rectification Campaign "more unified ideologically and united organizationally" and thus "much more competent" in confronting its enemies. Mao was determined to lead such a party to challenge the Nationalist government for Chinese political power.

• • •

In late spring 1945, the CCP held its Seventh Congress. Zhou was eager to show his respect for and obedience to Mao. Among the seven keynote speakers at the opening session of the Congress, he was the only one who ended by shouting "Long live Comrade Mao Zedong!"[71]

On April 30, Zhou gave a speech at the congress concerning the united front. He praised Mao's leadership and the brilliance of Mao Zedong Thought. Meanwhile, he also made another self-criticism of the mistakes that he had committed in "managing relations with the GMD":

> Those of us who had taken up leadership roles in Wuhan, myself included, gave too much credence to the belief that the Guomindang forces could win victories, and had ignored our own forces. Militarily I emphasized mobile war, without giving due attention to guerilla war.[72]

During the Rectification, Zhou had been accused of having committed "rightist capitulationism" in his handling of the CCP's united front with the GMD. Now, he was given the opportunity to report on the united front at the Seventh Congress. This meant that he had passed the test of the campaign, and also revealed that Mao still needed him to manage the united front work and other important assignments.

But Zhou's "old debt" was not forgotten. His influence in the party leadership withered. Although he was a top party leader, Zhou ranked twenty-third among the forty-four elected members of the Central Committee in votes cast. Among the thirteen who were named to the Politburo, Zhou received the third-fewest votes. Zhou received the fewest votes of the five Secretariat members.[73] He showed no sign of grievance.

After all, Zhou had never aspired to become a top leader. Even before Mao's Rectification, he had already established the principle that so long as Mao was the leader, he would never strive for that position. And so long as Mao was alive, he knew that the position was Mao's. After the Rectification Campaign in Yan'an, Zhou set for himself another principle: he would not pursue the party's number two position either. In the years to come, in addition to embracing Mao as the paramount leader, Zhou favored Liu Shaoqi as the second-in-command. After Liu's downfall in the Cultural Revolution, Zhou offered his unfailing support to Lin Biao, the next number two leader and Mao's designated successor.

Zhou knew well that only by doing so would it be possible for him to avoid another deadly clash with Mao.

13

THE VORTEX OF BIG POWER POLITICS

1944–1946

Zhou Enlai stayed in Yan'an for most of 1944. After the Rectification Campaign, he remained a member of the CCP's inner circle. But he was less powerful and busy than he had been in the previous years.

China's war against Japan entered its seventh year in 1944. Globally, it was evident that the Axis powers were losing the war. In China, however, the Japanese launched Operation Ichi-Go ("Number One"), a gigantic military offensive intended to open a transportation corridor through eastern China. The resistance put up by Chinese troops quickly collapsed. In a few short months, they yielded to the Japanese a large swath of territory, including many cities and transportation lines and links. Chiang's status as China's supreme leader was called into serious question.[1]

The Japanese offensive did not surprise Mao, Zhou, and their comrades. A few months earlier, US president Franklin Roosevelt, UK prime minister Winston Churchill, and Chiang had announced in their jointly issued Cairo Declaration that the war in the Asia-Pacific region would have to end with Japan's unconditional surrender. Mao thus recognized that it was no longer possible for Chiang and Japan to reach a compromise and predicted that Chiang's troops "might face a major Japanese attack."[2] Chiang made a similar prediction in a telegram to Roosevelt: "The Japanese bandits may soon launch a big offensive in China to consolidate their strategic rear."[3]

The CCP's talks with the GMD had stopped since Zhou had returned to Yan'an in the summer of 1943. At one point, Chiang even planned "to attack Yan'an," an idea he later abandoned to avoid provoking a negative reaction in China and abroad.[4] Before the Cairo Conference took place, Chiang had not planned to resume negotiations with the CCP, although he indicated that he might be willing to do so, especially if Zhou could return to Chongqing, which would make it "easier for the two sides to discuss any questions."[5] After the Cairo Conference, however, he showed a more positive attitude toward resuming negotiations with the CCP. In early January 1944, Mao told Guo Zhongrong, Chiang's liaison in Yan'an, that the CCP was then considering sending Zhou or another emissary to Chongqing. Guo quickly brought back a welcoming reply from Chongqing.[6] But Mao actually was not ready to follow his own suggestion, as he deemed it better to wait until "the second half of the year or the first half of the next" to resume the talks.[7] Mao was unwilling to send Zhou back to Chongqing either. He waited until February to inform Guo that the CCP would send Lin Boqu to Chongqing in mid-March, joining Dong Biwu there to meet with their GMD counterparts.[8]

Around the same time, Chiang took another initiative. Through Shao Lizi, an old friend of Zhou's and a high-ranking GMD official, he invited Zhou to attend a roundtable on constitutional politics in Chongqing. Although this was a subject that Zhou had long emphasized, he politely turned down Chiang's invitation, primarily because of Mao's objection to it.[9] In fact, Zhou believed that the CCP should be present at the event. "The constitutional movement was not a GMD invention," he explained at a Politburo meeting, "but was initiated by parties in the middle and joined by many provincial strongmen." Zhou argued that although Chiang intended to use the "constitutional movement" as a means to contain the CCP, the party should not avoid it. Rather, he contended, the CCP should "actively engage in it, thus demonstrating our eagerness to resolve the problems in political ways, which will also increase our influence among those middle-of-the-roaders."[10] With the support of the Politburo, Zhou delivered a public speech on constitutional politics on March 12, marking his debut after surviving the Rectification Movement. He declared that the CCP favored constitutional politics as the way to overcome its differences with the GMD. This meant, he stressed, that the Nationalist government should guarantee democracy and freedom for the people, lift the ban on other political parties, and allow local autonomy.[11]

This time Mao listened to Zhou. Although, unlike Zhou, he was never interested in constitutional politics in itself, he understood that verbal promotion of the subject was a "good political tactic" to attract third parties and gain the political upper hand over the GMD. Zhou stated at a CCP Secretariat meeting on April 15 that politics was a main area of competition between the CCP and the GMD and that it was in the CCP's interest to pursue détente with the GMD, while demanding that Chiang "respect democracy and freedom by practicing constitutional politics." Mao, who readily grasped Zhou's points, agreed that the CCP should not make the GMD feel threatened while "highlighting democracy with third parties and emphasizing fighting against Japan with the UK and the US."[12] This exchange between Mao and Zhou revealed, again, their intention to highlight "democracy" and "nationalism" in the CCP's public presentation of its domestic and international policies.

. . .

In early May, when Lin Boqu, representing the CCP on Zhou's behalf, conferred with Zhang Zhizhong, the chief GMD negotiator, Zhang invited Lin to present "a plan to resolve the current deadlock." Lin replied that Zhou and Lin Biao had already presented such a plan to the GMD the previous year, but the GMD had not responded. He suggested that he and Zhang take Zhou's recent speech on constitutional politics as the basis of the talks.[13] Mao, recognizing that Chiang faced a serious lack of credibility at home and abroad in the wake of the GMD's military defeats, called on the CCP "to be prepared to manage big changes in the near future." He thus devised new ideas for negotiations with the GMD that would go beyond the terms that Zhou had already introduced.[14] In late May, Lin submitted a series of new terms, including the "adoption of democratic politics by the government," "allowing other parties' activities," and "practicing genuine local autonomy by the people." The CCP also asked that its total troop strength be expanded to forty-seven divisions.[15] These new conditions were viewed as quite aggressive by Zhang, who even refused to convey them to Chiang.[16] However, the revised terms were only the CCP's new bottom line. The Communists' demands for "broadening democracy" grew louder with each military defeat the Nationalists endured. On August 18, Zhou dispatched a cable to CCP negotiators in Chongqing, in which he highlighted the proposition that "the government should be reorganized," a request that Mao ardently supported.[17] On September 15, the CCP formally proposed that the GMD "end one-party rule . . . and establish a coalition government by all anti-Japanese parties."[18]

Mao, in the final analysis, firmly believed that "political power comes out of the barrel of a gun," and that the CCP's conflict with the GMD would eventually have to be settled on the battlefield after the end of the war with Japan. He thus emphasized that the party should take establishing a strong military force, consolidating its base areas, and preparing to occupy big cities and key transportation lines as "a top-priority task."[19] Beginning in mid-1944, the CCP leadership ordered that several of the party's best units be dispatched to create new base areas south of the Yangzi River. Their tasks would include carrying out guerrilla operations in areas near Shanghai and Hangzhou and along the railway connecting the two cities, "tightly surrounding them with our guerrilla warfare."[20] In the autumn, the CCP leadership further directed a newly formed Southern March Column composed of its best troops to penetrate deep into regions south of the Yangzi.[21]

Mao and Zhou also focused a great deal of their attention on international diplomacy. As the most experienced CCP leader in this respect, Zhou now found in it another way to return to the party's innermost decision-making circle. The GMD's battlefield debacles provoked a strong negative reaction abroad. Roosevelt and his military planners were deeply worried. Chiang's relationship with Joseph Stilwell, the American general and chief of staff of Allied forces in the China Theater, also encountered huge difficulties. The cooperation between Chiang and Stilwell had enjoyed a brief honeymoon after Stilwell arrived in China in 1942. Before long, however, their relations cooled, then gradually deteriorated into mutual hostility. Chiang was offended by what he regarded as Stilwell's disobedience or even contempt of his authority as commander of the China Theater, and Stilwell was angry about the pervasive corruption in Chiang's government and the incompetence of the generalissimo's troops. At the start of 1944, Stilwell sent Roosevelt multiple highly critical reports on Chiang as GMD forces repeatedly collapsed in the face of Japanese offensives. He was by no means pro-Communist. However, he advocated US military cooperation with the CCP, which he saw as necessary to turn the tide of the War of Resistance in China.[22]

To urge Chiang to carry out political reforms, Roosevelt sent his vice president, Henry Wallace, to China in June 1944. Wallace held six meetings with Chiang in Chongqing over the course of three days. Chiang stressed that "the CCP's propaganda has been hypercritical" and that "the CCP has indeed been backed by the Comintern." He hoped that the United States would "clearly understand the vicious essence of the CCP challenge." However, Wallace, who had long harbored a pro-Soviet tendency, responded to Chiang that "if the CCP issue does have a Soviet background, China should have begun direct consultation with the Soviets at an earlier time." He urged Chiang to reform his government and pursue cooperation with the CCP. He also mentioned that the United States wanted to dispatch a group of military observers to Yan'an, to which Chiang gave his assent.[23]

Zhou and his comrades took note of these developments. Simultaneous to Wallace's arrival in China, *Jiefang ribao* (Liberation Daily) published an editorial essay accusing Chiang of being a dictator, and boasting that the CCP had realized the "Four Freedoms" championed by Roosevelt in its "Liberated Zone."[24] In early July, a mass rally was held at Yan'an to celebrate American Independence Day, an event unprecedented in CCP history. In his speech at the rally, Zhou praised American democracy, especially the American people's spirit in pursuing independence and national liberation.[25] A group of American military observers headed by Colonel David Barrett, known as the Dixie Mission, arrived in Yan'an on July 28. *Jiefang ribao* heralded their arrival in an editorial titled "Welcome, American Observers, Our Comrades-in-Arms!!" Mao added the words "our comrades-in-arms" to the essay's title.[26] Zhou frequently met with Barrett and other members of the group during their time at the Communist headquarters.[27]

On August 18, the CCP Center issued to the whole party an "Instruction on Foreign Affairs" drafted by Zhou and his associates. This was the first comprehensive CCP document on foreign policy. The party, the instruction asserted, faced major changes in domestic and international situations. Thus, the CCP had to give more attention to foreign affairs, using its experience in handling united front work at home to manage diplomacy with the United States in particular, since "compared with the Soviet Union and Britain, the United States has been more deeply involved in China's war against Japan." Zhou reasoned that as the CCP's united front policy had succeeded domestically, "to carry out such a policy internationally will likely lead to even greater achievements for us . . . thus creating many more favorable conditions for the victory of the Chinese revolution."[28]

Mao, together with Zhou, met with John S. Service, an American diplomat who was in Yan'an at the time, on August 23. Mao focused on the CCP's embrace of democracy and China's need for American support.

"China must industrialize," Mao emphasized. "This can be done in China only by free enterprise and with the aid of foreign capital. Chinese and American interests are correlated and similar. They fit together economically and politically. We can and must work together." He explained that the CCP was more democratic and, militarily, more competent than the GMD, stressing that "the United States would find us more cooperative than the Kuomintang (Guomindang). We will not be afraid of democratic American influence—we will welcome it. . . . We must have American help." He asked to "know what you Americans are thinking and planning. . . . We cannot risk any conflict with you." Zhou listened for most of the meeting. When it was his turn to speak, he told Service, "For the United States, the only way to be sure of decisively winning the war in China and avoiding civil war is to give arms to both [Guomindang] and Communists."[29]

Were Mao's and Zhou's words sincere? Did they genuinely plan to implement these ideas in China's postwar reconstruction as they set out to build a new nation? Or had their assurances merely been the lines of a political play? Any successful diplomacy includes an element of performance. Successful diplomats are also good actors. This was especially the case for Zhou, who loved the theater and had been an amateur actor in his student years. Diplomacy plays out on its own stage. Mao's and Zhou's expressions should be treated neither as a genuine reflection of their intentions nor as a total deception. After all, it was easier or more necessary for the CCP to favor democracy and strive for liberty as the political force in opposition. What truly matters is whether that political force will still embrace genuine freedom and democracy, and allow its power to be checked and balanced, once it takes power.

Genuine or not, Mao and Zhou's performance was effective. In its drive to dominate China's political discourse, the CCP seized two important banners—nationalism and democracy—forcing the GMD to go on the defensive. Service, as well many other Americans in China, listened to the two CCP leaders. In their reports to Washington, Service and other American diplomats described the Chinese Communists as being nationalists first and communists second. In some dispatches, they even viewed the CCP as being truly in favor of democracy.[30]

* * *

When the CCP leaders were working diligently to establish a rapport with the Americans, the relations between Chiang and Stilwell worsened dramatically. On July 7, at Stilwell's urging, Roosevelt asked Chiang to transfer "all responsibilities and power" of commanding Chinese troops to Stilwell; otherwise, Roosevelt warned, "our common cause will suffer a disastrous setback."[31] Chiang immediately took this as a brazen challenge to his authority and power. Rather than confront Roosevelt directly, he adopted a "moderate strategy": while agreeing to transfer military command to Stilwell, he also asked Roosevelt to send to China a "plebiscite representative in whom he can personally trust" to help "mediate" his relationship with Stilwell.[32] On August 10, Roosevelt informed Chiang that General Patrick J. Hurley would come to China as his personal representative, tasked with managing the Chiang-Stilwell controversy while mediating relations between the GMD and the CCP.[33] Zhou and his fellow CCP leaders saw the Hurley mission as both a challenge and an important opportunity. In an instruction Zhou drafted on behalf of the Party Center, he stressed that Hurley's coming, if properly handled, might promote the CCP's efforts "to seek American military support."[34]

Hurley was a general, not a diplomat. Before he came to China, he visited Moscow, where Vyacheslav Molotov, the Soviet foreign minister, told him that the CCP were "self-professed Communists" whom Moscow did not support. Instead, the Soviets were willing "to support US efforts to help unify China."[35] Hurley thus felt that if Chiang could develop a good relationship with Moscow, it would help settle the CCP question. When he met with Chiang on September 7, he told the generalissimo that Washington supported his efforts to unify China's military forces as well as to achieve political unification "on the basis of democracy."[36]

The rift between Chiang and Stilwell had by then spiraled out of control. Chiang met with Hurley on September 24, demanding that Stillwell be recalled and another commander "with the spirit of friendship and cooperation" be sent to China.[37] Hurley, seeing Chiang's demands as connected to his duty to mediate GMD-CCP relations, asked Chiang to allow him to meet with CCP representatives in Chongqing and to visit Yan'an. In his report to President Roosevelt, Hurley emphasized that the two countries' wartime cooperation lay at the center of America's China policy, and Chiang's role was of critical importance. Yet Roosevelt "was confronted by a choice between Chiang Kai-shek and Stilwell." In his opinion, Hurley told the President: "If you sustain Stilwell in his controversy, you will lose Chiang Kai-shek and possibly you will lose China with him." Hurley thus proposed that Stillwell be recalled if Chiang would agree to reforming China's government and military forces.[38] On October 18, Roosevelt announced that Stilwell would be recalled from China.[39]

Meanwhile, Hurley informed CCP representatives in Chongqing that Chiang had agreed to his plan to visit Yan'an. On October 21, Chiang handed Hurley a proposal to resolve the CCP question. Feeling that the proposal was "quite harsh," Hurley asked Chiang to revise it.[40] On November 7, Chiang gave Hurley an amended proposal, in which the term that the CCP should recognize Chiang as "commander of all Chinese troops" was changed, as Hurley requested, to one stipulating that "CCP troops obey and carry out" Chiang's orders on the condition that "CCP troops be reorganized by the Government."[41]

Hurley flew to Yan'an on November 7. Mao and Zhou welcomed him at the airport. Beginning the next day, the two CCP leaders held back-to-back talks with the American envoy. Zhou knew from his previous experience dealing with the Americans how to handle Hurley, a rookie diplomat. Along with Mao, he emphasized that the CCP favored democracy and nationalism, rather than Communism; that they were pursuing a political system following genuine democratic principles; and that they were also determined to cooperate with the Americans to defeat Japan.[42] Their words were music to Hurley's ears. After two days of meetings, Hurley reached a five-point agreement with Mao and Zhou. The terms of the agreement stipulated, among other conditions, that the CCP would join a coalition government, the GMD would carry out democratic reforms, and all Chinese troops would be placed under the command of a new united Military Council.[43] Hurley was quite satisfied with his achievement, as he believed "the basic principles are almost all ours." In particular, he believed that a coalition government was compatible with democratic principles and would not undermine Chiang's position.[44]

What Hurley failed to realize was that Mao and Zhou defined "coalition government" differently to him. In Hurley's view, Chiang's legitimacy and status would naturally be enhanced once the CCP committed to joining a coalition government led by Chiang. But for Mao and Zhou, a coalition government would check and balance Chiang's power, thus challenging the generalissimo's "one-party dictatorship." Zhou foresaw the difficulties that Hurley would face. He told other CCP leaders, "Chiang knows the difference between including us in his government and establishing a coalition government. But Hurley, confusing the two, thinks that Chiang will accept it. My prediction is that Chiang will inevitably demand that such an agreement be revised."[45]

Together, Zhou and Hurley arrived in Chongqing on November 10. As Zhou predicted, Chiang saw the five-point agreement as a serious challenge to his authority as China's paramount leader. Hurley, frustrated by Chiang's opposition to the agreement, reported the generalissimo's reaction to Roosevelt, who instructed him to further pressure Chiang to compromise with the CCP.[46] Chiang, while refusing to make any concessions, repeatedly warned the American general that he had fallen into the Communists' trap. Finally, Chiang persuaded Hurley to convey a new proposal to Zhou, according to which the CCP would give up command of its troops in exchange for joining the Military Council, and the GMD would retain its dominant position in the government.[47]

The next meeting between Hurley and Zhou ended in a heated quarrel. Hurley presented Chiang's counterproposal to Zhou, explaining that it should serve as the basis of further negotiation. Zhou immediately rebuffed him, claiming Chiang's apparent concession to allow the CCP to join the government and the Military Council was an empty gesture that would give the CCP no real power and ensure the continuation of the GMD's one-party dictatorship. He also sternly criticized Hurley for abandoning the agreement that the two of them had reached in Yan'an. Toward the end of the meeting, Zhou threatened to leave Chongqing at once.[48] On the margin of Zhou's telegram reporting the meeting, Mao commented that, if the CCP accepted Chiang's counterproposal, "the GMD's one-party reign will not change; the development of our troops will be restricted."[49] Mao's words encapsulated the key differences between the two parties.

Zhou also met with Chiang. The generalissimo argued that to preserve the dignity of the government, he had to reject the CCP's proposal to transform it. "The government is the cabinet, not the state. If it fails to fulfill its responsibility, why can it not be reorganized?" Zhou asked Chiang. The meeting ended in less than half an hour with the two failing to see eye to eye.

Zhou "was not as respectful and self-controlled as before," Chiang wrote in his diary, seemingly with a sigh.[50]

Afterward, Zhou considered "forcing Chiang to agree to a coalition government by demanding to establish Liberation Zone Councils" in CCP-controlled areas.[51] Mao instructed him not to submit this new proposal. Instead, he instructed Zhou to "adhere to the five-point agreement" and "return to Yan'an," while telling Hurley that he would "not return to Chongqing on the same plane," signaling him that his mediation effort was on the verge of failure.[52] Hurley, who had just been appointed US ambassador to China, was greatly embarrassed. He repeatedly urged the CCP to accept Chiang's counterproposal and "participate in the government." Zhou was unmoved. If the CCP was to join the government this way, he asserted, "it will become a mere guest, with no real voice and power."[53] Zhou flew back to Yan'an on December 7. In a cable to Hurley, he reiterated that unless Chiang's government was transformed, he would not return to Chongqing. Yet, in order not to completely cut off relations, Zhou also mentioned that the CCP would still consult with the Americans about concrete issues of military cooperation and keep in close contact with American military observers.[54]

Meanwhile, Mao and Zhou sought to bypass Hurley to establish direct connections with Washington. Mao even proposed a visit to Washington to meet with American leaders, especially President Roosevelt.[55] They never heard back from Washington.

Hurley still hoped to get Zhou back to Chongqing, but Zhou turned him down. The differences between the CCP and the GMD were great, Zhou stressed, and it was too early for him to return to Chongqing.[56] Hurley then tried another way. Shortly after New Year's Day in 1945, he cabled Mao and Zhou, suggesting that negotiations between the two parties resume in Yan'an and offering to attend the talks. Such a meeting would have no consequence, Mao replied.[57] But Hurley was persistent. He wrote Mao again, urging Zhou to return to Chongqing to resume the talks as "Chiang's attitude had changed."[58] This time, Zhou agreed, if only to avoid a deadlock with Hurley.

The resumed talks, as Zhou had predicted, quickly stalled. Zhou met with Chiang on February 13, in Hurley's presence. Chiang took a harsh stance. His party would only cede its power to a future National Assembly, he claimed, not to a gathering of various parties intent on "dividing the spoils." The coalition government favored by the CCP, Chiang contended, meant to "overthrow his government" and undermine his position as China's leader. Zhou rebutted

Chiang's points one by one, leading to a "heated quarrel" between them.[59] After the meeting, Zhou issued a statement criticizing Chiang's insistence on a one-party dictatorship, which he suggested had caused GMD-CCP negotiations to break down.[60] He flew back to Yan'an on February 16.

* * *

Underlying Zhou's tough approach toward Chiang and Hurley was the CCP leaders' belief that the international situation was turning decisively in their favor. As they observed the Soviet Red Army's rapid advance in Europe, Mao and his comrades expected to see the Soviets play a larger role in East Asian politics. They also believed that the Americans needed the CCP's support—logistical and otherwise—for their war against Japan. Early in February 1945, Stalin informed Mao that he would be meeting with Roosevelt and Churchill at Yalta. Mao judged that with the "strengthening of the Soviet Union's voice in determining important Eastern affairs, . . . both the United States and Chiang would be more willing to make political compromises with us."[61]

The Yalta Summit, however, did not develop as Mao had hoped. Stalin cut a deal with Roosevelt on China. He agreed to enter the war against Japan within two to three months of Germany's defeat and to recognize Chiang as China's sole leader while not supporting the CCP in China's internal conflict. In exchange, Roosevelt agreed to accept Outer Mongolia's independence and promised that all former Russian rights and privileges lost to Japan in the 1904–1905 Russo-Japanese War would be restored to the Soviet Union.[62]

Chiang pressed Roosevelt, successfully, to divulge the main contents of the Yalta agreement concerning China.[63] Though he was upset, Chiang still believed there was time for him to bargain with Stalin on the terms of a Chinese-Soviet treaty. On the Communist side, however, Stalin did not brief his CCP comrades about the deals he had made with the Americans, so Mao and Zhou knew nothing about them. They still thought that the Soviets' joining the war against Japan would greatly enhance the CCP's power at home. When, on April 4, Moscow announced that it would nullify its treaty of neutrality with Japan, Mao felt more confident that Moscow would soon declare war on Japan. In the future, he hoped, CCP troops would fight the Japanese in cooperation with the Soviets.[64]

Hurley had by then returned to the United States for a work report. On April 2, he announced at a press conference that the US government fully supported the Nationalist government and would not cooperate with "any armed warlords or armed political party."[65] Mao and his fellow CCP leaders were enraged, claiming that the CCP would "firmly oppose America's mistaken policy toward China," while "challenging those imperialists within the US government, such as Hurley."[66] By doing so, the CCP became entangled in the highly complex web of big power politics.

* * *

Meanwhile, both the GMD and the CCP were gearing up for a political and military showdown after the war. From Chiang's perspective, his leadership during the war should have strengthened the legitimacy of his position as China's supreme leader. Despite the GMD's military debacles, Chiang still believed that he should dominate China's political arena in the postwar era. At the GMD's Sixth Congress in May, Chiang announced, "Our main task today is to destroy the CCP. Japan is our enemy abroad, and the CCP is our enemy at home. Only by eliminating the Communists will our task be fulfilled."[67]

The CCP held its Seventh Congress around the same time. In his political report to the congress, Mao called on the CCP to become the dominant political force in China through cooperating with the Soviet Red Army. In analyzing the international situation facing the CCP, Mao pointed out that the United States, by "allying with Chiang to fight against Japan, rejecting the Soviet Union, and opposing Communism," was attempting to establish hegemony in East Asia. But Mao believed that support from the Soviet Union would play a more decisive role in the development of the Chinese revolution. "The international support to us surely will come," Mao promised. "If not, you may chop off my head!" Furthermore, the CCP's political influence and military strength had achieved rapid and unprecedented growth during the war years. Mao, with full confidence, announced, "This time we must take over China. We must be prepared for this prospect."[68]

Zhou gave a lengthy speech on the united front at the Seventh Congress. He narrated the CCP's relations with the GMD, emphasizing that the party must play a leadership role in the united front with a clear definition of enemies and friends. Zhou said that he had "committed many serious mistakes" in the past, which he would continuously work to correct.[69] By delivering such a speech, Zhou again demonstrated his embrace of the Rectification Movement while echoing the party's main task, which Mao had described as "striving to take over China."

Leaders of both the GMD and the CCP believed as their respective congresses got underway that the war against Japan would not end soon, and hence that there was enough time for them to prepare for a coming civil war. Zhou predicted in a June 16 telegram that "the War of Resistance will not reach its final stage this year, and dramatic changes are likely next year."[70] As late as August 4, a CCP internal directive still estimated that "the Japanese bandits will not be defeated until winter 1946." Accordingly, CCP leaders believed that they "would have about one year's time to get ready" for an "inevitable civil war" after Japan's defeat.[71]

Chiang's government began to negotiate with the Soviets after he learned of the deal concerning China that Roosevelt and Stalin had struck at Yalta. However, it was difficult for the two sides to agree on such issues as Outer Mongolia's independence and Soviet "rights and privileges" in China. Stalin remained committed to recognizing Chiang as China's sole leader and stopping its support for the CCP—two assurances he used as critical bargaining chips. However, in mid-July, negotiations in Moscow between T. V. Soong, Chiang's envoy, and Stalin were deadlocked.[72] Apparently, Chiang did not expect the war against Japan to end soon; therefore, he did not have a sense of urgency to cut a deal with Stalin.

* * *

The end of the war, however, came much faster than Mao, Zhou, and Chiang had predicted. On July 27, the Allies demanded Japan's unconditional surrender in the Potsdam Declaration. Then, after two American atomic bombs were dropped on Hiroshima and Nagasaki and the Soviet Red Army entered the war, Japan unconditionally surrendered to the Allies on August 15. Almost in an instant, China's war against Japan had come to a victorious end.

Mao was overjoyed by the news of the Soviet invasion of Northeast China (Manchuria). "It is such a huge delight that we now can fight the war in cooperation with the Soviet Army," he told Zhou and other comrades.[73] He ordered CCP regional commanders "with no hesitation, to occupy big and small cities and important transportation lines, seize weapons and resources, and go all out to mobilize and arm the masses."[74]

Chiang knew that the Nationalist government could ill afford the rapid expansion of CCP forces; hence, he immediately ordered Japanese troops not to surrender to them. Meanwhile, he decided to make major concessions in negotiations on a new treaty with the Soviets. By then, T. V. Soong had resumed talks with Stalin in Moscow. With great reluctance, Chiang made the painful decision to accept Outer Mongolia's independence, clearing the way to sign the Sino-Soviet treaty. Stalin, in return, promised not to support the CCP, and to channel Moscow's moral, military, and other material support to China "all to China's Central Government."[75] On August 14, the day that the Sino-Soviet treaty was signed, Chiang cabled Mao, inviting him to come to Chongqing to discuss "important international and domestic issues."[76]

Mao and the CCP were thus put in a very difficult position. Furthermore, Stalin repeatedly told Mao and his comrades that they must negotiate with Chiang to avoid a civil war in China. In an August 23 telegram, the Soviet dictator sternly warned his Chinese comrades, "China cannot afford a civil war. If a civil war were to erupt in China, the Chinese nation will be embarking on a path toward destruction."[77] From Stalin's perspective, this was fully compatible with the secret clauses on China in the Yalta accord. But Mao and his comrades saw it as a cruel betrayal. Moscow's support had been a vital part of their original plans to compete with Chiang for control of postwar China. With Stalin's refusal to provide such support, the CCP had no choice but to accept the Soviet leader's demands. On August 22, the CCP Center informed the whole party that "the Soviet Union, confined by the Sino-Soviet treaty and for the purpose of maintaining peace, is not in a position to support us. Chiang Kai-shek can use his legal position to accept the surrender of the enemy forces, and the Japanese and the puppet troops will hand big cities and vital transportation links to him." Mao and the CCP leadership thus decided to reexamine their perceptions and strategies, in order to "get prepared to deal with the changing situation in a long-term perspective."[78]

In considering Chiang's invitation, most CCP leaders preferred to send Zhou to Chongqing rather than Mao.[79] Zhou agreed. After all, one of his main tasks over the course of the war against Japan had been to deal with Chiang and the GMD, and he was in a good position to handle another mission to Chongqing. But Mao thought differently. He began a long speech at a Politburo meeting on August 23 by commenting on the Soviet position. "The war against Japan has ended, and the whole world, including Europe and the East, has entered an era of postwar peaceful reconstruction." Therefore, he reasoned, "if the Soviets were to assist us, the Americans certainly would support Chiang, and, as a result, international peace would suffer, and a world war might follow." The CCP thus had to adjust its strategies in accordance with the changing situation and "acknowledge that Chiang has the legitimate right to accept Japan's surrender" as well as "to take over big cities." The party, Mao suggested, while adopting "peace, democracy, unity" as its guiding principles for public representation, should not turn down Chiang's invitation. "I should go; this should not be delayed."[80]

Given his long history of dealing with the GMD, Zhou knew that Mao and others would give great weight to his opinions. He was willing to take up the challenging task of meeting with Chiang in Chongqing, he told them, and he was "not very certain" about whether it was the right time for Mao to go. He proposed to delay making a final decision on the matter that day, waiting instead until "after I have been there to engage in the negotiations with Chiang." He further warned that "we must also take into consideration that all this could just be a plot by Chiang."[81]

That day, Mao received another cable from Chiang, who welcomed Zhou to Chongqing. However, Chiang emphasized to Mao, "as for all the important questions that we face now, I hope to discuss them face to face with you." Clearly, he hoped that Mao and Zhou would come to Chongqing together.[82] Mao and Zhou knew that the meeting was to be a critical political showdown. The next day, Mao cabled Chiang, informing him that "Comrade (Zhou) Enlai will immediately come to Chongqing to see you, and I will come shortly afterward."[83]

Mao had obviously made up his mind by the time he talked with Zhou and several other Politburo members on August 25. He should go to Chongqing, he told his comrades, whom he persuaded to agree with him.[84] The next day, Mao chaired a full Politburo meeting, at which he stressed that, by his going to Chongqing, the CCP "will put all the political initiative in our hands." "Under four conditions," he elaborated, "namely our own strength after the end of the war, the hopes of the people of the whole country, Chiang's own difficulties, and international intervention, it is possible that this time we may resolve some problems."[85] Finally, the CCP Politburo approved Mao and Zhou's meeting with Chiang in Chongqing. Liu Shaoqi would be in charge of the party's routine decision-making during Mao's absence.[86]

Mao's decision, in retrospect, was an extraordinarily bold yet intelligent strategic move. By then, Chiang had invited him to negotiate, which Stalin also had urged him to do, giving Mao the initiative. Meanwhile, the Americans, as well as China's media and common people, were all watching to see if he was willing to negotiate. Mao's decision to go to Chongqing immediately placed his party in a hugely advantageous political position. Given the benefits associated with the mission, Mao felt it was worth taking the risk.

Mao arrived in Chongqing on August 28, accompanied by Zhou and Hurley. The negotiations between the two sides quickly began. Chiang's principles were rather straightforward: In addition to greatly scaling down the strength of CCP military forces and restricting the autonomy of CCP-controlled areas, he would make sure that political reforms should "not go beyond the legal tradition of the current government" and asserted that "military orders and

13.1 Zhou Enlai, Mao Zedong, Patrick J. Hurley, and Zhang Zhizhong, August 28, 1945. *Everett Collection / Alamy Stock Photo*

government decrees should be kept unified."[87] Mao's guidelines for the negotiations sharply contrasted with Chiang's. Among Mao's requirements were that representatives to the National Assembly be reelected, the existing decrees hindering "freedom enjoyed by the people" be nullified, political parties be granted legal status, and the elected local governments currently in existence in CCP-controlled "Liberated Zones" be recognized. Mao also mentioned that the CCP's troops should be reorganized into forty-eight divisions, to be commanded by CCP officers.[88] On September 3, Zhou presented to the GMD side a draft plan for discussion. Although it included no mention of a "coalition government," the plan stated that the CCP would "participate in the government" and "join the Military Council," provided that it could continue to control the Liberated Zones and command CCP troops.[89] If these terms were to be accepted, Chiang instantly understood, his emphasis on unifying China's political and military order would become an empty gesture.

Due to the two sides' dramatic differences, the negotiations were probably doomed to fail. Over the following six weeks, the two sides argued back and forth on many matters, but they simply could not make any progress on two key issues: the "democratization of politics" and the "nationalization of the military." As the talks wore on, the little mutual trust that might have existed between the two sides at the beginning was gradually exhausted. On September 27, Zhou proposed that the status of the Liberated Zones might be "temporarily maintained" pending a future settlement by the Political Consultative Conference. GMD representatives, with no better alternative, did not challenge Zhou's stopgap solution.[90]

Negotiations continued well into October, until both sides saw it as necessary to conclude them. They thus decided that on October 10, the official anniversary of the Republic of China's founding, the two sides would sign a "Summary of the Negotiations Between the Government and the CCP." The text was filled with empty rhetoric about "peace, democracy, unification, and unity." It also listed a series of yet-to-be-resolved issues which would be settled by a future Political Consultative Conference. The Chongqing negotiations, after six weeks, produced nothing more than this piece of paper. Zhou signed the summary on behalf of the CCP. The next day, Mao flew back to Yan'an, while Zhou stayed behind to deal with all remaining matters.

* * *

The civil war rapidly escalated as soon as Mao departed Chongqing. In fact, both sides had continued to fight each other even while the Chongqing negotiations took place. Shortly after Mao arrived at the wartime capital, the CCP Center ordered Communist troops in different regions to "continue the offensive from now on, and make the utmost effort to control as much territory as possible in North and Central China."[91] The party leadership decided to dispatch large numbers of cadres and troops to Northeast China to transform the region into a strategic base for the CCP. Mao fully knew that by coming to Chongqing he had seized the political initiative. He specifically instructed CCP military commanders to not be scared by the GMD troops, and to "resolutely and thoroughly wipe them out in the name of self-defense" if "our troops are in a position to win in battles." He added, "The better you fight, the safer I am in Chongqing."[92]

Internationally, this period witnessed the dramatic escalation of tensions between Washington and Moscow in both Europe and Northeast Asia. Stalin thus found it necessary to adopt a tougher policy toward the United States and Chiang's government in China. Lieutenant Colonel Belunosov, a representative of Marshal Rodion Malinovsky, commander of the Soviet forces in the Far East, arrived at Yan'an in mid-September. He told CCP leaders that so long as the party's troops in the Northeast did not enter big cities there, and provided that they did not "let the American and Nationalist side know about this," the Soviets would allow them to enter the Northeast unopposed. There, CCP troops could occupy the countryside and some small and medium-sized cities. When the Soviet troops withdrew from the Northeast, they would not hand the areas they had occupied over to the GMD but would "let the Chinese solve the matter by themselves."[93]

The CCP leadership hence decided on September 19 to adopt a grand strategy of "maintaining a defensive posture in the South while waging offensives in the North" for its confrontation with the GMD.[94] After Mao returned to Yan'an, the CCP leadership further decided to block GMD troops from entering the Northeast, while "striving to place the whole region under the CCP's control."[95] Mao calculated that the CCP should first win battles in the Northeast and strengthen its position there. After six months, if possible and necessary, they would face off with Chiang and the GMD in a showdown at the start of the Political Consultative Conference.

The escalation of hostilities between the CCP and the GMD presented President Harry Truman with a huge dilemma. On the one hand, it was preferable for the United States to support Chiang and the Nationalist government in order to check the expansion of Soviet influence in East Asia and maintain stability in China. On the other hand, America risked becoming directly involved in China's civil war or even provoking a confrontation with the Soviets if it intervened in China. After weighing the pros and cons, Truman announced on December 15 that the United States would continue to support the Nationalist government but would not use American military forces to intervene in China's internal affairs. Hurley had by then resigned his ambassadorship. Truman decided to send General George Marshall as his special envoy to China to mediate the conflict between the two Chinese adversaries.[96]

Mao's immediate reaction was that Marshall had come to China for the sake of "supporting Chiang, guarding against the Soviet Union, and suppressing the CCP."[97] But Zhou interpreted Marshall's appointment differently. It was most likely under Zhou's influence that, on December 19, the CCP Center issued an internal instruction, stating that Truman's statement meant that "the United States has decided not to directly intervene in the Chinese civil war, or to support Chiang's attempt to use force to unify China, but to support China's peaceful unification."[98]

Zhou welcomed Marshall at Chongqing Airport on December 22. They met the next day. "President Truman's statement is a very good one," Zhou told Marshall. "We support many of the main points in the statement." "There is much that we may learn from American democracy," he emphasized, "including the spirit of Washington's devotion to national independence, Lincoln's 'of the people, by the people, for the people' statement, and Roosevelt's 'four freedoms,' and we may also learn from America's agricultural reforms and industrialization."[99]

Zhou quickly realized that unlike Hurley, Marshall genuinely hoped to successfully mediate the CCP-GMD dispute.[100] Thus, he was willing to try his best to be impartial in dealing with the differences between China's two contending parties. On his part, Marshall thought Zhou an "honest and capable" counterpart in the negotiations.[101] Marshall and Zhou quickly established a basic level of mutual trust. One time, Zhou fell asleep in his seat while aboard Marshall's plane for a trip. When he disembarked from the plane, he left behind a notebook containing information about several top CCP spies. Zhou at once reported this "huge accident" to Mao along with "serious self-criticism." He formulated plans for the emergency evacuation of the agents, but he did not order them to act immediately. His instinct told him that Marshall, an "old-fashioned gentleman," was unlikely to hand the information to the GMD. Zhou's intuition proved correct. Within a few hours, Marshall sent a staff member to personally deliver Zhou a sealed envelope containing his lost notebook. None of Zhou's agents was exposed.[102]

Marshall planned to carry out his mediation task in three steps. The first would be to bring about a cease-fire between the two sides. The second would be to convene a Political Consultative Conference. Third, Marshall would see to it that troops were fully reorganized. It seemed that the plan harmonized with Zhou's stand that government reform should be pursued before military reorganization.

A three-person group including Marshall, who convened it; Zhou, acting as the chief CCP delegate; and Zhang Qun (later Zhang Zhizhong), serving as the GMD representative, was formed in late December to mediate "a cease-fire and all related issues." Marshall had already drafted a cease-fire agreement, according to which "all troops should stay where they have been" once the nationwide cease-fire took effect.[103] Zhou supported the draft agreement at once. But the two Chinese sides still differed on troop deployment in the Northeast. With Marshall mediating the disagreement, Zhou and Zhang Qun finally decided to let him save face, and on January 10, 1946, a truce agreement was signed.

Zhou was delighted. Other CCP leaders, including Liu Shaoqi, were also happy with the agreement. Mao agreed to let the party announce in his name that "China's new phase of peace and democracy has now begun."[104] The Political Consultative Conference held its first meeting on the same day that the truce was signed. Yet the two sides found it extremely difficult to agree on a concrete agenda for the conference. At the core of their disagreement lay the issue of reforming the government, which Chiang had been extremely reluctant to discuss. On January 14, the GMD announced a new "reform plan": additional members would be added to the Government Committee, but these added members would be nominated by Chiang, who would keep his veto power over the committee's decisions; and the GMD would still hold a majority in the committee.[105]

Zhou immediately dismissed the GMD's proposal as no more than an admission of Chiang's pursuit of one-party rule, and he described Chiang's reformist rhetoric as totally disingenuous. To Zhou's satisfaction, representatives from other parties also criticized the plan. Marshall did not like it either. He privately sent Chiang an alternative plan to reorganize the government, according to which a Provisional Governing Committee would be established, but would not be controlled by a GMD majority. Instead, all resolutions—which Chiang could not veto—would require a two-thirds majority to pass. Chiang regarded Marshall's plan as ridiculous, as Marshall, "with no understanding of our domestic situation or the CCP's plots," had proposed "what even the Communists dare not to raise" and thus had "created a very big mess."[106] Nonetheless, Chiang would not split with Marshall, in order to avoid another "Stilwell incident."[107] Although Marshall did not make his draft public, the plan still put pressure on Chiang to come up with several key concessions. In particular, he agreed to appoint only twenty GMD members to the Government Council, allowing the other twenty to be named by the CCP and other parties without the GMD's approval. It seemed that the door to a successful Political Consultative Conference had been reopened.

* * *

In retrospect, this was the most glorious and hopeful moment of Marshall's mission in China. On January 27, Zhou flew back to Yan'an to give a progress report on Marshall's mediation efforts. He emphasized at a meeting of top CCP leaders the next day that the question of the CCP-controlled Liberated Zones would now be resolved as a "normal issue of local autonomy"; the question of nationalizing the military would be settled in parallel with the process of political democratization; and furthermore, the CCP would be guaranteed veto power once the government was reformed.[108] Liu Shaoqi endorsed Zhou's work on behalf of the Party Center. In particular, Liu mentioned that although the CCP had made huge concessions on the nationalization of all troops, its doing so would stimulate the democratic movement around the country. Therefore, the concessions were worth it. All CCP leaders attending the meeting echoed Liu's praise of Zhou's achievement.[109] Mao, who was on a sick leave, missed the meeting, and he was thus not among those who lauded Zhou.

Excited, Zhou flew back to Chongqing, bringing Mao's letter of greetings to Marshall. On the evening of January 31, the Political Consultative Conference passed five resolutions and erupted in a standing ovation over the passage. Another lengthy standing ovation followed Chiang's concluding remarks endorsing these resolutions. The Marshall mission seemed to have been hugely successful.

The CCP leadership now appeared to be genuinely intent on pursuing political power through the parliament. The CCP Center issued an intraparty announcement that China, as indicated by the five resolutions adopted at the Political Consultative Conference, "will soon begin a new phase characterized by peace and democracy." Therefore, "the struggles to carry out the Chinese revolution will also change from the current form of violent ones to nonviolent struggles by mobilizing unarmed masses and through the parliament." The party "thus will stop directly leading the army . . . and will join the government."[110] Liu was quite supportive of this new line, and Zhou embraced it zealously. Other party leaders were also generally enthusiastic about the change of course.

Mao remained suspicious of the new emphasis on nonviolent struggle and parliamentary politics, however. On February 12, the CCP Central Secretariat met to discuss the issue of troop reorganization. The chairman, who had not yet fully recovered from his illness, attended the meeting, questioning whether China would go down "a French-style parliamentary path." Further, he warned that both the Americans and Chiang wanted to use the policy of "unifying troops" as a means to eliminate the Communists: "We must not fall into such a trap, and not be wiped out." He loudly reminded his colleagues that "China is not France!" Mao's remarks thus had the effect of dumping a bucket of cold water on his comrades' heads. "Yes, there is danger in exchanging the nationalization of troops for the democratization of the country," Liu acknowledged. "The prospect of democratization is far from certain."[111]

Soon, as Mao had predicted, the truce between the GMD and the CCP was broken again. On February 25, Zhou, Zhang Zhizhong, and Marshall signed a plan on the rectification of the army as a step toward nationalizing China's military forces. On its face, the plan represented a settlement of this contentious issue. In reality, however, when the two sides tried to implement the agreement, they immediately hit another impasse. Zhou assessed the problem facing the two sides as follows: "Although the plan is disadvantageous to us, it is not acceptable to Chiang either. This is why he immediately tried to use such means as establishing a Ministry of Defense, and changing the unit codes of an army to that of a division to attempt to bypass the restrictions the plan will impose on him."[112] In fact, this was exactly what the Communists themselves were doing. Just as the military rectification was about to begin, the CCP Center issued an order to the whole party: "In addition to changing half of our main force to local guardian units, we should also keep a portion (about one third) of our best officers, hiding them in various liberated zones without presenting them for appointment by the GMD."[113] Not surprisingly, efforts aimed at "reorganizing and nationalizing troops" were destined to fail.

Unsurprisingly, fierce fighting again broke out between the two sides, especially in the Northeast. The situation was made more complicated by the rapid deterioration of US-Soviet relations. In February 1946, Washington firmly opposed negotiations between Moscow and Nanjing on economic cooperation in the Northeast.[114] Meanwhile, the Americans intentionally leaked the secret agreements on China that Roosevelt and Stalin had reached at Yalta, which included terms that undermined Chinese sovereignty. Such a revelation immediately triggered a wave of anti-Soviet sentiment among Chinese intellectuals, followed by a series of anti-Soviet demonstrations and protests. The Soviets quickly implemented a tit-for-tat approach to deal with the situation. In early March, Moscow suddenly announced that Soviet troops would leave the Northeast. At the same time, the Soviet command there secretly informed the CCP of the date that Soviet troops would evacuate Shenyang and several other cities, urging the CCP to take control of the cities after the Soviets left. The Soviets also told their Chinese comrades that CCP troops should feel free to act at will in areas they took control of.[115]

These developments were undoubtedly good news for the CCP on the eve of a decisive showdown with the GMD in the Northeast. The CCP leadership immediately decided to go all out to gain control of Changchun and Harbin, two large cities located in central and northern Manchuria, as well as the entire Changchun Railway, to prevent the GMD troops from entering the region.[116]

Chiang knew full well that if the Communists were to control the vast areas north of Shenyang, they would gain a powerful strategic base from which to fight the GMD. He thus ordered GMD troops to quickly advance northward and prevent the Communists from taking over the central and northern regions of the Northeast after the withdrawal of Soviet troops. Meanwhile, CCP troops also gathered to stop the GMD forces. The two sides both found that the city of Siping was strategically critical. In early April, Chiang amassed a large force to attack Siping, while Lin Biao, the CCP commander in the Northeast, also deployed large forces there. A showdown between the two sides followed.

CCP leaders still hoped that Zhou's negotiations with Marshall might stop or at least delay the GMD troops' attack on Siping. Meanwhile, CCP troops occupied Changchun, near Siping, after the Soviets left the city. Marshall proposed that the CCP might give up Changchun in exchange for the GMD delaying its attack on Siping. However, neither party would listen to him. Facing a deadlock, Marshall informed Zhou that he had "exhausted my resource in an effort to compromise [between] the various positions" between the CCP and the GMD, and that he thus would stop his mediation on the Northeast.[117] This would mark the beginning of the end of his China mission.

After the end of negotiations, bloody fighting between the two sides in Siping went on for nearly a month. Finally, CCP troops suffered a shortage of supplies and reinforcements. On May 18, Lin Biao ordered CCP troops to give up on Siping; Changchun was now exposed to the GMD advance. Zhou immediately approached Marshall, proposing that if the GMD was willing to accept a truce in the Northeast, the CCP would hand it Changchun. However, before he and Marshall could work out a deal, Changchun had already fallen to GMD forces. Chiang then ordered his troops to continue their assault on the Northeast. In response, Mao ordered CCP troops south of the Great Wall to launch revenge offensives against GMD forces there. Chiang now realized that, by concentrating too much on the Northeast, he had probably overextended his fronts. As the civil war engulfed half of China, the "new phase of peace and democracy" evaporated.

Marshall refused to abandon his mediation efforts, though, and he hoped that Zhou would be cooperative. Marshall persuaded the GMD and CCP to reach several temporary cease-fire agreements. During one truce that would end on June 15, the GMD again raised the issue of the "rectification of the troops." When Zhou read its statement, he commented, "This is complete nonsense. Their intention for a total war is crystal clear."[118] Not surprisingly, large-scale fighting erupted between the two sides days before the June 15 truce expired.

13.2 Zhou Enlai and Deng Yingchao in Nanjing, 1946.
Historic Collection / Alamy

Chiang called Zhou to a meeting on July 2. The atmosphere of the meeting was extremely tense. Chiang demanded that CCP troops surrender to the GMD a series of cities, including Chengde, Andong, areas along a main railway line in Shandong, and the northern part of Jiangsu. Otherwise, Chiang said, "there is no need to continue the discussion." Zhou firmly rejected Chiang's demand and, as Chiang described it in his diary, "left the room in a rather cross and crusty mood." "A bandit like him is even worse than an animal," Chiang wrote.[119] This was the last time Zhou and Chiang met face to face. They would never see each other again.

The next day, Chiang announced—without consulting other parties—that the National Assembly would begin on November 12. This was a death sentence for GMD-CCP negotiations. Although Marshall would stay in China until January 1947, his mediation efforts had already failed. Zhou knew that there was nothing he could do to make the negotiations productive. He had not returned to Yan'an earlier largely to create the impression among the public that the CCP had strived for peace to the bitter end. As October turned to November, the civil war had spread to all areas north of the Yangzi River, and GMD troops were even preparing to attack Yan'an. Zhou knew that the time had come for him to leave Nanjing. On November 16, he called a press conference, at which he declared that Chiang should bear full responsibility for sparking the civil war, and that the CCP would "work together with the Chinese people and all genuine democratic parties to strive for genuine peace and democracy."[120]

Zhou fully understood that the CCP had in fact resolved to go all out to fight and win the civil war. The next day, Zhou wrote a letter to his old friend Guo Moruo, predicting that "the future will be decided on the battlefield."[121] Zhou and Deng Yingchao flew from Nanjing to Yan'an, in a plane provided by Marshall, on November 19, 1946.

14

THE CIVIL WAR

1946–1949

Autumn 1946 saw China engulfed in a bloody civil war.

Zhou Enlai met with Mao and Liu Shaoqi on November 21, two days after he returned to Yan'an. The chairman reiterated the claim he had made at the CCP's Seventh Congress—that civil war in China was inevitable.[1] Mao was implicitly reminding Liu and Zhou that they had been wrong about the "new phase of peace and democracy" they had favored in early 1946, and he had been right. Zhou reported on his negotiations with Chiang and Marshall: "In recent years, our party's calls for peace, democracy, unity and independence have won the people's support, and Chiang's dictatorship and the Americans' true intention to monopolize the occupation of China have been fully exposed." He believed that the party should continue to advocate publicly for democracy, peace and independence, while "striving to wage armed struggles." Although Chiang was eager to destroy the CCP, Zhou observed, his policies and strategies were seriously flawed. As Chiang had "no plans beyond six months," Zhou argued, his commanders had "little confidence in a prolonged war," and "pessimism and disgust for war" prevailed among his lower-level officers. Therefore, Zhou stressed, the CCP could fight the war and win it.[2]

Zhou's comments on the prospects of the war echoed exactly what Mao had long told the whole party. Delighted, the chairman immediately praised Zhou for his work in GMD-controlled areas, efforts that allowed the CCP "to seize the banners of peace and democracy while isolating Chiang." The CCP, Mao proclaimed, could defeat the GMD "in three to five years; otherwise, in ten to fifteen years at the most."[3]

Mao's optimistic outlook was undergirded by his understanding of the international situation that the CCP faced. Although he, like Zhou and Liu, was concerned about "whether the American reactionaries will intervene on Chiang's behalf," he saw favorable conditions that might prevent Washington from doing so. "The Soviet Union is on the rise and America is in decline," he observed. In two years, he asserted, "the Soviet Union will recover, Britain and France will turn left, and America will approach a crisis." He thus concluded that "if we can survive the next year, the situation will improve the year after next."[4] While much of Mao's analysis about Western countries would later prove wildly inaccurate, the Americans never did intervene in the Chinese civil war.

On the conceptual level, Mao's outlook on the international situation reflected his distinctive thesis of the "intermediate zone." According to Mao, in the postwar world, there existed a vast unaffiliated zone between the United States and the Soviet Union, and the US imperialists could not attack the Soviet Union until they had conquered that zone. He also believed that the "principal contradiction" in the world, rather than being the American-Soviet confrontation, was that which manifested itself in the struggles between peoples in the intermediate zone—especially in China—and the "reactionary American ruling class."[5] Apparent in the chairman's assertion was his belief that the CCP would play a central role in bridging the world revolution and the global trend of decolonization. Zhou embraced the Maoist "intermediate zone" thesis and urged every party member to "carefully study" the idea and apply it to their analysis of the world situation.[6]

These ideas of Mao's were totally unknown to Chiang. Yet the generalissimo believed he could "smash the Communists militarily in six months." Indeed, just as Mao and Chiang had expected, 1947 became the year that would determine the orientation, or even the result, of the civil war. But it was Chiang's troops who would be badly beaten, as the war turned decisively in the CCP's favor.

At first glance, however, Chiang seemed to hold the upper hand in the war in early 1947. His forces were far greater in number, substantially better equipped, and included an air force and a navy, both of which the CCP lacked; they also controlled almost all of China's big cities and major transportation lines. In comparison, the Communists were under pressure from superior GMD forces on every front. The fiercest fighting occurred in Manchuria, a region that neither side could afford to lose. There, as early as

May 1946, the Communists had lost Changchun after having abandoned strategically important Siping. GMD offensives extended even to Harbin, located in the far north of Manchuria. Elsewhere in China, CCP troops were all on the defensive. In mid-October 1946, Chiang's troops occupied the Communist stronghold of Zhangjiakou in northern China, an event that was widely regarded as the CCP's worst military defeat.

Even Shaanbei, where the CCP had situated its headquarters for the last decade, became a Nationalist target. In February 1947, Chiang decided to attack and occupy Yan'an for both political and military reasons. In the international context, he knew that the foreign ministers from Washington, Moscow, London, and Paris were planning to meet in March, and that they "would possibly discuss China." By occupying Yan'an, Chiang hoped to make Stalin feel it undesirable to continue supporting the CCP.[7] Militarily, Chiang had by then fallen short of his original goal of crushing the Communists in six months. Concerned that the war might shift in the CCP's favor, he sought to use the capture of Yan'an to boost his troops' morale.

Although Chiang's order to attack Yan'an was "absolutely confidential," Zhou, the spymaster, learned of it almost immediately through Xiong Xianghui, the mole he had strategically planted next to Hu Zongnan, the general in charge of Chiang's operation to attack Yan'an.[8] Mao and the CCP leadership had long considered abandoning Yan'an if necessary; now, they quickly decided to evacuate the red capital.[9] On March 18, Mao, Zhou, and the CCP Center left Yan'an, which fell to GMD troops the next day.

Chiang was overjoyed by the destruction of the "old nest of the Communist bandits."[10] Nanjing was soaked in an atmosphere of celebration. International observers generally took the fall of Yan'an as evidence that Chiang was winning the civil war. Stalin in faraway Moscow even invited the chairman to take refuge in the Soviet Union for the sake of his safety.[11] In hindsight, however, the implications of Yan'an's capture were much more complicated.

• • •

After they left Yan'an, the CCP leaders decided to divide themselves into two groups. One, led by Mao, Zhou, and Ren Bishi, would stay in Shaanbei. The other, headed by Liu and Zhu De, would cross the Yellow River and form a Central Work Committee in northwestern Shanxi to "carry out the work assigned by the Party Center."[12] This was an extremely important arrangement for Zhou. Since his time at the Yangzi River Bureau back in 1938, Zhou had seldom been directly involved in core strategy and policy-making at the Party Center. His power and influence in the party leadership had declined in the wake of the Yan'an Rectification Movement. This new arrangement, however, allowed him to work closely with Mao. In August 1947, he would be formally named acting chief of staff of the CMC.[13] In addition to making key military decisions, he would oversee the implementation of CCP strategies and policies. He would help draft most of Mao's war telegrams and dispatch them in Mao's name. Consequently, Zhou consolidated his powerful position within the CCP.

Mao and Zhou decided to stay in Shaanbei out of strategic and tactical considerations. Zhou explained that by remaining there, "we will attract Hu Zongnan's main force to Shaanbei, thus allowing other liberated zones to eliminate more enemies."[14] Further, the Communists had deep roots in Shaanbei after having ruled the region for over a decade. In Mao's words, "This is an area of mountainous terrain, where we have a good mass base and plenty of maneuvering space, so our security is guaranteed."[15] Indeed, Hu's units had on several occasions come close to Mao and Zhou's location after the occupation of Yan'an, but they were never able to pinpoint the exact whereabouts of the two "Communist bandit chieftains."

In addition to Xiong, Zhou and his intelligence organs had planted many other top-level agents next to key figures in the enemy camp over the years. Among them were Guo Ruhuai, chief of operations in Chiang's Ministry of Defense; Jia Yibing, a close associate of Chiang Ching-kuo; Han Liancheng, commander of the Forty-Sixth Army; Zhang Kexia, deputy commander of the Thirty-Third Army Corps; Yan Youwen, an assistant to General Fu Zuoyi, commander of GMD forces in northern China; and Wu Shi, deputy minister of defense (who was later exposed after moving to Taiwan and executed at Chiang's orders). These agents were swords with which Zhou cut deeply into Chiang's political and military machine.

Zhou also had support from a superb intelligence staff with an outstanding command of intelligence details. Shortly after evacuating Yan'an, Zhou learned that the GMD intelligence services possessed the technology to detect the CCP's radio activity and identify the location of its personnel. He immediately ordered the Party Center's radio transmitters to cease operations for three days.[16] Simultaneously, on behalf of the CMC, he instructed all People's Liberation Army (PLA) commanders "not to use radios to issue orders in prebattle deployment and during operations." Instead, they were to "use small transmitters, sending telegrams to large radio stations—which should be moved elsewhere—to dispatch them, so as to confuse the enemy."[17] Suddenly, the signals from the large radio stations at the CCP Center ceased, making the GMD's advanced signal tracking technology useless for monitoring Mao's and Zhou's movements.

Another major task for Zhou was to reorganize the CCP's lines of military command and the assignments of its intelligence personnel. To that end, he crossed the Yellow River and set out for northwestern Shanxi in late March 1947. After two weeks of close collaboration with Liu and the Central Work Committee there, he completed the job. On April 11, Zhou telegraphed Liu and others on behalf of the Party Center, informing them that the staff at the CMC headquarters would be divided into three groups: one staying in northwestern Shanxi; one moving to the Taihang Mountains; and one, composed of personnel at the central intelligence services, returning to Shaanbei with him and working under his direct supervision.[18] With this organizational reshuffling, Zhou strengthened his position in the CCP's military command while further enhancing his dominant role in its intelligence network.

* * *

Mao and Zhou treated the war from the outset as a contest of the two combating sides' political strategies. In their assessment, Chiang was "without a clearly defined political line" and "neither wanted to practice democracy nor dared to exert a dictatorship."[19] They thus saw an opportunity to seize the banners of "democracy" and "nationalism." Yet this was no easy task at the beginning. The Chinese people wanted peace after Japan's surrender. A civil war waged by the CCP against the government was a bad thing for many everyday Chinese.

In February 1946, Washington leaked the contents of the secret deals concerning China it had struck with Moscow in the Yalta accords. The revelation immediately triggered large-scale anti-Soviet protests in major Chinese cities. Zhou and his comrades were facing a dilemma: they certainly would not allow the protests to implicate the CCP; but they could not openly criticize the secret deals worked out at Yalta that involved the Soviets. Zhou, who was still in Chongqing at the time, contended that "patriotic actions should not be mixed up with xenophobia" in a bid to shield the CCP from the anti-Soviet furor. Zhou also perceived the difficult situation that Chiang was in; after all, it was Chiang's government that had signed the treaty with Moscow. Zhou demanded that Chiang suppress the protests, so that "a democratic order will be guaranteed."[20] The anti-Soviet protests were quelled after a few short weeks without doing much damage to the CCP.

Yet Zhou was not one to be satisfied by merely holding the party's political ground. When the time was right, he would take the offensive. Shortly after he returned to Yan'an in November 1946, he took over the party's Department of Urban Works, which was in charge of "all party activities in Chiang-controlled areas."[21] In late December 1946, he received a report from CCP organs in Beiping that, on December 24, Shen Chong, a female student at Peking University, had been raped by two American Marines on her way to a movie. Media coverage of the incident instantly triggered a massive public outcry, as students in Beiping, Shanghai, and other cities poured into the streets to protest the Americans' sexual assault of Shen. The uproar, Zhou observed, provided the CCP with a critical political opportunity. In an intra-party document issued on December 31, he instructed party organs in Beiping and other cities to actively participate in demonstrations and "demand a public trial of the American criminals by a Chinese court." Moreover, Zhou continued, the party organs should call for the "withdrawal of all American troops from China; opposition to America's interference in China's internal affairs; (opposition to) its sale of ammunition and providing of loans to the GMD to fight the civil war; and (demanding) the abolition of the Chinese-American treaty of commerce and the boycotting of American goods," to "lead the mass movement in the direction of isolating America and Chiang and opposing America's colonization of China."[22]

Zhou regarded the eruption and subsequent persistence of "anti-Chiang and anti-American" protests in GMD-controlled areas as having opened a "second battlefield" in the civil war.[23] To help the movement build momentum, Zhou ordered CCP organs in GMD-controlled areas to "expand propaganda, avoid frontal confrontations with the authorities, strive to attract the middle elements, and use legal means . . . to establish a broad united front" in support of the demonstrations.[24] Under Zhou's direction, the thrust of the "people's movement" shifted from such large themes as "opposing America and opposing Chiang" to more down-to-earth ones, such as "opposing civil war" and "opposing hunger." Later, Zhou articulated the party's political goals as "forming a democratic coalition government, and establishing a new China of peace, independence, and democracy."[25] In so doing, Zhou and the CCP forced Chiang and the Nationalist government to go on the defensive on both the political and moral fronts.

• • •

In the final analysis, though, Zhou and his fellow CCP leaders acutely understood that the civil war was a bloody military showdown, the result of which would ultimately be determined on the battlefield. The state of the war in early 1947 was far more complicated than the apparent "strong GMD and weak CCP" situation would suggest. From the beginning of the war, Mao, Zhou, and the CCP leadership had decided not to take as their primary operational goals the capture and consolidation of territory. Rather, they saw it as more desirable to mobilize Communist troops for a mobile war, in order to strike an isolated enemy and "defeat the enemy units one by one."[26] The situation, Mao reasoned, demanded that the Communists "temporarily give up a few places, a few cities. . . . Otherwise, the final victory will not be achieved."[27] Zhou was well acquainted with Mao's military thought. In the orders he gave to CCP troops on behalf of the CMC, Zhou frequently stressed that in fighting the enemy, it was essential to "find its weak spots while amassing our own forces to eliminate the enemy through constant mobile warfare."[28]

Chiang's military strategy, by contrast, emphasized "occupying important sites and controlling key transportation lines."[29] His troops thus took it as a top priority to capture cities, including Yan'an. Whenever GMD armies took a city, though, they eliminated relatively few Communist troops and had to leave more of their own forces behind to defend their gains. Consequently, Chiang's troops and the supply lines on which they depended became overextended, as Mao and Zhou had hoped. The Communists tactfully combined dramatic retreats with bold advances in accordance with the changing situation on the ground. Though they were outnumbered by the enemy, the Communists were often able to focus a superior force at the enemy's weak spots and eliminate isolated enemy units.

Mao and Zhou maximized the Communists' strategic advantage by making full use of the PLA's highly disciplined command structure. After Mao gained control over military decision-making power in the CCP, he gave his utmost attention to balancing relations between commanders of different backgrounds, establishing the ironclad rule that "all actions must be done in accordance with orders from the Party Center." Zhou was a master of coordinating different forces. As chief of staff in the CMC, he had repeatedly ordered CCP troops (though often inferior in numbers and equipment) to create a "fist" formation and overwhelm the enemy at specific points on the battlefield. In comparison, Chiang's armies were plagued by divisions between Chiang's own faction and those aligned with various other strongmen, impairing Chiang's ability to implement strategy and deploy troops. Indeed, Chiang often found it difficult to have his orders be properly conveyed, let alone effectively carried out. Consequently, Chiang's troops were repeatedly defeated on the battlefield.

* * *

Mao and Zhou fully understood that the civil war in China was also a contest of the two sides' ability to mobilize the Chinese public. In this respect, too, they held the upper hand. Despite Chiang's many advantages, Mao told his comrades in May 1946, before the outbreak of full-scale civil war, "he has huge weaknesses, as he cannot resolve the land problem."[30] Mao and the CCP thus strove to "mobilize the masses to seize land from landlords" to realize the vision that "all those who plough should have their own land" and lay the groundwork for a "fundamental transformation of land ownership." In September 1947, the CCP Center issued an "Outline of the Chinese Land Law," in which it reemphasized the principle of distributing "land to the tillers" and "abolishing the land ownership of all landlords."[31] Then, it used the slogan of "defending the fruits of land reform" to mobilize millions of "liberated peasants" to join the PLA, which greatly enhanced the Communists' military strength and prospects in the war.

In fact, "land to the tillers" had long been a Nationalist slogan, and the idea was an integral part of Sun Yat-sen's political vision. When Chiang learned of the CCP's efforts to mobilize the peasantry through land reform, he knew that it was a promising strategy. Therefore, he repeatedly tried to revise the Nationalist government's 1930 Land Law, in order to ensure that "the land system will be reformed." Unlike the CCP, however, the GMD lacked the organizational power to carry out such a policy, and its officials either did not know about or were unwilling to carry out land reform. As a result, none of Chiang's land reform plans ever left the page. As Chiang's troops lacked the capacity for mobilization, they inevitably performed poorly in battle.

* * *

By mid-1947, Mao and Zhou saw that the tide of the war had begun to turn in their favor. GMD offensives had been repulsed almost everywhere. March saw GMD troops occupy Yan'an in Shaanbei, but this "shining moment" was short lived. Within a few months of their having captured the former red capital, Hu Zongnan's units suffered several major defeats at the hands of the Communists. The same story happened elsewhere, including in the Northeast, northern China, and eastern China. At the PLA headquarters, report after report came to Zhou's desk from every battleground of the war, each proclaiming a Communist victory. Chiang's experience was different. He found that "the state of the war in the Northeast and northern China is extremely worrisome. . . . many of our comrades have lost confidence, showing signs of reluctance and fear."[32] In late July 1947, Zhou reported to a CCP leadership meeting that "the enemy's offensives have reached their limit." As for the Communists' response, Zhou proposed, "We must carry out the strategy of bringing the war to the enemy's rear. . . . and thoroughly destroy Chiang's reactionary rule."[33]

Reports of victory from every front continued to flow to Mao and Zhou during the remainder of 1947. At a late-December meeting of top party leaders and PLA commanders in the small Shaanbei village of Yangjiagou, Mao confidently announced, "The war has reached a turning point. For the first time in two decades, our troops have surpassed the GMD in the balance of forces."[34] Zhou echoed Mao in his briefing on the military situation: "In the second half of the year, without exception, we have held the initiative on all fronts." As a result, Zhou told his comrades, wholly one-third of the country's territory and population lay within the CCP's "Liberated Zones."[35] At another meeting of top party leaders a few days later, Zhou stated, "We should be confident that we will defeat Chiang and win nationwide victory in three to five years."[36]

Just as Mao and Zhou had expected, the PLA continued to carry out successful offensives from the start of 1948. Chiang even lamented in his diary that "everything is in turmoil and everywhere is in danger, as if an Armageddon could come at any time."[37] On April 21, the PLA recaptured Yan'an, and Chiang's troops were soon forced to abandon Shaanbei. Mao and Zhou had not left Shaanbei since they evacuated Yan'an one year earlier. But rather than return to Yan'an, on March 23, 1948, they crossed the Yellow River and entered Shanxi. In early May, they arrived at the village of Xibaipo in Pingshan County, Hebei Province; there, they joined up with the Central Work Committee headed by Liu Shaoqi. Mao, Zhou, and the CCP Center would call this small village home for the next six months.

Apart from their military defeats, Chiang and the Nationalist government faced precipitously deteriorating political conditions. To shore up support for his government, in late March, Chiang ordered that the National Constitutional Assembly convene. Zhou and the CCP immediately decried Chiang as "an absolute dictator." Zhou also leveraged all of his connections with those "parties in the middle," urging them not to attend the assembly. Thanks to Zhou's efforts, the assembly was attended only by two small parties and the GMD. Meanwhile, ugly internal battles raged within the GMD ranks, threatening to tear the party asunder. Chiang, as expected, was elected president. However, in the vote for vice president, Sun Ke, Sun Yat-sen's son and Chiang's pick for the position, was defeated by Li Zongren, the Guangxi warlord who had long been at odds with Chiang. Consequently, the divisions within the GMD leadership deepened. Chiang intended for the assembly to serve as a remedy for the GMD's disease, but it turned out to be a poison pill, bringing Chiang further political losses.

The economic and financial situation in GMD-controlled areas was also dire. Since the beginning of the civil war, Chiang had focused his attention on military affairs, failing to see the urgency of managing his regime's economic and financial challenges. Worst of all was hyperinflation. The Chinese currency had depreciated in value almost 370 times from August 1945 to June 1948. Chiang realized that the "economy is in such an awful state, which is more worrisome than the military situation."[38] To deal with the financial crisis, Chiang's government issued an emergency order on August 19 to launch a new currency, the gold yuan. The next day, Chiang dispatched his son Chiang Ching-kuo to Shanghai to "hunt the tigers" (*dahu*), those evil speculators who had stored scarce goods in the hopes of reaping megaprofits. However, the junior Chiang met his Waterloo in Shanghai. When his purge of "economic foes" touched the Yangzi Company—which was chaired by David Kung, nephew of Soong Mei-ling, the generalissimo's wife—Soong intervened. She demanded that Chiang Ching-kuo let his cousin off;

Chiang refused. At the time, Chiang senior was in Beiping to supervise a decisive military showdown with the Communists in Manchuria. He flew to Shanghai on October 8 after an urgent telephone call from his wife.[39] The young Chiang's "tiger hunting" campaign came to an abrupt end. Subsequently, the value of the golden yuan plunged, with the banknotes becoming little more than wastepaper within a few short months. Chiang and his government also lost whatever credibility they still had among the Chinese population. Even Chiang himself lamented, "This is the sign of a total collapse."[40] Zhou and other CCP leaders took note of every development. The Chiang regime's days, they now believed, were numbered.

In fact, however, Chiang and the Nationalist government did not approach collapse until the late summer and early fall of 1948, despite suffering repeated military defeats and other failures. From a military perspective, they still seemed to have hope. Zhou himself calculated that Chiang's government remained in the lead in military forces, territory, and the population of the areas under its control.[41] If Chiang could have sustained the GMD's war effort and carried out the necessary reforms at the right time, his government might not have been so quickly defeated. Mao and Zhou thus knew that it was necessary "to launch several decisive military campaigns" to expand the Communists' advantage in the civil war.[42] In a general evaluation of the war's trajectory, Mao still aimed to overthrow Chiang's regime within five years. Yet Zhou was even more optimistic than Mao, believing that "if we could give Chiang a few serious blows" in 1948 and 1949, "together with the effects of Chiang's financial collapse and internal conflicts, his downfall might come much earlier."[43] Mao and Zhou still feared that the Americans might stage a military intervention. But Mao also predicted that it was "impossible for the United States to send hundreds of thousands or even a million troops to China."[44] In their strategic planning, Mao and Zhou now shifted their main attention to the task of launching several "decisive campaigns" during the second half of 1948.

The CCP's "big operations" began in Jinan, capital of Shandong Province. On September 11, Zhou, representing the CMC, ordered PLA commanders in Shandong to capture Jinan. The Communist assault began eight days later. At a critical time in the battle, Wu Huawen, a GMD division commander whom Zhou had long worked on, defected to the Communists, completely reversing the balance of forces on the battlefield. The PLA occupied Jinan on September 24. Realizing that the war in eastern China was turning further in the CCP's favor, Zhou cabled PLA commanders there the next day, ordering them to immediately begin another, much larger operation, the Huaihai Campaign, in central and eastern China.[45]

At almost the same time, Communist forces in the Northeast had won several major victories. Under Lin Biao's command, PLA forces had confined GMD troops to the narrow strip between Shenyang and Changchun. Were Lin's troops to occupy strategically important Jinzhou, GMD forces in the Northeast would be totally isolated. On October 2, Zhou cabled Lin, ordering his troops to do their utmost to seize Jinzhou within ten days. By then, GMD troops in Changchun had been encircled for months.[46] On October 17, Zeng Zesheng, a GMD army commander, led his unit to defect to the PLA. Zheng Dongguo, the GMD commander in Changchun, found himself and his troops at a dead end. Zhou personally wrote Zheng—who was once a student of Zhou's at the Whampoa Military Academy—urging him to "recall the original revolutionary aspirations of Whampoa" and join the PLA's side in the fight.[47] Zheng was reluctant to defect; only when the city's defense was collapsing and at the urging of his subordinates did Zheng "honorably surrender" to the PLA. After seizing Jinzhou and Changchun, the PLA encircled the remaining GMD troops in the Northeast. Then, after foiling the GMD troops' attempt to break through the encirclement and return to areas south of the Great Wall, the PLA eliminated all opposition in Manchuria. On November 2, the PLA occupied Shenyang and "liberated" the Northeast.

Northern, central, and eastern China now became the main theaters of the war. In northern China, GMD troops commanded by General Fu Zuoyi had been pushed into a small area between Beiping and Tianjin. In eastern China, a decisive showdown between the two sides began on the battlefield at Huaihai. By late November, after a series of victories, the PLA had cut the main Nationalist forces in northern and eastern China into two large groups. Mao and Zhou decided to order the PLA in northern China not to go on the offensive against Fu's forces in Beiping and Tianjin, in order to prevent them from moving west or retreating to the south along maritime routes. They also ordered Lin Biao's troops in Manchuria to enter areas south of the Great Wall at an earlier date, around November 15, to reinforce PLA troops in northern China.[48] In late November, with Mao devising bold, creative ideas, and Zhou coordinating, CCP forces launched the Huaihai Campaign, their final offensive against GMD troops. The leads that Zhou had earlier planted within the ranks of GMD troops considerably aided the campaign. By early

January 1949, reportedly, the PLA had eliminated Chiang's force of eight hundred thousand soldiers.

Mao and Zhou now shifted their focus to northern China, where Chiang's troops were totally surrounded. On January 16, PLA troops occupied Tianjin after twenty-nine hours of fierce fighting. The window of opportunity for GMD troops in Beiping to flee south by sea was shut closed. Under Zhou's direct leadership, the Communists used both hard and soft tactics to pressure Fu Zuoyi, even in his own home through Fu's daughter, a Communist agent. On January 21, Fu accepted an agreement on the "peaceful liberation" of Beiping. The Communists had thus "liberated" all the land north of the Yangzi River. The shift in the war's trajectory had been "very fast indeed," Zhou commented, and the civil war "has virtually ended. . . . It is now certain that the GMD will be defeated in the coming year!" All that the PLA had left to do, he added, was "no more than cleaning up the battlefield."[49] Zhou was not an emotional person. But his confidence and excitement were evident when he made the statement.

* * *

The year was 1949. In his New Year's message, Mao raised a critical question, "whether to carry the revolution through to the end or to abandon it halfway." In Mao's view, the only solution was the former. He elaborated:

> We must use the revolutionary method to wipe out all reactionary forces resolutely, thoroughly, and completely; we must unswervingly persist in overthrowing imperialism, feudalism and bureaucratic capitalism; and we must overthrow the GMD's reactionary rule throughout the country.[50]

Chiang knew that he was losing the war. He called for peace in his New Year's address, asking his Communist enemies to preserve the Republic of China's constitution, its legal heritage, and its military forces as the basis for a fair settlement. Mao scoffed at Chiang's pleas, insisting that all GMD war criminals be punished, the old legal heritage and the constitution of Chiang's regime be abolished, and all reactionary troops be reorganized.[51] These terms, especially the first one, lay far beyond the limits of what Chiang could accept. Meanwhile, within the GMD, Vice President Li Zongren's feud with Chiang turned white hot. Facing huge pressure from inside and outside of the GMD, Chiang announced his resignation as president on January 21. After he had returned to his hometown of Xikou, Chiang wrote in his diary, "It is never too late to mend the fence after the sheep escape."[52] However, would there still be a future left for Chiang and the GMD on the mainland?

On the Communist side, Mao, Zhou, and their comrades were already preparing for the inauguration of a "New China." In early January, the CCP Politburo met at Xibaipo and passed a resolution coauthored by Zhou. While cheering "the GMD's military, political, and economic defeats by our hands," the resolution's authors stressed that the revolution "must not be aborted halfway."[53] A CCP Central Committee plenum was held at Xibaibo over the first half of March. Zhou personally arranged security measures for the gathering, which was attended by almost all of the party's top leadership. "You must make sure that the safety of the plenum is absolutely guaranteed," Zhou told Fang Zhichun, who had been put in charge of the plenum's security detail.[54]

At the plenum, Mao reiterated his exhortation to "carry the revolution through to the end." Rather than highlight the goal of "thoroughly defeating Chiang's reactionary regime," though, he defined the "end of the revolution" in wider, deeper, and longer terms. In his keynote speech, Mao stressed that

> To secure countrywide victory is only to complete the first step of a long march. . . . The Chinese revolution is great, but the road after the revolution will be longer, the work greater and more arduous. . . . We are not only good at destroying the old world, we are also good at building a new one.[55]

In retrospect, the chairman's statement reveals that he had already envisioned the "revolution" and its "end" at a high level. Moreover, his was a unique vision, if still a vague one. What did "destroying the old world" and "building a new one" mean? As later developments would make clear, Mao's words presaged his determination to launch a series of political, social, and cultural revolutions aimed at transforming the Chinese state, Chinese society, and the hearts and minds of the nation's people. Zhou also underscored the importance of "carrying the revolution through to the end" in his speech at the plenum. But unlike Mao, his attention remained focused on destroying the GMD's reactionary rule and then establishing and consolidating a new CCP-led regime. He discussed the challenges facing the CCP in the transition from war to reconstruction and in the reunification of a long-divided country. Rather than concentrate all political power at the center, Zhou stated, the new regime must stimulate provincial and local initiatives.[56] Zhou and other CCP leaders most likely failed to apprehend the deep significance and ambitious implications of Mao's lecture. In particular, Zhou and his colleagues would likely have found it unimaginable then that Mao would over the next quarter century define "revolution" in extraordinarily utopian terms and steer China into the disastrous Great Proletarian Cultural Revolution in the name of "continuous revolution."

* * *

The CCP leadership had by that time selected Zhou to negotiate with the GMD. He immediately sent a message to Li Zongren, emphasizing that "there is no middle path."[57] Working with Mao, Zhou compiled a list of GMD "war criminals"; Chiang's was the first name on the list. The Communist leadership insisted that "punishing war criminals" was the premise of any peace settlement between the two sides. Zhou conceived of three possible scenarios for the negotiations. First, the GMD would agree to reorganize its government in accordance with the CCP's terms. Second, the United States would stage a military intervention. And third, the war would continue. Zhou believed that while the CCP should be prepared for an American intervention, the most probable result of the negotiations was that the civil war would drag on.[58]

On April 1, Zhou, acting as the CCP's chief negotiator, began talks with Zhang Zhizhong, chief negotiator for the GMD, as well as other GMD representatives. Zhou and Zhang had long been counterparts at the negotiation table, and they had never resorted to shouting. Even when the GMD was much stronger than the CCP, Zhang never embarrassed Zhou during negotiations. This time, however, Zhou asked Zhang immediately after the two met, "Why did you go to see Chiang at Xikou before leaving Nanjing?" This was quite an unreasonable question in this situation. Although Chiang had stepped down as president, he still effectively controlled the Nationalist government; Li in Nanjing was a president in name only. Without Chiang's consent, the GMD would have been unable to enter into the peace talks and implement its resolutions. But when Zhang explained the situation to Zhou along these lines, Zhou promptly fired another volley at him: "We will not accept any fake peace directed by Chiang."[59] As this tense encounter revealed, the chances of the talks succeeding—that is, ending the civil war and bringing peace to China—were next to none.

The two sides then began "individual exchanges," which quickly highlighted impasses in three areas: the punishment of GMD war criminals, authority for CCP troops to cross the Yangzi River, and the reorganization of GMD forces. On the CCP side, Mao personally met with Zhang. In "a relaxed yet deeply touching manner," the chairman attempted to persuade Zhang and other GMD negotiators to agree to the CCP's terms. Yet the chasms between the two sides on the three key issues had not narrowed. Zhang felt that the CCP's terms were "in fact an ultimatum for surrender, which Nanjing absolutely will not accept."[60] On April 13, the two sides held the first formal meeting of the negotiations, at which Zhou handed Zhang the CCP's draft "agreement on domestic peace." If Nanjing sincerely accepted the CCP's principal terms, Zhou told him, all other matters would be easily settled. "The central issue," Zhou continued, was the matter of the CCP taking over and reorganizing the GMD military. This, Zhou claimed, "concerns whether the people's revolution will be carried out to the end, so there is no space for any compromise."[61] Zhou's rigid position on the military issue must have reminded Zhang of the GMD-CCP negotiations in which he had been so deeply involved. In those earlier discussions, Zhou persistently refused to yield on these very demands; nor would Chiang make a single concession. Now, with the situation reversed, these terms constituted Zhou's line in the sand with respect to the GMD.

On the second day, Zhou assigned Li Weihan, another CCP negotiator, to brief a group of "prodemocratic figures" in Beiping about the first round of peace talks.[62] For his part, Zhou had attempted to woo the GMD negotiators in an overnight conversation. That same evening, Zhou received Zhang's response to the CCP's terms, complete with over forty "suggestions for revisions." The two sides met for the second round of negotiations on April 15. Zhou handed Zhang the CCP's final version of the peace agreement, whose text had been carefully revised, with some "aggressive expressions" taken out. Not excised from the document, however, were the Communists' key terms, such as the PLA crossing the Yangzi, the reorganization of GMD troops, and the complete takeover of the Nationalist regime by the CCP. "This is the final version," Zhou told Zhang. If the GMD side failed to reply by April 20, Zhou warned, the PLA would cross the Yangzi.[63] Zhang and other GMD negotiators found themselves with no choice but to accept the CCP's terms and submit them to Nanjing for approval.

On April 20, Zhou received a formal rejection of the CCP's final conditions from Li Zongren and the Nationalist government. The Communists' terms, Li and the Nationalist government argued, amounted to no less than the "conquerors' mistreatment of the conquered."[64] Neither Zhou nor others in the CCP leadership were surprised by the rejection. That night, the PLA crossed the Yangzi, and a few short days later, they had occupied Nanjing. The Nationalist government decamped to Guangzhou. Thereafter, the rule of Chiang and the Nationalist regime in mainland China all but collapsed.

• • •

Over the years, Zhou had served as a main practitioner and, at times, decision-maker in the CCP's external affairs. In earlier times, he had dealt with diplomatic issues and challenges as the representative of the "revolutionary force" in opposition to the government. Now, he and the CCP were to become China's new rulers, facing new kinds of diplomatic challenges.

Zhou's first major diplomatic test came shortly after CCP troops occupied Shenyang in November 1948. Contrary to Zhou's and other CCP leaders' expectations, Angus Ward, the American consul general at Shenyang, had decided to stay in the city. Problems ensued. A few days after the PLA had taken Shenyang, Zhu Qiwen, director of the CCP's Shenyang Military Control Committee, invited Ward, the British and French consuls, and the Soviet trade representative to his office for a meeting. Then, without asking for the Party Center's approval, Zhu visited the American, British, and French diplomats for a separate discussion, during which he informed them that the CCP was willing to meet with American merchants "to resume trade activities in the Northeast on the basis of equality."[65] Zhou, upon receiving a report from Shenyang, realized immediately that Zhu's actions were quite troublesome. By then, news that the American, British, and French consulates had stayed in Shenyang had already alerted Soviet officials based in the city, who believed that the Westerners had not fled Shenyang for "political purposes."[66] Meanwhile, Zhu's unauthorized engagements with Western diplomats carried the risk of giving the Americans "unrealistic illusions." On top of that, as the CCP's spymaster, Zhou was worried that amid the ongoing civil war, the American consulate might be used as an intelligence station for the GMD. After discussing the matter with Mao, Zhou expressed in a November 10 telegram to the CCP's Northeast Bureau that "Zhu Qiwen's behavior was extremely inappropriate." Further, Zhou stressed that, "as the governments of the UK, the US, and France did not recognize our government, we naturally will not recognize their consulates." It was necessary, Zhou argued, to "use the current situation of military control" in Shenyang to "block and isolate American and British diplomatic agencies there" and "force them to evacuate." Zhou also emphasized that "the policies of the Party Center should be strictly followed" in all diplomatic matters, and noted that timely reports for further instruction were required in all contacts with foreign governments or their agents.[67]

For whatever reason, though, the Shenyang authorities failed to follow Zhou's orders. On November 15, without asking for approval in advance from the Party Center, they ordered "former American, British, and French consulates to hand over all radio transmitters in their possession to Shenyang authorities within 36 hours."[68] However, the Shenyang authorities did not immediately implement the order. On November 17, Mao cabled Gao Gang, secretary of the CCP's Northeast Bureau, and sternly criticized Zhu's "naïve behavior." The next day, Mao and Zhou ordered the Shenyang military authorities to "confiscate the transmitters of the American consulate," while restricting the activities of "former American diplomats," in order to "squeeze British, American, and French diplomats" out of Shenyang.[69] A few days later, Zhou received a report from Shenyang that the Americans at the consulate had been involved in espionage activities. Alerted, he instructed that Ward and other Americans be locked in the consulate building, severing their connections with the outside.[70] The events precipitated a diplomatic standoff between the CCP and the Americans that would not be settled for an entire year.[71]

In their management of the Ward case, Mao and other CCP leaders—especially Zhou—came face to face with the pressures of complicated diplomatic issues. The case was closely related to the CCP's relations with Moscow. Given the publicly known "special interests" claimed by the Soviets in the Northeast, Mao and Zhou repeatedly stressed the importance of carefully heeding the advice of the CCP's "Soviet brothers."[72] All this, naturally, would further push the Communist leadership to adopt a more deliberate, scrupulous approach to such critical issues for the "New China" as whether they should, and how they might, ally with the Soviet Union. The Ward case also provided Mao and Zhou an important opportunity to explore the intentions and possible policy orientations of Western powers, including the United States, the United Kingdom, and France. While they had no desire to retreat from the principles of anti-imperialism, the CCP leadership also realized that it would be unwise simply to reject the possibility of establishing diplomatic relations with Western countries if those countries took the initiative.[73]

Unsurprisingly, diplomacy became a major subject of discussion among CCP leaders during the January 1949 Politburo meeting. In his presentation, Zhou stated that the Chinese people had "suffered a century of oppression, and have now stood up. They should demonstrate a greater sense of self-dignity."[74] On January 19, the CCP Center issued a directive on diplomatic affairs drafted by Zhou and revised by Mao. The document formally stipulated the new regime's determination to "have a fresh start" in its diplomatic affairs. The directive emphasized that "the privileges of the imperialists in China must be abolished, and the independence and liberation of the Chinese nation must be realized." Therefore, the new regime should "not recognize those diplomats currently in China dispatched by imperialist countries as official diplomatic personnel." In so doing, the directive contended, "we will occupy a positive position in diplomacy, without being bound by the humiliating diplomatic legacies of the past."[75]

It was in this context that Soviet Politburo member Anastas Mikoyan arrived in Xibaipo on January 31, acting as Stalin's special envoy. Since the spring of 1948, there had been discussions about Mao visiting Moscow to meet with Stalin, but it was difficult for Mao to leave China during the civil war. In late 1948, Stalin offered to dispatch to China a member of the Soviet Politburo to hear Mao's views and convey them to Moscow. In January 1949, Stalin decided to send Mikoyan to China for the sake of avoiding misunderstandings between Mao and the CCP and as a means of obtaining a fuller picture of Mao's and the other CCP leaders' policies and intentions.

Prior to Mikoyan's arrival, a Soviet Politburo member had never come to China to meet with CCP leaders. Mao and his fellow CCP leaders hence regarded Mikoyan's visit as a matter of the utmost importance. Zhou personally arranged the security details for Mikoyan's visit, making sure that every thing, no matter how small, was attended to. Zhou accompanied Mikoyan throughout the latter's stay in Xibaipo.[76] He participated in every meeting that Mao and other CCP leaders held with Mikoyan, and he met one on one with the Soviet envoy on two occasions. Mao provided Mikoyan an overview of the CCP's historical development, emphasizing that at each phase of its growth, the party had benefitted from Moscow's guidance and support. During the civil war, Mao noted, "your support in Manchuria was of critical importance." Mao hoped that the Soviet party would "establish an agency of representatives at CCP headquarters." Zhou immediately echoed Mao, emphasizing that "we truly hope that the Soviet Union becomes closer to the CCP," as "the main problems" facing the Chinese revolution would "need to be resolved in Moscow." Mao repeatedly stressed that China would firmly stand on the Soviet side in the international struggle against imperialism, and that "there exists no middle path."[77]

In an individual meeting with Mikoyan on February 1, Zhou recalled in detail the CCP's exchanges with the United States, which began with the arrival of American military observers in Yan'an. The party's contacts with the United States were interrupted, however, after the CCP rejected General Marshall's proposal to mediate a resolution to the Chinese civil war. Zhou stressed that the CCP would not "provoke controversy with the Americans, but if the United States opposes us, we will firmly strike back." As Zhu De was present at the meeting, Zhou further requested that the Soviet Union "send us some experts and equipment to make weapons, and dispatch to China some advisors to help us train our troops, establish military schools, and organize logistical work including that of military industry." Zhou and Mikoyan also covered such topics as postwar economic reconstruction; the CCP's general plans for establishing a new government; China's foreign affairs and foreign trade; and issues concerning the Chinese diplomatic service. Further, Zhou discussed with Mikoyan the sharing of intelligence between the CCP and Moscow.[78] Mikoyan previously had had no direct contact with Zhou; after the visit, he commented that Zhou was the best choice to serve as prime minister in the new CCP regime.[79]

Upon his return to the Soviet Union, Mikoyan immediately reported to Stalin on his meetings with Mao, Zhou, and other CCP leaders. Stalin heard

Mao's and Zhou's promises, and he significantly increased Soviet support to the CCP.[80] On the Chinese side, when Mao delivered his concluding remarks at the plenum on March 13, he explicitly stated that

> The CCP-Soviet relationship is one between brothers. We should stand on the same front as the Soviet Union. We are allies. Whenever there is the opportunity, we should openly announce this.[81]

Mikoyan's visit thus became a new point of departure for the development and deepening of CCP-Soviet relations.

• • •

Interestingly, at the same time as the CCP was strengthening its relationship with the Soviets, the Americans made inquiries to gauge the Chinese Communists' appetite for cooperation. In late March, Zhou received a report from Shanghai. According to the report, Chen Mingshu, a pro-CCP "democratic figure" who had good personal relations with the Americans, had met with US ambassador to China John Leighton Stuart on March 25 and 26. The American ambassador described to Chen two of America's main concerns: first, that the CCP might stand on the Soviet side in an American-Soviet confrontation; and second, that after reunifying the country, the CCP might stop cooperating with other political parties and abandon a democratic coalition government. Stuart said that if the CCP could "establish a coalition government in favor of peace, independence, democracy and freedom" and "change its attitude toward the United States," Washington would surely "be willing to establish a friendly relationship with the CCP and provide aid to the new government for China's resurgence and reconstruction."[82] Zhou immediately reported the matter to Mao and the Party Center.

Unbeknownst to Stuart, however, Mao had stressed at the Central Committee plenum in March that "concerning the question of recognition of our country by imperialists, we should not be in a hurry to resolve it, and should not be in a hurry to resolve it even after the victory in the whole country."[83] Statements of this sort made by Mao had defined "making a fresh start" and "opposing US imperialism" as the fundamental principles that the new Communist regime would follow. All this, in retrospect, presaged the

New China's emergence as a "revolutionary country" that would challenge the existing international order in world affairs.

* * *

When the Communist forces occupied Nanjing, the Nationalist government relocated to Guangzhou. Mao and Zhou found the diplomatic situation facing the CCP curious. Nikolai Roshchin, the Soviet ambassador in China, went to Guangzhou with the Nationalists; Stuart, however, stayed in Nanjing. Mao and Zhou were both experienced practitioners of united front strategies. While not compromising with the Americans on matters of principle, they would not simply turn down every olive branch that the Americans presented them. They thus showed a willingness to monitor whether the United States' China policy would "turn toward the direction of establishing diplomatic relations with us." Mao and Zhou determined that "if the United States and United Kingdom cut off relations with the Nationalists," the CCP might even "consider the issue of establishing diplomatic relations with them."[84] Zhou was enraged to learn that several PLA soldiers had conducted a search of Stuart's residence after the liberation of Nanjing. He personally drafted instructions for the CCP committee in the city, ordering that "no actions of indoor search of foreign ambassadors, ministers, consulates, and members of diplomatic services and foreign residents be taken."[85]

Mao and Zhou had another problem on their hands: the closer the Communists came to victory in the civil war, the greater their concerns became about the threat of direct American military intervention in the conflict. As early as January 1949, the Party Center's directive on diplomatic affairs specifically warned all party members about the risk:

> We have always taken into account the possibility that the United States might directly send its troops to China to occupy several of our coastal cities and engage us in war. We should alert ourselves that this possibility still exists, lest we are caught unprepared if and when the intervention does take place.[86]

After Communist troops occupied Nanjing and Shanghai, Mao again cautioned PLA commanders in eastern China:

> There have been some signs recently that imperialist countries are preparing for a joint intervention against our revolution. . . . More American naval vessels have appeared in Qingdao, foreign embassies still in Nanjing are preparing to leave, Britain has increased its troops in Hong Kong, and the GMD in Guangzhou seems happy on some occasions. It is too early to judge if these signs will change into the reality [of foreign intervention]. We should get ready in advance, so that [our] preparedness will [allow us to] avert peril.[87]

In order to "gauge the intentions of the US government" as well as the orientation of its China policy, Zhou decided to name his associate Huang Hua as foreign affairs director at the Nanjing Military Control Committee. Zhou instructed Huang to "establish personal contact with Stuart in his role as a Yenching alumnus." Before Huang departed for Nanjing, Zhou further advised him "to give special attention to the US government's China policy," to "be cautious in managing everything, and to report and ask for instructions frequently."[88] On May 10, Zhou drafted a telegram, sent in Mao's name, to the CCP's East China Bureau and Nanjing City Committee. He specifically instructed Huang "to listen more and talk less" during his meetings with Stuart. Huang was absolutely not to "leave the Americans with an impression that the CCP was willing to accept American aid." In particular, Zhou emphasized, Huang should make it clear to Stuart that unless Washington "cease all support to the GMD and cut off its connections with the reactionary GMD remnants, and never interfere with China's internal affairs," the Chinese Communists would not consider developing relations with the United States.[89]

In his first conversation with Stuart on May 13, Huang straightforwardly requested that Washington "evacuate the American naval vessels and marines from Qingdao, so as to prevent any conflict from happening."[90] Stuart got Huang's message. In his next meeting with Huang, Stuart informed Huang that American troops had left Qingdao on May 21.[91] Zhou took this development seriously. In a June 3 telegram sent to Huang and the CCP's Nanjing Committee by Zhou on behalf of the Party Center, Zhou confirmed that "the American fleet in Qingdao has indeed gone." He instructed Huang to reciprocate by "personally revealing to Stuart" that the CCP would convene "a new political consultative conference after occupation of Guangzhou [by the PLA]."[92]

All the while receiving directions from Zhou, Huang held a series of meetings with Stuart and Stuart's secretary Philip Fugh, including three lengthy conversations with the American ambassador. Yet they, as well as Zhou in Beiping, quickly found that despite the cordial atmosphere of the talks, the Chinese Communists and the Americans lacked a shared political language or a consensus on international norms and codes of behavior. Stuart highlighted the legitimacy of America's interests in China and tried to persuade the Chinese Communists to accept "widely recognized international regulations and principles" as a precondition for diplomatic relations between the two sides. Huang demanded that America first cut off all its connections with the GMD, while conducting all its exchanges with China—economic, political, and cultural—"on the basis of equality and mutual benefit."[93] Consequently, the more the men talked, the more acutely they perceived the wide gap in their political perspectives.

On June 8, Fugh mentioned to Huang that Stuart wanted "to meet Zhou in Beiping before he departs for the United States."[94] Zhou showed interest in the message, seeing it as an opportunity for the CCP to further explore Washington's intentions while driving a wedge into the "anti-New China alliance" that Washington had tried to form. But he was wary not to let the Americans develop an "unrealistic illusion" about such an overture or take advantage of his response. Thus, he asked Lu Zhiwei, president of Yenching University, to "personally invite Stuart to Beiping as Yenching's former president." Lu did so. Meanwhile, he instructed the CCP Nanjing Committee that "if Stuart requests to come to Beiping, he may visit Yenching University before returning to America." Whether Stuart would meet with Zhou would "be decided after he arrives in Beiping."[95] On June 18, Huang learned from Fugh that Washington had approved Stuart's contact with the CCP. Zhou then instructed Huang to inform Stuart that the CCP "had agreed to his request to visit Yenching," and that it was also possible for him to "meet with the authorities there."[96] However, Stuart replied that because the US Congress would be adjourned by the end of July, there probably was not enough time for him to go to Beiping. Further, "[t]he US Congress contains many factions, and a trip to Beiping might cause inconvenient comments." He would let Secretary of State Dean Acheson decide whether he should go to Beiping.[97] Zhou was alerted and, on June 30, emphasized in a telegram to the CCP Nanjing Committee that, whether or not Stuart would come to Beiping, the CCP would "have no illusion that the U.S. imperialists might change their policies." He also reiterated that Stuart's Beiping trip was motivated by "his own initiative, not from our invitation. This point should be made very clear. . . . lest it be used for propaganda purposes."[98]

* * *

In fact, while the CCP was engaged in these secret exchanges with the Americans, its relationship with the Soviets was rapidly moving toward a major breakthrough. CCP leaders did not conceal Huang's contacts with Stuart from Moscow. Mao and Zhou briefed Stalin about the Huang-Stuart contacts through I. V. Kovalev, the general Soviet advisor at the CCP headquarters.[99] Most importantly, in response to Mikoyan's visit, the CCP leadership decided to dispatch a high-ranking delegation to Moscow. In early June, it was decided that Liu, the CCP's second-in-command, would head the delegation.

Liu arrived in Moscow on June 26 for what would be a two-month-long visit to the Soviet Union. Stalin met with Liu at the Kremlin the next day. The Soviet leader offered to provide the new CCP regime with a low-interest loan of US$300 million.[100] On July 4, Liu submitted a report to Stalin on behalf of the CCP, in which Liu stated that "the Soviet party is the headquarters of the world Communist movement, and the CCP is just the headquarters of a front of the movement."[101] Having read the report, Stalin showered praise on the Chinese revolution in his subsequent meetings with Liu, saying that the center of the world revolution was moving toward China and East Asia. He also agreed to provide China with various other kinds of aid, and dispatch to China military advisors as well as a large number of experts in other areas. He even apologized for some of the Soviet party's offenses against the Chinese revolution. In addition, he told Liu that the Soviet and Chinese parties should have a "division of labor" arrangement in promoting the world revolution. "You should play a larger role in the East and colonial and semicolonial countries," Stalin told Liu.[102] In mid-August, Liu returned to China bearing Moscow's promise of support.

All of this set the stage for a major breakthrough in the CCP's relations with the Soviet Union. On June 30, Mao issued a statement in which he announced that the "New China" would establish a special relationship with Moscow by adopting a policy of "leaning to one side," the side of the Soviet

Union and the Soviet bloc, in the polarized world. The chairman declared that the New China would

> Externally. . . . ally ourselves with the Soviet Union, with the people's democratic counties, and with the proletariat and the broad masses of the people in all other countries, and form an international united front (with them). . . . We must lean to one side.[103]

Huang's contact with Stuart and the latter's plans to visit Beiping had not gone well. On July 1, Acheson ordered Stuart "in no circumstance to make a visit [to] Beiping."[104] In the wake of Mao's "lean to one side" announcement, Stuart left China in early August. On the eve of his departure, the US State Department published a *China White Paper.*[105] Mao personally wrote five commentaries for the Xinhua News Agency, identifying US imperialism as China's most dangerous enemy.[106] A torrent of propaganda characterized by radical anti-US imperialism erupted on the heels of Mao's statements, as the era of total confrontation between China and the United States began.

* * *

All the while, the civil war continued in southern, southwestern, and western China. The wave of Communist victories continued as well. In the closing months of 1949, Chiang tried but failed to turn Sichuan—as he had done during China's war against Japan—into the last bastion of the GMD's resistance against massive Communist offensives. On December 12, Chiang flew from Chengdu, the second-largest city in Sichuan, to Taiwan. Never again would Chiang return to the Chinese mainland. For Mao, Zhou, and their fellow CCP leaders, the civil war was won, with the exception of the pending "liberation" of Taiwan and Hainan and of such outlying regions as Tibet. They were fully ready to embrace the birth of a New China.

PART III

BUILDING "NEW CHINA"

15

"WE, THE CHINESE, HAVE STOOD UP!"

1949–1950

Beijing is famous for its beautiful autumns, which usually begin in early September. Mao Zedong, Zhou Enlai, and their comrades gathered in Beijing in September 1949 for the founding of the People's Republic of China (PRC). This was for them a historic moment, a setting-off point that, they hoped, would lead to the unfolding of a wholly new era in Chinese and world history. They were in high spirits.

On September 22, Zhou chaired the opening session of the New People's Political Consultative Conference (NPPCC). Mao delivered a passionate speech, in which he proclaimed, "We, the Chinese, have stood up!"[1] This announcement was not only directed at the international community. It was, first and foremost, for the Chinese people to hear. Mao was making a sweeping claim about the legitimacy of the "New China" that he and the CCP would set out to build. Zhou delivered a report summarizing the draft Common Program of the NPPCC and its main features, promising that the New China would be a "country of new democracy" that was "independent, democratic, peaceful, unified, and rich and powerful," and that the NPPCC was the "best organizational form" of political participation for the new republic.[2]

Zhou awoke very early on the morning of October 1, 1949—the day of the ceremony marking the PRC's establishment. He arrived at Tiananmen, the Gate of Heavenly Peace, hours before the event began. In his characteristically fastidious style, he inspected the site's every detail, leaving nothing unchecked. Mao had long been accustomed to working through the night and sleeping during the day; but he too rose early that morning. At three

15.1 Zhou Enlai at the First Plenary Session of the Chinese People's Political Consultative Conference, late September 1949. *Bettmann Archive / Getty Images (515511618)*

o'clock in the afternoon, the ceremony began. From atop Tiananmen, Mao announced the founding of the People's Republic. Zhou, who stood next to Mao, wore a smile as he listened to the chairman's declaration. But upon a closer look, he also appeared lost in thought.

What might Zhou have been thinking about? Was he contemplating his dream, three decades before, of "China rising high in the world"? Did he feel that his vision was finally coming true? We have no way of knowing for certain. However, his experiences as the PRC's premier over the next

15.2 Mao Zedong and Zhou Enlai attending the founding ceremony of the People's Republic of China on the Tiananmen Rostrum, October 1, 1949. *Sovfoto / Universal Images Group via Getty Images*

twenty-seven years would reveal that there were no straight or simple answers to these questions.

• • •

Zhou and his comrades had been making preparations for the PRC's establishment since the spring. In his concluding remarks at the Central Committee plenum in March, Mao said, "It is certain that (Zhou) Enlai will take a position in the new government, which is that of premier of the cabinet."[3] Zhou took on an especially crucial responsibility in shaping the new government.

In March 1949, Mao and Zhou entered Beiping (the name of the city would be changed to Beijing in September). Their associates had prepared residences and offices for them at Xiangshan in Beijing's western suburbs. In May, they decided to requisition Zhongnanhai, the former imperial garden located in central Beiping, and turn the compound into the living and working quarters for top CCP leaders. From then on, Zhongnanhai would witness the formulation of China's most important strategies and policies.

Zhou and his wife, Deng Yingchao, first moved into a courtyard in the Fengze Garden in the middle of the Zhongnanhai complex. They loved their new abode. However, when Zhou learned that Mao had also taken a liking to the courtyard, he decided to let Mao have it. In November, Zhou and Deng moved into Xihuating—the West Flower Pavilion—located in the northwest corner of Zhongnanhai. The pavilion was a rectangular compound comprising two courtyards. Upon entering the compound, visitors first encountered a front yard. Here stood the hall in which Zhou met with guests. To the rear of the compound, in the middle of a courtyard, was Zhou's meeting room. Zhou and Deng's bedroom flanked the courtyard on the right, along with Deng's office. Zhou's office (where he kept important documents, including the intelligence reports he was in charge of, in a secure vault) was located on the left-hand side of the courtyard. Zhou and Deng would live and work here for the next quarter century. Zhou did not permanently leave the residence until June 1, 1974, when he was brought for cancer treatment to the 305th Hospital of the PLA. After Zhou's death, Deng continued to live at the West Flower Pavillion until July 1991, when she was admitted to the Beijing Hospital.

• • •

One of Zhou's key tasks after he arrived in Beiping was to work out the NPPCC's Common Program, a text that later would serve as the provisional constitution of the PRC. Zhou's colleagues had been working on an early version of the document, then titled "The Common Program of the Chinese People's Revolution," since 1948. By mid-1949 they had completed two drafts; however, the rapidly developing civil war made these drafts obsolete. When Zhou spoke at a preparatory meeting of the NPPCC on June 16, he mentioned that the two earlier drafts of the Common Program had emphasized "mobilizing the people of the whole country to support our war effort." Now, Zhou stated, "the work facing us has shifted to carrying out reconstruction" and "to building a China of new democracy." Therefore,

Zhou said, the program should be rewritten under a new title, "The Common Program of New Democracy."[4] Zhou spent an entire week in late June drafting the new program. Over the next two months, he solicited suggestions for revisions to the draft from a diverse group of people, including many non-Communist "democratic figures." Finally, a new version of the document was completed in late August, in which Zhou articulated his views on how the New China and its new government should be.

The "New China," according to the document, should concentrate on building a "society of new democracy"; only with "the consolidation and development of such a society should socialism begin to be pursued." On the subject of "the Chinese people's rights," Zhou's draft highlighted "freedom of thought, body, speech, publication, assembly, association, correspondence, domicile, doing business, to hold processions and demonstrations, [and of] religious belief." The government of the New China, according to Zhou, should be a "democratic coalition government" based on "a broad people's democratic united front" including the CCP and various democratic parties. The government, Zhou added, was to be "neither a dictatorship of one class," nor would "one party . . . dominate the government." Economically, China should adopt a "mixed mode of production," which would allow for capitalism to endure. Accordingly, the New China should implement an economic policy of "taking into account both public and private interests, of benefiting both labor and capital, of mutual aid between the cities and countryside, and circulation of goods between China and abroad." Internationally, Zhou continued, the New China would adhere to a foreign policy characterized by "leaning to one side" and anti-imperialism. With respect to the concepts of "China" and the "Chinese nation," Zhou believed that the New China would become "a federation of multiple nationalities."[5]

In mid-August, Zhou sent the draft to Mao for his review and approval. The chairman spent nearly six weeks from late August to mid-September reading and revising the program. While he accepted most of the document's contents, Mao made two important revisions. First, he removed the notion of "coalition government." Zhou's promise that no one party would dominate the government was also dropped. Second, the New China would no longer be defined as a "republic of federation."

These were crucial changes. When they vied with the GMD for the banner of "democracy" in the mid-1940s, Mao, Zhou, and the CCP had used the notion of "coalition government" to put Chiang on the political defensive. Zhou, in his negotiations with Chiang's representatives and the Americans, frequently accused Chiang of trying to pursue "the domination of the government by one party." Zhou obviously remembered this. Therefore, when he drafted the Common Program, he often used the term "coalition government" to define the new regime, promising that the CCP would not pursue its own "one-party domination" of the new government. Mao's deletion of the concept in his version of the Common Program clearly revealed the chairman's determination to ensure total control over the new regime by the CCP.

Since its founding, the CCP had championed the idea of China becoming "a republic of federation." To highlight the revolutionary nature of its nationality policy, the party had even argued that "while China proper . . . should be unified as a genuine democratic republic . . . Mongolia, Tibet, and Muslim Xinjiang should become autonomous, as democratic, free autonomies."[6] Indeed, CCP leaders even claimed that the GMD's promise of "unity between five nationalities" was designed to "conceal its policy of national oppression" targeted at the minority nationalities. The CCP, meanwhile, "acknowledges the rights of national self-determination of all minority nationalities. . . . Even leading to their separation from China."[7] Mao once proclaimed his support for the idea that Tibet, Outer Mongolia, and Xinjiang might "form autonomous republics attached to the Chinese federation" after "the people's revolution has been victorious."[8] Zhou held similar viewpoints. After the outbreak of the civil war between the CCP and the GMD, Zhou favored a CCP nationality policy that included "defending the right of self-determination by ethnic minorities," and he condemned Chiang's "abolishing" their "right of self-determination."[9] It was not accidental that Zhou used the phrase "federation of China's multiple nationalities" in his draft. However, Zhou's tone changed after Mao made his opinion clear. At the preparatory conference of the NPPCC on September 7, Zhou described the CCP's nationality policies, emphasizing the importance of "uniting all nationalities into a big family" in New China. "We must prevent the imperialists from sabotaging China's unification by utilizing the nationality issue," he said. Therefore, the "New China" would not become a federation, although it would allow for "autonomy in [minority] nationality regions."[10]

Although he abandoned the term "coalition government," Zhou still hoped that the new government would not only guarantee the CCP's leadership but also be defined by breadth and inclusiveness. As early as September 1948, Zhou secretly composed a list of seventy-seven prominent "democratic figures," based in Hong Kong and elsewhere, to be considered as candidates for the NPPCC. He instructed the CCP's Shanghai Bureau and Hong Kong Bureau branches to "confidentially arrange for them to travel to liberated zones in Northern China."[11] The person whom Zhou most diligently attempted to persuade to join the new regime was Song Qingling (Soong Chingling), Sun Yat-sen's widow. Song had long been a Communist sympathizer and had also worked for the Comintern. However, she had been living in Shanghai for many years and was not in good health. Song was apprehensive about going to Beijing, the city where Sun had died. Moreover, she probably felt concerned that joining the new regime would curb her political independence. Zhou wrote Song a touching letter, which Deng Yingchao delivered personally to her in Shanghai. Deng then stayed in Shanghai to continue persuading Song. Zhou thoughtfully arranged for Song to stay in Shanghai and, should she join the NPPCC, commute to and from Beijing conveniently.[12] Finally, Zhou's persistence paid off, as Song agreed to come to Beijing for the NPPCC. Later, she even agreed to serve as vice president of the PRC.

Zhou also strove to attract other "democratic figures" to serve the new regime. When the Council of Government Affairs was established, it resembled a product of "democratic cooperation." Zhou naturally became the council's premier. Two of the four vice premiers, Huang Yanpei and Guo Moruo, were non-Communist "democratic figures." Of the fifteen state councilors, Zhou had personally selected nine with non-Communist identities: Tan Pingshan, Zhang Bijun, Ma Xulun, Chen Shaoxian, Wang Kunlun, Luo Longji, Zhang Naiqi, Shao Lizi, and Huang Shaoxuan. Zhou also appointed over thirty non-CCP individuals to serve as ministers and vice ministers.

One exception was the Foreign Ministry. When Zhou was forming the new government, Mao asserted that the regime could continue existing practices in all domains except diplomacy, which must have a fresh start.[13] Accordingly, Zhou decided to make himself foreign minister, to ensure that he and the CCP would have direct control over China's foreign affairs. The new government's Foreign Ministry would comprise people from two groups. The first was the diplomatic team that Zhou had formed during his time in Chongqing, including Wang Bingnan, Qiao Guanhua, Gong Peng, Chen Jiakang, and Zhang Wenjin. Most of them had gone to Yan'an after the outbreak of the civil war. Prior to the CCP Center's evacuation from Yan'an, Zhou, along with Ye Jianying, had gathered the group together and transferred them to the Shanxi "Liberated Zone."[14] Zhou knew that the group's members had diplomatic experience and spoke foreign languages. "Do not let them be separated, and make it difficult to locate them," Zhou instructed. Under Zhou's guidance, a Foreign Affairs Group was established under the CMC in May 1947. Ye was to head the group and Wang Bingnan would serve as its second-in-command. Almost all of Zhou's former diplomatic staff joined the group.[15] In 1949, they were sent to Beijing, where they became core members of the Foreign Ministry.

Zhou also reassigned to the Foreign Ministry a group of PLA commanders from the army corps, making them candidates for China's foreign ambassadorships. Zhou explained his rationale for the move as follows: "Doing diplomacy is similar to fighting battles. Diplomacy is only nonviolent battles."[16] Although the commanders Zhou selected had no diplomatic background, they were absolutely loyal to the party and had abundant experience in dealing with complicated situations during the war against Japan and the civil war. Most of the PRC's first cohort of ambassadors came from this group of commanders.

* * *

On October 2, the day after the PRC's founding, Zhou was still buzzing with excitement. Late in the evening, the report he had been waiting for all day finally came: Moscow had recognized the People's Republic and would establish diplomatic relations with the new nation.[17] Zhou immediately phoned Mao to share the great news with the chairman. One of Mao's objectives when he unveiled the strategy of "leaning to one side" three months earlier was to win Moscow's speedy recognition of New China.[18] Now, Mao and Zhou welcomed the news that Stalin's government was the first to recognize the PRC, brimming with delight.

Mao believed that a face-to-face meeting with Stalin was crucial to maximize the benefits that China could gain from the Soviet Union. On his wish list for the visit were such items as securing substantial Soviet military and economic support. Mao's main goal, though, was to sign a new treaty of alliance with the Soviet Union, one that would replace the treaty Moscow had signed with Chiang Kai-shek's government in 1945. This new treaty would at once substantiate Mao's "leaning to one side" approach and facilitate the CCP leadership's designing of a path toward modernity for New China.

Mao wanted to bring Zhou with him on the trip, which would allow him to remain in the background, where he could sound out Stalin's intentions. On November 9, Mao cabled Wang Jiaxiang, the new PRC ambassador in Moscow, asking Wang to inform Stalin of his plan to visit the Soviet Union. In particular, Mao instructed Wang, "Please ask Stalin to decide whether Comrade [Zhou] Enlai should come with me, or if his coming should be decided after my arrival in Moscow."[19] In his reply, however, Stalin only confirmed his invitation for Mao and made no mention of Zhou. This was not a good sign for Mao and Zhou. On November 12, Mao informed Stalin that he would leave Beijing for Moscow in early December.[20] Zhou immediately put together a team of China's top experts in various fields to prepare for Mao's visit.

• • •

On the cold and sunny morning of December 6, Mao departed Beijing for Moscow by train. Zhou and other CCP leaders came to the station to see Mao off. After a ten-day journey across Siberia, Mao arrived in Moscow at noon on December 16, greeted at the train station by Vyacheslav M. Molotov, Nikolai Bulganin, and other Soviet leaders.[21] That evening, Stalin, joined by nearly every member of the Soviet Politburo, welcomed Mao at the Kremlin. The Soviet dictator had never hosted such a grand reception for a foreign leader; this represented Stalin's gracious gesture toward Mao.

Mao was not ungrateful, but he had come to Moscow in the hopes of obtaining something bigger and more substantial. When Stalin asked him what he hoped to achieve from the visit, Mao replied that he wanted to "bring about something that looks nice and tastes delicious." Shi Zhe, Mao's interpreter, explained that "'looking nice' means something with a good outlook, and 'tasting delicious' means something substantial." What Mao was actually referring to was a new Sino-Soviet treaty, but Stalin did not seem to understand Mao's message. Lavrentiy Beria, head of the Soviet secret police, could not help but laugh at Mao's expression.[22]

In fact, the cunning Soviet dictator's incomprehension probably was merely feigned. When the two leaders' formal discussion began, Mao directly raised the matter of signing a new Sino-Soviet treaty. Stalin did not reject Mao's request outright. Instead, he lectured the chairman at length about the difficulties he was facing. "The Soviet Union and China signed the treaty of 1945 in accordance with the Yalta agreements," he told Mao. It was desirable "not to change any provisions of the treaty, because even a single amendment could offer the United States and Britain legal excuses to change Yalta's provisions concerning the Kuril Islands and southern Sakhalin." Indeed, the Sino-Soviet treaty of 1945 was an integral part of the Yalta settlement. If it were nullified, the Yalta accords could also be overturned. So, Stalin proposed, rather than sign a new treaty, it would be preferable to "maintain the current treaty in format while revising it in substance."[23]

Stalin also mentioned Lüshun (Port Arthur) and the Chinese Eastern Railway (CER), which were of strategic importance to Stalin. From the time of Czarist Russia, securing access to the Pacific Ocean was central in Russian and Soviet security strategies in the Far East. After its defeat by Japan in 1904–1905, Russia had lost control over Lüshun and the CER. With the signing of the Sino-Soviet treaty at the end of World War II, the Soviets regained the right to station troops in Lüshun for thirty years and to "jointly use" the CER. "As Communists, it is inappropriate for us to station our troops in a friendly foreign country," Stalin told Mao. Therefore, while the treaty of 1945 "granted us the right to use Lüshun, we might not use the right and, instead, pull our troops out if the Chinese government so requests." Mao immediately detected the insincerity of Stalin's words. There is "no need for you to hurriedly withdraw your troops from Lüshun," he assured the Soviet dictator. Then, Mao brought Zhou's name into the conversation. Zhou should come to Moscow, Mao insisted, "in case there is the need to negotiate a new treaty and sign it." Stalin gently rebutted him, replying, "If we are not sure what we really want to work out, why should we call Zhou here?" Mao gave no direct answer.[24]

Mao left the meeting in a very bad mood. It took him almost two days to write and dispatch a telegram about the meeting to his colleagues in Beijing. Although he began the telegram by saying that "Stalin's attitude is really sincere," the content of his message indicated otherwise. Stalin was unwilling to sign a new treaty with the PRC, Mao told his colleagues. However, it seemed possible for the two countries to negotiate and sign agreements on Soviet loans and other support for China. As for Lüshun, Mao suggested that the two sides could resolve the issue by "not formally changing the current terms" and finding ways to lead up to "the actual withdrawal of Soviet troops." Mao also informed his comrades that Stalin found it "unnecessary for Foreign Minister (Zhou) to fly here just for the sake of signing a statement." However, Mao suggested, if the two countries were to "sign agreements on loans, aviation, and trade. . . . it might still be necessary for the Foreign Minister to come." Obviously, Mao still refused to abandon his hope of bringing "something that looks nice and tastes delicious" back to China. And the matter of Zhou coming to Moscow became a subtle yet crucial part of Mao's strategy in his negotiation vis-à-vis Stalin.[25]

CCP leaders in Beijing met on December 21. They specifically discussed whether Zhou should join Mao in Moscow, so that substantial Soviet support to China could be negotiated. After the meeting, Liu Shaoqi and Zhou jointly cabled Mao with a proposal: "If the Soviet side agrees to sign agreements on Lüshun, loans, aviation, and trade, Comrade (Zhou) Enlai might still go to Moscow. . . . But if the Soviets do not want to sign these agreements, and are only willing to make a statement on troops stationed in Lüshun as well as on general political issues, there would be no need for Comrade (Zhou) Enlai to go." If Mao found it necessary, Liu and Zhou emphasized, "Comrade (Zhou) Enlai can set off immediately after receiving your call."[26]

On the evening of December 21, Mao attended Stalin's birthday celebration, an event at the top of his official agenda. In public, Stalin tried his best to show respect for Mao, arranging for Mao to sit next to him and inviting the chairman to give a speech as the guest of honor. Although Stalin frequently glanced smilingly at Mao, the chairman "wore a stiff expression and said almost nothing throughout" the celebration.[27]

The next day, Mao summoned Stalin's liaison Ivan Kovalev to his quarters. Mao told Kovalev that he wanted to meet with Stalin in one or two days, declaring that "we would like to discuss and resolve the following issues: the Sino-Soviet treaty, and agreements on loans, trade and aviation; further, I plan to ask Zhou Enlai to come to Moscow for the signing ceremony." Mao also asked Kovalev to see to it that "the minutes of this conversation are given to Stalin."[28]

Two days later, the Chinese chairman and the Soviet dictator met again. They discussed a wide range of topics, including "the international Communist movement, Vietnam, Japan, India, Indonesia, a Communist information bureau in the East, Western Europe, [American politician] Henry Wallace, and revolutionary strategies in various Eastern countries." Neither Stalin nor Mao mentioned the signing of a new Sino-Soviet treaty. Mao once again suggested that Zhou should come to Moscow. Stalin replied, "As chairman of your government, you are already here; why should the premier of your cabinet also come? This may leave others with an unfavorable impression."[29] The meeting lasted over five hours, but Mao left it empty handed. In a telegram to his comrades in Beijing, he reported disappointedly that "the conclusion" from his talk with Stalin "is that it is better for Comrade [Zhou] Enlai not to come here."[30]

Over the following days, Mao stayed in his dacha, where he did nothing but watch Russian movies. He did not want to challenge Stalin directly. He proposed Zhou's coming to Moscow to remind the Soviet dictator of his desire for a new treaty; but Stalin, the wily old fox, repeatedly turned Mao down. Knowing that the Soviets had doubtlessly bugged his quarters, Mao loudly complained to his associates that he had nothing to do in Moscow besides "eating, sleeping, and shitting."[31] Meanwhile, he showed no intention to leave Moscow and return home without signing a new Sino-Soviet treaty. This was his tactic to prompt Stalin to act and—hopefully—cause him to change his mind. Stalin surely had received Mao's message. He wavered between a number of potential responses, carefully weighing the pros and cons of each.

Then, something rather strange happened. On December 24, Kovalev submitted a report to Stalin, detailing how the CCP's policies had diverged from Stalin's instructions. For example, the CCP had not given enough attention to the role of the working class in China, and it had not imposed any restrictions on foreign businesses. In particular, Kovalev observed, "despite the active support that Britain and the United States had given to Chiang," CCP leaders still hoped that the two Western powers would "recognize the People's Republic soon." The clearest evidence for this, Kovalev stressed, was Zhou's soft stance toward the West.[32] Stalin only shared the report with a few members of the Politburo. However, he decided to give a copy to Mao. "Kovalev is not political material, but a technician. It is quite inappropriate for him to involve himself in politics," commented the Soviet dictator.[33] Why did Stalin share the report with Mao nonetheless? He may have done so to confide in Mao, or to send him a warning. Meanwhile, Stalin's move probably conveyed an implicit explanation for his refusal to invite Zhou to Moscow, suggesting that Zhou had a "pro-West" tendency.

Finally, Stalin made up his mind. After all, with the Cold War escalating and the Soviet-American confrontation worsening, it was essential to make sure that Mao's China would stand on the side of the Soviet Union. Consequently, the turn of events that Mao had desired finally came.

On the evening of January 2, 1950, Molotov and Mikoyan knocked on Mao's door. They had been sent by Stalin, they told the chairman, to hear his opinions on what the two sides should do to make his visit to Moscow fruitful. Mao immediately recognized that his moment had arrived. The first and most ideal option, Mao said, was that "we might sign a new Sino-Soviet alliance treaty," as "this will greatly consolidate the Sino-Soviet relationship by placing it on the basis of a new treaty." There were also domestic advantages, elaborated the chairman: "China's workers, peasants, intellectuals, and leftist nationalist bourgeoisie will be greatly encouraged, while the rightist nationalist bourgeoisie will be isolated; internationally, we will have more political capital to deal with imperialist countries and to terminate all treaties they signed with China in the past." Mao's enthusiasm for the first option was palpable. In comparison, he was much more reluctant to present the other two options. The second was that the Chinese and Soviets might "issue a joint communiqué, stating that. . . . we have reached a consensus on all important issues under discussion." The third option was to "sign and issue a public statement but not a treaty . . . to list the principles underlying our relationship."

As he had done before, Mao linked the three options to whether Zhou should be called to Moscow. Mao made it clear that Zhou would only come if the first option was chosen. Molotov, who obviously had received instructions from Stalin prior to the meeting, immediately asserted that Mao's first option was the best, and that Zhou should join Mao in Moscow. "Will we sign a new treaty to replace the old one?" Mao asked, wanting confirmation. "Yes!" replied Molotov.[34]

Mao was jubilant. As soon as Molotov left, Mao dispatched a cable to Beijing. "Our work here has achieved a major breakthrough in the past two days," he told his comrades. "Comrade Stalin has finally agreed to invite Comrade Zhou Enlai to Moscow and sign a new Sino-Soviet Treaty of Friendship and Alliance and other agreements on credit, trade, and civil aviation." But Mao did not want to give the Russians an impression that he was in a hurry to negotiate the treaty, so he also instructed Zhou "to prepare for five days . . . and come here by train, not by airplane."[35] A few hours later, Mao sent another telegram to Beijing. "Comrade (Zhou) Enlai's visit to the Soviet Union should be formally approved by a State Council conference," Mao instructed, "and he should report that the visit is for signing a new Sino-Soviet Treaty of Alliance." Mao emphasized that Zhou should "point out that this will place the People's

Republic in a more favorable position, forcing capitalist countries to accept our terms, which will also force other countries to recognize China unconditionally, while abolishing old treaties and signing new treaties with us."[36]

Mao's colleagues in Beijing "completely endorsed" all of the chairman's ideas during an all-night meeting on January 3. Zhou "decided to leave Beijing by train on the evening of the ninth," to "arrive in Moscow on the nineteenth."[37] Heeding Mao's instructions, he gave a report at a State Council meeting on Sino-Soviet relations, in which he highlighted the recent progress made on that front as a major diplomatic achievement of New China.[38]

* * *

Zhou arrived in Moscow on January 20. The Soviets had already arranged for him to stay in his own dacha, but he chose to move into Mao's. To prevent Soviet agents from listening to their conversations, Mao and Zhou always held their important discussions in the garden.[39]

Two days later, Zhou joined Mao for a meeting with Stalin. The Soviet dictator was prepared, bringing with him drafts of the new treaty and a series of other agreements prepared by his assistants. He proposed that they begin the discussion by covering "various existing agreements between China and the Soviet Union," as well as "such practical issues as Manchuria and Xinjiang." Mao again mentioned that he hoped to sign a new Sino-Soviet treaty, which would "further confirm the friendly relationship between us." Stalin agreed immediately. When the two leaders discussed the content of the treaty, Mao, obviously thinking about his proclamation that "we, the Chinese, have stood up," stressed the treaty's political impact within China. "The new treaty should include a clause of mutual consultation and coordination on international issues," said Mao, "as this will strengthen our position at home." "Surely this should be included," Stalin replied without hesitation. When the discussion turned to the issue of revising the agreements on Lüshun, Dalian, and the CER, Mao mentioned that "changing these agreements will alter decisions made at the Yalta Conference." Stalin's attitude was clear and firm: "Yes, it will be touched upon. Let it go to hell. Since we have chosen to revise the treaty, we will go to the end. . . . We will have to struggle with the Americans."

"Who should be assigned to draft the treaty?" Stalin then asked. Before Mao gave his response, Stalin proposed, "I think this should be the job of Vyshinsky and Zhou." "I agree," Mao replied.[40]

On the Chinese side, the task of working out the details of the treaty and other agreements fell on Zhou's shoulders. This would be no easy feat. Zhou had participated in many negotiations, including some with the Nationalists and the Americans, but the negotiations with the Soviets would probably prove most challenging of all. Zhou knew not only that he needed to show high respect for the Soviet elder brothers, but that it was up to him to defend New China's vital national interests.

Zhou's meetings with Mikoyan, Vyshinsky, and other Soviet leaders began on January 23. The first item on the agenda was the new Sino-Soviet treaty. The Soviets brought a draft of the treaty that they had been working on since Stalin gave his approval for a new treaty. They also came with a dozen draft agreements on Lüshun, Dalian, the CER, and matters such as trade, loans, joint ventures, and the sending of Soviet experts to China. Zhou felt that "much important content" had "been omitted" from these documents, especially those pertaining to Lüshun, Dalian, and the CER. Mao, having heard Zhou's remark, suggested, "We should make drafts of our own."[41]

Almost immediately, Zhou began working on a treaty draft "under the chairman's direction." On January 24, the draft was ready. Upon comparison, Zhou's draft and the Soviets' draft were quite similar. The main change that Zhou made was to add the term "mutual assistance" to the treaty's title, making it the "Sino-Soviet Treaty of Friendship, Alliance, and Mutual Assistance." This reflected Zhou's determination to emphasize "equality" in creating the new treaty.

When the Soviets received Zhou's draft, they quickly found it to be "very close to" their own; other than the occasional textual change, they made no major revisions to the document. On January 25, Zhou cabled Liu, informing him that the text of the treaty had been "drafted and prepared by us," and that "the Soviets have made no major changes to it, except for language editing." Consequently, "it is already a done deal," Zhou stated.[42] Mao was satisfied, too. The next morning, he telegraphed Liu, reporting to his comrades in Beijing that "the work here has gone quite smoothly." However, it was not yet time to celebrate, so Mao instructed them to "keep [their] lips sealed" about the matter for the time being.[43]

Mao's precaution was not unjustified, as Zhou and his Soviet counterparts soon found themselves at loggerheads on Lüshun, Dalian, and the CER. These issues involved vital Soviet interests in the Far East, which had implications for the scope and essence of the new treaty. When Zhou received the Soviet draft agreements on these issues on January 23, he realized that his views were radically different from those of his Soviet counterparts. Zhou's realization was further confirmed when, on January 26, the Soviets handed him a draft agreement on Dalian. The Soviets requested that the Chinese waive tariffs on Soviet goods that passed through the Port of Dalian and permit them to use port facilities free of charge. They agreed to allow the Chinese to control the port, but they demanded that the directorship and deputy directorship of the Port of Dalian be filled by representatives from the two sides on a rotating basis. The Soviets also proposed that Dalian, along with Lüshun, be placed under martial law until a peace treaty had been signed with Japan.[44]

Zhou and Mao felt that the terms of the Soviet draft impinged on Chinese sovereignty. That same day, Zhou presented a Chinese counterdraft to the Soviets, in which he bundled Lüshun, Dalian, and the CER—which the Soviets previously had dealt with separately—into a single draft agreement.[45] The greatest difference, however, lay in the content of the counterdraft. Zhou proposed that the Soviet Union give up all its rights with respect to Lüshun, Dalian, and the CER, and return them to China; that all properties the Soviet Union had *temporarily* possessed on lease in Lüshun and Dalian be taken over by the Chinese; and that the Soviet Union commit to returning the CER and all properties attached to it to China without compensation.[46] Zhou and his associates had obviously prepared the draft well in advance and given careful consideration to its terms. The counterdraft reflected Zhou and Mao's insistence that the new Sino-Soviet treaty and other agreements be presentable to the Chinese public and thus enhance the New China's legitimacy at home and abroad by demonstrating that "we, the Chinese, have stood up."

But Zhou's counterdraft effectively pushed Stalin and the Soviets into a corner, forcing them to make some tough choices. Stalin and other Soviet leaders reviewed Zhou's draft, leaving large *X*s and question marks in the margins and between the lines of text and penning such comments as "Stalin disagrees."[47] But Stalin did not want to see negotiations break down simply on account of these disagreements. After all, the negotiations on a new treaty had already gone so far, and the rights to the three possessions in question would eventually be returned to China anyway. Would Stalin be willing to reject the Chinese terms and thus allow the negotiations to fail? In several later drafts that the Soviets produced, it was apparent that they were gradually, albeit begrudgingly, trying to align their terms with Zhou's.

Finally, Stalin made the agonizing decision to yield to the Chinese. Zhou received the Soviets' final response on January 29. They were willing to make substantial concessions: They agreed that after the signing of a peace treaty with Japan or no later than 1952, the Soviet Union would transfer, with no compensation, all of its rights to the CER to the Chinese; the Soviet troops would leave Lüshun, whose civil administration would be turned over to China; the two sides would "deal with the question of Dalian" after the signing of a peace treaty with Japan; and "the administration of the Port of Dalian will be completely overseen by China." If "either signatory [is] involved in a war," the two countries, with the approval of their governments, "may jointly use the naval bases in Lüshun, so as to benefit them in a common battle against the aggressor."[48] By this point, the Soviets' positions on the three issues were very close to those of the Chinese. That day, the Soviets produced the final version of the treaty, in which any differences between the two sides' wordings had been excised.[49]

On February 8, Zhou dispatched a lengthy telegram to Liu Shaoqi summarizing the progress he had made in his negotiations with the Soviets. Nearly every item on the agenda, he proudly told his comrades in Beijing, had been resolved. The time of the signing of a new treaty was near.[50]

Toward the end of the telegram, however, Zhou mentioned that there were still "individual issues" that he would "report in another telegram."[51] The "issues" Zhou referred to were the talks that he and his Soviet counterparts had held leading up to several secret agreements. At the end of January, once the two sides had made significant progress on Lüshun, Dalian, and the CER, Mikoyan broached the topic of the Soviet Union's "special interests" in Xinjiang. The USSR, Mikoyan asserted, favored an agreement on the region that barred any "personnel from a third country" from access to Xinjiang and the Northeast (Manchuria). Zhou discussed the matter with the Soviets. On February 10, Mikoyan handed Zhou a draft agreement in which the Soviets proposed that "no leases or concessions be allowed for foreigners" either in the Soviet Far East or Soviet Central Asia, or in China's Xinjiang and Northeast. Apparently, the Soviets were worried that the "influence of a third country" might penetrate into Manchuria and Xinjiang, which had been Soviet spheres of influence. Sensing the sensitivity of this matter, Zhou relayed the draft to Mao. The chairman felt deeply offended. "The Soviets are still interested in the Northeast and Xinjiang, and are still trying to repeat what they did at Yalta," he commented. By then, though, the signing date of the new treaty was fast approaching. Neither Zhou nor Mao wanted to find their path to a Sino-Soviet agreement blocked yet again. Mao decided to give his assent to the Soviet request. On February 11, Zhou informed the Soviets that Mao had approved the draft agreement presented by Molotov. The Soviets proposed that the draft be kept confidential, and Zhou agreed.[52]

The day of the treaty's signing came on February 14, 1950. Both Stalin and Mao attended the ceremony, while Zhou and Vyshinsky signed the documents. The treaty stipulated that Beijing and Moscow would "make every effort possible to stop Japan's aggression and the aggression by a third state which is directly or indirectly associated with Japan's act of aggression." And "in the event that one of the High Contracting Parties is attacked by Japan or states allied with it, and thus goes into a state of war, the other High Contracting Party will immediately render military and other assistance with all the means at its disposal." Zhou and Vyshinsky also signed an agreement regarding a US$300 million loan granted by the Soviet Union to China at an annual interest rate of 1 percent. In accordance with an understanding that Zhou had reached with the Soviets, the funds would largely be used to purchase Soviet military equipment. The Soviets also agreed to transfer the CER to China by the end of 1952 and to withdraw Soviet forces from Lüshun following the signing of a peace treaty with Japan, or failing that, no later than the end of 1952.[53]

On the evening of February 16, Stalin hosted a sumptuous state banquet at the Kremlin for Mao and Zhou. This was the most relaxing event that the two Chinese leaders had attended since they arrived in Moscow.

During and after their long trip back to Beijing by train, Mao and Zhou each delivered several speeches to high-ranking CCP cadres. The chairman stressed that the Sino-Soviet treaty had "united two great nations through an alliance" that would "produce a huge impact in the whole world." Further, Mao asserted that "the first socialist country in the world will provide us with the best experience and lessons for us to learn from."[54] In his view, Beijing's alliance with Moscow validated his choice to "lean to one side" and demonstrated that the strategy was already yielding significant dividends for China. Zhou explained that according to the treaty, "Lüshun and the Chinese Eastern Railway will be returned to China in 1952" and that "Lüshun and Dalian are already administered by us." Indeed, "only a China led by the CCP could achieve such a settlement with the Soviet

15.3 Zhou Enlai with Mao Zedong and Stalin at the signing of the Sino-Soviet Treaty of Friendship, Alliance, and Mutual Assistance, February 14, 1950. *Album / Alamy Stock Photo*

Union," he claimed.[55] Evidently, Zhou was making every effort to underscore the new Sino-Soviet treaty's resonance with Mao's statement that "we, the Chinese, have stood up."

But Mao was acutely aware that he and Stalin were highly dissimilar. Stalin was accustomed to wielding the language of power, raw and unrefined, at will. Moreover, he always placed Soviet strategic interests above all else. Mao's spirit abounded with revolutionary romanticism, and he liked to use philosophical language to discuss the Communists' ideals and historical mission. This was also true of Mao's attempt to define China's national interests. He never directly challenged Stalin's position as the leader of the world revolution, but he was extremely sensitive about the Soviet dictator's habit of treating him as his inferior. He did not relish meeting with Stalin in person, which was another reason why he had insisted on bringing Zhou to the talks in Moscow. The signing of the Sino-Soviet treaty made Mao's "lean to one side" approach the cornerstone of China's domestic and international policies. The way that it was worked out, however, presaged that the future development of Sino-Soviet relations was bound to be uneasy.

* * *

While Mao, Zhou, and their comrades were busy laying the groundwork for the new regime, they never forgot about Taiwan, which was still controlled by Chiang and had yet to be "liberated." Along with the steady mopping-up of GMD forces remaining on the mainland, Mao and the CCP leadership began to put the "liberation of Taiwan" at the top of their agenda. On June 14, 1949, Mao cabled Su Yu, commander of the PLA's Third Field Army, instructing Su and his comrades to consider "the issue of seizing Taiwan." Mao asked them to explore "how to divide the enemy troops in Taiwan, seeking to induce a part of them to shift to our side." "If we do not resolve the Taiwan issue," he emphasized, "it will be enormously harmful to Shanghai and other coastal ports."[56] Without waiting for Su's reply, Mao again cabled Su and the CCP East China Bureau, criticizing them for "not having paid sufficient attention" to Taiwan, and ordered them to "give high priority to [Taiwan] immediately." The chairman particularly mentioned intelligence work, which had been handled by Zhou. He instructed CCP organs in Shanghai and the PLA command in East China to establish "a special agency at every command branch to study how to resolve the Taiwan question." In addition to research, the agencies "should pay great attention to recruiting collaborators," including personnel from the "GMD army, navy, and air force; government officials; and the capitalists who have fled to Taiwan, Xiamen, and Hong Kong," so that they might provide assistance during the Taiwan campaign. "Without such help," Mao stressed, "it will be very difficult to occupy Taiwan."[57]

The chairman was impatient. A telegraph he dispatched to Zhou on July 10 most clearly spelled out his vision of general strategies to "liberate Taiwan" and a timeline for the campaign:

> We must prepare for conditions to attack Taiwan. In addition to the army, we should mainly rely on internal collaborators and an air force. If we have one of these two, we will succeed. And if we have both, we will be more certain to succeed. It is impossible for our air force to overwhelm the enemy's air force in a short time (such as a year). Thus, we might consider dispatching three to four hundred to study in the

> remote place (the Soviet Union) for six to eight months, while purchasing about one hundred planes, which will join the air force we have now to form an offensive force. They will support our cross-strait operations and be prepared to occupy Taiwan next summer.[58]

After he received Mao's instructions, Zhou immediately set out to prepare for "liberating Taiwan." However, Zhou and his comrades encountered insurmountable obstacles in their efforts to satisfy either of Mao's requirements. Mao and Zhou hoped that Moscow would provide the CCP with substantial aid in developing the PRC's naval and air combat capacities. During his trip to Moscow in summer 1949, Liu Shaoqi submitted to Stalin the CCP's request for naval support. The Soviet dictator was reluctant to grant the request, as he feared that doing so could risk a direct confrontation with the United States. Stalin did agree, though, to provide the CCP some naval vessels and to help the CCP train naval personnel.[59] In late July, Zhou assembled a Chinese delegation headed by Liu Yalou, the newly named air force commander, to visit the Soviet Union. In the delegation's meetings with the Soviets, Liu requested Soviet support in the form of three to five hundred fighters, with which China could establish an air force capable of supporting an invasion of Taiwan within one year. The Soviets pledged that they would "try their best to help."[60]

The situation facing Zhou and the CCP leadership dramatically worsened when, in the fall of 1949, the PLA suffered two major setbacks in its attempt to occupy the islands of Jinmen and Dengbu off the Fujian and Zhejiang coast. The PLA's Tenth Army Corps tried to rapidly occupy the Jinmen islands in late October. After they landed, however, the corps' three regiments were cut off from reinforcements due to the changing tide. The regiments were totally destroyed.[61] In November, the Sixty-First Division of the PLA suffered another major defeat in its failed occupation of Dengbu. After the division quickly landed on and almost seized control of the island in a single day, the GMD troops, aided by their side's naval and air superiority, launched a counterattack. Four GMD regiments landed on Dengbu, forcing the PLA to abandon the operation.[62]

The PLA's defeats at Jinmen and Dengbu were, in Mao's words, unprecedented in the Communist experience during the civil war.[63] The losses dealt a huge blow to the overall strategy of Mao, Zhou, and the CCP leadership to attack Taiwan. Earlier, Mao and the CCP leadership had planned to launch the Taiwan campaign in the summer of 1950.[64] But difficulties in naval and air development and the setbacks on Jinmen and Dengbu prompted them to reconsider the feasibility of their timetable for "liberating Taiwan." In a conversation with Nikolai V. Roshchin on December 5, Zhou told the Soviet ambassador that "it seems that the date for the Taiwan campaign will be no earlier than September and October of 1950."[65]

Chiang also launched a series of effective countermeasures to frustrate the CCP's plans to attack Taiwan. In early 1950, he dispatched bombers to bombard mainland coastal cities, including Shanghai. Although the bombardments were soon halted when Soviet air units quickly moved into eastern China, Chiang had already achieved his objective, which was to force the CCP to assign a higher priority to defense of airspace in coastal areas. This, in turn, would substantially delay the newly established CCP Air Force's preparations to invade Taiwan. Then, Chiang made further adjustments to his overall strategy for defending Taiwan. In April 1950, the PLA began a large-scale invasion of Hainan Island. Rather than send more reinforcements to defend Hainan, Chiang ordered the bulk of his troops to evacuate the island and contribute to the defense of Taiwan.[66] In late May, Chiang took the initiative to order GMD troops on the Zhoushan Islands off Zhejiang to be secretly transferred to Taiwan.[67] Consequently, the PLA easily took control of Hainan and the Zhoushan Islands, but it had failed to eliminate large numbers of GMD forces as Mao and Zhou had hoped.

In the face of mounting obstacles, Mao, Zhou, and the CCP leadership had to postpone the date on which the PLA was scheduled to launch the invasion of Taiwan. In April 1950, the PLA's Third Frontal Army, which had been designated as the main occupying force, decided to push back "the time for attacking Taiwan in a three-service coordinated operation" to spring 1951. The CMC approved the delay.[68] At the Third Plenum of the Central Committee in mid-June, the party leadership confirmed that the Taiwan campaign would not begin earlier than summer 1951.[69] Therefore, even if the Korean War had not broken out, the CCP could not feasibly have launched the Taiwan campaign in 1950.

A more fatal blow to the CCP's plans to liberate Taiwan came in the spring and early summer, with the arrest and betrayal of Cai Xiaoqian, secretary of the CCP's Taiwan Work Committee, and the exposure and execution of General

Wu Shi, the highest-ranked CCP agent in Chiang's military organization. The CCP's underground intelligence network in Taiwan collapsed.[70] Within the CCP leadership, it had long been Zhou's duty to plant and utilize collaborators within the GMD. Throughout the civil war, Zhou and the CCP had absolutely held the upper hand vis-à-vis Chiang and the GMD. But the situation completely changed when the GMD government moved to Taiwan. Chiang regarded the expunging of "bandit spies" as a matter of survival for his regime, and as soon as he moved to Taiwan, he spared no effort to uncover Communist spies. Indeed, CCP intelligence activities in Taiwan were beset by a number of challenges. In particular, Taiwan is separated from the mainland by a wide strait, which made it difficult for the CCP to dispatch intelligence agents to Taiwan and maintain communication with them. Cai snuck into Taiwan in 1945, but his efforts to develop underground CCP organs did not go smoothly. As of 1948, Cai's clandestine cells had only recruited several dozen members. After Chiang arrived in Taiwan, the whole island was soaked in a mood of impending doom. The CCP's underground organs on the island grew rapidly, building a membership of nearly two thousand. A turning point came in early 1950, when Chiang's special agents apprehended a key liaison between Wu and Cai. Wu was arrested in early March and executed on June 10. Cai quickly went into deep hiding; still, he was arrested in late April. Chiang's agents successfully broke down his mental defenses. Cai's surrender to the GMD resulted in the demise of the CCP's entire underground network in Taiwan. From then on, the CCP was unable to reestablish its underground intelligence cells in Taiwan, with the exception of a few strategic moles who had been in "single-line communication" with Zhou.[71] For years, Chiang had suffered one setback after another in his intelligence showdown with Zhou. In Taiwan, he took his revenge in a single, life-or-death showdown.

After the outbreak of the Korean War, US president Harry Truman announced that the United States would dispatch the US Navy's Seventh Fleet to "neutralize" the Taiwan Strait. It was no longer possible for the CCP to use military means to "liberate" Taiwan. When he later reflected on this episode of history, Mao confessed that he had made a "strategic mistake." "On the mainland," the chairman observed, "we won and Chiang lost. However, after crossing the Yangzi River . . . we failed to use the full strength of the Second and Third Field Armies to liberate Taiwan. . . . Instead, our troops were diverted. . . . At that time, we only saw that Hu Zongnan had a big force in the Southwest. However, Hu was a dead fish. . . . And in Taiwan, Chiang was given a second life."[72]

• • •

Mao and Zhou now turned their attention to the "liberation" of Tibet, another key region crucial to the CCP's goal of creating a multinational, unified New China. On July 8, 1949, the Tibetan government, in an effort to demonstrate neutrality in the civil war between the Communists and the Nationalists, closed the Nationalist government's mission in Lhasa and expelled all Han Chinese officials from Tibet.[73] On September 2, Beijing announced that the expulsion of Chinese officials from Tibet had been "planned and initiated by British and US imperialists and their follower, the Nehru government of India . . . and carried out by the reactionary local authorities of Tibet." The move, Beijing asserted, would "absolutely not be allowed."[74] In formulating their Tibetan strategy, CCP leaders realized that to "liberate Tibet," "it is impossible not to use force."[75] However, they believed that "fundamentally, Tibet is also a political issue," and that its resolution would require the combined use of "military, diplomatic, and united front means."[76] Naturally, Zhou would play a central role in the implementation of such a strategy.

In the fall of 1949, the CCP leadership began to make miliary preparations to invade Tibet. By early 1950, they had designated the PLA's Eighteenth Army and the CCP's Southwest Bureau to carry out "the march into Tibet" from Xikang and Sichuan.[77] Meanwhile, the PRC Foreign Ministry invited the "local government of Tibet" to dispatch representatives to Beijing for negotiations leading to Tibet's "peaceful liberation."[78] In response, the Kashag (the government in Lhasa) argued that Tibet had, over the course of history, become independent; that Tibet's relationship with China was one of priest and patron; and that no foreign imperialism existed in Tibet. It asked Beijing "not to use force to attack Tibet."[79] The Kashag also tried to solicit support from Britain, the United States, India, and the United Nations. Beijing immediately used all this as evidence to claim that the "Tibetan local government" was heavily under the influence of Western imperialists. Under pressure from Beijing, Kashag abandoned its plans to send missions to Washington and London.

In February 1950, the Kashag appointed a three-person group led by the high-ranking lay official Tsepon Shakabpa to pursue a dialogue with Beijing in order to "secure assurance that the territorial integrity of Tibet [will] not be violated." But when Shakabpa, having been in New Delhi, requested to speak with Beijing's representatives in Hong Kong, Beijing ignored him. It was not until late May that Shakabpa was invited to Beijing for "talks with the central government."[80] In August, the Tibetans still had not responded. Twice Zhou instructed Shen Jian, the Chinese chargé d'affaires in India, to urge the Tibetans to come to Beijing "in their capacity as representatives of the Tibetan local government."[81]

By then, the PLA's Eighteenth Army had nearly completed preparations to launch a "decisive strike" against the Tibetan troops at Chamdo, known as the "gate to Lhasa," where the main force of the Tibetan army was stationed. Following Zhou's orders, Yuan Zhongxian, the Chinese ambassador to India, sent an ultimatum to Shakabpa on September 17, demanding that the Tibetan negotiators "arrive in Beijing by September 20."[82] No Tibetan delegation came. Yuan sent Shakabpa another warning on September 23, emphasizing that as "the September 20 deadline has passed, the PLA will take action as planned," and that the Tibetans "will bear all responsibility for the consequences . . . unless they travel to Beijing immediately."[83] Two weeks later, on October 3, the PLA's Southwest Military Region issued the order for a military mobilization.[84] Bloody battles in Chamdo began three days later and lasted two weeks, in which the PLA won a clear victory. According to the report Zhou received, a total of 180 Tibetans were killed or wounded, about 900 were captured, and another 4,300 surrendered.[85] Zhou noted that the person who ordered the surrender was Ngapoi Ngawang Jigme, the most senior Tibetan political and military officer in Chamdo. Ngapoi's call for surrender marked the beginning of his long-term cooperation with the CCP.[86]

While the battles of Chamdo were still underway, Zhou instructed Yuan to inform Tibetan negotiators that their "intentional delay" in coming to Beijing was to blame for the bloodshed in Chamdo. However, the door to negotiation remained open, "if the Tibetans should come to Beijing immediately."[87] The defeat in Chamdo deepened divisions and even sparked panic among the Tibetan elites in Lhasa. On November 17, the sixteen-year-old Dalai Lama ascended the throne, two years before reaching the age at which a Dalai Lama traditionally took over actual leadership. At first, Tibetan leaders decided to appeal once more to the United Nations in order to "stop the Chinese invasion." However, their last-ditch effort to end the fighting through diplomacy proved fruitless.[88]

At this juncture, India entered the picture. For geopolitical reasons, New Delhi was gravely concerned about the PLA's "planned advance into Tibet."[89] The Indians also felt that "recent developments in Tibet have affected the friendly relations [between India and China] and the interest of peace all over the world," which, indeed, could "give an excuse for those countries to deny the People's Republic its seat at the United Nations."[90] "Tibet is Chinese territory," the PRC Foreign Ministry retorted, "and the Tibet issue belongs to China's internal affairs."[91] When Sardar K. M. Panikkar, the Indian ambassador to China, met with Zhou on October 21, Panikkar stressed that the PLA's military action in Tibet could produce a negative impact on Beijing's efforts to be accepted by the United Nations. Zhou was unmoved. "This is China's internal issue, and no foreign country has the right to interfere," Zhou reiterated.[92] Ten days later, when K. P. S. Menon, the Indian deputy foreign minister, expressed "regret" about the PLA's advance into Tibet, Zhou received instructions from Mao, which he stated as follows: "Our attitude [toward India] should be even tougher. We should say that Chinese troops will arrive in any part of Tibet they want, regardless of whether the Tibetan local government is willing to negotiate [with the central government] and what the result of the negotiations might be."[93] On November 16, Zhou informed India that the Chinese government was "greatly surprised" by New Delhi's attempt to "influence and obstruct the exercise of the PRC's sovereign rights in Tibet."[94] Although India's prime minister Jawaharlal Nehru, like many Indians, worried that the Chinese military presence in Tibet would nullify the region's function as a buffer between China and India, he believed that, "given the very nature of Tibetan geography, terrain and climate, a large measure of autonomy is almost inevitable."[95] Consequently, New Delhi did not take any action beyond expressing "regrets and concerns."

Lhasa had been pushed into a dead end in the wake of the Chamdo disaster. Now, the absence of international support and interference had left the Kashag with no other choice but to negotiate with Beijing. Thus voices for a "peaceful settlement" increasingly gained influence among the Tibetan elite, and Ngapoi in particular. In his reports to the Kashag, Ngapoi drew on his own experience to argue that a peaceful solution would save the Tibetan people and land from a destructive war, and that negotiating with Beijing represented Tibet's "only chance of preserving a degree of autonomy."[96] The young Dalai Lama took a cautious view of the situation. In early December 1950, he left Lhasa for Yadong, a town on the Tibetan-Indian border. On January 27, 1951, he wrote to Yuan, expressing his intention to negotiate with Beijing. On February 1, Yuan conveyed "Chairman Mao's warm regards to the Dalai Lama" and informed the Dalai Lama that the chairman "welcome[d] him to send representatives to Beijing to discuss questions concerning the peaceful liberation of Tibet."[97] Before he departed from Lhasa, the Dalai Lama (and the Kashag) had already "given Ngapoi full power to proceed with negotiations with the Chinese."[98] After learning that the United Nations had decided not to include Tibet on the General Assembly's agenda, the Dalai Lama and the Kashag decided that a group of negotiators headed by Ngapoi would travel to Beijing to hold negotiations there.

Zhou knew that the time to resolve the Tibetan question had arrived. When Ngapoi arrived in Beijing on April 22, Zhou greeted him and the other Tibetan negotiators at the train station. Five days later, the young Panchen Lama, Tibet's second-ranking spiritual and religious leader after the Dalai Lama, also came to Beijing, having been invited by Zhou. Likewise, Zhou greeted the Tibetan dignitary at the train station. Negotiations between the Tibetans and Li Weihan, Beijing's chief representative, began on April 29. The two sides held seven rounds of talks over the following three weeks. Three issues dominated the agenda: the PLA's role in Tibet, the status and power of the Dalai Lama, and the question of recognizing the Panchen Lama. Although Ngapoi and his colleagues tried to argue that there was no need for the PLA to advance into Tibet, Li heeded Zhou's instructions not to budge from Beijing's stance on the matter. Li did promise, however, that after the PLA entered Tibet, the Dalai Lama's status and power, as well as the religious and political systems of Tibet, would be maintained. Zhou's strategy of combining the carrot and the stick worked. The two sides reached an agreement on these issues without prolonged debate.

Then, negotiations nearly hit an impasse on the question of the Panchen Lama's status and role. Historically, the relationship between the Dalai Lamas and the Panchen Lamas had been tense. Zhou knew that by including the Panchen Lama, who was reputedly more patriotic than the Dalai Lama, Beijing would occupy a stronger position at the negotiating table and have more leverage to restrain the Dalai Lama in the long run. Li thus insisted on including cooperation between the Panchen Lama and the Dalai Lama in the agreement. Ngapoi refused to accept this term, contending that the agreement was one designated for defining the relationship between Beijing and Lhasa, not the relationship among Tibetans. But Li stressed that this was an important matter for Beijing, especially because "the Panchen Lama and his group had not done anything against the motherland in the history of the twentieth century." This was a subtle reminder—indeed, a warning—to the Dalai Lama and his group: Beijing had not forgotten their supposedly unpatriotic or even "traitorous" behavior in the past.[99] Ngapoi was willing to compromise; at his urging, the Dalai Lama and the Kashag agreed to Beijing's terms.

On May 23, 1951, an agreement on the "peaceful liberation of Tibet," with seventeen clauses, was signed in Beijing. The most important part of it was undoubtedly the first clause, which states that "the Tibetan people shall unite and drive imperialist forces from Tibet, and shall return to the big family of the motherland—the People's Republic of China." In exchange, Beijing agreed to maintain "the established status, functions, and powers of the Dalai Lama" and, for the time being, "not to alter Tibet's political, economic, and social systems that were by nature feudal and theocratic." Beijing also agreed not to push "various reforms" in Tibet unless the Tibetans so demanded and after consulting "leading Tibetan personnel." A secret text attached to the agreement stipulated that the PLA would enter Tibet and be stationed in "important locations for national defense and transportation," and that Tibetan troops would be reorganized into PLA units and commanded by the PLA headquarters in Tibet.[100]

This was a major victory for Beijing. But Zhou knew that without the Dalai Lama's endorsement, the agreements would not have the legitimacy necessary for their implementation. So, he dispatched Zhang Jingwu, a talented PLA political commissar, to Yadong to persuade the Dalai Lama to return to Lhasa. Zhang's efforts were successful. On October 24, 1951, the young Dalai Lama, having returned to Lhasa, dispatched a telegram to Beijing in which he formally endorsed the Seventeen Point Agreement.[101] The Panchen Lama then issued a similar statement, applauding "Tibet's return to the motherland."[102] With the two Holinesses' approval, Tibet officially became part of the PRC.

Mao, Zhou, and their comrades took the "liberation of Tibet" as another moment to assert that "we, the Chinese (a group in which the PRC now included the Tibetans), have stood up."

16

THE KOREAN WAR

1950-1953

Sunday, June 25, 1950, should not have been a stressful day for Zhou Enlai. He had attended many events since early June. Nothing important marked his calendar that day. He could have taken a break.

However, he was awakened early in the morning by a call about Korea. Large numbers of North Korean troops had begun an invasion of the South before daybreak, shattering the enemy's resistance in a few hours. They occupied Seoul, the South Korean capital, within three days of the attack. President Harry Truman quickly announced that American forces would come to South Korea's rescue and that the US Seventh Fleet would also be dispatched to "neutralize" the Taiwan Strait. The United Nations subsequently condemned North Korea as the aggressor in the conflict, thereby allowing America to carry out its intervention in Korea under the UN's banner.

Zhou and Mao knew that North Korea was planning to attack the South, but they did not know that the war would begin on June 25. Washington's speedy reaction came as an even greater shock to them. Zhou now needed to shift the bulk of his attention to the crisis in Korea.

• • •

A sheet of ice three feet thick does not form overnight. The war in Korea was engendered by accumulated tensions between communist revolutionaries and right-wing conservatives on the peninsula.[1] In late April 1949, Zhou secretly received Kim Il, political director of the Korean People's Army (KPA), with whom he held four meetings. Mao met with Kim, too, who requested that the Chinese send all ethnic Korean soldiers in the PLA to Korea; Mao and Zhou agreed. Mao also mentioned that if the North were to invade the South, it would be better to induce the South to attack first, and then begin a counteroffensive. The Chinese could dispatch "volunteers" to support them, Mao said. But the PLA, still fighting the civil war in China, did not have a free hand to intervene in Korea. Therefore, "if the North is to attack the South, it should be done in early 1950, when the international situation could change in our favor."[2]

As the PLA's chief of staff, Zhou was responsible for overseeing the repatriation of ethnic Korean soldiers. Under his effective management, by the summer of 1949, two PLA divisions, made up primarily of ethnic Koreans, had arrived in Korea.[3] These new troops bolstered North Korean leader Kim Il-sung's confidence. In fall 1949, he first asked Moscow—and then Beijing—to support him in unifying the peninsula by force. Stalin rejected Kim's request, not wishing to overturn the status quo in Northeast Asia.[4] Mao and Zhou had their own reservations. Kim had sought their aid at a time when the PLA was encountering difficulties in trying to "liberate Taiwan"; hence they hoped that Kim would wait until after "the settlement of the Taiwan question."[5]

But Kim was impatient, repeatedly raising his request with Stalin. At the end of January 1950, Stalin's attitude changed. He was now willing to meet with Kim in Moscow to discuss Kim's plan to attack South Korea. However, Stalin told Kim that "this matter should be kept confidential, and should not be shared with other North Korean leaders or the Chinese comrades."[6]

Mao and Zhou, however, were not totally incognizant of Kim's plan. At the end of March 1950, around the time of Kim's trip to Moscow, Mao and Zhou met with Yi Chu-yon, North Korea's ambassador to China, to discuss "the question of a meeting between Kim and Mao." Mao agreed to meet with Kim once the latter had visited Moscow. Not mincing words, he directly asked Yi, "When do you plan to unify the country?" Yi gave no answer. Mao continued, "If you plan to take military action against the South in the near future, my meeting [with Kim] should not be a formal one; he should come informally." Zhou, obviously trying to squeeze an answer out of Yi, suggested that Kim pay a public visit to Beijing. Again, Yi did not comment. Mao then said: "Korea's unification cannot be achieved in a peaceful way and must be realized by force. As for the Americans, do not fear them. They will not start a third world war over such a small place."[7]

On April 1, Zhou spoke at a national work conference of Chinese military intelligence. He emphasized China's duties of supporting Eastern revolutions—including the Korean revolution:

> We have won our victory today. We should have the aspiration of bearing larger responsibility, the responsibility of emancipating the whole world. In the future, we will help the oppressed brotherly people in the East, such as those in Korea, Indonesia, and Vietnam, to win their emancipation. If all these nations stood up, won't the strength of the people in the world be greater, and the collapse of imperialism be easier?[8]

With such thoughts in their minds, how could CCP leaders veto Kim's plan to use a revolutionary war to unify the Korean Peninsula, despite their disagreement with Kim about the timing of the plan's implementation?

During Kim's secret visit to Moscow, Stalin approved his plan to attack the South. But he also warned Kim, "If you should get kicked in the teeth, I shall not lift a finger. You have to ask Mao for all the help."[9] The Soviet dictator passed the buck to Mao.

On May 13, Kim covertly arrived in Beijing. In the context of the conversation between Mao, Zhou, and Yi in March, this arrangement suggested that Mao and Zhou already knew that Kim had come to discuss "taking military action against the South."[10] Moreover, they likely sensed that Kim would not have gone this far without Stalin's approval.

While meeting with Mao and Zhou, Kim indeed divulged that Stalin had endorsed his plan to attack South Korea. As soon as the meeting ended, Mao asked Zhou to cable Stalin to seek his "personal clarifications" of Kim's claim.[11] The Soviet dictator confirmed that he had discussed Kim's plan to attack the South. However, he also told Mao, "The question should be decided finally by the Chinese and Korean comrades together, and in case of disagreement by the Chinese comrades, the decision on the question should be postponed until a new discussion."[12]

Mao did not use this veto power. Instead, he asked Kim whether China should deploy several divisions along its border with Korea, so that they might provide the KPA with support "if necessary." Kim said "no." They also discussed whether the Americans might intervene, a prospect that Kim also dismissed. Mao said that while the possibility of American intervention could not be ruled out, more attention should be given to Japanese mercenaries.[13] As Zhou and Roshchin, the Soviet ambassador, listened on, Mao told Kim,

> It is not convenient for the Soviet Union to get involved in combat activities, because it is bound by the agreement with America on demarcation along the thirty-eighth parallel. China is not bound by similar obligations, so we can easily provide you with assistance.[14]

Zhou attended Mao's farewell banquet for Kim, where the two Chinese leaders overheard the North Korean leader tell Roshchin, "Our negotiations with Comrade Mao Zedong went very smoothly. He supported what had been agreed upon in Moscow with Comrade Stalin."[15] Mao and Zhou, though shocked, said nothing. They probably still had reservations about Kim's plan to attack the South, but they did not block it. Kim took this to be a demonstration of support. After returning to Pyongyang, he accelerated preparations for invading the South, without bothering to brief Mao and Zhou on his decision.

* * *

After the war broke out in Korea, Mao and Zhou first had to deal with Taiwan. On June 28, Zhou issued a statement condemning America's "invasion of Chinese territory, which completely violates the UN charter."[16] Two days later, Zhou informed Xiao Jingguang, commander of the PLA Navy, that "the Taiwan campaign is postponed."[17] Turning to Korea, Zhou found it troubling that he knew so little about the situation on the battlefield. On June 30, Zhou told Chai Chengwen, the designated Chinese military attaché in East Germany, that he would be reassigned to Korea, where he would serve as "a liaison with Kim Il-sung."[18]

On the morning of July 2, Zhou attended a Politburo meeting about Korea. In a meeting with Zhou that afternoon, Soviet ambassador Roshchin asked Zhou on behalf of Stalin if China would send troops to support North Korea in the event that US forces crossed the thirty-eighth parallel. The Chinese had already deployed a force of 120,000 soldiers in the Northeast, Zhou told Roshchin, which could be used if the Americans were to cross the parallel. Zhou also suggested that the KPA should rapidly march southward to occupy key ports there, while maintaining a powerful reserve force to guard against a potential sudden attack in their rear by the Americans.[19]

Stalin's response came on July 5. He supported the Chinese deployment of troops along the Korean border. If the Chinese were to enter operations in Korea *after* US troops crossed the thirty-eighth parallel, he promised, Moscow would "provide them with air support."[20] With this promise, however, Stalin effectively put the Chinese in a straitjacket: only if the Americans were to cross the thirty-eighth parallel would China send troops to Korea; otherwise, they would not. Zhou soon found out that Stalin would not budge from this stand over the next two months.

On July 7, the CMC decided at a meeting chaired by Zhou to establish a Border Defense Army to prepare to engage in operations in Korea.[21] Five days later, Mao and Zhou met with Lee Sang-jo, KPA's deputy chief of staff. China had amassed 320,000 troops along its border with Korea, the two Chinese leaders boasted, declaring that "if Korea is in need of support, China can send troops there." They asked Pyongyang to send "an authorized military delegation to Beijing" by August 1 and to confirm with China by August 10 whether it wanted China's support.[22] The next day, Zhou asked Pyongyang to provide Beijing with Korea's military maps and samples of KPA uniforms, and requested that the North Koreans keep Beijing informed of the situation in Korea.[23]

Zhou also managed diplomacy. On July 12, he formulated five conditions for settling the Korean question: withdrawal of all foreign troops from Korea; withdrawal of US forces from the Taiwan Strait; resolution of the Korean issue by the Koreans themselves; expulsion of the Nationalist regime in Taipei from the UN and the taking over of China's UN seat by Beijing; and the convening of an international conference for the signing of a peace treaty with Japan.[24] These terms became China's official position on settling the Korean question.

From this moment on, Zhou would oversee China's involvement in the Korean War. Informed by his own military experience, Zhou understood that logistical preparation should always precede military operations, especially for a war abroad. In mid-July, he assigned this important task to the government in the Northeast. He also convened several meetings of officials in Beijing and from the Northeast to resolve concrete logistical problems.[25]

Thanks to Zhou's coordination, by early August, more than 260,000 Chinese troops had amassed along the Korean border. Yet by then the war in Korea had reached a stalemate. At a Politburo meeting on August 4, Mao outlined his stance on the Korean War: "If the US imperialists are allowed to win the war, they will become more arrogant and will threaten us. We have to assist the Koreans. We must lend them a hand by sending our military volunteers there."[26] Zhou agreed, adding his comments:

> If the U.S. imperialists defeat Korea, the cause of peace would suffer and the Americans would become more aggressive. In order to win the war, China must bring its strength to bear. If China does so, the whole international situation will change. We must establish such a broad perspective.[27]

Apparently, both Mao and Zhou believed that China had to help North Korea win the war, or at least prevent the undoing of the North's battlefield gains.

As the days passed, Zhou's worries about a reversal of the war situation in Korea grew. He shared his concerns with Mao, giving particular emphasis to the danger of an enemy landing operation behind North Korean lines. He suggested that Inchon was a location deserving special attention. "This is a key question in the military situation in Korea," stressed Zhou, to which Mao agreed. Zhou then communicated with Pyongyang and Moscow, urging the Koreans to be mindful of the possibility of an enemy amphibious landing operation on their coastal flanks.[28] He did not hear back from the Koreans or the Soviets. Kim had held the Chinese military observers Zhou had dispatched to Korea in Pyongyang, where they were not briefed on the situation at the front.[29]

On August 26, Zhou made a comprehensive report at a CMC meeting. It was important, he said, to adopt a "positive attitude" toward Korea, which had become the "focus of a worldwide struggle." China should push forward its war preparations: "We should not disappoint the Korean people if we are not ready to go to Korea in a few months; and we should not let the enemy know about this at too early a time. This way, we will be victorious when we do act."[30]

Indeed, from early July to early September of 1950, Mao, Zhou, and the CCP leadership were eager to send Chinese troops to Korea, in order to help the North Koreans shore up their rear and coastal defense and allow Korean troops to engage all out in frontal battles. At the time, there were no significant differences of opinion on this plan among Mao, Zhou, and their comrades.

Along with their preparing for war, CCP leaders launched a "Great Movement to Resist America and Assist Korea" domestically, which took "defending our homes and safeguarding our country" as its central slogan. They used all propaganda means at their disposal to stir up "hatred of US imperialism" and "sympathy and support for the Korean people" among the Chinese population. Meanwhile, a campaign to "suppress reactionaries" also emerged, which quickly swept across the country.[31] These campaigns clearly indicated CCP leaders' overarching approach toward managing the Korean crisis. For them, China's security interests would be best served through simultaneously defending China's border safety, enhancing the CCP's power and authority at home, and promoting New China's international influence and reputation.

Kim did not invite the Chinese to intervene in Korea, largely because Stalin was unwilling to permit him to do so. Since early July, Kim had inquired with Moscow on multiple occasions about whether he should ask the Chinese to send troops to Korea, but he never heard back from Moscow.[32] Consequently, without an invitation from Kim and lacking Stalin's support, Mao and Zhou had to halt their plan to send troops to Korea.

· · ·

On September 15, 1950, Zhou's nightmare became reality. US and UN forces had landed at Inchon and begun to march northward, quickly splitting the Korean communist forces in two. The trend of the war reversed completely.

When Zhou learned of the landing at Inchon, he and other CCP leaders immediately began to consider how they might avert the further deterioration of North Korea's position. On September 18, Zhou told Roshchin that Pyongyang had provided Beijing with virtually no intelligence, and that Beijing thus knew little about the military situation in Korea. He asked for Moscow's help. He also mentioned the "grave worries" by Western countries that the Soviet Union and China might intervene in Korea, so "we should take advantage of this by taking steps that would be regarded as indicative of our intent [to intervene]."[33] Clearly, he was trying to ascertain where Moscow stood.

The next day, Zhou met with Yi and asked him, "What does the Korean government want us to do now?"[34] Zhou also instructed Ni Zhiliang, the Chinese ambassador to North Korea, to deliver a letter to Kim, in which he advised the Korean leader to "be prepared to fight a prolonged war," rather than risking everything on the battlefield.[35] Zhou was implying that the Koreans should try their best to hang on until Chinese assistance arrived.

But again, Kim did not have authority on the critical matter of involving the Chinese in the war. Stalin, who had the final say, said nothing. All the requests that the Koreans had made to Stalin for receiving Chinese support fell on deaf ears.[36] Two weeks passed, during which the KPA suffered one defeat after another, while Zhou and his fellow Chinese leaders could do nothing to help them.

• • •

Things changed on September 30, when South Korean forces crossed the thirty-eighth parallel. North Korean resistance was teetering on the brink of collapse. Kim again cabled Stalin for help; finally, Stalin replied, instructing Kim to turn to China for assistance. On October 1, Kim wrote Mao, formally requesting that China send troops to Korea. Stalin also cabled Mao, stating that without outside support, the Korean revolutionary regime would collapse; therefore, it was essential that Beijing come to Pyongyang's aid.[37]

Mao's reaction was swift. That evening, he called Zhou and other top party leaders to discuss the situation in Korea. The matter, which was not settled at the meeting, would be discussed further the next day by the Politburo.[38] Late that night and the next day, Zhou twice cabled Ambassador Ni, instructing him to tell Kim to divide his remaining troops into two groups, with one "retreating to the North in many small squadrons" and the other staying behind enemy lines "to drag down as many enemy troops as possible, slowing their northward advance."[39]

Mao too was burning the midnight oil. He personally drafted a telegram to Stalin, in which he stated that Chinese leaders had decided "to send a portion of our troops, under the name 'volunteers,' to Korea, aiding the Korean comrades in their fight against the troops of the United States and its running dog Syngman Rhee." It was necessary to do so, he explained, "as this is closely related to revolutions in Korea and the East, and would also have a huge impact on the development of China's domestic political situation." Mao added that China's entry into the war should "solve the problem, that is, we should be prepared to eliminate the invaders from the United States and other countries and drive them out [of Korea]." The most crucial part of the draft was the following paragraph:

> Since Chinese troops will fight American troops in Korea (although under the name "Chinese volunteers"), we must be prepared for the Americans to declare war on China. We must be prepared for the possible bombardment by the American air force of many Chinese cities and industrial bases, and for attacks by American naval forces on China's coastal areas.

Mao then asked Stalin to clarify whether—if China were to enter the war—"the Soviet Union could provide us with assistance by supplying us weapons, dispatching a volunteer air force into Korea, and deploying a large number of air units to aid us in strengthening our air defense in Beijing, Tianjin, Shanghai, and Nanjing if the United States uses its air force to bombard these places."[40]

These perspectives of Mao deviated significantly from his earlier idea, before the Inchon landing, of dispatching Chinese "volunteers" to Korea. In his plans in July and August, the Chinese would have entered Korea disguised as KPA units and would mainly have defended North Korea's rear and flanks. Thus, in that scenario, China was unlikely to engage in a direct military confrontation with America. In this draft telegram of October 2, however, Mao expected that China's entry into the war could result not only in a Chinese-American war in Korea but even in extensive American bombardment of the Chinese mainland. This would be a very different war for China.

Mao's approach inevitably prompted serious concerns from other Chinese leaders. At 3:00 P.M. on October 2, the Politburo met to discuss whether China should enter the war in Korea. Mao's colleagues conveyed their reservations about and even outright opposition to China's getting involved in a "total war" with America, which was completely different from the plan they had previously supported. Mao later recalled that "only one person and a half, myself plus half Zhou Enlai" voiced support for his idea of active intervention at the meeting.[41] This means that Zhou at least did not fully join the chorus of opposition to Mao's ideas.

Mao now had to shelve his draft telegram to Stalin. Instead, he met with Roshchin, asking him to send a different message to the Soviet leader. Citing his comrades' opinion, Mao mentioned that if China were to enter the war, it might "entail extremely serious consequences," including "provoking an open conflict between the United States and China." Therefore, Mao expressed, many CCP leaders believed it was necessary to "show caution," and they thus "have not decided whether to send troops to Korea."[42]

Around the same time, Zhou met with K. M. Pannikar, Indian ambassador to China, asking him to help convey a crucial message to Washington:

> The American forces are trying to cross the 38th parallel and to expand the war. If they really do this, we will not sit still without doing anything. We will intervene [*women yao guan*]."[43]

This was an important message, so Zhou prepared it with caution. In particular, he consulted Pu Shouchang, his English interpreter, to choose an accurate English gloss for "*yao guan,*" which could be translated as "to be concerned" or "to take care of." Zhou picked "intervene" as the term that best captured his original meaning.[44] In retrospect, Zhou had transmitted the message to kill two birds with one stone: If it indeed was to play a role of deterring the advance of the US / UN forces, Beijing would gain the much-needed space and time for Chinese troops to finish mobilizing and preparing for the war; and if Washington ignored the warning and continued to push the war toward the Chinese border, Beijing would be able to make a much more convincing case to the Chinese people and the world that China's intervention in Korea was necessitated by a severe threat to its national security.

Mao's heart was still set on intervention. Late on October 3, he asked Zhou to arrange a plane to Xi'an to transfer Peng Dehuai, the PLA's vice commander in chief, to Beijing.[45] Knowing that Mao intended to put Peng in command of the Chinese troops in Korea, Zhou immediately carried out the order.

When the Politburo held an enlarged meeting on October 4, Mao asked all those who had reservations about intervening in Korea to present their views. Zhou already knew what Mao had in mind, so he said nothing at the meeting. Toward the end, Mao said that although all dissenting voices were reasonable, he would still feel "very sad" if China did nothing "when a neighboring country was in danger." The meeting adjourned without a decision.[46]

The next morning, Mao sent Deng Xiaoping to see Peng. Deng relayed Mao's views to Peng, also telling him that Mao wanted him to command the troops to enter Korea. Mao then talked with Peng, clearly sharing with him his intention to send troops to Korea.[47] After the Politburo meeting resumed that afternoon, Mao skillfully steered the discussion toward the question of why China should enter the war. Peng did not disappoint Mao. When he finally spoke, he loudly announced, "It is necessary to send troops to support Korea." He even said that "if we were to lose, it would be no worse than winning the war of liberation a few years later." Zhou also "firmly supported Mao's ideas to send troops to assist Korea." Spurred by the changed atmosphere at the meeting, the Politburo adopted the decision to enter the Korean War.[48]

Zhou communicated the Politburo's decision at a CMC meeting with PLA commanders the next day. "The Korean government has repeatedly asked us to send our troops there, how can we fail to do so?" Zhou raised his voice, declaring, "The question we now face is no longer whether to enter the war, but how to pursue victory in it."[49]

• • •

On October 8, Mao formally issued the order to send "Chinese volunteers" to Korea and informed Kim of the order.[50] He reported to Stalin through the Soviet embassy in Beijing that the CCP leadership had decided to enter the war: "Comrades Zhou Enlai and Lin Biao will depart at 8:00 A.M. today to meet with you at your present location."[51]

Zhou was already on a plane, flying to see Stalin. He would personally explain to Stalin how difficult it had been for CCP leaders to decide to join the war, and he also planned to work out the details of Soviet military support to China, including air coverage for Chinese ground troops in Korea and safeguarding China's coastal airspace, with the Soviet dictator.

On October 11, Zhou, accompanied by Lin Biao, met with Stalin at the Soviet leader's villa on the Black Sea, for what was to be one of the most difficult meetings of his career. Throughout the meeting, Zhou persistently brought the discussion to the subject of Soviet military aid to China, especially in the form of air support. Yet Stalin's attitude was hesitant. He agreed to provide China with a substantial supply of weapons, equipment, and ammunition. However, he also told Zhou that it was impossible for the Soviet air force to engage in fighting over Korea during the early stages of China's involvement in the war. This posed a huge dilemma for Zhou, who was not authorized to tell Stalin that China would enter the war even without Soviet air support. Therefore, he switched the topic to what Moscow and Beijing might do if China did not send troops to Korea.[52] At the end of the meeting, Zhou pushed Stalin to do something that the Soviet dictator had never done before: he and Zhou would jointly dispatch a telegram to Mao to assert that "the Soviet Union will fully satisfy China's need for artillery, tanks, airplanes, and other military equipment," while cautioning that it would "take at least two or two-and-half months for the Soviet air force to prepare to support Chinese operations in Korea."[53]

Stalin's reneging on his promise of air support forced Mao to order Chinese troops to put their war preparations on hold.[54] On October 13, Mao chaired another Politburo meeting to discuss China's entry into the war. Under Mao's direction, CCP leaders again "reached the consensus that it is desirable to dispatch our troops to Korea." Mao immediately cabled Zhou, asking him to inform Stalin of the Politburo's decision. The chairman stressed that to enter the war was "extremely advantageous to the interests of China, Korea, the East, and the world as a whole." Conversely, if China refrained from getting involved in the war, "the international and domestic reactionary bluster would surely become louder; such a situation would be very unfavorable to us." Therefore, Mao contended, China "should enter the war and must enter the war; entering the war can be most rewarding; failing to do so may cause great harm."[55]

Mao also instructed Zhou to "stay in Moscow for a few more days" to iron out the details of Soviet financial and military assistance to China, along with other support. "So long as the Soviet Union dispatches its air force to support our war operations in Korea within two or two and a half months," Mao told Zhou, "and also sends their air units to help defend such cities as Beijing, Tianjin, Shenyang, Shanghai, Nanjing, and Qingdao, we shall not be afraid of a general air attack."[56] Zhou conveyed Mao's message to Stalin and also consulted with Molotov about Mao's requests. Molotov's response was positive.[57]

In the meantime, Mao also confided in Zhou that he had a "back-up plan." If, after they occupied Pyongyang, the US and UN forces paused there, instead of immediately resuming their march toward the Yalu River, Chinese troops would, after entering Korea, establish a defensive perimeter north of Pyongyang composed of two or three lines. If the enemies launched an offensive, the Chinese troops would wipe them out in front of the perimeter;

but if the enemies made no advance, the Chinese troops would not attack them. Only once all preparations had been made after six months would the Chinese start an overall counteroffensive.[58] This plan was aborted due to the rapid northward advance of the US and UN forces.

Zhou returned to Beijing on October 17. Mao again ordered a halt to the movement of Chinese troops so he could learn from Zhou about Stalin's exact position on Soviet aid to China.[59] After Zhou reported Stalin's stance, Mao said, "The decision to send the volunteers to Korea will not change."[60] On October 19, Chinese troops began crossing the Yalu.

* * *

China's entry into the war quickly altered the situation on the Korean battlefield. In late October, Chinese troops fought their first battle against South Korean units, forcing them to retreat from the vicinity of the Yalu River to the Chosin Reservoir. On Stalin's orders, beginning on November 1, Soviet air units based in Northeast China were also preemptively scrambled to help defend Chinese supply lines over the Yalu.[61] But General Douglas MacArthur, commander of US and UN forces, was too arrogant to heed all this. In mid-November, he launched an "ending the war" offensive; consequently, his troops fell into the traps that the Chinese had set for them. In late November, the Chinese began a powerful counteroffensive. By mid-December, they had recovered nearly all the territory north of the thirty-eighth parallel that had been previously lost to the enemy advance.

China's military victory in Korea put Zhou and his comrades in an opportune position to negotiate an end to the war, if they so desired. On December 5, thirteen non-Western countries, headed by India, handed a cease-fire proposal to Beijing, suggesting that the Chinese stop their advance at the thirty-eighth parallel and that "big powers with interests in Korea" meet to discuss a resolution to the conflict.[62] Nine days later, the UN passed the thirteen-nation resolution and assembled a three-person group to seek the "basis on which a satisfactory cease-fire in Korea could be arranged."[63] The Indians repeatedly promised the Chinese that the thirteen-country group did not originate in the West, and that in exchange for Beijing's acceptance of a ceasefire, other Chinese interests would be taken into account.[64]

But Mao and Zhou were unwilling to accept anything short of a total victory. On December 8, Zhou instructed his associate Chen Jiakang to ask the

Indians why the thirteen countries had failed to propose a cease-fire when the US / UN forces crossed the thirty-eighth parallel, and had submitted their proposal to the Chinese while Chinese forces were advancing. Three days later, Zhou told Panikkar that as the Americans had already violated the thirty-eighth parallel, there was no need for China to respect it either.[65]

In Korea, Peng saw a different picture. Despite their initial success, Chinese troops' poor supply lines and lack of air support rendered them vulnerable. Peng thus preferred to suspend the Chinese advance until reinforcements arrived from China.[66] But Mao was eager to "force the Americans out of Korea" and hoped that subjecting the Americans to even greater pressure might coerce them into seeking a cease-fire. If so, he instructed Zhou, China would demand that the Americans withdraw from Korea, beginning with the retreat of US forces south of the thirty-eighth parallel.[67] On December 21, Mao ordered Peng "to fight another campaign" and "to cross the thirty-eighth parallel."[68] The next day, Zhou formally rejected the thirteen-nation cease-fire resolution.[69]

On December 31, 1950, Chinese troops began another offensive, occupying Seoul five days later. Chinese advance units quickly reached the thirty-seventh parallel. The Soviet air force extended its coverage of Chinese supply lines to the northern part of Korea. On January 11, 1951, the UN three-person group made a series of new suggestions. In addition to an immediate cease-fire, it proposed that foreign troops gradually withdraw from Korea and a four-power meeting (comprising the Soviet Union, the United States, Britain, and China) be convened to settle outstanding Far East problems, including the Taiwan question and the PRC's representation in the UN.[70]

In retrospect, this might have been a golden opportunity for Beijing to end the war. An immediate cease-fire would have allowed the Chinese forces to retain their gains; likewise, if the cease-fire failed, the Chinese would earn a valuable respite with which to rebuild their offensive momentum. Further, Beijing's acceptance of the proposal would certainly have put Washington in a diplomatic quagmire. As US secretary of state Dean Acheson later stated, at the time, if the United States had supported the proposal, it might have resulted in "the loss of the Koreans and the fury of Congress and the press"; on the other hand, rejecting it could have led to "the loss of our majority and support in the United Nations." Washington's decision to support the proposal, Acheson confessed, was largely based on the hope that China would reject it.[71] So, if Zhou and his comrades had accepted the proposal, Beijing would have occupied a favorable position militarily as well as in international diplomacy.

But Mao and Zhou were overcome by a victorious mentality fueled by Chinese advances on the battlefield. The Chinese troops, they believed, had the capacity to march on until they won another glorious victory. Moreover, Zhou believed, albeit mistakenly, that the three-person group's proposal was crafted to promote Washington's aims. On January 17, Zhou introduced Beijing's own terms for negotiations, arguing that the proposal of the three countries was "designed to give the American troops some breathing room" in Korea. He called for a seven-power meeting to be held in China, for the PRC to take over China's seat in the UN, and for the withdrawal of all foreign troops from Korea and Taiwan.[72]

This misjudgment—one of the very few Zhou ever made in his career—had serious consequences. Soon after, Zhou actually had second thoughts, and he wanted to take back his refusal of the three-country group's proposal, but it was already too late.[73] This missed opportunity meant that the Korean War would rage on for another two and a half years, and that the PRC would become more isolated in the international community.

Zhou and his comrades' mistake stemmed largely from their overly optimistic outlook on the war situation. In a deeper sense, though, they were also driven by the desire to carry out more extensive social mobilization and state-society integration at home. As Mao had hoped, the "Great Movement to Resist America and Assist Korea" within China entered a new phase following China's entry into the war, and the "glorious Chinese victory" in Korea served as a powerful force for domestic mobilization. On February 2, 1951, the CCP leadership called on the whole country to echo the Chinese victory in Korea by supporting the party's domestic transformation campaign, in order to "heighten our nation's self-confidence and self-respect."[74] In mid-February, a Politburo meeting that Zhou attended again emphasized that "Resisting America and Assisting Korea" must be made a nationwide and long-term endeavor, and that "everyone in every corner of the country will be reeducated."[75]

However, Chinese forces lacked the capacity to turn Beijing's ambition into reality. On January 25, the US / UN forces began a counteroffensive, pushing back the Chinese advance. In late February, Peng rushed back to Beijing, where he reported to Mao that his troops had had to take up a defensive position and regroup to prepare for a counteroffensive in the spring.[76] In light of Peng's report, Mao realized that this would be a protracted war, a verdict that Zhou communicated to Stalin on Mao's behalf. Yet Mao and Zhou still believed that the Chinese could eventually force the Americans, who lacked the heart to sustain heavy losses, out of Korea in a war of attrition.[77]

Two months later, Chinese troops began another major offensive. Without adequate air support and reliable access to supplies, the offensive failed to push the combat line significantly southward. In the final phase of the campaign, several advanced Chinese units were encircled, and an entire Chinese division was lost.[78] Mao and Zhou had to reconsider China's objectives for the war. Realizing that a huge gap existed between Beijing's ambitions and the cruel reality on the battlefield, Mao was now willing to end the war short of a total Chinese victory.

In late May, Chinese leaders and military planners began an exhaustive review of strategies in Korea. Zhou was absent, as he had fallen ill from overwork. Mao permitted him to take a medical leave in the coastal city of Dalian.[79] Acting chief of staff Nie Rongzhen later recalled that during the strategy review, "the majority's opinion was that our forces should stop at the thirty-eighth parallel, continue fighting throughout the armistice talks, and strive to settle the war through negotiation."[80]

A main concern of Mao's was the impact that a compromise might have on China's domestic situation. He and other CCP leaders now found that by highlighting China's success in driving the enemy from areas close to the Yalu River back to the thirty-eighth parallel, they could justifiably claim that China had achieved a triumphant victory in the war. Kim Il-sung, who at the moment was unwilling to stop fighting, hoped to launch another major offensive before coming to the negotiation table. But Mao managed to convince Stalin to endorse Beijing's new strategy of "negotiating while fighting."[81]

• • •

Korean armistice talks began on July 10, 1951, first at Kaesong and then at Panmunjom. Zhou returned to Beijing to oversee the Chinese side during the negotiations. He, as well as Mao and other Chinese leaders, predicted that an agreement could be reached in a matter of weeks.

Negotiations, however, would go on for two years. Initially, Mao was personally involved in decision-making. Later, as talks wore on, Mao left the task of managing the negotiations to Zhou, who would report to Mao only on the most important matters. Zhou was also in charge of telegraphic communication with Moscow and Pyongyang. All of Beijing's telegrams to Stalin were dispatched in Mao's name, but almost all of them were drafted by Zhou.

The talks were difficult from the beginning. Not until July 26 did the two sides reach an agreement on a five-part agenda for continuing negotiations: adopting an agenda; fixing a military demarcation line; making concrete arrangements for an armistice in Korea; repatriating prisoners of war (POWs); and presenting recommendations on related issues to the governments of both sides.[82]

The next stage of negotiations proved even more difficult, as neither side was willing to make any concessions. In late August, Zhou chaired a series of discussions in Beijing about China's negotiation strategies. He and his comrades realized that their earlier expectations about the talks had been too optimistic. What had ultimately taken place at the negotiating table was a "serious political struggle" concerning the credibility and reputations of both sides, which neither side was willing to risk being damaged. With Mao's approval, Zhou and his comrades decided to employ a strategy of "aggressive defense" on the battlefield. They hoped that increasing casualties in a protracted war would eventually force the Americans to meet Beijing's minimum demands at the negotiation table.[83]

In the coming months, the two sides first agreed to accept the actual line of contact as the demarcation line. On February 19, 1952, the two sides also agreed to call a political conference within ninety days after an armistice was reached in order to settle the Korean question. Zhou and his comrades felt that the end of the talks was in sight.

However, Zhou soon discovered that the POW issue, which he had expected to be the easiest to revolve, had emerged as the greatest obstacle in the negotiations. Discussion on the issue began on December 11, 1951. Five months later, the US / UN side proposed that the repatriation of prisoners of war be carried out on a voluntary basis. Zhou immediately realized that the adoption of this proposal would mean that large numbers of Communist prisoners would not be repatriated. Treating this as a crucial issue related to whether China's war in Korea was just and justifiable, Mao and Zhou were determined not to make any concessions. This unyielding approach was met by an equally rigid American attitude, causing the negotiations as a whole to stall. In the meantime, fierce fighting continued on the battlefield, as the war lasted for another seventeen long months.

On July 12, 1952, the US and UN negotiators put forward a "final and unchangeable" proposal on "voluntary repatriation." Kim was willing to accept it. Mao, Zhou, and other Chinese leaders spent two days discussing the matter before concluding that "it would be extremely disadvantageous to us if we were to accept this solution." What the Americans had proposed was "by no means a concession," Zhou wrote Kim. "If we accept it in the face of the enemy's rampant air bombardment, . . . they will be more arrogant and our own morale will be damaged." Rather, "only by firmly holding our own ground will the enemy eventually make due concessions." Zhou asked Kim to "frankly share with us all of Korea's needs, and if they are beyond China's capacity, you and I will jointly ask Comrade Stalin to help us."[84] Apparently, Mao and Zhou were determined to dispel any illusion that the war would soon be over.

· · ·

Around the same time that the armistice talks began, the San Francisco Conference for making peace with Japan was convened. Following Zhou's rejection of the UN three-person group's proposal in January 1951, the PRC was not invited to attend the conference. Thus, the peace treaty with Japan signed at the conference lacked any input from Beijing. Zhou lambasted the treaty as being seriously flawed, and he announced that the San Francisco Conference System was not a binding peace settlement for China.[85] Here lay one of the most profound and enduring legacies of the Korean War, and one of the deepest underlying causes of the territorial disputes that now embroil China and other countries in the East and South China Seas.

· · ·

In mid-August 1952, Zhou traveled to Moscow with two goals. First, he wanted to share with Stalin Beijing's strategies for managing the war in Korea and confirm Moscow's pledge of enhanced military support. Second, he planned to discuss with the Soviet dictator China's "grand strategy" for domestic reconstruction. Zhou brought with him a long list of requests for massive Soviet aid. In addition to military support for the Chinese war effort in Korea, he hoped that Stalin would agree to provide support to China's industrialization drive, especially the crafting and implementation of its first five-year plan—indeed, support on a scale never before seen in history.

On August 20, Zhou met with Stalin at the Kremlin. He began by briefing the Soviet leader on China's domestic development and the war situation in Korea. The Chinese troops "now are sufficiently confident that they have the capacity and ability to fight a prolonged war," said Zhou. He explained why Mao and the CCP leadership had decided to stick to the principle of "repatriating all POWs." This was a battle of wills. China would be willing to end the war on agreeable conditions, Zhou added, but would not yield to unreasonable American terms. If the Communists could demonstrate greater resilience than the Americans, sooner or later they would squeeze some concessions from the enemy. Although Zhou acknowledged that a firm Communist stand might prolong the war in Korea, he asserted that it would not trigger a third world war. With respect to the POW issue, Zhou mentioned that if some POWs were indeed unwilling to be repatriated, they could be sent to a neutral country, and they would be repatriated or go to a third country after their intentions had been identified. However, Zhou stressed, the Chinese faced an uphill battle in fighting the war, especially as the Americans had a nine-to-one advantage over the Chinese in artillery firepower. Stalin agreed that it was impossible for the Americans to fight a prolonged war in Korea. If the Communists kept their patience at the negotiating table while maintaining a strong position on the battlefield, he said, the Americans would eventually have to cut a deal with them. To Zhou's delight, Stalin agreed to increase Soviet military support to China, including the dispatching of five Soviet antiaircraft artillery regiments to Korea, in order to bolster China's negotiating position.[86] Kim Il-sung, summoned by Stalin and Zhou, also came to Moscow. Stalin instructed him to heed Mao's and Zhou's advice.

Mao was now more determined to adhere to an unyielding position at the negotiating table. He and Zhou saw prolonging the war as unacceptable to the Americans: "First, it will result in American casualties; second, it will cost America money; third, it will cause insurmountable difficulties for them at home and abroad; and fourth, it will make them face a strategic dilemma as their strategic emphasis is in Europe," as Mao assessed the situation.[87] China should "further enhance our efforts to fight the war," Zhou said, in an echo of Mao, and should continuously "stabilize and consolidate our ground until the enemy is forced to quit."[88] On October 8, the Chinese negotiators formally rejected the US / UN "final proposal," causing the Americans to suspend the talks indefinitely. But Mao and Zhou were not shaken. Zhou assured Kim in a telegram that Beijing would "absolutely not abandon the principle of repatriating all POWs."[89]

Mao and Zhou did not take America's nuclear threat seriously, either. China should not be intimidated by America's firing the "empty cannon" of threatening to use the bomb, Zhou said. Rather, it was America's allies that "will be so scared that they turn the table upside down."[90]

On December 16, Zhou sent a telegram to Stalin on Mao's behalf. In summarizing China's negotiation strategy, Zhou wrote that "the losses of American troops in Korea have not reached the degree for them to stop the war," which "might become even more brutal in the next year or so." Only when "the enemy suffers more casualties," Zhou concluded, could the war situation "turn decisively in our favor."[91]

• • •

In these days, in addition to coping with the complicated situation in Korea, Zhou Enlai was confronted with the personal crisis that his stepdaughter, Sun Weishi, was facing in life. Weishi was a pretty girl, who was innocent yet also with her own mind. These were the qualities that Zhou and Deng Yingchao had liked very much. Even during her short time in Yan'an, she had been the target of the amorous pursuit of some prominent "revolutionary veterans." When she followed Zhou and Deng to travel to Moscow, Lin Biao was also there for medical treatment. Although he was a married man (his wife then was Zhang Mei), Lin still began to chase after Weishi. However, Weishi showed no interest in Lin, feeling that he was not her type. Later, Lin divorced Zhang and married another young woman, Ye Qun.[92]

After returning to China from the Soviet Union, Weishi devoted herself to stage acting. In 1950, when she was adopting and directing *Paul Korchagin,* a famous Soviet play, she fell in love with Jin Shan, China's "drama emperor" then. But Jin was married to his second wife, movie star Zhang Ruifang. When Weishi revealed her love for Jin and their plan to marry to Deng Yingchao, both Zhou and Deng immediately expressed their strongest opposition. Zhou knew both Jin and Zhang well. Jin was a "big spy" who had worked for CCP intelligence since the early 1940s, and Zhang was also a CCP activist personally recruited by Zhou in the Chongqing times. However, to Zhou and Deng's great disappointment and frustration, Weishi refused to listen to their serious advice, as she felt that she "shared so such in common" with Jin.

After Jin divorced Zhang, in October 1950, Weishi and Jin got married. Zhou did not attend their marriage ceremony. Only Deng attended the ceremony, making a brief presentation at it in her capacity as "the bride's parent."[93] In summer 1952, in order to make a film on Chinese–North Korean solidarity, Jin led a group that visited North Korea. When Kim Il-sung learned that Jin was Zhou's stepson-in-law, he specially arranged for his own secretary, a pretty and capable girl, to serve as Jin's guide and interpreter. Jin started a love affair with the girl. Learning of this, Weishi was shocked and heartbroken. Enraged, Zhou even said that Jin deserved nothing but execution.[94] Both Zhou and Deng believed that Weishi should immediately divorce Jin; however, Weishi again refused to listen to them. Deng then asked Weishi's best friend Lin Li to tell her that she should "turn herself back to the party's position."[95] However, although extremely sad, Weishi found that she was still in love with Jin, and so she decided to "give him another opportunity." Jin was expelled from the party and sent to accept "transformation through labor" in the countryside. A few years later, due to Weishi's efforts, Jin's party membership was restored, and he was also called back to Beijing to his old work unit.[96] Yet, due to Weishi's disobedience, her relationship with her stepparents could never return to those old days of intense intimacy.

• • •

By the beginning of 1953, the war in Korea had been raging for over two and a half years, with still no end in sight. The Chinese had amassed a military force of 1.35 million soldiers in Korea. With the delivery of an enormous volume of Soviet ammunition, weapons, and equipment, Zhou and his comrades believed, the Chinese logistical system had "already reached the best since the beginning of the war."[97]

On February 22, General Mark Wayne Clark, commander of the UN forces, put forward a proposal for exchanging sick POWs to serve as the first step toward breaking the stalemate. Mao and Zhou decided to delay their response to Clark's proposal, "waiting and observing for a while before taking any action."[98]

16.1 Zhou Enlai and Deng Yingchao with their stepdaughter, Sun Weishi, early 1950s.
Historic Collection / Alamy Stock Photo

But the situation soon changed, as Stalin died on March 5. Two days later, Zhou arrived in Moscow to attend the Soviet dictator's funeral. He and the Soviet leaders did not discuss the Korean issue in depth. He then flew to Prague to attend the funeral of Klement Gottwald, the president of Czechoslovakia.

When Zhou returned to Moscow on March 21, he found that the Soviet leaders had already developed a more specific plan for ending the Korean War. They prepared a letter to Mao and Kim, in which they suggested that Kim and Peng should "positively respond" to Clark's February 22 proposal. Then, "an authoritative representative of the PRC (preferably Comrade Zhou Enlai) will issue a statement" to demonstrate "a positive approach" toward the issue, which Kim and the Soviet government would support. On the POW issue, "a proposal should be made to repatriate all prisoners who are firm on repatriation, and other prisoners should be handed to countries of neutrality, so as to guarantee that the repatriation issue will be settled in a fair and just way." The Soviets asked Zhou to convey the letter to Beijing.[99]

On March 21, Zhou had an overnight meeting with almost all members of the new Soviet leadership, including Georgi M. Malenkov, Nikita Khrushchev, Beria, Molotov, and Bulganin, to discuss Sino-Soviet relations and the Korean War. The Communist side should "wait for a while" before resuming talks, said Zhou. "From our perspective, to strive for repatriating our POWs is a just struggle. It is the enemy who purposely tries to make trouble for us." Further, Zhou argued that prolonging the negotiations "can exhaust America's manpower and money, especially can place the enemy in a strategically disadvantageous position, and deepen contradictions within the Western camp." Soviet leaders disagreed, contending that "it is unfavorable to the Soviet Union and to the people of China and Korea to prolong the war. . . . Now is the right time for an armistice."

"Will the Americans adopt a drag-on policy [with the war]?" Zhou asked.

"It is possible," replied the Soviet leaders, "but this is a question for the Americans to answer." However, "if our side refuses to make any concessions," they reasoned, "it is more likely that they may allow the war to drag on. But if our side makes some concession, it will be more difficult for America to prolong the war, and more likely for them to compromise."

At the end, Zhou described the Soviets' proposal as a "big change" and a "new policy." He would need to receive instructions from Beijing, he said, before replying to the Soviets.[100]

Zhou immediately cabled Mao, conveying the opinions of the Soviets. Evidently inclining to accept the Soviet proposal, he explained that "central in the Soviet proposal is to get prepared to reach a compromise on the POW issue, so we will be able to claim the initiative in pursuing peace."[101] Mao's reply came the next day: "We agree to the policy as proposed [by the Soviets]. This is actually the same as one of the three proposals that we gave to Comrade Sheminov [Stalin], that is, to exchange POWs in accordance with the quota that had been worked out by the two sides, and to hand over all POWs whose exchanges have not been agreed upon to neutral countries, where they will await a settlement in the future. . . . The timing is now right to put forward this proposal."[102] Zhou immediately relayed Mao's reply to the Soviets.

After he returned to Beijing, Zhou briefed Mao on his meetings in Moscow.[103] He then cabled Kim to apprise him of his meetings with Soviet leaders. "Be prepared to compromise on the POW issue," he informed Kim, "for the sake of reaching an armistice in Korea. However, if this effort fails, be prepared to continue fighting."[104] On March 30, Zhou issued a statement in which he expressed his preference for an arrangement whereby those POWs who were unwilling to be repatriated would be transferred to a neutral state. This way, Zhou stressed, "a just solution to their repatriation will be ensured."[105]

The door to ending the war through negotiations had opened. But Mao and Zhou were still unsure if an armistice could be reached this time. On April 3, Zhou told a State Council meeting, "The possibility that the war will end is greatly increased, yet it is still possible that the war might be prolonged."[106] He believed that in order to push the enemy to treat negotiations more seriously, it remained "necessary to adopt a tit-for-tat strategy" while negotiating with the Americans.[107]

The armistice talks resumed on April 26. Although neither side had at any point abandoned preparations for another potential recess of the talks, negotiations moved forward slowly yet surely. On June 8, the two sides reached an agreement on the principle of voluntary repatriation of POWs.[108] Late in the evening, Zhou conveyed his congratulations to the Chinese negotiating team. By June 15, military staff representing both negotiating parties had worked out what was intended to be the final demarcation line. At 6:00 P.M. that evening, Peng Dehuai ordered all troops under his command to cease offensive operations beginning on June 16.

The situation suddenly changed on June 18, when South Korean president Syngman Rhee ordered the release of more than twenty-five thousand North Korean prisoners held by South Korea in order to make it an "established fact" that a large number of North Korean POWs would remain in South Korea. Mao and Zhou decided to seize this opportunity "to give South Korean troops another blow."[109] A Chinese offensive campaign began on July 13, inflicting heavy casualties on two of Rhee's elite divisions before the South Koreans were able to hold their ground. On July 26, Zhou announced that an "agreement had been reached on all issues" in the armistice talks.[110]

The next day, an armistice agreement was signed at Panmunjom. Although the war had raged for three bloody years, the demarcation line the two sides eventually drew was only marginally different from the one that existed at the war's beginning.

* * *

With the war over, Zhou was in high spirits. The night before the signing of the armistice, he joined Mao at a performance by a group of dancers from India.

Zhou knew well that China had paid a huge price for fighting the war. Hundreds of thousands of Chinese soldiers had lost their lives. China's ongoing confrontation with America had worsened. Huge sums of money had been spent on the war effort at the expense of China's economic development. Taiwan became a chronic headache for CCP leaders. Beijing's alliance with Moscow was significantly strengthened, but China's economic dependence and other forms of reliance on the Soviet Union also greatly increased. In the years to come, Mao and the CCP leadership would place extraordinary emphasis on defense and heavy industry in resource allocation. Consequently, a highly centralized planned economy emerged in China, leading to a "shortage economy" that endured for the remainder of the Mao era.

However, as Mao, Zhou, and their comrades viewed it, China's gains were substantial. The fact that Chinese troops had driven the US and UN forces from the Yalu River back to the thirty-eighth parallel had put China's leaders in a convincing position to tell their own people—and the world—that New China had won a glorious victory in Korea. During the war, the Communist regime penetrated into almost every facet of Chinese society through intensive mass mobilization campaigns under the banner of revolutionary nationalism. Three nationwide campaigns swept through China's countryside and cities: the suppression of counterrevolutionaries; land reform; and the movements for disciplining corrupt Communist cadres and regulating "national capitalists." Consequently, the CCP effectively enhanced its organizational control over Chinese society and dramatically strengthened its authority and reputation in the minds of everyday Chinese.

Mao's gains seemed even more extraordinary. As the main advocate of the decision to go to war, he saw his power become subject to even fewer checks and balances than before. In the ensuing years, he would wield this enormous and unrestricted power to pursue his dramatic utopian visions, including such campaigns as the Great Leap Forward and Great Proletarian

Cultural Revolution, which would culminate in disasters of a scale unprecedented in Chinese and world history alike.

During the war years, Mao and the CCP leadership took the nation's intellectuals as the main target of a "thought remodeling" campaign, in order to "wipe out the reactionary pro-American ideas and sentiments." By doing so, they certainly meant to maximize the political mobilization effect triggered by China's entry into the Korean War; they also hoped to use this campaign to allow the party's political agenda and revolutionary plans to penetrate deeply into the hearts and minds of all Chinese citizens, leading up to the "revolutionary transformation" of their innermost world. In the campaign, Zhou gave a seven-hour-long speech to more than three thousand university professors in Beijing and Tianjin. Zhou shared with the audience his own experience of "thought remodeling," which was painful yet inevitable.[111] Many listeners said that they had been deeply affected by Zhou's call, expressing their willingness to transform their own conceptual realm as Zhou had done. But was this a genuine reflection of their thinking? Among the listeners was Wu Ningkun, a Peking University professor and recent returnee after studying in the United States. Many years later, he described his true feeling then in his memoir: "My mind started wandering after the first hour (of Zhou's speech), and I gave up my perfunctory attempt at note-taking." He could not help but recall the advice that his former classmate T. D. Lee, later a Nobel laureate, had given him on the eve of his returning to China, warning him of minding his "brains be washed by others."[112] In 1957, Wu was designated a "reactionary rightist." Few of Wu's colleagues who applauded Zhou's speech were able to escape purges in the round after round of political campaigns in the following quarter century. Even Zhou himself would repeatedly become the target of political criticism and attacks.

Yet Zhou could not have foreseen any of this at the time. He was still totally overcome with joy over "China's glorious victory in Korea."

17

TRANSITION TO SOCIALISM

1952–1955

In the summer of 1952, the emphasis of Zhou's work turned to domestic affairs. The CCP Politburo had earlier picked him to head the drafting of China's first five-year plan.[1] In July 1952, Peng Dehuai took over Zhou's duties at the CMC.[2] Zhou's focus shifted to diplomacy as well as the critical task of drafting the five-year plan.[3]

How would this monumental project be done? Mao, Zhou, and the other CCP leaders saw the Soviet Union as a fitting model according to which China could design its own socialist economy. On July 26, Zhou cabled Stalin on Mao's behalf, informing the Soviet leader that he planned to visit Moscow in August. There, Zhou would talk with Stalin about "China's resistance against America and assistance to Korea,. . . and [China's] reconstruction plans in the next five years." Zhou provided Stalin with a long wish list in advance of the meeting. China needed Soviet support in "China's geological survey, industrial design, and ordering equipment and transferring technologies." Zhou also requested Soviet "loans to help cover the deficit in China's trade with the Soviet Union."[4]

Zhou assembled a large team to prepare for the visit. The group included Chen Yun and Li Fuchun, both of whom were regarded by CCP leaders as experts on economic affairs. On August 11, Zhou oversaw the team's completion of a strategic planning document, which set out China's goals for the next five years. The document featured three broadly defined goals: "laying the foundation of China's industrialization and consolidating its national defense, improving people's material and cultural life, and moving the Chinese economy toward socialism."[5] Mao and Zhou apparently hoped to convince Stalin of China's huge strategic value following its entry into the Korean War. If they could impress Stalin, they believed, China could obtain substantial support from the Soviets that could aid China's economic development. The document was immediately conveyed to Stalin.

On August 17, Zhou arrived in Moscow along with a large Chinese delegation. He held his first meeting with Stalin on August 20. On the topic of Soviet military aid to China, Stalin said that he would satisfy almost all of China's needs in Korea. He also took the opportunity to reply to China's other requests for assistance. "About the survey of industrial resources, industrial designs, supplies of industrial equipment and technological data, and the dispatching of trainees to the Soviet Union," Stalin said, the Soviets "definitely are willing to try their best to help China."[6]

On September 3, Zhou conferred with Stalin again to discuss China's five-year plan and Soviet support for the initiatives therein. The Soviet leader brought with him nearly all members of the Politburo. Zhou said candidly that Beijing hoped to get full-scale support from Moscow for the five-year plan. Stalin wasted no time in diving into the details of the plan. While he stressed that the plan had his full support, he also advised Zhou to provide for some leeway in the plan's implementation. Zhou was greatly pleased. "Comrade Stalin is quite satisfied with our work in the past three years," he reported to Mao and the CCP leadership. "He also confirmed the support for us in designing, equipment, experts, and loans in the next five years. They will do some comprehensive calculations before giving us the definitive aid figures."[7]

Two days later, Zhou wrote two letters to Molotov. In the first, he stated that over the next five years China wanted to import 18.43 billion rubles' worth of equipment and common goods from the Soviet Union for the purpose of "planning economic reconstruction and national defense development." However, China's income from exports and nontrade items was estimated to total 13.81 billion rubles, leaving a deficit of 4.62 billion rubles. Zhou asked the Soviets to provide China with a loan of 4 billion rubles over the next five years. China would pay the equivalent of 620 million rubles in cash, in the form of US dollars, Swiss francs, or British pounds, to cover the difference.[8]

In the second letter, Zhou put forward a series of crucial requests. In order to "rapidly upgrade China's technological standards," he wrote, Beijing requested that Moscow provide a series of key technological materials, including the following:

> 1.The Soviet Union's current standards of industrial projects and products of other economic branches, including state standards, all-Soviet standards, current technological conditions, and production specifications of various enterprises; 2. A few typical designs of mines, factories, schools, hospitals, and other projects; 3. Regulations and procedures for technical operations of industrial and transportation enterprises; 4. Manufacturing drawings of machines and electric motors; 5. Technological and economic standards adopted by advanced enterprises in the Soviet Union concerning the use of equipment and the consumption of raw materials, electricity, and fuel.[9]

Molotov's reply came on September 8, in which he unambiguously agreed to China's extensive requests for the transfer of intellectual property and advanced technology.[10] Further, as Zhou later described, all the transfers were free of charge, except for "the costs of paper and photocopying."[11]

Zhou met Stalin for the third time on September 19, when he gave the Soviet leader his "heartfelt thanks." Zhou left Moscow three days later, having accomplished his mission. Stalin had agreed to meet almost all of China's military needs for its war effort in Korea. Most importantly, he had honored nearly every one of Zhou's requests for comprehensive Soviet support in Beijing's ambitious plans to industrialize China.

Li Fuchun would stay in Moscow until the next summer. Zhou visited the Soviet Union again when he attended Stalin's funeral in March 1953, and he returned shortly thereafter for more extended discussions with the new Soviet leadership. After Zhou accepted their proposal to end the Korean War, Nikita Khrushchev and his colleagues demonstrated huge enthusiasm for supporting China. In May and June 1953, Beijing and Moscow signed accords that stipulated that the Soviet Union would provide comprehensive support for the development of China's national economy. The events that followed constituted no less than the transfer of modernity and industrialization from one country to another on a scale never before seen in human history. In a decade's time, China's industrialization would progress by several stages. However, economically and technologically China became more dependent on the Soviet Union, a development that planted in Mao a growing, yet inarticulable, sense of inequality, which would set in motion the schism that ended in the Sino-Soviet split.

On September 24, two days after Zhou returned to Beijing, Mao chaired a meeting of the Central Secretariat. Zhou reported that Stalin had committed to providing comprehensive support for China's economic development.[12] After listening to Zhou's report, Mao made an important announcement:

> From now on, we may complete the transition to socialism in ten to fifteen years, rather than beginning the transition after ten to fifteen years.[13]

With this, the chairman revealed a grand idea that he had developed over the past several years. At the time of the PRC's founding, the Common Program specified that conditions would not be ripe for the transition to socialism until a "society of new democracy" was established in China. Now, Mao implied, the phase of "new democracy" would be cut short and the transition to socialism would begin immediately.

How would Zhou and other CCP leaders respond to Mao's dramatic change in thought? Mao had already considered this question. He stressed at the Central Secretariat meeting that state-run enterprises already accounted for 70 percent of industry and 40 percent of commerce in the Chinese economy. "In another five years, the percentage of the private sector will be even smaller, although its size may increase." He asked, "What will the situation be like ten or fifteen years later?"[14] This question was for other CCP leaders, especially Liu Shaoqi and Zhou, to answer. For years, Mao had sensed that Liu and Zhou differed with him on the transition to socialism. Mao emphasized speed, while they preferred balance and stability. After this meeting, Liu and Zhou still did not treat the task of realizing Mao's vision as a major priority. Mao, though unhappy, did not confront them immediately.

• • •

At that time, Zhou devoted most of his attention to recent personnel changes in the CCP leadership. In June 1952, Deng Xiaoping, Deng Zihui, Xi Zhongxun, Rao Shushi, and Gao Gang, all heads of big regions, were transferred to Beijing to take up important positions in the central government. The most visible among them was Gao Gang, a rising star in Chinese high politics.

Zhou and Gao did not know each other well before 1949. They developed a close working relationship during the Korean War, when Gao was responsible for handling logistics suppliers for Chinese troops in Korea. After his arrival in Beijing, Gao was named chairman of the State Planning Council and took away part of Zhou's power. Still, Zhou showed great respect for Gao. When he sent documents for other leaders to review, Zhou would put Gao's name directly after Mao's and Liu's, and he occasionally would even write Gao's name immediately after Mao's. Upon his secretary's reminding him, Gao called Zhou, asking him to stop this practice.[15] Apparently, Zhou had already detected that Gao was a likely candidate for Mao's successor.

Mao's main concern was still the matter of achieving the party leadership's consensus on the transition to socialism in ten to fifteen years. The chairman mentioned this subject at several meetings in early 1953, but he needed a proper occasion to present the crucial matter to the whole party in a powerful way. At the time, Zhou and the State Council had introduced a new tax system, which gave Mao an excuse to loudly announce his "transition to socialism" agenda.

After 1949, the new Communist regime quickly established its own tax system. In early 1950, Zhou oversaw the implementation of a series of new tax policies. The policies granted tax exemptions or reductions to state-owned and cooperative enterprises, which were relatively weak at the time, as a means of supporting them. By 1953, state-run enterprises and cooperatives came to occupy a much larger share of the Chinese economy. A growing number of state-owned enterprises were doing business with private companies, many of which willingly served as their agents in order to share their tax benefits. Consequently, tax revenues collected by the state fell. It was in this context that the Ministry of Finance, with Zhou's support, introduced a plan of tax reforms. The reforms stipulated that tax collection would be integrated with the production process, and that public and private businesses would be taxed at the same rate.[16] Zhou probably felt that although the launching of the tax reforms was an important matter, his role as the premier of the State Council had authorized him to preside over it. Without reporting to Mao, Zhou approved the new tax law, and the State Council published it.

Severe price fluctuations occurred in Beijing, Shandong, and elsewhere in the wake of the tax reforms. Mao had long been unhappy with the highly hands-on way Zhou ran the State Council.[17] He was also upset with Zhou's

17.1 Zhou Enlai's official portrait, ca. 1954. *The Print Collector / Alamy*

(and Liu's) lack of enthusiasm for his ideas regarding the transition to socialism. Zhou's approval of the new tax law without reporting to him, coupled with the reforms' negative repercussions, gave Mao a good excuse to confront Zhou.

On January 15, 1953, Mao wrote to Zhou, Deng, Chen Yun, and Bo Yibo. "The new tax laws have not been discussed by the [Party] Center," he charged. "Without proper preparation, they were published in a rush." Indeed, even he, the chairman of the PRC, "did not know about them until [he] read the newspaper." The hasty and uncoordinated manner in which the reforms were rolled out, Mao implied, was to blame for the price fluctuations that had since roiled some markets in China. He demanded that Zhou explain "what, exactly, are the advantages and disadvantages of the new tax laws compared with the old ones, and why the new laws have caused price fluctuations," and report back to him.[18]

Shocked, Zhou immediately called a meeting of heads of various ministries to discuss Mao's criticism.[19] At Zhou's instruction, the Ministry of Finance quickly dispatched inspectors throughout the country to examine and resolve the problems caused by the new tax system. Then, the leaders of the ministries of finance, commerce, and food supplies jointly wrote to the Party Center to report on the new tax system and its impacts.[20]

It might have been improper for Zhou to launch the new tax system without first consulting Mao. But Mao's main concern was not the tax reforms, but the broad issues related to the transition to socialism. On February 10, Zhou and Bo Yibo, the minister of finance who was directly in charge of the tax reform, made self-criticism at the Politburo. Zhou claimed responsibility for the mistake; but Mao did not want to settle the matter this way. He seized on a statement that Bo had made—"public and private enterprises should pay taxes equally"—and claimed that Bo had violated the strategies and policies set by the party at the time of the PRC's founding. More seriously, Mao asserted, instead of reporting to the Party Center, Bo "had consulted with the capitalists" about the tax reforms. This was "a huge mistake of rightist-leaning opportunism."[21]

In a parallel move, Mao was acting to rein in Zhou's power. In December 1952, Mao had ordered that "all major and important policies and plans must be made by the Party Center."[22] In March 1953, the Party Center further decided that "all major and important strategies, policies, plans, and decisions in government work must be reported to the Party Center in advance and implemented after discussion and approval by the center."[23] According to this decision and following the transfer of five regional leaders to Beijing, Zhou stopped serving as secretary of the party organs at the State Council. Consequently, his overall administrative power was significantly reduced. Reportedly, Mao had even considered changing Zhou's appointment. On one occasion, he asked Gao Gang whether he was "willing to head the cabinet if Enlai no longer served as premier." Stunned, Gao did not know how to respond. "Maybe Lin Biao should be considered," he murmured.[24]

All of the above revealed Mao's dissatisfaction with Zhou. However, the chairman was even more unhappy with Liu. It was Mao who had made Liu the CCP's second-in-command. In recent years, however, he felt that Liu had failed to match his position on such big issues as what socialism was and how it should be pursued. Hence, while he criticized Zhou's flawed tax reforms, Mao also made a fuss about Liu's failure to report to him before "signing and issuing central documents." In a May 15 letter to Liu and Yang Shangkun, director of the CCP Central Administrative Office, Mao ordered that "from now on, all documents and telegrams issued in the name of the center must first be reviewed by me."[25] Four days later, he wrote to Zhou and Peng Dehuai, instructing them to examine all telegrams and documents issued by the center in the previous nine months to identify those that he had not personally reviewed and approved. "The central meetings," Mao stressed, "have passed several resolutions without my approval. This is wrong and violates the party's discipline."[26]

Meanwhile, a curious event occurred in Beijing. In March, An Ziwen, deputy chief of the Central Personnel Department, "privately composed" a list of candidates for Politburo positions. An's list probably originated from an idea that Mao shared with Gao in early 1953. The chairman said that he had considered dividing the central leadership into a first and second line, and that he intended to retreat to the second line. Gao then shared this with An, saying that "the chairman had discussed with him that the Politburo would be reorganized and that various central posts would be strengthened."[27] Without further clarification from Gao, An prepared a list of potential "Politburo members at the Eighth Congress and the division of labor between various ministries and commissions."[28] Mao obtained the list. In April, his secretary went to see Gao, showing Gao the list and then taking it back.[29] Gao noted that Bo Yibo, who, as Gao believed, belonged to Liu's "North China section," was included among the candidates for the Politburo. However, Lin Biao, of the "Northeast section," was not. He immediately suspected that Liu was behind the list, as An had long been known as "Liu's man." Without Liu's backing, Gao speculated, An would not have dared to compose such a list. Gao discussed the matter with Chen Yun, Lin Biao, and others who were close to him. Strangely, though, he did not report the issue to Mao, which he later acknowledged as "a sky-high mistake."[30]

Later, Liu firmly denied that he had had any advance knowledge of the list. Zhou did not know about the list until it became a big issue. Mao sternly criticized An, telling him, "As deputy head of the Personnel Department, what authority do you have to make a list of Politburo candidates?" An acknowledged his mistakes, submitted a written self-criticism, and was given a "serious warning." Mao did not dig further into the matter. He only ordered that "this thing stops here. No further spreading of it should be allowed!"[31] However, both Gao and Rao Shushi, director of the CCP's Central Personnel Department, disobeyed Mao's strict order and repeatedly shared the contents of the list with others. This was a formative moment in the emergence of what became known as the "Gao-Rao antiparty clique."[32]

* * *

Summer came. The controversy over the tax reforms was not over. At a Politburo meeting on June 1, 1953, Mao again charged that the tax reforms "had wrongly equated public elements with private elements" and "had not been reported to the Party Center for discussion." The Politburo decided to call a National Finance Conference in Beijing in mid-June, which Zhou would chair.[33]

When, on June 13, the Finance Conference held a preparatory meeting, Zhou briefly mentioned the party's general line on the transition to socialism in his opening remarks. Then he stressed that "the conference's central theme is financial issues."[34] Mao disagreed. It was the party's general line that should be highlighted at the conference, he reminded Zhou and others.[35] In order to reset the conference's theme, Mao called an enlarged Politburo meeting on June 15, which Liu and Zhou both attended, and at which Mao emphatically reiterated his "general line on the transition to socialism":

> From the PRC's founding to the basic completion of socialist transformation, there is a transition period. In ten to fifteen years or a little longer, the country's industrialization and socialist transformation of agriculture, handcrafts, and capitalist industry and commerce will be basically accomplished.[36]

Mao then picked several "wrong notions" to criticize. One of them was "consolidating the order of new democracy," which was Liu's idea (although Mao did not name Liu). "Why do some comrades try to adhere to 'the order of new democracy,' rather than pursue socialism?" Mao asked. "The notion . . . is a harmful one. Transition is happening every day, and socialist elements are emerging every day, too. How can the 'order of new democracy' be consolidated?"[37] Another expression that Mao criticized was actually Zhou's (although Mao did not name Zhou either). In early 1952, Zhou had said that the private economy should exist and develop under the leadership of the state-run economy, as this would help "China move from new democracy toward socialism."[38] "Move from new democracy toward socialism? . . . This is a vague formulation," Mao opined. "Moving toward a goal and no more . . . means that the goal has not been reached. The notion sounds plausible but does not bear scrutiny."[39] The Finance Conference was originally scheduled to last half a month. Following the June 15 Politburo meeting, with the conference's main theme shifting to endorsing Mao's general line on the transition to socialism, the conference would go on for more than two months.

Mao was a master of intraparty struggles. At the Finance Conference, instead of openly criticizing Liu and Zhou, he took Bo, a main associate of Liu's and a chief participant in Zhou's tax reforms, as the principal target of his criticism. Mao claimed that Bo had gone to "the side of the capitalist class and become their agent."[40] This was also his warning signal for Liu and Zhou. But he did not let Liu and Zhou off the hook: he tasked Zhou with handling criticism against Bo and asked Liu to make self-criticism. In so doing, Mao hoped to induce Liu and Zhou to wholeheartedly embrace his general line, allowing him to play an unchallengeable role in defining the CCP's mainstream political discourse.

Zhou intuited that he had to cooperate with Mao and make the conference a success according to the chairman's vision. Therefore, he wrote Bo, urging him to "examine himself more deeply." But despite Bo's best efforts, his self-criticism actually backfired, causing him to be labeled "a rightist opportunist." Gao fanned the flames of the controversy by encouraging participants to "criticize Bo while entangling Liu." In his speech at the conference, Gao sternly condemned Bo's mistakes, but he also cited many incidents that involved Liu.[41] Consequently, the conference's emphasis was derailed from the basic line that Mao wanted to emphasize during Bo's reckoning. There was even the possibility that Liu would come under an outright verbal assault, which was not the outcome Mao had hoped for. The chairman had targeted Liu (and Zhou) in order to pave the way for the whole party to embrace his general line. Once this was done, Mao still needed the cooperation of Liu, Zhou, and other party leaders. Gao had failed to apprehend Mao's intentions.

When the rumor began to circulate at the conference that it was Mao who wanted to target Liu, Zhou faced a big dilemma: he could not simply stop Gao, nor could he allow the conference to get out of control. Meanwhile, Zhou feared that he might also become a target of criticism; hence he took the initiative to consult with Mao. The chairman advised Zhou to invite Chen Yun and Deng Xiaoping, both sophisticated practitioners of intraparty politics, to speak at the conference. They did so after Zhou spoke with them. Chen and Deng's criticism of Bo was "adequately phrased," and they powerfully highlighted the importance of embracing the "general line in the transition period." The atmosphere at the conference changed.[42]

When the conference was underway, another thing happened. As director of the Central Personnel Department, Rao, who did not get along with An, had been kept completely in the dark by his deputy director about the "An List." When by chance Rao heard about the list, he was seriously offended, and he calculated that he might use the matter to strangle An politically. In addition, Rao was enraged when An told Liu about a clash of his with Rao. At a group meeting also attended by Liu and Zhou, Rao questioned An about the list he had composed in March. An did not know how to respond, as Mao had instructed that the list not be discussed further. After the meeting, Liu told Rao not to pursue the matter; but Rao refused to listen to Liu. Thus a seed of his own demise was sown.

The Finance Conference reached a climax on August 11, when Liu made self-criticism regarding his past mistakes. In addition to admitting that he was wrong about "consolidating the order of new democracy," he traced his other errors over the years. These missteps, Liu stated, included his idea of "a new phase of peace and democracy" in the mid-1940s and his suggestion that "the exploitation of capitalists could be beneficial" in 1949. Moreover, he had been wrong to show a rightist tendency during land reform, agricultural collectivization, and other campaigns.[43] He said all this for Mao to hear.

Zhou delivered the conference's concluding remarks, which Mao had reviewed and approved. He began by highlighting Mao's "general line on the transition to socialism." Though Zhou did not criticize himself overtly, his speech included several sentences added by Mao, encapsulating those episodes for which Mao found Zhou at fault. One such sentence read, "The mistake of revising the tax system, . . . is a manifestation of rightist opportunism on the economic front, which also reflects bourgeoisie thinking within the party."[44] In the chairman's own concluding remarks, he again emphasized that it was necessary "to carry out struggles against bourgeois thought within the party" to avoid "deviating from the party's general line in the transition period."[45] Yet when the conference ended, Zhou's sense was that the chairman was not fully satisfied with the progress made in promoting his "general line."

* * *

In the wake of the National Finance Conference, Zhou could clearly see that Gao's star was rising. A new leadership structure was emerging under Mao: Liu was in charge of party affairs, Zhou headed the government, and Gao supervised the planned economy.[46]

Gao was an ambitious and capable man. But he had never worked in the Party Center, and he was thus unfamiliar with CCP high politics. He felt that he shared Mao's vision and many of Mao's ideas, and hence he would naturally have Mao's support. In October 1953, Gao left Beijing to go on vacation in the south of China, stopping in Hangzhou, Guangzhou, and other cities. Acting as though Mao had personally authorized him, Gao talked with provincial leaders everywhere he went, gossiping that the chairman had grown disappointed with Liu ever since he became second-in-command. In recent years, Liu's ideological position had often oscillated between "ultraleftist" and "ultrarightist," which meant, Gao claimed, that Liu had not proved to be a reliable deputy for the chairman. Worse, Gao told others, Liu had developed a "small circle" of his own within the party, assigning important offices to those close to him while excluding others. Although Mao had clearly ordered him to cease talking about the "An List," Gao frequently brought it up as evidence with which to attack Liu.[47] Yet, during the tour, Gao never said anything negative about Zhou.[48] Finally, in Deng Xiaoping's words, Gao "had received support from four big regions," including from Lin Biao and Peng Dehuai.[49] In fact, Gao had put himself in a highly perilous position.

While Gao toured the South, another conference on personnel affairs was held in Beijing. There, Liu issued another self-criticism, listing his "rightist mistakes."[50] He did so, again, for Mao to see. The chairman indeed saw it. After all, Mao had bigger plans, and he would need help from Liu, Zhou, and other leaders to promote his "general line." After Liu had repeatedly made self-criticism following Mao's implicit suggestion that he do so, the chairman was willing to let him off. Gao, however, failed to see Mao's broader designs.

Gao's relations with Stalin and the Soviets also concerned Mao. When the chairman was visiting Moscow in December 1949, Stalin had handed him a report written by Kovalev, which highlighted Gao's pro-Soviet activities. Mao said nothing at the time. But on several occasions after Gao was in trouble, he mentioned Gao's "special relations" with the Soviets.[51] Mao never forgot about this sort of thing.

Mao was upset when he learned that Gao had repeatedly used the An List to attack Liu during his southern tour. On December 15, he told his colleagues at a Central Secretariat meeting that he planned to leave Beijing to go to the South, asking them to discuss whether Liu should be in charge of the Party Center's work during his absence. The majority, including Zhou, supported the motion. However, Gao insisted that "it is better to let all be in charge in turns." Liu echoed Gao's opinion. Ultimately, the meeting decided that while Mao was away, the Central Secretariat would "collectively discuss and resolve all problems."[52]

At the meeting, Mao suddenly asked who had exposed "that list of names," saying that the matter should be thoroughly investigated. After the meeting, Mao asked Gao to stay behind, and specifically asked him who had leaked the contents of the list. This was the last opportunity Mao gave Gao to confess. If Gao had admitted that the leak was his doing, Mao certainly would have blamed him, but he would not have gone so far as to dismiss him from his position. However, Gao did not tell Mao the truth. The chairman was greatly disappointed.[53]

Yet Gao failed to realize that he was already in serious danger. After the meeting, he talked with Chen Yun and Deng, separately. Deng alleged that Gao had asked him to "join forces to get rid of Liu." Chen later described a few of his private exchanges with Gao. "We should have several vice chairmen," Chen quoted Gao as saying. "One can be you, and another can be me, and we will take turns being in charge."[54]

Mao started talking to other leaders, beginning with Zhou. The contents of their conversation are unknown. However, in light of later events, most likely Mao had asked Zhou to help him control the confusing situation. It was probably during this meeting that Mao told Zhou, "Gao opposes not only Liu but also you!"[55] Later on, Zhou would become a central figure in Mao's efforts to settle the Gao case.

17.2 Zhou Enlai with Mao Zedong, Zhu De, and Chen Yun at Ziguang Pavilion, Zhongnanhai, 1954. *World History Archive / Alamy Stock Photo*

Chen and Deng came to see Mao, complaining to the chairman about Gao. Chen was a close friend of Gao's, and after they were both transferred to Beijing, Gao shared nearly all of his thoughts with Chen. In his attempt to take Liu down, Gao frequently consulted with Chen. However, when he saw Mao that day, Chen reported to Mao everything that Gao had told him, confirming that Gao had made many negative comments about Liu in Mao's name. Chen even told Mao that Gao had proposed that "we should take charge (of the Party Center) in turns." Deng added that Gao had once asked, "Who is China's Lenin, and who is China's Stalin?"; this implied that Gao coveted Mao's high position. The conversation went on for over two and a half hours. Mao also summoned Zhou to join the discussion.[56] It seemed that Mao, at once angry and embarrassed, was inclined to purge Gao. Zhou took note of all of this.

Mao's conversations with central and provincial leaders continued in the following days. He was most concerned about three things: getting further clarification of what Gao had said and done in the past months; determining how widely he had spread the contents of the "An List"; and deciding how, if necessary, to "rectify Gao." He met again with Chen and Deng late on December 19. By then, it was clear that the chairman had decided to "split with Gao." He asked Chen to travel to all the locations that Gao had visited on his tour and tell the leaders there, "Do not be fooled by Gao."[57] On the afternoon of December 20, Mao talked with Liu for the first time since the December 15 Central Secretariat meeting.[58] Evidently, the chairman had devised a plan to resolve the Gao problem, and he needed to work out a deal with Liu. It was most likely at this meeting that they agreed to bring Gao and Rao down together.

From December 17 to 23 Mao and Zhou met six times. Mao knew that Zhou had established numerous connections within the party leadership and controlled huge administrative resources as well as power. Zhou's cooperation, he understood, would be essential if he were to split with Gao, in order to shake off the embarrassment Gao had caused him. Gao's loss of Mao's trust did not surprise Zhou. Gao had been too outspoken and his knowledge of CCP high politics too superficial. Zhou had no bad feelings toward Gao; although Mao claimed that Gao had been against him, he knew this not to be the case. Now Gao was in big trouble, however, and it seemed that Mao and Liu had reached an agreement on how to deal with him. Zhou knew that he had to work with them to settle the case.

At 2:00 P.M. on December 24, Mao chaired an enlarged meeting of the Politburo attended by Liu, Zhou, Gao, and Rao, among others. Two headquarters existed in Beijing, the chairman claimed. "One is headed by me; it makes transparent statements and speaks in transparent ways. The other is commanded by someone else; it fans the flames of conspiracy." Mao then announced that he would travel to Hangzhou to supervise the drafting of the PRC constitution. The meeting endorsed Mao's proposal to prepare a resolution on enhancing the party's unity. During Mao's absence, Liu would be in charge of the Party Center's routine work.[59]

* * *

Zhou and Liu stayed in the capital while Mao was gone. Although Mao had announced that Liu would be in charge during his absence, Liu could not handle the Gao case at will, as he was one of its stakeholders. Zhou's role thus became crucial. Publicly Mao said that he had gone to Hangzhou to oversee the creation of the PRC constitution. But he was still preoccupied with resolving the Gao dilemma.

Three days after Mao left Beijing, Liu and Zhou worked out a draft resolution on intraparty unity and immediately sent it to Mao. After much deliberation, Mao wrote to Liu and Zhou on January 7, 1954, proposing that a Central Committee plenum be called in late January to pass the resolution.[60] Mao's proposed agenda for the plenum contained no mention of criticizing Gao. Rather, Mao specifically asked Liu to make self-criticism. Liu's notes should be "short and to the point," Mao instructed, and he should not admit to mistakes that he had not made. Moreover, once Liu had written his remarks, he was to let Mao read them first.[61] The next day, Liu wrote Mao, telling the chairman that he and Zhou had gotten along smoothly.[62] The Politburo decided to hold the plenum on January 30.

Liu telegraphed Mao the draft of his self-criticism on January 16, with Zhou's support. He stressed that Chen Yun, Peng Zhen, Deng, and others had revised and approved the text, which now awaited Mao's appraisal. Liu did not mention Gao by name; he merely implied that he had tried to defend himself "in a few places" in the draft's text, as he had faced fierce but groundless attacks. Thus, Liu argued, "some self-defense was necessary."[63] By this he was apparently referring to Gao.

Gao wrote to Mao on January 19. He admitted that he had made mistakes and expressed that he was willing to make self-criticism at the next plenum. He hoped to go to Hangzhou to talk with Mao.[64] Gao had asked Yang Shangkun to deliver the letter to Mao; instead, Yang gave it to Liu, who immediately called a meeting with Zhou and other leaders to discuss the letter. They concluded that Mao had four options: to permit Gao to meet with him in Hangzhou; to assign the Central Secretariat the task of talking with Gao;

to return to Beijing to handle the matter; or to appoint Liu and Zhou to talk to Gao. They found that the matter would be "difficult to handle" if Mao were to allow Gao to go to Hangzhou or if he returned to Beijing, and it would be "too big a deal" to make the secretariat talk to Gao. So, they suggested, it was most proper for Mao to appoint Liu and Zhou, along with Deng, to talk to Gao.[65] The suggestion was carefully laid out, covering all possible scenarios that Mao might encounter. Gao visiting Mao in Hangzhou, or the chairman returning to Beijing, could result in a face-to-face argument between the two. Mao absolutely wanted to avoid such an embarrassing situation. Who but Zhou could have assessed the situation so shrewdly?

Mao cabled Liu from Hangzhou after he heard Yang's report. The chairman agreed to Liu and Zhou's suggestion. "As the opening of the plenum is imminent," Mao said, "it would be inappropriate for Comrade Gao Gang to come here." But he particularly stressed that at the plenum, "self-criticism by any comrade should be welcome . . . so as to wait for the awakening of those who have made mistakes." He also instructed Liu and Zhou "to let Comrade Gao Gang read this telegram" and noted that he would "not reply to him directly."[66] Thus, Mao gave Liu and Zhou a free hand to manage the Gao case. Liu, Zhou, and Deng talked with Gao on January 25, having received Mao's telegram. Although Gao said he was willing to make self-criticism, actually he was deeply unwilling to do so.[67] Liu and Zhou reported to Mao that Gao had not "awakened."

On January 28, as Yang was about to return to Beijing, Mao again emphasized to him that criticism of Gao at the next plenum should be carried out with a "positive approach" following the principle of "learning from past mistakes to avoid them in the future." With the passage of the resolution on party unity, it was essential to "uproot the environment of activities that nurtured conspiracies" and "to enhance education and persuasion." "We should give Gao a way out, so he will not settle for a stalemate."[68] Apparently, Mao did not want to ruin Gao.

The plenum began on February 5 without Mao. This was the only time he had missed a plenum since he became the party's top leader. Liu and Zhou, who presided over the conference, did not explicitly name Gao, but they allowed the presenters to label Gao's behavior as "conspiracy activities against the party." Of those who spoke at the plenum, Zhu De's tone was the mildest. He emphasized the importance of preserving the party leadership's unity and claimed Gao's problems stemmed from the "spreading of individualism and the growth of self-exaltation and complacency among some comrades." Mao endorsed the notes of Zhu's speech upon reading them before the plenum.[69] However, no one echoed Zhu at the plenum. Though he and Zhu were old friends, not even Zhou stood up to back Zhu.

Gao made self-criticism on February 7, but he admitted only to have "lacked sufficient understanding of the importance of intraparty unity." Thus, Gao continued, he had made "mistakes in individualism and liberality."[70] Such a self-critique surely was not acceptable in this situation.

The two high points of the plenum came on February 10. The first was Liu's speech. After reporting on the work of the Central Secretariat and the Politburo, Liu made a series of accusations against Gao, but did not name him. Then, he offered his own self-criticism, highlighting several of his past mistakes.[71] By jettisoning all these "historical burdens," Liu put himself in a stronger position to oppose Gao. The second high point was the passage of a resolution to endorse the "general line on the transition to socialism."[72] This was the "most important matter" that Mao had repeatedly emphasized, and it was a crucial reason for the chairman's decision to cease protecting Gao. With the resolution adopted, Liu and Zhou had fulfilled the task that Mao most cared about.

• • •

The plenum did not produce any verdict on Gao. At the time, it might have seemed that the Central Committee had decided to simply wait for "Gao's self-awakening." Five days later, though, two roundtables, one on Gao's issues and another on Rao's, began. The roundtables were not part of the chairman's plan. There is no evidence to indicate that Liu and Zhou had consulted Mao, during or after the plenum, about convening them. Why they were held remains a mystery. In any case, the two roundtables thoroughly changed the essence of the Gao and Rao cases by grouping the two officials into what was called the "Gao-Rao antiparty clique."

Gao delivered further self-criticism on the first day of the roundtable about his case.[73] He simply repeated what he had said before, still refusing to fully incriminate himself. When, during the meeting, Chen Yun exposed Gao's "mistakes and crimes," he and Gao got into a heated quarrel, disputing a number of facts. Zhou defended Chen, accusing Gao of "spattering Chen with mud" and trying to drag Chen into the water while he himself was drowning.[74] Gao sat down and said nothing more.

On February 17, Gao tried to commit suicide by shooting himself, but he did not die. Prior to his suicide attempt, Gao had written separately to Mao and Zhou. In his letter to Zhou, Gao asked the premier to help take care of his wife, Li Li'an, and his children, "given the many years of friendship between the two of us."[75] When he learned of Gao's failed suicide attempt, Mao was thoroughly disappointed. Zhou and Liu proposed to put Gao "under supervision and education" and ramp up criticism of his "mistakes and crimes." The Politburo approved the proposal.[76] The tone of criticism against Gao escalated dramatically in the wake of his attempted suicide.

After careful preparation, Zhou delivered a harsh and methodical speech on February 25. He listed ten of Gao's "big crimes." First, Gao had devised the notion that "the party was created by guns," and he had attempted to split the party and seize power at an opportune moment. Second, Gao had carried out factional activities and opposed other leaders. Third, he had used "a list of names for the Politburo and various central departments" to spread rumors. Fourth, Gao had privately promised promotions to others to gain influence. Fifth, Gao had made the Northeast an independent kingdom. Sixth, he had usurped the name of the Party Center to damage Liu's and other leaders' reputations. Seventh, he had plagiarized others' texts to rise through the ranks. Eighth, he had created difficulties in Sino-Soviet relations. Ninth, he had conspired to seize state power. Tenth, Gao was corrupt in his personal life. Further, Zhou declared, after "his intentions were exposed," Gao "betrayed the party and the people by attempting to commit suicide."[77] Zhou then submitted the outline of his speech to Mao in order to have it circulated within the party, which Mao approved.[78]

Gao had long been known as the "king of the Northeast." After his downfall, the task of bringing that region back into the fold became a matter of the utmost importance. The job fell on Zhou's shoulders. Immediately after the roundtable on Gao, Zhou met with several leading cadres from the Northeast. "Gao has long been conducting antiparty activities in the Northeast," Zhou said. Therefore, it was necessary to convene a conference of cadres from the Northeast to "understand and expose Gao's mistakes."[79] The conference was held in Shenyang in late March; Zhou attended it along with Luo Ruiqing, the minister of public security. Zhou told the more than five hundred cadres gathered at the conference that Gao's problem was not one of "normal political, ideological, or organizational mistakes." Rather, he stressed, Gao was "a bourgeois careerist" who had tried to "split and oppose the party."[80] Zhou's speech inflamed passions at the conference, leading many to attack Gao and his like in a severe tone. After Zhou returned to Beijing, Luo chaired the conference. The attacks on Gao grew louder and louder; many of the claims had no factual basis whatsoever. Finally, five high-ranking cadres who had worked with Gao in the Northeast were labeled "five tigers" belonging to the Gao antiparty clique.[81]

Gao was then placed under house arrest to receive "disciplined reeducation." He wrote a detailed "self-examination," which he submitted to the Party Center on April 29. He waited day after day, hoping to hear back from Mao, Zhou, or someone else, but no reply came. With each passing day his will to live waned. On August 17, 1954, Gao committed suicide. Zhou rushed to Gao's home, still remembering the letter Gao had sent him after his first suicide attempt. Zhou ordered an autopsy of Gao's body and specifically instructed that a respectful funeral be arranged for Gao, and that Li Li'an, Gao's widow, be treated well.[82] Zhou probably gave these instructions because he did not want the negative impact of the Gao case to spread further.

By abandoning Gao, Mao had not only retained but even consolidated his control over intraparty high politics. Along with having elicited Liu's and Zhou's embrace of his "general line on the transition to socialism" and obtained a systematic self-criticism from Liu, Mao had regained the initiative on a series of big issues, especially that of defining and implementing the "general line."

Mao's attitude toward Gao's death was perplexing. He was unsatisfied with Gao and had hoped to teach him a serious lesson. But he did not mean to destroy Gao, who shared many of his political ideas and was a quite capable person. Mao had agreed to criticize Gao and had even allowed Liu and Zhou to label Gao as an "antiparty figure" largely because the Gao case had caused huge repercussions for top party leaders. After all, although by then Mao was already hugely powerful, he had not reached the level of simply doing anything he wanted at will. Several years later, Mao revealed that he had considered "sending Gao back to Shaanbei, preserving his party membership, and retaining him as a member of the Central Committee." But Mao "was one step behind," and Gao committed suicide. "I feel very sorry," Mao lamented.[83] Revealed here was Mao's intention to "freeze" Gao for a while and release him later. This is precisely what Mao did to Deng during the Cultural Revolution, years later.

· · ·

Rao Shushi's name gradually became linked to Gao beginning in December 1953, when top CCP leaders were dealing with Gao's problems. However, Rao still believed that there had been little connection, let alone any collusion, between him and Gao. It was true that both he and Gao had made the mistake of spreading the "An List." But this error, Rao thought, would result in nothing more than severe criticism, which he could deal with by making "serious self-criticism." Rao could not have imagined that he would not only come under withering attack after Gao's downfall, but would also be arbitrarily linked to Gao as another head of the "Gao-Rao antiparty clique." Indeed, the Gao case morphed into the "Gao-Rao case."

When, in mid-December, Mao decided to abandon Gao, he also made up his mind to throw out Rao. This was, in a sense, the result of tacit bargaining between Mao and Liu. Gao had been "Mao's man" in the arena of CCP high politics. And Rao, despite the rift that had begun to emerge between him and Liu, was still regarded as "Liu's person." Mao asked Chen Yi, an old adversary of Rao's, about Rao during a conversation on December 21. Chen, not knowing what Mao was after, provided only irrelevant answers. Yet, once Chen figured out the chairman's intentions, he immediately came up with a series of accusations regarding Rao's "mistakes and crimes."[84] At a meeting of central leaders on December 24, Mao mentioned that there were really two headquarters in Beijing, a comment that he aimed directly at Gao and Rao.[85]

On February 3, 1954, Rao was summoned to a meeting with Liu and Zhou, which Zhu De, Deng, and Chen Yun also attended. Liu was the main speaker. Zhou said almost nothing, but his presence added weight to Liu's words. Liu asked Rao to make self-criticism at the next Central Committee plenum, telling him that the resolution on enhancing party unity was made primarily in response to his and Gao's problems.[86] Rao realized that he was in big trouble. At the plenum, which was held a week later, Rao made self-criticism about his offenses, especially his issues with Chen Yi. He also touched on his problems with An at the Personnel Department, admitting that he had failed to heed Liu's advice.[87] Unsurprisingly, his self-criticism did not pass muster. With respect to the "An List," he admitted only that "I have developed some misunderstandings about a certain list of names put forward by An Ziwen." However, no one pursued this matter further at the plenum.

A roundtable concerning Rao began on February 15. Chen Yi delivered the keynote speech, in which he enumerated a host of Rao's past mistakes.[88] Two days later, Rao again made self-criticism. He began with a few old cases, noting in particular that he had feuded with An Ziwen after being transferred to Beijing and had "developed a wrong sense about a certain list of names put forward by An." Then, Rao continued, he "failed to follow Comrade [Liu] Shaoqi's advice to stop the dispute" and insisted on handling the matter his own way. Moreover, Rao claimed, he "even went so far as to express his grievance against Comrade [Liu] Shaoqi." Rao's statement was subtle. The causal relationship implicit in Rao's self-criticism was not necessarily evident to everyone at the session. One thing was clear, though: there had been no conspiracy or collusion between Rao and Gao. Nonetheless, in the roundtable's report to the Party Center, Rao was accused of "colluding with Gao to carry out activities to split the party."[89]

How could this have happened? In a way, Rao was merely a convenient victim of intraparty high politics. The key here was that historically, Rao's rapid rise in the party ranks began after Liu became secretary of the Central China Bureau and the head of the New Fourth Army. In Rao's own words, "My close relationship with Comrade Shaoqi has been well known."[90] However, he had seriously crossed the line in his management of the "An List," offending both Mao and Liu. Consequently, he became a victim of the deal between Mao and Liu. Mao purged Rao to remedy his loss from the purge and subsequent death of Gao. Liu abandoned Rao not just because Rao had offended him. Crucially, Liu did so to clear his connection to An's list while balancing the negative impact of Gao's death for Mao.

In January 1955, Rao was formally arrested when he tried to overturn the verdict given him. He went insane in prison and died there in 1974.

• • •

After Gao's death and Rao's arrest, Pan Hannian, vice mayor of Shanghai and CCP superspy, and Yang Fan, head of the Shanghai Public Security Bureau, were arrested on the charge that they were leaders of another "reactionary clique." A careful study of this case reveals its implications for Zhou. In particular, in the CCP's intraparty struggles, the purge of Pan and Yang greatly mitigated Zhou's apparent gains in the Gao case.

Pan's downfall was triggered by an accidental development. At a party conference held after the "exposure of the Gao-Rao antiparty clique," some confessed to their previously unknown "historical problems." Mao, approving of these admissions, announced that all high-ranking cadres should take the initiative to air their past transgressions in a written confession to the party. "All those who do so will be welcomed, and all those who still try to hide such problems will be severely punished."[91]

As he listened to Mao's announcement, Pan thought of a secret that he had kept for over a decade. During the war against Japan, he had exchanged information with Li Shiqun, the Shanghai intelligence chief of Wang Jingwei's puppet regime. In March 1943, Pan was "all of a sudden dragged by Li to see Wang," an incident he did not immediately report to the Party Center. When the Nationalist intelligence services obtained information concerning Pan's "collusion" with the Japanese and the Wang regime, they ran a sensational media campaign framing the revelation as evidence that the CCP had "betrayed China." Pan then found it more difficult to report the encounter to the party leadership.[92] Heeding Mao's instructions at the conference, Pan went to see Chen Yi to divulge his meeting with Wang over a decade earlier. Chen immediately reported the information to Mao, who commented, "This person can never be trusted."[93] Luo Ruiqing, minister of public security, personally went to Pan's hotel and arrested him on account of his status as a "long-hidden enemy agent."

Pan was a highly accomplished superspy for the CCP. He had made a big mistake by not disclosing his meeting with Wang, but that meeting alone did not warrant his being labelled an "enemy agent." Moreover, Pan had admitted to his mistake because Mao had promised at the party conference that cadres who confessed to their mistakes in the past would be pardoned and treated with leniency, regardless of the nature of their transgression. Nonetheless, Mao baselessly and arbitrarily claimed that Pan was an "enemy spy" and ruthlessly purged him. In fact, there was reason to believe that Mao purged Pan to entangle Zhou. Since the 1930s, Pan had been a top agent in Zhou's intelligence and united front network. If Pan indeed had been an enemy agent, that would mean that Zhou's intelligence network had been gravely compromised, with the enemy penetrating even the network's highest ranks. This was almost a slap at Zhou's face.

Zhou did not directly speak on Pan's behalf. Vouching for him would have put Zhou in a serious bind. He knew full well that both Mao and Liu had lost a key associate in the wake of the Gao-Rao affair. It so happened that Pan's confession delivered Mao a new case at this particularly delicate moment. It was not at all strange that Mao made a big deal out of Pan's case. However, Zhou was clever. Rather than confront Mao directly, he immediately instructed

Luo Qingchang, a close associate of his and a leading figure in the CCP's intelligence services, to assemble a special group that would perform a thorough review of the telegraphic exchanges between Pan and the Party Center from 1939 to 1948. The group concluded that Pan had reported all his activities, including his "penetration into the Japanese bandits' inner circle and use of its members," to the Party Center. Indeed, Luo concluded, everything that Pan had done fell within the guidelines of the party's "secret operation codes . . . long endorsed by the [Party] Center."[94]

On April 29, 1955, Li Kenong, another close associate of Zhou's and a CCP spymaster, submitted a report to the party leadership following Zhou's instructions. Li pointed out a series of problems with the allegation that Pan was an "enemy agent." For example, Li noted, the Party Center had approved all the intelligence links that Pan had pursued with Wang's puppet regime. Pan had provided the party with a large amount of highly valuable intelligence information. The intelligence network in which Pan operated, moreover, was never exposed or sabotaged, and as Mao and Zhou both knew, some of its agents were still active.[95] Li received no response to his report, but Zhou had achieved his objective. He never meant to whitewash Pan, which was beyond his capacity to do. What Zhou wanted was to protect himself and his control over the CCP's intelligence services. Li's report had at least prevented Mao from using the Pan case as an excuse to purge Zhou.

Pan was held in prison until January 1963, when a secret trial convened to rule on his alleged crimes. Zhou gave detailed instructions about who and how many people should attend the trial, while expressly ordering that the trial's proceedings be tape recorded. To this end, he approved the purchase of recording equipment from Hong Kong.[96] The trial, however, was just for show. Before it began, Pan was told that "if he accepted the verdict, he would be put on parole immediately after the sentencing." Indeed, Pan was granted parole shortly after he was sentenced to fifteen years in prison for being an "enemy agent."[97] He was allowed to settle with his wife in the suburbs of Beijing, and he was occasionally permitted to visit relatives and friends. Pan probably had Zhou to thank for these arrangements. In the Cultural Revolution, though, Pan was again imprisoned. In 1975, he was relocated to a farm in Hunan, where he died in 1977. He was exonerated in 1981.[98]

• • •

On March 31, 1955, the CCP Central Committee passed a resolution on "the antiparty alliance between Gao and Rao." All CCP leaders, including Zhou, heralded the resolution as a "great victory." It appeared that Liu had emerged as a major winner in the Gao case, especially since it consolidated his position as the party's second-in-command. Zhou also seemed to have won an important victory. With Gao's downfall, he reclaimed, and even enhanced, his administrative power. The reality, however, was far more complicated. The Gao case made Mao very uncomfortable, as he saw Liu and Zhou expand their power and influence in the party leadership. After weighing the pros and cons, he had opted to avoid a showdown with them over Gao; instead, he took the initiative to sacrifice Gao. Yet Mao's character meant that he could not tolerate this result. The Gao case thus sowed the seeds of Mao's eventual split with Liu, and it deepened Mao's longstanding distrust of Zhou. Two years later, Mao would use the "opposing rash advance" controversy to attack Zhou. To be sure, the tensions that would surface between Mao and Zhou were partly caused by their different views on how socialism should be pursued. On the level of intraparty politics, though, might these tensions also have had something to do with the way that the Gao case was settled?

From a longer perspective, the Gao-Rao case had a huge impact on the trajectory of CCP high politics. Liu, Zhou, and their fellow CCP leaders probably did not realize at the time that the Gao-Rao case had opened a Pandora's box, paving the way for ugly struggles among leaders in the party's upper echelon. Without any solid evidence, Gao and Rao were painted as heads of a supposed "Gao-Rao antiparty clique," and Pan, a CCP spymaster who had made monumental contributions to the party, was labeled a "hidden enemy agent." Their cases set a precedent for similar cases in the future. Zhou would inevitably be brought into each of those political struggles as a target of Mao's criticism.

• • •

As 1955 approached, China formally unfolded its comprehensive program for the transition to socialism. The same year also saw a collectivization movement—born from Mao's theory of "continuous revolution" and the need for massive capital to industrialize the economy—sweep across the Chinese countryside. In the process of collectivization, the state would extract excessive amounts of grain from the peasants, which was integral to accelerating the transition to socialism, as it was the only way for China to accumulate on its own the capital required for rapid industrialization. Against this backdrop, Zhou turned much of his attention to designing a system of "unifying purchases and unifying sales" in China.

Beginning in 1951, the Chinese state had tried to manage and exert control over the buying and selling of grain throughout the country. However, the existence of free grain markets made this a challenging task. The issue became more pressing when, over three months in the summer of 1953, the state collected a total of 4.9 million tons of grain but had sold more than 6.2 million tons. Zhou consulted with Chen Yun, who suggested that the problem could only be resolved through "unified buying of grain in the countryside and unified selling of grain in cities."[99] Zhou immediately gave his support to Chen's proposal, which he and Mao would both endorse at an enlarged meeting of the Politburo on October 2. In particular, the chairman stressed at the meeting that while the measures Chen proposed would "cause discontent among the peasants, urbanites, and foreign press, they should still be adopted."[100] The meeting decided that free grain markets would be abolished, and that the state would monopolize the buying and selling of grain throughout the country. This meant that the state would use the "price scissors" between agricultural and industrial products to extract excessively from the peasants, thus creating a long-lasting domestic source of capital accumulation for the country's ambitious industrialization plans. Meanwhile, by controlling all citizens' basic means of living, the program would tightly bind the population's lives to the state. Consequently, China saw the emergence of the world's most rigid household registration system.

In September 1953, Zhou chaired a session of the People's Political Consultative Conference (PPCC) to discuss the promotion of the party's general line on the transition to socialism. A verbal confrontation erupted between Mao and Liang Shumin, a distinguished "democratic figure" and an important target of the CCP's united front policies. Liang had lengthy experience in rural reconstruction, and thus he regarded himself as quite knowledgeable about rural problems and the suffering of the peasants. Liang and Mao had discussed rural issues several times since the PRC's founding, and they were, by all appearances, on good terms. At the start of the conference, Zhou delivered a report on the general line. In a group discussion, Liang praised Zhou's report, but he also stressed that the party and government should patiently listen to everyday people's opinions and resolve their problems.[101] Zhou then invited Liang to share his opinions with others at the plenary session. Liang agreed.

On September 11, Liang gave a carefully prepared presentation. He mentioned that Zhou's report highlighted only the "construction of heavy industry and the transformation of private industry and commerce," and he opined that more attention should be given to "developments in light industry and transportation." He then turned to "the countryside and villages." In the Chinese revolution, he emphasized, the CCP had depended on the peasants and took the countryside as its base. However, after the party liberated China's cities, Liang argued, the CCP shifted its focus to urban areas, while "the rural areas became marginalized." Liang asserted that "now the workers are living a life above the sky while the peasants' life is under the earth." "If you ignore the peasants today," Liang continued, "people will say that you have abandoned the peasants."[102]

Zhou did not rebut Liang. Indeed, Zhou likely agreed with many of Liang's views, including, for instance, the notion that the development of heavy industry should not be pursued at the expense of light industry and agriculture. Later Zhou expressed similar ideas in his "opposing rash advance" endeavor. But Liang had offended Mao. The next day, the chairman gave an extemporaneous presentation aimed at "someone who disagrees with our general line, believing that the peasants have lived a very poor life and asking for us to specifically take care of them." Mao raised his voice, saying, "We, the Communists, have been involved in mobilizing the peasants for decades. We do not understand the peasants? This is such a joke!"[103]

Liang, unconvinced, stood up to argue with Mao. Zhou did not intervene, but Mao became enraged, accusing Liang of "opposing the general line." At the time, Mao was vehemently pushing other CCP leaders to embrace the general line. He said to Liang the same thing he had told Zhou, thus leaving no room for Zhou to maintain an ambiguous stance on this crucial issue. Zhou delivered a lengthy speech at the conference's plenary session on September 17. Echoing Mao's tone, he insisted that Liang had meant to oppose the general line. To support his accusation, Zhou pointed to history. By quoting an essay that Liang wrote in 1949 (in which he criticized some of the CCP's policies), he claimed that Liang had long been an "anti-Communist and antipeople figure." Liang, utterly offended, stood up and asked Zhou why another essay of his, "Advising the GMD," was not mentioned.[104]

Mao interrupted Liang three times during his presentation, commenting that Liang was "a hypocrite," who "killed others by the pen, rather than by the knife." Liang still hoped to defend himself. Mao announced that the conference would be postponed for one more day, and that Liang would be permitted to speak later.[105] The next day, Liang's presentation was stopped after less than ten minutes. Everyone was mobilized to attack Liang, calling him "extremely reactionary." Liang tried to carry on with his speech, waiting, he said, "to see if Chairman Mao is truly magnanimous." "No, I probably lack the magnanimity you wish to see," replied Mao. Cries then broke out across the conference hall: "Reactionaries do not deserve democratic rights! Get out, Liang Shumin!"[106] Apart from CCP cadres, many "democratic figures" were among those who berated Liang. They failed to realize that by depriving Liang of the right to present his views, they were laying the groundwork for the deprivation of their own right to speak out in the future, opening the door to even graver consequences.

Liang refused to compromise. Finally, a vote was held, in which the majority (not including Mao) was against allowing Liang to continue his presentation. The drama ended. Zhou had invited Liang to speak, but he also presided over the barrage of criticism against Liang and even went so far as to dig into the historical origins of Liang's "reactionary behavior." In the circumstances of the time, Zhou had acted on Mao's instructions. However, by doing so, he created another dangerous precedent: when someone was being criticized, that person's history would be arbitrarily and distortedly used as "evidence" to justify groundless accusations against him. This method would be broadly used in the Cultural Revolution. The most notorious case was the one involving Chairman Liu Shaoqi, who would be vilified as a "traitor, renegade, and scab."

• • •

Compared with Liang, Zhou had a closer relationship with Hu Feng, a friend of Lu Xun and a CCP sympathizer. Zhou and Hu stayed in frequent contact during their years in Chongqing. Hu even called Zhou "Father Zhou."[107] To Zhou, however, Hu was only an ally in the united front, rather than a comrade. After 1949, Hu continued to see Zhou as his teacher, but Zhou thought of Hu differently. Although Hu had supported the CCP politically—even to the extent of calling 1949 the "beginning of time"—he believed that such a stand was compatible with his aspiration for the "liberation of individuality." During the CCP's first round of "thought reform" aimed at intellectuals, Hu's relationship with Zhou Yang, the CCP's czar of cultural affairs, became increasingly tense. The two had known each other and had a rocky relationship in the 1930s, when Hu repeatedly clashed with Zhou Yang and other CCP cultural officials due to his expression and defense of his own perspectives. After 1949, Zhou Yang continued to find Hu a writer alien to the party's cultural policies. In his eyes, Hu's worldview was profoundly penetrated by "bourgeois and petit bourgeois perspectives, a tendency that absolutely should be criticized."[108]

Zhou had no choice but to support Zhou Yang. In July 1952, he approved "the procedures (proposed by Zhou Yang) to criticize Hu's cultural and literary thought." Hu wrote many letters to Zhou and requested to meet with him. "I am in the middle of a busy schedule," Zhou replied, asking Hu to talk with Zhou Yang and "make some self-criticism about your own cultural thought and attitudes."[109] Clearly, Zhou still treated Hu's problems as "a contradiction among the people"; had Zhou been in charge of Hu's case, Hu would not have been labeled a "reactionary figure." However, Mao intervened. Upon reading Hu's diary and correspondence, the chairman determined that Hu and his confidants had formed an "antiparty clique," and he ordered the Public Security Bureau to take over the case. Mao personally wrote the preface to the materials on the "Hu reactionary clique," which were later published. In the preface, Mao accused Hu and his like of being "special agents of the GMD or the imperialists,. . . or CCP traitors."[110] Zhou fell silent, while Hu was arrested and placed in detention for over twenty years. When he was finally released from prison and "rehabilitated" after the Cultural Revolution (several years after Zhou's passing), Hu's physical and mental health had already been destroyed.

• • •

In retrospect, the years 1953–1955 mark an extremely important period in the PRC's history. With the end of the Korean War and the promise of massive Soviet economic and technological support, Mao felt that the time had come to cut "new democracy" short and accelerate the transition to socialism. Neither Zhou nor Liu seemed to show sufficient enthusiasm for Mao's initiative. Mao responded with bold ideological and organizational action, criticizing Liu and Zhou while simultaneously (even as he abandoned Gao Gang) pulling them to his side and compelling them to embrace his general political line. This demonstrated Mao's political wisdom and strength. He knew that once his general line was made the CCP leadership's consensus, and he thus would more firmly define the party's mainstream discourse, everything else would be easier to settle. Indeed, once the stage was set on his terms, no matter how Liu, Zhou, or any other CCP leaders performed, they would be actors on a stage of Mao's creation.

On the surface, the Gao-Rao affair, the Pan case, and the criticism against Liang and Hu were not interrelated. In fact, however, they were all integral parts of Mao's grand program of "continuous revolution." But there was a key difference between the Gao-Rao affair and the cases of Pan, Liang, and Hu. The settlement of the Gao-Rao case was the result of negotiation and bargaining among Mao, Liu, Zhou, and others. Thus, Zhou still had a major say in the process. A common feature of the latter three cases was that in defining them, Mao had ignored facts, laws, and the views of other party leaders; the judgments made on these fallen personages were primarily Mao's own. In these cases, Zhou often differed with Mao, yet he connived with Mao or even became Mao's accomplice. In the years that followed, Mao persistently pushed his "continuous revolution" forward, while constantly waging ridiculous struggles against supposed enemies of the revolution. The events of the mid-1950s were just the beginning.

Zhou's experience in these two years is difficult to summarize. He was severely criticized by Mao for his "mistakes" in designing the tax reforms and saw his power somewhat weakened. However, in the Gao-Rao case, he was able to recover much of his administrative power by helping Mao absolve himself of responsibility. Yet, hardly had he celebrated when he was dealt a bitter blow from Pan's purge. In retrospect, all this was a foretaste of similar encounters that Zhou would face over the next two decades.

18

FROM GENEVA TO BANDUNG

1954–1955

On a cold day in mid-February 1954, Zhou Enlai received a heart-warming report: At the end of a month-long meeting in Berlin, foreign ministers from Moscow, Washington, London, and Paris called for the convening of a conference at Geneva to bring peaceful settlements to war-torn Korea and Indochina. They invited Beijing to send a delegation to the conference.[1] For Zhou, this was a "huge international victory."[2] How could it not be one? The PRC would now attend an international gathering for the first time in the de facto capacity of one of the "five powers"! This was an unmistakable sign that New China had emerged as a major world power.

Zhou immediately carved time out of his full schedule to read copious quantities of documents, telegrams, and intelligence reports relating to the upcoming conference in Geneva.[3] In late February, he worked out a plan. Beijing's top-priority goals for Geneva, he believed, were to break up America's blockade and embargo against the PRC and highlight New China's accomplishments for the world to see. Therefore, Beijing "must actively participate in the conference" and "make it a success." Given America's rigid stance, the Geneva Conference was unlikely to reach a breakthrough on Korea. However, Zhou observed, the prospects for Indochina looked brighter, especially as Paris and Washington were not in complete agreement on the matter. Thus, Zhou asserted that China should try to "dangle the carrot in front of France while using the stick to deal with America," and make sure that the conference "will not end without any result." On March 2, the CCP leadership approved the plan.[4]

The war in Korea had been bloody, and the armistice there failed to quash hostilities between the opposing sides in the conflict. It is no wonder that Zhou thought a settlement of the Korean issue to be out of the question at Geneva. But he did see an opportunity for a settlement in Indochina, where 1954 marked the eighth year of the anticolonial war in Indochina waged by the League of Independence (Vietminh), led by Vietnamese Communists, against the French colonialists. Beijing had lent the Vietminh substantial support since 1950 and had even dispatched Chinese military and political advisors to Vietnam to aid them. After a series of battlefield victories in early 1954, the Vietminh had become more powerful than ever before. Policymakers in Paris were increasingly reluctant to continue fighting a war with such dubious prospects; yet they were also unwilling to allow the Vietminh to dominate Indochina. The Indochina issue was to figure prominently in discussions at Geneva. Zhou had not presided over China's support to the Vietminh; that was Liu Shaoqi's responsibility. Now, Vietnam's fate was to be negotiated through international diplomacy, a process over which Beijing would presumably exert significant influence. As China's chief negotiator in Geneva, Zhou knew that he had to be prepared.

As both premier and foreign minister of the PRC, Zhou had various other expectations for Geneva. During the revolution and the early years of the People's Republic, Zhou explained at a Foreign Ministry meeting in early April, the CCP had conducted diplomacy "as an outsider off the formal stage . . . observing neither rules nor codes, and fearing nothing at all." But now Beijing faced a different scenario: "We will step onto the international stage, and we are also a great power . . . we should play a formal drama in a measured way." To achieve this, Zhou emphasized, it was necessary to adjust Chinese foreign policy to accord with China's "changing identity" in the world.[5]

Zhou understood that he needed to coordinate strategies with Beijing's Communist allies. Vietminh troops, Zhou knew, would soon wage the final offensive of their months-long siege of the French stronghold at Dien Bien Phu. In early to mid-March, Zhou cabled Chinese military advisers working for Ho Chi Minh, calling their attention to the forthcoming "international struggle" at Geneva. "To achieve success in the diplomatic field," Zhou stressed, Vietminh troops should strive for a glorious victory on the battlefield. To this end, Beijing would greatly increase its military and other support to the Vietminh. Zhou also told Ho that the Communists should "actively participate in" the Geneva Conference and strive for a peaceful settlement to the conflict in Vietnam. For this, Zhou suggested, the Vietminh might consider accepting "a relatively fixed demarcation line in Vietnam," which would allow the Communists to "control an area that is linked together."[6] Ho, together with Pham Van Dong, foreign minister of the Democratic Republic of Vietnam (DRV), came to Beijing in late March. In his meetings with Ho, Zhou gave particular emphasis to the experience gained by China from the Korean War negotiations, stressing that it was necessary to maintain "realistic expectations" for Geneva. According to Chinese records, Ho agreed.[7]

In early April, Zhou, together with Ho and Dong, visited Moscow. He found that Soviet leaders supported settling the conflict in Indochina through negotiation. As this would be his first time attending a major international conference, Zhou told Soviet foreign minister Vyacheslav M. Molotov that he was eager to heed the opinions of Soviet comrades. In response, Molotov advised Zhou that if the Communists were reasonable, it would be possible to solve one or two problems at Geneva. Zhou expressed his complete agreement.[8]

• • •

The Geneva Conference began on April 26, 1954. As Zhou had predicted, "discussions on Korea have quickly entered a deadlock." However, he reported to Beijing that the prospects for resolving the matter of Indochina looked hopeful. Georges Bidault, the French foreign minister, was "eager to discuss the Indochina question," Zhou noted, and had already "approached Molotov" and expressed "the desire to meet with us." Thus, Zhou believed, "the discussion on Indochina could begin ahead of schedule."[9]

Zhou also had his eye on the Briton at the conference. With Molotov's arrangement, Zhou conferred with Anthony Eden, the British foreign secretary, in an "informal meeting" on April 30. This was Zhou's first face-to-face meeting with a leader of a major Western power. When Eden inquired about whether the Chinese would be willing to persuade the Vietminh to release wounded prisoners in their custody, Zhou immediately replied that this would not be a problem "if the concerned parties met directly." The meeting also confirmed Zhou's earlier speculation that the British, like the French, were more interested in Indochina than Korea.[10]

18.1 Zhou Enlai attending the Geneva Conference, April 1954. *Historic Collection / Alamy Stock Photo*

Formal discussions on the Indochina issue began in Geneva on May 8, the day after French troops in Dien Bien Phu surrendered to the Vietminh. Although the Vietnamese Communists had, in preconference consultations with Beijing and Moscow, agreed to a settlement based on temporarily dividing Vietnam into two zones, Zhou found that they now hoped to squeeze more concessions from their adversaries. Pham Van Dong, Vietnam's head negotiator at Geneva, stated that in order to end the war in Indochina, the Vietminh would ask to reestablish their virtual control over most of Vietnam. Moreover, Dong pushed for a package settlement that would include all three countries of Indochina and would also give "due rights and position" to the "resistance forces in Laos and Cambodia," who, despite Dong's denial, were mostly Vietnamese "volunteers."[11]

Zhou later admitted that he had been unaware of "the distinctions and differences between the three countries of Indochina" when he came to Geneva.[12] Therefore, both he and the Soviets had originally supported the Vietminh's pursuit of a package settlement treating Indochina as one entity. His meetings in Geneva with representatives from Laos and Cambodia made him realize that "the national and state boundaries demarcating the three associate countries in Indochina were quite distinctive," and that "the royal governments in Cambodia and Laos were seen as legitimate by the overwhelming majority of their people." Hence, Zhou reasoned, "we must treat them as three different countries."[13]

In early June, Zhou met with Molotov and Dong. The three reaffirmed that the Communists would commit to a strategy of partitioning zones of control between the two sides in a cease-fire agreement.[14] An on-site cease-fire "is not favorable to us," Zhou explained in a telegram sent to Beijing and also conveyed to top Vietminh leaders, as it would not allow the Vietminh to control the whole northern part of Vietnam. Conversely, dividing Vietnam into northern and southern zones would place a large, contiguous zone under Vietminh control, while making the cease-fire more enforceable.[15]

Discussions on Korea at Geneva ended inconclusively on June 15. Zhou feared that the conference's sessions on Indochina might also fail. At this critical moment, the French parliament replaced Prime Minister Joseph Laniel with Pierre Mendès-France, a longtime critic of the war in Indochina. Mendès-France promised that he would either bring the negotiations to a successful conclusion by July 20 or resign. Zhou saw this as a "window of opportunity" to make a deal with the French on Indochina.[16]

Zhou called another meeting with Molotov and Dong on June 15. He spoke straightforwardly. The Vietminh's rigid attitude would render the negotiations fruitless, Zhou told Dong, and the Vietnamese Communists themselves would also squander a golden opportunity to achieve a peaceful solution. Zhou proposed that all foreign forces—including the Vietminh's "volunteers"—withdraw from Laos and Cambodia, so that "our concessions on Cambodia and Laos will prompt the other side to concede on dividing Vietnam into two zones." Molotov strongly supported Zhou's proposal. Dong also gave his consent, albeit reluctantly.[17]

Zhou immediately relayed his new approach to the British and the French. If the United States did not maintain military bases in Laos and Cambodia, he told Eden, Beijing would be willing to recognize the two countries' respective royal governments, and it would also persuade the Vietminh to withdraw its "volunteers" from their soil.[18] Zhou also met with Bidault, apprising the French foreign minister about all that he had told Eden, and also mentioning that Beijing had no objection to Laos and Cambodia remaining in the French Union.[19] At the plenary session that afternoon, Zhou introduced a new proposal for a cease-fire in

Indochina that stipulated the withdrawal of *all* foreign forces from Laos and Cambodia.[20]

Zhou's efforts, coupled with the unwillingness of the French and British to let the conference fail, led the two contending sides to an agreement on June 19 concerning how military talks should proceed, thus opening the door to "the cessation of hostilities" in Laos and Cambodia.[21] Then, the Geneva Conference adjourned for three weeks, offering Zhou a valuable opportunity to further coordinate Communist strategies for the next round of negotiations at Geneva.

• • •

How to persuade the Vietnamese comrades to make the necessary concessions at Geneva remained Zhou's primary concern. In order to reach the best possible deal on Indochina, Zhou stated in a lengthy telegram to Beijing, the Vietminh would have to give up some of their claims. However, at Geneva, their perceptions and plans had "failed to match reality." If they were to stick to such an approach, warned Zhou, "the negotiations cannot go on, and our long-term interests will not be best served."[22] This was a complex matter, and it was difficult to reach a consensus with the Vietnamese "merely through telegraphic exchanges." Zhou thus proposed to travel back to China during the conference recess to meet with Ho in person, so that "a consensus can be worked out." Beijing immediately approved Zhou's plan.[23]

Zhou regarded Mendès-France as another key figure. On June 23, he met with the French prime minister at the French embassy in Bern, Switzerland. "I have lived in France and am with good feelings toward the French people," he told Mendès-France. "I also hope that France's international reputation will become higher." He then emphasized that Beijing definitely wanted peace to prevail in Indochina. At Mendès-France's request, Zhou agreed to help persuade the Vietnamese Communists to speed up the negotiations.[24]

Meanwhile, Zhou found time in his busy schedule to meet with Tep Phan, the head of the Cambodian delegation to the Geneva Conference, and Phoui Sananikone, the leader of the Laotian delegation. He promised them that Beijing would respect Cambodia's and Lao's sovereignty and independence with the hope that they would join the ranks of a "new type of country in the region—like India, Indonesia, and Burma—where no foreign military bases exist." He also encouraged them to establish a closer relationship with the Vietminh, and he said that he would help them establish such a relationship.[25] On June 24, Zhou left Geneva.

• • •

Zhou now turned all his attention to the upcoming meeting with Ho Chi Minh in Liuzhou. He knew that if he could not persuade Ho and other Vietminh leaders to accept the Chinese-Soviet line of making necessary compromises at Geneva, the conference as a whole, the PRC's debut on the world stage, and Zhou's own diplomatic endeavor would all fail. Therefore, Zhou arrived in Liuzhou determined and prepared.

The meeting began on July 3. General Vo Nguyen Giap, commander of the Vietminh forces, made a detailed report on the military situation in Vietnam. The enemy had suffered a huge setback at Dien Bien Phu, but was far from defeated, said Giap. New French reinforcements had arrived in Indochina, and the strength of the enemy forces, which now came to about 470,000 troops, was greater than that of the Vietminh's of approximately 300,000 soldiers. In addition, the enemy still controlled such major cities as Hanoi, Saigon, Hue, and Da Nang. Giap acknowledged that a fundamental change in the balance of force between the two sides on the battlefield had not taken place.[26]

Zhou interrupted Giap just as the Vietminh commander was wrapping up his lengthy presentation: "If the United States does not interfere, and France sends in more troops, how long will it take for us to seize the whole of Vietnam?" "Probably another two to three, or, more likely, even three to five years," replied Giap. General Wei Guoqing, the chief Chinese military advisor to the Vietminh, who was also present at the meeting, seconded Giap's estimate.[27]

Now came Zhou's turn. The war in Indochina had already been internationalized, he said, and the danger it posed "has even surpassed that of Korea." It was because neither Moscow nor Washington wanted to see the war in Korea expand that "a stalemate emerged between the two sides" there. In comparison, "the war in Indochina not only has engaged the three Indochina countries," stressed Zhou, "but also has influenced the whole of Southeast Asia—even Europe and the entire world." Zhou then highlighted the danger of America's possible intervention in Indochina. Because the imperialist countries feared the enormous influence of the Chinese revolution, they would not allow the Vietnamese revolutionaries to win a glorious victory. Therefore, Zhou stressed, "if we ask too much at Geneva, and if peace is not achieved, the United States surely will intervene," thus delaying the victory of the Vietminh. All things considered, Zhou emphasized, "we must isolate the United States and break up its plans; otherwise, we will fall into the trap set by the US imperialists." In order to bolster his argument, Zhou highlighted "the example of Korea" as supporting evidence: "The key to the Korea issue lay in America's intervention. It was completely beyond our expectation that American reinforcements would arrive so quickly. . . . If it had not been for America's intervention, the Korean People's Army would have driven Syngman Rhee's troops into the ocean." As the result of America's intervention, "we only achieved a draw at the end of the war, and were unable to win a victory." Therefore, Zhou concluded, the Vietminh must prevent what had happened in Korea from reoccurring in Indochina.[28]

In the last two days of the meeting at Liuzhou, Zhou outlined a desirable settlement based on four basic conditions: the enacting of a simultaneous cease-fire in all three countries of Indochina; the drawing of the demarcation line at the sixteenth parallel or, if necessary, the seventeenth parallel in Vietnam; the forbidding of weapon and ammunition shipments into Indochina once the settlement went into effect; and the shutting down of all military bases in Indochina. Given that Cambodia and Laos were different from Vietnam, Zhou elaborated, they should be allowed to pursue their own paths of development so long as they did not join a military alliance or permit the establishment of foreign military bases within their borders.[29]

Zhou's presentation seemed to have deeply impressed the Vietnamese, especially Ho. Toward the end of the meeting, Ho thanked Zhou for "not only carrying out the struggle in Geneva, but also coming here to present this important report." He was in "complete agreement" with Zhou, and he promised to adjust the Vietminh's aims and strategies in accordance with Zhou's advice, as "now Vietnam is standing at a crossroads, heading either to peace or to war, and the correct direction should be the pursuit of peace."[30]

Zhou fully achieved his goals set for the meeting. The Chinese and the Vietnamese leaders agreed that, for the next phase of the negotiations at Geneva, they would strive to pursue a settlement in Vietnam by temporarily partitioning the country along the sixteenth parallel, and they would tolerate the establishment of non-Communist governments in Laos and Cambodia.[31]

Ho kept his word. Vietnam's Party Central Committee issued a directive on July 5 endorsing a new strategy for solving the Indochina problem through a cease-fire based on the temporary partitioning of Vietnam into two parts, leading to Vietnam's reunification after the withdrawal of French forces and through a national plebiscite.[32] The directive clearly reflected the agreement that Ho and Zhou had reached at Liuzhou.

* * *

Zhou returned to Beijing on July 6. The next day, he reported at a CCP Politburo meeting that the Chinese delegation at Geneva had adopted "a policy line to pursue cooperation with France, Britain, Southeast Asian countries, and the three countries of Indochina—that is, to unite with all the international forces that can be rallied together and to isolate the United States—so that America's plans for expanding its world hegemony will be hindered and undermined." Mao and the Politburo fully backed Zhou's report.[33]

On July 9, Zhou flew from Beijing to Moscow. The next day, he met with a group of Soviet leaders headed by Georgi M. Malenkov. Zhou found that he and the Soviets had the same ideas; together, they agreed to introduce "fair and reasonable conditions that the French government is in a position to accept, so that the agreement on restoring peace in Indochina will be quickly achieved." In particular, it was crucial to prevent "the interference and sabotage of the United States."[34]

Zhou arrived in Geneva on the afternoon of July 12. At seven o'clock that evening, he met with Molotov, briefing the Soviet foreign minister on his meeting with Ho in Liuzhou. Molotov asked Zhou if he believed it was feasible to set the demarcation line at the sixteenth parallel. Zhou replied that he and Ho had agreed to aim for a solution that drew the demarcation line at the sixteenth parallel, but they would also accept the seventeenth parallel, if necessary.[35]

Zhou sensed Dong's lack of enthusiasm to carry out the "July Fifth Directive," however. Therefore, he held an overnight meeting with Dong, in which Zhou told Dong that the directive was based on a consensus between the Chinese, Soviet, and Vietnamese leaders. The danger of direct US military intervention in Indochina was serious and real, Zhou said. To avoid such intervention, he emphasized, the Communist side "must actively, positively, and quickly carry out negotiations to pursue a settlement, and must make the negotiations simple and avoid complicating them, so that Mendès-France will not step down." Zhou also promised Dong that "with the eventual withdrawal of the French, all of Vietnam will be yours." Dong finally yielded to Zhou's logic, if not necessarily to his pressure.[36]

Zhou did not get much sleep that night. At 10:30 A.M. on July 13, he was shaking hands with Mendès-France. He found that the French prime minister was now mainly concerned with the location of the demarcation line. Zhou told him that while the Communists preferred to draw the line along the sixteenth parallel, they were willing to compromise.[37] At 11:45 A.M., Zhou conferred with Eden, telling the British foreign secretary that the Chinese and Vietnamese had reached an agreement on pursuing peace in Indochina, and that the Vietminh were willing to compromise. "If France is willing to make further concessions on the question of dividing zones," he promised Eden, "the Vietnamese will also make due concessions."[38]

Zhou meant what he said. In the final round of negotiations at the conference, Mendès-France insisted that setting the demarcation line at the seventeenth parallel was the final limit of his concession, and that if he yielded any further on the matter, he would have to resign. Zhou, with Molotov's blessing, decided to change the Communist position on the demarcation line from the sixteenth to the seventeenth parallel to meet the French requirement.[39] Thus, the Geneva Conference reached a settlement on Indochina in the early morning of July 21. Officially speaking, Mendès-France had not exceeded his deadline, Zhou told him.

* * *

Zhou's agenda at Geneva, while centering on diplomacy about Indochina, also included efforts to expand China's trade relations with Western capitalist countries. Among the more than two hundred members of Zhou's entourage were a group of Chinese trade officials, whom Zhou had authorized to hold a series of private talks with representatives of capitalist countries, especially those from Britain, while Zhou was busy with meetings on high-profile diplomatic matters. Lei Renmin, one of Zhou's associates and China's first vice minister of foreign trade, oversaw these activities on the conference's sidelines. Beginning in early May, he had several meetings with Humphrey Trevelyan, the British chargé d'affaires in Beijing, and Peter Tennant, the overseas director of the Federation of British Industry, exploring trade opportunities between the two countries.[40]

In a follow-up to these meetings, on May 28, Lei met with two frontbench members of the British Parliament, Harold Wilson of the Labor Party and Robson Brown of the Conservative Party. Two days later, Zhou also met with the two MPs. Wilson proposed that Britain and China respectively set up trade offices in Beijing and London. "We will consider this," Zhou replied.[41] In a telegram to Mao on June 1, Zhou proposed that "in order to promote Chinese-British relations, we may formally raise the matter of setting up a permanent trade office in London, which should enjoy full diplomatic privileges and status." Mao and the CCP leadership approved Zhou's proposal in two days.[42] Zhou met with Eden on June 1, when they agreed that China and Britain would establish consulates in each other's capitals.[43] On June 17, China and Britain issued a joint statement announcing the establishment of consular-level diplomatic relations between the two nations. This was followed by a Chinese trade delegation's visit to Britain from late June to mid-July. To Zhou, these developments represented the "improvement of China's trade and diplomatic relations with Britain," which had served to further "isolate the United States" and "expand our achievements at the Geneva Conference."[44]

Even to the United States, Zhou also showed some flexibility whenever there was an opportunity. Undoubtedly, the United States was New China's principal enemy then; yet Zhou did not refuse to deal with the Americans, and he even regarded the Geneva Conference as an opportunity to open a channel of communication with Washington. He had a very bad impression of John Foster Dulles. But this was not primarily because the US secretary of state refused to shake hands with him (which actually was not the case), but because of Dulles's rigid attitude toward Beijing. In comparison, his impression of Walter Bedell Smith, Dulles's deputy, was much better. "The American imperialists are not the same, we should not view them in the same way," he told his associates.[45]

On May 19, Trevelyan met with Huan Xiang, one of Zhou's associates. Trevelyan said that he was willing, in a private capacity, to help devise a solution for Chinese and American nationals living in the other country to return to their own country. Huan replied that he would "report for instruction and reply later."[46] After hearing Huan's report, Zhou immediately realized the opportunity in Trevelyan's approach and decided to give a positive response.

On May 26, Huang Hua, then the spokesperson of the Chinese delegation, publicly announced that the Chinese and American sides should "have direct contact about these issues." In a telegram to the CCP Center on June 3, Zhou analyzed the situation as follows: "It seems that there exist differences inside the US government and the US delegation." Therefore, the Chinese side should "wait for a short period, and if the Americans indeed come to negotiate, we should follow our established policies to have contact with them and, then, according to the result of the contact, to decide where to hold the negotiation. . . . If the American side does not want to have contact with us, we may immediately issue a statement, making clear our consistent policy and the actual situation of our penalizing those Americans who had violated laws and protecting law-abiding American residents, while exposing and denouncing the groundless behavior of the American side to hold our students."[47]

There was a breakthrough on June 4, when Trevelyan informed Huan that the US side had agreed to begin negotiations on the issue of repatriation of foreign residents with the Chinese side, provided that Trevelyan would also be present. The US side would appoint its ambassador to Czechoslovakia, Ural Alexis Johnson, as its representative, and it hoped that China would make Wang Bingnan, China's ambassador to Poland, the Chinese representative. Further, the US delegation hoped that the talks would begin the next day.[48] Zhou immediately decided to accept Trevelyan's proposal. The same afternoon, Huan and Trevelyan met again, agreeing that "the initial contact will begin tomorrow."[49]

Beginning on June 5, under Zhou's direct guidance, Wang and Johnson held four consular-level meetings in Geneva. The two sides mainly discussed issues concerning their residents trapped in the other country. No substantial breakthrough occurred from these meetings; they nevertheless served as a channel of communication between Beijing and Washington. When these talks ended on June 21, the two sides agreed that they would keep in contact via "staff officers passing on information" upon repatriation of their nationals and students residing in the other country.[50] This left a narrow door open that would lead to the launch of Chinese-American ambassadorial-level talks a year later.

• • •

Zhou left Geneva having accomplished nearly all of his goals for the conference. Indeed, his international diplomatic debut had been a great success. The creation of a Communist-ruled North Vietnam would form a buffer zone between China and the capitalist world in Southeast Asia. The opening of new dialogues between China and such Western powers as France and Britain would help end the PRC's global isolation. More importantly, the crucial role played by China at the Geneva Conference implied that for the first time in modern history, China had been accepted by the international community—friends and foes alike—as a genuine world power. That these achievements seemed to echo Mao's proclamation that "we, the Chinese, have stood up" provided Mao, Zhou, and the Chinese Communist leadership with new authority to promote broader and deeper domestic mobilizations.

* * *

Zhou's glorious moment, however, soon came to an abrupt end. After the Geneva Conference, he visited several Eastern European countries to reinforce the PRC's solidarity with them. In late July, during a visit to Poland, Zhou received a telegram from Beijing that at once confused and shocked him. Mao had instructed Deng Xiaoping to draft and send the telegram to Zhou on behalf of the Central Committee. The premier was informed that "upon studying the situation after the Geneva Conference," the Central Committee had concluded that the United States, "unhappy with its failure at Geneva," would continue to be "hostile to our country" and carry out a policy of "creating tension in international affairs." Turning to Taiwan, the telegram stated that "now we are still facing the prospect of fighting a war against Chiang's bandit clique, and we still have to fulfill the task of liberating Taiwan." The telegram then claimed that "since the end of the Korean War, we have failed to highlight the task of liberating Taiwan to the people throughout the country in a timely manner (we have been late for about six months).... If we do not underscore and strive to fulfill the task now, we will be committing a serious political mistake."[51]

Although the telegram had been addressed to Zhou, his name did not appear anywhere in it. Nonetheless, in criticizing the failure of the Chinese delegation to bring up the Taiwan question before or during the Geneva Conference, the message clearly targeted Zhou. This was unfair. After all, had Zhou tried to tack the Taiwan question onto the agenda for the Geneva Conference, discussions on Indochina at the summit would inevitably have been derailed. In that event, would it still have been possible for a peace accord to be reached at the conference? Further, the tone of the telegram was incongruous with Zhou's efforts at Geneva to demonstrate that New China was a flexible and rational actor in international affairs. Rather than praising Zhou for such a resounding achievement at Geneva, Mao had elected to criticize the premier. Zhou's joy and excitement faded.

In this rebuke, Mao revealed some of his basic perceptions of China's external policies and strategies. No matter how hard Zhou had tried to relax international tensions, Mao saw abundant tension and the potential for confrontation in China's external environment. Mao also aspired to use that international tension to facilitate domestic mobilization. In the same telegram, he explicitly emphasized that

> the introduction of the task [of liberating Taiwan] is not just meant to undermine the American-Chiang plot to sign a military treaty; rather—and more importantly—by highlighting the task, we mean to raise the political consciousness and alertness of the people of the whole country; we mean to stir up our people's revolutionary enthusiasm, thus promoting our nation's socialist reconstruction.[52]

In a more subtle sense, Mao's sudden attack on Zhou probably carried another meaning. Zhou's performance at Geneva, while winning him a huge international reputation, was certain to further augment his influence and standing in China and within the CCP leadership in particular. Had Mao felt it necessary to do something to rein in Zhou's upward trajectory? Surely, it was unfair that in the telegram from the Central Committee Zhou was not credited for his triumphant diplomatic achievements at Geneva, but rebuked for his "mistakes." However, in criticizing Zhou, Mao had sent the premier a warning. Indeed, here we observe a revealing phenomenon that occurred on numerous occasions since the PRC's establishment: whenever Zhou made an outstanding contribution in state or diplomatic affairs, Mao would find an excuse to criticize or attack him.[53] This episode after Geneva was just one of those occasions.

• • •

By the time Zhou received the telegram, *Renmin ribao* had already published an editorial announcing that "the Chinese people must liberate Taiwan."[54] This move effectively placed the Taiwan question onto the chessboard of international confrontation. Zhou immediately issued a "serious self-criticism" for the "mistake" the chairman had accused him of committing. He also took action at once. On July 29, when Zhou met with Soviet leaders Khrushchev and Malenkov in Moscow, he explained the CCP's new policy toward Taiwan in detail. The meeting's prearranged theme, "striving to lessen international tensions after Geneva," was sidelined.[55]

Mao's were not empty words. Chinese media launched a summer-long propaganda campaign with "we must liberate Taiwan" as the main slogan. On September 3, PLA shore artillery batteries in Fujian shelled the Nationalist-controlled Jinmen Islands, heightening tensions in the Taiwan Strait. In response, Washington accelerated talks with the Nationalists on a treaty of mutual defense, which was formally signed on December 5. In internal discussions, military planners in Washington even considered using nuclear weapons if the crisis continued to escalate.[56] In early 1955, before the US Congress ratified the US-Taiwan treaty, the PLA occupied two Nationalist-controlled island chains off the coast of Zhejiang Province. Chinese-American relations further deteriorated.

Zhou's diplomacy at Geneva seemed to have sharply contrasted with Beijing's militant policies toward Taiwan, as Zhou was facing the dilemma of whether to favor a moderate international policy, as he had done at Geneva, or to adhere to the radical policy of anti-imperialism that the PRC had pursued ever since its founding, as demonstrated by Beijing's instigation of the Taiwan crisis. Yet in Mao's attempt to stimulate sustained domestic mobilization, the two aspects of China's external policies, one "soft" and another "hard," seemed to almost merge into one. Both served his purpose of stimulating everyday Chinese people's patriotic consciousness and revolutionary nationalism, thus promoting his "continuous revolution" programs.

There were few among Beijing's leaders, Mao knew, who had Zhou's ability to bring these "soft" and "hard" aspects together in a highly subtle and sophisticated fashion in China's foreign policy practice. Mao often criticized Zhou, but he always needed Zhou's services as New China's "diplomatic face."

* * *

In spring 1955, when the gunfire along the Taiwan Strait finally went quiet, Zhou was once more on his way to another major international event: the Asian-African Conference in Bandung, Indonesia.

If Geneva was Zhou's debut on the world scene, Bandung offered him another major opportunity to perform in the international spotlight. In April and May 1954, leaders from Burma, Ceylon, India, Indonesia, and Pakistan proposed to convene a summit of Asian and African countries. As concrete plans for the conference began to materialize, the question of whether to invite the PRC to the conference provoked serious disagreement among several Asian countries. When Zhou learned of this controversy, he instantly recognized that the Asian-African Conference provided an important opportunity for China to expand its influence among non-Western countries. He understood from the beginning that China's large population, vast size, long history, profound culture, and especially its experience as a "semicolonial country" in modern times meant that its presence alone would make it a central actor at the conference. What would follow promised to greatly impact not only China's international influence but also the CCP's domestic mobilization efforts. Therefore, it was vital that China attend the conference.[57]

Earlier, when the Geneva Conference adjourned in late June 1954, Zhou had made a detour on his flight back to Beijing to visit New Delhi and Yangon, where he met with Indian prime minister Jawaharlal Nehru and Burmese prime minister U Nu, respectively. "The main purpose of the visit," he reported to Beijing, "was to prepare to work out a kind of Asian peace pact, in order to give America's plot of organizing a bloc of aggression in Southeast Asia a serious blow, as well as to promote the restoration of peace in Indochina."[58]

Zhou stayed in New Delhi for two days, where he consulted with Nehru about the possibility of setting up "peace zones" in East Asia and South Asia. Despite the differences between the political and social systems of China and India, Zhou told Nehru, the two countries had similar historical backgrounds and both belonged to the "cultures of the East." Moreover, both countries had suffered from the oppression and exploitation of Western imperialism and colonialism. Given all this, Zhou reasoned, China and India should base their relationship on the principles of peaceful coexistence. If so, he further emphasized, Beijing and New Delhi would be setting up a "good model" for other Asian countries to follow. In order to convince Nehru of his sincerity, Zhou said that as a Communist, he believed in the necessity of revolution, but he did not support exporting revolution from one country to another.[59] Zhou and Nehru issued a joint statement, in which they announced that the "Five Principles of Peaceful Coexistence" should serve not only as the basic foundation undergirding state-to-state relations, but also as the foundation of international relations as a whole.[60] Following his India trip, Zhou visited Burma, where he and Prime Minister U Nu issued a similar joint statement.[61] Zhou secured both India's and Burma's firm support for Beijing's attending the Bandung Conference.[62]

Nehru and U Nu each visited Beijing in the fall of 1954. There, they met with Mao and had extended meetings with Zhou. Central to the dignitaries' discussions with Zhou was the matter of how to build unity among Asian and African countries. Zhou told them that he definitely wanted to attend the Asian-African Conference. Both Nehru and U Nu reassured Zhou that India and Burma firmly supported the PRC's—and especially Zhou's—participation in the conference at Bandung. They also hoped that China would play an important role in making the conference a success.[63]

Zhou headed a special task force to work out a "plan to participate in the Asian-African Conference." Zhou personally revised the plan, which was approved by the CCP Politburo.[64] The plan pointed out that the conference, "not attended by Western imperialist countries but by the majority of countries in Asia and Africa," was being convened in the context that "the struggles by peoples in Asia and Africa for national independence are rapidly developing." Among the states that would participate in the Bandung Conference were "such socialist countries as the PRC and the Democratic Republic of Vietnam, as well as many countries in favor of peaceful neutrality." According to the plan, by attending the conference, China should "strive to expand the united front for world peace, promote movements of national independence, and create conditions for establishing and enhancing our country's ties and diplomatic relations with various Asian and African countries."[65]

With respect to China's strategies for the conference, Zhou reasoned that China's attendance at the summit alone would represent a great victory for New China's diplomacy. Therefore, Chinese delegates should avoid making any radical statements at the conference. To ensure the success of the conference, instead of "discussing the question of Communism," the Chinese delegation would emphasize China's and other Asian and African countries' shared history, cultural legacies, and modern experience of suffering from imperialist and colonialist aggression.[66]

. . .

When Zhou was preparing to fly to Indonesia, he encountered the most serious assassination attempt of his career. His would-be assassins were special agents working for the Nationalist regime in Taiwan. The reasons for the Nationalists' attempt on Zhou's life were quite obvious; from Taiwan's perspective, if Zhou were allowed to appear at the Asian-African Conference, it would mean another major diplomatic victory for Beijing, diminishing Taiwan's influence among Asian and African countries, most of which still recognized Chiang's government as the legitimate representative of China. Taiwan's intelligence services had mobilized all of their resources in Hong Kong and other parts of Asia in a plot to assassinate Zhou. However, the PRC intelligence agencies under Zhou's command intercepted the enemy's plan. Originally, Zhou was supposed to take *Kashmir Princess,* an Air India–owned Lockheed L-749A aircraft chartered by the PRC government, to fly from Hong Kong to Indonesia. At the last minute, Zhou decided to take another route and plane to Indonesia.[67]

On April 11, agents working for Taiwan in Hong Kong successfully planted a bomb on the *Kashmir Princess.* Instead of Zhou, several staff members of the Chinese delegation and journalists boarded the plane. Despite warnings from Beijing, the British Hong Kong authorities had failed to discover the bomb and thus did not take effective action to stop the plot. The bomb exploded in the plane when it was in midair, en route from Hong Kong to Indonesia, and the *Kashmir Princess* crashed into the South China Sea. Of the nineteen crew members and passengers on the plane, sixteen died and three survived. Zhou, however, narrowly escaped falling victim to what would have been one of the most spectacular assassinations in the history of the Cold War.

Chinese sources have never revealed how Beijing had intercepted the information or, in particular, why Zhou, upon learning that Taiwanese agents would sabotage the plane, still used it to transport members of the Chinese delegation and Chinese and pro-PRC foreign reporters from Hong Kong to Indonesia. These questions still await definitive answers.

Zhou and his associates, however, capitalized on the crash in their dealings with the British; indeed, they managed to greatly enhance Beijing's influence, as well as its ability to conduct activities, in Hong Kong. In October 1955, Sir Alexander Grantham, governor of Hong Kong, "privately" visited Beijing. Zhou met with him for a three-hour "unofficial" meeting, in which he disclosed to Grantham China's willingness "to tolerate Britain's continued presence in Hong Kong." Zhou also "identified certain 'rules of conduct' for Hong Kong, for example that Britain should not steer the territory toward democracy or self-government; that foreign powers should not use it as a military base; that Nationalist subversion should be prevented and the safety of Chinese officials protected; and that China's economic interests should not be obstructed."[68] On March 12, 1956, the British government further promised Beijing that "Her Majesty's Government have no intention of permitting Hong Kong to be used as a base for hostile activities against anyone. . . . Her Majesty's Government wish to make it clear that if in future it is considered that Hong Kong's facilities are being deliberately abused, Hong Kong Government will hold itself free to take whatever action it deems necessary to deal with such abuse."[69] This was a response that Zhou was very much willing to receive.

• • •

Zhou arrived in Jakarta on April 16 and flew to Bandung the next day. Zhou's charismatic personality and diplomatic skills refined the predetermined tone of his participation in the Asian-African Conference. At public events, he carefully avoided using radical language in presenting Beijing's domestic and international policies. In private meetings, he repeatedly stressed that Beijing favored peace, and that New China would not export revolution to other countries. In particular, he cautiously avoided contradicting dissenting voices outright, and he crafted a public image that he was the most eager of the conference's attendees to see the summit succeed. Indeed, Zhou even broached the highly sensitive subject of Chinese-American relations. He announced that Beijing was willing to negotiate with Washington to reduce "tensions in the Far East" and iron out the differences between China and the United States.[70]

These lengths, however, were still insufficient to dispel widespread doubts among the conference's participants about Beijing's intentions for its appearance at Bandung. The tense atmosphere that was characteristic of the Cold War period prevailed—mainly implicitly though occasionally explicitly—at the conference. Representatives from several countries even attacked the People's Republic as a country of "red imperialism." Zhou knew that extraordinary means were necessary to overcome these circumstances. He had prepared a speech long before he departed for the conference that was scheduled to be delivered at its plenary session on April 19. Mao reviewed and revised multiple drafts of the speech before ultimately approving the final version, which stressed the possibility and necessity of cooperation between Asian and African countries—in accordance with the Five Principles of Peaceful Coexistence—due to their shared experience as victims of Western colonialism and imperialism.[71] After Zhou arrived in Bandung, however, he sensed that the leaders of pro-West or pro-America countries harbored deep suspicions about China's motives and purposes. What Zhou found most worrisome—even offensive—was that these leaders not only viewed New China as a vicious and expansionist Communist country but also regarded it as a Soviet puppet, one without an identity or aspirations of its own. Zhou felt increasingly concerned that this characterization would undermine the PRC's basic qualification for playing a central role at the conference as well as in the broader non-Western world, outcomes that he saw as the primary objective for the PRC's attendance at the conference.[72]

With no time to consult with Mao, Zhou took the initiative to make a last-minute change. He would distribute his prepared notes at the conference, but he would devise an edited version that placed greater emphasis on the PRC's desire and moral capacity to "seek common ground in spite of differences" among Asian and African countries, so that collectively they would play a larger role in world affairs.

On the afternoon of April 19, in the conference's packed assembly hall, Zhou took the podium. "The Chinese delegation has come here to seek common ground, not to create division," he loudly announced to his fellow Asian and African leaders. "Is there any reason to believe that there is common ground between us?" he asked rhetorically. Then he gave his answer: "Yes." He stressed that despite their differences (including sharp ideological divergences), they were all Asian and African countries that, in modern history, "have suffered and are still suffering from the calamities caused by colonialism" and had been linked together by the common cause of "continuing their struggle for complete independence." He emphasized that he was a Communist, and that he believed Communism should be the preferred means for modernizing China and transforming the world. Still, he asked the assembly, "Is there any reason why we cannot understand and respect each other, and give each other our support and sympathy?" Again, he answered his own question: "Sure." Zhou stated that "there is every reason to make the Five Principles the basis for establishing friendship, cooperation, and good-neighbor relations among us."[73]

Zhou's speech has been widely praised as one of the most important and successful of his long career. He made it clear that China, in the grand scheme of historical development, was one of the Asian and African countries standing in opposition to the global reign of imperialism and colonialism. Although revolutionary terms were absent from Zhou's speech, the context in which he delivered the address imparted it with profound revolutionary significance: Zhou had introduced what was in effect a new set of international norms and codes of behavior legitimized by China's shared experiences with other Asian and African countries. Thus, Zhou made it clear that China stood on the correct side of historical development.

Thus, on the afternoon of April 19, 1955, when Zhou gave up a nap to prepare—then to deliver—the speech, he again demonstrated to the world his qualities as a diplomatic giant and first-class statesman.

* * *

Following Bandung, Zhou turned more of his attention to developing relations with countries in Asia and Africa, while engaging more actively in international affairs in the larger non-Western world. Under his direction and, at times, close supervision or even personal involvement, the People's Republic established diplomatic relations with a series of Asian and African countries, including Afghanistan, Cambodia, Ceylon, Egypt, Guinea, Iraq, Morocco, Syria, Sudan, and Yemen, in a short time span.

When the Suez crisis erupted in 1956, Zhou made sure that Beijing loudly broadcast its support of Egyptian president Gamal Abdel Nasser's decision to nationalize the Suez Canal. He met twice with Hassan Ragab, the Egyptian ambassador to Beijing, emphasizing that "if President Nasser and the

Arabic people persist in their resistance, victory will surely be theirs. . . . And China will do its best to support them."[74] On November 10, Zhou telegraphed Nasser, announcing that China would give Egypt 20 million Swiss francs in cash for its struggle against imperialism.[75]

But Zhou did not ignore Western capitalist countries. After Geneva, he tried to take full advantage of the new channels that he had opened with Britain, France, and other Western countries. In the fall of 1954, he personally arranged the visit of Clement Attlee, former British prime minister and then leader of the Labor Party, to Beijing. Zhou promised Attlee that "China is willing to take all steps to promote peaceful cooperation with Britain" while urging the Briton to push his government to support the seating of Beijing in the UN and the expulsion of Taiwan from the UN, thus allowing China and Britain to upgrade their diplomatic relations to the ambassadorial level.[76] Zhou intentionally made no mention of Hong Kong to Attlee. He explained at a meeting of Foreign Ministry cadres, "As for issues not ripe for discussion, we should not discuss them. One example is the Hong Kong question. . . . Should we take back Hong Kong? And how might we take it back? Our government has not been able to consider the question, so we should not talk about it."[77]

Japan was another country that Zhou paid much attention to. In 1951, Zhou vehemently condemned the San Francisco Peace Treaty. In the meantime, however, he caught signs that some Japanese private businesses hoped to trade with China. In 1952, he instructed Nan Hanchen, the chief Chinese delegate attending an international economic conference in Moscow, to meet with three members of the Japanese Diet from opposition parties—Kora Tomi, Hoashi Kei, and Miyakoshi Kisuke. Then, with Zhou's support, they visited Beijing and, on June 1, signed with Nan (who represented China) an unofficial Chinese-Japanese trade agreement.[78] However, as the Korean War was still ongoing, the agreement was not implemented.

With the signing of the Korean armistice, the two houses of the Japanese Diet each passed resolutions to urge the Japanese government to relax restrictions on trade with China. Zhou immediately took advantage of this development to convey messages through various channels to "Japanese friends": "We are willing to restore peace with Japan, and establish trade relations with it on the equal and mutual-beneficiary basis."[79] In October 1953, when a group of Japanese legislators visited China, under Zhou's direction, the Chinese side signed with them another unofficial trade agreement.[80] In December 1954, Ichiro Hatoyama became Japan's prime minister, adopting a more flexible approach toward improving relations with Beijing. The next month, Shozo Murata, president of the Japan Association for the Promotion of International Trade, visited China in the capacity of a private citizen, and on January 23, 1955, Zhou met with him. Murata emphasized that he came to China to pave the way toward signing a new Japanese-Chinese trade agreement. He also raised a series of questions about Beijing's policy toward Japan, such as whether Beijing supported the Japanese Communist Party in carrying out subversive activities against the Japanese government and how to explain that Japan was regarded as a perceived target of the Sino-Soviet treaty of alliance. Zhou said that the Five Principles of Peaceful Coexistence should be "fully applied to Chinese-Japanese relations." Although Japan had invaded China in the past, Zhou stressed, China would not take revenge against Japan. Chinese-Japanese trade relations should develop on the basis of "equality and mutual benefit," to open the way toward normalization of Chinese-Japanese relations.[81]

When the Bandung Conference was to be held, Hatoyama considered personally attending it. However, concerned about involving himself in complicated political disputes at the conference while trying to highlight trade, he decided to send Tatsunosuke Takasaki, minister of international trade and industry, to attend the conference instead. On April 18, a half hour before the conference's opening, Zhou arrived at the conference hall and had a brief exchange with Takasaki. They agreed to find a better time and location to meet. On the morning of April 22, accompanied by Liao Chengzhi, a Japanese-speaking senior member of Zhou's delegation, Takasaki secretly arrived at Zhou's residence. Zhou began the conversation by recalling his experience of studying in Japan. Although he did not speak much Japanese then, he said, he could read Japanese newspapers. Taking this as a lead, he mentioned that China and Japan shared similar languages and had had a long history of cultural exchanges. Although their political systems were different, they should hold dialogues and develop economic and trade exchanges.[82] On May 4, representatives from China and Japan signed China's third unofficial trade agreement, with each side pledging to trade £30 million worth of commodities. Then the two sides issued a statement, pointing out that the signing of the agreement "had received support and assistance of the two governments" and that it "would be smoothly carried out."[83] In the wake of the Zhou-Takasaki meeting, Chinese-Japanese exchanges on economic affairs, trade, cultural activities, and other unofficial areas further expanded. In a series of Zhou's meetings with Japanese visitors, even the issue of "restoring diplomatic relations" was repeatedly discussed.[84]

Zhou even found it possible to open a dialogue with the United States. After Zhou stated in Bandung that Beijing was willing to "sit down and enter into negotiations with the US government," Washington responded on July 13, proposing that representatives of ambassadorial rank of the two sides meet in Geneva. Zhou accepted the US proposal two days later. He appointed Chinese ambassador to Poland Wang Bingnan as the Chinese representative to the talks with the Americans.[85]

A key issue at the start of the talks was the repatriation of stranded citizens in America and China to their native countries. Zhou very much wanted to see the talks move forward. Thus, following Zhou's instructions, on the first day of the talks, Wang "suddenly informed" Ambassador Johnson, his US counterpart for the talks, that Beijing had decided to release eleven "illegal US military personnel" detained in China.[86] On September 10, the two sides announced an agreement on the repatriation of Chinese and American nationals stranded in either country.[87]

Yet this turned out to be the sole agreement that Beijing and Washington were able to reach in the ambassadorial talks. In addition to such barriers as the two sides' different views on the status of Taiwan, the US-Taiwan treaty of mutual defense, and China's representation at the UN, there was one leftover matter, as Washington saw it, pertaining to the repatriation agreement. Two Americans, Jack Downey and Richard Fecteau, were still imprisoned in China on spying charges. They had been captured in the mountains of China's Jilin Province in late October 1952 after their plane was shot down. Washington claimed that they were UN servicemen who should be repatriated as Korean War POWs. Dag Hammarskjöld, the UN general secretary, visited Beijing in early 1955 to personally ask Zhou for their release. Zhou firmly rejected the request, asserting that as Downey and Fecteau "had committed the crime in China, they should be treated by Chinese law."[88] At the time, Zhou probably did not expect that almost two decades later, he would order their release as a goodwill gesture during the Chinese-American rapprochement in the early 1970s.

• • •

In the meantime, Zhou Enlai was involved in a major CCP policy change toward Taiwan, which was shifting from an emphasis on a military takeover to "peaceful liberation" through negotiations with Chiang Kai-shek. In July 1955, Zhou asserted at a full session of the People's Congress that "there are two ways for the Chinese people to liberate Taiwan, one military way and one peaceful way. If possible, the Chinese people are willing to liberate Taiwan peacefully."[89] A few months later, he reiterated that although the CCP was prepared to use military means to liberate Taiwan if necessary, it was now willing to consider "solving the Taiwan issue" through peaceful means.[90] After a series of probes, Zhou openly announced on June 28, 1956, that Beijing was "willing to discuss with the Taiwan authorities the concrete steps toward, as well as conditions for, the peaceful liberation of Taiwan." He invited the authorities in Taiwan to "dispatch representatives to Beijing, or to another proper location, to begin such a dialogue with us."[91]

These words were accompanied by back-channel activities. One such channel was a Hong Kong–based freelance journalist named Cao Juren, who had extensive connections with GMD leaders. In a meeting with Cao on October 7, 1956, Zhou outlined Beijing's conditions for a peaceful settlement of the Taiwan issue: after Taiwan's "return to the motherland," the island would continue to be governed by the GMD, and a "proper position" would be arranged for Chiang in the central government. Zhou also emphasized that in order to create an atmosphere conducive to negotiating with the GMD, Beijing had ceased its anti-Chiang propaganda campaign.[92] Until 1958, Cao continued to serve as a messenger between top leaders in Beijing and Taipei. On one occasion, Zhou expressed that in carrying out the moderate policy toward Taiwan, "we are sincere and patient, we can wait."[93]

Zhou did not know, at the moment, that this "moderate phase" of Beijing's policy toward Taiwan would again be interrupted, in 1958, during the fever pitch of Mao's Great Leap Forward.

19

TO RUSH OR NOT TO RUSH?

1956–1958

The year 1956 was an eventful one in Chinese and world history, as well as in Zhou Enlai's political career. In February, the Soviet leader Nikita Khrushchev condemned Stalin in a secret speech delivered at the Soviet Communist Party's Twentieth Congress, thus triggering de-Stalinization waves throughout the Communist world. A CCP delegation attending the congress was not invited to Khrushchev's closed-door speech. Afterwards, the Chinese were briefed on and given the text of the speech, but they received no further explanation.[1]

Khrushchev's denunciation of Stalin shocked Mao, Zhou, and other CCP leaders, who had long viewed Stalin as the leader of international Communism. Zhou attended a series of CCP leadership meetings beginning in mid-March to discuss Khrushchev's speech. Mao set the tone: Khrushchev had not just "lifted the lid" but "made a mess."[2] To start with, he applauded Khrushchev for shattering the myth that Stalin was "forever correct" and for exposing Moscow's "erroneous tendency to treat other parties as inferiors." He recalled that early in China's war against Japan, Stalin supported Wang Ming's "rightist policy" of placing the united front before the CCP's own interests. After the Second World War, Stalin had forced the CCP to come to terms with the GMD to avoid "the destruction of the Chinese nation." Mao particularly mentioned that when he visited Moscow after the PRC's establishment, Stalin was reluctant to sign a new treaty of alliance with the New China. Only after China entered the Korean War did the Soviet dictator regard the Chinese Communists as genuine proletarian internationalists.

Though Mao did not name him, Zhou was involved in nearly all the stories told by Mao.[3]

However, Mao also stressed that he strongly disagreed with Khrushchev's "total negation" of Stalin, claiming that despite all of his mistakes, Stalin remained "a great Marxist-Leninist." The chairman contended that in the final historical analysis, Stalin's achievements should account for 70 percent of his career and his mistakes for only 30 percent.[4]

Zhou's presentation at the meetings echoed Mao's tone. Citing his own experience, he stated that many of the CCP's mistakes "had not been our own doing, but had been caused by the Comintern's intervention."[5] By saying so, he meant to criticize himself for his share in these "mistakes" while also trying to defend himself.

Apart from the shockwaves of de-Stalinization, Zhou faced great domestic challenges at the time. The rapid advance of "socialist reconstruction and transformation" had caused China's economic production to overheat. Adjustment, Zhou felt, was necessary. Yet Zhou's vision and plans for the economy differed from Mao's. The chairman was a romanticist and believed that the faster China's economic development, the better. In 1955, when China had completed agricultural collectivization and nationalized industry and commerce, he asked, "America has a population of 100 million. China's is more than 600 million. . . . Why can't China catch up with and surpass America?"[6] Mao's words revealed his mentality that would nurture the disastrous Great Leap Forward.

Zhou, like Mao, was eager to pursue socialism in China, but he was more practical than Mao. In early 1956, he was alarmed to read reports and data indicating that excessive investments had overburdened the Chinese economy. "Our plans should be practical and workable, and should avoid the blind pursuit of a rash advance," he stressed at a State Council meeting.[7]

Mao disagreed with Zhou. At a Politburo meeting in late April, Zhou and Mao engaged in a face-to-face dispute when the chairman asserted that 2 billion yuan should be added to infrastructure investment to stimulate the economy. Remembering the myriad warning lights flashing for China's economy, Zhou told his colleagues, "To increase the budget may cause tension in material supplies, leading to an expansion in the urban population and a series of other difficulties." Offended, Mao adjourned the meeting before the premier could go any further with his presentation. Zhou immediately approached Mao, saying that "as China's premier, my conscience does not allow me to endorse your proposal." Mao became even more upset, and he soon left Beijing to "take vacation" in the south.[8]

Zhou probably thought that he merely differed with the chairman on an issue concerning his responsibilities as the premier. Moreover, the mid-1950s saw Zhou more capable and bolder in presenting his own opinions than at any time since the Yan'an Rectification Campaign. In fact, however, he had badly offended Mao, who would never forget this episode of his quarrel with Zhou.

Zhou continued to discourage a "rash advance" after Mao left Beijing. At a State Council meeting, he pointed out that too much effort had been spent on "opposing conservative approaches and rightist tendencies," a campaign that, Zhou stressed, should not "continue forever." Instead, he argued, "We must overcome the tendency of one-sidedly stressing speed and quantity in production. . . . And we must oppose the tendency of rash advance." When he introduced the draft budget for 1956 at a June 4 Politburo meeting chaired by Liu Shaoqi, Zhou again highlighted the tensions caused by "rash advance," stressing the necessity of continuously modulating spending and balancing infrastructure investment.[9]

Zhou's stance on the economy had a great impact on CCP leaders, especially during Mao's absence from Beijing. Liu instructed *Renmin ribao* to prepare an editorial opposing rash advance.[10] Following Zhou's suggestion, the Politburo agreed to "pursue steady economic development with comprehensive balance." One week later, the Politburo adopted another resolution stating that along with resisting conservative approaches, "we must simultaneously fight against rash advance, a tendency that has recently emerged in many regions and economic sectors. It will not help to promote socialist reconstruction. Rather, it will only cause severe losses."[11]

Mao, who was away from the capital, did not attend any of these meetings. But when he returned to Beijing, proofs of the *Renmin ribao* editorial had been circulated among party leaders for comments. Both Liu and Zhou approved the draft. Mao, however, refused to read it. When he later recalled the episode, he lamented that "the essay took me as its target, why should I have read it?"[12] The chairman's disgust—even anger—toward the premier was apparently nearing a breaking point. This was certainly because Zhou's ideas sharply contradicted Mao's political impulses. Moreover, the Politburo had decided to support Zhou in Mao's absence, which inevitably triggered the chairman's deep-seated fear of losing his authority and power. He did not lash out immediately. Rather, he waited for the right time to take his revenge.

* * *

The CCP held in late September its Eighth National Congress, an extremely important gathering in the party's history. The event brought Zhou a great deal of excitement, but it disquieted Mao.

Mao's eagerness to overcome China's backwardness in the shortest possible time was palpable when he spoke at the congress: "The United States has a population of only 170 million, and as we have a population several times larger, are similarly rich in resources, and have more or less the same kind of climate, it is possible for us to catch up with the United States!"[13] Zhou was not as enthusiastic as the chairman. In his speech, he talked about China's "great achievements," but he also repeatedly mentioned "flaws and mistakes in our work" and lessons still to be learned. Once more, he emphasized the importance of "setting up a reasonable pace of economic development." Only by weighing "the basic needs of our country's socialist industrialization against material, financial, and human conditions, as well as maintaining necessary reserves," Zhou stressed, "will our plans be workable."[14]

The term "Mao Zedong Thought" did not appear in the new party charter adopted by the congress. When Deng Xiaoping spoke on the issue at the congress, he stressed that "love of the leader, in essence, should be love of the party, the proletarian class, and the people, not worship of any individual."[15] Liu stated in his political report to the congress that "the contradiction between the proletarian and capitalist classes has basically been resolved" following the socialist transformation of privately owned means of production. Thus, Liu asserted, "the principal contradiction in our country" was now that "between an advanced socialist system and backward social production capacity."[16] Zhou, like Liu, Deng, and other party leaders, strongly supported these two important changes.

Mao, to be sure, did not wish to see the term "Mao Zedong Thought" omitted in the new party charter, but he did not challenge the change. Mao also joined his colleagues at the Eighth Congress in raising his hand to pass the report containing the new description of the "principal contradiction" in Chinese society. However, he had problems with the report. When he heard Liu reading the newly defined "principal contradiction," he murmured, "Not good, not good."[17] Mao told Liu a few days later that the congress's description of China's principal contradiction was incorrect. Shocked, Liu replied, "It has been passed. What can we do?" Mao acquiesced.[18] He was not ready to come up with an alternative formulation just yet.

• • •

Mao, Zhou, and their comrades also noted that de-Stalinization had triggered strong repercussions in Eastern European countries. A major indication came from Poznań, an industrial city in Poland, a member of the Soviet bloc. In June 1956, spurred by the tidal wave of de-Stalinization, workers in Poznań poured into the streets to protest high taxes and demand better wages. The demonstrations soon evolved into a large-scale patriotic and antigovernmental uprising. On June 28, the government used force to suppress the uprising, taking the lives of many demonstrators.[19]

The tragic event in Poznań exposed the profound crisis engulfing Communism in Poland and throughout the Soviet bloc, shocking the Soviet leaders in Moscow and deeply worrying CCP leaders in Beijing. Zhou paid close attention to reports from Warsaw, especially those from Wang Bingnan, the Chinese ambassador to Poland, and Xie Wenqing, the Xinhua reporter in Warsaw. They believed that underlying the uprising in Poznań was the confusion of party members and the masses with Khrushchev's report. Wang and Xie also identified as an important catalyst for the turmoil the Polish party's "mistakes and flaws," which Xie argued were the main source of discontent among Polish workers and everyday citizens.[20]

Mao and Zhou both read the reports, but the lessons they drew from them were different. To Zhou, the Poznań incident underscored the importance of ensuring that a socialist country's economic development be carried out in a balanced manner. At a Central Committee plenum, Zhou mentioned Poznań in particular, emphasizing that such events as "dozens or even hundreds of thousands holding protests in the streets" should not be allowed to happen in China.[21] Mao thought differently. For him, the most important lessons of Poznań were twofold. First, vigilance against sabotage by imperialists should never be relaxed. Second, the links between the party and the masses must be strengthened.

• • •

The shockwaves of de-Stalinization also buffeted the Korean Communists in Pyongyang, where Kim Il-sung had ruthlessly suppressed opposition factions within the Korean Workers' Party (KWP) while installing himself as dictator. In 1955, Kim introduced *Juche* ideology, which emphasized enhancing the role of the "indigenous Korean way" in all aspects of the Korean revolution. De-Stalinization created new space for Kim to establish North Korea as a unique Communist state following the *Juche* model. Yet Khrushchev's sharp criticism of "personality cults" posed a serious challenge to Kim's pursuit of his own cult. In June 1956, Kim visited the Soviet Union and several Eastern European countries to seek more economic support. However, in Moscow, Khrushchev and his colleagues not only criticized Kim's economic policies but also accused him of aspiring to a "personality cult" styled after Stalin's. Kim was embarrassed.[22] His opponents learned of Moscow's criticism of Kim through several channels (including Yi Sang-jo, the North Korean ambassador to the Soviet Union and a political opponent of Kim). They saw this as a good opportunity to act.

At a KWP Central Committee plenum on August 30, several prominent party leaders stood up to challenge Kim's personality cult and his economic and other policies. Kim, who had been informed of the attack by his pawns in advance, came up with effective rebuttals and began to purge the challengers. Then, several leading plotters fled Pyongyang overnight to seek asylum in China, while Yi sought asylum in Moscow. They complained to Chinese and Soviet leaders about Kim's "mistakes and crimes." Kim responded by expanding the purge. Two top party leaders, Choi Chang-ik and Pak Chang-ok—both vice premiers—were arrested.[23]

The "August crisis" in Pyongyang alarmed Beijing and Moscow. The tumult had begun on the eve of the CCP's Eighth Congress, which Kim had agreed to attend. He changed his mind at the last minute, however, and decided to send Choi Yong-gon, North Korea's number two leader, to Beijing. "Kim Il-sung is hostile to us," Mao and Zhou felt about Kim's decision.[24] On September 18, Mao, along with Liu and Zhou, held a three-hour-long meeting with Anastas Mikoyan, who was in Beijing for the CCP Congress.

Mao accused Kim of "continuously behaving like Stalin" and "killing anyone who opposes him." He believed it necessary for the Chinese and Soviets to act together to "help Kim correct his mistakes."[25] Then, Mao and Zhou met with Choi, informing him that both Beijing and Moscow believed that Kim had been completely wrong in managing intraparty matters. Given the close relationship between Beijing and Pyongyang, Mao said, "the problems in your country will also have an impact on China and the Soviet Union. Therefore, we cannot fail to intervene."[26]

A joint Chinese-Soviet delegation led by Peng Dehuai and Mikoyan flew to Pyongyang on September 19. Under pressure, Kim agreed to make some concessions. On September 23, the KWP Central Committee held another plenum, which decided to restore Choi Chang-ik's and Pak Chang-ok's membership of the Central Committee.[27] The story, however, was far from finished.

* * *

Eastern Europe again caught the attention of Mao and Zhou near the beginning of October 1956 as crises unfolded almost simultaneously in Poland and Hungary. The Polish leadership was reorganized after the Poznań incident, and Władysław Gomułka, who had a reputation as a courageous reformer, was elected first secretary of the Polish United Workers' Party. His reform measures, though, alarmed Khrushchev and the Soviet leadership, and Khrushchev flew to Warsaw on October 18 to warn the Polish leaders. Moscow then briefed Beijing, informing the Chinese leadership that the Soviet Union was preparing to intervene militarily in Poland given the highly unstable situation there.[28]

Mao immediately called an urgent meeting with Zhou and other leaders to discuss the Polish crisis. They concluded that Moscow indeed intended to intervene in Poland's internal affairs. Mao, accompanied by Zhou, summoned Pavel Yudin, the Soviet ambassador, to his quarters and warned that if Moscow were to militarily intervene in Poland, Beijing would use the "strongest language to publicly protest it."[29]

A reply from Moscow arrived on October 21. The Soviets had decided not to use force in Poland, and they invited the CCP to dispatch a delegation to Moscow to discuss how to handle the Polish crisis. CCP leaders immediately accepted the invitation.[30] Zhou should have been the best candidate for such a mission; however, he could not go as he had already scheduled visits to seven Asian countries. The responsibility fell to Liu Shaoqi and Deng Xiaoping. By the time Liu and Deng arrived in Moscow, the situation in Poland had stabilized. However, antigovernment demonstrations in Hungary had quickly turned into a violent uprising. Mao and Zhou, comparing the situations in Hungary and Poland, believed that the Polish crisis was mainly anti-Soviet, while the Hungarian uprising was primarily anti-Communist, and that both crises had their roots in Moscow's great power chauvinism.[31] In Moscow, Liu and Deng suggested to the Soviet leaders that they issue a statement about equal relations among Communist parties and states. Khrushchev agreed to the proposal. In the statement, which was issued on October 30, Moscow promised to abide by the principle of "more equal exchanges with fraternal states and parties."[32]

The same day, Mao and Zhou learned from Liu and Deng that the Soviet leaders were planning to withdraw their troops from Hungary. Mao and Zhao decided to oppose Moscow's "abandonment of Hungary to reactionary forces."[33] Liu and Deng then met with Khrushchev and other Soviet leaders, conveying to them Beijing's belief that the Soviet withdrawal would be tantamount to a betrayal of the Hungarian people and would make the Soviet leaders "historical criminals." As Liu and Deng were departing Moscow the next day, Khrushchev informed them on their way to the airport that the Soviet leadership would use force to suppress the "reactionary revolt" in Hungary.[34] Indeed, the Soviet Red Army went on to ruthlessly suppress the rebels in Budapest and other parts of Hungary. Mao, Zhou, and other CCP leaders thus believed that they had played a decisive role in helping Moscow correctly settle the Polish and Hungarian crises.

* * *

The Hungarian and Polish incidents had a huge effect on CCP leaders. Back in Beijing, Liu described his experiences in Moscow at a Central Committee plenum in November 1956. Zhou shared his thoughts on the Polish and Hungarian crises, highlighting "two major lessons" to be learned. First, the party must persistently oppose the "great power mentality abroad and 'big Han nationalism' and dictatorship over the people at home." Second, while it was correct to "give priority to the development of heavy industry," Zhou contended, it was essential not to "ignore the people's immediate interests." Therefore, Zhou emphasized,

> Light industry and agriculture are most closely related to the people's interests. Ignorance of them will result in bad consequences, leading up to a serious imbalance in economic development.

He again mentioned that "rash advance" in the two preceding years had upset the balance of China's national economy and industrial production. What was more important, he asked rhetorically, "heavy industry or the people?" He replied, "The people, of course." The 1957 economic plan that Zhou introduced would "properly downsize" production, placing China's economic development on a more solid foundation. "We must prevent an event like the Poznań incident from happening in China," Zhou warned.[35]

Mao did not subscribe to Zhou's perspectives. But he did not directly challenge Zhou either. Rather, he used philosophical language to rebut the premier: "All things are at once in motion and not in motion. . . . But motion is absolute while rest is temporary and conditional. Our planned economy is simultaneously in equilibrium and disequilibrium. Equilibrium is temporary and conditional. . . . Viewed in this light, is our economy advancing or retreating? We should tell the cadres and the masses that it is both advancing and retreating, but mainly advancing. . . . We must protect the enthusiasm of the cadres and masses, rather than pour cold water on them."[36] Though Mao had not mentioned him by name, each of Mao's words squarely targeted Zhou. A few months later at the Nanning Conference, Zhou's report would be subjected to severe criticism as an "example of rightism."[37]

* * *

Zhou began his planned visit of Vietnam, Cambodia, India, Burma, Pakistan, Nepal, and Afghanistan in mid-November. He had been abroad several times since the PRC's establishment, but this was the first time that he would visit so many countries in one trip abroad.

One issue at the top on Zhou's agenda was China's border disputes with neighboring countries, especially Burma and India, a matter that he had spent much time and energy studying over the previous two years. The Chinese leadership had been preoccupied with many urgent challenges since the PRC's establishment, and it had thus adopted an attitude of temporarily maintaining the status quo toward complicated border issues. In June 1954, Zhou paid a brief visit to India and Burma. Then, Nehru and U Nu visited Beijing in October and December, respectively, both mentioning China's border issues with their countries in their talks with Zhou.

Chinese and Burmese border garrisons clashed in November 1955 at a place known as Huangguo Yuan, resulting in casualties on both sides. Zhou saw it as necessary to "accelerate the resolving of the border disputes with Burma." In January 1956, Yangon proposed that the "1941 Line" serve as the basis for a settlement on the border issue.[38] Then, border negotiations between China and Burma began. Zhou spent many long hours poring over relevant documents and maps, finding that China's border issues with Burma and India—which had both been part of British India—involved the McMahon Line put forward by the British-Indian authorities at the Simla Conference of 1914. Upon a thorough examination of the sources, Zhou confirmed that no Chinese government had ever recognized the McMahon Line from the time of the Simla Conference to 1949. The "1941 Line" mentioned by the Burmese was part of the McMahon Line that covered the southern section of the China-Burma border. In 1941, while China faced the darkest hours in its war against Japan, the British demanded that the Chinese accept this line; otherwise, they would close the Yunnan-Burma Road, China's only overland route to the outside world at the time. The Nationalist Government yielded to the British demand. After much deliberation, Zhou told the Burmese ambassador U Hla Maung on June 22, 1956, that "the border issues could be settled on the basis of the status [of the border] at the time of the PRC's establishment and Burma's independence."[39] Here, Zhou put forward the initial version of the "Line of Actual Control," an important concept that he would further clarify and use to solve China's complicated border disputes with neighboring countries. In his offer to the Burmese ambassador, Zhou implied that Beijing was willing to recognize the "1941 Line."

On August 27, Zhou called a meeting of heads of various government departments to discuss the border issue with Burma. Under Zhou's direction, the meeting decided to accept the "1941 Line." Zhou shared his thoughts with the meeting's participants:

> Now, the "1941 Line" is the central issue in China-Burma border disputes. Thus, to define our attitude toward it is the key to a settlement. In the legal sense, the then Chinese and British governments had formally exchanged documents approving the line in 1941. According to international law, in the case of regime change in one country, only political and other treaties can be revised, not border demarcation treaties. If we do not recognize the "1941 Line," there is no legal reference to support [our stance]. In the political sense, we favor peaceful coexistence. If we reach a deadlock with Burma because of the border issue, we will gain little and lose much.[40]

Zhou called a meeting with U Hla Maung at nine thirty that evening. At the meeting, Zhou put forward a "package plan" to settle the China-Burma border issue: The Chinese, "in spite of difficulty," would take steps to practically recognize the "1941 Line" along the southern section of the border. The plan also stipulated that Burma take action to enable China to recover the "permanently leased" territory that the British-Burmese authorities had obtained in the middle section of the border. And along the northern part of the border, the Burmese side would return Hpimaw, Gawlum, and Kangfang, which "British documents had recognized as China's," to China. Zhou emphasized that, "from the south to the north, all sections should be resolved simultaneously."[41] Zhou reiterated the main contents of his package plan when U Nu visited China in October 1956. He also said that the Chinese would "use the same principle to deal with our border issues with India, Pakistan, Afghanistan, the Soviet Union, Mongolia, Korea, and Vietnam."[42]

* * *

Zhou's first stop on his international trip was Hanoi. His five meetings with Ho, Pham Van Dong, and other Vietnamese leaders highlighted two major issues. The first was the situation in Indochina after the collapse of the 1954 Geneva Accords. In accordance with the agreement, Vietnam was temporarily divided into two zones along the seventeenth parallel, and a plebiscite on national reunification was to be held within two years under international supervision. However, the Ngo Dinh Diem regime in the South, with Washington's support, not only blocked the election but also unleashed waves of "white terror" throughout South Vietnam. Zhou was a main architect of the Geneva Accords. Now, with the breakdown of the agreement and the prospects of reunification dim, what was Hanoi to do? Zhou advised his Vietnamese comrades that Vietnam's reunification would be "a prolonged struggle." They should concentrate on consolidating their regime in the North. Only by turning the North into "the base of people's democracy" would it be possible for Hanoi to strive to reunify the whole country.[43]

The flawed land reforms in North Vietnam and the financial difficulties facing Hanoi posed another big issue. Hanoi had carried out land reform largely by following the Chinese model, and Chinese advisors were involved in the making of many specific land reform policies. The Vietnamese naturally sought Zhou's advice to correct problems with their land reform. They also hoped to get financial support from China to cope with their serious economic and financial challenges. Zhou said that land reform was an accumulative process during which problems would inevitably appear, but these problems also would teach the Vietnamese Communists valuable lessons that would help them overcome their difficulties. Zhou believed the economic and financial challenges facing Hanoi were mainly caused by the war. With careful management, they could also be mitigated. Zhou agreed that China would offer Vietnam expedited support in addition to the 800 million yuan that Beijing had earlier promised Hanoi.[44]

Zhou visited Cambodia next. Then, on November 28, he arrived in New Delhi, the most important stop on his itinerary. In the 1950s, India was a major partner of China in international affairs. Their relations, said to be like those between *bhai-bhai* (brothers), were especially close. In June 1954, Zhou paid a short visit to India, during which he and Nehru formally introduced the Five Principles of Peaceful Coexistence. In October, Nehru visited China, where he was very warmly received. Zhou's visit, broken into two main phases (in addition to several other stopovers), lasted more than twenty days. His talks with Nehru went extremely well. They easily reached consensus on a series of international issues, such as the Suez Canal crisis and the situation in Eastern Europe, both of which had attracted worldwide attention. They also reiterated their shared determination to promote the Five Principles. Zhou had two meetings with Nehru in the first part of the visit, but the border issue did not come up in either one.

Zhou then visited Burma. His previous discussions with U Nu and others on the Burmese side had laid the foundation for solving their border issue. The main difficulty now facing both sides was how to properly explain the situation in their home countries. Zhou told U Nu that he had several major hurdles to clear. First, he needed to give the Chinese people a clear explanation. Second, if China were to accept the McMahon Line, he would need to persuade the Dalai Lama and the Panchen Lama to agree. Third, he had to rebut the GMD's accusation that the CCP had betrayed China's national interests. "For us to overcome these hurdles, we need time," Zhou said. "In order to permanently settle the entire border issue, by making big concessions for the interests of both [parties], we have come up with the current plans, and we will try our best to overcome all difficulties to make it work."[45] As Zhou talked with U Nu, he was obviously also considering how to settle China's border differences with India. However, Zhou could not have expected that his plans would work with Burma, but not with India.

Zhou spent ten days in Pakistan after he left Yangon, and he returned to India on December 30. Nehru, who had just returned from a visit to the United States and Canada, met him at the airport. In their meetings, Nehru raised the India-China border issue. According to Indian records, Zhou said that the McMahon Line, "established by British imperialists," had not been accepted by "the then Chinese Government" and also "was unfair." However, the "Chinese Government was of the opinion that they should give recognition to the McMahon Line" because it "was an accomplished fact" and in light of the friendly relationships among China, India, and Burma. But he needed to first "consult the Tibetan Government about it."[46] Nehru had since claimed that there existed no territorial disputes between India and China. Zhou, however, insisted that he had never accepted the McMahon Line, and that the Chinese government absolutely would not recognize it as the legal border with India.[47] According to Chinese records, though, Zhou did tell Nehru that the Chinese side had tried not to cross the McMahon Line, and that it was willing to take a "realistic approach," treating the line as a reference for negotiating with India.[48] Nehru later described Zhou's statement as a "deception" and "betrayal." At the moment, though, neither Zhou nor Nehru could have imagined that, in a few short years, China and India would fight a bloody war due to the border dispute.

Another of Zhou's missions in India was to persuade the Dalai Lama, who was then in India for the 2,500th Buddha Jayanti (the Buddha's birthday), to

19.1 Mao Zedong, with Zhou Enlai and Liu Shaoqi, meeting with the Dalai Lama and Panchen Lama, 1954. *Geopix / Alamy Stock Photo*

return to Tibet. At that time, the radical Communist "democratic reforms" in Tibetan-inhabited areas in Sichuan and Xikang had resulted in widespread armed resistance by ethnic Tibetans, causing strong repercussions among Tibetan political and religious elites in Lhasa. Zhou was afraid that the Dalai Lama might stay in India rather than return to Tibet. Zhou had already met with the Dalai Lama on November 29 during the premier's earlier stay in Delhi. The purpose of the meeting was mainly to "listen to the Dalai Lama's opinions and suggestions."[49] On December 30, Zhou met with the Dalai Lama again, promising that no further reforms would be carried out in Tibet without the consent of Tibetan leaders. "The main task now is to carry out reconstruction well, develop Tibet's economy, and upgrade the people's standard of living. Only when the economy has developed and people's livelihood, including that of the nobles and monks, has become better than it is now, will we discuss reforms in accordance with the situation at that time."[50] Two days later, Zhou met with the Dalai Lama once more. He promised on behalf of Mao that there would be no reforms in the next six years, and that "whether reforms will be introduced after six years, and how reforms will be introduced, will be yours to decide." Zhou further mentioned that Beijing had already sent inspectors to areas inhabited by Tibetans in Sichuan and Xikang to "help manage the situation there." He also suggested that the Dalai Lama send his own people there: "As you are also Tibetans, you should be in a better position to identify the shortcomings of our work."[51]

Nehru helped Zhou's cause, trying in a personal meeting to convince the Dalai Lama to return to Lhasa. Otherwise, Nehru cautioned, the Dalai Lama would become a "tree without roots."[52] Finally, the Dalai Lama returned to Lhasa at the end of March 1957, marking another big achievement for Zhou.

• • •

Originally, Zhou was to visit Afghanistan and Nepal after India. However, at the end of November, the Soviets suddenly invited Zhou to visit Moscow.[53] In early December, the government in Warsaw invited Mao to visit Poland, hoping that his coming would help enhance the Polish Communists' position in the forthcoming general election. Mao thought that Zhou was a more appropriate person to go and conveyed Warsaw's invitation to Zhou, who thus decided to postpone his trip to Afghanistan and Nepal and travel first to Moscow and Warsaw. The trip would allow Zhou not only to fulfill a mission assigned by the Party Center, but also to get firsthand information about the situation in these two countries in the wake of de-Stalinization. In early January 1957, Zhou received a call from Mao and rushed back to Beijing. A few days before, *Renmin ribao* had published an editorial that systematically addressed Mao's perspectives on the challenges facing international communism. Mao felt it necessary to communicate with Zhou so that the premier would be better prepared to engage in discussions with Soviet and Polish leaders in Moscow and Warsaw.[54]

Zhou arrived in Moscow on January 7, 1957. Khrushchev welcomed him at the airport, accompanied by nearly all the top Soviet leaders. When he met with the Soviet leaders, Zhou, following Mao's ideas, repeatedly emphasized the importance of "strengthening the unity of the socialist camp headed by the Soviet Union," while sternly criticizing Moscow's great power chauvinism.[55] Zhou noticed that Khrushchev and other top Soviet leaders never mentioned the editorial in *Renmin ribao,* which he saw as a sign of their disagreement with the viewpoints presented in it.[56]

Zhou's next stop was Poland. He told Gomułka and other Polish leaders that the CCP firmly supported Poland's pursuit of equality and sovereignty, stressing that "this is our responsibility." He also asked Gomułka to pay attention to the "revisionist tendency" within the Polish United Workers' Party.[57] Zhou originally had no plans to visit Hungary. However, the Hungarian leader János Kádár specifically traveled to Moscow while Zhou was there, and at Kádár's insistence, Zhou decided to pay a one-day visit to Hungary. After arriving in Budapest, Zhou found that "the situation here is better than what we had expected, and the leaders of Hungary are resolute and also quite united." Zhou's talks with Kádár also went "more smoothly and constructively than talks with the Soviet and Polish leaders." Zhou told Kádár that Beijing would provide Budapest with 100 million rubles in foreign currency and 100 million rubles' worth of material aid in addition to the aid that China had committed earlier.[58]

Zhou returned to Moscow on January 17, where he resumed meeting with Soviet leaders. Zhou emphasized that the events in Poland and Hungary were different in essence. By threatening to dispatch troops to Warsaw, Moscow had meant "to interfere in the internal affairs of a fraternal party and state." Zhou again stepped on Khrushchev's toes by mentioning Stalin, pointing out that Khrushchev and others had worked with Stalin for a long time, so that they also "bore some responsibility for tolerating Stalin's mistakes." Tension seeped into the atmosphere of the meeting. Zhou had planned to raise such important issues as signing long-term supply agreements with Moscow, the sending of more Soviet advisors to China, and Chinese-Soviet "cooperation on nuclear and missile technology." He decided not to raise these matters, "mainly because I do not want to let them feel that we are trying to take advantage of their difficulties to bargain with them."[59]

Zhou summarized his meetings with Soviet leaders in a lengthy telegram to Mao and the CCP Center on January 24. "Their main mistakes are related to their thought," Zhou wrote, as "they often separate the interests of the Soviet party from those of fraternal parties." Their views about Stalin "have changed, but, in my opinion, this is just for dealing with their current needs, and is not the product of deep reflection." In Chinese-Soviet relations, "we are now facing a great common enemy, so the Soviet comrades are eager to consolidate their unity with us. However, as I see it, their attitude does not necessarily come from the bottom of their hearts." In international affairs, they "lack a comprehensive perspective and good prediction of the situation, and their global strategies are poorly elaborated."[60] Zhou's critique of the Soviets mirrored Mao's understanding of China's position and influence in the international Communist movement. Mao thus liked Zhou's report very much, immediately recommending it to a conference of provincial party leaders that was being held in Beijing at the time.[61]

Zhou visited Afghanistan, Nepal, and Ceylon (a stop that was added at the last minute) after he left Moscow. It was not until February 6 that he flew back to Kunming, capital of Yunnan Province. This prolonged trip had lasted almost three months and covered eleven countries in Asia and Europe. Zhou was approaching sixty that year, but he seldom showed signs of fatigue.

• • •

When Zhou returned to Beijing in early February 1957, he found a fresh political atmosphere in the capital. At the end of the month, Mao gave a speech titled "On Managing Contradictions among the People" at the Supreme State Council. He spoke on the subject largely because the de-Stalinization trend had, since the spring of 1956, given rise in China to such critical appeals as "abolishing dictatorship at an early time." There were also mass strikes, demonstrations, and protests in different parts of China. Mao defined these as "problems within the people," stating that "contradictions are part of the existence of a socialist society." In the face of these "disturbances," Mao said, the most important step was "to overcome bureaucratism." Moreover, Mao continued, "we may just let the disturbances erupt. And this will become the process through which we may improve our work while, at the same time, educating our workers, peasants, and students." Mao also said, "There should be no dictatorship over the people. It is mistaken to talk about it."[62]

After he delivered the above statements in Beijing, Mao repeated them in other parts of China. On March 17, he told cadres in Tianjin that "by now, large-scale and massive class struggles have basically ended. As mentioned in the resolution of the Eighth Congress, our whole party should devote itself to reconstruction." Further, he said that to deal with the challenges, "we should adopt a policy of 'allowing one hundred flowers to blossom and letting one hundred schools of thought compete with each other' to deal with them. This is the only good method; all others will not work." The next day, he announced at a conference of cadres in Shandong that class struggle was basically over. "However, class struggle in the ideological sphere, that is, the struggle between proletarian and bourgeois thought will continue. The contest and debate in this respect will continue for several more decades."[63]

Zhou had just finished his trip to the Soviet Union, Poland, and Hungary, and so he shared many of Mao's views. When he spoke at a PPCC meeting on March 19, Zhou emphasized that "we should make the construction of our own socialist country a success; this is the most important. Thus, we must understand the contradictions at home, and correctly resolve them. . . . This is what we should learn from the Hungarian incident and from criticizing Stalin."[64]

A CCP Politburo meeting on April 19 passed a resolution on initiating a "Rectification Movement" aimed at "eliminating bureaucratism, factionalism, and subjectivism within the party."[65] Zhou explained that the whole party's acceptance of the measure was necessary to correctly manage contradictions among the people. Therefore, the CCP was to carry out, in a top-down manner, a rectification campaign within its own ranks. The campaign would begin at the very top of the party and would gradually be expanded; nonparty members would be welcome to participate in the campaign alongside party members.[66] Finally, the CCP began the Rectification Movement internally under the banner of "allowing one hundred flowers to blossom and letting one hundred schools of thought compete with each other," and people not belonging to the CCP, including the members of various democratic parties, were welcomed and encouraged to participate in the campaign.

Voices critical of the CCP emerged after the Rectification Movement began, however. Chu Anping, editor in chief of *Guangming ribao* (Guangming Daily), allegedly said that "the idea of 'all under heaven belonging to the party' is the ultimate origin of all factionalism." Zhou thought Chu's remarks "outrageous."[67] Later, some people reportedly asked the CCP to share power with the democratic parties. Although Mao had once asserted that "allowing people to speak out, the sky will not fall down," he could not tolerate such accusations and demands. On June 6, Mao drafted a set of "instructions on enhancing the rectification campaign," which he shared with the CCP Central Committee. He told Liu and Zhou that the Rectification Movement was intended to "expose the true face of those who had held reactionary or mistaken viewpoints." Therefore, it was desirable to allow "both constructive critiques and reactionary elements, as well as their destructive comments, to all be exposed, so that we may deal with them accordingly." When the time was right, Mao said, the genuine leftists should be mobilized to "repulse the attacks of the rightist and reactionary elements."[68]

The situation quickly turned around. On July 1, an essay written by Mao, "The Bourgeoisie Tendency of *Wenhui bao* Must Be Criticized," was published in *Renmin ribao.* In the essay, Mao named the Democratic League and the Workers and Peasants Democratic Party, whose members had been among the most outspoken participants in the Rectification Movement, as "parties against Communism and socialism." Furthermore, Mao defined "the rightists" as "bourgeoisie reactionaries against the people, against the Communist Party, and against socialism."[69] In a few short days, the direction of the political winds had changed completely. The Rectification Movement that grew out of Mao's call for "one hundred flowers to blossom" was suddenly replaced by the "antirightist" campaign.

Zhou supported the movement's dramatic change of course. After all, he was a Communist. He could not tolerate the CCP being scolded, and he did not want to see the CCP's control of power challenged and weakened. He and Mao held the same views when the CCP leadership was shifting its focus from rectification to antirightist activities. In his own words, the CCP decided to undergo rectification for the sake of "developing and constructing our country," yet those "friends on the right" saw the situation in a deeply pessimistic light. "For them, following the Polish and Hungarian incidents, China is almost finished. . . . The ship will sink, and the sky will turn dark. They have developed other plans and are thus derailed."[70] Zhou differed from Mao, however, on how to define and deal with the "rightists." He believed that although the rightists "stood against socialism," they still generally "belong[ed] to the people," so they were not enemies.[71] These comments, on a more fundamental level, revealed that Zhou's basic understanding of the relationship between the collective and the individual was different from Mao's. This was clearly evident in a "discursive encounter" between Zhou and Mao, in which they each gave opposite priority to the collective and the individual. In the summer of 1957, Mao defined "democratic centralism" as follows:

> Our goal is to create a political atmosphere of liveliness in which there is both centralism and democracy, discipline and freedom, unity of will and personal ease of mind, in order to promote socialist revolution and socialist reconstruction.[72]

Shortly after, Zhou also defined democratic centralism in a speech. He copied Mao's formula almost identically, but he reversed the order of the collective and the individual:

> The system of democratic centralism is one under which there will be both democracy and centralism, freedom and discipline, development of individuality and unity of will.[73]

Whether intentionally or not, Zhou put "democracy," "freedom," and the "development of individuality" (Mao's had used the term "personal ease of mind") first.

Zhou probably did not expect, however, that the transition from rectification to antirightism would see Mao begin to reckon with his mistake of "opposing rash advance" the year before. As the chilly winds of late autumn swept across China's vast expanse, Mao turned his attention back to the party itself. He was ready to fully vent his anger about the "opposing rash advance" affair, which he had kept to himself for over a year. Zhou was his target. The first thing Mao did was to come up with a new notion of the "principal contradictions" in China at a Central Committee plenum in late September. He announced that

> the contradiction between the proletariat and the bourgeoisie and the contradiction between the socialist and capitalist paths undoubtedly are the main contradictions in the society of our country now.[74]

In retrospect, this was a statement of extraordinary importance. This notion of "principal contradictions" would serve as the theoretical basis for a series of political campaigns that Mao would launch in the next two decades, including the Great Proletarian Cultural Revolution. Mao would also use this theory to justify his next purge of Zhou. At the moment, however, no CCP leader—including Zhou—stood up to question it.

• • •

Mao visited Moscow in November 1957 to celebrate the fortieth anniversary of the Russian Bolshevik Revolution and to attend a summit of leaders of Communist countries. Mao's mentality during this visit was different from that during his first visit to the Soviet Union eight years before. At that time, Stalin, as the indisputable leader of international Communism, never hid his sense of superiority when he met with others. Although Stalin agreed to sign a treaty of alliance with China and pledged substantial Soviet material support, Mao only remembered his feeling of profound inequality with the Soviet dictator.[75] Eight years had passed; the PRC had been consolidated and its international position greatly enhanced. More recently, as Mao saw it, Beijing had played a decisive role in settling the Polish and Hungarian crises. He had developed a superior moral and psychological sense that would now shape his attitude toward Khrushchev.

At the Moscow summit, Mao's arrogance was evident. He treated a lengthy speech he delivered on November 18 as though it were just another one of his intraparty presentations. During his discussion of the features of "our era" and the Communists' historical missions, he touched on the question of war and peace. In his unique style, he used vivid language to argue as follows:

> Now we should also think of another scenario, that is, those war monsters are to start a war, and they will drop A-bombs and H-bombs anywhere and everywhere. They will drop bombs, and we will also drop bombs. Thus, people will be killed. In the worst-case scenario, how many may die? There are 2.7 billion people in the world today. One third of them might be lost. . . . At the extreme, one half might be lost, and another half would survive. However, imperialism will then be eliminated, and the whole world will become socialist. Dozens of years from now, the world population will again reach 2.7 billion, and thereafter will certainly be much greater.[76]

This surely was an important speech. But Mao delivered it using only a brief outline, speaking spontaneously, freely expressing himself as he jumped from thought to thought. Li Yueran, the Chinese interpreter, had no advance knowledge of what Mao would say. He was extremely nervous when Mao spoke, and he had no time to come up with the best Russian expressions for the chairman's musings; he could only "literally translate for Mao word by word."[77] Mao's approach clearly demonstrated his sense that he already had become the "big boss" of international Communism. With an air of moral superiority, he talked about nuclear war in cynical language. His doing so, however, did not mean that he favored waging nuclear war or transforming the world through nuclear war. However, his intuitive presentation, conveyed in a poorly composed Russian translation, stunned the audience. Mao's grandiosity became crazed arrogance, and his views about nuclear slaughter descended into complete nonsense.[78] Yet Mao was totally unaware of the disastrous effects of his speech. Instead, he believed that Khrushchev, who had been eager to pursue "peaceful coexistence" with the United States, had been scared to death by the imperialists' bluffing about their readiness to use nuclear weapons.

Mao's attitude toward Kim Il-sung changed at the Moscow summit. On November 9, Mao met with Kim and told him that Beijing was preparing to pull all Chinese troops in Korea back to China. He also proposed that Kim pardon his political opponents in Korea, promising that China would never use them to challenge Kim. They decided that Zhou would soon pay a formal visit to Pyongyang to "strengthen the two countries' unity and friendship."[79] Zhou then briefed the Soviet ambassador Yudin of Mao's conversations with Kim, mentioning that when Mao first proposed to withdraw Chinese troops from Korea, Kim had worried that it was "not yet the right time" to do so but later agreed to it.[80]

Zhou visited Pyongyang in February 1958. He and Kim agreed that all Chinese troops would leave Korea by the end of the year.[81] On his way back to Beijing, Zhou shared his opinions about Kim with local leaders in Shenyang: "Kim is a talented person," but he "is not an ideal leader." Affected by "individualism and factionalism, he had also mistakenly treated and even killed some comrades." However, Zhou emphasized, "in Korea's current situation, there is no other option but to lift up the taller one among short people." Thus, Kim should be "evaluated from a comprehensive perspective. His weakness is just one of the ten figures, and his strength is the other nine."[82]

Mao and Zhou changed their attitude toward Kim largely because Mao had become more sympathetic toward Kim's suppression of opposition factions within the party amid China's own transition from "allowing one hundred flowers to blossom" to the "antirightist" campaign. Meanwhile, the Korean dissidents' behavior had also influenced Mao and Zhou's change of view. After arriving in China, the dissidents had been treated quite well, but they did not know how to act cautiously in the political arena. Zhou mentioned that during China's antirightist campaign, they made "all kinds of erroneous comments," "opposing not only the Korean Workers' Party but also the Soviet and Chinese Communist Parties." They also claimed that "the Chinese, Korean, and Soviet leaders were all dictators who were not democratic at all."[83] Consequently, they fell out of favor with Mao and Zhou.

Khrushchev mentioned at the Moscow summit that the USSR would surpass the United States in fifteen years. Impressed, Mao immediately announced that "in fifteen years, we can probably surpass the UK." Although the chairman chose Britain as a target for China to aim for, his true hope was to catch up with and surpass the Soviet Union. When he returned to China, he told his comrades, "It has taken more than four decades for the Soviet Union to produce that much grain and other stuff. If we can do the same in ten or even eight years, that would be great. We should be able to do that, as we have a large population, our political environment is more active, and we have better commanded Leninism."[84] The chairman thus believed that, given China's political and moral advantages, if it could accelerate its economic development, he and the CCP would naturally deserve the status of leader of the international Communist movement.

* * *

Mao was now ready to turn to Zhou. While in Moscow, he approved the publication of an editorial in *Renmin ribao,* which attacked in harsh language the "opposing rash advance" affair of 1956.[85] Mao moved to demonize the concept of "opposing rash advance" as soon as he returned to Beijing. In another *Renmin ribao* editorial personally revised by Mao, "opposing rash advance" was described as a policy of stagnation, one that sought to hinder the advance of China's socialist revolution and reconstruction. Zhou, the principal advocate of "opposing rash advance," was a primary target of Mao's attacks.[86]

Mao chaired a CCP work conference in Nanning in January 1958. When Zhou arrived, he found that the editorial published in *Renmin ribao* on June 20, 1956—the one that Mao disapproved of—along with his speech at the November 1956 Central Committee plenum, had been circulated among conference participants as a "reference for critiques."[87] The chairman dominated the conference, repeatedly claiming that Zhou's "opposing rash advance" campaign had "suppressed the revolutionary vigor of 600 million people." On one occasion, Mao even pointed his finger toward Zhou and announced, "You support opposing rash advance, I am against opposing rash advance!" In Mao's view, Zhou was on the verge of becoming a rightist, with a distance, Mao claimed, of "only fifty meters" separating him from the label. In the face of the chairman's fierce offensive, Zhou made "preliminary self-criticism" at the conference, acknowledging that he "should take the main responsibility" for the "opposing rash advance mistake."[88]

But this was just Mao's warm-up. In March, he called another central work conference in Chengdu at which he escalated his attacks on "opposing rash advance." He asserted that "rash advance is the Marxist way and 'opposing rash advance' is an anti-Marxist way." Therefore, "we shall commit to rash advance in the future."[89] Zhou made a more comprehensive self-criticism. In addition to his own mistakes on domestic issues, Zhou also blamed himself for his "conservative and rightist tendency" in handling the PRC's foreign relations. He admitted that the Foreign Ministry's work under his direction had neglected necessary struggles in its treatment of nationalist countries, showed wishful thinking toward imperialism (especially toward Japan and the United States), and failed to level necessary criticism at the revisionist policies of other socialist countries.[90] Acting in accordance with Mao's wishes, the Chengdu Conference decided to boldly revise China's economic development plans, which now included the new goal of "surpassing Britain in less than fifteen years."

Still, Mao continued his reckoning with Zhou. At a CCP National Congress in May, he again accused Zhou of "failing to get the bigger picture," claiming that if Zhou's mistakes were not corrected, "the party will be divided."[91] Zhou tried to make "deeper and more thorough self-criticism" in response to Mao's aggression toward him; but this was not an easy thing to do. A dozen years had passed since Zhou was purged during the Yan'an Rectification Movement. Although he had never meant to forget those lessons, he had not had another similar encounter with Mao. How could he satisfy Mao? He racked his brain but found no answer. One evening, he summoned Fan Ruoyu, his secretary, to his office and attempted to dictate something to Fan one sentence at a time. He "spoke very slowly, and sometimes would not utter a word for several minutes," Fan recollected. Fan quietly left Zhou's office, "so that he could think things through by himself." However, Zhou sat alone in his office until well after midnight, as if at a total loss. Finally, Deng Yingchao intervened, proposing that Zhou dictate a rough draft, which Fan would help edit and turn into a text for Zhou to review. Fan recalled that "during the fortnight that Zhou was working on the notes, his hair quickly turned grey." After this episode, Fan found, "Zhou was much less outspoken in similar situations."[92]

Zhou acknowledged in a May 17 speech at the party congress's plenary session that "I am the culprit of the serious mistake of opposing rash advance, and I should draw many lessons from it." While trying to "dig deep into the roots" of his wrongdoing, he said, "The conceptual origin of my mistake lies in the subjectivism and metaphysical nature of my thinking." He confessed that he had held a "conservative rightist attitude toward socialist reconstruction" that culminated in his violating Mao's "grand design for it." In addition to using harsh language to criticize himself, Zhou adopted the same method that he had used during the Yan'an Rectification to praise Mao:

> As proven by China's revolution and reconstruction, Chairman Mao has represented the truth. When we have deviated from his leadership, we lost our direction and committed mistakes, as is proven by all those that I have committed. In comparison, all the correct things that we have done are due to his leadership and thought. Therefore, we must diligently study his instructions, his glorious example of combining the universal truth of Marxism with the practice of the Chinese revolution, his method of the mass line, and his great work style and example as a great Communist.[93]

Mao, finally satisfied, announced, "The problem of opposing rash advance is now resolved. The Central Committee and the whole party are now united." He then introduced a new timetable—China would surpass the UK in seven years and catch up with the US in another eight. "In the next months," he announced, "there will be another big rash advance, one much more radical than the last."[94] The chairman thus gave marching orders for the Great Leap Forward.

Zhou was still in shock. At a Politburo meeting on June 9, he asked his colleagues to consider whether it was appropriate for him to continue to serve as the premier. In a sense, this was also Zhou's subtle way of testing Mao's continuing support. Zhou's colleagues, including Liu Shaoqi, Zhu De, Lin Biao, Chen Yun, and Deng Xiaoping, all opposed Zhou's resigning. Mao, who also attended the meeting, did not stop their opposition, and the Politburo decided that Zhou should remain the premier. Deng then drafted the meeting minutes, which confirmed that Zhou "should continue to hold his current position, and there is no need to make a change." The chairman approved the minutes.[95]

On June 8, Mao took a further step to reduce the State Council's power. He proposed changing the party and governmental decision-making structure by establishing five groups in charge of finance, legal matters, foreign affairs, science, and culture and education. The groups were to be headed by Chen Yun, Peng Zhen, Chen Yi, Nie Rongzhen, and Lu Dingyi, respectively. All five groups would "report directly to the Politburo and the Secretariat." Mao stipulated that "the power to make big decisions is in the hands of the Politburo, with concrete arrangements to be made by the Secretariat." To enhance his points, he emphasized that "the State Council and the party organs there only have the power to make suggestions; decision-making power is controlled by the Party Center."[96]

The five groups were established in two days. The Party Center reemphasized that "all party, government, and military organs should report to the Center through the Central Secretariat. The Secretariat's decisions on general matters should be immediately implemented. The Secretariat should, after discussing them, report important matters to the Politburo Standing Committee, which will make the final decision."[97] This new decision-making process completely bypassed the State Council headed by Zhou, leaving it with only the right to make suggestions.

Consequently, Zhou's power was greatly compromised. In the ensuing years, until the outbreak of the Cultural Revolution, he often found himself more a policy conveyer than a principal decision-maker among top CCP leaders. He had to treat Mao's sharp criticism as another crucial lesson and a serious warning: If he deviated from Mao's leadership and policy lines, he could come under attack by Mao at any time, or even be subject to his political demise. This fear would haunt Zhou until the last days of his life.

20

THE GREAT LEAP FORWARD

1958–1960

Zhou Enlai survived Mao's harsh criticism of his "opposing rash advance mistakes" campaign just as the Great Leap Forward was sweeping across China, fueled by enormous zeal instigated by Mao, who now believed that "in fifteen years we will not only catch up with Britain but also with America." Mao sought to surpass the Soviet Union as well, declaring, "We have such a large population, why can't we become the number one power in the world?"[1] By crushing the movement to "oppose rash advance," the chairman issued marching orders for the Great Leap.

Mao saw a dramatic increase in China's steel production as central to the Great Leap Forward's success. He aimed for China to produce twice as much steel in 1958 as it did in 1957. Zhou was named head of the task force for the new steel target, an assignment he had to accept.[2] The Great Leap's raging fires also burned throughout China's vast countryside, as production from the summer harvest "skyrocketed." Whereas the output from a typical harvest equaled a few hundred kilograms per *mu* (one-sixth of an acre), the harvest that summer reportedly yielded dozens, even hundreds, of times that amount. Such "victorious reports" of burgeoning crop production flooded Zhongnanhai daily. Delighted, Mao began to discuss how to consume the surplus grain.[3]

Zhou was the premier, so he was still responsible for supervising production. However, the authority of the five leading groups above him had tied his hands. Further, almost all CCP leaders were afraid of failing to keep pace with Mao. Deng later acknowledged, "It was not just Mao. All of us, including Liu,

Zhou, and I, were also enchanted."[4] Though Zhou might have had reservations and suspicions about the Great Leap, the tidal wave of fervor behind the campaign gave him no option but to sing its praises—which is exactly what he did in many of the speeches he gave during those months.

Still, Zhou did not waste any opportunity to remind others to keep calm amid the excitement. During a July inspection tour in Guangdong, Zhou advised local cadres that it was important to plant grain at a moderate density, instead of attempting to maximize yield by planting crops as closely together as possible. On another occasion, Zhou quoted one of Mao's recent remarks about not exaggerating the Great Leap, and emphasized that false reporting of grain production should be avoided and that peasants should keep sufficient rations.[5] He was suspicious of the reports of massive steel production. When a county in Henan claimed that it had produced over one million tons of steel, Zhou sent Gu Ming, one of his secretaries, to the county "to see with his own eyes." When Gu brought back several pieces of this "steel," Zhou inspected them and murmured, "This is not steel!"[6] However, he was unable to voice his dissent beyond the walls of his office.

CCP leaders gathered in mid-August for a central work conference at Beidaihe, a scenic coastal site ideal for summer retreats. Mao was in command. In his speeches, he boasted that "we must turn our country into a great industrial power in three, five, or seven years" after reaching the 1958 steel production target. Mao argued that it was necessary to establish people's communes in the countryside, as "the grain problem has basically been resolved." The chairman suggested that the people's communes should be big organizations "with many people, vast land, large production capacity, and big businesses combining government administration with social functions and providing public dining service." He asked, "If we could fight a war for twenty-two years and win it, why can't we succeed in building socialism?"[7] Zhou echoed Mao in his presentation, describing the situation as "excellent," as the Great Leap was "happening in all sectors of the national economy." He followed Mao's lead in predicting that China would establish "a basically complete industrial foundation," "modern agriculture," and "relatively advanced technology," as well as a "basic command of missile and nuclear technology," in three to five years. Although Zhou acknowledged that "some goals were too radical," the tone of his speech was decidedly positive.[8]

The Beidaihe Conference consequently finalized a series of highly ambitious goals for the Great Leap: steel production would double in 1958, reaching 10.7 million tons; and grain output would reach 300 to 350 million tons.[9] CCP leaders also decided to establish thousands of people's communes throughout the Chinese countryside.[10] After the conference, Mao continued to call for the Great Leap Forward to accelerate, as he believed that "we can surpass Britain next year." He called upon the whole party to "strive to achieve the goal of getting closer to the United States in five years and surpassing it in seven!"[11]

The Great Leap Forward had already swept the country in violent waves. The torrent of fervor unleashed at the Beidaihe Conference turned the Leap into a monstrous flood.

• • •

Several other matters seemingly unrelated to the Great Leap also occupied Zhou in the summer of 1958. In fact, the issues were interrelated. One of them was another crisis in the Taiwan Strait.

Zhou had led Beijing to significantly soften the tone of its policies toward Taiwan since the end of the First Taiwan Strait Crisis in 1955. Zhou stated at a plenary session of the People's Congress on July 30, 1955, that "if possible," Beijing would be "willing to liberate Taiwan peacefully."[12] One year later, in June 1956, Zhou openly announced that Beijing was "willing to discuss with the authorities in Taiwan the concrete steps and conditions for a peaceful liberation of Taiwan." He invited Chiang Kai-shek to "dispatch representatives to Beijing, or to another appropriate location, to begin such discussions with us."[13] Mao echoed Zhou, stating that if Taiwan did "return to the motherland," everything on the island would be kept as it was. Mao suggested he would allow the Taiwanese authorities to "continue to follow the 'Three Principles of the People'" after Taiwan reunited with the mainland.[14] Privately, Zhou also tried to communicate with Chiang, albeit unsuccessfully, through a series of unofficial backdoor channels.

Beijing's softened approach toward Taiwan was reversed almost overnight in the summer of 1958. On Mao's orders, PLA shore batteries began a massive artillery shelling of the GMD-controlled Jinmen Islands on August 23, firing about thirty thousand shells within ninety minutes. The shelling of Jinmen continued for six weeks, triggering a near war in the Taiwan Strait.

Mao's sudden change of policy reflected his frustration over Chiang's apparent ignorance of the "peace initiatives" that Beijing had staged in the past years. He thus found it necessary to "use fighting to promote negotiations." Also, the railway connecting Xiamen—a coastal city only a few kilometers from Jinmen—to other mainland cities was completed in spring 1957, allowing large quantities of heavy weaponry to be delivered to the Fujian front. In late 1957, Fujian saw the construction of several new airfields, which effectively nullified the GMD's control over the airspace there.[15] Mao believed that he now had the means to neutralize the chronic security threat posed by the GMD to China's coast.

In a deeper sense, though, Mao had decided to shell the Jinmen Islands to boost the Great Leap Forward. As a master of mass mobilization, he knew well that the added pressure generated by an external crisis could help to justify the heightened internal tensions caused by the Great Leap. "Tension may force people to think," he elaborated, "may help stimulate people's positive spirit, may help mobilize the masses, may even help mobilize those who have lagged behind, and may mobilize the middle-of-the-roaders to join the struggle."[16] Indeed, if the Great Leap Forward was like a Beijing opera performance to Mao, then the shelling and Taiwan Strait crisis were the booming drumbeats carrying the performance forward. Without them, the opera would lose its rhythm, dramaticism, and theatricality, and consequently, the meanings it had in the first place.

The outbreak of the Second Taiwan Strait Crisis dramatically increased Zhou's foreign policy responsibilities. Washington had signed a treaty of mutual defense with Taipei in 1954. Secretary of State John Foster Dulles publicly warned that Beijing would face "serious consequences" if it used force to occupy the GMD-controlled islands off the coast. President Dwight Eisenhower also stated that defending Jinmen was important for defending Taiwan.[17] By early September, as the Jinmen Islands were gradually cut off from their supply lines, an amphibious landing operation by the PLA seemed imminent. Pentagon planners even considered using tactical nuclear weapons to deal with the possible attack; the potential for a deadly Sino-American confrontation loomed large.[18]

Seeing this danger, Zhou tried to use the declaration of China's twelve-mile maritime boundary as a preemptive measure. Zhou had been involved in delineating China's territorial waters for several years.[19] He now felt it vital to finalize China's maritime boundary, and quickly. On September 3, Mao called a meeting of top CCP leaders to discuss Zhou's concerns. The leaders thought that Washington would defend Taiwan but was unwilling to defend minor coastal islands or to "engage in a military confrontation there with us." Zhou suggested that by "setting our territorial waters at twelve miles," China might ensure that American naval ships would "not dare come close to Jinmen." The participants in the meeting approved Zhou's suggestion.[20] On September 4, Zhou formally declared that China's territorial waters extended to a distance of twelve nautical miles, and that no foreign military aircraft or naval vessel could cross the boundary without Beijing's permission.[21]

Mao also believed that "military action should go hand in hand with diplomacy"; therefore, China should be prepared to resume the Sino-American ambassadorial talks in Warsaw, which had begun in late 1955.[22] At the end of 1957, when the US ambassador to Poland departed Warsaw at the end of his term, Washington proposed that an American chargé d'affaires be allowed to attend the talks instead. Beijing immediately attacked the proposal as an American plot to downgrade the talks, which were thus interrupted.

The same day that Zhou made the territorial waters announcement, Dulles reiterated that the United States would help defend GMD-controlled coastal islands. Notably, though, he also expressed willingness to negotiate with Beijing to resolve the crisis concerning Taiwan.[23] Zhou stressed in a response two days later that it was within China's sovereignty rights to use military means to deal with the GMD. But he also stated that Beijing was ready to resume the ambassadorial-level talks with Washington.[24] The Chinese and Americans quickly agreed to restart the talks at the Swiss embassy in Warsaw on September 15.

Mao saw this as an opportunity to make Washington force Taipei to give up the offshore islands, thus ending the crisis while keeping a channel open for future communication with Washington.[25] Zhou agreed with Mao. He personally prepared a draft note, which the Chinese side would present in Warsaw, in which he emphasized that Beijing had the right "to use all proper means" to liberate GMD-controlled islands and demanded that Washington "withdraw all of its armed forces from Taiwan and the Taiwan Strait." The note also stipulated that if "GMD troops are to take the initiative to withdraw from the offshore islands, the PLA will not pursue them." Further, after the PRC had recovered the offshore islands, "it will strive to liberate Taiwan and the nearby Penghu islands by peaceful means and will, for a certain period, avoid using force to liberate them."[26] These two points potentially amounted to a major concession since, if the terms outlined in the note were accepted, Beijing would commit to not using force to "liberate" Taiwan for an indefinite time.[27]

Mao initially approved Zhou's plan, which was conveyed to Wang Bingnan, the Chinese ambassador to Poland. But the chairman quickly changed his mind. On September 13, he instructed Zhou that during the first week of the Warsaw talks, Wang "should not lay out all of our cards on the table but should first test [the Americans]. It seems likely they will not lay out all of their cards and will try to test us too."[28] Zhou immediately informed Wang that, at the talks, he should "go around with the Americans to force them to lay out all of their cards first."[29]

The talks resumed in Warsaw on September 15. Jacob Beam, the American ambassador to Poland, spoke first, arguing for an immediate cease-fire in the Taiwan Strait.[30] Wang began his presentation by emphasizing that China had the right to use "all appropriate means" to liberate Taiwan. Then, failing to follow the new instructions given to him by Mao and Zhou, he stated that if the GMD forces took the initiative to abandon the offshore islands, the PLA would not pursue them, and that for recovering the offshore islands, Beijing would "strive to use peaceful means to liberate Taiwan, avoiding the use of force for a given period of time." Despite the novelty of the proposal, Beam's instinctive reaction was to rebut it, which he claimed "would mean surrender of territory" belonging to an American ally.[31]

Mao, who was in Anhui on an inspection tour at the time, flew into a rage upon receiving a report that Wang had revealed Beijing's bottom line before the Americans had shown their cards. "Wang Bingnan is worse than a pig," exclaimed the chairman. "Even a pig knows how to turn around when it hits a wall, but Wang does not even know how to turn around." He thought of firing Wang immediately. Zhou defended Wang, a main associate of his for many years, advising the chairman that firing Wang might cause more confusion; hence Mao agreed to let Wang stay.[32] But he did not let Zhou off the hook easily. He criticized Zhou's original instructions to Wang as being "too complex and not to the point" and "weak and powerless," thus having "caused a big mistake." Mao decided to call Chen Yi back to Beijing "to help Zhou in handling this matter." He further demanded that all of Wang's future presentation notes be drafted in Beijing, and that Wang should "not change a single word of them." The Chinese side, Mao ordered Zhou, should adopt an "offensive strategy" for the next ambassadorial-level meeting "to retake the initiative."[33]

Zhou wasted no time in implementing Mao's order. He then wrote Mao, beginning by acknowledging that his original plan "was presented at too early a time, leaving the other side with the impression that we are eager to pursue success at the talks." He then put forward several suggestions: The Foreign Minister would issue a statement rebutting Secretary Dulles's speech; Chinese media and public opinion would be mobilized to echo the rebuttal; and Moscow and Soviet bloc countries would be asked to support it. In the meantime, "while avoiding engaging the US navy and air force, we will wage a large-scale operation, using naval, air, and artillery forces, to deal a heavy blow to Jinmen garrisons and Chiang's naval and air power."[34] Mao liked Zhou's new plans, commenting that it was "what our diplomatic struggle should be."[35] Zhou then instructed Wang to handle his talks with the Americans in Warsaw in accordance with these new plans.[36]

When Wang and Beam met again on September 22, the Chinese ambassador was primed for a counteroffensive. Without mentioning the offer he had given one week earlier, Wang presented a new proposal, which demanded that the United States withdraw all its armed forces as the precondition to easing tensions in the Taiwan Strait. Beam immediately rejected Wang's proposal.[37] Consequently, the talks again became a battlefield of mutual accusations and denunciations, with each ambassador rebutting every point the other made. At least, however, the channel for dialogue between Beijing and Washington survived.

Meanwhile, the PLA's Fujian command devised a new plan to escalate military operations, according to which the PLA would coordinate its ground shelling and air bombardment of Jinmen to pursue a "bigger and more comprehensive victory."[38] But Zhou now felt the plan to be inappropriate. He wrote Mao, pointing out that it was difficult to "have good coordination in a land, air, and sea joint operation, and American ships and planes could also be hit." Further, this could "provide Chiang's air force with an excuse to bombard the mainland." Therefore, Zhou believed it better to continue the "shelling but not land on (Jinmen)" and "make the enemy panicky day and night without rest."[39] Mao approved Zhou's proposal.[40] The PLA continued its artillery shelling of the Jinmen Islands and GMD supply convoys, without taking any other action that would escalate the confrontation.

The crisis had gone on for over a month by the end of September, when Mao and Zhou noticed subtle changes in Washington's attitude. On September 30, in response to a question about whether the United States should support the withdrawal of GMD troops from the offshore islands, Dulles stated, "If there were a cease-fire in the area which seemed to be reasonably dependable, I think it would be foolish to keep these large forces on these islands."[41] This was probably Dulles's response to Wang's overture in Warsaw two weeks earlier. But it came too late.

Zhou was alarmed. At a meeting of top leaders on October 3, he assessed that Dulles was trying to induce Beijing to adopt a nonmilitary policy toward Taiwan. In turn, Zhou believed, Washington would persuade Chiang to trade the offshore islands for Taiwan's safety, thus perpetuating the separation between mainland China and Taiwan.[42] Mao agreed with Zhou's assessment, adding that if Beijing accepted the overture, "we will fall into Dulles's trap."[43] Instead of trying to occupy the offshore islands, Mao now considered using a "noose strategy" by leaving Jinmen in Chiang's hands. The offshore islands "are very close to the mainland," Mao elaborated, so if they were kept in Chiang's possession, they could serve as Beijing's "points of contact" with the GMD, which would become a "noose" around the Americans' neck. "Whenever we need tension, we may tighten the noose, and whenever we want to relax the tension, we may loosen it. We will let them hang there, neither dead nor alive, using them as means to deal with the Americans."[44]

On October 5, Mao ordered the PLA "not to fire a single shell" for two days. The next day, Beijing broadcast a "Message to the Compatriots in Taiwan," which was written by Mao but published in Peng Dehuai's name. The message announced that, beginning on October 6, on the condition of "no American escorts," the bombardment of Jinmen would cease for seven days, during which time the GMD troops and civilians on the islands could receive supplies. "We are all Chinese," Mao appealed to Chiang, "so reconciliation is the best course for us to take."[45] A de facto cease-fire followed with the repeated renewal of the order. The Second Taiwan Strait Crisis ended as suddenly as it began. It did, however, leave a deep and long-lasting impact on CCP-GMD relations. Chiang and the GMD had never trusted Mao and the Communists, but this episode of artillery shelling mixed with peace gestures shattered any illusions Chiang and his allies might have had about the CCP's "united front" policies. Zhou's apparent "peace initiatives" toward Taiwan had all been wasted.

* * *

Zhou was also involved in summer 1958 with managing emerging tensions in Beijing's relations with Moscow. The prospect of a Sino-American clash in the Taiwan Strait alarmed Moscow's leaders. On September 5, N. G. Sudarikov, counselor of the Soviet embassy in Beijing, urgently requested to meet with Zhou. He told Zhou that he had just received a phone call from Khrushchev, who wanted to dispatch Foreign Minister Andrei Gromyko to Beijing to learn more about the Taiwan crisis and coordinate the two countries' moves. Zhou immediately sensed the discontent in the Soviet diplomat's tone, and he invited Gromyko to visit Beijing. "By shelling Jinmen," he explained, "China does not mean to use armed force to liberate Taiwan." He also promised that Beijing would take full responsibility for its own actions and would not "drag the Soviet Union into the water" if the shelling engendered "big troubles."[46]

Zhou's exchange with Sudarikov revealed that the once seemingly unbreakable Sino-Soviet alliance was in trouble. Before the spring of 1958, however, the two countries had appeared to be enjoying a prolonged honeymoon in their relations. In June 1957, Soviet ambassador Yudin informed Zhou that Moscow was willing to help China establish a nuclear energy research center and develop a nuclear industry.[47] In early August, Zhou wrote Nikolai Bulganin, head of the Soviet state, stating that "after the establishment of our nuclear energy industry, we will need to produce nuclear weapons and their delivery instruments. We hope that the Soviet side will give us its full support."[48] Bulganin quickly informed the Chinese that "in principle there exists no problem" with Zhou's request.[49] On August 25, Moscow formally informed Beijing that the Soviet Union was ready to discuss with the Chinese "issues concerning nuclear industry, rocket weapons, and aviation technology."[50] A Chinese delegation visited Moscow the next month. On October 15, Beijing and Moscow signed an "Agreement on New National Defense Technology," according to which the Soviet Union would provide China with nuclear technology in the form of a sample atomic bomb.[51] On April 8, 1958, Zhou proposed to Khrushchev that the two sides begin implementing their agreement on nuclear cooperation. Khrushchev replied to Zhou on April 24, writing as follows:

> The Soviet Government agrees to the proposal that you raised in your letter dated April 8 this year about providing Beijing with those materials and the sample of extreme importance in accordance with the Soviet-Chinese agreement on October 15, 1957. The Commission of External Economic Exchanges of the Council of Ministers of the Soviet

> Union has been authorized to organize discussions of the concrete issues involved in this matter and to sign contracts related to it, so that, following your suggestion, the above materials and the sample can be provided to you in the shortest time. N. Khrushchev (signature)[52]

Given the highly sensitive nature of the matter, Khrushchev avoided using terms such as "nuclear technology" and "atomic bomb" in the letter. This was an extraordinary commitment from Moscow's perspective, as it touched on the exceedingly delicate issue of nuclear proliferation. Khrushchev and the Soviet leadership obviously felt that they were in a position to ask Beijing to return the favor to their utmost. Soviet defense minister Rodion Malinovsky proposed in an April 18 letter to Peng, the Chinese defense minister, that the Soviets cooperate with China on constructing a long-wave radio transmission and receiving center in southern China, which would enable Moscow to better communicate with Soviet submarines in the Pacific region. The Soviets pledged to cover 70 percent of the total construction cost of 110 million rubles, indicating that the two sides would jointly use the radio facility after its completion.[53]

Mao, however, was alarmed by the Soviet proposal, which he saw as detrimental to China's sovereignty and integrity. China would agree to the building of the station, he decided, only on the condition that it covered all the cost and retain exclusive ownership of it.[54] Peng's reply to Malinovsky followed the line Mao had dictated.[55] The Soviets failed to grasp the implications of Peng's reply; in a draft agreement they sent to the Chinese on July 11, the Soviets still insisted that the station be jointly constructed and managed by the two sides.[56] Beijing responded with a further clarification: China would construct the station, purchase the equipment it was unable to produce, invite Soviet experts to help build the facility, and, after its completion, solely own it while allowing it to be used jointly by the two countries.[57] The Soviets still did not understand what the Chinese meant. On July 11, Moscow presented the Chinese with another draft, which still insisted on sharing the cost of building the station and jointly managing it after its completion.[58]

Another dispute, one concerning the establishment of a joint Soviet-Chinese submarine flotilla, emerged between Beijing and Moscow before the radio facility issue was settled. As early as 1957, Xiao Jingguang, commander of the Chinese navy, had, after the signing of the Sino-Soviet agreement on new technology for national defense, discussed with his Soviet counterpart Sergey Gorshkov the prospect of Moscow providing Beijing with new naval technology and equipment.[59] Zhou wrote Khrushchev on June 28, 1958, requesting that Moscow, "in a step-by-step and planned fashion, provide us with blueprints of new types of battleships and ships equipped with rockets and missiles, as well as blueprints and calculation documents for mechanical supplies, parts, materials, radio equipment, and new weapons related to them."[60]

Soviet ambassador Yudin delivered Moscow's response on July 21. He explained at a meeting with Mao that the geography of the Soviet Union made it difficult for its navy to take full advantage of the new submarines. Because China had a long coastline and good harbors, Moscow proposed to establish a joint submarine flotilla with China. The Soviet leadership, Yudin said to the chairman, "hopes that Zhou and Peng, along with their experienced associates, may visit Moscow, where we will show them everything and have a more specific discussion." Mao immediately thought of China's sovereignty. "First, we should clarify the guiding principles," he told Yudin. "Must we do it with your assistance, or should we jointly do it? Otherwise, you will offer no assistance?" Mao emphasized that he had no interest in creating a Sino-Soviet "military cooperative."[61]

The chairman summoned Yudin to his quarters the next day, joined by Zhou and other top CCP leaders. They began to converse at 11:30 A.M. and continued until 4:30 P.M. Mao again delivered a lengthy monologue, giving Yudin almost no chance to comment. The chairman began by reviewing the history of CCP-Soviet relations, claiming that the Soviets had always treated their Chinese comrades from a posture of "great power chauvinism" and had even tried to develop a sphere of influence in China. He complained that the Soviet proposals to establish a long-wave radio station and a joint submarine flotilla were designed to control China. "You do not trust the Chinese. You only trust the Russians. The Russians are superior, and the Chinese are inferior, rough handed. Therefore, you want to have this joint venture," Mao charged. "You may accuse me of being a nationalist or another Tito, but I will say that you have extended Russian nationalism to China's coasts." He asked Yudin to "report all my comments to Comrade Khrushchev . . . telling him exactly what I have said without any polishing."[62]

Zhou said almost nothing at the meeting. However, when Mao, pointing at Zhou, told Yudin that the premier was probably less angry than he was,

Zhou immediately said, "This is the unanimous opinion of our Politburo."[63] Yudin was scared. His lips quivered, his face turned red and sweaty, and he stumbled over his words. A few days later, he suffered a major stroke and was rushed back to Moscow for emergency medical treatment.[64]

Khrushchev was "confused and shocked" by Mao's comments.[65] He rushed to Beijing on July 31 and held prolonged meetings with Mao over the next four days. When he saw Mao, he swore that Moscow had had absolutely no intention to control China. The idea of jointly constructing the long-wave station was Malinovsky's "personal opinion," Khrushchev claimed, not a decision by the Soviet Presidium. He promised that Moscow would let China have full ownership of the radio facility after its completion. Turning to the joint fleet, Khrushchev blamed Yudin for failing to accurately deliver Moscow's proposal. However, Mao would not easily accept Khrushchev's explanation, insisting that the Soviets' attitude toward China was steeped in "great power chauvinism."[66] Zhou attended all the meetings except those on the first day. He was mostly silent. Only when Mao and Khrushchev mentioned overseas Chinese in Southeast Asia and the Japan question did Zhou offer a few informational notes.[67]

By personally rushing to Beijing and trying his best to please Mao, Khrushchev had shown Mao respect. The chairman's anger seemed to have subsided. On August 3, Malinovsky and Peng signed an agreement on the construction of the long-wave radio station and the dispatching of Soviet experts to China.[68] The two sides also issued a communiqué declaring that they had "reached complete agreement on all issues discussed."[69]

Yet, as Zhou could clearly sense, the psychological gap between Mao and Khrushchev persisted and expanded. The memory of this experience stuck in Khrushchev's mind after he left Beijing. Although Mao had repeatedly emphasized that fraternal parties should be equals, Khrushchev felt deep down that Mao had never treated him (or anyone) as an equal.[70] Nor would Mao forget about this episode. He later called 1958 a turning point in Beijing's relations with Moscow, "because they wanted to control China militarily."[71]

Mao had already decided to shell Jinmen by the time the Soviet leader arrived in Beijing, though he had not briefed Khrushchev on the matter. One year later, Mao told Khrushchev that the decision had been made "after you had left Beijing."[72] Mao lied. Not surprisingly, Khrushchev flew into a rage upon learning of China's bombardment of Jinmen.[73] He thus decided to dispatch Gromyko to Beijing.

Zhou met with Gromyko on September 6. Echoing his talks with Sudarikov the day before, he told Gromyko that by shelling Jinmen, Beijing neither planned to liberate Taiwan nor to land on Jinmen. Instead, he asserted, "We have done so to suppress the arrogance of the GMD and the Americans, and to support the struggles of the Arab people." Finally, after listening to Zhou, Gromyko replied, "The Soviet Party Central Committee fully supports the stand and measures taken by the Chinese comrades." Zhou immediately expressed his "deep gratitude for the warm support" of the Soviets.[74] Mao, accompanied by Zhou, also met with Gromyko that evening. He emphasized, as Zhou had, that "we are shelling Jinmen not because we plan to attack Taiwan," and that "we will bear full responsibility, and will not involve you in it."[75]

After Mao decided to adopt the "noose strategy," Zhou met with Soviet chargé d'affaires S. F. Andonov, to whom he explained that Beijing had decided "it is better to leave Jinmen in Chiang's hands." The Americans, Zhou explained, were seeking to relieve themselves of the burden by trying to persuade Chiang to withdraw his troops from the offshore islands. The "noose strategy," Zhou continued, was aimed at breaking up America's "hands-off" policy. Originally, Beijing planned to take two steps. This first would be to recover the offshore islands, and the second would be to liberate Taiwan. "We now believe that it is better to let Chiang stay on the islands. As the Americans are now trying to get away, we will not let them do so. . . . Whenever we want tension, we will strike at them, and whenever we want an easing of tension, we will loosen [the noose] there. The initiative is in our hands."[76] Zhou hoped that Moscow would give Beijing's new policy its full support.

Khrushchev was not convinced. He later told Mao and Zhou, "As you had shelled the offshore islands, you should have attacked and occupied them. We cannot understand why you had shelled those islands without taking them over." A serious rift appeared between the Chinese and Soviet leaders.[77]

• • •

Zhou turned all his attention to the Great Leap Forward following the end of the Second Taiwan Strait Crisis. By then, over ninety million people had gotten involved in the mass movement to produce steel in China's cities and countryside. News of huge successes kept coming, and new records were reported every day. As head of the task force for steel production, Zhou had to give absolute priority to fulfilling the goal of producing 10.7 million tons of steel. He had to loudly encourage more steel production, although he knew that much of the "good news" could not have been true. He was exhausted.

Meanwhile, throughout China, dozens of thousands of people's communes that integrated production, study, consumption, and everyday life emerged almost overnight. Grain output reports continued to generate almost astronomical figures. All this spurred the revolutionary fever of Mao and other CCP leaders, who felt as though the establishment of a Communist society was rapidly approaching. Like everyone else, Zhou tried to emulate Mao's lofty rhetoric. At the end of the year, Beijing loudly announced that the main goals of the Great Leap, especially the production of 10.7 million tons of steel, had been surpassed.

Zhou felt no pleasure at all in the fulfillment of these targets. Although he said nothing about it, he suspected that the publicly reported figures were unreliable. Despite 1958's "best harvest in history," reports of food and cooking oil shortages poured into Zhou's office in early 1959. Supplies of grain, vegetables, and meat decreased significantly in the cities. Steel outputs, after "fulfilling and surpassing" the goals of 1958, dropped sharply in the first two months of 1959, falling to slightly more than half the amount of steel produced in the last months of 1958. It was apparent that the targets set at the Beidaihe Conference for steel production in 1959 would be impossible to reach. However, Zhou could do nothing without Mao's word. When he later recalled the circumstances he faced at that time, Zhou lamented, "I was the premier, but not even I could reduce the steel production plan by one thousand tons."[78]

In fact, Mao could not totally ignore tensions in the area of economic development, although he was in very high spirits. As a strategic master, Mao certainly understood the importance of keeping a balance between offense and defense. He called several central meetings starting at the end of 1958 to discuss how to maintain the momentum of the Great Leap Forward while not making it "too hot," although his emphasis remained on the former, not the latter. Zhou did not say much at these meetings. He focused on the specifics in several of his presentations, avoiding discussing major issues of policy or strategy.

From late February to early March 1959, Mao called and presided over an enlarged meeting of the Politburo in Zhengzhou. He mentioned at the meeting that the tendency to "make everything Communist overnight" and the phenomenon of "too much centralization" should be stopped. He also declared that those people's communes that had violated the socialist principle of "distribution according to work" in their practices should be rectified.[79] Zhou attended the meeting and was a member of the group that drafted a series of new regulations to manage the communes. The meeting had ostensibly been convened to lower the temperature of the Great Leap. Nevertheless, Mao announced at its conclusion that "we are surely able to achieve an even greater leap forward in 1959."[80] During the Maoist era, no matter how many times the chairman cited the need to restrain "leftist tendencies," he never did anything to mitigate them. This was because he was always the ultimate source and driving force of ultraleftism.

Not surprisingly, Mao steered the discussion at another central-level meeting shortly after the Zhengzhou Conference to focus exclusively on how to achieve and retain high levels of production in steel and other industrial sectors and how to consolidate people's communes. The meeting completely ignored the grave danger of serious nationwide shortages in grain production and supply.[81] However, reports detailing the grain shortage reached Beijing from time to time in spring 1959. On April 17, Mao conveyed to Zhou two reports, titled "Twenty-Five Million People in Fifteen Provinces Are Facing the Big Problem of Not Being Able to Feed Themselves."[82] The premier immediately wrote to the party secretaries of the fifteen provinces, instructing them "to quickly investigate and confirm the real situation, and take measures to transport grain to deal with the urgent crisis that more than twenty-five million people are temporarily being affected by a shortage of food supply."[83]

Meanwhile, when Zhou was making an inspection tour in Hebei, he used what he had just seen in the countryside to ask the local leaders to consider whether "six small freedoms" could be given to the peasants: "raising poultry, keeping small pieces of hilly land, owning trees around one's house, collecting firewood, and keeping some sideline production for family use." He further commented,

> This is about maintaining small "selves" in a big "collective," about walking by using both legs. There should be space reserved for "self." Without individuals, how can the "collective" come into being?[84]

Zhou made these comments almost intuitively, yet they represented a shocking revelation of his basic understanding—though usually kept only to himself as a Communist—about the ultimate relationship between the individual and the collective. His suggestion of giving the peasants "six small freedoms" was also otherwise unheard of during the heyday of the Great Leap Forward. Indeed, he probably was the first top CCP leader who had spoken of using these measures to deal with a potential crisis in the Chinese countryside.

However, Zhou had lost much of his administrative power by then; hence he no longer had the same authority as before to issue direct orders. Meanwhile, the deluge of exaggerated and fabricated reports of grain production and fake statistics showing ample grain reserves persisted. Zhou no longer knew for certain what the real status of grain production and supply was in the whole country. Every spring since the mid-1950s, there had been food shortages reported here and there within China. Thus, Zhou and the CCP leadership treated the new wave of grain shortage reports the same way as they had shortages in previous springs—as localized problems. They failed to treat the present shortage as an extraordinary and perilous situation with serious implications for the nation, let alone take powerful measures to deal with it. This was a huge mistake, and it was an important cause of the Great Famine that swept across the whole country.

* * *

Mao, Zhou, and the CCP leadership also ignored signs of the Great Famine because they were then preoccupied with a Tibetan rebellion in Lhasa. In addition, Zhou needed to work on improving China's deteriorating relations with India.

There had been some indications that turmoil in Tibet was imminent. Beijing had generally carried out gradualist reform policies in Tibet since the region's "peaceful liberation" in 1951. As described in Chapter 19, in India in 1956, Zhou promised the Dalai Lama that at least in the ensuing six years, "democratic reforms" would not be introduced in Tibet proper.[85] However, in the context of "socialist transformations" throughout China, in 1956 Beijing implemented radical "democratic reforms" in areas inhabited by ethnic Tibetans in Sichuan, Xikang, and elsewhere, triggering impassioned and powerful resistance from the ethnic Tibetans, who established the "Four

Rivers and Six Ranges" guerrilla force in 1958. After this force was suppressed by the PLA, many of the resistance fighters fled to Lhasa. But Mao was unconcerned, predicting that "if Tibet's reactionary elements dare to start a full-scale rebellion, the working people there will undoubtedly be liberated at an earlier time."[86]

On March 10, 1959, when a Tibetan rebellion did erupt in Lhasa, Mao, when was in Wuhan, contended that Tibet's "reactionary upper-class clique" was behind the revolt. He predicted that "we will be compelled to carry out the democratic reforms at an earlier time" if the turmoil escalated. He instructed the CCP Tibet Work Committee "to stay defensive militarily and offensive politically with the purpose of dividing the Tibetan elites, striving to attract more people to our side, educating the lower classes and the masses, and getting prepared to deal with the outbreak of rebellions on a larger scale." Beginning the next day, Liu chaired a series of meetings by CCP leaders in Beijing to discuss the situation in Tibet, which Zhou attended. Like Mao, they viewed the turmoil in Lhasa as not so much a crisis as an opportunity. They believed that until the situation in Lhasa became clearer, the PLA should "take up a posture of self-defense" and not "fire the first shot," so that the rebels would grow "more arrogant and, therefore, more exposed," giving the PLA "more sufficient reasons to thoroughly suppress them." They also decided to dispatch to Tibet more troops, who could be used to crush the revolt when necessary.[87]

Mao in Wuhan and Liu, Zhou, and other CCP leaders in Beijing also devoted much of their attention to the Dalai Lama. At first, they believed that "we should try to work more on the Dalai Lama himself."[88] But they did not believe it essential to keep him in Lhasa. It would be good if he stayed, Mao stated. But "if Dalai and his group are to escape, our troops should not stop them at all. Whether they are going to Shannan or to India, let them go."[89] Liu and other CCP leaders shared Mao's views. They believed that while it was better to try to keep the Dalai Lama in Lhasa, it would not matter much if he were to leave, for if the Dalai Lama fled, settling the unrest in Tibet would no longer depend on "the awakening of some upper-class members of the former Tibetan government, but on resolutely suppressing the rebellion and comprehensively carrying out reforms." On March 17, the Dalai Lama left Lhasa for India. The PLA did not make any major effort to stop him.[90]

Zhou had been contemplating the tensions in China's relations with India for months. Now, he particularly reminded other Chinese leaders that the events in Tibet had an Indian connection. "Both the British and American governments have been quite active behind the curtain," Zhou said, "and they have supported the Indian government, pushing India to the fore. The command center of the Tibetan rebellion is located in Kalimpong, India."[91]

Late in the evening of March 19, Beijing received a report from the PLA command in Lhasa that "the armed rebels are waging a full-fledged offensive against us." The next morning, Beijing ordered PLA troops to ruthlessly crush the rebellion. By the third day, Lhasa was fully under the control of the PLA.[92]

The CCP Politburo again discussed Tibet on March 22. Zhou proposed that specific policies related to "democratic reforms" be introduced although the rebellion was still being quelled. The meeting decided that as the Kashag (the Tibetan government in Lhasa) had "betrayed the motherland, it is no longer feasible to stick to the 'no reforms for six years' promise."[93] Zhou said at a State Council meeting on the same day that Tibet's feudal system was alien to "our socialist big family." Originally, Beijing was willing to not impose "democratic reforms "in Tibet itself, Zhou claimed, and to give [the Tibetans] the opportunity to change." However, Tibet's reactionary elites "have stubbornly tried to maintain this most reactionary system, and staged the rebellion. So, we are forced to suppress it." Zhou also stressed that those who had been involved in the rebellion should be treated differently, the reforms carried out gradually, and questions about religion handled with the utmost caution.[94]

On March 28, Zhou announced that the Kashag would be dissolved, and that political power in Tibet would be handed over to a "Preparatory Committee of the Tibet Autonomous Region." Zhou also called on the people of Tibet to "unite together" to "strive to construct a democratic and socialist new Tibet."[95] Then, the PLA expanded operations to suppress the rebels in other parts of Tibet. By 1962, Tibet was already effectively under Beijing's control.[96]

• • •

When the unrest erupted in Lhasa, Zhou immediately thought of the rebellion's connections to China's troubled relations with India. Since 1956, Zhou had begun to sense that the border issue could became a bottleneck in Chinese-Indian relations. Indeed, as 1958 neared, more signs of tension between Beijing and New Delhi emerged. In addition to the two sides' disagreement on the McMahon Line along the eastern section of their shared border, a separate dispute surfaced concerning the western border when New Delhi described Aksai Chin as Indian territory. In early 1958, the Indians found that the Chinese had constructed a motorway linking Xinjiang and Tibet in the region.[97] Nehru wrote to Zhou on December 14, describing in great detail India's position on its border with China. He contended that the Chinese-Indian agreement of 1954 on Tibet had "resolved all unsettled issues between us," meaning that there were "no border disputes between the two countries."[98] The letter shocked Zhou. Among the Chinese leadership, Zhou had had the most contacts with Nehru, and his relationship with the Indian prime minister had been amiable. Zhou realized after he read Nehru's letter, especially what he regarded as the prime minister's "obvious misrepresentation" of Zhou's description of the McMahon Line, that he probably did not truly understand Nehru, and that the Chinese-Indian border issue was much more complicated than he had previously imagined.

Zhou wrote to Nehru on January 23, 1959, systematically presenting China's stand on the border dispute with India: "The boundaries between China and India have never been formally established. . . . In history, the Chinese central government and the Indian government have never signed any treaty or agreement concerning the Chinese-Indian border." In terms of international law, Zhou argued, the McMahon Line "has not been a legal one" and "has never been recognized by any Chinese central government." Zhou proposed that before the border issue was settled, the two sides should try to keep the line where it presently stood to avoid any incidents.[99]

India's political elites and media almost unanimously placed the blame on Beijing when the Tibetan rebellion erupted in Lhasa. When the Dalai Lama and a group of his associates escaped from Lhasa on March 17, they quickly traveled toward India to seek asylum there. Mao and Zhou now more firmly believed that an "India factor" had played a role in the rebellion in Tibet. Tensions between China and India worsened further.

Zhou received another letter from Nehru on March 22. The Indian prime minister continued to insist that India's border with Tibet had been well established, and that China's maps had mistakenly included large parts of Indian territory on the Chinese side of the boundary.[100] For Zhou and the Chinese leadership, this was unacceptable; Zhou had to produce another comprehensive reply to Nehru.

At a conference of top CCP leaders, including Zhou, in Shanghai on March 25, India was the main subject of discussion. Zhou and the CCP leadership were facing a dilemma. They knew that India was not an imperialist country. If China criticized India directly, it could be further isolated internationally. But they also believed that New Delhi was behind the Tibetan rebellion and harbored expansionist territorial ambitions toward China. Zhou and his comrades saw it as necessary to expose and repulse India's supposed machinations. They concluded that they would "let the Indian authorities do more unjust things now, and, when the right moment comes, settle all our debts with them."[101]

The "right moment" soon came. On April 3, the Indian Foreign Ministry informed Pang Zili, the Chinese ambassador to India, that the Dalai Lama had come to India to seek political asylum, and that India would give him a "respectful reception" and allow him to stay.[102] Mao summoned a meeting of top leaders in Hangzhou on April 8. He noted that "now Britain, the United States, and India are making all kinds of noise, engaging in a big anti-China chorus, opposing China's suppression of the rebellion." He ordered Chinese propagandists to "wage an open counteroffensive" to justify Beijing's stand on Tibet.[103] Mao assigned Zhou to take charge of this matter. On April 15, *Renmin ribao* published an editorial essay, written under Zhou's direction, emphasizing that Nehru should not be allowed to damage the friendship between China and India.[104]

Zhou still hoped to keep some flexibility in criticizing India—and Nehru in particular—until then. On April 18, Zhou claimed at a meeting of the National People's Congress leadership that the Dalai Lama had been "kidnapped to India" in the hope that he would be able to escape the control of the rebels and "return to the motherland."[105] On the same day, however, the Dalai Lama issued a statement attacking Beijing, which was distributed with the help of Indian diplomats. Nehru met with the Dalai Lama, on April 24, followed by a press conference. Zhou's space for maneuvering was greatly diminished. At an April 25 meeting of the Politburo Standing Committee, Mao said, "To repulse India's anti-China activities, we should put emphasis on having a big debate with Nehru. We should sharply criticize him and not be afraid of offending him."[106] On May 4, Zhou followed Mao's lead, asserting that "it seems that Nehru has developed some illusions about using the Dalai Lama as a bargaining chip on the border issue."[107] Two days later, Zhou and Mao met with diplomats from the Soviet Union and the Soviet bloc. Zhou claimed that Nehru was seeking to turn Tibet into a "buffer country" while preventing democratic reforms there and forcing the PLA out of the region.[108]

The singing of "Hindi-Chini Bhai Bhai" ("India-China, brothers, brothers") had moved hundreds of millions of Chinese and Indians throughout the 1950s. Now, with the outbreak of the Tibetan rebellion and the flaring up of border disputes between the two countries, dark clouds had gathered over the prospects of Chinese-Indian relations in a few short months.

• • •

A new dilemma faced Sino-Soviet relations almost at the same time. As the Great Leap Forward began to take shape in China, many Soviet experts working in the country warned that the Great Leap could negatively impact the Chinese economy. But Khrushchev and the Soviet leadership generally still viewed the Leap in a positive light.[109] The difficulties of establishing the long-wave station and the joint submarine fleet, as well as the crisis in the Taiwan Strait, however, converged to erode the basis for such positive views. Moreover, the irrational, hyperbolic ways in which the Leap continued to evolve pushed Soviet leaders' opinions of Mao and the CCP leadership in a highly negative direction.

The Soviet Communist Party held its Twenty-First Congress in January 1959. Zhou led the CCP delegation to the congress, giving him an opportunity to help improve Chinese-Soviet relations, which he dearly hoped would happen. When Khrushchev spoke at the congress, although he praised Moscow's friendship with Beijing, he also declared, "Egalitarianism is not the way of transitioning to Communism but is detrimental to Communism's reputation." As if this had not been enough, he added, "It is wrong to think that a Communist society will arise overnight." Khrushchev's comments needed no footnote; anyone who heard them would have known that he was criticizing China's people's commune movement. Zhou did not directly confront Khrushchev. Following the directions that the CCP leadership had given to him, he still emphasized in his speech that the international Communist movement should be "headed by the Soviet Union."[110] When he met with Khrushchev and other Soviet leaders, he tried his best to open pathways for continuing Chinese-Soviet cooperation. As a result, his visit to Moscow concluded with an agreement on expanding Chinese-Soviet economic cooperation over the next eight years, under which Moscow agreed to provide China with equipment and technological aid for seven to eight large industrial projects with a total value of 5.7 billion rubles.[111]

Several of Moscow's earlier clashes with Beijing, however, had by then begun to cause some pushback from the Soviet leadership. On June 20, Moscow informed Beijing that as the Soviet Union was preparing to negotiate with the United States and United Kingdom on forbidding nuclear tests, and a summit of Soviet and American leaders would soon be held, it was an inopportune moment to provide China with nuclear technology. Moscow thus postponed its pledge to provide China with a sample atomic bomb and related technological documents, promising that it would reconsider the issue in two years according to the situation then.[112] Meanwhile, many Soviet experts had received orders not to return to China after taking vacations back home. This was a huge blow to the Chinese leadership as well as to Chinese-Soviet relations.

• • •

The Chinese economy continued its downward spiral as spring gave way to summer in 1959. Agriculture was particularly problematic. Indeed, the Great Famine was beginning to spread throughout the whole country. The political atmosphere in the party's upper echelon was complicated. In the words of Li Rui, who once served as Mao's political secretary, people generally felt that "there had been too much confusion and upheaval in 1958, which Mao knew that he was responsible for, but was unwilling to take the responsibility."[113] Zhou avoided saying anything about domestic issues at meetings of top leaders. Although the Party Center had decided to adjust its goals for steel, coal, grain, and cotton outputs, and to make people's communes less centrally managed, it still called for the Great Leap Forward to advance. CCP leaders simply ignored signs pointing to the coming Great Famine.

Mao spoke at a Central Committee plenum on April 5. He insisted that 1958 had progressed in the right direction. There had been shortcomings, of course, but none of them was serious. He blamed others for failing to communicate with him, emphasizing that "all power must be controlled by the Politburo Standing Committee and the Secretariat," with him as "the commander in chief and Deng Xiaoping as the deputy commander in chief."[114] Zhou and his State Council were sidelined once more.

It became clear by the end of the summer that many key production goals, especially the target of eighteen million tons of steel, could not be reached. Still, Mao was totally unwilling to abandon the Great Leap Forward banner or to scale down the people's communes in the Chinese countryside. Against this backdrop, an enlarged meeting of the Politburo was held at Lushan. By then, Mao had already sensed that many in the party had grown increasingly suspicious about the Great Leap. On June 28, he telephoned Zhou, saying that it was vital to calm things down in Lushan and spend more time studying political economy.[115] Four days later, Mao called a meeting with Liu, Zhou, and other top party leaders. He described the situation, asking if the domestic situation was good or bad. He answered the question himself: "The overall situation is good. A bit of it is not good." He believed that the party should stick to the existing policy line. "We have had great achievements," he said, setting an optimistic tone. "There are many problems, but the future is bright."[116]

Not surprisingly, most presentations at the Lushan Conference echoed Mao's tone. Zhou also emphasized in his presentation that the achievements of 1958 had been great. When he mentioned that some goals of production had been "a bit too high" and the scale of infrastructure construction "a bit too large," he carefully focused on concrete examples, to avoid making a big deal of them.[117]

Peng Dehuai arrived at Lushan on July 1. When he spoke, he also toasted the "great achievements" of the previous year; but he was bolder than others, including Zhou, in discussing the shortcomings. Mao was listening. The most offensive of Peng's comments was his claim that "it is very abnormal and even dangerous to only pursue the prestige and authority of a person, not the prestige and authority of the collective."[118] Peng's presentation did not produce much of an impact at first. However, seeing that the conference was approaching its end, Peng felt "very worried." On July 14, after back-and-forth deliberation, he wrote a letter to Mao, in which he outlined his assessment of the current situation and "the main lessons to be drawn." Although Peng affirmed that "the achievements of the Great Leap Forward are a sure fact" and that the people's communes were "of great significance," he dedicated much of the letter to discussing problems and lessons. In particular, he said that mass participation in steel production had come "with losses and gains," and that "petty bourgeoisie craziness" must be corrected. This was unacceptable to Mao.[119]

Mao did not act for two days. On July 16, he conveyed Peng's letter to other party leaders, including Zhou.[120] At the outset, Zhou did not consider the matter to be serious. He even thought that Peng's letter "has indeed reflected the real situation" and was thus "not much of an issue."[121] In fact, this was also the opinion of the majority at the conference, many of whom supported Peng's viewpoints.[122] All this had made Mao even more upset and angry. So many people echoing Peng posed a huge challenge to Mao's authority and power, seriously threatening the legitimacy of his grand enterprise of "continuous revolution."

Feeling uneasy with Mao's reaction, Peng told the chairman on July 19 that he had written his letter hurriedly, and he asked to withdraw it. But water spilled on the ground cannot be picked up again. Mao began his revenge on July 22, when he had a five-and-a-half-hour conversation with Liu, Zhou, and Lin Biao, during which he probably shared with his colleagues the course of action he would take, and also attempted to gauge their attitudes.[123] The next morning, he delivered a three-hour presentation at the conference. "We have been facing attacks from both within and outside the party," Mao claimed. Peng was a "careerist" and a "plotter," who tried to totally negate the Great Leap and overturn the party's general lines for socialist reconstruction. Mao even threatened that "if the PLA does not follow me, I will go to find the Red Army. I believe that the PLA will follow me." He accused Peng and those who supported him as having "repeated the path of those who had committed mistakes in late 1956 and early 1957. They have thrown themselves to the verge of becoming rightists, only thirty kilometers away."[124] Mao was referring to Zhou's experience. How could the premier fail to feel shocked?

At that point, however, Zhou still did not seem to believe that Mao meant to take Peng down. When Zhou saw Peng at a State Council meeting, he told Peng not to take Mao's criticism lightly, but not to treat it as a very big deal either. He compared Peng's letter with his own "opposing rash advance" mistakes, telling Peng, "You have not fallen as deep as I had then."[125] However, Mao saw Peng's problems as much more serious than the premier's. Backed by his huge authority and unchecked power, he orchestrated an all-out criticism of Peng's "coordinated antiparty plot." In addition to labeling Peng and his "accomplices" as "rightist opportunists," Mao also made the wild claim that Peng had somehow colluded with Khrushchev and the Soviets to challenge the CCP's policies in general, and the people's communes and the Great Leap Forward in particular.[126]

Zhou's attitude toward Peng changed. On July 26, he told a group of ministers and vice ministers to "clarify their attitudes" toward Peng's letter and "draw a clear line" on it. He criticized Peng's notion of "losses outweighing gains" while urging Peng to "thoroughly recognize his own fallibility."[127] At a Politburo meeting on August 1, he called Peng a sneaky plotter. Indeed, he said, Peng's criticism of "petty bourgeoisie craziness" was merely a pretext to attack the party's general lines and Mao's leadership role.[128] Peng later complained that Zhou was "too crafty and cunning."[129] This was probably too harsh a moral accusation. Zhou had just survived a fierce attack from Mao for his "opposing rash advance" mistakes, and he had his own unspeakable dilemmas.

The Central Committee held another plenum beginning on August 2. By the time the plenum concluded two weeks later, it had "exposed" an "anti-party clique" headed by Peng and joined by Zhang Wentian, Huang Kecheng, and Zhou Xiaozhou. Peng was dismissed as minister of defense. Mao boasted that "this plenum has resolved a big problem, and it is a big victory. In a timely manner, it has prevented the party from becoming divided."[130]

Mao also spoke at Lushan about "properly lowering" the extraordinary production goals.[131] This created a paradoxical situation for Zhou. Back in Beijing, Zhou repeatedly relayed the "spirit of Lushan" at a series of conferences, trying to adjust the main goals of the production plans for 1959.[132] But his mission was impossible to accomplish. The purge of Peng and his "rightist clique" at Lushan had generated powerful outcries throughout China, as people around the country reiterated the need to "continue the Leap." Mao also sang the praises of the Leap at a high pitch.[133] Thus, to stay politically correct, Zhou had to try hard not to commit mistakes that could be described as being rightist in nature. However, it was nonetheless necessary to "adjust production goals." What was the balancing point between these two conflicting goals? Zhou knew well that if he was unable to strike the right balance, he could become ensnared, thus committing another serious "political mistake."

More terrifying still, the changing political winds meant that such practices as boasting about "extraordinary successes," fabricating grain outputs, and extracting excessive amounts of agricultural products from the countryside prevailed, causing a serious discrepancy between grain production and supply nationwide. Yet, in the wake of Lushan, no CCP leader, including Zhou, dared to stand up in search of the truth. Consequently, although China's grain outputs decreased dramatically, state procurement increased significantly. Meanwhile, the public canteens in the people's communes kept grain consumption and losses at a very high level.

A disastrous Great Famine, unprecedented in Chinese or even human history, was about to engulf China's vast land and population.

21

MAO RETREATS TO THE "SECOND LINE"

1959–1962

Zhou Enlai was rather perplexed when he opened his 1960 work calendar. Despite the constant stream of "victory reports" that poured into his office, the Chinese economy was embarking on a path of sharp decline. Internationally, in addition to its confrontation with Washington, Beijing faced serious challenges in its relations with Moscow and New Delhi. Zhou's agenda was already overloaded with his duties as the premier. Yet he still had to treat reading as a top-priority task; other Chinese leaders were doing the same.

The "reading fever" owed its start to Mao. The chairman could not have failed to predict that dissenting voices would emerge among other party leaders in response to the Great Leap Forward's abysmal failure. In late 1959, he formally retreated to the "second line" of the party leadership, leaving Liu Shaoqi and Deng Xiaoping to assume leadership of the "first line." Meanwhile, Mao wrote Liu, asserting that it was time to study political economy. He summoned a group of his literary associates to a quiet location in Hangzhou, where they read *Textbook of Political Economy*.[1] His associates then compiled his comments and circulated them widely among the party elite. Mao said that the reading's purpose was to summarize the lessons of socialist reconstruction and "find its rules." But the reading doubled as an attempt by Mao to prevent his control of the party's mainstream discourse from slipping. In his reading comments, Mao contended that "with the relative development of capitalism, the more backward the economy is, the easier the transition to socialism will be." "Poverty," he reasoned, "is the vehicle for China's great leap. Because of poverty, there is momentum for making revolution."[2] This was Mao's attempt to justify the Great Leap and his thesis of "continuous revolution" in theoretical terms. In retrospect, Mao never lost power—especially discursive power—after he retreated to the second line, although Liu and Deng, on the first line, had enhanced their decision-making authority.

In early February, Zhou organized his own reading group, composed of Li Fuchun, Tao Zhu, and Song Renqiong, as well as several economists, philosophers, and historians, to study *Textbook of Political Economy* in Chonghua, Guangdong. The group finished the book's chapters on socialism in three weeks. In discussions on the volume, Zhou repeatedly praised the Great Leap, which he called Mao's "creative development of Marxism-Leninism" in China. But he also tried to qualify his acclaim by emphasizing that "it is impossible to leap every day. Some adjustment is needed."[3]

All the while, "continuing the Great Leap" remained the central theme in China. In January, Mao again set the tone at a Politburo meeting in Shanghai, declaring that "the Lushan Conference was good. Since then, production has increased month by month. This year will witness a leap even greater than last year's."[4] Zhou did not play a major role at the meeting. Since mid-1958, much of his economic decision-making power had been taken over by the Central Secretariat and the five central leading groups. At the meeting, Li Fuchun, the vice premier and head of the finance and economy leading group, introduced the economic development plans for 1960 and for the next three and eight years, respectively.[5] Zhou sat listening. The meeting reconfirmed the goal of catching up to Britain in three years and establishing China's own "comprehensive industrial system" in eight.[6]

The reality of the Chinese economy, however, was dramatically different from the rosy picture that Mao and other CCP leaders depicted. The announcement that economic goals for 1959 were "completed ahead of schedule" was largely false. Zhou knew this full well; his experience supervising steel production in the last three months of 1959 had been nightmarish. After the Lushan Conference, "guaranteeing steel production" became a task of absolute priority in the political sphere. As head of the steel production task force, Zhou found that even he had no power to reduce the projected steel output by a single ton. All activities throughout the country were forced to give way to a frenzy of steel production, which yielded mountains of low-grade scrap rather than quality steel. At the year's end, Beijing announced that steel production targets had been surpassed. However, entering the new year, steel output declined significantly, sinking again to less than half the level of the previous months. That the Great Leap Forward had failed was more evident than before.

More ruinous to the Great Leap was that the state substantially increased its extraction of grain in 1959 although grain output had fallen dramatically. People everywhere were starving. Even so, public dining services expanded after the Lushan Conference; in many places, even seeds were consumed as food. Consequently, the food shortage became even more serious.

Although he was the premier, Zhou lacked knowledge or understanding of the huge gaps between China's grain production, supply, and consumption. His thinking, widely shared by Chinese leaders, was still influenced by a long-standing trend: since 1949, reports had come almost every spring warning of food shortages; however, food supply usually would improve after the summer and autumn harvests. This time, however, Zhou—like Mao and other party leaders—clearly failed to recognize that reports of food shortages might foreshadow a great famine.

Mao simply ignored the reports. Beginning in late April, he went on inspection tours to Hebei, Shandong, and Henan. All the provincial leaders he met assured him that grain production and food supplies were quite good. On April 30, Mao spoke with Tan Zhenlin, the vice premier who had just hosted a conference on agriculture. Tan reported that "the deaths in Anhui were isolated cases. Most sick people have received good treatment. Few have left home for food. There is a lot of food there."[7] Tan and others attempted to tell Mao what he wanted to hear.

Mao and the Chinese leadership thus totally ignored the signs that a famine was engulfing China's vast countryside, let alone adopt any specific measures to remedy the crisis. A whole year would be wasted as a result. Materializing in China was a tragedy and disaster on a scale unseen in Chinese history, or even human history.

• • •

There was another reason for Zhou to fail to perceive warning signs of the Great Famine apart from his awkward position in the leadership. Beginning in mid-1959, he had to give much of his attention to emerging tensions along China's border with India.

On August 25, Chinese and Indian border garrisons clashed at Longju on the western section of the border. Both sides suffered casualties in the fighting. Zhou wrote Nehru two weeks later, delineating Beijing's stand on the border issue. The Chinese government, Zhou stated, "absolutely does not recognize the so-called McMahon Line, but Chinese troops have never crossed that line." And Beijing was willing to "face reality and take into consideration the friendly relationship between China and India, actively seeking for a settlement that is fair and reasonable to both sides." Zhou hoped that measures could be taken to "restore the long-standing state of the boundary between the two countries."[8]

However, on October 21, another, larger skirmish erupted between Chinese and Indian garrisons at the Kongka Pass, which also lay along the border's western extent. This incident further worsened China's image in the Indian media and among the Indian public. Right-wing parties even demanded that India's diplomatic relations with China be cut off.[9] All this added a great deal of urgency to the task of resolving the Sino-Indian border dispute.

Both Mao and Zhou believed that it was essential to prevent a third clash from taking place. Zhou attended a work conference in Hongzhou on November 3, at which Mao introduced a new idea. Nehru had proposed that the two sides withdraw from Longju, the chairman noted. In that case, Mao reasoned, why should the Chinese not expand the withdrawal to the whole border, with "each side's troops retreating ten, fifteen or even twenty, thirty, and forty kilometers" and only "unarmed personnel managing each side's business along the customary lines." Zhou and Nehru might meet in Beijing or New Delhi "just for peace," the chairman proposed. "Good, very good," Zhou replied, in complete agreement with Mao, and added that "the two sides might establish an arms-free zone before the negotiations."[10] The conference authorized Zhou to raise these ideas with Nehru.

Zhou sent a long letter to Nehru on November 7, proposing that Chinese and Indian troops "each withdraw twenty kilometers at once" from the line of actual control and refrain from sending their armed personnel back to disputed areas, "while still maintaining civil administrative personnel and unarmed police there."[11] The next day, Zhou further explained the logic of his proposal to Shri Parthasarathy, the Indian ambassador to China. "For each side to retreat twenty kilometers is just a proposal for positively opening a pathway," Zhou said. Despite their differences, China and India remained friendly toward each other, he emphasized: "There exists no fundamental conflict of interest between us."[12]

Nehru agreed in a November 16 response to meet with Zhou at "a suitable time and place." He agreed that the two sides should cease patrolling the eastern and middle sectors of the border.[13] The western sector, however, proved problematic. The line that Nehru proposed for the two sides to base their operations there, as renowned author Neville Maxwell pointed out, "would have involved Indian evacuation of one post," while for China, "it would have meant evacuating about twenty thousand square miles, an evacuation that would have left no land route from Sinkiang [Xinjiang] to Tibet."[14] In his December 17 reply, Zhou described Nehru's counterproposal as "unfair and unreasonable," arguing that it "represents a big step backward from the principle agreed upon earlier by the two countries of maintaining for the time being the actual, existing state of the border." Zhou suggested that he and Nehru begin talks on December 26.[15] But Nehru was not eager to see Zhou so soon. In a letter to Zhou on February 5, 1960, he agreed to meet Zhou in April but also insisted that India's boundaries with China had been demarcated; therefore he could not "negotiate" with Zhou about the issue.[16]

While Zhou communicated back and forth with Nehru, he simultaneously accelerated efforts to finalize China's border settlement with Burma. Since the mid-1950s, Zhou had tried to use the pending resolution of the Chinese-Burmese border dispute as a precedent to promote China's border negotiations with India. Beijing's border negotiations with Yangon began to move forward in 1956 after Zhou made a major concession to the Burmese by recognizing the "1941 Line." Negotiations were interrupted in 1958 and the first half of 1959 due to political turmoil in Burma and the Burmese opposition's challenge to Zhou's "package solution."[17] General Ne Win became the country's prime minister in October 1958 following U Nu's resignation. On June 4, 1959, after the political situation in Burma had stabilized, Ne Win presented to Beijing his "final proposal" for settling the border dispute with China, in which he generally accepted Zhou's "package solution" ideas.[18] Zhou's associates at the Foreign Ministry thus found that the proposal "matched our bottom line, showing that Ne Win sincerely hopes to resolve the problem." In December, Zhou invited Ne Win to visit China for "negotiations to finally settle the two countries' border issue."[19] Ne Win visited

Beijing in late January, and on January 28, Zhou and Ne Win signed the border agreement.[20]

* * *

In mid-March, Zhou began to prepare intensively for his visit to India as soon as he returned from Guangdong to Beijing. By then, he had come up with a package solution that "changed (the territory of) the western sector with that of the eastern sector" with India. The essence of Zhou's solution was that, along the eastern section of the border, both sides should "negate in principle" the legitimacy of the McMahon Line made unilaterally by the British colonists. Meanwhile, he adopted the concept of the Line of Actual Control (LAC), according to which China would recognize India's sovereignty over the area south of the McMahon Line, which was almost identical to the LAC, and India would recognize Chinese sovereignty in Aksai Chin on the western extent of the border. In the east, Zangnan (southern Tibet), south of the McMahon Line, had been under India's control since the early 1950s. And in the west, China had long controlled Aksai Chin, which the Xinjiang-Tibet motorway completed by the Chinese in 1958 passed through. This was the only road that linked Tibet's Ali (Ngari) area to China's interior, which was thus of extreme strategic importance to China. The "change the west with the east" plan, Zhou believed, would be mutually acceptable to both India and China by respecting the real situation on their borders while paying due attention to the vital interests of both sides.

Zhou's thinking revealed Chinese-style wisdom. In fact, his main purpose for introducing the LAC, which overlapped with the McMahon Line, was to clear the way for Beijing's de facto acceptance but de jure rejection of the line. This would allow Zhou to come up with an acceptable explanation for the border settlement to the Chinese populace. He also hoped that such a major concession would result in Nehru's recognition of Chinese sovereignty in Aksai Chin. Nehru thought differently, however, due to his background, knowledge, personality, and understanding of public opinion in India. Although India had never controlled Aksai Chin, Nehru insisted that the map unilaterally made by British colonists included the region within the Ladakh region of India. Nehru's assertion came as a surprise to Zhou, especially given the premier's recent success in settling China's border dispute with Burma by the same method.

Zhou had probably overlooked two important differences between India and Burma. First, Burma and its leaders, including U Nu and Ne Win, did not have the same kind of "great power consciousness" as did Nehru and the Indian political elite. Second, compared to Burma, India had adopted a more pluralistic parliamentary democracy. Consequently, India's leadership had to reflect a wider range of views in their decision-making and had to deal with more complicated domestic politics.

Zhou was uncertain before he left for India about whether his package plan would work. The plan, which had been drafted under Zhou's direction, stated that "it is possible for the talks to reach some consensus, but not complete success or total failure." At the very least, Zhou hoped, the talks would help "ease the current situation and prepare conditions for future meetings toward a reasonable settlement."[21]

Zhou first stopped in Burma to meet with U Nu, who by then had become Burma's prime minister again, in the hope of signing a border treaty with Burma before he went to India. However, U Nu told Zhou that there was not enough time for the Burmese parliament to pass legislation enabling the agreement.[22] The two sides issued a joint communiqué once Zhou left Yangon, announcing that they had reached "agreements in principle" on a border settlement. When U Nu proposed that China could resolve its border dispute with India by following the Chinese-Burmese example, Zhou immediately confirmed that this was what he "absolutely wanted to do." U Nu asked whether he could "share the conversation with Nehru." "I have no objection," replied Zhou.[23]

Zhou arrived in New Delhi on the evening of April 19. On his most recent trip to India, he had been greeted at the airport by tens of thousands of people. This time, he received no such welcome.[24] The difficulty of the talks exceeded even Zhou's worst expectations. At their first meeting on the morning of April 20, Nehru insisted that India's boundaries traced the Himalayas. In mountainous areas, the two countries had always treated the Greater Himalayan Watershed as the border, and no serious problems had occurred. However, Nehru noted, China had taken some steps that "for us were aggressions"; for instance, the motorway that China had constructed in the western section of the border cut through Indian territory. He also denied that India had intervened in China's internal affairs with respect to Tibet.[25]

Zhou delineated China's stance at the second meeting with Nehru. He said that China and India, as two old countries, had not demarcated the

21.1 Zhou Enlai and Indian prime minister Nehru in New Delhi, April 1960.
Everett Collection Historical / Alamy Stock Photo

boundaries between them as was commonplace among modern states, but that "traditional customary lines" had existed between them. The McMahon Line along the eastern section of the border was a relic of British imperialism. Historically, areas south of the Line, known as Zangnan or southern Tibet, were administered by the Tibetan government, but this was unilaterally changed by the Indians after 1949. Although the Chinese government had never recognized the McMahon Line, Zhou stressed, it had supported maintenance of the status quo there and adopted a realistic approach toward resolving the problem. Aksai Chin, on the western side of the border, had always been under China's control and was never controlled by India, and "China's maps had long included the region within its boundaries," while "India's maps had undergone many changes." India's territory claims there were for him a surprise. Zhou proposed that before they reached a formal settlement on the border, the two countries should maintain the status quo and keep their respective military units separate to avoid conflict.[26]

Zhou and Nehru debated back and forth during the third, fourth, and fifth meetings, with each leader reiterating his perspectives; it was exceedingly difficult for them to find common ground for a compromise. Zhou found that Nehru rebutted almost every point or proposal he made, or simply ignored them. Nehru even insisted on referring to his meetings with Zhou as "conversations" rather than "negotiations."[27] Zhou did not want the meetings to end in a state of such stark disagreement. At the sixth meeting, he proposed that the two sides establish a joint committee to identify their disputes, and that they maintain the LAC until the boundary was demarcated. Zhou also suggested that the two sides issue a joint communiqué announcing that their "meetings had made progress." Reluctantly, Nehru agreed.[28]

Zhou and Nehru held their seventh and last meeting on April 25. They found that they could not even agree on the content and wording of the joint communiqué. Did they agree on the location of their shared border? Was there a Line of Actual Control? Had the two sides achieved any progress apart from procedural business? They ultimately issued a brief communiqué, which expressed that there were differences between them, and that the talks would continue.[29]

Zhou's trip to India had failed. He had never felt so powerless. He realized that the border disputes were far more complicated than he had perceived. Moreover, his intuition told him that the optimal moment for resolving the border dispute with India was likely gone forever. On several later occasions, he said that Nehru was the "most arrogant" person and the person "most difficult to deal with" he had encountered in his career.[30] Zhou even said in a conversation with the Soviet ambassador to China that "Nehru was shameless, . . . and had devolved into an imperialist running dog."[31] Nehru also felt deeply disappointed, as he believed that Zhou had "betrayed" his trust and support. Later, when Han Suyin, who had maintained a friendship with both Zhou and Nehru, conveyed the former's "friendly message" to the latter, Nehru replied, "I've had enough of Zhou's friendship."[32] Zhou and Nehru had completely lost confidence in each other.

• • •

Meanwhile, Beijing's relations with Moscow also showed new signs of tension. In June 1959, Moscow announced that it would suspend the implementation of its agreement with China to cooperate on nuclear energy. Chinese-Soviet relations, which had once been so strong as to be likened to "the sun shining in the sky," were embarking on a path of sharp decline.

In September 1959, Khrushchev visited the United States and met with President Eisenhower at Camp David. He then flew directly to Beijing, where he attended the PRC's tenth anniversary celebrations. On the evening of September 30, he delivered a speech at the state dinner hosted by Mao, in which he boasted about the "Camp David spirit" of the Soviet-American summit, which he claimed would bring about a détente in East-West relations. Mao was unconvinced. When Khrushchev mentioned that "it is unwise to try to use force to test the stability of capitalism," Mao felt that Khrushchev was ridiculing China and him personally. The chairman immediately decided not to speak at the banquet, letting Zhou do so instead.[33]

Khrushchev and Mao met formally on October 2. Each leader brought with him a group of his own comrades. Zhou was among the Chinese contingent at the meeting, which, in theory, offered a good opportunity for him to help the Chinese and Soviet leaders bridge the chasm between them. However, the meeting went in the other direction and quickly broke down into a heated quarrel.

Khrushchev said at the beginning of the meeting that he had learned from the Americans that China had detained five US citizens. He told Mao, "For the sake of adopting a nonprovocative policy, . . . it is better to release them." "Release them?" Mao replied. "Yes, eventually we will release them, but we will not grant the Americans' request." Zhou explained that China had long since released all its prisoners of war in Korea, and that of the five Americans, three were "spies disguised as priests" and two were CIA agents who had been caught after their plane was shot down over China.

The discussion then turned to Taiwan. Khrushchev accused the Chinese of committing "adventurist mistakes" and asked why Beijing was unwilling to ease tensions in the Taiwan Strait. Mao rebutted Khrushchev's assertions, emphasizing that China did not want to fight a war with America, but that "we cannot, as the Americans want, state that we will not use force in the Taiwan area." Zhou intervened, saying that "the only way to improve our relations with the United States is for them to withdraw their troops from Taiwan. The relations between Taiwan and the mainland are China's internal affairs. How we may liberate Taiwan, in peaceful or military ways, is an issue in which no one may intervene."

Khrushchev pivoted to Sino-Indian relations. He blamed China for "killing Indians on the border" and asked, "Why do you want to compete for such a small piece of territory? It is such barren land, lying below the

Himalayas." Zhou launched into a battle of words with Khrushchev: "They attacked us first. What were we to do? Should we have only fired into the sky?" Khrushchev replied, "I have fought in a war. I do not know who opened fire first. I only know that no Chinese was killed, and the Indians were shot to death." Zhou ridiculed Khrushchev for "lacking the ability to tell right from wrong." Chen Yi echoed Zhou, exclaiming, "Your compromising attitude toward Nehru is a serious political mistake!" Enraged, Khrushchev shouted, "The Soviet Union has existed for forty-two years, and we have not compromised with anyone!"

Seeing that the quarrel was getting out of control, Zhou tried to lower the temperature, saying that "there might be disputes and unresolved issues between us, but publicly we always emphasize our solidarity with the Soviet Union."[34] Nonetheless, the meeting ended discouragingly.

Zhou did not want to see Beijing's relations with Moscow deteriorate further. All CCP leaders who attended an October 4 Politburo meeting called by Mao to discuss Sino-Soviet relations lambasted Khrushchev. Zhou criticized Khrushchev, too, but he also pointed out that despite Beijing's differences with Moscow, it was better to prevent the gulf between the two countries from widening. "We should not argue with them now, and should be patient," Zhou said. "We may wait to let the objective facts and the development of history educate them." The meeting decided that, in dealing with Moscow, "we still should adopt a policy emphasizing unity and avoiding disputes."[35]

Khrushchev was not an easygoing person, however. He delivered a speech at Vladivostok on his way back to Moscow, in which, after he praised Moscow's "fraternal solidarity" with Beijing, he claimed that it was unwise for one to "desire war like a rooster itching for a fight." Mao was genuinely offended, as he believed that Khrushchev was implicitly attacking him and China's policies toward the United States.[36] In January 1960, Mao claimed at a Politburo meeting in Shanghai that Khrushchev was a revisionist, and that the Soviet Union might go down the path of revisionism.[37]

In fact, the root cause of the Sino-Soviet rift lay in Beijing's and Moscow's respective definitions of their status in the international Communist movement. April 1960 marked the ninetieth anniversary of Lenin's birth. Mao and the CCP leadership decided to use the occasion to publish several lengthy essays highlighting the "correct perspectives" of Mao and the CCP on such subjects as imperialism, peace and war, and proletarian revolution, while criticizing (though not by name) the "modern revisionist" views held by

Khrushchev and the Soviet leadership. The essays were translated into Russian, English, German, French, Japanese, and many other languages, and widely circulated. Deeply insulted, Khrushchev and the Soviet leadership labeled Mao and the CCP as "dogmatists" and "factionalists."[38]

Within this context, at a June 1960 "gathering of fraternal parties" in Bucharest, Romania, the Soviets and representatives from multiple other parties scolded members of the CCP delegation led by Peng Zhen. Khrushchev and Peng even got into a public argument.[39] Peng then received from Beijing a set of detailed instructions drafted by Zhou, who, while instructing Peng to "firmly struggle with Khrushchev," advised him to pay attention to the big picture and still sign the communiqué for the gathering. After he received the telegram, Peng commented, "Only Zhou could author such a clear and comprehensive text. He has considered all the details for us."[40]

After the confrontation in Bucharest, Mao decided to further alert party cadres to the differences between the Chinese and Soviets, as well as the historical origins of their disjuncture. He asked Zhou to take the lead on this matter. Zhou delivered a lengthy report on the Comintern and CCP-Soviet relations at that year's Beidaihe Conference in mid-July.[41] He divided the CCP's relations with the Comintern and the Soviet Union into five periods, stating that Moscow was "good on the two ends but bad in the middle." The Soviets had greatly aided the Chinese revolution, he said, but had also made such mistakes as interfering with the CCP's internal affairs. At the Tehran Conference, Zhou noted, Stalin accepted that all of China, except for the Northeast, was under the American and British spheres of influence. After World War II, Stalin "used tough language to order us to negotiate with Chiang Kai-shek." During China's civil war, "he did not believe that we could win." Stalin's reception of Mao had been "very cold" when the chairman visited Moscow in late 1949 and early 1950. Prior to China's entering the Korean War, he "agreed to provide us with air support and then reneged." However, Zhou stressed, "Stalin was willing to criticize himself": for example, in summer 1949, when Liu visited Moscow, Stalin "implicitly acknowledged his mistakes toward China." His attitude changed with China's joining the Korean War, when Stalin "recognized," Zhou asserted, "that China was not a 'half-Tito,' but genuinely Communist" and committed major Soviet aid to China. After Stalin's death, Soviet leaders "wanted to end the Korean War quickly," revealing that they were "very much afraid of the Americans." At home, Khrushchev "put all power in his own hands, while boasting about himself abroad." Since 1958, "he has tried to control us," treating China as the "yellow peril." Toward the end of the report, Zhou stressed that although China's struggles with Khrushchev would be "long and complex," the CCP should not "struggle for a split" but strive "for unity."[42]

Apparently, Zhou did not want relations with the Soviet Union to break down any further. On July 16, however, Moscow decided to recall all Soviet experts in China while significantly reducing military and other forms of support to Beijing.[43] Zhou was surprised. With this move, Khrushchev meant to deal Mao and the Chinese leadership a serious blow at a time when the Great Leap Forward was wreaking economic and social havoc in China. Mao angrily criticized the "sudden attack" by Khrushchev, whom he called "untrustworthy." On July 31, Zhou spoke again at Beidaihe at Mao's request, accusing the Soviets of "pressuring us" by recalling their experts from China. "We must defend our honor and repay all the debts we owe them," he stressed.[44]

Meanwhile, Zhou still attempted, albeit unsuccessfully, to persuade Moscow to allow some experts to stay in China. On August 16, he hosted a farewell banquet for the departing Soviet experts, where he thanked them for their "enormous contributions" to China's reconstruction. "We are separated," he said, "but I believe that the friendship of our two peoples and two countries will be eternal."[45]

From Mao's perspective, the decision by Khrushchev and the Soviet leadership to recall all Soviet experts was not necessarily a bad thing. In fact, even though no one said as much, many within the party leadership knew that Mao was ultimately responsible for the disastrous failure of the Great Leap, which challenged the myth of his "eternal correctness" and his indisputable power and authority. Moscow's recall of all Soviet experts from the country provided Mao with a timely excuse to claim that all of China's difficulties stemmed from Moscow's betrayal. By simultaneously criticizing "Soviet great power chauvinism," Mao took up an even stronger position from which to dominate the CCP's mainstream political narrative with his discourse of "continuous revolution." No CCP leader, Zhou included, was able to challenge such a Maoist endeavor.

• • •

Mao, Zhou, and their comrades still faced daunting domestic challenges. Despite the fanfare heralding the "continuing leap forward," steel output decreased dramatically. The situation in the countryside was worse. There were signs that even basic production was in jeopardy there, to say nothing of a "Great Leap Forward." Throughout the spring, CCP leaders received reports warning of extreme food shortages in cities—a foreboding development that they still dismissed as a temporary phenomenon. An April 12 Party Center document read, "Now, we are about fifty days away from the entry of fresh grain into the market. This is a crucial period for grain extraction, transportation, and sales, while ensuring people's livelihood."[46] However, after mid-May, grain extraction did not pick up, and food supplies in cities continuously dwindled. As June neared, grain supplies in Beijing, Shanghai, Tianjin, and a dozen industrial cities in Liaoning Province had been almost completely exhausted, sending alarm bells ringing on a nearly daily basis. Reports of severe food shortages poured into Zhongnanhai. Interestingly, Mao's attitude toward Zhou's economic decision-making began to change subtly.

At a week-long enlarged Politburo meeting in Shanghai beginning on June 8, Mao's tone had shifted compared with the preceding months or even weeks. Rather than sing the praises of the Great Leap, he included some "self-criticism" in his speech at the opening session of the conference: "The time of our reconstruction is still quite short. Our experience is insufficient. . . . We should not cover up our mistakes, but should summarize our experiences, so that we can adjust our direction in a timely manner."[47] Two days before the meeting ended, Mao directly mentioned Zhou. Pointing to the premier, he said, "I like the speech you made at the CCP's Eighth Congress. It has given us much maneuvering space."[48] Then, Mao wrote a piece titled "Ten Year Summary," which was distributed at the conference on its last day. In addition to acknowledging that "I myself have committed many mistakes," Mao praised Zhou, "Most goals, such as steel output, set in the Second Five-Year Plan under the direction of Comrade Zhou Enlai have left us with the space of three more years. How good it is!"[49]

Here, Mao was obviously talking about Zhou's "opposing rash advance" endeavor in 1956–1957. As conditions had changed since then, Mao now viewed Zhou's former "wrongdoings" as a positive contribution. But he was not rehabilitating Zhou; the chairman simply aimed to delegate the responsibility of remedying the Great Leap crisis to others at a time that he found himself in political trouble. Superficially, Mao's words improved Zhou's political environment, giving him greater freedom to operate. In reality, however, Mao merely passed two hot potatoes—boosting steel production and resolving the grain crisis—to Zhou.

At the meeting, Mao asked Zhou to "talk about the situation of agriculture," although Zhou had never overseen agriculture. The chairman urged him "to reclaim the initiative in one go." Zhou declared that "the general situation is very good," but then discussed how aggressive goals had led to serious consequences for agriculture. Indeed, he said, "we now will not only lose the initiative but also face the danger of the plans for 1962 failing." Echoing Mao's instruction to "reclaim the initiative in one go," Zhou proposed to significantly lower production goals for grain, cotton, and meat (but not steel). Only by doing so, he stressed, would "it be possible for us to reclaim the initiative."[50]

With the partial restoration of Zhou's economic decision-making power, the financial and economic leading group halted its activities. Yet Zhou was at once facing two major challenges: to guarantee steel production and to secure supplies of grain. He knew that the former remained an absolute priority for Mao, and the latter was only of secondary importance. At the time, many cities were experiencing a dramatic decrease in food supplies even after the summer harvest. On July 13, Vice Premier Li Xiannian reported to Zhou that food supplies in Beijing and Tianjin would run out in four days, in Shanghai in two days, and in Liaoning in six. "Everything should give way to grain transportation," Li stressed, which should be "the number one task."[51]

But Zhou could not act on this matter without Mao's support. On July 25, Li wrote Mao directly, reporting the "dangerous situation" of food supplies in Beijing, Shanghai, Tianjin, and industrial cities in Liaoning, which would be exhausted in a matter of days.[52] However, Mao was still constrained by his statement that "everything else can be slowed, but not steel production."[53] Rather than address the root causes of the grain shortage, the CCP leadership responded to Li's serious warnings by emphasizing increased extraction of grain from the countryside. On August 10, the Party Center issued two instructions. One called on the whole party to strengthen foreign trade and promote agricultural production, while the other highlighted the "protection of grain and steel production."[54] However, as the instructions simultaneously emphasized both grain and steel production, in practice concern for steel production overwhelmed that for grain production, and steel thus became the top priority. This was made most evident in another central instruction issued on August 15, which ordered provincial leaders to do their utmost to guarantee the "execution of grain transportation and supply (in cities) in August and the ensuing months."[55]

. . .

In early September, Zhou received the draft economic plans for 1961 prepared by the National Planning Commission. He worked with Li Fuchun to decide on measures "to rectify, substantiate, consolidate, and upgrade" the Chinese economy.[56] However, these measures had nothing to do with controlling steel production, which remained a heavy burden on Zhou's shoulders. To "protect steel production," Zhou had to call many meetings and repeatedly emphasize that every effort should be made "to fulfill the task of producing eighteen million tons of steel in 1960." To accomplish this, it was necessary to protect supplies of food to industrial cities; thus, more grain had to be extracted from the countryside. Zhou called leaders of every province almost every day, urging them to meet their grain supply quotas.[57] When grain extraction in most provinces failed to pick up after the autumn harvest, the central leadership repeatedly pressed provincial leaders for more grain.[58] Consequently, the flames of the Great Famine consumed an even wider swath of China's vast land.

Zhou found the statistics he received in the process of coordinating food distribution throughout the country to be inaccurate and confusing. Although the Ministry of Food estimated that "the whole country's grain output would be around 140 million tons," the sum of the numbers provided by various provinces far surpassed that figure. It was difficult for the Ministry of Food and many provinces to agree on what the exact volume of grain output was. After discussing the discrepancy with all parties involved, Zhou decided that, "with respect to agricultural production, each department or province may come up with its own estimate. However, the national plan for grain purchasing and consumption must be based on numbers provided by the Ministry of Food."[59] By doing so, Zhou was trying to limit further damage caused by widespread false reporting.

The "Xinyang incident" now occurred. On October 21, four cadres at the Central Personnel Department and Censorship Committee submitted a detailed report to the Party Center, revealing that large numbers of people in the Xinyang District of Henan Province had died of starvation, and that rampant corruption existed among cadres there.[60] Three days later, Li

Fuchen conveyed the report to Mao, who delegated the matter to Liu and Zhou.[61] They soon confirmed that the four cadres' allegations were generally true.

The famine and high death toll in Xinyang were deeply tragic. However, the cadres who exposed it unintentionally did Zhou a big favor, allowing him to make comments that he otherwise would not have dared to utter. On October 29, Zhou told a Politburo meeting that "a famine as enormous as this one has not happened in the eleven-year history of our country. For a person of my age, we have not heard of a famine on this dramatic scale."[62] On November 3, with Mao's approval, the Party Center issued an instruction to correct "the mistakes of Communist egalitarianism" and allow the peasants to keep small parcels of reserved land and produce foods for their own households.[63] In his revisions to an urgent directive on the behalf of the Party Center, Zhou called for "including people with different opinions" in the implementation of the instruction.[64]

It became clearer as December approached that importing large amounts of grain from foreign countries would be necessary to mitigate the colossal disaster that was the Great Famine. But this was an unspeakable truth. In addition to exhausting China's limited foreign currency reserves, importing grain would be a tacit admission that the Great Leap Forward and people's communes had totally failed. Both Chen Yun and Zhou supported immediately importing grain, but they knew that this was a decision only Mao could make. Finally, at a central work conference on December 30, Mao told Chen that he endorsed Chen's proposal to import grain. He also asked Zhou and Chen to handle the details.[65] At that moment, Zhou was at Beijing Airport for a long-planned trip to Burma for the signing of the Chinese-Burmese border treaty. Learning of Mao's decision, Zhou called for a meeting at the airport with Chen and Ye Jizhuang, the minister of foreign trade, at which they decided to authorize the immediate import of 1.5 million tons of grain. A few hours later, Zhou had another phone meeting with Chen Yun and others in Beijing when he stopped in Kunming on his way to Burma, in which they agreed to increase the amount of grain to be imported to 2.5 million tons.[66]

The first thing Zhou did once he arrived in Yangon was to dispatch Lei Renmin, deputy minister of foreign trade, to Hong Kong to investigate channels and methods for importing, transporting, and paying for the grain. On January 8, 1961, Zhou heard back from Lei that grain supplies on the international market were "rich and sufficient," and that transportation and payment could be resolved "by leasing foreign ships and using the method of payment upon delivery" guaranteed by the Bank of China's Hong Kong branch.[67]

After he returned to Beijing, Zhou learned from Ye Jizhuang, Lei Renmin, and other Foreign Trade Ministry officials that on the international market, "one ton of rice is worth at least one and a half tons of wheat." He immediately decided to use the price differential to export rice while importing wheat. Consequently, although China later purchased one and half times more wheat than the rice it sold, it nearly broke even on the two transactions.[68] The first shipload of grain was delivered at the Port of Tianjin less than two months later. In 1960, China imported a total value of US$33.87 million of grain and cooking oil. The country's imports of the two commodities increased dramatically in 1961, rising to a value of US$517.7 million.[69] The imported grain greatly relieved the serious food shortage in China; otherwise, the effects of the Great Famine would have been even more devastating.

Meanwhile, Zhou also made a dubious decision. Reportedly, when he discovered that there were large numbers of "abnormal deaths" throughout the country, he ordered that the information be kept strictly confidential, and that related documents and statistics be destroyed.[70]

• • •

As 1961 began, Zhou and his colleagues in the Chinese leadership were in a dark and dismal place. They all knew that the Great Leap had been catastrophic, plunging Chinese society and the Chinese economy into the abyss. Mao, hiding in the shadows, let Liu and Deng handle the crisis. Zhou was pushed to the forefront, where he acted like the head of a fire brigade.

The Central Committee held its Ninth Plenum in January. Zhou began his presentation by stating that "the achievements of the past three years have been great—indeed, a leap forward at a very high speed." He then carefully described the daunting challenges of 1961. The serious drop in grain output "has compelled us to import grain as a temporary measure that must be carried out over the next three years." With respect to planning, Zhou suggested, "there should be leeway in production numbers and the correction of numbers should be allowed when mistakes are discovered." Zhou said that 1961 would become a "year of adjustment," and that "when leaping forward is no easy matter, making adjustments is even more difficult. This year will be another year of hard work."[71] After the plenum concluded, Zhou repeatedly spoke on the importance and the necessity of making "adjustments."[72] At a central work conference in March, Zhou favored fixing quotas of peasants' grain sales to the state in advance on an annual basis while allowing them to keep surplus grain for themselves. This way, Zhou contended, the peasants' incentive to produce grain would be stimulated. The conference decided to increase the yearly amount of imported grain to five million tons.[73]

Meanwhile, at Zhou's urging, the Party Center decided to close tens of thousands of factories and discontinue hundreds of large construction projects. Thus, more than twenty million urbanites would be resettled in the countryside. At one point, Zhou was greatly concerned that this resettlement, if improperly managed, could engulf Chinese society in a wave of turmoil.[74] Yet no such chaos came about. Within a few months, Zhou's push to adjust rural policies, along with the large-scale grain importation and evacuation of urban citizens, significantly reduced the prospect of a much larger famine.

When Zhou, as well as Liu, Deng, and other first-line leaders, strove to save China from disaster, Mao did not interfere with their efforts. However, he remained unwilling to recognize that the Great Leap had utterly failed. At a central work conference in May, Liu said that the disaster was caused "30 percent by natural causes and 70 percent by human error."[75] Mao stayed silent. At another conference in Lushan that August, Zhou repeatedly underscored the difficulties that China faced. Rather than challenge him, Mao commented that "the mistakes are just a few, which should not be overemphasized," and that "now we have reached the low ebb, and the situation will surely improve day by day."[76] Mao made these alarming statements for all the leaders on the first line—especially Liu, Zhou, and Deng—to hear.

* * *

The structure of China's foreign trade underwent profound changes in the wake of Moscow's recall of all Soviet experts in 1960 and China's mass importation of Western grain. At the Beidaihe Conference in August 1960, the Party Center decided to establish a three-person "foreign trade command" composed of Zhou, Li Fuchun, and Li Xiannian, led by Zhou. Zhou made an extremely important proposal: China should shift the emphasis of its foreign trade from the Soviet Union and the Soviet bloc to Western capitalist countries and Japan.[77]

Zhou wasted no time in implementing the proposal. That same month, he introduced "three political principles" and "three trade principles" for promoting China's stagnant trade relations with Japan. He stipulated that the Japanese government should cease its hostility toward China, not involve itself in the conspiracy to create two Chinas, and not obstruct the development and normalization of Chinese-Japanese relations. Meanwhile, he made it clear that Beijing would endorse China's trade with Japan in the form of government agreements, private contracts, and other special arrangements.[78] These new measures quickly revived Chinese-Japanese trade relations. Under Zhou's direction, similar measures were adopted to pave the way for China to develop trade relations with such Western capitalist countries as the United Kingdom, France, West Germany, Canada, and Australia.

Under Zhou's management, Beijing's Taiwan policy experienced major changes in 1960 following the crisis of 1958. At a Politburo meeting in May, CCP leaders decided to adopt a new policy line with the understanding that "it is better to put Taiwan in the hands of Chiang and his son than to allow it to be controlled by the Americans." They elaborated that "the liberation of Taiwan cannot be done in a hurry. If not by this generation, it could be done by the next generation once conditions have been gradually created and the right moment has come." They now envisioned that if Taiwan were to be reunified with the motherland, personnel decisions and all military and political power—except for diplomacy, which Beijing would handle—would be solely controlled by Chiang; Taiwan's military, governmental, and economic budgets, if strained, would be subsidized by the central government; Taiwan's social reformation would be postponed until conditions had become more suitable and only with Chiang's endorsement; and the two sides would agree not to dispatch special agents to the other side, and not to sabotage each other's internal unity and order. These were known as the "four concrete measures." Later, when Zhou tried to convey these measures to Chen Cheng, Taiwan's vice president, he added that if Taiwan were to return to the motherland, the central government would "properly deal with all issues by respecting the opinions" of Chiang and Chen Cheng. Zhou named this the "one major principle."[79]

Zhou knew that Chiang had a deep sentimental attachment to the village of his birth. In 1961, he instructed that photos of Chiang's family houses in

Fenghua, including the tombs of Chiang's ancestors, be taken and, through indirect channels, sent to Chiang. "The Chiang family tombs in Fenghua remain intact, and the flowers and grass there are as usual," Zhou inscribed on the back of one photo.[80]

* * *

As the year 1962 arrived, it was still winter in Beijing; however, the air of early spring could be felt in China's political life. From January 11 to February 7, the Party Center convened a large work conference in Beijing attended by seven thousand cadres at the central, provincial, and local levels. Thus, the event was also known as the "Seven Thousand Cadres Conference." According to Mao's plans, the conference's main theme was opposition to separatism. He hoped to unify thought throughout the entire party at a very difficult time.

The disastrous consequences of the Great Leap, however, were too big to be ignored. At the conference, some participants questioned—explicitly and implicitly—the Party Center's strategies and policies in previous years, while the majority either kept silent or offered only unsubstantial statements. Mao took note of all this. Sounding more sincere than ever before, he proposed that it was necessary for everyone to "unleash their anger and frustration." "We hold this conference in Beijing to solve problems," he said. "Now, we see that some comrades have been reluctant to candidly share their opinions. This is not good." He even acknowledged that "for the mistakes committed by the [Party] Center, I am directly or indirectly responsible." Unintentionally, though, Mao revealed his true purpose when he said, "Without allowing frustration to be released, there will be no unity; and without democracy, there will be no centralization." Ultimately, Mao's goal was still to strengthen "unity and centralization" within the party.[81] When he used such language to invite critique, he hinted at his next move.

Liu had played a leading role in the first line of China's central decision-making since late 1959. He believed that difficulties stemming from the Great Leap Forward were "30 percent" the result of "natural disasters" and "70 percent" caused by "human mistakes."[82] He maintained this position at the conference, claiming that "for the peasants," their suffering was "30 percent [the result of] natural disasters and 70 percent [that of] human mistakes. If we deny it, they will not be convinced."[83] Peng Zhen, the mayor of Beijing, had long been a close follower of Mao. At the conference, he noted that "it is impossible for Mao not to commit mistakes." Yet, he said, Mao's "reputation and credibility are like the Himalayas," while "his mistakes are like a few tons of earth, . . . only one percent or tenth of one percent of his achievements." Still, he asserted, these mistakes should be "examined and criticized." To do otherwise, Peng continued, "will leave a very bad impact on our party."[84] Although Peng was careful in making these comments, he suggested that Mao had also made mistakes and could thus be criticized.

Zhou was much more cautious and shrewder than Peng. At the conference, Lin Biao exaggeratedly hailed Mao's greatness, attributing the origins of the disaster China then found itself in to a "failure to follow Mao Thought." Zhou did almost the same. He knew Mao too well, and he still vividly remembered how Mao had ruthlessly attacked him for "opposing rash advance." He certainly had also noted Mao's comments about unity and centralism. Hence, he was determined not to utter a single word of discontent about Mao. When Peng commented that Mao also had committed mistakes, Zhou immediately replied, "It is we, not the chairman, who should take responsibility" for the fallout from the Great Leap.[85] Like Lin, Zhou also defended Mao in his speech. Yet unlike Lin, Zhou emphasized his own responsibility for the mistakes. He stressed that

> Chairman Mao should not take responsibility [for the mistakes]. If we had adhered to his thought and the three red flags, our achievements would be much greater. . . . The chairman has long recognized the problems. It is we who have made the mistakes. And the chairman alone was not in a position to stop us. Now, the whole party should unite wholeheartedly in an enhanced and more centralized way, listening to the helmsman and to the Party Center, and the center should listen to Chairman Mao. . . . Otherwise, we cannot move forward by a single inch.[86]

Viewed through the lens of the CCP's intraparty struggles, Zhou's way of handling this matter demonstrated exceptional political wisdom. As later developments showed, Mao remembered everyone who had criticized him at the conference. At the beginning of the Cultural Revolution, he described Liu Shaoqi's behavior then as "the rightist leaning of 1962." Peng had long been a Maoist. However, after the Seven Thousand Cadres Conference, Mao suspected that Peng was no longer loyal to him. In the Cultural Revolution, Peng became one of the first top CCP leaders to be purged; but Zhou would not face Mao's wrath.

* * *

Mao left Beijing after the Seven Thousand Cadres Conference. Liu and Deng wanted to continue to promote the conference's theme in the areas of strategy and policymaking. Liu called an enlarged meeting of the Politburo Standing Committee a few weeks later. As the meeting was held at the Xilou Building in Zhongnanhai, it was also called the "Xilou Conference." The main actors at the Xilou Conference were Liu and Chen Yun. During the discussion on economic difficulties, Chen highlighted the serious decline in agricultural production, excessive investment in infrastructure, high inflation, widespread speculation, and the dramatic decrease in living standards for city dwellers.[87] Chen's speech was warmly received. Liu told him, "I firmly support you."[88] Liu also made several bold and harsh comments. He believed that the Seven Thousand Cadres Conference "had failed to thoroughly explore the difficulties or to expose the problems," emphasizing that "it is not a normal time now, . . . so we cannot use normal methods, but have to adopt abnormal ones to thoroughly implement economic adjustments."[89]

Zhou echoed Chen and Liu, but he focused his presentations on potential ways to resolve the practical problems facing the country. He stated that "the financial difficulties now are very serious, and some of the difficulties we have not even seen before. . . . We need a period of recovery in the next decade."[90] Yet Zhou was still unsure about Mao's intentions, not knowing if the chairman would stay on the second line or return to the first.

* * *

The spring breeze also reached China's foreign service on the heels of the Seven Thousand Cadres Conference. On February 20, Wang Jiaxiang, head of the Central Liaison Department, wrote an "intraparty communication" to Zhou, Deng, and Chen Yi, with four suggestions: first, to issue a statement to "comprehensively describe and confirm that Chinese foreign policy favors peace"; second, to carry out a policy of détente, rather than one of exacerbating tensions, in order to avoid encountering enemies from all directions; third, in international struggles, to give emphasis to tactics, combining marching forward with retreating, offense with defense, and struggles with compromises; and fourth, not to give foreign aid "beyond our own capacity."[91]

Zhou made no comments to Wang's proposal when he received it. Deng handled the matter and conveyed the proposal to Liu and Peng Zhen, who took no action either. Earlier, Deng had received another report from Wang, which Deng had submitted to Mao for his opinion. The chairman responded by asking Deng to "discuss it first, and let me know of your preliminary opinions." Mao said that he was "still considering the issue" and was therefore "not in a position to make comments."[92] Mao's response implied that he did not agree with Wang's suggestions. Six months later, when the trajectory of Chinese politics swung dramatically leftward, Wang became the subject of severe criticism.

• • •

After the Xilou Conference, the Party Center decided to revive the central financial and economic leading group. Zhou named Chen Yun to lead it, but Chen said that for health reasons he should serve only as a member of the group. Li Fuchun thus was tapped to head the group, and Zhou would also join it as a member.[93] When the group met in March, Chen reiterated the need to adjust the budget and plan for 1962 by substantially cutting spending on heavy industry and infrastructure construction.[94] Zhou supported Chen, saying that "generally speaking, the most difficult time has passed," but, echoing Liu, he emphasized that "the financial and economic difficulties we now face remain quite serious, and there are also difficulties we have not encountered or expected." He thus proposed to "change the emphasis of economic planning from industry and transportation to agriculture and the market" while arranging production by "following the most urgent needs of the present time" and "pursuing comprehensive balancing from now on." Therefore, he stressed, "the scale of infrastructure construction should be further reduced, and investments should be further cut."[95]

Chen left Beijing the second day after the meeting to take medical leave in Hangzhou. At another Politburo Standing Committee meeting, Liu again proposed to name Chen to head the finance and economic group. Chen again turned the position down, which Liu, Zhou, and Deng brought to Mao's attention. The chairman decided to make Chen the group head, and Li Fuchun and Li Xiannian the deputy heads, while Zhou remained a member. Chen did not return to Beijing until late June. Why was he so reluctant to assume the role of group leader? Was he, like Zhou, also carefully observing Mao's moves?

22

THE CHAIRMAN RETURNS

1962–1963

The CCP leaders' moment of critical reflection in early 1962 and the flexible policies introduced by Liu, Zhou, and Deng were short lived. With the arrival of summer in Beijing, another chilly current permeated China's political atmosphere. Mao was returning to center stage in high politics.

There had been signs pointing to the chairman's coming back. He remembered the Seven Thousand Cadres Conference in a very negative light. After he returned to Beijing on April 9, Mao mentioned at a Supreme State Council meeting that differences of opinion existed among the party leadership about the "three red flags"—the Great Leap Forward, the people's communes, and the party's general line for building socialism. "Were they wrong or right?" he asked.[1] This was Mao's warning signal to other leaders, including Zhou.

In early spring, Mao had sent his secretary Tian Jiaying to Hunan to "conduct an investigation." Tian found that production increased significantly when land was distributed among local peasants and output was linked with each household's income. When he reported the results of his investigation to Mao, Liu Shaoqi, and Chen Yun, Liu and Chen were excited, but Mao was indifferent.[2] Tian personally briefed Mao, then in Shanghai, saying that even the peasants in Shaoshan, the chairman's home village, favored "household responsibility or evenly dividing land among households." The chairman, with a "cold face," told Tian, "To follow the mass line does not mean we should always listen to the masses. As regards linking output with household income, we should not listen to them."[3]

Zhou was watching attentively. He found that Chen Yun also supported the household responsibility option.[4] But Chen, a cautious person, was unwilling to speak publicly on this sensitive issue. Nor did Zhou openly voice his opinion; instead, he inquired with Tian, asking him "whether it is okay to give more space to private endeavors in the countryside."[5] Zhou was seeking to gauge Mao's views on the matter.

Tian was Mao's envoy. As the chairman had made clear his opposition to allowing more private initiatives, Tian should not have taken any further action. But he was an idealist, and he had received implicit and explicit support from Liu, Chen, and Zhou to continue his exploration of private enterprise in rural areas. During his next trip to Hunan, in addition to carrying out a "good investigation," he sent two of his own associates to Anhui to assess private initiatives there, with the hope of collecting "more cohesive data about the overall situation." Finally, Tian concluded that linking output with household income was a good way to boost agricultural production.[6] In late June, he reported his findings to Liu and Deng in Beijing, both of whom supported him. Deng made his famous comment, "Black cat or yellow cat, so long as it catches mice, it is a good cat." Liu told Tian to convey his assessment to Mao.[7] It is unclear whether Tian also spoke with Zhou. When Chen expressed to Zhou his opinion that redistributing land to individual households was worth trying as a means to stimulate peasants' productivity, Zhou agreed.[8]

Mao did not sit idly by. In the previous two months, he had traveled to southern China to gather information about the summer harvest there, returning to Beijing on June 6.[9] When Chen proposed to him that the "redistribution of land should be adopted to stimulate production," the chairman became "extremely upset," although he did not immediately rebuke Chen.[10] Tian also strongly recommended the "household responsibility" option to Mao. The land redistribution policy was only "a temporary measure," Tian explained, "and the peasants will be redirected to collective farming after production recovers." Mao pushed Tian to answer two questions: "Do you support a collective or private economy?" and "Is this your personal opinion, or is this the opinion of others?"[11]

Mao met with Liu, Zhou, Chen Boda, and Tian two days later. He began by discussing the summer harvest in Henan and Shandong, claiming that "the situation there is not so bad." Then, he made clear his firm opposition to "linking output with household income." He spoke very harshly to Tian, accusing him of having served as a "main advocate" of the wrong idea to redistribute land among peasants.[12]

Zhou remembered every one of Mao's words. One year later, he recalled in a speech, "Last July, when we all were worried that the situation was too difficult to be saved, the chairman went to two of the worst-hit provinces, Henan and Shandong. . . . After he returned to Beijing, he told us that the situation [in the two provinces] was not so bad."[13] Chen Yun quickly got cold feet, leaving Beijing on July 15 to go on "vacation" in Beidaihe. He wrote Mao two weeks later, asserting that he fully supported "consolidating a collective economy in the countryside." He then asked for sick leave, which Mao immediately approved.[14]

Liu's response was different. In early July, he encountered Mao at the Zhongnanhai swimming pool. When Liu greeted Mao, the chairman scolded him in a stern voice, asking, "Why have you been in such a hurry? Why have you failed to resist the pressure? Why did you paint such an utterly dark picture of the situation?" Liu lost control of his temper and rebutted Mao: "So many people have starved to death. Your name and mine will be recorded in history. People have been eating people. This will be recorded in history!" Enraged, Mao raised his voice and retorted, "The Three Red Flags have been dropped. Land has been redistributed. If you cannot resist the pressure, what will happen after I die?" Liu calmed down and stopped arguing with Mao.[15] However, the episode cast a dark shadow over Mao and Liu's already troubled relations. At the time of the encounter, Mao was probably determined to eventually remove Liu.

Throughout July, Mao continued to criticize decollectivization, making it a major issue that concerned "favoring socialism or capitalism."[16] On July 18, he talked with Yang Shangkun, chief of the Central Administrative Office, about "whether collective or private farming should be pursued." Mao mentioned Zhou, saying that he was unhappy with the State Planning Commission and Ministry of Commerce led by the premier. Feeling that Mao's criticism of Zhou was a "very serious matter," at 9:00 P.M. that evening, Yang relayed to Zhou "the chairman's points" about him.[17] Yang's information set alarm bells ringing for Zhou.

CCP leaders gathered again at Beidaihe in late July. Originally, they were supposed to discuss adjusting and consolidating the economy, an agenda for which Zhou had prepared a large packet of documents. However, Mao arrived at Beidaihe with a different objective, to highlight "class and class struggle."

The chairman emphasized the theme on the first day of the conference, announcing that the question of whether the revolution should be "led by the proletariat or the bourgeoisie" was "a common issue at home and abroad." For Mao, this was also a matter of "whether a proletarian dictatorship or capitalist dictatorship should be implemented" or "whether to pursue socialism or capitalism." "This," he warned, "will be a struggle for a very long time. Even after one hundred years, it will still continue."[18]

In a keynote speech on August 6, Mao asked all those attending the conference to contemplate "whether classes still exist in a socialist country." He also inquired, "Is the situation at home one of complete darkness, or are there still some bright spots?" Further, he asked the leaders gathered at the conference, "Do we still want to have collectivization in the countryside?" In a threatening tone, he announced that "some comrades have viewed the situation as one of complete darkness, seeing no light in it at all, which has caused confusion in the minds of others." This phenomenon, he suggested ominously, was "most rampant among top leaders."[19] No one dared to challenge him. Liu knew that he was Mao's target. On August 11, he made self-criticism, acknowledging that his earlier assessment of the situation had been totally wrong.[20]

Zhou missed the first few days of the conference, as he was preoccupied with state diplomatic business in Beijing. When he arrived at Beidaihe, he immediately sensed tension in the air. He spoke out in support of Mao on August 17. The issues that the chairman had highlighted, Zhou said, were "very sharp, very important, and very timely." Class struggles had indeed existed "in different eras, and will exist for a long time, . . . enduring even until the arrival of Communism." Zhou also echoed Mao's analysis of the situation: "Some comrades have talked too much about how difficult the situation is, producing a bad influence within our party. It had been a trying time, but was not a period of complete darkness."[21] Who were the "comrades" Zhou mentioned in his statement? Although he did not name them, he probably understood them to be Liu and himself. Meanwhile, Zhou also tried to defend his reputation. Since early 1962, he stated, the comrades at various central ministries had worked very hard, going all out to fulfill the tasks assigned to them by the Party Center. Their achievements should be recognized, Zhou emphasized.

The Central Committee held its Tenth Plenum in late September. From the outset, tension pervaded the conference hall. In his opening speech,

Mao reiterated these questions: Do classes still exist in a socialist country? Is there class struggle? "Yes," Mao answered. He stressed that "throughout the socialist phase of history, there is the danger of capitalist restoration." Therefore, "class struggle should never be forgotten." From now on, Mao told his comrades, "we should talk [about class and class struggle] every year, every month, and at every party plenum and congress."[22]

Zhou highlighted two points in his remarks, both of which Mao would have very much liked to hear. First, he emphasized that the situation was "better this year than last year, and better last year than the year before last." Second, he recapitulated and voiced his support for Mao's notion of "class struggle": "Chairman Mao, in leading us, has always emphasized the necessity of using the perspective of class struggle to analyze a situation and identify contradictions." This, Zhou stressed, had allowed the whole party to "comprehend the central task, know the direction, mobilize everyone and everything, and get problems solved." Zhou also clarified his attitude toward the household responsibility option. "The chairman has recognized it as a main problem and highlighted the consolidation of a collective economy as the central task in the cause of socialist reconstruction," Zhou asserted.[23]

Mao vociferously attacked the Soviet Union during the plenum's discussion of international issues, claiming that revisionism had taken over in Moscow. Zhou, likely in order to remedy his failure to rebut Wang Jiaxiang's reports early in the year, described the international situation in a rather positive light, announcing that "the truth of Marxism-Leninism and the center of the world revolution have indeed moved from Moscow to Beijing." He highlighted three main tasks for China's participation in class struggle abroad: "To fight against imperialism, to fight against revisionism, and to fight against reactionaries in various countries." "Our confrontation with US imperialism," Zhou elaborated, "is the main contradiction"; China's "direct confrontation with Khrushchev's revisionism in the Soviet Union has entered a new stage"; and the struggle against "reactionary nationalism" had also become intense.[24]

Despite the tense atmosphere at the plenum stemming from the emphasis on "class struggles," Zhou still reminded his comrades that it was crucial not to ignore such matters as the timely reaping of grain and cotton, the construction of irrigation works, the production of coal and wood products, the improvement of commercial networks, and the development of good industrial plans. He also suggested—courageously and, in retrospect, wisely—

that class struggle should not hinder efforts to consolidate the economy. "One lesson of the Lushan Conference of 1959 was that after [the conference], the antirightist struggle expanded to the grassroots level and entangled the masses. This time, when we oppose rightist tendencies, we must also take care to fend off ultraleftist tendencies. We should not make this another mass movement."[25] Not only did Mao not rebut Zhou's statements, he even endorsed Zhou's opinion that "routine work should not be sidelined."[26] The plenum thus adopted several documents prepared by Zhou on adjusting and consolidating China's national economy. But this was not Zhou's victory. Many of the things Zhou urged his colleagues to avoid, such as launching larger political campaigns or purging ordinary cadres and involving the masses, all eventually happened. The Tenth Plenum, which followed Mao's opinions, catalyzed the radical leftward turn in Chinese internal and external policies that presaged the coming of the Cultural Revolution.

• • •

As China's domestic political environment was experiencing huge changes in the spring and summer of 1962, its national security situation also faced an unusual set of challenges, especially to the east and the west.

Zhou saw with much worry that tensions along the Indian border had continued to worsen since the start of the year. After Zhou's visit to India in April 1960, Chinese troops stationed along the borders had tried not to cross or even get close to the Line of Actual Control between the two sides, thus fulfilling Zhou's promise to Nehru and avoiding direct encounters with Indian troops. However, the Indian prime minister misjudged the situation. Beginning in late 1960, he ignored the Indian military's assessment that Indian troops were far from ready for a war and launched a "forward policy" vis-à-vis China. With Nehru's approval, Indian troops advanced on the borders, forcing Chinese garrisons to continuously retreat and pushing the Line of Actual Control toward the Chinese interior.[27] Beijing's protests had no effect.

These developments placed great pressure on the Chinese leadership, especially Zhou, to act. Although Zhou was already extremely disappointed with Nehru in the wake of his failed trip to India in April 1960, he could not have imagined that, in addition to denying the existence of a border dispute, Nehru would launch the "forward policy" and allow Indian troops to aggressively change the status quo of the two countries' borders. Zhou's impression of Nehru became even more negative. "Nehru is arrogant, self-centered, and extremely unreasonable. In these respects, he has surpassed all negotiation counterparts I have ever met," Zhou told his close associate Huang Zhen.[28]

Zhou had long been a wholehearted supporter of settling China's border dispute with India through making mutual concessions based on mutual understanding. However, Nehru's launching of the "forward policy"—and New Delhi's adoption of an upgraded version of the policy in late 1961 in particular—had pushed the Line of Actual Control to deeper into Chinese territory, especially along the western extent of the border. Finally, Zhou found his diplomatic strategy at a dead end. Beginning in late 1961, the Chinese leadership increasingly referenced military deployment as a means to manage the border dispute. Zhou had not been involved in Beijing's military decision-making for almost a decade. Now, he was brought into deliberations regarding the use of military force to counter the Indian border threat.

As 1962 approached, Beijing's leaders agreed that China had to be prepared to take military action against India if necessary. On February 1, the CMC instructed the PLA commands in Tibet and Xinjiang to "make plans to carry out antiencroachment struggles against Indian troops." Zhou participated in the drafting of the directive. Heeding Zhou's suggestion, the CMC emphasized that Chinese garrisons should stringently adhere to the previous order to "not take provocative actions and not open fire within thirty kilometers of the Chinese side of the traditional line of control." The instruction also made it clear that the matter of "whether to fight or not to fight is a decision reserved by the CMC."[29]

In early May, Zhou received a report from PLA deputy chief of staff Yang Chengwu that asserted, citing a series of recent incidents, that the Indians were determined to continue encroaching on and gradually occupy the whole of Aksai Chin. Therefore, even though the Chinese were striving to avoid a bloody clash with the Indians, "military conflict is inevitable, so it is necessary to get fully prepared."[30] On May 14, Zhou met with chief of staff Luo Ruiqing and Yang, who gave him a detailed report on the situation. One week later, Zhou commented on a plan by the General Staff that "we should be fully prepared for provocative armed actions by India on the Chinese-Indian border. Preparations should be completed by the end of June. If the Indian side dares to open fire, we will fire back. And if we are to do so, we must win on the battlefield, and must recover the territory seized by Indian troops."[31] Although Zhou had persistently advocated resolving the border dispute with India through negotiation, by carrying out the "forward policy," Nehru had turned the Chinese premier into a reluctant supporter of using limited military action to stabilize the border if necessary.

* * *

As Beijing was gradually moving toward going to war with India, tensions suddenly spiked along China's eastern coast. Ever since the Nationalist regime had retreated to Taiwan, Chiang Kai-shek had never given up hope that one day he would return to the mainland. It was not until 1961, when Chiang saw that the Great Famine had engendered enormous economic difficulty and societal instability on the mainland, that he felt the moment had come. In early 1962, Chiang accelerated preparations for a large-scale operation to "recover the mainland."[32]

PRC intelligence timely detected Chiang's maneuvering, and Beijing's leaders quickly turned their main strategic attention to the Taiwan Strait. Zhou stressed in a May 22 response to the General Staff's plan regarding the Chinese-Indian border dispute that "our main attention should be aimed in the ocean direction."[33] On May 31, Luo briefed Mao about Chiang's intention and preparations to attack the mainland. "We should be prepared for Chiang to amass a force of four hundred thousand to land on the mainland in the fall," Mao said, adding that "we should not allow the threat in the west to attract our attention there. The primary strategic direction has remained in the east. This is where our vital interests lie." The next day, Luo announced in a report on preparing for war that "the threat from the west should be seriously dealt with. However, more deserving of being seriously dealt with is Chiang. Our principal strategic direction is in the east, rather than in the west."[34]

To confront the challenge from Taiwan, the CCP leadership decided to transfer large numbers of PLA troops from northern China to the Fujian coast, a move that would be completed by mid-June.[35] Meanwhile, Mao and Zhou also decided to use the Sino-American ambassadorial talks as a channel to send Washington a warning message while gauging the Americans' intentions. Mao ordered that the troop movement to Fujian be carried out openly, saying that he wanted Chiang to take note of the CCP's efforts to disrupt his plans and delay his action.[36] Mao also meant to send a warning signal to Chiang's American allies.

In late May, Zhou received Wang Bingnan, the Chinese ambassador to Poland, who was then taking home leave in Beijing. Zhou told Wang that Chiang saw the domestic and international challenges facing the CCP as a "once-in-a-thousand-years opportunity" and was "determined to take enormous action." He instructed Wang to rush back to Warsaw. "The key now is whether the Americans will support Chiang," Zhou said, "so we should strive to make the Americans play a role in stopping Chiang from attacking the mainland."[37]

In fact, the Americans were also trying to communicate with Wang in Warsaw at the time.[38] On June 14, Wang, who had returned to Warsaw, proposed to meet with John Cabot, the US ambassador to Poland, for an "informal tea chat" the next day. Cabot immediately accepted the invitation.[39] The same night, however, the Chinese Foreign Ministry instructed Wang "to use illness as an excuse to postpone the meeting with the US ambassador for a few days."[40] Zhou had ordered that the meeting be postponed because the mass movement of PLA troops to Fujian had been delayed by flooding.[41] To Mao and Zhou, the talks in Warsaw and the deployment of PLA troops to Fujian were interrelated. On June 22, the Foreign Ministry again instructed Wang to "make an appointment to meet with the US ambassador on the twenty-third or the twenty-fourth."[42] Wang immediately invited Cabot to meet the next day, which Cabot agreed to at once. A few hours later, the Foreign Ministry informed Wang that "at 23:00 on the twenty-third, Beijing time, the news of Chiang's plan to attack the mainland will be in the air."[43]

Cabot came to Wang's quarters for tea on June 23. Following Zhou's instructions, Wang accused Washington of encouraging Chiang's plans to attack the mainland. "America is playing with fire," Wang warned. "Once Chiang starts the war, the result will not bring any benefit to America, which must take full responsibility for Chiang's adventurous moves and all of their serious consequences." By then, US intelligence had detected that the PLA had amassed more than four hundred thousand troops in Fujian.[44] Cabot told Wang that Taipei had committed to Washington that "without our permission, it would not launch any attack on the Chinese mainland," and that he "was authorized" to say that "we have no intention to give such permission in the current situation." If Chiang were to invade the mainland, Cabot promised Wang, Washington would "clearly cut off any connection with these attacks." He further clarified that Washington's commitment to Taipei "will be involved" only if the mainland attacked Taiwan. Cabot even went so far as to state that "our two sides should keep in contact to prevent such an event from happening." Cabot then asked Wang if Beijing could make the same promise. "The issue of the PLA invading Taiwan through military means is nonexistent," replied Wang. This was exactly what Cabot wanted to hear. After the meeting, Wang immediately relayed to Beijing his conversation with Cabot, especially America's stance of "opposing the Chiang clique's attack on the mainland, while also opposing our attack on Taiwan."[45]

In a few days, Zhou received intelligence confirming that Chiang had stopped massing troops. On July 26, the CMC reported to Mao that as it was now much less possible for Chiang's troops "to carry out a large- or medium-scale invasion of the mainland," the troops in Fujian could be moved elsewhere. Mao approved the report.[46]

Beijing's policies toward Taiwan returned to the "one major principle and four concrete measures" line established in 1960. Zhou remained the main practitioner of the PRC's Taiwan policy. In the ensuing years, Zhou strove to maintain contact with Taiwan's leaders, especially Chiang himself, even while China's domestic and international policies were taking a dramatic turn toward ultraleftism. In July 1963, the political situation in Taiwan changed when Chen Cheng resigned his post as vice president, officially due to illness. Zhou was surprised, especially as he had hoped that Chen would adopt a more flexible approach toward the CCP if one day he were to succeed Chiang as Taiwan's supreme leader. On July 9, Zhou met with Zhang Zhizhong and Fu Zuoyi, two former Nationalist generals who had been CCP collaborators since 1949. Zhou doubted that Chen had actually resigned due to illness. He speculated that American intervention or infighting among the leadership in Taiwan might have brought about Chen's resignation. Zhou told Zhang and Fu that no matter how Taiwan's situation changed, "our policy is to try to pursue cooperation with the elder Chiang or his son."[47]

Zhou arrived in Guangzhou on December 6 on his way to a foreign visit. During the next forty-eight hours, he disappeared from public view. Accompanied by Zhang Zhizhong, Zhou visited the site of the former Whampoa Academy and then boarded Battleship No. 846 of the South China Sea Fleet. After a whole day of sailing, Zhou arrived at a "previously designated location" near Hong Kong, where he met with Zhang Xiqun, a Hong Kong businessman with close connections to Chiang and his son, Chiang Ching-kuo, in particular.

Zhou said that the United States had been more actively trying to turn Taiwan into an independent political entity. Therefore, the CCP and the GMD should form another "united front" on the basis of opposing the formation of "two Chinas." He elaborated as follows:

> We will not ignore Taiwan because we were the stronger side, and we will not cut deals at the expense of principles in the face of hardship. If one simply looks at the issue from our perspective, it would certainly be better if Taiwan returned to the motherland. However, if it does not return now, the powerful position of the motherland will not be jeopardized. We strive to serve the great virtue of the nation and the great cause of the motherland's unification, which should be accomplished by both the CCP and the GMD.

Zhou also asked Zhang Xiqun to bring Chiang Ching-kuo several bottles of Maotai liquor.[48] The meeting reportedly "connected Zhou with the authorities in Taiwan, including Chiang Kai-shek, Chiang Ching-kuo, and Chen Cheng." When the battleship arrived back at port the next day, Zhou told his associates that he had "had the best sleep in recent memory."[49]

• • •

Tensions caused by Chiang's plan to attack the mainland vanished by late June 1962. Meanwhile, the situation on the border between China and India deteriorated further. On July 7, Zhou learned that Indian troops had invaded the Galwan Valley, a route leading into Aksai Chin, two days before. Zhou believed that the development proved that India's goal was to gradually encroach on and occupy Aksai Chin.[50] He still hoped to use diplomatic means to settle the issue or at least prevent the situation from worsening. On July 8, the Chinese Foreign Ministry sent a stern letter of protest to India, drafted under Zhou's guidance: "The Chinese side has avoided direct conflict with the invading Indian troops. However, the Chinese side can no longer yield to India's ever-escalating military pushes and will not give up the right of self-defense in the face of wanton attacks. If Indian troops insist on invading and provoking, they will have to bear all the consequences."[51]

Zhou understood, however, that language alone, no matter how strong, would not be enough to stop the Indian troops from advancing further. On

July 9, with Mao's support, he approved the sending of a reconnaissance squadron to occupy two high points on the north bank of the Galwan River. Meanwhile, he reiterated in an instruction to the troops that "if the Indians do not open fire, we should not open fire first; if the Indians launch an attack on us and try to encircle us, we may fight back, but we should also try to limit casualties and to take more prisoners."[52] Thus, for the first time since 1959, Chinese border garrisons were authorized to open fire if pushed into a corner. Zhou was extremely nervous over the next two days. He demanded that the PLA Xinjiang Command brief him once every two hours.[53]

Zhou learned on the evening of July 10 that Indian troops had again approached Chinese garrisons from three sides along the western section of the border and, provocatively, had even come within fifty meters of Chinese posts.[54] The next day, Zhou received another report that "two Indian helicopters [had] transferred reinforcing units to their newly established strongholds, hovering over nearby areas to conduct reconnaissance activities while trying to scare away Chinese watch posts and patrol squadrons there." In addition, "another Indian squadron was moving further along the Galwan Valley, trying to establish another advance post of aggression." Zhou realized that a direct showdown could happen at any moment.[55] That evening, he called a meeting of leading military and diplomatic personnel to discuss how to deal with the situation. The meeting went on past midnight. As soon as it concluded, Zhou rushed to present Mao with two options for dealing with the invading Indian troops: either use armed force to expel the Indian troops and eliminate their strongholds, or continue to try other means to repulse the Indians.[56]

The time to fight, Mao said, had not yet come, as it was necessary to further expose Nehru's true intentions as well as allow the international community to better understand the situation on the Sino-Indian border. As Mao stressed, "Our struggle with India is a complicated international issue. It has not only involved India, but also the US imperialists and the Soviets, who have supported India. They all have tried to punish us while we are facing temporary difficulties. We should not fall into their trap. We should stick to not firing the first shot." Zhou immediately conveyed Mao's instructions to the General Staff, which came up with the following policies toward India: "While making absolutely no further concessions, striving to avoid bloodshed; coexisting with them over a prolonged period in an interlocked status between the two sides."[57]

Indian garrisons again approached Chinese posts on July 21 in the Chip Chap River valley. For the first time since 1959, Chinese soldiers fired warning shots to stop the Indian advance.[58] Zhou received a report on the developments at 1:30 A.M. and immediately conveyed the information to Mao.[59] Once more, they decided to abide by the "diplomacy first" policy for the moment. Zhou gave the following order to the PLA command in Xinjiang by way of the General Staff: "You should continue to follow the principle of not firing the first shot. When they try to encircle us, we should respond by encircling them; and when they try to cut us off, we should respond by cutting them off, thus effectively stopping their advance and encroachment." If and only if the Indians launch an offensive after ignoring repeated warnings, "we may fight to defend ourselves." However, Zhou stressed, "even in a situation like that, our troops still should leave Indian troops a way to evacuate. If they do so, we should not stop them; if they do not escape, we should maintain our standoff with them."[60]

That day, Zhou also received a report from Pan Zili, the Chinese ambassador to India. Pan informed Zhou that Nehru had said that India would not necessarily demand the withdrawal of all Chinese troops from territory claimed by India as the precondition to enter border negotiations with China. Zhou saw this as a new indication of Nehru's softening stance on the dispute.[61] On July 22, with Mao's approval, Zhou dispatched a telegram of the "highest urgency" to Chen Yi, who was then in Geneva for a conference on Indochina. Zhou instructed Chen to seize "the opportunity of Nehru's showing interest in resuming negotiations" to call a meeting with V. K. Krishna Menon, the Indian minister of defense who was also in Geneva at the time, telling him that China wanted to resume negotiations as "the border issue can only be resolved through direct talks." Zhou asked Chen to settle with Menon such details as the "procedure, timing, location, and level" of the talks.[62]

Chen had just met with Menon in Geneva that day. Nonetheless, he wasted no time in contacting Menon and inviting him to meet again the next day. Menon agreed at once.[63] When the two met the next morning, they clearly reached some form of agreement about resuming border talks and began preparing to issue a joint statement. However, as Menon was unable to contact New Delhi due to "technical reasons," the statement was not issued.[64] In fact, even if Menon had received permission from New Delhi, the negotiations probably would not have resumed. When Chen was with Menon, a paparazzo captured a photograph of the two officials together, which was published in an Indian newspaper. Some members of the Indian Parliament used the photo to accuse Nehru of appeasing China.[65] Zhou noted the Indian media's dramatic reaction to the "little bit of flexibility" demonstrated by Nehru. His disappointment had never been deeper, as the prospect of settling or even relaxing the border dispute with India through diplomacy was quickly fading away.

Mao, Zhou, and nearly the entire CCP leadership, when they gathered at Beidaihe in mid-August, also discussed the border dispute with India. They received a report from the CMC that emphasized that it was necessary to "wage tit-for-tat struggles against the Indian encroachment." Mao approved the report.[66] In early September, the CMC ordered Chinese troops stationed along both the western and eastern sections of the border to not retreat when Indian troops tried to push forward in a standoff scenario, while reiterating that they should not fire the first shot unless they were explicitly ordered to do so by the supreme leadership.[67]

Tensions along the Chinese-Indian border finally reached the verge of exploding in early October. On October 5, Zhou received an intelligence report from the General Staff quoting a report by the Associated Press and Agence France-Presse in New Delhi that Indian troops were likely to launch an offensive in the next several days.[68] Zhou commented in the margin of the report, "If the enemy begins taking action in the eastern sector of the border, we should not only give him a bitter strike there but also eliminate some of his strongholds in the western sector." This meant that the Chinese troops would carry out "counteroffensive operations" along the entire border. Zhou instructed Luo to "submit plans for the Party Center to consider."[69] Around the same time, the PLA delivered large quantities of military and other materials to areas along the Sino-Indian border.[70]

On October 8, Zhou attended an enlarged meeting of the Politburo Standing Committee, convened by Mao, to hear the General Staff's briefing on strategies for the conflict with India. Mao, after hearing the opinions of Luo and others, decided to wage a "war of self-defense against the invading Indian troops."[71] Luo immediately called a CMC work meeting, at which he conveyed Mao's instructions and ordered the beginning of final mobilization for the war.[72] That same day, Zhou met with Stepan Chervonenko, the Soviet ambassador to China, informing him that India might launch a large-scale offensive on the border with China. "If they indeed attack us, we will surely take action in self-defense," Zhou said.[73] A few days later,

Khrushchev met with the Chinese ambassador to Moscow, Liu Xiao, surprising both Mao and Zhou. Khrushchev told Liu that Moscow stood on Beijing's side in China's border dispute with India, a position that the Soviet Presidium had unanimously chosen in response to Zhou's discussion with Chervonenko. "We will take due diplomatic action," Khrushchev told Liu.[74]

Nehru obviously did not realize at such a critical moment that the Chinese leaders' patience had been exhausted, and that the Chinese would imminently wage a "war of self-defense." During an exchange with the press on October 12, a reporter asked Nehru what orders he had given to Indian troops on the border with China. Nehru boasted, "Our instructions are to free our territory."[75] Xinhua, in its report, translated Nehru's remark as "Our orders are to cleanse all of them from our territory."[76] Zhou and other Chinese leaders immediately saw this a revelation of Nehru's intentions for launching a big offensive, which also gave them a reason to act.

Mao called a meeting of top leaders at 1:30 P.M. on October 17 to have a final round of discussion of the proposed "war of self-defense against India." Luo reported that "now it seems that there is no way out for us unless we wage a war of self-defense. We should act immediately."

"Can we win the war?" asked Mao.

"Yes, we can," replied Luo.

"You must wait for the order from the supreme command to fire the first shot," Mao said, looking Luo in the eye. "After firing that shot, how to fight the war will be entirely your responsibility."[77] Chinese leaders had previously thought of taking military action only along the western sector of the border. The meeting decided that although most of the encounters were occurring in Aksai Chin, conditions in the eastern sector of the border were more suitable for the use of large forces. Mao reasoned that as the war must give a great and painful blow to the "Indian reactionaries," it should involve both the eastern and western sectors of the border. That evening, Mao signed an order detailing "operations to eliminate the invading Indian troops." The next afternoon, the CMC ordered Chinese troops to begin the "border campaign of self-defense."[78]

• • •

The Chinese offensive began early on the morning of October 20. The resistance of the Indian troops quickly collapsed. Within three short days,

Chinese troops eliminated all strongholds established by the Indians in the western sector under the Indian government's "forward policy." By October 29, they had approached the Line of Actual Control between the two sides in November 1959. In the eastern sector, Chinese troops approached and crossed the McMahon Line, occupied Tawang in the west, and approached Walong in the east.[79]

Zhou began thinking about the next step to be taken as soon as the war broke out. On October 21, he made this statement at a State Council meeting:

> We are in favor of settling international disputes through negotiation. But Nehru refused to negotiate, called for the war, and launched the attack. The conflict originated in India's embracing the legacy of British imperialism. We cannot make endless concessions, so we fight back. If Nehru remains stubborn and refuses to seek compromise with us, we have no other choice but teach him a bitter lesson.[80]

On October 24, the Chinese government issued a statement, drafted under Zhou's guidance, which outlined three proposals: settling the border issues between the two sides peacefully; stopping the conflict, followed by a mutual troop withdrawal; and resuming negotiations. "Before reaching a peaceful settlement, the two sides should respect the Line of Actual Control existing between them on November 7, 1959, and the armed forces of the two sides should respectively withdraw twenty kilometers from that line, so as to avoid direct contact."[81] The same day, Zhou wrote Nehru, stating that he was "extremely pained" about the border clashes between the two countries, while reiterating Beijing's three proposals.[82] Nehru replied that the precondition for ending all military action was to restore the border to where it stood on September 8, 1962. The difference between the line of November 7, 1959, proposed by Zhou and the line of September 8, 1962, insisted upon by Nehru, was 6,500 square kilometers of territory. This was the land that the Indians had occupied since early 1960, especially after Nehru's adoption of the "forward policy."

It was unthinkable to Zhou that Nehru, in the wake of the Indian troops' suffering a total defeat on the battlefield and having been pushed south of the line of November 7, 1959, would still reject this line as the basis for negotiation. Zhou explained at an October 29 meeting with Burmese ambassador to China Maung Maung Kyaw Win that Nehru's position meant that India would keep the territory that Indian troops had occupied in Aksai Chin in the past two years; and that, in the eastern sector, China had to retreat further north from positions already north of the McMahon Line. "How can this be called cease-fire? This is not cease-fire. This is to ask us to surrender," Zhou lamented.[83] Still, on October 29, Beijing ordered Chinese troops to halt all operations.

Zhou again turned his main attention to diplomacy. He personally communicated with leaders of countries with diplomatic relations with China about the origins and direct causes of the Sino-Indian border clashes. However, Indian troops launched a major offensive in the Walong area on November 14. Two days later, the Chinese began a powerful counteroffensive, quickly reversing the Indian attack. Now, even New Delhi was exposed to the Chinese offensive; Nehru announced a nationwide state of emergency.

Beijing did not intend to continue the offensive, however. On November 18, Mao read in *Cankao ziliao* (reference materials that top Chinese leaders had relied upon for foreign news reports) that the Indian president, Sarvepalli Radhakrishnan, had mentioned he was interested in resolving differences with China through negotiation. The chairman immediately conveyed the news to Zhou with his own remarks: "Why suddenly talk so loudly about a peaceful settlement? Please read this. The Foreign Ministry should study whether other Indian leaders have made similar comments in the past several days."[84] Zhou rushed to Mao's residence half an hour later, where he told Mao that this was something new.[85] At midnight, Zhou urgently called for a meeting with P. K. Banerjee, India's chargé d'affaires in Beijing. The premier said that he agreed with Radhakrishnan, and that the two sides should immediately resume negotiations. "Although the situation seems quite tense now," Zhou continued, "if we take a longer perspective and think more deeply, China and India should continue to be friends. I have been to New Delhi four times. I am willing to go there a fifth time." Zhou asked Banerjee to report to Nehru immediately.[86]

Mao and Zhou did not wait for Nehru's response. Instead, they took another giant step beyond almost all expectations. On November 21, Beijing announced that Chinese troops would unilaterally stop fighting beginning at 12:00 A.M. on November 22; furthermore, beginning on December 1, they would withdraw to twenty kilometers behind the Line of Actual Control between the two sides on November 7, 1959. The month-long war abruptly ended.

Why did the Chinese take the initiative to withdraw after having won a major victory in the war against India? In fact, withdrawing was what Mao, Zhou, and the rest of the Chinese leadership had planned to do before the war began. At the Tenth Plenum, Zhou had made it clear that if China was forced to fight a war with India, it would do so "for [the sake of] opening the path toward negotiation."[87] On October 20, the same day the war began, Zhou stated at a State Council meeting that, once Nehru's "head was broken and bleeding," the Chinese would return to the table to settle the border dispute with the Indians through negotiation.[88] From the outset, Mao and Zhou were hoping to "seize the right moment"—that is, "when the Indian reactionaries have been taught a bitter lesson"—to halt military operations. Seeing that the PLA had won a series of major victories in the second round of operations, Mao felt that Nehru and the "Indian reactionaries" had been badly beaten, and so a cease-fire became the logical next step.

Deeper domestic considerations had also played a part in Mao's decision to stop the war and pull Chinese troops back. When the war began, Zhou made it clear that "this war, first and foremost, is a political battle."[89] Mao saw the war as an important step, in the wake of the Beidaihe Conference and the Tenth Plenum, in his return to the first line in the Chinese decision-making circle. War decisions, indeed, are always the best touchstones for political power. Through being a decisive voice in determining when and how to fight and end the war, Mao also consolidated his position as the supreme commander of the Chinese military.

For Mao, the war also catalyzed a huge mobilization of everyday Chinese throughout the country. Zhou knew this well, which he stated as follows:

> The chairman has quoted Mencius and said that "a country without an enemy and outside threats will surely head toward destruction." One thrives by experiencing worries and suffering, and withers from enjoying pleasure and overly protecting himself. A nation emerges by overcoming many difficulties. The success of our use of this as a slogan to mobilize our people has proven how correct the chairman's thought is.[90]

The resounding Chinese victory in the war against India, combined with the CCP's successful military and social mobilization to "smash Chiang's plot to attack the mainland," greatly inspired China's massive population, who had yet to emerge from the dark shadow of the disastrous Great Leap

Forward and Great Famine. On November 14, the Party Center issued a formal document, boasting that the war against India had exposed "the true face of Indian reactionaries" while highlighting "the power and reputation of the Chinese military and the motherland."[91] After the Chinese victory in the war, propaganda groups composed of heroes from the war toured the whole country to make appearances, in order to stir up "patriotism and everyday people's love of and support for the socialist motherland."[92] All this was of utmost importance for Mao to launch mass mobilization campaigns throughout China on his terms.

* * *

The war was over; however, much more had to be done at home and abroad to follow up on China's military success. This again was Zhou's task. At home, Zhou needed to explain not only why it had been necessary to fight the war but also why the troops had been pulled back after winning a major victory on the battlefield. Indeed, many in the Chinese military believed that while it was acceptable to stop operations or even pull back troops, at least Tawang, the former capital of southern Tibet, and Walong, a strategically important town, should have been kept in Chinese hands.[93] Zhou explained the logic behind the government's decision. "Nehru has been unwilling to let go of his vision of a great Indian empire," Zhou told People's Congress leaders. "Thus, he has refused to give up the policy of aggression. Indeed, only by fighting a war of self-defense would it be possible to force him to retreat in the face of difficulty. For this, we needed to fight the war and to fight a big war, as a small war would not work." "Would it have worked if we did not pull back our troops after fighting the war?" Zhou asked. "Of course, this is a possibility," Zhou replied. "But doing so will give others a wrong impression, as if we had planned to use military means to change the status quo." He emphasized that "we fought the war for justice, not to change the status quo, which can only be changed through negotiation. . . . Therefore, we withdrew our troops."[94]

The international challenges facing Zhou were also serious. At first, he and Mao believed that the international community had probably noticed that China had tolerated Indian troops' repeated moves to encroach on territories claimed by China and under Chinese control. In addition, despite its total victory on the battlefield, China had taken the initiative to stop operations and unilaterally retreat to twenty kilometers behind the Line of Actual Control that stood before Nehru adopted the "forward policy." This was unprecedented in world history. However, not only Western countries, such as the United States and Britain, but also many Asian and African countries had accused China of resorting to the use of force. The key here was that India's implementation of the "forward policy" had been carried out in a series of small and unannounced moves. Despite China's repeated protests, the mainstream international media almost never reported these moves. By comparison, China's large-scale counteroffensive was so big that it immediately caught the world's attention. Nehru thus was able to present India as the victim on the international scene. Furthermore, Nehru had long been an influential fighter for anticolonialism, a leader of the Non-Aligned Movement, and an advocate of democracy. Consequently, India easily won the sympathy of countries friendly to both India and China, which was beyond Zhou's expectations.

Zhou wrote to leaders of dozens of Asian and African countries immediately after the war began. He narrated the evolution of the Chinese-Indian border dispute and the causes of the conflict, emphasizing that China did not mean to use force to obtain territory but was compelled to fight a war of self-defense after being pushed into a corner. China's purpose was still to return to the negotiation table and use peaceful means to settle the border disputes.[95] After the war ended with China's unilateral cease-fire and withdrawal, Zhou turned the emphasis of his diplomatic efforts to exchanges with the "Colombo Six"—Ceylon, Indonesia, Burma, Cambodia, the United Arab Republic (Egypt), and Ghana—which he hoped would support or at least be neutral toward the Chinese position.[96] With Zhou's tireless efforts, eventually the leaders of the Columbo Six developed an understanding of China's approach. This also made Zhou realize that it was crucial for Beijing to extend its diplomatic activities in the vast regions of Asia and Africa.

When almost the whole world condemned China after the outbreak of the Sino-Indian War, Moscow's attitude was exceptional. Keeping Khrushchev's promise to the Chinese ambassador Liu Xiao, the Soviet government changed its previous stance of neutrality and stood explicitly on China's side. In a memo to Beijing on October 22, Moscow stated that the Soviet Union endorsed China's position on the war. More specifically, regarding the "McMahon Line," Moscow declared that it "supports China's stand, that is, it is not an established borderline, but a legacy of the tragic historical past."[97] All this should have pushed Chinese-Soviet relations, which had been extremely tense in recent years, in a more positive direction.

Khrushchev, of course, had his own intentions. The Sino-Indian border war happened almost at the same time as the eruption of the Cuban Missile Crisis. By supporting China in its border dispute with India, Khrushchev apparently hoped that Beijing would return the favor by backing Moscow in the Cuban Missile Crisis.[98] He had miscalculated, as Mao refused to return Khrushchev's favor and instead gave the Soviet leader the cold shoulder. By then, Mao had drawn up a grand blueprint for his "continuous revolution" with the central theme of "antirevisionism" internationally and "preventing revisionism" domestically. The Sino-Indian border dispute did not matter as much in the context of such a grand plan. Following Mao's thought, Beijing publicly supported Cuba. On October 28, Zhou chaired a mass rally attended by over ten thousand people in support of "the heroic Cuban comrades" that dispatched a telegram of solidarity to Fidel Castro.[99] Yet Beijing also criticized Moscow, portraying its decision to withdraw missiles from Cuba as "kowtowing to U.S imperialism and a betrayal of the Cuban Revolution."[100] This instantly offended Khrushchev and the Soviet leadership, who began to attack China's "wrong policy toward India." What followed was a continuing deterioration of Sino-Soviet relations.

But this was exactly what Mao had hoped for. He thus was able to hold the banner of "antirevisionism" even higher aloft and more fiercely attack the Soviet leaders by linking them with the "Indian reactionaries."

* * *

Toward the end of 1962, Zhou knew that China had survived its most difficult episode since the failed Great Leap Forward. Yet he also knew that the task of economic recovery was huge. He had no time to relax. The Party Center held a work conference in Beijing beginning on February 11, 1963. Zhou drafted the conference's agenda, for which he listed the discussion topics of "grain, salaries, increasing production, reducing waste of raw materials, and opposing corruption." He expected that the conference would concentrate on these topics.[101]

The situation, however, changed before the conference began. At an enlarged Politburo and Central Secretariat meeting chaired by Liu, Mao intervened, raising another issue. "Will revisionism also appear in our country? There are two possibilities: possible or impossible," Mao announced, before replying to his question: "Only by carrying out a campaign of socialist education will revisionism in our country be avoided."[102] Mao had a long conversation with Zhou on the evening of February 9. What they discussed is unknown. However, judging from the context of the conversation and what happened after it, they most likely discussed changing the themes of the forthcoming central work conference.[103]

When the work conference began on February 11, its main focus was no longer on the topics set by Zhou, but on the subject of opposing revisionism at home and abroad. Mao attended the conference and put forward his favorite question again at the opening session: "Will revisionism appear in China?" He stressed that the only way "to prevent revisionism from appearing in China" was "to carry out socialist education."[104]

Zhou also discussed antirevisionism in his presentation, but he also managed to highlight grain production and curbing bureaucratism.[105] Mao tolerated Zhou's diverging from the antirevisionism theme. Although the chairman was eager to emphasize class struggle and "opposing revisionism," he did not want to repeat the practice of criticizing Zhou's "opposing rash advance" campaign. It seemed that he had not forgotten the disastrous consequences of the Great Leap. Thus, an interesting relationship was emerging between the chairman and the premier, which would persist in the years to come. While Mao stressed "opposing and preventing revisionism," he allowed Zhou to work on adjusting and developing the Chinese economy. Indeed, from time to time, Mao even praised Zhou's efforts on the economic front. From the Socialist Education Movement to the Cultural Revolution, Mao's "continuous revolution" advanced from one phase to another, eventually pushing China into a state of chaos. Zhou played a central role in managing the Chinese economy, using whatever means he had to sustain the livelihood of hundreds of millions of ordinary Chinese.

• • •

Shortly after New Year's Day 1963, the great Chinese-Soviet polemic witnessed a full-scale outburst. In February, the CCP leadership set two interrelated tasks for 1963: highlighting antirevisionism internationally and emphasizing preventing revisionism at home. It was thus necessary to carry out the Socialist Education Movement.

Due to Mao's efforts to push the topic to the forefront, the international struggle for antirevisionism was repeatedly discussed by Chinese leaders. Each round of discussion ratcheted up the tone of criticizing "Soviet revisionism" to a new level. In response, the Soviets spoke out more loudly against the Chinese attacks while mobilizing other Communist parties to join them. The international Communist movement was profoundly divided. In early July, Deng led a CCP delegation to meet his Soviet counterparts in Moscow. Heated debates ensued between the two sides on almost every issue they discussed; neither side was willing to make any concessions.[106] Consequently, as Mao had predicted, the relationship between the Chinese and Soviet parties was brought to the verge of total collapse.

As the international "antirevisionism" struggles escalated, the Socialist Education Movement was spreading across China. In early May, the CCP Center adopted a document announcing that "it is necessary to carry out socialist education throughout the countryside."[107] On May 7, Mao elaborated that "the essence of socialist education is about class, class struggle, socialist education, and relying on poor and lower-middle peasants" to carry out the movement in the countryside or, as he said on another occasion, about "unearthing the roots of revisionism."[108]

Zhou made one suggestion about the document after he read it: he proposed that the phrase "to unite with more than 90 percent" of cadres and masses be changed to "to unite with more than 95 percent." Mao agreed.[109] This was not an arbitrary change. It meant that, in practice, hundreds of thousands—or even millions—of people would not be targeted in the campaign. Zhou also tried to remind his comrades of the importance of maintaining the normal order of industrial and agricultural production. Zhou mentioned on another occasion on September 19 that "with the improvement of the situation, it is easy to wrongly think that everything is quite good and become overly optimistic. But China is still a backward country. For us to rise, much more effort is needed."[110]

Entering 1964, leftist-oriented political winds, unleashed by the Socialist Education Movement, became increasingly powerful in Chinese politics and society, as Mao more frequently stressed the importance of "fending off revisionism." In June, he put forward the issue of "raising qualified successors of the proletariat," as this was essential to prevent the restoration of capitalism in China.[111]

• • •

Meanwhile, Mao highlighted the importance of "third front" construction in China's industrial development. The State Planning Council, headed by Li Fuchun, had begun to draft the Third Five-Year Plan in early 1963 as the Chinese economy improved. Bearing in mind the lessons of the Great Famine, Li and his colleagues paid close attention to agriculture and light industry, so that "people's needs for grain, clothing, and other daily essentials" would be met. The council's draft plan received Zhou's full support.[112] But Mao abruptly intervened. On April 25, a General Staff report mentioned that the structure of the Chinese economy made it ill prepared for a sudden attack by the enemy. Indeed, China's main industries were all located in the east, and the country's major cities were almost all situated along the coast, rendering them exposed to attacks coming from the Pacific Ocean. Vital transportation lines and links were also vulnerable to bombardment, and reservoirs, with their insufficient discharge capacity, could cause enormous damage if destroyed by the enemy.[113] The report caught Mao's attention. On May 11, he commented at a meeting that "our nation's economy has two fists, agriculture and national defense, and one bottom, infrastructure and industry. But the draft five-year plan has failed to sit on the 'bottom.'"[114] On May 27, Mao further emphasized at a meeting of top leaders that in the nuclear age, it was essential to have a strategic rear. Therefore, the new five-year plan should divide the nation's industrial layout into a first, second, and third front, respectively representing coastal provinces and cities, provinces in central regions, and inland provinces in the Southwest. In no circumstance, Mao argued, should infrastructure and industry, the "bottom" of the national economy, be deemphasized.[115]

At a meeting the next day, Zhou expressed his support for developing the third front to occupy a central position in the next five years. But he also mentioned the need for comprehensive and long-term planning, declaring, "We must pay good attention to the third front, but we must also not ignore the first and second fronts." In the five-year plan, Zhou stated that "we should establish a third-front perspective, and should also know how continuously to promote the first and second fronts."[116] Clearly, Zhou did not want to see

China's national economy be disregarded as the result of overemphasizing the third front.

On June 8, Mao again emphasized the development of the third front, but he also highlighted the danger of revisionism emerging in China. He made an ominous statement: "In my opinion, one third of the power in our country is not controlled by us, but by our enemies." Zhou echoed Mao, positing that revisionists indeed "controlled the power of many grassroots units."[117] Three days later, Liu delivered a speech on "fighting against revisionism" that he based on Mao's rhetoric. He asked, If the Soviet Union could turn revisionist forty-some years after its formation, could China also become revisionist in the future? "It is possible," Mao answered. "If we do not pay sufficient attention, this will surely occur."[118] But unbeknownst to Liu—or other Chinese leaders including Zhou—Mao had already designated him as the target of his "opposing revisionism" campaign. And Liu had trapped himself politically by supporting Mao, paving the way for his being named "China's Khrushchev" in the coming Cultural Revolution.

23

REVOLUTIONS IN THE INTERMEDIATE ZONE

1962–1965

One day in January 1963, Zhou received a poem from Mao:

> So many deeds cry out to be done, forever with urgency;
> The world rolls on, pressed by time.
> Ten thousand years is too long,
> Seize the day, seize the moment!
> Revolutionary spirit stirs up the four seas,
> Workers and peasants wave their long spears.
> Our force is irresistible,
> Away with all pests![1]

Zhou had known Mao for almost a quarter century, but this was the first time Mao had sent him such a composition. In it, Mao articulated his view of the international situation while also revealing his deep concern and grand aspirations for China. The poem's final line—"Away with all pests!"—would reemerge in the form of the widespread Cultural Revolution slogan "Sweep away all monsters and ghosts." The conflation of Mao's international and domestic concerns was not unusual. In his conceptual realm, the "international" and the "domestic" were both integral parts of "all under heaven." As he attempted to decode the chairman's intentions in sending him this poem, Zhou likely would have sensed its relevance to the CCP's intraparty struggles.

The poem's chief concern, though, was Mao's international outlook. The United States was then China's most dangerous enemy. Mao's "antirevisionism" crusade meant that Moscow had also become Beijing's foe. A decade and a half earlier, during the Chinese Civil War, Mao had introduced his "intermediate zone" thesis. Now, in light of the dramatic changes to China's internal and external situations, the chairman presented a new version of the thesis highlighting the existence of "two intermediate zones" between the United States and the Soviet Union. According to Mao, "Asia, Africa, and Latin America belong to the first intermediate zone; Europe, North America and Canada, and Australia, as well as Japan, belong to the second intermediate zone." Both zones, the chairman stressed, were opposed to the two superpowers' attempts to control them.[2]

Zhou, reflecting Mao's international thought, had already stated at the Tenth Plenum in September 1962 that "the center of the world revolution has transferred from Moscow to Beijing."[3] After he received Mao's poem, Zhou stressed in several internal speeches that China was facing a promising "revolutionary international situation." As Chinese domestic politics swung dramatically to the left, Zhou harbored no doubt that China's external policies would also undergo a radical shift.

• • •

Zhou knew that Asia, Africa, and Latin America—and Southeast Asia and Indochina in particular—were central in Mao's global outlook. Indeed, Mao hoped to leverage the outbreak of war and revolution in Indochina as a pretext for the sweeping domestic mobilizations and mass campaigns that would promote his "continuous revolution" programs. This presented Zhou with a dilemma, however. As one of the leading proponents of the 1954 Geneva Accords, Zhou had sincerely hoped that the agreement would bring about the reunification of Vietnam while enhancing the security situation south of China's borders. However, blocked by the United States and the anti-Communist Ngo Dinh Diem regime in Saigon, the plebiscite on reunification prescribed by the Geneva Accords was never held, and Vietminh members who remained in the South were ruthlessly suppressed. Zhou's response was realistic. When he visited Hanoi in November 1956, Zhou advised Ho Chi Minh and other DRV leaders that their pursuit of reunification would be "a prolonged struggle." It thus was important to "improve the people's democracy in the North" while attracting people from the South.[4] In the summer of 1958, Hanoi sought Beijing's advice about relaunching the "Southern Revolution" in Vietnam. Zhou, representing the CCP leadership, reiterated that "the most fundamental, important, and urgent task" facing the Vietnamese revolutionaries was "how to carry out socialist revolution and reconstruction in the North." In South Vietnam, Zhou elaborated, "it is now impossible to achieve a revolutionary transformation," so the Communists there should "hide themselves for a long time while building their strength, connecting with the masses, and waiting for the coming of the right moment" to relaunch the revolution.[5] This time, the Vietnamese did not follow Beijing's advice. By then, land reform in North Vietnam, which imitated the Chinese model, had suffered serious setbacks, wounding the CCP's once-exalted reputation among the Vietnamese. Meanwhile, the former Vietminh members in the South who had survived Diem's bloody suppression had begun an armed resistance. In 1959, Hanoi decided to "relaunch the Southern Revolution."

When Zhou visited Hanoi in May 1960, he adopted a subtler attitude. Though he did not express opposition to the Southern Revolution concept, he advised his Vietnamese comrades to adopt a "flexible approach combining political and military struggles." Even when violence became inevitable, he stressed, "it is necessary not to abandon political action."[6] In June 1961, Pham Van Dong came to Beijing. While Mao said that Beijing supported the armed struggles in the South, Zhou adhered to the tone he had set in his earlier meetings with Dong. "The South must be liberated," he said. But "the tactics should be flexible and multiple. . . . Illegal struggles should be combined with legal ones, and armed struggles should be associated with political ones."[7] In practice, Beijing continued to supply Hanoi with massive amounts of economic aid (including substantial deliveries of grain) but did not substantially increase its military support for the Southern Revolution.

Things changed in the second half of 1962. The Vietnamese Communists' armed struggle in the South had gradually taken shape. Beijing's dispute with Moscow had escalated along with the dramatic leftward turn of China's domestic and international policies. Mao was more enthusiastic about the rise of Communist-led armed resistance in South Vietnam. He even made self-criticism regarding the 1954 Geneva Accords on Indochina, acknowledging that "we made a mistake then."[8] Mao's comments contained a veiled criticism of Zhou, who had taken pride in his contribution to the agreement.

Zhou quickly adjusted his own approach toward Vietnam. In the summer of 1962, he told Ho and Nguyen Chi Thanh, secretary of the Vietnamese Labor Party (Communist Party) Southern Bureau, that China fully supported the Southern Revolution. The Vietnamese leaders mentioned the increasing likelihood that the Americans would intervene in Vietnam with air or ground forces, or even attack the North.[9] Their comments struck a nerve with Zhou, who told Dong in late August that the South Vietnamese comrades "should mainly depend upon themselves in waging the armed struggles," and that serious attention should be given to Washington's reaction.[10] He did not promise that China would help defend the North. That was Mao's decision to make. On October 5, Mao and Zhou met with Giap. While he praised the guerrilla war in South Vietnam, Mao acknowledged that "in the past years, we have not thought much about the offensives by the imperialists. We now should give some good attention to it." Given that "the situation in South Vietnam is quite good," as the Vietnamese Communists had "caught one of the Americans' five fingers," the chairman reasoned, "it is not an easy decision for the United States to intervene." China, Mao promised, "will pay very close attention to the situation in South Vietnam and Laos."[11]

Beginning in early 1963, Beijing significantly increased its military and other aid to Hanoi. In March, Chinese chief of staff Luo Ruiqing met with DRV leaders in Hanoi to discuss "what China might do to support Vietnam if the enemy attacks the North, and how the two sides might cooperate in waging the war."[12] In May, Liu Shaoqi told Ho in Hanoi that "we stand together with you. If war breaks out, you can count China as your rear area."[13] On June 4, Mao admitted to Le Duan and others that "on South Vietnam, we have been wrong. Once we advised you to only wage political struggles rather than military struggles. . . . The US imperialists and Ngo Dinh Diem have taught us."[14] Though Zhou did not attend the meeting, what Mao had criticized was his position on Vietnam. Zhou could not fail to realize that the chairman, in so doing, was firing another warning shot across his bow.

Zhou acted immediately. In September 1963, he invited Ho, Laotian Communist leader Kaysone Phomvihane, and Indonesian Communist leader D. N. Aidit to Chonghua in Guangdong Province for a strategic discussion on "promoting revolutions in Southeast Asia." In his presentation, Zhou

23.1 Zhou Enlai and Ho Chi Minh in Beijing, early 1960s. *CPA Media Pte. Ltd. / Alamy Stock Photo*

called Southeast Asia a "focal point of contradictions in the world," where "imperialism and colonialism had had deep roots" yet the people there had awakened. Zhou promised that China would serve as "the Great Rear of Southeast Asian revolutions" and would do its "utmost to support the anti-imperialist struggles in various Southeast Asian countries."[15]

In June 1964, with the war in Vietnam escalating and Sino-Soviet relations growing ever more strained, Mao made a promise to Van Tien Dung, chief of staff of the People's Army of Vietnam. "If the Americans dare to bring the war to North Vietnam," the chairman said, "Chinese troops will be sent there . . . as volunteers spontaneously organized by our people and not controlled by our government. And you may send your volunteers to the South in the same way."[16] Mao thus set the tone for Zhou, who was about to attend a summit of Chinese, Vietnamese, and Laotian Communist leaders. In early July, Zhou conferred with Ho and Phomvihane in Hanoi. They all believed that the Americans were trying to use South Vietnam as a "base for attacking socialist countries." Zhou again saw Southeast Asia as the "focal point of all contradictions in the world." In his view, the US imperialists were trying to fight a "special war" in South Vietnam, Laos, and Thailand. "Their aggression in Southeast Asia will not stop," Zhou stressed, and "they might escalate the 'special war' or even expand it into a regional war by sending more troops to South Vietnam and Laos, or by bombarding or even attacking North Vietnam." To counter this threat, he pledged, China would increase military and economic aid to Vietnam. No matter what Washington might do, China would "resolutely support the struggles of Southeast Asian people." Meanwhile, Zhou advised Ho and Phomvihane to "try our best to confine the war to its current scope." As for Beijing, he assured them, "when America takes a step, China will also take a step. When America sends troops there, China will also send troops there."[17]

* * *

Less than one month after the Zhou-Ho-Phomvihane summit in Hanoi, a scenario that Zhou had long feared took place. On August 2, USS *Maddox* was conducting an intelligence surveillance operation in the Tonkin Gulf when it was attacked by three Vietnamese torpedo boats. Three days later, Washington announced that DRV forces again had torpedoed American ships. The Americans responded by bombing several strategic targets in North Vietnam. The US Congress passed the Gulf of Tonkin Resolution, authorizing President Lyndon Johnson to use force.

As soon as he learned of the Gulf of Tonkin Incident, Zhou, along with Luo Ruiqing, cabled Ho, Dong, and Dung to inquire about the details of the situation. Zhou advised the DRV leaders to "clarify the situation, make necessary policies, and get sufficiently prepared."[18] On August 6, with information provided by Chinese intelligence, Zhou confirmed that "the clash in Gulf of Tonkin on August 2 was genuine, but it was an unexpected encounter for both sides." However, the alleged second attack on August 4 "was made up by the Americans to find an excuse to justify their expansion of aggression in North Vietnam." He judged that six key motives lay behind the Johnson Administration's actions: "First, to save its defeats in South Vietnam, retaliating by befogging people's minds; second, to test the reactions of [the United States's] allies, including its subordinates; third, to test the strength of the Vietnamese resistance; fourth, to test Chinese-Vietnamese relations and China's reaction; fifth, to test the reaction of the socialist camp; and sixth, to gain the upper hand in the US presidential election."[19]

In mid-August, Le Duan made a secret trip to Beijing, in which he told Mao that Hanoi did not order the attack on August 2. The chairman echoed him, stating that the incident was not "an intentional offense" by the Americans but the result of misinformation. "It looks like the Americans do not want to fight a war," the chairman observed, "you do not want to fight a war, and we do not necessarily want a war. The war will not happen." When a member of Le Duan's delegation said that Washington was "making noise about attacking the North," Mao commented that "if the Americans attack North Vietnam, they must remember that we Chinese also have legs, which are for walking." He promised Duan that China would take "visible action" to demonstrate its support for Vietnam.[20] When Mao met with Dong in Beijing on October 5, he encouraged the Vietnamese to go all out to defeat the Saigon regime while trying their best to avoid direct conflict with the Americans. Zhou followed Mao's lead and discussed with Dong "how to focus on collapsing the Saigon regime."[21] In January 1965, Zhou proposed to a Vietnamese military delegation in Beijing that they should mobilize their main forces to begin a well-coordinated general offensive against the enemy's "strategic hamlets" in the South. He estimated that such offensives, combined with the "political collapse" of the Saigon regime, would lead to a Vietnamese Communist victory "earlier than we had originally expected."[22]

However, the Americans intervened. In early February, during the US secretary of defense Robert McNamara's visit to Saigon, the Vietnamese Communist guerrillas attacked American forces at Pleiku Air Base. In response, President Johnson ordered the launch of Operation Rolling Thunder to bombard the North, and the dispatching of large numbers of US ground forces to the South. The war in Vietnam quickly escalated. Over the next several years, the conflict would serve as a focal point in Chinese external policies and an enduring justification for Mao's domestic mobilizations.

* * *

The war in Vietnam did not, however, prevent Mao, Zhou, and other leaders in Beijing from keeping a close eye on developments in Africa, Latin America, and other parts of Asia. The global decolonization movement was rapidly gaining ground, as a number of former colonies in Asia and Africa had won independence. As Zhou observed, "the awakening of the people of Asia, Africa, and Latin America has begun and can never be stopped."[23]

The victory of the Cuban Revolution came as a pleasant surprise to Mao and Zhou, who were deeply impressed when Fidel Castro launched a series of radical political and social campaigns at home and Havana established diplomatic relations with Beijing. In November 1960, Che Guevara led a Cuban economic delegation to China. Zhou received Guevara and accompanied him in a meeting with Mao. The chairman praised the Cuban Revolution for its huge impact, not only in Latin America but also across Asia and Africa. Guevara said that "the victory of our revolution happened when imperialism was dozing off and failed to take concentrated action to deal with us," and that revolutionary Cuba was then facing daunting challenges. Zhou promised Guevara that "although we have suffered from a big natural disaster, so long as a fraternal country is experiencing greater difficulty than we are, we will try our best to support Cuba."[24] Beijing's cooperation with Havana developed rapidly after Guevara's visit. Following the Cuban Missile Crisis in 1962, Mao even regarded Cuba as "an international banner of anti-imperialism and antirevisionism."

Southeast Asia was another core focus of the Chinese leadership at the time. Apart from Vietnam, Mao, Zhou, and other Chinese leaders also devoted particular attention to President Sukarno's Indonesia and the rise of his New Emerging Forces movement. Jakarta established diplomatic relations with Beijing shortly after the PRC's founding. In 1955, Zhou attended the Bandung Conference and hosted Sukarno in China. By rejecting the concept of dual citizenship, an issue that had greatly bothered Sukarno and the Indonesian government, Zhou laid the foundation for Beijing's stable development of relations with Jakarta. In 1958, Sukarno secretly dispatched a military mission to China seeking assistance in suppressing an armed rebellion that had erupted in Sumatra. Mao and Zhou assured the Indonesian leader that China "firmly supports your just struggles" and provided Indonesia with weapons and other military equipment valued at $US20 million.[25] In the early 1960s, Indonesia sought China's support in its efforts to reclaim sovereignty in West Irian. In January 1962, Beijing offered Jakarta a special loan of 129.5 million Swiss francs.[26] From 1958 to 1960, during a series of attacks and exclusionary measures against ethnic Chinese in Indonesia, Zhou insisted on responding "with rationality and calmness," in order to preserve Chinese-Indonesian relations.[27] At the end of 1961, Sukarno confidentially asked Zhou for help in treating his serious kidney disease. Zhou arranged for a team of Chinese medical specialists, headed by Dr. Wu

Jieping, to go to Jakarta. Wu and his colleagues treated Sukarno with a combination of Chinese and Western medicine, greatly relieving his symptoms.[28]

After 1963, Sukarno shifted his political orientation dramatically to the left, allying with the Indonesian Communist Party at home while adopting increasingly radical foreign policies. He even ordered Indonesia to leave the International Olympic Committee and launch a "Games of the New Emerging Forces" to rival the Olympics. He also called Malaysia a "product of neocolonialism" and used Malaysia's election to the UN Security Council as an excuse to withdraw from the UN in December 1964. Beijing backed all these moves by Sukarno and was actively involved in the Sukarno-led New Emerging Forces movement. In January 1965, when Indonesia's first deputy prime minister Subandrio visited China, Zhou told him that Beijing would expand its "comprehensive political, economic, technological, and military cooperation" with Jakarta.[29] At the end of September, four high-level Indonesian delegations visited China simultaneously. Mao even said that China was willing to share its nuclear technology with Indonesia.[30] But this honeymoon would not last for long. The eruption of the September 30th Incident in Indonesia marked the beginning of the end of the Beijing-Jakarta alliance.

* * *

Zhou also strove to expand Beijing's influence and connections in Africa. After the outbreak of the Chinese-Indian border war, Zhou found that many Asian and African countries with diplomatic relations with PRC sympathized more with New Delhi than with Beijing. After the cease-fire between China and India took effect, Ceylon led six Asian and African countries in an effort to mediate the Sino-Indian dispute. Each of the states that participated had been friendly to China; however, one way or another, they all blamed Beijing once mediation got underway. Zhou deployed all of his political skill to explain China's perspective to the leaders of the "Colombo Six," explaining why China had introduced the concepts of "customary lines" and the "Line of Actual Control" and elucidating the concepts' legal, political, and historical as well as contemporary significance.[31] The experience made Zhou realize the necessity of enhancing China's exchanges with more Asian and African countries. In mid-December 1963, Zhou embarked on a three-month-long journey, visiting thirteen Asian and African countries, along with Albania.

Zhou's first stop was the United Arab Republic (then the official name of Egypt). At the official reception, hosted by President Gamal Abdel Nasser, Zhou recalled that "in 1924, when I was passing the Suez Canal on my way from Europe back home, the whole African continent was still under the dark rule of imperialism.... Forty years are just a flash in history. But the world, the Middle East, and Africa have changed greatly."[32] Zhou held three meetings with Nasser during his five-day stay in Egypt. China, Zhou told Nasser, supported the Arab countries' struggle against imperialism in their fight for national independence, as well as their implementation of policies of nonalignment. In response to Nasser's call for "Arab unity," Zhou said that China supported the "unity of Arab countries in their own ways." He spent much time explaining to Nasser Beijing's policy toward the United States. Washington was "responsible for the bad relations between our two countries," he charged. "To oppose China, the United States has turned Taiwan, South Korea, and Indochina into three areas of tension." "Some," Zhou continued, "have accused China of being a belligerent and expansionist country" despite the fact that "China does not have even one solider abroad, and the United States has deployed one million troops overseas." It was because Washington had been hostile toward Beijing and tried to encircle China that "we are forced to be anti-American." Still, he stressed, "we are friendly toward the American people," and "there exists no military conflict between the two countries." On the subject of China's border dispute with India, Zhou emphasized that "now there is peace.... If the Indians do not cross the Line of Actual Control, the two sides will not become involved in a military conflict." Zhou agreed to provide Egypt with a ten-year interest-free loan of 335 million Swiss francs to finance the purchase of equipment and raw materials.[33]

On December 21, Zhou arrived in Algeria, a country that Beijing saw as more socialist than Egypt in its orientation. Upon his arrival in Algiers, Zhou called the victory of the Algerian Revolution "almost a miracle" and "the great event of the 1960s" in the wake of the Chinese and Cuban revolutions.[34] Over the following six days, Zhou held four meetings with the Algerian president, Ben Bella. Zhou toured the country accompanied by Houari Boumédiène, Algeria's vice president and defense minister. When Ben Bella told Zhou that he was determined to pursue genuine socialism, Zhou praised him, yet advised him "not to strive for such a noble goal in a rush." To eliminate the impacts of imperialism, Zhou suggested, "it is important to avoid multidimensional confrontations, and to combine principle with flexibility in making strategies and policies." There were "two principal issues between us and the Americans," Zhou told Ben Bella. "First, that the relations between the two countries should be based on the Five Principles [of Peaceful Coexistence]; and second, that the Americans agree to withdraw from Taiwan and the Taiwan Strait." Although there was a chance that America might launch a war against China, Zhou said, "it is unlikely that such a war will occur immediately or lead to a third world war. This is because if America opens a new battlefield in China, its strength elsewhere will be greatly weakened. Its main concerns are still with Europe."[35]

After departing Algiers, Zhou visited Morocco from December 27 to 31, where he met with King Hassan II to discuss how China and Morocco might enhance their bilateral relations. During his stay, Zhou also "explored and studied the oil industry in North Africa" and visited an oil refinery built with French and Italian technology. In a special report to Beijing, he stressed that Egypt, Algeria, and Morocco "have used foreign aid to construct new industries using modern equipment. They are all enjoying the benefits of less investment, newer equipment, a higher level of automation, quicker returns, and the involvement of fewer laborers. This has presented us with a new subject in our importation of foreign industrial equipment and use of foreign aid."[36]

On New Year's Eve, 1963, Zhou flew over the Mediterranean to visit Albania, a firm ally of Beijing's in its heated rivalry with Moscow. His meetings with Albanian leader Enver Hoxha dealt almost exclusively with the matter of "fighting against Khrushchev and Soviet modern revisionism." Hoxha also put forth a series of hefty requests for Chinese aid, almost all of which Zhou accepted. Thus a highly asymmetrical alliance relationship began to form between the two countries, in which Albania, with a population of just two million, would receive more Chinese aid than any other nation. By the late 1970s, when Chinese-Albanian cooperation collapsed in the wake of Beijing's rapprochement with Washington, China's aid to Albania had exceeded RMB10 billion.[37]

Zhou then flew to Tunisia, where Zhou and President Habib Bourguiba signed a communiqué stating that China and Tunisia would establish diplomatic relations. According to Zhou's itinerary, his next stop was Ghana. However, he suddenly learned that Ghana's president, Kwame Nkrumah, had almost been assassinated in a failed coup. The security situation in Ghana was unclear, and all of Zhou's associates believed that he should cancel the visit. However, Zhou refused to "abandon the trip when the host is in temporary difficulty," not only deciding to go ahead with the visit to Ghana but also offering to meet with Nkrumah at his residence at Osu Castle.[38] On January 15, 1964, Zhou gave an announcement in Accra, Ghana's capital, on the eight principles that China would strictly follow in offering economic aid and technical assistance to other countries: to provide the aid on the principle of equality and mutual benefit, never regarding such aid as unilateral alms; to strictly respect the sovereignty of the recipient countries, never attaching any conditions or asking for any privileges; to provide aid in the form of interest-free or low-interest loans and to extend loan periods in order to lighten the burden on the recipient countries; not to make the recipient countries dependent on China but to help them achieve self-reliance; to help the recipient countries build projects that require less investment but yield quicker results; to provide the highest-quality equipment and materials, and to replace the equipment and materials if they are not up to the agreed specifications and quality; to see to it that the personnel of the recipient country fully master the technology provided by China; and to ensure that the experts dispatched by China have the same standard of living as the experts of the recipient country.[39]

In mid-January, Zhou went to West Africa, visiting Mali and Guinea, both of which had been quite friendly to China. In fact, Guinea was the first sub-Saharan country to establish diplomatic relations with the PRC. Moreover, Guinea's president, Ahmed Sékou Touré, was one of the few Asian and African leaders who had issued a statement describing the Chinese-Indian border war as "fair and reasonable" on China's part. Next, Zhou turned to Northeast Africa, visiting Sudan, Ethiopia, and Somalia. On February 5, Zhou flew back to China, concluding his fifty-day trip to Africa.

On February 14, after a ten-day break in Kunming and Chengdu, Zhou resumed his journey, going first to Burma, and then leaving for Pakistan. The tenor of Zhou's trip to Pakistan differed dramatically from that of his first trip to the country a few years before. Beijing's relations with Pakistan had made rapid progress since China's border clash with India. Ayub Khan, the Pakistani president, emphasized to Zhou that "no war and no conflict" existed between their respective countries, and that "we have been moving toward the same direction as revealed by history and desired by our peoples." Zhou got the message. He mentioned that in China's border disputes with India, "we have persisted in negotiations, but we cannot give up on [our] principles." He also said that China supported "Pakistan's struggle to maintain its own independence and sovereignty."[40] In the joint communiqué they signed, Zhou and Ayub expressed the hope that "the Kashmir disputes could be settled in accordance with the Kashmiri people's will."[41] This was the first time that China made a pro-Pakistan statement on the Kashmir issue. China and Pakistan were not allies; yet a relationship centered on solid trust and cooperation began to emerge between the two states.

On February 26, Zhou was joined in Dhaka, the capital of East Pakistan, by Song Qingling (Soong Chingling), widow of Sun Yat-sen and vice president of the PRC. Together they visited Ceylon. As Sirimavo Bandaranaike, Ceylon's prime minister, had convened the Columbo Six, Zhou reiterated to her China's stance in exhaustive detail. "We have retreated twenty kilometers from the Line of Actual Control, leaving there only a few civilian administrative sites," he said, "and we absolutely will not make provocations." Zhou added that "if Indian troops advance, we will ask the Columbo Six to mediate and will not directly clash with the Indians." Only in the event that "mediation has failed will we take action in self-defense."[42]

Zhou and Song returned to Kunming on March 1. In his report to the National People's Congress Zhou emphasized that his three-month trip "has further increased the friendship between China and Asian and African countries, which will also enhance the grand unity of anti-imperialism among the world's people." In particular, Zhou noted that "Africa today is no longer the Africa of the late nineteenth century or the early twentieth century. Africa is a continent of awakening, waging struggles, and making advances." He also stressed that "opposition to the aggression, intervention, sabotage, and control of them by imperialists has become a bright sign for the national revolutions in Asia."[43]

• • •

Mao was a shrewd strategist. He regarded US imperialism, Soviet revisionism, and Indian reactionaries as China's three most bitter enemies. Yet he exhibited a more flexible attitude toward the capitalist countries in the "second intermediate zone." Even as China's external policies were growing more radical by the day, Mao did not strike out in all directions at once. This gave Zhou the space to develop China's relations with capitalist countries.

The country that Zhou worked on the most diligently—with Mao's support—was Japan. At the Tenth Plenum in the spring of 1962, the chairman mentioned that "Japan has sold us chemical fertilizer, steel of special types, pesticides, and the world's finest vinylon production equipment, which socialist countries would not sell us. Tatsunosuke Takasaki, their representative, will probably come here next month."[44] It was Zhou who had invited Takasaki to China for trade negotiations. Zhou first met him in Bandung in 1955, thus opening the door for Chinese-Japanese trade.[45] However, economic and cultural exchanges between China and Japan almost completely stopped when in May 1958 right-wing Japanese in Hiroshima burned the flag of the PRC. On July 7, deputy director of the Foreign Affairs Office of the State Council Liao Chengzhi, acting on instructions from Zhou, introduced "three political principles: The Japanese government should cease its hostility toward China, not endeavor to create two Chinas, and not obstruct the normalization of Chinese-Japanese relations."[46] When Kishi Nobusuke, who had carried out a hostile policy toward Beijing, resigned from his post as Japan's prime minister in June 1960, Zhou saw an opportunity to resume China's trade relations with Japan. In an August 27 meeting with Suzuki Kazuo, senior director of the Japan-China Trade Promotion Council, Zhou reiterated the three political principles and introduced "three trade principles," which defined China's preference for developing Chinese-Japanese trade through governmental agreements, private contracts, and special arrangements.[47] Takasaki came to Beijing in mid-October. When he met with Takasaki, Zhou delineated three "minimum conditions" for improving Chinese-Japanese relations. The conditions stipulated that the two countries not engage in mutual hostility, that Japan not follow Washington in pursuing a "two Chinas" policy, and that Japan not block the progress of its relations with China toward normalization.[48]

Mao's positive comments on Japan at the Tenth Plenum motivated Zhou to further engage Japan. Also visiting China that month was Kenzo Matsumura, a senior Diet member from the ruling Liberal Democratic Party. Zhou suggested to Matsumura that the two countries should "not be bound by things of the past . . . but should look forward with a farsighted vision." "We need to adopt the promotional and gradual method," Zhou argued, and try to improve political and economic relations between China and Japan on the basis of the three political principles, the three trade principles, and the nonseparability of politics and the economy.[49] Liao and Matsumura signed a trade agreement on September 19, according to which the two sides would expand Chinese-Japanese trade through the use of barter, delayed payment, and long-term agreements. In late October, Takasaki led a huge delegation to China; Zhou spoke with Takasaki during the visit. On November 9, Liao and Takasaki signed a trade memorandum, which paved the way for what would be known as the L-T Trade Agreement between China and Japan. In June 1963, with Zhou's participation, China signed a semiofficial agreement with Japan, the first in PRC history, to import whole-set equipment for the production of vinylon. The deal would involve US$22.77 million in delayed payment.[50] In 1963, Chinese trade with Japan had already returned to 1956 levels. Within two more years, Chinese-Japanese trade would increase more than five times from 1963 levels.[51]

• • •

Zhou's greatest achievement in the "second intermediate zone" was the establishment of diplomatic relations between Beijing and Paris in early 1964. France held a special place in the premier's heart. He had lived in France in the early 1920s, and his revolutionary career began there. The 1954 Geneva Accords on Indochina were the product of Zhou's cooperation with French prime minister Pierre Mendès-France. Zhou's Geneva experience taught him that although France and the United States were allies, theirs was a complicated relationship, and it was possible to work with French politicians. In May 1957, former French prime minister Edgar Faure visited China on a trip arranged by Zhou. The two met on May 24. Zhou stated that the key to establishing formal diplomatic relations between China and France lay in whether they could reach an agreement on the Taiwan question. Should France find this too much of a stretch, Zhou told Faure, "we can wait."[52] On May 30, Zhou joined Faure for a meeting with Mao, who told Faure, "As Premier Zhou has told you, we want to establish diplomatic relations with France. This is beneficial to both countries." Mao stressed that "China is a country of independence, independence from the Soviet Union," explaining his dislike of the term "the Communist Bloc." "France has had a glorious history," Mao asserted, so it "should play a role of mediation and reconciliation" in international affairs. Zhou nodded in assent.[53]

After Charles de Gaulle became president of France in 1958, Zhou praised de Gaulle's "heroic action for maintaining France's independence and sovereignty." However, the war in Algeria had blocked the prospect of a breakthrough in French-Chinese relations until after Algeria became independent in July 1962. On October 21, 1963, Faure returned to China with a handwritten letter from de Gaulle, who explicitly authorized Faure to discuss establishing diplomatic relations with China on his behalf.

This development excited Zhou, who assigned Zhang Xiruo, head of the Chinese Diplomatic Association, to serve as Faure's official host. But Zhou would personally handle Faure's visit. Faure arrived in Beijing on October 22. When Zhou met with him the next morning, he presented Faure with three options. The first was to "recognize the PRC and support its seat at the UN, while exchanging ambassadors" with China. Alternatively, France could elect to "establish partial diplomatic relations like the UK and Holland." Finally, if "difficulties involving Taiwan" proved too great, France and China could "try to promote a relationship between the two countries" not by establishing formal diplomatic relations but through "setting up trade representative agencies and other semiofficial and civil agencies." Zhou also stressed that "China's opposition to two Chinas is firm and will not change." Faure understood, making it clear that under de Gaulle, France would "exclude the British way" in handling relations with China. "If we are to act, we want to exchange ambassadors."[54]

The second day, Zhou assigned Chen Yi to meet with Faure. The single most important message Chen conveyed to the Frenchman was that "unless France cut[s] off all relationships with Taiwan, no formal diplomatic relations can be established between China and France." If "you find it difficult to expel the Chiang clique's representatives," Chen said, "we can wait."[55] During an October 25 meeting with Faure, Zhou reiterated the three options Beijing had posed to France—formal recognition, conditional recognition, or the development of "a special status" with China without diplomatic recognition. Faure said he preferred that China and France establish diplomatic relations. He presented Zhou with a "personal proposal": France could issue a statement expressing its formal recognition of the PRC government, and "you could respond that you are quite satisfied with the French proposition while stating that this means that France has cut off relations with Taiwan." By doing so, "you do not impose a condition upon France, and no one can say that there exist two Chinas." Zhou immediately saw the novelty of the proposal. He pushed Faure to clarify that France would recognize only one China rather than "two Chinas" or "one China and one Taiwan, that Taiwan was a province of China, and that by establishing diplomatic relations with China, France would cut off relations with Taiwan." Faure's response was affirmative. "If so," Zhou said, "the way to settle this issue will be found sooner or later."[56]

Zhou assessed that the negotiations had reached a critical point. He arranged for Faure to visit Datong and the Yungang Grottoes in Shanxi while the Chinese and French sides awaited de Gaulle's response to Faure's report (in an unusual move, Faure had shared his report with his Chinese hosts). With Mao's approval, Zhou made a big decision: He would not ask France to cut off diplomatic relations with Taiwan as a prerequisite for establishing diplomatic relations with the PRC. On November 2, he submitted a three-step plan in writing to Faure: First, France would recognize the PRC in a formal note and propose that the two countries establish diplomatic relations and exchange ambassadors. Next, the PRC would reply that, as the sole legal government representing China, it welcomed France's proposition and would move to establish diplomatic relations with France immediately. Finally, the two governments would then agree to simultaneously publish the above notes, immediately establish embassies in each other's countries, and exchange ambassadors. Underlying the plan, Zhou stressed, were the understandings that he and Faure had reached: France's recognition of the PRC as China's sole legal government already "automatically meant that the 'government of the Republic of China'" was no longer recognized by France; France would support the PRC's legal rights and position in the UN; and, after establishing diplomatic relations with the PRC, France would withdraw its representatives from Taiwan. Faure told Zhou that although he was not authorized to sign any formal document, he would bring the plan to de Gaulle and immediately inform the Chinese side once the French president had made a decision.[57]

A few days later, Zhou learned that de Gaulle had approved Faure's report. Beginning on December 12, Chinese-French negotiations about "more concrete issues" continued in Bern, Switzerland, between Li Qingquan, the Chinese ambassador to Switzerland, and Jacques de Beaumarchais, head of the European Office of the French Foreign Ministry. Zhou directly supervised the proceedings. When de Beaumarchais told Li that Paris did not favor including in the communiqué the expression "the PRC is the sole legal government representing the whole of the Chinese people," as insisted upon by Beijing, Zhou, who was in Algeria at the time, ordered Li to fly there and report to him in person. Zhou decided that so long as France did not adhere to a "two Chinas" policy and the only language it could not accept was the above expression, China would be willing to remove that sentence from the communiqué. Furthermore, Zhou concluded, Beijing would publish an explanation of this issue after the issuance of the communiqué, and France would "confirm this Chinese way [of explaining the issue] by restating it."[58] The two sides then quickly finalized the text of the communiqué, which was issued on January 27. As Zhou had expected, de Gaulle kept his word. On February 10, Paris informed Taipei that after the PRC diplomats arrived in Paris, Taiwan would have had no reason to keep its embassy in the French capital. Taiwan cut off diplomatic relations with France that same day; Zhou had won another major diplomatic victory.

* * *

In the early 1960s, China's trade with the socialist bloc decreased dramatically alongside the rapid deterioration of Chinese-Soviet relations. Yet Zhou saw another opportunity: to expand trade relations with Western capitalist countries. As already mentioned, in June 1963, China signed an agreement with Japan for the importing of whole-set vinylon equipment. The establishment of diplomatic relations between Beijing and Paris also further weakened the American-led economic embargo on China, opening the door ever wider to Chinese-Western trade. Zhou quickly decided to promote China's trade relations with other Western capitalist countries using the same approach that had brought about trade with Japan and Japan's export to China of advanced technology. Under Zhou's direct leadership, China began in 1963 to import whole-set equipment and technology for use in the industries of oil production, mining, chemicals, metals, electronics, and precision instruments. Altogether China secured eighty-four such projects, valued collectively at US$2.2 billion.[59] Meanwhile, Western countries gradually began to replace the Soviet Union and the Soviet Bloc as China's leading source of foreign trade. In 1965, the total volume of Chinese exports and imports reached US$4.245 billion, 52.8 percent of which came from trade with

Western countries.[60] After China established diplomatic relations with France, Zhou oversaw agreements made with Italy and Austria permitting China to set up trade offices in Rome and Vienna. Were it not for the Cultural Revolution, new breakthroughs in China's economic, commercial, and even political relations with countries of the second intermediate zone might have come sooner.

* * *

China's relations with the Soviet Union presented Zhou with a series of challenges. After a brief thaw starting in late 1961, Beijing's relations with Moscow deteriorated rapidly beginning in late 1962 as a consequence of the Chinese-Indian border war and the Cuban Missile Crisis. The great Sino-Soviet feud quickly got out of hand, with each side branding the other as "revisionist" or "dogmatist." Not only did the volume of bilateral trade drop dramatically, but technological cooperation, as well as cultural and athletic exchanges, also stalled.

Zhou was not actively involved in the shouting match between Beijing and Moscow. Instead he devoted much of his time in 1963–1964 to border negotiations with the Soviets. This proved a difficult process, as the talks involved each side losing territory and the other side gaining some. By early summer in 1964, though, China and the Soviet Union finally reached an agreement on the eastern sector of the border after three rounds of intensive discussion and bargaining. However, Mao intervened. On July 10, he told a delegation from the Japanese Socialist Party, "The Soviet Union has occupied too many lands. At Yalta, Outer Mongolia got nominal independence and was taken away from China. In fact, it was controlled by the Soviet Union. The territory of Outer Mongolia is much bigger than that of your Kuril Islands. We have raised the question of whether Outer Mongolia should be returned to China. They said 'no.' We raised the issue with Khrushchev and Bulganin in 1954 when they were visiting China."[61] Mao did not consult with Zhou before he made these startling statements. On July 19, Zhou told a group of visitors from the Japanese Socialist Party that it was China's consistent policy and basic position to support Japan's demand for the Soviet Union to return the northern islands to Japan.[62] Mao's comments were quickly published by the Japanese media, provoking an angry response from Moscow, including a lengthy essay rebutting Mao's statement published in *Pravda*. Khrushchev personally denounced Mao's naked "territorial ambition."[63] Earlier, under Zhou's direction, Beijing and Moscow had made significant progress toward settling their border dispute; now, those negotiations were about to collapse.

On October 15, with Sino-Soviet relations at a low ebb, Khrushchev was ousted as the Soviet leader in a coup in Moscow. Late that night, Stepan Chervonenko, the Soviet ambassador to China, urgently requested to see Mao. Khrushchev had resigned, Chervonenko told Wu Xiuquan, deputy head of the CCP Central Liaison Department.[64] Zhou's initial reaction was that this was a "very good thing." He immediately reported the news to Mao and other CCP leaders, suggesting that they "hold a meeting to study this matter immediately."[65] The next afternoon, Mao commented at a Politburo Standing Committee meeting that "there will be changes in Moscow, but not very big or very rapid ones. We shall wait and see."[66] At another meeting of the Politburo Standing Committee five days later, Zhou and several others suggested that the CCP should "present our attitude from a positive perspective." Mao disagreed, saying, "My opinion is that we should let the dust settle first." He even said to Liu, Deng, and Zhou in a somewhat cynical tone, "I am a center-leftist. You are all leftists. They (the Soviets) are revisionists. But now they are concerned about America. So, they need to have China as their friend." Mao mused about "sending a vice premier to Moscow for the upcoming October Revolution celebrations."[67]

Mao had changed his mind by the time top CCP leaders met again a few days later. Seeing that Khrushchev's downfall had produced a strong reaction from other Communist parties, Mao realized that this could be a good opportunity to expand Beijing's influence in the international Communist movement. "We should act," he told Zhou and others, probably by "dispatching a delegation headed by [Zhou] Enlai to Moscow to attend the October Revolution celebrations." The CCP leadership, going along with Mao's idea, then decided that Zhou would travel to Moscow "to discuss with the Soviet leaders international Communism, Sino-Soviet relations, and other issues of mutual concern."[68] Mao cautioned Zhou, though, that he should "watch patiently" rather than "try to push the improvement of Sino-Soviet relations." It was unlikely that "there will soon be big changes [in Moscow]," the chairman predicted.[69]

Zhou's attitude was more positive than Mao's. He believed that it was possible and desirable to "work on the Soviets and push them to change." On

October 28, Zhou informed Chervonenko that he would lead a CCP delegation to Moscow and asked whether the Soviets were willing to use the October Revolution anniversary celebrations as an opportunity to invite representatives from all twelve socialist countries, including Albania, to Moscow for meetings.[70] That evening, Zhou met with ambassadors from North Korea, North Vietnam, Romania, Albania, and Cuba, countries all of which were either pro-Beijing or at least neutral in the international Communist movement. The socialist countries, Zhou proposed to the ambassadors, might all send to Moscow a delegation, ideally headed by their respective prime ministers, to meet the new Soviet leaders. "The situation in Moscow has changed," he observed, and this "would have an effect not only on the Soviet Union but also on other fraternal countries and parties, and on the entire international Communist movement, as well as on our common enemies, the imperialists, and their agents." While stressing "the need to wait and see," Beijing would "support positive changes (in Moscow) while pushing them to change in a good direction."[71] The next day, Zhou conveyed the same proposal to the ambassadors from East Germany, Bulgaria, Hungary, Czechoslovakia, Poland, and Mongolia.[72] Chervonenko made an urgent appointment with Zhou on October 31, during which he relayed the new Soviet leaders' response: they thanked Beijing for paying such close attention to the October Revolution celebrations and welcomed Zhou to Moscow. "The October Revolution opened the path for all of us," Zhou replied. "This is an international festival, not your festival alone."[73]

Zhou flew to Moscow on November 5 together with DRV prime minister Pham Van Dong. As the two discussed how Moscow might receive them, Zhou mentioned that he hoped Soviet prime minister Alexei Kosygin could be there, although it was possible that one of his deputies would greet them on the tarmac instead. When Zhou's plane landed in Moscow, none other than Kosygin greeted him at the airport. Zhou was delighted.[74]

Zhou began a series of meetings at 11:10 A.M. the next morning, with Leonid Brezhnev, Kosygin, and his "old friend" Mikoyan, respectively. To feel the Russians out, Zhou told Brezhnev that he wanted to speak at the rally commemorating the October Revolution. The new Soviet leader showed no interest in the matter. Mikoyan, however, touched on the real issue, asking Zhou, "Have you brought with you plans to recover our relationship to what it was ten or fifteen years ago?" Zhou replied, "We have expressed our goodwill in our congratulatory telegram. We hope that our two parties and two countries will unite on the basis of Marxism-Leninism and proletarian internationalism, and struggle against our common enemies and for our common cause. For this purpose, we have come here to participate in the celebrations while exchanging opinions with you. We hope to make this a good starting point for the future."[75]

The situation took an abrupt turn when Zhou attended a banquet held by Soviet leaders on the evening of November 7. After much drinking, Soviet defense minister Rodion Malinovsky approached He Long, deputy head of the Chinese delegation, and said, "We should not allow any Mao or any Khrushchev to disturb us again. . . . We have ousted Khrushchev. Why can't you get rid of Mao?"[76] Word of the encounter shocked Zhou, who, along with He Long, immediately went to see Brezhnev. "Malinovsky's words are a serious provocation," Zhou said with a firm voice, "which we absolutely oppose." Brezhnev, unprepared and surprised, at once told Zhou that Malinovsky did not represent the Soviet leadership, and dismissed his drunken utterance as pure nonsense. Zhou retorted, "This is not nonsense but a revelation of his true views after drinking."[77]

That evening, Zhou confirmed the contents of Malinovsky's comments with the Chinese interpreters and then notified the Party Center about the incident in a "telegram of the highest urgency." Beijing's reply arrived the next morning, containing instructions for Zhou to "take the offensive," and "tightly hold this matter . . . without allowing it to be distracted by anything else."[78] When Zhou met with Brezhnev and other Soviet leaders again the next day, he immediately put to them a series of tough questions, such as "Do you welcome us here in order to challenge us publicly?" and "Do you want the Chinese party to overturn Chairman Mao's leadership?" Brezhnev replied that he and other Soviet leaders were "utterly uneasy and angry" about the incident. Malinovsky was not a Soviet Presidium member; his words did not represent the position of the Soviet leadership, but were merely "the nonsense of a drunken man." Despite Brezhnev's repeated apologies, Zhou would not let him off the hook: "You cannot use 'nonsense after drinking' as the explanation. There is an old Chinese saying, 'When liquor goes in, the truth comes out.' I will report [this] conversation to our Party Center."[79]

Zhou's unyielding attitude revealed his sense of the incident's grave political sensitivity. He knew well that any reluctance to pursue the matter on his part could dramatically damage his relationship with Mao or, even worse, lead to his own political demise. Over the next three days, he held consecutive meetings with Brezhnev and other Soviet leaders, in which he maintained an aggressive approach and pushed for a "thorough and completely satisfactory explanation" from the Soviet leaders. Finally, Mikoyan was so offended that he said, "Regarding our attitude toward China, we are not different from Khrushchev." "If so," Zhou retorted, "what is there for us to discuss?"[80] On October 12, Zhou told Vietnamese leader Le Duan, "Following the contacts of the past few days, we find that the situation is worse than our earlier expectations."[81] Even so, when Zhou held his last meeting with Brezhnev, he still told the Soviet leader, "We have not been able to have extensive and comprehensive discussion this time. But the door to further consultation between our two parties is still wide open."[82] Nonetheless, Zhou was fully aware that this was a matter not for him, but for Mao to decide.

Mao greeted Zhou at the Beijing Airport, joined by nearly all the CCP leadership. This grand gesture was the chairman's reward to Zhou for his "heroic performance" in Moscow. That afternoon, Zhou related his experiences in Moscow to the Politburo Standing Committee. The new Soviet leadership was "unable to explain clearly why they brought Khrushchev down," Zhou asserted. "They were unhappy with his leadership style, not his policy line, and they differ from Khrushchev merely on some specific issues."[83] Beijing's cautious optimism about the prospects of Sino-Soviet relations darkened once again.

• • •

On October 16, nearly coinciding with Khrushchev's downfall, China successfully detonated its first atomic bomb. The two events were not directly related. Yet Mao, Zhou, and other Chinese leaders saw both as good news.

Zhou had long been involved in the development of China's nuclear industry. In fact, he had already taken an interest in nuclear technology before the PRC's founding. In February 1949, the CCP decided to dispatch a delegation to the World Peace Congress in Paris. From the list of candidates for the delegation, Zhou nominated Qian Sanqiang, who had completed a PhD in physics under the direction of professors Irène Joliot-Curie and Jean Curie. Zhou supported Qian's request to use the congress as an opportunity to purchase an electromagnet for a mid-size cyclotron and other equipment, and he gave Qian a large amount of US dollars with which to buy them.[84]

When Mao and Zhou met with Khrushchev during his visit to China in 1954, Zhou told him, "We need the truly big stuff," implicitly asking the Soviets to support China's efforts to develop an atomic bomb. The request caught Khrushchev off guard. When he realized what Zhou meant, Khrushchev replied, "That stuff is very expensive. It requires longer planning." He also commented that "our big socialist family needs only one nuclear umbrella." Mao and Zhou were not happy with Khrushchev's response.[85]

On January 14, 1955, Zhou met with Qian Sanqiang and Li Siguang, China's leading geologist, to inquire about the state of nuclear studies in China, the researchers involved, and storage of uranium mines.[86] The following day, Mao led a discussion at the CCP Central Secretariat on how China could develop its own nuclear industry. Zhou invited Li and Qian to the meeting. Qian brought uranium detection devices to the meeting and showed attendees how to use them. Mao announced at the meeting, "With the support of the Soviet Union, we must develop nuclear energy! . . . We have the people and the resources. What kind of miracles can we not create?" The meeting decided that China would develop its own nuclear industry.[87] On January 31, Zhou said at a State Council plenum that "on the one hand, we should oppose the use of nuclear weapons and, on the other, we should command nuclear energy."[88]

Zhou then met several times with Soviet ambassador Yudin to discuss Moscow's sending experts to China and providing China with major technological support.[89] This was during the heyday of the Sino-Soviet alliance, when the Soviet leaders demonstrated great enthusiasm for supporting China. In June 1957, Yudin informed Zhou that the Soviet Union was willing to help China establish a nuclear energy research center.[90] On August 6, Zhou wrote Bulganin, asking Moscow to provide "major support" to China for the production of nuclear weapons and their delivery systems. The Soviets swiftly agreed to discuss with the Chinese "the establishment of nuclear industry and such issues as producing nuclear weapons, rockets, and aviation technology."[91] Nie Rongzhen then led a Chinese delegation to Moscow, whose negotiations with the Soviets went quite smoothly. On October 15, the two sides signed an "Agreement on New Technology for National Defense," according to which the Soviet Union would share nuclear technology with China and even provide the Chinese with a sample bomb.[92] On April 8, 1958, Zhou wrote Khrushchev, suggesting they begin implementing the October 15, 1957, agreement. Two weeks later, Khrushchev informed Zhou that Moscow had agreed to the proposal of providing Beijing with the "materials and samples of extreme importance."[93]

With the worsening of Chinese-Soviet relations, however, Khrushchev's attitudes changed. In June 1959, Moscow suspended the agreement on nuclear cooperation with Beijing. In July 1960, Moscow went further, recalling all Soviet experts working in China and canceling all agreements and related contracts on nuclear cooperation. The experts would also take back to the Soviet Union all their blueprints and other materials. This breakdown in Sino-Soviet cooperation took place under grim circumstances in China; the Great Leap Forward had failed and the Great Famine was engulfing China's vast population. Nonetheless, the Chinese leadership resolved not to abandon the nuclear project. Zhou announced the party leadership's decision: "We plan to make our own bomb in eight years."[94] On July 16, 1961, the CCP leadership decided to mobilize the whole country's resources to enhance the development of China's nuclear industry.[95] To implement the decision, Zhou concluded that funding and resources for the development of missiles and the bomb should be guaranteed, even as other budgets were being cut due to the devastation wrought by the Great Leap.[96] In a speech at the National Science Commission, Zhou emphasized that the nuclear industry should be shielded from the sweeping adjustments that China's national economy was about to undergo. "To have our own missiles and nuclear weapons," he said, "is the only way to prevent them from being used against us."[97] With Zhou's approval, an office of the national defense industry was established in the State Council, which would report directly to him and the Party Center.[98]

China's efforts to develop nuclear weapons hit a bottleneck in the second half of 1962 due to critical technological difficulties. On October 10, Luo Ruiqing proposed to Zhou that it was necessary to "establish a special committee under the center's direct leadership" in advance of the first bomb test slated for 1964. Luo further proposed that Zhou lead the committee, whose duties would include "enhancing guidance over the nuclear industry, playing a supervisory role and examining execution of the plan at any time, allocating manpower and resources, and timely resolving any problem that emerges in the process of research, design, and construction."[99] Mao approved the proposal on November 3, instructing that the committee should tackle its work "by going all out in coordination."[100] On November 17, the special committee was formally established, with Zhou at the helm.[101] The committee met three times before the month was out. Zhou placed particular emphasis on the principles of "respecting facts, pursuing progress gradually, being persistent, and staying modest."[102]

As Zhou and the CCP leadership strove to develop the bomb, the nuclear issue became a focal point in the dispute between China and the Soviet Union. In August 1962, Moscow informed Beijing that the Soviet government had agreed to Washington's proposal about nuclear nonproliferation. Beijing immediately accused Moscow of trying to "monopolize nuclear technology" and demanded that the Soviets "not sabotage Chinese sovereignty or take responsibility for China."[103] In July 1963, Washington, Moscow, and London signed the Partial Test Ban Treaty on nuclear weapons. Beijing condemned it as an attempt "to bind others' arms and legs" while allowing the nuclear powers "to continuously build, store, and use nuclear weapons." In an open letter, Beijing claimed that "the more countries possess the bomb, the more likely the bomb will not be used."[104]

Zhou and the CCP leadership decided to accelerate their nuclear project. The theoretical design of the atomic bomb was completed in March 1963. That July, Zhou argued that detonation aside, China needed to acquire the means for "practical use of the nuclear weapon." At the end of the year, he stressed that the "development of missiles should be taken as the main task and air-dropping [atomic bombs] the supplementary task."[105] On December 24, the bomb passed a comprehensive examination and test at the base where it was being developed in the Northwest. On January 14, the condensed uranium product that could be used for the bomb also passed tests. Zhou hailed the achievements, urging all involved in the project to "continuously fulfill all the tasks in the future with persistence."[106]

The nuclear project thus entered its final phase. On April 11, 1964, a meeting of the special commission chaired by Zhou decided that preparations for the detonation of the first bomb should be completed by September 10 "in one test."[107] On June 6, the trial explosion succeeded. Assembly of the bomb finished on August 19, and an exercise imitating the test went without a hitch on September 1. In mid-September, Zhou told another special committee meeting that he "preferred to have the test earlier than later"; the exact date of the test, he continued, should "be determined before National Day [October 1]" in accordance with the situation then, which would be reviewed and approved by the Party Center.[108] Mao backed Zhou up, commenting that "the bomb is a thing used to scare others. Therefore, it is better to have the detonation earlier."[109] Zhou wrote Mao on September 21, proposing that the test be held no later than October 24. The chairman's approval came the same day.[110] Zhou conveyed the decision in a message to the officials in charge of the test, bringing up other important details. "There will be four good days in October," he wrote. "If a day in mid-October cannot be seized upon, there is another one in late October." He instructed those carrying out the test "to carefully calculate changes in the direction of the wind, and the spreading radius of radioactive debris," and to make sure that "confidentiality is maintained absolutely."[111] On October 11, Zhou reported to Mao. "Now everything is ready. . . . The exact date and time of the detonation will be determined in accordance with the weather conditions between October 15 and 20."[112]

Zero Hour came on October 16. The bomb exploded at 15:00. Zhang Aiping, the commander on site, waited four minutes before dispatching a telegraph to Zhou declaring simply, "It is a success!" Zhou asked, "Is it a genuine explosion?" Zhang responded, "Yes." A few minutes later, Zhou forwarded to Zhang instructions from the chairman: "Confirm whether it was a genuine nuclear explosion." Zhang replied with another "Yes."[113]

That evening, Zhou, joined by Mao, announced with visible excitement at the Great Hall of the People, "We have successfully tested our first atomic bomb!"[114] For Zhou and Mao, the detonation was another moment that bore witness to Mao's declaration of nearly fifteen years prior that "we, the Chinese, have stood up."

24

GATHERING STORMS IN GUSTY WINDS

1965–1966

By the end of 1964, Zhou Enlai could clearly sense the coming of a political tempest on a scale unprecedented in CCP history, especially after witnessing Mao in a rare fit of rage toward Liu Shaoqi and Deng Xiaoping. At a central work conference, Liu spoke on the Socialist Education Movement, while Mao interrupted him repeatedly. When Liu asked if the movement should adopt the term "new bourgeois elements," Mao interjected, "What does 'bourgeois' mean here? The peasants do not understand it." Liu suggested that the concept of "rectifying the party" not be used; otherwise many members could be expelled from the party. "I support rectifying the party," Mao said in rebuttal, as millions of party members were "not true Communists."[1] No matter how hard Liu tried, he could not come up with an expression that would please Mao. Zhou, like others at the conference, kept silent.

The tension between Mao and Liu became more obvious at another meeting of top leaders in late December. On the topic of "the principal contradictions" to be addressed by the Socialist Education Movement, Liu asked, "Might we say that the essence of the contradictions is a mixture of those among the people and those between us and the enemy?" Mao rejected Liu's notion: "What else could it be?. . . . It is anticapitalist in essence."[2] In Mao's eyes, Liu was totally wrong to take ordinary cadres and the masses, rather than those "capitalist roaders in power," as the main targets of the Socialist Education Movement. Again, Zhou looked on wordlessly.

December 26 was Mao's seventy-first birthday. He asked Jiang Qing, his wife, to arrange a banquet on his behalf, and he made a list of three dozen invitees. In addition to Liu, Deng, Zhou, and other central and provincial leaders, Mao also invited to the banquet scientist Qian Xuesheng, model peasant Chen Yonggui, and pioneer educated young peasants Dong Jiageng and Xing Yanzi. Mao asked Qian, Chen, Dong, and Xing to sit at his table; Liu, Deng, Zhou, and other leaders were seated at the other two tables.[3] The atmosphere at the banquet was bizarre. Mao opened the conversation by saying, "We should not just eat but should also talk." He then launched into a monologue featuring merry laughs mixed with sour comments. He mentioned once more that someone had argued that the essence of the Socialist Education Movement was contradictions within and outside the party. "This is not Marxism," he said, again targeting Liu. When Mao warned, "There is the danger of revisionism emerging within the party," the whole room fell into "dead silence."[4] The grassroots guests did not understand what the chairman meant. But Zhou, as well as Liu, Deng, and other leaders, knew why Mao made these comments. They had to take Mao's words seriously.

The banquet was only a warm-up for Mao. Two days later, he attacked Liu and Deng at a Politburo meeting. He came prepared, bringing with him a copy of the PRC constitution and the CCP charter. "Am I a party member? Am I a citizen?" he asked. "If so, why do I have no freedom of speech, and am not allowed to say a few words?" Mao was accusing Liu and Deng of having violated his rights as a party member and citizen by barring him from one meeting and not inviting him to speak at another. Mao again stated that the Socialist Education Movement should "expose those capitalist roaders in power." Liu and Deng were at a loss for words.[5]

Zhou should have realized by then that Mao was planning a huge political offensive involving him. Months before, Mao had suddenly mentioned the nine essays he wrote in 1941 to criticize the "wrong lines of the early 1930s." Mao asked Zhou and other top party leaders for comments on the essays, claiming that he wanted to revise them.[6] Why did the chairman want to revisit them almost a quarter century later? Zhou had been a main target of Mao's criticism in the essays. Mao had thus sent Zhou a warning signal.

Near the end of 1964, Mao again let Zhou know that he was watching him, mentioning Qi Yanming, deputy minister of culture and a longtime close associate of Zhou, in a conversation with Liu, Zhou, and Deng. "Qi is not a good person," he told Zhou. "Is he the chief of your office? He is not the right man for the role."[7] Alarmed, Zhou soon decided to let Qi go. Qi was later purged during the Cultural Revolution.

Mao mentioned the nine essays once more after the new year of 1965 began. This time, he specifically commented that they "included the premier's name, which should be deleted, as the premier has in his career done more correct things than he has made mistakes."[8] Mao's words were pregnant with cryptic meaning. On the one hand, he implied that Zhou would not be a main target of the next intraparty purge. On the other hand, Mao reminded Zhou that his past mistakes were not forgotten, although they were outnumbered by his correct actions. However, whenever necessary, Mao could bring up and highlight Zhou's mistakes at any time, as he already had in the past.

Had it not been for these ominous occasions, 1964 would have been a time of celebration for Zhou. The Chinese economy grew significantly that year after its 1963 recovery from the disastrous Great Leap Forward. The darkest hours for China were over, Zhou knew. In late December, Zhou was again named premier at a plenary session of the National People's Congress. He delivered a speech on government work at the congress, the highlight of which was Zhou's assertion that "in not too long a historical period," China would likely become "a socialist power, with modern agriculture, modern industry, modern national defense, and modern science and technology."[9] Mao reviewed Zhou's speech and added a paragraph: "We cannot repeat the old path of technological development of other countries, and thus creep one step after another behind others. We must break up the norms and try our best to adopt advanced technology, building our country into a modern socialist power before long. This is what we have called the 'Great Leap Forward.'"[10] Mao meant to defend the disastrous Great Leap, as well as to consolidate the agenda of his "continuous revolution." These weighty words must have been distressing for Zhou to read.

Indeed, the events of the times did little for Zhou's peace of mind. At the work conference in December 1964, Mao easily won the upper hand in an encounter with Liu. Then, Liu took a step back by withdrawing a Socialist Education document written under his leadership. Mao's offensive, however, did not stop there. In January 1965, he personally chaired another central work conference, which produced a new document on Socialist Education—the Twenty-Three Articles. In his final edits to the document, Mao continued to criticize Liu's view that the Socialist Education Movement's key mission was to resolve "contradictions within or outside the party." Such a definition, Mao commented, failed to capture the essence of the principal contradictions in Chinese society. The focal point of Socialist Education, Mao wrote, was to "purge the capitalist roaders with power within the party."[11] This was the first time that the phrase—which would later be used to define the central mission of the Cultural Revolution—was formally included in a CCP document. In this sense, the issuance of the Twenty-Three Articles was the opening act of the Cultural Revolution.

* * *

The dramatic changes in China's domestic political landscape took place while the Vietnam War was rapidly escalating. On February 7, Vietcong guerrillas raided Pleiku Air Base in the suburbs of Saigon. US president Lyndon Johnson immediately decided to set in motion Operation Rolling Thunder, launching a massive bombardment of strategic targets in North Vietnam. Meanwhile, Washington began to dispatch large numbers of American ground forces to South Vietnam.

Mao, Zhou, and the CCP leadership faced a series of questions: Would the United States expand the war to North Vietnam? Could the war even be brought to Chinese soil? How would Mao assess the impact of the Vietnam War while simultaneously leading China into the Cultural Revolution? And how should China cope with the challenge the war presented? In retrospect, Mao wanted to control the crisis while taking full advantage of the international pressure that it would generate to justify intensive domestic mobilization in China. Mao was not afraid of fighting a war. However, he did not want a war at a time when he was guiding China toward the Cultural Revolution—especially not a major war with the United States.

Mao's first move targeted Moscow. The escalation of the Vietnam War made it possible for the deeply divided international Communist movement to come together under the banner of anti-imperialism. In early February 1965, Soviet prime minister Kosygin visited China, the first such visit by a Soviet leader since Khrushchev's downfall. A moderate in Moscow, Kosygin hoped to persuade the CCP to attend a Communist Party summit in Moscow scheduled to begin on March 1.[12] Zhou and Kosygin held four meetings over two days. To improve Sino-Soviet relations, they agreed to celebrate the fifteenth anniversary of the Sino-Soviet Treaty of Friendship and Alliance, promote bilateral trade, complete all delayed Soviet projects in aid of China, and send students to each other's countries, in addition to coordinating their support for Vietnam's anti-American war. But Zhou rejected Kosygin's request for the CCP to attend the Moscow summit: "This is unilaterally called by the Soviet Party, so we will not attend it."[13]

Kosygin next visited Hanoi, and then, on February 10, he stopped for one day in Beijing on his way to Pyongyang. Zhou met Kosygin at the airport and went with him to the guesthouse where the Soviet prime minister would stay. In the car, they discussed concrete measures that Beijing and Moscow would take to support Vietnam. For example, they would jointly mobilize world opinion to condemn America's aggression, and China would help deliver Soviet weapons to Vietnam via Chinese railways. They agreed to sign relevant agreements the next morning.[14]

The situation changed overnight, however. Instead of having another one-on-one meeting with Kosygin, Zhou—along with Liu, Deng, and other Chinese leaders—joined Mao to meet with the Soviet prime minister. Mao dominated the discussion with a monologue. Zhou gave a few brief comments when Mao called on him. Kosygin told Mao that Moscow had provided Hanoi with ground-to-air missiles, artillery pieces, torpedo boats, and other weapons, all for free. The Soviets hoped to cooperate with the Chinese comrades in supporting Vietnam, he said, and "the Vietnamese comrades also welcome such cooperation." Mao did not follow Kosygin's lead. Instead, he said that in addition to supporting North Vietnam, it was important to give more support to the guerrillas in South Vietnam. Kosygin mentioned the forthcoming Communist summit in Moscow. Mao immediately replied that Beijing would not attend it. When Kosygin suggested that the two parties stop their open dispute, Mao rebutted his suggestion: "I support an open dispute. The open dispute will last for another ten thousand years." "It should not last so long," said Kosygin. "OK," replied the chairman, "I will shorten it by one thousand years, with only nine thousand years left." Zhou then joined the debate. When Kosygin said that "every effort should be made to avoid war," Zhou responded, "If the imperialists try to impose a war on us, we will surely fight." Kosygin emphasized that Moscow had given more support to Vietnam than Beijing. "Have we not given enough support?" Zhou fired back. He also mentioned that Moscow "had supported the Indian reactionaries against China. This is your biggest problem."[15]

Kosygin left Beijing in despair, his hope of improving Sino-Soviet relations after Khrushchev's downfall having been dashed.

In hindsight, it was not strange that Mao had been so hostile toward Kosygin. At the time, Mao was trying to push China toward the Cultural Revolution; the last thing he wanted was an improvement in Sino-Soviet relations. Otherwise, the legitimacy of his "continuous revolution," which took opposition to Soviet revisionism as a central objective, would be compromised or even undermined.

Mao fully supported one of Zhou's other initiatives—ensuring that the war in Vietnam would remain a limited one. They both hoped that while the flames of the war continued to burn, they would not get out of control and spread to China. To this end, Zhou wanted to "communicate" with the Americans. Zhou met with Pakistani President Mohammad Ayub Khan in Karachi on April 2, 1965. He asked Khan to convey to President Johnson a three-point message during his forthcoming trip to Washington: "China will not take the initiative to provoke a war against the United States; China means what it says; China is prepared."[16]

Zhou remembered the "lesson from Korea" when he used this "Pakistani channel." Back in 1950, amid the threat of a military showdown in Korea between Beijing and Washington, Zhou told the Americans that if they crossed the thirty-eighth parallel, "we will intervene." That message was delivered through the Indians, whom the Americans did not trust, and "the Americans did not listen to us." This time, Zhou emphasized, "our friend has changed; it is no longer India but Pakistan," so that the message could at least reach Washington.[17] But Zhou failed to anticipate that Johnson would abruptly postpone Ayub Khan's visit to the United States.[18] Hence Khan was unable to deliver Zhou's message to the Americans in person.[19]

Zhou repeated the same three-point warning to the Americans in his meetings with Burmese, Indonesian, and Tanzanian leaders.[20] But he had no way of knowing if Washington heard him. Eventually he thought of Britain, an American ally that had maintained a consulate in Beijing. On May 31, Donald Hopson, the British chargé d'affaires in China, received a rare summons from Foreign Minister Chen Yi. Chen told Hopson that Premier Zhou had asked President Ayub Khan to convey a message to Washington about the war in Vietnam. However, as Johnson had postponed Khan's visit, Zhou's message had likely not been delivered. Beijing would "be grateful," Chen said, if London would help convey the three-point

24.1 Zhou Enlai with Indonesian president Sukarno and Egyptian president Nasser in Cairo, 1965. *Keystone Press / Alamy Stock Photo*

message to Washington while "pressuring the Americans to withdraw from South Vietnam."[21] The British acted immediately.[22] A few days later, Zhou learned that top American leaders had received his message.[23] Hopson hoped that, in exchange, London would be able to discuss with Beijing matters pertaining to Hong Kong and British-Chinese trade. Instead, he found himself once again "customarily isolated" in Beijing.

Zhou's warnings and Washington's response enabled China and the United States to avoid a military showdown. In the ensuing years, American ground forces never invaded North Vietnam, and air bombardment of the North never crossed the twentieth parallel, keeping a safe distance from China's borders. Beijing provided Hanoi with large amounts of military and other material support, including the sending of Chinese engineering troops and antiaircraft artillery units, but Chinese combat troops were never sent to Vietnam. Consequently, China and America did not become involved in another military face-off.[24] This was exactly the result Mao and Zhou sought.

• • •

24.2 Zhou Enlai and Deng Xiaoping, ca. 1965. *Imaginechina Limited / Alamy Stock Photo*

In early 1965, Zhou established, at Mao's instruction, four "small planning commissions" to serve the specific needs of construction of the third front. The draft text of the Third Five-Year Plan prepared by Li Fuchun and his associates was abandoned, and Zhou decided to make a new plan emphasizing war preparation and third-front construction.

Meanwhile, CCP leaders held a series of meetings to discuss how to deal with the escalating Vietnam War. At an April 12 Politburo meeting chaired by Liu, Deng outlined four possibilities for a coming war: "First, the war will be fought in South Vietnam; second, the war will be fought in both South and North Vietnam, and will be linked to the war in Laos; third, the war will be fought in our provinces neighboring Vietnam; and fourth, the US imperialists will fight a larger regional war with us, even involving Korea." China had to be prepared for all four prospects.[25]

Zhou had already called a meeting about war preparation before the April 12 Politburo meeting took place. At that meeting, he stated that although a world war was unlikely for the moment, the flames of the Vietnam War could possibly spread to China. It was thus vital that China give as much support to Vietnam as possible while ramping up production at home and getting ready for war. Zhou stressed that, while the third front was being constructed, the first and second fronts should not be ignored, since if a war were to soon break out, these fronts would still need to shoulder the main burden.[26] Zhou followed the same line of thought in his Politburo presentation, in which he endorsed Deng's opinions. In preparing for war, he said, "military industry, the third front, and foreign aid all need to be accelerated." However, "some moves," he cautioned, "should be slower than others, and some should even be postponed." International representation of China's policies "should reserve leeway, and some statements should be made incrementally. We should strike the enemy only after he strikes us first. With respect to putting forward the slogan of 'assisting Vietnam and resisting America,' the sentence can be divided in two in practice, first to 'assist Vietnam,' and then to 'resist America.'"[27]

Mao continuously stressed in the months that followed that the construction of the third front must be regarded as a top priority regardless of whether China became involved in a war.[28] For Zhou, the key question remained how to balance the third front and the other two fronts. He told a Politburo meeting that while it was essential to guarantee war preparation and the construction of the third front, other "key aspects of the national economy," especially agriculture and food supply, should not be ignored. He believed that "some control should be exerted" on infrastructure development, war preparation, and foreign aid, and that "unlimited expansion should not be allowed." In no circumstance should "the situation of 1958 and 1959 be repeated," he emphasized.[29]

Against this backdrop, Zhou selected several expressions from Mao's talks to make up a brief and straightforward Mao quotation: "To be prepared for war, to be prepared for famine, and to do everything for the people."[30] In composing the quotation, Zhou certainly remembered the Great Famine a of few years before. Thus, he equated "preparing for famine" with "preparing for war" to avoid an imbalance in China's economic development. In particular, agriculture must be taken as the first area to protect.[31] This time, Mao accepted Zhou's endeavor.[32] The new five-year plan that Zhou had spent much time working on was never finalized, but the quotation about being prepared for war and famine was made a "supreme instruction" that the whole country would follow. Over the next decade or so, this Mao quotation equipped Zhou with a veritable "emperor's sword" (*shangfang baojian*) with which to preserve the bottom line in China's economic development, and agricultural development in particular, which proved especially crucial when China descended into the chaos of the Cultural Revolution.

• • •

Another subject that Zhou frequently discussed with foreign leaders in the summer of 1965 was the planned Second Asian-African Conference. Indonesian president Sukarno introduced the idea for the conference in April 1964, which he proposed to hold in Indonesia on the tenth anniversary of the 1955 Bandung Conference. Zhou immediately supported the idea, but he suggested that it would be better if the conference were held in an African country. Sukarno accepted Zhou's proposal. In April 1965, Zhou visited the Indonesian capital, Jakarta, to celebrate the tenth anniversary of the Bandung Conference, where he also met with many foreign leaders. They decided collectively that the Second Asian-African Conference would be held in Algeria. For Zhou, this would be a good opportunity to strengthen and spread China's international influence.

The path toward the conference was bumpy. One obstacle was the different positions held by China and India on whether to invite Moscow. Beginning in early June, Zhou and Chen Yi visited Pakistan, Tanzania, and Egypt, before traveling to Algeria for the conference. Zhou insisted in meetings with foreign leaders that all participants of the conference should be Asian and African countries, "countries of other regions, with no exception, will not be invited," and "puppet regimes of imperialists cannot attend either."[33] A coup erupted in Algeria when Zhou arrived in Cairo on June 19, in which President Ben Bella was overthrown. Zhou did not want to give up on the conference. He stayed in Cairo and sent Chen to Algiers for the meeting of foreign ministers in preparation for the conference. However, the situation in Algeria remained confusing and uncertain, and the conference was ultimately postponed to "avoid a split among Asian and African countries."

But Zhou's engagement with the Asian and African countries was not without positive results. In November 1965, a vote by the UN General Assembly on whether Beijing or Taipei should occupy China's UN seat ended in a draw for the first time in UN history. This represented an enormous achievement in international diplomacy for Zhou.

Meanwhile, however, China's external relations witnessed the emergence of a strong countercurrent. When Zhou was hosting a National Day reception on the evening of September 30, he learned that "something very big" had happened in Indonesia.

Zhou was not surprised. In early August, Mao and Zhou had met with D. N. Aidit, chairman of the Indonesian Communist Party (ICP), when he visited China. Aidit told Mao and Zhou that if the Indonesian right-wing forces tried "to strike us," the ICP would "establish a military committee and strike back."[34] Zhou assigned Yao Zhongmin, the Chinese ambassador to Indonesia, to be Beijing's "sole contact" with Aidit. In mid-August, Aidit informed Yao that the ICP "is determined to take resolute action to seize political power in Indonesia." In early September, Yao delivered Beijing's reply to Aidit, advising the ICP to "be determined and well prepared and move forward resolutely; in the event of setbacks, be determined to persist in struggles in the countryside." Then, Aidit informed Yao that the ICP would make the "decisive move" on September 30. Zhou cabled Aidit a few days later, supporting the ICP's decision and advising him that "after the success of the uprising, the ICP should continue to recognize Sukarno as the president and maintain 'Nasakom,' which might be useful internationally."[35]

On October 2, Zhou told an Indonesian delegation visiting Beijing that he had learned from foreign news reports that "the coup by a committee of right-wing generals had failed" in Jakarta and that President Sukarno's "guards had organized a revolutionary committee to control the situation."[36] Over the next two days, Zhou told two other Indonesian delegations that Sukarno remained "quite safe"; however, Zhou told the delegations he was unable to make any further judgment of Indonesia's situation.[37] However, Beijing's telegraphic communication with the Chinese embassy in Jakarta was never interrupted. Zhou instructed Yao "to be cautious, not to make comments, and not to publicly search for information, while maintaining normal contact with Indonesian officials." Zhou also reminded Yao "to get mentally prepared for sudden changes, including an attack on the embassy by the military."[38]

Not until two weeks later did Zhou and the CCP leadership confirm that right-wing forces had indeed seized control of Indonesia, "although massacres of ICP members and supporters had not begun."[39] However, as Sukarno had informed the Chinese embassy in early November that "if he were to be given some time, he should be able to control the situation," CCP leaders, including Zhou, remained hopeful that "the ICP and left-wing forces would amass their strength" and begin a counteroffensive.[40] Chen Yi, accompanying

Zhou in a meeting with a North Korean delegation, even claimed that "the ICP has a membership of three million. If only dozens of thousands resist resolutely, that will be fine. . . . If the right-wing forces overthrow Sukarno, that might turn out to be a good thing." This way, the ICP would "firmly turn toward carrying out armed struggles."[41]

However, the situation in Indonesia did not develop as Zhou and other CCP leaders had hoped. Aidit was executed in late November, and by the end of the year, no "resolute counteroffensive" by the ICP had taken place. The Indonesian military, by gradually marginalizing Sukarno, a very old friend of Zhou's, had gained complete control of power. Within a few short months, the ICP was destroyed, and the "Beijing-Jakarta Revolutionary Axis" collapsed. In March 1966, the CCP leadership ordered all records of confidential telegraphic exchanges between Beijing and the ICP leadership to be destroyed.[42]

The dramatic reversal of the situation in Indonesia also put an end to Zhou's pursuit of the second Asian-African Conference. In a letter to leaders of the Asian-African countries in late October, he acknowledged that "rather than forcefully pursuing the conference in violation of the principle of consensus, it is better to temporarily table it."[43] But Zhou knew, as he told several foreign visitors in November, that it was now impossible to hold the conference.[44]

* * *

Zhou's biggest headache as summer turned to fall in 1965, apart from his obsession with China's international challenges, remained China's domestic political situation, which was becoming increasingly tense. CCP leaders held a series of meetings in Beijing that began on September 18 and continued for nearly a month. Mao's speeches and comments at these meetings were highly provocative. "Before long I will depart to see Marx," he lamented. "How may I report to him? You make me carry a capitalist tail with me; I will not accept that! . . . If the Central Committee becomes revisionist, I will rebel!"[45] Zhou and other leaders could clearly sense that the chairman was about to take political action on a scale unprecedented in CCP history.

On November 10, 1965, the Shanghai-based *Wenhui bao* published a lengthy essay written by a previously little known author named Yao Wenyuan, titled "On the New Historical Drama 'Hai Rui Dismissed from Office.'"

At first glance, the article seemed to be a normal academic piece. If there was something unusual about the subject of the essay, it was that the author of the drama was Wu Han, vice mayor of Beijing. Yet for Mao, the article represented an important step toward the Cultural Revolution. Early in the spring, Jiang Qing had traveled to Shanghai and commissioned Yao to write the essay.[46] After the essay's publication, few in the party's top leadership paid much attention to it. The CCP's Beijing Committee, and particularly Peng Zhen, who headed the committee, attempted to protect Wu by describing the situation as an academic debate. They also blocked newspapers in Beijing from reprinting the essay.[47]

Zhou had no prior knowledge of Yao's essay, but his intuition probably told him that it was not a simple matter. He was extremely cautious from the beginning, carefully watching Mao's moves. Meanwhile, he tried not to let the matter spin out of control until Mao made his position on the essay clear. On November 26, Zhou arrived in Shanghai to attend the eightieth birthday celebrations of Anna Louise Strong, a leftist American journalist who had long lived in China. Chen Pixian, Shanghai's party secretory, asked Luo Ruiqing to brief Zhou on Yao's essay, telling him that "the chairman has been quite unhappy about Beijing's refusing to publish it in local papers." Zhou thanked Chen when he saw him the next day.[48]

After he returned to Beijing, Zhou immediately called Peng to force newspapers in Beijing to publish Yao's essay.[49] Additionally, he and Peng wrote an "editor's note" to accompany the essay when it was published in *Renmin ribao*. The note emphasized that "there should be the freedom to criticize and countercriticize. As for wrong opinions, we should reason with them, respect the facts, and try to persuade others through reasoning."[50] Apparently, at that time Zhou still tried his best to treat the matter as an academic issue.

Soon, however, more events unfolded. On December 21, Mao stated in a talk in Hangzhou that "the crux of 'Hai Rui Dismissed from Office' was the question of dismissal. Emperor Jiajing dismissed Hai Rui, and in 1959 we dismissed Peng Dehuai. Peng Dehuai is Hai Rui."[51] Mao's words clearly indicated that criticism of the Hai Rui case was not, as Zhou had expected, merely an "academic issue." It was a political case, one that the chairman would use to entangle his political enemies.

Zhou was suddenly notified by the Central Administrative Office in early December that he was to attend "an extremely important conference" in Shanghai. No agenda, however, was attached to the notice. Zhou knew at once that something highly unusual had happened. He rushed to Shanghai, where he found that Luo, the chief of staff, would become the target of a new purge.

Lin Biao initiated the purge. After Lin became China's minister of defense, he and Luo had enjoyed a brief honeymoon. But when Lin struggled to engage in routine CMC work due to poor health, Mao assigned Marshal He Long to help Lin. Gradually, however, Lin began to feel that, with He Long's presence, Luo had gradually alienated him while becoming increasingly closer to He. Lin wrote Mao on November 30, saying that he had "some important matters to report," but that he would like to first send Ye Qun, his wife, to see Mao for a preliminary briefing.[52] Ye flew to Hangzhou the same day for a "briefing" that lasted five hours.[53] On December 2, Mao commented on a report that Lin had sent him, endorsing Lin's approach of "highlighting politics" and denouncing "those who have spread eclecticism [that is, opportunism]" in the PLA.[54] Mao thus indicated that he agreed to Luo's purge. He also relayed the remarks to Zhou, Liu, and other top leaders.[55]

It seems that Mao decided to side with Lin for two reasons: He needed Lin's firm support to launch the Cultural Revolution, and he felt that Luo had been too close to Liu and Deng.[56] He knew that Zhou's services would be required to arrange and complete Luo's removal. Mao spoke with Zhou in Shanghai late on the night of December 5, when he must have shared with the premier his plans to purge Luo.[57] This should have come as a huge surprise to Zhou, especially because he had seen Luo just a few days before in Shanghai, and Luo had conveyed to him Chen Pixian's message about Mao's connection with the Yao essay. After the meeting, Zhou immediately acted on the chairman's instructions.

The conference on the Luo case began on December 8, and it would go on for an entire week. When the Politburo Standing Committee first met about the case, Mao set the tone for its discussion by referring to Luo as an "ambitious schemer" whose "worldview is different from ours." In particular, the chairman emphasized that "Luo has virtually treated Comrade Lin Biao as an enemy." Then, the conference was expanded to include Politburo members, heads of various ministries, and high-ranking PLA commanders. Ye Qun delivered on Lin's behalf three speeches lasting a total of ten hours. She claimed that "Luo's individualism has reached such a degree that he would not be satisfied unless Comrade Lin Biao let him be the minister of defense."[58]

Zhou and Deng had a conversation with Luo outside the meeting. They informed him that Mao believed he was "against Lin, but not me," and that if Luo did not oppose Lin or the theme of "highlighting politics," and did not ask for more power, his case could be tabled for the moment. Luo did not believe that it was Mao who had decided to purge him, and hence he asked to confront Lin face to face in Mao's presence. Zhou looked at Luo, not knowing what to say. After a long while, he told Luo, "How can you be so naïve?" and he asked Luo to "calm down." There was no need to talk to Mao or Lin, Zhou said.[59]

Luo's purge was not an isolated incident. Around the same time, Yang Shangkun was dismissed after many years as head of the Central Administrative Office, also at Mao's behest. Yang's replacement was Wang Dongxing, a longtime head of Mao's bodyguards. With the reshuffling, Mao further concentrated power in his own hands. Yang, as a party cadre and state bureaucrat, was in theory still responsible to the party and the state, whereas Wang, a close associate of Mao's, would be first and foremost responsible to Mao. Zhou had maintained a close relationship with Yang, who frequently informed Zhou about Mao's whereabouts. His relationship with Wang had not been close, and he had to develop a rapport with Wang almost from scratch.

The high-level personnel change brought to the fore the organizational structure and operational system of the party and the state. Zhou, as well as Liu, Deng, and other party leaders, should have at least tried to question the decision to replace Yang with Wang. However, they kept silent. This probably meant that they had all by then realized that no space was left for them to speak out against any of Mao's decisions.

• • •

In early 1966, Mao accelerated preparations for the Cultural Revolution. Two seemingly unrelated events occurred in February. First, a "Group of Five" headed by Peng Zhen drafted the "Outlines of Current Discussions on Scholarly Issues" (known as the "February Outlines"). Almost at the same time, Jiang Qing called in Mao's name a roundtable discussion on literary and arts work by the PLA. In fact, the two events were closely connected.

The making of the February Outlines was largely the work of the party establishment, represented by Peng Zhen in this case, who racked their brains to devise a series of norms and regulations for channeling the emerging mass movement in the direction they envisioned. On the one hand, the authors of the February Outlines asserted that the criticism of "Hai Rui Dismissed from Office" represented a "big struggle in the sphere of ideology," which was "part of the struggles between socialism and capitalism." On the other hand, the document called for adherence to Mao's teaching on "allowing all different opinions to be presented and to persuade others by reasoning" in the spirit of "all being equal before the truth."[60]

Zhou did not take part in the drafting of the February Outlines. However, he paid close attention to the document from the beginning. On February 5, he attended a Politburo Standing Committee meeting chaired by Liu and Deng, at which Peng reported on how the outlines had been composed. He insisted that Wu Han's problems were an academic issue, rather than a political case, and that no connection existed between Wu and Peng Dehuai. Liu and Deng endorsed Peng's verdict, and Zhou concurred. Consequently, the meeting approved the February Outlines. Deng immediately relayed the decision to Mao along with the text of the outlines.[61]

Peng went to Wuhan with Kang Sheng and Lu Dingyi on February 8 to report to Mao. Knowing that Liu, Deng, Zhou, and others had approved the February Outlines, Mao did not voice any opposition to the document. Still, he asked, "Can Wu Han be considered an anti-Party and antisocialist figure?" "No, he cannot, but he has been very nervous," replied Peng. Mao said that Wu might continue to serve as vice mayor of Beijing, so that there was no need for him to be nervous.[62] Mao's words gave Peng and others the impression that he had approved the outlines. On February 12, the February Outlines was relayed to the whole party after Deng signed the document.[63]

But Mao had actually assigned Jiang Qing to another mission. On February 20, Jiang organized a roundtable on the PLA's literary and arts work. After repeated revisions—with Mao's input—a summary of the roundtable took shape, which emphasized that since 1949, "there have been fierce class struggles on the cultural front, and an anti-Party and antisocialist black line had excised its dictatorship." To "thoroughly uproot this line," it was necessary "to wage a great socialist revolution on the cultural front."[64] Lin Biao was not involved in the roundtable at all. However, when Mao was revising the summary, he added a few words to its title indicating that it was done "with Comrade Lin Biao's entrustment."[65] By doing so, Mao meant to give more strength and legitimacy to the document while forcing Lin to support its conclusions.

The roundtable was an important debut for Jiang Qing on China's political stage. In previous years, she had actively promoted what was billed as a "revolution of Peking Opera." Then, with Mao's support, she coordinated Yao's essay and its publication. Now she formally stepped into the forefront of Chinese politics, and soon she would become the "banner woman" of the Cultural Revolution. Previously Zhou had not had much direct contact with her. After this event, Zhou's working relationship with Jiang would become very close in the years to come.

Once Lin's name was attached to Jiang's summary, Mao quickly rewarded him and decided to conclude the Luo case, which had been pending since the previous December. Beginning on March 4, Deng, Peng, and Ye Jianying chaired a CMC meeting, at Mao's instruction, to continue criticizing Luo and to settle his case. Luo, who felt the proceedings "truly intolerable," attempted suicide on March 18. He did not die, but his leg was broken and he became permanently disabled.[66]

* * *

Mao again raised the issue of antirevisionism in mid-March. From March 17 to 20, he held a meeting in Hangzhou attended by top CCP leaders to discuss whether the party should dispatch a delegation to attend the Soviet Communist Party's Twenty-Third Congress. In fact, Liu, Zhou, Deng, and other leaders had already discussed the matter. After deliberating back and forth, and repeatedly guessing Mao's intentions, they had decided to send a CCP delegation to Moscow.[67] However, when Mao spoke at the Hangzhou conference, he categorically rejected the decision. The Soviets were convening the congress in the context of huge domestic and international difficulties, Mao said. "We should not go there. We should not leave them with any illusions. There is no need for us to even send them a congratulatory telegram. We only need to tell them that we are not coming."[68]

Mao had to firmly adhere to "antirevisionism," because only by constantly emphasizing that the Soviet Union had deteriorated into a "revisionist country" would his efforts to take dramatic action in China to fight against revisionism be justified. Furthermore, over the years, Mao had always linked the struggles of "anti–Soviet revisionism" with opposition to the Soviet Union's great power chauvinism against China, imbuing "anti–Soviet revisionism" with the spirit of revolutionary nationalism and Chinese patriotism.

It became even more difficult for other CCP leaders to challenge him on this issue.

Unsurprisingly, Mao was willing to do anything to enhance his domestic and international "antirevisionism" agenda. It so happened that Miyamoto Kenji, general secretary of the Japanese Communist Party (JCP), was then visiting China in an effort to establish an "international united front of assisting Vietnam and resisting America." Although this was an area long managed by Liu and Deng, Mao intervened in an utterly arbitrary way.

Miyamoto arrived in China in mid-February, where he held a series of meetings with Peng Zhen in Shanghai and Guangzhou before traveling to Hanoi. Miyamoto returned to Beijing at the end of February, holding consecutive meetings with Liu and Deng from March 4 to 8. In the international Communist movement, the JCP had firmly supported the CCP's struggles against Soviet revisionism. However, Miyamoto told his Chinese comrades, this time was different, as supporting Vietnam should be a mission of the highest priority. After Khrushchev's downfall, he explained, Moscow had begun providing more support to Vietnam, thus laying the foundation for establishing a broader united front including Moscow against US imperialism. Liu and Deng were unmoved, and they still insisted that anti-imperialism had to be linked with antirevisionism, and that the Chinese and Japanese parties should not have too many illusions about the new Soviet leadership. The meetings deadlocked.[69]

Miyamoto spent eleven days in North Korea beginning on March 11. There, he and Kim Il-sung also agreed to establish an anti-American front.[70] He then returned to Beijing for further meetings with Liu and Deng. He reported that both the Vietnamese and Korean comrades endorsed including Moscow in an anti-American international front. Finally, Liu and Deng reached a last-minute compromise with Miyamoto, agreeing to issue a joint communiqué to criticize revisionism without naming the Soviets.[71] Associates of the two sides began to draft and revise the joint communiqué.

Liu and Deng's handling of the matter was not without precedent. In the great polemic between Beijing and Moscow, the CCP, to attract more support, usually did not force other parties to name the Soviets in criticizing revisionism. The JCP was a major actor in international Communism and a longtime CCP ally. The ICP, another CCP ally, had collapsed in the wake of the September 30 incident. The JCP's support thus became even more important for the CCP than before. Furthermore, Hanoi and Pyongyang, both of which had sided with the CCP in the "antirevisionism" struggles, clearly supported including Moscow in an anti-US front. Beijing's continued opposition to such a united front could cause China to become isolated internationally. Liu and Deng thus compromised with Miyamoto.

Zhou did not attend the meetings with Miyamoto. While the joint communiqué neared completion, he chaired a mass rally attended by over sixteen thousand people to welcome the JCP delegation. Once the two sides had worked out every detail of the text of the communiqué, Zhou again met with the JCP delegation, giving them his "warm congratulations." He told Miyamoto that the text of the communiqué had been urgently sent to Mao for approval, and that a formal signing would be held "at a time that the Japanese comrades feel appropriate." Zhou then hosted a farewell banquet for Miyamoto at the Great Hall of the People.[72]

Mao, however, turned the whole matter on its head. Mao commented after reviewing the communiqué that by failing to name "Soviet revisionism," it missed the most important point and thus was only a "nameless announcement." He immediately revised the text, adding sentences referring to the "Soviet-led clique" in three places.[73] On March 28, Mao met with Miyamoto in Shanghai, telling him that all the agreements that the JCP had reached with Liu and Deng did not count, and that the joint communiqué should not be issued. Miyamoto repeatedly tried to explain that both the JCP and CCP "have carried out struggles against imperialism and revisionism, and it would be desirable if a joint communiqué could be issued based on a consensus on these two matters." Mao replied, "I would only like to say two things. First, your attitude is what the Soviet leadership welcomes. And second, it is what we do not welcome." Consequently, Mao killed the communiqué that Liu, Deng, and Miyamoto had worked so hard to put together.[74]

Mao's behavior came with big consequences. In addition to exposing the contradictions between him and Liu and Deng, he also created a serious crisis in the CCP's relationship with the JCP. Miyamoto left China enraged. Later, after the JCP had tried unsuccessfully to obtain a satisfactory explanation and apology from the CCP, it formally cut off relations with the CCP, which thus lost one of its most important allies in international Communism.[75]

To Zhou, Mao's highly abnormal move was another severe warning. Although the chairman had been known for acting in unpredictable ways, this time his actions had implications for the CCP's international reputation and credibility. Mao's behavior had broken all codes and protocol. This was an indication that for him the countdown had begun to the "very big action" that he had long planned.

* * *

Mao, a master of intraparty struggles, knew it was now the time to make Zhou more clearly pick a side. In late March, he summoned Kang Sheng to Shanghai and talked with him over three consecutive days. Both the party's Beijing Committee headed by Peng Zhen and the Central Propaganda Department directed by Lu Dingyi, the chairman claimed, had "protected the bad guys" and "stood on the side of revisionism." Therefore, they should be dissolved. He announced that "if revisionism has emerged at the Party Center, rebellions against it should arise everywhere."[76] After he returned to Beijing on March 31, Kang immediately conveyed Mao's explosive opinions to Zhou and Peng Zhen.[77]

Zhou should have realized at once that Mao had presented him with a big challenge. He did not respond for two days, in part because he was managing the aftermath of a large earthquake in Xingtai, Hebei Province. But the untypical delay of his response to the chairman also reveals how difficult it was for him psychologically to decide how to respond to Mao.

Zhou finally wrote Mao on the evening of April 2. He reported that "by consulting with Peng Zhen and Kang Sheng," he was determined to "follow the chairman's instructions and hold high the banner of proletarian cultural revolution, thoroughly criticizing reactionary academic thought in literature, history, and philosophy and exposing the antiparty and antisocialist bourgeois stands held by those academic authorities." Indeed, he claimed, "this is a question concerning the seizure of the leadership position in the cultural sphere." He further stated that "the report by the Group of Five (e.g., the February Outlines) is wrong," and that it was necessary to "replace it with another Central Committee notice with the chairman's examination and approval" to "energize the proletariat while suppressing the bourgeoisie."[78]

Mao liked Zhou's response. The premier had clearly declared that he would stand on Mao's side in the enormous struggles on the horizon. We have no way of knowing what went through Zhou's mind in the forty-eight hours that ended in his writing this letter to express his loyalty to Mao. But it likely was a painful process for him, even one of soul-searching. Ultimately, he decided to stand on Mao's side in a political storm unprecedented in CCP history. Zhou's response also fit well with the principles that he had followed since the Yan'an Rectification Campaign.

In retrospect, spring 1966 was probably the last window of opportunity for Liu, Zhou, Deng, and others in the party establishment to collectively block Mao from leading China toward the disastrous Cultural Revolution. Indeed, it was the sort of moment that, once missed, never comes again. However, in the face of an increasingly daring and unscrupulous Mao, Zhou and his colleagues were vulnerable, reluctant to act, and lacking courage and imagination. Consequently, it became impossible for them to resist Mao's unreasonable, rampant, and crazy offensives.

Why, then, were they and the whole party and state establishment so powerless against Mao? Why did they fail to show any guts or capacity to push back on Mao's extraordinarily provocative moves? Was this because of Mao's despotic power and semidivine authority? Or was this due to the 1943 resolution providing him with the final authority on all important decisions? Both of these reasons are true. But the key probably also lay in the inability of either Liu, Zhou, Deng, or any other CCP leader to come up with an alternative grand legitimacy narrative for the Chinese revolution and "continuous revolution." From opposing Soviet revisionism to preventing revisionism from claiming dominance in China, Mao had assembled a whole set of theories that would lead China toward the Cultural Revolution. Meanwhile, he also linked such theories to the sensitive subject of opposing Soviet great power chauvinism against China. In fact, since 1964, he had begun to claim that China should be prepared against the threat of a Soviet attack on China.[79] Indeed, Mao had established his ideological and discursive dominance by combining his Communist utopian vision with Chinese patriotism and revolutionary nationalism, which took "we, the Chinese, have stood up" as its motto. In China's political development, this dynamic, combined with his unchecked political power and unchallengeable authority, thus made Mao invincible.

• • •

Now, Peng Zhen became the next target of Mao's purge. Among the CCP leadership, Peng had long been regarded as a confidant of Mao. Indeed, he was even thought to possess the power of a "half general secretary." However, the chairman grew increasingly suspicious of Peng after he said at the Seven Thousand Cadres Conference that Mao could also be criticized.

Purging Peng was another of Mao's personnel shake-ups in preparation for the Cultural Revolution.

Zhou remained quite cautious in dealing with Peng, always trying to involve Peng when making a decision. But in early April, the situation quickly changed. Beginning on April 9, the Central Secretariat, chaired by Deng, met for three days. Zhou, though not a member of the secretariat, also attended the meeting. On April 12, Zhou, along with Deng and Peng Zhen, wrote Mao, reporting the decision to brand Luo as a criminal who had "opposed Mao and Mao Thought," and "forced Lin to step down" while "managing his own independent kingdom."[80]

Although Peng signed the letter, Mao had already identified him as a "Luo accomplice." When the Central Secretariat met in mid-April, Kang Sheng conveyed Mao's harsh criticism of Peng and the February Outlines, immediately exposing Peng to fierce attacks from his comrades.[81] Mao appeared at the meeting on April 23. He claimed that Peng, as the person backing Wu Han, had made the criticism of Wu extremely difficult. Then, in a loud voice, the chairman warned that "revisionism has not only appeared in the cultural circles but has also emerged in the party, the government, and the military, which is a very big problem."[82] The conference officially linked Peng Zhen with Luo Ruiqing, Lu Dingyi, and Yang Shangkun as a "counterrevolutionary clique."

There was absolutely no evidence to support the allegation that the four belonged to the same faction. Indeed, they did not even interact much beyond what is normal for a working relationship. Still, they were arbitrarily brought together as the members of a "counterrevolutionary clique." When Gao Gang and Rao Shushi were purged, they were groundlessly referred to as a "clique." At the Lushan Conference of 1959, Peng Dehuai, Zhang Wentian, Huang Kecheng, and Zhou Xiaozhou, in the same baseless way, had also been identified as a "clique." No factual evidence was presented to support any of these accusations, yet the verdicts were reached anyway. None of the accused was allowed to defend himself. Ironically, Peng, Luo, Lu, and Yang were actively involved in the invention of those previous cases. Now, the gate to the hell that they had opened for others was theirs to walk through.

• • •

Two monumental documents of the Cultural Revolution came into being toward the beginning of May 1966. The first, the "May Seventh Instruction," was a letter that Mao wrote to Lin about the PLA's involvement in agricultural production. The story began with the army's difficulty in maintaining an adequate supply of food after the Great Leap Forward. Following Zhou's instructions and with Lin's support, soldiers were mobilized to produce grain, which greatly improved the army's food supply. From then on, the army continued to participate in agricultural production. While praising the army's practice of grain production, Mao put forward a series of "big ideas": All organizations in China—the army, factories, people's communes, schools, commercial and service businesses, and party and government agencies—should be made into "big schools." Each "should learn politics, military affairs, and culture, and engage in agricultural production, and should build up its own medium- and small-sized workshops to produce goods for its own use and the exchange of other goods of equal value." In addition, the army should "take part in mass work, factory work, and rural socialist education. After socialist education, there are always other kinds of mass work for it to do, to unite the army and people as one. The army should also participate in the revolutionary struggle against capitalist culture."[83]

Mao's remarks revealed his imagined "ideal status" of China's party, state, and society. His vision was utopian in essence, and it reflected the ways the chairman hoped to transform China and the Chinese people. In this sense, Mao's vision also revealed his intention to begin the process of "grand reconstruction" simultaneously with the process of "grand destruction" in his "continuous revolution."

The Politburo held a series of enlarged meetings chaired by Liu that began on May 9. Mao did not attend them, but the whole process was under his control. Zhou was scheduled to visit Romania and Albania in mid-May. Romania's leader, Nicolae Ceaușescu, very much hoped to use Zhou's visit to highlight Bucharest's "independent foreign policy" that resisted the pressure of Moscow's influence.[84] He thus dispatched Emil Bodnăraș, Romania's first vice premier, to Beijing to confirm Zhou's visit. Until May 13, the Chinese had promised Bodnăraș that Zhou's trip to Romania would go ahead as scheduled. However, on May 14, Beijing suddenly informed Bodnăraș that Zhou's visit would be postponed.[85]

Zhou put off his trip, violating normal diplomatic protocol, because the political struggles among top CCP leaders had reached another critical point. On May 15, Zhou reported to Mao that a "Capital Work Group" headed by Marshal Ye Jianying had been established to enhance "security in the capital area."[86] Meanwhile, following Mao's orders, Zhou deployed additional "reliable military units" to secure the "safety of Beijing and the surrounding areas."[87] Taking note of these highly unusual measures, Zhou knew that he had to stay in Beijing.

In mid-May, the CCP Central Committee issued the "May Sixteenth Notice," a constitutional document of the Cultural Revolution. Mao personally revised and edited its text. The most noticeable of Mao's additions to the notice was the following paragraph:

> Those representatives of the bourgeoisie who have sneaked into the party, the government, the army, and various cultural circles are a bunch of counterrevolutionary revisionists. Once the conditions are ripe, they will seize political power and turn the proletariat dictatorship into a bourgeoisie dictatorship. We have discovered some of them, but not some of the others. Some are still trusted by us and are being trained as our successors. People like Khrushchev are still nestling beside us. Party committees at all levels must pay full attention to this danger.[88]

In the above paragraph, Mao most clearly identified the missions and goals that he would pursue in the coming "Great Proletarian Cultural Revolution." Zhou knew that he had to more clearly and firmly demonstrate his support for Mao. Thus, he and Lin Biao became two main players at the Politburo meeting. Their presentations were most unusual and most influential.

Lin highlighted the danger of a "reactionary coup d'état" in China and how to prevent it. In boasting that every one of Mao's words represented the truth, he stated that "one word of Mao's counts for ten thousand words of others," and that "whoever opposes Mao will be put to death by the whole party and cursed by the whole country."[89]

Zhou delivered his speech on May 21, in which he fully endorsed Lin's views on preventing a "reactionary coup d'état" from happening by fighting against revisionism. He warned that even with the party's best efforts, "revisionism will come into being on both the central and local levels." Therefore, it was essential to not allow "revisionism to take over our control of power." He then pivoted to the subject of "keeping one's political integrity in his senior years," pledging his eternal loyalty to Mao:

> We must follow Chairman Mao. Chairman Mao is our leader today, and he will remain our leader one hundred years later. If one fails to be loyal to him in one's later years, all of one's past contributions will be completely nullified. Even after one's coffin is sealed or [one's] corpse is cremated, one will still be doomed.[90]

None of the top CCP leaders had ever made such a statement. Given Zhou's status in the Chinese leadership, the impact of these words was beyond extraordinary. This was a hugely crucial statement for Mao, in both the political and symbolic sense.

Indeed, the attitudes of Zhou and Lin were of critical importance while Mao pushed China toward the Cultural Revolution, but Zhou's was probably even more essential for the chairman. After his return to the first line in the CCP, Mao began to work on Zhou, giving Zhou the respect he had withheld from him since the premier's opposition to rash advance. After all, Zhou controlled China's administrative and executive power. Mao knew well that both in staging a political showdown with Liu and other "capitalist roaders in power" and in maintaining the routine operation of China's party and state in a time of great political turmoil, Zhou's service was indispensable.

But this did not mean that Zhou could have checked and balanced Mao at will. If he were to use his administrative and executive power to challenge Mao, he would need not only the determination and courage to "sacrifice oneself to preserve one's ultimate virtue" (*shashen chengren*) but also, and more importantly, the support of a grand legitimacy narrative to counter Mao's narrative and underpin his challenge to the chairman. But it was Mao who held absolute control over such a narrative, which had been profoundly intertwined with Mao's thoughts and ideas and propelled by his unlimited political power. As a result, when the tidal wave of the Cultural Revolution was engulfing Chinese society and the country's political landscape, Zhou chose almost intuitively to go along with the trend. This, it turns out, was exactly what Mao had expected.

PART IV

SURVIVING THE CULTURAL REVOLUTION

25

THE OPENING SALVOES OF THE CULTURAL REVOLUTION

1966–1967

On the evening of June 1, 1966, China's central radio service delivered the text of a "big character poster" written by seven Peking University (PKU) faculty members, who fiercely attacked the university leadership for its "conspiratorial activities against the Cultural Revolution." Kang Sheng brought the content of the poster to Mao's attention; the chairman read it, then ordered the Xinhua News Agency to "broadcast this text in its entirety."[1] These were Mao's marching orders for the Great Proletarian Cultural Revolution.

Zhou was unprepared for such a dramatic turn of events. He knew that the Socialist Education Movement at PKU had caused huge tension between the faculty and university leaders, and he had advised them to moderate their actions, especially considering that the campus hosted students from dozens of foreign countries.[2] Only a few days before, he, Liu Shaoqi, and Deng Xiaoping had discussed the situation at PKU, and they had decided to dispatch a work team there to "direct the movement," a decision endorsed by the chairman.[3] Now, Mao had suddenly changed his mind, and Zhou was alarmed.

Mao was in Hangzhou at the time, while Liu handled the Party Center's routine decision-making in Beijing. Liu and other CCP leaders, including Zhou, wanted to dispatch work teams to high schools and colleges in Beijing to regulate the mass activities taking place on campuses. They kept Mao informed of the developments in Beijing, and they asked him to return to the city to take charge.[4] On June 9, Liu, Zhou, and Deng flew to Hangzhou to see

Mao, who told them not to fear chaos and to go all out to mobilize the masses. Thus, he said, work teams would probably not be needed "until the dust has settled."[5] Liu again asked Mao to return to Beijing; the chairman said "no."

Back in Beijing, Zhou immediately began preparing for his long-planned, twice-postponed visit to Romania and Albania. Now, Zhou did not want to delay the trip any further, as this would allow him to stay away from the swirling political vortex in Beijing. Mao approved Zhou's travel plan.[6]

Zhou returned from abroad on July 1. Among those who welcomed him at Beijing Airport was Kang Sheng, who joined Zhou on the car ride back to the city. He suggested that Zhou not engage too deeply in the Cultural Revolution, but instead give more attention to the new Central Cultural Revolution Group (CCRG). Kang also told Zhou, "Liu and Deng may fall. . . . You should not get involved in dispatching work teams."[7] Kang was very close to Mao and had also long maintained a close friendship with Zhou. He probably would not have given Zhou these crucial suggestions without Mao's consent. It seemed that Mao did not want the premier to fall into the political trap he had set for Liu and Deng.

Mao kept his distance from Beijing. On June 15, he left Hangzhou to hide in a remote place, the Dripping Water Cave, not far from his hometown of Shaoshan. He needed a quiet environment to think about "some big issues" before the brewing political storm made landfall. At the end of June, he moved to Wuhan.

The situation in Beijing was murky. Although apparently the Cultural Revolution was being vigorously promoted, Liu and Deng were extremely cautious, as they did not know what exactly the Cultural Revolution was for. Around this time, a "June Eighteenth Incident" occurred at PKU when a serious conflict erupted between the work team assigned to the university and people who opposed it.[8] Liu and Deng believed that they should send more work teams to various schools in Beijing to guide the mass movement. They reported to Mao every decision they made for his approval, but received no substantial response.[9] Liu and Deng had no choice but to take one step, look around, then take another. Mao suddenly summoned Zhou to Wuhan on July 11. They met for three hours that afternoon; the next morning they talked for another two hours.[10] In these conversations, Mao was most likely sharing his thoughts and plans with Zhou.

Mao surprised the whole country on July 16 when he swam in the Yangzi River. Tens of thousands had gathered along the river that day to celebrate the tenth anniversary of Mao's 1956 swim in the Yangzi. Many of them witnessed Mao appear unexpectedly in the river as if "strolling in the backyard." The scene was widely publicized throughout China, accompanied by a Mao quotation: "Violent storms and waves are not frightening at all. Human society has developed despite them."[11] With his words and actions, the chairman sent a powerful message to the entire nation, especially the young generation: if he, at seventy-three, could still swim in the Yangzi, he was capable of virtually anything.

Mao returned to Beijing two days later. Liu rushed to see him. Mao was inside, talking with several CCRG members. The chairman, knowing that Liu was waiting outside, told his secretary, "I do not want to see him."[12] The next day, Liu chaired an enlarged meeting of the Politburo Standing Committee, which Zhou attended. Chen Boda, who was now head of the CCRG, proposed that all work teams be immediately recalled from schools around the capital. The majority at the meeting, including Liu and Deng, opposed the motion. Zhou tactfully suggested that the work teams might be "temporarily recalled and the masses thus be allowed to carry out the movement by themselves."[13] Mao joined the meeting that evening. He listened to Liu's and Deng's reports and said nothing about the work teams.[14]

The enlarged meeting continued the next day. Deng, likely spurred by the fact that Mao had not made any negative comments on the work teams, firmly opposed withdrawing them. In a rare moment of impetuousness, Deng yelled at Chen Boda, "If all the work teams are to be recalled, how can the party lead?" Liu supported Deng, both claiming that most work teams were good. Zhou kept silent, and the motion to withdraw the work teams was tabled.[15] Though Mao missed the meeting, he quickly learned every detail about it. Deng's cooperation with Liu was, in the chairman's view, a huge offense. Later in the Cultural Revolution, Deng would bear the label of China's "second-largest capitalist roader in power."

Mao now felt it time to act. He announced on July 23—after listening to reports from Beijing leaders about the situation at the city's schools—that "it was a mistake to dispatch work teams," which had become "barriers of the mass movement."[16] The next day, he reiterated at a CCRG meeting that "all work teams should be recalled."[17] The third day, he emphasized again at an enlarged meeting of the CCRG that "the policy of dispatching work teams should change," so that "teachers and students will be able to carry out revolutionary activities by themselves."[18]

Zhou had a long conversation with Liu and Deng after he was apprised of Mao's unequivocal support for recalling the work teams. Then he sent them a letter, in which he wrote that their differences in opinion with the chairman "have mainly been caused by different evaluations and understandings of the current situation." The premier acknowledged that he had once shared Liu and Deng's "general understanding" of dispatching work teams, as they all believed that "there was the need to do so" at the time. But "every work team has had its specific experience in the place it has been." Therefore, Zhou advised Liu and Deng, "it is necessary to investigate and concretely analyze each case."[19] Zhou made these comments to free himself from the burden of the work team issue, as well as to help Liu and Deng climb out of the abyss their defense of the work teams had plunged them into. On July 26, the Politburo decided that all work teams would be recalled and dissolved.[20]

On July 29, the CCP's Beijing Committee convened a rally for college and high-school activists at the Great Hall of the People, at which Liu, Zhou, and Deng spoke. Zhou conveyed Mao's instruction to fulfill three tasks at schools: "To struggle, to criticize, and to transform." The Cultural Revolution was a new phenomenon, Zhou said. As a "veteran revolutionary," he had now "encountered new problems."[21] Liu and Deng said the same at the rally.[22] They were all telling the truth.

Mao came to the rally without informing anyone, staying behind the curtain while Liu, Zhou, and Deng spoke. After the last speech, the people attending the rally began to shout, "We want to see Chairman Mao!" As if by magic, Mao walked from behind the curtain onto the stage. He waved to the crowd and said nothing. The students responded with thunderous applause.[23]

News of the scene quickly spread to every school in Beijing and then across campuses nationwide. The word of the chairman's appearance instantly excited young students around the country. On August 1, to stoke the excitement even more, Mao wrote to the Red Guards at the high school affiliated with Tsinghua University the following message: "I express my warm support to you. In carrying out the Cultural Revolution throughout the whole country, we will warmly support all those who adopt the same revolutionary attitude as yours."[24] The chairman made this highly unusual move to boost support for the Cultural Revolution.

• • •

The CCP Central Committee's Eleventh Plenum began on August 1. Liu delivered a work report on the first day. While he was talking about the work teams, Mao repeatedly interrupted him. "Over 90 percent of the work teams have been completely wrong," Mao claimed. "They cannot wage struggles, cannot make criticism, and cannot pursue transformation. They have only played the role of suppressing and blocking the masses."[25]

Zhou spoke the next day. He told the plenum that he had just come back from a meeting at Mao's residence. Then, he reviewed the development of the Cultural Revolution, from the Yao essay to the big character poster written by seven PKU faculty members and "the chairman's decision to recall all work teams." "The political line," Zhou emphasized, was "at the center of all of them." More specifically, this concerned "whether or not to dare to struggle against revisionism and the capitalist roaders by mobilizing the masses." Emulating Mao's tone, he encouraged everyone to have "the determination to rebel by joining the masses to make revolution." All this, he acknowledged, might "temporarily bring Beijing into a chaotic situation" or even "disturb the order of our regime." However, he stressed, "we have nothing to fear, as to fear is not compatible with the chairman's thought." Zhou also made self-criticism for participating in the decision to dispatch work teams to Beijing schools in early June. Although he, Liu, and Deng had reported the decision to Mao, he said, they had acted to "preserve the old order."[26]

The chairman was now ready to take center stage. On August 4, he summoned a meeting of the Politburo Standing Committee. He and Liu, sitting next to each other, "got into a quarrel on some issues in an inflammatory mood."[27] Mao opened fire on Liu at the meeting, claiming that "the party leadership has violated its own commitments." He shouted, "Mass line? Trusting the masses? Believing in Marxism-Leninism? All are false!" Liu tried to calm down, saying, "I am in Beijing, so I should bear the main responsibility." Mao ridiculed him, exclaiming, "What have you done? You have established a bourgeois dictatorship in Beijing!" As if all this were not enough, Mao declared, "Among those sitting here today are evil elements and monsters!"[28]

The chairman summoned Zhou for another confidential discussion the next day. Zhou then called Liu, suggesting that he not attend public events or meet with foreign guests.[29] Mao also wrote a big character poster titled "Bombarding the Headquarters," in which he sternly accused Liu and Deng of "taking a reactionary, bourgeois stand; implementing bourgeoisie dictatorship; and trying to suppress the Cultural Revolution so spectacularly carried out by the proletariat."[30]

Lin Biao, who had been on vacation in Dalian, rushed back to Beijing on August 6 on Mao's orders in order to reinforce the chairman at the plenum.[31] Indeed, the orientation of the plenum was about to change completely. Mao's big character poster was distributed at the plenum on August 7, causing Liu and Deng to immediately become the targets of fierce attacks. The plenum, which originally had been scheduled for five days, was prolonged to twelve. The party leadership was reorganized during the last several days of the plenum in a series of promotions and demotions.

A new central leadership came into being on August 12. Mao was named the chairman of the Central Committee, and Lin Biao was named the vice chairman. Mao, Lin, Zhou, Tao Zhu, Chen Boda, Deng, Kang Sheng, Liu, Zhu De, Li Fuchun, and Chen Yun formed the new Politburo Standing Committee. With this new structure, in addition to becoming the sole vice chairman of the Central Committee, Lin was also designated as Mao's successor. Zhou was no longer vice chairman but stayed on the Politburo Standing Committee.[32] The Central Secretariat would no longer meet independently; its replacement was a central liaison meeting convened by Zhou and attended by Jiang Qing, Chen Boda, Kang Sheng, and other CCRG members. Ye Qun would also attend the meeting as Lin's representative and as a liaison between Lin and Zhou.[33] The change seemed to be a promotion for Zhou. Indeed, his status as convenor of the central liaison meeting, which integrated the power of the party, the government, and the military, suggested that he occupied a central position in the new power structure. In fact, however, it was Mao who controlled all the power. Zhou knew well that the new structure was a source of both safety and danger for him. His position was like that of a single tree standing above the rest of the forest. A strong and unforeseen wind could bring him down at any time.

Mao next had the idea of hosting a mass parade of young activists from Beijing and all over the country. Zhou managed to organize and complete all preparations for the gathering in a few short days after Mao introduced his idea. Mao intended to inspire the youngsters' revolutionary fervor and spirit, encouraging them to boldly partake in "revolutionary, rebellious actions." He shared with his associates the logic behind the grand parade: "We must draw lessons from the Soviet Union, where few people have had the opportunity to see Lenin. Thus, they have dropped Lenin's banner."[34] Mao would not make the same mistake.

Mao arrived at Tiananmen, the Gate of Heavenly Peace, in military uniform shortly after 5:00 A.M. on August 18 to review the parade of a million Red Guards and young students. When the parade began, a female student put a Red Guard armband on Mao's left arm. Zhou also wore a military uniform that day, a departure from his usual attire.[35]

• • •

The Cultural Revolution entered a phase of total mania in the wake of the August 18 rally. The chaos swept through the capital under the slogan "Down with all vicious monsters." Red Guard units in Beijing, which mostly comprised the children of revolutionary cadres and other "red category" families, began to take violent "revolutionary action" across the city, beating people identified as belonging to "black categories" and raiding their homes. Such "revolutionary behavior" then spread to other parts of the country. For a few days, Red Guards in Beijing even demanded that, to "make the whole world red," traffic lights should be changed, with green signaling drivers to stop and red meaning "go." Zhou immediately called a meeting with their representatives, in which he spent hours explaining to them why the proposed change was dangerous. Finally, they gave in.[36]

In the ensuing months, the Cultural Revolution movement was generally still under the control of the party and state apparatus. Most leaders of central ministries and almost all top officials in the provinces and municipalities were not attacked. In the main, the Red Guards' "rebellious actions" targeted designated "bad elements" in society rather than "capitalist roaders in power." The result was a near replay of the antirightist movement, albeit on a much larger scale.

Zhou faced a major dilemma. On the one hand, he had to follow what he understood as Mao's intention to "light a fire," and he repeatedly called for the Cultural Revolution to be carried out in the "spirit of revolutionary rebellion." On the other hand, he strove to regulate the movement, in order not to allow the flames to spread out of control. In late August, Zhou and Tao Zhu drafted ten measures to regulate the movement and protect key party and state agencies and their leaders. At the same time this was also another of Zhou's attempts to gauge Mao's intentions and bottom line.[37] If

Mao vetoed the measures, this would give Zhou insight into Mao's vision for the movement. If Mao approved them, though, Zhou would have a series of regulations to follow. Mao rejected the measures, ordering Zhou and others to "let the movement go by itself with no restrictions placed on the masses."[38] In early September, Zhou called for a second document to be drafted to propose disciplinary restrictions aimed at curbing the Red Guards' excesses. On September 3, he was summoned to a meeting with Tao Zhu, Chen Yi, Li Fuchun, and CCRG members to discuss the document. Those from the CCRG, who had an acute sense of what Mao liked and disliked, firmly opposed it. The document was dead before the chairman even saw it.[39]

Beginning in August, hundreds of thousands of Red Guards and young students traveled for free throughout China to "spread revolutionary ideas." This put the nation's transportation system under enormous pressure; the influx of students tested the limits of Beijing and other cities' capacity to accommodate new arrivals. Zhou, unable to block the nationwide trend, could only try his best to keep China's transportation infrastructure and national economy from becoming paralyzed. On September 15, when Mao—for the third time—reviewed a parade of one million young students at Tiananmen Square, Zhou delivered a speech standing next to Mao. He emphasized that it was crucial to guarantee healthy levels of production in the nation's industrial and agricultural sectors. Therefore, "Red Guards and revolutionary students should not make liaison efforts at factories and enterprises," Zhou shouted to the huge crowd. Also, he stressed, "Factories and rural areas should not make revolution by suspending production."[40] While the Great Helmsman was steering China into a raging storm, Zhou was doing all he could to prevent it from striking a reef.

By the time northerly winds brought down the last leaves in Beijing in fall 1966, the Cultural Revolution had paralyzed many of the capital's party and government agencies. Throughout the country, chaos was spreading continuously. Yet overall, the existing party and government institutions had not totally lost control. At one point, Mao told Zhou that the Cultural Revolution at the central level might conclude by the end of the year.[41]

Despite the chairman's words, however, the last three months of 1966 witnessed the further escalation and expansion of the Cultural Revolution. On October 2, *Renmin ribao* published an editorial essay titled "Thoroughly Criticize the Bourgeois Reactionary Line." Here, the notion of "bourgeois reactionary line" was a new invention, revealing Mao's intention to further

25.1 From left to right, Jiang Qing, Zhou Enlai, Lin Biao, and Mao Zedong at the Tiananmen Rostrum, September 15, 1966. *World History Archive / Alamy Stock Photo*

fan the flames of the Cultural Revolution. After he read the essay, Zhou discussed this new concept with Mao: Throughout the party's history, whenever a political line had to be defined, it would usually include an adjective such as "leftist" or "rightist." Never before had a term like "bourgeois reactionary" been used. What did it mean? Zhou asked. Mao replied that using "reactionary line," rather than "counterrevolutionary line," meant that those who had participated in that line would not necessarily be defined as enemies. Mao's oblique response to Zhou's question made it more complicated and confusing for Zhou to handle his routine work as the premier.[42]

Mao convened a central work conference on October 9 to discuss how to criticize the "bourgeois reactionary line."[43] The conference was scheduled for seven days, but it would not end until three weeks later. On October 16, Chen Boda delivered a keynote speech, which Mao had revised and approved.

Chen mentioned that in the party's history, the struggles between two lines had been complicated and fierce. Therefore, he emphasized, it was essential to dispel fear and strive to mobilize the masses, deepening the Cultural Revolution.[44] Both Liu and Deng made self-criticism at the conference, acknowledging that they had committed "serious mistakes by carrying out bourgeois reactionary lines."[45] The attitude of most in attendance, however, was lukewarm, even openly resentful. Mao noticed all of this. When he spoke, he said that the Cultural Revolution had lasted only six months, and it was understandable that many had failed to see its necessity. However, Mao told them, "revolutionary movements are naturally legitimate."[46]

Zhou was extremely cautious at the conference. Since the Eleventh Plenum, he had been closely watching Mao's every move, especially those that revealed his attitude toward Liu and Deng, and trying to figure out what Mao's next steps would be, but in vain. When he spoke at the work conference, Zhou mentioned that "the current situation shows that we are still at an early stage of the movement, which may continue for another five to ten years, as the chairman has said we will gain some experience over the next five years." But he also discussed "the need to set up a timetable for the Cultural Revolution." In particular, he hoped that the movement at central agencies might "come to an end by the coming Chinese New Year."[47] Indeed, Zhou could not determine what exactly the Cultural Revolution was meant to accomplish. This was not strange in the slightest. After all, if not even Mao could clearly answer this question, how could Zhou?

Mao appeared to have won a major victory in the Cultural Revolution with the close of the October work conference. Liu and Deng, after making self-criticism of their mistakes, had been thoroughly sidelined, and Mao's authority and power had risen to unprecedented heights. In reality, though, Mao was faced with a quandary: was it time already to proclaim the "victorious conclusion" of the Cultural Revolution? Mao was unwilling to end the movement so soon. He could clearly sense that the power of the existing party and state structures endured, if only invisibly. Moreover, his goal of "revolutionizing the people's spiritual world" through the Cultural Revolution was far from accomplished. It was true that the political power he now enjoyed was almost unlimited. But it was also true that he often felt he still had to yield to unseen forces beyond his control.

What Mao had sensed was the deep-rooted unwillingness of so many high-ranking cadres to carry the movement forward. They paid allegiance to him by mouth, not by heart. The party and state bureaucracy—the very elements that, in theory, should have served as the driving force for his vision—stood between what Mao intended the Cultural Revolution to be, and what it had become. Mao did not seem to fear that Liu would reemerge during his lifetime, and he remained confident in his ability to skillfully control intra-party political struggles. His biggest worry was whether his grand enterprise of "continuous revolution" would be undermined or even reversed after his passing. Given all this, what was to be the end of the Cultural Revolution? Mao was unable to come up with a clear answer. But he was certain of one thing: the storm this time had been huge, yet the victories he had won were only superficial. What should be his next steps? In fact, not even Mao himself could answer this question, let alone come up with good answers for other, less straightforward ones.

Zhou's situation was precarious. His intuition should have told him that politically he probably was in his safest position since the "opposing rash advance" attacks, as he was for the moment indispensable to Mao. Nonetheless, Zhou still felt uneasy. Mao was a person who followed neither rules nor conventional logic. Now, as Zhou could sense, Mao was attempting to play a card game on a scale absolutely unprecedented in history. But the premier did not know what cards Mao was holding, or how immense the card game would become.

• • •

The mass movements of the Cultural Revolution grew even more unrestrained in the last two months of 1966. Increasingly, they broke norms and regulations established during the CCP's previous political campaigns. Mao embraced—or even encouraged—such breakthroughs. This was most apparent in his attitude toward the "Anting Incident." On November 10, over a thousand members of the newly established "Shanghai Workers' Revolutionary Rebellion Headquarters" (SWRRH) arrived at Anting, a minor train station about twenty kilometers from Shanghai. They intended to travel to Beijing to obtain support and recognition from the CCRG for their organization, but Shanghai party authorities stopped the group at Anting. In protest, the workers lay across the rail tracks, blocking the Shanghai-Beijing Railway for more than twenty hours.[48]

No such event had ever occurred in the history of the People's Republic. Party leaders in Shanghai reported the incident to Beijing. Zhou found the workers' behavior undesirable, as it had the potential to trigger a new wave of chaos in Shanghai and even throughout China. But he did not intervene directly; instead, he persuaded Chen Boda to cable the workers, requesting that they return to Shanghai, as their protest "[would] influence the productivity of their own work units or even that of the whole country."[49] The turning point came on November 11, when Zhang Chunqiao, deputy head of the CCRG, flew to Shanghai to negotiate with the workers' leaders. At first, he asked them to return to Shanghai, assuring the workers that "everything can be discussed there." Gradually, however, his attitude changed. He described the workers' planned trip to the capital as a "revolutionary move" and promised that once they returned to Shanghai, all their requests would be satisfactorily resolved.[50] After most of the workers had arrived back in Shanghai, Zhang signed an agreement with their leaders—going against a resolution passed by the Shanghai CCP committee—to "recognize that the SWRRH is a legitimate revolutionary organization, and that their effort to travel to Beijing is a revolutionary move."[51]

Zhang had taken bold action largely because he had perceived the chairman's eagerness to engage the workers in the Cultural Revolution. When Zhang returned to Beijing, Tao Zhu, who was also a CCRG advisor, expressed doubts about Zhang's behavior.[52] But Mao approved of the way Zhang had settled the matter. At a Politburo meeting, the chairman asked, holding a copy of the PRC constitution, "Do the workers have the freedom of assembly? Have you read the constitution?" "It is fine to act first and obtain authorization later," he claimed, "as a concept always comes into being after there is a fact."[53] Zhou had paid close attention to the situation at Anting, and he acted quite shrewdly in response. When the incident began, he pushed Chen Boda to the front to handle it, and he supported Tao Zhu in questioning Zhang's management of the event but did not raise objections of his own.[54] Thus, it was easy for him to change his stance after Mao declared his support for Zhang.

Also underway in Beijing at the time was a national planning conference on industry and transportation. Chen Boda drafted for the conference a document permitting workers to establish their own organizations and allow students to make "revolutionary connections" at factories.[55] The party and government officials attending the conference almost unanimously opposed the document, complaining that "if the students and the workers were to join forces in a 'revolutionary rebellion,' the nation's economy will fall into complete disorder."[56] The conference reviewed a second document written with Zhou's support, which stipulated that workers could only "make revolution in their spare time" and that students would not be allowed to "pursue revolutionary connections" in factories.[57] Mao immediately rejected the proposal. A further document was needed, the chairman instructed, which would support workers' right to establish revolutionary organizations.[58]

The conference went on for nearly three weeks, despite being originally scheduled for just five days. Lin Biao joined the conference on December 6, announcing that it had not gone well. Indeed, he claimed, it was time for the Cultural Revolution in the industrial and transportation sectors to change direction completely.[59] The orientation of the conference was transformed. With Chen Boda acting as coordinator, a new document was drafted on "making revolution and promoting production." The proposal, which was based on the document that Chen had drafted earlier, allowed workers to participate in revolution during their off-work time, to establish their own organizations, and to make "revolutionary connections" with students. After Mao gave his approval, the document was relayed to the whole country.[60]

Zhou made some rather interesting and revealing comments at the conference. On the subject of the "tide of rebellions" that had emerged in the Cultural Revolution, he said, "As we cannot stop it, we may try to channel it." He viewed this as a "punishment," lamenting that "the punishment is created by our own behavior in the past. If we do not bear responsibility for it, who will? If we do not go into hell, who will? If we do not enter the tiger's cave, who will? We must be spiritually prepared for all of this."[61]

This was a rare confession from Zhou in those hectic days of the Cultural Revolution. Since the beginning of the movement, Zhou had largely been pushed to take action. But he had also tried to seize the initiative by reading Mao's intentions. After all, Zhou was facing and working alongside a veritable demigod, whose power and authority reached their zenith during the Cultural Revolution, and whose grand narrative of the "continuous revolution" dominated mainstream discourse in the CCP. Zhou had no choice but stay with Mao while China sailed into rapids and storms.

• • •

December 26, 1966, was Mao's seventy-third birthday. He and Jiang Qing summoned Chen Boda, Zhang Chunqiao, Yao Wenyuan, Wang Li, Qi Benyu, and Guan Feng—all members of the CCRG—to his home for dinner. But this was not simply a banquet. Mao had things to say. He was worried that capitalism would come back after he died, asserting "this is why we must carry out the Cultural Revolution" and must "struggle against the capitalist roaders in power." The struggle had begun long ago, he elaborated, but now it would culminate in a "great showdown, involving the whole country."[62] Suddenly, the chairman stood up. Holding his wine glass high, he said something completely beyond the expectations of anyone at the dinner: "Cheers to the victory of the full-scale civil war in the whole country next year!"[63]

Mao was seventy-three. His words were more than shocking; they were practically an outcry of hysteria. But he did give the toast. This was a "supreme instruction," which the whole country would put into practice unreservedly.

Several CCRG members gathered in the wake of the dinner to discuss the drafting of the 1967 New Year's editorial essay. After much deliberation, they decided to replace the phrase "full-scale civil war in the whole country" with "full-scale class struggle in the whole country." They also decided to focus on what the "end" of the Cultural Revolution should be, titling the essay "To Carry the Great Proletarian Cultural Revolution through to the End."[64] Mao approved the essay. It delivered an extremely important message to the nation: the Cultural Revolution would soon enter a new phase, characterized by even greater chaos.

Zhou did not attend Mao's dinner, but Jiang Qing conveyed Mao's words to him the next day. He likely sensed that the Cultural Revolution would continue in ways far beyond anything he had ever experienced.

Ironically, despite Mao's aggressive language, he could not completely sever his connections with the existing party and state structure, of which he had been the foremost creator and beneficiary. Even with his seemingly unlimited power, in the face of the existing structure he was just like the Monkey King, who could never escape from the Buddha's palm.[65] No matter how hard Mao tried to destroy the prevailing party and state structure, he would remain its prisoner. Zhou personified the existing structure's power, both detectable and undetectable. In this sense, when Mao sought to challenge the existing structure, he needed Zhou's cooperation more than ever before.

• • •

The first sign that Mao would take extraordinary new steps to lead the Cultural Revolution to the deeper levels was his abrupt purge of Tao Zhu, then still a Cultural Revolution star. The day after Mao's birthday banquet, Jiang Qing suddenly attacked Tao at a central briefing meeting, accusing him of being "China's biggest defender of the old order." Zhou was shocked, but still wanting to protect Tao, he shared Mao's notion of "full-scale civil war in the whole country" with Tao so that he could better prepare for the challenge.[66] On December 29, Mao criticized Jiang, saying that she had acted on her own initiative and moved forward too quickly.[67] In hindsight, Mao probably rebuked Jiang because he had not made up his mind about Tao's fate. After New Year's Day, however, Tao faced a continuous barrage of attacks. On January 4, 1967, Jiang Qing and Chen Boda publicly announced that Tao was "a true carrier of reactionary bourgeois lines."[68] Zhou remained committed to protecting Tao; early the next morning, he advised Tao to stay at home for several days.[69] However, the situation worsened rapidly. On January 8, Mao said that he would "not protect Tao anymore."[70] Almost overnight, Tao had become another major target of fierce attacks in the Cultural Revolution, next only to Liu and Deng.

In retrospect, Tao's downfall was not sudden. As an important party leader in Guangdong and southern China, he seemed to have long enjoyed Mao's trust and support. When the Cultural Revolution began, he was transferred to Beijing and quickly became China's number four leader, outranked only by Mao, Lin, and Zhou. He was put in charge of the routine operation of the party and the government and thus established a close working relationship with Zhou, while serving as a barrier between Zhou and all kinds of challenges that the premier would otherwise have to personally deal with. They shared similar political perspectives. Neither of them seemed to have fully understood Mao's ideas and plans for the Cultural Revolution, but they were both willing to act in accordance with what they understood as Mao's intentions. Neither of them believed that Mao meant to use the Cultural Revolution to destroy the entire party and state structure. Rather, they believed that party and government organs, as well as cadres and officials on all levels, would become the main drivers of the Cultural Revolution. It was completely beyond their imagination that Mao would go so far as to mobilize the masses to destroy China's party and state system.

Mao decided to purge Tao as a critical step in his drive to deepen the Cultural Revolution. By then, although mass movements had emerged across the country, party and government organs were still capable of controlling the overall situation. By bringing down Tao, Mao sent out an explicit signal that he was willing and ready to launch attacks on party and government organs throughout China. The chairman had an innate desire to see the world in disarray, as, to him, "only by bringing the world into great disorder can it be turned into a place of great order."[71]

When Mao moved to attack Tao, Jiang Qing finished him off at center stage. This period also saw Jiang, as well as the CCRG, begin to consolidate extraordinary political power in China, as Jiang emerged as the queen of the CCRG. Thus, the Cultural Revolution became, in a sense, a husband-and-wife enterprise comprising Mao and Jiang.

Tao's political demise put Zhou in an extremely difficult and complex situation. When Mao explained on January 8 why he had abandoned Tao, he said that he had done so because "this guy is not trustworthy."[72] There is no way of knowing how Zhou felt hearing Mao's comments. It is very likely that he would have thought Mao also saw him as a potential target. What did "not trustworthy" mean? Did the phrase refer to Tao's failure to thoroughly follow Mao's ideas and intentions? However, at that time, it was nearly impossible for anyone, including Zhou, to infer the chairman's wishes precisely. Mao's claim of Tao being "not trustworthy" was also a serious warning to Zhou, who represented the "old government" and embodied its power.

* * *

The purge of Tao Zhu was not an isolated event. Marshal He Long, another major figure in the party and military, was attacked almost simultaneously. Again, Lin Biao had pushed for the purge. In the CCP's military system, He Long and Lin Biao commanded armies on two separate fronts. The two leaders' relationship was not close, but it was not hostile either. In 1959, Lin became the minister of defense. He Long served in an interim role in the CMC to handle the organization's routine affairs beginning in late 1963 while Lin dealt with poor health. Conflicts began to emerge between the two, which became a key factor leading to the purge of Luo Ruiqing. Initially, He Long was not a target of the Cultural Revolution. But Lin constantly complained about him to Mao, signaling to the chairman that he would not feel safe until He Long was destroyed. It so happened that Mao himself had felt unhappy about He Long's close relationship with Liu and Deng. All this led to the chairman's decision to abandon He Long.

This was a highly unusual move, however—even for Mao. In managing personnel matters within the party and the military, Mao always took great care to balance different factions and groups. Historically, He Long had never opposed Mao, and he had been an enthusiastic supporter of the marriage between Mao and Jiang Qing. When Mao purged He, though, he violated the informal yet crucial rules that he had devised and long followed to manage intraparty struggles. This demonstrated that the chairman desperately needed Lin Biao's support, which in turn meant that the Cultural Revolution would see the further breaking of political norms amid the movement's rampant chaos.

Mao, by deciding to purge He Long, also sent another warning signal to Zhou. Historically, Zhou's relationship with the marshal had been quite close. When the CCP launched the Nanchang Uprising in 1927, Zhou persuaded He to take part in the resistance and join the CCP. In the many years that followed, He Long had always treated Zhou as an elder brother. Now, with He Long's political career in pieces, how could Zhou not feel that he too was in danger?

On January 11, He Long and his wife arrived in despair at West Flower Pavilion, Zhou's home and office at Zhongnanhai. Zhou had a brief talk with them. Then, however, he did not see them for a whole week "due to an extremely full working schedule."[73] Zhou and Li Fuchun formally met with the He couple at 4:00 P.M. on January 19. Zhou told He about Lin Biao's allegation that he had spread negative rumors about him behind his back and destroyed his network throughout the military command. Lin had said that as long as He Long was there, "he cannot be at ease." He Long tried to defend himself, but Zhou interrupted him, saying, "There is no need for you to say more. The chairman is defending you. I am also defending you. I will find a place for you to rest for a while. I will bring you back in the fall."[74] Zhou's words actually contained a veiled message: only if Mao defended He Long would Zhou also defend him. At 4:00 A.M. the next morning, He Long and his wife moved to a compound near Xiangshan in Beijing's western suburbs. Although He Long never forgot Zhou's promise that he would be brought back to Beijing in the fall, Zhou failed to act on his promise.[75] He Long had long suffered from severe diabetes, which worsened dramatically with the poor living conditions and lack of medical care he endured in isolated detention. He passed away in 1969.

Zhou's attitude toward He Long seemed so cold and heartless. He Long began to complain about Zhou, saying on several occasions, "If others do not know me, don't you, Zhou Enlai, know me well?"[76] But Zhou faced his own, unspeakable dilemma. Given that Lin Biao had tried his utmost to put He Long to political death, and that Mao had already decided to abandon him, it would have been impossible and useless for Zhou to try to protect He by changing Mao's mind.

Zhou met with Foreign Ministry representatives after the downfall of Tao Zhu and He Long. After he asked the attendees of the meeting about their whereabouts, he suddenly declared, "This movement we are now experiencing is the cruelest in our party's history."[77] This was a rare glimpse of Zhou's private thoughts on the Cultural Revolution. He had to act even more cautiously, while trying his best to align his every move with Mao's obscure ideas and intentions.

* * *

At almost the same time that Tao Zhu and He Long were purged, revolutionary rebels in Shanghai seized all power from the city's party and government authorities. The event was immediately given the name of "the January Revolution." In hindsight, the rebellion served as the opening act of the Cultural Revolution's evolution into a "full-scale civil war," as Mao had ordained.

Mao had been paying close attention to Shanghai. On January 2, 1967, he dispatched Zhang Chunqiao and Yao Wenyuan to the city, who communicated confidentially with Mao through a secure phone line.[78] On January 5, after Zhang and Yao arrived in Shanghai, they supported efforts by revolutionary rebels at *Wenhui bao* and *Jiefang ribao,* mouthpieces of the Shanghai party committee, to take over the two papers. The next day, revolutionary rebels in Shanghai held a rally attended by one hundred thousand people with Zhang and Yao's blessing. The rebels announced that they would strip the Shanghai party committee and government of their power.[79] This was the first case of revolutionary rebels seizing power from provincial and municipal authorities in the People's Republic.

Mao made no immediate comment on the January Revolution in Shanghai. *Renmin ribao* was also silent.[80] When Mao called a meeting of

CCRG members two days later, he did not mention the Shanghai rebels' January 6 rally to seize power. Instead, he stressed the significance of their takeover of *Wenhui bao* and *Jiefang ribao.* "This is a national matter," Mao said. "We should support their rebellious action. It is good that the leftists have seized power. The direction of it is correct. This is a great revolution, one in which one class has overthrown another. It will play a huge promotional role in pushing forward the Great Proletarian Cultural Revolution in East China, as well as in provinces and municipalities all over the country."[81]

Mao's behavior revealed the huge quandary he was facing in trying to balance "destruction" and "construction" with respect to the existing party and state order. How should the existing party, government, and military establishment be treated? Should they all be destroyed, then rebuilt from scratch? At the moment, Zhou remained unclear about Mao's real intentions. But did Mao know any better than the premier? He had made the statement in favor of a "full-scale civil war." Now, when his words were turning into actions, exactly what should this "civil war" become, and to what extent should it be fought? Not even Mao had clear answers to these questions.

When the January Revolution erupted in Shanghai, a growing number of everyday people throughout the country were putting forward a wide range of economic demands, resulting in a trend that was called the "vicious wind of economism." The movement then spread along with the trends of rebelling and "seizing political power." This was not the least bit strange. After all, the rise of mass rebellions during the Cultural Revolution was stimulated not just by top-down mobilizations, but also by bottom-up forces, representing the outburst of pent-up social, political, and economic tensions that had steadily grown since the CCP came to power in China. Amid the gathering storms of rebellion, it was inevitable that everyday people would seek out economic benefits and try to advance their own interests. This was particularly true for those who had lived on the margins of society, such as part-time workers and contract workers.

On January 9, *Wenhui bao* and *Jiefang ribao* published an "Urgent Notice" written by thirty-two rebel organizations headed by the SWRRH. In the notice, the groups emphasized the importance of adhering to the general direction of revolutionary rebellion and "seizing political power," and they declared that the "vicious wind of economism," demonstrated for example by freely increasing wages, widely issuing subsidies, and seizing and occupying public housing, should stop at once. The authors of the notice also claimed that the trend was "a form of the bourgeois reactionary line persistently pursued by the party's old Shanghai Municipal Committee."[82] The next day, Jiang Qing brought the "Urgent Notice" to Mao's attention. Mao immediately realized that, by relaying the notice to the whole country, he would show his support for the revolutionary rebels in Shanghai while preventing the situation from going completely out of control. The notice was "very good," he remarked, and he commented that the "policies and actions" in Shanghai "are correct" and should be followed by others throughout the country.[83] Following Mao's instructions, the Party Center, State Council, CMC, and CCRG immediately sent a joint congratulatory telegram to Shanghai.[84]

Mao's response to the "Urgent Notice" in Shanghai was exactly what Zhou had wanted to see, and so his reaction was swift. On January 10, Zhou, along with Chen Boda, Jiang Qing, Kang Sheng, and other CCRG members, met with representatives of revolutionary rebel groups in Beijing and elsewhere. He specifically asked Wang Li to read the "Urgent Notice," as well as a *Renmin ribao* editorial essay which expressed strong support for it.[85] It was the chairman, Zhou stressed, who had discovered the notice and decided to broadcast it to the whole country.[86]

Mao was jubilant. At a central liaison meeting on January 16, he said, "It is good that the leftist masses have mobilized to seize political power." But he also added that "they should only oversee politics and play a supervisory role, and should not manage everyday business."[87] Zhou found this "supreme instruction" eminently useful. Henceforth, he would loudly voice his support for the "seizure of political power" by revolutionary rebels, but he would also "follow the chairman's instructions" to place various restrictions on the rebels' activities. In particular, he would repeatedly remind them that it was wrong to sabotage production in the name of revolution. In late January, Zhou dictated, with Mao's approval, four guidelines for "seizing political power": it should be pursued by genuine revolutionary leftists; it should be an action of unity by the left; it should be conducted within one's own work unit; and it should be carried out in steps, not all at once.[88]

Under the direction of Zhang and Yao, the revolutionary rebels in Shanghai announced the establishment of the "Shanghai People's Commune" on February 5. The commune's origins could be traced to Mao himself. In mid-January, Mao said that he was considering whether to establish a "Beijing Commune."[89] In fact, the term "commune" had long enchanted the chairman, who admired the Paris Commune of 1871. During the Great Leap

Forward, he loudly announced that "people's communes are good."[90] Now, a commune was born in Shanghai that, in theory, realized Mao's vision of smashing the old state authority and also initiated the larger process of establishing a new state apparatus that Mao had dreamed of. Therefore, Zhang and Yao, as well as the revolutionary rebels in Shanghai, had every reason to expect the chairman's full endorsement and support.

Mao's response to the declaration, however, was equivocal. Beijing kept silent after the Shanghai Commune came into being, and *Renmin ribao* did not report the development. As Mao later explained that if news of the Shanghai People's Commune were published, "communes will appear everywhere. Then, do we still need the party, the government, or the military? Will communes run everything?" Mao further reasoned, "In that case, we also need to change the name of the state to 'The People's Commune of China.'" He thus concluded that the "Shanghai People's Commune's name should be dropped. It is better to call it a revolutionary committee."[91]

Mao's deliberation and ultimate decision revealed his true thoughts on "new types of state apparatuses." This was very much like a modern version of the classic story "Lord Ye's Love for a Dragon," a fable in which Lord Ye, a professed lover of dragons, was frightened when a real dragon appeared in front of him. Like Lord Ye, Mao talked enthusiastically about communes, his imagined "dragon." But once a commune was actually formed, he was scared. To rule China, he found, he could not cast away such institutional forces as the party, the government, and the military. Thus, he required Zhou's services and support now more than he ever had in the past.

Mao would also find it next to impossible to control the demon that was "full-scale civil war" after he unleashed it upon the country. All mass movements have their own dynamics and developmental trajectories. Mao could not get a firm grip on the rebellions, even with his huge authority and power. In the wake of the January Revolution in Shanghai and similar "revolutionary actions" elsewhere, mass movements to "seize political power" spread like wildfire across China. Meanwhile, the movements were accompanied by widespread factional conflict, resulting in bloody armed struggles that even involved the use of small arms and artillery. A real "full-scale civil war" would quickly engulf China's vast landscape. This monster had been Mao's creation; now, it was beyond his power and capacity to lock it in its cage. Mao thought that he had sown dragon's teeth, but it appeared he might reap only fleas.

26

GREAT CHAOS ALL UNDER HEAVEN

1967–1968

Spring 1967 arrived as another fraught moment in Zhou Enlai's political career. Between him and the party and state apparatus there had long existed an interdependent relationship, which served as a pillar of his administrative and executive power. Now, the violent storms of the Cultural Revolution threatened to topple that pillar. He had to proceed with extreme caution.

Great chaos indeed unfolded "all under heaven" as the tsunami set off by Mao's calls to "seize political power" made landfall. In October 1966, Mao predicted that the Cultural Revolution "would probably last another ten months, if not longer." Later, in February 1967, he said that the Cultural Revolution needed "three more months" to attain "an overall victory."[1] The chairman thus contemplated bringing in the PLA to help the "leftist revolutionary rebels" seize power and secure a rapid victory. In late January, he wrote Lin Biao regarding "dispatching troops to support the leftist masses." He contended that "it was false in the past to ask the PLA to stay away from the Cultural Revolution. They actually have been involved anyway." Thus, he continued, "in the future, the PLA should honor the requests of genuine revolutionaries for support."[2] Heeding Mao's instructions, the CMC ordered the entire military to "support the leftist masses."[3] Zhou embraced this new development enthusiastically, probably seeing the PLA's involvement as a way to bring a degree of order to China's chaotic political landscape while clearing the way for the Cultural Revolution to end.

Mao's decision, however, was a double-edged sword for himself. On the one hand, like Zhou, he believed the PLA's participation could effectively keep the mass movement from getting out of control. On the other hand, mobilizing troops would inevitably enhance Lin's position and influence, further disturbing the fragile balance between different military factions—whose coexistence was already tenuous—and Lin's dramatically increasing power. After prolonged consideration, Mao decided to go ahead and engage the PLA in the Cultural Revolution, confident that the military remained firmly under his control. Although Lin was China's second-in-command, in theory he could not move a single squadron without Mao's approval. Further, by then Mao had already named Marshal Xu Xiaoqian, who had previously belonged to a different PLA faction, as head of the PLA's Cultural Revolution leading group, in a move to check and balance Lin's military power.

Mao had failed to expect, however, that a group of marshals and veteran party leaders would participate in an effort later known as "the February Countercurrent" around the same time, upsetting his strategic plans. Chen Yi, Li Xiannian, Tan Zhenlin, and others gathered at Li Fuchun's home after New Year's Day 1967 to discuss their dissatisfaction with the Cultural Revolution.[4] On January 20, top PLA leaders met at the Jingxi Hotel to deliberate whether Xiao Hua, director of the PLA's political department, should be subjected to public denunciation at a mass rally—an idea that Jiang Qing and the CCRG supported. Marshal Ye Jianying became so angry during a heated debate with Jiang that he injured a finger when slamming his palm against a table.[5] Zhou intervened, and Xiao would not have to attend the rally and be denounced.[6]

The marshals did not take any follow-up action in the wake of the "Jingxi Hotel Encounter," but Zhou found it necessary and opportune to act. On February 2, he proposed to establish two liaison groups that would meet on a regular basis. The first, composed of CCRG members and Zhou himself, would discuss and decide on issues concerning "the situation, policy-making, and drafting related documents." The second would include Zhou, Chen Boda, Kang Sheng, and Li Fuchun (all of whom were members of the Politburo Standing Committee), several marshals and veteran leaders, and Jiang Qing and several CCRG members. This group's main task would be to discuss and handle "routine issues concerning party and government operations."[7] Through this proposal, Zhou probably meant to test Mao and attempt to clarify the confusing political situation.

Mao immediately vetoed Zhou's proposals.[8] However, he also sensed the need to take some balancing action. On February 6, the chairman called a meeting with Zhou, Jiang, and other members of the CCRG. To Zhou's surprise, Mao sternly reproached Jiang: "You should be criticized. You have no political experience, no experience as a worker or a peasant, and no experience in military struggles. . . . If you try to knock down all the veteran cadres, you yourself will be brought down sooner or later."[9] It seemed that Mao was trying to appease the marshals while demonstrating that he was impartial toward those close to him. But he also could have been playing a trick on the marshals: by criticizing Jiang, he might have hoped to induce them to further expose their true colors. If he indeed had such a design, the marshals, who had observed Mao's chilly response to the Shanghai People's Commune, took the bait. They believed they could act more boldly. At a February 11 Politburo briefing meeting chaired by Zhou, the marshals rebuked Jiang and other CCRG members. Ye pointed his finger at Jiang, exclaiming, "You have caused chaos in the party, in the government, and in factories and the countryside! Now, you even try to bring chaos to the military." He then attacked Zhang and Yao for initiating "such a great matter concerning the structure of our state as the Shanghai Commune . . . without going through the Politburo."[10] Xu Xiangqian echoed Ye: "The army is a pillar of the revolution; do you still want it? If not, I will quit!"[11] In fact, Ye and Xu were just repeating what Mao had said a few days before. Yet they had violated an unspoken rule: Mao's words could not necessarily be repeated by others. Zhou kept calm, neither joining nor stopping Ye, Xu, and others when they attacked the CCRG.[12]

Zhou and the marshals were even more surprised when, days later, Mao urged Jiang to make self-criticism, claiming that she had "high aspirations but low capacity." The chairman even called the CCRG an "independent kingdom that has ignored the Politburo and its Standing Committee." He also claimed that he had no intention of "bringing down all cadres," as this would be "anarchism in action." Again, Mao mentioned the Shanghai People's Commune. "This is a huge matter," he said, "but it was not discussed in advance."[13] The marshals and other veteran leaders thought that their time had come to take further action.

On February 16, Zhou chaired a meeting of all CCRG members (except Jiang), as well as the marshals and veteran leaders, to discuss "making revolution and promoting production." The veterans began to attack the stars of the Cultural Revolution as soon as the meeting began. Tan Zhenlin targeted Zhang Chunqiao, accusing Zhang and his like of using "mobilizing the masses" as a pretext to challenge the party's leadership and purge veteran cadres. In Jiang's absence, Tan said, "I do not want her to protect me. I do not work for her. I work for the party." He complained that "the struggles now are the most ruthless in our party's history. Even though you may chop off my head or put me in prison, I will struggle to the end." Zhou listened. Only when Tan stood up to leave the room did Zhou order him to stay. Chen Yi, who had been quiet at previous meetings, urged Tan on, exclaiming, "Do not leave! Stay and struggle against them!" Chen then voiced his own complaints in an indignant tone: "In the Yan'an Rectification Movement, the premier, I, and many others were purged." He then named Liu Shaoqi, Deng Xiaoping, and Peng Zhen as the ones who had purged them. "However," he continued, "as has been proven today, who are the opponents of Chairman Mao?"[14] One after another, the marshals and veteran leaders echoed Tan and Chen in their protestations. Zhou did not join them. The harshest statement that he made was a rebuttal of Chen Boda: "Why didn't you consult with us when *Hongqi* published the essay calling for the downfall of all veteran cadres?"[15] Clearly, he stood on the side of the veterans. Zhou also made several phone calls to Mao for instructions.[16] It seemed that Mao had not asked him to silence the veterans.

Zhou did not immediately brief Mao about the meeting once it ended. He probably hoped to let the dispute cool down on its own. Jiang Qing missed the meeting; but when she heard about it from Zhang Chunqiao, Yao Wenyuan, and Wang Li, she immediately compelled them, along with Kang Sheng, to see Mao.[17] The chairman listened with "a smiling face" until Kang mentioned Chen Yi's complaints about the Yan'an Rectification. Mao became enraged, shouting, "Was the Rectification wrong? Should I ask Wang Ming to come back?" To the chairman, Chen Yi's words posed a fundamental challenge to the legitimacy of the Cultural Revolution.[18] Mao was unhappy with Zhou, too. When Zhang cited Zhou's comments on the *Hongqi* essay, Mao retorted, "There is nothing in the party charter that requires the essay to be approved by him!"[19]

Mao waited for three days. On February 19, he called Lin Biao, Zhou, the marshals, and veteran leaders, and all the members of the CCRG to a meeting. He was in a state of "thunderous anger."[20] What had happened three days before, he claimed, was a "huge matter," and those who complained at the meeting were "big troublemakers." Then, contradicting his remarks about Jiang and the CCRR a few days prior, he declared that "only 1,

2, or 3 percent of what CCRR has done is incorrect, and 97 percent is correct. I will firmly oppose whoever opposes them. Do you want to discredit them? No way!"[21] The chairman's words stunned everyone. Zhou immediately took responsibility for the February 16 meeting going so wrong. Mao ordered him to host meetings to settle the matter: "If one meeting does not work, a second will follow; if one month is not enough, it will be extended to two months; if the Politburo cannot resolve [the issue], the whole party will be mobilized to handle it."[22]

Following Mao's orders, Zhou chaired a series of meetings over the ensuing weeks to deal with the aftermath of the incident, which was now known as "the February Countercurrent." With Mao's backing, Jiang and her CCRG comrades acted aggressively, calling the marshals and veteran leaders "conspirators who have opposed Chairman Mao and longed for a capitalist restoration." Scared, the veterans in turn criticized themselves relentlessly.[23] Zhou also acknowledged that he was politically "insensitive" and "dumb." Jiang told Zhou, "You are just a wavering element."[24]

Mao, however, did not mean to oust these veteran leaders. After all, he was no longer in a position to do so. The marshals were heads of PLA factions with historic pedigrees. By then, He Long had been purged, and if now the marshals also fell, Lin's power and influence would expand further. Mao, a master of the divide and conquer method, certainly did not want Lin's faction to become the dominant force in the military. Still, the February Countercurrent had effectively reshaped Beijing's decision-making structure. Over the next two years, until the party's Ninth Congress in 1969, the CCRG would replace the Politburo and the Central Secretariat as the body responsible for handling important party and state business, which it did through a "central liaison meeting." Mao named Zhou to serve as the convenor of the meeting.[25] This was a rather subtle and dangerous assignment for Zhou, who held a lofty title in the new group, but no real power. Often, it was Jiang Qing who had the final say. Zhou had to tolerate her. After all, he knew that she was not only the chairman's wife but also his most trusted agent.

* * *

Despite all the trouble associated with the February Countercurrent, Zhou still hoped that the Cultural Revolution would end sooner than later. On several occasions in March, he speculated that if revolutionary committees were established in more provinces, the Cultural Revolution would be pushed much closer to a victorious end.[26] Yet the chairman felt differently, seeing in the February Countercurrent the extraordinary unwillingness of the veteran leaders to embrace the Cultural Revolution. He thus responded with two sweeping moves. First, he ordered the PLA to impose military rule where it was necessary to "support the leftist forces" in "seizing political power."[27] Clearly, Mao hoped to use this extraordinary measure to help place the dramatically escalating Cultural Revolution under his control. Once more, Zhou was quite supportive of Mao's initiative. He revealed his thinking in a speech at a conference attended by high-ranking PLA commanders, in which he pointed out that Mao's action would pave the way for "the great unity of the revolutionaries through 'grasping revolution and promoting production.'" He also emphasized "the necessity of creating opportunities for the revolutionary cadres to split with the capitalist roaders," freeing them to join in the establishment of new revolutionary committees at provincial and local levels.[28] Evidently, Zhou hoped that military rule would allow some sidelined cadres to reclaim power while bringing the Cultural Revolution to a close.

Zhou's support for a military takeover at the central level, however, was conditional. He firmly supported the military taking over those ministries overseeing traffic, transportation, communication, finance and the economy, and production—and even urged that the takeover of these ministries occur "without any delay."[29] However, he strongly opposed allowing "revolutionary rebels to seize power" or to implement military rule at the Foreign Ministry. Otherwise, he worried, there could be serious international consequences.

The second major action Mao took was to dramatically escalate charges against Liu Shaoqi, whom he now formally named China's "largest capitalist roader." Mao faced a dilemma: Liu was undoubtedly his main political enemy, but the chairman had launched the Cultural Revolution to achieve ends far greater than the purging of Liu. If his sole aim was to bring Liu down, he could have concluded the Cultural Revolution at the October 1966 work conference, and the January Revolution would have been unnecessary. Ultimately, the February Countercurrent awakened his deep sense of anxiety about his posthumous legacy. Mao feared that if he neglected to destroy Liu, he might give Liu an opportunity to reemerge after his passing. More crucially, Mao probably also hoped that by proclaiming Liu to be an enemy of the utmost wickedness, he would create among the masses a shared sense of hatred toward a common adversary, sentiment he could harness to consolidate his lasting dominance. Mao was thus determined to sentence Liu's political career to death. He no longer called Liu a "comrade." He even supported—and personally edited—a *Renmin ribao* article by Qi Benyu that described Liu as the "biggest traitor" of the Chinese revolution.[30]

Mao named Zhou to head the Central Office on Special Cases and tasked him with overseeing the Liu case. Zhou could not refuse his new duty, although he must have been extremely unwilling to accept it. Historically, Zhou had never been close to Liu, who became the CCP's second-in-command while Zhou was being purged in the Rectification Movement. But Zhou never saw Liu as an enemy. Zhou knew that he was less likely to be regarded as a competitor for Mao's power as long as Liu stood between him and the chairman. After 1949, Zhou never engaged in a direct confrontation with Liu. They cooperated with each other in handling the Gao Gang case, for instance. When Mao criticized Zhou for his mistake of "opposing rash advance," Liu joined other top CCP leaders who supported retaining him as the premier. The two leaders' work to deal with the fallout of the disastrous Great Famine further strengthened their working relationship. When, during the Cultural Revolution, Zhou realized that Liu was Mao's main target, he took up a strategy of extreme caution. This matter did not concern Liu alone, he knew, but potentially threatened everyone. If Liu, as head of the state, could be purged so easily, who else was safe?

Mao killed two birds with one stone by making Zhou oversee the Liu case. He understood that the case would prove highly contentious, and that only Zhou, with his extensive connections and extraordinary political skills, could manage to push the case through without stirring up too much controversy. Furthermore, by making Zhou sign all the documents associated with the case, Mao probably calculated that if the prosecution of Liu were successful, future historical accounts would depict Zhou as merely a participant in the case, and not its primary architect. But if the case went wrong, Zhou could not extricate himself from his huge responsibility in the matter. He had no way of escaping this fate.

Zhou's situation was made more complicated when, in late spring, big character posters attacking him appeared at several Beijing universities. At the Beijing Steel and Iron College, a certain "May Sixteenth Corps" published "An Open Letter to Zhou," accusing him of being "a representative of rightist opportunist lines" in the Cultural Revolution. Then, a citywide "May Sixteenth Red Guards Corps" was established with the main goal of criticizing Zhou.[31] Meanwhile, Red Guards at Nankai University, Zhou's alma mater, discovered "Wu Hao's Statement on Splitting with the Communist Party," published in late February 1932 by the Shanghai-based publication *Shenbao.* They quickly found that Wu Hao was an alias used by Zhou, and they immediately submitted the paper to the CCRG as evidence that "Zhou is a traitor." Jiang Qing conveyed it to Zhou.[32]

If he were only attacked by students, Zhou did not have much to worry about. It was Mao's attitude that was key. The chairman defended Zhou's performance in the Cultural Revolution, saying that "the views (about Zhou) of the extraleftists are wrong. The comrades of the CCRG should persuade the students." Mao relayed these particular comments to Zhou.[33] The CCRG then proclaimed that the May Sixteenth Corps was a "reactionary organization controlled by bad elements."[34] The Wu Hao case, however, posed bigger trouble for Zhou. When Zhou received the paper that Jiang sent him, he immediately told Jiang that this was a rumor "made up and circulated by the enemy." He then, along with his associates, pored over old editions of *Shenbao* from February 1932. After Zhou located "Wu Hao's Statement" and its rebuttal, he personally compiled a chronology and sent all the documents to Mao with a handwritten note. "Wu Hao's Statement," Zhou emphasized, was a fabrication by the enemy, which had appeared after he left Shanghai and arrived in Jiangxi.[35] The chairman's response was strange. Although he should have been quite familiar with the matter, he instructed Zhou to "convey the materials to the comrades of the CCRG for reading, and keep them in the file."[36] By doing so, Mao allowed the case to linger without a verdict. Mao was apparently protecting Zhou, but he was also putting a noose around the premier's neck.

Attacks on Liu escalated, prompting Mao to adjust his attitude toward the marshals and veteran leaders involved in the February Countercurrent. Zhou, heeding Mao's request, arranged for the veteran leaders to review that year's May Day (or International Workers' Day) parade from atop the Gate of Heavenly Peace. But Zhou knew full well that Mao's mind could change at any time. He thus reminded Chen Yi and others that under no circumstances should they "become cocky"; otherwise, Zhou warned, there could be "another turnaround."[37] These words also revealed Zhou's assessment of his own position. Indeed, he was sharing with Chen and other members of the old guard his own feelings and experience.

• • •

The "full-scale civil war" that Mao had unleashed showed no sign of ending as summer 1967 arrived. Throughout China, the main themes of the Cultural Revolution had mixed with all kinds of complicated factional and local disputes, creating deep divisions among the "revolutionary rebels" and resulting in violent factional struggles everywhere.

Zhou was having a very difficult time, facing criticism from various mass organizations from time to time. Many of his colleagues and associates at the State Council and the Foreign Ministry had come under huge pressure. He often found himself powerless to protect them, but nevertheless, he still tried to shield his colleagues from the barrage of criticism. The person he gave his utmost to defend was Marshal Chen Yi. Drawing lessons from Tao Zhu's downfall, Zhou sought to act before Mao could intervene. So long as the chairman did not explicitly oppose it, he would stand in support of Chen. Zhou came to a rally that Foreign Ministry rebels organized to denounce Chen, and he protested when the crowd shouted "Down with Chen Yi!" He declared, "If you dare take Marshal Chen away, you will have to step over my body!"[38] By defending Chen, Zhou was also protecting his last line of administrative and executive power.

Great chaos was rampant all under heaven, but Mao, sitting in his quarters at Zhongnanhai, only had vague knowledge of the turmoil. However, even if he had known how out of control the situation was, he probably would not have worried too much. He still firmly believed that, with his absolute authority and godlike power, he could easily turn great chaos into a "great settlement." There was no sign that he was planning to bring the Cultural Revolution to a speedy end.

The turmoil in Wuhan was the worst in the country. Early that year, the masses there had divided into two huge factions. One was the "One Million Heroes," which opposed attacking party committees in Hubei Province and Wuhan. The other faction, the "Workers' Rebellion Headquarters," favored destroying the "old power structure" associated with the provincial and city authorities. Confrontations between the two factions grew increasingly violent throughout the spring. The PLA command in Wuhan sided with the One

Million Heroes. The Workers' Rebellion Headquarters, supported by the CCRG, responded by adding the military to its list of targets for fierce attacks. Consequently, the situation in Wuhan devolved into even greater chaos.

Near the start of July, Mao suddenly came up with the idea of traveling to Wuhan to inspect the situation there. On July 13, he summoned Lin Biao, Zhou, and members of the CCRG to a meeting, at which he informed them that he would go to Wuhan to see "how the masses are doing there." Zhou tried to persuade Mao to drop the idea, citing the potential threat to his safety. But the chairman was determined to go. He ordered Wang Dongxing to get his personal train ready for the trip.[39]

Mao departed Beijing for Wuhan before dawn the next morning, accompanied by Yang Chengwu, the PLA's acting chief of staff. Zhou flew from Beijing to Wuhan half an hour before.[40] Mao arrived in Wuhan the next afternoon, when Zhou had already made all arrangements for the chairman's tour of the city. Over the next two days, Mao and Zhou heard reports from Xie Fuzhi, the minister of public safety, and Wang Li, a CCRG member, who had traveled to Wuhan to try to solve the problems. Mao thought that he knew how to end the factional conflict in Wuhan. The first order of business, he instructed, was to "rehabilitate the reputation of the Workers' Headquarters." Meanwhile, the One Million Heroes should also be recognized as a legitimate mass organization, Mao argued, and the two factions should be pushed to end their conflict. Meanwhile, Chen Zhaidao and Zhong Hanhua, respectively the commander and political commissar of the PLA's Wuhan headquarters, should change their attitude toward the Workers' Headquarters and acknowledge that they had made serious mistakes. Mao believed that as both factions "now are trying to use my name," it should not be difficult to settle the problems in Wuhan and Hubei with these instructions of his.[41]

Zhou also encouraged Chen and Zhong to come out in support of the "leftist workers," telling them that if they did so, Mao would not purge them.[42] On the evening of July 18, Zhou joined Mao for a talk with Chen and Zhong. The chairman explicitly asked them to "change their viewpoints" and "help persuade the 'One Million Heroes' to change their positions." Then, Mao advised that they should host a meeting of the two warring factions and bring about "a grand unity" between them. Chen and Zhong promised that they would resolutely carry out Mao's instructions.[43] Believing that the crisis in Wuhan would soon be resolved, Zhou flew back to Beijing that evening. Mao was delighted. "After the end of the Cultural

Revolution next spring," he told his associates, "we shall convene the party's Ninth Congress." He even mentioned that those "veteran comrades" who had been purged, such as He Long and Deng Xiaoping, would be reelected to the Central Committee.[44]

Both Mao and Zhou, however, miscalculated. Mao's instructions were easy for him to issue but difficult for others to follow. On July 19, Chen and Zhong accompanied Xie Fuzhi and Wang Li to a conference of commanders above the division level, where they made self-criticism. Wang then delivered a lengthy speech in which he referred to the One Million Heroes as a "conservative organization" that had made "directional mistakes."[45]

Wang's speech, however, angered members of the One Million Heroes. On July 20, a crowd of people belonging to the organization and many PLA officers and soldiers who supported them surrounded and then broke into the East Lake Guest House, where Wang Li was staying. Room by room, they searched for Wang. When they found him, they dragged him to the compound to denounce and torture him. Unbeknownst to the mob, Mao was in a nearby room, "frightened."[46]

Zhou was shocked to hear that Mao "was almost attacked." He immediately reported this to Lin Biao and Jiang Qing, who wrote Mao to suggest that he leave Wuhan immediately.[47] Zhou flew back to Wuhan on the afternoon of July 20, where he wasted no time arranging an evacuation operation for Mao. Early the next morning, Mao hurriedly left Wuhan and flew to Shanghai from a military airport dozens of miles away from Wuhan.[48] Mao's experience in Wuhan had a profound impact on him. He had assumed that people all under heaven would listen to and obey his every instruction, but such was not the case. Judging by Mao's later behavior, he would apparently lose much of his admiration for mass movements following his escape from Wuhan.

Mao remained in Shanghai until mid-September 1967. China's largest city was then also witnessing fierce confrontations between two contending mass organizations. The feud originated in factional struggles at the Shanghai Diesel Engine Factory, where the "United Headquarters" and the "Red East" had been fighting each other since earlier that year. Like the One Million Heroes in Wuhan, the United Headquarters was also regarded as a "conservative organization"; unlike the One Million Heroes, however, it did not have the support of the military. The Red East, on the other hand, was backed by the Shanghai Revolutionary Committee headed by Zhang Chunqiao and Yao Wenyuan. By the time Mao arrived in Shanghai, the Diesel Engine Factory's factional struggles had spilled out and spread to the whole city. Dissident "rebellious organizations" collectively formed a citywide alliance (mostly spurred by their feeling marginalized in other revolutionary committees) to support the United Headquarters. The alliance's existence challenged Zhang, Yao, and the Shanghai Revolutionary Committee.

On August 4, Shanghai's mainstream "revolutionary organizations" mobilized, with the support of Zhang and Yao, hundreds of thousands of workers to attack the United Headquarters. By the end of the day, members of the United Headquarters surrendered, and the Shanghai-wide alliance that supported it subsequently collapsed. Having vanquished these opposition forces, the Shanghai Revolutionary Committee no longer faced any serious challengers. When Mao watched the footage of the event, he became excited. "Good, good. Very good," he told Zhang and Yao.[49] Mao's words revealed that his previous love of mass rebellions was being subtly replaced in the wake of his experience in Wuhan by a distrust of or even a sense of disgust toward mass movements not under his control.

* * *

During Mao's absence, Zhou stayed in Beijing, where the Cultural Revolution had also spun out of control. Liu Shaoqi was subjected to an onslaught of denunciations. Beginning in early July, tens of thousands of Red Guards and other rebels, with the CCRG's blessing, surrounded Zhongnanhai, trying to expel Liu from the central leadership's compound. Zhou's situation was rather difficult. On the one hand, he knew that Mao was determined to destroy Liu; hence he could not simply interfere with the siege of Zhongnanhai by the emboldened masses. On the other hand, he understood that the security of Zhongnanhai—and even the general order in the capital—could be jeopardized if the siege continued. He had to take extraordinary caution at every move.

This was the time that Wang Li became a Cultural Revolution superstar. He was an ambitious person. Wang delivered speech after speech after he returned from Wuhan to Beijing, acting as the hero who had brought the crisis in the city to an end. Zhou had had no problem with Wang in the past, but he became alarmed when Wang began, intentionally or not, to extend his reach into the Foreign Ministry. Indonesia was a hot subject at the Foreign Ministry at the time. China's relations with Indonesia had deteriorated rapidly since the September 30th Incident nearly two years before. In April 1967, Jakarta announced that Yao Dengshan, the Chinese chargé d'affaires there, was no longer welcome in the country. Yao returned to Beijing on April 30, greeted at the airport by Zhou, Jiang Qing, and all the members of the CCRG. On May Day, Mao met with Yao—an encounter not arranged by Zhou—at the Gate of Heavenly Peace, and a photograph was taken with Yao standing between Mao and Jiang Qing. All of a sudden, Yao had become a celebrity of the Cultural Revolution. Yao bumped into Qi Benyu, another CCRG member, at a meeting on August 4, who told him that it was all right for the revolutionary rebels to seize power at the Foreign Ministry and criticize Chen Yi. Yao relayed Qi's opinion to cadres at the Foreign Ministry.[50] On August 7, Wang delivered a speech at the ministry, in which he fully supported Qi's viewpoints as communicated by Yao, as well as the actions by the rebels to "seize power" at the Foreign Ministry, including their attacks on Chen Yi.[51] Zhou was greatly offended, although he did not immediately take action against Wang. He was patiently waiting for the right moment.

The siege of Zhongnanhai was lifted around the same time. On August 5, a "mass rally one million strong" was held at Tiananmen Square to denounce Liu, after which the size of the crowd gathered outside Zhongnanhai shrank significantly. Many Red Guards now protested at the British office in Beijing due to the explosive situation in Hong Kong. Since the beginning of the year, the ardor of the Cultural Revolution had been spreading to Hong Kong, which was still a British colony, buffeted by wave after wave of anti-British protests. How to control the worsening situation in Hong Kong presented Zhou with a daunting challenge. Since 1949, Hong Kong had served as a key window to international trade for the PRC, as well as one of its suppliers of foreign currency and bases for intelligence collection. Zhou fully understood that "in no circumstance should we be pushed to reclaim Hong Kong." He thus had repeatedly reminded CCP agencies in Hong Kong that unlike in the mainland, they should not pursue Cultural Revolution–style mobilizations in the colony. Meanwhile, he instructed them to actively participate in the "anti-British patriotic activities" led by the leftist masses to put pressure on the British authorities while expanding the CCP's position and influence in Hong Kong.[52] Obviously, the line separating the two sets of instructions was extremely thin.

In early May, workers at an artificial flower factory in Kowloon went on strike over a dispute with the factory owners and subsequently clashed with riot police. Many were injured and twenty-one union representatives were arrested. With Zhou's approval, the Chinese Foreign Ministry issued a "most urgent and vehement protest" on May 15, demanding that the Hong Kong authorities acknowledge their serious mistakes, apologize to the purged masses, punish those responsible, and promise not to commit similar acts in the future.[53] Three days later, Zhou attended a mass rally in Beijing in support of the "struggles in Hong Kong" and approved mobilizing people to protest continuously outside the British office in Beijing. Meanwhile, he also made it clear that protesters should absolutely not be allowed to enter the office building or to block office members from entering or leaving it, let alone torture any British diplomats or office employees.[54] When Zhou learned that Red Guards in Shanghai had broken into a British official's residence, destroyed furniture, written insulting messages on the wall, and dragged British representatives into the yard to "receive denunciations," he demanded angrily, "Why have you failed to share the regulations that we have made for mass demonstrations at the British office in Beijing with the masses in Shanghai?"[55]

The anti-British struggles by the leftist masses in Hong Kong continued to spread over the following days and weeks. When the British Hong Kong authorities made virtually no concessions, the situation gradually got out of control. On May 22, a large protest by the leftist masses in front of the Hong Kong governor's house turned violent. The riot police opened fire; several protesters were wounded, and dozens arrested. A Xinhua report on the incident claimed that as many as two to three hundred protestors had been wounded or killed; *Renmin ribao* called it a "bloody massacre."[56] On the same day, Zhou held an urgent meeting to learn about the situation in Hong Kong. He sternly criticized Xinhua and *Renmin ribao* for their severely exaggerated reports on the number of casualties. This would result in a "serious loss of credibility," Zhou declared, which would produce nothing positive and only "ignite people's rage." He asked those at the meeting why they had failed to get his approval before running such a big story. When the officials in charge of Hong Kong affairs proposed to "kill several Hong Kong policemen to send them a serious warning," Zhou lost his temper, shouting, "This is anarchy!" He reasoned that "although we do not recognize Hong Kong as foreign territory, it is now under British rule." As "we do not plan to reclaim Hong Kong now, or to fight a war with Britain, our struggles there should be reasonable, advantageous to us, and controllable, and we should not take the initiative to go on the offensive." Therefore, "our work in Hong Kong cannot copy the Red Guards' ways in the mainland."[57] The officials in charge of Hong Kong affairs were persistent, however. At another meeting on May 30, they again proposed to carry out armed attacks on police stations in Hong Kong and "kill several of the worst police officers." Zhou scolded them, exclaiming, "This is ridiculous!" He added, "As Communists we carry out political struggles, not assassinations."[58]

But what exactly was Beijing to do about Hong Kong? Not even Zhou had the answer. The only option was to escalate the tone of propaganda about Hong Kong. *Renmin ribao* had been preparing an editorial essay about Hong Kong. On June 2, Zhou reviewed the draft of the essay, but he did not make any comments on it. Later, he asked Chen Boda to help revise and polish the essay's language, to ensure that its tone would not be "too high." The essay, titled "Firmly Repulse the Provocation of the British Imperialists," was published the next day. Its tone, though, was still quite intense.[59] Zhou's lack of an explicit and consistent approach toward Hong Kong indicated that he was still waiting for Mao to give the final word on the matter.[60]

The situation in Hong Kong deteriorated dramatically in early July, when, on July 8, an armed skirmish erupted between Chinese militia and British police at Sha Tau Kok, a town on the border with Hong Kong, resulting in two Chinese and five British deaths. This time, Mao gave definitive instructions: "Hong Kong should remain what it has been.... It is better not to use force there." Zhou wasted no time to convey Mao's words to the General Staff and the officials in charge of Hong Kong affairs. Regarding the skirmish at Sha Tau Kok, Zhou said, "There should not be a next time. It is not in line with our current policy of not using force in Hong Kong." He further elaborated that "the struggle in Hong Kong will be a long one. We should not rush it. It is not in our interest to rush it. We must act by unanimously following the policy line set by the chairman."[61]

Hong Kong's situation, however, did not develop as Zhou had hoped. The mood of the radical leftists in Hong Kong reached a fever pitch. In addition to continuing their protests, they planted bombs, real and fake, throughout the city. British Hong Kong authorities imposed emergency laws, banning left-wing newspapers, shutting down left-wing schools, and arresting a number of leftist leaders and activists. Against this backdrop, the Chinese Foreign Ministry drafted in mid-August an ultimatum demanding that the Hong Kong authorities lift the ban on three left-wing papers and release nineteen reporters from prison. This time, Zhou approved the ultimatum, which Beijing delivered to the British on the afternoon of August 20.[62] However, the Chinese side had not prepared any strong follow-up measures if the ultimatum was rejected. According to one account, China's final option was to expel a second secretary in charge of media work at the British office in Beijing.[63] This last resort was clearly incompatible with the content and language of the ultimatum. Thus, the plan was either a gamble or merely a bluff.

Zhou usually took extreme precautions in handling such matters. Why and how, then, could he have approved the ultimatum? Zhou probably did so because by then he had no better option. He could not allow the situation in Hong Kong to deteriorate further, perhaps forcing Beijing to "take back Hong Kong prematurely," but he could not allow himself to be labeled as a "rightist surrenderist" either. By approving the ultimatum, he was likely counting on luck, hoping that the British authorities in Hong Kong would be scared into making some concession—if only a symbolic one—thus providing him with a reason to order an end to the chaos in Hong Kong. Again, Zhou miscalculated. The British did nothing. After the August 22 deadline passed, the situation in Beijing went out of control, as the crowds surrounding the British office broke in and set it on fire.[64] Zhou knew that he could not avoid his share of responsibility for the growing political quagmire. Indeed, Mao "sternly criticized him, as well as Chen Boda and Kang Sheng."[65] Zhou knew that he had to act immediately to prevent the situation from getting even worse.

• • •

Hours after the fire at the British office was put out, Zhou summoned a meeting of leaders of "revolutionary rebels" at the Foreign Ministry. He called the arson "a typical case of rampant anarchism" that must be thoroughly investigated.[66] This was also Zhou's way of defending himself; although his position remained extremely perilous, he refused to wait to meet his doom. After much deliberation, he decided to take a risky action. Close to midnight on August 24, he called Yang Chengwu, who had been with Mao in Shanghai, urging him to fly back to Beijing. Early in the morning of August 25, the two had a one-on-one conversation. Zhou told Yang that Wang Li had delivered an outrageous speech at the Foreign Ministry in which he encouraged the rebels there to seize power, and that it had also been Wang who had supported the siege of Zhongnanhai and encouraged the protestors to set fire to the British office. Indeed, Zhou stressed, Wang had even called for "digging out capitalist roaders within the military. . . . My biggest concern is the chain reaction from all this." Zhou gave Yang a copy of Wang's August 7 speech and asked him to report everything to Mao.[67]

Zhou knew this was a dangerous move, as Wang had been celebrated as a hero of the CCRG. Hence he tactfully highlighted Wang's August 7 speech, mixing with it references to the seizure of power at the Foreign Ministry, the fire at the British office, and Wang's call for "attacking capitalist roaders in the PLA." Still, what Zhou did was akin to corralling a lion in its den. The result depended on Mao's unpredictable response. Following Zhou's instructions, Yang immediately flew back to Shanghai, where at nine o'clock in the morning, he conveyed Zhou's report to the chairman.[68]

Zhou did not hear a word from Mao or Yang for the rest of August 25. His anxiety peaked. In the evening, Shirley Graham, the widow of Dr. W. E. B. Du Bois, who had lived in Beijing for years and was about to leave, came to say farewell to Zhou. She observed that Zhou looked "depressed and exhausted." In a despondent, even despairing voice, Zhou said,

> The whole Chinese revolution may be defeated for a while. We may lose everything. But never mind. If we are defeated here, you in Africa will learn from our mistakes, and you will develop your own Mao Zedong, and you will learn to do it better. And so, in the end, we shall succeed.

Graham asked Zhou "what he meant." Zhou only said that "the situation was very complex, and the future looked uncertain."[69]

Zhou's bad mood lingered until the next day. At 9:00 A.M. on August 26, Mao summoned Yang and told him, "Wang Li, Guan Feng, and Qi Benyu are not good people. They are trying to sabotage the Cultural Revolution." He instructed Yang to immediately fly back to Beijing and report directly to Zhou. Wang and Guan should be arrested at once, Mao ordered, and Qi was to be put on probation pending his later arrest.[70] Around noontime, Yang conveyed Mao's decision to Zhou "word by word." Zhou was greatly relieved. That evening, he called a meeting, which was attended by Jiang Qing, Chen Boda, Kang Sheng, and other CCRG members. Word by word, sentence by sentence, he read Mao's instructions as delivered to him by Yang.[71] Wang and Guan were promptly arrested. The following January, Qi would also be detained. Although Jiang Qing consented to the purge of Wang, Guan, and Qi, this development was still a huge blow to the CCRG.

In hindsight, it is clear that Zhou had used the full extent of his political wisdom and skill. The moment at which he had chosen to act was precisely right. At that point, on the one hand, conflict had emerged between Jiang Qing and Wang, Guan, and Qi within the CCRG for various reasons. On the other hand, in the wake of his experience in Wuhan, Mao was willing to consider ending the Cultural Revolution's "full-scale civil war" in order to restore political and social order. Equipped with his sharp political intuition, Zhou detected these subtle changes. When he put his bold plan in motion, he had no way of guaranteeing its success. This was a rare gamble in his political career, which ended in a win for Zhou.

Mao decided to abandon Wang, Guan, and Qi not just to appease Zhou, but also to stabilize the PLA. After Wuhan, Mao had sensed that widespread discontent existed among PLA commanders about the Cultural Revolution. He had seized and consolidated his political power by holding "the barrel of a gun," and he was determined to keep firm control of the military. Therefore, under no circumstances would he tolerate Wang's challenges to the military. Zhou had accurately perceived the chairman's thinking.

The CCRG had been the primary institutional instrument Mao used to carry out the Cultural Revolution. Now, he decided to sacrifice one of the group's arms to protect its body. This was an important sign. Mao certainly did not mean to abandon the CCRG; nor did he intend to abruptly end the Cultural Revolution. But he had realized that the Cultural Revolution, as a practical political process, had gone much too far. The "revolutionary rebels" were no longer willing to listen to him or blindly follow his instructions. To Mao, the revolution—his own brainchild—had gone down the wrong path.

Mao also found that he depended on Zhou more at that moment than ever before. At the end of 1968, when Mao read a letter a PKU student had written about the Wu Hao affair, he wrote, "This matter has been clarified. It was a rumor made by the Guomindang."[72] This was what Zhou had been waiting for, although it would not be Mao's final response to the Wu Hao matter.

• • •

Revolutionary committees had been established in only nine of China's twenty-nine provinces and regions by the start of 1968. Despite the PLA's intervention, the nationwide civil war showed no sign of abating. Mao announced repeatedly that "there exists no fundamental contradiction among the working class," and he called for the "suppression of factionalism" throughout the country. Yet these appeals had only a limited effect. Zhou had to work with the CCRG and the military to try to "settle factional problems" in one province after another, but progress was slow. The end of the great chaos of the Cultural Revolution still lay beyond the horizon.

The struggles among top CCP leaders also became increasingly unpredictable. One day's noble could become the next day's prisoner. In March, Yang Chengwu, the acting chief of staff; Yu Lijin, political commissar of the Air Force; and Fu Chongbi, commander of the Beijing Military Garrison, were arrested with no forewarning. On March 22, they were fired from their positions. Two days later, Lin Biao announced at a mass rally that the three leaders had been ousted. Standing in front of Mao, Lin listed their crimes, asserting that they had made the serious mistake of participating in factionalism while opposing Mao Thought. But Lin also said their mistakes were "neither very big nor very small," failing to specify what exactly these mistakes had been.[73] Only in retrospect can the true reasons for the purge be suggested: Fu might have offended Jiang Qing, Yang might have alienated Lin Biao, and Yu had been feuding with Wu Faxian, Air Force commander and a confidant of Lin. There was no evidence to show that they had been involved in any underground activities or had formed a clique in any way.

Zhou, like others, knew nothing about why and how these purges had so suddenly occurred. When he spoke at the rally to support Mao and Lin's judgment of the three disgraced leaders, he concentrated on praising Jiang Qing, highlighting "the extraordinary role" that Jiang had played in the Cultural Revolution. "Comrade Jiang Qing is a resolute and brave member of the party and a proletarian soldier," Zhou said. "She has been so . . . ever since the 1930s, when she was already a resolute and brave Communist, and a female soldier fighting against all kinds of enemies."[74] These words were meant for Mao and Jiang to hear.

Mao announced at a meeting on March 28 that there was no need for the CMC to meet anymore, and that its role would be filled by an executive military group headed by Lin Biao.[75] Mao was rewarding Lin. However, this decision seemed to hand part of Mao's absolute power over the military to Lin, which sowed another seed of the future Mao-Lin split.

* * *

Mao had finally tired of seeing "chaos all under heaven" by the time the summer of 1968 arrived. Even the notion of China being the center of the world revolution—an idea in which Mao had been engrossed—had lost its appeal to the chairman, who now saw it as necessary to restore order.[76] Zhou did not fail to notice the subtle change in Mao's mind-set. The premier's attention was fixed on Guangxi, where rampant "armed struggles" between factions had become notorious throughout China. Abutting Vietnam, Guangxi served as the corridor through which material aid sent to Vietnam by the Soviet Union and several Eastern European countries traveled. Large-scale violent confrontations between different factions in Guangxi inevitably hampered the normal delivery of aid to Vietnam. The situation became even worse when the "revolutionary rebels" stole ammunition and weapons from the shipments. Vietnam, the Soviet Union, and Eastern European nations repeatedly complained to Beijing about the impact of unrest in Guangxi on aid shipments.[77] Yet, despite Zhou's attention and personal intervention, the "Guangxi problem" had continuously worsened.

Now, Zhou decided to use Guangxi as a typical case to make a guiding document not only for settling the disorder in that province, but for suppressing disturbances around the country. Zhou personally supervised the drafting of the document, which Mao quickly approved. On July 3, the document, known as the "July Third Order," was issued. The order claimed that the epidemic of violence in various parts of Guangxi, where railway transport was disrupted, material aid bound for Vietnam was robbed, and PLA barracks were attacked, was absolutely "reactionary activity."[78] Zhou then met with representatives of the two warring factions in Guangxi, whom he ordered in stern language to allow order to prevail. Otherwise, Zhou warned, they would be "committing crimes of the most serious nature."[79] The military authorities in Guangxi immediately launched a bloody crackdown on mass organizations in the province, ultimately making Guangxi the region where the most people were murdered during the Cultural Revolution.

The July Third Order, however, failed to curb the chaos that was raging in other parts of China. Zhou then spent a whole week drafting the "July Twenty-Fourth Notice," which addressed the situation in Shaanxi Province. He personally revised the document, emphasizing the need to "immediately stop armed struggles; dismantle armed patrols, strongholds, and passes; and dissolve professional armed squadrons." He added, "All interrupted land and water transportation lines, postal services and telegraphic communications must be resumed unconditionally," and "all weapons and other equipment deprived from the PLA must be returned immediately and unconditionally."[80]

Finally, there came a decisive turning point on July 27. That morning thousands of members of the "Workers' Mao Thought Propaganda Team," on orders from Mao, entered the campus of Tsinghua University, where violence had raged for months. They demanded that the two rival factions there stop fighting, dismantle their strongholds, and hand over their weapons. One faction, Mount Jinggang, refused to obey the commands; then they opened fire on the Workers' Team. Five died, and hundreds were wounded.[81]

Early on the morning of July 28, Mao summoned to a meeting the "five big leaders" of the Red Guards at Beijing's universities and colleges, including Nie Yuanzhi from PKU and Kuai Dafu from Tsinghua. Zhou also attended the meeting. The chairman gave the student leaders a long lecture in which he placed particular emphasis on the July Third Order and the July Twenty-Fourth Notice. He stressed that these two documents did not concern just Guangxi and Shaanxi, but all of China. "If anyone is to continuously violate these regulations by attacking the PLA, disrupting transportation, killing people, or setting fires, . . . they are bandits; they are Guomindang. And they will be rounded up. If they resist, they will be wiped out."[82]

Mao's statement clearly indicated that he was ready to split with the rebellious mass movement that had so far prevailed in the Cultural Revolution. On July 30, Zhou, along with Jiang Qing, Chen Boda, and Kang Sheng, proposed that Mao's July 28 speech be relayed to the whole country, and that workers' and soldiers' teams be sent to all colleges, high schools, and work units where chaos had taken root.[83] Beginning at that moment, all Red Guard organizations virtually collapsed, and the Red Guard movement died.

• • •

While the Cultural Revolution was receding at home, on August 20, the Soviet Red Army invaded Czechoslovakia. Zhou immediately instructed the Foreign Ministry to discuss how China should respond.[84] On August 22, Mao called a meeting with Zhou and other top leaders to discuss the matter. The chairman regarded the Soviet invasion as evidence of Moscow facing "an extremely difficult time." He also was worried about whether the Soviets would invade China. The meeting decided that China would condemn the invasion in the strongest terms and would offer its firm support to the "anti-aggression efforts" of Romania and Albania, both of which were under the threat of Soviet invasion too.[85]

When Zhou learned that Aurel Duma, Romania's ambassador to China, would host a Romanian National Day reception on August 23, he immediately decided to attend it and deliver a speech. Late in the night on August 22, he discussed the content of the speech with members of his speech drafting group. The next morning, he spent two hours revising his notes for the address.[86] On August 23, *Renmin ribao* published an editorial essay arguing that the Czechoslovakia invasion had revealed that "the Soviet renegade clique has long since degenerated into a gang of social-imperialists," and that "Soviet social-imperialism" was as dangerous to the people of the world as US imperialism.[87] At Duma's reception that evening, Zhou denounced the Soviet invasion of Czechoslovakia as being "exactly the same as Hitler in the past, in his aggression against Czechoslovakia, and as US imperialism today in its aggression toward Vietnam." He also called the Soviet Union "a country of social-imperialism and social-fascism."[88]

Zhou's claim was laden with meaning. Since the establishment of the PRC, anti-US imperialism had dominated political discourse in the New China, and it served as a major theme for legitimizing Maoist programs and policies that sought to transform China's state, society, and international outlook. Mao had launched the Cultural Revolution to prevent a "Soviet-style capitalist restoration" in China. However, until then, Beijing had never used the label of "social-imperialism" to refer to Moscow. Now, by calling the Soviet Union a social-imperialist country, a theoretical door was opened for Beijing to define the Soviet Union as China's most dangerous enemy in the world.

* * *

By early September, "new revolutionary authorities" had emerged in every province, following the establishment of revolutionary committees in Tibet and Xinjiang. The "full-scale civil war" had come to an end. On September 7, a crowd of one hundred thousand rallied in Beijing to celebrate "the whole country turning red." Zhou delivered a speech at the rally, in which he noted that twenty months had passed since the January Revolution. The Cultural Revolution had achieved great victories by "successfully seizing power from capitalist roaders" around the country.[89] However, as Zhou would soon know, the Cultural Revolution was far from over.

The CCP Central Committee held in October its Twelfth Plenum, which was meant to wrap up the "great revolution reckoning." Yet, even according to the party's own charter, the plenum was illegal due to the lack of a quorum. Among the members and alternate members of the Central Committee elected at the party's Eighth Congress, eighty-seven were still alive, but most of them had been purged. Zhou arranged for a group of "sidelined" Central Committee members to be rushed to Beijing, some directly from prison cells. Still, only forty of the members elected at the Eighth Congress attended the plenum—fewer than half. Thus, the first act at the plenum was to make ten alternate Central Committee members full members, in order to legitimate the gathering.[90] Several dozen stars of the Cultural Revolution who were not Central Committee members also attended the plenum.

The number one task of the plenum was to "permanently expel" Liu from the party. Mao made Zhou play a central role in this ridiculous drama. For many months, the Central Office on Special Cases had been preparing for this moment, putting together a report thousands of pages in length, alleging that Liu was a "renegade, traitor, and scab." Given his abundant experience, Zhou should have easily found numerous flaws in the document. He was extremely unwilling to put his signature on such a phony report. Therefore, he let it sit on his desk for almost two weeks. However, because he was head of the office that produced the report, he knew that he had no choice but to sign it, as Mao intended him to do. Finally, he made the most difficult decision in his life and career. He signed the report, and left this comment:

> Liu is indeed a big traitor, a renegade, a spy, an enemy agent, and a treasonous person. By committing all kinds of crimes, he is an unpardonable reactionary. We cheer for the Great Proletarian Cultural Revolution launched and led by our great leader, Chairman Mao. Without it, how could the crimes of Liu and his like of betraying the party and the country be so thoroughly exposed?

Zhou also mentioned, as he had done on the eve of the Cultural Revolution, the importance of maintaining loyalty in one's later years: "This is a test for us about whether we are qualified to be Communists, and whether we can maintain our revolutionary loyalty in our later years. In this respect, we all should learn from you, Comrade Jiang Qing."[91] At the plenum, Zhou delivered a speech about the Liu case on the party's behalf.

Zhou did all this for Mao to see. Had he not yielded to the pressure, he would have been seen as differing with Mao on the legitimacy of the Cultural Revolution. He probably also hoped that the settling of the Liu issue would bring the Cultural Revolution to a close. Although it was absolutely contradictory to his own conscience, he still sacrificed Liu in the end. Years later, after Liu's widow Wang Guangmei was released from prison, she refused to forgive Zhou. She was certainly entitled to do so. Yet, although this was a dark moment in Zhou's life and political career, there are reasons for history to pardon Zhou as a beleaguered politician and an entrapped person. After all, this was a time when Zhou was very much like a small boat, caught in stormy weather, that could be capsized at any moment. Yet without Zhou, the big ship that was China, carrying hundreds of millions of passengers, might have sunk.

* * *

Zhou experienced another tragedy while the plenum was underway: on October 14, Sun Weishi, his stepdaughter, died in prison. Zhou and Deng Yingchao had no children. Despite the fissure caused by Weishi's failure to listen to their advice about her marriage with Jin Shan, they still loved Weishi very much (and Jin Shan never had another affair). During the Cultural

Revolution, however, Weishi was imprisoned on March 1, 1968, for "involving [herself] in counterrevolutionary activities" and "spying for the Soviet Union." Reportedly, the case was concocted by Jiang Qing, and Lin Biao's wife, Ye Qun.[92] After secretly collecting materials against Weishi, Jiang suddenly brought the "evidence" to Zhou Enlai, forcing him to sign the arrest warrant. When Zhou learned of Weishi's death, he wrote on October 17, "Did she commit suicide or was she murdered? This should be investigated. Her body should go through an anatomic exam to identify the exact cause of her death." However, before an autopsy could be performed, Weishi's body was cremated. When Deng Yingchao heard of this, she burst into a loud sob, lamenting, "How miserably has she died!"[93] Weishi was not rehabilitated until after the end of the Cultural Revolution.

Sun Weishi's tragic experience was not an isolated incident. In January 1968, Zhou's own younger brother, Zhou Enshou, was also arrested and imprisoned. Before the Cultural Revolution, Enshou had been a member of a dining group organized by Wang Guangqi, the brother of Wang Guangmei, Liu Shaoqi's wife. When Jiang Qing received materials collected by some Red Guards about Enshou's "wrongdoings," she conveyed them to Zhou. Seeing that Liu's brother-in-law was involved in the matter, Zhou at once sensed its complications. He immediately reported the matter to Mao, whose response was that Zhou might "handle it in accordance with the situation." Zhou then instructed the PLA's Beijing Garrison to arrest Enshou and place him in "protective detention." Zhou Enshou would not be released until May 1975, and he would not be "thoroughly rehabilitated" after Zhou's death and the end of the Cultural Revolution.[94] In these two cases, Zhou Enlai, as China's premier, still had to agree to put his loved ones into prison. This was Zhou Enlai's tragedy. In a broad sense, this was also the tragedy of Mao's Great Proletarian Cultural Revolution, as well as the tragedy of China's whole revolutionary era.

• • •

Both Mao and Zhou knew that to end the Cultural Revolution, they needed to thoroughly stamp out the Red Guard movement. On December 21, the Chinese Central Broadcast announced Mao's "latest instructions": "It is necessary for educated youths to go to the countryside to be reeducated by poor and lower-middle peasants."[95] This was a crucial step taken by Mao to conclude the Cultural Revolution, which was launched first in schools. For three years, students above the junior high school level had been kept in their schools to "carry out revolution." Now, as the end of the Cultural Revolution neared, the decision to send millions of urban youth to the countryside would simultaneously serve three purposes. First, the move would undermine the political energy and capacity of the Red Guards. Second, it would greatly reduce the huge employment pressure that had built up in the cities. Further, at least in terms of logic, it could be presented as an important step in the Cultural Revolution's manifesting the vision Mao outlined in his May Seventh Instruction, that is, transitioning from a phase of destruction to one of construction.

Renmin ribao published a quotation of Mao's after the Twelfth Plenum adjourned: "The Great Proletarian Cultural Revolution, for consolidating the proletarian dictatorship, preventing capitalist restoration, and constructing socialism, was completely necessary and very timely."[96] The statement seemingly was intended to secure the historical position of the Cultural Revolution. However, the Cultural Revolution would not end for another seven years, after both Mao and Zhou had gone "to see Marx."

27

LIN BIAO DIES

1969–1971

Late in the afternoon on April 1, 1969, Zhou Enlai arrived at the Great Hall of the People for the CCP's Ninth Congress. Mao opened the gathering at 5:00 P.M., proclaiming that the congress would be a memorable event of "unity and victory" and would bring the Cultural Revolution to a "victorious conclusion."[1] However, the Ninth Congress would not culminate in a resounding success for Mao's "continuous revolution." Rather, it saw profound division among those who had supported the Cultural Revolution, catalyzing a process that would doom the turbulent movement.

Worrying signs foreshadowed the upheaval in the party. The drafting of the congress's political report had been underway since early 1969. At first, Mao asked Chen Boda to lead the task along with Zhang Chunqiao; but Chen and Zhang disagreed about the themes that should be covered in the report. While Chen believed it time for the party to turn its attention to economic development, Zhang stressed that the revolution was not over. Mao agreed with Zhang and instructed him to prepare his own draft. Chen nevertheless finished his version of the report, which Mao ignored. Finally, Zhang's draft was adopted with the chairman's endorsement.[2] Although Zhou was not involved in the drafting of the report, the premier must have noticed Mao's cooling attitude toward Chen.

Chen consulted with Lin Biao in preparing his report. Chen's emphasis on the economy in his draft reflected Lin's preference to give priority to that subject.[3] Mao repeatedly shared Zhang's drafts with Lin for comment. Lin never objected to the content of the drafts; in fact, he had not read any of them. He delivered Zhang's report at the congress in "broken sentences."[4] Mao, though annoyed, said nothing, but Zhou saw everything.

Lin nonetheless was the star of the congress, which adopted a new party charter formally confirming him as Mao's successor. Zhou was duty bound to justify the choice. He highlighted Lin's history of supporting Mao in all intraparty struggles. When Mao launched the Cultural Revolution, Zhou stressed, Lin had played "an essential role in spreading Mao's thought to the whole party, the whole army, and the people of the whole country—even the whole world."[5] Zhou, who had long excluded himself as a candidate for the party's second-in-command, embraced Lin's ascendance.

Lin's position and power rose to new heights. Yet, a tree towering above the rest of the forest inevitably invites violent gusts of wind. In retrospect, Lin probably started down the path to his eventual demise the moment he was officially made Mao's heir.

Different forces vied for power at the Ninth Congress, despite Mao's calls for unity. Zhou, as chief of the congress's secretariat, handled the nomination of candidates for leadership posts. Although Zhou was skilled at balancing the desires of various factions, this time he found it difficult to come

27.1 Mao Zedong posting his vote, followed by Lin Biao, Zhou Enlai, Chen Boda, Kang Sheng, Jiang Qing, Zhang Chunqiao, and Yao Wenyuan at the CCP's Ninth Congress, April 1969. *World History Archive / Alamy Stock Photo*

up with solutions agreeable to all. Jiang Qing was his biggest headache. Zhou and the nomination group included Jiang in their list of candidates for Politburo seats, but this was not enough to satisfy Mao's wife. She believed that she was entitled to join the Politburo Standing Committee, since she had "contributed enormously to the Cultural Revolution." Zhou knew that she was unqualified for such a role, but, as always, Mao had the final say in the matter. Despite the chairman's occasional criticism of Jiang, he remained her staunchest supporter. Hence, Zhou added Jiang's name to the preliminary list for the Standing Committee. He was relieved when Mao removed Jiang's name from the list, commenting that "she does not deserve it."[6]

Mao was unanimously elected to the Central Committee. Lin fell two votes short of Mao, probably because he (along with Ye Qun, his wife) had not voted for himself, to avoid giving himself the same status as Mao. Zhou also fell two votes short, which was likely his and Deng Yingchao's doing. The trouble was that Jiang fell short by a dozen or so votes. She suspected that this was the work of Lin's generals. Zhang Chunqiao proposed to "investigate the matter," but Mao stopped him.[7] Different factions were at odds with each other even before the congress ended.

The political structure established at the congress comprised three forces. The first was Jiang Qing's Cultural Revolution faction, whose ranks included Chen Boda, Kang Sheng, Zhang Chunqiao, and Yao Wenyuan, in addition to many Cultural Revolution stars. The second was the military faction headed by Lin, which was made up of multiple army commanders who had gained positions in the Central Committee. Four generals close to Lin—Huang Yongsheng, Wu Faxian, Li Zuopeng, and Qiu Huizuo—even became Politburo members. However, Lin did not have full control of the PLA, as Mao remained chairman of the CMC. The third group comprised veteran officials who either had not been purged in the Cultural Revolution or had recently been rehabilitated. Broadly speaking, Zhou also belonged to this group.

Mao stood at the top of the structure, but his control of power was not absolutely secure, as Lin was visibly gaining influence. After all, it was Mao who had elevated Lin to his current level of prominence. However, when he promoted Lin, the chairman overturned his long-standing rule that control of the military should be balanced among forces from different backgrounds. In retrospect, the task of resolving problems that arose from the resulting tensions accounted for much of the difficulty Mao faced in ending the Cultural

Revolution. Pandora's box had been flung open, kicking off another round of intraparty struggle.

* * *

Mao faced a big dilemma after the CCP's Ninth Congress. Although he wanted to end the Cultural Revolution, at the same time he launched a series of new political campaigns, driven by some of his "fresh ideas" and the continued party infighting.

The most mysterious and ridiculous of the new campaigns was the movement to purge "May Sixteenth elements." The May Sixteenth Corps was a small group of young students who had targeted Zhou in their attacks, but which by 1969 had long since dissolved. However, Mao repeatedly made vague references to "May Sixteenth elements" in several talks after 1969, claiming that the extraordinary turmoil of the Cultural Revolution was the result of their conspiracies.[8] In practice Mao often invoked "May Sixteenth elements" as a pretext to get rid of yesterday's "revolutionary rebels" or Red Guards, thus serving his intention to reestablish state control over society. In the Foreign Ministry, Zhou cited "May Sixteenth elements" to justify the removal of the radical rebels who had tried to seize power there.[9] By doing so, Zhou effectively renormalized policy implementation in China's external relations.

Meanwhile, Zhou turned much of his attention to revitalizing the Chinese economy, which had suffered serious setbacks in the previous years of the Cultural Revolution. He frequently quoted Mao's instruction of "making revolution, promoting production" to validate his efforts to resuscitate the floundering economy.[10] His hard work paid off. In 1969, China's gross industrial and agricultural production increased 23.8 percent from 1968's lows, with industrial production growing 34.3 percent.[11] The Chinese economy continued to improve in the following years although the Cultural Revolution had not yet come to a close, growing by more than 10 percent in five of the seven years from 1969 to 1976, the year that the Cultural Revolution finally ended.

The contradictions between Jiang's Central Cultural Revolution Group and the military faction persisted, albeit at a low simmer, as the economy recovered. At the heart of the dispute was Mao's suspicion that his designated heir might betray him. He also sensed subtle ideological differences between him and his second-in-command. Despite all this, however, Mao unintentionally enhanced Lin's power and influence when he stirred up a nationwide mobilization push aimed at "preparing for war."

After two border clashes between Chinese and Soviet garrisons at Zhenbao Island on the Ussuri River in March 1969, Mao called on the whole country to "prepare for war." He did so not because he believed that China would become involved in a major war, but mainly to provoke a sense of national mobilization ahead of the Ninth Congress. As tensions between Beijing and Moscow worsened, in August, Soviet troops eliminated a squadron of Chinese soldiers at a border garrison in Xinjiang. Meanwhile, rumors spread that Moscow was gearing up for a preemptive strike on China's nuclear facilities.[12] On August 28, Beijing ordered a general mobilization in the Chinese provinces and regions that bordered the Soviet Union and Outer Mongolia.[13] In late September, with China's National Day fast approaching, Mao decided that no provincial civilian or military leaders should travel to Beijing to join in the holiday celebrations, as "the enemy may use that opportunity to wipe out our leadership."[14] On September 30, Lin ordered that Beijing go into a state of military emergency. He even considered preemptively destroying the main dam at the Miyun Reservoir in the suburbs of Beijing, lest the Soviets target it in a nuclear strike. Fortunately, Zhou stopped the plan, and the reservoir was saved.[15]

No Soviet attack came on National Day. Moreover, Beijing and Moscow had agreed to resume border negotiations; a Soviet delegation was scheduled to arrive in Beijing on October 19. Yet Mao, consumed by the war scare he had provoked, feared that the Soviets might use the negotiations as an opportunity to launch a sneak attack on Beijing. He told Zhou, "It is not good for all our central leaders to stay in Beijing. Many will die in the attack by one atomic bomb. They should be dispersed."[16] On the evening of October 14, Mao left Beijing for Wuhan, and all other central leaders evacuated from Beijing by October 20.[17] Zhou stayed in the capital. A "frontal command" headed by Chief of Staff Huang Yongsheng, along with Wu, Li, and Qiu (who were all Lin Biao's longtime subordinates and vice chiefs of staff), moved into an underground shelter in the western suburbs of Beijing.[18]

The war scare also affected Lin, who was away in Suzhou. On October 18, Lin dictated—without notifying Mao—an "urgent instruction" to his secretary on "guarding against a sudden attack by the enemy."[19] Lin's secretary then dictated the order to Huang by telephone, and in turn, Huang instructed that the order be relayed to the whole PLA. Yan Zhongchuan, the vice chief of staff on duty that evening, titled it "Vice Chairman Lin's Order Number One," allegedly "for the sake of convenience."[20] The PLA immediately entered a status of war readiness.

Lin's issuing the order without Mao's knowledge presented an extraordinary challenge to the chairman's absolute control over the Chinese military. By the time Zhou received the transcript of Lin's order, it already had been dispatched. Zhou immediately reported it to the chairman. When Wang Dongxing, head of the garrison guarding Mao, handed Lin's order to Mao, the chairman yelled, "Set it on fire!" He seized the document from Wang and burned it himself; Wang was only able to save the envelope.[21] That evening, Zhou called Wang, asking about Mao's reaction to Lin's order. "He burned it to ashes," replied Wang. "It was burned?" Zhou asked. "Yes," confirmed Wang.[22] Zhou must have realized that the chasm between Mao and Lin had drastically widened.

* * *

The first half of 1970 saw no apparent deterioration of the Mao-Lin relationship, but signs of trouble gradually began to appear. It started with a seemingly innocuous matter: preparing for the convening of the next National People's Congress (NPC), China's rubber-stamp parliament.

Mao was still in Wuhan. On March 7, all of a sudden he raised the question of whether it was necessary to keep the positions of president and vice president of the state. Their roles were nominal, he said, and could be taken over by heads of the NPC.[23] The second day, Zhou conveyed Mao's opinion at a Politburo meeting; the chairman's perspective received "unanimous support." Accordingly, the Politburo named Zhou to head a group that would select NPC representatives and come up with its agenda, putting Kang Sheng and Zhang Chunqiao in charge of revising the PRC's constitution.[24]

Ten days later, a central work conference chaired by Zhou again endorsed abolishing the presidency of the state. At that moment, Lin, who was still in Suzhou, intervened. He sent a message to Mao's secretary, in which he proposed that "Chairman Mao should be president of the state." Mao, making no comment on the proposal, asked his secretary to "convey his regards to Comrade Lin Biao."[25]

Lin sent another message to Mao and the Politburo in mid-April, on the eve of another Politburo meeting, in which he reiterated his proposal that

Mao should assume the role of PRC president. "Such a move matches the expectations within and outside the party, and also meets the hopes of the people at home and abroad," Lin emphasized.[26] Zhou and his colleagues endorsed Lin's proposal at the Politburo meeting the next day. When Zhou reported the events to Mao, the chairman's response was swift: "I cannot do this anymore. This proposal is inappropriate."[27] Mao returned to Beijing a few days later and restated his position at a Politburo meeting: "I will not be the president of the state. There is no need to have that post."[28] But did Mao mean what he said? Zhou was not sure.

Lin persisted with this idea despite Mao's refusal. Shortly after the meeting, Lin said during a private conversation with General Wu Faxian, "It is inconceivable for a big country like China not to have a head of state." Further, Lin emphasized that he, being "in poor health," could not take up the role, and that Mao was "the only person who can serve in the position." Wu felt that Lin was "very sincere."[29] But this contradicts China's official narrative about the matter that emerged after Lin died, which claimed that Lin raised the issue of maintaining the state presidency because he wanted to use the position to "cut into the line" and to "divide the party and seize the power."[30] This accusation, however, is not convincing. President of the PRC was a mostly symbolic post with little real power. As Lin had already been designated as Mao's successor, he had no need whatsoever to seek the position.

Zhou seemed to waver between Mao and Lin all the while, demonstrating the great lengths he went to avoid taking a side on such a sensitive matter—especially one about which the chairman and the vice chairman disagreed. He probably also hoped that the issue would be settled at the forthcoming Central Committee plenum at Lushan.

Zhou witnessed another clash between Lin's generals and the Cultural Revolution stars on August 13. At a Politburo meeting that Zhou chaired, Wu Faxian pointed out that Zhang Chunqiao had, in the draft constitution he produced, deleted three adjectives that Lin had "invented" to describe Mao's contribution to the development of Marxist-Leninism: "ingenious," "creative," and "comprehensive." Wu alleged that Zhang had done so to belittle Mao while assailing Lin. Zhou blamed neither Wu nor Zhang and tried his best to settle the quarrel.[31] At another meeting on the second day, Zhang conceded—heeding the advice Zhou had given him privately—and the Politburo decided to add the three adjectives to the draft.[32]

Zhou was still quite uneasy, however. A poem he hand-copied from a classic text clearly reflected his ambivalence:

> February weather is the hardest to satisfy in the whole year;
> Silkworms like it warm, ginseng likes it cold.
> Boys growing vegetables need rain;
> Girls picking mulberry leaves want it clear and dry.[33]

These lines vividly revealed the huge dilemma that Zhou faced as the result of the standoff between Lin's generals and Mao's wife and her associates. Zhou could not throw his support behind either side, as he knew well that Lin and Mao, respectively, stood behind the feuding factions. Zhou could not afford to offend either of them.

* * *

Lushan was an eventful place in CCP history. Eleven years earlier, Peng Dehuai had suffered ruin and shame at the Lushan Conference of 1959, and Lin, taking advantage of Peng's downfall, would ascend dramatically in his political career. Now, in late August 1970, another Central Committee plenum would be held at Lushan.

At a preparatory meeting Mao chaired on the eve of the plenum, almost all the top leaders supported retaining the state presidency. Chen Boda contended that it was necessary to unify the positions of party chairman and state president. Lin and even Zhou also endorsed the stance. Mao's face turned pale. "If you want to keep the position," Mao said, "I will not take it." In a threatening tone, he stated that "this should be a plenum of unity and success, not one of division and failure."[34]

Zhou's attitude was strange. Since the Yan'an Rectification and, especially, after his "opposing rash advance" ordeal, he had consistently followed the rule of never challenging Mao. Whenever he found himself at odds with the chairman, he would hasten to make self-criticism until Mao absolved him. It was thus quite unusual that Zhou supported retaining the state presidency—and having Mao serve in the role—despite Mao's repeated opposition to keeping the position. Had Mao said something different to Zhou privately? Or were Mao's real intentions too obscure for even Zhou to judge? Zhou might have thought it safe to support retaining the post until

Mao thoroughly clarified his opinion on the matter. Now, however, Zhou got Mao's message.

The plenum was scheduled to begin at 3:00 P.M. on August 23, but Mao and Lin did not appear until 3:45 P.M., having talked in a nearby room while everyone else, including Zhou, waited. No one knew what they had discussed.[35] Lin's opening presentation—poorly organized and repetitious, impressing few in the audience—lasted over an hour. He flattered Mao as a "genius." Without mentioning whether the state presidency should be retained, he stressed that "the status of Chairman Mao as the great leader, the head of the state, and the supreme military commander should be formalized in a legal sense." He also implied that a certain person was trying to oppose Mao's status as the indisputable leader of the party and the state.[36] For the majority of the audience, the vice chairman's speech was just another litany of clichés. They all applauded in a routine demonstration of respect.

Lin's flattery toward Mao was familiar to the chairman, who smiled as he listened to the presentation. However, Mao's face stiffened when Lin began to implicitly attack the Cultural Revolution stars. When the chairman declared that "the meeting [was] adjourned," he left the room immediately.[37] Zhou, sitting next to Mao and Lin, was alarmed.

Lin's speech did not provoke much of a reaction at first. Almost all who attended the meeting failed to grasp the implications of his words. But Chen Boda knew that Lin had targeted Zhang Chunqiao. Chen thus approached Lin after the meeting, asking him if the chairman knew what he would say prior to his delivering the speech. "Yes, he knew," replied Lin. Chen was jubilant. He had been at odds with Zhang for some time, and now he saw an opportunity to get revenge. He went at once to exchange information and opinions with Wu Fuxian. They were ready to open fire on Zhang the next day.[38]

Those present at the plenum on August 24 listened in groups to the recording of Lin's speech from the day before. Chen eagerly participated in his group, boasting in flowery language about Mao's greatness and emphasizing his own thesis that "a genius makes a huge difference in history." Chen's praise of Mao contained veiled accusations against Zhang. Ye Qun and Wu Faxian also spoke enthusiastically about Lin's speech in their respective groups. The most noteworthy endorsement came from Wang Dongxing, who loudly voiced his support for the vice chairman. Wang's words had a big impact, given his close relationship with Mao.[39] The Cultural Revolution faction had been unpopular among the delegates, but no one had dared to challenge them directly. Now, a barrage of accusations bombarded Zhang from all directions. Tension soon pervaded the political atmosphere at Lushan.

Zhou looked on coolly, attempting neither to encourage nor to stop the attacks on Zhang. That evening, Wang Dongxing called Zhou, asking the premier whether a collection of quotations on genius that Chen had compiled should be distributed. "No, do not do it now," replied Zhou.[40] He had a political hunch that this was no simple matter.

The next morning, a widely distributed newsletter carrying a transcript of Chen's presentation further fanned the flames of the plenum fracas. People rushed to speak out in support of retaining the state presidency. Many also clamored for the "anti-Mao plotters," whose existence Chen had implied in his speech, to be exposed. Zhang was a sitting duck in the face of such vociferous criticism.[41] Around noontime, Zhang and Yao Wenyuan, accompanied by Jiang Qing, went to see Mao. They burst into tears, describing to the chairman Zhang's miserable experience at the plenum.[42] The conversation was a virtual replay of a scene that had occurred during the February Countercurrent, when Jiang Qing led Zhang and others to report their complaints about veteran officials to Mao. Jiang, Zhang, and Yao went to see Zhou immediately after they met with the chairman. The aggrieved group must have conveyed to Zhou what Mao had said to them.[43]

The chairman went into action. At 3:00 P.M., he called a meeting of top leaders. With a somber expression on his face, he demanded that discussion about the state presidency be dropped immediately. Once again, he refused to take the position. "If you continue to make noise," he asserted, "I will let you do it. . . . And I may just resign as chairman of the Central Committee." The meeting decided to archive Lin's speech, while ordering Chen and Wu to make self-criticism.[44]

Zhou conferred with Jiang and Kang Sheng right after the meeting adjourned, clearly in order to discuss how to carry out Mao's instructions.[45] Then, Chen and Wang Dongxing also spoke with Zhou. According to Wang's recollection, Zhou urged him to be "the first one to make self-criticism." Wang submitted such a letter to Mao the next day.[46]

The plenum adjourned for two days beginning on August 26. Mao repeatedly summoned Zhou for one-on-one talks that lasted late into the night. In turn, Zhou talked to people individually or hosted small-group meetings day and night.[47] Mao summoned Chen and "sternly scolded him."[48] Zhou asked Lin's generals, particularly Wu, to make self-criticism immediately.[49]

But Lin was resentful. "You have done nothing wrong," he told Wu, implying there was no need for Wu to blame himself.[50] Lin had almost never challenged Mao in the past. This time, however, he did. Lin's standing up to Mao probably indicated that he felt the chairman had deceived him. Also, Lin likely overestimated his own political might.

Zhou chided Chen and Wu at an enlarged meeting of the Politburo on August 29, claiming that they had "presented mistaken viewpoints at group discussions" and asserting that it was "Chairman Mao who has realized this dangerous trend." But Zhou stated that "it should be allowed for a comrade to commit mistakes, who should be given the opportunity to correct them." Apparently, he did not want to punish Lin and his generals too harshly. Nor did he want to blow the matter out of proportion.[51]

Mao, for his part, showed no intention to settle the "storm over Lushan" easily. He circulated a short essay titled "Some of My Opinions" on August 31, which echoed his move at the Central Committee's plenum in August 1966, when he wrote "Bombarding the Headquarters" to challenge Liu and Deng. At this moment, Mao's essay took Chen, rather than Lin, as its target. The chairman even wrote that he and Lin "both believed" it was wrong for Chen to spread the phony thesis about genius.[52] The chairman's dramatic act decisively changed the direction of the plenum. Zhou was tasked with coordinating the chairman's "counteroffensive" at the plenum. On September 1, Zhou informed Chen that he would be criticized.[53] Ye and Wu, whose arguments against Zhang had been the loudest at the plenum, would also be subjected to criticism.

The plenum concluded on September 6. Mao announced at the closing session that "Lushan will not be leveled to the ground in one explosion, and the Earth will continue to rotate," thus sending another warning to Lin.[54] Zhou emphasized in his speech that the plenum remained "one of unity and victory," and he did not mention whether the push to "criticize Chen" would continue.[55] When Zhou spoke with Lin's generals, Wu, Li, and Qiu, before he departed Lushan, he conveyed to them Mao's assertion that "it is better to have unity, so all problems should be settled at Lushan."[56]

Mao had another one-on-one talk with Zhou just two days later, in which he assigned the premier to take charge of a special investigation of Chen.[57] The "struggles at Lushan," Zhou realized, had not ended.

• • •

Hardly had Zhou settled back in Beijing when he received additional instructions from Mao: a "criticize Chen campaign" would be launched immediately to resolve "unsettled issues at Lushan." Zhou's first move was to "liberate" Wang Dongxing. Although Wang had already made self-criticism at the plenum, Zhou now tried his best to coach Wang to come up with a "more profound" line of self-criticism, which Mao quickly accepted.[58] Zhou then turned to Lin's generals, especially Wu, urging them to "sincerely criticize" themselves. He also met with Lin and proposed that Lin ask his generals to write to Mao and Lin, "completely separating themselves from Chen Boda."[59] This was Zhou's way of helping Lin's generals while allowing Lin to pass Mao's test.

Zhou did all this not just for Lin, but for himself too. He and Lin had known and worked alongside each other since the mid-1920s. Zhou showed Lin a growing amount of respect as Lin rose ever higher in the CCP military apparatus, especially after he became the defense minister in 1959. During the Cultural Revolution, Zhou wholeheartedly endorsed Lin as China's second-in-command, support that accorded with Zhou's principle of not competing for that position under Mao. More importantly, both he and Lin believed in giving more emphasis to economic development. Indeed, in CCP intraparty politics, Zhou had allied himself more with Lin and his military group than he had with the Cultural Revolutionists.

Zhou knew as soon as the Mao-Lin rift emerged that he had to side with Mao in the matter. But he also understood the uniqueness of the Mao-Lin contradiction; after all, it was Mao who had chosen Lin as his successor. Lin also had deep roots and influence in the military. Although the standoff between Lin's generals and Jiang Qing and her followers presented Zhou with new challenges, Zhou's ample political experience would, in theory, enable him to overcome them. Simultaneously, Zhou saw that the feud might provide him with an additional buffer for political maneuvering, thus increasing his political safety. If Lin fell, Zhou would lose this buffer and become more exposed to Mao's deep-seated suspicion and desire for absolute control. Therefore, it was in Zhou's best interest not to let the Mao-Lin dispute escalate beyond control.

Mao's deep distrust of Lin, however, would make it difficult or even risky for Zhou to continue his attempt to straddle both sides of the dispute. By then, Mao had almost certainly decided not to keep Lin as his successor. Nonetheless, he did not want to openly split with Lin either. So he targeted Chen Boda instead, criticizing Chen's notions about genius—which Lin had first introduced. Mao calculated that avoiding a direct confrontation with Lin would give him more space to determine when, and how, to entangle the vice chairman in his snares.

Lin did not cooperate, as he was highly suspicious of Mao's intentions. He had established three principles for himself after Lushan: no matter how much Mao pressured him, he would "say nothing, do nothing, and blame nothing about himself."[60] Although Zhou repeatedly, albeit implicitly, beseeched Lin to yield to Mao, Lin stubbornly refused to submit.

Mao and Lin stood next to each other atop the Gate of Heavenly Peace on October 1, 1970, China's National Day. They did not mention Lushan or the drive to "criticize Chen" at all. Mao had a rather friendly conversation with Ye Qun when he saw her—another of the chairman's signals of goodwill to Lin.[61] A few days later, Ye produced a note of self-criticism. Wu submitted his at nearly the same time.[62]

But what Mao cared most about was Lin's attitude. Therefore, he treated Ye's and Wu's self-criticisms extremely harshly, accusing Ye of being overly influenced by "back-alley information" and castigating Wu for his indirect and enigmatic style. "This (what happened at Lushan) was a plot, initiated by a few, to deceive more than two hundred Central Committee members," Mao alleged.[63] Although Mao did not name Lin in his tirade, he intended for Lin to hear it, thus pressuring Lin to admit his "mistakes." Two days after Mao made his remarks, Zhou, joined by Kang Sheng, visited Lin and handed him a copy of Mao's comments.[64] Lin was unmoved.

On December 18, Mao was interviewed by the American journalist Edgar Snow. It was "rather disgusting," Mao told Snow abruptly, for others to refer to him as "great leader, great commander, great helmsman, and great teacher."[65] This was another encoded message, as this naming was originated by Lin. By attacking these honorary titles in a conversation with a foreign journalist, Mao demonstrated that his antagonism toward Lin was rounding the corner.

• • •

The rifts between Mao and Lin did not visibly worsen in winter 1970–1971. Yet this lull in their dispute was just the quiet before the storm. Zhou called a Politburo meeting according to Mao's instructions the same evening the chairman met with Snow. The Politburo decided to convene a conference of PLA commanders in North China.[66] The gathering, known as the "North

China Conference," began on December 12, 1970, and lasted for several weeks. Mao personally called on Ye, Huang (although he did not attend the Lushan conference), Wu, Li, and Qiu to attend the event, of which Zhou was put in charge. He kept in close communication with Mao, briefing the chairman while receiving instructions from him. Initially, Zhou endeavored to persuade the four generals to self-criticize, in order to "drag" them away from Lin. However, the generals "neither criticized Chen nor made self-critique."[67] Zhou concluded the conference on January 24, 1971. "Through exposing and criticizing Chen Boda," the premier announced, "all participants have gained a better sense of his antiparty crime."[68]

Although Mao's desired outcome for the conference had not materialized, he still allowed the conference to end. He did so largely because by then he had already rushed to call another "criticize Chen" meeting, which began on January 9 and was attended by about 150 PLA commanders, including the four generals. Mao hoped to use the new meeting to explore their attitudes while isolating Lin, but the generals remained unwilling to follow his agenda. Mao's patience was wearing thin. On February 19, Zhou followed Mao's order in announcing at the conference that no one would be allowed to "adopt a lukewarm attitude" toward the meeting's agenda of "criticizing Chen" and "let time elapse without achieving anything."[69] The next day, Mao personally picked on the four generals, demanding of them, "Why have you been so passive about criticizing Chen? Why have you failed to act positively without being pushed? . . . You must change your attitude."[70]

Huang, who served as chair of the conference, did not know what to say, as he had not even attended the Lushan Conference. To persuade Huang and others to speak out, Zhou made a long presentation at a Politburo meeting on February 22. The premier divulged that he himself had committed many mistakes in history, and that it was painful to admit them—which made self-criticism even more necessary.[71] Huang kept silent. Zhou stopped him after the meeting, asking, "Why have you been so quiet at the meeting?" "To the chairman, it does not matter what you say. What matters most is your attitude toward him. What he wants to wipe out is your factionalism!"[72] Finally, Huang, along with Wu, Li, and Qiu, acknowledged that they had all committed "serious mistakes in political lines" at Lushan, that they should have recognized their errors, and that their inaction was even more serious a mistake, which they were willing to correct. Zhou reported the generals' statement to Mao. "Very good!" exclaimed Mao. "This is a positive sign. All of you must keep your word!"[73] A few days later, the generals made another round of self-criticism, with which Mao seemed even more pleased, responding, "Well written! The key is how to thoroughly resolve the problems in the future."[74] Clearly, Mao now saw the prospect of driving a wedge between the generals and Lin.

Mao and Zhou met with the four generals on March 24. Mao asked Ye Qun and Wu to resubmit their self-criticisms. He also sent Zhou to Beidaihe to see Lin there and ask Lin to read the generals' self-criticisms.[75] By doing so, Mao implied that he was waiting for Lin's self-criticism, too.

Lin disappointed Mao. He proved elusive when Zhou, joined by the four generals, met with him. Lin asserted that he was "in full support of all of Mao's instructions" and said that he was also glad to see the self-criticism from Ye and the four generals.[76] Lin even expressed regret that he had unwittingly been "used by Chen Boda." But this was as far as he was willing to go. Before he spoke at Lushan, Lin told Zhou, he "had consulted with the chairman" and had said at the plenum "exactly what he had shared with him."[77] Lin doubtlessly was seeking to remind Mao that since the chairman had advance knowledge of his speech at Lushan, Mao should not press him too hard.

Lin's response was not what Zhou had hoped for. When Mao received Zhou's written report, he summoned Zhou and the four generals for their verbal briefing.[78] Toward the end of the conversation, Mao pointed to the four generals and told Zhou, "As far as I'm concerned, all their problems have now been resolved." Zhou looked pleased, saying that Mao's words were "of great significance for the whole party to unite together."[79]

Mao had not told the truth, however. In his mind, the Lin affair was far from settled. Mao called for another rectification conference, which began on April 15. Zhou, who chaired it, set the tone of the conference in his opening speech, in which he attested that Ye, as well as the four generals, had repeatedly passed up "the opportunity to educate themselves" after the Lushan Conference. Only with the chairman's "persistent pushing have they made self-criticism." It was necessary to convene this further meeting, Zhou continued, because their "disease needed to be further treated, and they themselves could thus be saved." They should use the conference as another chance to "educate themselves through better understanding the reality" of the situation, the premier emphasized, so that "new unity" could be achieved "on a more solid basis."[80]

Zhou carefully phrased his speech to not make it sound overly harsh toward Ye and the four generals. Still, they became the targets of fierce accusations at the conference. The most enthusiastic critics were the stars of the Cultural Revolution and a few PLA commanders who had jumped in rank during the Cultural Revolution. Veteran leaders, such as Zhu De, Nie Rongzhen, and Li Xiannian, said almost nothing at all. Deng Yingchao, Zhou's wife and a Central Committee member, even stood up to stop the "excessive accusations" being hurled at Ye and the generals, something that she had virtually never done on similar occasions in the past.[81] Clearly, she spoke out on Zhou's behalf, revealing Zhou's eagerness to let the five under attack pass the test.

Ye and the four generals made a final round of self-criticism in late April. Afterward, Zhou immediately reported to Mao that they had shown willingness to "pursue unity" by "more actively involving themselves in the 'criticize Chen' campaign."[82] Zhou also tried to lure Lin into giving a presentation that included "some self-criticism" at the conference. Once more, Lin declined the invitation. Though he was deeply disappointed, Zhou knew that there was nothing more he could do.

Zhou concluded the conference on April 29. In a deliberately worded speech, he said that Ye and the four generals had been seriously wrong in their political lines and their decision to partake in factionalism. Unlike Chen Boda, who was cast as an antiparty figure, however, Ye and the generals were portrayed as misled but essentially good party members, whose problems were "ones within our own ranks." Zhou also argued that the generals had made mistakes because they had failed to follow the chairman's instructions, but that now, they should be encouraged to rectify their errors. This, Zhou stressed, would lead to "unity on the basis of Marxism-Leninism and Mao Thought," allowing the party "to strive to achieve greater victories."[83] Though Zhou's address ended on a positive note, he knew that for Mao, the Lin Biao affair was not over.

• • •

When the Rectification Campaign was underway, Lin Liguo, Lin Biao's son, drafted a document, titled "571 Outline," with the aid of a group of young PLA officers in his inner circle. The outline contained cutting attacks on the political lines and personnel and economic development strategies under

Mao. Lin Liguo and the officers claimed in the outline that "for more than a decade, the national economy has been stalled," and that "the actual living standard of everyday masses and grass-level cadres has declined, and there is growing discontent among them." The group further asserted that "the political life of the party and the state has been made a feudal autocratic dictatorship." They lambasted Mao, calling him "B-52," an insulting way to name the chairman in the Chinese context, and describing him as "paranoid and a sadist" who had ruthlessly purged his political enemies while "putting the blame for all bad things on the victims." Overall, though, the outline was more a preamble to a denunciation of Mao than a sophisticated political program. Although the authors of the document had implied that it was a plan for "armed uprising" (571, pronounced "wu-qi-yi" in Chinese, sounds like "armed uprising"), it was by no means a workable coup scheme, as it did not detail the organization of and participants in a coup, or how it would be carried out.[84] Young Lin's main concern was to defend his father's gravely endangered status and power.

No evidence shows that Lin Biao knew about the plan. Furthermore, with Lin's deep political experience, such a rough and unworkable plan would not likely have been produced had he been involved in it. Yet the content of the plan undoubtedly revealed some of Lin's thoughts. When Mao repeatedly pushed Lin's wife, Ye Qun, to make self-criticism, Lin inevitably felt this to be repulsive. There is no evidence to suggest that the four generals knew about the plot, either, let alone helped devise it. When the Lin case finally came to trial in 1980, the four generals, as defendants, were accused of being involved neither in the drafting of the "571 Outline" nor in the plot to assassinate Mao. The generals' main crime was to have sided with Lin against Mao.

• • •

The failure of the rectification conference caused Mao and Lin to drift even further apart. Lin's "say nothing, do nothing, and blame nothing" attitude genuinely offended or even enraged Mao, and Mao's aggressive urgings to make self-criticism scared Lin and made him depressed. The chairman and the vice chairman's relationship had reached an ominous dead end.

Lin viewed that year's May Day—or International Workers' Day—celebrations from atop Tiananmen Gate. He had virtually no interaction with either Mao or Zhou that day, though he sat next to the chairman. In fact, he left the celebrations after only a few minutes. When Zhou learned that the Xinhua photographer present did not even have time to take an official photo documenting Lin's presence, he lost his temper and yelled at the photographer for his "failure to fulfill his responsibility." Then, Zhou personally went through video footage to find an image to be published in the papers the next day in which Lin was with Mao, but only the backside of the vice chairman's face was visible.[85] The image showed unity among the country's two top leaders. No matter how untrue the narrative conveyed by the photo was, Zhou still wanted to show it to the whole country and the whole world.

Mao probably saw Lin's behavior as revealing the vice chairman's intense arrogance. In fact, Lin was consumed by fear—which was vividly reflected in a letter he wrote but never sent. Three weeks after the May Day celebrations, Lin had a conversation with Zhou about the "unity of the party and safety of its leaders." Then, he drafted a letter to Mao, in which he stated that following "the great victory of the Cultural Revolution," it was crucial to guarantee that "the Central Committee and the Politburo will stay solid in unity for a prolonged period." He proposed that a policy be established stipulating that all current Politburo members and commanders of PLA regional headquarters and above "should not be arrested, detained, executed, or fired for the next ten years." Lin suggested that the policy be relayed to "every soldier of the garrisons in Beijing and other cities," to ensure that it would be faithfully carried out. Lin explained that he had decided to formulate the policy because "after reading the documents of the criticize Chen conference, some comrades have been greatly worried about their own safety," which had thus become a "crucial matter deserving of good attention." Lin asked Mao to consult with Zhou about the matter and "instruct the premier to find ways to settle these worries."[86]

Lin did not send the letter to Mao. Perhaps he knew after writing it that the ideas it contained were "not perfect or even incorrect."[87] More likely, however, was that Lin never sent the letter because Zhou had advised him not to, and Lin took the advice. The letter was discovered in Lin's secret archives after his death.

The continuing deterioration of the Mao-Lin relationship put Zhou in an increasingly perilous situation. When Zhou discovered that Zhang Chunqiao had not included any praise for Lin in a draft editorial he wrote for *Renmin ribao* to celebrate the party's anniversary, the premier added a sentence to the draft highlighting Lin's contributions to "promoting the study of Chairman Mao's quotations."[88] Zhou racked his brain for ideas to create and consolidate a public impression that CCP leaders were still in complete unity. As it soon turned out, though, it was beyond Zhou's capacity to halt the breakdown in relations between Mao and Lin.

* * *

Mao went on another tour of southern China beginning in August 1971. By then, he was most likely determined to remove Lin as China's second-in-command. The challenge he faced was not whether, but how and when, to do so. It seems that he had two goals for the tour. First, he hoped to send Lin and his associates a series of warning signs to see how they would respond. Second, he would meet with provincial party and military leaders, with the intention of mobilizing them for a showdown with Lin at the next Central Committee plenum. He was confident in his ability to achieve both goals. In the past, he had confronted Zhang Guotao; criticized Zhou Enlai, Wang Ming, and Bo Gu; purged Gao Gang, Peng Dehuai, Peng Zhen, Luo Ruiqing, Lu Dingyi, and Yang Shangkui; and, finally, undermined Liu Shaoqi and Deng Xiaoping during the Cultural Revolution. In none of these episodes had he encountered an adversary who could be called his equal. Nor would Lin prove an especially formidable opponent for him. After all, Mao still controlled China's party, military, media, and mainstream discourse. He thus believed that he could bring Lin down if he so wished.

Mao's biggest dilemma did not lie in high politics, but in how to justify Lin's downfall to the party as well as the entire country. Mao had already declared after Liu Shaoqi's demise that the Cultural Revolution had led to "unity" and "victory." If now he were to purge Lin, who was known as his "closest comrade-in-arms," it would be difficult for him, even with his extraordinary authority and power, to produce a convincing explanation. Therefore, rather than bringing Lin down directly, Mao sought to find a way to show Lin some respect (in fact, this was also Mao's own self-respect) while forcing him to step aside "voluntarily."

Mao spoke with group after group of civilian and military leaders at every stop on the tour. He stated that "the scandal at Lushan [was] not over," and that "other plotters" with "their plans, organizations, and programs" were "behind Chen Boda." Their effort to "retain the presidency of the state," Mao claimed, was a pretext for their "anxiously attempting to seize supreme power." It would have been impossible for those listening to the chairman not to recognize that Lin was the target of his accusations. Mao mentioned Lin's name more frequently in the latter phase of the tour, asserting that Lin had delivered the speech at Lushan "without consulting with me." Therefore, Lin "certainly should take some responsibility for the struggle at Lushan."[89] Mao kept Zhou informed of his activities. On September 4, Wang Dongxing sent a special messenger to deliver to Zhou the transcripts of Mao's talks.[90] Zhou was alarmed and deeply worried by what he read.

Lin, who was in Beidaihe, reacted to the news that Mao had repeatedly named and criticized him as he had done ever since Lushan—he put his fate in heaven's hands. He was an introverted person who almost never socialized with others. Now, he did not even leave his dark living room, where he sat for hours without uttering a word.[91]

Lin Liguo, however, felt compelled to act. He and several confidantes from his small clique quickly came up with a plan to murder Mao by destroying his train near Shanghai or elsewhere on the chairman's way back to Beijing. The young Lin also considered asking his father to flee Beidaihe to establish another Party Center in southern China in case the coup attempt failed.[92] There is no evidence, however, to indicate that Lin Biao was aware of his son's plot. Nor did the four generals know anything about it. Moreover, the young Lin and his fellow plotters lacked the means to carry out their assassination plan, which never took shape.

Mao's moves in southern China grew increasingly more mysterious. He arrived in Shanghai on the evening of September 10 and spent the night on his train. At 1:00 P.M. the next day, he abruptly ordered the train to leave Shanghai and head straight to Beijing.[93] The train arrived at Fengtai Station in the Beijing suburbs around noontime on September 12. Zhou learned of Mao's return through a phone call from Wang Dongxing. "Why has the chairman returned so quietly and suddenly?" asked Zhou. "Not even I received an advance notice."[94] Mao then greeted several Party officials and PLA commanders at the train, to whom he emphasized that the "struggles between different lines within the party are still underway."[95] He finally returned to his Zhongnanhai residence around 4:00 P.M.

Lin Biao learned sometime that afternoon that Mao was back in Beijing. Lin Liguo, realizing that his plot to assassinate the chairman had failed, began weeping loudly. He and Ye Qun discussed asking Lin Biao to take a plane—Trident jet no. 256, which he had moved to the nearby Shanhaiguan

Airport—to Guangzhou and "take some decisive action" there. The young Lin also shared this plan with a few innermost members of his circle. Lin Biao, on the other hand, was extremely calm throughout the afternoon and most of the evening; he showed no signs of unease. He and Ye Qun even discussed the engagement ceremony for Lin Doudou, their daughter, which their associates were busy preparing for.[96] Things would change dramatically after the young Lin, joined by his mother, walked into his father's room for an hour-long private talk.

* * *

September 12 was a normal working day for Zhou. Nothing out of the ordinary happened during the daytime. Early in the evening, he chaired a long-planned meeting to discuss the government's report to the NPC. However, around 10:00 P.M., he received a call from Wang Dongxing, who reported that Lin Doudou had rushed to the central garrison guarding Lin Biao at Beidaihe, telling the officers there that Lin Biao, Ye Qun, and Lin Liguo were preparing to escape.[97] After checking with the air force, Zhou learned that a Trident jet was docked at Shanhaiguan Airport. At 11:30 P.M., he received a phone call from Ye Qun, who said that "Lin Biao would like to make an inspection tour to Dalian." Zhou asked, "Does he want to travel by air or by ground?" "By air," replied Ye. Zhou immediately advised Ye that it was not safe for Lin to do so at night. He also offered to meet Lin and Ye before their departure, but Ye responded vaguely to the offer.[98] Alarmed, Zhou ordered that no plane at Shanhaiguan Airport should be allowed to take off, and that any order to move a plane must be issued collectively by Zhou, Huang Yongsheng, Wu Faxian, and Li Zuopeng.[99] What Zhou did not expect was that only ten minutes later, Lin, together with his wife and son, would pile into a car and rush to Shanhaiguan Airport. They boarded Trident jet no. 256 at 12:32 A.M. on September 13, joined by a five-person crew (with only one pilot) who had been hurriedly called to the site, and took off.

Zhou was shocked to learn that Lin's plane had departed. He reported the news to Mao and asked the chairman to leave his Zhongnanhai residence and move into a shelter at the Great Hall of the People.[100] Meanwhile, he ordered that all airfields in the country close, and that all radar units be put into operation to monitor the skies. He also instructed all air traffic control centers to continuously call Lin's plane, asking it to return. Zhou would "personally be at the airport to welcome them."[101]

No reply came. The radar showed that initially Lin's plane was not flying in any one direction, but was making a big circle in the air. The plane turned northwest nearly twenty minutes later. As the plane approached the Mongolian border, Zhou went to the chairman, asking him if the plane should be intercepted or shot down. "Clouds want to rain and girls want to marry," Mao lamented, quoting an old Chinese saying. "Let him go!"[102] Around 1:50 A.M., Lin's plane crossed the border and entered Mongolian airspace.

"Traitor!" Zhou murmured when he learned that Lin's plane had left China. He reported the development to Mao at once. Then, he summoned all Politburo members in Beijing to a meeting. Lin had flown abroad, he told them.[103]

Zhou began a telephone marathon shortly after midnight, personally calling all commanders of the PLA's eleven regional headquarters and the heads of all twenty-nine provinces and municipalities to inform them of Lin's flight. Over the span of twenty-four hours, he dozed off several times for a few minutes each. Following Mao's orders, the PLA in the whole country went on high alert.[104] Lin's four generals, Huang, Wu, Li, and Qiu, were placed "under observation for ten days."[105]

The next afternoon, Zhou called a Politburo meeting to discuss how to prepare a diplomatic response to Lin's flight. He listed four possible scenarios: Lin might issue a public statement "betraying the motherland"; issue a neutral statement through a third party; stay silent; or simply disappear. Ye Jianying suggested that a preemptive statement might be issued, lest Lin tell his side of the story abroad first. Mao vetoed the suggestion. Late that evening, Zhou received an intelligence briefing from Air Force Headquarters, which had intercepted a telegram sent by a Mongolian radar officer. The telegram stated that at 2:30 A.M., an unidentified Chinese plane had caught fire and crashed about sixty kilometers northeast of Öndörhaan. Mongolia's defense minister had thus ordered all troops to go into maximum combat readiness. Zhou conveyed his own judgment of the situation to Mao: "Perhaps that plane has crashed, or perhaps it is just a trick by the enemy."[106]

The next day, Zhou finally went to sleep with the aid of sleeping pills after having worked nonstop for forty-eight hours. At 2:00 P.M., a phone call from the Foreign Ministry awoke him. The Mongolian Foreign Ministry had just informed the Chinese embassy that a Chinese plane had crashed in Öndörhaan; all on board had died.[107]

Zhou hurriedly reported the information to Mao. "Is this information reliable?" the chairman asked. "Yes," Zhou replied.[108] Mao could not help but tell Wang Dongxing, "Lin Biao has done me a big favor."[109] Indeed, Lin's dying on foreign soil gave Mao the best possible excuse to deprecate him, letting the chairman himself off the hook for the darkest implications and consequences of the Lin affair. Zhou shared Mao's sentiment. But Lin's death posed another grave problem for Mao: How could Mao convincingly explain why Lin, his hand-picked successor, had betrayed the country?

A few days later, Zhou carried out the chairman's order to deal with the aftermath of the Lin affair. He oversaw the writing of a draft notice detailing Lin's "escape from the country after his betrayal of it." With the chairman's approval, the notice began to circulate within the nation's party and military apparatus on September 18.[110] Zhou placed Huang, Wu, Li, and Qiu in detention on September 24, as Mao demanded, and Ye Jianying would take over the work of the CMC.[111] Lin's military faction was destroyed.

The biggest challenge that faced Mao and Zhou was how to craft a convincing explanation for Lin's downfall. Zhou repeatedly called Politburo meetings to discuss the dilemma. On October 24, they worked out a draft circular emphasizing that Lin was a traitor who "had made all kinds of beautiful statements while making vicious plots in dark corners." Mao assented to the Party Center's relaying to the entire nation the narrative about Lin's betrayal of the country and the party.[112] Investigators discovered the "571 Outline" at Lin Liguo's residence, which shocked both Mao and Zhou. Zhou's immediate reaction was that the document should be kept totally confidential. However, Mao ordered that it should be relayed in its entirety to the party and all the country, to expose the "true face of Lin and his like."[113]

When Zhou learned there were rumors in circulation that it was he who had ordered the downing of Lin's plane, he assured a group of senior military officers he had had nothing to do with Lin's death: "Let me repeat, I did not order shooting down Lin Biao's plane; it went down and crashed during a forced landing. Lin destroyed himself. . . . How can I order the troops to kill the vice chairman of the Party Central Committee and the deputy commander in chief of the army? He was the designated successor in the party constitution adopted at the Ninth Congress! . . . The chairman was generous with him. Why should I kill him?"[114]

Mao's revolution was a semireligious cause. People's belief in the revolution was necessary to propel and sustain it, and the worst-case scenario for it was for the populace to lose faith in it. Although Mao would remain the country's "great leader" in everyday life, in the wake of Lin's death, his heavenly image came crashing to the ground in the minds of ordinary Chinese. Indeed, the myth of Mao's "eternal correctness" had shattered for the first time in the PRC's history. Mao sensed this change. After Lin's death, the chairman began to make some self-criticism. Gradually many "capitalist roaders" who had been purged in the Cultural Revolution returned to the political stage. In hindsight, this was a sign that the Cultural Revolution would be doomed after Mao died.

Marshal Chen Yi—a legendary figure among CCP leaders—passed away on January 6, 1972. Chen's early relationship with the future chairman was not smooth. However, he wholeheartedly embraced Mao's authority and power once Mao became the CCP's top leader, slowly but surely winning Mao's trust. He had met and befriended Zhou during their shared time in Europe in the 1920s; he thus treated Zhou as his superior as well as an elder brother. In the Cultural Revolution, Zhou tried his best to protect Chen, especially after Zhou found that Mao did not seem to want to destroy Chen. Nonetheless, Chen had been sidelined from decision-making in Beijing until Lin's death.

Mao initially did not plan to attend Chen's memorial service, which, therefore, was not planned as a top-level event. On the day of the service, however, the chairman suddenly decided to attend it. Zhou immediately grasped the weighty political meaning of the chairman's change of heart toward Chen. This was a signal that other veteran officials who had been purged in the Cultural Revolution might be rehabilitated. Zhou upgraded the priority level of the event without delay and informed all senior leaders in Beijing that they should attend it. He also issued a last-minute invitation to Cambodia's Prince Sihanouk, an old friend of Chen's who was then in exile in Beijing. Zhou then rushed to the site of the service to supervise the final preparations. Ye Jianying had been designated to read Chen's eulogy at the service, but after Mao arrived, Zhou took the notes Ye had prepared and delivered the speech himself.[115]

* * *

The impact of Lin's death severely damaged Mao's health. He seemed to age more with each day. He caught a bad cold upon returning from Chen's service but, long skeptical of medical doctors, refused to be treated. As Mao's health continued to deteriorate, on January 25, Zhou wrote a note to the chairman, attempting to persuade him to accept treatment.[116] It did not work, and Mao's condition worsened further.

Early on the morning of February 12, Zhou received an urgent call. Mao had suddenly collapsed. As he rushed to Mao's quarters, Zhou's "legs were so powerless, and it took quite a while for him to step out of the car."[117] The chairman was still unconscious when Zhou saw him. Zhou, who was in total shock, "lost control of his bladder and bowels, soiling his pants."[118] The doctors and nurses were trying to save Mao. After several long minutes, the chairman regained consciousness. Zhou told him, "Chairman, the power is still in your full command!"[119]

Mao survived. He was now willing to accept medical treatment, and he gradually recovered. But he would not forget the moment he lay on the brink of death. His suspicion of and uneasiness with Zhou deepened. The relationship between the chairman and the premier in the years to come was destined to be bumpy.

28

NIXON AND KISSINGER COME TO CHINA

1969–1972

For almost two years, from 1969 to 1971, Zhou Enlai's overriding concern was the rift between Mao and Lin Biao. Yet he never lost sight of America. He had a long history of dealing with the Americans, going back to his encounters with the journalist Edgar Snow, President Franklin Roosevelt's envoy Lauchlin Currie, and the diplomat John Service, as well as his negotiations with generals Hurley and Marshall. China and the United States became bitter enemies during the Korean War; their enmity persisted after the war. Zhou was a principal architect and practitioner of China's domestic and international agenda, at the heart of which lay anti–US imperialism. But he also attempted to ease tensions between the two countries whenever possible. Indeed, it was he who pushed Beijing to engage in ambassadorial talks with Washington, and who ultimately directed Beijing's talks with the Americans.

During the Cultural Revolution, Zhou saw that China's relations with America had sunk to a low ebb. In late 1968 and early 1969, however, as Sino-Soviet relations were rapidly worsening, an undercurrent of change began to impact Sino-American relations. When Richard Nixon became US president in January 1969, Washington proposed to resume the Chinese-American ambassadorial talks in Warsaw, which had stopped by then. Beijing sent an affirmative response with "unprecedented speed."[1] It was Zhou who made the decision. He, like Mao, was closely studying whether America's policies in Asia in general and toward China in particular would change if Nixon were elected president. Shortly after Nixon's victory, Zhou told a foreign Communist leader that, in dealing with the United States and the Soviet Union, China should "catch and try to take advantage of the contradiction between them."[2] Around the same time, Zhou received a report from Marshal Chen Yi, the sidelined foreign minister, who contended that US global strategy had continued to emphasize America and Europe while regarding the Soviet Union as its main enemy. Therefore, Chen argued, "It is wrong to think that the US imperialists' main attention had moved East because of the Vietnam War, or that no contradiction exists between the United States and the Soviet Union because they both were against China."[3] Zhou immediately referred the report to Mao.

On February 19, Zhou participated in a meeting attended by Mao, Lin Biao, members of the Cultural Revolution Group, and four marshals, including Chen Yi, Xu Xiangqian, Nie Rongzhen, and Ye Jianying. Mao, who had read Chen's report, particularly mentioned that there was a need to study the international situation.[4] Two days later, Zhou instructed the four marshals to discuss international issues, and he tapped Chen to convene the discussions. By mid-March, the marshals had held four meetings.[5]

• • •

Before the marshals could continue work on Mao and Zhou's assignment, though, a clash erupted on March 2 between Chinese and Soviet border garrisons at Zhenbao Island (known as Damansky in Russian) on the Ussuri River.[6] When the two sides moved additional troops there, Zhou kept in close contact with the front commanders via telephone.[7] On March 15, a larger, fiercer fight between the two sides resulted in heavier casualities on both sides.[8]

The Zhenbao battles brought Sino-Soviet relations to a crisis point. In Moscow, Prime Minister Alexei Kosygin, a moderate in the Soviet government, did not wish to see the conflict with China spiral out of control. On March 21, he called Beijing through a hotline that had not been used in years, asking to talk to either Mao or Zhou. The young Chinese operator, however, refused to connect him.[9] Kosygin did not give up. He called the Soviet Embassy in Beijing to connect with the Chinese Foreign Ministry. Li Lianqing, head of the ministry's Soviet and Eastern European Department, received the call and replied, "I will report to the premier."[10]

At a Foreign Ministry meeting the next morning, Zhou sternly criticized the operator who refused to put Kosygin's call through and praised Li for not turning Kosygin down. Nonetheless, Zhou did not believe that it was a good time to have a direct phone conversation with Kosygin. Instead, he decided, if "the Soviets had something to say," they should "formally raise it through diplomatic channels." Mao approved Zhou's position.[11] Beijing and Moscow exchanged a series of diplomatic notes accusing each other of responsibility for the Zhenbao battles, yet both sides became more restrained in their actions. The crisis situation had subsided for the moment.

In fact, Mao did not want a war to break out between China and the Soviet Union. He hoped, rather, to use the clash to promote a domestic mobilization drive to coincide with the CCP's Ninth Congress. He thus did not want to see the conflict with the Soviets escalate unchecked. "That is enough, no more fighting," he ordered after the second battle at Zhenbao.[12] At a meeting with Zhou and other Chinese leaders about the party congress, the chairman confessed that "it is advantageous to get mobilized and prepared if we are facing a strong enemy." He instructed Zhou to give an internal speech on preparing for war and launching nationwide mobilizations.[13]

Waves of mobilizations to "prepare for war" emerged across China beginning in late March. Zhou personally supervised the making of two documentary films about the Zhenbao battles, which would be shown throughout the country.[14] Heeding Mao's directive to "dig deep into the earth," men and women in cities all over China set about building underground air raid shelters. In a sense, this was a near replay of the mass movement to "make steel" during the Great Leap Forward.

• • •

In the wake of the Zhenbao clashes, the four marshals focused their discussion on analyzing Soviet strategic intentions toward China. On March 18, they finished a report in which they cast doubt on the notion that Moscow was ready to wage a major war against China, as this would "require the mobilization of at least three million troops." They, however, made no mention of the sensitive topic of Chinese-American relations.[15] As the situation at Zhenbao began to stabilize following Kosygin's phone call, Zhou turned his main attention to the upcoming Ninth Congress. The marshals thought that they had completed Mao's assignment.

But Mao had not forgotten about the marshals. In May, Zhou informed the marshals that they should continue their study of international issues and report to him once they had developed "mature ideas"; then he would submit their report to the chairman. Zhou also assigned two of his close associates, Xiong Xianghui and Yao Guang, to aid the marshals in their discussions and help them draft reports.[16]

The marshals submitted another report to Mao and Zhou on June 11. They contended that the US imperialists, with their strategic emphasis in the West, could not easily launch an attack against China. Thus, they argued, the United States had tried to push Asian countries into the first line against China. By comparison, "the Soviet revisionists see us as the main enemy, so they are a more serious security threat." Nonetheless, even "the Soviets would . . . face great difficulty if they tried to wage a big war with China."[17] The marshals stopped short of suggesting how China's international policies should be adjusted.

Some new signs of potential improvement of Sino-American relations appeared around that time. On July 21, the US State Department announced that it would loosen restrictions on Americans traveling to China. Five days later, Prince Sihanouk of Cambodia relayed to Zhou a letter from US senator Mike Mansfield, who wanted to visit Beijing to seek a "solution to the twenty-year confrontation" with China.[18] The marshals, after receiving Zhou's briefing about these new developments, observed that both Washington and Moscow might want to take advantage of China's contradictions with each other. Therefore, "we should deliberately try to make use of US-Soviet contradictions too." But they cautioned that there was no need to act too soon. "We should table Mansfield's request to visit China. As the Americans are eager to contact us," the marshals suggested, "we should let them wait."[19] Zhou did not extend Mansfield an invitation to come to China.

• • •

In late summer, Sino-Soviet tensions escalated again when Soviet troops slaughtered a Chinese border squadron of thirty soldiers in Xinjiang.[20] For months, Beijing had been receiving reports warning that the Soviets might launch a preemptive strike on China's nuclear facilities.[21] Now, Mao and Zhou were genuinely alarmed. On August 23, at Zhou's suggestion, Beijing decided to establish a Leading Group on Air Defense led by the premier to prepare for the sudden outbreak of nuclear war.[22] Five days later, the CCP Center ordered all provinces and regions bordering the Soviet Union and Outer Mongolia to enter a state of war alertness.[23] Another wave of mass mobilization campaigns to "prepare for war" swept across China.

On September 2, while the specter of war loomed over Beijing, Zhou learned that Ho Chi Minh had passed away. He immediately decided to fly to Hanoi. The Vietnamese responded that, as Ho's funeral would not be held for several days, it would be inconvenient to receive Zhou at that time. But Zhou insisted on going. Finally, an unusual arrangement was made: Zhou would make a short trip to Hanoi to pay respects to Ho, who was lying in state, and Vice Premier Li Xiannian would then attend Ho's funeral as China's special envoy.[24] Zhou's move diverged from diplomatic norms, which he justified by emphasizing that "the intimate relationships between China and Vietnam, as well as between Ho and me" had prompted his visit. But his intention to avoid an embarrassing encounter with the Soviet leaders at Ho's funeral probably played a part in his decision.

Moscow dispatched Prime Minister Kosygin to Hanoi. Beyond Zhou's expectations, Kosygin inquired with Beijing via Hanoi whether he might "stop over in Beijing to meet with Premier Zhou."[25] With Mao's belated approval, Zhou decided to meet Kosygin at Beijing Airport. But when the Chinese response reached Hanoi, Kosygin was already in the air on his way back to Moscow. He learned of the Chinese message while his plane was refueling in Dushanbe, capital of the Tajik Soviet Republic. Kosygin's plane turned around and flew to Beijing.[26]

There was some common ground between Zhou's and Kosygin's mindsets. In particular, neither man wanted to see relations between Beijing and Moscow break down further. Yet they were both constrained by the broader environment that their countries were facing.

On September 11, Zhou and Kosygin met at Beijing Airport. Zhou began by conveying Mao's greetings to "Comrade Kosygin." The Soviet prime minister immediately replied, "Comrade Brezhnev and all members of the Soviet Politburo also asked me to convey their greetings to you and Comrade Mao Zedong." Zhou straightforwardly raised the question of the Soviet nuclear threat to China: "You threaten that you will use preemptive means to destroy our nuclear bases. If you do so, we will announce that this is war, this is aggression, and we will firmly resist, and resist to the end." Then Zhou changed the tone of the discussion, explaining to Kosygin that as China was not even able to handle all of its own affairs, Beijing absolutely did not want to go to war with the Soviet Union. In fact, China favored normalizing relations between the two countries. These words were music to Kosygin's ears. "The Soviet Union does not want to fight a war against China either," he replied emphatically.

Zhou made three proposals: maintaining the border at its present location, avoiding a new armed conflict, and keeping troops from both sides away from disputed areas. Kosygin accepted all three proposals, adding that the two sides' border agencies should consult with each other in advance if a tense situation were to arise. Zhou immediately voiced his support for this suggestion. The two leaders also agreed that they would formally exchange letters confirming their agreement to these terms. In addition, each country would soon send an ambassador to the other's capital, and the two countries would expand their trade relations. They further agreed to resume negotiations on border issues soon.[27] Mao approved of Zhou's handling of his meeting with Kosygin.[28]

The briefing Zhou gave to the four marshals further convinced them that the Soviet Union was unlikely to launch a large-scale attack on China. In a report to Mao and Zhou, they proposed that "at a proper time," China might consider playing the "American card" in dealings with the Soviets.[29] Chen Yi confided some of his "unconventional thoughts" to Zhou, suggesting that in addition to the ambassadorial talks in Warsaw, China might "take the initiative to hold talks with the Americans at the ministerial or even higher level, so that basic and related problems in Sino-American relations can be resolved."[30]

But Mao was still deeply worried about the possibility of a Soviet sneak attack on China. On September 17, he added a sentence to the official slogans that had been created for the PRC's anniversary celebrations: "Be prepared to cope with a war of aggression using nuclear weapons."[31] Zhou noted that Kosygin was greeted at the airport upon his return to Moscow "only by figures of second or third levels," and that the Soviets had not taken any follow-up action either.[32] On September 18, Zhou wrote Kosygin, listing the agreements that they had reached. "After you have confirmed them," stated Zhou, "they will become the agreements between the Chinese and Soviet governments . . . and will be immediately implemented."[33] Kosygin's reply was equivocal. He merely expressed that "our side has taken practical measures to normalize the situation along the border," without confirming the terms that he and Zhou had verbally agreed to.[34] As a result, the war scare persisted among top CCP leaders.

By then it was late September, near the date of the PRC's twentieth anniversary. According to custom, this was to be a grander celebration than usual, one attended by all the country's top leaders. But Mao felt uncertain about how the festivities should be celebrated. He told local leaders and military commanders, "For National Day this year, provincial civilian and military leaders should not come to Beijing. I am afraid that the enemy may use that opportunity to wipe out our leadership."[35] Zhou shared Mao's concern, saying, "The current international situation is very tense. We must be prepared for war. In particular, we must be prepared to deal with a sudden attack by the enemy."[36]

The closer National Day came, the wilder the war scare became. On September 30, Lin Biao inspected a military airport in Beijing's suburbs, where he ordered all planes to be evacuated and the runways barricaded. Late in the evening, he sent an urgent message to Zhou, proposing to discharge the water kept at Miyun Reservoir near Beijing, as he saw the possibility that the enemy "might bombard the reservoir during the holidays, collapsing its huge dam." Zhou knew that such an extreme measure would catastrophically flood the surrounding low-lying areas. At Zhou's urging, no action was taken.[37]

* * *

The Soviets took no action against China on October 1. But another thing happened that Mao and Zhou had not anticipated: China's relations with North Korea, which had sunk to a low-water mark during the Cultural Revolution, saw a dramatic improvement. On the afternoon of September 30, Beijing received an inquiry from Pyongyang asking whether China would invite Choi Yonggun, North Korea's number two leader, to the Chinese National Day celebration. Zhou immediately reported the inquiry to Mao. At 6:00 P.M., Beijing sent Pyongyang a response welcoming Choi to Beijing; at 11:00 P.M., Choi's plane touched down at Beijing Airport.[38]

Mao, accompanied by Zhou, met with Choi the next day atop the Gate of Heavenly Peace. Choi told Mao that Pyongyang's relationship with Beijing was "like one between lips and teeth made by thick blood," and he also explained that Pyongyang had always been closer to Beijing than to Moscow in the "struggles against revisionism." "Yes," Mao replied, "you are different from them." The chairman told Choi that the Americans "intend to attack you. But their target is not just you; their main target is China. Therefore, our two countries must be united." Mao invited Kim Il-sung to visit China, "either publicly or secretly." He pointed to Zhou and said, "we may dispatch Premier Zhou to visit Korea."[39] The next day, Zhou confirmed to Choi that he would soon visit Pyongyang.[40]

• • •

By then Beijing and Moscow had agreed to move forward with border negotiations, which would begin in Beijing on October 20. This was a good thing, as the two countries had finally taken a step toward relaxing the tensions between them. Yet leaders in Beijing were consumed with deep suspicion prompted by the war scare. They remained worried that the Soviets might use this opportunity as a pretext for a large-scale sudden attack on China, just as they had done against Czechoslovakia.

No matter how ridiculous these notions may seem, Mao took them quite seriously. "It is not good for all our central leaders to stay in Beijing," he told Zhou. "Many will die in the attack by one atomic bomb. They should be dispersed."[41] Zhou and the Politburo then decided that only Zhou and Chief of Staff Huang Yongsheng would stay in Beijing to handle the routine operations of the government and military. All other top leaders, including Mao and Lin Biao, would leave Beijing by October 20.[42] Zhou then worked out an evacuation plan, according to which Mao would move to Wuhan, and Lin to Suzhou. The four marshals would be relocated to different places, and so their discussions would come to an end.[43]

On October 18, unbeknownst to Mao, Lin Biao verbally dictated an urgent instruction on preparing for war and guarding against a sudden attack by the enemy from Suzhou. The same evening, Huang Yongsheng relayed the directive, now named "Vice Chairman Lin's Order Number One," to military commands nationwide, which were thus sent into a state of war readiness. As described in Chapter 27, Mao was outraged. This became a crucial moment leading up to the chairman's eventual split with his designated successor.

Nothing out of the ordinary took place as the Soviet delegation arrived in Beijing, and the border negotiations began as scheduled. Mao and Zhou realized that they had merely raised a false alarm. The extremely tense situation between China and the Soviet Union began to relax.

• • •

In Washington, Beijing was still on President Nixon's mind, but as he had no direct channel of communication with Beijing, he had to take a circuitous path to contact the Chinese. During his world tour in summer 1969, Nixon spoke with Pakistani president Mohammad Yahya Khan and Romanian leader Nicolae Ceaușescu, both of whom had maintained good relations with Beijing. Nixon asked them to convey to the Chinese leaders his belief that "Asia could not 'move forward' if a nation as large as China remained isolated."[44] When, in November 1969, Zhou received Yahya Khan's message from the Chinese ambassador to Pakistan, he reported it to Mao and commented, "The direction of the movement of Nixon and Kissinger is noteworthy."[45] Yet at that moment, neither Zhou nor Mao was ready to capitalize on Washington's shift.

Nixon did not wait for the Chinese to act, however. On December 3, all foreign diplomats were invited to a Yugoslavian fashion show in Warsaw. Walter Stoessel, the American ambassador to Poland, came to the event with a mission. When he found the Chinese diplomats, he quickly approached them and told the Chinese interpreter, in "broken Polish," that President Nixon wanted to have an "important and concrete conversation" with China.[46]

Zhou immediately reported to Mao the telegram from the Chinese embassy in Poland about the American ambassador's "unusual behavior." "The opportunity now is coming," he commented. "We now can knock on the Americans' door."[47] Zhou found a safe way to respond. Two Americans had been held in China for months after their yacht had strayed into Chinese territorial waters near Hong Kong. The Foreign Ministry had proposed to release the yachters "at a suitable time." On December 4, Zhou approved the proposal after a long delay.[48] Three days later, the two Americans were freed. Nixon's national security advisor, Henry Kissinger, on the other side of the Pacific Ocean, immediately picked up on this signal, guessing that this was Zhou's work.[49]

On December 11, the Chinese chargé d'affaires in Poland, Lei Yang, met with Stoessel "informally" in Warsaw. When Zhou received Lei's report, he asked Yahya Khan to inform Washington that "if President Nixon intends to resume contacts with China," he should use the "official channel in Warsaw." Washington received the message the next week.[50] On January 8, 1970, Lei and Stoessel had another "informal meeting," which was held at the US embassy in Warsaw, the first time in the Sino-American ambassadorial talks' history. They agreed to resume the formal talks on January 20, which would take place in turn in the two countries' embassies.[51] When Lei and Stoessel formally met at the Chinese embassy on January 20, they discussed the possibility of the two sides holding "meetings at 'higher level' or through 'other channels'" in the future.[52]

On February 12, Zhou presided over a Politburo meeting to discuss Lei's talking points for the ambassadorial dialogue. They decided that if Washington was to send a representative of the ministerial rank or a special presidential envoy to Beijing, "the Chinese government will *receive* him." In the original text prepared by the Foreign Ministry, the expression was that the Chinese government "will *consider receiving*" the American official. Zhou changed the text to "will receive," commenting, "If we use 'will consider,' it is too light a statement; therefore I changed it to 'will receive,'" in order to make the message more affirmative." Mao approved the meeting notes the next day.[53]

Lei met with Stoessel again on February 20. Following Zhou's instructions, he again highlighted the Taiwan question, emphasizing that any improvement of Sino-American relations must begin with withdrawal of American troops from Taiwan. But he also informed the American ambassador that the Chinese government would "be willing to receive" a high-ranking American representative in Beijing.[54] This was to be the last meeting of the decade-long Sino-American ambassadorial talks. President Nixon, eager to elevate his communication with Beijing to a higher level, once again sent a message to the Chinese leadership through Yahya Khan. This time, Nixon stated that, since it was difficult "to control speculation in the American press about the Warsaw talks," he "therefore would be prepared to open a direct White House channel to Peking [Beijing], if Peking would agree."[55] Upon reading the message, Zhou commented, "Nixon intends to adopt the method of the [American-Vietnamese] negotiations in Paris, and let Kissinger make the contact."[56]

But Nixon's message came at a bad time. Just a few days earlier, Cambodia's Prince Sihanouk had been removed in a coup by the pro-American general Lon Nol while the prince was abroad on his yearly vacation. Sihanouk arrived in Beijing from Moscow on March 19. Zhou greeted Sihanouk at the airport and told the prince that China would absolutely continue to recognize him as the head of the Cambodian state. "The only thing I need to know," said Zhou, "is whether you are determined to fight to the end." "Yes," replied Sihanouk. "We firmly support you," Zhou promptly assured the prince.[57] In the following days, Zhou invited the Vietnamese prime minister Pham Van Dong to join his meetings with Sihanouk in Beijing, and he also met with Pol Pot—the leader of the Khmer Rouge who was then also in Beijing—and urged him to cooperate with Sihanouk.[58] On March 23, an anti-American exile government headed by Sihanouk was established in Beijing. Zhou proposed to Mao that the next meeting with the Americans should be postponed in light of the situation in Cambodia, a proposal that Mao approved.[59]

The prospect of a Beijing-Washington diplomatic opening was made darker in the following months. In early May, Nixon ordered American troops in South Vietnam to carry out a major operation aimed at destroying Vietnamese Communist safe havens in Cambodia. A Politburo meeting chaired by Zhou on May 16 decided that the talks with the Americans had to be postponed.[60] Four days later, one million Chinese demonstrated at Tiananmen Square. Mao issued a statement calling for "the people of the world to unite and defeat the US aggressors and all their running dogs."[61]

However, neither Beijing nor Washington meant to abandon their dialogue. On June 15, Vernon Walters, the American military attaché in Paris, proposed to the Chinese military attaché that a "confidential channel of communication" should be opened, as the "Warsaw forum was too public and too formalistic." Beijing was not ready to accept the proposal at the time.[62] But Zhou decided to send Washington another signal. On July 10, he ordered the release of Bishop James Walsh, an American who had been imprisoned in China since 1958 on espionage charges.[63]

However, not until early fall would Mao and Zhou refocus their attention on the Americans. Mao, like Nixon, was unhappy with the "formalistic" nature of the Warsaw channel. Unlike the US president, though, Mao probably had another layer of subtle concerns about domestic explanation and mobilization in mind when he considered receiving Nixon or a high-level US official in Beijing. Therefore, the chairman was unwilling to allow the process of Chinese-American détente to be determined by Washington's intentions. At this critical point, Zhou read Mao's mind with remarkable clarity. Mao favored détente with Washington, but he would not rush to achieve it.

* * *

In October and November, Zhou received more overtures from Washington through the Pakistani and Romanian channels, indicating that Nixon remained willing to dispatch a high-ranking representative to China. This time, Mao and Zhou were ready to give an affirmative response.[64] In mid-November, Zhou told President Yahya Khan in Beijing that if the Americans were truly willing to resolve the Taiwan question, the Chinese government would "receive a representative of President Nixon in Beijing." This was the first time, Zhou emphasized, that Beijing's response "has come from a head, through a head, to a head."[65] One week later, Zhou met with Gheorghe Radulescu, Romania's vice prime minister, asking "the Romanian friends to tell Washington" that the Chinese government would welcome President Nixon's representative or even the president himself to Beijing.[66] Zhou also asked the Pakistanis and Romanians not to convey the message to Washington right away. Consequently, the Pakistanis delivered the message to Washington on December 9, and the Romanians delayed sending the message to the Americans until January 11, 1971.[67]

Zhou requested that sending the message be put off probably because Edgar Snow, an American writer, was then visiting Beijing. Snow was an old friend of Mao, Zhou, and many other Chinese leaders, whom he had interviewed in the Red Zone in the 1930s. Snow later published *Red Star over China,* helping to cultivate a highly positive image of the Chinese Communists in China and abroad. Snow visited China twice after the PRC's establishment. During the Cultural Revolution, he again applied to visit China but could not obtain a visa. In August 1970, Snow, who was living in Switzerland then, suddenly received several calls from Huang Zhen, China's ambassador in France, who had known Snow since the 1930s. When Snow saw Huang in Paris, he complained about Beijing's rebuffs of him in previous years. Huang urged him to reapply to visit China. "Premier Zhou has personally handled the matter," Huang told Snow, "and you will be treated as Chairman Mao's distinguished guest."[68]

Snow arrived in China in late August. Zhou personally arranged his itinerary. On October 1, Zhou invited Snow and his wife to view the National Day celebration from atop the Gate of Heavenly Peace and personally escorted him to stand by Mao. Zhou arranged for a "good photograph to be taken" of Snow and Mao talking to each other, which would later be printed on the front pages of major newspapers throughout China.[69] With this, Zhou meant to transmit a key signal to the Americans. Yet the message went unnoticed by Kissinger, who later acknowledged that the Chinese "overestimated our subtlety."[70]

28.1 Zhou Enlai with Mao Zedong, Edgar Snow, and Lois Wheeler Snow at the Tiananmen Rostrum, October 1, 1970. *CPA Media Pte. Ltd. / Alamy Stock Photo*

Yet from the perspective of Mao and Zhou, it was even more crucial that the Chinese people take note of the photo. For over two decades, the United States had been thoroughly demonized in the minds of millions and millions of everyday Chinese by anti-American propaganda. Now, as Mao was planning to forge a new relationship with the United States, he would need to create a new image of America in the minds of the Chinese populace. Subtle signals such as this one would gradually ready the Chinese people for the coming about-face in China's relations with America.

On December 18, Mao met with Snow for five hours. Before that, on November 5, Zhou had a lengthy conversation with Snow that focused on international issues. Zhou told Snow that the Sino-American ambassadorial talks had not resolved a single issue since their inception. In order to settle the problems between the two countries, Zhou stressed, they should first discuss America's military aggression and occupation of Taiwan. All other issues were of secondary importance. "Our attitude toward negotiation has not changed. It is the US government that should change," asserted Zhou.[71]

Though Zhou's comment may have smacked of cliché, he had crafted his wording in order not to take away the spotlight from Mao. When the chairman met with Snow, he covered many topics in the areas of domestic and international affairs. Mao told Snow that he liked the Republicans more than the Democrats in US politics. "I welcome Nixon becoming the president, as he is less deceptive. If he wants to come to Beijing, please send a message to him: He should come secretly, rather than publicly. He just needs to board a plane, and he can come . . . I am willing to talk to him. He may come as a tourist, or as the president."[72] Washington, according to Nixon, "learned of Mao's statement within days after he made it."[73]

• • •

In the first months of 1971, the exchanges between Beijing and Washington went silent. In fact, both the Chinese and the Americans were waiting for the right opportunity to take the next step. This was especially important for Mao, who, in addition to weighing the pros and cons of rapprochement with Washington in strategic and geopolitical senses, needed a triggering event that would allow him to bring about and mobilize the Chinese people's *inner* support for a new relationship with America.

In late March 1971, almost all of a sudden an opportunity appeared in Nagoya, Japan, where the Chinese national table tennis team was competing in the Table Tennis World Championships. The Chinese players, who were the best in the world, had missed the event in 1967 and 1969 due to the Cultural Revolution. In early 1971, Koji Goto, president of the Japanese Table Tennis Association, made the utmost effort to invite the Chinese to the forthcoming championships in Nagoya. With Zhou's personal intervention and Mao's approval, China accepted the invitation.[74]

Zhou paid special attention to the Chinese players' activities in Japan, instructing their leaders to "call Beijing by telephone at least twice a day." Mao also showed great interest, asking his head nurse Wu Xujun to brief him every day.[75] During the event, Zhuang Zedong, the former Chinese world champion, accidentally encountered an American player, Glenn Cowan, on the shuttle bus. They exchanged greetings and small gifts. When the Chinese players met the Americans at a reception, one American player courteously said that he hoped to visit China one day. The Chinese team leaders reported these developments to Beijing as indications of the Americans' willingness to visit China.[76]

After much deliberation, the Chinese Foreign Ministry and sports officials concluded that "the timing is not yet right for the Americans to visit China." Zhou endorsed the report and sent it to Mao for approval.[77] The chairman did not respond for two days. Late in the evening on April 6, he was in bed after having taken sleeping pills. Suddenly, he called Wu Xujun and asked her to call the Foreign Ministry to "invite the American team to visit China." Wu could not believe her own ears, but Mao, despite being under the influence of sleeping pills, urged Wu to make the call.[78]

Zhou and many of his associates had a sleepless night on account of Mao's sudden change of mind. The next morning, the leader of the Chinese team, Zhao Zhenghong, found the Americans and extended them an invitation to visit China. According to Zhou's instructions, he told them that China would subsidize their travel expenses if they were short of funds.[79] Zhou was personally in charge of making arrangements to receive the American players. Before the first "friendly game" in Beijing, he ordered the Chinese players not to beat the Americans in every game, but to let them win a few.[80] As for the audience, Zhou instructed that they "should be informed in advance to applaud when there is the atmosphere to do it."[81] He also met with the American players. To avoid making the event seem overly dramatic and shift the focus away from the Americans, he decided to invite players from Canada, Colombia, England, and Nigeria to the meeting as well.[82] Virtually overnight, this "ping-pong diplomacy" completely changed the political atmosphere between China and the United States, making the theme of improving relations between the two countries "an international sensation," as Kissinger put it, that "captured the world's imagination."[83]

Zhou knew it was now time to push the process of Chinese-American rapprochement further along. On April 21, again by way of the Pakistani channel, Zhou sent a message to Nixon, emphasizing that Taiwan was "the principal and prerequisite problem that had to be resolved before any relations could be restored." He made it clear that China was "now interested in direct discussions" as a means of settling the Taiwan question and thus was willing to "receive publicly in Beijing a special envoy of the president of the US (for instance, Mr. Kissinger) or the US secretary of state or even the president of the US himself for a direct meeting and discussion."[84] In his reply, Nixon clearly stated that he was prepared to accept Zhou's invitation to visit Beijing "for direct conversations" with PRC leaders. He also proposed that Kissinger might secretly visit Beijing to begin a preliminary exchange of views and arrange an agenda for the president's visit.[85]

Zhou called a Politburo meeting in late May to discuss Beijing's strategies for improving Sino-American relations. In his report, Zhou summarized eight "basic principles" regarding Kissinger's and Nixon's proposed visits to China:

> All US armed forces and military installations should be withdrawn from Taiwan and the Taiwan Strait; Taiwan is China's territory, and the liberation of Taiwan belongs to the domain of China's internal affairs; China will strive to liberate Taiwan peacefully; activities promoting "two Chinas" or "one China and one Taiwan" should be firmly opposed; China and the United States cannot establish diplomatic relations if the previous three conditions are not fully realized, and instead may set up a liaison office in each other's capital; China will not bring up the matter of China's seat at the UN; China will not take the initiative to raise the question of Sino-American trade; all US armed forces should withdraw from Indochina, Korea, Japan, and Southeast Asia.[86]

Zhou also considered the challenge to the CCP's legitimacy that the opening of China's relations with America might bring about. To this end, he specifically enumerated a handful of concerns. Would Sino-American rapprochement negatively influence the American people's struggle against the "monopoly capitalist ruling class"? Would it weaken Hanoi's position at the Paris peace talks? What would be its impact on US-Soviet relations? Zhou contended that thawing Chinese-American relations might further compel American troops to withdraw from Indochina. Indeed, this would represent the "victorious result of our struggles against imperialism, revisionism, and reactionary forces." If the efforts to open relations between the two countries succeeded, the "competition between the two superpowers" would become fiercer; if it failed, the "reactionary face" of US imperialism would be further exposed, and "our people's consciousness" would be further heightened.[87]

On May 29, after Mao approved his report, Zhou once again used the Pakistani channel to send a formal response to Washington:

> Premier Chou [Zhou] Enlai has seriously studied President Nixon's messages of April 29, May 17, and May 22, 1971, and has reported with much pleasure to Chairman Mao Tse Tung [Mao Zedong] that President Nixon is prepared to accept his suggestion to visit Peking for direct conversations with the leaders of the People's Republic of China.

By HB NARA Date

Message from Premier Chou en Lai to President Nixon
May 29, 1971

Premier Chou En Lai sincerely thanks His Excellency President Yahya Khan for most rapidly transmitting the three messages from President Nixon.

Premier Chou En Lai has seriously studied President Nixon's messages of April 29, May 17th and May 22nd 1971, and has reported with much pleasure to Chairman Mao Tse Tung that President Nixon is prepared to accept his suggestion to visit Peking for direct conversations with the Leaders of the People's Republic of China. Chairman Mao Tse Tung has indicated that he welcomes President Nixon's visit and looks forward to that occasion when he may have direct conversations with His Excellency the President, in which each side would be free to raise the principal issue of concern to it. It goes without saying that the first question to be settled is the crucial issue between China and the United States which is the question of the concrete way of the withdrawal of all the US Armed forces from Taiwan and Taiwan Straits Area.

Premier Chou En Lai welcomes Dr Kissinger to China as the US representative who will come in advance for a preliminary secret meeting with high level Chinese officials to prepare and make necessary arrangements for President Nixon's visit to Peking.

28.2 Zhou Enlai's Message to President Nixon via the Pakistanis, May 1971. *Gongheguo wushinian zhengui dangan (Fifty-Year Precious Archives of the People's Republic), ed. Chinese Central Archive (Beijing: Zhongguo dangan, 1999), 2:1030; Zhou Manuscript Collection; National Archive*

> Chairman Mao Tse Tung has indicated that he welcomes President Nixon's visit and looks forward to that occasion when he may have direct conversations with His Excellency the President, in which each side would be free to raise the principal issue of concern to it.[88]

When Nixon received Zhou's message, he commented, "This is the most important communication that has come to an American president since the end of World War II."[89]

Beginning on June 4, Zhou presided over a work conference attended by more than two hundred leading cadres from all over China to discuss the new policy toward the United States. Though it was originally scheduled for five days, the conference lasted two weeks. Zhou delivered a lengthy keynote speech, in which he detailed the history of Sino-American relations. He criticized the Democrats for having "initiated war repeatedly," including the wars in Korea and Vietnam. As president, Nixon was "eager to establish normal relations with us," an ambition "pushed by the situation, and to collect political capital for his reelection." He thus was willing to send high-ranking officials, even Kissinger, to negotiate with China. Beijing, while welcoming Nixon's special envoy, would adhere to "its stand and principles," Zhou emphasized. "If indeed Kissinger comes to China, the negotiation may result in something, in order to open the way for Nixon's visit, or may not result in anything, and that will not harm us a bit." Zhou concluded by stressing that "the situation today is the result of our continuous struggle against the imperialists and the revisionists." Whether the negotiations succeeded or failed, China had nothing to lose.[90]

During the conference, the CCP leadership relayed to the whole country Mao's conversation with Snow, requesting that "the text be verbally conveyed to all party members, and [that] serious study about it should be organized."[91] In another speech at the central work conference, Zhou further stressed that Snow's interview with Mao should be relayed to the whole country, "which should be studied by the masses through careful organization, in order to get the masses educated."[92] The entire nation now knew that Nixon would be welcomed in China.

• • •

On July 9, Kissinger secretly arrived in Beijing via Pakistan, becoming the first high-ranking US official to visit China since the PRC's establishment. Zhou carefully prepared for Kissinger's trip. He sent a longtime associate of his, Zhang Wenjin, along with Tang Wensheng (Nancy Tang) and Mao's grandniece Wang Hairong, to Istanbul to meet and accompany Kissinger to Beijing. Zhou knew that Zhang was not a talkative person, so he particularly asked him to be "more active, not to make the guests feel alienated in their first trip to China."[93] In order to maintain complete confidentiality, he decided that Kissinger's plane would land at Nanyuan, the military airport in Beijing's southern suburbs. Kissinger would be staying at the Diaoyutai State Guest House, where all meetings would also be held. If the discussion were successful, the two sides would announce that it had taken place after Kissinger left Beijing. But if it failed, they would say nothing about it, letting it disappear as if it had never happened.

Zhou arranged for Marshal Ye Jianying to meet Kissinger at the airport. Over the next forty-eight hours, Zhou and Kissinger would have six meetings, lasting for a total of seventeen hours.[94] The two men quickly came to respect each other. While Zhou found Kissinger "very intelligent—indeed a doctor," Kissinger regarded Zhou as "one of the two or three most impressive men I have ever met."[95]

At 4:25 P.M. on July 9, Zhou's first meeting with Kissinger began. He asked Kissinger to speak first, as he was the guest. The purpose of his visit, Kissinger said, was a preliminary discussion on "issues of concern of both sides" and Nixon's prospective visit to China. President Nixon was committed to ending the war in Vietnam through negotiation, he said, and American troops would withdraw from Vietnam if America's honor and self-esteem were protected. He appeared slightly nervous as he pivoted to discuss Taiwan. After the end of the Vietnam War, he told Zhou, the United States would withdraw two-thirds of its armed forces in Taiwan from the island, and it would continue to withdraw more troops from Taiwan as Sino-American relations further improved. He also stated that Washington recognized Taiwan as part of China and would not support Taiwan's independence, and he emphasized that the United States firmly supported resolving the Taiwan question through peaceful means. Zhou listened attentively, immediately realizing that, to pave the way for Nixon's China visit, Kissinger had already made critical concessions on Taiwan. In particular, he noted Kissinger's acknowledgement of Taiwan as being part of China. He regarded Kissinger's linking Taiwan with Vietnam, however, as an attempt to bargain with Beijing.

When it was his turn to speak, Zhou highlighted Taiwan. All US forces must withdraw from Taiwan, he stressed, and the treaty between the United States and Chiang Kai-shek's government must be abolished. But he also stated that "the continuing existence of differences between China and the United States on Taiwan should not become the barrier blocking the two countries from improving bilateral relations."[96]

Zhou briefed Mao on the meeting as soon as it concluded. When the premier mentioned that the Americans were willing to accept that there was only one China and that Taiwan was part of China, Mao nodded in approval. When Zhou reported that Washington would withdraw some, but not all, American troops from Taiwan, Mao smiled and commented, "It would take time for a monkey to evolve into a human. They are now at the stage of an ape." The Indochina issue, Mao stressed, was of greater importance: "We are not in a hurry on the Taiwan issue because there is no fighting there. There is a war in Vietnam and people are being killed. We should not invite Nixon to come just for our own interests." Mao instructed Zhou not to focus on specific issues in speaking with Kissinger the next day, but to "brag to" Kissinger about the "big strategic picture" that "although all under heaven is in great chaos, the situation is wonderful."[97]

Thus Zhou's approach changed completely the next day. Using ideologically aggressive language to paint a picture of a world in great disorder, he presented Beijing's "principal stands" on a series of international issues, including Vietnam, India, Japan, Korea, and Taiwan, each of which defied Washington's corresponding policies.

Kissinger was stunned by Zhou's "fierce litany." But when he began a point-by-point rebuttal of Zhou's presentation, he found that the premier's attitude softened again. He would not have been so nervous if he had realized that Zhou's "empty words" were primarily not for him, but for China's everyday people, to hear. Toward the end of the meeting, Zhou proposed that they start discussing the date of Nixon's visit to China. They agreed that Nixon should come to Beijing in spring 1972.[98] On July 15, Beijing and Washington simultaneously announced that Nixon would be visiting China. The world was shocked.

• • •

Shortly after Kissinger's departure, Zhou also set off from China, flying to Hanoi late in the day on July 13, where he held three meetings within twenty-four hours with Vietnamese leaders. He expressed to the Vietnamese that he had "made it very clear to Kissinger that Beijing is not the place to negotiate peace for Vietnam." Beijing truly believed that its improved relations with Washington, Zhou said, would make it less important for America to stay in Vietnam, thus enhancing Hanoi's bargaining power at the negotiation table.[99] Zhou was known by many Vietnamese leaders as a persuasive negotiator and trusted friend. But this time, the premier apparently failed to convince them. They did not rebuff him to his face; after all, China's robust support was crucial for them to continue fighting the war against the Americans. However, they were very doubtful of Beijing's intentions. Thus it was not surprising that internal Vietnamese instructions described Beijing's contacts with Washington as "throwing a life preserver to Nixon, who had almost been drowned."[100]

With nearly no time to rest after he landed back in Beijing, Zhou flew to Pyongyang late on July 14. After two meetings lasting a total of seven hours, Zhou persuaded the North Korean leader, Kim Il-sung, to accept Beijing's endeavor to improve its relations with Washington. But in return, Kim requested that the Chinese "help put Pyongyang's proposal for relaxing tensions on the Korean Peninsula on the table." Zhou said he would.[101] One month later, when Kim secretly visited China, Zhou described to him how the CCP had carried out its "united front" strategy in the past. "We will persistently carry out the struggle, without refusing to compromise when necessary and possible," Zhou told Kim.[102]

Zhou's next interlocutor was Prince Sihanouk, the leader of Cambodia's anti-American exile government in Beijing. Zhou promised Sihanouk, "Under no circumstance will China abandon our old friend." He also predicted that a détente between Beijing and Washington would help engender conditions suitable for the prince to return to Cambodia.[103]

When Zhou met with Xhorxihi Ropo, Albania's ambassador to China, he faced a steep challenge. Although he tried his best to emphasize that Beijing's anti-imperialist and antirevisionist attitude would not change at all on account of the Chinese-American contacts, Ropo refused to listen. In August, the Albanian Labor Party wrote to the CCP leadership, firmly opposing Beijing's détente with Washington and claiming that the Chinese had "betrayed" the cause of the world proletarian revolution.[104]

This was also the time that Mao and Zhou were fully occupied with the Lin Biao affair and its aftermath. Once they had gotten the political situation in Beijing firmly under control, though, they again turned their attention to Chinese-American relations. Ambassador Huang Zhen and US ambassador Walter Stoessel were taking full advantage of the newly opened "Paris channel" to ensure that the most important messages from the top leadership of one side would be delivered to the top leadership of the other side as safely and swiftly as possible.[105]

* * *

On October 20, 1971, Zhou again welcomed Kissinger in Beijing; this time, the reception took place in public. The ten meetings Zhou held with Kissinger during the next six days lasted a total of twenty-three hours and forty minutes.[106]

During the first half of their meetings, Zhou and Kissinger concentrated on the situation and on policies. Then, they pivoted in the second half to discuss, at Kissinger's suggestion, preparing a joint communiqué for Nixon's visit. The Chinese side had not thought of this, Zhou said. Therefore he asked Kissinger to compose a draft communiqué, which Kissinger handed to him on the evening of October 22. Upon perusing the draft, Zhou instantly knew that it required significant revision. Still, he told Kissinger that it could be used as the basis for further discussion.

Mao was not interested in Kissinger's proposal. But the Americans truly wanted a joint communiqué, Zhou explained, so it was better to have one. "OK, then let us do it," Mao replied. "I have said many times that all under heaven is great chaos, so it is a good way to let each side speak out for itself." Mao instructed Zhou that if the Americans wanted to talk about "peace, security, and rejecting the pursuit of hegemony," then the Chinese should emphasize "revolution, liberation of the world's oppressed peoples, and big powers having no right to bully and humiliate small countries." Yes, this was no more than "firing an empty cannon," Mao admitted. But he insisted that "all of these points must be highlighted; anything short of that is unacceptable."[107]

Kissinger's first reaction upon receiving the Chinese draft was disbelief. It was impossible, he told Zhou, for a US president to sign a document featuring such harsh language condemning US imperialism. However, once he had finished reading the document full of "empty cannons," he recognized its novelty, which "might resolve our own perplexities" in keeping Washington's credibility.[108] Zhou and Kissinger sat down again and completed another version based on the Chinese draft. It not only defined common grounds but also used clear yet well-controlled language to state each side's views on important issues. Gradually, a draft communiqué came into being that both sides found acceptable.

The most difficult matter was that of articulating the status of Taiwan. A breakthrough on the Taiwan question was achieved when Kissinger came up with a proposal that stated, "The United States acknowledges that all Chinese on either side of the Taiwan straits maintain there is but one China and that Taiwan is part of China. The United States Government does not challenge that position."[109] Zhou liked it. He later commented that this paragraph was "Kissinger's contribution as none of us could figure out the proper expression. After all, a doctor is indeed useful as a doctor."[110] Unbeknownst to Zhou, however, this expression was not Kissinger's invention. As early as 1968, Senator Mansfield, in a public speech, had already used an expression on the Taiwan question that bore a close resemblance to the one used by Kissinger.[111] There had been bipartisan support in the United States for pursuing a new relationship with China, the Taiwan question notwithstanding. When Kissinger left Beijing on October 26, Zhou and Kissinger had reason to be satisfied about the progress that they had made in just six days.

While Kissinger was on his way to the airport, he learned that the United Nations General Assembly had voted by an overwhelming majority to expel Chiang's Nationalist regime and restore the PRC's representation at the UN and in its Security Council. This exceeded Kissinger's expectations. The development also came as a surprise to Zhou, who immediately called a meeting of Foreign Ministry officials to discuss whether China should send a delegation to the UN. At first, Zhou and his associates were inclined to wait until the next year. When Zhou went to report to Mao, the chairman was joking with Brooklyn-born Tang Wensheng, "Miss Nancy Tang, your country has been defeated!"[112] Zhou told Mao that although China had won a clear victory at the UN, "we were totally unprepared for such a result." Zhou suggested that a small group might be sent to the UN "to investigate the situation on site, and to make preparations for future action." "No," Mao said. "Isn't it true that the UN Secretary-General has already telegraphed us? We should send our delegation there, to be headed by Qiao Guanhua."[113] Zhou wasted no time in carrying out Mao's order.

As the date of Nixon's visit neared, Zhou was faced with another great concern: he was uncertain whether Mao would be able to meet with the US president. Mao's health had begun to rapidly deteriorate since Lin Biao's death. Early in the morning on February 12, 1972, just nine days before Nixon was scheduled to arrive in Beijing, Mao lost consciousness before being rescued from the brink of death.[114] "Make sure the chairman is well enough to see him," Zhou told the doctors.[115] However, neither Zhou nor the doctors knew if this could be done. Zhou could only pray.

• • •

On February 21, the forecast called for snowy weather, but no snow fell that day. Zhou arrived at Beijing's Capital Airport around noontime. After Nixon's

28.3 Zhou Enlai and Nixon at Beijing Airport, February 21, 1972. *AFP via Getty Images*

plane, Air Force One, had landed and finished taxiing off the runway, Zhou approached the tarmac, where he stood motionless while Nixon and the First Lady, Pat Nixon, walked down the steps of the plane. Zhou waited for Nixon to initiate a handshake, only extending his hand once the president had already done so. In this historic moment, which was captured by Zhou's official photographer, Zhou knew that he was playing the roles of both a statesman and an actor. The implication of the handshake was clear: after twenty years of total confrontation between China and the United States, it was Nixon who had flown halfway around the earth to shake hands with the premier in Beijing. The symbolic import of this encounter between Nixon and Zhou likely reminded all Chinese that they "[had] stood up."

For days, Zhou had been worried that Mao's health would prevent him from meeting with Nixon. But Mao was in good spirits that day, repeatedly asking about Nixon since the early morning. Almost as soon as he knew that Nixon had arrived in Beijing, he instructed his associates to inform Zhou that he wanted to see Nixon right away.[116]

So, hardly had Nixon settled in at the Diaoyutai Guesthouse when Kissinger rushed in, telling him that Mao wanted to see him and that Zhou was waiting downstairs.[117] Nixon left hurriedly with Zhou. The president brought

Kissinger and Winston Lord, Kissinger's assistant, along with him. He did not bring Secretary of State William P. Rogers to meet the chairman, however.

Mao received Nixon in his study at Zhongnanhai. "I am not good at speaking today," he told Nixon. But he actually spoke a lot. He refused to discuss "concrete issues"; instead, he said, he would talk about "questions of philosophy." Indeed, the chairman seemed eager to demonstrate his broad vision, showing the Americans that he not only was in total control of all affairs relevant to China, but was also intellectually qualified to comprehend and deal with *anything* of significance in the known universe. That Nixon and Kissinger had come such a long way to listen to his teachings was, for Mao, enormously gratifying. Zhou sat there, glancing at his watch from time to time. He had told Nixon that the meeting would be short, no more than ten to fifteen minutes long. It lasted one hour and five minutes.[118]

In Zhou's meetings with Nixon, the question of Taiwan still presented a crux to finalizing the text of the joint communiqué, which was up to Kissinger and Qiao Guanhua, the Chinese vice foreign minister and Zhou's main associate, to resolve. The key challenge was to find a mutually acceptable expression of the US stance on the linkage between Washington's timetable for withdrawing US troops from Taiwan and Beijing's commitment to settling the Taiwan issue peacefully. This was a crucial issue for the Chinese, since they insisted that any matter concerning Taiwan "belonged to China's internal affairs." However, under Zhou's leadership, the Chinese demonstrated flexibility and compromises were found on this issue.

The last troubling episode of Nixon's visit was triggered by tensions among the Americans themselves. When Nixon went to meet with Mao, Secretary of State Rogers was left behind. Kissinger, in finalizing the joint communiqué, did not consult with Rogers and his colleagues. On February 25, Rogers told Zhou that he would like to bid Mao farewell. The request bucked ritual procedure, Zhou knew; neither would Mao's health allow him to see Rogers. Zhou consulted with Kissinger, who told him, "It is totally unnecessary." Zhou realized that Rogers had made the request because Nixon "did not bring him to see Mao."[119] Then, after Kissinger and Qiao had settled the text of the joint communiqué, Rogers and his associates identified a series of "niches" in it, demanding that the document be further revised. Zhou decided to propitiate them by "giving them face," to use the Chinese expression. The next day, Zhou suddenly appeared on the floor where Rogers was staying, greeting Rogers and thanking him for the contributions he and his associates had made to America's détente with China.[120] Zhou also instructed Qiao to meet with Kissinger again for a final round of revisions to the text of the communiqué. On the eve of Nixon's scheduled departure, the communiqué was completed.

On February 28, the China-US joint communiqué was formally issued in Shanghai. It announced that neither China nor the United States "should seek hegemony in the Asia-Pacific region and that each is opposed to efforts by any other country or group of countries to establish hegemony." The Soviet Union, though unnamed, was the apparent target of this assertion. In many ways, this was one of the most important historical documents of the twentieth century, as well as one of Zhou's most significant diplomatic accomplishments.

Zhou was good at drinking, but he seldom drank very much on diplomatic occasions. At his farewell banquet for Nixon, however, he drank one glass of Maotai after another. Nixon also drank a lot. Their faces turned red.[121]

* * *

After seeing Air Force One take off from Shanghai, Zhou immediately flew back to Beijing, where he briefed Mao on his meetings with Nixon and the issuance of the Shanghai Communiqué. On March 3, he delivered a speech to leading cadres from the Party Center and the State Council. Paragraph after paragraph, he explained the articles of the communiqué, emphasizing that "the Soviet Union, Japan, and Chiang Kai-shek are the big losers" of the document, and that "we have opened the door of America."[122]

This was Zhou's moment, and also an extremely important moment in Chinese and world history. It ended the nearly quarter century of outright confrontation between the PRC and the United States, opening a new chapter in the relations between the world's most populous nation and its most powerful country. It also changed the essence of the Cold War, obscuring the distinctions between socialist and capitalist approaches toward achieving modernity, burying the shared consciousness among the world's Communists that their ideology offered preferred solutions to the problems facing the world. Equally important, it altered China's own trajectory toward development. Might we argue that, with the Shanghai Communiqué's issuance, China had already taken its first step down a path that would eventually lead to the era of "reform and opening up"?

29

GLORY REAPS TEARS

1972–1974

In the wake of Lin Biao's death, Zhou Enlai emerged as China's de facto number two leader. His role in the opening of relations with America had won him enormous international fame and domestic admiration. He seemed to be enjoying a golden moment as a politician and a statesman. However, a vague sense of uneasiness lurked behind his cheerful demeanor.

One day, Ji Dengkui, a Politburo member, witnessed Zhou totally lose control over himself in an unusual episode:

> The premier was sitting alone in his temporary office as if in a trance, taken over by a dark sentiment. Li Xiannian and I did not know why he looked so glum, so we approached him to try to comfort him. He listened, saying nothing. I said, "Lin Biao has destroyed himself. From now on we can give good attention to the country's economic reconstruction. This is a happy moment." These words were obviously too much for his overburdened mind. His tears flew down, quickly turning into a cry. Louder and louder, he wailed, choked with sobs. . . . Finally, he calmed down. After quite a while, he said, "You do not understand, it is not so simple. It has not finished yet." He stopped and did not utter another word.[1]

Zhou was a man of iron will. Almost never in his whole life had he had such an outburst in front of his associates. Why this time?

No one is able to enter Zhou's innermost world and answer that question. We may, however, consider the question from a few different angles. In those days, Zhou had probably been subjected to extreme stress; by the time he could relax, the dual sensation of enormous joy mingled with deep sorrow proved too much for his reeling mind, and, as a result, he lost control of his emotions. It is also likely that Zhou believed that Mao's Cultural Revolution was a catastrophe, and understanding that he could be seen as an accomplice of Mao's, he foresaw the difficulty he would encounter in facing the judgment of the Chinese people and of history. Alternatively, Zhou may have had a terrible hunch as, after Lin's downfall, he had risen to become China's virtual second-in-command. Lin had been known as Mao's "closest comrade-in-arms" and successor, yet his life had come to an abrupt, miserable end. Was Zhou gripped by the fear that he might follow Lin's path? What did Zhou mean by "it has not ended yet"? Nobody can say for sure. What is certain, though, is that his intuition told him the path ahead would be difficult.

• • •

In any event, the spring following Lin's death saw Zhou's power and position within the Chinese leadership grow. The winter snow of China's domestic and international situation was melting; the sweet fragrance of spring was in the air. The Chinese-American rapprochement, along with the PRC claiming China's seat at the UN and in its Security Council, brought about new breakthroughs in China's external relations. Within one and a half years from mid-1971 to the end of 1972, almost thirty countries, including almost all the major Western powers except the United States, established diplomatic relations with the PRC.

Britain was the first of the Western powers to recognize the People's Republic. However, relationships between China and Britain had remained on the consular level for almost two decades, with the Taiwan question obstructing progress. In early 1972, the Chinese and British held a series of meetings about upgrading their relations, in which Zhou was personally involved. On March 2, two days after Nixon left China, Zhou called a meeting with John Denson, the British chargé d'affaires in Beijing. By then, the British mission in Beijing had moved back into its previous office building that had been damaged during the height of the Cultural Revolution. Zhou told Denson apologetically, "It was the bad elements who set fire to your office, which the Chinese government opposed, so we covered the expense of its repair." Zhou also told Denson that, in order to upgrade Sino-British relations, London must not keep a consulate in Taiwan and must clearly reject such notions as "Taiwan's legal status being unsettled," "two Chinas," and "one China and one Taiwan."[2] London responded positively. On March 13, the diplomatic relations between Beijing and London were elevated to the ambassadorial level.

Zhou also paid great attention to West Germany. In the early years of the PRC, following the "leaning to one side" principle, Beijing refused to recognize the Federal Republic of Germany. After Moscow established diplomatic relations with Bonn, China also declared an end to war status with Germany. However, no progress was made in diplomatic relations between Beijing and Bonn. In 1969, the Social Democratic Party's Willy Brandt became West Germany's prime minister. Beginning in the early 1970s, Beijing and Bonn began to discuss establishing diplomatic relations. Brandt was then actively pursuing détente with the Soviet Union; improving relations with China was not his priority. Brandt's apparently pro-Soviet diplomacy also made Beijing uneasy.

Around that time, Zhou read several reports by Wang Shu, a Xinhua reporter stationed in Bonn. Wang emphasized that West Germany was not a revisionist country, and that its NATO membership was intended to fend off the Soviet threat. Wang mentioned that the Christian Democratic Union, the opposition party, had also expressed support for establishing diplomatic relations with China. Zhou noted Wang's analysis and mentioned it at several Foreign Ministry meetings.[3] In July 1972, Gerhard Schröder, vice chairman of the Christian Democratic Union, visited China. During his meeting with Schröder, Zhou recalled his time living in Berlin in the 1920s. He particularly mentioned that because of Konrad Adenauer's farsighted vision, West Germany—unlike Japan—had not developed direct relations with Taiwan. As a result, there existed no outstanding obstacles that would prevent China and West Germany from establishing diplomatic relations.[4]

On July 21, Zhou received Wang, who had been called back to Beijing from Germany, and heard his report about the prospects of diplomatic ties between Beijing and Bonn.[5] Three days later, Zhou brought Wang to see Mao. The chairman, who fully supported establishing diplomatic relations with Bonn, said that internationally he "like[d] the rightists in particular, such as Nixon and his kind."[6] Wang rushed back to Bonn and, in an unusual move, was appointed China's chief negotiator with West Germany. The discussions progressed quietly, but steadily. On September 29, the two countries reached a draft agreement to establish diplomatic relations; the document was formally signed in Beijing on November 11.

Zhou also set his eyes on improving relations with France. Beijing and Paris had established diplomatic relations in 1964, but those ties were frozen during the Cultural Revolution. In 1969, Charles de Gaulle resigned as France's president in the wake of the May 1968 events. With Mao's support, Zhou continued to plan a trip by de Gaulle to China; but de Gaulle passed away in 1970, before the visit could take place. By then, Beijing's relations with Paris had begun to thaw. In July 1972, French foreign minister Maurice Schumann visited Beijing to prepare for a trip to China by Georges Pompidou, the then president of France. Zhou emphasized to Schumann that both China and France favored independence and self-determination. He recalled his time in France in the 1920s: "'La Marseillaise' and 'L'Internationale,' which we have been so familiar with and have sung so often, are all from France. We cherish this intimate connection."[7] In September 1973, Pompidou visited China at last. Zhou met with Pompidou along with Mao and accompanied the French leader throughout his visit. In formal meetings, Zhou repeatedly stressed that both China and France adhered to an independent foreign policy, "not allowing any superpower in the world to control us." Pompidou's last stop in China was for sightseeing in Hangzhou, with no formal meetings arranged for him there. On a tour of the scenic West Lake, Zhou periodically spoke with the French president in the French that he had learned almost half a century before, to Pompidou's delight.[8] Zhou could turn any occasion into a diplomatic performance at will.

• • •

A half century earlier, Zhou had been living and working in Britain, Germany, and France, an experience whose influence extended even into his later years. But nothing could compare with Zhou's memory of living in Japan as a student, during which time he had developed a special feeling toward Japan that would stay with him throughout his life. He always regarded Japan as an important country, and he had long hoped that China and Japan would establish diplomatic relations. In the 1950s, when the worst moments of the

Cold War opened a chasm between China and Japan, Zhou still tried his best to seize every opportunity to promote trade, cultural, and athletic exchanges with Japan. A turning point came in the early 1970s. Washington had not briefed Tokyo in advance of Kissinger's secret visit to China in July 1971, even though Japan was America's major Asian ally. This incident, known as the "Nixon shock," was a huge blow to Japan, and especially to Prime Minister Sato Eisaku, who had been extremely pro-America. In October, Zhou introduced three principles for normalizing Chinese-Japanese diplomatic relations: the PRC government was the sole legal government of China; Taiwan was an inseparable part of China; and the Japanese-Taiwan treaty was illegal and invalid and had to be nullified.[9] In July 1972, Satō resigned as Japan's prime minister. Zhou immediately realized that the moment for a breakthrough in Chinese-Japanese relations had arrived.[10]

In April 1972, Miki Takeo, a candidate for the chairman of the ruling Liberal Democratic Party, visited China. Before he departed for Beijing, Miki announced that he supported Zhou's "three principles." Zhou assigned his close associate Wang Guoquan, the chairman of the Chinese Association of International Friendship, to hold preliminary talks with Miki. If progress were achieved in these talks, Zhou would meet with Miki. Wang and Miki quickly reached a consensus on a series of issues. Then, Wang abruptly mentioned the Diaoyu Islands (Senkaku Islands in Japan), asking Miki to accept that "the Diaoyu had been China's territory since ancient times." Wang even implied that if Miki refused to concede on the matter, "it would be impossible for his China visit to be successful." Miki, unprepared for the sudden change of subject, was stunned. When Zhou learned of this, he immediately decided to meet with Miki. "Wang is such a radical leftist," he told Miki. "He is much more radical than I am. He has put in front of you a big dilemma. How can he do so without taking into consideration the purpose of your visit and the situation that you have been facing? On this front, he does not represent me." Zhou acknowledged that there were "apparent differences between us" about which country the Diaoyu Islands belonged to, which was "an important issue." However, Zhou stressed, the issue "can only be resolved when the timing is right, through negotiations between our two governments." Now, Zhou continued, "the most urgent question that we are both facing is how to overcome all the difficulties and remove all the barriers, in order to restore diplomatic relations between our two countries in the shortest possible time."[11]

Sasaki Kozo, a Japanese Socialist Party leader, visited Beijing in mid-July. Zhou told him that if Japan's new prime minister, Tanaka Kakuei, and foreign minister, Ohira Masayoshi, were willing to visit China to discuss forming diplomatic relations with the PRC, he would warmly welcome them. "We now must look forward," Zhou said, "rather than look backward, resolving problems for the future."[12]

In late July, Takeiri Yoshikatsu, chairman of the Japanese Komeito party, arrived in Beijing on his own initiative, but he presented himself as an unofficial envoy of the Japanese government. Zhou had three lengthy meetings with him over three days. A focal point of their dialogue was how to deal with Taiwan if the PRC and Japan were to establish diplomatic relations. Zhou insisted that Japan would have to recognize the PRC as China's "sole legal government" and also cut off formal relations with Taiwan. About the Diaoyu Islands, Zhou told Takeiri, "There is no need to involve the question. Compared to the restoration of diplomatic relations, it is not a real issue." Takeiri said that he would truthfully report Zhou's opinion to Tanaka.[13]

Tanaka and Ohira visited China in late September. Zhou had already planned a strategy for his discussions with the Japanese leaders. In particular, Mao had long decided that China would give up its request for war reparations from Japan, a decision that Zhou fully supported. Chiang Kai-shek, in signing his "Chinese-Japanese peace treaty," had already given up his request for reparations. Mao and Zhou, same as Chiang, wished to adopt an approach of "responding to wrongdoing with virtue" to demonstrate the magnanimity of China as a great power.

On the Taiwan question, Zhou had made it clear that his "three principles" should serve as the basis for establishing diplomatic relations. It was thus impossible for Tanaka to come to Beijing if he did not accept these principles. Given all this, Zhou was quite confident that Tanaka's visit would lead to an improvement in Chinese-Japanese diplomatic relations. Zhou was involved in all the talks with Tanaka. As both Zhou and Tanaka were eager to see the negotiations succeed, one after another, the two sides' various problems were resolved.

One big obstacle, especially for the Chinese side, was an expression by Tanaka at the welcome banquet hosted by Zhou.[14] In describing Japan's war against China, Tanaka said, "In the past, Japan had made much trouble for the Chinese people, about which I again express my regret." Listening to this, almost all Chinese present, including Zhou, felt confused and unhappy.

29.1 Zhou Enlai with Japanese prime minister Tanaka, late September 1972. *Bettmann Archive / Getty Images (514871852)*

Could the huge disaster of Japan's aggression against China be summarized in such a light expression as "making trouble"? Zhou's face darkened. The next day, in his formal meeting with Tanaka, Zhou spent almost a whole hour to explain why "making trouble" was not an acceptable phrase to be used here, as it was often used, for example, when "someone in the street spilled water on a woman's skirt." Tanaka listened carefully. Finally, he told Zhou, if the Chinese side had a more suitable phrase, he was willing to accept it.[15]

On the evening of September 27, Mao and Zhou met with Tanaka and Ohira. "The problems that had been there and could not be resolved for decades or even a hundred years were resolved in a few short days," commented the chairman. This was because "now we are both in need of this result."[16]

Mao's meeting with Tanaka created a positive atmosphere for Ohira and Ji Pengfei, the Chinese foreign minister, to settle all remaining issues in their meetings. Ohira most sincerely told Ji that both he and Tanaka had experienced that war of aggression and fully understood "the essence of it." But they had to take into consideration Japan's national condition, sentiment, and interests. In the evening of the last day of their meetings, when the text of the joint statement had to be finalized, Ohira, sentence by sentence, read a paragraph to Ji, saying that this was the limit to which he could go: "The Japanese side is keenly aware of its responsibility for causing serious damage to the Chinese people through the war in the past, and deeply regrets it." After a long pause, Ji proposed adjourning the meeting for ten minutes, and then went to the next room to report to Zhou. Someone in the room proposed that the term "war" should be changed to "war of aggression." Zhou rebutted him, noting that anyone reading the joint statement would know that the "war" in it was "the war of aggression." Otherwise, why should the Japanese government "deeply regret it" and be "keenly aware of its responsibility"?[17] Ji immediately returned to the meeting room and told Ohira that his suggested expression was accepted.

Tanaka raised the Senkaku / Diaoyu issue. According to the Japanese minutes of the meeting, he asked Zhou, "What is your view on Senkaku? Many have asked me about it." Zhou replied, "I do not want to discuss Diaoyu at this time. It is not good to discuss the issue now. This has now become a problem because oil was discovered there. If there had not been oil discovered, neither Taiwan nor the United States would have regarded [the Diaoyu Islands] as a serious matter." However, according to Chinese records, the conversation did not end there, but continued as follows:

> TANAKA: "Good! There is no need to discuss this issue. We can come back to it later."
>
> ZHOU: "Let us come back to it later. This time we will resolve those basic questions that can be resolved now. For example, the normalization of relations between our two countries should be solved first. This is the most urgent question. Some questions need to be discussed later, once the situation has changed."
>
> TANAKA: "Once diplomatic relations have been established, I believe other questions can also be resolved."[18]

Thus, both Zhou and Tanaka, demonstrating their political wisdom, came to an agreement over the course of a few exchanges to table the disputes over the Diaoyu / Senkaku Islands.[19]

On September 29, Zhou and Tanaka signed a joint statement announcing the establishment of diplomatic relations between China and Japan. Zhou had accomplished another big mission. Amid the repeated disturbances, both minor and major, to Chinese-Japanese relations as the twenty-first century unfurls, it is appealing to recall the time when the sky over the two countries appeared to be awash with sunlight.

• • •

Zhou also played a central role in launching and promoting the "Four-Three Project," which involved importing US$4.3 billion in whole-set factory equipment and advanced technology from Western capitalist countries. The foundation for the project was actually laid before Nixon's China visit. In late 1971, as Chinese-American relations relaxed and the PRC joined the UN, major Western countries were facing economic tension caused by excess production capacity. Meanwhile, in China, grain outputs had stagnated, there was a nearly constant shortage of cotton and other raw materials, and a limited fertilizer production capacity slowed the pace of agricultural development. Even Mao mentioned these problems in a conversation with Zhou, which Zhou instantly seized on as an opportunity to discuss the prospect of importing whole-set equipment and technology for fertilizers and chemical fibers with Vice Premier Li Xiannian.[20]

On January 23, 1972, Li, Hua Guofeng, and Yu Qiuli jointly proposed to Zhou in a report that four sets of equipment for manufacturing chemical fibers and two sets for manufacturing fertilizers be imported, along with key equipment and parts from France and Japan that would be used to transform outdated factories. The total value of the imported supplies would be around US$400 million.[21] Zhou approved the proposal, as did Mao.[22]

The launch of the project prompted competition among many provinces for hosting the equipment. Several other industrial sectors also put forward proposals for imported supplies. For instance, on August 6, the State Planning Council submitted a report on importing 1,700mm rolling mills from West Germany, which Zhou quickly approved.[23] In the meantime, Li worked with his colleagues to balance the various importation proposals.[24] On January 2, 1973, the State Planning Council submitted a report on "increasing equipment importation and expanding economic exchanges" to Zhou. The report proposed the adoption of twenty-six projects of importation of whole-set equipment and technology in order to "introduce new technology, support agriculture, and enhance basic industry and light industry." These projects were expected to cost US$4.3 billion in total. Zhou unhesitatingly embraced the report. Subsequently, Mao gave his approval, too.[25]

In the early 1970s, the value of China's annual foreign trade was less than US$5 billion, of which imports accounted for about US$2 billion. Zhou's support for the launching of the Four-Three Project was thus a weighty move. While it can hardly be compared, in size and purpose, to the sweeping policy of "reform and opening up" that Beijing adopted in the late 1970s, the importation project was nevertheless an important prelude to China's coming embrace of the larger global capitalist market.

* * *

Mao, a master politician, possessed an extraordinary capacity to detect changes in political situations and the balance of power. In the wake of Lin's death, he sensed the tremendous headwinds facing the Cultural Revolution, and he knew that he had to take some action to deal with them. Therefore, early in 1972, he agreed to rehabilitate certain veteran cadres who had been purged during the Cultural Revolution. He now put all the blame on Lin, claiming that it was the dead marshal who had ultimately been responsible for the purges.

Zhou was more than willing to agree with Mao on rehabilitating cadres. Once Mao gave the green light, Zhou immediately proceeded with the plan. One by one—and, later, one group after another—purged officials reemerged on China's political scene, many of whom reclaimed their previous positions. Zhou was involved in almost all the cases that required examination and approval at the central level. There is no evidence to suggest that Zhou played a negative role in any of them.

The most noteworthy among the rehabilitated cadres was Deng Xiaoping, China's "second-largest capitalist roader," who had been disgraced during the Cultural Revolution. Deng had long been someone whom Mao liked and trusted within the CCP leadership. In the late 1950s, Mao even called Deng his "second-in-command" in the party.[26] However, as the 1960s began, Mao became disappointed with Deng on a series of occasions, even feeling that Deng had become an opponent, thus leading to Deng's purge in the Cultural Revolution. But Mao still remembered Deng's time as a Maoist; indeed, he held distinct attitudes toward Liu Shaoqi and Deng. When the Cultural Revolution reached its peak, Deng, unlike Liu, was treated relatively leniently by Mao. While Liu was labeled a "traitor, spy, and renegade" and "permanently expelled from the party," Deng retained his party membership after Mao spoke on his behalf.[27] In 1969, Deng was sent to Jiangxi Province. Zhou personally called the chairperson of the Jiangxi Revolutionary Committee, and Deng was assigned to a location near Nanchang, Jiangxi's capital city, where living conditions were better.[28] Zhou clearly had perceived the subtleties of Mao's attitude toward Deng. In a political sense, Mao sought to leave the door open to working together with Deng later.

At the memorial service for Chen Yi in early January 1972, Mao told Chen's widow that Deng's problem was a "contradiction among the people." When Zhou learned of this, he immediately leaked Mao's remarks to Deng's family.[29] At a Politburo meeting on January 24, Zhou said that Lin and his gang had tried to purge and put Deng to death, which ran counter to the chairman's intentions.[30] However, Deng's rehabilitation was delayed after that, and Zhou did not take further action in the ensuing months.

Mao was actually waiting for Deng to clarify his attitude toward the Cultural Revolution. After all, Deng was notorious for being the "second-largest capitalist roader." To allow him to stage a reemergence in the realm of Chinese high politics could undermine the legitimacy of the Cultural Revolution. This was a complicated matter even for Mao. Meanwhile, Zhou would not move forward unless Mao authorized him to do so.

On August 3, 1972, Deng wrote to Mao, asking for permission to "come out to do some technical work." The most important message contained in the letter, however, was a paragraph that read, "In the autobiography that I wrote in June and July of 1968, I made self-criticism about myself and the mistakes and crimes that I had committed. As of now, I still stand by everything that I said in the self-criticism. I once again confirm the promise that I made to the Party Center, which is that I will never reverse the verdict on me."[31]

This was exactly what Mao had been waiting for. A few short days later, Mao responded in an instruction to Zhou as follows: "The mistakes committed by Comrade Deng Xiaoping are serious. However, he is different from Liu Shaoqi." Mao then highlighted several of Deng's major contributions in the history of the party.[32] The same day, Zhou chaired a Politburo meeting, at which he conveyed Mao's comments on Deng.[33] When Zhou found that Deng's rehabilitation had not been carried out immediately, on December 18 he again raised the matter at a Politburo meeting, emphasizing that "Comrade Deng Xiaoping has requested to come out to do some work, please consider his request. The chairman has also mentioned this several times."[34] Finally, in January 1973, Deng received a note permitting his return to Beijing. On February 20, he arrived in the capital. On March 9, Mao approved a report by Zhou on behalf of the Politburo that reinstated Deng's party membership and reinstalled him as vice premier of the State Council.[35]

On April 9, Zhou had a long conversation followed by a dinner with Deng and his wife. Zhou "advised Deng about how challenging his working environment could become." He also gave Deng a real trump card, telling him that "Zhang Chunqiao was a traitor, but the chairman won't let us investigate him."[36] Deng, who would later transform China and the world, had reappeared on China's political stage.

• • •

Just as Zhou was experiencing one of the busiest chapters of his long political career, alarm bells rang: two to four red blood cells were found in a sample of Zhou's urine taken during a routine exam on May 12, 1972. After further examination, the premier was diagnosed with early-stage gallbladder cancer.[37] A task force headed by Dr. Wu Jieping and comprising top medical experts quickly came up with a proposal: Zhou should be thoroughly examined immediately and, if necessary, undergo surgery as soon as possible. Wu sent a report to the Party Center on behalf of the task force, requesting permission to conduct a cystoscope exam on Zhou at once.[38]

At the Party Center, a group composed of Ye Jianying, Zhang Chunqiao, and Wang Dongxing was established to supervise Zhou's medical treatment. The group wasted no time in conveying Dr. Wu's report to Mao. A few days later, Mao's reply came: "First, no surgery should be performed. Second, Zhou himself and Deng Yingchao should not be informed. And, third, there is the need for good nutrition."[39] Mao's explanation to his associates was that "a surgery might cause the cancer to spread, and thus could be dangerous. Chinese medicine should be used to control the illness."[40] Upon learning of Mao's instructions, the members of the task force were all "very troubled and extremely worried." They repeatedly voiced their concerns, emphasizing the importance of giving Zhou timely treatment and the possible serious consequences of delaying it. However, their urgings were futile, and the doctors could only give Zhou "conservative treatment."[41]

Why had Mao responded so unreasonably? Did he do so out of sheer ignorance or did his orders betray some ulterior purpose? This is a question that we will never be able to answer. In any case, the doctors had to obey

Mao. No matter what Mao's true intentions were, he delayed timely medical treatment for Zhou. Less than four years later, Zhou would die of cancer.

• • •

In the meantime, Zhou had had to turn his attention to another matter. On May 3, Mao summoned him to a meeting, at which the chairman asked him to consider "convening a central rectification conference focusing on criticizing Lin Biao." Mao also requested that Zhou "talk about the history of political line struggles within the party," taking his own experience as a reference.[42] Zhou, with his keen political sense, instantly realized that Mao's move was pregnant with deep political implications. He called a Politburo meeting the same day, at which the attendees decided to convene a "rectification conference" to criticize Lin. Mao approved the decision three days later.[43]

Soon afterwards, Zhou would be diagnosed with gallbladder cancer. However, from mid-May to early June, he had to devote much of his time to organizing the conference for criticizing Lin, all the while reflecting on his own "political mistakes." Dr. Zhang Zuoliang, Zhou's physician, vividly described the premier's condition around that time:

> All of a sudden, he began to lock himself in his office to write. He was in a very low mood; he neither met with any foreign visitors nor attended any meetings. For more than ten days, he sat at his desk and seldom went out for a walk. . . . Writing day and night and getting little sleep, his eyelids and even his whole face were swollen. He no longer played ping-pong, and did not even have a haircut or shave . . . I have never seen him so slovenly since I had arrived at the West Flowers Pavilion.[44]

On May 21, the conference for criticizing Lin began, attended by more than three hundred cadres from the Party Center and the provinces. Zhou chaired the conference, and spoke at the first session. "We are engaged in the tenth struggle of political lines in our party's history," Zhou said. "Our main goal is now to expose, criticize, and smash Lin Biao's antiparty clique." In introducing documents distributed at the conference, Zhou particularly highlighted a letter by Mao to Jiang Qing from July 1966, in which Mao had revealed "some uneasiness" about "certain notions held by Lin Biao." This letter, Zhou claimed, indicated that Mao had long sensed Lin's deeply hidden evil intentions. However, "for the sake of launching the Cultural Revolution and mobilizing the masses," Mao did not immediately expose him. As "it now seems," Zhou stressed, "only our great leader Chairman Mao could have foreseen things in such a penetrating way."[45]

These were comments of which not even Zhou himself would be convinced, let alone the more than three hundred high-ranking cadres in attendance at the conference. Nevertheless, he still had to deliver those words. Indeed, he was probably the only person in a position to make such comments. The rectification conference would last a whole month, but it would not resolve any actual problems.

Beginning on June 10, Zhou made self-criticism over the course of three consecutive evenings. He described and explained in detail six major mistakes pertaining to political lines that the party had made in the 1920s and 1930s. In discussing the mistakes of Wang Ming and others, Zhou also referred to his personal experience, and he made a harsh self-criticism. Indeed, he even called himself a "criminal," saying that "when I committed these mistakes, if it had not been for Chairman Mao's efforts to rescue me, educate me, and give me the opportunity to correct my mistakes, I would not be standing in front of you today!" Zhou also told the audience that "by knowing my past mistakes, you will no longer be bound by any blind faith in me. You have the right to ask me to correct my mistakes. If I do not and again make big mistakes, you have the right to call the Party Center's attention to them, either warning me or, if the mistakes are serious, dismissing me."[46]

Mao mentioned the "Wu Hao affair" when he instructed Zhou to "talk about history." On June 23, Zhou gave a presentation about the "Wu Hao incident"; the presentation was recorded, and the tape was transcribed. The Politburo, at Mao's instruction, asked Zhou to sign the transcript. Both the tape and the transcript were to be permanently kept at the Central Archives.[47] However, Zhou did not sign the transcript at that time, and it was kept in his office until his death.[48]

Thus Zhou experienced another extremely difficult chapter in his political career within the CCP leadership just as his good name and reputation were gaining global recognition following Nixon's visit to China. Ultimately, however, he survived once again.

• • •

At the conference, the participants, all of whom were high-ranking officials, raised many questions about the party's general strategies and policies in the aftermath of Lin's death. Zhou thus took the initiative to tell those in attendance, "All those ultraleftist statements by Lin were leftist in appearance and rightist in essence." This was Zhou's best effort to mold how the Lin Biao affair would be defined and criticized. It again provoked in Zhou's mind a question that he was unable to answer on his own: this time, would the Cultural Revolution finally come to an end?

In early August, Zhou spoke to a group of Chinese diplomats. As he had done at the conference for criticizing Lin, he emphasized the danger of ultraleftism. This was a global phenomenon, he said, spreading even within the Foreign Ministry and infiltrating Chinese embassies abroad. What, then, was ultraleftism? It had to do with making exaggerated statements without respecting facts, Zhou asserted. Therefore, ultraleftism was leftist in appearance yet rightist in essence. "If ultraleftism is not thoroughly criticized," Zhou emphasized, "right-leaning tendencies will prevail again."[49]

Zhou's speech, however, offended the radical leftists within the party leadership. After she learned of Zhou's speech, Jiang Qing, the leftists' representative, immediately voiced her disagreement. A few days later, Zhang Chunqiao and Yao Wenyuan, two of Jiang's allies, openly expressed their support for Jiang.[50]

Since the beginning of the Cultural Revolution, Zhou had differed on many issues with Jiang and her allies. Despite this, his efforts to work with them were generally successful. This time, though, was different, as the rift that emerged between him and them concerned an issue of fundamental importance. This rift potentially also lay between Zhou and Mao, who had consistently lent support to Jiang and her allies. In retrospect, this was the prelude to Zhou's deeply fraught relationship with Mao during the last years of his life. However, by late 1972, Mao himself had not yet clarified how to define the essence of "criticism of Lin."

Before the chairman explicitly revealed his opinion on the matter, Zhou continued to act in accordance with his own ideas. In late November, Zhou received a proposal from the Chinese foreign service about convening a conference to "thoroughly criticize the ultraleftism and anarchism in foreign affairs," which Zhou approved.[51] But Zhang Chunqiao raised a question: "Is the problem that we are facing now still criticism of ultraleftism and anarchism?" Jiang echoed Zhang's sentiment, commenting that "what we should criticize is Lin Biao's ultrarightism as a traitor to China."[52] Jiang and Zhang thus blocked the proposed conference. This was a warning signal to Zhou. Without Mao's backing, he likely realized, Jiang and Zhang would not have challenged him in such a way.

A new development came soon after. On December 5, Wang Ruoshui, a *Renmin ribao* editor, wrote a letter to Mao in which he reported that a dispute had recently flared up between Zhou and Zhang regarding the criticism of ultraleftism. Wang commented, "This has raised the question of whether ultraleftism has been sufficiently criticized. I believe that the premier is correct, and Zhang Chunqiao and Yuan Wenyuan are wrong."[53] Mao promptly responded that Lin Biao had been an ultrarightist the whole time. He asked Jiang to convey Wang's letter to Zhou, Zhang, and Yao, who, Mao advised, should all meet with Wang to "settle this matter."[54]

On December 19, Zhou, Jiang, Zhang, and Yao met with Wang. Hewing to the tone set by Mao, Zhou said, "When I said that ultraleftism must be thoroughly criticized, I was referring to foreign policy and some problems in our work. I did not refer to Lin Biao's entire policy line. Lin betrayed the party and the country, which was ultrarightist." Zhou then said that Wang's views were wrong, "which is confusing theoretically and not fact-based practically." Zhou concluded that "Lin was a reactionary, and this is what we should expose and criticize."[55] Zhou's comments on how to define the Lin Biao affair revealed that Jiang, Zhang, and Yao had won the upper hand in their dispute with Zhou. This was the beginning salvo in what was to be a series of repeated attacks on Zhou's "rightist-leaning behavior" in the last years of his life.

* * *

Zhou's medical treatment was continuously delayed. After May 1972, the doctors tried to control Zhou's illness through conservative methods. They did not inform Zhou of his illness; but Zhou was accustomed to getting to the bottom of things. "In the past," recalled Dr. Wu, "whenever we gave him an exam, he always thoroughly explored the reason for the exam with us. But this time, after several exams, he no longer asked us anything. He only concentrated on his work."[56] On November 11, the doctors suggested in a report that Zhou "should pay special attention to getting good rest, increasing sleep time, and reducing his workload." The next day, Mao remarked about the report that Zhou "should get good rest, limit his workload, and must not be ignorant."[57]

In early 1973, suddenly Zhou had gross hematuria. Dr. Wu rushed to see Marshal Ye Jianying; the doctor appealed to Ye to administer an exam and give treatment to Zhou without further delay. A few days later, Ye went to see Mao and showed the chairman a tube of Zhou's urine tinged with blood. The second day, the Party Center approved Dr. Wu's request to further examine Zhou.[58]

However, the exam was delayed for another two months. On March 9, Zhou disclosed his illness at a Politburo meeting and requested two weeks' medical leave. Mao approved Zhou's request the next day.[59] Then, Zhou was admitted to a temporary medical facility for a cystoscope exam. The day before the exam, the doctors received additional instructions from Mao. For the sake of caution, the chairman advised, the exam should be done "in two steps," that is, "first the exam, and then the treatment." Wu met with Deng Yingchao to hear her opinion. Deng told him, "If you see that small thing there, just take it out. It is simple." Wu now knew what he should do.[60]

On March 10, nearly ten months after he was initially diagnosed with cancer, Zhou underwent his first cystoscope exam. Dr. Wu found that the situation was better than expected; the cancer was still in an early stage. There were three lesions, each smaller than a green bean. Ignoring Mao's orders to conduct the exam and treatment in two steps, Wu took the lesions out right away. The treatment was effective, and Zhou's hematuria disappeared.[61] Beginning in July, the doctors gave Zhou intravesical therapy in order to consolidate the treatment.[62] At the moment, Zhou's prognosis seemed quite optimistic.

• • •

While the premier's health was improving, Mao's discontent about him simmered. The arena in which he was to spar with Zhou was that of China's external relations. Chinese-American rapprochement brought about big changes in China's domestic and international policies. To establish a new legitimacy narrative for China and help the country cope with new international challenges, Mao put forward his "Three Worlds Theory," in which he provided a new definition of the changing world structure. But just what, exactly, were Mao's new international narratives? Even Zhou, who had worked with Mao for almost a half century, found it difficult to grasp their essence.

In June, "New Situation," an internally circulated Foreign Ministry newsletter, published a piece by one of the ministry's research groups. In the article, the group contended that competition and collaboration coexisted between the two superpowers, and that the "possibility of joint American-Soviet dominance in the world has increased." Zhou liked the report, commenting that the questions raised in it were "worth further study." Mao, however, took issue with the report's claims, arguing that it had understated the problems between Washington and Moscow. Although Zhou did not know why Mao had criticized the report, he immediately ordered the Foreign Ministry to recall the newsletter once he learned of the chairman's response, asserting that "I am the one who should take the main responsibility."[63]

But Mao did not stop there. On July 4, he met with Zhang Chunqiao and Wang Hongwen, when he again criticized the research group's analysis of the world situation. "The Foreign Ministry's handling of several issues recently is not to my satisfaction," claimed the chairman. "I often have emphasized great turmoil, great division, and great transformation, but the Foreign Ministry has suddenly come up with something like great deception and great shared dominance (by the two superpowers)." Mao also said that this indicated the Foreign Ministry's inability to see through the outside appearance of something to discover its essence. In fact, Zhou was the implicit target of the chairman's criticism: "[There is] no discussion about big issues; daily reports cover only small matters; if this tendency is not to be turned around, revisionism will necessarily follow." As if these cutting remarks were not strong enough, the chairman added darkly, "If revisionism is to rise in the future, no one should allege that I have not issued a warning in advance."[64]

Zhang informed Zhou immediately following the conversation that a Politburo meeting should be held to discuss Mao's comments. Zhou agreed right away.[65] The next day, at a Politburo meeting chaired by Zhou, Zhang relayed Mao's criticism of the Foreign Ministry. Zhou described in detail to his Politburo colleagues how Mao had criticized the Foreign Ministry since late June. He also made self-criticism, again acknowledging that it was he who should take responsibility for the mistake. On July 12, he called a meeting of leading Foreign Ministry officials to discuss the writing of another essay to criticize and correct the newsletter's mistakes. He also submitted a report to Mao in which he analyzed those mistakes. Adhering to what he understood to be Mao's points, Zhou accepted that the competition between the superpowers was "a prolonged commitment of both," and that their collusion was just a "surface-level phenomenon" that served "their competition in larger areas."[66] Mao then told Zhou that there was no need for him to make more self-criticism. It seemed that this matter was over; but it was not.

* * *

In August 1973, the CCP held its Tenth National Congress. Zhou delivered the main political report and was elected vice chairman of the Central Committee, which meant that he had maintained the de facto number two position in the party hierarchy. Deng Xiaoping also attended the congress and was elected to the Central Committee.

The person who had caught everyone's attention, though, was Wang Hongwen. Mao introduced Wang as a man who, having been a peasant, a soldier, and a worker, was eminently qualified to become a party leader. At the Tenth Congress, Wang jumped several ranks in leadership to be elected vice chairman of the Central Committee, the same rank as Zhou. On repeated occasions following the congress, Wang accompanied Mao to meet with foreign leaders visiting China. This showed that Mao was providing Wang with opportunities to showcase his qualifications while continuously observing and testing him with the eventual prospect of making Wang his successor.

Zhou supported Wang's rise from the beginning. The newsreel made of the congress included footage of Zhou insisting that Wang should walk ahead of him in a show of great respect for the rising political star. This was almost a replay of a scene from the early part of the Cultural Revolution—when Lin was designated as Mao's successor, Zhou had also insisted that Lin walk ahead of him.

After the congress, Zhou turned his focus to the task of preparing for the Fourth National People's Congress. Zhou chaired a September 12 Politburo meeting that decided to set up three groups to organize the People's Congress, revise the PRC constitution, and draft a governmental report, respectively. Zhou then informed Mao of this decision. On October 11, the Party Center issued a notice about convening the People's Congress, which conveyed a recent instruction from the chairman: "This Great Proletarian Cultural Revolution has been carried out for eight years. Now it is time for stability and unity. The whole party and whole country should be united."[67]

Was this the signal that the Cultural Revolution would finally come to an end?

• • •

One evening in late October, Zhou went to the restroom during a break of a Politburo meeting. He saw that his urine was totally red, indicating that his cancer had recurred. Dr. Wu called several meetings attended by dozens of experts, who concluded unanimously that Zhou must undergo surgery, and that Zhou should have two blood infusions per week while their proposal to perform surgery on the premier to stop his blood loss was pending approval.[68] Zhou was desperately in need of good rest and timely treatment.

However, Zhou would get neither, as he soon found himself at the center of another political vortex. In mid-November, Zhou had to devote his attention to receiving Henry Kissinger, who was paying another visit to China, this time in his new capacity as US secretary of state. Given his status within the party leadership as "a lone tree standing above the rest of the forest," as an old Chinese proverb puts it, he knew that he had to act even more cautiously than ever before.

Kissinger arrived in Beijing on November 10, and he stayed in the capital for four days. Altogether Zhou had five formal meetings with him, which, in Kissinger's words, touched on a series of bilateral, regional, and global issues and were "a success on all planes."[69] On November 12, Mao, accompanied by Zhou, met with Kissinger for two hours and forty-five minutes. The conversation, which was quite easygoing, covered a wide range of topics, including international issues, Taiwan, the Watergate scandal, the Middle East, and even philosophy. Mao mentioned Watergate with disdain. He asked why the Americans had allowed such a "crock of shit" balloon to turn into a very big matter.[70]

One part of the conversation dealt with a very serious issue. When Mao said that it was necessary to contain Soviet expansionist ambitions, Kissinger immediately emphasized that Washington would not collude with Moscow in dealing with Beijing. He promised Mao, "There is nothing we are doing with the Soviet Union that you don't know. You can count on that for the future." Kissinger echoed Mao's assertion that "the Soviet Union wants to attack China," saying that, indeed, the Soviets "want to destroy your nuclear capability." Mao joked, "But our nuclear capability is no bigger than a fly of this size." Kissinger responded in a serious tone, "We believe that if this eventually were to happen, it would have very serious consequences for everybody. And we are determined to oppose it as our own decision without any agreement with China."[71]

Zhou did not participate in this part of the conversation, as he already knew that Kissinger would raise this topic with Mao. Kissinger had told Zhou during their first meeting two days before that Washington had rejected the Soviets' proposal to exchange strategic intelligence about China. The Americans did so, Kissinger stressed, "not out of altruism," but because they believed that "it is in our interest" to prevent "a massive attack on China by the Soviet Union." Prompted by this interaction with the Soviets, Kissinger moved to investigate the matter:

> I ordered some studies in our government that only four or five people know about, of what we know about what such a threat could be, and what from our knowledge could be done to prevent it, and of what help we could be in ways that are not obvious, because I don't think a formal relationship is desirable for either of us. These would be of a technical nature. . . . We have some ideas on how to lessen the vulnerability of your forces and how to increase the warning time, and I repeat that it has to be done in such a way that it is very secret and not obvious.

Kissinger further said that he "could mention the details in a small group, either to the Prime Minister or someone he designates." He also emphasized that "this is not something that involves reciprocity or any formal relationship, but advice based on our experience and some regularized intelligence information."[72]

Zhou instantly recognized that the issue raised by Kissinger was of the utmost importance; it was what Mao would call a "big matter." Hence, it is hard to imagine that he would have failed to report the issue to Mao after the meeting.

On the evening of November 13, after all formal meetings had been concluded, Zhou and Kissinger had a special conversation, in which they discussed at length how China and the United States would cooperate in the event that a Sino-Soviet war broke out. The United States would provide help in two ways, Kissinger told Zhou. First, the Americans would supply "equipment and other services"; and second, they would help China establish an early warning capacity, so that China would receive "sound warning of missile launch." Kissinger specifically described the second way:

> Now any help we would give you in our mutual interest should be in a form that is not easily recognizable. With respect to missile launches, we have a very good system of satellites which gives us early warning. The problem is to get that information to you rapidly. We would be prepared to establish a hotline between our satellite and Beijing by which we could transmit information to you in a matter of minutes.

Zhou asked, "Through the satellites?" Kissinger replied, "Well, the information goes to Washington and then to Peking." He then explained his proposal in detail:

> We could do that in one or two ways that would not attract attention. We could just announce the establishment of a hotline just as we have with Moscow, Japan, etc. But yours would be of a special nature but that would not be generally known. This would enable you to move your bombers and if possible you could move your missiles if you knew an attack was coming. You would then need good communications from Peking to your various bases, but we could probably help with that in some guise. Another way is to sign between ourselves an agreement on accidental nuclear war, the same as we have signed with the Soviet Union, and also establish a hotline.

Kissinger further clarified, "I am simply thinking of methods of establishing a hotline to Peking that would not attract attention. We could also give you the technology for certain kinds of radars but you would have to build them yourselves." Zhou listened. When the two said good night, he told Kissinger, "As for the specific matter you wished to discuss, I will have to study it. And tomorrow morning before your leave, I will pay you a visit and bid you farewell. I think there are some things that would be useful to us."[73]

What did Zhou do after that? A widely circulated Chinese account was that Zhou immediately rushed to Mao's quarters to personally report to Mao. However, the chairman had fallen asleep after taking sleeping pills. Not daring to wake Mao, Zhou did not report to him.

However, Zhang Hanzhi, the wife of Vice Foreign Minister Qiao Guanhua, who herself once was close to Mao, told a different story. After Zhou's meeting with Kissinger, according to Qiao, he asked Zhou "if there was anything left to do. The premier replied that he was in a hurry, as Kissinger's questions had to be answered immediately, and he thus needed to report to the chairman." The next morning, Zhou told Qiao that "Kissinger has proposed to have formal military cooperation between China and the United States. The Americans will use their advanced satellite technology to monitor Soviet military activities in the Far East, and they and we will also exchange military intelligence. The chairman had given him the green light to go ahead."[74] Zhang's recollection, if reliable, means that Zhou actually had reported to Mao and received the chairman's approval.

Zhou arrived at Kissinger's guesthouse early the next morning. They had a brief discussion about Japan; then they had a one-on-one meeting. Zhou told Kissinger, "If as you envisioned it would be possible for you to cooperate with warnings, that would be greatly helpful. And, of course, there are also communications networks. But this must be done in a manner so that no one feels we are allies." Kissinger agreed, then pointed out, "There is no way we can establish a hotline secretly." Zhou said that he understood. Kissinger continued, "Once the line is established, we can give it the purpose you described yesterday and that can be kept secret."

Finally, Zhou told Kissinger that as they had broached "so concrete and complex an issue, we need to study it before we can consult you further." Future consultations between the two sides should be carried out at "authoritative levels." Zhou suggested, "Besides your coming in person, we will have contact with each other through the Liaison Office. That would be Ambassador [David] Bruce here and Huang Chen (Huang Zhen) there. And that would be done only through him and one interpreter. . . . And on our part here, I, Marshall Yeh (Ye), and the Vice Minister, Tsai Hung-ching (Cai Hongqing), whom you met the other day, would be the only ones involved." Kissinger agreed, emphasizing that "your ambassador should talk only with me. Because those who know do not know what I have told you. And, frankly, so that you understand, I will tell my colleagues only each step as we decide it—not more. In that way there is the least danger of a leak." Zhou added, "Yes. Because we know that you can keep secrets, but you must be very strict when you do so." "Yes," replied Kissinger.[75]

Kissinger brought with him two draft documents. One was a draft treaty linking "a hotline and an accidental war," and another was an MOU (memorandum of understanding) about "simply the hotline."[76] Kissinger explained that "we don't care about the treaty, we just wanted an excuse to sign a hotline agreement." He left both drafts with Zhou, saying that he was "prepared to establish a hotline directly without a treaty." Zhou's final words betrayed much caution: "We will have to study these issues because, given the nature of our country, if we want to adopt such a course of action that would have great impact internationally . . . if it is too inconvenient, it can wait."[77]

After Kissinger's departure, however, no one on the Chinese side ever approached him.[78] This important matter thus ended inconclusively without a follow-up.

* * *

Zhou's trouble began as soon as Kissinger left Beijing. When Mao learned from "the two young ladies" Nancy Tang and Wang Hairong that Zhou had been "too soft" toward the Americans, he became enraged, claiming that the premier had made "wrong statements" in his meetings with Kissinger.[79]

On November 17, Mao summoned Zhou to a meeting, at which the chairman commented on Zhou's talks with Kissinger, warning, "Be careful not to be deceived by the Americans. They are trying to get a straw from China to save their own lives. In dealing with America we should remember that when we are struggling against them, it is easy for us to be left-leaning; and when we are trying to unite with them, it is easy for us to lean toward the right." Mao further said that China "should not be involved in such matters as making a military alliance with them."[80] These remarks virtually closed the door to Chinese-American military cooperation. Mao instructed the Politburo to meet to discuss his opinions.

Zhou acted without delay. At a Politburo meeting that evening, he conveyed Mao's instruction, and he also briefed his colleagues on his meetings with Kissinger. Jiang Qing immediately accused Zhou of avoiding "the essence of the matter," which was his "rightist capitulationism." Zhou, breaking from his usual response to such criticism, openly rebutted Jiang's accusation: "I, Zhou Enlai, have committed many mistakes in my career, but the label of 'rightist capitulationism' does not fit me at all!"[81] The second day, Zhou submitted two reports to Mao about the Politburo meetings. In making self-criticism, he only acknowledged that he had "not done enough" in his meetings with Kissinger.[82]

On November 18, Mao gave the Politburo another, clearer instruction: to meet to criticize the serious mistakes that Zhou had committed in his meetings with Kissinger. In the meantime, Mao also mentioned Marshal Ye Jianying (who had been in charge of the routine work of the CMC after Lin's death), calling for criticism of his "serious mistakes in handling discussions on military affairs during Kissinger's visit."[83]

The Politburo held consecutive meetings from November 21 to early December, each of which principally targeted Zhou. Nancy Tang gave the opening presentation on Mao's behalf. According to Zhang Hanzhi's recollection, Mao's thirty-year-old interpreter talked for almost three hours. All members of the Politburo, including Zhou, Ye, and the "Gang of Four," sat listening. Mao was quite harsh toward Zhou: "If the Soviets were to invade China, Zhou would become a puppet emperor of theirs! And if the US imperialists were to invade China, Zhou would be no more than a lowly capitulationist."[84] These words held the potential to destroy Zhou's political career.

Over the next several days, members of the Politburo attacked Zhou in turn, accusing him of having "humiliated the nation and jeopardized its sovereignty" and of going down the path of "rightist capitulationism" in his meetings with Kissinger. Zhang Hanzhi, as a "backbencher" named by Mao, also attended the meetings. She recalled that people vied with one another to level repetitious and hollow accusations against Zhou.[85] Jiang Qing and Yao Wenyuan, who were among the most active participants at the meetings, even branded Zhou as the "vicious head of a wrong political line."

To Zhou, this was all total nonsense. Ever since the Rectification Campaign in Yan'an, he had responded to Mao's criticism of him by making repeated self-criticism until Mao let him off the hook. But this time, as he faced accusations of being a "traitor to China," he refused to tolerate the attacks and tacitly admit to wrongdoing by making "self-criticism." Before they received further instructions from Mao, the attendees at the meetings could only repeat the same accusations in a louder and louder voice. The meetings deadlocked. Meanwhile, Zhou's medical treatment was disturbed. On several occasions, he had to interrupt a blood transfusion to attend a meeting.[86]

• • •

Deng Xiaoping was also at the meetings, which was Mao's idea. By bringing Deng back into the Chinese decision-making circle, Mao intended for him to check and balance Zhou. Now, he asked Deng to attend the meetings in order to observe and test Deng's attitudes. Deng, who knew Mao very well, could have easily understood Mao's intentions. He did not say anything until that moment, as he had been waiting for the most suitable time to speak. He knew well that while his presentation should not go so far as to topple Zhou, it should be robust enough to satisfy Mao. At this critical point, he learned from the two young ladies that Mao, who was waiting for him to "stand out," meant to give Zhou a bitter lesson short of wiping him out. Deng was ready to speak.

Deng did not accuse Zhou of being a "traitor to China." Instead, he highlighted Zhou's failure to report to Mao before his final meeting with Kissinger. The essence of Zhou's problem, Deng told the premier, was that "your position is just one step below the chairman's. For others, the chairman's position is within sight, but beyond reach. For you, however, it is within sight and within reach. This is the essence of your problem."[87]

Deng's claim that Zhou sought to attain Mao's status seemed serious, yet it would not spell political ruin for Zhou. After all, many might have quite reasonably assumed that after Mao's death, Zhou would succeed Mao to become China's paramount leader. This was neither too wild an expectation nor a violation of the party constitution and the party's practices. After Deng finished his presentation, Jiang and others strove to paint Zhou as a person who "had been most impatient in trying to replace Mao." But this was not what Deng meant, and Zhou firmly rejected this characterization too. Later, Mao also dismissed the charge. The accusation that Zhou had "betrayed China" was different. In an era when patriotism and revolutionary nationalism had become the foundation of the legitimacy narrative of the CCP and the state, if Zhou were to be identified as having "betrayed and humiliated the country," he would surely face the same fate as Lin Biao, who had suffered a shameful death.

It seemed that Zhou was quite clear about the distinction between Jiang's accusation and Deng's comments. After Deng's presentation, Zhou mirrored Deng's tone, making "serious self-criticism."[88] When Mao heard about Deng's remarks from the two young ladies, he was quite satisfied. "I know he will speak," said Mao. He praised Deng as being more politically skillful than Jiang Qing and others.[89]

Zhou's apparent surrender at the Politburo meeting seemed to signal that his political career had come to an end. In those days, recalled Zhou's bodyguard, the premier was deeply lonely. No one would greet him whenever he entered or left the meeting room.[90]

Yet the political winds changed overnight, as Mao suddenly sheathed his sword. Mao and Zhou met with the visiting King Birendra of Nepal on December 9. The chairman and the premier exchanged a "warm and long handshake." Mao also pointed to the two young ladies who were there as interpreters, telling Zhou, "Premier, these little soldiers are difficult to handle. We have promoted them, but they have made trouble for you, as well as for me."[91] In a few words, Mao seemed to suggest to Zhou that he had not originally intended for the Politburo to criticize Zhou so harshly. Thus, Mao took a break from criticizing Zhou.

After the meeting, Mao talked to Zhou and Wang Hongwen. He praised the Politburo meetings of the previous two weeks, commenting that they "went very well." Therefore, "criticizing Zhou" had not been a mistake after all. At a Politburo meeting three days later, Mao again charged that "the Politburo [under Zhou] fails to discuss politics," and that "the Central Military Commission [under Ye] fails to discuss military matters." Mao warned Zhou and Ye, "If you do not change, I will call another meeting here."[92] Zhou received Mao's message: First, Mao would always exert absolute dominance; second, Zhou had to be vigilant at all times, and under no circumstances allow himself to overshadow Mao.

The tempest had passed. Zhou resumed his role as convener of Politburo meetings. In accordance with Mao's instruction, on December 22, 1973, Zhou drafted a notice for the Party Center, announcing that Deng would be "a member of the Politburo and participate in Central leadership work," as well as "a member of the Central Military Commission, playing a leading role at the commission."[93]

But Mao did not forget the "Zhou-Kissinger scandal," which he again brought up in a conversation with Deng at the end of 1974. Mao told Deng, "It was about a protective umbrella, (the Americans) want to lend us a protective umbrella."[94] Evidently, Mao had merely shelved the matter; if he found it necessary, he could take it out to bring Zhou to a reckoning at any time.

30

LAST DAYS

1974–1976

Alarm bells rang again for Zhou's health in the spring of 1974. Beginning in early March, large amounts of blood, more than one hundred milliliters a day, were found in his urine. On March 11, he had a comprehensive medical exam at the PLA's 305th Hospital. The results stunned Zhou's doctors. The premier's cancer had recurred. They immediately performed another electrocautery procedure on him, but it failed to control his illness. In early May, another exam showed that Zhou's cancer had come back.[1]

On June 1, Zhou arrived at his office early in the afternoon, scanning the surroundings intently. Then, joined by Deng Yingchao, he left the West Flower Pavilion, where he had lived and worked for almost a quarter century, and then he was admitted to the 305th Hospital. He would never set foot again in the pavilion before his death a year and a half later.

The same day, the doctors performed a surgery to remove the part of Zhou's gallbladder affected by cancer. The procedure went well. Zhou quickly recovered, and the blood in his urine also disappeared.[2] But the doctors hardly had time to celebrate when Zhou's cancer came back yet again. Zhou had another surgery on August 10, but his situation did not improve.[3] Both Zhou and his doctors knew that he would probably never be able to leave the hospital again.

• • •

Even in the hospital, Zhou was still involved in top-level decision-making, and he chaired Politburo meetings. However, he also fully understood that he was just a transitional figure during a transitional period.

Beginning in early 1974, a rather strange campaign of "criticizing Lin Biao and criticizing Confucius" had swept across China. After he died, Lin had become the central target of criticism and attacks in China's political discourse. Why, then, was the ancient Chinese sage Confucius also condemned? The answer eluded Zhou.

The genesis of the campaign lay in a conversation between Mao and Jiang Qing, back in August 1973. "All accomplished politicians in Chinese history were Legalists," Mao said, "They all advocated rule by law, and all emphasized the present over the past. By comparison, the Confucians stressed virtue and morality, placed more emphasis on the past over the present, and tried to turn back the wheel of history."[4] Jiang did not necessarily understand why Mao had said this, but she conveyed Mao's words at a Politburo meeting, requesting that they be incorporated into the political report of the CCP's Tenth Congress. Zhou did not know Mao's purpose, but he had a hunch that this was no simple matter. As it was necessary to take time to digest Mao's ideas, he replied to Jiang, the chairman's comments should not be publicized immediately.[5]

Beginning in late 1973, the Chinese official media, directed by Yao Wenyuan, published a series of articles criticizing Confucius. Almost at the same time, a group of teachers from two Beijing universities, whom Mao had tasked to go through Lin Biao's collections, found many objects indicating Lin's reverence for Confucius. In particular, Lin possessed a piece of calligraphy that contained a quotation from Confucius: "To control oneself and return to rituals are the most important of the myriad things." Mao instructed the Politburo to link condemnation of Lin with criticism of Confucius, which, from Mao's perspective, would prove that Lin had tried to "go back to the past." Thus, Lin's problems could be characterized as ultrarightist in essence. Both Confucius and Lin consequently became the targets of an onslaught of attacks.

Mao had big plans for the wave of criticism against Lin and Confucius that he had kicked off. After Lin's death, it became evident that the Cultural Revolution had reached a dead end. But Mao was unwilling to let it end on that note. By demonizing Lin and Confucius, Mao hoped to cultivate a political atmosphere that reflected his idea that "revolution still continues," while the chairman built a transitional power structure—with Deng as the main pillar—in alliance with the "Gang of Four." Thus the campaign to criticize Lin and Confucius was very different from the criticism of "Hai Rui Dismissed from Office" on the eve of the Cultural Revolution. Although both were Mao's attempts to create a particular political environment to serve his purposes, the latter was designed to launch the Cultural Revolution, while the former was meant to conclude it. Jiang Qing, however, did not grasp the distinction between the two.

Criticizing Lin and Confucius figured prominently in the first directive issued by the CCP Center in 1974. Mao's words, which Zhou had been reluctant to publicize a few months before, became the directive's central theme.[6] On January 25, without consulting Zhou, and without any discussion by the Politburo, Jiang Qing called for a mobilization rally by cadres associated with administrative offices of the Central Committee and the State Council. She asked Zhou to chair the rally. Though he was unhappy about it, Zhou agreed to Jiang's request. Mao's wife acted extremely aggressively at the rally. One by one, she cited the names of a list of individuals whose actions she then condemned. In a fit of excitement, she even attacked Marshal Ye Jianying for having "opened a back-door access" to privileges for his relatives. Zhou, sitting on the rostrum and watching Jiang's excessive performance, did not say a thing.[7] He knew well that behind Jiang was Mao.

Geng Biao, then head of the party's Central Liaison Department, was among those named and criticized at the rally. Afterward, Geng found Zhou and complained about his experience. "I have three words of advice for you," Zhou told Geng. "No matter how hard they try to undermine you, you should not be undermined; no matter how desperately they try to kick you out, you should stay; and regardless of how uglily they insult you, you should not commit suicide."[8] Zhou's advice to Geng revealed his own ways of coping with similar situations.

But Jiang already had mishandled Mao's plans. From Mao's perspective, to criticize Lin and Confucius was a weighty endeavor that concerned political lines. His wife, however, had mistook the main thrust of the campaign by focusing on such trivial things as access to privileges, thus making it more difficult for Mao to deal with major political issues while also managing personnel matters. This displeased Mao, who blamed Jiang for "deemphasizing the importance of criticizing Lin and Confucius" and "messing it up with small things."[9] This was a prelude to Mao's later criticism of the Gang of Four.

By then, Mao had become such a lone person that not even his wife could easily see him. If Jiang Qing wanted to visit Mao, she needed Wang Dongxing's approval, or she had to go through Wang Hairong and Nancy Tang, the two young ladies who were then still the liaisons between Mao and the Politburo.

Zhou continued to chair Politburo meetings. In early February, he sent a report to Mao about criticism of Lin and Confucius. This certainly was an important campaign, he emphasized, yet it was also crucial to "accumulate experience for it." His unspoken message was that this campaign should not be allowed to run out of control. Zhou was good at reading Mao's mind. He knew that, this time, what Mao wanted was to create an atmosphere of "continuing the revolution" in the ideological sphere, rather than to again bring "great chaos" to spheres "all under heaven." Mao approved the report with no further instructions.[10]

* * *

In personnel matters, the chairman focused his attention on Deng Xiaoping, whom he had been watching for a year since Deng reemerged in China's political scene in early 1973. At the same time, Mao also kept an eye on Wang Hongwen, who he quickly realized was by no means the right choice for his successor. In December 1973, at the Politburo's meetings for criticizing Zhou, Mao again tested Deng, who passed the test. In March 1974, Mao further thought of letting Deng attend a special assembly of the United Nations in New York, which would be a big step by the chairman to boost Deng.

It was around this time that Mao introduced his Three Worlds Theory. In a series of talks with visiting foreign leaders from late 1973 to mid-1974, Mao contended that "the U.S. and the Soviet Union belong to the First World. The middle elements, such as Japan, Europe, Australia and Canada, belong to the Second World. We are the Third World."[11] Instead of using the word "revolution," Mao used levels of "development" to define the "three worlds." This was actually Mao's response to the ever-deepening legitimacy crisis facing his concept of "continuous revolution" after Lin Biao's death. Making China strong, and enabling the country to stand up among all nations in the world, had served as a powerful engine for the legitimacy narrative of Mao's New China ever since he announced that "we, the Chinese, have stood up" at the PRC's establishment. By introducing the Three Worlds Theory, Mao meant to tell the Chinese people that China was still playing a central role in transforming the world, thus sustaining and cultivating the sense that they had indeed "stood up."

Mao thus believed that it was critical to introduce the Three Worlds Theory at the UN special assembly. Naturally, the best person to take up the mission was Zhou; however, the premier was too sick to make the trip. (Even if Zhou's physical condition had allowed him to travel, would Mao have let him go anyway?) Aside from Zhou, who else could have been more qualified than Deng? In addition to the huge media impact associated with the international reappearance of such an important figure as Deng, this mission would also serve Mao's purpose of enhancing Deng's stature in Chinese domestic politics.

Through Wang Hairong and Nancy Tang, Mao first had the Foreign Ministry suggest in a report that Deng might lead the Chinese mission to the UN.[12] Interestingly, Mao asked the two ladies not to reveal that this was his idea, probably because he wanted to gauge Zhou's reaction. Zhou approved the Foreign Ministry report without hesitation, after which Mao also approved the report.[13] When it was brought to the Politburo, however, Jiang Qing stood out in opposition to the suggestion.[14] Upon learning of Jiang's response, Mao instructed the two ladies to tell Zhou, "It is my opinion that Deng should attend the UN assembly. However, if the comrades at the Politburo disagree, this matter can be tabled."[15] Zhou would not table the proposal. At another Politburo meeting that he chaired, the majority favored having Deng serve as the head of the Chinese delegation to the UN. However, Jiang continued to cast a "nay" vote against the idea.[16] The two ladies reported this to Mao. "Comrade Deng Xiaoping going abroad is my idea," the chairman wrote his wife, "and you'd better not oppose it." After the next Politburo meeting had concluded, Zhou was able to report to Mao, "The Politburo is unanimous in supporting the chairman's decision to send Comrade Deng Xiaoping to the UN special assembly."[17]

A few days later, the Politburo discussed and approved the speech that Deng would be delivering at the UN, a speech at the center of which was Mao's Three Worlds Theory. Jiang asked for sick leave and did not attend the meeting.[18] On April 6, Zhou, along with other top leaders, personally saw Deng off at the airport.

Deng's speech at the UN special assembly made a huge media splash. He articulated Mao's Three Worlds Theory, emphasizing that the Third World was composed of developing countries in Asia, Africa, and Latin America, a group of nations that counted China among its ranks.[19] Deng's reputation abroad and good image at home were simultaneously enhanced.

When Deng returned to Beijing via Paris, he shared several French croissants with Zhou. Those had been the food they liked the most almost half a century before, when they were both engaged in revolutionary activities in France.

· · ·

Shortly after Zhou was admitted to the 305th Hospital, alarm bells also rang for Mao's health, which had been deteriorating since the crisis in February 1972. New symptoms appeared in mid-June 1974. He could not move his tongue; his mouth could not close; his words were garbled; and the muscles in his right hand and his legs were atrophying. The Politburo summoned medical specialists in cardiology, neurology, anesthesiology, otolaryngology, respiratory medicine, general surgery, and intensive care, who formed a special team to examine and treat the chairman. For several years, doctors had suspected that Mao had Parkinson's disease. But this time, they found that Mao's illness was much more complicated and difficult to deal with than expected. Mao was suffering from a kind of motor neuron disease—the cells that controlled his body's voluntary muscles were dysfunctional and gradually dying.[20] Those with the disease usually died within two years of being diagnosed; hence both the doctors and Mao knew that his days were numbered. The chairman often murmured, "I have been invited by the King of Hell to drink hard liquor with him."[21]

The dramatic deterioration of Mao's health made it all the more urgent for him to make posthumous arrangements for China. "The Proletarian Cultural Revolution has lasted eight years," he said. "It is now better to have stability and unity."[22] To achieve this, Mao wanted to see a political alliance develop between Deng and the Cultural Revolution faction headed by his wife, which would also form a new power structure within the party leadership.

However, for months, all Mao saw was a Jiang Qing who understood neither his dilemma nor his intentions. Mao certainly knew that his wife and her close associates were the most devoted to his "revolutionary lines." Of all the top party leaders, they were the only ones he could trust completely. After all, Jiang had obtained her political status and power because she was his wife, so under no circumstances would she betray him. But in terms of political skill, vision, and personality, Jiang was completely lacking in sophistication. Often her behavior disappointed Mao, especially when she deviated from the "big issues" that he sought to highlight.

At the time, Mao was planning another tour of the South of China. On July 17, the day before his departure, he chaired a Politburo meeting at his Zhongnanhai residence, where he criticized his wife. "Comrade Jiang Qing, you should be careful. You should not form a small clique of four people," Mao told her. "Others have had complaints about you, but they do not dare to tell you in person, so you do not know about this. You should not set up two factories, one for iron sticks, and one for big labels. This is not good. You should be careful."[23] Mao would reiterate his criticism of Jiang on several other occasions.

Mao, however, certainly did not mean to destroy Jiang and her close associates. He did not link her behavior with such labels as revisionism, left- or right-leaning opportunism, dogmatism, factionalism, or empiricism, as he had often done with other rivals in past intraparty struggles. The main problem of Jiang and those with her, said the chairman, was their inability to work with others. Jiang should be viewed through a dialectical lens, Mao emphasized, suggesting that "part of her was very good, and part of her was not so good."[24] Mao still hoped that the Gang of Four would cooperate with Deng, who would serve as the core of a new power structure. However, Jiang and her allies did not seem to understand Mao's ideas and objectives. Politically, they failed to grasp the importance of "uniting with the majority." In criticizing Lin and Confucius, they missed the "key points" and often acted foolishly. Mao thus found it necessary to criticize them, but this was as far as Mao was willing to go. His words revealed nothing more than his disappointment in his wife's failure to live up to his expectations.

Zhou did not miss a single word Mao said at the meeting. What should have immediately caught his attention, though, was another statement Mao made: "I am no longer in need of the nine essays. I have burned them to ashes." (In fact, he had not.)[25] These essays, written by Mao during the Yan'an Rectification Movement, included two that directly criticized Zhou. Thus, Zhou knew that he was still being targeted by Mao.

All the while, the campaign to criticize Lin and Confucius continued to grow. In mid-June, at a meeting with the Gang of Four's ghostwriters, Jiang made a strange comment: "Why do you only criticize Lin Biao and Chen Boda? Why do you fail to mention the Confucius of our times? Why does the contemporary Confucius disappear in your critical articles?"[26] With this, Jiang pointed her spear at Zhou, albeit implicitly. She knew that she had Mao's support on this matter.

On September 30, the eve of the twenty-fifth anniversary of the founding of the PRC, Zhou hosted a National Day reception in what turned out to be the last time he would perform such a role. When he entered the banquet hall of the Great Hall of the People, many people in attendance at the reception jumped to their feet to give the premier a standing ovation several minutes long. By then, quite a few of the guests knew that Zhou was terminally ill. The sight of his skinny frame brought them to tears. As Zhou's cancer was spreading throughout his body, slowly killing him, his reputation in the hearts of the Chinese seemed to have reached a new height. Mao did not attend the reception, and when he received the report about it, he probably had no reason to feel happy.

• • •

In late 1974, the focal point of top-level Chinese politics shifted to the planning of the Fourth National People's Congress. As top governmental positions would be assigned at the congress, it represented another step in the ongoing power transition. Who would be named to head the new cabinet, and how would cabinet positions be allocated? These were key questions to answer.

Mao had already decided to let Deng take center stage in Chinese high politics. On October 4, he instructed Wang Hongwen to inform the Politburo that Deng should be named first vice premier.[27] This was another critical move by Mao to establish a new power structure with Deng as a main pillar. By choosing Wang to deliver the message, he obviously hoped that Jiang Qing would not voice any opposition to Deng's appointment.

However, Jiang challenged the arrangement anyway. At a Politburo meeting on October 17, she became involved in a heated quarrel with Deng. "I used my iron fist to deal with hers," Deng later claimed.[28] He probably felt emboldened to do so because Zhou had informed him that both Jiang and Zhang Chunqiao had been considered "traitors." Also, at the time, Deng believed that he had Mao's trust and support.

With Jiang's backing, Wang Hongwen flew to Changsha the next day to personally complain to Mao about Deng. But Mao refused to listen to him. The chairman even warned Wang not to "mingle with Jiang Qing" so often and instead "develop a relationship of unity with Comrade Deng Xiaoping."[29] Though it seemed Mao was warning Wang, in reality he was also giving Wang advice.

Zhou supported Deng. The two shared similar political perspectives, and Zhou also knew that Deng's rise meant that politically he would be more protected from a Mao who never truly trusted him. Deng paid more frequent visits to Zhou in the premier's hospital room to seek his advice. Zhou also frequently had long conversations with Wang Hairong and Nancy Tang, who were still Mao's liaisons. "Those people have planned to attack Comrade Xiaoping for quite a while," Zhou told them, "and he has been extremely patient and tolerant."[30] Zhou knew that the two would convey his words to Mao.

Just as Zhou expected, the two ladies were soon summoned by Mao, who was then in Changsha, to serve as his interpreters for a meeting with the Danish prime minister, Poul Hartling. Deng also attended the meeting. The two ladies took the opportunity to convey Zhou's message to Mao. The following day, Mao told Deng that he fully trusted him to be involved in the organizing of a new cabinet. The chairman also told the two ladies that "the premier should remain our premier," and that "so long as his health allows, he may work together with Comrade Wang Hongwen to consult with others, and come up with a list of personnel arrangements." Mao particularly reiterated that "Deng should take up the positions of first vice premier and chief of the general staff." All in all, Mao stressed, "The policy should be for unity and stability."[31]

In late December, Zhou was temporarily discharged from the hospital and flew to Changsha, where he met with Mao to finalize the appointments for top positions that would be announced at the forthcoming People's Congress. In a sense, Zhou agreed to make the trip because he was already keenly aware of Mao's intention to assign important missions to Deng. Zhou knew well that his time was running out. If he wanted to maintain his good name after his death, who could be a better choice to carry the torch for him than Deng, who shared his key perspectives? At the time, however, Zhou could not have foreseen that just a year later Mao would purge Deng for the second time and would choose Hua Guofeng as his nominal successor. Nor would Zhou see it. By the time Deng was purged again, Zhou had already gone "to see Karl Marx."

While Zhou was en route to Changsha, Wang Hongwen also traveled to the city to see Mao. The chairman received Zhou and Wang shortly after they arrived, and he talked with them for two hours. The chairman would meet Zhou and Wang again over the next two days. Obviously, Mao had already given much thought to the personnel arrangements at the People's Congress. "The premier will remain the premier," he said. Deng was "politically very strong"; so, in addition to assuming the position of first vice premier, he should also be appointed vice chairman of the CCP Central Committee, vice chairman of the Central Military Commission, and chief of staff of the PLA. To balance Deng's new authority, Zhang Chunqiao, who had no military experience at all, would become director of the PLA's Department of Political Affairs, as well as second vice premier. Mao told Wang, "You should not continuously mingle with Jiang Qing and others. The Party Center is made up of only these few people. You should unite together, and should not make factions. Otherwise you will fall down."[32] Mao's advice to Wang once again revealed his way of balancing political power at the top.

December 26, 1974, was Mao's eighty-first birthday. Zhou was called to Mao's quarters past midnight, where the two talked through the night. Mao again confirmed his approval of Zhou's work on assigning government posts. Then, he changed the topic and began to expound his theory of continuing the revolution under a proletarian dictatorship. "China is a socialist country," Mao said, "so there still exist such bourgeoisie rights as salaries being divided into eight levels, distribution according to labor contribution, and exchanges by currency." All of this, emphasized the chairman, "can only be restricted under a proletarian dictatorship." The current Cultural Revolution would soon end. However, Mao predicted, a similar revolution would "happen again once every seven to eight years," for many times to come.[33] Zhou listened. He also took the opportunity to tell Mao that Zhang Chunqiao had "serious historical problems." "That I already know," said Mao.[34]

Zhou's trip to Changsha and his conversations with Mao revealed the dilemma that the chairman had always faced and was never able to resolve, even with his unlimited power: On the one hand, he absolutely did not want to hand power and his grand "revolutionary enterprise" over to Zhou. But, on the other hand, he had to rely on Zhou's remarkable administrative talent to maintain the routine functioning of the party-state that he had founded. At the end of 1974, in particular, he knew that Zhou was one of the few people who could help him bring about the endgame of the Cultural Revolution. In other words, this was a clear revelation that the dragnet of Zhou's personalized administrative capacity had trapped Mao's seemingly unlimited power.

• • •

Zhou was exhausted and extremely weak by the time he returned to Beijing, but he could not afford to rest. On December 28, he called a meeting with Wang Hongwen, Ye Jianying, Zhang Chunqiao, and Deng Xiaoping, in which he relayed to them his conversations with the chairman in Changsha. In particular, he told them that Mao had approved the arrangements for top-level government positions for the People's Congress. This was the "supreme instruction." No one, of course, would raise a dissenting voice.[35]

The next day, Zhou chaired a Politburo meeting at which he asked his colleagues to discuss and approve the nominations for top governmental positions that he and Mao had worked out. Zhou would keep his position as premier. He also conveyed to those in attendance Mao's theory of "continuing the revolution under proletarian dictatorship."[36] The revolution was not over, Zhou informed his colleagues.

New Year's Day 1975 began for Zhou with a confidential discussion with Deng and Li Xiannian in his hospital room.[37] Then, the three arrived together at the Great Hall of the People for another Politburo meeting, where governmental appointments to be made at the People's Congress in mid-January were approved. Zhou and Deng would serve as premier and first vice premier, respectively. As Zhou was terminally ill, Deng would assume his duties as acting premier. To balance Deng's appointment, Zhang Chunqiao would be named second vice premier.[38] Zhou personally drafted the reports to Mao about these conclusions. He was very cautious, so he asked Wang Hongwen to cosign the reports.[39] Zhou also included a particular sentence in the report: "I plan to make self-criticism for not having done an excellent job of criticizing Lin and Confucius." A few days later, he received Mao's response, which was conveyed to him by the two young ladies: "No self-criticism is needed."[40]

Prior to the People's Congress, a Central Committee plenum approved the arrangement of government positions that had been decided by Mao, Zhou, and the Politburo. Central Committee members also heard from Zhou that Mao emphasized the need to pay attention to "the question of theory," and that the whole party and whole country should "better pursue stability and unity."[41]

On January 13, the Fourth National People's Congress began at the Great Hall of the People. Zhou delivered the speech on government work.

30.1 Zhou Enlai speaking at the First Plenary Session of the Fourth National People's Congress in January 1975. *Imaginechina Limited / Alamy Stock Photo*

According to one eyewitness account, he "looked skinny and quite ill, but his steps were steady. All representatives stood up, and the applause lasted as if forever." Zhou's speech was about five thousand words long, which was brief by Chinese standards. Still, he was too weak to deliver it, so he only read its opening and concluding paragraphs. He left the platform "in another round of thunderous standing ovation."[42] When Zhou's speech was published, the most noteworthy part of it was his reiteration of what he had said twelve years before at the last People's Congress: China would "realize four modernizations in industry, agriculture, national defense, and science and technology by the end of the twentieth century."[43]

China was still in the abyss of the Cultural Revolution at the time, and the rhetoric of "continuous revolution" remained the mainstream discourse of

Chinese politics. Zhou would likely have received Mao's permission to speak in this way at the congress. His speech was also an expression of his own beliefs. Otherwise, why would he have summoned his remaining strength to speak at the congress when he already knew that he would not live much longer? As it turned out, the speech would be Zhou's last public appearance in his long political career.

Zhou then chaired a State Council working meeting, which would also be his last. "My health has been failing me," he announced. "From now on, my work at the State Council is handed over to Comrade Deng Xiaoping."[44]

* * *

This extremely busy time for Zhou was finally over with the conclusion of the People's Congress. Meanwhile, his health had worsened further. A fecal test found occult blood in his stool; a subsequent sigmoidoscope procedure revealed that a tumor had grown in his colon. This was not an outgrowth of Zhou's gallbladder cancer, but an unrelated and much more malicious case of squamous cell carcinoma.[45] The doctors, stunned and speechless, knew that this meant Zhou would die even sooner than expected.

On February 4, Zhou had another surgery, which took four hours. But it had little effect. On March 6, doctors gave Zhou a colonoscopy, finding a tumor the size of a walnut in Zhou's large intestine close to the liver. The Politburo permitted the doctors to perform another surgery on Zhou, which was done on March 26 and lasted eight hours. As before, the surgery had almost no effect, leaving Zhou one step closer to death.

By that time, the Gang of Four were enthusiastically pushing another nationwide political campaign, this time based on Mao's instructions on "the question of theory," which Zhou had originally relayed to the Politburo. On March 1, Zhang Chunqiao suddenly raised the question of criticizing empiricism, asserting that, though empiricism was as damaging as dogmatism, it had not been criticized since 1949. Thus, Zhang reasoned, its danger should not be underestimated.[46] Jiang Qing immediately echoed Zhang. In their dictionary, "empiricism" was a label specifically reserved for Zhou. In his hospital room, Zhou made no reaction.

On May 3, 1975, Mao chaired a Politburo meeting for the last time in his life. Zhou temporarily left the hospital to attend the meeting. "How are you? How is your health condition?" Mao inquired as he greeted the premier. The meeting turned out to be another of Mao's efforts to try to bridge Deng and the Gang of Four. Mao set the tone for the meeting, stating, "We need stability and unity. Dogmatism or empiricism is trying to revise Marxism-Leninism, and both need to be corrected through education."[47] Mao commented that "Jiang Qing is a little empiricist," then advised Jiang and those with her "not to continuously act like a 'Gang of Four'; not continuously do it." He reminded them that he had highlighted this problem several times before. "Why don't you try to unite with the over two hundred members of the Central Committee?" he asked. But Mao also emphasized that this was "not a big problem, which, as a small issue, should not be made into a big one." Mao added that patience and unity were needed to resolve the problem.[48]

The next day, Deng visited Zhou in the hospital. The details of their discussion have never been declassified. What we know is that they "exchanged opinions about how to carry out Mao's instructions at the Politburo meeting on May 3."[49]

• • •

Although Zhou was dying, Mao still could not set his mind at ease. In the summer of 1975, Mao reread and revised the nine essays he had written during the Yan'an Rectification. As previously mentioned, Zhou had been a target of criticism from Mao in some of these essays.[50] Zhou had no illusions about Mao's feelings toward him. On June 16, he wrote Mao a letter in which he virtually insulted himself:

> Since the Zunyi Conference, forty years have passed. Despite the chairman's endless teaching, I have still repeatedly made mistakes or even committed crimes. About all this, I feel tremendous shame and regret. Now, in my illness, I have repeatedly recalled those mistakes. In addition to maintaining my loyalty in my old age, I am willing to complete a qualified summary of my career.[51]

Zhou died before he was ever able to complete such a summary, however.

On June 9, Zhou dragged his extremely frail body to the Babaoshan Revolutionary Funeral House to attend the memorial service for Marshal He Long, who had died six years before. This was a matter of enormous importance to Zhou. By attending the service, he meant not only to show his remorse for not doing more to defend a very old friend but also to further push for the rehabilitation of veteran leaders who had been purged in the Cultural Revolution. Upon arriving at the memorial hall, Zhou bowed eight times in front of He's portrait. He loudly told He Long's widow that he was so sorry that he had failed to protect the marshal.[52] Such a scene, especially when Zhou said that "I will not live long myself," could not but bring almost everyone there to tears.

• • •

In the summer of 1975, Deng went full steam ahead on what he called a "rectification and consolidation campaign." He selected three sentences from Mao's sayings and packaged them into what he named "Mao's three important instructions": "To study theory and fight against revisionism, to pursue stability and unity, and to develop the national economy." Taking these "three instructions" as the lodestar of his campaign, Deng began by attempting to restore order to railway transportation, and then by trying to rectify the military, the national defense system, the science and technology sector, and the steel and iron industry. These efforts quickly showed positive results, as demonstrated in China's industrial production statistics. During this period, although Deng was repeatedly challenged by the Gang of Four, he did not compromise with them. Instead, he used his own "iron way" to deal with Jiang Qing's. At one point, with Mao's support, he even forced Jiang to carry out self-criticism at the Politburo for her mistake of "making a Gang of Four."[53]

In hindsight, Mao gave Deng the space to do all of this for two intertwined purposes, one explicit and one implicit. The explicit purpose was that in order to end the Cultural Revolution, Mao would have to reestablish—through "rectification and consolidation"—the CCP's control over China's state and society, while simultaneously reinvigorating China's long-stagnant economy. After all, Mao understood that if the Chinese economy did not develop substantially, his statement that "we, the Chinese, have stood up," his chief claim to legitimacy, would not be convincing. The implicit purpose was that Mao understood that giving people power was the best way to induce them to reveal their true selves. Mao wanted to further test Deng by making him powerful, in order to find out his true opinion of the Cultural Revolution.

In fact, Mao did not unleash Deng completely. While Deng was diligently working on his "rectification and consolidation campaign," Zhang Chunqiao and Yao Wenyuan, members of the Gang of Four, published two lengthy essays, one on "comprehensive dictatorship over the bourgeoisie class," the other on "the social foundation of Lin Biao's antiparty clique," clearly demonstrating their desire to control and manipulate the propaganda sphere. Early in the fall, the Gang of Four launched a "revolution on the education front" to counterbalance Deng's consolidation efforts. Although Mao had repeatedly emphasized "stability and unity," the political struggles within the CCP leadership were becoming increasingly fierce.

Deng had kept a very close relationship with Zhou, the closest of his postrehabilitation career. He visited Zhou at the hospital almost every week, sometimes even once every few days. The length of their conversations depended on the subjects discussed and on Zhou's health. A few conversations lasted as long as one hour or even two hours or more. Zhou supported Deng wholeheartedly. However, with his deep knowledge and understanding of Mao, he repeatedly advised Deng "not to push too hard."[54] Zhou and Deng's close relationship made the Gang of Four extremely uncomfortable. They told Mao that "Deng often visits the premier."[55] Mao did not comment at the time; but he was listening, and he heard them.

Zhou's caution was not groundless. Before the end of the summer of 1975, Chinese political life was confronted with new campaigns of "commenting on *Water Margin*" and "criticizing capitulationism." Mao mentioned the classic novel *Water Margin* in an August conversation. "This is a good book as a negative example," he commented. "It is a good book because it describes those heroes who surrendered to the enemy, so it can be used as a negative example."[56] Yao Wenyuan, after learning of Mao's opinion on *Water Margin,* immediately wrote Mao, saying that "this is a very important issue," and that "for opposing and preventing revisionism, it should produce very positive effects if *Water Margin* is to be discussed and criticized." Mao wrote in his response that he "agreed with" Yao's ideas.[57]

As the autumn winds were beginning to blow, an exceedingly bizarre political ghost again roamed China's vast landscape. On the one hand, Deng Xiaoping was still trying earnestly to push forward "comprehensive consolidation." On the other hand, a campaign, led by newspapers on the central level, of commenting on and criticizing *Water Margin* emerged with the purpose of "letting all know that within our party there are capitulationists."[58]

Zhou, with his sharp political sense, immediately realized that this was no simple matter. The day after Mao approved Yao's report, Zhou instructed his associates to bring him several different versions of *Water Margin,* which he began to read.[59] After reading several "crazy essays" about *Water Margin* that had been published in papers controlled by Yao, Zhou remarked, "They are too outrageous. What is the target of such comments on *Water Margin* and criticism of capitulationism? It is self-evident."[60] In one conversation with Deng, Zhou again advised Deng not to push his consolidation efforts too quickly. However, it seemed that Deng did not heed Zhou's advice.[61] "He is just such a person, never patient," Zhou lamented.

As Zhou's health continued to deteriorate, his international diplomatic activities as China's premier were finally approaching their end. In April, North Korean leader Kim Il-sung visited Beijing. Zhou was in very poor health at the time; nonetheless, he met briefly with Kim in the hospital's reception room. His feet were so swollen that his shoes no longer fit. On the day of the meeting, a pair of cotton shoes was hastily made for him. The meeting—at which Deng Xiaoping was also present—was a ritual one, lasting about fifteen minutes.[62] After Kim left, Zhou had a conversation with Deng. No one knows what the two discussed.

On April 18, Mao met with Kim. The chairman told Kim, "Our premier has been ill. He has had three operations in the past year. The first two were for the bladder. Then something appeared outside his colon, and he had another operation." "Vice Chairman Deng Xiaoping has mentioned this to me," replied Kim. The chairman murmured, "The premier is ill, I am ill. I am already eighty-two. I will not live much longer."[63]

One day in late August, Prince Sihanouk of Cambodia came to Zhou's hospital room to bid him farewell. Sihanouk would soon be returning to Cambodia, which was then ruled by the Khmer Rouge. Knowing that there was great uncertainty in Sihanouk's future, Zhou turned to Khieu Samphan, the nominal leader of the Khmer Rouge who was there too, and said, "I most sincerely hope that you will be in unity with the prince, in order to enhance your victory!" In a sad voice, he said to Sihanouk, "I am sorry that I won't be able to see you off at the airport. Let us say good-bye now."[64]

On September 7, Zhou met with Ilie Verdeţz, the vice prime minister of Romania. All of Zhou's doctors advised him not to have the meeting, which Verdeţz had persistently requested. Nonetheless, Zhou decided that he would meet with his "old Romanian friend." He clearly knew that this would probably be his very last meeting with a foreign visitor. He was given only fifteen to twenty minutes, but the meeting lasted forty-five minutes. He made sure to mention that he had passed the torch to Deng, telling Verdeţz, "You can fully trust Comrade Deng, who will continue to carry out our party's domestic and international policies." Zhou recalled that only ten years before, when he attended Romanian leader Gheorghe Gheorghiu-Dej's funeral, he was able to walk in the freezing cold for four hours wearing a light overcoat. "I even cannot walk by myself for four minutes now. I am approaching the moment to see Karl Marx."[65]

* * *

In mid-September, doctors found a large tumor in Zhou's lower abdomen. On the afternoon of September 20, he was to have another major surgery, one that, if it went wrong, could take his life. Before he entered the operating room, Zhou mustered all of the energy and strength he could manage to write something. He asked his secretary to bring him the transcript of his recorded description of the "Wu Hao case" that he had made on June 23, 1972. His hand trembling, he signed his name, Zhou Enlai, on the first page of the file, and next to his signature he wrote, "before entering the operating room." Then he asked to see Deng Xiaoping. Zhou shook Deng's hand and told him, "You have done an excellent job in the past year, much better than what I have done." While Zhou was being pushed into the operating room, he raised his voice and shouted, "I am loyal to the party and the people! I am not a capitulationist!"[66] The shadows of the "Wu Hao case" and the "Kissinger scandal" still lingered in his mind. Deng Yingchao immediately asked Wang Dongxing, who was also there, to report Zhou's "last words" to Mao.[67]

The surgery lasted five hours. Although Zhou survived, the doctors found that Zhou's cancer had spread to his whole body and that there was really nothing more they could do. Deng Xiaoping, who was waiting outside, instructed the doctors to do everything possible to "reduce his pain and prolong his life."[68]

Zhou's health continued to worsen over the following days and weeks. His immune system had virtually collapsed. He could no longer go on a morning walk, even just for a few minutes. On October 12, he had another surgery, which was fruitless. But Zhou was still meeting with people. He also remembered the accusation that he was a "capitulationist." On November 15, when he was feeling a little better, he asked his secretary to bring him a piece of paper. "I have been loyal to Chairman Mao, to the party, and to the people," he wrote. "I have made many mistakes, but I am not a capitulationist."[69] This was his desperate response to the attacks that the "commenting on *Water Margin*" campaign had leveled at him.

• • •

In the fall of 1975, when chilling winds from the north were sweeping away the last leaves from Beijing's trees, China's political atmosphere shifted again. After observing Deng for several months, Mao began to withdraw his support for him.

Early in October, the liaison channel between Mao and the Politburo changed. Wang Hairong and Nancy Tang had lost Mao's trust, probably because Mao felt that they had been too close to Zhou and Deng. Beginning on October 10, Mao's nephew, Mao Yuanxin, was transferred from Liaoning to Beijing to serve as the liaison officer between Mao and the Politburo.[70]

The young Mao grew up in his uncle's home, and he had a good relationship with Jiang Qing. During the Cultural Revolution, he had been the head of the revolutionary rebels in Liaoning. After he became Mao's personal liaison, Jiang and the Gang of Four had better access to Mao, which suggested that the chairman's attitudes toward Deng and the Gang of Four had shifted.

Around that time, Liu Bing, a cadre at Tsinghua University, wrote two letters to Mao, in which he complained about the behavior of two Tsinghua leaders who previously had worked for Mao. Deng helped deliver Liu's letters to the chairman. The first letter reached Mao in August, to which he gave no response. But when Mao received the second letter in late October, he became enraged. He summoned Deng to his quarters and blamed Deng for helping to convey Liu's letters.[71] The next day, Mao had a conversation with his nephew, who mentioned that Deng seldom talked about the achievements of the Cultural Revolution. "He was unhappy with the Cultural Revolution," Mao replied, and this was "why he stood on Liu Bing's side." "This is not an isolated issue," Mao further commented, "but a reflection of the struggles between two political lines."[72]

Mao Yuanxin, according to his uncle's instructions, had several conversations with Deng, in which the younger Mao attempted to "help him" correct his attitude toward the Cultural Revolution. The talks did not go well.[73] Finally, the elder Mao decided that Deng should not be confronted with "small matters." He only needed to do one thing: to lead the Politburo to adopt a resolution on the Cultural Revolution. Mao set the tone for the resolution: "Generally, it should conclude that the Cultural Revolution is 70 percent correct and 30 percent wrong."[74]

Deng and Zhou spoke several times over the following days. Zhou advised Deng to avoid confronting Mao; he knew Mao too well. Whether Deng would be kept in his position or fired depended entirely on a single slip of Mao's lips. Zhou saw clearly that the task of crafting a resolution on the Cultural Revolution was in fact Mao's final test for Deng or, indeed, the last opportunity he would give Deng.

However, after much deliberation, Deng decided not to take on Mao's assignment. When the Politburo met on November 20, Deng made an extensive self-criticism about how he lacked an understanding of the great significance of the Cultural Revolution. Thus, he reasoned, it would be inappropriate for him to preside over the process of adopting a resolution on the Cultural Revolution. "I was in the Peach Blossom Grove. I did not even know what happened in the Han Dynasty, how can I talk about what followed later during Wei and Jin times?"[75]

Deng's response deeply disappointed the chairman, as Deng had stepped on the most sensitive part of his toes. A few years before, when Mao approved Deng's political reemergence, he was moved by Deng's promise that "I will never reverse the verdict on me" in the Cultural Revolution. Mao lamented, "He has said that he will never reverse the conclusion. That does not count!"[76] Deng's second purge was now a certainty.

Learning of Deng's response, Zhou sighed, "He always acts too much in a hurry." However, could it be that Deng was actually more farsighted than Zhou on this critical matter? Deng had already said once that he would never reverse his endorsement of the Cultural Revolution. He did not want to repeat it. Otherwise, after Mao's death, if he were to stage another political reemergence, how could he face a future beyond the disastrous Cultural Revolution?

* * *

Zhou's condition worsened further as November turned to December, and he was more often comatose. But his desire to live had never been stronger. When he could eat, he would force himself to swallow even one or two more spoonfuls of food, so that he would have more energy to fight the cancer. Early on the morning of December 20, he suddenly awoke. He wanted to see

Luo Qingchang, a longtime associate of his who had been in charge of China's intelligence network and the "united front" policy toward Taiwan. According to the rules at the time, since Luo was a spymaster, this meeting had to be approved by the Politburo. When Deng received the report, he commented, "What a time is this? The Premier is so ill. Let him see anybody he wants. There is no need to ask for approval!"[77] When Luo rushed to Zhou's room, the premier murmured a few words about names related to Taiwan. Before he could go further, he again lost consciousness. Luo waited, but Zhou did not awaken.[78]

As 1976 began, Zhou was fast approaching the end of his life. He was now comatose most of the time. Early in the morning of January 5, he underwent his sixth procedure since he had been admitted to the hospital. It was useless. At eleven o'clock in the evening of January 7, Zhou regained consciousness for the last time in his life. In an extremely weak yet still clear voice, he said to Dr. Wu Jieping, "There is nothing left here. You may go to take care of Comrade Kang Sheng. He needs you more."[79]

Deng Yingchao, who had been accompanying Zhou for several days, went back to the West Flower Pavilion to sleep. That night, she received a call from the hospital: Zhou was dying. A few minutes later, she rushed to Zhou's bedside, but he had already fallen into a deep coma. No matter how persistently she, and others around her, called his name, he could not hear them.[80]

On January 8, 1976, as the clock read 9:57 A.M., Zhou Enlai passed away at the age of seventy-seven.

• • •

Deng Yingchao, now Zhou's widow, would live for another sixteen years. When Zhou was alive, she was never granted any critical party or government leadership position, although she was elected to the CCP Central Committee at three party congresses. After her husband's passing, she entered the Politburo in 1977 and became chairperson of the National Political Consultative Committee, a position Zhou had held for twenty-seven years, in 1982. In order to preserve her late husband's reputation and, probably, cover up some of the darkest episodes of his service under Mao, she demanded that all records of the 1973 "criticize Zhou" Politburo meetings be destroyed, which the party leadership accepted. She passed away in 1992, at the age of eighty-seven.

ABBREVIATIONS IN NOTES

NOTES

ACKNOWLEDGMENTS

INDEX

Abbreviations in Notes

Archives and Database

APRF	Russian Presidential Archive
AVPRF	Archive of Foreign Policy of the Russian Federation
CCA	Chinese Central Archive
CFMA	Chinese Foreign Ministry Archive
FPA	Fujian Provincial Archive
GSPA	Gansu Provincial Archive
HBPA	Hubei Provincial Archive
HPA	Hebei Provincial Archive
JLPA	Jilin Provincial Archive
JSPA	Jiangsu Provincial Archive
LBJL	Lyndon B. Johnson Presidential Library
NA	National Archive of the U.S.
NMML	Nehru Memorial and Museum Library
NSA	National Security Archive
PLAA	Chinese People's Liberation Army Archive
RGANI	Russian State Archive of Contemporary History
RGASPI	Russian State Archive of Social and Political History
SHMA	Shanghai Municipal Archive
TsAMO RF	The Central Archives of the Ministry of Defence of the Russian Federation
UKNA	United Kingdom National Archive
WWCDA	Woodrow Wilson Center Digital Archive

ZGWGWK	Song Yongyi et al., *Zhongguo wenhua dageming wenku* (Chinese Cultural Revolution database)

Other Sources

CYNP	Zhu Jiamu et al., *Chen Yun nianpu* (Chronological records of Chen Yun) (Beijing: Zhongyang wenxian, 2000)
DNP-A	Yang Shengqun and Yan Jianqi et al., *Deng Xiaoping nianpu, 1904–1974* (Chronological records of Deng Xiaoping, 1904–1974) (Beijing: Zhongyang wenxian, 2009)
DNP-B	Leng Rong and Wang Zuoling et al., *Deng Xiaoping nianpu, 1975–1997* (Chronological records of Deng Xiaoping, 1975–1997) (Beijing: Zhongyang wenxian, 2004)
DWX	*Deng Xiaoping wenxuan* (Selected Works of Deng Xiaoping) (Beijing: Renmin, 1993)
FRUS	*Foreign Relations of the United States*
GCGJZGGM	*Gongchan guoji, liangong (bu), he zhongguo geming dang'an ziliao congshu* (Series of archival materials on the Comintern, the Bolshevik Party, and the Chinese Revolution), 21 volumes (Beijing: Zhongyang wenxian, 1997–2012)
JDYLZYWX	*Jiangdang yilai zhongyao wenxian xuanbian, 1921–1949* (A collection of important documents since the founding of the CCP, 1921–1949), 26vols. (Beijing: Zhongyang wenxian, 2011)
JGYLZYWX	*Jianguo yilai zhongyao wenxian xuanbian* (Selected important documents since the PRC's founding) (Beijing: Zhongyang wenxian, 1994)
LNP	Liu Chongwen and Chen Shaoshou et al., *Liu Shaoqi nianpu, 1898–1969* (Chronological records of Liu Shaoqi, 1898–1969) (Beijing: Zhongyang wenxian, 1996)
LWG	*Jiangguo yilai Liu Shaoqi wengao* (Liu Shaoqi's manuscripts since the founding of the People's Republic) (Beijing: Zhongyang wenxian, 2005–)
MJSHDJS	Yuan Wei et al., *Mao Zedong junshi huodong jishi* (Major events in Mao Zedong's military activities) (Beijing: Jiefangjun, 1994)
MJSWG	*Jianguo yilai Mao Zedong junshi wengao* (Mao Zedong's military manuscripts since the founding of the People's Republic) (Beijing: Junshi kexue and Zhongyang wenxian, 2009)

MJSWJ	*Mao Zedong junshi wenji* (A collection of Mao Zedong's military papers), 6 vols. (Beijing: Junshi kexue and Zhongyang wenxian, 1993)
MNP-A	Pang Xianzhi et al., *Mao Zedong nianpu, 1898–1949* (Chronological records of Mao Zedong, 1898–1949)(Beijing: Zhongyang wenxian, 1993)
MNP-B	Pang Xiaozhi and Feng Hui et al., *Mao Zedong nianpu, 1949–1976* (Chronological records of Mao Zedong, 1949–1976), 6 vols. (Beijing: Zhongyang wenxian, 2013)
MWG	*Jiangguo yilai Mao Zedong wengao* (Mao Zedong's manuscripts since the founding of the PRC) (Beijing: Zhongyang wenxian, 1987–1999)
MWJ	*Mao Zedong wenji* (A collection of Mao Zedong's works), 8 vols. (Beijing: Renmin, 1993–1999)
MWJWX	*Mao Zedong waijiao wenxuan* (Selected diplomatic papers of Mao Zedong) (Beijing: Zhongyang wenxian, 1994)
MXJ	*Mao Zedong xuanji* (Selected works of Mao Zedong), 5 vols. (Beijing: Renmin, 1977)
MXZWX	*Mao Zedong Xizang gongzuo wenxuan* (Selected works on Tibet by Mao Zedong) (Beijing: Zhongyang wenxian and Zhongguo zangxue, 2001)
MZ-A	Jin Chongji et al., *Mao Zedong zhuan, 1898–1949* (A biography of Mao Zedong, 1898–1949) (Beijing: Zhongyang wenxian, 1996)
MZ-B	Pang Xiaozhi et al., *Mao Zedong zhuan, 1949–1976* (A biography of Mao Zedong, 1949–1976) (Beijing: Zhongyang wenxian, 2003)
MZWTWX	*Minzu wenti wenxian huibian* (A collection of documents on nationality issues) (Beijing: Zhongyang dangxiao, 1991)
PNP	Wang Yan et al., *Peng Zhen nianpu* (Chronological records of Peng Zhen) (Beijing: Renmin, 1998)
RMRB	*Renmin ribao* (People's daily)
WGYJZL	Party History Teaching and Research Group at National Defense University comp., *Wenhua dageming yanjiu ziliao* (Cultural Revolution research materials) (Beijing: Guofang daxue, 1988)
ZGDSJXCKZL	*Zhonggong dangshi jiaoxue cankao ziliao* (CCP history teaching reference materials) (Beijing: Guofang daxue, 1986)

ZGZYKRTYZXWX	Editorial Group, *Zhonggong zhongyang kangri minzu tongyi zhanxian wenjian xuanbian* (Selected CCP Central Committee documents on Anti-Japanese national united front during the War of Resistance against Japan) *Zhonggong Zhongyang kangri tongyi zhanxian wenjian xuanbian* (Beijing: Dang'an, 1986)
ZGZYWJXJ-A	*Zhonggong zhongyang wenjian xuanji, 1921–1949* (Selected documents of the CCP Central Committee, 1921–1949), 20 vols. (Beijing: Zhongyang dangxiao, 1991)
ZGZYWJXJ-B	*Zhonggong zhongyang wenjian xuanji, 1949–1966* (Selected documents of the CCP Central Committee, 1949–1966), 50 vols. (Beijing: Renmin, 2013)
ZGZYWXZLHB	*Zhonggong zhongyao lishi wenxian ziliao huibian* (A collection of CCP's important historical documents and materials) (Los Angeles, CA: Chinese Publication Service Center, 2006–)
ZHMGZYSL	Qin Xiaoyi chief, ed., *Zhonghua minguo zhongyao shiliao chubian* (A collection of important historical materials of the Republic of China) (Taipei: Party History Compilation Commission under Guomindang Central Committee, 1970–)
ZJSHDJS	Editorial Group, *Zhou Enlai junshi huodong jishi* (Factual records of Zhou Enlai's military activities) (Beijing: Zhongyang wenxian, 2000)
ZJSWX	*Zhou Enlai junshi wenxuan* (Selected military papers of Zhou Enlai), 4 vols. (Beijing: Zhongyang wenxian, 1997)
ZNP-A	Li Ping and Fang Ming et al., *Zhou Enlai nianpu, 1898–1949* (Chronological records of Zhou Enlai, 1898–1949, revised and expanded edition)(Beijing: Zhongyang wenxian, 2007)
ZNP-B	Li Ping and Ma Zhisun et al., *Zhou Enlai nianpu, 1949–1976* (Chronological records of Zhou Enlai, 1949–1976) (Beijing: Zhongyang wenxian, 1998)
ZSXXJ	*Zhou Enlai shuxin xuanji* (Selected correspondence of Zhou Enlai) (Beijing: Zhongyang wenxian, 1988)
ZTYZXWX	*Zhou Enlai tongyi zhanxian wenxuan* (Selected works on the united front by Zhou Enlai) (Beijing: Renmin, 1984)
ZWG	*Jianguo yilai Zhou Enlai wengao* (Zhou Enlai's manuscripts since the founding of the PRC) (Beijing: Zhongyang wenxian, 2008–)

ZWJHDDSJ	Pei Jianzhang et al., *Zhou Enlai waijiao huodong dashiji, 1949–1975* (Major events in Zhou Enlai's diplomatic activities, 1949–1975) (Beijing: Shijie zhishi, 1993)
ZWJWX	*Zhou Enlai waijiao wenxuan* (Selected diplomatic papers of Zhou Enlai) (Beijing: Zhongyang wenxian, 1990)
ZXJ	*Zhou Enlai xuanji* (Selected works of Zhou Enlai) (Beijing: Renmin, 1984)
ZYBJWTWJHB	Chinese Foreign Ministry, *Zhongguo he yindu guanyu liangguo zai zhongguo Xizang defang de guanxi wenti zhongyin bianjie wenti he qita wenti laiwang wenjian huibian, 1950nian 8 yue–1960nian 4yue* (A collection of documentary exchanges between China and India on issues concerning China's Tibet region, Chinese-Indian borders and other matters, August 1950–April 1960)
ZZ-A	Jin Chongji et al., *Zhou Enlai zhuan, 1898–1949* (A biography of Zhou Enlai, 1898–1949 (Beijing: Zhongyang wenxian, 1998)
ZZ-B	Jin Chongji et al., *Zhou Enlai zhuan, 1898–1949* (A biography of Zhou Enlai, 1898–1949) (Beijing: Zhongyang wenxian, 1998)
ZZQWJ	Liu Yan, ed., *Zhou Enlai zaoqi wenji* (A collection of Zhou Enlai's early writings) (Tianjin: Nankai daxue, 1993)

Notes

Prologue

1. Even then, many Chinese speculated that Mao's failure to attend Zhou's memorial service revealed an odd relationship between the two. Li Zhisui, Mao's doctor, recalled that "there was little reaction in Group One (Mao and his staff)" to Zhou's death, and "life continued as usual. The staff still watched movies . . . each night." Li Zhisui, *The Private Life of Chairman Mao* (New York: Random House, 1994), 609–610.

2. *Renmin ribao* (People's daily, hereafter *RMRB*), January 16, 1976, 1.

3. *Wenhui bao* (Wenhui daily), March 25, 1976.

4. For good accounts of the Nanjing Incident of 1976, see Shi Yun and Li Danhui, *Nanyi jixu de jixu geming—cong pilin dao pideng* (The continuous revolution that was difficult to continue: From criticize Lin to criticize Deng) (Hong Kong: Chinese University Press, 2008), 624–628; Roderick MacFarquhar and Michael Schoenhals, *Mao's Last Revolution* (Cambridge, MA: Harvard University Press, 2006), 423–425; Frederick C. Teiwes and Warren Sun, *The End of the Maoist Era: Chinese Politics during the Twilight of the Cultural Revolution, 1972–1976* (Armonk, NY: M. E. Sharpe, 2008), 466–488.

5. Pang Xiaozhi et al., *Mao Zedong zhuan, 1949–1976* (A biography of Mao Zedong, 1949–1976, hereafter *MZ*-B) (Beijing: Zhongyang wenxian, 2003), 1774.

6. For excellent accounts of the Tiananmen Incident of 1976, see MacFarquhar and Schoenhals, *Mao's Last Revolution*, chap. 24; and Teiwes and Sun, *End of the Maoist Era*, 463–488.

7. Tong Huaizhou, ed., *Tiananmen shichao* (The Tiananmen poems) (Beijing: Renmin wenxue, 1978), 282.

8. Pang Xiaozhi and Feng Hui et al., *Mao Zedong nianpu* (A chronological record of Mao Zedong, 1949–1976, hereafter *MNP*-B) (Beijing: Zhongyang wenxian, 2013), 6:645–646.

9. For a thoughtful and informative study on the subject, see Ezra Vogel, *Deng Xiaoping and the Transformation of China* (Cambridge, MA: Harvard University Press, 2011); see also Odd Arne Westad and Chen Jian, *The Great Transformation: China's Road from Revolution to Reform* (New Haven, CT: Yale University Press, forthcoming).

10. See, for example, Editorial Group, ed., *Jing'ai de Zhou zongli, women yongyuan huannian nin* (Our beloved premier Zhou: We will forever commemorate you) (Beijing: Renmin, 1977).

11. Han Suyin, *Eldest Son: Zhou Enlai and the Making of Modern China, 1898–1976* (New York: Kodansha America, 1994), v.

12. Frank Dikötter, *The Cultural Revolution: A People's History, 1962–1976* (London: Bloomsbury, 2016), 68.

13. See, for example, Gao Wenqian, *Wannian Zhou Enlai* (Zhou Enlai in his later years) (Hong Kong: Mingjing, 2003); Sima Qingyang and Ouyang Longdou, *Xinfaxian de Zhou Enlai* (Newly discovered Zhou Enlai) (Carle Place, NY: Mingjing, 2009).

14. Jung Chang and Jon Halliday, *Mao: The Unknown Story* (New York: Anchor Books, 2005). Chang and Halliday also paint a very negative picture of Zhou in the book. However, historians have sharply challenged their way of citing sources, and the volume has been "criticized in the academic community on the grounds of unreliability and distorted judgments." See Alexander V. Pantsov with Steven I. Levine, *Mao: The Real Story* (New York: Simon & Schuster, 2012), 5.

15. See, for example, Gao Wenqian, "The Last Days: Comrade Zhou Enlai in Hospital," *Renmin ribao* (People's daily), January 4, 1986; Gao Wenqian, "Zhou Enlai and the Three 'Leftist-Leaning' Mistakes within the CCP," in Lu Xingdou and Bai Yuntao, eds., *Zhou Enlai he ta de shiye* (Zhou Enlai and his cause) (Beijing: Zhongyang dangxiao, 1990), 30–51.

16. Andrew J. Nathan, "Introduction," in Gao Wenqian, *Zhou Enlai: The Last Perfect Revolutionary* (New York: PublicAffairs, 2007), ix–xiv.

17. Gao, *Wannian Zhou Enlai,* 10. The book, although banned in mainland China, has been hugely influential among Chinese readers, and Chinese intellectuals in particular.

18. Barbara Barnouin and Yu Changgen, *Zhou Enlai: A Political Life* (Hong Kong: Chinese University Press, 2006), 317.

1. Childhood (1898–1910)

1. The name of the city has experienced a series of changes in modern times. At the time of Zhou Enlai's birth, it was located in Shanyang County. In 1912, its name was changed from Shanyang to Huai'an and has remained so since. In order to avoid confusion, I use "Huai'an" throughout this volume.

2. Deng Yingchao, Zhou's wife, described Zhou as "a descendant of a declined mandarin-bureaucratic family." Deng, "About Comrade Zhou Enlai," submitted to the Comintern on February 22, 1940, f. 495, op. 225, d. 139, RGASPI.

3. Although Zhou Enlai was born in Huai'an, as the Zhou clan, including Enlai's grandfather, originally hailed from Shaoxing in Zhejiang Province, he always regarded Shaoxing as his *yuanji* or native place, following a long-standing Chinese tradition.

4. Li Haiwen et al., *Zhou Enlai jiashi* (Zhou Enlai's family genealogy) (Beijing: Dangjian duwu, Zhongguo qingnian, 1998), 1–6.

5. Zhou Enlai's speech at the second anniversary of Lu Xun's death in *Xinhua Ribao* (New China daily), October 20, 1938, cited from Jin Chongji et al., *Zhou Enlai zhuan, 1898–1949* (A biography of Zhou Enlai, 1898–1949, hereafter ZZ-A) (Beijing: Zhongyang wenxian, 1998), 1.

6. Li et al., *Zhou Enlai jiashi,* 142–149.

7. Ibid., 177–191.

8. Ibid., 191–196; Zhou Enlai, *Zhou Enlai zishu* (Zhou Enlai's autobiography) (Beijing: Jiefangjun wenyi, 2002), 2.

9. Ibid., 2.

10. Zhou Enlai later told the American journalist Edgar Snow that she "became my real mother when I was a baby. I did not leave her for even one day until I was ten years old, when she and my mother both passed away." Edgar Snow, *Red Star over China* (New York: Random House, 1938), 46.

11. This is a Confucian expression about the perfect way of being a "Junzi" (true gentleman). It is from one of the four books, *The Great Learning*.

12. "Comrade Zhou Enlai recalls his personal and revolutionary history: Talks with American journalist Henry R. Lieberman," *Zhonggong dangshi ziliao* (CCP history material), no. 1 (1982): 5.

13. ZZ-A, 5.

14. "Comrade Zhou Enlai Recalls," 5; Deng Yingchao, "About Comrade Zhou Enlai"; Editorial Group, ed., *Zhou zongli yu guxiang* (Premier Zhou and his hometown) (Nanjing: Jiangsu renmin, 1985), 17–18.

15. ZZ-A, 6; Li et al., *Zhou Enlai jiashi*, 272–273; Editorial Group, *Zhou zongli yu guxiang*, 19–21.

2. Manchuria to Nankai (1910–1917)

1. Li et al., *Zhou Enlai jiashi*, 273–274.

2. Ibid., 206–207; Jin Chongji et al., *Zhou Enlai zhuan, 1898–1949* (A biography of Zhou Enlai, 1898–1949, hereafter ZZ-A) (Beijing: Zhongyang wenxian, 2008), 6.

3. "Comrade Zhou Enlai recalls," 6.

4. For Zhou's own discussion of how these events damaged China's sovereignty and integrity as a student at Nankai School, see Zhou Enlai, "On how crises may help consolidate the nation and state" (winter 1915), in Liu Yan, ed., *Zhou Enlai zaoqi wenji* (A collection of Zhou Enlai's Early Writings, hereafter *ZZQWJ*) (Tianjin: Nankai daxue, 1993), 1:61–63.

5. *ZNP*-A, 1:9.

6. ZZ-A, 1:10.

7. "Comrade Zhou Enlai recalls," 6.

8. ZZ-A, 1:11; *ZNP*-A, 1:11.

9. ZZ-A, 1:13.

10. *ZZQWJ*, 1:2.

11. ZZ-A, 1:10; *ZNP*-A, 10.

12. ZZ-A, 1:14; Li et al., *Zhou Enlai Jiashi*, 211.

13. Li Dongjun, *Zhongguo sixue bainian ji: Yan Xiu xin sixue yu jindai zhongguo zhengzhi wenhua xinian* (A century of private education in China: Yan Xiu's new private education and modern Chinese political culture) (Tianjin: Nankai daxue, 2004).

14. Zheng Zhiguan et al., *Zhang Boling zhuan* (A biography of Zhang Boling) (Tianjin: Tianjin renmin, 1989).

15. Tianjin Nankai School, ed., *Zhou Enlai nankai zhongxue suiyue* (Zhou Enlai's Nankai years) (Beijing: Zhongyang wenxian, 2017), 216–217.

16. ZZ-A, 1:23; Li Aihua, "Was Zhou Enlai the Only Tuition-waived Student at Nankai?" *Dangde wenxian* (Party history documents), no. 2 (1997): 95–96.

17. Li, *Zhou Enlai nankai zhongxue suiyue*, chap. 2.

18. "Comrade Zhou Enlai recalls," 6–7; ZZ-A, 1:20.

19. Li, *Zhou Enlai nankai zhongxue suiyue*, 58.

20. Ibid., 60–61, 138–139.

21. *ZZQWJ*, 1:55–56; *Zhou Enlai nankai zhongxue suiyue*, 188–193.

22. Stephen R. MacKinnon and Oris Friesen, eds., *China Reporting: An Oral History of American Journalism in the 1930s and 1940s* (Berkeley: University of California Press, 1987), 81.

23. *ZZQWJ*, 1:21–22.

24. *ZZ-A*, 1:25.

25. Immanuel C. Y. Hsu, *The Rise of Modern China*, 5th ed. (New York: Oxford University Press, 1995), 494.

26. Wu Guozhen, *Ye Lailin: Wu Guozhen jianzheng de guogong zhengdou* (Night comes: The Guomingdang-CCP struggles as witnessed by Wu Guozhen) (Hong Kong: Zhongwen daxue, 2009), 24–25.

27. *ZZQWJ*, 1:57.

28. *ZNP-A*, 1:15; *ZZQWJ*, 1:45–48.

29. *ZZQWJ*, 1:169–172.

30. *ZNP-A*, 1:22.

31. *ZZQWJ*, 1:14, 75.

32. Li, *Zhou Enlai nankai zhongxue suiyue*, 328–332.

33. *ZNP-A*, 1:23.

3. Japan (1917–1919)

1. *ZZ-A*, 1:24; *ZNP-A*, 1:23.

2. Li Aihua, ed., *Zhou Enlai zhongxue shidai jishi changbian* (A chronological and factual record of Zhou Enlai's high school years) (Beijing: Zhongyang wenxian, 2011), 470–471.

3. Editorial Group, *Zhou Enlai qiannian shidai shixuan* (Selected poems of young Zhou Enlai) (Beijing: Renmin wenxuan, 1978). This is a retranslation on the basis of the English translation of the poem in Nancy T. Lin, *In Quest: Poems of Chou Enlai* (Hong Kong: Joint Publications, 1979), 9.

4. This was the first of the many rented places where Zhou had lived in Tokyo and other parts of Japan, such as Kyoto. For a good and thorough examination of this place, see Mayumi Itoh, *The Origins of Contemporary Sino-Japanese Relations: Zhou Enlai and Japan* (New York: Palgrave Macmillan, 2016), 43–45.

5. Deng Yingchao, in a report to the Comintern dated February 22, 1940, entitled "About Comrade Zhou Enlai," described that Zhou went to study in Japan "with the continuous support" of his relatives, teachers, and good friends (f. 495, op. 225, d. 139, RGASPI); for a good summary of the major financial support that Zhou's friends and others had pledged to him, see Itoh, *Zhou Enlai and Japan*, 201.

6. Zhou diary, January 11, 1918, in *Zhou Enlai luri riji, yingyin ben* (Zhou Enlai's Japan diaries, photocopy edition) (Beijing: Zhongyang wenxian, 1998), no page numbers, photos of diaries printed in chronological order.

7. Zhou diary, January 29, 1918.

8. Ibid., February 15, 1918.

9. In Zhou's diaries during these days, there were descriptions of him mingling with his Nankai friends almost every day.

10. Chen Duxiu, "A Letter to the Youth," *Qingnian zazhi* (The journal of the youth) 1, no. 1 (September 15, 1915): 1. The name of the journal would be changed to *Xin Qingnian* (The new youth) beginning with the next issue.

11. Zhou diary, February 15, 1918.

12. Ibid., February 15, 1918.

13. Ibid., February 9, 1918.

14. Neither in Zhou's diaries, nor in recollections of Zhou's friends or in any other sources, is there anything to indicate that he was gay. The claim that Zhou was gay is no more than an eye-catching speculation.

15. Zhou diary, February 14, 1918.

16. Ibid., February 11, 1918.

17. Ibid., February 15, 1918.

18. Ibid., February 17, 1918.

19. Ibid., February 18, 1918.

20. Ibid., February 20, 1918.

21. Ibid., February 20, 1918.

22. Ibid., February 4, 1918.

23. Ibid., March 10, 1918.

24. *ZZ-A*, 36–37.

25. Zhou diary, April 4, 1918.

26. Ibid., May 2, 1918.

27. *ZNP-A*, 1:27.

28. Zhou diary, May 10, 1918.

29. Ibid., May 19, 1918.

30. Ibid., July 4, 1918.

31. Ibid., July 5, 1918.

32. Ibid., April 23, 1918.

33. Ibid., October 20, 1918.

34. *ZZQWJ*, 1:300. This is a retranslation based on the English translation of the poem in Lin, *Poems of Chou Enlai*, 11–12.

35. *ZNP-A*, 15.

4. May Fourth Activist (1919–1920)

1. Chen Duxiu, *Duxiu wencun* (Chen Duxiu's writings) (Hefei: Anhui renmin, 1987), 388.

2. One of the best and quite thoughtful studies on this subject, in my view, remains Lin Yusheng, *Crisis of Chinese Consciousness: Radical Antitraditionalism in the May Fourth Era* (Madison: University of Wisconsin Press, 1978).

3. See, for example, Li Dazhao, "Wilson and Peace," in *Li Dazhao wenji* (A collection of Li Dazhao's writings) (Beijing: Renmin, 1984), 1:285; Tang Baolin, *Chen Duxiu quanzhuan* (A complete biography of Chen Duxiu) (Hong Kong: Chinese University Press, 2011), 113–114.

4. Gu Weijun, *Gu Weijun huiyilu* (Willington Koo's memoirs) (Beijing: Zhonghua shuju, 1982), 1:164, 170–171.

5. Chow Tse-tsung, *The May Fourth Movement: Intellectual Revolution in Modern China* (Stanford, CA: Stanford University Press, 1967), 86.

6. Xu Guoqi, *China and the Great Wars: China's Pursuit of a New National Identity and Internationalization* (New York: Cambridge University Press, 2005), 261–262.

7. See Zhou's letters to Nankai alumni in Japan, May 1919, *Zhou Enlai shuxin xuanji* (Selected Correspondence of Zhou Enlai, hereafter *ZSXXJ*), 3–4. "I now go to Nankai every day, as I love Nankai," Zhou wrote.

8. *ZZQWJ*, 302–303.

9. *ZZ-A*, 1:47–48.

10. Jin Feng, *Deng Yingchao zhuan* (A biography of Deng Yingchao) (Beijing: Renmin, 1993); for Deng's May Fourth experience, see chapter 2 of the book; for Deng's own description, see Deng Yingchao's autobiography, January 21, 1940, f. 495, op. 225, d. 139, RGASPI.

11. *ZZ-A*, 1:48.

12. *ZZQWJ*, 304–305.

13. *ZZ-A*, 50.

14. *ZNP-A*, 1:32.

15. *ZZQWJ*, 310.

16. *ZNP-A*, 1:32–33.

17. *ZZ-A*, 1:52.

18. *ZZQWJ*, 332.

19. Tianjin History Museum et al., eds., *Wusi yundong zai Tianjin: lishi ziliao xuanji* (May Fourth Movement in Tianjin: Selected historical documents) (Tianjin: Tianjin renmin, 1979), 364–365.

20. *ZZ-A*, 1:54.

21. *ZNP-A*, 1:35.

22. Ibid., 1:36.

23. Li Ping, *Zhou Enlai yisheng* (Zhou Enlai: A life) (Beijing: Zhongyang wenxian, 2001), 39.

24. Zhojian offers a detailed account about this event. See *ZZQWJ*, 1:338–340.

25. See Zhou Enlai's account in ibid., 345–347.

26. *ZNP-A*, 1:43.

27. *ZZ-A*, 1:58–59.

28. *ZNP-A*, 1:41.

29. Zhou provides a list of presentations that he and his inmates had given in prison. See *ZZQWJ*, 1:419–421.

30. Ibid., 1:474–475.

31. "Comrade Zhou Enlai recalls," 7.

32. Zhou to Chen Shizhou, January 30, 1921, *ZSXXJ*, 23–24.

5. Becoming a Communist in Europe (1920–1924)

1. Huai En, ed., *Zhou zongli qingshaonian shidai shiwen shuxin ji* (A collection of Premier Zhou's poems, essays, and letters during his youth years) (Chengdu: Sichuan renmin, 1979), 258.

2. Yan Rengeng, "Zhou Enlai and Yan Xiu," *Dangde wenxian* (Party history documents), no. 4 (1990): 86; see also Yan's own records in Yanxiu diary, February 27 and March 13, 1921, Xiao Zhanpeng and Lu Xingsu et al., *Yanxiu riji* (Yan Xiu's diaries) (Tianjin: Nankai daxue, 2003), 4:2354, 2356.

3. Zhou to Chen Shizhou, January 30, 1920, *ZSXXJ*, 24.

4. *ZNP-A*, 1:44.

5. Zhou to Yan Xiu, February 8, 1921, *ZSXXJ*, 29.

6. Xie Shuying, "Taking the Same Ship to France with Zhou Enlai," cited from Li PingPing, *Zhou Enlai yisheng*, 44; Xie Shuying, "Recalling the Past at the Age of Eighty-Seven," *Beijing wenshi ziliao xuanji* (Selected entries of Beijing literature and history materials) 36 (Beijing: Beijing, 1989).

7. *ZZQWJ*, 1:390–485; *ZNP-A*, 1:44–45.

8. Zhou to Yan Xiu, January 25, 1921, *ZSXXJ*, 17.

9. Zhou to Yan Xiu, February 8, 1921, *ZSXXJ*, 28.

10. Ibid., 28.

11. *Zhou Enlai tongzhi luou wenji, xu bian* (A collection of essays by Comrade Zhou Enlai during his time in Europe, supplementary volume) (Beijing: Wenwu, 1982), 70.

12. Zhou Enlai, "Crisis in Europe after the War," *Yishi Bao*, February 1, 1921, cited from *ZZQWJ*, 1:493–498.

13. Zhou to Yan Xiu, January 25, 1921, *ZSXXJ*, 20.

14. Zhou to Chen Shizhou, January 30, 1921, *ZSXXJ*, 23–27. Chen was a nephew of Madame Chen, Zhou's adoptive mother. He was about ten years Zhou's senior, and he had had a very close relationship with Zhou during the latter's childhood years.

15. Ibid., 23–24.

16. Zhou to Yan Xiu, February 9, 1921, *ZSXXJ*, 28.

17. Zhou to Chen Shizhou, February 23, 1921, *ZSXXJ*, 30–31. Zhou mentioned in the letter that living in Paris would "reduce expenses 60–70 percent."

18. They arrived in France on December 27, 1920, and reached Paris on New Year's Day of 1921. See *ZNP-A*, 1:45; "Zhang Shenfu's Recollection of Activities of Party and League Organizations in Europe," *Tianjin wenshi ziliao xuanji* (Selected entries of literature and history materials of Tianjin), no. 15 (May 1981): 86–87; Vera Schwarcz, *Time for Telling Truth Is Running Out: Conversations with Zhang Shenfu* (New Haven, CT: Yale University Press, 1992), 94.

19. Zhang Shenfu, "Recollections on the Circumstances before and after the Founding of the Chinese Communist Party," in *Yida Qianhou: Zhongguo gongchandang diyici daibiao dahui qianhou ziliao xuanbian* (Before and after the First Congress: Selected documents surrounding the First Congress of the Chinese Communist Party) (Beijing: Renmin, 1980); Schwarcz, *Conversations with Zhang Shenfu*, 97–99.

20. Schwarcz, *Conversations with Zhang Shenfu*, 100.

21. Schwarcz, *Conversations with Zhang Shenfu*, chap. 4; in a recollection of Zhang as the person who motivated him to join the Communist Party, Zhou also mentioned that "he wanted to fuse the ideas of Russell, Marx, Freud, and Einstein." Zhou Enlai, "On the Question of Intellectuals," *ZXJ*, 2:357.

22. "Zhang Shenfu's Recollection," 87–92.

23. *ZNP-A*, 1:48.

24. "Zhang Shenfu's Recollection," 87.

25. Zhou Enlai to Chang Ce'ou, March 25, 1922, *ZSXXJ*, 34. In the letter, Zhou, then in France, asked Chang, then in London, to subscribe to the *Times* for him.

26. *Zhou Enlai tongzhi luou wenji*, 71.

27. Ibid., 5–21.

28. Ibid., 109–111; *ZNP-A*, 1:49.

29. *Zhou Enlai tongzhi luou wenji*, 133–153; *ZNP-A*, 1:50–51.

30. *Zhou Enlai tongzhi luou wenji*, 5–21, 83–85, 109–111, 133–153.

31. *ZNP-A*, 1:51.

32. For a good discussion of Zhou's gradual conversion to Marxism, see Marilyn A. Levine, *The Found Generation: Chinese Communists in Europe during the Twenties* (Seattle: University of Washington Press, 1993), 147–149. Levine's study about why and how the generation of Zhou and his comrades became active and committed Communists in Europe, in my view, remains the best on the subject that any scholar has written.

33. Zhou to Chen Xiaocen and Li Yitao, March 1922, *ZSXXJ,* 35–41.
34. Zhou to Li Xijing and Zheng Jiqing, March 1922, *ZSXXJ,* 48.
35. Ibid., 46–48.
36. *ZZ-A,* 1:81–82.
37. *ZNP-A,* 1:60.
38. *ZZ-A,* 1:82.
39. *ZNP-A,* 1:61.
40. *ZSXXJ,* 49. The translation is a revised version of the one in Lin, *Poems of Zhou Enlai,* 27–28.
41. *ZNP-A,* 1:57–58; Wu Dianyao et al., *Zhu De nianpu* (A chronological record of Zhu De), rev. ed. (Beijing: Zhongyang wenxian, 2006), 1:59.
42. *ZNP-A,* 1:61.
43. *ZZ-A,* 1:87.
44. Wu Hao, "Religious Spirit and Communism," August 1922, *ZZQWJ,* 2:85.
45. Alexander V. Pantsov and Steven I. Levine, *Deng Xiaoping: A Revolutionary Life* (New York: Oxford University Press, 2015), 31–33; Richard Evans, *Deng and the Making of Modern China* (New York: Penguin Books, 1995), 19; Yang Shengqun et al., *Deng Xiaoping zhuan, 1904–1974* (A biography of Deng Xiaoping, 1904–1974) (Beijing: Zhongyang wenxian, 2014), 1:47; *Tianjin wenshi ziliao,* 15:117.
46. Deng Xiaoping's autobiography (in Chinese), January 1926, f. 530, op. 2, d. 5, RGASPI; see also Pantsov and Levine, *Deng Xiaoping: A Revolutionary Life,* chap. 1; *DNP-A,* 1:17–18.
47. *ZZ-A,* 84.
48. In his diary on November 8, 1921, Yan Xiu recorded that he sent 720 yuan (about 100 British Pounds) to Zhou for subsidizing his tuition for the next year. *Yan Xiu riji,* 4:2404.
49. Han, *Eldest Son,* 52–53, 422.
50. "Zhang Shenfu's Recollection," 87.
51. Ibid., 84.
52. "The CCP's Attitudes toward the Current Situation," June 1922, *Zhonggong zhongyang wenjian xuanji* 1 (1989): 45–46. The best accounts about how the CCP leadership, with the urging and support of the Comintern, established an alliance with the Guomindang remain Tony Saich, *The Origins of the First United Front in China: The Role of Sneevliet (Alias Maring),* 2 vols. (Leiden: Brill, 1991); and Hans J. van de Ven, *From Friends to Comrades: The Founding of the Chinese Communist Party, 1920–1927* (Berkeley: University of California Press, 2012).
53. *ZZ-A,* 1:89.
54. *ZZ-A,* 1:90.
55. Ibid., 90.
56. Li, *Zhou Enlai yisheng,* 60; *ZNP-A,* 1:61–63.
57. Li, *Zhou Enlai yisheng,* 60.
58. *ZZQWJ,* 1:347–350.
59. Zhou Bingde, *Wo de bofu Zhou Enlai* (My uncle Zhou Enlai) (Shenyan: Liaoning renmin, 2000), 168–169; *ZZ-A,* 1:96.
60. Huang Yanli, ed., *Zhang Ruoming yan jiu ji ziliao jiji* (A collection of researches and research materials about Zhang Ruoming) (Hong Kong: Asian Studies Center of the University of Hong Kong, 1997), 54–55.
61. Zhou Enlai's talk with his niece Zhou Bingde, 1956, cited from *ZZ-A,* 1:96.
62. Deng Yingchao, "Remembering the Life at the West Flower Hall," *RMRB,* March 5, 1997. See also *ZZ-A,* 97.
63. *ZZ-A,* 97–98.

6. Into Storms of the Great Revolution (1924–1927)

1. For two excellent recent studies on the Opium War and its impact upon modern China, see Mao Haijian, *The Qing Empire and the Opium War: The Collapse of the Heavenly Dynasty* (Cambridge, UK: Cambridge University Press, 2016); Julia Lovell, *The Opium War: Drugs, Dreams, and the Making of Modern China* (New York: The Overlook Press, 2014).

2. Hans J. van de Ven, *War and Nationalism in China, 1925–1945* (London: Routledge Curzon, 2003), chaps. 2–3; See also Arthur Waldron, *From War to Nationalism: China's Turning Point, 1924–1925* (New York: Cambridge University Press, 2003).

3. Every top CCP leader and those with close connections with the Comintern and Moscow were given an alias.

4. Both Mao and Zhou recalled that they first met in Guangzhou. In July 1973, Mao and Zhou met with Yang Zhenning (Chen-Ning Yang), a Nobel laureate in physics. Yang asked, "Premier Zhou, when did you begin to know Chairman Mao?" Zhou replied, "I first met him in 1925." Mao and Zhou's meeting with Yang Zhenning, July 17, 1973, CCA.

5. In addition to the Mao biographies by Chang and Halliday, and by Pantsov and Levine, cited in this book's Prologue, there are two others that I would like to mention here: Philip Short, *Mao: The Man Who Made the World*, rev. ed. (London: I. B. Tauris, 2017); Jonathan D. Spence, *Mao Zedong: A Life* (New York: Penguin Books, 2006).

6. Zhou Enlai to Chinese Socialist Youth League Central Committee, September 1, 1924, *ZSXXJ*, 69.

7. *ZNP-A*, 1:70.

8. Ibid., 1:70.

9. "Zhang Shenfu's Recollection of Activities of Party and League Organizations in Europe," 88.

10. *ZNP-A*, 1:70.

11. Cheng Shuwei and Zheng Ruifeng, *Zhou Enlai yu Huangpu junxiao* (Zhou Enlai and Whampoa Military Academy) (Beijing: Zhongyang wenxian, 2014), 16–17.

12. Wang Yichang, "Zhou Enlai and the Whampoa Military Academy's Department of Political Affairs," in *Huangpu junxiao shiliao, 1924–1927* (Historical materials of the Whampoa Military Academy), ed. Guangdong Museum of Revolutionary History (Guangzhou: Guangdong renmin, 1985), 181; Li Ping and Peng Hong, *Zhou Enlai junshi shengya* (Zhou Enlai's military career) (Beijing: Huawen, 1999), 12.

13. Zhou Enlai, "Our Party's Relations with Guomindang in 1924–1926," *ZXJ*, 1:116; Bao Huisheng, *Bao Huisheng huiyi lu* (Bao Huisheng's memoir) (Beijing: Renmin, 1983), 156.

14. About Chiang's life and career, see two outstanding biographies: Jay Taylor, *The Generalissimo: Chiang Kai-shek and the Struggle for Modern China* (Cambridge, MA: Harvard University Press, 2009); Alexander Pantsov, *Victorious in Defeat: The Life and Times of Chiang Kai-shek, 1887–1975* (New Haven, CT: Yale University Press, 2022).

15. *ZNP-A*, 1:78.

16. Taylor, *Struggle for Modern China*, 45.

17. For an informative study on the subject, see C. Martin Wilbur, *Sun Yat-Sen, Frustrated Patriot* (New York: Columbia University Press, 1976), especially chaps. 5–7.

18. Zhang Guotao, *Wo de huiyi* (My recollections) (Beijing: Dongfang, 1992, for internal circulation only), 2:5; Chang Kuo-t'ao (Zhang Guotao), *The Rise of the Chinese Communist Party, 1928–1938* (Lawrence: University Press of Kansas, 1972), 1:451.

19. Sophie Quinn-Judge, *Ho Chi Minh: The Missing Years* (Singapore: Horizon Books, 2003), 98; see also Huang Zheng, *Hu Zhiming yu zhongguo* (Ho Chi Minh and China) (Beijing: Jiefangjun, 1987), 26–27.

20. Cheng and Zheng, *Zhou Enlai yu huangpu junxiao,* chap. 5.

21. Jin Feng, *Deng Yingchao zhuan* (A biography of Deng Yingchao) (Beijing: Renmin, 1993), 80–81.

22. Han, *Eldest Son,* 58. In the English edition of Han's book, however, it is not mentioned that the number of letters Zhou wrote to Deng reached more than 250. In the book's Chinese version, which was prepared with "extensive help" by CCP scholars, the number is given. See Han Suyin, *Zhou Enlai he ta de shiji* (Zhou Enlai and his century) (Beijing: Zhongyang wenxian, 1992), 66.

23. Barnouin and Yu Changgen, *Zhou Enlai: A Political Life,* 33.

24. Jin, *Deng Yingchao zhuan,* 1:93–94.

25. Zhao Wei, *Xihuating suiyue* (My years at West Flower Pavilion) (Beijing: shehui kexue wenxian, 2009), 145–146; Gao, *Zhou Enlai,* 47.

26. After Mao's death, Deng Yingchao requested that all documentary materials about the Politburo's enlarged meeting in November 1973, the main theme of which was "criticize Zhou," as well as documents concerning Zhou's involvement in the Central Office on Special Cases (which Zhou headed), be destroyed.

27. Zhou, *Wo de bofu Zhou Enlai,* 172–176.

28. *ZNP*-A, 1:81.

29. *ZZ*-A, 1:84–85.

30. *ZNP*-A, 1:85.

31. *ZZ*-A, 1:128–129.

32. Ibid., 130.

33. Zhou Enlai, "The Party's Relations with the Guomindang, 1924–1926," spring 1944, *ZXJ,* 1:118.

34. Ibid., 119.

35. Chiang Kai-shek diary, March 19, 1926, Hoover Institute Library, Stanford, CA (hereafter Chiang diary; unless identified otherwise, Hoover Institute Library is the source).

36. Chiang diary, March 19, 1926.

37. "Rogachev's Written Report on the March 20, 1926 Incident in Guangzhou" (April 28, 1926), *Gongchan guoji, liangong (bu), he zhongguo geming dang'an ziliao congshu* (Series of archival materials on the Comintern, the Bolshevik Party and the Chinese Revolution, hereafter *GCGJZGGM*), 21 volumes (Beijing: Zhongyang wenxian, 1997–2012), 3:233. For a detailed discussion of actions that Chiang took from the night of March 19 to March 20, see Yang Tianshi, "The Mysterious Zhongshan Gunboat Incident," *Lishi yanjiu* (Historical research), no. 2 (1988): 122–123.

38. *ZXJ,* 1:120. See also Bao Huisheng, *Bao Huiseng huiyi lu* (Bao Huisheng's memoir) (Beijing: Renmin, 1983), 210–211. Bao was Zhou's successor as Whampoa's director of political affairs and had a very close working relationship with both Chiang and Zhou.

39. Yang Tianshi, "Mysterious Gunboat Zhongshan Incident," 119–122. In this study, Yang further identified Ouyang Zhong, a right-wing Guomindang officer working at the Bureau of the Navy, who played a "key role" in giving the order in Chiang's name to move the Gunboat Zhongshan, prompting misunderstanding between various parties involved in the incident(120–121).

40. Van de Ven, *War and Nationalism in China,* 97–100; Yang, "Mysterious Zhongshan Gunboat Incident," 116–118; Yang Kuisong, *Zhongjian didai de geming: guoji da Beijing xia kan zhonggong chenggong zhidao* (Revolution in the intermediate zone: Understanding the CCP's path toward success in the light of the international background) (Taiyuan: Shanxi renmin, 2010), 112.

41. Yang, "Mysterious Zhongshan Gunboat Incident," 124.

42. *ZZ*-A, 132–133; *ZNP*-A, 1:94.

43. Zhou's presentation at a CCP politburo meeting, November 27, 1943, cited from Gao, *Wannian Zhou Enlai,* 18–19.

44. Chiang diary, March 21, 1926.

45. Yang Tianshi, "Three Issues Related to the Zhongshang Gunboat Incident," *Bainianchao* (Hundred-year tide), no. 2 (1997): 73–74.

46. Yang, *Zhongjian didai de geming,* 115.

47. The Second Historical Archive, ed., *Zhongguo guomindang diyi, dierci quanguo daibiao dahui shiliao* (Documentary materials of the Chinese Nationalist Party's first and second national congresses) (Nanjing: Jiangsu guji, 1986), 2:712–716.

48. Yang Tianshi, "After the Zhongshan Gunboat Incident," *Lishi yanjiu* (Historical research), no. 5 (1992): 22–25.

49. Yang, *Zhongjian didai de geming,* 115–116.

50. Liu Wusheng and Du Hongqi et al., *Zhou Enlai junshi huodong jishi* (Records of Zhou Enlai's military activities) (Beijing: Zhongyang wenxian, 2000), 1:35.

51. *ZNP-A,* 1:94.

52. Ibid., 98.

53. *ZZ-A,* 1:145.

54. Minutes of Zhou's speech, March 19, 1927, *Shanghai gongren sanci wuzhuang qiyi* (The armed uprisings of Shanghai's workers) (Shanghai: Shanghai renmin, 1983), 335–336.

55. Minutes of Zhou's speech at the meeting of the Special Committee, March 30, 1927, *Shanghai gongren sanci wuzhuang qiyi,* 436.

56. Taylor, *Struggle for Modern China,* 65–66; Pantsov, *Victorious in Defeat,* 139–140.

57. *ZZ-A,* 1:158–159.

58. Minutes of Zhou's speech, December 22, 1957, cited from *ZZ-A,* 1:160.

59. *ZZ-A,* 1:160–161.

60. Minutes of Zhou's speech at the Special Committee, April 19, 1927, *Shanghai gongren sanci wuzhuang qiyi,* 458.

61. *ZXJ,* 1:6–7.

62. *ZZ-A,* 1:164–165.

63. Ibid., 165.

64. *ZNP-A,* 1:116–117.

65. Comintern Central Executive Committee to CCP Central Committee, May 1927, *GCGJZGGM,* 5:446–447.

66. Yang Kuisong, *Guomindang de liangong yu fangong* (Guomindang: Unity with Communists and anti-Communism) (Beijing: Shehui kexue wenxian, 2008), 222–228.

67. *ZNP-A,* 1:121.

68. Ibid., 1:119.

69. *ZZ-A,* 1:174.

70. Ye Ting, "From Nanchang Uprising to Chaoshan Defeat," in Xiao Ke et al., *Nanchang qiyi* (The Nanchang Uprising) (Beijing: Renmin, 1979).

71. Li Lisan, "On Processes and Lessons of the August 1 Revolution," October 1927, *Zhonggong zhongyang wenjian xuanji* (Selected documents of CCP Central Committee) (Beijing: Zhongyang dangxiao, 1988), 3:408–411; *ZZ-A,* 1:185–187.

72. *ZZ-A,* 1:189; *Nie Rongzhen huiyilu* (Nie Rongzhen's memoirs) (Beijing: Jiefangjun, 1983), 74.

73. *ZNP-A,* 1:129.

7. Shanghai Underground (1927–1931)

1. An excellent summary of the emergence and demise of Shanghai as a "revolutionary center" in the late 1920s and early 1930s is offered in Tony Saich, *From Rebel to Ruler: One Hundred Years of the Chinese Communist Party* (Cambridge, MA: Harvard University Press, 2022), 83–84.

2. *JDYLZYWX,* 4:616–633; *ZNP-A,* 1:127–130; *MNP-A,* 1:224.

3. ZZ-A, 1:266, 285–286.

4. Frederik Wakeman, *Policing Shanghai, 1927–1937* (Berkeley: University of California Press, 1995), chaps. 1–3.

5. Liang Kan, "The *Te Ke* in Shanghai: A Study of the Chinese Communist Secret Service, 1927–1934," *Chinese Historians* 6, no. 2 (Fall 1993): 27–44; Mu Xin, *Yinbi zhangxian tongshuai Zhou Enlai* (Zhou Enlai, commander of the secret front, hereafter *Yinbi zhangxian*) (Beijing: Zhongguo qingnian, 2013), chap. 1; about Gu, see Liu Yugang, *Gu Shunzhang: zhonggong lish shang zui weixian de pantu* (Gu Shunzhang: The most dangerous traitor in CCP history) (Beijing: Dangdai zhongguo, 2014).

6. Liang, "*Te Ke* in Shanghai," 30–33; Liu, *Gu Shunzhang,* chap. 4.

7. *ZNP-A,* 1:150.

8. *ZZ-A,* 1:197.

9. Deng Yinchao, "An Experience of Meeting a Mishap and Getting Out of It," in *Bujin de sinian* (Endless memory) (Beijing: Zhongyang wenxian, 1987), 46–47.

10. See Stephen Kotkin, *Stalin: Paradoxes of Power, 1878–1928* (New York: Penguin, 2014), 627–633, 640, 655.

11. Zhou's note on a meeting by Stalin and Qu Qiubai and other CCP leaders (in Chinese), June 9, 1928, *GCGJZGGM,* 7:477–482; *Dangde wenxian* (Party history documents), 1988, 1:3–6.

12. *ZZ-A,* 1:184–185.

13. Yang, *Zhongjian didai de geming,* 192.

14. Nikolai Bukharin, "The Current Situation of the Revolution and Our Tasks," June 29, 1928, *Dangde wenxian,* 1988, 1:19–25; see also Yang, *Zhongjian didai de geming,* 193–194.

15. *ZNP-A,* 1:145.

16. Qu Qiubai's political report at CCP's Sixth Congress, June 28, 1928, *JDYLZYWX,* 5:329–334.

17. *ZZ-A,* 1:185–187; *ZNP-A,* 1:146.

18. Zhou Enlai, "Report on Personnel Matters at the Sixth Congress," June 30, 1928, *JDYLZYWX,* 5:335–352.

19. Zhou Enlai, "Main Tasks in Military Work after the Sixth Congress," July 3, 1928, *JDYLZYWX,* 5:353–362 (quote is from 362); *GCGJZGGM,* 7:501–503.

20. *ZZ-A,* 1:144.

21. *Zhou Enlai xuanji* (Selected works of Zhou Enlai, hereafter *ZXJ*) (Beijing: Renmin, 1984), 1:157–187.

22. *ZZ-A,* 1:144.

23. *ZZ-A,* 1:192–193.

24. Luo Qingchang recollection, June 26, 1997, cited from *Zhonggong dangshi yanjiu* (CCP history study), no. 1 (1998): 68.

25. *ZNP-A,* 1:151.

26. About the "three outstanding heroes," see Mu, *Yinbi zhangxian tongshuai Zhou Enlai,* chap. 5.

27. Ibid., 77–88.

28. Wakeman, *Policing Shanghai,* 139–142.

29. Mu, *Yinbi zhangxian tongshuai Zhou Enlai,* 154–166.

30. Editorial Group, ed., *Peng Bai zhuan* (A biography of Peng Bai) (Beijing: Beijing, 1984).
31. Pantsov with Levine, *Mao: The Real Story,* 223.
32. *ZZ-A,* 1:210.
33. CCP CC to Mao and Zhu, February 7, 1929, *JDYLZYWX,* 6:31–38.
34. CCP CC to Runzhi (Mao Zedong), April 7, 1929, *JDYLZYWX,* 6:125–139.
35. CCP Red Fourth Army Committee to CCP CC, April 5, 1929, *JDYLZYWX,* 6:116–123 (quote is from 116–117).
36. *ZNP-A,* 1:164; *MNP-A,* 1:276.
37. *MNP-A,* 1:278–279.
38. Ibid., 281.
39. *ZZ-A,* 1:212.
40. Ibid., 213.
41. Liu Shufa et al., *Chen Yi nianpu* (A chronological record of Chen Yi) (Beijing: Renmin, 1995), 1:137.
42. CCP CC's Instruction to the Red Fourth Army Frontal Committee, September 28, 1929, *ZXJ,* 1:29–42 (citation at 32).
43. Mao to CCP CC, November 28, 1929, *MJSWJ,* 1:84; *MZ-A,* 209.
44. *MJSWX,* 1:86–125; see *MNP-A,* 1:290–291.
45. *ZNP-A,* 1:184; Huang Shaoqun, *Zhou Enlai zai 1927–1935 nian* (Zhou Enlai in 1927–1935) (Beijing: Zhongyang wenxian, 2006), 83.
46. *ZNP-A,* 180.
47. In CCP documents, they were called "Polish Barbarian" and "German Barbarian," demonstrating a sense of contempt on the part of CCP leaders for these "foreign comrades."
48. *ZZ-A,* 1:232–233.
49. Ibid., 233.
50. Ibid., 233.
51. Zhang Ying, *Zouzai xihuating de xiaolu shang* (Walking on the trails of the West Flower Pavilion) (Beijing: Shehui kexue wenxian, 2014), 1–2; *ZNP-B,* 3:538.
52. *ZNP-A,* 1:184.
53. Zhou Enlai's introduction to the CCP Center's contradiction with the Comintern Far Eastern Bureau, May 3, 1930, f. 514, op. 1, d. 1121, RGASPI.
54. Zhou's report on meeting with Stalin to the CCP Politburo, August 22, 1930, cited from Yang, *Zhongjian didai de geming,* 226. See also *ZNP-A,* 1:189; *ZZ-A,* 1:237; Zhou's recollection at the Beidaihe Conference, July 14–18, 1960, 855-5-1798, HPA.
55. Comrade Su (Zhou Enlai) presentation at the Sixteenth Congress of the Bolshevik Party, July 15, 1930, *GCGJZGGM,* 12:203–208; *ZNP-A,* 1:187.
56. Comintern Executive Committee's resolution on the China question, July 23, 1930, *GCGJZGGM,* 12:209–211.
57. Yang Kuisong, "A Study of Comintern's Financial Support to the CCP," pt. 1, *Dangshi yanjiu ziliao* (Party history research materials), no. 1 (2004): 1–18.
58. Yang Kuisong, "A Study of Comintern's Financial Support to the CCP," pt. 2, *Dangshi yanjiu ziliao,* no. 2 (2004): 20–21.
59. *ZZ-A,* 1:247.
60. *JDYLZYWX,* 7:183–201.
61. CCP Politburo's resolution on the current situation, June 11, 1930; CCP Center's letter to Comintern Presidium, June 12, 1930, *GCGJZGGM,* 9:257–273, 202–203.

62. FEB's letter to CCP Politburo, June 20, 1930, *GCGJZGGM,* 9:177–182.

63. CCP Politburo's report to Comintern Presidium, August 5, 1930, *GCGJZGGM,* 9:227–229.

64. FEB's telegram to Comintern Presidium, August 7, 1930, *GCGJZGGM,* 9:255–256.

65. *ZNP*-A, 1:189.

66. Ibid.

67. CCP CC to Executive Committee of Comintern Presidium, August 25, 1930, *GCGJZGGM,* 9:333–334; *ZNP*-A, 1:192–193.

68. (Zhou) Enlai, "A Report Relaying the Comintern's Resolution," September 24, 1930, *JDYLZYWX,* 7:405–428.

69. Te Sheng (Xiang Zhongfa), "Work Report of the Politburo," September 1930, *ZGZYWJXJ*-A, 6:351–358.

70. *ZZ*-A, 1:245.

71. Ibid., 245.

72. Comintern Executive Committee's letter to CCP CC, October 1930 (received on November 16, 1930), *Zhonggong Zhongyang wenjian xuanji, 1921–1949* (Selected documents of the CCP Central Committee, 1921–1949, hereafter *ZGZYWJXJ*-A) (Beijing: Zhongyang dangxiao, 1991), 6:644–655.

73. Zhou's speech at the Beidaihe Conference, July 14–18, 1960, 855-5-1798, HPA.

74. *JDYLZYWX,* 7:405.

75. Zhou Enlai, "Personal Understanding Our Party's Six Line Struggles during the New Democracy Phase of the Revolution" (outline), June 10, 1972, cited from *ZZ*-A, 1:285.

76. "Conclusion of the Representative of the Comintern at the Fourth Plenary Session," *ZGZYWJXJ*-A, 7:28.

77. *ZZ*-A, 1:255.

78. Yang, *Zhongjian didai de geming,* 249.

79. Cai Mengjian, "A Tale that Could Have Changed China's Modern History," *Zhuanji wenxuan* (Biographical literature, Taipei) 37, no. 5 (November 1980): 39–48.

80. Ibid.

81. Mu, *Yinbi zhangxian tongshuai Zhou Enlai,* 358–359.

82. Ibid., 360–361; *ZZ*-A, 1:291–292.

83. Wu Ji'min, *Shengxi bosha: Zhou Enlai yu Gu Shunzhang* (Life and death fight: Zhou Enlai and Gu Shunzhang) (Beijing: Zuojia, 1993); Liu, *Gu Shunzhang.*

84. Chen Yangshan recollection, oral history transcript in author's possession.

85. Yang, *Zhongjian didai de geming,* 258.

86. Yang Kuisong, "What Kind of General Secretary Is Xiang Zhongfa," *Jindaishi yanjiu* (Modern history study), no. 1 (1994).

87. Wakeman, *Policing Shanghai,* 147–151; Yang Kuisong, "The Noulens Incident and the Comintern's Secret Network in China," *Minguo renwu guoyanlu* (A study of Republican historical figures) (Chengdu: Sichuan renmin, 2013), 77–99.

88. *ZZ*-A, 1:293.

89. Zhang Wenqiu, *Mao Zedong de qingjia Zhang Wenqiu huiyilu* (Mao Zedong's in-law Zhang Wenqiu's memoir) (Guangzhou: Guangdong jiaoyu, 2002), 135–136.

90. Resolution 152, Political Secretariat of Comintern Executive Committee, July 3, 1931, *GCGJZGGM,* 10:340.

91. *ZNP*-A, 1:222; *ZZ*-A, 1:306.

92. Zeng Xianxin, *Wuhao Shijian shimo* (A complete account of the Wuhao Incident) (Beijing: Zhongyang wenxian, 2011).

8. Jiangxi Countryside (1931–1934)

1. Huang Ping, *Wangshi huiyi* (Remembering the past experience) (Beijing: Renmin, 1981), 79–80.

2. *ZNP*-A, 1:219.

3. Wu Hao (Zhou) to CCP Center, December 25, 1931, cited from *ZZ*-A, 1:297.

4. Gao Hua, "A Historical Examination of the Cleansing the AB-Clique Incident," *Lishi biji* (Notes on history) (Hong Kong: Oxford University Press, 2014), 103–123; see also Stephen C. Averill, "The Origins of the Futian Incident," in *New Perspectives on the Chinese Revolution,* ed. Tony Saich and Hans J. van de Ven (New York: Routledge, 1995), 79–115; Chen Yung-fa, "The Futian Incident and the Anti-Bolshevik League: The 'Terror' in the CCP Revolution," *Republican China* 19, no. 2 (April 1994): 1–54.

5. CCP General Frontal Committee to Jiangxi Provincial Committee, December 3, 1930, cited from Dai Xiangqing et al., *AB tuan yu futian shijian shimo* (The AB Clique and the Futian Incident) (Zhengzhou: Henan renmin, 1996), 98.

6. In June 1930, Mao's Red Fourth Army, by merging with two other Red Army units, was renamed First Frontal Army.

7. Dai et al., *AB tuan,* 113–126.

8. Circular No. 2 by Soviet Area Bureau, Resolution on the Futian Incident, January 16, 1931, *Zhonggong dangshi jiaoxue cankao ziliao* (CCP history teaching reference material) (Beijing Guofang daxue, 1986), 14:639–642.

9. *ZNP*-A, 1:207–208.

10. CCP Politburo Resolution on the Futian Incident, March 28, 1931, *JDYLZYWX,* 8:317–322.

11. Gao Hua, *Hong taiyan shi zenyang shengqi de* (How the Red Sun rose) (Hong Kong: Chinese University Press, 2003), 30.

12. Li Zhiying, *Bo Gu zhuan* (A biography of Bo Gu) (Beijing: Dangdai Zhongguo, 1994), 93–96; *MNP*-A, 1:356.

13. This was exactly how Zhou would label himself in his "self-criticism" during the Yan'an Rectification Movement.

14. Zhang Xuexin et al., *Ren Bishi zhuan* (A biography of Ren Bishi), rev. ed. (Beijing: Zhongyang wenxian, 2000), 263–264.

15. CCP CC's instruction to CCP Soviet Area Bureau and Red Army Frontal Committee, August 30, 1931, *ZGZYWJXJ*-A, 7:355–375. In 1989, the authoritative *Zhou Enlai nianpu* and *Zhou Enlai zhuan* confirmed that Zhou was the letter's author (*ZNP*-A, 1:216, *ZZ*-A, 1:293–294). In the past two decades, however, many publications in Mainland China have mentioned that the letter was a product of the Provisional Central Committee, omitting the fact that Zhou was its author.

16. Yang Ruiguang et al., *Ren Bishi nianpu* (A chronological record of Ren Bishi) (Beijing: Zhongyang wenxian, 1993), 173; *MNP*-A, 1:357.

17. *MNP*-A, 1:358.

18. Telegram No. 4, CC to Soviet Area Bureau, ca. October 20, 1931; Yang et al., *Ren Bishi nianpu,* 174–175; *JDYLZYWX,* 8:606–607.

19. Zhang et al., *Ren Bishi zhuan,* 270–272; Yang et al., *Ren Bishi nianpu,* 176; *MZ*-A, 272.

20. *MNP*-A, 1:357–358.

21. *JDYLZYWX,* 8:641–646.

22. *MZ*-A, 273.

23. CCP Provisional CC to SAB, late October 1931, cited from *MNP*-A, 1:358.

24. Zhou to CCP Politburo, December 18, 1931, *ZSXXJ*, 76–77.

25. SAB's Resolution on Suppression of Reactionaries in the Soviet Area, January 7, 1932, *ZGZY-WJXJ*-A, 8:18–28.

26. Gao, *Wannian Zhou Enlai*, 78.

27. Zhou, "Personal Understanding of Our Party's Six Line Struggles during the Phase of New Democracy Revolution," June 10, 1972, CCA.

28. CCP CC's resolution on pursuing victory first in one or a few provinces, January 9, 1932, *JDYL-ZYWX*, 9:34–44.

29. *ZNP*-A, 1:220–221.

30. *ZZ*-A, 1:273.

31. *MZ*-A, 283.

32. Ibid., 283–284.

33. *ZNP*-A, 1:222; *MNP*-A, 1:368.

34. *MNP*-A, 1:368; *ZNP-A*, 1:222–223.

35. Mao to Zhou, March 30, 1932, *Mao Zedong junshi wenji* (A collection of Mao Zedong's military papers) (Beijing: Junshi kexue and Zhongyang wenxian, 1993, hereafter cited as *MJSWJ*), 1:263.

36. *ZNP*-A, 1:223.

37. *MZ*-A, 290; *JDYLZYWX*, 9:235–252.

38. Mao to SAB, May 3, 1932, *MJSWJ*, 1:271–272.

39. *ZNP*-A, 1:224.

40. *ZGZYWJXJ*-A, 8:209–219.

41. *MZ*-A, 292.

42. Mao, "Rebutting the Third Left-Leaning Line," ca. first half of 1941, CCA; see also *MZ*-A, 294; Zhang et al., *Ren Bishi zhuan*, 1:287.

43. Zhou, Mao, Zhu De, and Wang Jiaxiang to SAB, July 25, 1932, *ZJSWX*, 1:153; *JDYLZYWX*, 9:394.

44. Zhou to SAB, July 29, 1932, *ZJSWX*, 1:159.

45. *MNP*-A, 1:380.

46. Ibid., 384–385.

47. Zhang et al., *Ren Bishi zhuan*, 297.

48. Zhou, Mao, Zhu De, and Wang Jiaxiang to SAB, September 23, 1932, *ZJSWX*, 1:183–184.

49. SAB to Zhou, Mao et al., September 25, 1932, cited from Zhang et al., *Ren Bishi zhuan*, 1:297; see also *ZJSWX*, 1:190–191, note 1.

50. Zhou, Mao, Zhu, and Wang to SAB, September 25, 1932, *ZJSWX*, 1:189–190.

51. Zhang et al., *Ren Bishi zhuan*, 1:298; Yang et al., *Ren Bishi nianpu*, 192.

52. Zhang et al., *Ren Bishi zhuan*, 1:299.

53. Accounts and Explanation of the Ningdu Conference by Ren Bishi, Xiang Ying, Gu Zuolin, and Deng Fa, November 12, 1932, cited from *Ren Bishi zhuan*, 300.

54. Decades later, Mao commented when recalling the situation of the time, "Well, at the very least, my head had not been chopped off." So it was at least possible that Mao could have been killed if the matter were pursued to the extreme. See minutes of conversation between Chairman Mao and the Indonesian Communist Party delegation led by Aidit, August 5, 1965, CCA.

55. Zhou's speech at Beidaihe Conference, July 14–18, 1960, 855-5-1798, HPA.

56. *ZNP*-A, 1:235–236.

57. *ZZ*-A, 1:316.

58. Accounts of the disputes at the Ningdu Conference, by Ren, Xiang, Gu, and Deng Fa, November 12, 1932, Zhang et al., *Ren Bishi zhuan,* 301.

59. *ZNP*-A, 1:237–238.

60. Ibid., 1:238.

61. Zhou, "Personal Understanding," June 10, 1972, CCA.

62. *JDYLZYWX,* 9:555–557; *ZZ*-A, 1:316.

63. Mao's conversation with Aidit, August 5, 1965, CCA; see also *MNP*-B, 5:518.

64. Zhou to SAB and CCP CC, January 26, 1933; Zhou to SAB and convey to CCP CC, January 30, 1933, *ZJSWX,* 1:239–240, 244–245.

65. Zhou to SAB and convey to CCP CC, February 7, 1933, *ZJSWX,* 1:250–251.

66. Zhou to SAB and convey to CCP CC, February 13, 1933, *ZJSWX,* 1:258–259.

67. Huang Daoxuan, *Zhangli he xianjie: Zhongyang suqu de geming* (Tension and limits: revolution in Central Soviet Areas) (Beijing: Shehui wenxian, 2011).

68. *ZJSHDJS,* 1:203; *ZZ*-A, 1:336.

69. Zhou and Zhu to Bo Gu, Xiang Ying, and Braun, November 14, 1933, *ZJSWX,* 1:315; *ZJSHDJS,* 1:198–199.

70. Political Secretariat of Comintern Executive Committee to CCP CC, January 2, 1934, *GCGJZGGM,* 14:7–8.

9. The Long March (1934–1935)

1. Wu Xiuqua, *Huiyi yu huainian* (Recollection and reflection) (Beijing: Zhonggong zhongyang dangxiao, 1991), 113–114.

2. According to Zhou's recollection during the Rectification Movement in Yan'an, in making decisions on who might leave or stay behind, Bo Gu and Braun sought for Zhou's input. *ZZ*-A, 1:307.

3. The Political Committee of the Secretariat of Comintern Executive Committee to Arthur Ewert and CCP CC, June 16, 1934, *GCGJZGGM,* 14:143–144; see also *ZZ*-A, 1:306. Arthur Ewert was then the Comintern's representative to the CCP CC.

4. Otto Braun, *A Comintern Agent in China* (Stanford, CA: Stanford University Press, 1982), 76. Other Red Army commanders, however, said that the plan of "total evacuation" came from Brown. See, for example, Nie Rongzhen, *Inside the Red Star: The Memoirs of Marshal Nie Rongzhen* (Beijing: New World Press, 1988), 183.

5. Zhu De and Zhou to Zhou Zikun and Huang Kaixiang, concerning dispatch of representatives to negotiate with Guangdong's representatives, October 5, 1934, *ZJSWX,* 1:346–347.

6. He Changgong, *He Changgong huiyi lu* (He Changgong's memoirs) (Beijing: Jiefangjun, 1987), 325–328; *ZJSWX,* 1:346, note 1.

7. Braun, *Comintern Agent in China,* 76.

8. Chiang diary, October 17, 1934.

9. Chiang to his generals, October 31, 1934; Chiang to Ministry of Foreign Affairs and convey to Liu Wendao, November 4, 1934, *Jiang Zhongzheng xiansheng nianpu changbian* (A long chronological record of Mr. Chiang Kai-shek) (Taipei: Academia Historica, 2015), 4:461, 464.

10. Wang Xinsheng, "An Examination of the CCP Center's Telegraphic Communication with the Comintern before and during the Long March," *Dang de wenxian* (Party history documentation) 2 (2010): 77–82.

11. Zhang Wentian's notes during the Rectification Movement, December 16, 1943, *Zunyi huiyi wenxian* (Documents on the Zunyi Conference) (Beijing: Renmin, 1985), 78–79; Mao's recollection

of the Zunyi Conference, June 1963, cited from Wang Li, *Xianchang lishi: wenhua da geming jishi* (Making of history on site: Notes on the Cultural Revolution) (Hong Kong: Oxford University Press, 1993), 126.

12. Qin Fuquan, *Bo Gu he Mao Zedong: ji zhonghua suweiai de lingxiu men* (Bo Gu and Mao Zedong: The leaders of the Chinese Soviet Republic) (Hong Kong: Dafeng, 2009), 128. The author is Bo Gu (Qin Bangxian)'s nephew.

13. Braun, *Comintern Agent in China,* 92–93.

14. *MZ-A,* 337.

15. *MZ-A,* 341; *ZZ-A,* 1:310–311. Braun recalled that Mao "brusquely rejected" his suggestion and "insisted that we continue to move westward into the interior of Kweichow (Guizhou)." And Zhou was "shifting allegiance to the 'Central Triad.'" Braun, *Comintern Agent in China,* 92–93.

16. Braun, *Comintern Agent in China,* 93.

17. Zhou's presentation at a Politburo meeting in Yan'an, November 27, 1943, *Zunyi huiyi wenxian,* 64.

18. The Politburo's decision on strategic moves, December 18, 1934, *JDYLZYWX,* 12:656–657.

19. Zhou's presentation, *Zunyi huiyi wenxian,* 64.

20. Ren Bishi's note during Yan'an Rectification Movement, December 2, 1943, cited from *MZ-A,* 342.

21. *ZNP-A,* 1:292.

22. After losing their base area straddling Hubei, Henan, and Anhui to GMD forces in 1932, Zhang Guotao's Red Army troops, which were renamed the Red Fourth Frontal Army, moved to western Sichuan and created new base areas there.

23. During the Nanchang Uprising of 1927, Zhou already had worked together with and debated with Zhang. Hence, he had firsthand experience about Zhang as a tough person to get along with.

24. Zhou Meihua et al., *Jiang Zhongzheng zongtong dangan, shilue gaoben* (President Chiang Kai-shek's archives: Draft chronology of events) (Taipei: Academia Historica, 2017), 28:684.

25. *ZZ-A,* 1:313; Qin, *Bo Gu he Mao Zedong,* 123.

26. The conference has not left detailed minutes. Our knowledge of it comes mainly through an outline about the Zunyi Conference written by Chen Yun after the conference, as well as recollections of several participants.

27. Chen Yun, "An Outline about the Politburo Enlarged Meeting in Zunyi," in *Zunyi huiyi wenxian,* 42–43; Braun, *A Comintern Agent in China,* 94–95.

28. Zhou Enlai, "Lessons in Party History," June 1972, in *Zunyi huiyi wenxian,* 67; see also *MZ-A,* 341–342.

29. Qin, *Bo Gu he Mao Zedong,* 128–129; Braun, *Comintern Agent in China,* 96–97.

30. Chen, "Outline," 42.

31. Ibid., 42, 43.

32. Qin, *Bo Gu he Mao Zedong,* 124–132.

33. Chen, "Outline," 43.

34. *MNP-A,* 1:445; *JDYLZYWX,* 10:483.

35. Nie, *Inside the Red Star,* 222.

36. *Li Zuopeng huiyilu* (Li Zuopeng's memoir) (Hong Kong: Beixing, 2011), 16–20; Cao Suofei, "The Decoding Work that My Father Did during the Long March," *Renmin zhengxie bao* (People's consultative committee bulletin), August 17, 2006.

37. Qin, *Bo Gu he Mao Zedong,* 151–152.

38. *MZ-A*, 347.

39. *MZ-A*, 353; *ZNP-A*, 1:281.

40. Editorial Group, *Hongjun Changzheng: wenxian* (The Red Army's Long March: Documents) (Beijing: Jiefangjun, 1995), 280; *MNP-A*, 1:449.

41. A main achievement of Chiang's during this period was his success in removing Wang Jialie as Guizhou's provincial governor. Chiang wrote, "The provincial government of Guizhou was completely reorganized, . . . and Wang resigned in face of difficulties. The military and political power has since been controlled by the Central Government." Chiang diary, May 1, 1935.

42. Chiang diary, April 24 and May 31, 1935.

43. See Chiang diary, April 22, April 27, and May 12, 1935. On May 11, Chiang told Liu Xiang, Sichuan's strongman, that he was "deeply worried as there was no telegram from northern China the whole day."

44. Xu Xiangqian, *Lishi de huigu* (History in retrospect) (Beijing: Jiefangjun, 1988), 411–413.

45. Li Manchun et al., *Liu Bocheng zhuan* (A biography of Liu Bocheng) (Beijing: Dangdai zhongguo, 1992), 117–122.

46. Chang, *Rise of the Chinese Communist Party*, 2:377; Zhang, *Wo de huiyi*, 1:220–221.

47. *ZJSWX*, 1:399; *ZNP-A*, 1:287.

48. Chang, *Chinese Communist Party*, 2:403–405; Zhang, *Wo de huiyi*, 1:248–250.

49. *ZZ-A*, 1:357.

50. *ZNP-A*, 1:289.

51. *JDYLZYWX*, 12:256.

52. Mao's presentation at a Politburo meeting, August 6, 1935, cited from Yang, *Zhongjian didai de geming*, 322; see also *MNP-A*, 1:464.

53. Chang, *Rise of the Chinese Communist Party*, 2:418–419; Zhang, *Wo de huiyi*, 3:263.

54. Wei Guolu, *Sui Zhou fuzhuxi changzheng* (Following Vice Chairman Zhou in the Long March) (Beijing: Zhongguo qingnian, 1976), 55–58; Li Zuofu, "Vice Chairman Zhou in Sickness for Forty Days," in Editorial Group, *Huainian Zhou Enali* (Remembering Zhou Enlai) (Beijing: Renmin, 1986), 313–316; *ZNP-A*, 1:293; Jin Feng, *Deng Yingchao zhuan* (Beijing: Renmin, 1993), 202–203, 288.

55. See, for example, Mao's talks with Wei Guoqing, Ding Sheng, and Liu Xingyuan, August 28, 1971, *MNP-B*, 6:394–395.

56. *ZNP-A*, 1:295–296; *MNP-A*, 471.

57. CCP CC to Zhang Guotao, Xu Xiangqian, and Chen Changfeng, September 9, 1935, *JDYL-ZYWX*, 12:304.

58. Chang, *Rise of the Chinese Communist Party*, 2:422–423.

59. Mao's report and conclusion at the E'jie Conference, September 12, 1935, *Zhongguo gongnong hongjun disi fangmianjun zhanshi ziliao xuanbian, changzheng shiqi* (The war materials of the fourth frontal army of the Chinese Workers and Peasants Red Army) (Beijing: Jiefangjun, 1992), 150–151; *MNP-A*, 1:472–473.

60. *MNP-A*, 473; *ZNP-A*, 1:297.

61. *MNP-A*, 1:477; *ZNP-A*, 1:298.

62. Nie, *Inside the Red Star*, 248; *MNP-A*, 1:476.

63. Chiang to Zhu Shaoliang et al., September 29, 1935, *Jiang Zhongzheng xiansheng nianpu changbian*, 4:693.

64. *MNP-A*, 1:488.

65. *ZNP-A*, 1:299.

10. "As Chinese, We Must Fight as One Nation" (1935–1937)

1. *MNP*-A, 1:465–466; Ding Zhi, "The Central Red Army's Changing Policies of Northward Marching," *Wenxian yu yanjiu* (Documents and studies) 5 (1985); Mao to Luo Pu, December 1, 1935, *MJSWJ*, 1:408–409; see also Mao's report on the military situation, December 23, 1935, cited from Yang Kuisong, *Xi'an shibian xintan: Zhang Xueliang yu zhonggong guanxi zhimi* (A new study on the Xi'An Incident: The secrets of Zhang Xualiang's relationship with the CCP) (Nanjing: Jiangsu renmin, 2006), 41.

2. See, for example, Zhang Guotao to Peng Dehuai and Mao, December 5, 1935, *JDYLZYWX*, 12:520.

3. Li Haiwen et al., *Zhanghao zhuan* (A biography of Zhang Hao) (Beijing: Danghai zhongguo, 2001), 109.

4. Cited from Yang, *Xi'an shibian xintan*, 30.

5. Li et al., *Zhanghao zhuan*, 126.

6. Lin Yuying to Zhang Guotao, January 16, 1936; Lin Yuying to Zhang Guotao and Zhu De, January 24, 1936, *Zhongguo gongnong hongjun disi fangnianjun*, 321, 328.

7. Zhang Guotao to Lin Yuying and Zhang Wentian, January 27, 1936; Lin Yuying and Zhang Wentian to Zhang Guotao, February 14, 1936, *Zhongguo gongnong hongjun disi fangnianjun*, 331–332, 371–372.

8. Li et al., *Zhanghao zhuan*, 109–110.

9. *JDYLZYWX*, 12:473–474.

10. *ZNP*-A, 1:301.

11. *JDYLZYWX*, 12:531–551.

12. *ZZ*-A, 1:376; *ZNP*-A, 1:303.

13. *ZNP*-A, 1:301.

14. Yang Kuisong, *Kangzhan qianhou guogong tanpan shilu* (A factual account of GMD-CCP negotiations before and after the War of Resistance), rev. ed. (Beijing: Xinxing, 2013), 5–7.

15. Chiang diary, December 31, 1935.

16. Ibid., October 2, 1935.

17. Ibid., February 20, 1936.

18. Yang, *Kangzhan qianhou guogong tanpan shili*, 15–16.

19. *MJSWJ*, 1:413–422; *MNP*-A, 1:507.

20. *ZJSWX*, 1:437–439.

21. *ZNP*-A, 1:302.

22. Ibid., 304.

23. Ibid., 304–305.

24. *ZZ*-A, 1:378.

25. Yang, *Kangzhan qianhou guogong tanpan shilu*, 14–15.

26. Zhou to Luo Pu and Mao, March 2, 1936, cited from ibid., 9.

27. Yang, *Xi'an shibian xintan*, 63.

28. *ZZ*-A, 1:378; ibid., 63.

29. *ZNP*-A, 1:309–310; *ZZ*-A, 1:378–379.

30. Zhou to Zhang Wentian, Mao, and Peng Dehuai, April 10, 1936, *Zhonggong dangshi ziliao* (CCP history materials), 33 (February 1990): 3–4.

31. Zhang Youkun et al., *Zhang Xueliang nianpu* (A chronological record of Zhang Xueliang) (Beijing: Shehui kexue wenxian, 2009), 1000.

32. Zhou to Zhang Xueliang, April 22, 1936, *ZSXXJ*, 87.

33. Liu Ding's report to Li Kenong, April 30, 1936, cited from Zhang, *Zhang Xueliang nianpu*, 998–999.

34. Cited from Yang, *Xi'an shibian xintan*, 107.

35. Lin Yuying, Zhang Wentian, and Mao to Zhu De, Liu Bocheng, and Xu Xiangqian, May 20, 1936, *Zhonggong zhongyang kongri minzu tongyi zhanxian wenjian xuanbian* (Selected documents on anti-Japanese united front of the CCP CC) (Beijing: Dangan, 1985), 2:147–148.

36. After surviving the GMD forces' suppression campaign in 1932, He Long led his troops, later renamed the Red Second Frontal Army, to try to create base areas in the peripheries of Hunan, Hubei, Sichuan, Guizhou, and Yunnan Provinces.

37. *Zhonggong zhongyang*, 2:147–148.

38. *ZNP-A*, 1:316.

39. Yang, *Kangzhan qianhou guogong tanpan shilu*, 25.

40. *Zhongguo gongnong hongjun disi fangmianjun*, 533–540.

41. CCP Central Secretariat to Wang Ming and Kang Sheng, June 16, 1936, f. 495, op. 74, d. 249, RGASPI; Alexander Dallin and F. I. Firsov, eds., *Dimitrov and Stalin: Letters from the Soviet Archives, 1934–1943* (New Haven, CT: Yale University Press, 2000), 96–100.

42. Zhou's speech at a Politburo meeting, August 10, 1936, cited from Jin Chongji, *Shengsi guantou* (Life-and-death moment) (Beijing: Sanlian, 2016), 220.

43. *MNP-A*, 1:567–568.

44. Secretariat of Comintern Executive Committee to CCP Central Secretariat, August 15, 1937, *GCGJZGGM*, 17:465–468.

45. *ZNP-A*, 1:324.

46. Ibid., 324.

47. Zhou to Chen Guofu and Chen Lifu, September 1, 1936, *ZTYZXWX*, 17–18.

48. CCP CC's instruction on compelling Chiang to resist Japan, September 1, 1936, *JDYLZYWX*, 13:276–277.

49. Dimitrov diary, September 7 and 11, 1936, in Georgi Dimitrov and Ivo Banac, eds., *The Diary of Georgi Dimitrov, 1933–1949* (New Haven, CT: Yale University Press, 2012), 29–30.

50. *MJSWJ*, 1:578–579, 583, 592–594, 598–599.

51. *ZNP-A*, 1:327; see also Yang, *Xi'an shibian xintan*, 196.

52. *JDYLZYWX*, 13:282–288.

53. Pan Hannian's report to CC, November 12, 1936, cited from ZZ-A, 1:329.

54. Yang Kuisong, "Why Did the Xi'an Incident Happen?" in *Tanwang yuejin* (Discussing the past, understanding the present) (Beijing: Jiuzhou, 2012), 83–85.

55. Chiang diary, November 22, 1936.

56. Yang, *Kangzhan qianhou guogong tanpan jishi*, 40.

57. Xu Yongchang diary, October 17, 1936, *Xu Yongchang riji* (Diaries of Xu Yongchang) (Taipei: Institute of Modern History, Academia Sinica, 1990), 3:480–481.

58. Zhang et al., *Zhang Xueliang nianpu*, 1121–1122.

59. *MNP-A*, 1:621; *ZZ-A*, 1:399.

60. CCP CC to Secretariat of Comintern Executive Committee, December 12, 1936, f. 495, op. 74, d. 280, RGASPI.

61. Cited from Yang, *Tanwang yuejin*, 104.

62. Zhang Peisen et al., "Zhang Wentian and the Xi'an Incident," *Dang de wenxian* (Party documents), 3 (1988): 7–8.

63. *ZNP*-A, 1:338–339; Zhang et al., "Zhang Wentian," 8.

64. "The China Incident," *Pravda*, December 14, 1936.

65. Yang, *Xi'an shibian xintan*, 334; Chiang diary, December 14, 15, and 16, 1936.

66. *ZNP*-A, 1:341.

67. Ibid.; Wu Dianyao, *Liu Ding zhuan* (A biography of Liu Ding) (Beijing: Zhongyang wenxian, 2012), 289–290.

68. *ZZ*-A, 1:405–406; *ZNP*-A, 1:341–342.

69. Zhou to Mao and CCP CC, December 17, 1936, *Zhongguo gongchandang guanyu xian shibian dangan shiliao xuanbian* (Selected CCP archival documents about the Xi'an Incident, hereafter *Xi'an shibian*) (Beijing: Zhongguo dang'an, 1997), 213–214.

70. Zhou to Mao and CCP CC, December 17, 1936, *Xi'an shibian*, 214.

71. CCP CC to GMD CC, December 18, 1936, *Xi'an shibian*, 218–219.

72. *ZNP*-A, 1:342.

73. Zhang Peisen, *Zhang Wentian nianpu* (A chronological record of Zhang Wentian) (Beijing: Zhonggong dangshi, 2000), 1:398; CCP CC's instruction on the Xi'an Incident and our tasks, December 19, 1936, *Xi'an shibian*, 222–224.

74. Comintern Executive Committee Secretariat to CCP CC, December 16, 1936, *GCGYZGGM*, 15:265–266.

75. *ZNP*-A, 1:343.

76. Zhou to Mao and Zhang Wentian, December 21, 1936, *Xi'an shibian*, 246.

77. T. V. Soong (Song Ziwen) diary, December 20, 1936, Hoover Institute, Stanford, CA.

78. Soong diary, December 22, 1936. See also *ZXJ*, 1:70.

79. Chiang diary, December 23, 1936.

80. Meeting with Song Ziwen, *ZXJ*, 1:70–71; Soong diary, December 23, 1936.

81. Zhou and Bo Gu to CCP Central Secretariat, December 24, 1936, *Xi'an shibian*, 269.

82. Chiang diary, December 24, 1936; Soong diary, December 23, 1936.

83. Soong diary, December 25, 1936.

84. Chiang diary, December 25, 1936.

85. Zhou to CCP CC, December 25, 1936, *ZTYZXWX*, 34.

86. Ibid.

87. Ibid.; Soong diary, December 25, 1936.

88. Long Feihu, "Recalling Zhou Enlai's Peaceful Resolution of the Xi'an Incident," *Wenshi jinghua* (Digest of history and literature) 12 (2001).

89. Zhang, *Zhang Xueliang nianpu*, 1025–1026.

90. Yang, *Guomindang de liangong yu fangong*, 349.

91. Secretariat of Comintern Executive Committee to CCP CC, January 19, 1937, *GCGJZGGM*, 15:270–271.

92. Zhou to Zhang Wentian and Mao Zedong, January 26, 1937; Mao, Zhu De, and Zhang Guotao to Zhang Wentian and Zhou Enlai, January 27, 1937, *Xi'an shibian*, 351–352, 354.

93. *ZHMGZYSL*, 5th ser., 1:262–263.

94. *ZHMGZYSL*, 5th ser., 1:251–253, 264.

95. *ZNP*-A, 1:358–359.

96. Chiang diary, March 6, 1937.

97. CCP Central Secretariat's report to the Comintern on talks with Chiang, April 5, 1937, *JDYLZYWX*, 14:137–142; Chiang diary, March 26, 1937.

98. *ZNP-A*, 1:369.
99. *ZNP-A*, 1:372.
100. Chiang diary, June 1, 1937.
101. CCP CC's report to the Comintern, June 17, 1937, *JDYLZYWX*, 14:334–336.
102. Yang, *Kangzhan qianhou guogong tanpan shilu*, 77–78.
103. For an excellent description and explanation of how and why the July 7th Incident evolved into a full-scale war between China and Japan, see Rana Mitter, *Forgotten Ally: China's World War II, 1937–1945* (Boston: Houghton Mifflin Harcourt, 2013), 79–85; van de Ven, *War and Nationalism in China*, 187–200.
104. *MNP-A*, 2:12; Jin Chongji, "From the December Conference to the Sixth Plenum," *Dang de wenxian*, no. 4 (2014): 57.
105. *MNP-A*, 2:14–15; Zhang et al., *Ren Bishi zhuan*, 493–494. See also Yang Kuisong, "An Examination of the CCP's Changing Military Policies in the Early Phase of the War of Resistance," *Jindaishi yanjiu* (Modern history studies), 6 (2015).
106. *ZNP-A*, 386–387; see also Zhang Guotao, *Wo de huiyi*, 3:389–390; Chang, *Rise of the Chinese Communist Party*, 2:537–538.
107. *MNP-A*, 2:15–16; *ZNP-A*, 1:386.
108. *ZNP-A*, 1:391.
109. Zhou Guoquan and Guo Dehong, eds., *Wang Ming nianpu* (A chronological record of Wang Ming) (Hefei: Anhui renmin, 1991), 92–93.
110. *ZNP-A*, 1:401–402.
111. Li Weihan, *Huiyi yu yanjiu* (Recollection and study) (Beijing: Dangshi ziliao, 1986), 1:443.
112. *JDYLZYWX*, 14:736–737.

11. Chongqing Fog (1938–1943)

1. Speech by Chiang, September 23, 1937, *ZHMGZYSL*, 5th ser., 1:285–286.
2. Chiang diary, October 25, 1937.
3. Chen Shaoyu and Zhou Enlai's report to the CC on talks with Chiang, December 21, 1937, *JDYLZYWX*, 14:757–758.
4. Chiang diary, February 25, 1938.
5. Chen Lifu to Chiang, February 1, 1938, *ZHMGZYSL*, 5th ser., 1:325.
6. *ZZ-A*, 2:485–486.
7. Chen Shaoyu and Zhou to CCP Secretariat, February 10, 1938, *Kangzhan chuqi zhonggong zhongyang Changjiangju* (CCP Yangzi River Bureau in the early phase of the War of Resistance) (Wuhan: Hubei renmin, 1991), 156–157; Chiang diary, February 10, 1938.
8. *ZNP-A*, 1:412.
9. Ibid., 1:415; Yu Shi, "Zhou Enlai and the Yangzi River Bureau in the early phase of the War of Resistance," *Zhonggong dangshi yanjiu* (CCP history research), no. 2 (1988): 17.
10. Wang Jiaxiang, Report on the Comintern's Instruction, September 14, 1938, *JDYLZYWX*, 15:555–556.
11. *ZNP-A*, 1:429–430.
12. Zhou to CCP Central Secretariat, October 28, 1938, *Kangzhan chuqi*, 295.
13. *ZNP-A*, 1:435; Tong Xiaopeng, *Fengyu sishi nian* (In wind and rain for forty years) (Beijing: Zhongyang wenxian, 1996), 1:186–188.

14. *JDYLZYWX,* 15:785–786.

15. Elizabeth J. Perry, "Reclaiming the Chinese Revolution," *Journal of Asian Studies* 67, no. 4 (2008): 1147–1164.

16. Report by Chen Shaoyu and Zhou Enlai to CCP CC on negotiations with Chiang about a big party, December 13, 1938, *ZGZYWJXJ*-A, 12:5–6; *ZZ*-A, 2:534.

17. Zhou's report to CC about talks with Chiang, January 21, 1939, *JDYLZYWX,* 16:25–26.

18. *MNP*-A, 2:105–106.

19. Zhou's letter of reply to Chiang, January 25, 1939, *JDYLZYWX,* 16:34–37.

20. *Jiang Zhongzheng xiansheng nianpu changbian,* 6:14.

21. *ZNP*-A, 2:448.

22. Tong Xiaopeng et al., *Nanfangju dangshi ziliao* (Materials of CCP Southern China Bureau) (Chongqing: Chongqing chubanshe, 1990), 3:329–330; also see Ling Qing, *Cong yanan dao lianheguo: Ling Qing waijiao shengya* (From Yan'an to the United Nations: Ling Qing's diplomatic career) (Fu Zhou: Fujian renmin, 2008), 20–21.

23. Ibid., 1:158.

24. Ibid., 193.

25. Tong Xiaopeng, *Shaoxiao lijia laodahui: Tong Xiaopeng huiyilu* (Leaving home young and returning old: Tong Xiaopeng's memoirs) (Fuzhou: Fujian renmin, 2000), 225–226.

26. *MWJ,* 2:207.

27. Mao's report on situation and our tasks, June 8, 1939, cited from Yang, *Guomindang de liangong yu fangong,* 416; *MWJ,* 2:196–234.

28. Chiang diary, June 10, 1939.

29. Shi Zhe, *Zai lishi juren shenbian: Shi Zhe huiyilu* (On the side of historical giants: Shi Zhe's memoirs) (Beijing: Zhongyang wenxian, 1998), 119; Liu Jiuzhou, "On the Side of Vice Chairman Zhou," in *Ceng yu weiren tongxing* (Experience with a great person) (Beijing: Zhongguo wenshi, 2002); *ZNP*-A, 2:454; *ZZ*-A, 2:563. B. K. Basu, a member of the Indian medical team, offers a different account of the accident. Zhou's horse "apparently shied at the sight of a dark hole on the road caused by an exploded bomb," causing Zhou to fall off. B. K. Basu, *Call of Yenan: Story of the Indian Medical Mission to China* (New Delhi: All India Kortnis Memorial Committee, 1986), 174.

30. Basu, *Call of Yanan,* 175.

31. Outline of Zhou's report at a Politburo meeting, August 4, 1939, *Nanfangju dangshi ziliao,* 3:18–37; *ZJSWX,* 2:240–249; *ZTYZXWX,* 43–47.

32. *MNP*-A, 2:134; *ZNP*-A, 2:457.

33. *ZZ*-A, 2:561–562; *ZNP*-A, 457.

34. Basu, *Call of Yanan,* 183; *ZZ*-A, 2:564.

35. CCP Central Secretariat to Stalin and Dimitrov, August 1, 1939, *GCGJZGGM,* 18:244.

36. Dimitrov to CCP CC, August 11, 1939, *GCGJZGGM,* 18:247.

37. Diagnosis of the condition of Comrade Zhou Enlai's fractured right arm, September 16, 1939, f. 495, op. 225, d. 139, RGASPI; Dimitrov to CCP CC, October 8, 1939, *GCGJZGGM,* 18:289.

38. Dimitrov to CCP CC, October 8, 1939, *GCGJZGGM,* 18:289.

39. Zhou to Stalin, January 23, 1940, f. 495, op. 225, d. 139, RGASPI.

40. Dallin and Firsov, eds., *Dimitrov and Stalin,* 122. Stalin told Dimitrov that "he was too busy."

41. Zhou's report at a Politburo meeting, November 27–December 2, 1943, cited from Yang Kuisong, "On Zhou's Summaries and Assessments on the Comintern's roles," Xu Xing et al., ed., *Zhou Enlai he ershi shiji de zhongguo he shijie* (Zhou Enlai and 20th-century China and the world) (Beijing: Zhongyang wenxian,2015), 272.

42. Shi, *Zai lishi juren shenbian,* 124.

43. Pantsov and Levine, *Mao: The Real Story,* 451.

44. *GCGJZGGM,* 18:302–341.

45. Dimitrov's letter to Stalin about providing financial support to the CCP, February 23, 1940, *GCGJZGGM,* 19:27–30; f. 495, op. 74, d. 317, RGASPI; Dallin and Firsov, eds., *Dimitrov and Stalin,* 122–125.

46. Dallin and Firsov, eds., *Dimitrov and Stalin,* 111–112.

47. Comintern Executive Committee's resolution in response to CCP delegation's report, March 3, 1940, *GCGJZGGM,* 19:40–41.

48. Shi, *Zai lishi juren shenbian,* 124.

49. Applications by Zhou Enlai and Ren Bishi to return to China, January 20, 1940; Travel clearance for Zhou, Ren, and Deng Yinchao, January 27, 1940, f. 495, op. 225, d. 2835, RGASPI.

50. Qin Jiufeng, "The Mother-Daughter Endearment between Deng Yingchao and Sun Weizhi," *Dangshi Zongheng* (About the party history), no. 6 (2004): 26.

51. Autobiography of Sun Weishi, April 2, 1941, f. 495, op. 225, d. 1235, RGASPI; see also Ren Jun, *Wo zhe jiushinian: yiduan geming jiating de siren jiyi, 1920–2010* (The ninety years of mine: A personal recollection of a revolutionary family, 1920–2010) (Beijing: Huawen, 2010), 135. Ren Jun was Sun Weishi's aunt.

52. Shen Guofan, *Zhou Enlai yang'nu Sun Weishi* (Zhou Enlai's stepdaughter Sun Weishi) (Beijing: Danghai zhongguo, 2014), 140–146.

53. Li Peng, PRC premier of the late 1980s to late 1990s, was not Zhou's and Deng's stepson. As he himself states, his relationship with Zhou and Deng was one between "old revolutionary leaders and a revolutionary martyr's child." See *Li Peng huiyilu, 1928–1982* (Li Peng's memoirs, 1928–1982) (Beijing: Zhongyang wenxian, Zhongyang dianli, 2014), 303.

54. Zhou Enlai to Deng Yingchao, March 7, 1948, *Zhou Enlai Deng Yingchao tongxin xuanji* (Selected correspondence between Zhou Enlai and Deng Yingchao) (Beijing: Zhongyang wenxian, 2014), 70.

55. Dimitrov to CCP CC, March 17, 1940, *GCGJZGGM,* 19:62.

56. Shi Zhe interview, August 1992; Shi, *Zai lishi juren shenbian,* 127–132. See also Zhang et al., *Ren Bishi zhuan,* 545.

57. Yang, *Kangzhan qianhou guogong tanpan shilu,* 146.

58. Mao to Peng Dehuai, April 4, 1940, *MNP-A,* 2:183.

59. *MJSWJ,* 2:547; *MNP-A,* 2:189; Editorial Committee, *Xinsijun wenxian* (New Fourth Army documents) (Beijing: Jiefangjun, 1995), 2:159–162.

60. Zhou to CCP CC, June 4, 1940, *ZJSHDDSJ,* 1:484; *ZZ-A,* 2:578–579.

61. Yang, *Kangzhan qianhou guogong tanpan shilu,* 153–154.

62. *ZHMGZYSL,* 5th ser., 3:506–509.

63. *ZNP-A,* 2:470.

64. *ZZ-A,* 2:581–582; *ZNP-A,* 2:470–472; see also CCP CC to Dimitrov, August 3, 1940, *GCGJZGGM,* 19:77–79.

65. *ZNP-A,* 2:472–473; CCP Central Secretariat to Peng Dehuai et al., August 12, 1940, *JDYLZYWX,* 17:459–460, 470–472.

66. *MNP-A,* 2:201; *ZZ-A,* 2:582.

67. *ZNP-A,* 2:473; see also "Zhou Enlai's Three Suggestions about Adjusting Guerilla Areas and Guerillas," September 1, 1940, *ZHMGZYSL,* 5th ser., 2:508–509.

68. *ZHMGZYSL,* 5th ser., 2:504–505.

69. Mao's instruction, November 1, 1941; Mao and Wang to Peng Dehuai, November 3, 1941, Zhongyang dang'an guan (Central archives), ed., *Wannan shibian: ziliao xuji* (The Southern Anhui Incident: Selected documents, hereafter *Wannan shibian*) (Beijing: Zhonggong Zhongyang dangxiao, 1982), 71–72, 76; *Hu Qiaomu huiyi Mao Zedong* (Hu Qiaomu remembers Mao Zedong, rev. ed.) (Beijing: Zhongyang wenxian, 2003), 119.

70. *Hu Qiaomu huiyi Mao Zedong* (rev. ed.), 119; *ZNP*-A, 2:482.

71. *MNP*-A, 2:215.

72. Zhou to Mao, November 1, 1940, *ZJSWX*, 2:277–278.

73. Zhu De, Peng Dehuai, Ye Ting, and Xiang Ying to He Yingqin and Bai Chongxi, November 9, 1940, *Wannan shibian*, 83–87.

74. Liu Wei's conversation with Zhou and Ye Jianying, November 30, 1941, *ZHMGZYSL*, 5th ser., 4:230–231.

75. Zhou's report to Mao and CCP CC regarding talks with Chiang, December 26, 1940, *Wannan shibian*, 121–122; see also Chiang diary, December 25, 1940.

76. *ZNP*-A, 2:491.

77. Mao and Zhu De to Ye Ting and Xiang Ying, December 30, 1940, *Wannan shibian*, 125.

78. Xu Yongchang diary, January 8, 1941, *Xu Yongchang riji*, 6:6.

79. Yang, *Guomindang de liangong yu fangong*, 440.

80. CCP CC's instruction to Zhou and Ye Jianying, January 12, 1941, *Wannan shibian*, 137.

81. Zhou and Ye Jianying to Mao, January 13, 1941, *Wannan shibian*, 140.

82. Mao, Zhu, and Wang Jiaxiang to Liu Shaoqi and Ye Ting, January 14, 1941, *Wannan shibian*, 144.

83. Mao, Zhu, and Wang Jiaxiang to Zhou, January 14, 1941, *Wannan shibian*, 145.

84. *MNP*-A, 2:256; see also Yang, *Guomindang de liangong he fangong*, 442.

85. Mao to Zhou and Ye Jianying, January 15, 1941, *Wannan shibian*, 147.

86. Zhou to Mao on military strategies, January 16, 1941, cited from Yang, *Guomindang de liangong yu fangong*, 444.

87. Liu Shaoqi to Mao, January 15, 1941, *Wangnan shibian*, 148–150.

88. *Zhongyang ribao* (Central daily), January 17, 1941.

89. *MNP*-A, 2:257.

90. Mao to Peng Dehuai and Liu Shaoqi, January 19, 1941; Mao's briefing for Liu, January 23, 1941; Mao to Zhou, January 25, 1941, *Wannan shibian*, 180, 187.

91. Mao to Peng Dehuai and Liu Shaoqi, January 19, 1941; Mao's briefing for Liu, January 23, 1941; Mao to Zhou, January 25, 1941, *Wannan shibian*, 180, 187.

92. *Xinhua ribao* (New China daily), January 18, 1941.

93. *MXJ*, 2:775.

94. Mao to Zhou, January 25, 1941, *Wannan shibian*, 190.

95. Mao to Zhou, Peng Dehuai, and Liu Shaoqi, January 20, 1941, *Wannan shibian*, 183–184.

96. Mao to Zhou, January 25, 1941; Mao to Zhou, January 27, 1941, *Wannan shibian*, 190, 191–192, 193–194.

97. Cited from Yang, *Guomindang de liangong yu fangong*, 445.

98. *ZNP*-A, 2:501; see also *Wannan shibian*, 203.

99. CCP CC's instruction, February 2, 1941; Mao's briefing to Zhou, February 7, 1941; Mao to Zhou, February 14, *Wannan shibian*, 202–203, 205–206, 207–209.

100. *ZHMGZYSL*, 3rd ser., 1:533–535.

101. Chiang diary, February 1, 1941.

102. *ZHMGZYSL*, 3rd ser., 1:542–545; *FRUS*, 1941, 5:82–83, 607.

103. *FRUS*, 1941, 5:608; *ZHMGZYSL*, 3rd ser., 1:552–553; *ZNP-A*, 2:503.

104. Chiang diary, February 22, 1941.

105. Zhou to Mao, February 10, 1941, *ZNP-A*, 2:503.

106. Mao to Zhou, February 14, 1941; CCP Central Secretariat to Zhou, February 14, 1941, *Wannan shibian*, 208, 212.

107. Zhou's report to CCP CC, February 25, 1941, *Wannan shibian*, 217–218.

108. CCP CC's instruction to Zhou, February 26, 1941, *Wannan shibian*, 219–220.

109. CCP CC's instruction to Zhou, February 28, 1941, *Wannan shibian*, 222–223.

110. Zhou's report to CCP CC regarding negotiation with Zhang Chong, March 1, 1941, *Wannan shibian*, 224.

111. Zhou's report to CCP CC regarding attending the Assembly, March 1, 1941, *Wannan shibian*, 225.

112. CCP CC's instruction to Zhou, Dong Biwu, and Deng Yingchao, March 1, 1941; Mao to Zhou, March 2, 1941, *Wannan shibian*, 226, 228–229.

113. Zhou's report to CCP CC regarding negotiating with Chiang, March 15, 1941, *Wannan shibian*, 235–236.

114. Xu Yongchang diary, May 5, 1941, *Xu Yongchang riji*, 6:101.

115. *ZNP-A*, 2:512; Mao to Peng et al., May 9, 1941, *JDYLZYWX*, 18:263–264.

116. Zhou to CCP CC, May 10, 1941; Zhou's report to CCP CC, May 11, 1941, *JDYLZYWX*, 18:278–282.

117. Zhou's report to CCP CC, May 11, 1941, *JDYLZYWX*, 18:278–282.

118. Mao to Zhou, May 10, 1941; Mao to Zhou, May 14, 1941, CCA.

119. Mao to Peng Dehuai, May 15, 1941, CCA; Mao to Peng Dehuai, May 14, 1941, *MJSWJ*, 2:641.

120. *ZNP-A*, 2:512–513.

121. Ibid., 2:515.

122. Soviet Bolshevik Party Politburo meeting's resolution No. 34, July 3, 1941, *GCGJZGGM*, 19:197.

123. Mao to Zhou, July 15, 1941, *MJSWJ*, 2:651–653.

124. CCP CC to Dimitrov, July 18, 1941, *GCGJZGGM*, 19:206–207; *Diary of Georgi Dimitrov*, 182.

125. Mao to Zhou, December 12, 1941, *MJSWJ*, 2:672–673; Mao to Dimitrov, December 12, 1941, *GCGJZGGM*, 19:247.

126. *ZNP-A*, 2:538.

127. Zhou to Mao, May 4, 1942; Zhou to Mao, June 19, 1942, *ZJSWX*, 2:398–399, 402.

128. *Nanfangju dangshi ziliao*, 1:172–173.

129. Tong, *Fengyu sishi nian*, 1:248–253; *Nanfangju dashi ziliao*, 1:194–196.

130. Tong, *Fengyu sishi nian*, 1:252.

131. *ZZ-A*, 2:630–631; *Nanfangju dashi ziliao*, 1:195–196.

132. Dekanozov to Dimitrov, June 7, 1942, *GCGJZGGM*, 19:282.

133. Dimitrov to Mao, June 15, 1942, *GCGJZGGM*, 19:285; *Diary of Georgi Dimitrov*, 227.

134. Mao to Dimitrov, June 24, 1942, *GCGJZGGM*, 19:287; *Diary of Georgi Dimitrov*, 228. Dimitrov conveyed Mao's telegram to "Comrades Stalin, Molotov, and Dekanozov."

135. Wang Shijie diary, July 5, 1943, *Wang Shijie riji*, 1:442.

136. *ZZ-A*, 2:671.

137. *ZHMGZYSL*, 5th ser., 4:234–235; *ZZ-A*, 2:671.

138. Zhou to Mao, August 14, 1942, *ZZ-A*, 2:672.

139. Zhou to Mao, August 19, 1942, *ZZ-A*, 2:672.

140. Mao to Zhou, September 3, 1942, *MNP-A*, 2:402.

141. Zhou to Mao, September 5, 1942, *ZNP-A*, 2:551.

142. *ZHMGZYSL*, 5th ser., 4: 236–242, 243–246; Zhou to Mao and CCP Secretariat, October 26, 1942, *ZNP-A*, 2:553–554; Mao to Zhou, October 28, *MNP-A*, 2:410–411.

143. Lin to CCP CC, December 16, 1943, cited from *ZZ-A*, 2:676.

144. *ZNP-A*, 2:569.

145. *ZNP-A*, 2:569; Chiang diary, June 7, 1943, Huang Zijin and Pan Guangzhi, eds., *Shen-ke ji* (Self-reflection and self-correction [in Chiang Kai-shek's diaries]) (Taipei: Academia Historica, 2011) 234–235.

12. Yan'an Sunrise (1941–1945)

1. For an excellent and insightful recent study on why and how Shaanbei and Yan'an became the Chinese Communist "holy land," see Joseph W. Esherick, *Accidental Holy Land: The Communist Revolution in Northwestern China* (Berkeley: University of California Press, 2022).

2. Chen Shaoyu (Wang Ming) and Zhou Enlai's report to the CC, December 21, 1937, *ZGZYKRTYZXWX*, 3:61–62.

3. *ZNP-A*, 1:415.

4. *MNP-A*, 2:51; *MZ-A*, 483–484. Comparing Mao's and Zhou's representations of CCP's military and political strategies, the differences were obvious.

5. *ZNP-A*, 1:415.

6. Yu Shi, "Zhou Enlai and the Yangzi River Bureau in Early Days of the War of Resistance against Japan," *Zhonggong dangshi yanjiu* (CCP history study), no. 2 (1988): 17.

7. Mao's presentation at a Politburo meeting, August 24, 1939, cited from *MZ-A*, 541.

8. Zhang et al., *Ren Bishi Zhuan*, 522–526.

9. Ibid., 521; Yang et al., *Ren Bishi nianpu*, 370.

10. *ZGZYKRTYZXWX*, 3:104–113, 121–133.

11. Yang et al., *Ren Bishi nianpu*, 370–372.

12. Ibid.

13. Ibid., 372; Xu Zehao et al., *Wang Jianxiang nianpu* (A chronological record of Wang Jiaxiang) (Beijing: Zhongyang wenxian, 2001), 190.

14. *Mao Zedong zai qida de baogao he jiangyan ji* (Mao and speeches and reports at the Seventh Party Congress) (Beijing: Zhongyang wenxian, 1995), 231.

15. *Wang Jiaxiang xuanji* (Selected works of Wang Jiaxiang) (Beijing: Renmin, 1989), 141; see also *MNP-A*, 2:90.

16. *Mao Zedong zai qida*, 231–232.

17. Zhou's speech at a Politburo meeting, September 26, 1938, *ZZ-A*, 2:522; *ZNP-A*, 1:429.

18. Zhou's speech at the Sixth Plenum of the Sixth CCP CC, September 30, 1938, *ZZ-A*, 523; *ZNP-A*, 1:429–430.

19. Liao Xinwen, "Organizational Change of the CCP Yangzi River Bureau during the Early Phase of the War of Resistance," *Wenxian yu yanjiu* (Documents and studies), 1987 (one-volume edition), 285.

20. Zhou and Guo, *Wang Ming nianpu*, 103.

21. Shi, *Zai lishi juren shenbian*, 141.

22. *MXJ*, 3:795–803.

23. *JDYLZYWX*, 18:443–446, 534–535.

24. *MWJ*, 2:372–377.

25. *MNP*-A, 2:329.

26. CCP Central Secretariat's decision on establishing advanced-level study groups, September 26, 1941, *JDYLZYWX*, 18:623–624.

27. *Nanfangju danshi ziliao*, 1:176; *ZZ*-A, 2:684.

28. Wang Ming, *Zhonggong wushi nian* (Fifty years of the Chinese Communist Party) (Beijing: Dongfang, 2004), 38.

29. *Hu Qiaomu huiyi Mao Zedong*, 200.

30. *MZ*-A, 633.

31. Minutes of CCP Central Secretariat meeting, October 13, 1941, cited from *MZ*-A, 633–634.

32. *MNP*-A, 2:333.

33. *Hu Qiaomu huiyi Mao Zedong*, 213.

34. Mao to Zhou (with top confidentiality), April 30, 1943, CCA.

35. Li, *Huiyi yu yanjiu*, 2:513.

36. *MZ*-A, 2:655.

37. *JDYLZYWX*, 20:531–537.

38. *Hu Qiaomu huiyi Mao Zedong*, 187.

39. *MXJ*, 3:811–829, 830–846.

40. Mao, "Rectifying Party Conduct, and Writing and Study Styles," February 1, 1942, *Zhengdun xuefeng de 22ge wenjian* (Twenty-Two documents in the Three Rectification Movement) (Yan'an, 1942), 4–5. After major revision and deletion, the essay's title was changed to "Transforming Our Study" and included in *MXJ*. However, the text cited here was deleted. See discussion in Gao Hua, *Lishi biji* (Notes on history) (Hong Kong: Oxford University Press, 2014), 1:190–191.

41. *MNP*-A, 2:381.

42. *MNP*-A, 2:386. CCP Central Propaganda Department's Instruction on Carrying out Rectification in the Whole Party to Correct the Three Wrong Trends, June 8, 1942; Instruction by Central Military Commission and General Political Department about Carrying out Rectification to Correct the Three Wrong Trends with the Troops, June 16, 1942, *JDYLZYWX*, 19:326–330, 336–341.

43. Mao to Zhou, June 13, 1942, *JDYLZYWX*, 19:331–332; *ZNP*-A, 2:546.

44. Cheng Zhongyuan, *Zhang Wentian zhuan* (A biography of Zhang Wentian) (Beijing: Dangdai zhongguo, 1993), 480–493.

45. Xu Zehao, *Wang Jiaxiang zhuan* (A biography of Wang Jiaxiang) (Beijing: Daidai Zhongguo, 1996), 360–362; Xu et al., *Wang Jiaxiang nianpu*, 305–306.

46. *LNP*, 1:373, 377.

47. "The CC's Decision on Adjusting and Simplifying Central Offices," March 20, 1943, *JDYLZYWX*, 20:171–176.

48. Shi, *Zai lishi juren shenbian*, 179; Shi Zhe interview, August 1992.

49. CCP Central Secretariat to Zhou, May 24, 1953, cited from *ZNP*-A, 2:567.

50. *ZNP*-A, 2:568, 569; Chiang diary, June 7, 1943.

51. *ZNP*-A, 2:570; *ZZ*-A, 2:679.

52. Tang Zong, *Zai Jiangjieshi shenbian banian: Shicongshi gaoji muliao Tang Zong riji* (At the side of Chang Kai-shek: Diary of Chang's senior associate Tang) (Beijing, Qunzhong, 1991), 359–360.

53. Xiong Xianghu, *Wo de qingbao he waijiao shengya* (My intelligence and diplomatic career) (Beijing: Zhonggong dangshi, 1999), 13–14.

54. *JDYLZYWX,* 20:468–469.
55. *MNP*-A, 2:452.
56. *ZNP*-A, 2:572.
57. *Hu Qiaomu huiyi Mao Zedong,* 289.
58. *ZNP*-A, 2:577–579.
59. *Hu Qiaomu huiyi Mao Zedong,* 295.
60. Ibid., 283–284.
61. *MNP*-A, 2:482.
62. *ZNP*-A, 1:579.
63. Outline of Zhou's presentation at the Politburo meeting, November 15, 1943, *ZZ*-A, 2:623–624.
64. Yang Kuisong, "Summaries and Assessments on the Comintern's Roles," in Xu Xing et al., *Zhou Enlai yu ershi shiji de zhongguo he shijie* (Beijing: Zhongyang wenxian, 2015), 1:271; Gao, *Wannian Zhou Enlai,* 78.
65. Cited from Gao, *Wannian Zhou Enlai,* 78–79.
66. Outline of Zhou's speech at CCP Politburo meetings, November 15, 1943, cited from Gao, *Wannian Zhou Enlai,* 79.
67. *Diary of Georgi Dimitrov,* 290.
68. Mao to Dimitrov, January 2, 1944, *Diary of Georgi Dimitrov,* 294–295.
69. *ZXJ,* 1:157–187; *Hu Qiaomu huiyi Mao Zedong,* 298.
70. Resolution on Several Historical Issues, April 20, 1945, *JDYLZYWX,* 22:73–112.
71. Zhou's remarks at the opening session of the Seventh Party Congress, April 1945. *Zhonggong qida wenjian xuan* (Selected documents of the CCP's Seventh Congress) (n.p., n.d., copy in author's possession), 10–12.
72. Zhou, "On the United Front," April 30, 1945, *JDYLZYWX,* 22:291–319 (quote is from 297).
73. *Zhonggong qida wenjian xuan,* 91.

13. The Vortex of Big Power Politics (1944–1946)

1. For a good account of the Chinese military debacle in the face of the Japanese Ichigo offensive and how it eroded American confidence in Chiang, see Rana Mitter, *Forgotten Ally: China's World War II, 1937–1945* (Boston, MA : Houghton Mifflin Harcourt, 2013), 318–325.
2. Mao and Peng Dehuai to Deng Xiaoping, December 16, 1943, *JDYLZYWX,* 20:673–674.
3. Chiang to Roosevelt, December 10, 1943, *Jiang Zhongzheng xiansheng nianpu changbian,* 7:519; see also van de Ven, *War and Nationalism in China,* 46.
4. Chiang diary, August 25, 1943, Huang Zijin and Pan Guangzhe, eds., *Kunmianji* (Hardship and diligence [in Chiang Kai-shek's diaries]) (Taipei: Academia Historica, 2011), 2:920–921; Xu Yongchang diary, September 1, 1943, *Xu Yongchang riji,* 7:157.
5. Chiang diary, November 12, 1943.
6. *ZHMGZYSL,* 5th ser., 4:261–262.
7. Mao to Dong Biwu, February 4, 1944, in Tong et al., *Nanfangju danshi ziliao,* 3:96.
8. *MNP*-A, 2:496; *ZHMGZYSL,* 5th ser., 4:262.
9. *ZNP*-A, 2:583.
10. Ibid., 585.
11. Zhou Enlai, "On The Question of Constitutional Politics and Unity," March 12, 1944; *Jiefang ribao* (Liberation daily), March 14, 1944, 1; *ZNP*-A, 2:585–586.

12. *MNP-A,* 2:508; *ZNP-A,* 2:586.

13. Wang Shijie diary, May 4 and May 6, 1944, *Wang Shijie riji* (Diaries of Wang Shijie) (Taipei: Institute of Modern History, Academia Sinica, 2013) 601–602; *ZNP-A,* 574.

14. Mao's work report at the Seventh Plenum of the CCP's Sixth CC, May 21, 1944, *MWJ,* 3:141.

15. Mao to Lin Boqu, May 15, 1944, *MWJ,* 3:130–134.

16. Wang Shijie diary, May 22, 1944, *Wang Shijie riji,* 606.

17. *ZNP-A,* 2:593; *MNP-A,* 536.

18. *JDYLZYWX,* 21:505.

19. *MNP-A,* 2:517–518.

20. Mao to CCP Central China Bureau, August 3, 1944; Mao and Liu to Rao Shushi et al., November 2, 1944, *MJSWJ,* 2:728, 733–734.

21. CMC to Zheng Weisan, Li Xiannian et al., October 14, 1944, *MJSWJ,* 2:731–732.

22. Ch'i Hsi-sheng. *The Much Trouble Alliance: US-China Military Cooperation during the Pacific War, 1941–1945* (Singapore: World Scientific, 2016), 581–582.

23. Wang Shijie diary, June 22 and 23, 1944, *Wang Shijie riji,* 614–615; Lyman P. Van Slyke, ed., *The China White Paper, August 1949* (Stanford, CA: Stanford University Press, 1967), 55–57; see also the discussion of the impact of Wallace's China visit upon Chiang in Mitter, *Forgotten Ally,* 327.

24. "Welcome Mr. Wallace," *Jiefang ribao,* June 23, 1944, 1.

25. *ZNP-A,* 2:591.

26. *Hu Qiaomu huiyi Mao Zedong,* 333.

27. David D. Barrett, *Dixie Mission: The United States Army Observer Group in Yenan, 1944* (Berkeley: Center for Chinese Studies, University of California, 1970).

28. CCP CC's instruction on diplomatic work, August 18, 1944, *ZGZYWJXJ-A,* 14:315.

29. Joseph W. Esherick, ed., *Lost Chance in China: The World War II Dispatches of John S. Service* (New York: Random House, 1974), 307, 313–314; *ZNP-A,* 2:594.

30. *FRUS,* 1944, 6:562–567; see also Mitter, *Forgotten Ally,* 328–329.

31. Van Slyke, *China White Paper,* 66.

32. Chiang diary, July 7, 1944; *ZHMGZYSLCB,* 3rd ser., 3:637.

33. *China White Paper,* 67.

34. *ZNP-A,* 2:595.

35. *China White Paper,* 72.

36. *FRUS,* 1944, 6:259.

37. Chiang diary, September 24, 1944; *ZHMGZYSLCB,* 7th ser., 3:662–671, 673–674.

38. Michael Schaller, *The U.S. Crusade in China, 1938–1945* (New York: Columbia University Press, 1979), 173–174.

39. Message from Roosevelt to Chiang, October 18, 1944, Charles F. Romanus and Riley Sunderland, *Stilwell's Command Problems* (Washington, DC: Government Printing Office, 1956), 468–469.

40. *FRUS,* 1944, 6:659.

41. Ibid., 666.

42. Schaller, *U.S. Crusade in China,* 195–196.

43. *China White Paper,* 19; *ZHMGZYSL,* 5th ser., 4:293.

44. *FRUS,* 1944, 6:699.

45. *ZNP-A,* 2:600–601.

46. *FRUS,* 1944, 6:703.

47. *ZHMGZYSL,* 5th ser., 4:294.

48. *ZNP*-A, 1:602.

49. *MNP*-A, 2:560.

50. *ZNP*-A, 2:603; Chiang diary, November 23, 1944.

51. *Hu Qiaomu huiyi Mao Zedong*, 353; *ZNP*-A, 2:603.

52. *MNP*-A, 2:561.

53. *ZNP*-A, 2:604.

54. Zhou to Hurley, December 8, 1944, *ZNP*-A, 2:604–605.

55. See Barbara Tuchman, "If Mao Had Come to Washington: An Essay in Alternatives," *Foreign Affairs* 51 (October 1972): 44–62.

56. *ZNP*-A, 2:607.

57. Ibid., 2:610.

58. Ibid., 2:610–611.

59. Wang Shijie diary, February 14, 1945, *Wang Shijie riji*, 1:677; *ZNP*-A, 2:616, and *ZZ*-A, 2:718.

60. *ZZ*-A, 2:719.

61. Mao to Zhou, February 3, 1945, *Zhonggong zhongyang kangri minzu tongyi*, 2:790.

62. *ZHMGZYSL*, 7th ser., 2:541.

63. Chiang diary, March 15, 1944, and the attachment, "Telegram by Ambassador Wei Daoming," Qin Xiaoyi ed., *Zongtong Jiangong dashi changbian chugao* (A preliminary compilation of long records of important events of President Chiang) (Taipei: Chiang Kai-shek Foundation of Culture and Education, 1978), 5A:685–687.

64. Cited from Niu Jun, *Cong yan'an zouxiang shijie* (Beijing: Zhongyang dangshi, 2008), 180.

65. *FRUS*, 1945, 7:317–322.

66. *MNP*-A, 589; *MXJ*, 3:1111–1114.

67. Li Yong and Zhang Zhongtian, *Jiang Jieshi (Chiang Kai-shek) nianpu* (Beijing: Zhongong dangshi, 1995), 311.

68. Mao Zedong, Concluding Remarks at the CCP's Seventh Congress, May 31, 1945, CCA; see also *MWJ*, 3:376–421.

69. Zhou, "On United Front," April 30, 1945, *ZTYZXWX*, 77–110.

70. CCP CC to CCP Guangdong Regional Committees, June 16, 1945, *ZGZYWJXJ*-A, 15:145.

71. CCP CC to Zheng Weisan, Li Xiannian, and Chen Shaomin, August 4, 1945, *ZGZYWJXJ*-A, 15:200.

72. *ZHMGZYSL*, 7th ser., 2:571–635.

73. Cited from Yang Kuisong, *Zhonggong he mosike de guanxi* (The relationship between the CCP and Moscow) (Taipei: Dongda, 1997), 521.

74. CCP CC (drafted by Mao) to Zheng Weishan et al. and convey to CCP Central China Bureau, August 10, 1945; CCP CC's resolution on the party's tasks after Japan's surrender, August 11, 1945; CCP CC (drafted by Mao) to Wang Zhen and Wang Shoudao, August 11, 1945, *MNP*-A, 3:1–2.

75. Wang Tieya, ed., *Zhongwai jiu yuezhang huibian* (A collection of old Chinese and foreign treaties) (Beijing: Sanlian, 1957), 3:1329; *ZHMGZYSL*, 7th ser., 2:613–620.

76. *Zhongyang ribao* (Central Daily, Chongqing), August 16, 1945.

77. *Zhonggong dangshi dashi ji* (Important events in CCP history) (Beijing: Renmin, 1981), 78; Shi, *Zai lishi juren shenbian*, 274; f. 45, op. 1, d. 322, APRF.

78. CCP CC and CMC's instruction on changing strategic policies, August 22, 1945, *JGYLZYWX*, 22:645.

79. *ZZ*-A, 2:727.

80. Mao's speech to the Politburo meeting, August 23, 1945, *MNP-A,* 3:10–11.

81. *Hu Qiaomu huiyi Mao Zedong,* 395; *ZZ-A,* 2:630.

82. *Zhongyang ribao* (Chongqing), August 25, 1945.

83. *MNP-A,* 3:12.

84. *MNP-A,* 3:13; *ZNP-A,* 2:630.

85. *MNP-A,* 3:14.

86. *MNP-A,* 3:16–17; *ZZ-A,* 729.

87. Chiang diary, August 19 and September 2, 1945.

88. *ZHMGZYSL,* 7th ser., 2:39–41.

89. Ibid.

90. "GMD-CCP Negotiations," September 27, 1945, Party History Work Commission of CCP Chongqing Municipal Committee et al., eds., *Chongqing tanpan jishi* (A factual record of Chongqing negotiations) (Chongqing: Chongqing, 1984), 219; *ZNP-A,* 2:636.

91. *MNP-A,* 3:13.

92. *MXJ,* 4:1151; *MNP-A,* 3:13–15.

93. See Yang, *Zhongong he mosike de guanxi,* 531–532; Zeng Kelin, *Zeng Kelin jiangjun zishu* (General Zeng Kelin's autobiography) (Shenyang: Liaoning renmin, 1997), 108–111. Zeng accompanied Lieutenant Colonel Belunosov to visit Yan'an and thus was an important witness of this important event.

94. CCP CC's instruction "Maintaining Defensive in the South and Waging Offensive in the North," September 19, 1945, *JDYLZYWX,* 22:685–686.

95. CCP CC's instruction to the CCP Northeast Bureau, October 19, 1945, *JDYLZYWX,* 22:753–754.

96. Statement by President Truman on United States Policy toward China, December 15th, 1945, in Van Slyke, *China White Paper,* 607–609.

97. Cited from Yang, *Zhongjian didai de geming,* 485.

98. CCP Center instruction on changing US policy toward China and our responses, December 19, 1945, *JDYLZYWX,* 22:870–871.

99. *ZNP-A,* 2:647; for a vivid account of the meeting, see Daniel Kurtz-Phelam, *The China Mission: George Marshall's Unfinished War, 1945–1947* (New York: W.W. Norton, 2018), 65–66.

100. Zhou's interview with Lieberman, *New York Times* correspondent in Nanjing, September 1946, *Zhou Enlai wenda lu* (Dialogues with Zhou Enlai) (Beijing: Renmin, 2016), 169.

101. Marshall even agreed to the comments by a Nationalist general that Zhou was "an extremely able and liberal-minded man with high integrity." *FRUS,* 1946, 9:1506.

102. Xiong Xianghui, *Wo de waijiao yu qingbao shengya* (My diplomatic and intelligence career, revised and expanded edition) (Beijing: Zhonggong dangshi, 2006) 31–34.

103. *ZHMGZYSL,* 7th ser., 3:64.

104. *MNP-A,* 3:54.

105. Meng Guanghan et al., *Zhengzhi xieshang huiyi jishi* (Factual accounts of the Political Consultative Conference) (Chongqing: Chongqing, 1989), 2:344–349.

106. *FRUS,* 1946, 9:139–141.

107. Chiang diary, January 23, 1946.

108. *ZNP-A,* 2:656.

109. Liu's speech, cited from Yang, *Zhongjian didai de geming,* 492; *LNP,* 2:14–15; *ZNP-A,* 2:656.

110. CCP CC's instruction on current situation and tasks, February 1, 1946, *JDYLZYWX,* 23:108.

111. *MNP-A*, 3:57; *LNP*, 2:20; see also Yang, *Zhongjian didai de geming*, 496.

112. *Zhou Enlai 1946nian tanpan wenxaun* (Selected documents of Zhou Enlai's negotiations in 1946) (Beijing: Zhongyang wenxian, 1996), 696.

113. CCP CC to Ye Jianying, Rao Shushi and convey to Zhou, February 28, 1946, cited from Yang, *Zhongjian didai de geming*, 497.

114. *ZHMGZYSL*, 7th ser., 1:453–454.

115. See Yang, *Zhonggong yu mosike de guanxi*, 559–560.

116. CCP CC (drafted by Mao) to CCP Northeast Bureau, March 24, 1946, *MNP-A*, 3:62–63.

117. *FRUS*, 1946, 9:802–805.

118. *Zhou Enlai 1946nian tanpan wenxuan*, 442.

119. Chiang diary, July 2, 1946.

120. *ZNP-A*, 2:722–723.

121. Zhou to Guo Moruo and Yu Liqun, November 1946, *ZSXXJ*, 356.

14. The Civil War (1946–1949)

1. Mao's talks with Zhou and Liu, November 21, 1946 (notes taken by Hu Qiaomu), CCA.

2. *ZNP-A*, 1:723–724; *JDYLZYWX*, 23:556–559.

3. Mao's talks with Zhou and Liu, November 21, 1946, CCA; see also *MNP-A*, 3:150–151; *MWJ*, 4: 196–200.

4. Mao's talks with Zhou and Liu, November 21, 1946, CCA.

5. Mao, "Talks with Anna Louis Strong," *Mao Zedong xuanji* (Selected Works of Mao Zedong, hereafter *MXJ*) (Beijing: Renmin, 1991), 4:1191–1192; *RMRB*, January 4, 1947.

6. Zhou and Lu Dingyi to Fang Fang and others, January 20, 1947, *JDYKZYWX*, 24:41.

7. Chiang diary, March 2, 1947; see also *Hu Zongnan xiansheng riji* (Mr. Hu Zongnan's diary) (Taipei: Academia Historica, 2015), 632; Kenneth W. Rea and John C. Brewer, eds., *The Forgotten Ambassador: The Reports of John Leighton Stuart, 1946–1949* (Boulder, CO: Westview Press, 1981), 70–71.

8. Xiong Xianghui, *Lishi de zhujiao* (Footnotes to history) (Beijing: Zhongyang dangxiao, 1995), 100–101.

9. In his talks with Liu and Zhou on November 21, 1946, Mao already mentioned that "it is now possible that we may lose Yan'an." Mao's talks with Zhou and Liu, November 21, 1946, CCA.

10. Chiang diary, March 19, 1947.

11. Stalin to Dr. Alof, June 15, 1947, f. 39, op. 1, d. 31, APRF; Shi Zhe, *Zai lishi juren shenbian: Shi Zhe huiyilu*, rev. ed. (At the side of historical giants: Shi Zhe's memoir) (Beijing: Zhongyang dangxiao, 1998), 308; interview with Shi Zhe, August 1992.

12. *ZNP-A*, 1:746; CCP Notice on Defending Shaan-Gan-Ning Border Region, April 9, 1947, *JDYLZYWX*, 24:130–131.

13. *ZNP-A*, 1:765.

14. *JDYLZYWX*, 24:115.

15. *JDYLZYWX*, 24:126, 130.

16. Tong, *Fengyu sishinian*, 1:500.

17. *ZJSWX*, 3:193.

18. *ZNP-A*, 1:758; Liu Jixian et al., *Ye Jianying nianpu* (Chronological records of Ye Jianying) (Beijing: Zhongyang wenxian, 2007), 1:474–475; Wang Yazhi, "Zhou Enlai and the Intelligence, Confidential and Communication work in Shanbei," in Li Qi, ed., *Zai Zhou Enali shenbian de rizi* (Time at the side of Zhou Enlai) (Beijing: Zhongyang wenxian, 1998), 597; interview with Wang Yazhi, August 1992.

19. *Hu Qiaomu huiyi Mao Zedong*, 422.

20. *ZNP-A*, 1:662.

21. Ibid., 1:726.

22. *Zhonggong zhongyang jiefang zhanzheng shiqi tonghyi zhanxian wenjian xuanbian* (Selected united front documents of the CCP CC during the War of Liberation) (Beijing: Dang'an, 1988), 139–140; *JDYLZYWX*, 24:22–23.

23. Zhou's speech at a Politburo meeting, February 1, 1947, cited from Jin Chongji, *Zhuanzhe niandai: Zhongguo de 1947* (Transformative years: China in 1947) (Beijing: Zhongyang wenxian, 2017), 86; *ZNP-A*, 1:736–737.

24. *ZXJ*, 1:268–270; *JDYLZYWX*, 24:98–100.

25. *ZNP-A*, 1:758.

26. *MJSWX*, 3:348.

27. *MXJ*, 4:1187.

28. *ZJSWX*, 3:181.

29. Qin Xiaoyi, ed., *Zongtong jianggong yanlun zongji* (A collection of President Jiang Jieshi's speeches and writings) (Taipei: GMD Party History Committee, 1984), 22:112, 113.

30. *MNP-A*, 3:78.

31. *JGYLZYWX*, 24:246, 256.

32. Chiang diary, June 22, 1947.

33. *ZJSWX*, 3:323; *ZNP-A*, 2:760.

34. *MWJ*, 4:333.

35. Zhou's speech at a CCP CC meeting, December 26, 1947, *ZZ-A*, 863–864; *ZNP-A*, 2:775–776.

36. *ZJSWX*, 3:304.

37. Chiang diary, February 23, 1948.

38. Chiang diary, June 10, 1948.

39. Xu Yongchang diary, November 12, 1948, *Xu Yongchang riji*, 9:138–139.

40. Chiang diary, September 3, 1948.

41. *ZJSWX*, 3:425–426.

42. Zhou's speech at a Politburo meeting, September 13, 1948, *ZJSWX*, 3:437; *Hu Qiaomu huiyi Mao Zedong* (2003), 523.

43. *MWJ*, 5:133; *ZJSWX*, 3:425–426; Jin Chongji, *Ershi shiji zhongguo shigang* (A 20th-century history of China) (Beijing: Shehui kexue wenxian, 2009), 2:645.

44. *Hu Qiaomu huiyi Mao Zedong*, 523.

45. *ZNP-A*, 2:809.

46. Ibid., 809.

47. Zhou to Zheng Dongguo, October 18, 1948, *ZSXXJ*, 415.

48. *ZJSWX*, 3:530–531, 538–540; see also *ZZ-A*, 902.

49. *ZNP-A*, 2:828. *ZZ-A*, 927; Yu Zhanbang, "The Whole Story of the GMD-CCP Peace Negotiation in Beiping in 1949," *Wenshi ziliao xuanji* (Selected Collections of History and Literature Materials) 67: 56–57.

50. *MXJ*, 4:1375.

51. *MXJ*, 4:1391–1394.

52. Chiang diary, February 1, 1949.

53. *JDYLZYWX*, 26:24.

54. *ZZ-A*, 2:913.

55. *MXJ,* 4:1438.

56. ZZ-A, 2:826.

57. Huang Qihan, "Recollections of the 1949 Peace Negotiation," *Wenshi ziliao xuanji* (Selected materials of literature and history) 67:13.

58. Zhou's speech at a roundtable attended by democratic figures, January 16, 1949, ZZ-A, 2:922.

59. Yu, "GMD-CCP Negotiations," 56–57.

60. Yang, *Guomindang de liangong yu fangong,* 724.

61. Li, *Huiyi yu yanjiu,* 2:512.

62. Ibid., 2:513.

63. Ibid., 2:513–514.

64. Yang, *Guomindang de liangong yu fangong,* 729.

65. Chen Jian, *Mao's China and the Cold War* (Chapel Hill, NC: University of North Carolina Press, 2001), 38–39.

66. Yang Kuisong, *Zhonghua renmin gongheguo jianguo shi yanjiu* (Studies on the history of the founding of the PRC) (Nanchang: Jiangxi renmin, 2010), 54.

67. CCP CC to CCP Northeast Bureau (drafted by Zhou), November 10, 1948, CCA; see also *ZNP*-A, 2:816.

68. Ward to Marshall, November 15, 1948, *FRUS,* 1948, 7:834–835; CCP Northeast Bureau to CCP CC, November 15, 1948, CCA.

69. Mao to Gao Gang, November 17, 1948; Mao to CCP Northeast Bureau (drafted by Zhou), November 18, 1948, CCA.

70. CCP Northeast Bureau to CCP CC, 12:00, November 21, 1948; CCP CC to CCP Northeast Bureau (drafted by Zhou), November 23, 1948, CCA; Stuart to Marshall, November 21, 1948, and Clubb to Marshall, November 26, 1948, *FRUS,* 1948, 7:838–839, 840.

71. Chen Jian, "The Ward Case and the Emergence of Sino-American Confrontation, 1948–1950," *Australian Journal of Chinese Affairs,* no. 30 (July 1993): 149–170.

72. Mao to Gao Gang, November 17, 1948, CCA.

73. CCP CC to CCP Northeast Bureau, November 23, 1948, CCA.

74. *ZNP*-A, 2:825–826.

75. CCP CC's directive on diplomatic affairs, January 19, 1949, *JDYLZYWX,* 26:55–60; *ZNP*-A, 2:829.

76. Interview with Shi Zhe, August 1992.

77. "Memorandum of Conversation between Anastas Mikoyan and Mao Zedong," January 30, 1949, No. 112416, WWCDA, https://digitalarchive.wilsoncenter.org/document/112416; Shi, *Zai lishi juren shenbian,* 334–344.

78. "Memorandum of Conversation between Anastas Mikoyan and Zhou Enlai," February 1, 1949, No. 110003, WWCDA, https://digitalarchive.wilsoncenter.org/document/110003; see also *ZNP*-A, 2:831.

79. Shi, *Zai lishi juren shenbian,* 346.

80. Shen Zhihua and Xia Yafeng, *Mao and the Sino-Soviet Partnership, 1945–1959* (Lanham, MD: Lexington Books, 2015), 27.

81. Mao's concluding remarks at the CCP Seventh CC's Second Plenum, March 13, 1949, CCA.

82. Mr. Chen Mingshu's report on American ambassador's two secret visits to Shanghai, March 26, 1949, CCA; Stuart diary, March 25 and 26, 1949.

83. *MXJ,* 4:1436.

84. CCP CMC to CCP General Front Committee, April 28, 1949, *MWJ,* 5:280.

85. CCP CC and CCP CMC to CCP General Frontal Committee, April 26, 1949, *ZJSWX,* 3:638–639.

86. *JDYLZYWX,* 26:23–24.

87. *MJSWJ,* 5:600.

88. Huang Hua, *Qinli yu jianwen: Huang Hua huiyilu* (Personal experience: Huang Hua's memoirs) (Beijing: Shijie zhishi, 2007), 79; interview with Huang Hua, October 1997.

89. CCP CC to CCP Nanjing Committee, May 10, 1949, *JDYLZYWX,* 26:397–398.

90. Huang, *Qinli yu jianwen,* 81.

91. Ibid., 82.

92. CCP CC to CCP Nanjing Committee, June 3, 1949, *JDYLZYWX,* 26:438–439.

93. *FRUS,* 1949, 8:741–767; Huang, *Qinli yu jianwen,* 81–83.

94. *ZWG,* 1:21.

95. Ibid., 21–22.

96. Ibid., 22.

97. Ibid., 23.

98. Ibid., 20.

99. Kovalev to Stalin, May 23, 1949, f. 45, op. 1, d. 331, ARPF.

100. Stalin's meeting with Liu on June 27, 1949: support to China, July 28, 1949, f. 45, op. 1, d. 329, APRF; Shi, *Zai lishi juren shenbian,* 361.

101. *Jianguo yilai Liu Shaoqi wengao* (Liu Shaoqi's manuscripts since the founding of the People's Republic, hereafter *LWG*) (Beijing: Zhoungyang wenxian, 2005–), 1:1–22; Liu's report to Stalin, f. 45, op. 1, d. 328, APRF.

102. Shi, *Zai lishi juren shenbian,* 368–369; interview with Shi Zhe, August 1992.

103. *MXJ,* 4:1477.

104. Secretary of State to the Ambassador in China, 6 P.M., July 1, 1949, *FRUS,* 1949, 8:766.

105. *United States Relations with China, with Special Reference to the Period 1944–1949,* issued by the US Department of State, Washington, DC, August 1949.

106. *MXJ,* 4:1486–1520.

15. "We, the Chinese, Have Stood Up!" (1949–1950)

1. *MWJ,* 5:343.

2. *ZWG,* 1:389–396.

3. Mao, Conclusion at the Second Plenum of the Seventy CC, March 13, 1949, CCA.

4. *ZNP-A,* 2:850–851.

5. Zhou, preliminary draft of "Common Program of New Democracy," August 22, 1949, *ZWG,* 1:291–316.

6. *Zhonggong Zhongyang wenjian xuanji, 1949–1966* (Selected documents of the CCP Central Committee, 1949–1966, hereafter *ZGZYWJXJ*-B) (Beijing: Renmin, 2013), 1:62–63.

7. Editorial Group, *Minzu wenti wenxian huibian* (A collection of documents on nationality issues, hereafter *MZWTWX*) (Beijing: Zhongyang dangxiao, 1991), 177–180, 185–186.

8. Edgar Snow, *Red Star over China* (New York: Random House, 1938), 444.

9. *Zhou Enlai 1946nian tanpan wenxuan,* 723.

10. *MZWTWX,* 1266–1267.

11. *ZNP-A,* 2:808; *ZZ-A,* 2:940–941.

12. Zhou to Song Qingling, June 21, 1949, *ZSXXJ,* 418; *ZZ-A,* 2:950–951.

13. Yun Shui, *Chushi qiguo jishi: Jiangjun dashi Wang Youping* (On diplomatic missions to seven countries: General and Ambassador Wang Youping) (Beijing: Shijie zhishi, 1996), 5; Luo Guibo interview, August 1992.

14. Zhou to Wang Bingnan, July 29, 1947; Zhou to Ye Jianying and convey to Wang Bingnan and others, November 10, 1947, *ZSXXJ,* 401–404; *ZNP*-A, 1:744.

15. Ling, *Cong Yan'an dao Lianheguo,* 58–60.

16. *Zhou Enlai waijiao wenxuan* (Selected diplomatic papers of Zhou Enlai, hereafter *ZWJWX*) (Beijing: 1990), 7.

17. Gromyko to Zhou, October 2, 1949, *RMRB,* October 4, 1949, 1; and Gromyko to Stalin, October 2, 1950, f. 07, op. 22a, p. 13, d. 198, AVPRF.

18. *MXJ,* 4:1477–1478.

19. CCP CC to Wang Jiaxiang, November 9, 1949, *Jianguo yilai Mao Zedong wengao* (Mao Zedong's manuscripts since the founding of the People's Republic, hereafter *MWG*), 13 vols. (Beijing: Zhongyang wenxian, 1987–1998), 1:131.

20. Mao to Stalin, November 12, 1949, *MWG,* 1:135.

21. Shi Zhe, *Zai lishi juren shenbian: Shi Zhe huiyilu* (At the side of historical giants: Shi Zhe's memoir), rev. ed. (Beijing: Zhongyang dangxiao, 1998), 387; *RMRB,* December 19, 1949, 1.

22. Shi, *Zai lishi juren shenbian,* 389–390; interview with Shi Zhe, August 1992.

23. Conversation between Stalin and Mao, Moscow, December 16, 1949, *Cold War International History Project (CWIHP) Bulletin,* nos. 6–7 (Winter 1995–1996), 5–7; *MNP*-B, 1:59; f. 45, op.1, d. 329, APRF.

24. Conversation between Stalin and Mao, Moscow, December 16, 1949, *CWIHP Bulletin,* nos. 6–7 (Winter 1995–1996), 5–7; f. 45, op. 1, d. 329, APRF; Shi, *Zai lishi juren shenbian,* 389–390.

25. Mao to Liu, December 18, 1949, *MNP*-B, 1:60.

26. Liu, Zhu De, and Zhou to Mao, December 21, 1950, *LWG,* 1:218–219.

27. Shi, *Zai lishi juren shenbian,* 394.

28. *MNP*-B, 1:62.

29. *MNP*-B, 1:62–63.

30. Mao to CCP CC, December 25, 1949, *MNP*-B, 1:63.

31. Interview with Shi Zhe, August 1992; Shi, *Zai lishi juren shenbian,* 391.

32. Kovalev's report to Stalin, "Several Questions of CCP Policies," December 24, 1949, f. 3, op. 65, d. 584, APRF.

33. *Wang Dongxing riji* (Wang Dongxing's diary) (Beijing: Zhongguo shehui kexue, 1993), 166–168.

34. Mao to CCP CC, January 2, 1950, *MWG,* 1:211; interview with Shi Zhe, August 1992.

35. Mao to CCP CC, 11 P.M., January 2, 1950, *MWG,* 1:211–212.

36. Mao to CCP CC, 4:00 A.M., January 3, 1950, *MWG,* 1:213.

37. Liu, Zhu De, and Zhou to Mao (drafted by Zhou), 7:30 P.M., January 4, 1951, *ZWG,* 2:8–9.

38. Li Ping and Ma Zhisun et al., *Zhou Enlai nianpu, 1949–1976* (Chronological records of Zhou Enlai, 1949–1976, hereafter *ZNP*-B) (Beijing: Zhongyang wenxian, 1998), 1:20.

39. Interview with Shi Zhe, August 1992.

40. Stalin and Mao meeting, January 22, 1950, f. 45, op. 1, d. 319, APRF; see also *MNP*-B, 1:84–85; Zhou to Liu and CCP Politburo, February 8, 1950, *ZWG,* 2:91–92.

41. *MNP*-B, 1:85–86.

42. Zhou to Liu and CCP Politburo, February 8, 1950, *ZWG,* 2:92.

43. Mao to Liu, 5:00 A.M. January 25, 1950, *MWG,* 1:251.

44. Soviet draft on Dalian, January 26, 1950, f. 07, op. 23a, p. 20, d. 248, AVPRF.

45. Chinese draft agreements on Lüshun, Dalian, and CER, January 26, 1950, f. 07, op. 23a, p. 20, d. 248, AVPRF.

46. Sino-Soviet Treaty of Friendship and Alliance (draft), January 24, 1950, *ZWG,* 2:53–54.

47. Shen Zhihua, *Zhongsu guanxi shigang* (A history of Chinese-Soviet relations) (Beijing: Shehui kexue, 2011), 119–120.

48. Soviet draft of PRC and USSR agreements on Lüshun, Dalian, and CER, January 28, 1950, f. 07, op. 23a, p. 20, d. 248, AVPRF.

49. Soviet revised version on the Chinese draft of the Sino-Soviet Treaty of Friendship, Alliance, and Mutual Assistance, January 29, 1950, f. 07, op. 23a, p. 18, d. 235, AVPRF.

50. Zhou to Liu and CCP CC, February 8, 1950, *ZWG,* 2:91–96.

51. Ibid., 95.

52. Report by Vyshinsky to Stalin, February 12, 1950, f. 3, op. 65, d. 369, APRF.

53. *Zhonghua renmin gongheguo duiwai guanxi wenjianji* (A collection of documents of PRC foreign relations) (Beijing: Shijie zhishi, 1957), 1:75–77.

54. *MNP*-B, 1:98–99; *MWG,* 1:291.

55. Zhou's speech at a Northeast cadres meeting, March 3, 1950, cited from Jin Chongji et al., *Zhou Enlai zhuan, 1949–1976* (A biography of Zhou Enlai, 1949–1976, hereafter ZZ-B) (Beijing: Zhongyang wenxian, 1998), 1:41.

56. Mao to Su Yu and CCP East China Bureau, June 14, 1949, CCA.

57. Mao to Su Yu and CCP East China Bureau, June 21, 1949, CCA.

58. Mao to Zhou, July 10, 1949, CCA.

59. For discussions, see Sergei Goncharov, John Lewis, and Xue Litai, *Uncertain Partners: Stalin, Mao and the Korean War* (Stanford, CA: Stanford University Press, 1993), 69; see also Lü Liping, *Tongtian zhilu* (The path leading to the sky) (Beijing: Jiefangjun, 1989), 132–169.

60. Lü, *Tongtian zhilu,* 137–156.

61. Michael Szonyi, *Cold War Island: Quemoy on the Front Line* (New York: Cambridge University Press, 2008), chap. 2; for a Chinese Communist account of the PLA's Jinmen defeat, see *Ye Fei Huiyilu* (Ye Fei's memoirs) (Beijing: Jiefangjun, 1988), 597–609.

62. Xu Yan, *Jinmen zhizhan* (Battles of Jinmen) (Beijing: Zhongyang guangbo dianshi, 1992), 94–102.

63. *MWG,* 1:100–101.

64. Mao to Zhou, July 10, 1949, CCA; *ZNP*-A, 1:854.

65. Roshchin's meeting with Zhou, December 5, 1949, f. 100, op. 42, d. 288, AVPRF.

66. Hong Xuezhi et al., *Zhongguo renmin jiefangjun disi yezhanjun zhanshi* (A war history of the Fourth Field Army of the PLA) (Beijing: Jiefangjun, 1998), chap. 12.

67. Xu, *Jinmen zhizhan,* 111–116.

68. *Zhongguo renmin jiefang jun zhashi* (War history of the Chinese People's Liberation Army) (Beijing: Junshi kexue, 2011), 4:114.

69. He Di, "The Last Campaign to Unify China," *Chinese Historians* 5, no. 1 (1992): 12; Xu, *Jinmen zhizhan,* 116–125, esp. 124–125.

70. Wu Shi et al.'s case of treason, Bureau of Martial Law under the Ministry of Defense, April 11, 1950–June 29, 1953, B3750347701/0039/3132034/34,accessed at Taiwan's official "Archive Access Service" (https://aa.archives.gov.tw).

71. Information gained from interviews with a senior Chinese military historian and two senior party historians.

72. Wang, *Xianchang lishi,* 135–136.

73. Melvyn Goldstein, *A History of Modern Tibet: The Demise of the Lamaist State* (Berkeley: University of California Press, 1989), 613–614.

74. *RMRB,* September 3, 1949, 1.

75. *MWG,* 1:152.

76. *LWG,* 1:2; *Heping jiefang xizan* (Peaceful liberation of Tibet) (Lhasa: Xizang renmin, 1995), 59–60; *Mao Zeodong Xizang gongzuo wenxuan* (Selected works on Tibet by Mao Zedong, hereafter *MXZWX*) (Beijing: Zhongyang wenxian and Zhongguo zangxue, 2001), 9–10.

77. For more detailed discussion, see Chen Jian, "The Chinese Communist 'Liberation' of Tibet, 1949–1951," in *Dilemma of Victory: The Early Years of the People's Republic of China,* ed. Jeremy Brown and Paul Pickowicz (Cambridge, MA: Harvard University Press, 2007), 136–138.

78. *RMRB,* January 21, 1950.

79. Goldstein, *History of Modern Tibet,* 623–624.

80. Chen, "Chinese Communist 'Liberation' of Tibet," 143–145.

81. Party History Office of Tibet Autonomous Region, eds., *Zhou Enlai yu Xizang* (Zhou Enlai and Tibet) (Beijing: Zhongguo zangxue, 1998), 6–7.

82. Ibid., 16.

83. Ibid., 16–17.

84. Ibid., 17.

85. Goldstein, *History of Modern Tibet,* chap. 18.

86. Ibid., 687.

87. *MWG,* 1:549.

88. Goldstein, *History of Modern Tibet,* 707–708.

89. Indian note, October 26, 1950, in Margaret Carlyle, ed., *Documents on International Affairs, 1949–1950* (London: Oxford University Press, 1953), 550–551.

90. Indian note, October 31, 1950, in Carlyle, *Documents on International Affairs,* 552–554.

91. *MWG,* 1:549.

92. *Mao Zedong Xizang gongzuo wenxuan* (Selected works on Tibet by Mao Zedong, hereafter *MXZWX*) (Beijing: Zhongyang wenxian and Zhongguo zangxue, 2001), 33.

93. Ibid., 34–35.

94. *Heping jiefang Xizang,* 176–178; see also Carlyle, *Documents on International Affairs,* 554–556.

95. B. N. Mullik, *My Years with Nehru: The Chinese Betrayal* (Bombay: Allied Publishers, 1971), 80.

96. *Heping jiefang Xizang,* 213–214; see also Goldstein, *History of Modern Tibet,* 742–743.

97. *Heping jiefang Xizang,* 119; CCP History Research Office of Tibetan Autonomous Region, ed., *Zhou Enlai he Xizang* (Zhou Enlai and Tibet) (Beijing: Zhongguo zangxue, 1998), 11–12.

98. Tsering Shakya, *The Dragon in the Land of Snow* (New York: Columbia University Press, 1999), 62.

99. Dan Zeng and Zhang Xiangming et al., *Dangdai zhongguo de Xizang* (Tibet of contemporary China) (Beijing: Dangdai zhongguo, 1991), 1:164; Shakya, *Dragon,* 69.

100. *Heping jiefang Xizang,* 129–130.

101. *MXZWX,* 56.

102. *Heping jiefang Xizang,* 207.

16. The Korean War (1950–1953)

1. Bruce Cumings offers detailed and insightful description and analysis of the origins of the Korean War. See *Origins of the Korean War,* 2 vols. (Princeton, NJ: Princeton University Press, 1981, 1990).

2. Shtykov to Vyshinsky, May 15, 1949; Kovalev to Stalin, May 18, 1949, doc. 121117, 114898, WWCDA, https://digitalarchive.wilsoncenter.org/document/121178, https://digitalarchive.wilsoncenter.org/document/114898.

3. Chen Jian, *China's Road to the Korean War* (New York: Columbia University Press, 1994), chap. 6; Kim Dong-jil, "Prelude to War? The Repatriation of Koreans from the Chinese PLA, 1949–50," *Cold War History* 12, no. 2 (June 30, 2011): 227–244.

4. "Politburo Decision to Confirm the Directive to the Soviet Ambassador in Korea," September 24, 1949, *CWIHP Bulletin*, no. 5 (Spring 1995): 6–7.

5. Mao to Stalin, October 21, 1949; Stalin to Mao, October 26, 1949, f. 45, op. 1, d. 332, APRF.

6. Stalin to Stykov, January 30, 1950, No. 112136, WWCDA, https://digitalarchive.wilsoncenter.org/document/112136; Stalin to Stykov, February 2, 1950, f. 45, op. 1, d. 347, APRF.

7. A. Ignatiev to Vyshinsky, April 10, 1950; Shtykov to Vyshinsky, May 12, 1950, f. 059, op. 5, p. 11, d. 4; f. 0102, op. 6, p. 22, d. 49, AVPRF.

8. Zhou's speech at the national work conference of the Second and Fifth Bureaus of the Intelligence Department of the CMC, April 1, 1950, *ZWG*, 2:249.

9. Sergey Goncharov, John Lewis, and Xu Litai, *Uncertain Partners: Stalin, Mao, and the Korean War* (Stanford, CA: Stanford University Press, 1993), 145.

10. Shtykov to Vyshinsky, May 12, 1950, No. 112980, WWCDA, https://digitalarchive.wilsoncenter.org/document/112980.

11. Roshchin to Stalin, May 13, 1950, No. 115977, WWCDA, https://digitalarchive.wilsoncenter.org/document/115977.

12. Vyshinsky, on behalf of Stalin, to Mao, May 14, 1950, No. 115976, WWCDA, https://digitalarchive.wilsoncenter.org/document/115976.

13. Interview with Shi Zhe, August 1992; Roshchin to Stalin, May 16, 1950, cited from Evgeniy P. Bajanov and Natalia Bajanova, "The Korean Conflict, 1950–1953: The Most Mysterious War of the 20th Century—Based on Secret Soviet Archive" (unpublished manuscript, copy in author's possession), 52–53.

14. Roshchin to Stalin, May 16, 1950, ibid., 52–53.

15. Ibid., 53.

16. *RMRB*, June 29, 1950, 1.

17. *Xiao Jingguang huiyilu* (Xiao Jingguang's memoir) (Beijing: Jiefangjun, 1988), 2:8, 2:26.

18. *ZNP-B*, 1:51.

19. Roshchin to Fillipov (Stalin), July 2, 1950, f. 45, op. 1, d. 331, APRF.

20. Stalin to Roshchen, July 5, 1950, *CWIHP Bulletin*, nos. 6–7 (Winter 1995–1996): 43.

21. Nie Rongzhen's report to Mao, July 7, 1950, 173-1-1, PLAA; Mao to Nie, 20:00, July 7, 1950, *MWG*, 1:428.

22. Shtykov to Stalin, July 20, 1950, f. 5, op. 918795, d. 122, pp. 352–353, TsAMO RF (Central Archives of the Ministry of Defense of the Russian Federation); see also *ZJSHDJS*, 2:131; *ZNP-B*, 1:55.

23. Shtykov to Stalin, July 15, 1950, f. 5, op. 918795, d. 122, pp. 303–305, TsAMO RF.

24. Chai Chengwen and Zhao Yongtian, *Kangmei yuanchao jishi* (A factual record of the war to resist America and assist Korea) (Beijing: Zhongyang dangshi ziliao, 1987), 47.

25. *ZWG*, 3:36–37; *ZNP-B*, 1:55, 1:66–67.

26. *MNP-B*, 1:168.

27. *ZNP-B*, 1:62.

28. *ZNP-B*, 1:67.

29. Chai and Zhao, *Panmendian tanpan* (Negotiations at Panmunjom) (Beijing: Jiefanjun, 1992), 77.

30. *ZJSWX,* 4:43–50.

31. *Weida de kangmian yuanchao yundong* (The great movement to resist America and assist Korea) (Beijing: Renmin, 1954), 7–8; *JGYLZYWX,* 1:358–360.

32. Shtykov to Stalin, July 15, 1950; Shtykov to Stalin, July 20, 1950; Shtykov to Vyshinsky, August 28, 1950, f. 5, op. 918795, d. 122, pp. 303–305, 352–355; f. 5, op. 918795, d. 127, pp. 666–669, TsAMO RF.

33. Roshchin to Stalin, September 18, 1950, f. 45, op. 1, d. 331, APRF; Qi Dexue et al., *Kangmei yuanchao zhanzheng shi* (A history of the war to resist America and assist Korea) (Beijing: Junshi kexue, 2000), 1:124.

34. Roshchin to Stalin, September 21, 1950, f. 45, op. 1, d. 331, APRF.

35. *ZNP*-B, 1:80.

36. Roshchin to Stalin, September 21, 1950; Roshchin to Stalin, September 22, 1950, f. 45, op.1, d. 331, APRF; Shtykov to Gromyko, September 21, 1950, f. 5, op. 918795, d. 125, pp. 86–88, TsAMO RF.

37. Kim Il-song and Pak Hon-yong to Stalin, September 29, 1950, *CWIHP Bulletin,* nos. 6–7 (Winter 1995–1996): 111–112; Kim Il-song and Pak Hon-yong to Mao, October 1, 1950, Qi et al., *Kangmei yuanchao zhanshi,* 1:148–149; Stalin to Mao and Zhou, October 1, 1950, see *CWIHP Bulletin,* nos. 6–7 (Winter 1995–1996): 114.

38. No record is available about the meeting. The account here is based upon a 1984 interview transcript by the Peng Dehuai biography group with Yang Shangkun. Interview with Zhang Xi and Wang Yazhi, August 1992.

39. *ZJSWX,* 4:64; *ZNP*-B, 1:83.

40. Mao to Stalin, October 2, 1950, *MWG,* 1:539–540. The quotation in the paragraph is not included in the telegram's published version in *MWG,* but is taken from a photocopy of the telegram's original text that the author obtained from CCA.

41. Interview with Shi Zhe, August 1992.

42. Roshchin to Stalin, October 3, 1950, *CWIHP Bulletin,* nos. 6–7 (Winter 1995–1996): 114–116.

43. Zhou's talks with Panikkar, October 3, 1950, 105-00009-01, CFMA. Panikkar offers a detailed description of Zhou's conversations with him. Zhou told him, "If the Americans crossed the 38th parallel, China would be forced to intervene in Korea." K. M. Panikkar, *In Two Chinas: Memoir of a Diplomat* (London: Allen & Unwin, 1955), 109–110; see also K. M. Panikkar, *An Autobiography,* trans. K. Krishnamurthy (Madras: Oxford University Press, 1977), 235–236; for an American reading of the message, see *FRUS,* 1950, 7:864–865.

44. Pei Jianzhang et al., *Xinzhongguo waijiao fengyun* (New China's diplomatic experiences) (Beijing: Shijie Zhishi, 1990), 97.

45. Zhang Yangwu (Peng's secretary) notes, October 4, 1950 (copy in author's possession); Wang Yan et al., *Peng Dehuai zhuan* (A biography of Peng Dehuai) (Beijing: Dangdai zhongguo, 1993), 400.

46. Wang et al., *Peng Dehuai zhuan,* 401–402; *Peng Dehuai zishu* (An autobiography of Peng Dehuai) (Beijing: Renmin, 1981), 257.

47. *MNP*-B, 1:250; Wang Yan et al., *Peng Dehuai nianpu* (Chronological records of Peng Dehuai, hereafter *PNP*) (Beijing: Renmin, 1998), 441; interview with Yang Shangkun by Peng Dehuai biography group, July 20, 1984, cited from *Peng Dehuai zhuan,* 402; interview with Zhang Xi and Wang Yazhi, August 1993.

48. *Peng Dehuai zishu,* 258; *ZNP*-B, 1:84.

49. *ZNP*-B, 1:84.

50. Mao's Order to Establish the Chinese People's Volunteers, October 8, 1950; Mao to Kim Il-sung, October 8, 1950, *MWG*, 1:543–544, 545.

51. Mao to Stalin via Soviet Embassy, October 8, 1950, f. 558, op. 11, d. 334, RGASPI.

52. Shi, *Zai lishi junren shenbian*, 442–449; interview with Shi Zhe, August 1992.

53. Stalin and Zhou to Soviet embassy in Beijing and convey to Mao, October 11, 1950, f. 558, op. 11, d. 334, RGASPI.

54. Mao to Peng and others, October 12, 1950, *MWG*, 1:552; Mao to Stalin, October 12, 1950, f. 558, op. 11, d. 334, p. 141, TsAMO RF.

55. Mao to Zhou, October 13, 1950, *Jianguo yilai Mao Zedong junshi wengao* (Mao Zedong's military manuscripts since the founding of the People's Republic, hereafter *MJSWG*) (Beijing: Junshi kexue and Zhongyang wenxian, 2009), 1:252–253; *MWG*, 1:556.

56. Mao to Zhou, October 13, 1950, *MWJ*, 6:103–104; *MJSWG*, 1:253.

57. Zhou to Stalin, October 14, 1950, *ZWG*, 3:404–405; Shi, *Zai lishi juren shenbian*, 447–448.

58. Mao to Zhou, October 14, 1950, *MWG*, 1:560.

59. Mao to Peng and Gao Gang, October 17, 1950, *MWG*, 1:567.

60. Mao to Deng Hua et al., October 18, 1950, *MWG*, 1:567–568; *MNP*-B, 1:216.

61. Zhou to Mao and Liu, October 29, 1950, *ZWG*, 3:427; Saharov to Stalin, November 2, 1950, f. 45, op. 1, d. 335, APRF.

62. William Stueck, *The Korean War: An International History* (Princeton, NJ: Princeton University Press, 1995), 139–140.

63. *FRUS*, 1950, 7, pt. 1:1542.

64. Stueck, *Korean War*, 140–141.

65. Zhou's conversation with Panikkar, December 12, 1950, 105-00009-01, CFMA; Panikkar, *In Two Chinas*, 118.

66. Peng to Mao, December 8, 1950, *PNP*, 453–454.

67. Mao's talks with Kim Il-sung, December 3, 1950, *MJSWG*, 1:388.

68. Mao to Peng, December 21, 1950, *MWG*, 1:731–732.

69. *ZNP*-B, 1:108; *FRUS*, 1950, 7:1594–1598.

70. For the text of the proposal, see *FRUS*, 1951, 7:64.

71. Dean Acheson, *Present at the Creation: My Years in the State Department* (New York: North, 1969), 513; see also Stueck, *Korean War*, 153–154.

72. *RMRB*, January 18, 1951; Zhou's conversation with Pannikar, January 17, 1951, 113-00068-01, CFMA; *FRUS*, 1951, 7:91–92.

73. On January 22, the PRC Foreign Ministry, in a note to the Indian ambassador, raised a revised proposal: if the withdrawal of all foreign troops from Korea was accepted "in principle," a limited cease-fire could then be adopted, while all other terms could be settled in further negotiation in relation to political issues. (See *RMRB*, January 24, 1951, 1.) Washington did not respond to this proposal.

74. CCP CC's instruction on Further Carrying out the Resisting American and Assisting Korea Patriotic Movement, February 2, 1951, *ZGZYWJXJ*-B, 5:93–96.

75. Main points of CCP Politburo enlarged meeting, February 18, 1951, *MWG*, 2:126.

76. *PNP*, 480–481; Wang et al., *Peng Dehuai zhuan*, 451–453.

77. Mao to Stalin, March 1, 1951, *MWG*, 2:151–153.

78. Du Pin, *Zai zhiyuanjun zongbu* (At the headquarters of the Chinese volunteers) (Beijing: Jiefangjun, 1988), 237–253.

79. *ZNP*-B, 1:155.

80. *Nie Rongzhen huiyilu,* 741–742.
81. Chen, *Mao's China and the Cold War,* 97–98.
82. *FRUS,* 1951, 7:735.
83. *ZJSWX,* 4:234–235; Chai and Zhao, *Kangmei yuanchao jishi,* 159–160.
84. Mao to Kim Il-sung (drafted by Zhou), July 15, 1952, *ZJSXW,* 4:289–291.
85. Zhou's statements on the peace treaty with Japan, August 15, 1951, 118-00087-01; September 18, 1951, 118-00306-39, CFMA; see also *RMRB,* August 15, 1951.
86. Conversation between Stalin and Zhou, August 20, 1952, *CWIHP Bulletin,* nos. 6–7 (Winter 1995–1996), 9–14; f. 45, op. 1, d. 329, APRF; Shi, *Zai lishi juren shenbian,* 455–456; *ZNP*-B, 256.
87. *MNP*-B, 1:582; *ZJSWX,* 4:292–297.
88. *ZNP*-B, 1:272–273.
89. *ZNP*-B, 263.
90. *ZWJWX,* 61.
91. Mao to Stalin (drafted by Zhou), December 16, 1952, *ZJSWX,* 4:308–313.
92. Lin Li, *Wangshi suoji* (Random notes on past events) (Beijing: Zhongyang wenxian, 2006), 56–57; Shen, *Zhou Enlai yangnu Sun Weishi,* 86–91.
93. Shen, *Zhou Enlai yangnu Sun Weishi,* 160–161.
94. Ren, *Wo zhe jiushinian,* 141.
95. Lin, *Wangshi suoji,* 216.
96. Ren, *Wo zhe jiushinian,* 142–143; Shen, *Zhou Enlai yangnu Sun Weishi,* 169–170.
97. Qi, *Kangmei yuanchao zhanzheng shi,* 3:358–372.
98. Ibid., 380.
99. Soviet Government to Mao and Kim, March 19, 1953, f. 3, op. 65, d. 830, APRF.
100. Minutes, Zhou's meeting with Soviet leaders, March 21, 1953, cited from Shen, *Mao Zedong, Sidalin he chaoxian zhanzheng* (Mao Zedong, Stalin and the Korean War) (Guangzhou: Guangdong renmin, 2013), 403–404.
101. Zhou to Mao, March 21, 1953, *ZWG,* 8:200–204.
102. Mao to Zhou, March 22, 1953, *MJSWG,* 2:133.
103. *ZNP*-B, 291.
104. Mao to Kim (drafted by Zhou), March 27, 1953, *ZNP*-B, 1:291.
105. *ZWG,* 8:217; *RMRB,* March 31, 1953.
106. *ZNP*-B, 1:293.
107. Zhou's report at a foreign affairs meeting, June 5, 1953, 102-00163–01, CFMA; see also *ZWJWX,* 59, 61–62; *MJSWJ,* 6:348.
108. *FRUS,* 1952–1954, 15:1151.
109. *MNP*-B, 2:118.
110. *ZNP*-B, 1:316.
111. Zhou, "On Remolding of Intellectuals," September 29, 1951, *ZXJ,* 2:69–80.
112. Wu Ningkun, *A Single Tear: A Family's Persecution, Love, and Endurance in Communist China* (New York: Atlantic Monthly Press, 1993), 6–7.

17. Transition to Socialism (1952–1955)

1. *MNP*-B, 1:302–303; *ZNP,* 1:130–131.
2. *ZNP*-B, 1:233.

3. Zhou's report to Mao, July 10, 1952, *ZWG*, 7:14–15.

4. Mao's letter to Filipov (Stalin) (drafted by Zhou), July 26, 1952, *ZWG*, 4:37–39; *MNP*-B, 5:576–577.

5. *ZNP*-B, 1:255.

6. Stalin-Zhou meeting, August 20, 1952, f. 45, op. 1, d. 329, APRF; Zhou to Mao and CCP Center, August 21, 1952, cited from Fang Weizhong and Jin Chongji et al., *Li Fuchun zhuan* (A biography of Li Fuchun) (Beijing: Zhongyang wenxian, 2001), 424–425.

7. Stalin-Zhou meeting, September 3, 1950, f. 45, op. 1, d. 329, APRF; Zhou's report to Mao and CCP CC, September 6, 1952, *ZWG*, 7:113–119.

8. *ZNP*-B, 1:258.

9. Zhou to Molotov, September 6, 1952, *ZWG*, 7:120–121.

10. *ZNP*-B, 1:258; Zhou's report to Mao and CCP CC, September 16, 1952, *ZWG*, 7:143–147.

11. Zhou's speech at the Chengdu Conference, March 1958, cited from Luo Pinghan, *Wenge qianye de zhongguo* (China on the eve of the Cultural Revolution) (Beijing: Renmin, 2007), 112.

12. *ZNP*-B, 1:261.

13. *MNP*-B, 1:603; Bo Yibo, *Ruogan zhongda juece he shijian de huigu* (Recollections on important decisions and events, hereafter *Ruogan zhongda juece*) (Beijing: Zhongyang dangxiao, 1993), 1:213; see also *MZ*-B, 38.

14. Bo, *Ruogan zhongda juece*, 1:213.

15. Zhao Jialiang, *Gao Gang zai Beijing* (Gao Gang in Beijing) (Hong Kong: Dafeng, 2008), 104–105.

16. *ZNP*-B, 1:275.

17. Wang Haiguang, "Struggles for Policies or Power: Reinterpreting Origins of the Gao-Rao Affair," *Lingdaozhe* (Leaders), no. 26 (February 2009).

18. Mao to Zhou et al., January 15, 1953, *MWG*, 4:27.

19. *ZNP*-B, 1:280.

20. Bo, *Ruogan zhongda juece*, 1:235, 237–238.

21. Ibid., 1:235.

22. *MWJ*, 6:252.

23. *ZGZYWJXJ*-B, 11:289–294.

24. Zhao, *Gao Gang zai Beijing*, 51.

25. *MWG*, 4:229.

26. *MWG*, 4:229–230.

27. *MZ*-B, 278; An Ziwen's speech at the 1955 CCP national convention, March 1955, cited from Lin Yunhui, *Congkao Gao-Rao fandang shijian* (Revisiting the Gao-Rao "antiparty" incident) (Hong Kong: Chinese University Press, 2017), 135–137.

28. Zhao, *Gao Gang zai Beijing*, 117–120.

29. Ibid., 118.

30. Ibid., 51, 120.

31. Dai Maolin and Zhao Xiaoguang, *Gao Gang zhuan* (A biography of Gao Gang) (Xi'an: Shaanxi renmin, 2011), 316–317; Zhao, *Gao Gang zai Beijing*, 118.

32. Gao later acknowledged that he had "failed to listen to Mao's advice and privately circulated the name list as well as my own wrong ideas." Zhao, *Gao Gang zai Beijing*, 50–51, 118–119.

33. *MNP*-B, 2:107–108.

34. Zhou's speech at the preparatory meeting for the second national conference on finance, June 12, 1953, 684-1-185–3, HPA; *ZNP*-B, 1:307; *ZWG*, 8:344–345.

35. *MWJ*, 6:304.

36. *MNP*-B, 2:116; *Dangde wenxian* (Party history documents), no. 4 (2003): 20.

37. *MWG*, 4:251; *Dangde wenxian*, 20–22; *MXJ*, 5:81–82.

38. *ZXJ*, 2:82.

39. *Dangde wenxian*, no. 4 (2003): 21; *MXJ*, 5:81–82.

40. Bo, *Ruogan zhongda juece*, 1:240.

41. *MZ*-B, 259.

42. Jin Chongji and Chen Qun et al., *Chen Yun zhuan* (A biography of Chen Yun) (Beijing: Zhongyang wenxian, 2015), 2:882–884; Yang et al., *Deng Xiaoping zhuan*, 2:964; Bo, *Ruogan zhongda juece*, 1:243–244.

43. Lin Yunhui, *Congkao Gao-Rao fandang Shijian*, 80.

44. Zhou Enlai's conclusion at the preparatory meeting for the second national conference on finance, June 12, 1953, 684-1-185–3, HPA; *Zhonggong dangshi jiaoxue cankao ziliao* (CCP History Teaching Reference Materials, hereafter *ZGDSJXCKZL*) (Beijing: Guofang daxue, 1986), 20:132–143.

45. Mao's speech at a central work conference, August 12, 1953, 855-2-249–2, HPA; see also *MXJ*, 5:90–94.

46. Wang Haiguang, a renowned party historian, raised this point in his "Struggles for Policies or Power: Reinterpreting Origins of the Gao-Rao Affair."

47. Lin Yunhui, *Xiang shehuizhuyi guodu* (Transition to socialism) (Hong Kong: Chinese University Press, 2008), 309; Zhao, *Gao Gang zai Beijing*, 149–154.

48. Zhao, *Gao Gang zai Beijing*, 51–52.

49. Ibid., 99–100.

50. *LWG*, 5:299–310.

51. Mao's speech at CCP Eighth CC's Second Plenum, November 15, 1956, CCA.

52. *MNP*-B, 2:209; Lin, *Congkao Gao-Rao fandang Shijian*, 118–120.

53. Lin, *Xiang shehuizhuyi guodu*, 302; also see Zhao, *Gao Gang zai Beijing*, 121.

54. *CYNP*, 2:191; *MNP*-B, 2:209, note 2; *Deng Xiaoping wenxuan* (Selected Works of Deng Xiaoping, hereafter *DWX*) (Beijing: Renmin, 1993), 2:257.

55. Zhao, *Gao Gang zai Beijing*, 52.

56. *MNP*-B, 2:209; *CYNP*, 2:191; *DNP*-A, 2:1150.

57. *MNP*-B, 2:210; *CYNP*, 2:191–192.

58. *MNP*-B, 2:210.

59. Ibid., 211.

60. *MWG*, 4:432–433.

61. *MNP*-B, 2:216.

62. Ibid.

63. Ibid., 218.

64. Ibid.

65. *Yang Shangkun riji* (Yang Shangkun's diary) (Beijing: Zhongyang wenxian, 2001), 1:100–103; *MNP*-B, 2:218.

66. *MNP*-B, 2:221.

67. *ZNP*-B, 1:348; *LNP*, 2:320; *DNP*-A, 2:1156.

68. *MNP*-B, 2:221; *Yang Shangkun riji*, 102.

69. *MNP*-B, 2:221; Jin Chongji et al., *Zhu De zhuan* (A biography of Zhu De) (Beijing: Renmin, 1993), 647–648.

70. Gao Gang's speech at the Fourth Plenum of the Seventh CC, February 1954.

71. *ZGDSJXCKZL*, 20:252–260; *LWG*, 6:78–92.

72. *ZGZYWJXJ*-B, 15:249–250.

73. Lin, *Congkao Gao-Rao fandang Shijian*, 207.

74. Zhu Jiamu et al., *Chen Yun nianpu* (Chronological records of Chen Yun, hereafter *CYNP*) (Beijing: Zhongyang wenxian, 2000), 1:197; Lin, *Xiang shehuizhuyi guodu*, 313.

75. Zhao, *Gao Gang zai Beijing*, 207.

76. *ZNP*-B, 1:355.

77. Outline of Zhou's speech at the roundtable on the Gao Gang problem, February 25, 1954, *ZGDSJXCKZL*, 20:267–269.

78. *MWG*, 4:451–452.

79. Zhao, *Gao Gang zai Beijing*, 217–221.

80. Zhang Mingyuan, *Wo de huiyi* (My recollection) (Beijing: Zhonggong dangshi, 2004), 389–391; Zhao, *Gao Gang zai Beijing*, 217–221; Lin, *Congkao Gao-Rao fandang Shijian*, 264–270.

81. Lin, *Congkao Gao-Rao fandang Shijian*, 281–285.

82. Zhao, *Gao Gang zai Beijing*, 240–244; Zhao Jialiang, "Questions and Rebuttals of 'Recalling the Gao-Rao Affair,'" *Yanhuang Chunqiu*, no. 12 (2009): 29–36.

83. Li Rui, *Lushan huiyi shilu* (A factual record of the Lushan Conference) (Zhengzhou: Henan renmin, 1994), 310.

84. Liu Shufa et al., *Chen Yi zhuan* (A biography of Chen Yi) (Beijing: Dangdai zhongguo, 2006), 494.

85. *MNP*-B, 2:211.

86. *LNP*, 2:320; Jing Yuchuan, *Rao Shushi zhuan* (A biography of Rao Shushi) (Hong Kong: Shidai guoji, 2010), 242.

87. Rao's self-criticism, February 9, 1954, *ZGZYWXZLHB*, 6th ser., 1:18–24.

88. Chen Yi's speech at conference on the Rao problem, February 23, 1954, *Zhonggong zhongyao lishi wenxian ziliao huibian* (A collection of CCP's important historical documents and materials, hereafter *ZGZYWXZLHB*) (Los Angeles, CA: Chinese Publication Service Center, 2006), 6th ser., 1:18–24, 51–58.

89. The report by Deng, Chen Yi, and Tan Zhenlin about the Rao problem roundtable, March 1, 1954, SZ15–3371, Hubei Provincial Archive; also see *LWG*, 6:148–149.

90. Rao's second self-criticism, February 23, 1954, *ZGZYWXZLHB*, 6th ser., 1:31–51.

91. Zhang Yun, *Pan Hannian zhuanqi* (Legendary life of Pan Hannian) (Shanghai: Shanghai renmin, 1996), 353–354.

92. Ibid., 236–242.

93. *Chen Yi zhuan*, 494.

94. Mao's comments on "The Essence and Tasks of the Central Intelligence Department," 1941, cited from Luo Qingchang, "Glorifying Tradition of the Intelligence Work, Settling All Remaining Issues," April 14, 1993, *Qingbao shi yanjiu* (Studies of intelligence history), no. 1 (1994).

95. Luo, "Glorifying Tradition"; Kai Cheng, *Li Kenong: Zhongong yingbi zhanxian de zhuoyue lingdaoren* (Li Kenong: outstanding leader of CCP's secret front) (Beijing: Zhonggong dangshi, 2018), 390–396.

96. Peng Shuhua, *Pan Hannian an shenpan qianhou* (Before and after trial of the Pan Hannian case) (Beijing: Zhongguo qingnian, 2010), 39–40.

97. Zhang Yun, *Pan Hannian chuanqi* (The legendary stories of Pan Hannian) (Shanghai: Shanghai renmin, 1996), 363–364.

98. Ibid., 378–383.

99. Jin and Chen et al., *Chen Yun zhuan,* 1:842.

100. *MNP*-B, 2:172–173.

101. Wang Donglin, *Liang Shuming wenda lu* (Dialogues with Liang Shuming) (Hong Kong: Sanlian, 1998), 135; Wang Donglin, *Liang Shuming he Mao Zedong* (Liang Shuming and Mao Zedong) (Changchun: Jilin renmin, 1989), 20.

102. Cited from Wang, *Liang Shuming he Mao Zedong,* 21–22.

103. Ibid., 22–23.

104. Liang Peishu, *Zhongguo zuihou yige daru: Ji fuqing Liang Shuping* (China's last great Confucian) (Nanjing: Jiangsu wenyi, 2012), 307.

105. Wang, *Liang Shuming wenda lu,* 140.

106. *MXJ,* 5:107–115; Wang Donglin, *Liang Shuming wenda lu,* 141–142.

107. Wu Yongping, "Hu Feng's Changing Naming of Zhou Enlai in His Correspondence," *Xin wenxue shiliao* (Historical materials of new literature), no. 3 (1989), 131–142.

108. Lin Mohan, "Before and After the Hu Feng Incident (1)," *Xin wenxuan shiliao,* no. 3 (1989), 4–28.

109. *ZNP*-B, 1:251.

110. *MWG,* 5:174.

18. From Geneva to Bandung (1954–1955)

1. Materials provided by Yudin on Berlin Foreign Ministers' Conference, February 17, 1951, 109-00396-01, CFMA; see also *FRUS,* 1952–1954, 16:415.

2. Shi Zhe, *Zai lishi juren shenbian: Shi Zhe huiyilu* (At the side of historical giants: Shi Zhe's memoir), rev. ed. (Beijing: Zhongyang dangxiao, 1998), 479; *ZNP*-B, 1:356–357.

3. Materials provided by Yudin on inviting China to attend the Geneva Conference, March 2, 1954, 109-00396–01, CFMA; *ZNP*-B, 1:355; Shi, *Zai lishi juren shenbian,* 480.

4. "Preliminary Assessment of and Preparation for the Geneva Conference," February 1954, 206-Y0054, CFMA; *ZNP*-B, 1:356–357; *ZZ*-B, 1:154–156.

5. Zhou's conversation with Li Kenong, Li Chuli, and Luo Guibo, April 13, 1954, CCA; interview with Luo Guibo, August 22, 1992; *ZNP*-B, 1:361; see also Zhou's speech to the Chinese delegation attending the Geneva Conference, June 21, 1954, in Lian Zhengbao et al., *Zhonghua renmin gongheguo waijiao dang'an xuanbian: 1954nian rineiwa huiyi* (Selected diplomatic documents of the People's Republic of China: The Geneva Conference of 1954, hereafter *Rineiwa huiyi*) (Beijing: Shijie zhishi, 2006), 453–454; Xiong Huayuan, *Zhou Enlai chudeng shijie wutai* (Zhou Enlai's first appearance on the world stage) (Shenyang: Liaoning renmin, 1999), 19–20.

6. *ZNP-B,* 1:355; Xiong, *Zhou Enlai chudeng shijie wutai,* 12–13.

7. Xiong, *Zhou Enlai chudeng shijie wutai,* 13; Li Lianqing, *Da waijiaojia Zhou Enlai: shezhan rineiwa* (Great diplomat Zhou Enlai: The Geneva debate) (Hong Kong: Tiandi tushu, 1994), 2:85–86.

8. Zhou to CCP CC, April 23, 1954, 206-00048-08, CFMA; Shi, *Zai lishi juren shenbian,* 480–486; Lian et al., *Rineiwa huiyi,* 18–19; Xiong, *Zhou Enlai chudeng shijie wutai,* 13.

9. Zhou to Mao and the CCP CC, April 28, 1954, cited from *ZNP*-B, 1:363.

10. Conversation between Zhou and Eden at the banquet by Molotov, April 30, 1954, 206-00091-01; Zhou to CCP CC, May 1, 1954, 206-00045-03, CFMA; Lian et al., *Rineiwa huiyi,* 97–98; Li, *Da waijiaojia Zhou Enlai,* 4:58–62; see also the Secretary of State (Dulles) to the Department of State, May 1, 1954, *FRUS,* 1952–1954, 16:648.

11. Zhou to Mao, Liu and CCP CC, May 12, 1954, Lian et al., *Rineiwa huiyi,* 122; Xiong, *Zhou Enlai chudeng shijie wutai,* 81–82; see also *FRUS,* 1952–1954, 16:755–756.

12. Minutes of Zhou-Ho meetings in Liuzhou, July 3, 1954, CCA.

13. Zhou to Mao, Liu and the CCP CC, May 30, 1954, cited from ZZ-B, 1:168–169; see also Xiong, *Zhou Enlai chudeng shijie wutai,* 98.

14. *ZNP*-B, 377–378, 380–382, 383–384; Xiong, *Zhou Enlai chudeng shijie wutai,* 90–91.

15. Zhou to Mao and the CCP CC, June 8, 1954 (two telegrams were dispatched on that day), *ZNP*-B, 1:377–378.

16. Zhou to Mao, Liu, and CCP CC, June 14, 1954; Zhou to Mao, Liu, and CCP CC, June 21, 1954, Lian et al., *Rineiwa huiyi,* 166–167, 176–177.

17. Xiong, *Zhou chudeng shijie wutai,* 90–91; *ZNP*-B, 1:383–384.

18. Zhou's conversation with Eden, June 16, 1954, 207-0005-05, CFMA; *ZNP*-B, 1:383; ZZ-B, 169; see also Anthony Eden, *Full Circle: the Memoirs of Anthony Eden* (Boston: Houghton, 1960), 145; *FRUS,* 1952–1954, 16:1158.

19. Zhou's report on his meeting with Bidault, June 18, 1954, 206-00046-22, CFMA; Lian et al., *Rineiwa huiyi,* 281; *ZNP*-B, 1:387.

20. Zhou's speech about Laos and Cambodia at the Geneva Conference, June 16, 1954, 206-00013-11; see also *FRUS,* 1952–1954, 16:1158.

21. Zhou to Mao, Liu and CCP CC, June 21, 1954, Lian et al., *Rineiwa huiyi,* 176; *FRUS,* 1952–1954, 16:1204–1205.

22. Zhou to Mao et al., June 19, 1954, cited from Xiong, *Zhou Enlai chudeng shijie wutai,* 98.

23. Ibid., 98; *ZNP*-B, 1:385–386; CCP CC to Zhou, June 20, 1954, 206-00049-01, CFMA; CCP CC to Wei Guoqing and Qiao Xiaoguang for delivery to Vietnamese Workers' Party CC, June 20, 1954, 206-00049-01, CFMA.

24. Zhou's conversation with Mendès-France, June 23, 1954, 206-00006-06, CMFA.

25. Zhou's conversation with Sananikone, June 21, 1954, 206-00007-03, CFMA; Zhou to CCP CC about meetings with Cambodian and Laotian delegations, June 24, 1954, 106-00046-29, CFMA; *ZNP*-B, 1:388–389.

26. Minutes of the Zhou-Ho meetings at Liuzhou, July 3–4, 1954, CCA.

27. Ibid.

28. Ibid.

29. Ibid.

30. Ibid.; interview with Luo Guibo, August 22, 1992.

31. *ZNP*-B, 1:394–395.

32. Ho Chi Minh, "Report to the Sixth Meeting of the Vietnamese Workers' Party CC, July 15, 1954, *Selected Works of Ho Chi Minh* (Beijing: Foreign Language Press, 1960), 2:290–298.

33. *ZNP*-A, 1:395; *MNP*-A, 2:255; Mao's speech at an enlarged Politburo meeting, July 7, 1954, *MWJ,* 6:332–337.

34. Zhou to Mao, Liu, and convey to Ho, July 11, 1954, cited from Xiong, *Zhou Enlai chudeng shijie wutai,* 147–148; see also *ZNP*-B, 1:396–397.

35. Xiong, *Zhou Enlai chudeng shijie wutai,* 150.

36. Zhou's conversation with Dong (excerpt), July 12, 1954, Lian et al., *Rineiwa huiyi,* 190–191; Xiong, *Zhou Enlai chudeng shijie wutai,* 151–152; *ZNP*-A, 1:397.

37. Zhou's conversation with Mendès-France, July 13, 1954, 206-Y0007, CFMA.

38. Zhou's conversation with Eden, July 13, 1954, 206-00091-10, CFMA.

39. Zhou to Mao, Liu, and CCP CC, July 20, 1954, Lian et al., *Rineiwa huiyi,* 313–315; *ZNP*-B, 1:398–402.

40. Record of meeting between Lei Jen Min and Trevelyan and Tennant, May 7, 1954, Trade Relations between CPG and UK (Folder 2) (1954), FO 371 / 110288, UKNA.

41. Zhou's conversation with Wilson and Brown, May 30, 1954, 206-00046, 01, CFMA.

42. Zhou's report to CCP CC, June 1, 1954, 206-00046-01, CFMA; CCP Center's reply to Zhou, June 3, 1954, Lian et al., *Rineiwa huiyi,* 416.

43. Zhou's conversation with Eden, June 1, 1954, 110-00023-08; Zhou's report to CCP CC, June 3, 1954, 206-00046-03, CMFA.

44. Zhou speech on diplomatic issues, August 12, 1954, 101-5-542, FPA.

45. Interview with Shi Zhe, August 1992.

46. Conversation between Huan Xiang and Trevelyan, May 19, 1954, 206-00011-03, CFMA.

47. Zhou's report to CCP CC, June 3, 1954, 206-00046-05, CMFA.

48. Conversation between Huan Xiang and Trevelyan, June 4, 1954, 206-00011-05, CFMA.

49. Conversation between Huan Xiang and Trevelyan, afternoon, June 4, 1954, 206-00011-05, CFMA.

50. Lian et al., *Rineiwa huiyi,* 401; *FRUS,* 1952–1954, 14:478.

51. CCP CC to Zhou, July 27, 1954, 206-00048-11(1), CFMA; see also *MNP*-B, 2:262–263.

52. CCP CC to Zhou, July 27, 1954, 206-00048-11(1), CFMA.

53. Several of Zhou's associates, after learning the content of the telegram, all felt that "this is truly unfair to the premier." Interview with Xue Mouhong, August 1994.

54. *RMRB,* July 23, 1954, 1.

55. *ZNP*-B, 1:405.

56. See discussion in Chen, *Mao's China and the Cold War,* chap. 7; Gordon H. Chang, *Friends of Enemies: The United States, China and the Soviet Union, 1948–1972* (Stanford, CA: Stanford University Press, 1990), 126–128.

57. PRC Foreign Ministry to various embassies on attitudes toward the Asian-African conference, December 25, 1954, Lian Zhengbao et al., *Zhonghua renmin gongheguo waijiao dang'an xuanbian: Zhongguo daibiao tuan chuxi 1955nian yafei huiyi* (Selected diplomatic archival documents of the People's Republic of China: Chinese delegation attending the Asian-African Conference, hereafter *Yafei huiyi*) (Beijing: Shijie zhishi, 2007), 25.

58. Zhou to Mao, Liu, and CCP CC, June 22, 1955, cited from Xiong, *Zhou Enlai chudeng shijie wutai,* 125.

59. Records of meetings between premiers of the two countries during Premier Zhou's visit to India, June 1954, 203-00006-1, CFMA; Xiong, *Zhou Enlai chudeng shijie wutai,* 128–129; see also first meeting between Zhou and U Nu, June 28, 1954, CFMA, 203-00007-03.

60. Pei Jianzhang, ed., *Zhonghua renmin gongheguo waijiaoshi, 1949–1956* (A diplomatic history of the People's Republic of China, 1949–1956) (Beijing: Shijie zhishi, 1994), 100, 121–122; Xue Mouhong et al., *Dangdai zhongguo waijiao* (Contemporary Chinese diplomacy) (Beijing: Zhongguo shehui kexue, 1988), 80–81.

61. First and second meetings between Zhou and U Nu, June 28, 1954, 203-00007-03, CFMA.

62. Lian et al., *Yafei huiyi,* 25.

63. Ibid., 14, 25.

64. Plans for Participating in the Asian-African Conference," April 5, 1955, 207-0004-01(1), CFMA.

65. Ibid.; see also "Draft Plan for Participating in the Asian-African Conference," January 16, 1955, 2007-00005-3(1); Asian Department, PRC Foreign Ministry comp., "Issues about the Asian-Afro Conference," December 15, 1954, 207-00085-17(1), CFMA.

66. Paragraph added by Zhou to the text of the "Plans for Participating in the Asian-African Conference," April 5, 1955, 207-0004-01(1), CFMA.

67. A substantial portion of Chinese Foreign Ministry archival documents related to the *Kashmir Princess* incident have been published in Lian et al., *Yafei huiyi,* 144–260; see also Steve Tsang, "Target Zhou Enlai: The 'Kashmir Princess Incident' of 1955," *China Quarterly* 139 (September 1994): 766–782.

68. Robert Cottrell, *The End of Hong Kong: The Secret Diplomacy of Imperial Retreat* (London: John Murray, 1993), 27.

69. On March 12, 1956, in a note to the PRC Foreign Ministry, the British Office in Beijing made the promise: FO 371-120966, UKNA.

70. Zhou's speech at the Asian-African conference, April 23, 1955, *ZWJWX,* 134.

71. The text of the written speech was published in *RMRB,* April 30, 1955.

72. Zhou to Zhang Wentian and report to CCP Center, April 25, 1955; Zhou to CCP Center and report to the Chairman, April 30, 1955, Lian et al., *Yafei huiyi,* 78–79, 87–90.

73. Zhou's supplementary remarks at the Asian-African Conference, April 19, 1954, *ZWJWX,* 120–125.

74. Zhou's conversation with Egyptian ambassador Hassan Ragab, November 7, 1956, 107-00075-02, CFMA.

75. Pei et al., *Zhonghua renmin gongheguo waijiao shi, 1949–1956,* 283.

76. Zhou's meeting with the British Labor Party delegation, August 14, 1954, 110-00027-03, CFMA.

77. Zhou's speech on diplomatic affairs, August 12, 1954, 101-5-542, pp. 1–10, FPA.

78. Pei et al., *Zhonghua renmin gongheguo waijiao shi, 1949–1956,* 160.

79. *ZNP*-B, 1:323–324.

80. Pei et al., *Zhonghua renmin gongheguo waijiao shi, 1949–1956,* 158–159.

81. Zhou's conversation with Shozo Murata, 1:30 P.M., January 23, 1955, 105-00210-03, CFMA; see also Shozo Murata, "Conversation with Premier Zhou," A-0133, pp. 122–148, Diplomatic History Archive, Japanese Foreign Ministry.

82. Zhou's conversation with Tatsunosuke Takasaki, April 22, 1955, 105-00211-04, CFMA.

83. Pei et al., *Zhonghua renmin gongheguo waijiao shi, 1949–1956,* 158–159.

84. See, for example, Premier Zhou's conversation with Tajima Masao, head of Japanese industrial and commercial delegation, October 14, 1955, 105-00210-06; Premier Zhou's conversation with Japanese industrial and commercial delegation, July 28, 1956, 105-00500-06, CFMA.

85. *FRUS,* 1955–1957, 2:643; Premier Zhou Enlai's conversation with British chargé d'affaires Douglas Walter O'Neill, July 15, 1955, 110-00141-04, CFMA.

86. Wang, *Zhongmei huitan jiunian huigu,* 46–49; *RMRB,* August 2, 1955.

87. *FRUS,* 1955–1957, 3:85–86.

88. Thomas Christensen, *Lost in the Cold War: The Story of Jack Downey, America's Longest-Held POW* (New York: Columbia University Press, 2022), chap. 14.

89. *ZWG,* 12:333.

90. *ZZ*-B, 1:477; *ZNP*-B, 1:542–543.

91. *RMRB,* June 29, 1956; *ZTYZXWX,* 320.

92. *ZNP*-B, 1:623.

93. *ZNP*-B, 1:624; Li Wei, *Cao Juren zhuan* (A biography of Cao Juren) (Zhengzhou: Henan renmin, 2004), chap. 16–17.

19. To Rush or Not to Rush? (1956–1958)

1. *MNP-*B, 2:536, 545; Zhao Zhongyuan. "Accompanying Zhu De to Attend the Soviet Party's Twentieth Congress in 1956," *Zhonggong dangshi ziliao,* no. 2 (2004): 89.

2. *MNP-*B, 2:545; *MZ-*B, 496; Wu Lengxi, *Shinian lunzhan, 1956–1966: zhongsu guanxi huiyilu* (Ten-year polemic debate, 1956–1966: A memoir on Sino-Soviet relations) (Beijing: Zhongyang wenxian, 1999), 6.

3. *MNP-*B, 2:545, 549–550; Wu, *Shinian lunzhan,* 12–14, 18.

4. *MZ-*B, 501–502; Wu, *Shinian lunzhan,* 12.

5. Wu, *Shinian lunzhan,* 9–10.

6. *MWJ,* 6:500.

7. Bo, *Ruogan zhongda juece,* 1:532; Shi Zhongquan, *Wo guan Zhou Enlai* (My observation of Zhou Enlai) (Beijing: Zhonggong dangshi, 2008), 240.

8. *ZZ-*B, 1:269.

9. *ZNP-*B, 1:575.

10. Shi, *Wo guan Zhou Enlai,* 241; Bo, *Ruogan zhongda juece,* 1:634.

11. *LNP,* 369; Bo, *Ruogan zhongda juece,* 1:536.

12. *MNP-*B, 2:587; Shi, *Wo guan Zhou Enlai,* 248.

13. *MXJ,* 5:296.

14. *ZXJ,* 2:218–219.

15. *DWX,* 1:223.

16. *JGYLZYWX,* 9:341.

17. Chen Xiaonong, comp., *Chen Boda zuihou koushu huiyi* (Chen Boda's final oral recollections) (Hong Kong: Thinker, 2011), 138.

18. Wang Guangmei and Liu Yuan, *Ni suo buzhidao de Liu Shaoqi* (The Liu Shaoqi you do not know) (Zhengzhou: Henan renmin, 2000), 25–26.

19. Pawel Machcewicz, *Rebellious Satellite: Poland 1956* (Washington, DC, and Stanford, CA: Woodrow Wilson Center Press and Stanford University Press, 2009), 118, 143–144; see also a report by the Chinese embassy in Warsaw, 109-01141-01, CFMA.

20. Chinese Embassy in Poland to Foreign Ministry, June 29, 1956; Wang Bingnan to Foreign Ministry, July 5, 1956; Chinese Embassy in Poland, "Opinions about the Poznan Violent Incident," July 25, 1956, 109-00761-02, 109-00761-04, 109-00761-01, CFMA; Xie Wenqing, "Causes of the Poznan Reactionary Insurgence," July 12, 1956, *Neibu cankao* (Internal reference), no. 1945 (July 28, 1956): 591–604; Xie Wenqing, "Situation and Opinions: Concerning the Poznan Violent Incident," *Neibu cankao,* no. 1952 (July 25, 1956): 75–89.

21. Zhou's report at the Second Plenum of CCP's Eighth Central Committee, November 10, 1956, CCA; Shi, *Wo guan Zhou Enlai,* 244.

22. Mao, Liu, and Zhou's conversation with Mikoyan, September 18, 1956, 18:00–21:00, CCA.

23. Shen Zhihua, *Zuihou de tianchao* (The last heavenly dynasty: Mao, Kim Il-sung and Chinese-Korean relations) (Hong Kong: The Chinese University Press, 2017), 333–334.

24. Mao, Liu, and Zhou's conversation with Mikoyan, September 18, 1956, 18:00–21:00, CCA.

25. Ibid.

26. Mao and Zhou's conversation with Choi Yong-gon, September 18, 1956, 22:30–24:00, CCA.

27. Mao and Zhou's conversation with Mikoyan, September 23, 1956, 19:30–21:00, CCA.

28. Lin Ke diary, October 20, 1956 (Lin Ke was Mao's secretary); *MNP-*B, 3:14–15; Wu, *Shinian lunzhan,* 37–42.

29. Wu, *Shinian lunzhan,* 35–36; see Shi, *Zai lishi juren shenbian,* 551; Jin Chongji et al., *Liu Shaoqi zhuan* (A biography of Liu Shaoqi) (Beijing: Zhongyang wenxian, 2008), 803–804.

30. Wu, *Shinian lunzhan,* 44.

31. Lin Ke diary, January 16, 1957.

32. Shi, *Zai lishi juren shenbian,* 551; "The Malin Notes on the Crises in Hungary and Poland, 1956," *CWIHP Bulletin* (Washington, DC, Woodrow Wilson International Center for Scholars), nos. 8–9 (Winter 1996–1997): 392.

33. *MNP*-B, 3:18–19; Liu Shaoqi's report on situation at Second Plenum of CCP's Eighth Central Committee, November 10, 1956, CCA.

34. Liu's report at Second Plenum of CCP's Eighth Central Committee, November 10, 1956, CCA; Shi, *Zai lishi juren shenbian,* 562; Wu, *Shinan lunzhan,* 53.

35. Zhou Enlai's report at the Second Plenum of the CCP's Eighth Central Committee, November 10, 1956, CCA; *ZWG,* 13:444; *ZXJ,* 2:229–238; Bo, *Ruogan zhongda juece,* 1:556.

36. *MXJ,* 5:313–329; *MNP*-B, 3:32–35.

37. Shi, *Wo guan Zhou Enlai,* 248.

38. Burmese note about border clashes, January 27, 1956, 105-00745-01, CFMA.

39. Zhou's conversation with Burmese ambassador U Hla Maung, June 22, 1956, 105-00307-02, CFMA; see also Yang Mingwei, *Zouchu kunjing* (Going out of the difficult situation: Zhou Enlai in 1960–1965) (Beijing: Zhongyang wenxian, 2000), 95.

40. Zhou's speech on the Chinese-Burmese border issue at a meeting by leaders of various departments and department branches, August 27, 1956, cited from *Zhonggong dangshi ziliao,* no. 4 (2004): 100–101; see also Zhou's internal speech on the Chinese-Burmese border issue at the fourth session of the People's Congress, July 9, 1957, 1057-8-44, pp. 102–141, HPA.

41. Main points of Premier Zhou's two talks with Burmese ambassador U Hla Maung, August 7 and August 28, 1956, 105-00757-02, CFMA; see also *ZNP*-B, 1:614.

42. Main points of Zhou's talks with Burmese leaders, September 5–December 24, 1956, 203-00019-02, CFMA; see also Li, *Da waijiaojia Zhou Enlai,* 4:238–239.

43. Topics of discussions during Premier Zhou's visit to Vietnam, November 17, 1956, 203-00016–02, CFMA; see also *ZNP*-B, 1:639–642; Li, *Da waijiaojia Zhou Enlai,* 4:138.

44. Second Asian Section of the Foreign Ministry, "Our Country's Assistance to Vietnam," April 1960, 203-00147-07, CFMA.

45. Main points of Zhou's conversations with Burmese leaders in Burma, September 15–December 24, 1956, 203-00019-02, CFMA; see Li, *Da waijiaojia Zhou Enlai,* 4:180–181.

46. Talks with Chou Enlai, January 1, 1957, *Selected Works of Jawaharlal Nehru* (New Delhi: Oxford University Press, 2005), 2nd ser., 36:614.

47. Nehru to Zhou, December 14, 1958, in *Select Documents on India's Foreign Policy and Relations, 1947–1972,* ed. A. Appadorai (New Delhi: Oxford University Press, 1982), 1:495–501.

48. Zhou's conversation with Chervonenko, October 8, 1962, 109-03804-01, CFMA; see also ZZ-B, 1:534.

49. Zhou's conversation with Dalai Lama, November 29, 1956, *Zhou Enlai he Xizang* (Zhou Enlai and Tibet) (Beijing: Zhongguo zangxue, 1998), 142–148.

50. Zhou's conversation with Dalai Lama, December 30, 1956, 105-00329-02, CFMA; see also *Dang de wenxian* (Party History Documents) no. 2 (1994): 36–37.

51. *Dang de wenxian,* no. 2 (1994): 37–39.

52. *Selected Works of Jawaharlal Nehru,* 2nd ser., 36:618–619.

53. *MWG,* 6:250.

54. *MNP*-B, 3:60; *ZNP*-B, 2:2.

55. Shi, *Wo guan Zhou Enlai*, 228–230; Shen Zhihua, *Wu'nai de xuanze: Lengzhan he zhongsu tongmeng de mingyun* (A reluctant choice: The Cold War and the fate of the Sino-Soviet alliance) (Beijing: Shehui kexue wenxian, 2013), 485–487.

56. *ZNP*-B, 2:5.

57. Shen, *Wu'nai de xuanze*, 488–489.

58. Shi, *Wo guan Zhou Enlai*, 233; Shen, *Wu'nai de xuanze*, 489–490.

59. Shi, *Wo guan Zhou Enlai*, 229; *ZNP*-B, 2:13.

60. Shi, *Wo guan Zhou Enlai*, 228–230; *ZNP*-B, 2:15.

61. *MNP*-B, 3:72.

62. *MWJ*, 7:236; *MNP*-B, 3:84, 92.

63. *MNP*-B, 3:112–113, 116–117.

64. *ZNP*-B, 2:27; *ZZ*-B, 1:369.

65. *ZNP*-B, 2:37; *RMRB*, April 27, 1957, 1.

66. *ZNP*-B, 2:36.

67. *ZZ*-B, 1:386.

68. *MNP*-B, 3:169.

69. *RMRB*, July 1, 1957; *MXJ*, 5:456–457.

70. *ZZ*-B, 1:387.

71. *RMRB*, June 27, 1957.

72. *MXJ*, 5:456–457.

73. Zhou's speech at a roundtable on nationality work, August 4, 1957, SZ1-1-12, Hubei Provincial Archive; for an edited version, see *ZXJ*, 2:266–267.

74. *MXJ*, 5:475; *MWG*, 6:595; *MNP*-B, 3:113.

75. *MWG*, 6:628.

76. *MWG*, 6:635–636.

77. Li Yueran, who interpreted for Mao then, told me that he had known nothing about what Mao would say in advance. When Mao spoke, he was extremely nervous and had no time at all to carefully think about the Russian expressions of Mao's words. He could only "literally translate them word by word." Interview with Li Yueran, October 1997.

78. Khrushchev recalled in his memoirs that Mao's "remarks were followed by a deathly stillness. . . . After the session the delegations began to swap impressions. I remember that Comrade (Antonín) Novotny (first secretary of the Czech party) said, 'Comrade Mao Zedong says that they're ready to lose 300 million of their 600 million people, but what would it be like for us? We have 12 million. We would lose everyone. There would be no one left to restore the population to its previous numerical strength." *Memoirs of Nikita Khrushchev*, vol. 3, *Statesman (1953–1964)* (University Park: The Pennsylvania State University, 2007), 436.

79. Shen, *Zuihou de tianchao*, 418–419.

80. Zhou's conversation with Yudin, January 8, 1958, 109-00828-01, CFMA.

81. *ZNP*-B, 127–129; Shen, *Zuihou de tianchao*, 428.

82. Zhou's speech on Chinese-Korean Relations, February 21, 1958, 1-1411-1958–94, JLPA.

83. Ibid.

84. Mao, speech at the Chengdu Conference, March 20, 1958, copy kept at East Asian Library, Cornell University.

85. *RMRB*, November 13, 1957.

86. *RMRB,* December 12, 1957.

87. *MNP*-B, 5:276.

88. *MNP*-B, 3:276–287; *ZNP*-B, 2:120; Tong, *Fengyu sishi nian,* 356–357.

89. *MNP*-B, 5:309–327.

90. *ZZ*-B, 1:424–425; Chen Xiaolu, "Chen Yi and China's Diplomacy," in *Chinese Communist Foreign Relations, 1920s–1960s,* ed. Michael Hunt and Niu Jun (Washington, DC: Wilson Center, 1994), 91–92.

91. Xiong Huayuan and Liao Xinwen, *Zhou Enlai zongli shengya* (Zhou Enlai's premier career) (Beijing: Zhongyang wenxian, 1997), 248.

92. Li Ping, *Kaiguo zongli Zhou Enlai* (Zhou Enlai as the republic's inaugural premier) (Beijing: Zhonggong zhongyang dangxiao, 1994), 361–362.

93. Zhou Enlai's speech at the second plenary session of the CCP's Eighth Congress, May 30, 1958, 855-4-1573–3, HPA.

94. Mao's speech at the second plenary session of the CCP's Eighth Congress, May 17, 1958, *ZZ*-B, 2:417.

95. *MNP*-B, 3:368; Xiong and Liao, *Zhou Enlai zongli shengya,* 249.

96. *MWG,* 7:268–269.

97. CCP CC's notice on establishing five leading groups, June 11, 1958, 91-004–0283, GSPA.

20. The Great Leap Forward (1958–1960)

1. Mao's speech at the second plenum of the CCP's Eighth Congress, May 8, 1958, 855-4-1262–1, HPA. See also *MZ*-B, 815–817.

2. *ZNP*-B, 2:169–170.

3. *MWG,* 7:394.

4. *DWX,* 2:260.

5. *ZNP*-B, 2:152.

6. Cheng Hua et al., *Zhou Enlai he tade mishumen* (Zhou Enlai and his secretaries) (Beijing: Zhongyang guangbo dianshi, 1992), 19.

7. Mao's speech at Beidaihe Conference, August 17, 1958, 91-018-0495, pp. 311–333, GSPA; see also *MNP*-B, 3:411–420.

8. *ZZ*-B, 1:453–454.

9. A Collection of Documents of the Beidaihe Conference, September 20, 1958, 177-001-0408, pp. 1–95, GSPA.

10. *RMRB,* September 1, 1958.

11. *MWG,* 7:381, 368.

12. *ZWG,* 12:333.

13. *RMRB,* June 29, 1956; Zhou, "Taiwan's Liberation Will Surely Be Achieved," June 28, 1956, *ZXJ,* 2:202.

14. *MNP*-B, 3:4.

15. Ye Fei's report to Peng Dehuai and CCP CMC, January 16, 1958, FPA, 101-12-221, pp. 1–14; *Ye Fei huiyilun,* 635–642; Han Huaizhi et al., *Dangdai zhongguo jundui de junshi gongzuo* (Military affairs in contemporary Chinese Army) (Beijing: Zhongguo shehui kexue, 1989), 2:387.

16. Mao's speech at an enlarged Politburo meeting at Beidaihe, August 17, 1958, 91-018-0495, pp. 311–333, GSPA; see also *MWG,* 7:386.

17. *Public Papers of the Presidents of the United States: Dwight D. Eisenhower, 1958* (Washington, DC: Government Printing Office, 1959), 639–650.

18. Department of State *Bulletin,* September 10, 1958; *FRUS,* 1958–1960, 19:115–122; see also Dwight Eisenhower, *Waging Peace: The White House Years, 1956–1961* (London: William Heinemann, 1965), 298.

19. *ZNP*-B, 2:163.

20. Wu Lengxi, *Yi Mao Zhuxi: wo qinshen jingli ruogan zhongda lishi shijian piandou* (Remembering Chairman Mao: Episodes of important historical events that I experienced) (Beijing: Xinhua, 1994), 79–80; *MNP*-B, 3:433.

21. *RMRB,* September 5, 1958, 1.

22. Wu, *Yi Mao Zhuxi,* 79–80.

23. *FRUS,* 1958–1960, 19:134–136.

24. *RMRB,* September 7, 1958, 1.

25. Wu, *Yi Mao Zhuxi,* 79–80.

26. Draft Chinese-American agreement, September 10, 1958, 111-00146-01, CFMA.

27. Zhou to Wang Bingnan, September 9, 1958, cited from Wang Bingnan, *Zhongmei huitan jiunian* (Nine years of Chinese-American negotiations) (Beijing: Shijie zhishi, 1985), 73–74.

28. *MWG,* 7:416; *MZ*-B, 1:872.

29. Zhou to Mao, September 13, 1958, cited from *ZZ*-B, 1:470.

30. *FRUS,* 1958–1960, vol. 19, *China,* 186–187.

31. Wang to Foreign Ministry, September 15, 1958, 111-00146-02, CFMA; *FRUS,* 19:191–196.

32. Interviews with Xue Mouhong, August 1994; see also *ZNP*-B, 2:470.

33. *MNP*-B, 3:448.

34. *Mao Zedong waijiao wenxuan* (Selected diplomatic papers of Mao Zedong, hereafter *MWJWX*) (Beijing: Zhongyang wenxian, 1994), 353.

35. Ibid.

36. Mao to Zhou, September 19, 1958, *MWJWX,* 353; Foreign Ministry to Wang, September 22, 1958, 111-00147-01, CFMA.

37. Wang to Foreign Ministry, September 22, 1958; Wang to Foreign Ministry, September 23, 1958, 111-00147-01, CFMA.

38. *ZZ*-B, 2:471.

39. Zhou to Mao, September 22, 1958, *ZJSWX,* 4:403.

40. *ZNP*-B, 2:471–472; Mao to Zhou, September 22, 1958, *MWG,* 7:424.

41. *FRUS,* 1958–1960, 19:301.

42. *ZNP*-B, 2:177; *ZJSHDJS,* 2:472.

43. *MZ*-B, 878–879.

44. *MNP*-B, 3:456–457.

45. *RMRB,* October 6, 1958; *MWG,* 7:439–441.

46. Zhou's conversation with Sudarikov, September 5, 1958, 109-00833-04, CFMA; *ZNP*-B, 2:166.

47. Zhou's conversation with Yudin, June 14, 1957, 109-00786-14, CFMA.

48. *ZNP*-B, 2:67.

49. Liu Xiao to Foreign Ministry and convey to CCP CC, August 15, 1957, 109-01726-02, CFMA.

50. Exchanges between Zhou and Bulganin concerning revision of Chinese-Soviet Agreements on Economic Cooperation in 1953 and 1956, August 25, 1957, 109-00792-01; Zhang Wentian's conversation with Soviet chargé d'affaires, August 24, 1957, 109-01787-04, CFMA.

51. Zhou Junlun et al., *Nie Rongzhen nianpu* (A chronological record of Nie Rongzhen) (Beijing: Renmin, 1999), 2:623; Li Jue et al., *Dangdai zhongguo de hegongye* (Contemporary Chinese nuclear industry) (Beijing: Dangdai zhongguo, 1987), 43.

52. Khrushchev's letter to Zhou (utmost confidential), April 24, 1958, 109-00838-03, CFMA.

53. *Peng Dehuai nianpu*, 681; Wang Taiping et al., *Zhonghua renmin gongheguo waijiaoshi, 1957–1969* (Beijing: Shijie zhishi, 1999), 224; *Xiao Jingguang huiyilu*, 2:201.

54. Yuan Wei et al., *Mao Zedong junshi huodong jishi* (Major events in Mao Zedong's military activities, hereafter *MJSHDJS*) (Beijing: Jiefangjun, 1994), 907.

55. Xue Mouhong et al., *Dangdai zhongguo waijiao* (Contemporary Chinese diplomacy) (Beijing: Zhongguo shehui kexue, 1990), 112–113; Wang et al., *Zhonghua renmin gongheguo waijiaoshi*, 224.

56. Xue et al., *Dangdai zhongguo waijiao*, 113.

57. Wang et al., *Zhonghua renmin gongheguo waijiao shi*, 224–225; Xue, *Dangdai zhongguo waijiao*, 113.

58. Xue et al., *Dangdai Zhongguo waijiao*, 113.

59. *Xiao Jingguan huiyilu*, 2:176–181.

60. Zhou to Khrushchev, June 28, 1958, 109-00838-03, CFMA; see also *ZNP*-B, 2:149.

61. Mao's first conversation with Soviet ambassador Yudin, July 21, 1958, CCA.

62. Mao's second conversation with Yudin, July 22, 1958, CCA; for an abridged version of the conversation, see *MWJWX*, 322–334; for an English translation, see *CWIHP Bulletin*, nos. 6–7 (Winter 1995–1996): 155–159.

63. Mao's second conversation with Yudin, July 22, 1958, CCA; *MWJWX*, 329.

64. Wu, *Shinian lunzhan*, 162.

65. Cited from Shen, *Zhongsu guanxi shigang*, 230.

66. Conversations between Mao and Khrushchev, July 31–August 3, 1958, CCA; "Conversation of N. S. Khrushchev with Mao Zedong," July 31, 1958, in Dimitry Volkoganov Collections, Manuscript Division, Library of Congress, Washington, DC.

67. Conversations between Mao and Khrushchev, July 31, 1968, CCA.

68. Wang et al., *Zhonghua renmin gongheguo waijiaoshi*, 226–227; Xue, *Dangdai zhongguo waijiao*, 114.

69. *RMRB*, August 4, 1958, 1.

70. *Memoirs of Nikita Khrushchev*, 3:423–424.

71. Cong Jin, *Quzhe fazhan de suiyue* (The years of tortuous development) (Zhengzhou: Henan renmin, 1989), 350.

72. *MNP*-B, 4:186.

73. Vladislav Zubok and Constantine Pleshakov, *Inside the Kremlin's Cold War: From Stalin to Khrushchev* (Cambridge, MA: Harvard University Press, 1996), 220–221; Nikita Khrushchev, *Khrushchev Remembers: The Last Testament* (Boston: Little, Brown, 1970), 403–405.

74. Yan Mingfu, "Shelling of Jinmen in 1958 and Gromyko's Secret Visit to China," *Bainianchao* (One hundred year tide), no. 5 (2006): 15; Wu, *Shinian lunzhan*, 178–179.

75. Wu, *Shinian lunzhan*, 179–180.

76. Zhou's conversation with Antonov, October 5, 1958, CFMA; Shi, *Wo guan Zhou Enlai*, 284.

77. "Memorandum of Conversation of Comrade N. S. Khrushchev with Chairman of the CC CCP Mao Zedong," October 2, 1959, in Dimitry Volkoganov Collections, Manuscript Division, LC; Yang Mingfu and Zhu Ruizhen, "Before and After Khrushchev's Visit to China in 1959," *Zhonggong dangshi ziliao*, no. 4 (2006): 35–52.

78. Qian Xiangli, *Lishi de bianju: Cong wanjiu weiji dao fanxiu fangxiu* (History's changing landscape: From saving crisis to antirevisionism and preventing revisionism) (Hong Kong: The Chinese University Press, 2008), 306.

79. *MNP*-B, 3:602–606.

80. *MWG*, 8:75.

81. Lin Yunhui, *Wutuobang yundong: Cong dayuejin dao da jihuang* (Utopian movement: From Great Leap Forward to Great Famine) (Hong Kong: The Chinese University Press, 2008), 426–427.

82. *MNP*-B, 4:21–22.

83. *ZZ*-B, 599.

84. Zhou's talks during an inspection tour in Hebei, May 24, 1959, 855-1551-1, HPA.

85. Zhou's conversation with the Dalai Lama, December 30, 1956, 105-00329-02, CFMA; see also *Dang de wenxian*, no. 2 (1994): 36–37.

86. Mao's comments on report of CCP Qinghai Provincial Committee, August 24, 1958, cited from *MZ*-B, 926.

87. CCP CC to CCP Tibet Work Committee, March 12, 1959, 855-1563-22, HPA; Wu, *Yi Mao Zhuxi*, 119–120.

88. CCP CC to CCP Xizang Work Committee, March 12, 1959, 855-5-1563-22, HPA; *Yang Shangkun riji*, 364.

89. Mao to CCP CC, March 11, 1959, Editorial Committee, *Zhongguo gongchandang xizan lishi dashiji, 1949–2004* (Major Events of the CCP's history in Tibet, 1949–2004) (Beijing: Zhonggong dangshi, 2005), 1:130–131; *Yang Shangkun riji*, 364.

90. *Xizang dangshi gongzuo dashiji*, 91.

91. *ZNP*-B, 2:212.

92. Yang Shaokun diary, March 20, 1959, *Yang Shaokun riji*, 367.

93. *LNP*, 2:452.

94. *ZNP*-B, 2:213.

95. *RMRB*, March 28, 1959.

96. For a detailed and vivid account of the PLA's bloody suppression of Tibetan "rebels" based on extensive research and many interviews, see Li Jianglin, *When the Iron Bird Flies: China's Secret War in Tibet* (Stanford, CA: Stanford University Press, 2022).

97. Informal Note given by the Foreign Secretary of India to the Chinese Ambassador, October 18, 1958, *Notes, Memoranda and Letters Exchanged and Agreements Signed between the Governments of India and China, 1954–1959* (New Delhi: Ministry of External Affairs, Government of India, n.d.), 26–27.

98. Nehru to Zhou, December 14, 1958, Madhavan K. Palat, ed., *Selected Works of Jawaharlal Nehru*, 2nd ser., vol. 45 (New Delhi: Jawaharlal Nehru Memorial Fund, 2014), 702–706.

99. Zhou to Nehru, January 23, 1959, Chinese Foreign Ministry, *Zhongguo he yindu guanyu liangguo zai zhongguo Xizang defang de guanxi wenti zhongyin bianjie wenti he qita wenti laiwang wenjian huibian, 1950nian 8 yue -1960nian 4yue* (A collection of documentary exchanges between China and India on issues concerning China's Tibet region, Chinese-Indian borders and other matters, August 1950–April 1960, hereafter cited as *ZYBJWTWJHB*) (Beijing: for internal circulation only, 1960), 176–179.

100. Nehru to Zhou, March 22, 1959, *Selected Works of Jawaharlal Nehru*, 2nd ser., 47:451–454.

101. Wu, *Shinian lunzhan*, 195.

102. *ZYBJWTWJHB*, 55.

103. Wu, *Shinian lunzhan*, 195.

104. *RMRB,* April 15, 1959.
105. *RMRB,* April 19, 1959, 2.
106. Wu, *Yi Mao Zhuxi,* 125; *MNP*-B, 4:28–29.
107. *ZJSHDJS,* 2:496.
108. Chairman Mao and Premier Zhou's conversation about the Tibetan issue and Chinese-Indian relations with delegates and diplomats from fraternal countries, May 6, 1959, *Waishi dongtai* (Developments in diplomatic affairs), no. 49 (May 9, 1959): 2–5 (internal newsletter distributed by the Chinese Foreign Ministry); *ZWJWX,* 268–276; *MXZGZWX,* 193.
109. *Neibu cankao* (Internal reference), no. 2575 (September 5, 1958); no. 2581 (September 12, 1958): 3–4; no. 2581 (November 5, 1958): 23–24.
110. *Yan Mingfu huiyilu* (Yan Mingfu's memoirs) (Beijing: Renmin, 2015), 1:522–523.
111. Ibid., 523.
112. Li et al., *Dangdai zhongguo de hegongye,* 32; *Nie Rongzhen nianpu,* 2:680.
113. Li Rui, *Dayuejin qinli ji* (Personal experience in the Great Leap Forward) (Haikou: Nanfang, 1999), 2:473.
114. *MWG:* 8:196.
115. *MNP*-B, 4:80.
116. *MWJ,* 8:75–82.
117. *ZNP*-B, 2:241, 242.
118. Cited from *Peng Dehuai zhuan,* 588–590.
119. *PNP,* 741.
120. *MWG,* 8:358.
121. *ZZ*-B, 518; Li, *Lushan huiyi shilu,* 119.
122. *Zhang Wentian wenji,* 4:322–342.
123. *MNP*-B, 4:111.
124. Mao's speech at the Lushan Conference, July 23, 1959, 102–116, GSPA.
125. *ZZ*-B, 518; Shi, *Wo guan Zhou Enlai,* 274–275.
126. *MNP*-B, 4:116; *MWG,* 8:391.
127. *ZNP*-B, 2:245.
128. Shi, *Wo guan Zhou Enlai,* 276.
129. Li, *Lushan huiyi shilu,* 163.
130. Shi, *Wo guan Zhou Enlai,* 276.
131. *MWG,* 4:121–122.
132. Zhou's speech, "Current Situation and Future Tasks," August 22, 1958, SZ1-02-0489-001, Hubei Provincial Archives.
133. Mao's speech at a military and foreign affairs conference, September 11, 1958, 91-008-0238, pp. 62–80, GSPA.

21. Mao Retreats to the "Second Line" (1959–1962)

1. *Textbook of Political Economy,* especially its socialist part, was an official Soviet textbook endorsed by Stalin.
2. Lin Ke, Notes on Mao reading *Soviet Socialist Political Economy,* 1959 (copy of manuscript in author's possession); *MNP*-B, 4:315–327; Lin, *Wutuobang yundong,* 532–533.
3. *ZZ*-B, 1:580.
4. Mao's talk at the Shanghai conference, January 17, 1960, 855-5-1793–5(2), HPA.

5. Fang and Jin, *Li Fuchun zhuan,* 536.

6. *MNP*-B, 4:303.

7. Ibid., 382.

8. Zhou to Nehru, September 8, 1959, *ZYBJWTWJHB,* 184–190; *Documents on the Sino-Indian Boundary Question* (Beijing: Foreign Language Press, 1960), 1–13.

9. Chinese Embassy in India to Foreign Ministry, October 27, 1959, 105-00408-01, CFMA.

10. *MNP*-B, 4:232–233; *ZZ*-B, 1:551.

11. Zhou to Nehru, November 7, 1959, *ZYBJWTWJHB,* 212–213; *Documents on the Sino-Indian Boundary Question,* 14–17.

12. Zhou's talk with Indian ambassador Parthasarathy, November 8, 1959, cited from ZZ-B, 1:553.

13. Reply to Chou En-lai, November 16, 1959, Palat, *Selected Works of Jawaharlal Nehru,* 2nd ser., 54:490; *ZYBJWTWJHB,* 214–219.

14. Neville Maxwell, *India's China War* (Garden City, NY: Anchor Books, 1972), 138.

15. Zhou to Nehru, December 17, 1959, *ZYBJWTWJHB,* 220–225; *Documents on Sino-Indian Boundary Question,* 18–28.

16. Nehru to Zhou, February 5, 1960, *ZYBJWTWJHB,* 228–229; *Documents on Sino-Indian Boundary Question,* 142–144.

17. Viewpoints of different factions of the Burmese Liberal Alliance about the Chinese-Burmese border issue, May 25, 1958, 105-00858-02, CFMA.

18. Summary of the Burmese plan to settle Chinese-Burmese border issue by the First Asian Department of the Foreign Ministry, *Waishi dongtai* (Developments in diplomatic affairs), no. 60 (June 6, 1959), 2–3.

19. Zhou's letter to Ne Win, December 22, 1960, 204-00114-03, CFMA; *Waishi dongtai,* no. 118 (December 24, 1959), 2; Ne Win's reply to Zhou, January 3, 1960; Zhou's letter to Ne Win, January 12, 1960; Ne Win's letter to Zhou, January 18, 1960, *Wasishi dongtai,* no. 1 (January 6, 1960), 2; no. 3 (January 17, 1960), 4; no. 4 (January 23, 1960), 2.

20. Ne Win's six-day visit to China, *Waishi dongtai,* no. 9 (February 4, 1960), 2; Yang, *Zouchu kunjing,* 110–112.

21. Premier Zhou to visit five countries in Asia, *Waishi dongtai,* no. 22 (April 13, 1960), 2–3; *ZNP*-B, 2:302; *ZZ*-B, 1:557.

22. *Waishi dongtai,* no. 22 (April 13, 1960), 3.

23. Second meeting between Zhou and U Nu, 203-00036-02, CFMA; U Nu's inquiry about Chinese-Indian border problems, *Waishi dongtai,* no. 25 (April 25, 1960), 2–4.

24. "Chou in New Delhi; Gets Cool Welcome," April 20, 1960, *New York Times,* 1.

25. "First Talk," n.d., NMML, P. N. Haksar Papers, Installments I and II, Subject Files, #24; see also *ZNP*-B, 2:307.

26. Talks between PM and Premier Chou held on 20th April 1960, from 5 P.M. to 7 P.M., P. N. Haksar Papers, Installments I and II, Subject Files, #24, pp. 17–26, NMML; see also *ZNP*-B, 2:308.

27. Talks between PM. and Premier Chou Enlai held on 21st April 1960, 4:00–6:30 P.M.; Talks between PM. and Premier Chou Enlai held on 22nd April 1960 from [?] A.M. to 1:10 P.M.; Talks between PM. and Premier Chou Enlai held on 24th April 1960, from 10:30 A.M. to 1:45 P.M.; Talks between PM. and Premier Chou Enlai held on 23th April 1960, from 4:30–7:45 P.M.; P. N. Haksar Papers, Installments I and II, Subject Files, #24, pp. 27–39, 40–53, 54–68, NMML; see *ZNP*-B, 2:309–312.

28. Talks between PM and Premier Chou Enlai held on 24th April 1960, from 10:30 A.M. to 2:40 P.M., n.d., P. N. Haksar Papers, Installments I and II, Subject Files, #24, pp. 69–85, NMML; see *ZNP*-B, 2:312.

29. Talks between PM and Premier Chou held on 25th April 1960, from 11 A.M. to 2:40 P.M., P. N. Haksar Papers, Installments I and II, Subject Files, #24, pp. 86–103, NMML; *ZNP*-B, 2:313; Joint Communiqué by Chinese Premier and Indian Prime Minister, *RMRB*, April 26, 1960, 1.

30. Zhou once told Sirimavo Bandaranaike, Ceylon's prime minister, that "I have never met a negotiation counterpart more difficult than Nehru," 204-01493-09, 79, CFMA.

31. Zhou's conversation with Chervonenko, May 9, 1961, 109-03757-01, CFMA.

32. Han, *Eldest Son*, 294.

33. Yan Mingfu and Zhu Ruizhen, "Before and After Khrushchev's 1959 Visit to China," *Zhonggong dangshi ziliao*, no. 4 (2006): 33–34; Wu, *Shinian lunzhan*, 220; *RMRB*, October 1, 1949, 5.

34. For an English translation of the Russian record of the meeting, see "Discussion between N. S. Khrushchev and Mao Zedong, October 2, 1959," No.112088, WWCDA, https://digitalarchive.wilsoncenter.org/document/112088; for Chinese accounts, see Yan Mingfu, *Qinli zhongsu guanxi: Zhongyang bangongting fanyizu de shinian, 1957–1966* (Personally witnessing Chinese-Soviet relations: Ten-year experience at the translation group of the Central Administrative Office, 1957–1966) (Beijing: Zhongguo renmin daxue, 2015), 189–204; Yan and Zhu, "Khrushchev's 1959 Visit to China," 34–52; Wu, *Shinian lunzhan*, 221–227. There are quite a few differences in the Chinese and Russian records of the meeting.

35. Wu, *Shinian lunzhan*, 227–228.

36. On October 9, 1959, the Chinese embassy in Moscow sent to Beijing a detailed report about Khrushchev's speech, *MWG*, 8:564–565; Yan and Zhu, "Khrushchev's 1959 Visit to China," 53.

37. Wu, *Shinian lunzhan*, 238–239.

38. Chinese Embassy in Moscow to Foreign Ministry, "An Unfriendly Note from the Soviet Foreign Ministry," July 21, 1960, 109-00921-01, CMFA.

39. Wu, *Shinian lunzhan*, 277; Yan, *Qinli zhongsu guanxi*, 234–235.

40. Yan, *Qinli zhongsu guanxi*, 240.

41. Zhou's speech at Beidaihe Conference, July 14–16, 1960, 855-5-1798, HPA; also see *ZXJ*, 2:300–312; Wu, *Shinian lunzhan*, 314–332.

42. Ibid.

43. Soviet embassy's note to Chinese Foreign Ministry about recalling all Soviet experts in China, July 16, 1960, 109-00924-01, CFMA.

44. Zhou's speech at Beidaihe conference, July 31, 1960, 855-5-1798, HPA; *MZ*-B, 1089.

45. *ZZ*-B, 3:588; Shi, *Wo guan Zhou Enlai*, 306.

46. Wang Weizhen et al., *Li Xiannian nianpu* (Chronological records of Li Xiannian) (Beijing: Zhongyang wenxian, 2011), 3:226.

47. *MNP*-B, 4:414–416.

48. *MNP*-B, 4:415.

49. *MWG*, 9:213–216.

50. Zhou's speech at a Politburo enlarged meeting, June 14, 1960, cited from ZZ-B, 1:583–584.

51. Li Xiannian's urgent report to Zhou, July 13, 1960, *Jianguo yilai Li Xiannian wengao* (Li Xiannian's manuscripts since the founding of the PRC) (Beijing: Zhongyang wenxian, 2011), 2:122–123.

52. Ibid., 123–124.

53. Cited from Lin, *Wutuobang yundong*, 585.

54. *JGYLZYWX*, 13:516–526, 512–515, 527–536.

55. Ibid., 537–538.

56. *CYNP*, 3:38.

57. *ZZ*-B, 2:601–604.

58. *ZGZYWJXJ*-B, 35:12–13, 41–44, 75–78, 79–81, 98–101, 253–255, 275–277, 492–497.

59. *ZNP*-B, 2:365; Yang Shaoqiao and Zhao Fasheng, "Zhou Enlai and Our Country's Grain Production," in *Bujin de sinian,* 230.

60. Qiao Peihua, *Xinyang Shijian* (The Xinyang incident) (Hong Kong: Kaifang chubanshe, 2009), 155–156.

61. *MWG,* 9:326.

62. Zhou's speech at an enlarged politburo meeting, October 29, 1960, *ZZ*-B, 2:600.

63. *JGYLZYWX,* 13:677–681.

64. *ZNP*-B, 2:363–364.

65. The chairman's comments during reports by leaders of various central bureaus, December 30, 1960, 855-6-2047–3, HPA; *Chen Yuan zhuan,* 1224, 1226; *CYNP,* 3:51–52.

66. *CYNP,* 3:55; Lei Renmin, "Recalling the Premier's Care and Instruction of Foreign Trade Work," *Bujin de sinian,* 254.

67. *ZNP*-B, 2:384; *CYNP,* 1230–1231; Lei, "Recalling the Premier's Care," 254.

68. Shen Jueren et al., *Dangdai zhongguo duiwai maoyi* (Foreign trade of contemporary China) (Beijing: Dangdai zhongguo, 1992), 2:38; Lin Haiyun, "Recollection of Zhou Enlai's Conception of Foreign Trade," in *Bujin de sinian,* 259.

69. *Dangdai zhongguo duiwai maoyi,* 393.

70. Zhou Boping, *Liangshibu shiernian jishi* (Twelve years of my experience at the Ministry of Food Supplies) (Beijing: Lantian shangwu, 2008).

71. Zhou's speech at the Ninth Plenum of the Eighth CC, January 19, 1961, 91-6-79–1961, GSPA.

72. Zhou's speech at a cadres' meeting at the Northeast Bureau, February 25, 1961, 1-1-17–171, JLPA; Zhou speech at a roundtable at the Central United Front Department, February 26, 1961, 91-018-0560, GPA; Zhou speech on the situation and domestic tasks, April 3, 1961, 91-018-0560, GSPA.

73. *ZZ*-B, 2:629, 608.

74. Ibid., 685.

75. *LNP,* 2:524.

76. Bo, *Ruogan Zhongda juece,* 2:1073.

77. *JGYLZYWX,* 13:512–515.

78. Zhou's talk with Kazuo Suzuki, Senior Director of Japan-China Trade Promotion Council, August 27, 1960, 105-00735-02, CFMA; see also *ZWJWX,* 289–290, *Peking Review,* no. 37 (September 14, 1960): 25–26.

79. Liao Xinwen, "Zhou Enlai and the Policy of Peaceful Liberation of Taiwan," *Dangde wenxian,* no. 5 (1994): 35.

80. Ibid.

81. *MNP*-B, 5:75–77; *ZZ*-B, 659.

82. *Liu Shaoqi xueji* (Selected works of Liu Shaoqi) (Beijing: Renmin, 1981), 2:337.

83. *Liu Shaoqi xueji,* 2:421.

84. Bo, *Ruogan zhongda juece,* 1026; Editorial Group, *Peng Zhen zhuan* (A biography of Peng Zhen) (Beijing: Zhongyang wenxian, 2012), 3:1063.

85. Wang Haiguang, *Shiguo jing weiqian: Zhongguo dangdai shi caiwei* (Times have changed but not the circumstances: Revisiting episodes of modern Chinese History) (Chengdu: Sichuan renmin, 2014), 197.

86. Zhang, *Bianju,* 109–110; Bo, *Guogan Zhongda juece,* 1027–1028.

87. *CYNP,* 3:110–113.

88. *Deng Liqun guoshi jiangtanlu* (Deng Liqun discussing the country's history) (Beijing: The Compilation Committee of Draft History of PRC, 2000), 2:456.

89. *LNP,* 2:549.

90. *ZZ*-B, 2:674.

91. Xu et al., *Wang Jiaxiang nianpu,* 486–489; Xu, *Wang Jiaxiang zhuan,* 557–564.

92. Yang Shengqun and Yan Jianqi et al., *Deng Xiaoping nianpu, 1904–1974* (Chronological records of Deng Xiaoping, 1904–1974, hereafter *DNP*-A) (Beijing: Zhongyang wenxian, 2009), 3:1692.

93. *CYNP,* 3:113; *Deng Liqun guoshi jiangtanlu,* 2:456.

94. *CYNP,* 3:133–135.

95. *ZNP*-B, 2:462–463.

22. The Chairman Returns (1962–1963)

1. *MNP*-B, 5:96.

2. Dong Bian et al., *Mao Zedong he tade mshu Tian Jiaying* (Mao Zedong and his secretary Tian Jiaying) (Beijing: Zhongyang wenxian, 1996), 90–91; *Deng Liqun guoshi jiangtanlu,* 6:364; *CYNP,* 3:118.

3. *MNP*-B, 5:102–103.

4. *CYNP,* 3:119.

5. *ZNP*-B, 2:481; Dong et al., *Mao Zedong he tade mshu Tian Jiaying,* 91.

6. Dong, *Mao Zedong he tade mshu Tian Jiaying,* 91.

7. Dong, *Mao Zedong he tade mshu Tian Jiaying,* 91–92; *DNP*-A, 3:1714; see also Qian, *Lishi de bianju,* 5, 203–204.

8. *ZNP*-B, 2:488.

9. *MNP*-B, 5:101–107.

10. *MNP*-B, 5:111; *CYNP,* 3:120.

11. *MNP*-B, 5:111. Tian later commented, "The chairman is truly sharp." What he meant was that Mao was "quite capable at catching the essence of others' statements, and putting forward questions outside of others' expectations, making it difficult for others to come up with a good answer." Dong, *Mao Zedong he tade mshu Tian Jiaying,* 93.

12. *MNP*-B, 5:112; *CYNP,* 3:120; Dong, *Mao Zedong he tade mshu Tian Jiaying,* 93.

13. Zhou's speech at the Secretariat of CCP Heilongjiang Provincial Committee, June 18, 1963, cited from *MBP*-B, 5:112.

14. *CYNP,* 3:121; *MNP*-B, 5:120.

15. Wang Guangmei and Liu Yuan, *Lishi yingyou renmin lai xie: ni suo buzhidao de Liu Shaoqi* (History should be written by the people: The Liu Shaoqi you do not know) (Hong Kong: Tiandi, 1999), 49.

16. *MZ*-B, 1234; *MNP*-B, 5:116.

17. *Yang Shangkun riji,* 2:196; *MNP*-B, 5:115.

18. *MZ*-B, 1235; *MNP*-B, 5:122.

19. Mao's first speech at the Beidaihe Conference, August 6, 1962, 855-6-2609, HPA; see also *MNP*-B, 5:128–129; *MZ*-B, 1236–1237; *ZNP*-B, 2:492.

20. *LNP,* 2:558; Bo, *Ruogan zhongda juece,* 2:1074–1075.

21. Zhou's speech at the Beidaihe Conference, August 17, 1962, 855-6-2257–9, HPA; see also *ZZ*-B, 691; *ZNP*-B, 2:492.

22. Mao's speech at the Tenth Plenum of the Eighth CC, September 24, 1962, 101-12–119, pp. 22–27, FPA; *MNP*-B, 5:151–153.

23. Zhou's speech at the Tenth Plenum of CCP Eighth CC, September 26, 1962, 855-6-2008-14, 855-6-2262-2, HPA.

24. Ibid.

25. Zhou's speech at the Tenth Plenum of the Eighth CC, September 16, 1962, 855-6-2008-14, HPA; see *ZZ-B*, 694.

26. Ibid.

27. Maxwell, *India's China War,* chap. 2.

28. Zhu Hong, *Huang Zhen zhuan* (A biography of Huang Zhen) (Beijing: Renmin ribao, 2000), 253.

29. Editorial Committee, *Zhongyin bianjie ziwei fanji zuozhan shi* (A history of the war of self-defense on Chinese-Indian borders) (Beijing: Junshi kexue 1994), 122.

30. Zhang Zishen et al., *Yang Chengwu nianpu* (Chronological records of Yang Chengwu) (Beijing: Jiefangjun, 2014), 362.

31. *ZJSHDJS,* 2:564.

32. Lin Xiaoting (Lin Hsiao-ting), *Kunshou yu fangong: Lengzhan zhong de taiwan xuanze* (Defense or counteroffensive: Taiwan's choices in the Cold War) (Beijing: Jiuzhou, 2017), chap. 5.

33. *ZJSHDJS,* 2:564.

34. Huang Yao and Zhang Mingzhe, *Luo Ruiqing zhuan* (A biography of Luo Ruiqing) (Beijing: Dangdai zhongguo, 1991), 369–370.

35. Ibid., 371–372.

36. Ibid., 370.

37. Wang Bingnan, *Zhongmei huitan jiunian huigu* (Nine years of Chinese-American negotiations) (Beijing: Shijie zhishi, 1985), 86.

38. Chinese embassy in Warsaw to Foreign Ministry, May 31, 1962, 111-00605-01, CFMA.

39. Wang Bingnan to Foreign Ministry, June 14, 1962, 111-00605-01, CFMA.

40. Foreign Ministry to Wang Bingnan, 23:00, June 14, 1962; Wang to Foreign Ministry, June 15, 1965, 111-00605-01, CFMA; Wang, *Zhongmei huitan jiunian huigu,* 87.

41. Wang, *Zhongmei huitan jiunian huigu,* 87.

42. Foreign Ministry to Wang, June 22, 1962, 111-00605-01, CFMA.

43. Foreign Ministry to Wang, 16:00, June 22, 1962, 111-00605-01, CFMA.

44. Clough to Rusk, June 21, 1962, No. 799.00 / 6-2162, in USSD 1960–1963 Internal, reel 6; Clough to Rusk, June 22, 1962, No. 792.00 / 6-2262, NA.

45. Wang to Foreign Ministry, June 23, 1962, 111-00605-01, CFMA; see also Wang, *Zhongmei huitan jiunian,* 86–90; Cabot to the [US] Department of State, June 23, 1962, *FRUS,* 1961–1963, 22:273–275.

46. *MJSWG,* 3:142; *MNP-B,* 5:119.

47. Liao Xinwen, "Zhou Enlai Secretly Met Messenger for Taiwan in 1963," *Baixing shenghuo* (Life of everyday people), no. 10 (2016): 50–51; interview with Liao Xinwen, October 2017.

48. Interview with Liao Xinwen and Gao Zhenpu, October 21, 2017; see also *ZNP-B,* 2:599.

49. Geng Zhonglin, ed., *Wu Ruilin shiliao* (Historical material of Wu Ruilin) (self-pub., n.p., n.d.), 2:1335–1341, 1348–1349; Luo Qingchang, "He Has Escorted a Voyage by Zhou Enlai, Recalling Comrade Wu Ruilin," in *Zui keai de ren: Wu Ruilin tongzhi jinian wenji* (Most beloved person: in commemoration of comrade Wu Ruilin) (Beijing: Gaige, 1997).

50. *ZNP-B,* 2:488.

51. *Zhonghua renmin gongheguo duiwai guanxi wenjianji,* 9:61.

52. *Zhongyin bianjie ziwei fanji zuozhan shi,* 139.

53. Ibid., 140–141.
54. *MNP*-B, 5:113; *ZNP*-B, 2:489.
55. *ZNP*-B, 2:488; Zhang et al., *Yang Chengwu nianpu*, 366.
56. *MNP*-B, 5:113; *ZNP*-B, 2:489.
57. Zhang et al., *Yang Chengwu nianpu*, 367; *Zhongyin bianjie ziwei fanji zuozhan shi*, 143.
58. *Zhongyin bianjie ziwei fanji zuozhan shi*, 146–147.
59. *ZNP*-B, 2:490; *MNP*-B, 5:117.
60. *Zhongyin bianjie ziwei fanji zuozhan shi*, 141.
61. Ambassador Pan Zili's farewell conversation with Nehru, July 13, 1962; Foreign Ministry to Ambassador Pan Zili (revised by Zhou), July 16, 1962, 101-01807-01; see Allen Whiting, *The Chinese Calculus of Deterrence: India and Indochina* (Ann Arbor : University of Michigan Press, 1975), 80; "The Afterthoughts of Premier Chou," interview with Neville Maxwell, *Sunday Times*, December 19, 1971.
62. *MNP*-B, 5:117; *ZNP*-B, 2:490; citation is from Li, *Da waijiaojia Zhou Enlai*, 4:316.
63. *CYNP*, 2:926; *MNP*-B, 5:117; *ZNP*-B, 2:490; citation is from Li, *Da waijiaojia Zhou Enlai*, 4:316.
64. Sarvepalli Gopal, *Jawaharlal Nehru: A Biography* (New Delhi: Oxford University Press, 2014), 213; Allen Whiting, *Chinese Calculus for Deterrence*, 264n19, quoting Arthur Lall's review of Maxwell's book *The Asian Student*, November 27, 1971.
65. Maxwell, *India's China War*, 251; *ZNP*-B, 2:490.
66. *MNP*-B, 5:138.
67. *Zhongyin bianjie ziwei fanji zuozhan shi*, 159–160; *ZNP*-B, 2:496n.
68. *ZNP*-B, 2:500.
69. *ZZ*-B, 699; *ZNP*-B, 2:500.
70. Logistics Office in Qinghai and Tibet of PLA General Staff, "Work summary of transportation of war materials during the War of Self-Defense along Chinese-Indian Borders," January 14, 1963; see also *Dangdai zhongguo jundui de houqin gongzuo* (The logistical affairs of the contemporary Chinese army) (Beijing: Zhongguo shehui kexue, 1990), chap. 7.
71. *Yang Chengwu nianpu*, 368; *ZNP*-B, 2:500; *MNP*-B, 5:164.
72. *Yang Chengwu nianpu*, 368.
73. Zhou's conversation with Soviet ambassador Chervonenko, October 8, 1962, 109-03804-01, CFMA.
74. Khrushchev's conversation with Liu Xiao, October 13, 1962, 109-03809-06; see also Khrushchev's talk at the farewell banquet for Liu Xiao, October 14, 1962, 109-03809-04, CFMA; Liu Xiao, *Chushi sulian banian* (Serving as ambassador in the Soviet Union for eight years) (Beijing: Zhonggong dangshi ziliao, 1986), 121.
75. Maxwell, *India's China War*, 369–371; *Statesman*, October 13, 1962.
76. *RMRB*, October 15, 1962.
77. *MNP*-B, 5:165; *PNP*, 4:220; see also Lei Yingfu, *Zai zuigao tongshuaibu dang canmou: Lei Yingfu jiangjun huiyilu* (Serving on the staff of the supreme headquarters: General Lei Yingfu's memoirs) (Nanchang: Baihuazhou wenyi, 1997), 209–210. (Lei wrongly stated in the memoir that the meeting was held on October 18.)
78. *MNP*-B, 5:165; *Zhongyin bianjie ziwei fanji zuozhan shi*, 179–180.
79. *Zhongyin bianjie ziwei fanji zuozhan shi*, 233–253.
80. *ZNP*-B, 2:504.
81. *RMRB*, October 25, 1962.
82. *ZNP*-B, 2:504.

83. Zhou's conversation with Burmese ambassador Kyaw Win, October 29, 1962, 105-01781-02, CFMA; *ZNP*-B, 2:571.

84. *MNP*-B, 5:169.

85. *MNP*-B, 5:169; *ZNP*-B, 2:513–514.

86. *ZNP*-B, 2:513–514; *MNP*-B, 5:169; Purnendu Kumar Banerjee, *My Peking Memoire of the Chinese Invasion of India* (New Delhi: Clarion Books, 1990), 72.

87. Zhou's speech at the Tenth Plenum of the Eighth CC, September 26, 1962, 855-6-2008-14, HPA.

88. *ZNP*-B, 2:504.

89. Zhou's speech at the Tenth Plenum of the Eighth CC, September 26, 1962, 855-6-2008-14, HPA.

90. Ibid.

91. CCP CC's Notice on the Chinese-Indian Border Clashes and Questions Concerning Chinese-Indian Relations, November 14, 1962, 855-6-2288-4, HPA.

92. Editorial Committee, *Zhongguo renmin jiefangjun junshi* (A history of the Chinese People's Liberation Army) (Beijing: Junshi kexue, 2010), 5:337–338; Han et al., *Dangdai zhongguo jundui de junshi gongzuo*, 1:633–634.

93. Interviews with two leading Chinese military historians.

94. Zhou's speech at a meeting of the Standing Committee of the People's Congress, November 24, 1962, 1057-8-44, HPA; see also *ZJSHDJS*, 575–577; *ZJSWX*, 4:469–477.

95. Zhou to President Nasser and other leaders of Asian and African countries, October 26, 1962, 107-00528-11, CFMA.

96. See, for example, Zhou's letter to leaders of the "Columbo Six," November 26, 1962, 105-01786-04; Zhou's conversation with Madam Bandaranaike and Subandrio, January 3, 1963, 105-01792-02, CFMA.

97. Memo of the Soviet government to the Chinese government, October 22, 1962, 109-03801-02, CFMA.

98. Khrushchev's conversation with Liu Xiao at Liu's farewell banquet, October 13, 1962, 109-03809-06, CFMA.

99. *RMRB*, October 29, 1962.

100. CCP CC's notice on the situation of Cuba's anti-American-imperialism struggles, December 4, 1962, 855-19-884, HPA.

101. Qian, *Lishi de bianju*, 294–295.

102. *MZ*-B, 1271.

103. *MNP*-B, 5:189.

104. *MZ*-B, 1272, 1311; *MNP*-B, 5:196–198, 200; Cong Jin, *Quzhe fazhan de suiyue*, 527.

105. *ZNP*-B, 2:533.

106. *Yan Mingfu huiyilu*, 2:797–842.

107. Editorial Group, *Nongye jitihua zhongyao wenjian huibian* (A collection of important documents of agricultural collectivization) (Beijing: Zhongyang dangxiao, 1981), 2:692.

108. *MZ*-B, 1317.

109. Qian, *Lishi de bianju*, 299.

110. *ZNP*-B, 2:580.

111. *MWG*, 11:85–87.

112. Bo, *Ruogan zhongda juece*, 2:1193–1194.

113. Editorial Committee, *Zhongguo renmin jiefangjun junshi*, 5:396.

114. *MNP*-B, 5:347–348.

115. Ibid., 5:354–355.

116. *ZZ*-B, 2:812–813; *MNP-B*, 5:355.
117. *MNP-B*, 5:358.
118. *LNP*, 2:592; *MNP*-B, 4:358.

23. Revolutions in the Intermediate Zone (1962–1965)

1. *MZ*-B, 1267–1268; *MNP*-B, 5:184.
2. *MWJWX*, 506–508.
3. Zhou's speech at the Tenth Plenum of the Eighth CC, September 26, 1962, 855-6-2008-14, HPA.
4. The subjects of Premier Zhou's meetings during his visit to Vietnam and the PRC-DRV joint communique, 203-00016-02, CFMA; Shi, *Wo guan Zhou Enlai*, 216; Guo Ming, *Zhongyue guanxi yanbian sishinian* (Forty years of Sino-Vietnamese relations) (Nanning: Guangxi renmin, 1992), 65–66.
5. Zhu Liang, "Some Important Matters in Chinese-Vietnamese Relations," *Zhonggong duiwai guanxi shiliao* (History materials of CCP's external relations, for strict internal circulation only) (2002), 5:164; Guo, *Zhongyue guanxi yanbian sishinian*, 66. For a Vietnamese account, see *The Truth about Vietnamo-Chinese Relations over the Past Thirty Years* (Hanoi: Ministry of Foreign Affairs, 1979), 29–33.
6. Summary of Premier Zhou's meetings with Phạm Van Dong during his visit to Vietnam, May 11, 1960, 203-00039-01, CFMA; Zhou Enlai's second conversation with Ho Chi Minh, Le Duan, and others, May 12, 1960, 1057-8-44, HPA; *ZWJHDDSJ*, 279–280.
7. Mao's conversation with Dong, June 15, 1961, 204-01445-04; Zhou Enlai's first and third conversations with Dong, June 12 and June 15, 1961, 204-01445-01, CFMA; see also *ZWJHDDSJ*, 313–314; Guo, *Zhongyue guanxi yanbian sishinian*, 67.
8. Mao's conversation with Vo Nguyen Giap, October 5, 1962, CCA; Mao's conversation with Le Duan et al., June 4, 1963, CCA.
9. Guo, *Zhongyue guanxi yanbian sishinian*, 67; Qu Aiguo et al., *Yuanyue kangmei: zhongguo zhiyuan budui zai yuenan* (Assisting Vietnam and resisting America, Chinese support force in Vietnam) (Beijing: Junshi kexue, 1995), 8.
10. Zhou and Chen's meeting with Dong, August 27, 1962, 106-01386-01; Zhou's conversation with Dong about Southern Revolution and support to Laos, August 28, 1962, 106-01394-14, CFMA; *ZJSHDJS*, 2:567.
11. Mao's conversation with Giap, October 5, 1962, CCA; *MNP*-B, 5:163–164.
12. Qu, *Yuanyue kangmei*, 9.
13. *LNP*-B, 2:577; Qu, *Yuanyue kangmei*, 8–9.
14. Mao's conversation with a VLP delegation, June 4, 1963, CCA.
15. Tong, *Fengyu sishi nian*, 2:219–220.
16. Mao's conversation with Van Tien Dung et al., June 24, 1964, 18:30–19:45, CCA.
17. Tong, *Fengyu sishi nian*, 2:220–221.
18. Li Ke and Hao Shengzhang, *Wenhua dageming zhong de jiefangjun* (The PLA in the Cultural Revolution) (Beijing: Jiefangjun, 1988), 408.
19. Zhou's meeting with North Korean and Romanian ambassadors, August 6 and August 8, 1964, 106-00788-05, CFMA.
20. Mao's conversation with Le Duan, August 13, 1964, 16:00–18:00, CCA.
21. Mao's conversation with Dong and Hoang Van Hoan, October 5, 1964, Odd Arne West et al., *77 Conversations between Chinese and Foreign Leaders on the Wars in Indochina, 1964–1977* (Washington, DC: The Wilson Center, 1998), 74–77.

22. Zhou's conversation with a Vietnamese military delegation, January 22, 1965, 106-00862-01, CFMA.

23. *ZWJWX,* 393.

24. Zhou's conversation with Che Guevara, October 18, 1960, 111-00163-03, CFMA.

25. Mao's and Zhou's letters to Sukarno, June 1958, 105-00363-06, CFMA; Wang Taiping et al., *Zhonghua renmin gongheguo waijiaoshi* (A diplomatic history of the PRC) (Beijing: Shijie zhishi, 1998), 2:57–58.

26. Wang et al., *Zhonghua renmin gongheguo waijiaoshi,* 2:58; Liu Shaoqi to Sukarno, April 27, 1963, 105-01834-01, CFMA.

27. Zhou Taomo, "The Political Swirl of the Overseas Chinese Issue in Indonesia," *Lengzhan guoji shi yanjiu* (Cold War international history studies) 9 (June 2010): 155–174.

28. Chen Yang, "Wu Jieping Treated Sukarno as a Medical Ambassador," *Shiji fengcai* (Century style), no. 1 (2017): 9–15; Olivia Cox-Fill, *Walking a Tightrope: Memoirs of Wu Jieping, Personal Physician to China's Leaders* (Bloxham, UK: Skyscraper Publications, 2019), 145.

29. Zhou's series of meetings with Subandrio, January 1965, 105-01319-01, CFMA.

30. Mao and Liu's conversation with an Indonesian delegation, September 30, 1965, 105-01917-03, CFMA.

31. See, for example, Zhou's conversations with Madame Bandaranaike and Subandrio, January 5, 1963, 204-01493-08, CFMA.

32. *RMRB,* December 16, 1963.

33. Zhou's one-on-one meeting with Nasser, December 20, 1963, 107-01027-08; Zhou's third meeting with Nasser, December 19, 1963, 107-01027-06, CFMA.

34. Zhou's third meeting with Ben Bella, December 24, 1963, 203-614–07, CFMA.

35. Zhou's fourth meeting with Ben Bella, December 26, 1963, 203-00614-06, CFMA.

36. Zhou and Chen Yi's report on visit to Morocco, January 5, 1964, 203-00381-01, CFMA; Li, *Da waijiaojia Zhou Enlai,* 5:145.

37. Wang, *Zhonghua renmin gongheguo waijiaoshi,* 3:271–273.

38. Premier Zhou plans to visit Ghana as originally scheduled, January 6–9, 1964, 108-00387-03, CFMA.

39. *ZWJWX,* 388–389.

40. Li, *Da waijiaojia Zhou Enlai,* 5:214–218.

41. PRC-Pakistan joint communiqué, February 23, 1964, *Zhonghua renmin gongheguo guowuyuan gongbao* (Bulletin of the State Council of the PRC), no. 5 (March 12, 1964): 84.

42. Zhou's third conversation with Madame Bandaranaike, February 29, 1964, 105-01890-02, CFMA.

43. Li, *Da waijiaojia Zhou Enlai,* 5:227–228.

44. *MZ-B,* 1256.

45. Zhou's conversation with Tatsunosuke Takasaki, April 22, 1955, 105-00211-04, CFMA.

46. Wang et al., *Zhonghua renmin gongheguo waijiaoshi, 1957–1969,* 20.

47. Zhou's meeting with Suzuki Kazuo, August 27, 1960, 105-00735-02, CFMA; *ZWJWX,* 289–290.

48. Zhou's conversation with Takasaki, October 13 and November 1, 1960, 105-00736-01, CFMA.

49. Zhou and Chen Yi's conversations with Matsumura, September 16–19, 1962, 105-01152-04, CFMA.

50. *Zhonghua renmin gongheguo jingji dang'an ziliao xuanbian, 1958–1965, Duiwai maoyi juan* (Selected materials from PRC Economic Archives, 1958–1965, foreign trade volume, hereafter *Zhonghua renmin gongheguo jingji dang'an ziliao xuanbian*) (Beijing: Zhongguo caijing jingji, 2011), 432–433, 469–471; *MZ-B,* 1256–1257.

51. Shen et al., *Dangdai zhongguo duiwai maoyi,* 1:30–31.

52. Edgar Faure, *Serpent and the Tortoise: Problems of the New China* (New York: St. Martin's Press, 1958), 22.

53. *MNP*-B, 3:168; Faure, *Serpent and the Tortoise,* 31–32.

54. Zhou's first conversation with Faure, October 23, 1963, 110-01982-08, CFMA.

55. Chen Yi's conversation with Faure, October 24, 1964, 110-01982-09, CFMA.

56. Zhou and Chen Yi's conversation with Faure, October 25, 1964, 110-01983-11, CFMA.

57. Zhou's letter to Mao, Liu, and Deng et al., November 1, 1963, 110-01982-06, CFMA; Zhou and Chen Yi's conversation with Faure, November 1, 1963, 21:15–22:00, 110-01982-14, CFMA.

58. Li, *Da waijiaojia Zhou Enlai,* 5:77–78; Wang, *Zhonghua renmin gongheguo waijiaoshi,* 3:368–369.

59. *Zhonghua renmin gongheguo jingji dang'an ziliao xuanbian,* 9.

60. Lu Shiguang et al., *Dangdai zhongguo maoyi* (Foreign trade of contemporary China) (Beijing: Dangdai zhongguo), 1:31, 32.

61. Mao's conversation with a delegation of Japanese Socialist Party, July 10, 1964, 105-01897-01, CFMA.

62. Zhou's conversation with a group of Japanese Socialist Party, July 19, 1964, 105-01897-04.

63. *Pravda,* September 2, 1964.

64. *Yan Mingfu huiyilu,* 2:859.

65. Li, *Da waijiaojia Zhou Enlai,* 5:275.

66. *MNP*-B, 5:419; Zhou's speech on situation, October 19, 1964, 1 / 1–20 / 145, Jilin Provincial Archive.

67. *MNP*-B, 5:422.

68. *MNP*-B, 5:425.

69. *MNP*-B, 5:425, 429.

70. PRC Foreign Ministry and CCP Central Liaison Department to Ambassador Pan Zili, about Zhou's conversation with Soviet ambassador, October 29, 1964, 109-02678-01, CFMA; Chervonenko's meeting with Zhou, October 29, 1964, f. 0100, op. 57, p. 508, d. 7, AVPRF.

71. Zhou's conversation with Vietnamese, Romanian, Albanian, Cuban, and North Korean ambassadors, October 29, 1964, 109-02678-04, CFMA.

72. Zhou's conversation with Bulgarian, Hungarian, Czechoslovakian, Polish, Mongolian, and East German ambassadors, October 30, 1965, 109-02678-05, CFMA.

73. Zhou's conversation with Chervonenko, October 30, 1965, 109-02678-0, CFMA.

74. Chinese Embassy in Moscow to Chinese Foreign Ministry, November 6, 1964, 203-00294-01, CFMA.

75. *Yan Mingfu huiyilu,* 2:862.

76. Ibid., 2:864.

77. Ibid., 2:864–865.

78. Ibid., 868.

79. Brezhnev and Zhou meeting records, November 8, 1964, f. 3, op. 16, d. 562, RGANI; *Yan Mingfu huiyilu,* 2:865–866; *ZNP*-B, 2:686.

80. *Yan Mingfu huiyilu,* 2:866–867.

81. *ZNP*-B, 2:686–687.

82. *MNP*-B, 5:434.

83. *MNP*-B, 5:434–435.

84. Li et al., *Dangdai zhongguo de hegongye,* 9.

85. Shi, *Zai lishi juren shenbian,* 511; interview with Shi Zhe, August 1992.

86. Zhou to Mao, January 14, 1955, *ZWG*, 12:15; Li et al., *Dangdai zhongguo de hegongye*, 13.

87. *ZWHWX*, 530.

88. Zhou Enlai's speech at the fourth plenary session of the State Council, January 31, 1955, *Dang de wenxian*, no. 3 (1994): 18–20.

89. Zhou's meeting with Yudin, March 22, 1956, 109-00743-03, CFMA.

90. Zhou's conversation with Yudin, June 14, 1957, 109-00786-14, CFMA.

91. *ZNP*-B, 2:67; Liu Xiao to Foreign Ministry and convey to CCP Center, August 15, 1957, 109-01726-02, CFMA.

92. *Nie Rongzhen nianpu*, 623; Li et al., *Dangdai zhongguo de hegongye*, 43.

93. Khrushchev to Zhou, April 24, 1958, 109-00838-03, CFMA.

94. Song Renqiong, "Silkworm Works until End of Life," in Editorial Group, *Women de Zhou zongli* (Our premier Zhou) (Beijing: Zhongyang wenxian, 1990), 69.

95. CCP CC's decision on strengthening building of nuclear industry, July 16, 1961, *ZGZYWJXJ*-B, 37:222–224.

96. *ZZ*-B, 787.

97. *ZJSWX*, 4:421; *ZZ*-B, 787.

98. Conveying Rui Ruiqing's report on establishing Office of National Defense Industry by CCP CC, November 29, 1961, GSPA.

99. Huang and Zhang, *Luo Ruiqing zhuan*, 393–394; *ZZ*-B, 788–789.

100. *MNP*-B, 5:167.

101. *ZGZYWJXJ*-B, 41:426–427.

102. *ZZ*-B, 796.

103. Xue et al., *Dangdai zhongguo waijiao*, 119–120.

104. Xie Yixian et al., *Zhongguo waijiao shi, 1949–1979* (A diplomatic history of the PRC, 1949–1979) (Zhengzhou: Henan renmin, 1988), 302–303.

105. Liu Jie, "An Outstanding Decisionmaker and Organizer of Our Country's Nuclear Project," in *Bujin de sinian*, 321.

106. *ZZ*-B, 796.

107. Li et al., *Dangdai zhongguo de hegongye*, 54; *ZZ*-B, 796.

108. *ZJSWX*, 4:484; *ZZ*-B, 797–798.

109. Dongfang He, *Zhang Aiping zhuan* (A biography of Zhang Aiping) (Beijing: Renmin, 2000), 2:776.

110. *ZJSWX*, 4:484–485; *MNP*-B, 5:409; *ZZ*-B, 798.

111. Dongfang, *Zhang Aiping zhuan*, 2:776–778; *ZZ*-B, 799–800.

112. Zhou Enlai's letter to Mao Zedong, Liu Shaoqi, Lin Biao, Deng Xiaoping, Peng Zhen, He Long, Nie Rongzhen, and Luo Ruiqing, October 11, 1964, *Dang de wenxian*, no. 3 (1994): 23.

113. Liu, "Outstanding Decisionmaker," 322–323.

114. *ZZ*-B, 2:806.

24. Gathering Storms in Gusty Winds (1965–1966)

1. *MNP*-B, 5:449.

2. *MNP*-B, 5:452–453; see also Lin Xiaobo and Guo Dehong, *Wenge de yuyan* (Prelude to the Cultural Revolution) (Beijing: Renmin, 2013), 171.

3. Zeng Zhi, *Yige geming de Yingcunzhe: Zeng Zhi huiyi shilu* (A lucky survivor of the revolution: Zeng Zhi huiyilu) (Guangzhou: Guangzhou renmin, 1999), 433.

4. *MZ-B*, 1371–1372; *MNP-B*, 5:456; Bo, *Ruogan zhongda juece*, 2:1131.

5. The chairman's speech, December 28, 1964, 101-12-255, pp. 1-9, FPA; *Yang Shangkun riji*, 478–482; *MZ-B*, 1372–1375; *MNP-B*, 5:457–458.

6. *MNP-B*, 5:329–330; *Hu Qiaomu huiyi Mao Zedong*, 212.

7. *MNP-B*, 5:438; Xiao Donglian, *Qiusuo zhongguo: wenge qian shinian shi* (In search of China: A ten-year history before the Cultural Revolution) (Beijing: Zhonggong dangshi, 2011), 2:1090; Zhang Guangyu, "Naming and Criticism," *Zuotian* (Yesterday), no. 42 (October 20, 2014): 4–5.

8. *MWG*, 11:50; *MNP-B*, 5:330.

9. *Zhou Enlai jingji wenxuan* (Selected economic papers of Zhou Enlai) (Beijing: Zhongyang wenxian, 1993), 563.

10. *MWJ*, 8:325, 341.

11. Bo, *Ruogan zhongda juece*, 1132.

12. Sergey Radtchenko, *Two Suns in the Heavens: The Sino-Soviet Struggle for Supremacy, 1962–1967* (Washington, DC, and Stanford, CA: Woodrow Wilson Center Press and Stanford University Press, 2009), 131, 140–141.

13. Zhou's four conversations with Kosygin, February 4 and February 5, 1965, 109-03957-06; Foreign Ministry's circular on Premier Zhou and Vice Premier Chen Yi's conversations with Kosygin, February 10, 109-03958-01, CFMA.

14. Zhou's fifth conversation with Kosygin, February 10, 1965, 109-03957-06, CFMA.

15. Mao conversation with Kosygin, February 12, 1965, 109-03957-07, CFMA; "Minutes from a Conversation between A. N. Kosygin and Mao Zedong," February 11, 1965, KC PZPR, XI A / 10, 517, 524, Polish Archive of Modern Records, No. 118039, WWCDC, https://digitalarchive.wilsoncenter.org/document/118039.

16. Zhou conversation with Ayub Khan, April 2, 1965, 106-01267-02, CFMA.

17. Ibid.

18. Richard N. Goodwin, *Remembering America: A Voice from the Sixties* (New York: Harper & Row Perennial, 1989), 394–395; Robert J. McMahon, *The Cold War on the Periphery* (New York: Columbia University Press, 1996), 318–324.

19. The Pakistani president actually delivered the message to Washington through a diplomatic channel. FO371 / 180 / 990, Foreign Policy, May-June 1965, folder 3, UKNA.

20. Pei Jianzhang et al., *Zhou Enlai waijiao huodong dashiji, 1949–1975* (Major events in Zhou Enlai's diplomatic activities, 1949–1975, hereafter *ZWJHDDSJ*) (Beijing: Shijie zhishi, 1993), 456–457.

21. Vice Premier Chen Yi's conversation with British chargé d'affaires Hopson, May 30, 1965, 110-01254-03; Chinese Foreign Ministry's circular about Vice Premier Chen Yi's conversation with British chargé d'affaires Hopson, June 20, 1965, 110-01254-01, CFMA; see also Peking (Mr. Hopson) to FO, No. 721, Priority / Confidential, May 31, 1965, FO 371 / 180996.

22. Washington (Sir P. Dean) to FO, No. 1460, priority / confidential, June 4, 1965, FO 371 / 180996, UKNA; McGeorge Bundy, Memorandum to the President, "Subject: Ch'en Yi message on Vietnam," Saturday, June 5, 1965, 6:50 P.M., NSF-CO, folder "Vietnam Memos (B), Vol. XXXV, 6 / 1–6 / 15 / 65," LBJL.

23. Peking (Mr. Hopson) to FO, No. 746, confidential, June 7, 1965, FO 371 / 180996, UKNA.

24. Chen, *Mao's China and the Cold War*, chap. 8.

25. Deng's speech at a Politburo meeting, April 12, 1965, 101-4-384, FPA; see also *DNP-A*, 1855–1856.

26. Zhou's instruction on preparing against war, April 10, 1965, 101-4-384, FPA; 855-8-3112-5, HPA; see also *ZNP-B*, 724.

27. Zhou's speech at a Politburo meeting, April 12, 1965, 101-4-384, FPA.

28. *MZ-B*, 1391–1392.

29. Comrade Duan Yun conveys the spirit of a Politburo meeting, May 15, 1965, 91-009-0576, GSPA; *ZNP-B*, 729–730.

30. *ZNP-B*, 751; *MNP-B*, 5:502.

31. Zhou's speech at a national planning conference, November 23, 1965, 855-8-3113-3, HBPA.

32. *MZ-B*, 1398.

33. Second conversation between Zhou and Tanzanian President Nyerere, June 6, 1965, 106-01269-05; conversation between Zhou and President Ho Chi Minh, June 15, 1965, 106-00861-02; Zhou's meeting with Algeria's presidential envoy, June 2, 1965, 107-00927-06, CFMA.

34. Mao's conversation with Aidit, August 5, 1965, CCA.

35. Zhu Liang, "Indonesia's September 30 Movement," *Zhonggong duiwai guanxi shiliao*, no. 5 (2000): 144–146; interview with Zhu Liang, January 2009. (Nasakom was an alliance of nationalism, religion, and communism favored by Sukarno in Indonesia.)

36. Premier Zhou's second conversation with delegation of Indonesian Provisional People's Consultative Conference, October 1, 1965, 105-01687-02, CFMA.

37. Zhou's conversation with an Indonesia Air Force Academy delegation, October 3, 1965, 105-01687-02; Zhou's conversation with an Indonesian Association of National Defense delegation, October 3, 1965, 105-01688-05; Zhou's third conversation with an Indonesian Provisional People's Consultative Conference delegation, October 4, 1965, 105-01917-01, CFMA.

38. Zhu, "Indonesia's September 30 Movement," 147; Liu Yibin, "After Indonesia's September 30 Incident," *Shijie zhishi* (World affairs), no. 1 (2006): 26.

39. Zhou speech at a central work conference, October 12, 1965, 855-8-3112-2, HPA.

40. Zhou speech at a central planning conference, November 13, 1965, 855-8-3113-3, HPA.

41. Second conversation by Zhou and Chen Yi with DPRK vice prime minister Yi Chu-yon, November 11, 1965, 106-01476-06, CFMA.

42. Zhu, "Indonesia's September 30 Movement," 148.

43. Zhou's letter to leaders of Asian and African countries, October 22, 1965, 107-00934-02, CFMA.

44. Second conversation by Zhou and Chen Yi with DPRK vice prime minister Yi Chu-yon, November 11, 1965, 106-01476-06, CFMA.

45. *MZ-B*, 1396.

46. Mao's conversation with Kabo and Balluku, February 3, 1967, CCA.

47. Editorial Group, *Peng Zhen nianpu* (A chronological record of Peng Zhen, hereafter *PNP*) (Beijing: Zhongyang wenxian, 2012), 4:448.

48. *ZNP-B*, 2:767; *Chen Pixian huiyilu* (Chen Pixian's memoirs) (Shanghai: Shanghai renmin, 2005), 34.

49. *PNP*, 4:450.

50. *RMRB*, November 30, 1965, 5.

51. *MNP-B*, 5:547–548.

52. Lin Biao's letter to Mao, November 30, 1965, cited from Huang and Zhang, *Luo Ruiqing zhuan*, 538; *MZ-B*, 1399; *MNP-B*, 5:544.

53. Zhang Yaoci, *Zhang Yaoci huiyi Mao Zedong* (Zhang Yaoci's recollection of Mao Zedong) (Beijing: Zhongyang dangxiao, 1996), 30–31.

54. *MWG*, 11:486.

55. *PNP*, 4:451.

56. See *Qiu Huizuo huiyilu* (Qiu Huizuo's memoirs) (Hong Kong: New Century Press, 2011), 377–379; *Li Zuopeng huiyilu* (Li Zuopeng's memoirs) (Hong Kong: Beixing, 2011), 537–538.

57. Gao Zhenpu, *Zhou Enlai weishi huiyilu* (Recollections of Zhou Enlai's bodyguard) (Shanghai: Shanghai renmin, 2000), 77–78.

58. Pu Weihua, *Zalan jiu shijie: Wenhua dageming de dongluan yu haojie* (Smashing the Old World: The turmoil and catastrophe in the Cultural Revolution) (Hong Kong: The Chinese University Press, 2008), 28.

59. Huang and Zhang, *Luo Ruiqing zhuan*, 547; Qian, *Lishi de bianju*, 431.

60. CCP CC Document (66), No. 267, February 12, 1966.

61. *PNP*, 4:486–487.

62. *MNP*-B, 5:557; *PNP*, 4:468–469.

63. *DNP*-A, 1893; Yang et al., *Deng Xiaoping zhuan*, 1326.

64. *MNP*-B, 5:554–555; 562–563.

65. *MNP*-B, 5:562; *MWG*, 12:23–30.

66. Huang and Zhang, *Luo Ruiqing zhuan*, 566–572.

67. Wu, *Shinian lunzhan*, 935–936.

68. *MNP*-B, 5:567; Wu, *Shinian lunzhan*, 937–939; *Yan Mingfu huiyilu*, 2:885–887.

69. Masaru Kojima, ed., *The Record of the Talks between the Japanese Communist Party and the Communist Party of China: How Mao Zedong Scrapped the Joint Communique* (Tokyo: JCP Central Committee, 1980), 137–160; see also *DNP*-A, 2:1897; *PNP*, 4:469–470.

70. Masaru, *Record of the Talks*, 163–168.

71. Ibid., 169–173.

72. Ibid., 188–189; see also *ZWJHDDSJ*, 491; *MNP*-B, 5:570.

73. Mao's comments on the CCP-JCP delegations' joint communiqué (draft), March 28, 1966, CCA; *MNP*-B, 5:570–571.

74. Mao's first and second conversations with the JCP delegation led by Miyamoto, March 28 and March 29, 1966, CCA; *MNP*-B, 5:571–572.

75. Masaru, *Record of the Talks*, 1–4.

76. *MNP*-B, 5:572–573.

77. *ZZ*-B, 2:879.

78. *MNP*-B, 5:373.

79. Mao's conversation with Korean Party and Government delegation, October 7, 1964, CCA. Mao asked, "Will the Soviet Union attack us?"

80. *ZNP*-B, 3:27.

81. *PNP*, 4:480; *MNP*-B, 5:573–574.

82. *MZ*-B, 1407–1408; *MNP*-B, 5:580.

83. *MWG*, 12:53–54.

84. Jiang Benlian, *Gei gongheguo lingdaoren zuo fanyi* (Interpreting for leaders of the republic) (Shanghai: Shanghai cishu, 2007), 35–36.

85. Ibid., 37–42.

86. *ZNP*-B, 3:31.

87. *ZJSHDJS*, 628–629; *ZNP*-B, 3:31–32.

88. CCP CC Notice, May 16, 1966, Party History Teaching and Research Group at National Defense University eds., *Wenhua dageming yanjiu ziliao* (Cultural Revolution research materials, hereafter *WGYJZL*) (Beijing: Guofang daxue, 1988), 1:1–4.

89. Lin's speech at a Politburo enlarged meeting, May 18, 1966, *WGYJZL*, 1:16–23.

90. Zhou's speech at a Politburo enlarged meeting, May 21, 1966, Song Yongyi et al., *Zhongguo wenhua dageming wenku* (Chinese Cultural Revolution database, hereafter *ZGWGWK*).

25. The Opening Salvoes of the Cultural Revolution (1966–1967)

1. *MWG*, 12:62.

2. Wang Nianyi, *Dadongluan de niandai* (Years of great turmoils) (Zhengzhou: He'nan renmin, 1989) 29.

3. *ZNP*-B, 3:34; *MNP*-B, 5:589.

4. Huang Zheng: *Fengyu wuhui: duihua Wang Guangmei: Duihua Wang Guangmei* (No regrets in storms: A dialogue with Wang Guangmei) (Beijing: Renmin wenxuan, 2015)407.

5. *MNP*-B, 5:593; see also *LNP*, 2:641.

6. *MNP*-B, 5:591, 594.

7. Wang Li, "Memoirs of a Year and Two Months, June 1966–August 1967," *Chinese Law and Government*, no. 6 (1994): 27.

8. About the June Eighteenth Incident, see MacFarquhar and Schoenhals, *Mao's Last Revolution*, 75–76; Wang, *Daduanluan de niandai*, 39–40; *WGYJZL*, 1:51–52.

9. *MNP*-B, 5:594–595.

10. Ibid., 5:598–599.

11. *RMRB*, July 26, 1966, 1; *MNP*-B, 5:599–600.

12. Huang, *Fengyu wuhui*, 411; *Qi Benyu huiyilu* (Qi Benyu's memoirs) (Hong Kong: Zhongguo wenge lishi, 2016), 444.

13. *MNP*-B, 5:600; *Qi Benyu huiyilu*, 445.

14. *MNP*-B, 5:600.

15. Li Xuefeng, "Recalling the First Fifty Days of the Cultural Revolution," *Zhonggong dangshi yanjiu* (CCP History Research), no. 4 (1998): 5; *Qi Benyu huiyilu*, 445–446; *DNP*-A, 3:1924–1925; Jin et al., *Liu Shaoqi zhuan*, 1027–1028.

16. *MNP*-B, 5:601.

17. *MBP*-B, 5:601; *Qi Benyu huiyilu*, 447.

18. *MNP*-B, 5:602.

19. *ZNP*-B, 3:41–42.

20. *MNP*-B, 5:603.

21. *ZNP*-B, 3:41–42.

22. *LNP*, 646–647; *DNP*-A, 3:1926; *MNP*-B, 5:603.

23. Mu Xin, *Jiehou changyi: shinian dongluan jishi* (A painful recollection of surviving the catastrophe: A factual account of the ten-year turmoils) (Hong Kong: Tiandi, 1997), 152; Li, *Private Life of Chairman Mao*, 470.

24. *MWG*, 12:87–88.

25. Jin et al., *Liu Shaoqi zhuan*, 1032–1033; *MNP*-B, 5:604–605.

26. *ZNP*-B, 3:45; Jin et al., *Liu Shaoqi zhuan*, 2:1033–1034; Xie Xuegong, "Diary on the Eleventh Plenum of the Eighth CC," *Yanhuang Chunqiu*, no. 5 (2015): 52–53.

27. *Qi Benyu huiyilu*, 456.

28. *MNP*-B, 5:606; Jin et al., *Liu Shaoqi zhuan*, 2:1035–1036.

29. Huang, *Fengyu wuhui*, 414; *ZNP*-B, 3:46.

30. *MWG*, 12:90.

31. *MNP*-B, 5:609.
32. Ibid., 611; *ZNP*-B, 3:48–49.
33. *ZNP*-B, 3:51, note 1; *Qi Benyu huiyilu*, 461–462.
34. *Wang Li fansilu* (Reflections by Wang Li) (Hong Kong: Beixing, 2001), 950.
35. *RMRB*, August 19, 1966, 1.
36. Gao, *Zhou Enlai weishi huiyilu*, 83.
37. *ZNP*-B, 3:51.
38. *MWG*, 12:112.
39. *ZNP*-B, 3:57.
40. *RMRB*, September 16, 1966, 1.
41. Gu Mu, "Remembering Our Beloved Premier Zhou," in Editorial Group., *Women de Zhou zongli* (Our premier Zhou) (Beijing: Zhongyang wenxian, 1990), 16; *ZZ*-B, 2:1692.
42. *MNP*-B, 6:2.
43. Ibid., 2–3.
44. Chen Boda's speech at the Central Work conference, October 16, 1966, *ZGWGWK*.
45. Liu Shaoqi's and Deng Xiaoping's self-criticism at the Central Work Conference, October 23, 1966, *ZGWGWK*.
46. Mao's speech at the Central Work Conference, October 25, 1966, *WGYJZL*, 1:150–151.
47. Zhou's speech at the Central Work Conference, October 28, 1966, *ZGWGWK*.
48. See Wang, *Daduanluan de niandai*, 127–128; Li Xun, *Geming zaofan niandai: Shanghai wenge yundong shigao* (Years of revolutionary rebellions: A history of the Cultural Revolution in Shanghai) (Hong Kong: Oxford University Press, 2015).
49. Li, *Geming zaofan niandai*, 317–318.
50. Shi Yun, *Zhang Chunqiao Yao Wenyuan shizhuan* (A factual account of Zhang Chunqiao and Yao Wenyuan) (Hong Kong: Sanlian, 2012), 368–360.
51. Li, *Geming zaofan niandai*, 333.
52. Ibid., 321–322; *Wang Li fansilu*, 954–955.
53. Cited from Pu, *Zalan jiu shijie*, 310; *Wang Li fansilu*, 955–956; *Qi Benyu huiyilu*, 536.
54. Li, *Geming zaofan niandai*, 321–322.
55. Shi, *Zhang Chunqiao Yao Wenyuan shizhuan*, 351.
56. Wang, *Dadongluan de niandai*, 135–137.
57. *ZNP*-B, 3:92.
58. Cited from Shi, *Zhang Chunqiao Yao Wenyuan shizhuan*, 351.
59. *ZNP*-B, 3:99.
60. *WGYJZL*, 1:182–183.
61. Zhou speech at the conference on political work in industry and transportation of the whole country, November 24, 1966, *ZGWGWK*; *ZNP*-B, 3:99.
62. *Qi Benyu huiyilu*, 541–544; see also Wang, *Xianchang lishi*, 100–104.
63. The account here is based upon critical reading of the following sources: *Qi Benyu huiyilu*, 541–544;Wang, *Xianchang lishi*, 100–104; Zhang Chunqiao's recollection in his letter to his daughter Zhang Weiwei, December 1, 1992, in *Zhang Yuzhong jiashu* (Zhang Chunqiao's letters to family from prison) (Hong Kong: Chinese University Press, 2015), 128; Yao Wenyuan's description in Xu Jingxian, *Shinian yimeng: Xu Jingxian huiyilu* (A ten-year dream: Xu Jingxian's memoir) (Hong Kong: Shidai guoji, 2003), 8. Those in attendance at the dinner had different recollections about whether Mao had said "full-scale civil war." Wang Li claimed that Mao said "cheers to full-scale class struggle in the whole country." Qi asserted that "Wang Li is wrong." Zhang remembered that Mao "cheered for the full-scale

civil war." Yao, according to Xu, said in a phone call to Shanghai the next day that Mao "cheered for the beginning of a full-scale civil war in the whole country!" If Mao had not said "full-scale civil war," it would have been impossible for Qi, Zhang, and Yao, at different times and in different circumstances, to all recall him saying so.

64. *Qi Benyu huiyilu,* 544–545; *RMRB,* January 1, 1967, 1.

65. This is a story from the Chinese classic novel *Journey to the West.*

66. *Qi Benyu huiyilu,* 544.

67. *MNP*-B, 6:27.

68. Wang, *Dadongluan de niandai,* 149–150.

69. *ZNP*-B, 3:108.

70. *Qi Benyu huiyilu,* 563.

71. Mao's letter to Jiang Qing, July 8, 1966, *MWG,* 12:71.

72. Zeng, *Yige geming de Yingcunzhe,* 449; *Qi Benyu huiyilu,* 562–563; Wang, *Daduanluan de niandai,* 150.

73. Li Lie et al., *He Long nianpu* (Chronological records of He Long) (Beijing: Zhongyang dangxiao, 1988), 787.

74. *ZNP-B,* 3:114–115; Li et al., *He Long nianpu,* 787–788.

75. Li et al., *He Long nianpu,* 788.

76. Ibid., 788.

77. Ling, *Cong yanan dao lianheguo,* 119.

78. *MNP*-B, 6:28; *Wan Li fansilu,* 764.

79. Li, *Geming zaofan niandai,* 580–606.

80. Ibid., 606.

81. *MNP*-B, 6:30; *MWG,* 12:185.

82. Li, *Geming zaofan niandai,* 658–659.

83. *MWG,* 12:186.

84. *Wang li fansilu,* 794.

85. *RMRB,* January 12, 1967, 1.

86. *ZNP*-B, 3:111–112; *Wang Li fansilu,* 793–794.

87. *MNP*-B, 6:34; *ZNP*-B, 3:113.

88. Zhou's speech to representatives of the industrial and transportation areas, January 16, 1967, *ZGWGWK;* see also Pu, *Zalan jiu shijie,* 356.

89. *Wang Li fansilu,* 764.

90. *MNP*-B, 3:403.

91. *MNP*-B, 6:51–52; MacFarquhar and Schoenhal, *Mao's Last Revolution,* 170–171.

26. Great Chaos All under Heaven (1967–1968)

1. *MNP*-B, 6:10; Mao's conversation with Kabo and Baluku, February 3, 1967, CCA.

2. *MWG,* 12:197.

3. *WGYJZL,* 1:258–259.

4. Shi, *Zhang Chunqiao Yao Wenyuan shizhuan,* 356; Fang and Jin et al., *Li Fuchun zhuan,* 667.

5. Liu Jixian et al., *Ye Jianying nianpu* (Chronological records of Ye Jianying) (Beijing: Zhongyang wenxian, 2007), 2:956; *Xu Xiangqian nianpu* (A chronological record of Xu Xiangqian) (Beijing: Jiefan, 2016), 2:185.

6. *ZNP*-B, 3:115.

7. *ZNP*-B, 3:122; *ZZ*-B, 954–955.
8. *ZNP*-B, 3:122.
9. *MNP*-B, 6:47–48.
10. Fan Shuo et al., *Ye Jianying zhuan* (A biography of Ye Jianying) (Beijing: Dangdai zhongguo, 1995), 586–587; Jixian et al., *Ye Jianying nianpu*, 2:959–960.
11. Pu, *Zalan jiu shijie*, 449–450; Liu Zhi et al., *Xu Xiangqian zhuan* (A biography of Xu Xiangqian) (Beijing: Dangdai zhongguo, 1991), 532.
12. Liu Wusheng, *Wenge zhong de Zhou Enlai* (Zhou Enlai in the Cultural Revolution) (Hong Kong: Sanlian, 2006), 192.
13. *MNP*-B, 6:51–52.
14. Wang, *Daduanluan de niandai*, 209–211; *Wang Li fansilu*, 977–978; *Qi Benyu huiyilu*, 2:576–577; *ZNP*-B, 3:127.
15. *ZNP*-B, 3:127; *ZZ*-B, 2:956.
16. Pu, *Zalan jiu shijie*, 449–450.
17. *Wang Li fansilu*, 979–980.
18. Ibid., 980–981, 983.
19. *ZNP*-B, 3:127; *Wang Li fansilu*, 981.
20. *Wang Li fansilu*, 983.
21. Liu, *Wenge Zhong de Zhou Enlai*, 198; *Wang Li fansilu*, 982–984.
22. Wang, *Dadongluan de niandai*, 216; *MNP*-B, 6:56.
23. *MNP*-B, 6:56.
24. *Wang Li fansilu*, 987.
25. *ZNP*-B, 3:127; *Wang Li fansilu*, 984.
26. Zhou's speech at a meeting by commanders of army level and above, March 13, 1967, *ZGWGWK*; see Wu Qingtong, *Zhou Enlai zai wenhua dageming zhong: huiyi Zhou zongli tong Lin Biao Jiang Qing lian'ge fangeming jituan de touzheng* (Zhou Enlai in the Cultural Revolution: Recalling premier's struggles against Lin Biao and Jiang Qing antiparty cliques) (Beijing: Zhonggong dangshi, 2013), 92.
27. *WGYJZL*, 1:361–362.
28. Zhou's speech at a meeting by commanders of army level and above, March 13, 1967, *ZGWGWK*.
29. *ZNP*-B, 3:137, 139; *MNP*-B, 6:87–88.
30. *MNP*-B, 6:68; *Qi Benyu huiyilu*, 2:606–607.
31. Pu, *Zalan jiu shijie*, 504–506; Wang Nianyi, "Some Materials about the May Sixteenth Corps," *Dangshi yanjiu ziliao* (Party history research materials), no. 1 (2002): 31–45.
32. *ZNP*-B, 3:154.
33. *MWG*, 12:359; *MNP*-B, 6:87.
34. The announcement by Jiang Qing, Chen Boda, and Kang Sheng at a mass meeting, August 11, 1967, *ZGWGWK*.
35. *ZNP*-B, 3:154–155.
36. *MNP*-B, 6:85; *ZNP*-B, 3:155.
37. *ZNP*-B, 3:150.
38. Zhou's talks with representatives of revolutionary rebels at the Foreign Ministry, May 12, 1967, and June 28, 1967, *ZGWGWK*; *ZZ*-B, 2:965.
39. *MNP*-B, 6:98; *Yang Chengwu jiangjun zishu* (An autobiography of General Yang Chengwu) (Shenyang: Liaoning renmin, 1997), 268–270.
40. *ZNP*-B, 3:170.

41. *MNP*-B, 6:99–100.

42. Zhou's speech at the conference of officers above division level in Hubei Military Command, July 18, 1967, *ZGWGWK; ZNP*-B, 3:170.

43. *MBP*-B, 6:101–103.

44. Ibid., 6:103.

45. Xie Fuzhi and Wang Li's instruction at a conference of officers of the Wuhan Military Command above division level, July 19, 1967; Xie and Wang's speech at Wuhan Water Works and Electricity College, July 19, 1967, *ZGWGWK*.

46. *MNP*-B, 6:103.

47. Ibid.

48. *MNP*-B, 6:103; *ZNP*-B, 3:171.

49. Xu, *Shinian yimeng*, 276.

50. *Qi Benyu huiyilu*, 2:661; Ma Jisun, *Waijiaobu wenge jishi* (A factual account of the Cultural Revolution in the Foreign Ministry) (Hong Kong: Chinese University Press, 2002), 167–169.

51. Ma, *Waijiaobu wenge jishi*, 169–171; *Wang Li fansilu*, 1015–1026; *Qi Benyu huiyilu*, 2:661–662.

52. Wu Dizhou's work notes, Wu Hui ed., *Wu Dizhou Xianggang wencun* (Wu Dizhou's Hong Kong manuscripts) (Hong Kong: Oxford University Press, 2022), 145–146.

53. *RMRB*, May 16, 1967.

54. Chen Yangyong, *Kucheng weiju: Zhou Enlai zai 1967* (Striving to sustain in the dangerous situation: Zhou Enlai in 1967) (Beijing: Zhongyang wenxian, 1999), 353.

55. Ibid., 353.

56. *RMRB*, May 24, 1967, 8.

57. Chen, *Kucheng weiju*, 353–354; *ZNP*-B, 3:155; Wu ed., *Wu Dizhou Xianggang wencun*, 159.

58. Ma, *Waijiaobu wenge jishi*, 158.

59. *RMRB*, June 3, 1967, 1.

60. Chen, *Kucheng weiju*, 355–356; *ZNP*-B, 3:155.

61. Chen, *Kucheng weiju*, 355–356.

62. *RMRB*, August 21, 1967, 2.

63. Ma, *Waijiaobu wenge jishi*, 161.

64. Mr. Hopson to Mr. Brown, "The Burning of the British Office in Peking," confidential, September 8, 1967, FC1 / 14, FCO 21 / 34, UKNA.

65. Wu Faxian, *Suiyue jianan: Wu Faxian huiyilu* (Difficult times: Wu Faxian's memoirs) (Hong Kong: Beixing, 2007), 694.

66. Zhou's talks with leaders of various organizations of revolutionary rebel units related to foreign affairs, 3:00 A.M., August 23, 1967, *ZGWGWK*; see also *ZNP*-B, 3:181; Ma, *Waijiaobu wenge jishi*, 179–180.

67. *ZNP*-B, 3:182; *ZZ*-B, 2:967; Zhang et al., *Yang Chengwu nianpu*, 455.

68. Zhang et al., *Yang Chengwu nianpu*, 455.

69. Sidney Rittenberg, *The Man Who Stayed Behind* (Durham, NC: Duke University Press, 2001), 381. Graham's files, kept at Radcliffe College at Harvard University, have nothing about this meeting. However, an official Chinese source recorded that Zhou indeed met with Graham on the evening of August 25 (*ZWJHDDSJ*, 515). Rittenberg would not have known about the meeting if Graham had not told him about it.

70. Zhang et al., *Yang Chengwu nianpu*, 455; *ZNP*-B, 3:182–183.

71. *ZNP*-B, 3:183; Zhang et al., *Yang Chengwu nianpu*, 455–456.

72. *MWG*, 12:464.

73. Lin Biao's speech at a conference of commanders above army level, March 24, 1968, *ZGWGWK*.

74. Zhou's speech at a conference of commanders of army level and above, March 24, 1969, *ZGWGWK*.

75. *MNP*-B, 6:157.

76. *MWG*-B, 12:276.

77. Zhou Enlai and Li Xiannian's instruction about the Railway Transportation Ministry's statement on the meeting by transportation heads from the Soviet Union and six other countries, July 17, 1968, 1-1-7403, CTDA.

78. *ZNP*-B, 3:242–243; The "July Third Order," *WGYJZL*, 2:138–139; *MWG*, 12:506.

79. *ZNP*-B, 3:248.

80. The "July Twenty-Fourth Notice," *WGYJZL*, 2:152–153; *ZNP*, 3:247.

81. Wang, *Dadongluan de niandai*, 301–302.

82. *MWG*, 6:175–177.

83. *ZNP*-B, 3:249.

84. Jiang, *Gei gongheguo lingdaoren zuo fanyi*, 80; *ZNP*-B, 3:252–253.

85. *MNP*-B, 6:185; *ZNP*-B, 3:252.

86. Jiang, *Gei gongheguo lingdaoren dang fanyi*, 80.

87. *RMRB*, August 23, 1968, 1.

88. *ZNP*-B, 3:252–253; see also "Premier Chou (Zhou) En-lai's Important Speech at Romania's National Day Reception," August 22, 1968, supplement, *Peking Review*, no. 34 (August 23, 1968): iii–iv.

89. Zhou's speech at the celebration rally of revolutionary masses in Beijing, September 7, 1968, *WGYJZL*, 2:197–199.

90. Zhou speech at the opening session of the Twelfth Plenum of the CCP's Eighth CC, October 13, 1968, *ZGWGWK*; see also Wang, *Dadongluan de niandai*, 311.

91. Zhou to Jiang Qing, September 25, 1968, cited from Gao, *Wannian Zhou Enlai*, 251.

92. Jiang Qing probably had been obsessed by the rumor that Mao was once romantically interested in Sun, and Ye Qun had been alert about Lin Biao's chase after Sun in Moscow.

93. Shen, *Zhou Enlai yangnu Sun Weishi*, 228; *ZNP-B*, 3:264.

94. Zhou Bingde, *Wo de bofu Zhou Enlai*, 263–281.

95. *RMRB*, December 22, 1968, 1.

96. *RMRB*, November 2, 1968, 1; *MWG*, 12:593.

27. Lin Biao Dies (1969–1971)

1. *MWG*, 13:23–24.

2. *MZ*-B, 1545; Wang Wenyao and Wang Baochun, *Wenge qianhou shiqi de Chen Boda: mishu de zhengyan* (Chen Boda in late Cultural Revolution years: Secretaries' testimony) (Hong Kong: Tiandi tushu, 2014), 136–142.

3. Chen, *Chen Boda zuihou koushu huiyi*, 363; Zhang Yusheng, *Maojiawan jishi: Lin Biao mishu huiyilu* (Maojiawan's true story: Memoir of Lin Biao's secretary) (Beijing: Chuqiu, 1988), 214.

4. Zhang, *Maojiawan jishi*, 214–215; *Qiu Huizuo huiyilu*, 2:620.

5. Zhou's speech at the Ninth Congress, April 14, 1969, 91-019-0006, GSPA.

6. *MWG*, 13:4.

7. *Qiu Huizuo huiyilu*, 2:646–647.

8. See, for example, Mao's conversation with a DPRK delegation, June 27, 1970; Mao's conversation with Ne Win, August 7, 1971, CCA.

9. Ma Jisen, *The Cultural Revolution in the Foreign Ministry of China: A True Story* (Hong Kong: The Chinese University Press, 2005), chaps. 11–12.

10. Zhou's speech at the National Planning Work Conference, March 14, 1960, 921-5-31, HPA; B246-2-385–91, SHMA.

11. Wang, *Dadongluan de niandai,* 360.

12. State Department Memorandum of Conversation, "US Reaction to Soviet Destruction of CPR Nuclear Capability," August 18, 1969, SN 67–69, Def 12 Chicom, NA; see also Henry Kissinger, *White House Years* (New York: Little, Brown, 1978), 183. On August 30, *Cankao ziliao* published a report published by the *Washington Star* two days before about Moscow's preparation for launching a preemptive nuclear strike on China, which Mao and Zhou could not have failed to note.

13. CCP CC order, August 28, 1968, *WGYJZL,* 2:365–367.

14. *MNP-B*, 6:267.

15. More detail about this will be covered in Chapter 28.

16. *MNP-B*, 6:270.

17. Ibid., 6:270–271; *ZNP-B*, 3:329.

18. Li Genqing, "Before and After Lin Biao's Urgent Instruction," *Yanhuang chunqiu,* no. 11 (2015): 47.

19. Ibid., 47; Zhang Yunsheng et al., *Wenge qijian wo gei Lin Biao dang mishu* (I served as Lin Biao's secretary during the Cultural Revolution) (Hong Kong: Zhonghua er'nu, 2003), 568.

20. Zhang Songjia, "Yan Zhongchuan and Order Number One," *Yanhuang chunqiu,* no. 9 (2015) 50.

21. Wang Dongxing, *Mao Zedong yu Lin Biao fangeming jituan de douzheng* (Mao's struggles against Lin Biao's counterrevolution clique) (Beijing: Dangdai zhongguo, 2010), 14–15.

22. Ibid., 15.

23. *MNP-B*, 6:283.

24. *ZNP-B*, 3:353; *MNP-B*, 6:283.

25. *MNP-B*, 6:285.

26. Ibid., 6:291.

27. *MWG,* 13:94; *ZNP-B*, 3:361.

28. *MNP-B*, 6:295.

29. Wu, *Suiyue jianan,* 777–778.

30. *MWG,* 13:244–245.

31. *Qiu Huizuo huiyilu,* 684; *MNP-B*, 6:318.

32. *ZNP-B*, 3:385; *MNP-B*, 6:318–319; Wu, *Suiyue jianan,* 783–784.

33. Ji Dong, *Nanwang de banian: Zhou Enlai mishu huiyilun* (Unforgettable eight years: The memoir of Zhou Enlai's secretary) (Beijing: Zhongyang wenxian, 2007), 139.

34. *MNP-B*, 6:319–320; *ZNP-B*, 3:386–387.

35. Chen Xiaonong, comp., *Chen Boda yigao: Yuzhong zishu ji qita* (Chen Boda's posthumous manuscript: autobiography written in prison and other matters) (Hong Kong: Tiandi tushu, 1998), 118. Several of Lin's associates recalled that, according to Ye Qun, Lin briefed Mao on what he wanted to say, and that Mao only told Lin that he should not mention Zhang's name.

36. Lin Biao's speech at the Second Plenum of CCP's Ninth CC, August 23, 1970, *ZGWGWK.*

37. *MZ-B*, 1573.

38. Chen, *Chen Boda yigao,* 118.

39. Wang Dongxing's presentation at the North China group at the Second Plenum of CCP's Ninth CC, August 24, 1970, *ZGWGWK.*

40. *MNP-B*, 6:325.
41. Xu, *Shinian yimeng*, 213–214; Briefing at the Plenum No. 6, August 24, 1970, *ZGWGWK*.
42. *MNP-B*, 6:326.
43. *ZNP-B*, 3:388.
44. *MNP-B*, 6:326–327; *ZNP-B*, 3:388.
45. *ZNP-B*, 3:389.
46. *ZNP-B*, 3:389; Wang, *Mao zuxi yu Lin Biao*, 48.
47. *MNP-B*, 6:329–331; *ZNP-B*, 3:389.
48. *MNP-B*, 6:327; Chen, *Chen Boda zuihou koushu huiyi*, 375.
49. *MNP-B*, 6:328.
50. Wu, *Suiyue jianan*, 806.
51. *ZNP-B*, 3:389–390; *MNP-B*, 6:329.
52. Mao, "Some of My Opinions," August 31, 1970, *MWG*, 13:114–115.
53. *MNP-B*, 6:331; *ZNP-B*, 3:391.
54. *MWG*, 13:126.
55. *MNP-B*, 6:333.
56. *Qiu Huizuo huiyilu*, 777.
57. *MNP-B*, 6:335–336; *Li Desheng huiyilu* (Li Desheng's memoirs) (Beijing: Jiefangjun, 1997), 404.
58. Wang, *Mao Zedong he Lin Biao*, 59–65.
59. *MNP-B*, 6:338; *ZNP-B*, 3:395–396.
60. *Qiu Huizuo huiyilu*, 775.
61. Ibid., 733.
62. Wu Faxian's first written self-criticism, September 29, 1970; Ye Qun's first written self-criticism, October 12, 1970, *ZGWGWK*.
63. *MWG*, 13:143, 137.
64. *ZNP-B*, 3:403.
65. *MWG*, 13:174.
66. *ZNP-B*, 3:422; *MNP-B*, 6:361.
67. Reference Materials of the North China Conference, January 17, 1971, 919-6-102–5, HPA; ZZ-B, 1028.
68. Outline of Zhou speech at the North China Conference, January 24, 1971, CCP CC Document, No. 6 (1971), 919-6-103–3, 855-10-2-2, HPA.
69. *MNP-B*, 6:369; *MWG*, 13:206–207.
70. *MNP-B*, 6:369; *MWG*, 13:208.
71. *ZNP-B*, 3:438.
72. *Qiu Huizuo huiyilu*, 747.
73. *MNP-B*, 6:374; *Qiu Huizuo huiyilu*, 2:754.
74. *MNP-B*, 6:374.
75. Ibid., 6:375.
76. *Qiu Huizuo huiyilu*, 2:758–759; *Li Desheng huiyilu*, 409.
77. Zhou Enlai's conversation with Lin Biao, March 30 and 31, 1971, cited from Gao, *Wannian Zhou Enlai*, 314–315; see also *Qiu Huizuo huiyilu*, 2:779; *ZNP-B*, 3:447; *MNP-B*, 6:376.
78. *MNP-B*, 6:377; *Qiu Huizuo huiyilu*, 2:759–762.
79. *Qiu Huizuo huiyilu*, 2:760.
80. *ZNP-B*, 3:453.
81. *Qiu Huizuo huiyilu*, 2:763–765; Wu, *Suiyue jianan*, 2:841.

82. *MWG,* 13:231.

83. *ZNP*-B, 3:454.

84. CCP CC's notice about printing and distributing "Outline of 571 Project," November 14, 1971, CCP Center Document, No. 74 (1971).

85. *ZNP*-B, 3:455; Du Xiuxian, "Lin Biao's 'Leaving without Saying Goodbye' to Mao Zedong," in *Lin Biao fangeming jituan fumie jishi* (True records of the demise of Lin Biao's reactionary clique), Xiong Huayuan et al. (Beijing: Zhongyang wenxian, 1995), 63–72.

86. "Wu Zhong talks about the September 13 Incident," *Yanhuang chuanqiu,* no. 1 (2012): 26.

87. Ibid., 27.

88. Zhang Chuanqiao's letter to Zhang Weiwei, May 24, 1991, *Zhang Chuanqiao yuzhong jiashu* (Zhang Chuanqiao's letters to home from prison) (Hong Kong: The Chinese University Press, 2015), 97.

89. *MWG,* 13:242–250.

90. *ZNP*-B, 3:478, 480.

91. Li Wenpu, "Lin Biao's Chief Bodyguard Has Things to Say," in *Zhonggong zhongda lishi shijian qinli ji* (Personally experiencing CCP's important historical events), ed. Li Haiwen (Chengdu: Sichuan renmin, 2006).

92. *Lishi de shenpan* (Trial of history) (Beijing: Qunzhong, 1981), 40–42.

93. *MNP*-B, 6:403; Zhang Yaoci, *Zhang Yaoci Huiyi Mao Zedong,* 105.

94. Wang, *Mao Zedong he Lin Biao,* 197.

95. *ZNP*-B, 3:480; *MNP*-B, 6:404.

96. Li, "Lin Biao's Chief Bodyguard."

97. *ZNP*-B, 3:480.

98. *ZNP*-B, 3:481.

99. Ibid.

100. *MNP*-B, 6:405; *ZNP*-B, 3:481.

101. *ZNP*-B, 3:481.

102. *MNP*-B, 6:405; *Wu Faxing huiyilu,* 863.

103. *ZZ*-B, 1041; Ji, *Nanwang de banian,* 125.

104. *ZNP*-B, 3:483; *ZZ*-B, 2:1040.

105. *ZNP*-B, 3:483.

106. *MNP*-B, 6:406; *ZNP*-B, 3:482; *Qiu Huizuo huiyilu,* 797–798.

107. *ZNP*-B, 3:482.

108. *MNP*-B, 6:406; *ZNP*-B, 3:482–483; Wang, *Mao Zedong yu Lin Biao,* 212.

109. *Qiu Huizuo huiyilu,* 788.

110. CCP CC Notice, September 18, 1971; CCP CC notice, October 6, 1971, *WGYJZL,* 2:557–559, 643–645; *MNP*-B, 6:406–407.

111. CCP CC notice, September 29, 1971, *WGYJZL,* 2:642.

112. CCP CC notice about relaying Lin Biao's case of betraying the party and the country to the masses of the whole country, October 24, 1971, *ZGWGWK.*

113. *WGYJZL,* 2:649–657, 658–667.

114. Zhou's report to leading cadres of the Guangzhou Military Region, October 1971, cited from Xue Qingchao, *Mao Zedong nanfang juece* (Mao Zedong's decision-making in the South) (Beijing: Huawen, 2013), 245; see also *ZNP,* 3:488–489.

115. Chen Yangyong, *Zhongquan chuji: Zhou Enlai zai 913 shijian zhihou* (Strike with heavy punches: Zhou Enlai after the September 13 Incident) (Chongqing: Chongqing, 2006), 48.

116. *ZNP*-B, 3:510; see also Gao, *Wannian Zhou Enlai,* 447.

117. *MZ-B*, 1616.

118. Zhang Zuoliang, *Zhou Enlai de zuihou shinian: yiwei baojian yisheng de huiyi* (Zhou Enlai's last ten years: Recollections of a doctor) (Shanghai: Shanghai renmin, 1997), 245–247; Li, *Private Life of Chairman Mao*, 560.

119. Zhou, *Wo de bofu Zhou Enlai*, 330.

28. Nixon and Kissinger Come to China (1969–1972)

1. *RMRB*, November 27, 1968, 5; Luo Yisuo, *Zai fengqi yunyong de niandai* (In years of dramatic changes) (Beijing: Xinhua, 2011), 120; John H. Holdridge, *Crossing the Divide: An Insider's Account of Normalization of U.S.-China Relations* (Lanham, MD: Rowman and Littlefield, 1997), 25.

2. *ZNP-B*, 3:267.

3. Cen Xiaolu, "Chen Yi and Chinese Diplomacy," in *Huanqiu tongci liangre: Yidai lingxiumen de guoji zhanlue sixiang* (The Whole World shares the same temperature: The international strategic thinking of the Mao generation) (Beijing: Zhongyang wenxian, 1993), 155.

4. *MNP-B*, 6:229–230; Zhou et al., *Nie Rongzhen nianpu*, 2:1107.

5. *Xu Xiangqian nianpu*, 2:250; Shufa et al., *Chen Yi nianpu*, 1213; Chen, "Chen Yi and Chinese Diplomacy," 155.

6. Xu Yan, "Chinese-Soviet Border Clash of 1969," *Dangshi yanjiu ziliao* (Party history research materials), no. 5 (1994): 6–8.

7. Transcript of Chen Xiliang interview, July 1995 (copy in author's possession).

8. Xu, "Chinese-Soviet Border Clash of 1969," 8–9.

9. Wang et al., *Zhonghua renmin gongheguo waijiaoshi, 1957-1969*, 273; Li, *Da waijiaojia Zhou Enlai*, 6:137.

10. Li, *Da waijiaojia Zhou Enlai*, 6:137.

11. Ibid., 138; *MNP-B*, 6:236–237; *MWG*, 13:21.

12. Yang, *Zhonghua renmin gongheguo jianguo shi yanjiu*, 2:358.

13. *MNP-B*, 6:234; see also Mao's speech at a Central Leadership Group meeting, March 15, 1969, *ZGWGWK*; Mao's speech at the First Plenum of CCP's Ninth CC, April 28, 1969, *MWG*, 13:35–41.

14. Li, *Da waijiaojia Zhou Enlai*, 6:143.

15. Fan et al., *Ye Jianying zhuan*, 598–599; Wei et al., *Nie Rongzhen zhuan*, 614; Liu et al., *Xu Xiangqian zhuan*, 541–542; Zheng Qian, "War Preparations around the Ninth Congress," *Zhonggong dangshi ziliao*, no. 41 (1992): 211.

16. Xiong Xianghui, "Prelude to Opening of Chinese-American Relations," *Zhonggong dangshi ziliao*, no. 42 (1992): 61–62.

17. Report by Four Chinese Marshals to the CC, "A Preliminary Evaluation of the War Situation," July 11, 1969, *CWIHP Bulletin*, no. 11 (Winter 1998): 166–168.

18. *ZNP-B*, 3:312; Xiong, "Prelude," 76–77.

19. Xiong, "Prelude," 78–79.

20. Xu, "Chinese-Soviet Border Clashes of 1969," *Zhonggong dangshi ziliao*, no. 5 (1994): 10.

21. *MJSWG*, 3:357.

22. CMC administrative office, "Report on Strengthening People's Anti-Air Attack Preparation in the Whole Country," August 27, 1969, *ZNP-B*, 3:316–317.

23. CCP CC's Order for General Mobilization in Border Provinces and Regions, August 28, 1969, *CWIHP Bulletin*, no. 11 (Winter 1998): 168–169.

24. *ZNP*-B, 3:319; Wang Weizhen et al., *Li Xiannian nianpu* (Chronological records of Li Xiannian) (Beijing: Zhongyang wenxian, 2011), 4:620.

25. Wang et al., *Li Xiannian nianpu*, 4:620.

26. Li, *Da waijiaojia Zhou Enlai*, 6:145; *ZZ*-B, 2:1083.

27. Information about A. N. Kosygin's Conversation with Zhou Enlai on September 11, 1969, https://digitalarchive.wilsoncenter.org/document/116973; Zhou's letter to Kosygin, September 18, 1969, *ZWJWX*, 462–464; *ZZ*-B, 1840.

28. *MNP*-B, 6:266.

29. Report by Four Chinese Marshals, "Our Views about the Current Situation," September 17, 1969, *CWIHP Bulletin*, no. 11 (Winter 1998): 170.

30. Xiong, "Prelude," 87.

31. *MNP*-B, 6:266.

32. Xiong, "Prelude," 83.

33. Zhou's letter to Kosygin, September 18, 1969, *ZWJWX*, 462–464.

34. *ZNP*-B, 3:323–324.

35. *MNP*-B, 6:267.

36. *ZJSHDJS*, 2:699; *ZNP*-B, 3:322.

37. Zhang, *Maojiawan jishi*, 308; Zheng Qian, "Preparations for War in the Whole around the CCP's Ninth Congress," *Zhonggong dangshi ziliao*, no. 41: 219; *ZNP*-B, 3:325.

38. Wang et al., *Zhonghua renmin gongheguo waijiaoshi, 1970–1978* (A diplomatic history of the People's Republic of China, 1970–1978) (Beijing: Shijie zhishi, 1999), 36–37.

39. Mao's conversation with Choi Yonggun, October 1, 1969, CCA.

40. *ZNP*-B, 3:325.

41. *MNP*-B, 6:270.

42. *MNP*-B, 6:270–271; *ZNP*-B, 3:329.

43. Li Genqing, "Before and After Lin Biao's Urgent Order," *Yanhuang chuqiu*, no. 11 (2015): 47; Liu Chongwen et al., *Liu Shaoqi nianpu* (Chronological records of Liu Shaoqi) (Beijing: Zhongyang wenxian, 1996), 2:661; *DNP*-A, 3:1948–1950.

44. Editorial Note, *FRUS*, 1969–1976, 17:51–52.

45. *ZZ*-B, 1088; *ZNP*-B, 3:334.

46. Luo Yisuo, "My Years in Poland," in *Dangdai zhongguo shijie waijiao shengya*, ed. Wang Taiping (Beijing: Shijie zhishi, 1996), 179–180; Stoessel to Secretary of State, December 3, 1969, Record Group (RG) 59, Department of State Records, Subject-Numeric Files, 1967–1969, POL 23-8 US, NA.

47. *ZZ*-B, 1087; Geng Biao, "A Glorious Banner of the New China's Diplomacy," in *Lao waijiaoguan huiyi Zhou Enlai* (Veteran diplomats remembering Zhou Enlai), ed. Tian Zengpei and Wang Taiping (Beijing: Shijie zhishi, 1998), 18.

48. *ZNP*-B, 3:336; *ZZ*-B, 1088.

49. Kissinger, *White House Years*, 188.

50. *ZNP*-B, 3:338; *ZWJHDDSJ*, 546; Kissinger, *White House Years*, 191.

51. Stoessel to Secretary of State, January 8, 1970, Subject-Numeric files, 1970–1973, Pol Chicom US RG 59, NA.

52. Stoessel to the Department of State, January 20, 1970, *FRUS*, 1969–1976, 17:167–169.

53. *ZNP-B*, 3:348; *ZZ*-B, 1089; *MNP*-B, 6:281.

54. Stoessel to Department of State, February 20, 1970, *FRUS*, 1969–1976, 17:180–183; Gong Li, *Kuayue honggou: 1969–1979 nian zhongmei guanxi de yanbian* (Crossing the chasm: Changing Chinese-American relations, 1969–1979) (Zhengzhou: He'nan renmin, 1992), 50–51.

55. F. S. Aijazuddin, *From a Head, Through a Head, to a Head: The Secret Channel between the US and China through Pakistan* (New York: Oxford University Press, 2000), 31–32; *ZNP*-B, 3:356.

56. *ZNP-B,* 3:356; *ZZ*-B, 4:1089–1090.

57. *ZNP*-B, 3:355–356; Pei Jianzhang and Wang Taiping et al., *Zhonghua renmin gongheguo waijiaoshi, 1970–1978,* 72.

58. *ZNP*-B, 3:356; Philip Short, *Pol Pot: The History of a Nightmare* (London: John Murray, 2004), 197–200.

59. *ZNP*-B, 3:357; *MWG,* 13:86.

60. *ZNP*-B, 3:367.

61. *RMRB,* May 20, 1970, 1.

62. Kissinger, *White House Years,* 696; *FRUS,* 1969–1976, 17:220–221; *ZNP-B,* 3:372; Gong, *Kuayue honggou,* 59.

63. *RMRB,* July 11, 1970.

64. Richard Nixon, *Memoirs of Richard Nixon* (New York: Grosset and Dunlap, 1978), 546–547; *ZNP-B,* 3:406.

65. Aijazuddin, *From a Head,* 43; *ZZ*-B, 4:1091; *ZNP-B,* 3:410–411; see also Nixon, *Memoirs,* 546–547.

66. *ZNP*-B, 3:417; Yang Mingwei and Chen Yangyong, *Zhou Enlai waijiao fengyun* (Zhou Enlai in diplomatic storms) (Beijing: Jiefangjun wenyi, 1995), 244.

67. Kissinger, *White House Years,* 700–703; Nixon, *Memoirs,* 546–547.

68. Yin Jiamin, *Huang Zhen jiangjun de dashi shengya* (General Huang Zhen's career as an ambassador) (Nanjing: Jiangsu renmin, 1998), 205–206.

69. *RMRB,* December 25, 1970, 1; Zhou even intervened in the size of the photo to be published in *Renmin ribao.* See Yang and Chen, *Zhou Enlai waijiao fengyun,* 243.

70. Kissinger, *White House Years,* 698.

71. *ZNP*-B, 3:407–408.

72. Mao's talks with Edgar Snow, December 18, 1970, *MWG,* 13:163–187; see also *Mao Zedong on Diplomacy* (Beijing: Foreign Language Press, 1998), 449–451; Edgar Snow, "A Conversation with Mao Tse-tung [Mao Zedong]," *Life,* April 30, 1971, 46–48.

73. Nixon, *Memoirs,* 547.

74. *ZNP*-B, 3:443–444; *MWG,* 12:284–285; *MNP*-B, 6:373.

75. Zhao Zhenghong, "The Ping-Pong Diplomacy As I Know," *Zhonggong dangshi ziliao,* no. 39 (1991): 144; Li Ke, Xu Tao, and Wu Xujun, *Lishi de zhenshi* (The truth of history) (Hong Kong: Liwen, 1995), 302; *MNP*-B, 6:373.

76. Qian Jiang, *Ping Pong waijiao muhou* (Behind the ping-pong diplomacy) (Shanghai: Dongfang, 1997), 170–172.

77. *ZNP*-B, 3:449; Ling, *Cong yanan dao lianheguo,* 129; Qian, *Ping Pong waijiao muhou,* 211.

78. Lin, Xu, and Wu, *Lishi de zhenshi,* 308–309.

79. Zhao, "Ping-Pong Diplomacy," 144–145.

80. Ling, *Cong yanan dao lianheguo,* 131.

81. Premier Zhou's remarks on the agenda of activities by foreign table tennis teams, April 11, 1971, B126-2-107.1, SHMA.

82. *ZNP*-B, 3:450–451; *ZWJWX,* 469–475; John Roderick, "Chou (Zhou) Says 'New Page' Has Opened," *New York Times,* April 15, 1971.

83. Kissinger, *White House Years,* 710.

84. *ZNP*-B, 3:452–453; Kissinger, *White House Years,* 714.

85. Message from the US Government to the PRC Government, May 10, 1971, *FRUS*, 1969–1976, 17:318–319; Kissinger, *White House Years*, 723–724; see also ZZ-B, 1095–1096; Gong, *Kuaiyue honggou*, 97–98.

86. CCP Politburo's report on Chinese-American negotiation (drafted by Zhou Enlai), May 26, 1971, CCP Center Document (1971) No. 40.

87. Ibid.

88. Premier Zhou's oral message to President Nixon, May 29, 1971 (photocopy of Zhou's handwritten message), in *Gongheguo wushinian zhengui dangan* (Fifty-year precious archives of the People's Republic), ed. Chinese Central Archive (Beijing: Zhongguo dangan, 1999), 2:1030–1032; Message from Premier Chou En-lai to President Nixon, *FRUS*, 1969–1976, 17:332–333.

89. Nixon, *Memoirs*, 552.

90. Zhou's speech at the Central Work Conference, June 4, 1971, 91-007-0028-0001, GSPA.

91. Transcript of Chairman Mao's conversation with Edgar Snow, May 31, 1971, CCP CC document for discussion (1971), No. 133.

92. Zhou's speech at a central work conference, June 18, 1971, 91-007-0028-0001, GSPA.

93. Kong Dongmei, *Gaibian shijie de rizi: He Wang Hairong tan Mao Zedong waijiao wangshi* (The time that the world was changed: Conversation with Wang Hairong about Mao Zedong's diplomatic activities) (Beijing: Zhongyang wenxian, 2006), 92; Tang Longbing, "A Mysterious Diplomatic Mission: Receiving Kissinger during His Secret China Visit," *Shijie zhishi*, no. 6 (1995): 30–31.

94. Transcripts of these meetings are now published in *FRUS*, 1969–1976, 17:359–452, and are available at RG 59, Policy Planning Staff (Director's) Files, 1969–1977, NA; for an informative Chinese record, see Wei Shiyan, "The Inside Story of Kissinger's Secret Visit to China," in Pei et al., *Xinzhonnguo waijiao fengyun*, 2:33–45.

95. Zhou, "Explaining the Sino-American Communiqué," March 3, 1972, CCA (an excerpt of the speech is published in *ZNP*-B, 3:515); Kissinger, *White House Years*, 745.

96. Haig to Eliot, 28 January 1972, enclosing Kissinger to the President, "My Talks with Chou Enlai [Zhou Enlai]," 17 July 1971, RG 59, Top Secret Subject-Numeric Files, 1970–1972, POL 7 Kissinger, NA; Wei, "Kissinger's Secret Visit to China," 41–42.

97. Wei, "Kissinger's Secret Visit to China," 41–42.

98. Kissinger, *White House Years*, 750; see also Wei, "Kissinger's Secret Visit to Beijing," 42–43.

99. *ZWJHDDSJ*, 596–597; *ZNP*-B, 3:469.

100. *ZNP*-B, 469–470; Guo et al., *Zhongyue guanxi yanbian sishinian*, 102–103.

101. *ZWJHDDSJ*, 597; *ZNP*-B, 3:469.

102. Excerpt of Zhou's conversations with Kim Il-sung, August 10, 1971, HPA.

103. *ZWJHDDSJ*, 597; *ZNP*-B, 3:469.

104. Albania Central National Archive (1971), F. 14. / AP-MPKK, File, No. 3, cited from Gjon Borici, "The Fall of the Albanian-Chinese Relations, 1971–1978," *ILIRIA International Review* 6.1 (2016), 108–109; *ZNP-B*, 3:474; Fan Chengzuo, "The Spring, Summer, Autumn and Winter in Chinese-Albanian Relations," in Wang, *Dangdai Zhongguo shijie waijiao shengya*, 4:245–246.

105. Cao Guisheng, "Recalling the Secret Chinese-American 'Paris Chanel,'" in Pei, *Xinzhongguo waijiao fengyun*, 2:46–55.

106. *FRUS*, 1969–1976, 17:498–558; Haig to Eliot, January 28, 1972, RG 59, Top Secret Subject-Numeric Files, 1970–1973, POL 7 Kissinger, NA; Wei Shiyan, "Kissinger's Second Visit to Beijing," in Pei et al., *Xinzhongguo waijiao fengyun*, 3:59–70.

107. Wei, "Kissinger's Second Visit to Beijing," 66–67.

108. Kissinger, *White House Years*, 782.

109. Wei, "Kissinger's Second Visit to Beijing," 69–70; Kissinger, *White House Years,* 787.

110. Zhou's Explanation of the Chinese-American Communiqué, March 3, 1972, 1057-8-44, 206, HPA.

111. See Chen Jian, commentary on "Mike Mansfield on Cross-Strait Relations," *Asia Perspective* 2, no. 3 (Spring 2003): 17–18.

112. Gong Li, *Mao Zedong he meiguo* (Mao Zedong and America) (Beijing: Shijie zhishi, 1999), 301.

113. *MNP*-B, 6:412–413.

114. *MNP*-B, 6:426; Li, *Private Life of Chairman Mao,* 560.

115. Li, *Private Life of Chairman Mao,* 562.

116. Wu Xujun, "I Eyewitnessed Details of Chinese-American Opening," *Shenzhou* (China).

117. Nixon, *Memoirs,* 500.

118. Mao's conversation with Nixon, February 21, 1972, CCA; Memorandum of Conversation, Beijing, February 21, 1972, 2:50–3:55 P.M., *FRUS,* 1969–1972, 17:677–684.

119. Zhou's Explanation of the Shanghai Communiqué, March 3, 1972, 1057-8-44, pp. 194–217, HPA.

120. Ibid.

121. Luo Yinsheng, *Hongse mingyuan Zhang Hanzhi* (Yinchuan: Ningxia renmin, 2009), 165.

122. Zhou's Explanation of the Shanghai Communiqué, 1057-8-44, HPA.

29. Glory Reaps Tears (1972–1974)

1. Interview with Ji Dengkui by CCP Central Institute of Documentary Studies, spring 1988, cited from Shi and Li, *Nanyi jixu de jixu geming,* 10.

2. Zhou's conversation with Denson, March 2, 1971, *Waishi dongtai,* March 18, 1971; Mr. Denson's meeting with Chou En-lai on March 3 (1971), FCO-21 / 839, UKNA; Pei and Wang et al., *Zhonghua renmin gongheguo waijiaoshi, 1970–1978,* 301–302.

3. Wang Shu, "From Reporter to Ambassador," in Wang Shu et al., *Bu xunchang de tanpan* (Unusual negotiations) (Nanjing: Jiangsu renmin, 1994), 26–29.

4. *ZNP*-B, 3:538; Wang, "From Reporter to Ambassador," 31; see also Zhou's conversation with Chinese ambassadors and foreign affairs officials, August 1, 1972, 1057-8-44, HPA.

5. *ZNP*-B, 3:538.

6. *MNP*-B, 6:440–442; Wang, "From Reporter to Ambassador," 38.

7. *ZNP*-B, 3:535.

8. Gu Baozi, *Zhou Enlai zuihou liubaitian* (Zhou Enlai's last six hundred days) (Beijing: Zhongguo qingnian, 2015), 180–181.

9. Pei and Wang et al., *Zhonghua renmin gongheguo waijiaoshi, 1970–1978,* 20.

10. Zhou's conversation with Chinese ambassadors and Foreign Ministry leading cadres, August 1, 1972, 1057-8-44, HPA.

11. Zhou Bin, *Wo wei zhongguo lingdaoren dang fanyi: jianzheng zhongri waijiao mixing* (I interpreted for Chinese leaders: Witnessing secret Chinese-Japanese diplomatic exchanges) (Hong Kong: Dashan wenhua, 2013), 236–237.

12. *ZNP*-B, 3:536.

13. Main points of the second meeting between Premier Zhou Enlai and Takeiri Yoshikatsu, chairman of the Japanese Kōmeitō, July 28, 1972, cited from *Zhanhou Zhongri guanxi wenxian ji, 1971–1995* (Collected documents of postwar Chinese-Japanese relations, 1971–1995), ed. Tian Heng (Beijing: Zhongguo shehui kexue, 1997), 89–95; *ZNP*-B, 3:540.

14. Mayumi Itoh, in *The Making of China's Peace with Japan: What Xi Jinping Should Learn from Zhou Enlai* (Singapore: Palgrave Macmillan, 2017), 129–131, offers a detailed and excellent description

of the incident. Itoh points out the incident was also caused by a wrong interpretation of the Chinese interpreter, who mistakenly used *mihuo* (which refers to light trouble), instead of *meiwaku* (which points to more serious trouble), for Tanaka's expression.

15. Zhou Bin, *Wo wei Zhou Enlai zongli dang fanyi: jianwen he fanwu* (I interpreted for Premier Zhou Enlai: What I saw, heard and understood) (Hong Kong: Tiandi, 2018), 111–112.

16. Mao's conversation with Tanaka, September 27, 1972, CCA; *MNP*-B, 6:449.

17. Zhou, *Wo wei Zhou Enlai zongli dang fanyi,* 121–122.

18. Zhang Xianshan, "Recollections of the Chinese-Japanese Negotiation on Restoring Diplomatic Relations," *Riben xuekan* (Journal of Japan studies), no. 1, (1998): 47; according to the note of Hiroshi Hashimoto, a Japanese diplomat who attended the Zhou-Tanaka meeting, Tanaka followed Zhou's comments and said, "That is right. Let us wait for another opportunity."

19. The Chinese transcript of the conversation has not been declassified. The accounts here follow the description of Zhang Xiangshan, which is based upon the Chinese transcript of the meeting.

20. Wang Weicheng et al., *Li Xiannian zhuan* (A biography of Li Xiannian) (Beijing: Zhongyang wenxian, 2009), 763–764.

21. Li Xiannian, Hua Guofeng, and Yu Qiuli to Zhou Enlai, January 23, 1972, *Zhonggong dangshi ziliao,* 90 (2004): 4–8; *Jianguo yilai Li Xiannian wengao* (Li Xiannian's manuscripts from the founding of the PRC) (Beijing: Zhongyang wenxian), 3:158–159; Wang et al., *Li Xiannian zhuan,* 764.

22. *ZNP*-B, 3:511.

23. State Planning Council's report on importing 1,700mm rolling mills, August 6, 1972, *Zhonggong dangshi ziliao,* 90:9–10; Chen Jinghua, *Guoshi yishu* (Recollection of my experience with state affairs) (Beijing: Zhonggong dangshi, 2005), 10–14; Wang et al., *Li Xiannian zhuan,* 766–767; Wang et al., *Li Xiannian nianpu,* 5:208–209.

24. Wang et al., *Li Xiannian zhuan,* 767.

25. State Planning Council's report on increasing equipment importation and expanding economic exchanges, January 2, 1973, *Zhonggong dangshi ziliao,* 90:12–19; *ZNP*-B, 3:570–571; Chen, *Guoshi yishu,* 14–15.

26. *MWG,* 8:196.

27. Cited from Yang et al., *Deng Xiaoping zhuan,* 2:1363.

28. Ibid., 2:1368–1369.

29. *DNP*-A, 3:1958.

30. Ibid., 2:1958.

31. Deng's letter to Mao, August 3, 1973, *ZGWGWK.*

32. *MWG,* 13:308; *MNP*-B, 6:445.

33. *ZNP*-B, 3:545.

34. *ZNP*-B, 3:567.

35. *MWG,* 13:347; *ZNP*-B, 3:583; *DNP*-A, 3:1972.

36. Deng Rong, *Deng Xiaoping and the Cultural Revolution: A Daughter Recalls the Critical Years* (Beijing: Foreign Languages Press, 2002), 245.

37. Zhang Zuoliang, *Zhou Enlai de zuihou shinian: yiwei baojian yisheng de huiyi* (Zhou Enlai's last ten years: Recollections of a doctor) (Shanghai: Shanghai renmin, 1997), 295–300.

38. Li Jing, "Wu Jieping: The Doctor of the Country of a Whole Generation," *Sanlian shenghuo zhoukan,* no. 12 (2011).

39. Zhou, *Wo de bofu Zhou Enlai,* 335–336; Li Jing, "Wu Jieping."

40. *MZ*-B, 1618.

41. Li Jing, "Wu Jieping."

42. *ZNP*-B, 3:523; *MNP*-B, 6:433, 436.

43. *MNP*-B, 6:433; *ZNP*-B, 3:523–524; CCP Center's Notice on Convening a "Criticize Lin Rectification Conference," CCP Central Institute of History Documents Research. ed., *Wenge shinian ziliao xuan* (Selected documents of ten-year Cultural Revolution) (internal publication, n.d.), 1st ser., 2:172–175.

44. Zhang, *Zhou Enlai de zuihou shinian,* 308–309.

45. Zhou's speech at the plenary session of the "Criticize Lin Rectification Conference" (excerpt), CCP Central Institute of History Documents Research. ed., *Wenge shinian ziliao xuan,* 1st ser., 1:176–189; see also Shi and Li, *Nanyi jixu de jixu geming,* 34–35.

46. Cited from Shi and Li, *Nanyi jixu de jixu geming,* 35–36.

47. Zhao Wei, *Xihuating suiyue* (My years at West Flower Pavillion) (Beijing: Shehui kexue wenxian, 2009), 211–212.

48. Ibid., 211.

49. Zhou's conversation with Chinese ambassadors and leading cadres of Chinese foreign services, August 1 and 2, 1972, 1057-8-44, HPA; see also *ZNP*-B, 3:541–542.

50. *MZ*-B, 1646.

51. *ZNP*-B, 3:565.

52. *MZ*-B, 1647; *ZNP*-B, 3:565.

53. Wang Ruoshui's letter to Mao, in *Weibei weineng wang youguo: Wenhua dageming shangshuji* (Humble yet never dare not to worry about the country: Petition letter in the Cultural Revolution), comp. Yu Xiguang (Changsha: Hunan renmin, 1989), 178–180.

54. *ZNP*-B, 3:566.

55. Chen, *Zhongquan chuji,* 280.

56. Li, "Wu Jieping."

57. *ZZ*-B, 1056.

58. Zhang, *Zhou Enlai de zuihou shinian,* 301; Zhou, *Wo de bofu Zhou Enlai,* 337–338; Li, "Wu Jieping."

59. *ZNP*-B, 3:583–584.

60. Li, "Wu Jieping."

61. Zhou, *Wo de bofu Zhou Enlai,* 336–337; Zhang, *Zhou Enlai de zuihou shinian,* 327; Gao, *Zhou Enlai weishi huiyilu,* 166.

62. Gao, *Zhou Enlai weishi huiyilu,* 166.

63. *ZNP*-B, 3:603; *MNP*-B, 6:484; Ma, *Waijiaobu wenge jishi,* 328.

64. *MNP*-B, 6:485.

65. *ZNP*-B, 3:604.

66. *ZNP*-B, 3:604; *MNP*-B, 6:485–486.

67. *MWG,* 13:402

68. Zhang, *Zhou Enlai de zuihou shinian,* 321.

69. *FRUS,* 1969–1976, 17:431.

70. Minutes, Mao's conversation with Kissinger, November 12, 1973, Chinese Foreign Ministry, Mao talk collections, 17:273–306; Memorandum of conversation, Mao with Kissinger, November 12, 1973, 5:50–8:25 P.M., *FRUS,* 1969–1976, 17:380–400. To translate the term *pi shi,* which literally meant "a matter like letting go the air," Tang made a long explanation.

71. Memorandum of conversation, Mao with Kissinger, November 12, 1973, 5:40–8:25 P.M., *FRUS,* 1969–1976, 17:384. Kissinger's last sentence above is different from the Chinese transcript of the conversation, which is, "Therefore we are determined to oppose it. We have decided that we will not allow

China's security to be sabotaged." See *MZ-B*, 1669; Chinese Foreign Ministry, Mao talk collections, 17:273–306.

72. Memorandum of conversation, Zhou with Kissinger, November 10, 1973, 9:25–10:00 P.M., *FRUS*, 1969–1976: 326–331.

73. Memorandum, Zhou with Kissinger, November 13, 1973, 10:00 P.M.–12:30 A.M., NSA.

74. Transcript of interview with Zhang Hanzhi, April 3, 1998 (copy in author's possession), 1–2.

75. Memorandum of conversation, Zhou with Kissinger, November 14, 1973, 7:25–8:25 A.M., Kissinger files, NSA.

76. Ibid.

77. In the Chinese record of the meeting, Zhou told Kissinger, "We have to consider, and will have to report to Chairman Mao, and everything will be decided by Chairman Mao." See Zhou Enlai's third one-on-one meeting with Kissinger, November 14, 1973, cited from *MZ-B*, 1669.

78. Author's exchange with Kissinger, March 31, 2012.

79. *ZNP-B*, 3:634.

80. Mao conversation with Zhou, November 17, 1973, cited from Li Jie, "From Rapprochement to Normalization: China's Political Change and Chinese-American Relations," in *Cong Jiedong dao jianjiao: zhongmei guanxi zhengchanghua zaitantao* (From détente to diplomatic relations: Reexamining normalization of Chinese-American relations), ed. Gong Li et al. (Beijing: Zhongyang wenxian, 2004), 274.

81. Transcript of interview with Zhang Hanzhi, April 3, 1998, 3.

82. *ZNP-B*, 3:634.

83. Transcript of interview with Zhang Hanzhi, 6; Liu et al., *Ye Jianying nianpu*, 2:1066.

84. Transcript of interview with Zhang Hanzhi, 4.

85. Transcript of interview with Zhang Hanzhi, 9–10.

86. Zhang, *Zhou Enlai de zuihou shinian*, 310–314.

87. Transcript of interview with Zhang Hanzhi, 6; *Xu Jingxian zuihou huiyi* (Xu Jingxian's final recollections) (Hong Kong: Thinker, 2013), 305.

88. Transcript of interview with Zhang Hanzhi, 114; Gao, *Wannian Zhou Enlai*, 474.

89. Deng, *Deng Xiaoping and the Cultural Revolution*, 255–256.

90. Zhang, *Zhou Enlai de zuihou shinian*, 312.

91. *MZ-B*, 1671.

92. *ZNP-B*, 3:636; *MZ-B*, 1672.

93. CCP CC notice, December 22, 1973, Zhongfa (Document issued by the CCP Central Committee) (1973), no. 44; *ZNP-B*, 3:638.

94. Mao's conversation with Deng, November 28, 1974, cited from Li Jie, "From Rapprochement to Normalization," 274.

30. Last Days (1974–1976)

1. Zhang, *Zhou Enlai de zuihou shinian*, 321–323; *ZNP-B*, 3:657.

2. Zhang, *Zhou Enlai de zuihou shinian*, 334.

3. Gao, *Zhou Enlai weishi huiyilu*, 167.

4. *MNP-B*, 6:480.

5. Ibid.

6. CCP CC Document No. 1 (1974); Mao approved issuance of the document, *MWG*, 13:371.

7. *ZNP-B*, 2:647–648; Wu, *Zhou Enlai zai wenhua dageming*, 255–256.
8. *Geng Biao huiyilu* (Geng Biao's memoirs) (Nanjing: Jiangsu renmin, 1998), 270; *ZZ-B*, 1130.
9. Mao to Jiang Qing, March 20, 1974, *MWG*, 13:372; *MNP-B*, 6:523.
10. *ZNP-B*, 3:649.
11. *Mao Zedong on Diplomacy*, 454.
12. *MNP-B*, 6:523.
13. Liu Wusheng, *Zhou Enlai de wannian suiyue* (Zhou Enlai's later years) (Beijing: Renmin, 2006), 291; *ZZ-B*, 2:1134.
14. Liu, *Zhou Enlai de wannian suiyue*, 291.
15. *MNP-B*, 6:523.
16. *ZZ-B*, 2:1134.
17. *ZNP-B*, 3:658.
18. *ZNP-B*, 3:661.
19. *RMRB*, April 11, 1974.
20. Li, *Private Life of Chairman Mao*, 580–581; see also *MNP-B*, 6:539.
21. *MNP-B*, 6:545–546.
22. *MWG*, 13:402.
23. *MNP-B*, 6:540–541.
24. Ibid., 540.
25. *Hu Qiaomu huiyi Mao Zedong*, 215.
26. *MNP-B*, 6:538–539.
27. *MNP-B*, 6:549.
28. *DNP-A*, 3:2058.
29. *MNP-B*, 6:662; *ZNP-B*, 3:679.
30. *ZNP-B*, 3:679; *MNP-B*, 6:552; Gao Zhenpu, *Peiban bingzhong Zhou Enlai de riri yeye* (The days and nights that I accompanied Zhou Enlai in his illness) (Beijing: Zhongguo qingnian, 2016), 353.
31. *MNP-B*, 6:554; *DNP-A*, 3:2060; Deng, *Deng Xiaoping and the Cultural Revolution*, 280.
32. *MNP-B*, 6:562.
33. *MWG*, 13:413–414; *MNP-B*, 6:564; *ZNP-B*, 3:687; *MZ-B*, 1713–1714.
34. *ZNP-B*, 3:687–688; Deng, *Deng Xiaoping and the Cultural Revolution*, 286–287.
35. *ZNP-B*, 3:688.
36. Ibid.
37. *ZNP-B*, 3:689; Wang et al., *Li Xiannian nianpu*, 5:394; *DNP-A*, 3:1.
38. *ZZ-B*, 2:1137; *ZNP-B*, 3:689; Leng Rong and Wang Zuoling et al., *Deng Xiaoping nianpu, 1975–1997* (Chronological records of Deng Xiaoping, 1975–1997, hereafter *DNP-B*) (Beijing: Zhongyang wenxian, 2004), 1:1.
39. Reports, Zhou to Mao, January 2 and 4, 1975, cited from *ZZ-B*, 2:1157.
40. *MNP-B*, 6:566–567.
41. *ZNP-B*, 690; *MZ-B*, 1716.
42. Mao Huahe, "Secret Convening of the First Session of the Fourth People's Congress," *Yanhuang chunqiu*, no. 2 (2013): 37.
43. *RMRB*, January 21, 1975, 1.
44. *ZNP-B*, 3:693–694.
45. Gao, *Zhou Enlai weishi huiyilu*, 167; Zhang, *Zhou Enlai de zuihou shinian*, 345.
46. *MNP-B*, 6:577.

47. *MNP-B*, 6:582–583.

48. Wu De, *Shinian Fengyu jishi: wo zai Beijing de yixie gongjing* (A factual record in stormy times: My working experience in Beijing) (Beijing: Dangdai zhongguo, 2008), 163.

49. *DNP-B*, 1:41.

50. *Hu Qiaomu huiyi Mao Zedong*, 215.

51. Zhou to Mao, June 16, 1975, cited from Gu, *Zhou Enlai zuihou liubaitian*, 399–400.

52. *ZNP-B*, 711; Xue Ming, "Zhou Enlai and He Long," in *Bujin de sinian*, 617–618; Li et al., *He Long nianpu*, 804; Gao, *Peiban bingzhong Zhou Enlai de riri yeye*, 211.

53. *MNP-B*, 6:593; *DNP-B*, 1:61–62.

54. Wu, *Shinian Fengyu jishi*, 162.

55. *MZ-B*, 2:1704; *ZNP-B*, 3:679.

56. *MNP-B*, 6:603.

57. *MWG*, 13:457; *MNP-B*, 6:603.

58. *MNP-B*, 6:607–608.

59. *ZNP-B*, 717.

60. *ZNP-B*, 720.

61. Cheng Zhongyuan, comp., *Deng Xiaoping de 24ci tanhua* (Deng Xiaoping's twenty-four conversations) (Beijing: Renmin, 2004), 104.

62. *ZWJHDDSJ*, 709; Gao, *Peiban bingzhong Zhou Enlai de riri yeye*, 197.

63. Mao's conversation with Kim Il-sung, 4:00 P.M., April 18, 1975, CCA.

64. Zhang Qing, "A Factual Account of Exchanges between Zhou Enlai and Sihanouk," in Tian and Wang, *Lao waijiaoguan huiyi Zhou Enlai*, 172.

65. *ZNP-B*, 719–720; Jiang, *Gei Gongheguo lingdaoren zuo fanyi*, 112–116.

66. *ZNP-B*, 3:721.

67. Wu, *Zhou Enlai zai wenhua dageming zhong*, 184.

68. *DNP-B*, 102; Zhang, *Zhou Enlai de zuihou shinian*, 350; Gao, *Zhou Enlai weishi huiyilu*, 181.

69. Zhao, *Xihuating suiyue*, 266.

70. *MNP-B*, 6:613.

71. *MNP-B*, 6:619; *DNP-B*, 1:125.

72. *MNP-B*, 6:619.

73. *DNP-B*, 1:127.

74. *MWG*, 13:488; *MNP-B*, 6:620–621.

75. *DNP-B*, 1:131–132; *MNP-B*, 6:625.

76. Chairman Mao's Important Instructions (October 1975–January 1976), *ZGWGWK; MWG*, 13:486–490 (one sentence was deleted, though, in the text published in this volume).

77. Deng, *Deng Xiaoping and the Cultural Revolution*, 373.

78. Luo Qingchang, "Remember Forever," *RMRB*, January 9, 1979; Gao, *Peiban bingzhong Zhou Enlai de riri yeye*, 265–268; Zhang, *Zhou Enlai de zuihou shinian*, 370; *ZZ-B*, 1192.

79. According to the account in ZZ-B (2:1193), Zhou told the doctors that "you should go to take care of other comrades." In fact, instead of "other comrades," he said, "Comrade Kang Sheng," who actually had died by then. Information gained from several interviews with senior party historians, 2008–2017.

80. Zhao, *Xihuating suiyue*, 271, 274.

Acknowledgments

Almost twenty years ago, Melvyn Leffler suggested this project to me when he invited me to write a short biography of Zhou Enlai for a "shapers of international history" series that he was editing. Without his initiative, this book (much larger than what was originally proposed by Mel) would probably never have come into being.

I am the author of the book, but its intellectual and academic foundation was constructed with the guidance and support of many teachers of various kinds. When I was still a graduate student and young faculty member at East China Normal University, Li Julian, Pan Renjie, Wang Side, and Feng Jixian not only taught me how to do historical research but also instilled in me a genuine sense of critical thinking. At Southern Illinois University, David Wilson, William Turley, and Wu Tienwei directed me to write a Ph.D. dissertation on China's road to the Korean War and the making of the Chinese-American confrontation. In the thirty-plus years since then, I have received support from many renowned scholars, including Warren Cohen, John Lewis Gaddis, Michael Hunt, Philip Kuhn, Roderick MacFarquhar, Jonathan Spence, Nancy Tucker, Ezra Vogel, Frederic Wakeman, and Marilyn Young. Several of them have since passed away, yet my memory of them and their inspiration will remain with me for the rest of my life.

I wish to specifically thank a number of friends, colleagues, and fellow scholars who read and made comments on various parts of the manuscript, shared documents and other source materials with me, or provided the forums at which I presented my research and received invaluable feedback. Among them are David Atwill, Chen Donglin, Thomas Christensen, Sherman

Cochran, Gu Yunshen, Han Gang, James Hershberg, Ram Guha, Jin Chongji, Jin Guangyao, Sulmaan Kahn, Jason Kelly, William Kirby, Mark Kramer, Charles Kraus, Marilyn A. Levine, Li Danhui, Li Haiwen, Li Xiaobing, Liao Xinwen, Frederic Logevall, Lu Hanchao, Lorenz Lüthi, Rana Mitter, Niu Jun, Christian Ostermann, Elizabeth Perry, Qin Hong, Sergey Radchenko, Priscilla Roberts, Mark Selden, Shen Zhihua, Joanna Waley-Cohen, Wang Feiling, Wang Haiguang, Wang Xi, Wei Chengsi, Odd Arne Westad, David Wolff, Xia Yafeng, Xiao Donglian, Xiao Gongqin, Xu Guoqi, Xu Jilin, Xu Xing, Xu Yan, Yang Kuisong, Yi Shensi, Yu Weimin, Zhai Qiang, Zhang Baijia, Zhang Shuguang, Zhang Sulin, Zhang Yang, Zhou Zhixing, and Zhu Xueqin.

I also would like to acknowledge the assistance that I have received from Gao Bei and Zhao Han at UVA; Jason Kelly, Christopher Tang, Wang Xinyi, Wang Yuanchong, and Zhou Taomo at Cornell University; Jiang Huajie at East China Normal University; and Cai Lechang and Wang Yilin at NYU-Shanghai. I also would like to thank John Payne for his meticulous preliminary copyediting of the manuscript.

I have received generous support, financial and otherwise, from various institutions. At the University of Virginia, the C. K. Yen Professorship of US-China Relations funded my early research on Zhou. At Cornell University, my research and writing benefited enormously from the Michael J. Zak Professorship for History of U.S.-China Relations and the Hu Shih Professorship of History. I will never forget the moral support of Michael Zak. At NYU-Shanghai, the continuing assistance that I have received is invaluable. I am most grateful to Mr. Ding Jingsong, Chancellor Yu Lizhong, Chancellor Tong Shihun, Vice Chancellor Jeffrey Lehman, and especially Provost Joanna Waley-Cohen. I am also indebted to the administrative assistance provided by Casey Owens, Joyce Yang, Sally Ni, Xiong Xinyi, and Almee Wang.

At Harvard University Press I most sincerely thank my editor, Sharmila Sen, for her insightful advice and steadfast trust and support, even when I repeatedly delayed the submission of a completed manuscript; I am grateful as well for the superb work of Heather Hughes and Samantha M. Mateo. I also thank Kathleen McDermott for the encouragement she has given me over the years, and Stephen Beitel for excellent editing of the manuscript. I also thank Mary Ribesky for shepherding the manuscript through production.

My deepest gratitude goes to my family. My beloved father, Chen Liqiang, helped me collect published Chinese source materials until well into his nineties. My wife, Chen Zhihong, has done much more than always caring about my health; as a language genius and a fellow scholar of twentieth-century international history, she helped me check all the translations of Russian documents cited in this volume. She was also the first critical reader of various versions of my manuscript. I thus dedicate this book to her.

Index